UK BUILDING BLACKBOOK

THE COST AND CARBON GUIDE

HUTCHINS' 2011

SMALL AND MAJOR WORKS

UK BUILDING BLACKBOOK

THE COST AND CARBON GUIDE

HUTCHINS' 2011 Edition

Compiled and written
by Franklin & Andrews Limited
Mott MacDonald House, 8-10 Sydenham Road, Croydon CR0 2EE

© 2011 Franklin & Andrews Limited

First Published 1945

Printed and bound in Great Britain by
CPI Antony Rowe, Chippenham and Eastbourne

Typeset by: Franklin & Andrews Limited

ISBN 978-1-901856-25-5 (Hard Copy)
ISBN 978-1-901856-26-2 (eBook)

A catalogue record for this book is available from the British Library.

Contents

Albania Tirana

Australia Adelaide Canberra Melbourne Sydney

Bahrain Manama

Bangladesh Dhaka

Botswana Gaborone

Bulgaria Sofia

Canada Burlington ON Calgary AB Clarenville NL Cornerbrook NL Edmonton AB Halifax NS Markham ON Mississauga ON Moncton NB Montreal QC Niagara Falls ON St John NB St John's NL Sydney NS Vancouver BC

China Beijing Hong Kong Shanghai Shenzen

Czech Republic Brno Prague

France Paris

Hungary Budapest

India Ahmedabad Bangalore Chennai Delhi Hyderabad Kochi Kolkata Mumbai

Indonesia Jakarta

Ireland Cork Dublin

Japan Tokyo

Kazakhstan Almaty

Kenya Nairobi

Libya Tripoli

Malaysia Kuala Lumpur

Netherlands Arnhem Utrecht

Nigeria Lagos Port Harcourt

Norway Stavanger

Oman Muscat

Pakistan Islamabad Karachi Lahore

Philippines Manila

Poland Gdansk Krakow Warsaw

Qatar Doha

Romania Bucharest

Russian Federation Moscow St Petersburg Surgut

Serbia Belgrade

Singapore

South Africa Johannesburg

Spain Barcelona

Taiwan Kaohsiung Taipei

Thailand Bangkok

Turkey Istanbul

Uganda Kampala

Ukraine Kiev

UAE Abu Dhabi Dubai Fujairah

UK Aberdeen Belfast Birmingham Brighton Bristol Cambridge Cardiff Colwyn Bay Croydon Derby Durham Edinburgh Exeter Glasgow Inverness Leeds Lerwick Liverpool London Manchester Newcastle Norwich Reading Sheffield Southampton York

USA Arlington VA Atlanta GA Baltimore MD Birmingham AL Bonifay FL Boston MA Buffalo NY Cape May NJ Charleston WV Chicago IL Cleveland OH Daphne AL Denver CO Freehold NJ Gilroy CA Hattiesburg MS Holyoke MA Houston TX Jersey City NJ Los Angeles CA Millburn NJ Mobile AL Monroe LA Morgantown WV New York NY Orange CA Pace FL Panama City FL Pensacola FL Philadelphia PA Phoenix AZ Pittsburgh PA Pleasanton CA Portland OR Rockville MD Sacramento CA Salt Lake City UT San Diego CA San Jose CA Seattle WA Tallahassee FL Tampa FL Tulsa OK

Uzbekistan Tashkent

Zambia Lusaka

Head Office
Mott MacDonald Limited
8-10 Sydenham Road
Croydon CR0 2EE
United Kingdom

T +44 (0)20 8774 2000
F +44 (0)20 8681 5706
W www.mottmac.com

This book is the first within the industry to estimate costs and carbon emissions for construction activities for buildings. This has been possible due to the incredible hard work and dedication of the specialist Economic Research Unit of Franklin + Andrews.

James Fiske, the director of the Economic Research Unit, would particularly like to thank and recognise the efforts of the following people:

Nang Vo Kham Murng
Aaron Wright
Karl Horton
Sam Wenham
Emma Will
Rachael Ogden
Jingxin Shen

Franklin + Andrews would also like to thank the many manufacturers, suppliers, merchants, contractors and specialist sub-contractors for their continued and valued assistance in the production of the costs and embodied CO_2 within this publication.

Finally a special thanks to those readers who have taken the trouble to contact us with suggestions for new sections and content generally, much of which has been incorporated within the current publication. The editing team constantly review the content of this publication and welcome suggestions from readers for its improvement.

Franklin + Andrews Limited

January 2011

Through government commitments to reduce greenhouse gas emissions by 80% before 2050 (26% by 2020), there is a need in the industry to measure and control the impact of carbon emissions from construction activities.

As a result we now often see two teams on construction projects, one quantifying cost and one quantifying embodied carbon. Both of these teams have to undertake a measurement process in order to produce their outputs. Unfortunately often these teams work in isolation and the measurement process is conducted twice, leading to inefficiencies and often inconsistencies in what is being measured.

This latest edition of the UK Building Blackbook (The Cost and Carbon Guide) has been developed to address this issue and try to improve efficiencies within the construction industry. The ultimate goal resulting in a quicker, cheaper and consistent way of evaluating both cost and carbon.

As well as retaining the accurate pricing that has made this price book a definitive guide for all construction trades and professions, this publication now also contains a carbon emission estimate for every activity of work.

The format of each section in Major Works follows that of previous editions with items generally measured in accordance with SMM7 measurement rules whilst Small Works is measured in accordance with SMM6 measurement rules.

The Appendices section provides valuable cost and other relevant data including construction indices, location factors, sustainability and average building costs for refurbishment and fit-out projects for works of a medium to large size.

We hope that this publication of data will assist the industry improve performance, reduce costs and limit any environmental impacts.

We look forward to your receiving feedback.

James Fiske
Head of Economic Research Unit
Franklin + Andrews

This exciting new edition of the Hutchins UK Building Costs Blackbook sets a new standard in the construction industry. This is the first construction price book series to include an estimate of Carbon Dioxide (CO_2) emissions for all activities of work – as well as retaining the accurate pricing that has made this price book a definitive guide for all construction trades and professions. The change of title now reflects its full content: UK Building Blackbook – The Cost and Carbon Guide – Small and Major Works.

The combined publication of the Hutchins Small and Major Works marks an exciting time in the industry, one where we can begin to quantify the environmental impacts of our building decisions with greater ease. Building owners, operators and businesses are being placed under pressure to reduce their carbon emissions. This measure is going to become increasingly important as we move into times of taxation and Carbon trading to support the UK Climate Change Act.

There have been numerous published sources of embodied CO_2 data for materials, none of these are truly comprehensive or relate to measured rates. We hope that this publication will go some way to providing CO_2 data in a useable format and help minimise the levels of interpretation that are currently causing reporting inconsistencies in the industry.

The complete content of the Small and Major Works section has been compiled in accordance with the requirements of professional quantity and building surveyors, architects, property developers, building contractors and specialists in need of reliable and informative cost and environmental information.

Introduction to small works section

Background

The edition for this year has retained the basic content as for previous years' publications and maintains the additional enhancements to the format, introduced in previous works, in order to improve the value to the reader. These improvements will, hopefully, ensure that the production of estimates and cost appraisals is made easier and more effective than before.

The measured rates sections are, wherever possible, generally trade based ensuring that the task of locating prices is made more simple. These measured rates sections are presented with pricing information displayed at both Net and Gross cost levels. The Memoranda section provides general information relating to material statistics including required quantities for selected work elements, specification information generally and other useful data.

Labour costs

Labour outputs used in this section remain unaltered and are derived from outputs used for previous editions

The wage rates agreed by the Building and Allied Trades Joint Industrial Council for the industry as of 30th June 2010 are as follows:-

All areas

Advanced craftsman	£405.99 per 39 hour week	£10.41 per hour
Adult general operative	£301.47 per 39 hour week	£7.73 per hour

Computation of hourly cost

	Advanced craftsman	Adult general operative
(a) Labour	£ p	£ p
Basic weekly wage	405.99	301.47
Overtime say 9 hours	93.69	69.57
Non-productive overtime, say 4.5 hours	46.85	34.79
Plus rate say 50%	273.27	202.92
	£819.80	£608.75
(b) Contributions and levies	£ p	£ p
Sickness and injury benefit	3.10	3.10
National insurance	93.41	66.40
CITB levy	4.10	3.04
Public Holidays	14.21	10.53
Holiday pay scheme	51.17	38.55
Retirement benefit	3.07	3.07
Death benefit	1.66	1.66
Trade supervision	39.95	33.43
Travel allowance, say	17.69	17.69
	£228.36	£177.47
(c) Computation of hourly cost	£ p	£ p
Operatives weekly rate as (a) above	819.80	608.75
Contributions etc as (b) above	228.36	177.47
	£1,048.16	£786.22
Inclement weather, say 2%	20.96	15.72
Redundancy reserve, say 2%	20.96	15.72
	£1,090.08	£817.66
Employers liability insurance @ 2%	21.80	16.35
	£1,111.88	£834.01
Site on-costs, say 6.75%	75.05	56.30
Overheads, say 13.25%	147.32	110.51
	£1,334.25	£1,000.82
Cost per hour	£27.80	£20.85

The wage rates agreed by the Joint Industry Board for Plumbing, Mechanical Engineering Services in England and Wales as of June 2010 are as follows:-

All Areas

Trained Plumber	£409.13 per 37.5 hour week	£10.91 per hour
Advanced Plumber	£477.38 per 37.5 hour week	£12.73 per hour

Computation of hourly cost

	Trained Plumber	Advanced Plumber
(a) Labour	£ p	£ p
Basic weekly wage per 37.5 hours	409.13	477.38
Additional 1.5 hours	16.37	19.10
Overtime say 9 hours	147.29	171.86
Non-productive overtime say 4.5 hours	49.10	57.29
	£621.89	£725.63
Plus rate 50%	310.95	362.82
	£932.84	£1,088.45
(b) Contributions, levies and expenses	£ p	£ p
Public holidays	20.48	23.43
Welding supplement	41.30	41.30
Travel allowance, say	37.33	37.33
National insurance	122.26	143.35
Industry pension scheme	60.82	70.38
Holiday pay scheme	55.11	61.90
CITB levy	4.98	6.07
Trade supervision	48.71	54.47
	£390.99	£438.23
(c) Computation of hourly cost	£ p	£ p
Operative's weekly rate as (a) above	932.84	1,088.45
Contributions etc as (b) above	390.99	438.23
	£1,323.83	£1,526.68
Inclement weather, say 2%	26.48	30.53
Redundancy reserve, say 2%	26.48	30.53
	£1,376.79	£1,587.74
Employers liability insurance @ 2%	27.54	31.75
	£1,404.33	£1,619.49
Site on-costs, say 6.75%	94.79	109.32
Overheads, say 13.25%	186.07	214.58
	£1,685.19	£1,943.39
Cost per hour	£35.11	£40.49

General Introduction

Material costs

Material prices used in this publication have been supplied by manufacturers and merchants, they include delivery to site and are current at second quarter 2010. Considerable variation can occur in material prices arising from load size, geographic area and also the trading status of the builder. It is important, therefore, that before entering into contractual situations confirmation is obtained from local merchants of material costs relevant to the project. This advice would equally apply to the rising trading costs of metals recently recorded on the world markets in particular steel and copper products where recent price rises have been dramatic

Plant hire costs

Plant hire rates used in this publication reflect locally hired machines, with possible savings arising from long term hire rate reduction or situations where the contractor's own plant is used. Rates are current at second quarter 2010.

Plant and tool hire

The following products with rates are based on information provided by HSS Hire Service Group Ltd., 25 Willow Lane, Mitcham, Surrey CR4 4TS, www.hss.com, with over 400 branches nationwide.

The rates per week are the maximum charge for each 7–day period and exclude VAT and delivery charges.

	per week £
Access and support	
Alloy access towers:	
2.2m platform height	94.00
4.2m platform height	133.00
6.2m platform height	172.00
Lightweight staging:	
2.4m long	35.00
3.6m long	39.00
Steel trestles – each	5.50
Scaffold board – each	4.00
Decorators trestles	
1.8m high	20.00
2.4m high	24.00
Ladders, double section:	
lightweight, push-up	
3.5m closed, 6.3m extended	31.00
5.0m closed, 9.0m extended	44.00
Combination ladder – 3.6m	56.00
Roof ladder – 4.6m double	49.00
Steps, 6 tread	27.00
Steps, 8 tread	30.00
Steps, 10 tread	32.00

General building

Super prop	20.00
Steel props – each:	
1.1m closed, 1.8m extended	4.00
1.8m closed, 3.0m extended	4.00
2.6m closed, 3.9m extended	4.00
Bolt croppers	19.00
Wheelbarrow, tyred, heavy-duty	10.00
Paving mallet	10.00
Tarpaulin, 5m x 4m	18.00

Concreting and compaction

Surface scaler:	
heavy duty, petrol	204.00
light duty, petrol	204.00
Concrete floor grinder, electric	148.00
Indent roller	18.00
Needle gun for keying, air operated	46.00
Poker vibrator, 47mm head, electric	74.00
Poker vibrator, 50mm head, petrol	46.00
Beam screed, petrol, per unit	195.00
Cement mixers:	
diesel	68.00
electric	24.00
Vibrating plate, light	55.00
Vibrating plate, medium	58.00
Vibrating roller, 560mm wide	128.00
Rammer	94.00

Plumbing, pumping and drain clearing

Pipe vice	27.00
Pipe cutters, 100mm	27.00
Clay pipe cutter, up to 150mm	33.00
Steel pipe bender, manual	78.00
Copper pipe bender	20.00
Drain clearer, power jet, petrol	366.00
Centrifugal pump, 50mm	64.00

Heating, cooling and drying

Building dryers, portable, 10ltr	84.00
Building dryers, warm air, 17ltr	102.00

Welding, lighting and power

Plasterers light	34.00
Telescopic floodlight, twin head	27.00

Breaking and drilling

Hydraulic breaker, medium duty	139.00
Breaker, medium duty	65.00

Fixing, carpentry and sanding

Cartridge hammer	52.00
Floor edging sander	60.00
Floor sander	74.00

Sawing and cutting

Chasing machine, light	78.00
Door trimming saw	55.00
Chain saw, petrol, safety kit	110.00
Chain saw, electric, safety kit	85.00

Painting and decorating

Air compressor, 9cfm, electric	96.00
Air compressor, 15cfm, electric or petrol	140.00
Tyrolean roughcast machine	27.00

Cleaning and floor maintenance

Mini hot washer	174.00
Electric steam cleaner	62.00
Carpet cleaner	80.00
Carpet cleaner upholstery tool	5.00
Floor scrubber-dryer, single	215.00
Surface scaler, heavy duty	216.00
Floor tile stripper	106.00

Lifting and materials handling

Compact excavator 1.5T	264.00
Compact excavator 3.0T	396.00
Skidsteer loader	309.00
Hi-Lift skip dumper, diesel	360.00
Rubbish chute	7.70
Rubbish chute hopper	11.40
Rubbish chute Y-section	12.60

Gardening

Turf cutter	116.00
Petrol brush cutter	140.00
Rotary mower, 500mm, petrol	31.00
All-terrain mower, 660mm, petrol	202.00
Electric lawn raker	22.00
Brush cutter, petrol	57.00
Lawn scarifier, petrol	80.00
Lawn aerator, petrol	134.00
Hedge trimmer, electric	24.00
Light duty tiller	50.00
Power digger	89.00

Cultivator	199.00
Post hole borer, manual	18.00
Post hole borer, one-man, petrol	95.00
Post hole borer, two-man, petrol	104.00
Post hole borer, hydraulic	184.00
Chain saw and safety kit, petrol	110.00
Chain saw and safety kit, electric	85.00
Logging saw	76.00
Stump grinder, petrol	214.00
Chipper/shredder, petrol	93.00
Leaf sucker/blower, petrol	54.00
Garden shredder, petrol	40.00

All costs displayed in this publication exclude VAT.

Explanatory notes

Constants of labour

For the greater convenience of readers wishing to calculate bonus targets etc., a column headed 'Labour Hours' is included throughout this edition, indicating the man-hours required per unit. The time given is for all employees, irrespective of the ratio of craft and general operatives or the number of employees in a gang.

For example, in bricklaying the ratio varies according to the conditions of work or availability of labour. Ratio of bricklayer to general operative may be 1-1, 2-1, 3-1 or even 4-1. This means that if two hours per unit is given, the proportion of hours would be as follows:-

Ratio	Bricklayer(s)	General operative(s)	Hours per Unit
1-1	1.00 hour	1.00 hour	2 hours
2-1	1.33 hour	0.67 hour	2 hours
3-1	1.50 hour	0.50 hour	2 hours
4-1	1.60 hour	0.40 hour	2 hours

Taking another trade – painting; on new work, a general operative's time is almost negligible, but on the other hand on repair or redecorating work involving washing down and preparatory work, one general operative may be required to service every four craft operatives. If the labour hours per unit for such an item were shown at 2.50 hours, this would mean four craft operatives and one general operative at 0.50 hours each.

Labour hours – Conversion table for decimal hours to hours and minutes; figures along the top and down left-hand side of table represent decimal hours to two decimal places, other figures are minutes.

	0.00	0.01	0.02	0.03	0.04	0.05	0.06	0.07	0.08	0.09
0.00	-	1	2	2	3	3	4	5	5	6
0.10	6	7	7	8	9	9	10	11	11	12
0.20	12	12	13	13	15	15	16	17	17	18
0.30	18	19	19	20	21	21	22	23	23	24
0.40	24	25	25	26	27	28	28	29	29	30
0.50	30	31	31	32	33	34	34	35	35	36
0.60	36	37	37	38	38	39	40	41	41	42
0.70	42	43	43	44	44	45	46	47	47	48
0.80	48	49	49	50	50	51	52	52	53	54
0.90	54	55	55	56	56	57	58	58	59	60

Worked example 1

Labour hours column shows 0.75. To obtain equivalent minutes: read down the left hand column to 0.70, then across the line to the column headed 0.05.
Answer: 45 minutes.

Worked example 2

Labour Hours column shows 1.44

Read down the left hand column to 0.40, then across the line to the column headed 0.04 = 27 minutes. Add 1 hour:

  Answer: 1 hour 27 minutes.

Labour hours – The time taken for the fixing of each of the items is expressed as a decimal portion of an hour, therefore 0.50 labour hours equals thirty minutes. The times are average and include for unloading distributing and subsequent fixing in position.

Labour hours – Conversion table for hours and minutes to decimal hours, to two decimal places. Figures along the top and down the left side of table represent minutes.

Mins	0	1	2	3	4	5	6	7	8	9
0	-	0.02	0.03	0.05	0.07	0.08	0.10	0.12	0.13	0.15
10	0.17	0.18	0.20	0.22	0.23	0.25	0.27	0.28	0.30	0.32
20	0.33	0.35	0.37	0.38	0.40	0.42	0.43	0.45	0.47	0.48
30	0.50	0.52	0.53	0.55	0.57	0.58	0.60	0.62	0.63	0.65
40	0.67	0.68	0.70	0.72	0.73	0.75	0.77	0.78	0.80	0.82
50	0.83	0.85	0.87	0.88	0.90	0.92	0.93	0.95	0.97	0.98

Worked example 1

Man takes 45 minutes to complete a job. To obtain decimal hours: Read down the left hand column to 40, then across the line to column headed 5.

  Answer: 0.75 hours.

Worked example 2

Man takes 1 hour 27 minutes to complete a job. To obtain decimal hours; Read down the left hand column to 20 then across the line to column headed 7. = 0.45 hours. Add 1 hour:

  Answer: 1.45 hours.

Establishment charges and profit

20% has been included in the net cost of labour to cover "site-on-costs", "establishment charges", for both new; repairs and alteration work and is made up of:-

Site-on-costs	6.75%
Establishment charges (overheads)	13.25%

10% has been added to net cost of labour and material to cover profit on both new and repair and alteration work.

It is considered that these percentages represent average overhead costs on competitive contracts of say £10,000 - £50,000, but they will necessarily vary according to the size and scope of the contract and the type of work involved.

The extra payments to which operatives are entitled under the Working Rule Agreement for executing certain types of work have been considered in the appropriate labour cost columns.

The following tables give the main items included in the assessment of the respective percentages.

Site on costs 6.75%

Setting out; cartage.
Protection and timekeeping.
Sanitary conveniences
Welfare arrangements and safety precautions.
Watching and lighting.
Sheds and site offices and record keeping.
Deterioration of non-chargeable plant.
Removal of debris and other cartage.
Site telephone; attendance; incidentals.
Gauge boxes; profiles; screeds; templates; samples; trial holes.
Replacements, making good and maintenance.

Establishment charges (overheads)

Third Party (about 0.4% on wages)	}	0.25%
Fire	}	
Bond fees (if any): Federation fees	}	
Estimating costs	}	
Rent, rates and taxes	}	13.00%
Lighting, heating, telephones	}	
Other office and overhead costs	}	
		13.25%

Cost of water

Cost of water is included in the materials columns. When water has to be separately priced in Bills of Quantities the rate is about £0.24% of contract figure, but district charges vary, and the rate can also vary with type of work.

Ratio – labour: material

	Percentage Labour	Material	Site on-costs Estab. charges
Excavation	75	5	20
Concrete and drainage	28	52	20
Brickwork	42	38	20
Woodwork	30	50	20
Plasterwork	57	23	20
Plumbing	24	56	20
Decorating	67	13	20
Glazing	17	63	20
Repair work	66	14	20
Roofing	27	53	20

In total, labour with materials, work out nearly equal but as certain trades (such as brickwork and woodwork) are disproportionate to other trades, it would be found that in average new work, the relative proportions will approximate to labour - 43%; material - 43%; with 'other items' - 14%.

Repairs and alterations section.

Important notes concerning establishment charges etc.

Most work of a repair and alteration nature is estimated on a specification only, or plan and specification without Bills of Quantities basis. The Schedules set out at the rear of each trade section therefore adhere in some cases to measurements and trade headings which are established and familiar; but where suitable standard measurement rules have been adopted.

Cost depends very much on size of job and distance from workshop (read remarks hereunder).

The repair sections of the publication are designed for the pricing of repair, adaptation and conversion work; and prices are based on the average conditions under which such work may be executed. Adjustments to prices should be made for exceptional working conditions of any work, for a very small or large job, simplicity or complexity of work, accessibility and weather conditions (season of year, especially in respect of external work). Circumstances necessitating adjustments as thus recommended will be apparent. For instance, if a tradesman has to travel especially to a job, such as re-hanging a door or repairing a burst pipe, it will obviously cost much more by comparison than if the tradesman was already on the site for other work.

Percentages where shown in the work section should be added for pricing work in occupied premises. This is for working in furnished rooms where the necessary extra care and protection retards speed of execution; but no allowance has been made for the removal and replacement of furniture, carpets etc.

It is possible for prices for many other items of repair work to be calculated from the items provided.

Unit prices have been built up as follows:

Labour including (a) site-on-costs and (b) establishment charges and material at cost, with allowances for waste and making good. Materials have been assessed on current prices as detailed in the preamble to each new work section, but with appropriate increases for small quantities and cost of cartage. Labour rates used are detailed under 'Labour costs – wage rates'.

Removal of existing
All items of removal include for:-
The hiring of a skip; delivery to site; wheeling and loading debris into and the removal of skip when full; disposal of contents; payment of charges

A basis for the estimate without quantities
It is not usual practice for tenders for small jobbing or alteration work to be priced on a Bill of Quantities. The absence of measured details and contract rates may not be of great importance at the estimating stage (except perhaps on the occasion of making an application for a House Renovation Grant). Such matters can, however, become complicated at the final account stage, especially when, as so often happens, there is a long list of variation orders to be agreed with the quantity surveyor acting on behalf of the Local Authority or the building owner.

Contractors using these schedules as a basis for their estimating could save a great deal of time and expense when agreeing an estimate, or settling the final account, if the following simple procedure is adopted when submitting the estimate. The following or similar wording could be printed or written, as a footnote to the estimate:–

Analysis of estimate

This estimate is based on Hutchin's Small Works and rates and prices used are those contained in that edition, and the following percentage adjustments shall apply to this job only....

General building work	Add or Deduct* .....%
Specialist sub-contractors listed below	
Trade	Add or Deduct* .....%
Trade	Add or Deduct*......%
Trade	Add or Deduct* .....%

* Delete whichever is not applicable.

The foregoing percentage adjustments are subject to the order to commence work being given within .....months from the date of this estimate. If the order to commence work is given after the expiry of the stated period, the Contractor reserves the right to revise the percentage adjustments. The foregoing adjustments do not preclude the Contractor from making any subsequent claim for increased cost arising from either national wage agreements, or agreed increases in the cost of materials occurring after the date of the estimate.

Advisory notes on the foregoing

Note 1: The number of months is left to individual contractors' discretion; six months is a reasonable interval, three or four months perhaps on small jobs.

Note 2: The percentage adjustment decisions are the absolute prerogative of the Contractor. This will depend on extra over payments, extra travel time, material costs, profit margin and a number of other factors.

Note 3: It is essential to enter the year of the edition of the price book used. The fact that a new edition might be published during the course of a contract, could cause misunderstanding if the edition year was not specified.

Note 4: Percentage adjustments stated are binding only to the contract to which they apply and are not obligatory on any succeeding contract.

Note 5: Percentage adjustments on specialist sub-contractors' work. rates included in the various sections are a general guide, quotations received from specialist firms may be substantially different from those quoted. It is, therefore, advisable to consider each specialist trade separately.

Note 6: Contractors must never lose sight of the fact that at some time they may, through no fault of their own, find that a contract may be the subject of dispute in a Court of Law. If the dispute revolved around the final account and/or the cost of building work, it is quite probable that both the judge and barristers will use the rates in the sections as a 'guiding light', it is understandable, therefore, that if the Contractor used certain percentage additions in the estimate and omitted to state the additions in writing he stands to forego what may have been a justifiable claim for extra cost, if, on the other hand, the percentage adjustments were written on the estimate, then such adjustments would have to be taken into consideration by all concerned. In this event the Contractor would not have to be subjected to a long and difficult cross-examination on estimating. This, in turn, would save litigation time and attendant costs, and could ensure a more generous settlement to the Contractor than might otherwise have been possible.

Dayworks – advisory notes for use when there is no standard form of contract

From time to time building contractors may have the good fortune to have the opportunity to carry out either part or the whole of the contract on a daywork basis.

This may be due to extreme urgency (e.g. repair after fire, flood or storm damage), complexity of the work or the impatience of the owner, when of course, there is not sufficient time for an estimate to be prepared.

These notes are primarily intended for jobs in the £500 - £25,000 range for private owners: too small to justify the services (and fees) of an architect and/or quantity surveyor, and any suggestion of a standard form of contract would be superfluous.

It is, however, essential that the contractors should ensure that there will be no misunderstanding about payment when the final account stage is reached. A letter to the owner on the following lines should suffice.

…I/we confirm your written/verbal instructions to carrying out sundry repairs and reinstatement work. The cost of the work shall be based on an inclusive hourly rate of £… per hour for each operative engaged on the work. The cost of all materials shall be current local costs.

To the sum total of the foregoing wages and material costs shall be added …………% to cover overheads and profit. Unless we receive your instructions to the contrary it will be assumed that our terms and conditions are acceptable. – End of letter.

If the total value of the work is expected to exceed £1,000 and/or more than one month's duration, add the following paragraph.

… On the last day of each month a detailed account will be forwarded to you and payment shall be made within 15 days. In the event of any inadmissibility or otherwise of any charges the whole matter shall be referred to ………..Esq., Quantity Surveyor, whose decision shall be final and binding.

The nomination of a quantity surveyor does not mean that the contractor has to pay the cost of a retaining fee for a quantity surveyor's services that may never be called on.

It does mean that, if necessary, there is a local quantity surveyor who would be prepared to examine all relevant documents for the contractor for an appropriate fee.

The hourly rate for operatives may be based on the cost to employ, that is standard wage rates, plus extra over rate, plus bonus, plus all employers' levies and contributions.

The percentage to be charged is a matter for individual firms. Taking into consideration the overall cost of wages and material is recoverable in full. Something between 120% and 150% should suffice.

Wage rates and percentage additions chargeable are the subject of a decision by the contractor and must be stated at the outset of the contract. The foregoing recommendations regarding hourly wage rates and percentage additions are not mandatory and may be varied from contract to contract.

How to prepare your own unit rate from the Schedules.

To help you to calculate your own Unit Price for each item, I have set out below, suggestions for adjusting the figures and costs in the columns to suit your particular requirements.

(a) Unit column
   m^3 - means the measurement per cubic metre.
   m^2 - means the measurement per square metre.
   m - means the measurement per linear metre.
   Each - means the measurement per each or number.

(b) Labour Hours column
   Labour hours for the time taken for the fixing of the item described, expressed as a decimal fraction of an hour. (e.g. 0.75 hours equals 45 minutes).

   The times given are average and include for unloading, distribution and fixing.

(c) Labour Net column
   Gives the total net labour cost by multiplying the labour hours by the all-in labour rate (inclusive of 6.75% site-on-costs and 13.25% overhead charges).

(d) Plant Net column
   Provides the average net cost of the hire of plant per unit of measure.

(e) Materials Net column
   Gives the discounted cost of materials plus an allowance for waste for materials used in each rate per unit of measure.

(f) Unit Net column
   Shows the total net cost of the labour, plant and materials columns.

(g) Labour Gross column
   Gives the gross labour cost by adding a profit of 10% to the net labour cost.

(h) Plant Gross column
   Shows the gross plant cost by adding a profit of 10% to the net plant cost.
(i) Materials Gross column
   Gives the gross material cost by adding a profit of 10% to the net material cost .

(j) Unit Price column
   Gives the total gross cost of the labour, plant and materials columns.

A profit level of 10% of the total of the net labour, plant and material columns in both the new work and the repair and alterations sections is assessed as a reasonable return on expenditure.

Suggestions in adjusting labour costs taken from the work sections to suit your own requirements.

(a) To assess the percentage adjustment to be applied to the work section rates:-

$\dfrac{\text{Your labour rate} - \text{Work section rate} \times 100}{\text{Schedule rate}}$ = % to add or deduct from the sections

(b) Multiply the man hours given by your own labour rate.

(c) A Unit Cost example could be as follows:-
   Description of item: Hutchins' ref. 310106A

Carcassing; sawn softwood; noggins; 38 mm x 50 mm – per m

Suggestion 1

Labour:
   0.30 man hours x £27.80 per hour (Hutchins' craft rate)   £8.34
   If your labour rate is £30.00, then

$\dfrac{£30.00 - £27.80}{£27.80} \times 100\%$ = +7.91%   £0.66

                                                          £9.00

Materials:
taken from the work section   +   £0.62

                                                                        £9.62

Profit:
given in the work section   + 10%   £0.96

Therefore the **Unit Price** is   **£10.58**

Alt. Suggestion 2

Labour
0.30 man hours x £30.00 (say your craft rate)   £9.00

Materials/Plant
As above   +   £0.62

                                                                        £9.62

Profit
Given in the work section   +10%   £0.96

Therefore the **Unit Price** is   **£10.58**

All costs displayed in this publication exclude VAT.

Introduction to major works section

The rates contained within this cost handbook have been derived from competitive estimates. It is intended that those using the prices within this price book will add an allowance for overheads and profit and for preliminaries. A suggested enhancement of 10% has been used for gross unit rate examples in both sections.

The rates do not include for other on-costs such as might be included under the preliminaries and general costs sections of bills of quantities. Sample preliminary build-ups are given in the publication to assist the reader in identifying these other costs for Major works and each provides a simple checklist for guidance.

Generally outputs used in the Major Works publication are based on the assumption of reasonable quantities of repetitive work. In the event that small quantities exist, which can happen on even the largest of projects, suitable adjustment would be appropriate to reflect anticipated performance. Similarly where site conditions are poor, adjustments to outputs would also be necessary to reflect the likely loss of productivity.

Labour costs

Labour rates used in the Major Works publication are calculated on the basis that most builders and contractors pay in excess of the minimum national wage rate. In respect of larger scale construction sites supply and demand dictates labour costs more than wage agreements. Therefore, from our experience, we have used, for the Major Works section, a net cost labour rate for trade Craftsmen of £16.98 per hour and for General Operatives £12.70 per hour.

These rates are compiled generally in accordance with the Code of Estimating Practice published by the Chartered Institute of Building. Labour rates do not include for supervision.

In support of customer requests, Labour gangs used in the measured rates now reflect a different calculation method, e.g. a 2 and 1 bricklaying gang comprising two bricklayers and one labourer. The cost of the gang is recovered by adding together the total cost of the three members of the gang and this generates the hourly rate used in the measured rates section of this publication.

Labour costs do not include any allowance for travelling time to and from the place of work; this is more usually calculated and costed within the preliminary sections of the tender documents.

Plant hire

Plant hire rates are typical of those being charged for the second quarter of 2010 and include for fuel in use and operators costs for plant normally hired with a plant operator. Travelling costs to and from site are not included and would normally be costed and included within the preliminary section of the tender documents. Small hand plant and tools are deemed included within the labour rates, being an essential part of a tradesman's tool bag on modern construction sites.

Materials

Material prices used within the Major Works section are at a national average level and are based on manufacturers' and merchants' price lists for the second quarter of 2010. They reflect average trade discounts for direct delivery loads and will generally, therefore, be at or near the lowest price available. Adjustment will be necessary to suit each specific project and location and we would, therefore, urge all to seek accurate quotations if submitting competitive tenders. Measured rates include an allowance for wastage in use and unloading costs.

VAT

Value Added Tax has not been included in the compilation of Net or Gross rates.

Introduction to carbon dioxide emissions

Climate change is considered to be one of the greatest environmental threats facing the world today. Carbon Dioxide (CO_2) is the most significant of the greenhouses gases contributing to this threat and the construction industry is one of the worst contributors to the creation of it.

Simplistically speaking there are two measures of CO_2 emissions, embodied and direct. Embodied relates to the CO_2 emissions made during the production of something, direct is that produced physically during a process or activity.

Materials used in the construction industry will generally have an embodied CO_2 measure. This demonstrates the CO_2 emissions during the extraction of the material and the production of the component. Plant will have a direct CO_2 impact during the running of the plant and burning of the fuel.

Study boundaries

It is essential to understand the boundaries of any study, and it is important to understand what boundaries the data has that you are using if you want to ensure that you are not double counting or missing elements of the measure.

Generally, published embodied CO_2 data will have one of four boundaries:
1)   Cradle to Gate
2)   Cradle to Site
3)   Cradle to Grave
4)   Cradle to Cradle

Cradle to gate measures all of the CO_2 emissions relating to the material to get it to factory gate ready for transportation to site. Cradle to site also contains an estimate of the transport. Cradle to grave also makes an allowance for its final disposal and cradle to cradle also includes elements of recycling.

As the latter three boundaries make allowances for project specific issues such as how for to transport to site, the authors only use the Cradle to Gate boundary for the materials. Further allowances can then be made by the user for transport and if needed disposal.

Labour

The CO_2 impact of labour is not included within the calculations as these impacts would occur regardless of if undertaking construction activity. Allowances for hand tools are made within the plant totals. Please see the 'Transportation' section with regard to quantification of labour transportation.

Materials

The authors have developed their own estimates of embodied CO_2 data for materials with a Cradle to Gate boundary. Reference was been made to published UK CO_2 figures for materials from a variety of sources in order to achieve this.

In particular, the publishers wish to acknowledge the research carried out by Professor Geoff Hammond and Craig Jones from the Department of Mechanical Engineering (University of Bath) on the embodied energy and carbon of a large number of building materials. The research publication, Inventory of Carbon and Energy (ICE), which is publicly available for download from the University web site have been invaluable source of data used to verify and supplement the primary research and composite item build-ups.

With any material the embodied CO_2 figures will be different for each material supplier depending on the manufacturing process adopted e.g. a supplier adopting a renewable energy source will have a lower figure than another. The figures used therefore represent an estimate of likely embodied CO_2 for materials, as with any estimate the figures should be superseded with actual manufacturer data when available.

The use of recycled materials will also have an impact on the embodied CO_2 for materials. For these estimated guides typical recycled content has been used but allowances or adjustments should be made in the instances of specific data being known.

As with the estimates of cost, elements of waste have been included, but additional allowance would need to be made for any project specific issues.

Please see the 'Transportation' section with regard to quantification of material transportation.

Plant

The embodied CO_2 of the production and maintenance of plant is not included within the guide figures. The plant elements are therefore quantified using the fuel consumption. The plant selected for the guide uses what the author considers the more traditional sources. Reductions will be recorded if alternate sources of renewable energy or biofuels are used.

As with the estimates of cost, elements of non-productive standing time have been included, but additional allowance would need to be made for project specifics such as ground conditions and weather.

Please see the 'Transportation' section with regard to quantification of the transportation of plant.

Transportation

The CO_2 impact for transporting labour, materials and plant resources has not been included within the unit rate data. This is due to the levels of disparity that will be recorded on projects. It is recommended that this is either excluded from the studies or quantified additionally.

It is important that quantification of transport is included when you are considering procurement options for locations with variations in transportation distance as this will have a significant impact on the final result, especially when quantifying international procurement options.

General Introduction

To quantify the transport of labour additionally the following table has been included to allow estimates of the kilograms of CO_2 produced per kilometre travelled:

Method	CO_2 emissions (kg/km)
Train	0.0400
Underground	0.0560
Bus	0.0930
Aeroplane: Short Haul	0.1800
Aeroplane: Long Haul	0.1120
Water	0.0755
Hatchback: Petrol	0.1750
Hatchback: Diesel	0.1350
Saloon: Petrol	0.2050
Saloon: Diesel	0.1580
People carrier: Petrol	0.2420
People carrier: Diesel	0.1960
SUV: Petrol	0.2910
SUV: Diesel	0.2380
Smaller Van	0.1430
Transit Van	0.2090
Motorbike	0.1000
Bicycle	0.0000

To quantify the transport of materials and plant additionally the following table has been included to allow estimates of the kilograms of CO_2 produced per tonne of weight transported per kilometre travelled:

Method	CO_2 emissions (kg/t/km)
Road	0.32
Rail	0.04
Water	0.01

Both tables above have been provided to allow estimates only, actual data will vary depending on age and state of repair of vehicle, weather conditions and numbers of people being transported.

Feedback and data requests

Your feedback is important to us. Please contact us with any comments or requests using the email: eru@franklinandrews.com

Pricing guidelines

If the reader is unfamiliar with the use of price books it is suggested that a few moments are taken to study the introduction section of this publication to help understand the approach taken in compiling the cost information used prior to attempting to use the data.

Definition of Terms and Symbols Used

m = lineal metre
m^2 = square metre
m^3 = cubic metre
Nr = number
mm = millimetre
PC = Prime Cost
Labour Cost = Net cost of labour per unit of measure
Plant Cost = Net cost of plant hire per unit of measure
Material Cost = Net cost of material per unit of measure
Unit Cost = Total cost per unit of measure excluding overheads and profit
Unit Price = Total Unit Cost per unit of measure plus 10% for profit

Measured unit rates

This section identifies the build-up cost of labour, plant and material per unit of measure for an item of work. The Net unit rate column presents costs at an average value for the UK with no addition of a profit element. The Gross rate column shows rates inclusive of 10% for profit, this should be adjusted if an alternative mark-up for profit is required.

Location factors

This section identifies current location factors for the whole of the UK in accordance with the values prepared by Franklin + Andrews. The publication establishes rates at an average unit value for the Net rate column with application of an average location factor for the Gross rates columns, inclusive of a mark-up of 10% to cover profit.

In order to fully utilise the location factors provided in this publication, to generate a more locally appropriate rate specific to a region, it will be necessary to compare and adjust the value for the selected region with the location value given for that region within the United Kingdom and applying the differential accordingly. For example, the average location value for the United Kingdom has been established as 1.00, therefore a project situated in, say, East Midlands, which has a location value of 0.94, would give a location true adjustment factor of 94% of the unit price shown in the unit rates section.

Similarly, a development in Wales, location factor 0.91, would require adjustment against the rates of 91% in order to reflect the cost variance for Wales. Readers requiring to adjust rates for local authority areas within Scotland will need to adjust against the factor current for Scotland of 0.99.

Pricing Guidelines

The prices shown are for guidance only, in determining any adjustments to the Unit Cost values shown it will be necessary to consider other related factors, such as the actual location of the site in terms of the area infrastructure. Locations well served by roads would make for ease of delivery of materials but where a site is situated in an area of restricted access this would add to the costs for supplies to that site. Local project related issues may also impact on the cost of the project and due care should be exercised in using the guide prices shown in this publication.

Small works preliminaries

Generally

The measured rates contained within the Small Works section of this publication do not include for those costs referred to as Preliminaries.

Unlike the measured rates that are directly affected by quantity changes, certain costs are not so affected and require a different approach to recovery. Examples might be scaffolding hire or the provision of a telephone, neither of which are affected by small changes in work quantity. These costs are recovered by adding a sum in the Preliminaries section of the tender documents.

The following are examples of the range of items that may be included in the Preliminaries section. The list is not exhaustive but will identify those common items that, if not allowed for in the tender elsewhere, should be included under the Preliminaries section.

Conditions of contract

Careful notice should be taken of the contract conditions in order to establish onerous obligations, restrictions or liabilities that may be imposed by the Employer. Particular care should be given to non-standard clauses. Many client bodies have developed contract forms for their own use. If presented with such contract forms the contractor should take legal advice on the significance of the conditions under which the works will be let.

Those items that should be evaluated with all contract forms may be considered under the following headings:

1)   Access to and possession or use of the site
2)   Limitations of working space
3)   Limitations of working hours
4)   The maintenance of existing services on, under or over the site
5)   The carrying out of the work in any specific order
6)   The requirement to provide Bonds
7)   The requirement to provide Insurance cover

Building contractors administrative arrangements

An assessment of the builders' site management requirements will normally include allowances for the following:

1)   Site supervision and administration
2)   Safety, health and welfare of work people
3)   Transport of work people

Plant hire

A bar chart programme may be prepared in order to establish the quantity and type of plant required on site, as well as the hire periods involved. Items of plant required for general usage and not already included in the measured rates can be included under the following headings, together with an allowance for transport and maintenance costs.

1)   Small plant and tools
2)   Scaffolding
3)   Cranes and lifting plant
4)   Site transport
5)   Plant required for specific trades

Employers facilities

The contract may well require facilities to be provided by the contractor, these may include the following:

1)   Temporary accommodation (e.g. offices)
2)   Telephones
3)   Programme or progress charts
4)   Signboards

Contractors facilities

The contractor should establish the extent of facilities required for his own operations and the cost of providing them against the following headings:

1)   Office, compounds, mess-rooms
2)   Hoardings and guard-rails
3)   Temporary roads, hard-standings and crossings
4)   Water for the works; temporary plumbing and distribution
5)   Lighting and power for the works; temporary installations
6)   Temporary telephones and the cost of calls

Temporary works

Temporary works can best be considered under the following headings:

1)   Traffic diversion
2)   Access roads
3)   Pumping and dewatering

Sundry items

Items that do not fall easily under the above headings can be included under this heading, for example:

1)   Testing of materials
2)   Testing of the works
3)   Protecting the works from inclement weather
4)   Removing rubbish and cleaning
5)   Maintenance of roads and services
6)   Drying the works
7)   Control of noise and pollution
8)   Statutory requirements

Sample preliminaries example

Every Building Contractor will treat the requirement for Preliminaries differently depending upon a number of factors. In addition each project will have its own special requirements in respect of Preliminaries and should be carefully assessed.

Preliminary costs for a small building project of 12 weeks duration, for example the construction of a domestic extension, approximate value £175,000, might be priced as follows:

Supervision and administration	£2,300.00
Site accommodation	£490.00
Light and power	£130.00
Insurances	£740.00
Water for the works	£80.00
Scaffolding	£4,650.00
Small plant	£380.00
Transport and travelling costs	£465.00
Total Preliminaries	**£9,235.00**

This represents **5.28%** of the tender sum.

Project overheads and profit

Every building contractor will need to recover from his activities sufficient income to fund overheads. In addition the builder will look to receive a fair return (profit) on the capital invested in the project. Therefore, in addition to the measured rates net cost and the preliminaries mentioned before, a sum of money will need to be added to recover profit.

The recovery of overheads and profit can be achieved in a number of ways. Some contractors prefer to add a lump sum to the tender, others will prefer to apportion the value across the range of measured work items by means of a percentage adjustment to the rates.

The method adopted in these schedules is to add overheads and profit equally on each rate by the addition of a percentage amount to the rate shown. Net rates include an addition of 20% on labour for overheads, Gross rates include a further 10% addition on labour, plant and materials for profit.

Pricing of scaffolding

As a guide for pricing scaffolding and access equipment the following rates may be considered a guide to likely costs involved for hired equipment, erected and dismantled by a specialist company and for weekly hire of both putlog and independent scaffolds.

Guide prices per square metre of structure scaffold.

Erection, dismantling and initial 4-week period of hire for scaffolding up to 8 m above ground level:

Putlog scaffold	£9.75 m²
Independent scaffold	£10.40 m²
Chimney access	£250.00 Nr

Rental per additional week:

Putlog scaffold	£1.45 m²
Independent scaffold	£1.60 m²
Chimney access	£26.00 Nr

Major works preliminaries and general conditions

Generally

Items within the scope of the works required but which are not specifically priced under measured work element are normally included under the SMM7 section headed Preliminaries/ General Conditions and are arranged as follows:

A10: Project particulars
States the name, nature and location of the Works and the names and addresses of the Employer and Consultants.

A11: Tender and Contract documents
Lists all documents that were used in the production of the bills of quantities.

A12: The site
Describes the site/existing buildings and any pertinent information in respect of boundaries, existing services, access and the like.

A13: Description of the work
Indicates the extent of the contract work involved with particular reference to physical shape and dimensions of each element where not indicated on the drawings and details of related work by others.

A20: The Contract/Sub-contract
Specifies the particular Form of Contract to be used with a schedule of clause headings of standard conditions and any special conditions or amendments to such. Points out the Employer's insurance responsibility and the need or otherwise for a performance guarantee bond.

A30: Employer's requirements: Tendering/Sub-letting/Supply
Describes the requirements and limitations laid down by the Employer and specifies any fixed or time related charges which may be requested in respect of the works.

A31: Employer's requirements: Provision, content and use of documents.
Describes the general requirements of the Employer in respect of the provision, content and use of all documents relating to the specific works.

A32: Employer's requirements: Management of the Works
Relates to the Employer's requirements for the administration of the Contract and proper conduct of the site activities.

A33: Employer's requirements: Quality standards/control
Sets out the expected degree of work standard and quality of materials utilised in the works.

A34: Employer's requirements: Security/Safety/Protection
Dictates the standard of provision of security of the Works and the extent of safety requirements that are to be provided. Any requirements in respect of maintaining adjacent structures, public and private roads and services and the like are specifically noted.

A35: Employer's requirements: Specific limitations on method/sequence/timing/use of site
Specifies the constraints relating to design of the Works and the method and sequence of the work .The access to the site and the use of the site during the Works are determined and the use or disposal of materials found on site are stated. The requirements in respect of working periods are also set out in this section, setting out daily working hours, specific start and finish times for the site staff.

A36: Employer's requirements: Facilities/Temporary works/Services
This item sets out the requirements in respect of all site accommodation that will be required to be provided by the contractor for the use of the Employer during the Works. It also sets out the needs in respect of all temporary services including toilet facilities, telephone and facsimile installation, fences, hoardings, screens and the like. The costs for heating, lighting, cleaning and maintenance will need to be included as required.

A37: Employer's requirements: Operation/Maintenance of the finished building
Draws attention to the requirements for the maintenance of the fabric of the structure and the engineering services during the work and following completion.

A40: Contractor's general cost items: Management and staff
This section allows for contractor's costs in respect of general site staff requirements, and costs of employment of such, specifically to control the Works and for support and supervision. It includes programming and production, quantity Surveying support staff and the like.

A41: Contractor's general cost items: Site accommodation
The costs for the contractor's own accommodation should be allowed for in respect of this item and to include offices, laboratories, cabins, stores, compounds, canteens, sanitary facilities and the like. Setting up or fixed costs and time related charges should all be considered in the build up of the total cost to be included.

A42: Contractor's general cost items: Services and facilities
Allowance can be included here for power, lighting, water, site telephone, safety, health and welfare, protection of the work, drying out, cleaning etc, small tools and plant, security and contractor specific costs in general respects. General attendance on nominated sub-contractors and the provision for use by such of contractor's own access equipment, hoists, lighting, power, plant and the like is deemed to be allowed for in this section.

A43: Contractor's general cost items: Mechanical plant
The cost for providing all heavy plant and equipment, transport and the like including bringing to site, maintaining and removing on completion should be allowed for in this item.

A44: Contractor's general cost items: Temporary works
Allowance can be included here for all items of temporary works required: roads, walkways, access and support scaffolding, hoardings, fencing and general compliance with all traffic regulations.

A50: Work/Products by/on behalf of the Employer
The extent of the works by others directly employed by the Employer are stated and detailed in this item, the attendance required on such and details of materials provided by the Employer are set out for consideration by the contractor.

A51: Nominated sub-contractors
Describes the work of the sub-contractors and allows for the main contractor's profit and special attendance on same when such sub-contract is given as a prime cost sum and has not been included within a measured work schedule. The provision of specific access and other requirements should be included.

A52: Nominated suppliers
Specifies the requirements for material provision by nominated suppliers including any costs for conveying the goods to site and details of special packing or similar, unloading, storing and hoisting of materials, placing in position and the return of packaging items to the supplier. Where a prime cost sum has been allowed the contractor would include an element of profit, the fixing of any item is allowed for within the measured work section.

A53: Work by statutory authorities/under takers
Work by statutory authorities includes that carried out by public companies responsible for statutory work during the execution of their statutory duty. A provisional sum is normally included to cover the cost of such work.

A54: Provisional work
Where work can be specifically detailed a provisional item is allowed for to cover unforeseen or unmeasurable work elements at pre-tender stage.

A55: Dayworks
Labour, materials and plant for works carried out under dayworks is allowed for under this section as a provisional sum.

Pricing

Each and every project will have its own unique requirements in respect of preliminaries and general conditions and these should be carefully considered and assessed.

As an example the following might be appropriate for, say, a new building project of traditional construction for an office structure with an expected contract period of nine months and carried out partially during winter months, the approximate value of the works being £1,500,000. Items are listed with their specific SMM7 reference code:

A20:	Bond	£5,625.00
A40:	Supervision and administration	£26,875.00
A41:	Site accommodation	£5,450.00
A42:	Heat, light and power	£3,625.00
A42:	Insurances	£3,750.00
A42:	Small plant	£3,125.00
A42:	Water for the works	£3,500.00
A43:	Transport and travelling costs	£6,500.00
A44:	Winter working	£3,150.00
A44:	Site dewatering	£7,000.00
A44:	Scaffolding	£11,250.00
	Total preliminaries	**£79,850.00**

This represents 5.32% of the tender sum

The inclusion or otherwise of the above scheduled costs is often left to the adjudication pre-tender meeting for discussion and decision which may be affected by current workload and competitive demands.

Pricing of scaffolding

As a guide for pricing scaffolding and access equipment the following rates may be considered a guide to likely costs involved for hired equipment, erected and dismantled by a specialist company and for weekly hire of both putlog and independent scaffolds.

Guide prices per square metre of structure scaffold.

Erection, dismantling and initial 4-week period of hire for scaffolding up to 8m above ground level:

Putlog scaffold	£10.25 m²
Independent scaffold	£10.90 m²
Chimney access	£262.50 Nr

Rental per additional week:

Putlog scaffold	£1.50 m²
Independent scaffold	£1.70 m²
Chimney access	£27.25 Nr

HUTCHINS'
SMALL WORKS

Excavation, Earthwork
and Concrete Work

Small Works 2011		Unit	Labour Hours	Labour Net £	Plant Net £	Materials Net £	Unit Net £	Unit with 10% £	CO₂ Kg
101	**NEW WORK**								
10101	**SITE PREPARATION**								
1010101	**Form temporary site road; 150 mm hardcore; maintain during period of contract**								
1010101A	3.00 m wide	m	2.70	56.30	-	10.78	67.08	73.79	6.950
1010102	**Break up and remove temporary site road 150 mm hardcore**								
1010102A	3.00 m wide	m	2.25	46.91	-	-	46.91	51.60	-
1010103	**Temporarily enclose site; fencing up to twenty times used**								
1010103A	1.35 m chestnut fencing	m	0.25	5.21	-	-	5.21	5.73	-
1010103B	2.70 m chainlink fencing	m	0.45	9.38	-	-	9.38	10.32	-
1010104	**Clear site of bushes, scrub and undergrowth; cut down small trees and grub up roots; burn or deposit in skip**								
1010104A	average 1.50 m high	m²	0.30	6.25	-	-	6.25	6.88	-
1010105	**Cut down hedging and grub up roots; burn or deposit in skip; hedge height**								
1010105A	600 mm	m	1.97	41.07	-	-	41.07	45.18	-
1010105B	900 mm	m	2.63	54.84	-	-	54.84	60.32	-
1010105C	1200 mm	m	3.12	65.05	-	-	65.05	71.56	-
1010105D	1500 mm	m	4.27	89.03	-	-	89.03	97.93	-
1010105E	1800 mm	m	5.74	119.68	-	-	119.68	131.65	-
1010106	**Cut down trees, lop off branches and grub up roots; burn or deposit in skip; fill hole with excavated material; girth and dia**								
1010106A	450 mm girth 140 mm dia	Each	16.00	333.60	-	-	333.60	366.96	-
1010106B	900 mm girth 290 mm dia	Each	28.00	583.80	-	-	583.80	642.18	-
1010106C	1350 mm girth 430 mm dia	Each	42.00	875.70	-	-	875.70	963.27	-
1010106D	1800 mm girth 570 mm dia	Each	56.00	1,167.60	-	-	1,167.60	1,284.36	-
1010106E	2250 mm girth 720 mm dia	Each	69.00	1,438.65	-	-	1,438.65	1,582.52	-
1010106F	2700 mm girth 860 mm dia	Each	81.00	1,688.85	-	-	1,688.85	1,857.74	-
1010106G	3150 mm girth 1000 mm dia	Each	92.00	1,918.20	-	-	1,918.20	2,110.02	-
1010106H	3600 mm girth 1150 mm dia	Each	102.00	2,126.70	-	-	2,126.70	2,339.37	-
1010107	**Excavate top soil to be preserved; by hand; average depth**								
1010107A	150 mm	m²	0.64	13.34	-	-	13.34	14.67	-
1010107B	225 mm	m²	0.93	19.39	-	-	19.39	21.33	-
1010107C	300 mm	m²	1.26	26.27	-	-	26.27	28.90	-
1010108	**Excavate top soil to be preserved; by machine; average depth**								
1010108A	150 mm	m²	-	-	0.30	-	0.30	0.33	0.260
1010108B	225 mm	m²	-	-	0.30	-	0.30	0.33	0.260
1010108C	300 mm	m²	-	-	0.30	-	0.30	0.33	0.260
10102	**EXCAVATION BY HAND**								
1010201	**Excavate to reduce levels; maximum depth not exceeding 0.25 m**								
1010201A	loose soil	m³	2.63	54.84	-	-	54.84	60.32	-
1010201B	firm soil; sand	m³	3.15	65.68	-	-	65.68	72.25	-
1010201C	light clay; compact soil; gravel	m³	3.94	82.15	-	-	82.15	90.37	-
1010201D	stiff heavy clay	m³	5.25	109.46	-	-	109.46	120.41	-
1010201E	soft chalk	m³	7.88	164.30	-	-	164.30	180.73	-
1010202	**Excavate to reduce levels; maximum depth not exceeding 1.00 m**								
1010202A	loose soil	m³	2.71	56.50	-	-	56.50	62.15	-
1010202B	firm soil; sand	m³	3.25	67.76	-	-	67.76	74.54	-
1010202C	light clay; compact soil; gravel	m³	4.06	84.65	-	-	84.65	93.12	-

Small Works 2011		Unit	Labour Hours	Labour Net £	Plant Net £	Materials Net £	Unit Net £	Unit with 10% £	CO₂ Kg
101	**NEW WORK**								
10102	**EXCAVATION BY HAND**								
1010202	**Excavate to reduce levels; maximum depth not exceeding 1.00 m**								
1010202D	stiff heavy clay	m³	5.42	113.01	-	-	113.01	124.31	-
1010202E	soft chalk	m³	8.13	169.51	-	-	169.51	186.46	-
1010203	**Excavate to reduce levels; maximum depth not exceeding 2.00 m**								
1010203A	loose soil	m³	2.88	60.05	-	-	60.05	66.06	-
1010203B	firm soil; sand	m³	3.46	72.14	-	-	72.14	79.35	-
1010203C	light clay; compact soil; gravel	m³	4.33	90.28	-	-	90.28	99.31	-
1010203D	stiff heavy clay	m³	5.77	120.30	-	-	120.30	132.33	-
1010203E	soft chalk	m³	8.65	180.35	-	-	180.35	198.39	-
1010205	**Excavate for basement; maximum depth not exceeding 0.25 m**								
1010205A	loose soil	m³	2.63	54.84	-	-	54.84	60.32	-
1010205B	firm soil; sand	m³	3.15	65.68	-	-	65.68	72.25	-
1010205C	light clay; compact soil; gravel	m³	3.94	82.15	-	-	82.15	90.37	-
1010205D	stiff heavy clay	m³	5.25	109.46	-	-	109.46	120.41	-
1010205E	soft chalk	m³	7.88	164.30	-	-	164.30	180.73	-
1010206	**Excavate for basement; maximum depth not exceeding 1.00 m**								
1010206A	loose soil	m³	2.71	56.50	-	-	56.50	62.15	-
1010206B	firm soil; sand	m³	3.25	67.76	-	-	67.76	74.54	-
1010206C	light clay; compact soil; gravel	m³	4.06	84.65	-	-	84.65	93.12	-
1010206D	stiff heavy clay	m³	5.42	113.01	-	-	113.01	124.31	-
1010206E	soft chalk	m³	8.13	169.51	-	-	169.51	186.46	-
1010207	**Excavate for basement; maximum depth not exceeding 2.00 m**								
1010207A	loose soil	m³	3.37	70.26	-	-	70.26	77.29	-
1010207B	firm soil; sand	m³	4.04	84.23	-	-	84.23	92.65	-
1010207C	light clay; compact soil; gravel	m³	5.05	105.29	-	-	105.29	115.82	-
1010207D	stiff heavy clay	m³	6.73	140.32	-	-	140.32	154.35	-
1010207E	soft chalk	m³	10.10	210.59	-	-	210.59	231.65	-
1010209	**Excavate pit to receive bases of stanchions, isolated piers etc; maximum depth not exceeding 0.25 m**								
1010209A	loose soil	m³	2.71	56.50	-	-	56.50	62.15	-
1010209B	firm soil; sand	m³	3.25	67.76	-	-	67.76	74.54	-
1010209C	light clay; compact soil; gravel	m³	4.06	84.65	-	-	84.65	93.12	-
1010209D	stiff heavy clay	m³	5.42	113.01	-	-	113.01	124.31	-
1010209E	soft chalk	m³	8.13	169.51	-	-	169.51	186.46	-
1010210	**Excavate pit to receive bases of stanchions, isolated piers etc; maximum depth not exceeding 1.00 m**								
1010210A	loose soil	m³	2.97	61.92	-	-	61.92	68.11	-
1010210B	firm soil; sand	m³	3.56	74.23	-	-	74.23	81.65	-
1010210C	light clay; compact soil; gravel	m³	4.45	92.78	-	-	92.78	102.06	-
1010210D	stiff heavy clay	m³	5.93	123.64	-	-	123.64	136.00	-
1010210E	soft chalk	m³	8.90	185.57	-	-	185.57	204.13	-
1010211	**Excavate pit to receive bases of stanchions, isolated piers etc; maximum depth not exceeding 2.00 m**								
1010211A	loose soil	m³	3.72	77.56	-	-	77.56	85.32	-
1010211B	firm soil; sand	m³	4.46	92.99	-	-	92.99	102.29	-
1010211C	light clay; compact soil; gravel	m³	5.58	116.34	-	-	116.34	127.97	-
1010211D	stiff heavy clay	m³	7.43	154.92	-	-	154.92	170.41	-
1010211E	soft chalk	m³	11.15	232.48	-	-	232.48	255.73	-

Small Works 2011		Unit	Labour Hours	Labour Net £	Plant Net £	Materials Net £	Unit Net £	Unit with 10% £	CO2 Kg
101	**NEW WORK**								
10102	**EXCAVATION BY HAND**								
1010213	**Excavate trenches to receive foundations; exceeding 0.30 m in width; maximum depth not exceeding 0.25 m**								
1010213A	loose soil	m³	2.71	56.50	–	–	56.50	62.15	–
1010213B	firm soil; sand	m³	3.25	67.76	–	–	67.76	74.54	–
1010213C	light clay; compact soil; gravel	m³	4.06	84.65	–	–	84.65	93.12	–
1010213D	stiff heavy clay	m³	5.42	113.01	–	–	113.01	124.31	–
1010213E	soft chalk	m³	8.13	169.51	–	–	169.51	186.46	–
1010214	**Excavate trenches to receive foundations; exceeding 0.30 m in width; maximum depth not exceeding 1.00 m**								
1010214A	loose soil	m³	2.97	61.92	–	–	61.92	68.11	–
1010214B	firm soil; sand	m³	3.56	74.23	–	–	74.23	81.65	–
1010214C	light clay; compact soil; gravel	m³	4.45	92.78	–	–	92.78	102.06	–
1010214D	stiff heavy clay	m³	5.93	123.64	–	–	123.64	136.00	–
1010214E	soft chalk	m³	8.90	185.57	–	–	185.57	204.13	–
1010215	**Excavate trenches to receive foundations; exceeding 0.30 m in width; maximum depth not exceeding 2.00 m**								
1010215A	loose soil	m³	3.72	77.56	–	–	77.56	85.32	–
1010215B	firm soil; sand	m³	4.46	92.99	–	–	92.99	102.29	–
1010215C	light clay; compact soil; gravel	m³	5.58	116.34	–	–	116.34	127.97	–
1010215D	stiff heavy clay	m³	7.43	154.92	–	–	154.92	170.41	–
1010215E	soft chalk	m³	11.15	232.48	–	–	232.48	255.73	–
1010217	**Excavate trenches to receive foundations; not exceeding 0.30 m in width; maximum depth not exceeding 0.25 m**								
1010217A	loose soil	m³	0.28	5.84	–	–	5.84	6.42	–
1010217B	firm soil; sand	m³	0.34	7.09	–	–	7.09	7.80	–
1010217C	light clay; compact soil; gravel	m³	0.43	8.97	–	–	8.97	9.87	–
1010217D	stiff heavy clay	m³	0.57	11.88	–	–	11.88	13.07	–
1010217E	soft chalk	m³	0.85	17.72	–	–	17.72	19.49	–
1010218	**Excavate trenches to receive foundations; not exceeding 0.30 m in width; maximum depth not exceeding 0.50 m**								
1010218A	loose soil	m³	0.54	11.26	–	–	11.26	12.39	–
1010218B	firm soil; sand	m³	0.65	13.55	–	–	13.55	14.91	–
1010218C	light clay; compact soil; gravel	m³	0.81	16.89	–	–	16.89	18.58	–
1010218D	stiff heavy clay	m³	1.08	22.52	–	–	22.52	24.77	–
1010218E	soft chalk	m³	1.63	33.99	–	–	33.99	37.39	CO2
1010219	**Excavate trenches to receive foundations; not exceeding 0.30 m in width; maximum depth not exceeding 0.75 m**								
1010219A	loose soil	m³	0.78	16.26	–	–	16.26	17.89	–
1010219B	firm soil; sand	m³	0.93	19.39	–	–	19.39	21.33	–
1010219C	light clay; compact soil; gravel	m³	1.16	24.19	–	–	24.19	26.61	–
1010219D	stiff heavy clay	m³	1.55	32.32	–	–	32.32	35.55	–
1010219E	soft chalk	m³	2.33	48.58	–	–	48.58	53.44	–
1010220	**Excavate trenches to receive foundations; not exceeding 0.30 m in width; maximum depth not exceeding 1.00 m**								
1010220A	loose soil	m³	1.00	20.85	–	–	20.85	22.94	–
1010220B	firm soil; sand	m³	1.20	25.02	–	–	25.02	27.52	–
1010220C	light clay; compact soil; gravel	m³	1.50	31.28	–	–	31.28	34.41	–
1010220D	stiff heavy clay	m³	2.00	41.70	–	–	41.70	45.87	–
1010220E	soft chalk	m³	3.00	62.55	–	–	62.55	68.81	–

Small Works 2011		Unit	Labour Hours	Labour Net	Plant Net	Materials Net	Unit Net	Unit with 10%	CO₂
				£	£	£	£	£	Kg
101	**NEW WORK**								
10103	**EXCAVATION BY MACHINE**								
1010301	**Excavate to reduce levels; maximum depth not exceeding 0.25 m**								
1010301A	loose soil	m³	-	-	5.01	-	5.01	5.51	4.420
1010301B	firm soil; sand	m³	-	-	6.23	-	6.23	6.85	5.490
1010301C	light clay; compact soil; gravel	m³	-	-	7.68	-	7.68	8.45	6.770
1010301D	stiff heavy clay	m³	-	-	10.35	-	10.35	11.39	9.120
1010301E	soft chalk	m³	-	-	15.66	-	15.66	17.23	13.800
1010302	**Excavate to reduce levels; maximum depth not exceeding 1.00 m**								
1010302A	loose soil	m³	-	-	4.12	-	4.12	4.53	3.630
1010302B	firm soil; sand	m³	-	-	5.01	-	5.01	5.51	4.420
1010302C	light clay; compact soil; gravel	m³	-	-	6.23	-	6.23	6.85	5.490
1010302D	stiff heavy clay	m³	-	-	8.27	-	8.27	9.10	7.290
1010302E	soft chalk	m³	-	-	12.39	-	12.39	13.63	10.920
1010303	**Excavate to reduce levels; maximum depth not exceeding 2.00 m**								
1010303A	loose soil	m³	-	-	5.01	-	5.01	5.51	4.420
1010303B	firm soil; sand	m³	-	-	6.23	-	6.23	6.85	5.490
1010303C	light clay; compact soil; gravel	m³	-	-	7.68	-	7.68	8.45	6.770
1010303D	stiff heavy clay	m³	-	-	10.35	-	10.35	11.39	9.120
1010303E	soft chalk	m³	-	-	15.66	-	15.66	17.23	13.800
1010305	**Excavate for basement; maximum depth not exceeding 0.25 m**								
1010305A	loose soil	m³	-	-	5.90	-	5.90	6.49	5.200
1010305B	firm soil; sand	m³	-	-	7.09	-	7.09	7.80	6.250
1010305C	light clay; compact soil; gravel	m³	-	-	8.87	-	8.87	9.76	7.810
1010305D	stiff heavy clay	m³	-	-	11.83	-	11.83	13.01	10.430
1010305E	soft chalk	m³	-	-	18.03	-	18.03	19.83	15.890
1010306	**Excavate for basement; maximum depth not exceeding 1.00 m**								
1010306A	loose soil	m³	-	-	5.60	-	5.60	6.16	4.940
1010306B	firm soil; sand	m³	-	-	6.79	-	6.79	7.47	5.980
1010306C	light clay; compact soil; gravel	m³	-	-	8.27	-	8.27	9.10	7.290
1010306D	stiff heavy clay	m³	-	-	10.91	-	10.91	12.00	9.620
1010306E	soft chalk	m³	-	-	16.55	-	16.55	18.21	14.580
1010307	**Excavate for basement; maximum depth not exceeding 2.00 m**								
1010307A	loose soil	m³	-	-	5.90	-	5.90	6.49	5.200
1010307B	firm soil; sand	m³	-	-	7.09	-	7.09	7.80	6.250
1010307C	light clay; compact soil; gravel	m³	-	-	8.87	-	8.87	9.76	7.810
1010307D	stiff heavy clay	m³	-	-	11.83	-	11.83	13.01	10.430
1010307E	soft chalk	m³	-	-	18.03	-	18.03	19.83	15.890
1010309	**Excavate pit to receive bases of stanchions, isolated piers etc; maximum depth not exceeding 0.25 m**								
1010309A	loose soil	m³	-	-	8.27	-	8.27	9.10	7.290
1010309B	firm soil; sand	m³	-	-	10.02	-	10.02	11.02	8.830
1010309C	light clay; compact soil; gravel	m³	-	-	12.39	-	12.39	13.63	10.920
1010309D	stiff heavy clay	m³	-	-	16.55	-	16.55	18.21	14.580
1010309E	soft chalk	m³	-	-	25.12	-	25.12	27.63	22.130
1010310	**Excavate pit to receive bases of stanchions, isolated piers etc; maximum depth not exceeding 1.00 m**								
1010310A	loose soil	m³	-	-	6.49	-	6.49	7.14	5.720
1010310B	firm soil; sand	m³	-	-	7.98	-	7.98	8.78	7.030
1010310C	light clay; compact soil; gravel	m³	-	-	10.02	-	10.02	11.02	8.830
1010310D	stiff heavy clay	m³	-	-	13.28	-	13.28	14.61	11.710

Small Works 2011		Unit	Labour Hours	Labour Net	Plant Net	Materials Net	Unit Net	Unit with 10%	CO₂
				£	£	£	£	£	Kg
101	**NEW WORK**								
10103	**EXCAVATION BY MACHINE**								
1010310	**Excavate pit to receive bases of stanchions, isolated piers etc; maximum depth not exceeding 1.00 m**								
1010310E	soft chalk	m³	-	-	20.10	-	20.10	22.11	17.720
1010311	**Excavate pit to receive bases of stanchions, isolated piers etc; maximum depth not exceeding 2.00 m**								
1010311A	loose soil	m³	-	-	8.27	-	8.27	9.10	7.290
1010311B	firm soil; sand	m³	-	-	10.02	-	10.02	11.02	8.830
1010311C	light clay; compact soil; gravel	m³	-	-	12.39	-	12.39	13.63	10.920
1010311D	stiff heavy clay	m³	-	-	16.55	-	16.55	18.21	14.580
1010311E	soft chalk	m³	-	-	25.12	-	25.12	27.63	22.130
1010313	**Excavate trenches to receive foundations; exceeding 0.30 m in width; maximum depth not exceeding; 0.25 m**								
1010313A	loose soil	m³	-	-	5.01	-	5.01	5.51	4.420
1010313B	firm soil; sand	m³	-	-	6.23	-	6.23	6.85	5.490
1010313C	light clay; compact soil; gravel	m³	-	-	7.68	-	7.68	8.45	6.770
1010313D	stiff heavy clay	m³	-	-	10.35	-	10.35	11.39	9.120
1010313E	soft chalk	m³	-	-	15.66	-	15.66	17.23	13.800
1010314	**Excavate trenches to receive foundations; exceeding 0.30 m in width; maximum depth not exceeding; 1.00 m**								
1010314A	loose soil	m³	-	-	4.12	-	4.12	4.53	3.630
1010314B	firm soil; sand	m³	-	-	5.01	-	5.01	5.51	4.420
1010314C	light clay; compact soil; gravel	m³	-	-	6.23	-	6.23	6.85	5.490
1010314D	stiff heavy clay	m³	-	-	8.27	-	8.27	9.10	7.290
1010314E	soft chalk	m³	-	-	12.39	-	12.39	13.63	10.920
1010315	**Excavate trenches to receive foundations; exceeding 0.30 m in width; maximum depth not exceeding; 2.00 m**								
1010315A	loose soil	m³	-	-	5.01	-	5.01	5.51	4.420
1010315B	firm soil; sand	m³	-	-	6.23	-	6.23	6.85	5.490
1010315C	light clay; compact soil; gravel	m³	-	-	7.68	-	7.68	8.45	6.770
1010315D	stiff heavy clay	m³	-	-	16.55	-	16.55	18.21	14.580
1010315E	soft chalk	m³	-	-	25.12	-	25.12	27.63	22.130
1010317	**Excavate trenches to receive foundations; not exceeding 0.30 m in width; maximum depth not exceeding; 0.25 m**								
1010317A	loose soil	m³	-	-	3.53	-	3.53	3.88	3.110
1010317B	firm soil; sand	m³	-	-	4.42	-	4.42	4.86	3.890
1010317C	light clay; compact soil; gravel	m³	-	-	5.34	-	5.34	5.87	4.700
1010317D	stiff heavy clay	m³	-	-	7.09	-	7.09	7.80	6.250
1010317E	soft chalk	m³	-	-	10.65	-	10.65	11.72	9.380
1010318	**Excavate trenches to receive foundations; not exceeding 0.30 m in width; maximum depth not exceeding; 0.50 m**								
1010318A	loose soil	m³	-	-	5.90	-	5.90	6.49	5.200
1010318B	firm soil; sand	m³	-	-	7.09	-	7.09	7.80	6.250
1010318C	light clay; compact soil; gravel	m³	-	-	8.87	-	8.87	9.76	7.810
1010318D	stiff heavy clay	m³	-	-	11.83	-	11.83	13.01	10.430
1010318E	soft chalk	m³	-	-	18.03	-	18.03	19.83	15.890
1010319	**Excavate trenches to receive foundations; not exceeding 0.30 m in width; maximum depth not exceeding; 0.75 m**								
1010319A	loose soil	m³	-	-	8.27	-	8.27	9.10	7.290
1010319B	firm soil; sand	m³	-	-	10.02	-	10.02	11.02	8.830
1010319C	light clay; compact soil; gravel	m³	-	-	12.39	-	12.39	13.63	10.920

Excavation, Earthwork and Concrete Work

Small Works 2011		Unit	Labour Hours	Labour Net	Plant Net	Materials Net	Unit Net	Unit with 10%	CO_2
				£	£	£	£	£	Kg
101	**NEW WORK**								
10103	**EXCAVATION BY MACHINE**								
1010319	**Excavate trenches to receive foundations; not exceeding 0.30 m in width; maximum depth not exceeding; 0.75 m**								
1010319D	stiff heavy clay	m³	-	-	16.55	-	16.55	18.21	14.580
1010319E	soft chalk	m³	-	-	25.12	-	25.12	27.63	22.130
1010320	**Excavate trenches to receive foundations; not exceeding 0.30 m in width; maximum depth not exceeding; 1.00 m**								
1010320A	loose soil	m³	-	-	10.65	-	10.65	11.72	9.380
1010320B	firm soil; sand	m³	-	-	12.99	-	12.99	14.29	11.440
1010320C	light clay; compact soil; gravel	m³	-	-	16.25	-	16.25	17.88	14.320
1010320D	stiff heavy clay	m³	-	-	21.59	-	21.59	23.75	19.020
1010320E	soft chalk	m³	-	-	32.20	-	32.20	35.42	28.380
10104	**BREAKING UP BY HAND**								
1010401	**Extra over excavation for breaking up**								
1010401A	brickwork in lime mortar	m³	4.00	83.40	-	-	83.40	91.74	-
1010401B	brickwork in cement mortar	m³	5.33	111.13	-	-	111.13	122.24	-
1010401C	concrete	m³	8.00	166.80	-	-	166.80	183.48	-
1010401D	reinforced concrete	m³	10.00	208.50	-	-	208.50	229.35	-
1010401E	semi-hard rock (sandstone etc)	m³	7.50	156.38	-	-	156.38	172.02	-
10105	**BREAKING UP BY MACHINE**								
1010501	**Extra over excavation for breaking up using compressed air equipment**								
1010501A	concrete average thickness; 150 mm	m²	0.17	3.54	2.50	-	6.04	6.64	11.780
1010501B	concrete average thickness; 300 mm	m²	0.50	10.43	7.35	-	17.78	19.56	34.700
1010501C	reinforced concrete average thickness; 150 mm	m²	0.25	5.21	3.68	-	8.89	9.78	17.350
1010501D	reinforced concrete average thickness; 300 mm	m²	0.75	15.64	11.03	-	26.67	29.34	52.050
1010501E	brickwork in lime mortar	m³	0.50	10.43	7.35	-	17.78	19.56	34.700
1010501F	brickwork in cement mortar	m³	0.67	13.97	9.85	-	23.82	26.20	46.480
1010501G	concrete	m³	3.35	69.85	49.30	-	119.15	131.07	232.590
1010501H	reinforced concrete	m³	5.00	104.25	73.57	-	177.82	195.60	347.150
1010501I	semi-hard rock (sandstone etc)	m³	2.60	54.21	38.26	-	92.47	101.72	180.540
10106	**EARTHWORK SUPPORT**								
1010601	**Earthwork support in firm ground to opposing faces not exceeding 2.00 m apart; maximum depth not exceeding**								
1010601A	1.00 m	m²	0.64	13.34	-	2.61	15.95	17.55	1.320
1010601B	2.00 m	m²	0.70	14.60	-	2.88	17.48	19.23	1.460
1010602	**Earthwork support in loose ground to opposing faces not exceeding 2.00 m apart; maximum depth not exceeding**								
1010602A	1.00 m	m²	4.98	103.83	-	20.66	124.49	136.94	10.460
1010602B	2.00 m	m²	4.98	103.83	-	20.66	124.49	136.94	10.460
10107	**DISPOSAL OF EXCAVATED MATERIAL**								
1010701	**Fill barrows; deposit**								
1010701A	wheel up to 20 m	m³	1.00	20.85	-	-	20.85	22.94	-
1010701B	add; wheel each additional 20 m	m³	0.45	9.38	-	-	9.38	10.32	-

Small Works 2011		Unit	Labour Hours	Labour Net	Plant Net	Materials Net	Unit Net	Unit with 10%	CO$_2$
				£	£	£	£	£	Kg
101	**NEW WORK**								
10107	**DISPOSAL OF EXCAVATED MATERIAL**								
1010702	Excavated material moved by hand from spoil heap or side of excavations; deposit in skip ; average distance from spoil heap or excavation								
1010702A	25 m	m^3	3.78	78.81	-	-	78.81	86.69	-
1010702B	50 m	m^3	4.40	91.74	-	-	91.74	100.91	-
1010703	Hand loading; transporting; depositing in spoil heaps; average distance from excavation								
1010703A	25 m	m^3	3.78	78.81	-	-	78.81	86.69	-
1010703B	50 m	m^3	4.40	91.74	-	-	91.74	100.91	-
1010704	Hire of skip; delivery to site; removing when full; disposal of contents; payment of tipping charges skip size								
1010704A	4.5 m^3	m^3	-	-	33.60	-	33.60	36.96	-
1010705	Excavated material loaded from spoil heaps or side of excavation into lorry and cart to contractor's tip								
1010705A	by hand	m^3	1.75	36.49	24.02	-	60.51	66.56	1.740
1010705B	by machine	m^3	-	-	26.98	-	26.98	29.68	4.350
10108	**FILLING**								
1010801	Excavated material as filling to excavations; by hand; deposited; compacted								
1010801A	in 250 mm layers	m^3	1.50	31.28	-	-	31.28	34.41	-
1010802	Excavated material as filling in making up levels; by hand; wheeling average 25 m; deposited; compacted; thickness								
1010802A	over 250 mm	m^3	2.20	45.87	-	-	45.87	50.46	-
1010802B	average 100 mm	m^2	0.36	7.51	-	-	7.51	8.26	-
1010802C	average 150 mm	m^2	0.46	9.59	-	-	9.59	10.55	-
1010802D	average 200 mm	m^2	0.55	11.47	-	-	11.47	12.62	-
1010803	Imported soil filling to make up levels by hand; wheel average 25 m; deposited; compacted; thickness								
1010803A	over 250 mm	m^3	1.30	27.11	-	19.91	47.02	51.72	53.390
1010803B	average 100 mm	m^2	0.17	3.54	-	2.00	5.54	6.09	5.360
1010803C	average 150 mm	m^2	0.26	5.42	-	2.99	8.41	9.25	8.020
1010803D	average 200 mm	m^2	0.35	7.30	-	3.98	11.28	12.41	10.680
1010804	Imported hardcore filling to make up levels; by hand; wheel average 25 m; deposited; compacted; thickness								
1010804A	over 250 mm	m^3	2.70	56.30	-	24.80	81.10	89.21	15.430
1010804B	average 75 mm	m^2	0.27	5.63	-	1.87	7.50	8.25	1.160
1010804C	average 100 mm	m^2	0.36	7.51	-	2.48	9.99	10.99	1.550
1010804D	average 150 mm	m^2	0.54	11.26	-	3.73	14.99	16.49	2.320
1010804E	average 200 mm	m^2	0.72	15.01	-	4.97	19.98	21.98	3.090
1010805	Hand packing hardcore to form vertical or battering faces; thickness								
1010805A	over 250 mm	m^2	1.26	26.27	-	-	26.27	28.90	-
1010805B	average 100 mm	m	0.20	4.17	-	-	4.17	4.59	-
1010805C	average 150 mm	m	0.30	6.25	-	-	6.25	6.88	-
1010805D	average 200 mm	m	0.34	7.09	-	-	7.09	7.80	-

Excavation, Earthwork and Concrete Work

Small Works 2011		Unit	Labour Hours	Labour Net	Plant Net	Materials Net	Unit Net	Unit with 10%	CO₂
				£	£	£	£	£	Kg
101	**NEW WORK**								
10109	**SURFACE TREATMENTS**								
1010901	**Level and compact**								
1010901A	bottoms of excavation	m²	0.12	2.50	-	-	2.50	2.75	-
1010902	**Grade and compact bottom of excavation or surface of filling to**								
1010902A	falls	m²	0.15	3.13	-	-	3.13	3.44	-
1010902B	crossfalls	m²	0.27	5.63	-	-	5.63	6.19	-
1010903	**Blind surfaces of soil or hardcore filling with sand; thickness**								
1010903A	25 mm	m²	0.10	2.09	-	0.81	2.90	3.19	0.190
1010903B	50 mm	m²	0.14	2.92	-	1.62	4.54	4.99	0.380
1010904	**Blind surfaces of soil or hardcore filling with ash; thickness**								
1010904A	25 mm	m²	0.12	2.50	-	0.65	3.15	3.47	0.630
1010904B	50 mm	m²	0.16	3.34	-	1.29	4.63	5.09	1.270
10110	**CONCRETE WORK**								
1011001	**Concrete (1:3:6) in**								
1011001A	foundation trench	m³	4.50	93.83	-	117.44	211.27	232.40	293.070
1011001B	bed, spread over site, and levelled 100 mm thick	m³	7.50	156.38	-	117.44	273.82	301.20	293.070
1011001C	bed, spread over site, and levelled 150 mm thick	m³	7.00	145.95	-	117.44	263.39	289.73	293.070
1011001D	bed, spread over site, and levelled 300 mm thick	m³	5.00	104.25	-	117.44	221.69	243.86	293.070
1011002	**Concrete (1:2:4) in**								
1011002A	foundation trench	m³	4.50	93.83	-	123.47	217.30	239.03	393.810
1011002B	treads, risers and landings (formwork measured separately)	m³	5.25	109.46	-	123.47	232.93	256.22	393.810
1011002C	isolated pier holes	m³	5.40	112.59	-	123.47	236.06	259.67	393.810
1011002D	small quantities to hearths (including formwork) 125 mm thick	m²	3.00	62.55	-	16.07	78.62	86.48	51.270
1011003	**Fill cavity with fine concrete**								
1011003A	50 mm	m²	0.65	13.55	-	6.76	20.31	22.34	21.550
1011004	**Labour tamped finish surface of unset concrete to**								
1011004A	levels	m²	0.15	3.13	-	-	3.13	3.44	-
1011004B	falls	m²	0.16	3.34	-	-	3.34	3.67	-
1011004C	crossfalls	m²	0.18	3.75	-	-	3.75	4.13	-
1011004D	cambers	m²	0.19	3.96	-	-	3.96	4.36	-
1011004E	slopes	m²	0.16	3.34	-	-	3.34	3.67	-
1011005	**Labour spade finish surface of unset concrete to**								
1011005A	levels	m²	0.22	4.59	-	-	4.59	5.05	-
1011005B	falls	m²	0.25	5.21	-	-	5.21	5.73	-
1011005C	crossfalls	m²	0.29	6.05	-	-	6.05	6.66	-
1011005D	cambers	m²	0.32	6.67	-	-	6.67	7.34	-
1011005E	slopes	m²	0.25	5.21	-	-	5.21	5.73	-
1011006	**Labour trowelled finish surface of unset concrete to**								
1011006A	levels	m²	0.29	6.05	-	-	6.05	6.66	-
1011006B	falls	m²	0.34	7.09	-	-	7.09	7.80	-
1011006C	crossfalls	m²	0.41	8.55	-	-	8.55	9.41	-
1011006D	cambers	m²	0.45	9.38	-	-	9.38	10.32	-
1011006E	slopes	m²	0.34	7.09	-	-	7.09	7.80	-
1011007	**Labour power floating finish surface of unset concrete to**								
1011007A	levels	m²	0.24	5.00	0.78	-	5.78	6.36	1.440
1011007B	falls	m²	0.27	5.63	0.88	-	6.51	7.16	1.620
1011007C	crossfalls	m²	0.32	6.67	1.04	-	7.71	8.48	1.920
1011007D	cambers	m²	0.35	7.30	1.14	-	8.44	9.28	2.100

Small Works 2011		Unit	Labour Hours	Labour Net	Plant Net	Materials Net	Unit Net	Unit with 10%	CO$_2$
				£	£	£	£	£	Kg
101	**NEW WORK**								
10110	**CONCRETE WORK**								
1011007	**Labour power floating finish surface of unset concrete to**								
1011007E	slopes	m^2	0.27	5.63	0.88	-	6.51	7.16	1.620
1011008	**Extra for working concrete around**								
1011008A	pipes or cables	m^2	0.20	4.17	-	-	4.17	4.59	-
1011010	**Carborundum non-slip grain surfacing to**								
1011010A	concrete steps etc	m^2	0.25	5.21	-	1.23	6.44	7.08	0.080
1011011	**Sizalcraft building sheets and laying**								
1011011A	under concrete floors	m^2	0.04	0.83	-	1.83	2.66	2.93	2.770
1011012	**Polythene building film and laying**								
1011012A	under concrete floors	m^2	0.04	0.83	-	1.09	1.92	2.11	5.880
1011013	**Treat concrete floors with three applications of**								
1011013A	silicate of soda solution	m^2	0.10	2.09	-	-	2.09	2.30	-
1011014	**Groove in concrete for and including galvanised steel water bar**								
1011014A	25 mm x 6 mm	m	0.75	15.64	-	7.43	23.07	25.38	2.770
1011015	**Groove including pinning lugs for**								
1011015A	sliding door track (track fittings measured separately)	m	0.55	11.47	-	-	11.47	12.62	-
1011016	**Hack face of concrete for key**								
1011016A	by hand	m^2	0.50	10.43	-	-	10.43	11.47	-
1011016B	by machine	m^2	0.25	5.21	0.79	-	6.00	6.60	-
1011017	**Bitumen expansion joint 9 mm**								
1011017A	100 mm deep seal top edge	m	0.50	10.43	-	3.04	13.47	14.82	3.270
1011018	**Form holes for pipes through 100 mm concrete and make good**								
1011018A	small	Each	0.30	6.25	-	-	6.25	6.88	-
1011018B	large	Each	0.35	7.30	-	-	7.30	8.03	-
1011019	**Form hole for pipes through 150 mm concrete and make good**								
1011019A	small	Each	0.35	7.30	-	-	7.30	8.03	-
1011019B	large	Each	0.38	7.92	-	-	7.92	8.71	-
1011020	**Form mortices in concrete for iron dowels and ragbolts and grout in**								
1011020A	100 mm deep	Each	0.50	10.43	-	0.43	10.86	11.95	0.750
1011021	**Grouting in**								
1011021A	foundation bolts and stanchion bases	Each	0.50	10.43	-	0.86	11.29	12.42	1.500
10111	**READY-MIXED PLAIN CONCRETE**								
1011101	**Foundations**								
1011101A	exceeding 300 mm thick	m^3	3.00	62.55	-	118.21	180.76	198.84	396.860
1011101B	not exceeding 300 mm thick	m^3	3.30	68.81	-	118.21	187.02	205.72	396.860
1011102	**Floors or oversite concrete**								
1011102A	100 mm thick	m^3	6.00	125.10	-	118.21	243.31	267.64	396.860
1011102B	150 mm thick	m^3	5.50	114.68	-	118.21	232.89	256.18	396.860
1011102C	300 mm thick	m^3	4.80	100.08	-	118.21	218.29	240.12	396.860

Excavation, Earthwork and Concrete Work

	Unit	Labour Hours	Labour Net £	Plant Net £	Materials Net £	Unit Net £	Unit with 10% £	CO₂ Kg

	Unit	Labour Hours	Labour Net £	Plant Net £	Materials Net £	Unit Net £	Unit with 10% £	CO_2 Kg
101 **NEW WORK**								
10112 **READY-MIXED REINFORCED CONCRETE (REINFORCEMENT AND FORMWORK MEASURED SEPARATELY)**								
1011201 **Foundations**								
1011201A exceeding 300 mm thick	m³	4.00	83.40	-	118.21	201.61	221.77	396.860
1011202 **Suspended floors or roofs**								
1011202A 100 mm thick	m³	7.50	156.38	-	118.21	274.59	302.05	396.860
1011202B 150 mm thick	m³	7.00	145.95	-	118.21	264.16	290.58	396.860
1011202C 300 mm thick	m³	6.00	125.10	-	118.21	243.31	267.64	396.860
1011203 **Walls**								
1011203A 100 mm thick	m³	8.00	166.80	-	118.21	285.01	313.51	396.860
1011203B 150 mm thick	m³	7.50	156.38	-	118.21	274.59	302.05	396.860
1011203C 300 mm thick	m³	6.50	135.53	-	118.21	253.74	279.11	396.860
1011204 **Columns; sectional area**								
1011204A not exceeding 0.05 sq.m	m³	10.00	208.50	-	118.21	326.71	359.38	396.860
1011204B 0.05 sq.m - 0.10 sq.m	m³	9.00	187.65	-	118.21	305.86	336.45	396.860
1011204C exceeding 0.10 sq.m	m³	8.00	166.80	-	118.21	285.01	313.51	396.860
1011205 **Beams; sectional area**								
1011205A not exceeding 0.05 sq.m	m³	9.00	187.65	-	118.21	305.86	336.45	396.860
1011205B 0.05 sq.m - 0.10 sq.m	m³	8.00	166.80	-	118.21	285.01	313.51	396.860
1011205C exceeding 0.10 sq.m	m³	7.00	145.95	-	118.21	264.16	290.58	396.860
10113 **SAWN SOFTWOOD FORMWORK**								
1011301 **Horizontal soffit to floors, landings and the like**								
1011301A first use	m²	2.70	75.06	-	6.06	81.12	89.23	7.400
1011301B each subsequent use	m²	2.70	75.06	-	0.11	75.17	82.69	0.140
1011302 **Sloping soffit of floors, roofs, staircases and the like**								
1011302A first use	m²	3.60	100.08	-	6.06	106.14	116.75	7.400
1011302B each subsequent use	m²	3.60	100.08	-	0.11	100.19	110.21	0.140
1011303 **Vertical or battering sides of foundations, ground beams, large machine bases and the like**								
1011303A first use	m²	3.45	95.91	-	2.02	97.93	107.72	2.470
1011303B each subsequent use	m²	3.45	95.91	-	0.11	96.02	105.62	0.140
1011304 **Vertical or battering sides of walls, solid balustrades and the like**								
1011304A first use	m²	3.45	95.91	-	6.06	101.97	112.17	7.400
1011304B each subsequent use	m²	3.45	95.91	-	0.11	96.02	105.62	0.140
1011305 **Vertical or battering sides of stanchion casings, columns, piers, pilasters and the like**								
1011305A first use	m²	3.60	100.08	-	5.85	105.93	116.52	7.140
1011305B each subsequent use	m²	3.60	100.08	-	0.11	100.19	110.21	0.140
1011306 **Sides and soffits of openings in walls, recesses in walls, projecting panels on walls and the like**								
1011306A first use	m²	3.60	100.08	-	6.06	106.14	116.75	7.400
1011306B each subsequent use	m²	3.60	100.08	-	0.11	100.19	110.21	0.140
1011308 **Sides and soffits of horizontal beam casings, beams, lintels and the like**								
1011308A first use	m²	3.90	108.42	-	6.06	114.48	125.93	7.400
1011308B each subsequent use	m²	3.90	108.42	-	0.11	108.53	119.38	0.140

Small Works 2011		Unit	Labour Hours	Labour Net	Plant Net	Materials Net	Unit Net	Unit with 10%	CO$_2$
				£	£	£	£	£	Kg
101	**NEW WORK**								
10113	**SAWN SOFTWOOD FORMWORK**								
1011309	**Sides and soffits of sloping beam casings, staircase strings and the like**								
1011309A	first use	m^2	4.65	129.27	-	6.06	135.33	148.86	7.400
1011309B	each subsequent use	m^2	4.65	129.27	-	0.11	129.38	142.32	0.140
1011310	**Sloping upper surface of beam casings, beams, staircase strings and the like; exceeding 15 deg from the horizontal**								
1011310A	first use	m^2	3.90	108.42	-	6.06	114.48	125.93	7.400
1011310B	each subsequent use	m^2	3.90	108.42	-	0.11	108.53	119.38	0.140
1011311	**Isolated beam casings and isolated beams**								
1011311A	first use	m^2	4.20	116.76	-	6.06	122.82	135.10	7.400
1011311B	each subsequent use	m^2	4.20	116.76	-	0.11	116.87	128.56	0.140
1011312	**Edges or faces of beds and the like not exceeding 250 mm high**								
1011312A	first use	m	0.38	10.56	-	0.49	11.05	12.16	0.600
1011312B	each subsequent use	m	0.38	10.56	-	0.03	10.59	11.65	0.030
1011313	**Edges of suspended floors, landings, roofs and the like not exceeding 250 mm wide**								
1011313A	first use	m	0.75	20.85	-	1.53	22.38	24.62	1.870
1011313B	each subsequent use	m	0.75	20.85	-	0.06	20.91	23.00	0.070
1011314	**Sides of kerbs and upstands and the like not exceeding 250 mm high**								
1011314A	first use	m	0.68	18.90	-	0.49	19.39	21.33	0.600
1011314B	each subsequent use	m	0.68	18.90	-	0.06	18.96	20.86	0.070
1011315	**Risers of steps and staircases not exceeding 250 mm wide**								
1011315A	first use	m	0.60	16.68	-	1.53	18.21	20.03	1.870
1011315B	each subsequent use	m	0.60	16.68	-	0.06	16.74	18.41	0.070
1011316	**Edges and soffits of projecting eaves not exceeding 600 mm girth**								
1011316A	first use	m	2.25	62.55	-	3.69	66.24	72.86	4.510
1011316B	each subsequent use	m	2.25	62.55	-	0.06	62.61	68.87	0.070
1011317	**Projecting or sunk cornices, bands and the like not exceeding 250 mm girth**								
1011317A	first use	m	0.60	16.68	-	1.53	18.21	20.03	1.870
1011317B	each subsequent use	m	0.60	16.68	-	0.06	16.74	18.41	0.070
1011318	**Throats, grooves, chases, rebates, chamfers and the like not exceeding 100 mm wide**								
1011318A	first use	m	0.20	5.56	-	0.63	6.19	6.81	0.770
1011318B	each subsequent use	m	0.20	5.56	-	0.07	5.63	6.19	0.090
1011319	**Labours on formwork**								
1011319A	raking cutting	m	0.20	5.56	-	0.21	5.77	6.35	0.260
1011319B	curved cutting	m	0.65	18.07	-	0.49	18.56	20.42	0.600
10114	**PLYWOOD FORMWORK**								
1011401	**Horizontal soffit of floors, landings and the like**								
1011401A	first use	m^2	2.84	78.95	-	16.56	95.51	105.06	4.550
1011401B	each subsequent use	m^2	2.84	78.95	-	0.24	79.19	87.11	0.240
1011402	**Sloping soffit of floors, roofs, staircases and the like**								
1011402A	first use	m^2	3.74	103.97	-	16.56	120.53	132.58	4.550
1011402B	each subsequent use	m^2	3.74	103.97	-	0.24	104.21	114.63	0.240

Small Works 2011		Unit	Labour Hours	Labour Net	Plant Net	Materials Net	Unit Net	Unit with 10%	CO₂
				£	£	£	£	£	Kg
101	**NEW WORK**								
10114	**PLYWOOD FORMWORK**								
1011403	**Vertical or battering sides of foundations, ground beams, large machine bases and the like**								
1011403A	first use	m²	3.59	99.80	-	14.12	113.92	125.31	4.000
1011403B	each subsequent use	m²	2.39	66.44	-	0.24	66.68	73.35	0.240
1011404	**Vertical or battering sides of walls, solid balustrades and the like**								
1011404A	first use	m²	3.59	99.80	-	14.12	113.92	125.31	4.000
1011404B	each subsequent use	m²	2.39	66.44	-	0.22	66.66	73.33	0.220
1011405	**Vertical or battering sides of stanchion casings, columns, piers, pilasters and the like**								
1011405A	first use	m²	3.74	103.97	-	14.12	118.09	129.90	4.000
1011405B	each subsequent use	m²	2.54	70.61	-	0.15	70.76	77.84	0.150
1011406	**Sides and soffits of openings in walls, recesses in walls, projecting panels on walls and the like**								
1011406A	first use	m²	3.74	103.97	-	14.46	118.43	130.27	4.100
1011406B	each subsequent use	m²	3.74	103.97	-	0.24	104.21	114.63	0.240
1011408	**Sides and soffits of horizontal beam casings, beams, lintels and the like**								
1011408A	first use	m²	4.04	112.31	-	14.12	126.43	139.07	4.000
1011408B	each subsequent use	m²	2.84	78.95	-	0.24	79.19	87.11	0.240
1011409	**Sides and soffits of sloping beam casings, staircase strings and the like**								
1011409A	first use	m²	4.79	133.16	-	14.12	147.28	162.01	4.000
1011409B	each subsequent use	m²	3.29	91.46	-	0.24	91.70	100.87	0.240
1011410	**Sloping upper surface of beam casings, beams, staircase strings and the like, exceeding 15 deg from the horizontal**								
1011410A	first use	m²	4.04	112.31	-	14.12	126.43	139.07	4.000
1011410B	each subsequent use	m²	2.84	78.95	-	0.24	79.19	87.11	0.240
1011411	**Isolated beam casings and isolated beams**								
1011411A	first use	m²	4.34	120.65	-	14.12	134.77	148.25	4.000
1011411B	each subsequent use	m²	3.14	87.29	-	0.24	87.53	96.28	0.240
1011412	**Edges or faces of beds and the like not exceeding 250 mm high**								
1011412A	first use	m	0.38	10.56	-	1.79	12.35	13.59	0.860
1011412B	each subsequent use	m	0.38	10.56	-	0.06	10.62	11.68	0.060
1011413	**Edges of suspended floors, landings, roofs and the like not exceeding 250 mm wide**								
1011413A	first use	m	0.75	20.85	-	3.62	24.47	26.92	1.030
1011413B	each subsequent use	m	0.75	20.85	-	0.07	20.92	23.01	0.070
1011414	**Sides of kerbs and upstands and the like not exceeding 250 mm high**								
1011414A	first use	m	0.68	18.90	-	1.75	20.65	22.72	0.840
1011414B	each subsequent use	m	0.68	18.90	-	0.07	18.97	20.87	0.070
1011415	**Risers of steps and staircases not exceeding 250 mm wide**								
1011415A	first use	m	0.60	16.68	-	3.87	20.55	22.61	1.100
1011415B	each subsequent use	m	0.60	16.68	-	0.07	16.75	18.43	0.070

Small Works 2011		Unit	Labour Hours	Labour Net	Plant Net	Materials Net	Unit Net	Unit with 10%	CO$_2$
				£	£	£	£	£	Kg
101	**NEW WORK**								
10114	**PLYWOOD FORMWORK**								
1011416	**Edges and soffits of projecting eaves not exceeding 600 mm girth**								
1011416A	first use	m	2.25	62.55	-	9.30	71.85	79.04	2.630
1011416B	each subsequent use	m	2.25	62.55	-	0.14	62.69	68.96	0.140
1011417	**Projecting or sunk cornices, bands and the like not exceeding 250 mm girth**								
1011417A	first use	m	0.60	16.68	-	3.87	20.55	22.61	1.100
1011417B	each subsequent use	m	0.60	16.68	-	0.07	16.75	18.43	0.070
1011418	**Throats, grooves, chases, rebates, chamfers and the like not exceeding 100 mm wide**								
1011418A	first use	m	0.20	5.56	-	1.44	7.00	7.70	0.410
1011418B	each subsequent use	m	0.20	5.56	-	0.03	5.59	6.15	0.030
1011419	**Labours on formwork**								
1011419A	raking cutting	m	0.20	5.56	-	1.68	7.24	7.96	0.480
1011419B	curved cutting	m	0.65	18.07	-	3.36	21.43	23.57	0.950
10115	**REINFORCEMENT**								
1011501	**Plain round mild steel bar reinforcement; BS 449; supplied, cut, bent, labelled and fixed including tying wire, distance blocks and ordinary spacers**								
1011501A	6 mm	m	0.12	3.34	-	0.24	3.58	3.94	0.510
1011501B	8 mm	m	0.10	2.78	-	0.39	3.17	3.49	0.900
1011501C	10 mm	m	0.09	2.50	-	0.59	3.09	3.40	1.410
1011501D	12 mm	m	0.08	2.22	-	0.80	3.02	3.32	2.030
1011501E	16 mm	m	0.07	1.95	-	1.42	3.37	3.71	3.610
1011501F	20 mm	m	0.07	1.95	-	2.06	4.01	4.41	5.630
1011501G	25 mm	m	0.07	1.95	-	3.11	5.06	5.57	8.800
1011502	**Mild steel bar links, stirrups and binders; cut, bent, labelled and fixed including tying wire and special spacers**								
1011502A	6 mm	m	0.14	3.89	-	0.24	4.13	4.54	0.510
1011502B	8 mm	m	0.12	3.34	-	0.39	3.73	4.10	0.900
1011503	**Fabric reinforcement; BS 4483; in slabs including tying wire and distance blocks, with allowance for 200 mm laps**								
1011503A	A98	m^2	0.14	3.89	-	1.46	5.35	5.89	3.640
1011503B	A142	m^2	0.14	3.89	-	1.90	5.79	6.37	5.250
1011503C	A193	m^2	0.14	3.89	-	2.58	6.47	7.12	7.140
1011503D	A252	m^2	0.16	4.45	-	3.35	7.80	8.58	9.340
1011503E	A393	m^2	0.18	5.00	-	5.32	10.32	11.35	14.560
1011503F	B283	m^2	0.14	3.89	-	3.30	7.19	7.91	8.820
1011503G	B385	m^2	0.16	4.45	-	3.90	8.35	9.19	10.710
1011503H	B503	m^2	0.18	5.00	-	5.16	10.16	11.18	14.020
1011503I	B785	m^2	0.20	5.56	-	7.04	12.60	13.86	19.240
1011503J	C283	m^2	0.14	3.89	-	2.38	6.27	6.90	6.170
1011503K	C385	m^2	0.14	3.89	-	3.07	6.96	7.66	8.060
1011503L	C503	m^2	0.16	4.45	-	3.79	8.24	9.06	10.260
1011504	**Fabric reinforcement; BS 4483; in casings to steel columns and beams including bending tying wire and distance blocks, with allowance for 200 mm laps**								
1011504A	D49	m^2	0.30	8.34	-	1.20	9.54	10.49	1.820
1011504B	D98	m^2	0.35	9.73	-	1.46	11.19	12.31	3.640

Small Works 2011		Unit	Labour Hours	Labour Net £	Plant Net £	Materials Net £	Unit Net £	Unit with 10% £	CO₂ Kg
101	**NEW WORK**								
10116	**PRECAST CONCRETE**								
1011601	**Copings; weathered and throated; bedded in gauged mortar; pointed**								
1011601A	300 mm x 75 mm	m	0.50	24.42	-	9.39	33.81	37.19	12.600
1011601B	356 mm x 75 mm	m	0.85	41.55	-	11.89	53.44	58.78	14.890
1011602	**Jambs and heads; bedded in gauged mortar; pointed**								
1011602A	100 mm x 75 mm	m	0.20	9.78	-	8.32	18.10	19.91	5.630
1011602B	225 mm x 75 mm	m	0.28	13.43	-	9.06	22.49	24.74	11.180
1011602C	350 mm x 75 mm	m	0.38	18.34	-	12.86	31.20	34.32	17.210
1011603	**cills; weathered; throated; grooved; bedded in gauged mortar; pointed**								
1011603A	225 mm x 75 mm	m	0.30	14.64	-	9.06	23.70	26.07	11.180
1011603B	275 mm x 100 mm	m	0.33	15.86	-	10.83	26.69	29.36	18.010
1011603C	275 mm x 150 mm	m	0.38	18.34	-	12.86	31.20	34.32	26.860
1011604	**Thresholds; weathered; bedded in gauged mortar; pointed**								
1011604A	275 mm x 75 mm	m	0.28	13.43	-	12.86	26.29	28.92	13.590
1011605	**Duct covers; placed in floor rebates**								
1011605A	300 mm x 50 mm	m	0.06	2.92	-	6.93	9.85	10.84	8.180
1011605B	300 mm x 63 mm	m	0.06	2.92	-	8.31	11.23	12.35	10.310
1011605C	300 mm x 75 mm	m	0.07	3.16	-	10.39	13.55	14.91	12.280
1011605D	300 mm x 100 mm	m	0.09	4.14	-	13.85	17.99	19.79	16.370
1011606	**Lintels; rectangular; purchased from manufacturer; reinforced; hoisted; bedded in gauged mortar 100 mm x 65 mm; length**								
1011606A	450 mm	Each	0.05	2.43	-	2.32	4.75	5.23	1.880
1011606B	600 mm	Each	0.07	3.16	-	3.13	6.29	6.92	2.510
1011606C	750 mm	Each	0.09	4.14	-	3.83	7.97	8.77	3.140
1011606D	900 mm	Each	0.10	4.87	-	4.63	9.50	10.45	3.760
1011606E	1050 mm	Each	0.12	5.64	-	5.41	11.05	12.16	4.390
1011606F	1200 mm	Each	0.13	6.37	-	6.17	12.54	13.79	5.020
1011606G	1350 mm	Each	0.15	7.35	-	6.96	14.31	15.74	5.640
1011606H	1500 mm	Each	0.17	8.08	-	7.68	15.76	17.34	6.270
1011607	**Lintels; rectangular; purchased from manufacturer; reinforced; hoisted; bedded in gauged mortar; 100 mm x 150 mm length**								
1011607A	450 mm	Each	0.12	5.64	-	3.47	9.11	10.02	4.340
1011607B	600 mm	Each	0.15	7.35	-	4.62	11.97	13.17	5.790
1011607C	750 mm	Each	0.19	9.29	-	5.77	15.06	16.57	7.240
1011607D	900 mm	Each	0.23	10.99	-	6.93	17.92	19.71	8.680
1011607E	1050 mm	Each	0.27	12.94	-	8.08	21.02	23.12	10.130
1011607F	1200 mm	Each	0.30	14.64	-	9.24	23.88	26.27	11.580
1011607G	1350 mm	Each	0.34	16.64	-	10.39	27.03	29.73	13.020
1011607H	1500 mm	Each	0.38	18.34	-	11.54	29.88	32.87	14.470
1011608	**Lintels; rectangular; purchased from manufacturer; reinforced; hoisted; bedded in gauged mortar; 150 mm x 65 mm; length**								
1011608A	450 mm	Each	0.08	3.65	-	2.78	6.43	7.07	2.820
1011608B	600 mm	Each	0.10	4.87	-	3.70	8.57	9.43	3.760
1011608C	750 mm	Each	0.13	6.13	-	4.65	10.78	11.86	4.700
1011608D	900 mm	Each	0.15	7.35	-	5.57	12.92	14.21	5.640
1011608E	1050 mm	Each	0.18	8.56	-	6.48	15.04	16.54	6.580
1011608F	1200 mm	Each	0.20	9.78	-	7.40	17.18	18.90	7.530
1011608G	1350 mm	Each	0.23	10.99	-	8.35	19.34	21.27	8.470
1011608H	1500 mm	Each	0.25	12.21	-	9.26	21.47	23.62	9.410

Small Works 2011		Unit	Labour Hours	Labour Net	Plant Net	Materials Net	Unit Net	Unit with 10%	CO₂
				£	£	£	£	£	Kg

101 **NEW WORK**

10116 **PRECAST CONCRETE**

1011609 **Lintels; rectangular; purchased from manufacturer; reinforced; hoisted; bedded in gauged mortar; 215 mm x 65 mm; length**

Code	Description	Unit	Labour Hours	Labour Net £	Plant Net £	Materials Net £	Unit Net £	Unit with 10% £	CO₂ Kg
1011609A	450 mm	Each	0.11	5.16	-	3.62	8.78	9.66	4.050
1011609B	600 mm	Each	0.14	6.86	-	4.81	11.67	12.84	5.390
1011609C	750 mm	Each	0.18	8.56	-	6.02	14.58	16.04	6.740
1011609D	900 mm	Each	0.21	10.27	-	7.39	17.66	19.43	8.090
1011609E	1050 mm	Each	0.25	11.97	-	8.43	20.40	22.44	9.440
1011609F	1200 mm	Each	0.28	13.67	-	9.79	23.46	25.81	10.790
1011609G	1350 mm	Each	0.32	15.62	-	10.83	26.45	29.10	12.140
1011609H	1500 mm	Each	0.36	17.37	-	12.05	29.42	32.36	13.480

1011610 **Lintels; rectangular; purchased from manufacturer; reinforced; hoisted; bedded in gauged mortar 255 mm x 65 mm; length**

Code	Description	Unit	Labour Hours	Labour Net £	Plant Net £	Materials Net £	Unit Net £	Unit with 10% £	CO₂ Kg
1011610A	450 mm	Each	0.13	6.13	-	3.98	10.11	11.12	4.230
1011610B	600 mm	Each	0.17	8.08	-	5.42	13.50	14.85	6.400
1011610C	750 mm	Each	0.21	10.02	-	6.62	16.64	18.30	8.000
1011610D	900 mm	Each	0.25	12.21	-	8.12	20.33	22.36	9.590
1011610E	1050 mm	Each	0.29	14.16	-	9.27	23.43	25.77	11.200
1011610F	1200 mm	Each	0.33	16.10	-	10.76	26.86	29.55	12.790
1011610G	1350 mm	Each	0.37	18.10	-	11.90	30.00	33.00	14.390
1011610H	1500 mm	Each	0.42	20.29	-	13.24	33.53	36.88	15.990

1011611 **Lintels; rectangular; prepared on site by contractor reinforcement; formwork; hoisted; bedded in gauged mortar**

Code	Description	Unit	Labour Hours	Labour Net £	Plant Net £	Materials Net £	Unit Net £	Unit with 10% £	CO₂ Kg
1011611A	150 mm x 112 mm 2 No. - 10 mm rods	m	0.23	10.99	-	2.78	13.77	15.15	15.170
1011611B	150 mm x 150 mm 2 No. - 12 mm rods	m	0.28	13.43	-	3.34	16.77	18.45	20.320
1011611C	225 mm x 112 mm 2 No. - 12 mm rods	m	0.33	15.86	-	3.62	19.48	21.43	22.760
1011611D	225 mm x 150 mm 2 No. - 19 mm rods	m	0.43	20.77	-	4.17	24.94	27.43	30.480
1011611E	225 mm x 225 mm 3 No. - 19 mm rods	m	0.55	26.85	-	6.26	33.11	36.42	45.720

1011612 **Lintels; boot; prepared on site by contractor; reinforcement; formwork; hoisted; bedded in gauged mortar**

Code	Description	Unit	Labour Hours	Labour Net £	Plant Net £	Materials Net £	Unit Net £	Unit with 10% £	CO₂ Kg
1011612A	338 mm x 225 mm extreme; 3 No. - 19 mm rods	m	0.85	41.55	-	11.13	52.68	57.95	68.680

1011613 **Padstones; bedded in gauged mortar**

Code	Description	Unit	Labour Hours	Labour Net £	Plant Net £	Materials Net £	Unit Net £	Unit with 10% £	CO₂ Kg
1011613A	225 mm x 225 mm x 150 mm	Each	0.30	14.64	-	4.75	19.39	21.33	4.140
1011613B	350 mm x 225 mm x 150 mm	Each	0.45	21.99	-	7.15	29.14	32.05	6.440
1011613C	450 mm x 225 mm x 150 mm	Each	0.60	29.34	-	9.50	38.84	42.72	8.290
1011613D	450 mm x 450 mm x 225 mm	Each	1.26	61.06	-	14.28	75.34	82.87	24.860

1011614 **Pier caps; bedded in gauged mortar**

Code	Description	Unit	Labour Hours	Labour Net £	Plant Net £	Materials Net £	Unit Net £	Unit with 10% £	CO₂ Kg
1011614A	300 mm x 300 mm x 75 mm for 225 mm piers	Each	0.50	24.42	-	6.80	31.22	34.34	3.680
1011614B	400 mm x 400 mm x 75 mm for 337 mm piers	Each	0.65	31.77	-	9.18	40.95	45.05	6.550

Small Works 2011		Unit	Labour Hours	Labour Net £	Plant Net £	Materials Net £	Unit Net £	Unit with 10% £	CO$_2$ Kg
102	**REPAIRS AND ALTERATIONS**								
10201	**EXCAVATION**								
1020101	**Excavate by hand over site area; wheel 18 m; deposit in skip**								
1020101A	average 300 mm deep	m^2	1.86	38.78	-	-	38.78	42.66	-
1020102	**Excavate by hand for trenches to receive foundations; wheel 18 m; deposit in skip**								
1020102A	not exceeding 1.0 m deep	m^3	6.52	135.94	-	-	135.94	149.53	-
1020102B	exceeding 1.0 m deep and not exceeding 2.0 m deep	m^3	8.02	167.22	-	-	167.22	183.94	-
1020103	**Excavate by hand for basement; wheel 18 m deposit in skip**								
1020103A	not exceeding 1.0 m deep	m^3	6.00	125.10	-	-	125.10	137.61	-
1020103B	exceeding 1.0 m deep and not exceeding 2.0 m deep	m^3	6.72	140.11	-	-	140.11	154.12	-
1020104	**Excavated material as filling to excavations deposited and compacted by hand in**								
1020104A	250 mm layers	m^3	2.00	41.70	-	-	41.70	45.87	-
1020105	**Extra over excavation for breaking up by hand brickwork in**								
1020105A	old foundations	m^3	7.09	147.83	-	-	147.83	162.61	-
1020106	**Hire of skip, delivery to site removing when full, disposal of contents, payment of tipping charges skip size**								
1020106A	4.5 m^3	m^3	-	-	43.48	-	43.48	47.83	
1020107	**Earthwork support in firm ground to opposing faces not exceeding 2.00 m apart maximum depth not exceeding**								
1020107A	1.00 m	m^2	0.85	17.72	-	2.61	20.33	22.36	1.320
1020107B	2.00 m	m^2	0.93	19.39	-	2.88	22.27	24.50	1.460
1020108	**Earthwork support in loose ground to opposing faces not exceeding 2.00 m apart maximum depth not exceeding**								
1020108A	1.00 m	m^2	6.62	138.03	-	20.66	158.69	174.56	10.460
1020108B	2.00 m	m^2	6.62	138.03	-	20.66	158.69	174.56	10.460
1020109	**Imported hardcore compacted to receive concrete to finished thickness**								
1020109A	100 mm	m^2	0.48	10.01	-	2.48	12.49	13.74	1.550
1020109B	150 mm	m^2	0.72	15.01	-	3.73	18.74	20.61	2.320
1020109C	225 mm	m^2	1.08	22.52	-	5.60	28.12	30.93	3.480
10202	**CONCRETE WORK**								
1020201	**Portland cement concrete in foundations**								
1020201A	1:2:4 mix	m^3	6.00	125.10	-	135.82	260.92	287.01	433.190
1020201B	1:3:6 mix	m^3	6.00	125.10	-	129.19	254.29	279.72	322.380
1020202	**Concrete (1:3:6) oversite; thickness**								
1020202A	100 mm	m^3	9.00	187.65	-	129.19	316.84	348.52	322.380
1020202B	150 mm	m^3	8.50	177.23	-	129.19	306.42	337.06	322.380

Small Works 2011		Unit	Labour Hours	Labour Net	Plant Net	Materials Net	Unit Net	Unit with 10%	CO$_2$
				£	£	£	£	£	Kg
102	**REPAIRS AND ALTERATIONS**								
10202	**CONCRETE WORK**								
1020203	**Concrete (1:3:6) oversite in patches not exceeding 4 sq.m in area including jointing to existing; thickness**								
1020203A	100 mm	m^3	14.00	291.90	-	129.19	421.09	463.20	322.380
1020203B	150 mm	m^3	13.50	281.48	-	129.19	410.67	451.74	322.380
1020204	**Extra over site concrete for**								
1020204A	preparing to receive asphalt, tiling etc including extra cement	m^2	0.45	9.38	-	3.54	12.92	14.21	20.920
1020204B	trowelling to smooth surface	m^2	0.55	11.47	-	-	11.47	12.62	-
1020205	**Sprinkling surface of concrete with**								
1020205A	coarse carborundum at 1 kg per sq.m and lightly trowelling	m^2	0.55	11.47	-	1.30	12.77	14.05	0.090
1020206	**Clean existing concrete or rendered floors and treat with**								
1020206A	application of silicate of soda solution	m^2	0.30	6.25	-	0.42	6.67	7.34	0.010
1020207	**Reinforced concrete lintels cast in situ including reinforcement and formwork; size**								
1020207A	113 mm x 150 mm	m	0.38	18.34	-	5.84	24.18	26.60	13.620
1020207B	113 mm x 225 mm	m	0.45	21.99	-	7.30	29.29	32.22	17.420
1020207C	225 mm x 150 mm	m	0.65	31.77	-	9.15	40.92	45.01	22.290
1020207D	225 mm x 225 mm	m	0.73	35.42	-	11.79	47.21	51.93	29.810
1020208	**Precast concrete lintels including reinforcement and formwork; size**								
1020208A	113 mm x 150 mm	m	0.23	10.99	-	2.78	13.77	15.15	15.170
1020208B	113 mm x 225 mm	m	0.33	15.86	-	3.62	19.48	21.43	22.760
1020208C	225 mm x 150 mm	m	0.43	20.77	-	4.17	24.94	27.43	30.480
1020208D	225 mm x 225 mm	m	0.55	26.85	-	6.26	33.11	36.42	45.720
1020209	**Needle through 225 mm brickwork with 150 mm x 100 mm shore with one pair Acrow or other adjustable struts to every linear metre or part thereof (maximum span 2.70 m). Cut out and remove defective lintel and supply, hoist and build in precast reinforced concrete lintel and make good all brickwork and plaster disturbed; lintel size**								
1020209A	225 mm x 150 mm	m	2.44	118.51	5.78	12.11	136.40	150.04	45.380
1020209B	225 mm x 225 mm	m	2.56	124.59	5.78	14.21	144.58	159.04	60.620
1020210	**Cut away triangular area of brickwork above lintel. Cut out and remove defective lintel and supply, hoist and build in precast reinforced concrete lintel, rebuild brickwork over including facing bricks to match existing and make good internal plaster; lintel size**								
1020210A	225 mm x 225 mm	m	5.12	249.19	-	19.69	268.88	295.77	94.710
1020210B	225 mm x 338 mm	m	7.28	354.22	-	34.01	388.23	427.05	129.780
1020211	**Take out stone or concrete cill. Supply and build in cast concrete cill including all making good; cill size**								
1020211A	225 mm x 75 mm	m	0.55	26.85	-	9.06	35.91	39.50	11.180
1020212	**Pier caps**								
1020212A	300 mm x 300 mm x 75 mm for 225 mm piers	Each	0.50	24.42	-	6.93	31.35	34.49	4.000
1020212B	400 mm x 400 mm x 75 mm for 338 mm piers	Each	0.65	31.77	-	9.31	41.08	45.19	6.870

Small Works 2011		Unit	Labour Hours	Labour Net	Plant Net	Materials Net	Unit Net	Unit with 10%	CO$_2$
				£	£	£	£	£	Kg
102	**REPAIRS AND ALTERATIONS**								
10202	**CONCRETE WORK**								
1020213	**Break up and remove old concrete steps, form new steps in**								
1020213A	concrete 1:3:6, including wrought formwork to risers and ends, and surfaces of treads trowelled smooth	m^3	9.54	464.17	-	147.16	611.33	672.46	344.320
1020214	**Break up and remove concrete floors, pavings etc, at ground level and load into skip**								
1020214A	not exceeding 150 mm	m^2	2.25	46.91	-	-	46.91	51.60	-
1020214B	150 mm - 225 mm	m^2	4.00	83.40	-	-	83.40	91.74	-
1020214C	225 mm - 300 mm	m^2	6.00	125.10	-	-	125.10	137.61	-
1020215	**Break up and remove reinforced concrete floors, pavings, etc, at ground level and load into skip**								
1020215A	not exceeding 150 mm	m^2	3.40	70.89	-	-	70.89	77.98	-
1020215B	150 mm - 225 mm	m^2	6.00	125.10	-	-	125.10	137.61	-
1020215C	225 mm - 300 mm	m^2	9.00	187.65	-	-	187.65	206.42	-
1020216	**Break up concrete paving 750 mm wide for new wall and remove. Excavate trench and part return, fill in and ram and remove remainder. Make good concrete paving. (Foundation concrete measured separately)**								
1020216A	100 mm thick	m	2.85	59.42	-	7.20	66.62	73.28	17.970
1020217	**Hack up broken or sunken areas of concrete paving, spread and consolidate hardcore 150 mm, lay new concrete to falls, joint to existing including trowelling to form smooth surface**								
1020217A	100 mm	m^2	1.08	52.54	-	16.89	69.43	76.37	35.020
1020217B	150 mm	m^2	1.23	59.84	-	23.32	83.16	91.48	51.060
1020218	**Hack surface of existing paving or floors and grout and render in**								
1020218A	19 mm cement mortar (1:2:5)	m^2	0.50	24.42	-	1.99	26.41	29.05	7.710
1020219	**Hack off defective cement rendering to steps (treads and risers) and make out in**								
1020219A	25 mm cement and sand (1:3) trowelled including nosings and arrises	m^2	1.26	61.06	-	3.70	64.76	71.24	12.650
1020220	**Clean and hack existing concrete surface to form key for**								
1020220A	granolithic paving	m^2	0.40	8.34	-	-	8.34	9.17	-
1020221	**Roughen and grout edge of existing concrete paving to new**								
1020221A	100 mm	m	0.40	8.34	-	-	8.34	9.17	-
1020221B	150 mm	m	0.50	10.43	-	-	10.43	11.47	-
1020222	**Breaking up reinforced concrete walls, columns, beams, suspended floors or roofs and loading into**								
1020222A	skip	m^3	27.00	562.95	-	-	562.95	619.25	-

Small Works 2011		Unit	Labour Hours	Labour Net	Plant Net	Materials Net	Unit Net	Unit with 10%	CO₂
				£	£	£	£	£	Kg
102	**REPAIRS AND ALTERATIONS**								
10202	**CONCRETE WORK**								
1020223	**Cutting holes through concrete for pipes, bars etc per 25 mm depth of cut and making good**								
1020223A	area not exceeding 0.003 sq.m	Each	0.20	4.17	-	0.25	4.42	4.86	0.840
1020223B	0.003 - 0.023 sq.m	Each	0.40	8.34	-	0.25	8.59	9.45	0.840
1020224	**Cutting holes through reinforced concrete for pipes, bars, etc., per 25 mm depth of cut and making good**								
1020224A	area not exceeding 0.003 sq.m	Each	0.30	6.25	-	0.25	6.50	7.15	0.840
1020224B	0.003 - 0.023 sq.m	Each	0.60	12.51	-	0.25	12.76	14.04	0.840
1020225	**Forming concrete (1:2:4) curbs and channels including all necessary formwork but excluding excavation**								
1020225A	average 0.047 sq.m sectional area	m	0.50	24.42	-	6.41	30.83	33.91	20.430

Brickwork and Blockwork

Brickwork and Blockwork

Small Works 2011		Unit	Labour Hours	Labour Net	Plant Net	Materials Net	Unit Net	Unit with 10%	CO$_2$
				£	£	£	£	£	Kg
201	**NEW WORK**								
20101	**CLASS B ENGINEERING BRICKWORK IN CEMENT MORTAR (1:3)**								
2010101	**Walls**								
2010101A	half brick thick	m^2	0.58	44.11	-	29.33	73.44	80.78	121.550
2010101B	one brick thick	m^2	0.98	74.92	-	57.38	132.30	145.53	238.390
2010102	**Skins of hollow walls**								
2010102A	half brick thick	m^2	0.58	44.11	-	29.33	73.44	80.78	121.550
2010102B	one brick thick	m^2	0.98	74.92	-	57.38	132.30	145.53	238.390
2010103	**Honeycomb sleeper walls**								
2010103A	half brick thick	m^2	0.44	33.87	-	22.27	56.14	61.75	92.250
2010104	**For every £10 per 1000 variation in the price of bricks, add or deduct as follows**								
2010104A	half brick walls	m^2	-	-	-	0.74	0.74	0.81	90.530
2010104B	one brick walls	m^2	-	-	-	1.49	1.49	1.64	181.060
2010105	**Extra over Class B engineering brickwork in cement mortar (1:3) for fair face and flush pointing one side as the work proceeds**								
2010105A	stretcher bond	m^2	0.16	12.00	-	-	12.00	13.20	-
2010105B	Flemish bond	m^2	0.17	12.84	-	-	12.84	14.12	-
2010105C	margins	m	0.04	2.83	-	-	2.83	3.11	-
20102	**COMMON BRICKWORK IN GAUGED MORTAR (1:1:6)**								
2010201	**Walls**								
2010201A	half brick thick	m^2	0.56	42.58	-	22.17	64.75	71.23	53.650
2010201B	one brick thick	m^2	0.91	69.49	-	42.54	112.03	123.23	103.010
2010202	**Skins of hollow walls**								
2010202A	half brick thick	m^2	0.56	42.58	-	22.58	65.16	71.68	54.620
2010202B	one brick thick	m^2	0.91	69.49	-	47.16	116.65	128.32	113.990
2010203	**Honeycomb sleeper walls**								
2010203A	half brick wall	m^2	0.43	32.80	-	17.74	50.54	55.59	42.910
2010204	**Projections of footings and chimney breasts**								
2010204A	half brick thick	m^2	0.62	47.70	-	22.58	70.28	77.31	54.620
2010204B	one brick thick	m^2	1.02	78.21	-	47.16	125.37	137.91	113.990
2010204C	one and a half brick thick	m^2	1.22	93.57	-	71.50	165.07	181.58	172.800
2010205	**Isolated piers and chimney stacks**								
2010205A	one brick thick	m^2	1.13	86.62	-	47.16	133.78	147.16	113.990
2010205B	one and a half brick thick	m^2	1.36	103.59	-	71.50	175.09	192.60	172.800
2010205C	two bricks thick	m^2	1.67	127.44	-	95.31	222.75	245.03	230.330
2010206	**Projection of attached piers, plinths, bands, oversailing courses and the like**								
2010206A	215 mm x 102.5 mm	m	0.19	14.14	-	5.76	19.90	21.89	13.950
2010206B	215 mm x 215 mm	m	0.48	36.93	-	11.22	48.15	52.97	27.150
2010206C	327.5 mm x 102.5 mm	m	0.27	20.26	-	8.19	28.45	31.30	19.800
2010206D	327.5 mm x 215 mm	m	0.91	69.49	-	17.12	86.61	95.27	41.420
2010207	**For every £10 per 1000 variation in the price of bricks, add or deduct as follows**								
2010207A	half brick walls	m^2	-	-	-	0.74	0.74	0.81	0.905
2010207B	one brick walls	m^2	-	-	-	1.49	1.49	1.64	1.810
2010207C	one and a half brick walls	m^2	-	-	-	2.23	2.23	2.45	2.715
2010207D	two brick walls	m^2	-	-	-	2.98	2.98	3.28	3.621
2010208	**Extra over commons for**								
2010208A	keyed bricks	m^2	-	-	-	1.26	1.26	1.39	-

Small Works 2011		Unit	Labour Hours	Labour Net	Plant Net	Materials Net	Unit Net	Unit with 10%	CO$_2$
				£	£	£	£	£	Kg
201	**NEW WORK**								
20102	**COMMON BRICKWORK IN GAUGED MORTAR (1:1:6)**								
2010209	**Extra over common brickwork in gauged mortar (1:1:6) for fair face and flush pointing one side as the work proceeds**								
2010209A	stretcher bond	m²	0.13	10.24	-	-	10.24	11.26	-
2010209B	Flemish bond	m²	0.15	11.24	-	-	11.24	12.36	-
2010209C	margins	m	0.03	2.60	-	-	2.60	2.86	-
20103	**FACING BRICKWORK (PC £390 Per 1000), IN GAUGED MORTAR (1:1:6)**								
2010301	**Walls**								
2010301A	half brick thick; stretcher bond	m²	0.69	52.52	-	28.73	81.25	89.38	103.470
2010301B	one brick thick; double stretcher bond	m²	1.31	99.77	-	58.56	158.33	174.16	209.030
2010301C	one brick thick; English bond	m²	1.38	105.12	-	58.97	164.09	180.50	210.000
2010301D	one brick thick; English garden wall bond	m²	1.33	101.75	-	58.97	160.72	176.79	210.000
2010301E	one brick thick; English cross bond	m²	1.45	110.55	-	60.53	171.08	188.19	215.840
2010301F	one brick thick; Flemish bond	m²	1.42	108.41	-	58.83	167.24	183.96	209.680
2010301G	one brick thick; Flemish garden wall bond	m²	1.35	103.05	-	58.83	161.88	178.07	209.680
2010302	**Skins of hollow walls**								
2010302A	half brick thick; stretcher bond	m²	0.69	52.52	-	28.59	81.11	89.22	103.150
2010302B	half brick thick; English bond (snapped headers)	m²	0.78	59.25	-	41.60	100.85	110.94	151.660
2010302C	half brick thick; Flemish bond (snapped headers)	m²	0.80	60.78	-	37.31	98.09	107.90	135.590
2010304	**For every £10 per 1000 variation in the price of bricks, add or deduct as follows**								
2010304A	half brick walls; stretcher bond	m²	-	-	-	0.79	0.79	0.87	0.964
2010304B	half brick walls; Flemish bond	m²	-	-	-	1.07	1.07	1.18	1.299
20104	**ARCHES AND COPINGS**								
2010401	**Extra over brickwork for flat arch, 112 mm soffit**								
2010401A	commons 112 mm high	m	0.20	15.37	-	0.31	15.68	17.25	0.740
2010401B	commons 225 mm high	m	0.27	20.57	-	0.31	20.88	22.97	0.740
2010401C	facings 112 mm high	m	0.25	19.19	-	3.15	22.34	24.57	10.700
2010401D	facings 225 mm high	m	0.34	25.61	-	5.78	31.39	34.53	19.610
2010402	**Extra over brickwork for camber arch, 112 mm soffit**								
2010402A	commons 225 mm high	m	0.57	43.58	-	0.31	43.89	48.28	0.740
2010402B	facings 225 mm high	m	0.60	46.18	-	5.78	51.96	57.16	19.610
2010403	**Extra over brickwork for segmental arch; 225 mm deep in two half brick rings**								
2010403A	commons	m	0.64	48.70	-	0.61	49.31	54.24	1.490
2010403B	facings	m	0.70	53.82	-	5.78	59.60	65.56	19.610
2010404	**Extra over brickwork in rough relieving arches**								
2010404A	commons 112 mm high	m	0.10	7.72	-	0.31	8.03	8.83	0.740
2010404B	commons 225 mm high	m	0.17	12.84	-	0.31	13.15	14.47	0.740
2010405	**Brick-on-edge coping to one brick wall; double tile creasing course; two small fillets; pointed all round**								
2010405A	commons	m	0.81	61.54	-	13.46	75.00	82.50	13.520
2010405B	facings	m	0.84	64.14	-	14.71	78.85	86.74	24.250

Brickwork and Blockwork

		Unit	Labour Hours	Labour Net £	Plant Net £	Materials Net £	Unit Net £	Unit with 10% £	CO₂ Kg
201	**NEW WORK**								
20106	**CILLS AND STEPS**								
2010601	**Heatherbrown quarry tile cill rounded on one edge, bedded, jointed and pointed in cement mortar**								
2010601B	194 mm x 194 mm x 12.5 mm	m	0.12	9.48	-	4.85	14.33	15.76	3.680
2010601C	150 mm x 150 mm x 12.5 mm	m	0.11	8.49	-	3.81	12.30	13.53	3.030
2010601D	150 mm x 150 mm x 19 mm	m	0.12	8.94	-	5.25	14.19	15.61	4.350
2010602	**Red quarry tile cill rounded on one edge, bedded, jointed and pointed in cement mortar**								
2010602B	200 mm x 200 mm x 19 mm	m	0.13	9.71	-	9.21	18.92	20.81	5.290
2010602C	150 mm x 150 mm x 20 mm	m	0.12	8.94	-	5.25	14.19	15.61	4.350
2010602D	150 mm x 150 mm x 12.5 mm	m	0.11	8.49	-	3.81	12.30	13.53	3.030
2010603	**Two courses roofing tiles set sloping to form**								
2010603A	external window cills; including pointing	m	0.45	34.63	-	8.94	43.57	47.93	3.070
2010604	**Brick-on-edge step in hard red paviors; bedded and pointed**								
2010604A	225 mm wide	m	0.47	35.93	-	17.52	53.45	58.80	23.590
2010604B	338 mm wide	m	1.01	76.91	-	25.71	102.62	112.88	34.650
2010604C	Extra for bullnosed paviors	m	-	-	-	55.81	55.81	61.39	4.610
2010605	**Brick-on-edge cill; bedded and pointed**								
2010605A	225 mm in facing bricks	m	0.44	33.33	-	6.39	39.72	43.69	23.190
2010605B	225 mm in single bullnosed engineering bricks	m	0.44	33.33	-	73.38	106.71	117.38	27.290
20108	**ARC CONBLOC DENSE AGGREGATE BLOCKS**								
2010801	**Blockwork in walls; partitions or skins of hollow walls**								
2010801A	75 mm solid	m²	0.37	28.44	-	14.68	43.12	47.43	23.440
2010801B	100 mm solid	m²	0.44	33.64	-	18.62	52.26	57.49	29.710
2010801C	140 mm solid	m²	0.52	39.45	-	33.12	72.57	79.83	39.740
2010801D	140 mm hollow	m²	0.55	42.05	-	24.25	66.30	72.93	18.110
2010801E	190 mm hollow	m²	0.62	47.48	-	35.16	82.64	90.90	22.920
2010801F	215 mm hollow	m²	0.68	52.29	-	34.00	86.29	94.92	25.330
2010801G	Extra for fair face and flush pointing blockwork as the work proceeds; any thickness; one face	m²	0.04	3.36	-	0.54	3.90	4.29	1.290
2010801H	Extra for fair face and flush pointing blockwork as the work proceeds; any thickness; both faces	m²	0.11	8.72	-	0.54	9.26	10.19	1.290
20109	**CELCON/THERMALITE CONCRETE BLOCKS**								
2010901	**Standard blockwork in walls; partitions or skins of hollow walls**								
2010901C	75 mm	m²	0.34	25.61	-	12.65	38.26	42.09	8.470
2010901E	100 mm	m²	0.40	30.73	-	16.36	47.09	51.80	10.110
2010901H	150 mm	m²	0.50	38.45	-	23.77	62.22	68.44	13.390
2010901K	215 mm	m²	0.64	48.70	-	34.41	83.11	91.42	17.660
2010901L	Extra for fair face and flush pointing blockwork as the work proceeds; any thickness; one face	m²	0.04	3.36	-	1.09	4.45	4.90	2.580
2010901M	Extra for fair face and flush pointing blockwork as the work proceeds; any thickness; both faces	m²	0.11	8.72	-	1.09	9.81	10.79	2.580
2010902	**Solar/High insulation blockwork in walls; partitions or skins of hollow walls**								
2010902A	115 mm	m²	0.51	38.68	-	19.29	57.97	63.77	22.790
2010902B	125 mm	m²	0.53	40.82	-	29.96	70.78	77.86	27.610

Small Works 2011		Unit	Labour Hours	Labour Net	Plant Net	Materials Net	Unit Net	Unit with 10%	CO$_2$
				£	£	£	£	£	Kg
201	**NEW WORK**								
20109	**CELCON/THERMALITE CONCRETE BLOCKS**								
2010902	**Solar/High insulation blockwork in walls; partitions or skins of hollow walls**								
2010902E	150 mm	m^2	0.60	46.18	-	27.90	74.08	81.49	32.420
2010902G	215 mm	m^2	0.79	60.01	-	39.35	99.36	109.30	44.930
2010902H	Extra for fair face and flush pointing blockwork as the work proceeds; any thickness; one face	m^2	0.04	3.36	-	1.09	4.45	4.90	2.580
2010902I	Extra for fair face and flush pointing blockwork as the work proceeds; any thickness; both faces	m^2	0.11	8.72	-	1.09	9.81	10.79	2.580
20113	**DAMP PROOF COURSES**								
2011301	**Polythene; horizontal; bedded in gauged mortar (1:1:6)**								
2011301A	112.5 mm wide	m	0.01	1.07	-	0.30	1.37	1.51	0.910
2011301B	225 mm wide	m	0.03	2.06	-	0.74	2.80	3.08	2.200
2011301C	over 225 mm wide	m^2	0.12	8.94	-	3.23	12.17	13.39	9.750
2011301D	over 225 mm wide; forming cavity gutter in hollow wall	m^2	0.19	14.37	-	3.23	17.60	19.36	9.750
2011302	**Polythene; vertical; bedded in gauged mortar (1:1:6)**								
2011302A	over 225 mm wide	m^2	0.35	26.91	-	3.23	30.14	33.15	9.750
2011303	**Fibre based bitumen; horizontal; bedded in gauged mortar (1:1:6)**								
2011303A	112.5 mm wide	m	0.01	1.07	-	0.93	2.00	2.20	0.910
2011303B	225 mm wide	m	0.03	2.06	-	1.94	4.00	4.40	1.880
2011303C	over 225 mm wide	m^2	0.12	8.94	-	10.00	18.94	20.83	10.720
2011303D	over 225 mm wide; forming cavity gutter in hollow wall	m^2	0.19	14.37	-	10.00	24.37	26.81	10.720
2011304	**Fibre based bitumen; vertical; bedded in gauged mortar (1:1:6)**								
2011304A	over 225 mm wide	m^2	0.35	26.91	-	10.00	36.91	40.60	10.720
2011305	**Hessian based bitumen; horizontal; bedded in gauged mortar (1:1:6)**								
2011305A	112.5 mm wide	m	0.01	1.07	-	1.32	2.39	2.63	0.910
2011305B	225 mm wide	m	0.03	2.06	-	2.88	4.94	5.43	2.200
2011305C	over 225 mm wide	m^2	0.12	8.94	-	13.85	22.79	25.07	10.720
2011305D	over 225 mm wide; forming cavity gutter in hollow wall	m^2	0.19	14.37	-	13.85	28.22	31.04	10.720
2011306	**Hessian based bitumen; vertical; bedded in gauged mortar (1:1:6)**								
2011306A	over 225 mm wide	m^2	0.35	26.91	-	13.85	40.76	44.84	10.720
2011307	**Hyload pitch polymer; horizontal; 100 mm laps sealed with Hyload contact adhesive; bedded in gauged mortar (1:1:6)**								
2011307A	112.5 mm wide	m	0.01	1.07	-	1.35	2.42	2.66	0.910
2011307B	225 mm wide	m	0.03	2.06	-	2.93	4.99	5.49	2.200
2011307C	over 225 mm wide	m^2	0.12	8.94	-	14.11	23.05	25.36	10.720
2011307D	over 225 mm wide; forming cavity gutter in hollow wall	m^2	0.19	14.37	-	14.11	28.48	31.33	10.720
2011308	**Hyload pitch polymer; vertical; bedded in gauged mortar (1:1:6)**								
2011308A	over 225 mm wide	m^2	0.35	26.91	-	14.11	41.02	45.12	10.720
2011311	**Fibre based lead lined; horizontal; bedded in gauged mortar (1:1:6)**								
2011311A	112.5 mm wide	m	0.02	1.30	-	2.97	4.27	4.70	0.910

Small Works 2011		Unit	Labour Hours	Labour Net £	Plant Net £	Materials Net £	Unit Net £	Unit with 10% £	CO_2 Kg
201	**NEW WORK**								
20113	**DAMP PROOF COURSES**								
2011311	**Fibre based lead lined; horizontal; bedded in gauged mortar (1:1:6)**								
2011311B	225 mm wide	m	0.03	2.60	-	6.33	8.93	9.82	2.200
2011311C	over 225 mm wide	m^2	0.15	11.77	-	30.33	42.10	46.31	10.720
2011311D	over 225 mm wide; forming cavity gutter in hollow wall	m^2	0.25	18.96	-	30.33	49.29	54.22	10.720
2011313	**Fibre based lead lined; vertical; bedded in gauged mortar (1:1:6)**								
2011313A	over 225 mm wide	m^2	0.35	26.91	-	30.33	57.24	62.96	10.720
2011314	**Hessian based lead lined; horizontal; bedded in gauged mortar (1:1:6)**								
2011314A	112.5 mm wide	m	0.02	1.30	-	3.12	4.42	4.86	0.910
2011314B	225 mm wide	m	0.03	2.60	-	6.36	8.96	9.86	2.140
2011314C	over 225 mm wide	m^2	0.15	11.77	-	31.81	43.58	47.94	10.720
2011314D	over 225 mm wide; forming cavity gutter in hollow wall	m^2	0.25	18.96	-	31.81	50.77	55.85	10.720
2011315	**Hessian based lead lined; vertical; bedded in gauged mortar (1:1:6)**								
2011315A	over 225 mm wide	m^2	0.35	26.91	-	31.81	58.72	64.59	10.720
2011318	**Welsh slates; two courses; horizontal; bedded in cement mortar (1:3)**								
2011318A	over 225 mm wide	m^2	0.69	52.83	-	759.88	812.71	893.98	21.870
2011319	**Welsh slates; two courses; vertical; bedded in cement mortar (1:3)**								
2011319A	over 225 mm wide	m^2	1.06	80.73	-	759.88	840.61	924.67	21.870
2011320	**Synthaprufe; vertical membrane; three coats brushed on; final covering dusted with clean sharp sand**								
2011320A	not exceeding 150 mm wide	m	0.04	2.83	-	1.20	4.03	4.43	1.280
2011320B	150 mm - 300 mm wide	m	0.06	4.59	-	2.40	6.99	7.69	2.570
2011320C	over 300 mm wide	m^2	0.13	10.01	-	7.95	17.96	19.76	8.490
20115	**AIR BRICKS AND SOOT DOORS**								
2011501	**Air bricks; terracotta; building in**								
2011501A	225 mm x 75 mm	each	0.07	5.66	-	3.91	9.57	10.53	0.540
2011501B	225 mm x 150 mm	each	0.10	7.72	-	5.18	12.90	14.19	1.080
2011501C	225 mm x 225 mm	each	0.11	8.49	-	14.67	23.16	25.48	1.620
2011502	**Air bricks; galvanised; building in**								
2011502A	225 mm x 75 mm	each	0.07	5.66	-	5.81	11.47	12.62	0.400
2011502B	225 mm x 150 mm	each	0.10	7.72	-	10.68	18.40	20.24	0.800
2011502C	225 mm x 225 mm	each	0.11	8.49	-	15.65	24.14	26.55	1.200
2011503	**Louvred ventilators; aluminium; screw fixed**								
2011503A	225 mm x 75 mm	each	0.07	5.66	-	3.26	8.92	9.81	15.770
2011503B	225 mm x 150 mm	each	0.10	7.72	-	3.86	11.58	12.74	31.540
2011503C	225 mm x 225 mm	each	0.11	8.49	-	5.40	13.89	15.28	47.310
2011504	**Air ventilators; plaster; flyproof; set in plastering**								
2011504A	225 mm x 75 mm	each	0.07	5.66	-	2.84	8.50	9.35	0.230
2011504B	225 mm x 150 mm	each	0.10	7.72	-	3.40	11.12	12.23	0.450
2011504C	225 mm x 225 mm	each	0.11	8.49	-	5.58	14.07	15.48	5.980
2011505	**Air brick extension cavity liners; terracotta; 300 mm long; building in**								
2011505A	225 mm x 75 mm	Each	0.10	7.72	-	5.52	13.24	14.56	2.690
2011505B	225 mm x 150 mm	Each	0.13	9.71	-	6.65	16.36	18.00	5.380

Small Works 2011		Unit	Labour Hours	Labour Net	Plant Net	Materials Net	Unit Net	Unit with 10%	CO₂
				£	£	£	£	£	Kg
201	**NEW WORK**								
20115	**AIR BRICKS AND SOOT DOORS**								
2011505	**Air brick extension cavity liners; terracotta; 300 mm long; building in**								
2011505C	225 mm x 225 mm	Each	0.19	14.14	-	17.59	31.73	34.90	8.070
2011506	**Soot doors; double cover; frame; cast iron; building in**								
2011506A	225 mm x 150 mm	Each	0.13	10.24	-	23.82	34.06	37.47	25.810
2011506B	225 mm x 225 mm	Each	0.15	11.54	-	33.16	44.70	49.17	38.720
20117	**CHIMNEY FLUE LININGS, BENDS, POTS ETC**								
2011701	**Parge and core flues**								
2011701A	225 mm x 225 mm	m	0.34	25.61	-	1.98	27.59	30.35	6.750
2011702	**Clay flue linings; BS 1181; bedded and jointed in cement mortar (1:3)**								
2011702A	125 mm dia	m	0.17	12.84	-	35.34	48.18	53.00	17.130
2011702B	150 mm dia	m	0.19	14.14	-	35.67	49.81	54.79	24.590
2011702C	185 mm dia	m	0.20	15.37	-	35.39	50.76	55.84	22.990
2011702D	200 mm dia	m	0.20	15.37	-	56.71	72.08	79.29	32.770
2011702E	225 mm dia	m	0.21	15.90	-	69.89	85.79	94.37	28.390
2011702F	300 mm dia	m	0.24	17.97	-	139.99	157.96	173.76	42.770
2011702G	185 mm x 185 mm	m	0.20	15.37	-	52.59	67.96	74.76	26.050
2011702H	200 mm x 200 mm	m	0.20	15.37	-	56.77	72.14	79.35	24.790
2011702I	225 mm x 225 mm	m	0.21	15.90	-	67.61	83.51	91.86	43.570
2011704	**Clay flue bends; BS 1181; bedded and jointed in cement mortar (1:3)**								
2011704A	125 mm dia	Each	0.19	14.75	-	33.23	47.98	52.78	4.790
2011704B	150 mm dia	Each	0.21	16.05	-	34.41	50.46	55.51	5.200
2011704C	185 mm dia	Each	0.24	17.97	-	37.58	55.55	61.11	6.250
2011704D	200 mm dia	Each	0.25	18.73	-	47.00	65.73	72.30	9.700
2011704E	225 mm dia	Each	0.25	19.19	-	52.93	72.12	79.33	6.990
2011704F	300 mm dia	Each	0.34	25.61	-	133.12	158.73	174.60	9.800
2011704G	185 mm x 185 mm	Each	0.23	17.20	-	51.72	68.92	75.81	23.100
2011704H	200 mm x 200 mm	Each	0.24	17.97	-	55.78	73.75	81.13	21.410
2011704I	225 mm x 225 mm	Each	0.24	18.20	-	66.62	84.82	93.30	40.190
2011714	**Chimney pots; clay; roll top or cannon head; set and flaunched in cement mortar (1:3); height**								
2011714A	300 mm	Each	0.39	29.51	-	37.03	66.54	73.19	11.420
2011714B	450 mm	Each	0.46	35.40	-	44.81	80.21	88.23	13.310
2011714C	600 mm	Each	0.55	41.82	-	64.27	106.09	116.70	13.990
2011714D	900 mm	Each	0.80	61.01	-	102.53	163.54	179.89	16.080
2011723	**Damp course to stacks (measured overall flues)**								
2011723A	double slate	m²	1.01	76.91	-	759.88	836.79	920.47	21.870
20118	**FIREPLACES**								
2011801	**Building in only**								
2011801A	continuous burning fire	Each	1.21	92.28	-	10.50	102.78	113.06	35.850
2011801B	back boiler	Each	2.40	183.33	-	10.50	193.83	213.21	35.850
2011801C	underfloor draught fire	Each	2.68	205.12	-	10.50	215.62	237.18	35.850
2011801D	tiled surround and hearth including assembling, jointing and setting in cement mortar 1:3	Each	2.85	217.96	-	6.54	224.50	246.95	22.350
20120	**TURNING PIECES AND CENTERING**								
2012001	**Turning pieces to flat arches; 112 mm soffit**								
2012001A	first use	m	0.15	11.54	-	1.11	12.65	13.92	1.360
2012001B	each subsequent use	m	0.13	10.24	-	-	10.24	11.26	-
2012002	**Turning pieces to flat arches; 225 mm soffit**								
2012002A	first use	m	0.19	14.14	-	3.27	17.41	19.15	4.000
2012002B	each subsequent use	m	0.15	11.54	-	-	11.54	12.69	-

Brickwork and Blockwork

	Unit	Labour Hours	Labour Net £	Plant Net £	Materials Net £	Unit Net £	Unit with 10% £	CO₂ Kg
201	**NEW WORK**							
20120	**TURNING PIECES AND CENTERING**							
2012003	**Centering to segmental arches; 225 mm wide soffit**							
2012003A	1.2 m span; first use	Each	0.42	32.03	-	7.17	39.20	43.12	8.760
2012003B	1.5 m span; first use	Each	0.44	33.33	-	8.99	42.32	46.55	10.970
2012003C	1.8 m span; first use	Each	0.49	37.15	-	10.80	47.95	52.75	13.180
2012003D	each subsequent use	Each	0.13	10.24	-	-	10.24	11.26	-
20122	**SUNDRIES**							
2012201	**Forming cavity not exceeding 100 mm between skins of hollow wall**							
2012201A	no wall ties	m²	0.03	2.06	-	-	2.06	2.27	-
2012201B	butterfly ties; galvanised wire; 5 No. per sq.m	m²	0.04	3.36	-	0.85	4.21	4.63	0.790
2012201C	twin triangular ties; galvanised wire; 5 No. per sq.m	m²	0.04	3.36	-	1.57	4.93	5.42	0.790
2012201D	twisted ties; galvanised wire; 5 No. per sq.m	m²	0.04	3.36	-	0.85	4.21	4.63	0.790
2012201E	Catnic ties; stainless steel; 5 No. per sq.m	m²	0.04	3.36	-	2.78	6.14	6.75	1.720
2012202	**Close cavity not exceeding 100 mm between skins of hollow wall at ends, jambs or cills of openings**							
2012202A	common brickwork half brick thick	m	0.12	9.25	-	2.42	11.67	12.84	5.860
2012202B	common brickwork half brick thick; bituminous felt	m	0.16	12.31	-	3.22	15.53	17.08	6.450
2012202C	common brickwork half brick thick; slate	m	0.20	15.37	-	36.79	52.16	57.38	6.700
2012202D	blockwork 100 mm thick	m	0.10	7.72	-	5.11	12.83	14.11	3.310
2012202E	blockwork 100 mm thick; bituminous felt	m	0.12	9.25	-	5.91	15.16	16.68	3.900
2012202F	blockwork 100 mm thick; slate	m	0.16	12.31	-	78.75	91.06	100.17	5.110
2012202G	Thermabate 50; 50-60 mm cavity width	m	0.04	3.06	-	7.20	10.26	11.29	46.640
2012202H	Thermabate 65; 65-75 mm cavity width	m	0.05	3.82	-	7.93	11.75	12.93	60.630
2012202I	Thermabate 75; 75-85 mm cavity width	m	0.06	4.36	-	8.69	13.05	14.36	69.960
2012202J	Thermabate 85; 85-95 mm cavity width	m	0.07	5.12	-	9.48	14.60	16.06	79.290
2012202K	Thermabate 90; 90-100 mm cavity width	m	0.07	5.66	-	10.18	15.84	17.42	83.950
2012203	**Close cavity not exceeding 100 mm wide at top of hollow wall with single course of blocks laid flat in gauged mortar (1:1:6)**							
2012203A	75 mm	m	0.09	7.03	-	2.66	9.69	10.66	1.700
2012203B	100 mm	m	0.11	8.49	-	3.46	11.95	13.15	2.050
2012203C	150 mm	m	0.15	11.54	-	6.49	18.03	19.83	3.390
2012204	**Rake out joints of brickwork**							
2012204A	to form key for plaster work	m²	0.17	12.84	-	-	12.84	14.12	-
2012204B	and point in cement mortar	m²	0.40	30.73	-	0.54	31.27	34.40	1.290
2012205	**Prepare top of brick wall**							
2012205A	for raising	m²	0.67	51.30	-	-	51.30	56.43	-
2012207	**Setting brickwork up to 50 mm forward or backward**							
2012207A	raised or sunk panels	m²	0.22	16.67	-	-	16.67	18.34	-
2012208	**Jablite expanded polystyrene board; cavity wall insulation; wedging in position between wall ties; fixing with insulation retaining discs**							
2012208A	25 mm thick	m²	0.07	5.12	-	3.67	8.79	9.67	8.780
2012208B	50 mm thick	m²	0.07	5.12	-	6.90	12.02	13.22	17.520
2012208C	75 mm thick	m²	0.07	5.66	-	10.67	16.33	17.96	26.270

Small Works 2011		Unit	Labour Hours	Labour Net	Plant Net	Materials Net	Unit Net	Unit with 10%	CO$_2$
				£	£	£	£	£	Kg
201	**NEW WORK**								
20122	**SUNDRIES**								
2012209	**Dritherm cavity wall insulation; wedging in position between wall ties**								
2012209A	50 mm thick	m^2	0.05	3.82	-	5.86	9.68	10.65	12.420
2012209B	75 mm thick	m^2	0.06	4.36	-	7.00	11.36	12.50	18.630
2012210	**Rockwool cavity wall insulation; wedging in position between wall ties**								
2012210A	50 mm thick	m^2	0.05	3.82	-	3.27	7.09	7.80	7.010
2012210B	75 mm thick	m^2	0.06	4.36	-	9.98	14.34	15.77	10.520
2012211	**Fill bottom of cavity wall with fine concrete; 50 mm cavity**								
2012211A	300 mm high	m	0.04	3.36	-	1.96	5.32	5.85	4.850
2012212	**Double tile creasing course; nibless flat tiles; red; machine made; projecting 50 mm from wall face in cement mortar 1:3**								
2012212A	half brick wall	m	0.32	24.39	-	10.21	34.60	38.06	7.690
2012212B	one brick wall	m	0.42	32.03	-	19.73	51.76	56.94	14.910
2012214	**Set one course of brickwork**								
2012214A	forward or backward (strings)	m	0.05	4.13	-	-	4.13	4.54	-
2012214B	dentil course up to 50 mm projection	m	0.11	8.49	-	-	8.49	9.34	-
2012214C	oversailing per course	m	0.07	5.12	-	-	5.12	5.63	-
2012214D	plinth course per course to 50 mm projection	m	0.03	2.60	-	-	2.60	2.86	-
2012215	**Wedge and pin up brickwork to underside of existing construction with slates in cement mortar 1:3**								
2012215A	half brick thick	m	0.14	10.78	-	4.74	15.52	17.07	12.830
2012215B	one brick thick	m	0.29	21.79	-	7.81	29.60	32.56	20.270
2012215C	one and a half brick thick	m	0.44	33.33	-	11.19	44.52	48.97	28.460
2012216	**Bed wood frames and cills in mortar and point up**								
2012216A	one side	m	0.14	10.78	-	0.54	11.32	12.45	1.290
2012216B	both sides	m	0.22	16.90	-	0.95	17.85	19.64	2.260
2012217	**Pointing in gun-grade polysulphide based mastic sealant**								
2012217A	one side	m	0.08	5.89	-	1.71	7.60	8.36	1.730
2012217B	both sides	m	0.15	11.77	-	3.34	15.11	16.62	3.380
2012218	**Bed plate in**								
2012218A	mortar	m	0.07	5.66	-	1.36	7.02	7.72	4.640
2012222	**Beam filling to**								
2012222A	one brick wall	m	0.22	16.90	-	-	16.90	18.59	-
2012223	**Cut chases in brickwork for**								
2012223A	small pipe or conduit	m	0.30	23.09	-	-	23.09	25.40	-
2012224	**Cut groove in brick cill for**								
2012224A	water bar	m	0.27	20.57	-	-	20.57	22.63	-
2012225	**Rake out joints in brickwork for**								
2012225A	turn in of asphalt skirting or metal horizontal flashings	m	0.13	10.24	-	-	10.24	11.26	-
2012225B	turn in of asphalt skirting or metal stepped flashings	m	0.20	15.37	-	-	15.37	16.91	-
2012226	**Cut and bond ends of wall in engineering bricks to existing**								
2012226A	half brick thick	m	0.16	12.31	-	0.84	13.15	14.47	3.500
2012226B	one brick thick	m	0.24	17.97	-	1.67	19.64	21.60	7.010
2012226C	one and a half brick thick	m	0.35	26.38	-	2.51	28.89	31.78	10.510
2012227	**Cut and bond ends of wall in common bricks to existing**								
2012227A	half brick thick	m	0.16	12.31	-	0.61	12.92	14.21	1.490

Brickwork and Blockwork

	Unit	Labour Hours	Labour Net	Plant Net	Materials Net	Unit Net	Unit with 10%	CO₂
			£	£	£	£	£	Kg
201	**NEW WORK**							
20122	**SUNDRIES**							
2012227	**Cut and bond ends of wall in common bricks to existing**							
2012227B	one brick thick	m	0.24	17.97	-	1.23	19.20	21.12	2.980
2012227C	one and a half brick thick	m	0.35	26.38	-	1.84	28.22	31.04	4.470
2012228	**Cut and bond ends of wall in facing bricks to existing**							
2012228A	half brick thick	m	0.16	12.31	-	0.60	12.91	14.20	2.920
2012228B	one brick thick	m	0.24	17.97	-	1.20	19.17	21.09	5.840
2012228C	one and a half brick thick	m	0.35	26.38	-	1.80	28.18	31.00	8.760
2012229	**Quoin up jambs in common bricks in gauged mortar 1:1:6**							
2012229A	half brick	m	0.40	30.73	-	3.92	34.65	38.12	9.480
2012229B	one brick	m	0.60	46.18	-	7.40	53.58	58.94	17.890
2012229C	one and a half brick thick	m	0.79	60.01	-	11.46	71.47	78.62	27.700
2012230	**Quoin up jambs in facing bricks in gauged mortar 1:1:6**							
2012230A	half brick	m	0.51	38.61	-	4.83	43.44	47.78	17.350
2012230B	one brick	m	0.60	46.18	-	9.14	55.32	60.85	32.920
2012230C	one and a half brick thick	m	0.93	70.79	-	14.11	84.90	93.39	50.600
2012232	**Mesh reinforcement in walls**							
2012232A	65 mm wide	m	0.09	6.65	-	0.83	7.48	8.23	1.970
2012232B	175 mm wide	m	0.11	8.72	-	2.22	10.94	12.03	5.480
2012233	**Angle fillets**							
2012233A	cement mortar	m	0.13	10.24	-	0.49	10.73	11.80	1.690
2012234	**Raking and cutting**							
2012234C	fair raking or splay cutting	m	0.11	8.49	-	3.30	11.79	12.97	16.060
2012234D	fair curved cutting	m	0.22	16.90	-	3.30	20.20	22.22	16.060
2012234E	fair squint or birdsmouth angle	m	0.11	8.49	-	4.20	12.69	13.96	20.440
2012234F	fair chamfered or round angle	m	0.15	11.54	-	3.30	14.84	16.32	16.060
2012240	**Catnic stainless steel stronghold wall connector system; plugging to wall with plugs and coach screws provided; twist and sliding arms to 225 mm centres and building into joints of walls**							
2012240A	60 mm - 250 mm thick	m	0.10	7.95	-	9.61	17.56	19.32	2.090
2012244	**Unload hoist; build in metal windows; door frames; pinning lugs; to brickwork; pointing externally**							
2012244A	not exceeding 0.5 sq.m	Each	0.37	28.21	-	0.37	28.58	31.44	1.270
2012244B	0.5 - 1.0 sq.m	Each	0.49	37.15	-	0.74	37.89	41.68	2.530
2012244C	1.0 - 1.5 sq.m	Each	0.67	51.30	-	1.23	52.53	57.78	4.220
2012244D	exceeding 1.5 sq.m	Each	0.76	57.72	-	1.61	59.33	65.26	5.480
2012245	**Hole for small pipe (not exceeding 55 mm dia) through walls and make good**							
2012245A	half brick wall	Each	0.13	10.24	-	0.37	10.61	11.67	1.270
2012245B	one brick wall	Each	0.22	16.90	-	0.62	17.52	19.27	2.110
2012245C	one and a half brick wall	Each	0.36	27.67	-	0.37	28.04	30.84	1.270
2012245D	blockwork 100 mm thick	Each	0.12	9.25	-	0.25	9.50	10.45	0.840
2012246	**Hole for large pipe (55 mm - 110 mm dia) through walls and make good**							
2012246A	half brick wall	Each	0.16	12.31	-	0.37	12.68	13.95	1.270
2012246B	one brick wall	Each	0.28	21.56	-	0.49	22.05	24.26	1.690
2012246C	one and half brick wall	Each	0.44	33.87	-	0.62	34.49	37.94	2.110
2012246D	blockwork 100 mm thick	Each	0.14	10.78	-	0.37	11.15	12.27	1.270
2012247	**Hole for extra large pipe (exceeding 110 mm dia) through walls and make good**							
2012247A	half brick wall	Each	0.20	15.37	-	0.37	15.74	17.31	1.270
2012247B	one brick wall	Each	0.34	26.15	-	0.49	26.64	29.30	1.690
2012247C	one and half brick wall	Each	0.04	3.13	-	0.62	3.75	4.13	2.110
2012247D	blockwork 100 mm thick	Each	0.18	13.84	-	0.37	14.21	15.63	1.270

Small Works 2011		Unit	Labour Hours	Labour Net	Plant Net	Materials Net	Unit Net	Unit with 10%	CO$_2$
				£	£	£	£	£	Kg
201	**NEW WORK**								
20122	**SUNDRIES**								
2012250	**Cut mortices for iron bolts, stays etc in brickwork and grout in cement mortar**								
2012250A	per 25 mm depth of mortice	Each	0.03	2.06	-	0.12	2.18	2.40	0.420
2012252	**Cut and pin in brickwork**								
2012252A	sink bearers, radiator brackets, holder bats etc	Each	0.25	19.19	-	0.49	19.68	21.65	1.690
2012252B	end of steel joists; not exceeding 250 mm high	Each	0.30	23.09	-	0.74	23.83	26.21	2.530
2012252C	end of steel joists; 250 mm - 500 mm high	Each	0.45	34.63	-	1.23	35.86	39.45	4.220
2012253	**Galvanised frame ties screwed to wood frame and built into brickwork**								
2012253A	203 mm girth	Each	0.07	5.12	-	0.69	5.81	6.39	0.280
2012253B	254 mm girth	Each	0.07	5.66	-	0.73	6.39	7.03	0.350

Small Works 2011		Unit	Labour Hours	Labour Net £	Plant Net £	Materials Net £	Unit Net £	Unit with 10% £	CO_2 Kg
202	**REPAIRS AND ALTERATIONS**								
20201	**DEMOLISHING BRICKWORK**								
2020101	**Demolish brickwork, any height, and set aside arisings**								
2020101A	half brick walls	m^2	0.75	15.64	-	-	15.64	17.20	-
2020101B	one brick walls	m^2	1.35	28.15	-	-	28.15	30.97	-
2020101C	one and a half brick walls	m^2	1.85	38.57	-	-	38.57	42.43	-
2020101D	two brick walls	m^2	2.40	50.04	-	-	50.04	55.04	-
2020102	**Sort, clean and stack sound bricks for reuse; in**								
2020102A	lime mortar	1000	14.00	291.90	-	-	291.90	321.09	-
2020102B	composite mortar	1000	17.00	354.45	-	-	354.45	389.90	-
2020102C	cement mortar	1000	22.00	458.70	-	-	458.70	504.57	-
2020103	**Hand load rubble to skip, cart away to tip**								
2020103A	and pay all tipping fees	m^3	2.00	41.70	33.60	-	75.30	82.83	-
20203	**CHIMNEY STACK REMOVAL**								
2020301	**Pulling down chimney stacks, clean sound whole bricks for reuse and remove remainder**								
2020301A	up to 9 m high or two storeys; lime mortar	m^3	9.39	717.94	-	-	717.94	789.73	-
2020301B	up to 9 m high or two storeys; cement mortar	m^3	12.07	923.06	-	-	923.06	1,015.37	-
2020301C	Extra over for each additional 3 m or storey height; lime mortar	m^3	2.35	179.50	-	-	179.50	197.45	-
2020301D	Extra over for each additional 3 m or storey height; cement mortar	m^3	3.02	230.73	-	-	230.73	253.80	-
20205	**CHIMNEY STACK REBUILDING**								
2020501	**Rebuild single flue chimney in common bricks, in cement mortar 1:3, including building in 185 mm dia socketed and rebated clay flue liners, BS 1181; up to 9 m or two storeys high; overall plan dimensions**								
2020501A	450 x 450 mm	m	2.01	153.82	-	79.55	233.37	256.71	134.880
2020501B	675 x 675 mm	m	3.24	247.70	-	109.07	356.77	392.45	199.640
2020502	**Rebuild double flue chimney in common bricks, in cement mortar 1:3, including building in 185 mm dia socketed and rebated clay flue liners, BS 1181; up to 9 m or two storeys high; overall plan dimensions**								
2020502A	450 x 750 mm	m	1.74	133.33	-	113.37	246.70	271.37	152.760
2020502B	675 x 675 mm	m	2.92	223.08	-	144.48	367.56	404.32	221.120
2020503	**Take off loose chimney pot and reset including flaunching**								
2020503A	up to two storeys or 9 m high	Each	0.67	51.30	-	0.86	52.16	57.38	2.950
2020504	**Take down and remove chimney pot, supply, set and flaunch new pot; up to two storeys or 9 m high**								
2020504A	300 mm pot	Each	0.84	64.14	-	35.30	99.44	109.38	5.510
2020504B	450 mm pot	Each	0.87	66.66	-	43.08	109.74	120.71	7.400
2020504C	600 mm pot	Each	0.91	69.26	-	62.54	131.80	144.98	8.090
2020504D	add for each additional storey or 3 m high; 300 mm pot	Each	0.09	6.96	-	-	6.96	7.66	-
2020504E	add for each additional storey or 3 m high; 450 mm pot	Each	0.13	9.71	-	-	9.71	10.68	-
2020504F	add for each additional storey or 3 m high; 600 mm pot	Each	0.17	12.84	-	-	12.84	14.12	-
20206	**DAMP PROOFING**								
2020601	**Treating with silicone or similar damp-proofing liquid**								
2020601A	external brick walls	m^2	0.07	5.66	-	0.88	6.54	7.19	0.080

Small Works 2011		Unit	Labour Hours	Labour Net	Plant Net	Materials Net	Unit Net	Unit with 10%	CO$_2$
				£	£	£	£	£	Kg
202	**REPAIRS AND ALTERATIONS**								
20207	**BRICKWORK REPAIRS**								
2020701	**Cut out defective brickwork and reface with new facing bricks (PC £390 per 1000), in**								
2020701A	cement mortar	m^2	1.91	146.17	-	28.09	174.26	191.69	104.380
2020701B	lime mortar	m^2	1.68	128.21	-	28.32	156.53	172.18	102.500
2020702	**Cut out single facing bricks and reface with new facing bricks (PC £390 per 1000), in**								
2020702A	cement mortar	Each	0.17	12.84	-	0.51	13.35	14.69	1.880
2020702B	lime mortar	Each	0.12	8.94	-	0.53	9.47	10.42	1.780
2020703	**Rake out mortar and repoint**								
2020703A	perished mortar	m^2	0.29	22.09	-	0.54	22.63	24.89	1.290
2020703B	sound mortar	m^2	0.72	55.12	-	0.54	55.66	61.23	1.290
2020704	**Cut out fractures in brickwork and lace in common bricks approximately 405 mm wide, 225 mm thick in**								
2020704A	cement mortar	m	1.21	92.28	-	20.84	113.12	124.43	53.200
2020704B	lime mortar	m	0.81	61.54	-	20.97	82.51	90.76	50.700
2020705	**Cut out fractures in brickwork, and lace in facing bricks (PC £390 per 1000), approximately 405 mm wide, 225 mm thick in**								
2020705A	cement mortar	m	1.33	101.30	-	25.86	127.16	139.88	92.930
2020705B	lime mortar	m	0.92	70.49	-	25.86	96.35	105.99	92.930
2020706	**Take down segmental arch and rebuild in facing bricks (PC £390 per 1000), 225 mm high on face, including centering**								
2020706A	113 mm wide soffit	m	2.01	153.82	-	6.53	160.35	176.39	23.520
2020706B	225 mm wide soffit	m	2.62	199.99	-	12.24	212.23	233.45	45.100
20209	**OPENINGS IN BRICK WALLS**								
2020901	**Cut opening through brickwork in cement mortar for doors, windows etc, including all necessary shoring and making good, in**								
2020901A	half brick walls	m^2	0.92	42.46	0.41	15.07	57.94	63.73	55.580
2020901B	one brick walls	m^2	1.84	84.99	0.83	27.49	113.31	124.64	88.260
2020901C	one and a half brick walls	m^2	2.76	127.45	1.14	40.04	168.63	185.49	121.360
2020901D	two brick walls	m^2	3.18	159.48	1.50	52.15	213.13	234.44	153.300
2020903	**Infill openings in brickwork in common bricks (PC £300 per 1000), in gauged mortar; in small areas and bond to existing**								
2020903A	half brick walls	m^2	0.82	62.84	-	22.92	85.76	94.34	103.790
2020903B	one brick walls	m^2	1.51	115.36	-	45.68	161.04	177.14	206.450
2020903C	one and a half brick walls	m^2	2.26	173.08	-	68.61	241.69	265.86	310.240
20210	**DAMP PROOF COURSES**								
2021001	**Damp-proof course in short lengths in existing walls including cutting out brickwork and building in with new bricks**								
2021001A	half brick wide; two course slate	m	0.62	47.48	-	131.19	178.67	196.54	5.780
2021001B	half brick wide; bitumen felt	m	0.52	39.75	-	1.48	41.23	45.35	2.750
2021001C	one brick wide and over; two course slate	m^2	2.18	166.66	-	898.43	1,065.09	1,171.60	28.660
2021001D	one brick wide and over; bitumen felt	m^2	1.78	135.85	-	30.47	166.32	182.95	11.040

Brickwork and Blockwork

	Unit	Labour Hours	Labour Net	Plant Net	Materials Net	Unit Net	Unit with 10%	CO₂
			£	£	£	£	£	Kg
202	**REPAIRS AND ALTERATIONS**							
20215	**FRAME REBEDDING**							
2021501	**Take out and rebed door or window frame including**							
2021501A	point externally and make good internally	m	0.19	14.14	-	0.49	14.63	16.09	1.690
2021502	**Rake out defective pointing around door or window frame and repoint in**							
2021502A	cement mortar	m	0.15	11.54	-	0.14	11.68	12.85	0.320
2021502B	mastic	m	0.20	15.37	-	0.74	16.11	17.72	1.420
20216	**FIRE AND HEARTH REPAIRS**							
2021601	**Take out existing fireplace including surround and hearth**							
2021601A	small iron	Each	1.34	102.60	-	-	102.60	112.86	-
2021601B	large tiled	Each	1.73	132.03	-	-	132.03	145.23	-
2021601C	free standing	Each	1.07	82.03	-	-	82.03	90.23	-
2021602	**Take out and reset existing fireplace including surround and hearth**							
2021602A	small iron	Each	3.35	256.41	-	13.09	269.50	296.45	44.700
2021602B	large tiled	Each	4.11	314.13	-	17.66	331.79	364.97	60.310
2021602C	free standing	Each	2.75	210.24	-	5.19	215.43	236.97	17.710
20218	**VENTILATION**							
2021801	**Air ventilator cut out and remove**							
2021801A	plaster fly proof 225 mm x 75 mm	Each	0.10	7.72	-	-	7.72	8.49	-
2021801B	plaster fly proof 225 mm x 150 mm	Each	0.12	9.48	-	-	9.48	10.43	-
2021801C	terracotta 225 mm x 75 mm	Each	0.11	8.18	-	-	8.18	9.00	-
2021801D	terracotta 225 mm x 150 mm	Each	0.14	10.78	-	-	10.78	11.86	-
2021801E	galvanised iron 225 mm x 75 mm	Each	0.11	8.18	-	-	8.18	9.00	-
2021801F	galvanised iron 225 mm x 150 mm	Each	0.14	10.78	-	-	10.78	11.86	-
2021803	**Air ventilator cut through brick wall (any thickness) build in and make good**							
2021803A	plaster fly proof 225 mm x 75 mm	Each	0.16	12.31	-	2.84	15.15	16.67	0.230
2021803B	plaster fly proof 225 mm x 150 mm	Each	0.19	14.14	-	3.40	17.54	19.29	0.450
2021803C	terracotta 225 mm x 75 mm	Each	0.17	12.84	-	3.91	16.75	18.43	0.540
2021803D	terracotta 225 mm x 150 mm	Each	0.20	15.37	-	5.18	20.55	22.61	1.080
2021803E	galvanised iron 225 mm x 75 mm	Each	0.17	12.84	-	5.81	18.65	20.52	0.400
2021803F	galvanised iron 225 mm x 150 mm	Each	0.20	15.37	-	10.68	26.05	28.66	0.800

Woodwork

Small Works 2011		Unit	Labour Hours	Labour Net	Plant Net	Materials Net	Unit Net	Unit with 10%	CO$_2$
				£	£	£	£	£	Kg
301	**NEW WORK**								
30101	**CARCASSING SAWN SOFTWOOD**								
3010101	**Floors**								
3010101A	50 mm x 100 mm	m	0.12	3.34	-	2.00	5.34	5.87	1.650
3010101B	50 mm x 125 mm	m	0.14	3.75	-	2.51	6.26	6.89	2.070
3010101C	50 mm x 150 mm	m	0.47	13.07	-	2.99	16.06	17.67	2.480
3010101D	50 mm x 175 mm	m	0.17	4.75	-	3.51	8.26	9.09	2.890
3010101E	50 mm x 200 mm	m	0.20	5.45	-	4.01	9.46	10.41	3.310
3010101F	50 mm x 225 mm	m	0.22	6.12	-	4.66	10.78	11.86	3.720
3010101G	63 mm x 125 mm	m	0.15	4.28	-	5.69	9.97	10.97	2.600
3010101H	63 mm x 150 mm	m	0.19	5.14	-	6.81	11.95	13.15	3.120
3010101I	63 mm x 175 mm	m	0.22	6.00	-	7.96	13.96	15.36	3.640
3010101J	63 mm x 200 mm	m	0.25	6.84	-	9.02	15.86	17.45	4.170
3010101K	63 mm x 225 mm	m	0.28	7.70	-	10.14	17.84	19.62	4.690
3010101L	75 mm x 125 mm	m	0.18	5.09	-	4.23	9.32	10.25	3.100
3010101M	75 mm x 150 mm	m	0.22	6.12	-	4.97	11.09	12.20	3.720
3010101N	75 mm x 175 mm	m	0.26	7.12	-	5.77	12.89	14.18	4.340
3010101O	75 mm x 200 mm	m	0.29	8.15	-	6.61	14.76	16.24	4.960
3010101P	75 mm x 225 mm	m	0.33	9.17	-	7.71	16.88	18.57	5.580
3010102	**Partitions**								
3010102B	38 mm x 100 mm	m	0.21	5.84	-	1.76	7.60	8.36	1.260
3010102C	50 mm x 75 mm	m	0.22	6.12	-	1.60	7.72	8.49	1.240
3010102D	50 mm x 100 mm	m	0.27	7.51	-	2.00	9.51	10.46	1.650
3010103	**Flat roofs**								
3010103A	50 mm x 150 mm	m	0.29	8.06	-	2.99	11.05	12.16	2.480
3010103B	50 mm x 175 mm	m	0.32	8.90	-	3.51	12.41	13.65	2.890
3010103C	50 mm x 200 mm	m	0.36	10.01	-	4.01	14.02	15.42	3.310
3010103D	75 mm x 100 mm	m	0.29	8.06	-	3.54	11.60	12.76	2.480
3010104	**Pitched roofs including ceiling joists**								
3010104A	25 mm x 100 mm	m	0.12	3.34	-	1.18	4.52	4.97	0.830
3010104B	25 mm x 125 mm	m	0.14	3.89	-	1.44	5.33	5.86	1.030
3010104C	25 mm x 150 mm	m	0.14	3.89	-	1.71	5.60	6.16	1.240
3010104D	38 mm x 75 mm	m	0.14	3.89	-	1.30	5.19	5.71	0.940
3010104E	38 mm x 100 mm	m	0.14	3.89	-	1.76	5.65	6.22	1.260
3010104F	38 mm x 125 mm	m	0.14	3.89	-	2.18	6.07	6.68	1.570
3010104G	38 mm x 150 mm	m	0.15	4.17	-	2.60	6.77	7.45	1.880
3010104H	50 mm x 75 mm	m	0.14	3.89	-	1.60	5.49	6.04	1.240
3010104I	50 mm x 100 mm	m	0.15	4.17	-	2.00	6.17	6.79	1.650
3010104J	50 mm x 125 mm	m	0.15	4.17	-	2.51	6.68	7.35	2.070
3010104K	50 mm x 150 mm	m	0.15	4.17	-	2.99	7.16	7.88	2.480
3010104L	63 mm x 100 mm	m	0.15	4.17	-	4.55	8.72	9.59	2.080
3010104M	63 mm x 125 mm	m	0.15	4.17	-	5.69	9.86	10.85	2.600
3010104N	63 mm x 150 mm	m	0.16	4.45	-	6.81	11.26	12.39	3.120
3010104O	63 mm x 175 mm	m	0.16	4.45	-	7.96	12.41	13.65	3.640
3010104P	75 mm x 100 mm	m	0.15	4.17	-	3.54	7.71	8.48	2.480
3010104Q	75 mm x 125 mm	m	0.16	4.45	-	4.23	8.68	9.55	3.100
3010104R	75 mm x 150 mm	m	0.17	4.73	-	4.97	9.70	10.67	3.720
3010104S	75 mm x 175 mm	m	0.18	5.00	-	5.77	10.77	11.85	4.340
3010104T	100 mm x 150 mm	m	0.18	5.00	-	7.33	12.33	13.56	4.960
3010104U	100 mm x 175 mm	m	0.20	5.56	-	7.33	12.89	14.18	4.960
3010104V	100 mm x 200 mm	m	0.21	5.84	-	9.12	14.96	16.46	6.610
3010104W	100 mm x 225 mm	m	0.22	6.12	-	10.64	16.76	18.44	7.440
3010105	**Kerbs, bearers and the like**								
3010105A	25 mm x 100 mm	m	0.20	5.56	-	8.28	13.84	15.22	5.780
3010105B	38 mm x 75 mm	m	0.05	1.39	-	1.30	2.69	2.96	0.940
3010105C	38 mm x 100 mm	m	0.07	1.95	-	1.76	3.71	4.08	1.260
3010105D	50 mm x 75 mm	m	0.07	1.95	-	1.60	3.55	3.91	1.240
3010105E	50 mm x 100 mm	m	0.09	2.50	-	2.00	4.50	4.95	1.650
3010105F	75 mm x 100 mm	m	0.14	3.89	-	3.54	7.43	8.17	2.480
3010106	**Noggins**								
3010106A	38 mm x 50 mm	m	0.30	8.34	-	0.99	9.33	10.26	0.630
3010106B	50 mm x 50 mm	m	0.35	9.73	-	1.08	10.81	11.89	0.830
3010106C	50 mm x 75 mm	m	0.40	11.12	-	1.60	12.72	13.99	1.240
3010107	**Herringbone strutting between joists (measured over joists)**								
3010107A	38 mm x 50 mm	m	0.45	12.51	-	0.99	13.50	14.85	0.630
3010107B	50 mm x 50 mm	m	0.50	13.90	-	1.08	14.98	16.48	0.830
3010109	**Solid strutting between joists (measured over joists)**								
3010109A	50 mm x 100 mm	m	0.35	9.73	-	2.00	11.73	12.90	1.650
3010109B	50 mm x 125 mm	m	0.40	11.12	-	2.47	13.59	14.95	2.070
3010109C	50 mm x 175 mm	m	0.50	13.90	-	3.41	17.31	19.04	2.890

Woodwork

Small Works 2011		Unit	Labour Hours	Labour Net	Plant Net	Materials Net	Unit Net	Unit with 10%	CO₂
				£	£	£	£	£	Kg
301	**NEW WORK**								
30101	**CARCASSING SAWN SOFTWOOD**								
3010110	**Sprocket pieces**								
3010110A	50 mm x 50 mm x 200 mm	Each	0.17	4.73	-	0.22	4.95	5.45	0.170
3010110B	50 mm x 100 mm x 600 mm	Each	0.20	5.56	-	1.20	6.76	7.44	0.990
3010111	**Extra labour trimming to openings**								
3010111A	500mm x 1000mm; joist 50mm x 100mm	Each	1.35	37.53	-	-	37.53	41.28	-
3010111B	750mm x 1000mm; joist 50mm x 100mm	Each	1.58	43.92	-	-	43.92	48.31	-
3010111C	600mm x 1200mm; joist 50mm x 175mm	Each	1.62	45.04	-	-	45.04	49.54	-
3010111D	900mm x 1800mm; joist 50mm x 175mm	Each	2.43	67.55	-	-	67.55	74.31	-
3010111E	600mm x 1200mm; joist 50mm x 200mm	Each	1.62	45.04	-	-	45.04	49.54	-
3010111F	900mm x 1500mm; joist 50mm x 200mm	Each	1.62	45.04	-	-	45.04	49.54	-
3010111G	600mm x 1200mm; joist 75mm x 175mm	Each	1.62	45.04	-	-	45.04	49.54	-
3010111H	1000mm x 2000mm; joist 75mm x 175mm	Each	2.70	75.06	-	-	75.06	82.57	-
3010112	**Trussed rafters; stress graded; sawn softwood; pressure impregnated; raised through two storeys; fixed in position; 450 mm eaves overhang Fan truss 22.5 deg pitch; span over wall plates**								
3010112A	5.00 m	Each	1.36	66.12	-	27.31	93.43	102.77	16.080
3010112B	6.00 m	Each	0.83	40.33	-	48.17	88.50	97.35	28.980
3010112C	7.00 m	Each	0.86	42.03	-	54.33	96.36	106.00	31.840
3010112D	8.00 m	Each	0.86	42.03	-	63.13	105.16	115.68	34.700
3010112E	9.00 m	Each	0.90	43.74	-	74.54	118.28	130.11	37.560
3010112F	10.00 m	Each	0.90	43.74	-	88.63	132.37	145.61	40.430
3010113	**Trussed rafters; stress graded; sawn softwood; pressure impregnated; raised through two storeys; fixed in position; 450 mm eaves overhang Fan truss 35 deg pitch; span over wall plates**								
3010113A	5.00 m	Each	0.86	42.03	-	46.90	88.93	97.82	26.120
3010113B	6.00 m	Each	0.86	42.03	-	51.03	93.06	102.37	28.980
3010113C	7.00 m	Each	0.90	43.74	-	56.79	100.53	110.58	31.840
3010113D	8.00 m	Each	0.90	43.74	-	65.04	108.78	119.66	34.700
3010113E	9.00 m	Each	1.86	51.71	-	75.76	127.47	140.22	37.560
3010113F	10.00 m	Each	0.93	45.20	-	88.98	134.18	147.60	40.430
3010114	**Trussed rafters; stress graded; sawn softwood; pressure impregnated; raised through two storeys; fixed in position; 450 mm eaves overhang Fink or W truss 22.5 deg pitch; span over wall plates**								
3010114A	5.00 m	Each	0.83	40.33	-	43.76	84.09	92.50	26.120
3010114B	6.00 m	Each	0.83	40.33	-	48.17	88.50	97.35	28.980
3010114C	7.00 m	Each	0.86	42.03	-	54.33	96.36	106.00	31.840
3010114D	8.00 m	Each	0.86	42.03	-	63.13	105.16	115.68	34.700
3010114E	9.00 m	Each	0.90	43.74	-	74.54	118.28	130.11	37.560
3010114F	10.00 m	Each	0.90	43.74	-	88.63	132.37	145.61	40.430
3010115	**Trussed rafters; stress graded; sawn softwood; pressure impregnated; raised through two storeys; fixed in position; 450 mm eaves overhang Fink or W truss 35 deg pitch; span over wall plates**								
3010115A	5.00 m	Each	0.86	42.03	-	46.90	88.93	97.82	26.120
3010115B	6.00 m	Each	0.86	42.03	-	51.03	93.06	102.37	28.980
3010115C	7.00 m	Each	0.90	43.74	-	56.79	100.53	110.58	31.840

Small Works 2011		Unit	Labour Hours	Labour Net £	Plant Net £	Materials Net £	Unit Net £	Unit with 10% £	CO$_2$ Kg
301	**NEW WORK**								
30101	**CARCASSING SAWN SOFTWOOD**								
3010115	**Trussed rafters; stress graded; sawn softwood; pressure impregnated; raised through two storeys; fixed in position; 450 mm eaves overhang Fink or W truss 35 deg pitch; span over wall plates**								
3010115D	8.00 m	Each	0.90	43.74	-	65.04	108.78	119.66	34.700
3010115E	9.00 m	Each	0.93	45.20	-	75.76	120.96	133.06	37.560
3010115F	10.00 m	Each	0.93	45.20	-	88.98	134.18	147.60	40.430
30103	**FIRST FIXINGS CHIPBOARD**								
3010301	**Boarding to floors; butt joints; thickness**								
3010301A	18 mm	m^2	0.35	9.73	-	7.13	16.86	18.55	7.720
3010301B	18 mm raking cutting	m	0.54	15.01	-	0.88	15.89	17.48	0.960
3010301C	18 mm curved cutting	m	0.93	25.85	-	2.04	27.89	30.68	2.210
3010301D	22 mm	m^2	0.42	11.68	-	5.64	17.32	19.05	9.440
3010301E	22 mm raking cutting	m	0.60	16.68	-	0.70	17.38	19.12	1.170
3010301F	22 mm curved cutting	m	0.99	27.52	-	1.61	29.13	32.04	2.700
3010302	**Boarding to floors; tongued and grooved joints; thickness**								
3010302A	18 mm	m^2	0.44	12.23	-	4.58	16.81	18.49	7.720
3010302B	18 mm raking cutting	m	0.54	15.01	-	0.61	15.62	17.18	1.030
3010302C	18 mm curved cutting	m	0.93	25.85	-	1.35	27.20	29.92	2.280
3010302D	22 mm	m^2	0.48	13.34	-	5.86	19.20	21.12	9.440
3010302E	22 mm raking cutting	m	0.60	16.68	-	0.78	17.46	19.21	1.260
3010302F	22 mm curved cutting	m	0.99	27.52	-	1.68	29.20	32.12	2.700
3010303	**Boarding to floors; moisture resistant; butt joints; thickness**								
3010303A	18 mm	m^2	0.35	9.73	-	5.36	15.09	16.60	7.720
3010303B	18 mm raking cutting	m	0.54	15.01	-	0.71	15.72	17.29	1.030
3010303C	18 mm curved cutting	m	0.93	25.85	-	1.58	27.43	30.17	2.280
3010303D	22 mm	m^2	0.42	11.68	-	6.41	18.09	19.90	9.440
3010303E	22 mm raking cutting	m	0.60	16.68	-	0.85	17.53	19.28	1.260
3010303F	22 mm curved cutting	m	0.99	27.52	-	1.83	29.35	32.29	2.700
3010304	**Boarding to floors; moisture resistant; tongued and grooved joints; thickness**								
3010304A	18 mm	m^2	0.44	12.23	-	5.40	17.63	19.39	7.720
3010304B	18 mm raking cutting	m	0.54	15.01	-	0.72	15.73	17.30	1.030
3010304C	18 mm curved cutting	m	0.93	25.85	-	1.54	27.39	30.13	2.210
3010304D	22 mm	m^2	0.48	13.34	-	6.41	19.75	21.73	9.440
3010304E	22 mm raking cutting	m	0.60	16.68	-	0.85	17.53	19.28	1.260
3010304F	22 mm curved cutting	m	0.99	27.52	-	1.83	29.35	32.29	2.700
3010306	**Boarding to roofs; butt joints; thickness**								
3010306A	12 mm	m^2	0.33	9.17	-	3.99	13.16	14.48	5.150
3010306B	12 mm raking cutting	m	0.33	9.17	-	0.60	9.77	10.75	0.770
3010306C	12 mm curved cutting	m	0.73	20.29	-	1.20	21.49	23.64	1.550
3010306D	18 mm	m^2	0.37	10.29	-	7.13	17.42	19.16	7.720
3010306E	18 mm raking cutting	m	0.54	15.01	-	1.07	16.08	17.69	1.160
3010306F	18 mm curved cutting	m	0.93	25.85	-	2.14	27.99	30.79	2.320
3010306G	25 mm	m^2	0.49	13.62	-	5.64	19.26	21.19	9.440
3010306H	25 mm raking cutting	m	0.65	18.07	-	0.85	18.92	20.81	1.420
3010306I	25 mm curved cutting	m	1.04	28.91	-	1.69	30.60	33.66	2.830
3010307	**Boarding to roofs; sloping; butt joints; thickness**								
3010307A	12 mm	m^2	0.35	9.73	-	3.99	13.72	15.09	5.150
3010307B	12 mm raking cutting	m	0.33	9.17	-	0.60	9.77	10.75	0.770
3010307C	12 mm curved cutting	m	0.73	20.29	-	1.20	21.49	23.64	1.550
3010307D	18 mm	m^2	0.46	12.79	-	7.13	19.92	21.91	7.720
3010307E	18 mm raking cutting	m	0.54	15.01	-	1.07	16.08	17.69	1.160
3010307F	18 mm curved cutting	m	0.93	25.85	-	2.14	27.99	30.79	2.320
3010307G	25 mm	m^2	0.64	17.79	-	5.64	23.43	25.77	9.440
3010307H	25 mm raking cutting	m	0.65	18.07	-	0.85	18.92	20.81	1.420
3010307I	25 mm curved cutting	m	1.04	28.91	-	1.69	30.60	33.66	2.830

Woodwork

	Unit	Labour Hours	Labour Net £	Plant Net £	Materials Net £	Unit Net £	Unit with 10% £	CO₂ Kg
301	**NEW WORK**							
30105	**FIRST FIXINGS STERLING BOARD**							
3010501	**Boarding to floors; butt joints; thickness**							
3010501A	18 mm	m²	0.32	8.90	-	7.08	15.98	17.58	5.840
3010501B	18 mm raking cutting	m	0.49	13.62	-	1.06	14.68	16.15	0.880
3010501C	18 mm curved cutting	m	0.84	23.35	-	2.12	25.47	28.02	1.750
3010501D	11 mm	m²	0.27	7.51	-	4.26	11.77	12.95	3.570
3010501E	11 mm raking cutting	m	0.27	7.51	-	0.64	8.15	8.97	0.540
3010501F	11 mm curved cutting	m	0.63	17.51	-	1.28	18.79	20.67	1.070
30106	**FIRST FIXINGS PLYWOOD**							
3010601	**Boarding to roofs; butt joints; thickness**							
3010601A	18 mm	m²	0.44	12.23	-	16.19	28.42	31.26	10.520
3010601B	18 mm raking cutting	m	0.40	11.12	-	2.43	13.55	14.91	1.580
3010601C	18 mm curved cutting	m	1.06	29.47	-	4.86	34.33	37.76	3.160
3010601D	25 mm	m²	0.50	13.90	-	23.16	37.06	40.77	14.600
3010601E	25 mm raking cutting	m	0.43	11.95	-	3.47	15.42	16.96	2.190
3010601F	25 mm curved cutting	m	1.13	31.41	-	6.95	38.36	42.20	4.380
3010602	**Boarding to roofs; sloping; butt joints thickness**							
3010602A	18 mm	m²	0.46	12.79	-	16.19	28.98	31.88	10.520
3010602B	18 mm raking cutting	m	0.40	11.12	-	2.43	13.55	14.91	1.580
3010602C	18 mm curved cutting	m	1.06	29.47	-	4.86	34.33	37.76	3.160
3010602D	25 mm	m²	0.52	14.46	-	23.16	37.62	41.38	14.600
3010602E	25 mm raking cutting	m	0.43	11.95	-	3.47	15.42	16.96	2.190
3010602F	25 mm curved cutting	m	1.13	31.41	-	6.95	38.36	42.20	4.380
3010605	**Boarding to dormers; tops or cheeks; butt joints; thickness**							
3010605A	18 mm over 300 mm wide	m²	0.73	20.29	-	16.19	36.48	40.13	10.520
3010605B	18 mm not exceeding 150 mm wide	m	0.11	3.06	-	2.43	5.49	6.04	1.580
3010605C	18 mm 150 mm to 300 mm wide	m	0.22	6.12	-	4.86	10.98	12.08	3.160
3010605D	18 mm raking cutting	m	0.40	11.12	-	2.43	13.55	14.91	1.580
3010605E	18 mm curved cutting	m	1.06	29.47	-	4.86	34.33	37.76	3.160
3010605F	25 mm over 300 mm wide	m²	0.83	23.07	-	23.16	46.23	50.85	14.600
3010605G	25 mm not exceeding 150 mm wide	m	0.13	3.61	-	3.47	7.08	7.79	2.190
3010605H	25 mm 150 mm to 300 mm wide	m	0.25	6.95	-	6.95	13.90	15.29	4.380
3010605I	25 mm raking cutting	m	0.43	11.95	-	3.47	15.42	16.96	2.190
3010605J	25 mm curved cutting	m	1.13	31.41	-	6.95	38.36	42.20	4.380
3010606	**Boarding to gutters; bottoms or sides; butt joints; thickness**							
3010606A	18 mm over 300 mm wide	m²	2.76	76.73	-	16.19	92.92	102.21	10.520
3010606B	18 mm not exceeding 150 mm wide	m	0.41	11.40	-	2.43	13.83	15.21	1.580
3010606C	18 mm 150 mm to 300 mm wide	m	0.83	23.07	-	4.86	27.93	30.72	3.160
3010606D	18 mm raking cutting	m	0.40	11.12	-	2.43	13.55	14.91	1.580
3010606E	18 mm curved cutting	m	1.06	29.47	-	4.86	34.33	37.76	3.160
3010606F	25 mm over 300 mm wide	m²	3.14	87.29	-	23.16	110.45	121.50	14.600
3010606G	25 mm not exceeding 150 mm wide	m	0.47	13.07	-	3.47	16.54	18.19	2.190
3010606H	25 mm 150 mm to 300 mm wide	m	0.94	26.13	-	6.95	33.08	36.39	4.380
3010606I	25 mm raking cutting	m	0.43	11.95	-	3.47	15.42	16.96	2.190
3010606J	25 mm curved cutting	m	1.13	31.41	-	6.95	38.36	42.20	4.380
3010607	**Boarding to eaves; verges; fascias and the like; butt joints; thickness**							
3010607A	18 mm over 300 mm wide	m²	1.52	42.26	-	16.19	58.45	64.30	10.520
3010607B	18 mm not exceeding 150 mm wide	m	0.23	6.39	-	2.43	8.82	9.70	1.580
3010607C	18 mm 150 mm to 300 mm wide	m	0.46	12.79	-	4.86	17.65	19.42	3.160
3010607D	18 mm raking cutting	m	0.40	11.12	-	2.43	13.55	14.91	1.580
3010607E	18 mm curved cutting	m	1.06	29.47	-	4.86	34.33	37.76	3.160
3010607F	25 mm over 300 mm wide	m²	1.66	46.15	-	23.16	69.31	76.24	14.600
3010607G	25 mm not exceeding 150 mm wide	m	0.25	6.95	-	3.47	10.42	11.46	2.190
3010607H	25 mm 150 mm to 300 mm wide	m	0.50	13.90	-	6.95	20.85	22.94	4.380
3010607I	25 mm raking cutting	m	0.43	11.95	-	3.47	15.42	16.96	2.190
3010607J	25 mm curved cutting	m	1.13	31.41	-	6.95	38.36	42.20	4.380

Small Works 2011		Unit	Labour Hours	Labour Net	Plant Net	Materials Net	Unit Net	Unit with 10%	CO₂
				£	£	£	£	£	Kg

301   **NEW WORK**

30108   **FIRST FIXINGS SOFTWOOD**

3010801	**Boarding to roofs; 150 mm wide boards; butt joints; thickness**								
3010801A	19 mm	m²	0.70	19.46	-	18.63	38.09	41.90	6.280
3010801B	19 mm raking cutting	m	0.20	5.56	-	2.80	8.36	9.20	0.940
3010801C	19 mm curved cutting	m	0.60	16.68	-	5.59	22.27	24.50	1.880
3010801D	25 mm	m²	0.75	20.85	-	21.29	42.14	46.35	8.260
3010801E	25 mm raking cutting	m	0.20	5.56	-	3.19	8.75	9.63	1.240
3010801F	25 mm curved cutting	m	0.60	16.68	-	6.39	23.07	25.38	2.480
3010802	**Boarding to roofs; sloping; 150 mm wide boards; butt joints; thickness**								
3010802A	19 mm	m²	1.05	29.19	-	18.63	47.82	52.60	6.280
3010802B	19 mm raking cutting	m	0.20	5.56	-	2.80	8.36	9.20	0.940
3010802C	19 mm curved cutting	m	0.60	16.68	-	5.59	22.27	24.50	1.880
3010802D	25 mm	m²	1.13	31.41	-	21.29	52.70	57.97	8.260
3010802E	25 mm raking cutting	m	0.20	5.56	-	3.19	8.75	9.63	1.240
3010802F	25 mm curved cutting	m	0.60	16.68	-	6.39	23.07	25.38	2.480
3010803	**Boarding to dormers; tops or cheeks; 150 mm wide boards; butt joints; thickness**								
3010803A	19 mm	m²	0.99	27.52	-	18.63	46.15	50.77	6.280
3010803B	19 mm raking cutting	m	0.20	5.56	-	2.80	8.36	9.20	0.940
3010803C	19 mm curved cutting	m	0.60	16.68	-	5.59	22.27	24.50	1.880
3010803D	25 mm	m²	1.07	29.75	-	21.29	51.04	56.14	8.260
3010803E	25 mm raking cutting	m	0.20	5.56	-	3.19	8.75	9.63	1.240
3010803F	25 mm curved cutting	m	0.60	16.68	-	6.39	23.07	25.38	2.480
3010804	**Boarding to gutters; bottoms or sides; sloping; thickness**								
3010804A	19 mm over 300 mm wide	m²	1.51	41.98	-	18.63	60.61	66.67	6.280
3010804B	19 mm not exceeding 150 mm wide	m	0.76	21.13	-	2.80	23.93	26.32	0.940
3010804C	19 mm 150 mm to 300 mm wide	m	0.98	27.24	-	5.59	32.83	36.11	1.880
3010804D	19 mm raking cutting	m	0.20	5.56	-	2.80	8.36	9.20	0.940
3010804E	19 mm curved cutting	m	0.60	16.68	-	5.59	22.27	24.50	1.880
3010804F	25 mm over 300 mm wide	m²	1.51	41.98	-	21.29	63.27	69.60	8.260
3010804G	25 mm not exceeding 150 mm wide	m	0.76	21.13	-	3.19	24.32	26.75	1.240
3010804H	25 mm 150 mm to 300 mm wide	m	0.98	27.24	-	6.39	33.63	36.99	2.480
3010804I	25 mm raking cutting	m	0.20	5.56	-	3.19	8.75	9.63	1.240
3010804J	25 mm curved cutting	m	0.60	16.68	-	6.39	23.07	25.38	2.480
3010805	**Boarding to verges; fascias; soffits, thickness**								
3010805A	19 mm over 300 mm wide	m²	1.34	37.25	-	18.63	55.88	61.47	6.280
3010805B	19 mm not exceeding 150 mm wide	m	0.68	18.90	-	2.80	21.70	23.87	0.940
3010805C	19 mm 150 mm to 300 mm wide	m	0.87	24.19	-	5.59	29.78	32.76	1.880
3010805D	19 mm raking cutting	m	0.20	5.56	-	2.80	8.36	9.20	0.940
3010805E	19 mm curved cutting	m	0.60	16.68	-	5.59	22.27	24.50	1.880
3010805F	25 mm over 300 mm wide	m²	1.34	37.25	-	21.29	58.54	64.39	8.260
3010805G	25 mm not exceeding 150 mm wide	m	0.68	18.90	-	3.19	22.09	24.30	1.240
3010805H	25 mm 150 mm to 300 mm wide	m	0.60	16.68	-	6.39	23.07	25.38	2.480
3010805I	25 mm raking cutting	m	0.20	5.56	-	3.19	8.75	9.63	1.240
3010805J	25 mm curved cutting	m	0.60	16.68	-	6.39	23.07	25.38	2.480
3010810	**Firrings; 50 mm wide; average depth**								
3010810A	38 mm	m	0.15	4.17	-	1.07	5.24	5.76	0.830
3010810B	50 mm	m	0.15	4.17	-	0.83	5.00	5.50	0.830
3010810C	75 mm	m	0.17	4.73	-	1.63	6.36	7.00	1.240
3010811	**Bearers**								
3010811A	25 mm x 50 mm	m	0.12	3.34	-	0.59	3.93	4.32	0.410
3010811B	38 mm x 50 mm	m	0.12	3.34	-	0.99	4.33	4.76	0.630
3010811C	50 mm x 50 mm	m	0.12	3.34	-	1.08	4.42	4.86	0.830
3010811D	50 mm x 75 mm	m	0.14	3.89	-	1.60	5.49	6.04	1.240
3010812	**Angle fillets**								
3010812A	38 mm x 38 mm	m	0.13	3.61	-	0.55	4.16	4.58	0.480
3010812B	50 mm x 50 mm	m	0.13	3.61	-	0.68	4.29	4.72	0.830
3010812C	75 mm x 75 mm	m	0.15	4.17	-	1.40	5.57	6.13	1.860

Woodwork

		Unit	Labour Hours	Labour Net £	Plant Net £	Materials Net £	Unit Net £	Unit with 10% £	CO$_2$ Kg
301	**NEW WORK**								
30108	**FIRST FIXINGS SOFTWOOD**								
3010813	**Tilting fillets**								
3010813A	19 mm x 38 mm	m	0.12	3.34	-	0.36	3.70	4.07	0.240
3010813B	25 mm x 50 mm	m	0.12	3.34	-	0.59	3.93	4.32	0.410
3010813C	38 mm x 50 mm	m	0.12	3.34	-	0.99	4.33	4.76	0.630
3010813D	50 mm x 75 mm	m	0.14	3.89	-	1.60	5.49	6.04	1.240
3010813E	75 mm x 100 mm	m	0.16	4.45	-	3.49	7.94	8.73	2.480
3010814	**Grounds or battens**								
3010814A	19 mm x 38 mm	m	0.07	1.95	-	0.36	2.31	2.54	0.240
3010814B	19 mm x 50 mm	m	0.07	1.95	-	0.48	2.43	2.67	0.310
3010814C	25 mm x 50 mm	m	0.07	1.95	-	0.59	2.54	2.79	0.410
3010815	**Framework to bath panel at 500 mm centres both ways**								
3010815A	25 mm x 50 mm	m^2	1.09	30.30	-	3.57	33.87	37.26	2.520
3010818	**Framework to walls at 300 mm centres one way; 600 mm centres other way**								
3010818A	25 mm x 50 mm	m^2	1.54	42.81	-	2.94	45.75	50.33	2.070
3010818B	38 mm x 50 mm	m^2	1.54	42.81	-	4.94	47.75	52.53	3.140
3010818C	50 mm x 50 mm	m^2	1.54	42.81	-	5.41	48.22	53.04	4.130
3010818D	50 mm x 75 mm	m^2	1.56	43.37	-	8.01	51.38	56.52	6.200
3010818E	75 mm x 75 mm	m^2	1.58	43.92	-	12.82	56.74	62.41	9.300
3010819	**Framework as bracketing and cradling around steelwork**								
3010819A	25 mm x 50 mm	m^2	1.70	47.26	-	4.30	51.56	56.72	3.030
3010819B	50 mm x 50 mm	m^2	1.80	50.04	-	7.92	57.96	63.76	6.050
3010819C	50 mm x 75 mm	m^2	1.90	52.82	-	11.74	64.56	71.02	9.080
3010820	**Blockings wedged between flanges of steelwork**								
3010820A	50 mm x 50 mm x 150 mm	Each	0.14	3.89	-	0.16	4.05	4.46	0.120
3010820B	50 mm x 75 mm x 225 mm	Each	0.15	4.17	-	0.36	4.53	4.98	0.280
3010820C	50 mm x 100 mm x 300 mm	Each	0.16	4.45	-	0.60	5.05	5.56	0.500
3010821	**Floors fillets fixed to floor clips**								
3010821A	38 mm x 50 mm	m	0.12	3.34	-	2.43	5.77	6.35	0.890
3010821B	50 mm x 50 mm	m	0.12	3.34	-	2.52	5.86	6.45	1.090
3010822	**Floor fillets set in concrete**								
3010822A	38 mm x 50 mm	m	0.14	3.89	-	0.99	4.88	5.37	0.630
3010822B	50 mm x 50 mm	m	0.14	3.89	-	1.08	4.97	5.47	0.830
30109	**FIRST FIXINGS SOFTWOOD BOARDING**								
3010901	**Boarding to floors; 100 mm wide boards; butt joints; thickness**								
3010901A	19 mm	m^2	0.60	16.68	-	18.63	35.31	38.84	6.280
3010901B	19 mm raking cutting	m	0.20	5.56	-	2.80	8.36	9.20	0.940
3010901C	19 mm curved cutting	m	0.60	16.68	-	5.59	22.27	24.50	1.880
3010901D	25 mm	m^2	0.60	16.68	-	21.29	37.97	41.77	8.260
3010901E	25 mm raking cutting	m	0.20	5.56	-	3.19	8.75	9.63	1.240
3010901F	25 mm curved cutting	m	0.60	16.68	-	6.39	23.07	25.38	2.480
3010901G	32 mm	m^2	0.66	18.35	-	23.96	42.31	46.54	10.580
3010901H	32 mm raking cutting	m	0.22	6.12	-	3.60	9.72	10.69	1.590
3010901I	32 mm curved cutting	m	0.63	17.51	-	7.19	24.70	27.17	3.170
3010902	**Boarding to floors; 150 mm wide boards; butt joints; thickness**								
3010902A	19 mm	m^2	0.50	13.90	-	18.63	32.53	35.78	6.280
3010902B	19 mm raking cutting	m	0.20	5.56	-	2.80	8.36	9.20	0.940
3010902C	19 mm curved cutting	m	0.60	16.68	-	5.59	22.27	24.50	1.880
3010902D	25 mm	m^2	0.50	13.90	-	2.12	16.02	17.62	0.820
3010902E	25 mm raking cutting	m	0.20	5.56	-	3.19	8.75	9.63	1.240
3010902F	25 mm curved cutting	m	0.60	16.68	-	6.39	23.07	25.38	2.480
3010902G	32 mm	m^2	0.55	15.29	-	23.96	39.25	43.18	10.580
3010902H	32 mm raking cutting	m	0.20	5.56	-	3.60	9.16	10.08	1.590
3010902I	32 mm curved cutting	m	0.60	16.68	-	7.19	23.87	26.26	3.170

Small Works 2011		Unit	Labour Hours	Labour Net	Plant Net	Materials Net	Unit Net	Unit with 10%	CO$_2$
				£	£	£	£	£	Kg
301	**NEW WORK**								
30109	**FIRST FIXINGS SOFTWOOD BOARDING**								
3010903	**Boarding to floors; 125 mm wide boards; tongued and grooved joints, thickness**								
3010903A	22 mm	m^2	0.65	18.07	-	17.56	35.63	39.19	7.270
3010903B	22 mm raking cutting	m	0.20	5.56	-	2.64	8.20	9.02	1.090
3010903C	22 mm curved cutting	m	0.60	16.68	-	5.27	21.95	24.15	2.180
3010903D	25 mm	m^2	0.65	18.07	-	18.63	36.70	40.37	8.260
3010903E	25 mm raking cutting	m	0.20	5.56	-	2.80	8.36	9.20	1.240
3010903F	25 mm curved cutting	m	0.60	16.68	-	5.59	22.27	24.50	2.480
3010904	**Boarding to floors; 150 mm wide boards; tongued and grooved joints; thickness**								
3010904A	25 mm	m^2	0.60	16.68	-	18.63	35.31	38.84	8.260
3010904B	25 mm raking cutting	m	0.20	5.56	-	2.80	8.36	9.20	1.240
3010904C	25 mm curved cutting	m	0.60	16.68	-	5.59	22.27	24.50	2.480
3010905	**Mitred margin**								
3010905A	25 mm x 75 mm	m	0.40	11.12	-	2.43	13.55	14.91	0.620
3010906	**Boarding to integral walls; 125 mm wide boards; tongued and grooved and V jointed; thickness**								
3010906A	19 mm	m^2	0.91	25.30	-	15.31	40.61	44.67	6.280
3010906B	19 mm raking cutting	m	0.20	5.56	-	2.30	7.86	8.65	0.940
3010906C	19 mm curved cutting	m	0.60	16.68	-	4.59	21.27	23.40	1.880
3010906D	25 mm	m^2	0.91	25.30	-	18.63	43.93	48.32	8.260
3010906E	25 mm raking cutting	m	0.20	5.56	-	2.80	8.36	9.20	1.240
3010906F	25 mm curved cutting	m	0.60	16.68	-	5.59	22.27	24.50	2.480
3010907	**Boarding to internal ceilings; 125 mm wide boards; tongued, grooved and V jointed; thickness**								
3010907A	19 mm	m^2	1.16	32.25	-	15.31	47.56	52.32	6.280
3010907B	19 mm raking cutting	m	0.20	5.56	-	2.30	7.86	8.65	0.940
3010907C	19 mm curved cutting	m	0.60	16.68	-	4.59	21.27	23.40	1.880
3010907D	25 mm	m^2	1.16	32.25	-	18.63	50.88	55.97	8.260
3010907E	25 mm raking cutting	m	0.20	5.56	-	2.80	8.36	9.20	1.240
3010907F	25 mm curved cutting	m	0.60	16.68	-	5.59	22.27	24.50	2.480
3010908	**Boarding to internal walls; Knotty Pine; 100 mm wide boards; tongued and grooved; thickness**								
3010908A	12 mm	m^2	0.97	26.97	-	19.70	46.67	51.34	4.690
3010908B	12 mm raking cutting	m	0.20	5.56	-	2.96	8.52	9.37	0.700
3010908C	12 mm curved cutting	m	0.60	16.68	-	5.91	22.59	24.85	1.410
3010908D	16 mm	m^2	0.97	26.97	-	26.28	53.25	58.58	6.250
3010908E	16 mm raking cutting	m	0.20	5.56	-	3.94	9.50	10.45	0.940
3010908F	16 mm curved cutting	m	0.60	16.68	-	7.89	24.57	27.03	1.880
3010908G	19 mm	m^2	0.97	26.97	-	31.21	58.18	64.00	7.420
3010908H	19 mm raking cutting	m	0.20	5.56	-	4.68	10.24	11.26	1.110
3010908I	19 mm curved cutting	m	0.60	16.68	-	9.37	26.05	28.66	2.230
3010909	**Boarding to internal ceilings; Knotty Pine; 100 mm wide boards; tongued and grooved; thickness**								
3010909A	12 mm	m^2	1.21	33.64	-	19.70	53.34	58.67	4.690
3010909B	12 mm raking cutting	m	0.20	5.56	-	2.96	8.52	9.37	0.700
3010909C	12 mm curved cutting	m	0.60	16.68	-	5.91	22.59	24.85	1.410
3010909D	16 mm	m^2	1.21	33.64	-	26.28	59.92	65.91	6.250
3010909E	16 mm raking cutting	m	0.20	5.56	-	3.94	9.50	10.45	0.940
3010909F	16 mm curved cutting	m	0.60	16.68	-	7.89	24.57	27.03	1.880
3010909G	19 mm	m^2	1.21	33.64	-	31.21	64.85	71.34	7.420
3010909H	19 mm raking cutting	m	0.20	5.56	-	4.68	10.24	11.26	1.110
3010909I	19 mm curved cutting	m	0.60	16.68	-	9.37	26.05	28.66	2.230

Woodwork

		Unit	Labour Hours	Labour Net	Plant Net	Materials Net	Unit Net	Unit with 10%	CO$_2$
				£	£	£	£	£	Kg
301	**NEW WORK**								
30110	**SECOND FIXINGS SHEET LININGS**								
3011001	**3.2 mm Hardboard linings to walls**								
3011001A	over 300 mm wide	m²	0.36	10.01	-	2.08	12.09	13.30	3.230
3011001B	not exceeding 300 mm wide	m	0.15	4.17	-	0.66	4.83	5.31	1.020
3011002	**3.2 mm Hardboard linings to ceilings**								
3011002A	over 300 mm wide	m²	0.41	11.40	-	2.08	13.48	14.83	3.230
3011002B	not exceeding 300 mm wide	m	0.17	4.73	-	0.66	5.39	5.93	1.020
3011002C	raking cutting	m	0.16	4.45	-	0.10	4.55	5.01	0.160
3011002D	curved cutting	m	0.53	14.73	-	0.21	14.94	16.43	0.320
3011003	**12 mm Chipboard lining to walls**								
3011003A	over 300 mm wide	m²	0.46	12.79	-	2.99	15.78	17.36	5.150
3011003B	not exceeding 300 mm wide	m	0.19	5.28	-	0.94	6.22	6.84	1.620
3011004	**12 mm Chipboard lining to ceilings**								
3011004A	over 300 mm wide	m²	0.53	14.73	-	2.99	17.72	19.49	5.150
3011004B	not exceeding 300 mm wide	m	0.22	6.12	-	0.94	7.06	7.77	1.620
3011004C	raking cutting	m	0.33	9.17	-	0.45	9.62	10.58	0.770
3011004D	curved cutting	m	0.73	20.29	-	0.90	21.19	23.31	1.550
3011006	**12 mm Insulation board lining to walls**								
3011006A	over 300 mm wide	m²	0.29	8.06	-	5.06	13.12	14.43	7.450
3011006B	not exceeding 300 mm wide	m	0.12	3.34	-	1.59	4.93	5.42	2.340
3011007	**12 mm Insulation board lining to ceilings**								
3011007A	over 300 mm wide	m²	0.33	9.17	-	5.06	14.23	15.65	7.450
3011007B	not exceeding 300 mm wide	m	0.14	3.89	-	1.59	5.48	6.03	2.340
3011007C	raking cutting	m	0.14	3.89	-	0.76	4.65	5.12	1.120
3011007D	curved cutting	m	0.40	11.12	-	1.52	12.64	13.90	2.240
3011008	**6 mm Sanded surface non-asbestos board lining to walls**								
3011008A	over 300 mm wide	m²	0.40	11.12	-	16.92	28.04	30.84	3.070
3011008B	not exceeding 300 mm wide	m	0.16	4.45	-	5.32	9.77	10.75	0.960
3011009	**6 mm Sanded surface non-asbestos board lining to ceilings**								
3011009A	over 300 mm wide	m²	0.46	12.79	-	16.92	29.71	32.68	3.070
3011009B	not exceeding 300 mm wide	m	0.18	5.00	-	5.32	10.32	11.35	0.960
3011009C	raking cutting	m	0.33	9.17	-	2.54	11.71	12.88	0.460
3011009D	curved cutting	m	0.93	25.85	-	5.08	30.93	34.02	0.920
3011010	**9 mm Sanded surface non-asbestos board lining to walls**								
3011010A	over 300 mm wide	m²	0.43	11.95	-	25.71	37.66	41.43	4.600
3011010B	not exceeding 300 mm wide	m	0.18	5.00	-	8.08	13.08	14.39	1.450
3011011	**9 mm Sanded surface non-asbestos board lining to ceilings**								
3011011A	over 300 mm wide	m²	0.50	13.90	-	25.71	39.61	43.57	4.600
3011011B	not exceeding 300 mm wide	m	0.21	5.84	-	8.08	13.92	15.31	1.450
3011011C	raking cutting	m	0.33	9.17	-	3.86	13.03	14.33	0.690
3011011D	curved cutting	m	0.93	25.85	-	7.72	33.57	36.93	1.380
3011014	**4 mm Plywood WBP Birch faced lining to walls**								
3011014A	over 300 mm wide	m²	0.44	12.23	-	8.80	21.03	23.13	2.340
3011014B	not exceeding 300 mm wide	m	0.18	5.00	-	2.77	7.77	8.55	0.740
3011016	**4 mm Plywood WBP Birch faced lining to ceilings**								
3011016A	over 300 mm wide	m²	0.51	14.18	-	8.80	22.98	25.28	2.340
3011016B	not exceeding 300 mm wide	m	0.21	5.84	-	2.77	8.61	9.47	0.740
3011016C	raking cutting	m	0.27	7.51	-	1.32	8.83	9.71	0.350
3011016D	curved cutting	m	0.60	16.68	-	2.64	19.32	21.25	0.700

Small Works 2011		Unit	Labour Hours	Labour Net	Plant Net	Materials Net	Unit Net	Unit with 10%	CO$_2$
				£	£	£	£	£	Kg
301	**NEW WORK**								
30110	**SECOND FIXINGS SHEET LININGS**								
3011018	**6.5 mm Plywood WBP Birch faced lining to walls**								
3011018A	over 300 mm wide	m²	0.48	13.34	-	12.98	26.32	28.95	3.500
3011018B	not exceeding 300 mm wide	m	0.20	5.56	-	4.08	9.64	10.60	1.100
3011019	**6.5 mm Plywood WBP Birch faced lining to ceilings**								
3011019A	over 300 mm wide	m²	0.55	15.29	-	12.98	28.27	31.10	3.500
3011019B	not exceeding 300 mm wide	m	0.23	6.39	-	4.08	10.47	11.52	1.100
3011019C	raking cutting	m	0.27	7.51	-	1.95	9.46	10.41	0.530
3011019D	curved cutting	m	0.60	16.68	-	3.90	20.58	22.64	1.050
3011021	**12 mm Blockboard lining to walls**								
3011021A	over 300 mm wide	m²	0.56	15.57	-	14.06	29.63	32.59	4.790
3011021B	not exceeding 300 mm wide	m	0.23	6.39	-	4.42	10.81	11.89	1.510
3011022	**12 mm Blockboard lining to ceilings**								
3011022A	over 300 mm wide	m²	0.64	17.79	-	14.06	31.85	35.04	4.790
3011022B	not exceeding 300 mm wide	m	0.27	7.51	-	4.42	11.93	13.12	1.510
3011022C	raking cutting	m	0.33	9.17	-	2.11	11.28	12.41	0.720
3011022D	curved cutting	m	0.73	20.29	-	4.22	24.51	26.96	1.440
3011024	**18 mm Blockboard lining to walls**								
3011024A	over 300 mm wide	m²	0.60	16.68	-	13.88	30.56	33.62	7.190
3011024B	not exceeding 300 mm wide	m	0.25	6.95	-	4.36	11.31	12.44	2.260
3011025	**18 mm Blockboard lining to ceilings**								
3011025A	over 300 mm wide	m²	0.69	19.18	-	13.88	33.06	36.37	7.190
3011025B	not exceeding 300 mm wide	m	0.29	8.06	-	4.36	12.42	13.66	2.260
3011025C	raking cutting	m	0.33	9.17	-	2.08	11.25	12.38	1.080
3011025D	curved cutting	m	0.85	23.63	-	4.16	27.79	30.57	2.160
30112	**SECOND FIXINGS SHEET CASINGS**								
3011201	**Cupboards; 3.2 mm hardboard sides; softwood framing**								
3011201A	25 mm x 25 mm	m²	6.45	179.31	-	11.25	190.56	209.62	4.610
3011201B	32 mm x 32 mm	m²	6.70	186.26	-	12.59	198.85	218.74	5.490
3011201C	38 mm x 38 mm	m²	6.70	186.26	-	14.10	200.36	220.40	6.410
3011202	**Cupboards; hardboard backs**								
3011202A	3.2 mm	m²	0.40	11.12	-	2.08	13.20	14.52	3.230
3011204	**Cupboards; 3.2 mm hardboard doors; softwood framing**								
3011204A	25 mm x 25 mm	m²	7.50	208.50	-	11.25	219.75	241.73	4.610
3011204B	32 mm x 32 mm	m²	7.80	216.84	-	12.59	229.43	252.37	5.490
3011204C	38 mm x 38 mm	m²	7.80	216.84	-	14.10	230.94	254.03	6.410
3011206	**Cupboards; 6.5 mm plywood sides; softwood framing**								
3011206A	25 mm x 25 mm	m²	6.45	179.31	-	22.15	201.46	221.61	4.880
3011206B	32 mm x 32 mm	m²	6.70	186.26	-	23.49	209.75	230.73	5.760
3011206C	38 mm x 38 mm	m²	6.70	186.26	-	25.00	211.26	232.39	6.680
3011208	**Cupboards; plywood backs**								
3011208A	6.5 mm	m²	0.50	13.90	-	10.48	24.38	26.82	3.800
3011209	**Cupboards; 6.5 mm plywood doors; softwood framing**								
3011209A	25 mm x 25 mm	m²	7.50	208.50	-	19.66	228.16	250.98	5.180
3011209B	32 mm x 32 mm	m²	2.62	199.99	-	20.99	220.98	243.08	6.050
3011209C	38 mm x 38 mm	m²	7.80	216.84	-	22.50	239.34	263.27	6.980

Small Works 2011	Unit	Labour Hours	Labour Net	Plant Net	Materials Net	Unit Net	Unit with 10%	CO$_2$
			£	£	£	£	£	Kg
301	**NEW WORK**							
30112	**SECOND FIXINGS SHEET CASINGS**							
3011212	**Boxed pipe casings; 300 mm girth; 19 mm x 25 mm sawn softwood framing; front fixed with brass screws and cups**							
3011212A	3.2 mm hardboard front	m	1.15	31.97	-	1.47	33.44	36.78	1.580
3011212B	6.5 mm plywood front	m	1.30	36.14	-	4.11	40.25	44.28	1.760
3011212C	25 mm softwood front	m	1.40	38.92	-	27.03	65.95	72.55	8.510
3011213	**Pelmet casings 225 mm girth; 75 mm x 25 mm sawn softwood framing; 19 mm x 100 mm softwood top; 6.5 mm plywood front 125 mm deep**							
3011213A	over 1.00 mm long	m	1.25	34.75	-	3.98	38.73	42.60	1.130
3011213B	short lengths; not exceeding 0.90 m long	Each	1.30	36.14	-	3.83	39.97	43.97	1.090
3011213C	short lengths; not exceeding 1.20 m long	Each	1.50	41.70	-	4.65	46.35	50.99	1.290
3011213D	extra for boxed ends	Each	0.45	12.51	-	0.20	12.71	13.98	0.070
3011214	**Pelmet casings 225 mm girth; 75 mm x 25 mm sawn softwood framing; part plugged and screwed to brick or concrete; 19 mm x 100 mm softwood top; 6.5 mm plywood front 125 mm deep**							
3011214A	over 1.00 m long	m	1.50	41.70	-	3.98	45.68	50.25	1.130
3011214B	short lengths; not exceeding 0.90 m long	Each	1.60	44.48	-	3.83	48.31	53.14	1.090
3011214C	short lengths; not exceeding 1.20 m long	Each	1.80	50.04	-	4.65	54.69	60.16	1.290
3011214D	extra for boxed ends	Each	0.45	12.51	-	0.20	12.71	13.98	0.070
3011216	**Plastic curtain track including**							
3011216A	brackets, gliders, stops and the like	m	0.65	18.07	-	6.73	24.80	27.28	1.270
30113	**SECOND FIXINGS PVC-u CLADDING**							
3011301	**Swish profiled cladding; fixed in accordance with manufacturers instructions; 38 x 25 mm sawn softwood framing at 450 mm centres**							
3011301A	to walls over 300 mm wide	m²	0.50	24.28	-	50.33	74.61	82.07	28.740
3011302	**Extra over cladding for**							
3011302A	edge trim	m	0.11	5.45	-	1.56	7.01	7.71	4.000
30116	**SECOND FIXINGS WROUGHT SOFTWOOD**							
3011601	**Skirtings**							
3011601A	19 mm x 100 mm chamfered or pencil rounded	m	0.12	3.34	-	4.25	7.59	8.35	0.630
3011601B	25 mm x 150 mm Torus-Ovolo; Torus-Ogee	m	0.14	3.89	-	7.85	11.74	12.91	1.240
3011601C	25 mm x 225 mm Torus	m	0.17	4.73	-	10.82	15.55	17.11	0.210
3011601D	returned ends	Each	0.19	5.28	-	-	5.28	5.81	-
3011601E	mitres	Each	0.12	3.34	-	-	3.34	3.67	-
3011602	**Picture rails**							
3011602A	25 mm x 50 mm	m	0.12	3.34	-	3.29	6.63	7.29	0.410
3011603	**Dado rails**							
3011603A	32 mm x 63 mm	m	0.19	5.28	-	4.10	9.38	10.32	0.670
3011604	**Architraves**							
3011604A	19 mm x 50 mm chamfered and rounded	m	0.14	3.89	-	0.93	4.82	5.30	0.310
3011604B	19 mm x 63 mm chamfered and rounded	m	0.14	3.89	-	2.59	6.48	7.13	0.400
3011604C	19 mm x 75 mm chamfered and rounded	m	0.14	3.89	-	1.86	5.75	6.33	0.620
3011604D	19 mm x 50 mm Ogee	m	0.14	3.89	-	2.24	6.13	6.74	0.310

Small Works 2011		Unit	Labour Hours	Labour Net	Plant Net	Materials Net	Unit Net	Unit with 10%	CO$_2$
				£	£	£	£	£	Kg
301	**NEW WORK**								
30116	**SECOND FIXINGS WROUGHT SOFTWOOD**								
3011604	**Architraves**								
3011604E	19 mm x 63 mm Ogee	m	0.14	3.89	-	2.86	6.75	7.43	0.400
3011604F	19 mm x 50 mm Ovolo	m	0.14	3.89	-	2.59	6.48	7.13	0.310
3011604G	25 mm x 75 mm Torus	m	0.14	3.89	-	4.10	7.99	8.79	0.620
3011604H	38 mm x 150 mm Edwardian	m	0.14	3.89	-	17.80	21.69	23.86	1.880
3011604I	19 mm x 50 mm twice rounded	m	0.14	3.89	-	2.23	6.12	6.73	0.310
3011604J	returned ends	Each	0.19	5.28	-	-	5.28	5.81	-
3011604K	mitres	Each	0.12	3.34	-	-	3.34	3.67	-
3011606	**Stops**								
3011606B	16 mm x 38 mm Ovolo	m	0.12	3.34	-	1.62	4.96	5.46	0.200
3011606C	16 mm x 50 mm Ovolo	m	0.12	3.34	-	2.10	5.44	5.98	0.260
3011606G	32 mm x 38 mm fire check	m	0.14	3.89	-	1.99	5.88	6.47	0.400
3011607	**Glazing beads**								
3011607A	8 mm x 12 mm	m	0.06	1.67	-	0.63	2.30	2.53	0.030
3011607B	8 mm x 16 mm	m	0.06	1.67	-	0.63	2.30	2.53	0.060
3011607C	25 mm x 45 mm fire check	m	0.12	3.34	-	2.79	6.13	6.74	0.370
3011608	**Quadrants**								
3011608A	12 mm	m	0.07	1.95	-	0.33	2.28	2.51	0.040
3011608B	16 mm	m	0.07	1.95	-	0.92	2.87	3.16	0.070
3011608C	19 mm	m	0.07	1.95	-	0.72	2.67	2.94	0.090
3011608E	25 mm	m	0.07	1.95	-	1.40	3.35	3.69	1.270
3011609	**Half rounds**								
3011609A	19 mm	m	0.07	1.95	-	0.91	2.86	3.15	0.190
3011609B	25 mm	m	0.07	1.95	-	1.04	2.99	3.29	0.320
3011609C	12 mm x 25 mm	m	0.07	1.95	-	0.92	2.87	3.16	0.070
3011611	**Scotia**								
3011611A	19 mm	m	0.07	1.95	-	1.10	3.05	3.36	0.190
3011611B	25 mm	m	0.07	1.95	-	1.68	3.63	3.99	0.810
3011611D	38 mm	m	0.07	1.95	-	2.14	4.09	4.50	0.240
3011611E	50 mm	m	0.07	1.95	-	3.22	5.17	5.69	0.410
3011615	**Window boards**								
3011615A	32 mm x 150 mm	m	0.24	6.67	-	9.39	16.06	17.67	1.590
3011615B	32 mm x 200 mm	m	0.27	7.51	-	12.55	20.06	22.07	2.120
3011615C	32 mm x 225 mm	m	0.32	8.90	-	14.37	23.27	25.60	2.380
3011617	**Shelves; worktops**								
3011617A	19 mm x 150 mm	m	0.19	5.28	-	5.98	11.26	12.39	1.460
3011617B	19 mm x 175 mm	m	0.22	6.12	-	6.93	13.05	14.36	1.700
3011617C	25 mm x 150 mm	m	0.19	5.28	-	7.56	12.84	14.12	1.920
3011617D	25 mm x 200 mm	m	0.26	7.23	-	10.20	17.43	19.17	2.560
3011617E	32 mm x 150 mm	m	0.19	5.28	-	8.35	13.63	14.99	2.450
3011617F	32 mm x 175 mm	m	0.22	6.12	-	9.72	15.84	17.42	2.860
3011619	**Shelves; worktops; cross tongued joints**								
3011619A	19 mm x 300 mm	m	0.33	9.17	-	12.50	21.67	23.84	2.910
3011619B	19 mm x 450 mm	m	0.40	11.12	-	18.82	29.94	32.93	4.370
3011619C	25 mm x 300 mm	m	0.33	9.17	-	15.77	24.94	27.43	3.830
3011619D	25 mm x 450 mm	m	0.40	11.12	-	26.18	37.30	41.03	5.750
3011619E	32 mm x 300 mm	m	0.33	9.17	-	17.50	26.67	29.34	4.900
3011619F	32 mm x 450 mm	m	0.40	11.12	-	26.18	37.30	41.03	7.360
3011621	**Shelves; worktops; slatted with 50 mm wide slats at 75 mm centres; thickness**								
3011621A	19 mm	m^2	1.56	43.37	-	21.19	64.56	71.02	4.180
3011621B	25 mm	m^2	1.56	43.37	-	22.97	66.34	72.97	5.520
3011621C	32 mm	m^2	1.56	43.37	-	25.82	69.19	76.11	7.050
3011623	**Bearers**								
3011623A	19 mm x 38 mm	m	0.12	3.34	-	1.23	4.57	5.03	0.240
3011623B	25 mm x 50 mm	m	0.12	3.34	-	1.72	5.06	5.57	0.410
3011623C	50 mm x 50 mm	m	0.12	3.34	-	2.87	6.21	6.83	0.830
3011623D	50 mm x 75 mm	m	0.12	3.34	-	6.54	9.88	10.87	1.240
3011624	**Bearers; framed**								
3011624A	19 mm x 38 mm	m	0.15	4.17	-	1.23	5.40	5.94	0.240
3011624B	25 mm x 50 mm	m	0.15	4.17	-	1.72	5.89	6.48	0.410
3011624C	50 mm x 50 mm	m	0.15	4.17	-	2.87	7.04	7.74	0.830
3011624D	50 mm x 75 mm	m	0.15	4.17	-	6.54	10.71	11.78	1.240

Woodwork

		Unit	Labour Hours	Labour Net	Plant Net	Materials Net	Unit Net	Unit with 10%	CO$_2$
				£	£	£	£	£	Kg
301	NEW WORK								
30116	SECOND FIXINGS WROUGHT SOFTWOOD								
3011626	Framing; framed								
3011626A	19 mm x 38 mm	m	0.19	5.28	-	1.23	6.51	7.16	0.240
3011626B	25 mm x 50 mm	m	0.19	5.28	-	1.72	7.00	7.70	0.410
3011626C	50 mm x 50 mm	m	0.19	5.28	-	2.87	8.15	8.97	0.830
3011626D	50 mm x 75 mm	m	0.19	5.28	-	6.54	11.82	13.00	1.240
3011630	Doors; wrought softwood 1.95 m x 0.75 m								
3011630A	38 mm two panel square both sides	Each	5.25	145.95	-	36.55	182.50	200.75	14.260
3011630B	50 mm two panel moulded both sides	Each	6.20	172.36	-	53.30	225.66	248.23	20.790
3011630C	38 mm four panel square both sides	Each	7.00	194.60	-	52.41	247.01	271.71	17.590
3011630D	50 mm four panel moulded both sides	Each	8.00	222.40	-	134.46	356.86	392.55	34.800
3011630E	38 mm six panel square framed	Each	8.00	222.40	-	44.92	267.32	294.05	17.520
3011630F	50 mm six panel moulded both sides	Each	9.00	250.20	-	79.19	329.39	362.33	30.890
3011630G	50 mm half glazed	Each	8.00	222.40	-	32.74	255.14	280.65	12.770
3011630H	38 mm half glazed	Each	7.20	200.16	-	33.50	233.66	257.03	13.070
3011630I	38 mm skeleton flush	Each	3.20	88.96	-	47.21	136.17	149.79	18.410
3011630J	38 mm solid flush	Each	4.80	133.44	-	53.30	186.74	205.41	20.790
3011630K	ledged and braced with 100 mm x 25 mm ledging and bracing covered with matchboarding 19 mm	Each	3.30	91.74	-	36.73	128.47	141.32	13.250
3011630L	framed, ledged and braced with 100 mm x 50 mm framing and 100 mm x 32 mm ledging and bracing, covered with matchboarding 19 mm	Each	10.00	278.00	-	53.54	331.54	364.69	16.850
3011630M	50 mm casement divided into eight panes open for glass	Pair	16.20	450.36	-	63.96	514.32	565.75	24.950
3011630N	50 mm casement divided into eight panes open for glass	Each	8.70	241.86	-	31.98	273.84	301.22	12.470
3011630O	38 mm casement divided into eight panes open for glass	Pair	15.60	433.68	-	57.87	491.55	540.71	22.570
3011630P	38 mm casement divided into eight panes open for glass	Each	8.00	222.40	-	28.93	251.33	276.46	11.290
3011631	Garage door								
3011631A	1200 mm x 2100 mm high, with 125 mm x 50 mm framing, lined externally with 25 mm V jointed matchboarding to form solid front	Pair	17.50	486.50	-	143.82	630.32	693.35	45.920
3011640	Frames; at jambs or heads								
3011640A	32 mm x 75 mm	m	0.25	6.95	-	4.87	11.82	13.00	0.790
3011640B	32 mm x 100 mm	m	0.25	6.95	-	6.32	13.27	14.60	0.980
3011640C	32 mm x 150 mm	m	0.25	6.95	-	9.16	16.11	17.72	1.470
3011640D	50 mm x 75 mm	m	0.28	7.78	-	6.37	14.15	15.57	1.150
3011640E	50 mm x 100 mm	m	0.28	7.78	-	8.28	16.06	17.67	1.530
3011640F	50 mm x 150 mm	m	0.28	7.78	-	12.55	20.33	22.36	2.300
3011641	Frames; once rebated; at jambs or heads								
3011641A	50 mm x 75 mm	m	0.28	7.78	-	6.97	14.75	16.23	1.150
3011641B	50 mm x 100 mm	m	0.28	7.78	-	8.87	16.65	18.32	1.530
3011641C	50 mm x 150 mm	m	0.31	8.62	-	13.09	21.71	23.88	2.300
3011641D	75 mm x 100 mm	m	0.35	9.73	-	13.60	23.33	25.66	2.300
3011641F	75 mm x 150 mm	m	0.35	9.73	-	19.07	28.80	31.68	3.450
3011642	Frames; once rebated; once grooved; at jambs or heads								
3011642A	50 mm x 100 mm	m	0.28	7.78	-	9.46	17.24	18.96	1.530
3011642B	50 mm x 125 mm	m	0.28	7.78	-	11.73	19.51	21.46	1.920
3011642C	50 mm x 150 mm	m	0.31	8.62	-	13.72	22.34	24.57	2.300
3011642D	75 mm x 100 mm	m	0.35	9.73	-	14.20	23.93	26.32	2.300
3011642F	75 mm x 150 mm	m	0.35	9.73	-	19.66	29.39	32.33	34.480
3011643	Frames; at mullions or transomes								
3011643A	32 mm x 75 mm	m	0.19	5.28	-	6.01	11.29	12.42	0.740
3011643B	32 mm x 100 mm	m	0.19	5.28	-	7.45	12.73	14.00	0.980
3011643C	32 mm x 150 mm	m	0.19	5.28	-	10.31	15.59	17.15	1.470

Small Works 2011		Unit	Labour Hours	Labour Net	Plant Net	Materials Net	Unit Net	Unit with 10%	CO$_2$
				£	£	£	£	£	Kg
301	**NEW WORK**								
30116	**SECOND FIXINGS WROUGHT SOFTWOOD**								
3011644	**Frames; twice rebated; at mullions or transomes**								
3011644A	38 mm x 100 mm	m	0.28	7.78	-	8.23	16.01	17.61	1.160
3011644B	38 mm x 150 mm	m	0.28	7.78	-	11.50	19.28	21.21	17.470
3011644C	50 mm x 100 mm	m	0.28	7.78	-	9.44	17.22	18.94	1.530
3011644D	75 mm x 100 mm	m	0.35	9.73	-	14.14	23.87	26.26	2.300
3011644E	75 mm x 150 mm	m	0.35	9.73	-	19.65	29.38	32.32	3.450
3011645	**Frames; once sunk weathered; once rebated; three times grooved; at cills**								
3011645A	75 mm x 150 mm	m	0.35	9.73	-	24.35	34.08	37.49	3.450
3011645B	75 mm x 175 mm	m	0.35	9.73	-	31.07	40.80	44.88	4.020
3011646	**Linings; tongued at angles**								
3011646A	25 mm x 75 mm	m	0.25	6.95	-	5.49	12.44	13.68	0.570
3011646B	25 mm x 100 mm	m	0.25	6.95	-	6.73	13.68	15.05	0.770
3011646C	25 mm x 125 mm	m	0.25	6.95	-	7.97	14.92	16.41	0.960
3011646D	25 mm x 150 mm	m	0.25	6.95	-	9.44	16.39	18.03	1.150
3011646E	32 mm x 100 mm	m	0.27	7.51	-	7.45	14.96	16.46	0.980
3011646F	32 mm x 125 mm	m	0.27	7.51	-	8.90	16.41	18.05	1.230
3011646G	32 mm x 150 mm	m	0.27	7.51	-	10.31	17.82	19.60	1.470
3011647	**Linings; once rebated; tongued at angles**								
3011647A	38 mm x 100 mm	m	0.28	7.78	-	8.81	16.59	18.25	1.160
3011647B	38 mm x 150 mm	m	0.28	7.78	-	12.05	19.83	21.81	1.750
30118	**SECOND FIXINGS WROUGHT HARDWOOD**								
3011801	**Threshold**								
3011801A	50 mm x 150 mm sunk, weathered and grooved	m	0.40	11.12	-	20.49	31.61	34.77	2.300
30120	**WINDOWS SOFTWOOD - PURPOSE MADE**								
3012001	**Casement window; side hung; rebated, moulded and grooved frame, mullions and transomes; 175 mm x 75 mm weathered, moulded and grooved cill; 45 mm sashes with 75 mm deep bottom rail**								
3012001A	100 mm x 75 mm	m^2	8.40	233.52	-	46.45	279.97	307.97	18.120
3012001B	sashes only - casement 45 mm without bars	m^2	2.60	72.28	-	15.23	87.51	96.26	5.940
3012001C	sashes only - casement 45 mm with bars	m^2	3.30	91.74	-	24.37	116.11	127.72	9.500
3012001D	frame only 100 mm x 75 mm	m	1.00	27.80	-	8.38	36.18	39.80	3.270
3012002	**Double hung sash window; 32 mm beaded inner lining; 25 mm outer lining; 32 mm pulley stile and bead; 25 mm back lining; 25 mm parting slip; all grooved tongued and blocked together and framed into hardwood sunk weathered, throated and check throated cill and fitted in with 50mm rebated and moulded double hung sashes with splay rebated meeting rails hung on and including steel axle pulleys with brass plate and screws, sash lines and weights**								
3012002A	175 mm x 100 mm	m^2	11.50	319.70	-	67.77	387.47	426.22	26.430
3012002B	175 mm x 100 mm sashes divided into small squares	m^2	12.25	340.55	-	70.05	410.60	451.66	27.320
3012003	**Frame for metal windows**								
3012003A	75 mm x 50 mm	m	0.75	20.85	-	3.81	24.66	27.13	1.490

Small Works 2011		Unit	Labour Hours	Labour Net	Plant Net	Materials Net	Unit Net	Unit with 10%	CO$_2$
				£	£	£	£	£	Kg
301	**NEW WORK**								
30122	**SECOND FIXINGS STANDARD DOORS**								
3012201	**Flush door; internal quality; skeleton or cellular core; hardboard faced both sides**								
3012201A	35 mm thick; 1981 mm high; 686 mm wide	Each	1.54	42.81	-	45.72	88.53	97.38	23.780
3012201B	35 mm thick; 1981 mm high; 762 mm wide	Each	1.54	42.81	-	46.36	89.17	98.09	26.410
3012201C	35 mm thick; 1981 mm high; 838 mm wide	Each	1.54	42.81	-	48.82	91.63	100.79	29.040
3012201D	40 mm thick; 2040 mm high; 626 mm wide	Each	1.54	42.81	-	48.44	91.25	100.38	25.540
3012201E	40 mm thick; 2040 mm high; 726 mm wide	Each	1.54	42.81	-	49.38	92.19	101.41	29.610
3012201F	40 mm thick; 2040 mm high; 826 mm wide	Each	1.54	42.81	-	51.67	94.48	103.93	33.690
3012202	**Flush door; internal quality; skeleton or cellular core; plywood faced both sides, lipped on two long edges**								
3012202A	35 mm thick; 1981 mm high; 686 mm wide	Each	1.54	42.81	-	61.37	104.18	114.60	22.330
3012202B	35 mm thick; 1981 mm high; 762 mm wide	Each	1.54	42.81	-	62.20	105.01	115.51	24.800
3012202C	35 mm thick; 1981 mm high; 838 mm wide	Each	1.54	42.81	-	65.04	107.85	118.64	27.280
3012202D	40 mm thick; 2040 mm high; 626 mm wide	Each	1.54	42.81	-	64.63	107.44	118.18	23.980
3012202E	40 mm thick; 2040 mm high; 726 mm wide	Each	1.54	42.81	-	66.04	108.85	119.74	27.810
3012202F	40 mm thick; 2040 mm high; 826 mm wide	Each	1.54	42.81	-	68.22	111.03	122.13	31.640
3012204	**Flush door; half hour fire resisting (FD30); hardboard faced both sides**								
3012204B	44 mm thick; 1981 mm high; 762 mm wide	Each	2.15	59.77	-	102.74	162.51	178.76	33.200
3012204C	44 mm thick; 1981 mm high; 838 mm wide	Each	2.15	59.77	-	107.28	167.05	183.76	36.510
3012205	**Flush door; half hour fire resisting; plywood faced both sides; lipped on two long edges**								
3012205A	44 mm thick; 2040 mm high; 726 mm wide	Each	2.15	59.77	-	106.94	166.71	183.38	29.710
3012205B	44 mm thick; 2040 mm high; 826 mm wide	Each	2.15	59.77	-	106.94	166.71	183.38	33.800
3012206	**Flush door; external quality; skeleton or cellular core; plywood faced both sides**								
3012206A	44 mm thick; 1981 mm high; 762 mm wide	Each	1.82	50.60	-	129.86	180.46	198.51	31.180
3012206B	44 mm thick; 1981 mm high; 838 mm wide	Each	1.82	50.60	-	135.63	186.23	204.85	34.290
3012206C	44 mm thick; 1994 mm high; 806 mm wide	Each	1.82	50.60	-	132.75	183.35	201.69	32.980
3012207	**Flush door; external quality; skeleton or cellular core; plywood faced both sides; opening for glass**								
3012207A	44 mm thick; 1981 mm high; 762 mm wide	Each	2.15	59.77	-	135.42	195.19	214.71	31.180
3012207B	44 mm thick; 1981 mm high; 838 mm wide	Each	2.15	59.77	-	138.95	198.72	218.59	34.290
3012208	**Flush door; external quality; half hour fire resisting; solid infill of flame retardant material; plywood faced both sides**								
3012208A	44 mm thick; 1981 mm high; 762 mm wide	Each	2.43	67.55	-	107.81	175.36	192.90	31.180

Small Works 2011		Unit	Labour Hours	Labour Net	Plant Net	Materials Net	Unit Net	Unit with 10%	CO₂
				£	£	£	£	£	Kg
301	**NEW WORK**								
30122	**SECOND FIXINGS STANDARD DOORS**								
3012208	**Flush door; external quality; half hour fire resisting; solid infill of flame retardant material; plywood faced both sides**								
3012208B	44 mm thick; 1981 mm high; 838 mm wide	Each	2.43	67.55	-	112.43	179.98	197.98	34.290
3012208C	44 mm thick; 1994 mm high; 806 mm wide	Each	2.43	67.55	-	112.43	179.98	197.98	32.980
3012209	**Panelled door; external quality; upper panel open for glass**								
3012209A	44 mm thick; 1981 mm high; 762 mm wide	Each	2.15	59.77	-	182.20	241.97	266.17	38.440
3012209B	44 mm thick; 1981 mm high; 838 mm wide	Each	2.15	59.77	-	189.44	249.21	274.13	42.270
3012209C	44 mm thick; 1994 mm high; 806 mm wide	Each	2.15	59.77	-	184.69	244.46	268.91	40.660
3012210	**Panelled door; external quality; fully glazed; ten panels open for glass**								
3012210A	44 mm thick; 1981 mm high; 762 mm wide	Each	2.15	59.77	-	155.59	215.36	236.90	38.440
3012210B	44 mm thick; 1981 mm high; 838 mm wide	Each	2.15	59.77	-	149.36	209.13	230.04	42.270
3012210C	44 mm thick; 1994 mm high; 806 mm wide	Each	2.15	59.77	-	152.23	212.00	233.20	40.660
3012211	**Matchboarded door; external quality; ledged and braced; 25 mm ledges and braces; 19 mm tongued, grooved and V jointed; one side vertical boarding**								
3012211A	36 mm thick; 1981 mm high; 762 mm wide	Each	1.77	49.21	-	139.39	188.60	207.46	22.740
3012211B	36 mm thick; 1981 mm high; 838 mm wide	Each	1.77	49.21	-	149.99	199.20	219.12	25.010
3012212	**Matchboarded door; external quality; framed, ledged and braced; 25 mm intermediate and bottom rails; 44 mm framing; 19 mm tongued, grooved and V jointed one side vertical boarding**								
3012212A	44 mm thick; 1981 mm high; 762 mm wide	Each	2.15	59.77	-	180.36	240.13	264.14	27.800
3012212B	44 mm thick; 1981 mm high; 838 mm wide	Each	2.15	59.77	-	189.39	249.16	274.08	30.570
3012213	**Stable matchboarded door; external quality; framed, ledged and braced; 25 mm intermediate and bottom rails; 44 mm framing, 19 mm tongued, grooved and V jointed one side vertical boarding; in two leaves**								
3012213A	44 mm thick; 1981 mm high; 762 mm wide	Each	2.53	70.33	-	227.45	297.78	327.56	27.800
3012213B	44 mm thick; 1981 mm high; 838 mm wide	Each	2.53	70.33	-	231.83	302.16	332.38	30.570
30124	**SECOND FIXINGS STANDARD DOOR FRAMES**								
3012401	**External door frames; treated and primed; hardwood cills; opening inwards or outwards; to suit door**								
3012401A	806 mm x 1994 mm	Each	0.76	21.13	-	120.31	141.44	155.58	15.440
3012401B	838 mm x 1981 mm	Each	0.76	21.13	-	125.53	146.66	161.33	15.760

Woodwork

		Unit	Labour Hours	Labour Net £	Plant Net £	Materials Net £	Unit Net £	Unit with 10% £	CO₂ Kg
301	**NEW WORK**								
30124	**SECOND FIXINGS STANDARD DOOR FRAMES**								
3012402	**External door frames; firecheck; rebated; intumescent strip; hardwood cill; opening inwards or outwards; to suit door**								
3012402A	806 mm x 2100 mm	Each	0.76	21.13	-	165.11	186.24	204.86	16.440
3012402B	762 mm x 2047 mm	Each	0.76	21.13	-	164.16	185.29	203.82	15.950
3012402C	838 mm x 2047 mm	Each	0.76	21.13	-	162.80	183.93	202.32	16.100
3012403	**Internal door frames; firecheck; rebated; intumescent strip; no cill; opening inwards or outwards; to suit door**								
3012403A	726 mm x 2040 mm	Each	0.63	17.51	-	146.36	163.87	180.26	15.780
3012403B	826 mm x 2040 mm	Each	0.63	17.51	-	149.26	166.77	183.45	16.110
3012403C	726 mm x 2017 mm	Each	0.63	17.51	-	138.33	155.84	171.42	15.630
3012403D	826 mm x 2017 mm	Each	0.63	17.51	-	139.26	156.77	172.45	15.960
30126	**SECOND FIXINGS STANDARD WINDOWS**								
3012601	**Casement windows including frames; side hung; double glazed opening casements and ventilators; hung on rust proof hinges; fitted with aluminium anodised casement stays and fasteners; knot and primed before delivery**								
3012601A	W107C height 750 mm x 630 mm	Each	0.88	24.46	-	145.68	170.14	187.15	3.120
3012601B	W109C height 900 mm x 630 mm	Each	0.99	27.52	-	147.28	174.80	192.28	3.390
3012601C	W110C height 1050 mm x 630 mm	Each	1.15	31.97	-	154.98	186.95	205.65	3.670
3012601D	W2N10CC height 1050 mm x 915 mm	Each	1.25	34.75	-	228.72	263.47	289.82	4.720
3012601E	W210C height 1050 mm x 1200 mm	Each	1.50	41.70	-	198.74	240.44	264.48	6.210
3012601F	W212C height 1200 mm x 1200 mm	Each	1.50	41.70	-	208.30	250.00	275.00	6.620
3012601G	W312CC height 1200 mm x 1770 mm	Each	2.00	55.60	-	368.32	423.92	466.31	6.950
3012601H	W310CC height 1050 mm x 1770 mm	Each	1.55	43.09	-	316.63	359.72	395.69	8.750
3012601I	W409CMC height 900 mm x 2339 mm	Each	2.15	59.77	-	307.73	367.50	404.25	8.440
3012601J	W410CMC height 1050 mm x 2339 mm	Each	2.15	59.77	-	454.10	513.87	565.26	7.620
3012601K	W412CMC height 1200 mm x 2339 mm	Each	2.25	62.55	-	454.24	516.79	568.47	8.060
3012602	**Velux roof windows; centre pivot; laminated Nordic red pine frame and sash; sealed unit double pre-glazing; 3 mm clear float glass; exterior aluminium cladding; natural brownish-grey finish; type EDZ flashings and soakers; for tiles and pantiles screwed to softwood (GGL); type**								
3012602A	GGL C02 height 780 mm x 550 mm	Each	6.05	168.19	-	251.70	419.89	461.88	31.130
3012602B	GGL C04 height 980 mm x 550 mm	Each	6.05	168.19	-	277.93	446.12	490.73	36.310
3012602C	GGL F06 height 1180 mm x 660 mm	Each	7.26	201.83	-	232.09	433.92	477.31	72.910
3012602D	GGL M04 height 980 mm x 780 mm	Each	6.65	184.87	-	314.83	499.70	549.67	43.870
3012602E	GGL M08 height 1400 mm x 780 mm	Each	7.87	218.79	-	265.49	484.28	532.71	88.430
3012602F	GGL P10 height 1600 mm x 940 mm	Each	7.87	218.79	-	454.37	673.16	740.48	69.110
3012602G	GGL S06 height 1180 mm x 1140 mm	Each	8.47	235.47	-	291.96	527.43	580.17	96.330

Small Works 2011		Unit	Labour Hours	Labour Net £	Plant Net £	Materials Net £	Unit Net £	Unit with 10% £	CO$_2$ Kg
301	**NEW WORK**								
30126	**SECOND FIXINGS STANDARD WINDOWS**								
3012602	**Velux roof windows; centre pivot; laminated Nordic red pine frame and sash; sealed unit double pre-glazing; 3 mm clear float glass; exterior aluminium cladding; natural brownish- grey finish; type EDZ flashings and soakers; for tiles and pantiles screwed to softwood (GGL); type**								
3012602H	GGL U04 height 980 mm x 1340 mm	Each	8.47	235.47	-	432.77	668.24	735.06	62.280
3012602I	GGL U08 height 1400 mm x 1340 mm	Each	9.08	252.42	-	1,793.37	2,045.79	2,250.37	117.250
30128	**SECOND FIXINGS STANDARD KITCHEN UNITS**								
3012801	**Base units; depth 600 mm**								
3012801A	500 mm wide x 900 mm high	Each	1.54	42.81	-	140.40	183.21	201.53	24.460
3012801B	600 mm wide x 900 mm high	Each	1.71	47.54	-	150.05	197.59	217.35	27.320
3012801C	1000 mm wide x 900 mm high	Each	1.98	55.04	-	210.16	265.20	291.72	38.770
3012802	**Sink units; depth 600 mm**								
3012802A	1000 mm wide x 900 mm high	Each	2.00	55.60	-	210.16	265.76	292.34	38.770
3012802B	1200 mm wide x 900 mm high	Each	2.20	61.16	-	224.38	285.54	314.09	44.490
3012803	**Wall units; depth 300 mm**								
3012803A	500 mm wide x 580 mm high	Each	1.54	42.81	-	99.61	142.42	156.66	11.740
3012803B	600 mm wide x 580 mm high	Each	1.71	47.54	-	109.54	157.08	172.79	13.430
3012803C	1000 mm wide x 580 mm high	Each	1.96	54.49	-	177.65	232.14	255.35	20.220
3012803D	500 mm wide x 780 mm high	Each	1.69	46.98	-	122.04	169.02	185.92	13.980
3012803E	600 mm wide x 780 mm high	Each	1.90	52.82	-	136.31	189.13	208.04	15.960
3012803F	1000 mm wide x 780 mm high	Each	2.20	61.16	-	197.80	258.96	284.86	23.890
3012804	**Store units; depth 600 mm**								
3012804A	500 mm wide x 2056 mm high	Each	2.97	82.57	-	336.57	419.14	461.05	52.400
3012804B	600 mm wide x 2056 mm high	Each	3.14	87.29	-	470.42	557.71	613.48	58.220
3012805	**Laminated plastic worktop; cut to size; lipped all round; fixed to worktops of base units with adhesive**								
3012805A	600 mm x 500 mm	Each	0.48	13.34	-	28.07	41.41	45.55	3.520
3012805B	600 mm x 600 mm	Each	0.55	15.29	-	.33.70	48.99	53.89	4.220
3012805C	600 mm x 1200 mm	Each	0.85	23.63	-	56.16	79.79	87.77	7.040
30142	**SOFTWOOD STAIRCASES COMPONENTS**								
3014201	**Treads**								
3014201A	25 mm nosed and risers 19 mm tongued	m^2	5.40	150.12	-	28.17	178.29	196.12	10.990
3014201B	32 mm nosed and risers 25 mm tongued	m^2	6.00	166.80	-	31.98	198.78	218.66	12.470
3014201C	Extra for bullnose step	Each	2.25	62.55	-	4.57	67.12	73.83	1.780
3014201D	Extra for double bullnose step	Each	4.00	111.20	-	9.90	121.10	133.21	3.860
3014202	**Winders**								
3014202A	25 mm cross-tongued and risers 19 mm	m^2	7.50	208.50	-	38.07	246.57	271.23	14.850
3014202B	32 mm cross-tongued and risers 25 mm	m^2	8.00	222.40	-	41.88	264.28	290.71	16.340
3014203	**Landings**								
3014203A	25 mm cross-tongued, including bearers	m^2	5.30	147.34	-	37.31	184.65	203.12	14.550
3014203B	32 mm cross-tongued, including bearers	m^2	5.30	147.34	-	41.12	188.46	207.31	16.040
3014205	**Strings**								
3014205A	275 mm x 38 mm	m	0.75	20.85	-	11.42	32.27	35.50	4.460
3014205B	ends of string framed to newel	Each	0.65	18.07	-	-	18.07	19.88	-
3014206	**Handrails**								
3014206A	50 mm mopstick	m	0.40	11.12	-	3.90	15.02	16.52	0.770
3014206B	75 mm x 50 mm	m	0.75	20.85	-	5.61	26.46	29.11	1.240
3014206C	75 mm x 50 mm hardwood	m	1.65	45.87	-	7.61	53.48	58.83	2.970

Woodwork

	Unit	Labour Hours	Labour Net £	Plant Net £	Materials Net £	Unit Net £	Unit with 10% £	CO₂ Kg

301	**NEW WORK**							
30142	**SOFTWOOD STAIRCASES COMPONENTS**							
3014206	**Handrails**							
3014206D	Extra for ramps	Each	4.00	111.20	-	12.18	123.38	135.72	4.750
3014207	**Newels**							
3014207A	100 mm x 100 mm framed	m	1.65	45.87	-	62.91	108.78	119.66	3.070
3014207B	half, 100 mm x 60 mm framed	m	1.10	30.58	-	6.85	37.43	41.17	2.670
3014207C	newel caps, splayed on four sides, 125 mm x 125 mm x 50 mm	Each	0.20	5.56	-	5.33	10.89	11.98	2.080
3014207D	newel caps, half splayed on three sides 125 mm x 63 mm x 50 mm	Each	0.20	5.56	-	4.57	10.13	11.14	1.780
3014208	**Framed spandrel**							
3014208A	38 mm with plywood panelling	m²	6.50	180.70	-	24.37	205.07	225.58	9.500
3014209	**Balusters**							
3014209A	38 mm x 38 mm	m	0.33	9.17	-	1.52	10.69	11.76	0.590
3014211	**Apron lining; chamfered and beaded**							
3014211A	225 mm x 19 mm	m	0.45	12.51	-	5.33	17.84	19.62	2.080
3014211B	225 mm x 25 mm	m	0.50	13.90	-	7.61	21.51	23.66	2.970
30144	**SOFTWOOD STAIRCASES PURPOSE MADE UNITS**							
3014401	**Staircase comprising 25 mm treads, 19 mm risers, 38 mm strings, 100 mm x 100 mm newels, 75 mm x 63 mm handrail and 31 mm balusters and apron lining but excluding spandrel framing below stairs**							
3014401A	900 mm wide x 2620 mm rise	Each	73.00	2,029.40	-	443.92	2,473.32	2,720.65	173.150
3014401B	add for 25 mm quarter space landing and extra newel	Each	5.50	152.90	-	63.20	216.10	237.71	24.650
3014401C	add for three winders and extra newel	Each	8.00	222.40	-	47.21	269.61	296.57	18.410
3014401D	deduct if stairs are built between enclosing walls with handrail fixed to one wall with brackets and without balusters, newel posts, or balustrade to upper floor	Each	25.00	695.00	-	128.68	823.68	906.05	50.190
30146	**SOFTWOOD STAIRCASES STANDARD UNITS**							
3014601	**Staircase with 25 mm treads and 19 mm risers, glued, wedged and blocked with 25 mm wall string, 38 mm x 38 mm turned balusters, 32 mm x 63 mm grooved string capping, 13 mm x 38 mm distance pieces (type B10 balustrade) and 50 mm x 75 mm hardwood handrail between 75 mm x 75 mm newels; in one flight**							
3014601A	855 mm wide x 2600 mm rise	Each	18.00	500.40	-	781.27	1,281.67	1,409.84	31.320
3014602	**Closed tread, half straight flight; 864 mm wide; 1421 mm rise; balustrade fixed one side; fixing to walls with screws**							
3014602A	855 mm wide x 1421 mm rise	Each	10.00	278.00	-	522.34	800.34	880.37	29.700

Small Works 2011		Unit	Labour Hours	Labour Net	Plant Net	Materials Net	Unit Net	Unit with 10%	CO$_2$
				£	£	£	£	£	Kg
301	**NEW WORK**								
30146	**SOFTWOOD STAIRCASES STANDARD UNITS**								
3014604	**Landing balustrade with 50 mm x 75 mm hardwood handrail, 38 mm x 38 mm turned Regency balusters, 32 mm x 140 mm baluster knee rails, 2 No. 32 mm x 50 mm stiffeners, one end joined to newel post, other end built into half newel**								
3014604A	3 m long	Each	12.00	333.60	-	200.18	533.78	587.16	0.410
30148	**SUNDRY ITEMS**								
3014802	**Trap door; 9 mm plywood panel; rebated softwood lining 35 mm x 107 mm**								
3014802A	750 mm x 750 mm	Each	1.60	44.48	-	53.36	97.84	107.62	11.620
3014803	**Softwood weather mould, throated; screwed to door**								
3014803A	50 mm x 75 mm	m	0.60	16.68	-	6.97	23.65	26.02	1.150
3014805	**Hat and coat rails, chamfered edges, plugged to brickwork**								
3014805A	125 mm x 25 mm	m	0.34	9.45	-	3.77	13.22	14.54	1.200
3014805B	125 mm x 25 mm in short lengths	m	0.50	13.90	-	3.77	17.67	19.44	1.200
3014806	**Perforated zinc; safe or larder apertures**								
3014806A	fixed with beads; in small areas	m^2	1.90	52.82	-	52.48	105.30	115.83	12.700
30150	**SUNDRY LABOURS**								
3015001	**Extra over fixing with nails for**								
3015001A	steel screws	m	0.04	1.11	-	0.03	1.14	1.25	0.150
3015001B	steel screws; sinking; filling heads	m	0.07	1.95	-	0.03	1.98	2.18	0.150
3015001C	steel screws; sinking; pellating over	m	0.19	5.28	-	0.03	5.31	5.84	0.150
3015001D	brass cups and screws	m	0.12	3.34	-	0.36	3.70	4.07	0.240
3015002	**Plugging blockwork**								
3015002A	300 mm centres; one way	m	0.08	2.22	-	0.04	2.26	2.49	0.020
3015002B	300 mm centres; both ways	m	0.14	3.89	-	0.13	4.02	4.42	0.060
3015003	**Plugging brickwork**								
3015003A	300 mm centres; one way	m	0.12	3.34	-	0.04	3.38	3.72	0.020
3015003B	300 mm centres; both ways	m	0.24	6.67	-	0.13	6.80	7.48	0.060
3015004	**Plugging concrete**								
3015004A	300 mm centres; one way	m	0.22	6.12	-	0.04	6.16	6.78	0.020
3015004B	300 mm centres; both ways	m	0.44	12.23	-	0.13	12.36	13.60	0.060
3015006	**Holes for pipes, bars etc; through softwood thickness**								
3015006A	12 mm	Each	0.05	1.39	-	-	1.39	1.53	-
3015006B	25 mm	Each	0.08	2.22	-	-	2.22	2.44	-
3015006C	50 mm	Each	0.12	3.34	-	-	3.34	3.67	-
3015006D	75 mm	Each	0.16	4.45	-	-	4.45	4.90	-
3015006E	100 mm	Each	0.19	5.28	-	-	5.28	5.81	-
3015007	**Head or nut in softwood**								
3015007A	let in; flush	Each	0.07	1.95	-	-	1.95	2.15	-
3015009	**Head or nut in hardwood**								
3015009A	let in; flush	Each	0.10	2.78	-	-	2.78	3.06	-
3015009B	let in; pellated	Each	0.24	6.67	-	-	6.67	7.34	-
3015010	**Mortice**								
3015010A	for and including metal dowel	Each	0.11	3.06	-	-	3.06	3.37	-
3015011	**Notching and fitting**								
3015011A	timber to steel	Each	0.33	9.17	-	-	9.17	10.09	-
3015012	**Planing**								
3015012A	by hand	m^2	0.40	11.12	-	-	11.12	12.23	-

Woodwork

	Unit	Labour Hours	Labour Net £	Plant Net £	Materials Net £	Unit Net £	Unit with 10% £	CO$_2$ Kg
301	**NEW WORK**							
30150	**SUNDRY LABOURS**							
3015014	**Hand labours on softwood**							
3015014A	chamfers	m	0.19	5.28	-	-	5.28	5.81	-
3015014B	rounds	m	0.25	6.95	-	-	6.95	7.65	-
3015014C	grooves	m	0.36	10.01	-	-	10.01	11.01	-
3015014D	rebates	m	0.39	10.84	-	-	10.84	11.92	-
3015014E	throats	m	0.39	10.84	-	-	10.84	11.92	-
3015014F	mouldings per 25 mm girth	m	1.13	31.41	-	-	31.41	34.55	-
3015014G	rebate in bottom of rail or door	m	0.30	8.34	-	-	8.34	9.17	-
30151	**INSULATION AND VENTILATION**							
3015101	**13 mm glass fibre sound insulating quilt type PF**							
3015101A	laid between joists	m^2	0.15	4.17	-	6.49	10.66	11.73	3.280
3015101B	fixed vertically between softwood battens	m^2	0.15	4.17	-	6.49	10.66	11.73	3.280
3015102	**Glass fibre thermal insulating quilt laid over ceiling joists**							
3015102A	60 mm	m^2	0.17	4.73	-	3.29	8.02	8.82	15.150
3015102B	80 mm	m^2	0.17	4.73	-	4.07	8.80	9.68	20.190
3015102C	100 mm	m^2	0.17	4.73	-	3.58	8.31	9.14	25.240
3015103	**Glass fibre thermal insulating quilt laid between joists**							
3015103A	60 mm	m^2	0.19	5.28	-	3.29	8.57	9.43	15.150
3015103B	80 mm	m^2	0.19	5.28	-	4.07	9.35	10.29	20.190
3015103C	100 mm	m^2	0.19	5.28	-	3.58	8.86	9.75	25.240
3015104	**Vermiculite granular loose fill insulation laid between joists**							
3015104A	50 mm	m^2	0.20	5.56	-	6.76	12.32	13.55	18.650
3015104B	75 mm	m^2	0.30	8.34	-	10.16	18.50	20.35	28.020
3015104C	100 mm	m^2	0.40	11.12	-	1.35	12.47	13.72	3.720
3015106	**Expanded polystyrene insulation board**							
3015106A	53 mm	m^2	0.38	10.56	-	6.18	16.74	18.41	17.700
3015106B	83 mm	m^2	0.38	10.56	-	10.47	21.03	23.13	27.710
3015107	**Bitumen impregnated insulating board**							
3015107A	13 mm	m^2	0.25	6.95	-	4.23	11.18	12.30	3.280
3015107B	raking cutting	m	0.36	10.01	-	-	10.01	11.01	-
3015107C	curved cutting	m	0.60	16.68	-	-	16.68	18.35	-
3015108	**PVC-u push-in soffit ventilators, 70 mm dia, including cutting hole through timber soffit board and installing discs at**							
3015108A	140 mm centres	m	1.20	33.36	-	10.59	43.95	48.35	9.760
3015109	**PVC-u type C slotted soffit ventilator and screwing to**							
3015109A	back of timber fascia	m	0.33	9.17	-	5.18	14.35	15.79	0.530
30152	**METALWORK**							
3015201	**Galvanised steel water bars including grooves in timber**							
3015201A	30 mm x 6 mm	m	0.30	8.34	-	9.90	18.24	20.06	5.290
3015201B	40 mm x 6 mm	m	0.32	8.90	-	11.82	20.72	22.79	7.050
3015202	**Black cup square carriage bolt with hexagon nut and washer**							
3015202A	M10 x 50 mm	Each	0.12	3.34	-	0.32	3.66	4.03	0.070
3015202B	M10 x 75 mm	Each	0.14	3.89	-	0.37	4.26	4.69	0.100
3015202C	M10 x 100 mm	Each	0.14	3.89	-	0.56	4.45	4.90	0.130
3015202D	M10 x 150 mm	Each	0.16	4.45	-	1.17	5.62	6.18	0.200
3015202E	M12 x 50 mm	Each	0.14	3.89	-	1.34	5.23	5.75	0.090
3015202F	M12 x 75 mm	Each	0.14	3.89	-	1.68	5.57	6.13	0.140
3015202G	M12 x 100 mm	Each	0.15	4.17	-	0.71	4.88	5.37	0.190
3015202H	M12 x 150 mm	Each	0.17	4.73	-	1.27	6.00	6.60	0.290

Small Works 2011		Unit	Labour Hours	Labour Net	Plant Net	Materials Net	Unit Net	Unit with 10%	CO$_2$
				£	£	£	£	£	Kg

301   **NEW WORK**

30152   **METALWORK**

3015204   Galvanised mild steel joist restraint straps, twice bent, one end drilled and screwed to timber, other end built in

3015204A	30 mm x 5 mm 700 mm girth bent at 75 mm	Each	0.40	11.12	-	3.18	14.30	15.73	3.360
3015204B	30 mm x 5 mm 800 mm girth bent at 100 mm	Each	0.48	13.34	-	3.66	17.00	18.70	3.780
3015204C	30 mm x 5 mm 1000 mm girth bent at 100 mm	Each	0.52	14.46	-	5.34	19.80	21.78	5.460

3015206   Galvanised steel joist hangers built in

3015206A	50 mm x 100 mm	Each	0.20	5.56	-	1.74	7.30	8.03	0.920
3015206B	50 mm x 125 mm	Each	0.21	5.84	-	1.74	7.58	8.34	1.120
3015206C	50 mm x 150 mm	Each	0.22	6.12	-	1.90	8.02	8.82	1.320
3015206D	50 mm x 175 mm	Each	0.23	6.39	-	1.90	8.29	9.12	1.510
3015206E	50 mm x 200 mm	Each	0.24	6.67	-	2.04	8.71	9.58	1.710
3015206H	75 mm x 100 mm	Each	0.27	7.51	-	2.11	9.62	10.58	1.470
3015206I	75 mm x 175 mm	Each	0.28	7.78	-	2.72	10.50	11.55	1.900
3015206J	75 mm x 200 mm	Each	0.29	8.06	-	2.72	10.78	11.86	1.900

3015207   Double sided galvanised timber connectors

3015207A	M12 x 50 mm	Each	0.05	1.39	-	0.51	1.90	2.09	0.540
3015207B	M12 x 64 mm	Each	0.06	1.67	-	0.67	2.34	2.57	0.650

3015208   Bulldog single sided round tooth-plate timber connectors

3015208A	63 mm	Each	0.07	1.95	-	0.85	2.80	3.08	0.280

3015209   Bulldog double sided round toothed- plate timber connectors

3015209A	50 mm	Each	0.05	1.39	-	0.59	1.98	2.18	0.170
3015209B	63 mm	Each	0.09	2.50	-	0.85	3.35	3.69	0.280
3015209C	75 mm	Each	0.11	3.06	-	1.11	4.17	4.59	0.400

3015210   Floor clips inserted in concrete when green

3015210A	50 mm	Each	0.05	1.39	-	0.43	1.82	2.00	0.080

3015211   Gallows bracket; 50 mm x 50 mm mild steel angle; support width

3015211A	350 mm	Each	1.04	28.91	-	47.51	76.42	84.06	16.130
3015211B	450 mm	Each	1.14	31.69	-	53.33	85.02	93.52	19.360
3015211C	600 mm	Each	1.24	34.47	-	57.98	92.45	101.70	25.820

30154   **IRONMONGERY**

3015401   Light pattern pressed steel butts and labour hanging door

3015401A	50 mm	Pair	0.58	16.12	-	0.94	17.06	18.77	0.800
3015401B	75 mm	Pair	1.17	32.53	-	0.79	33.32	36.65	0.460
3015401C	100 mm	Pair	1.42	39.48	-	1.35	40.83	44.91	1.040
3015401D	50 mm sheradised	Pair	0.58	16.12	-	1.73	17.85	19.64	0.460
3015401E	75 mm sheradised	Pair	1.17	32.53	-	2.67	35.20	38.72	0.850
3015401F	100 mm sheradised	Pair	1.42	39.48	-	4.51	43.99	48.39	0.980

3015404   Strong pattern steel butts and labour hanging door

3015404A	75 mm	Pair	1.17	32.53	-	3.48	36.01	39.61	0.850
3015404B	100 mm	Pair	1.42	39.48	-	5.18	44.66	49.13	0.980
3015404C	75 mm sheradised	Pair	1.17	32.53	-	4.63	37.16	40.88	0.850
3015404D	100 mm sheradised	Pair	1.42	39.48	-	5.57	45.05	49.56	0.980

3015406   Steel rising butts and labour hanging doors

3015406A	75 mm x 70 mm	Pair	1.45	40.31	-	2.98	43.29	47.62	0.710
3015406B	100 mm x 81 mm	Pair	1.70	47.26	-	4.01	51.27	56.40	1.040
3015406C	75 mm x 70 mm sheradised	Pair	1.45	40.31	-	5.98	46.29	50.92	0.850
3015406D	100 mm x 81 mm sheradised	Pair	1.70	47.26	-	6.12	53.38	58.72	1.030

3015409   Steel washered brass butts and labour hanging door

3015409A	76 mm	Pair	1.17	32.53	-	6.86	39.39	43.33	1.050
3015409B	102 mm	Pair	1.42	39.48	-	9.23	48.71	53.58	1.250

Woodwork

	Unit	Labour Hours	Labour Net £	Plant Net £	Materials Net £	Unit Net £	Unit with 10% £	CO$_2$ Kg
301 **NEW WORK**								
30154 **IRONMONGERY**								
3015411 **Brass rising butts and labour hanging door**								
3015411A 76 mm x 60 mm	Pair	1.45	40.31	-	5.98	46.29	50.92	1.050
3015411B 102 mm x 67 mm	Pair	1.70	47.26	-	8.82	56.08	61.69	1.250
3015412 **Hurlinge steel butts and labour hanging door**								
3015412A 76 mm	Pair	0.33	9.17	-	3.51	12.68	13.95	0.850
3015412B 102 mm	Pair	0.42	11.68	-	2.64	14.32	15.75	0.990
3015412C 76 mm sheradised	Pair	0.33	9.17	-	2.23	11.40	12.54	0.850
3015412D 102 mm sheradised	Pair	0.42	11.68	-	6.48	18.16	19.98	0.990
3015415 **Steel tee hinges and labour hanging door**								
3015415A 305 mm	Pair	0.83	23.07	-	3.24	26.31	28.94	1.840
3015415B 457 mm	Pair	0.92	25.58	-	4.83	30.41	33.45	2.280
3015416 **Steel light reversible hinges and labour hanging door**								
3015416A 305 mm	Pair	1.05	29.19	-	9.15	38.34	42.17	2.140
3015416B 457 mm	Pair	1.15	31.97	-	12.72	44.69	49.16	2.950
3015418 **Steel heavy reversible hinges and labour hanging door**								
3015418A 305 mm	Pair	1.33	36.97	-	11.68	48.65	53.52	2.140
3015418B 457 mm	Pair	1.50	41.70	-	15.86	57.56	63.32	2.950
3015418C 610 mm	Pair	1.67	46.43	-	23.11	69.54	76.49	3.750
3015419 **Interior straight sliding door gear; top track with wheel hangers; door guides; stops; finger pulls; steel pelmet and labour hanging**								
3015419A 35 mm to 44 mm thick single softwood door	Each	3.50	97.30	-	47.88	145.18	159.70	25.340
3015420 **Locks and latches**								
3015420A rim lock and furniture	Each	1.25	34.75	-	38.67	73.42	80.76	5.740
3015420B mortice lock and furniture	Each	1.45	40.31	-	44.98	85.29	93.82	5.630
3015420C mortice dead lock	Each	1.00	27.80	-	42.17	69.97	76.97	19.250
3015420D cylinder rim night latch	Each	1.20	33.36	-	41.57	74.93	82.42	3.970
3015420E Suffolk latch	Each	1.00	27.80	-	7.07	34.87	38.36	1.130
3015420F escutcheon	Each	0.30	8.34	-	1.60	9.94	10.93	0.560
3015420G Bales catch	Each	0.50	13.90	-	3.57	17.47	19.22	0.020
3015420H cupboard catch	Each	0.30	8.34	-	5.77	14.11	15.52	11.450
3015420I cupboard or drawer lock	Each	0.60	16.68	-	5.77	22.45	24.70	0.160
3015420J cupboard button	Each	0.25	6.95	-	0.96	7.91	8.70	1.200
3015422 **Door closers**								
3015422A overhead door closer; surface fixing	Each	1.75	48.65	-	113.11	161.76	177.94	3.940
3015422B Perko closer	Each	1.75	48.65	-	14.17	62.82	69.10	2.480
3015422C coil gate spring	Each	0.40	11.12	-	5.01	16.13	17.74	4.110
3015424 **Bolts**								
3015424A 150 mm barrel; straight	Each	0.45	12.51	-	4.40	16.91	18.60	0.450
3015424B 255 mm barrel; straight	Each	0.55	15.29	-	7.31	22.60	24.86	1.010
3015424C 150 mm tower; straight	Each	0.45	12.51	-	2.68	15.19	16.71	0.890
3015424D 255 mm tower; straight	Each	0.55	15.29	-	5.23	20.52	22.57	1.390
3015424E 455 mm monkey tail	Each	0.55	15.29	-	23.02	38.31	42.14	2.700
3015424F 225 mm flush	Each	0.85	23.63	-	25.44	49.07	53.98	1.010
3015424G indicator	Each	1.20	33.36	-	11.35	44.71	49.18	1.010
3015424H single door panic	Each	1.75	48.65	-	61.87	110.52	121.57	3.940
3015424I double door panic	Each	2.30	63.94	-	75.21	139.15	153.07	7.880
3015426 **Handles and pulls**								
3015426A door handle	Each	0.30	8.34	-	8.60	16.94	18.63	0.560
3015426B drawer pull	Each	0.20	5.56	-	8.60	14.16	15.58	0.120
3015426C cupboard knob	Each	0.20	5.56	-	8.23	13.79	15.17	2.250
3015428 **Plates**								
3015428A door push plate	Each	0.40	11.12	-	8.10	19.22	21.14	0.840
3015428B letter plate and opening through door	Each	1.75	48.65	-	11.91	60.56	66.62	3.940
3015430 **Window fittings**								
3015430A casement stay; 305 mm; with two pins	Each	0.40	11.12	-	5.53	16.65	18.32	0.300

Small Works 2011		Unit	Labour Hours	Labour Net	Plant Net	Materials Net	Unit Net	Unit with 10%	CO$_2$
				£	£	£	£	£	Kg
301	**NEW WORK**								
30154	**IRONMONGERY**								
3015430	**Window fittings**								
3015430B	casement fastener; wedge pattern	Each	0.50	13.90	-	5.41	19.31	21.24	0.290
3015430C	casement fastener; locking with keys	Each	0.55	15.29	-	6.41	21.70	23.87	18.290
3015430D	sliding sash fastener	Each	1.20	33.36	-	6.41	39.77	43.75	28.630
3015430E	sash lift	Each	0.30	8.34	-	3.59	11.93	13.12	1.480
3015430F	quadrant stay	Each	0.40	11.12	-	5.65	16.77	18.45	2.900
3015432	**Sundry items**								
3015432A	hat and coat hooks	Each	0.21	5.84	-	3.59	9.43	10.37	1.480
3015432B	cabin hook and eye	Each	0.30	8.34	-	4.70	13.04	14.34	1.720
3015432C	padlock hasp and staple	Each	0.30	8.34	-	3.67	12.01	13.21	3.190
3015432D	swivel locking bar	Each	0.40	11.12	-	46.57	57.69	63.46	6.900
3015432E	rubber door stop	Each	0.20	5.56	-	0.62	6.18	6.80	0.300
3015432F	door buffer	Each	0.30	8.34	-	9.16	17.50	19.25	0.080
3015432G	shelf bracket	Each	0.40	11.12	-	3.11	14.23	15.65	0.470
3015432H	security door chain	Each	0.30	8.34	-	3.98	12.32	13.55	0.320
3015432I	numerals; 75 mm high	Each	0.20	5.56	-	3.32	8.88	9.77	0.560

Woodwork

	Unit	Labour Hours	Labour Net	Plant Net	Materials Net	Unit Net	Unit with 10%	CO$_2$
			£	£	£	£	£	Kg
302	**REPAIRS AND ALTERATIONS**							
30201	**REMOVE TIMBERS**							
3020101	**Roof timbers**							
3020101A	complete including rafters, purlins, ceiling joists, plates and the like (measured flat on plan)	m^2	0.37	7.71	-	-	7.71	8.48	-
3020102	**Floor construction**							
3020102A	joists; softwood ; at ground level	m^2	0.28	5.84	-	-	5.84	6.42	-
3020102B	joists; softwood; at first floor level	m^2	0.55	11.47	-	-	11.47	12.62	-
3020102C	joists; softwood; at roof level	m^2	0.77	16.05	-	-	16.05	17.66	-
3020102D	individual floor or roof members	m	0.30	6.25	-	-	6.25	6.88	-
3020102E	extra for cutting off end flush with wall	Each	0.50	10.43	-	-	10.43	11.47	-
3020102F	decayed or infected floor plates	m	0.40	8.34	-	-	8.34	9.17	-
3020102G	tilting fillet or roll	m	0.17	3.54	-	-	3.54	3.89	-
3020102H	fascia or barge board	m	0.65	13.55	-	-	13.55	14.91	-
3020103	**Boarding and flooring; softwood; including withdrawing nails; at**							
3020103A	ground floor	m^2	0.42	8.76	-	-	8.76	9.64	-
3020103B	first floor	m^2	0.68	14.18	-	-	14.18	15.60	-
3020103C	roof, softwood	m^2	0.80	16.68	-	-	16.68	18.35	-
3020103D	gutter, softwood	m^2	0.88	18.35	-	-	18.35	20.19	-
3020103E	ground level; chipboard	m^2	0.17	3.54	-	-	3.54	3.89	-
3020103F	first floor level; chipboard	m^2	0.42	8.76	-	-	8.76	9.64	-
3020103G	ground level; plywood	m^2	0.25	5.21	-	-	5.21	5.73	-
3020103H	first floor level; plywood	m^2	0.48	10.01	-	-	10.01	11.01	-
3020104	**Stud partition; softwood; including finishings both sides**							
3020104A	solid	m^2	0.50	10.43	-	-	10.43	11.47	
3020104B	glazed, including removal of glass	m^2	0.67	13.97	-	-	13.97	15.37	
3020105	**Wall linings; including battening behind**							
3020105A	plain sheeting	m^2	0.33	6.88	-	-	6.88	7.57	-
3020105B	matchboarding	m^2	0.45	9.38	-	-	9.38	10.32	-
3020106	**Ceiling linings; including battening behind**							
3020106A	plain sheeting	m^2	0.50	10.43	-	-	10.43	11.47	-
3020106B	matchboarding	m^2	0.67	13.97	-	-	13.97	15.37	-
3020107	**Skirtings etc**							
3020107A	skirtings, picture rails, dado rails architraves and the like	m	0.12	2.50	-	-	2.50	2.75	-
3020108	**Shelves etc**							
3020108A	shelves, window boards and the like	m	0.35	7.30	-	-	7.30	8.03	-
3020109	**Doors**							
3020109A	single	Each	0.45	9.38	-	-	9.38	10.32	-
3020109B	single with frame or lining	Each	0.88	18.35	-	-	18.35	20.19	-
3020109C	pair	Each	0.77	16.05	-	-	16.05	17.66	-
3020109D	pair with frame or lining	Each	1.32	27.52	-	-	27.52	30.27	-
3020109E	Extra for taking out spring box	Each	0.83	17.31	-	-	17.31	19.04	
3020110	**Windows**							
3020110A	casement; with frame	Each	1.32	27.52	-	-	27.52	30.27	-
3020110B	double hung sash; with frame	Each	1.77	36.90	-	-	36.90	40.59	-
3020110C	pair; french with frame	Pair	4.40	91.74	-	-	91.74	100.91	-
3020111	**Staircase; balustrade**							
3020111A	single straight flight	Each	3.85	80.27	-	-	80.27	88.30	-
3020111B	dogleg flight	Each	5.50	114.68	-	-	114.68	126.15	-
3020111C	handrail and brackets	m	0.12	2.50	-	-	2.50	2.75	-
3020112	**Bath panels**							
3020112A	including frame	Each	0.45	9.38	-	-	9.38	10.32	-
3020114	**Kitchen fittings**							
3020114A	wall units	Each	0.50	10.43	-	-	10.43	11.47	-

Small Works 2011	Unit	Labour Hours	Labour Net	Plant Net	Materials Net	Unit Net	Unit with 10%	CO$_2$
			£	£	£	£	£	Kg
302	**REPAIRS AND ALTERATIONS**							
30201	**REMOVE TIMBERS**							
3020114	**Kitchen fittings**							
3020114B	floor units	Each	0.33	6.88	-	-	6.88	7.57	-
3020114C	larder units	Each	0.45	9.38	-	-	9.38	10.32	-
3020114D	built in cupboards	Each	1.55	32.32	-	-	32.32	35.55	-
3020115	**Casings**							
3020115A	for pipes	m	0.33	6.88	-	-	6.88	7.57	-
30202	**ERECT TEMPORARY HOARDING**							
3020201	**Second-hand timber posts, rails and struts, cover with second-hand close boarding or corrugated iron sheets and dismantle on completion**							
3020201A	1.8 m high	m	1.37	66.80	-	11.81	78.61	86.47	9.440
3020201B	Extra for 0.75 m wide door	Each	0.33	15.81	-	1.77	17.58	19.34	1.370
3020201C	Extra for pair of gates approx 2.4 m wide overall	Each	1.05	51.03	-	5.15	56.18	61.80	4.080
3020202	**Enclose frontage to site with chestnut fencing with posts at 1.8 m intervals and dismantle on completion**							
3020202A	1.2 m high	m	0.14	6.81	-	7.19	14.00	15.40	11.040
30204	**REMOVE DEFECTIVE AND RENEW**							
3020401	**Take up defective gutter boards and bearers and supply and fix**							
3020401A	new	m^2	1.85	89.86	-	20.80	110.66	121.73	10.530
3020402	**Take off defective rounded wood rolls to flats and supply and fix**							
3020402A	new	m	0.11	5.35	-	1.67	7.02	7.72	0.830
3020403	**Renew roof timbers**							
3020403A	100 mm x 50 mm	m	0.08	3.65	-	2.00	5.65	6.22	1.650
3020403B	125 mm x 50 mm	m	0.10	4.87	-	2.51	7.38	8.12	2.070
3020403C	150 mm x 50 mm	m	0.13	6.08	-	2.99	9.07	9.98	2.480
3020404	**Take down defective hips and ridges and supply and fix new**							
3020404A	175 mm x 31 mm	m	0.20	9.73	-	2.54	12.27	13.50	1.850
3020405	**Take down defective fascia and supply and fix new**							
3020405A	150 mm x 25 mm	m	0.20	9.73	-	4.42	14.15	15.57	1.240
3020406	**Take down defective soffit and bearers and supply and fix new**							
3020406A	225 mm x 19 mm	m	0.30	14.59	-	4.92	19.51	21.46	1.450
3020407	**Take off front gate, remove defective timber posts, grub up concrete, supply new post approximately 1.5 m long set in new concrete and rehang gate**							
3020407A	150 mm x 150 mm creosoted fir post	Each	1.50	72.88	-	29.13	102.01	112.21	47.090
3020407B	150 mm x 150 mm oak post	Each	1.62	78.96	-	102.57	181.53	199.68	50.860
3020408	**Excavate for and bolt to wood gate post**							
3020408A	concrete or oak spur set in concrete	Each	1.00	48.60	-	33.85	82.45	90.70	41.320

Woodwork

		Unit	Labour Hours	Labour Net £	Plant Net £	Materials Net £	Unit Net £	Unit with 10% £	CO₂ Kg
302	**REPAIRS AND ALTERATIONS**								
30204	**REMOVE DEFECTIVE AND RENEW**								
3020409	**Take down and remove all temporary weatherproofing together with all associated timber work to windows and doors and make good all existing joinery work including withdrawing all nails**								
3020409A	polythene sheet, hardboard, chipboard and the like	m²	0.60	29.14	-	1.99	31.13	34.24	0.360
3020409B	galvanised iron sheet or corrugated asbestos covering including all timber backing and make good	m²	0.85	41.30	-	2.39	43.69	48.06	0.430
30206	**TEMPORARY SCREENS**								
3020601	**Temporary screen comprising**								
3020601A	100 mm x 50 mm framing lined both side with building paper	m²	0.13	6.32	-	4.32	10.64	11.70	4.060
3020601B	100 mm x 50 mm framing lined one side with 19 mm matchboard	m²	0.30	14.59	-	6.41	21.00	23.10	3.860
3020601C	50 mm x 50 mm framing lined one side with hardboard	m²	0.23	10.95	-	2.67	13.62	14.98	2.880
3020602	**Strut up ceiling and remove struts on completion**								
3020602A	floor to ceiling average 2.6 m	m	0.55	26.71	-	1.24	27.95	30.75	1.030
3020603	**Strut and support window openings; area of window**								
3020603A	1.0 sq.m	Each	0.23	10.95	-	1.57	12.52	13.77	1.210
3020603B	1.5 sq.m	Each	0.25	12.16	-	2.35	14.51	15.96	1.820
3020603C	2.0 sq.m	Each	0.28	13.38	-	2.35	15.73	17.30	1.820
30208	**REPAIRS TO FLOORS**								
3020801	**Remove all grease and dirt from existing flooring, remove all projecting lino nails or tacks, punch down all floor brads, resecure any loose boards, plane off and leave smooth**								
3020801A	generally	m²	0.43	20.68	-	-	20.68	22.75	-
3020801B	in small areas; less than 1 sq.m	m²	0.55	26.71	-	-	26.71	29.38	-
3020801C	take up loose floor blocks and relay in mastic; single block	Each	0.18	8.51	-	0.20	8.71	9.58	0.460
3020801D	take up loose floor blocks and relay in mastic; in patches up to six blocks	Each	0.11	5.35	-	0.20	5.55	6.11	0.460
3020802	**Smooth hardwood floor with**								
3020802A	electric sanding machine	m²	0.50	24.28	-	-	24.28	26.71	-
3020803	**Take off existing skirting and refix**								
3020803A	replug grounds	m	0.18	8.76	-	-	8.76	9.64	-
3020804	**Take off existing softwood skirting and supply and fix new**								
3020804A	25 mm x 150 mm	m	0.25	12.16	-	7.85	20.01	22.01	1.240
3020806	**Take up existing shrunk or worn flooring, any thickness. Draw all nails, relay, cramp up, make up width or length with extra boarding of same thickness and clean off on completion; areas exceeding 0.5 sq.m**								
3020806A	plain edge	m²	0.45	21.84	-	2.39	24.23	26.65	0.870
3020806B	tongued and grooved	m²	0.55	26.71	-	2.10	28.81	31.69	0.870

Small Works 2011		Unit	Labour Hours	Labour Net	Plant Net	Materials Net	Unit Net	Unit with 10%	CO₂
				£	£	£	£	£	Kg
302	**REPAIRS AND ALTERATIONS**								
30208	**REPAIRS TO FLOORS**								
3020807	**Remove damaged 25 mm softwood floor boards; clean joists and renew**								
3020807A	plain edge	m²	0.43	20.68	-	19.97	40.65	44.72	7.270
3020807B	tongued and grooved	m²	0.50	24.28	-	17.56	41.84	46.02	7.270
3020807C	plain edge; in small detached areas not exceeding 1.0 sq.m	m²	1.10	53.42	-	19.97	73.39	80.73	7.270
3020807D	tongued and grooved in small detached areas not exceeding 1.0 sq m	m²	1.35	65.58	-	17.56	83.14	91.45	7.270
3020807E	plain edge exceeding 1.0 sq.m, not exceeding 2.5 sq.m	m²	1.00	48.60	-	19.97	68.57	75.43	7.270
3020807F	tongued and grooved exceeding 1.0 sq.m, not exceeding 2.5 sq.m	m²	1.25	60.72	-	17.56	78.28	86.11	7.270
3020809	**Renewing softwood joists and flooring including treating joists and underside of boards with creosote or other preservative**								
3020809A	100 mm x 50 mm floor joists; 25 mm plain edge flooring	m²	1.00	27.80	-	29.22	57.02	62.72	17.950
3020810	**Oak strip flooring pinned and glued to existing softwood floor; clean off and wax polish**								
3020810A	13 mm	m²	0.90	25.02	-	61.49	86.51	95.16	5.710
30210	**REPAIRS TO DOOR FRAMES, LININGS ETC**								
3021001	**Take down door**								
3021001A	cut 13 mm off bottom edge and rehang	Each	1.60	44.48	-	-	44.48	48.93	-
3021002	**Cut down architraves (one side)**								
3021002A	reduce length by 13 mm and refix	Set	0.55	15.29	-	-	15.29	16.82	-
3021002B	reduce length by 13 mm without removal	Set	0.50	13.90	-	-	13.90	15.29	-
3021003	**Take off skirting**								
3021003A	refix at higher level	m	0.30	8.34	-	-	8.34	9.17	-
3021004	**Hardwood border to hearth**								
3021004A	mitred	Each	0.60	16.68	-	4.00	20.68	22.75	0.920
3021004B	Add if sheet metal inner lining	Each	0.40	11.12	-	4.73	15.85	17.44	14.390
3021006	**Take down door, take out lining or frame, realign and refix. Refix existing architraves and make good work disturbed**								
3021006A	ease and adjust and rehang door	Each	5.00	139.00	-	-	139.00	152.90	-
3021010	**Take down, ease and rehang**								
3021010A	door	Each	1.80	50.04	-	-	50.04	55.04	-
3021010B	door on new butt hinges; remove lock and furniture and supply and fit new rim lock and furniture	Each	3.00	83.40	-	45.67	129.07	141.98	6.530
3021010C	door on new butt hinges; remove lock and furniture and supply and fit new mortice lock and furniture	Each	3.50	97.30	-	51.98	149.28	164.21	6.420
3021010D	door; take apart and fit new panel or rail	Each	4.80	133.44	-	5.33	138.77	152.65	3.510
3021010E	renew weatherboard to external softwood door	Each	1.00	27.80	-	5.79	33.59	36.95	1.150
3021010F	casement sash	Each	1.20	33.36	-	-	33.36	36.70	-
3021010G	defective staff and parting beads to double hung sash window and renew	Each	0.80	22.24	-	3.39	25.63	28.19	0.310
3021010H	double hung sashes; including new cords	Each	1.35	37.53	-	1.17	38.70	42.57	0.360
3021010I	cut out defective glazing bars to skylights, windows, doors or greenhouses and renew	m	0.90	25.02	-	0.65	25.67	28.24	0.070

Woodwork

		Unit	Labour Hours	Labour Net	Plant Net	Materials Net	Unit Net	Unit with 10%	CO$_2$
				£	£	£	£	£	Kg
302	**REPAIRS AND ALTERATIONS**								
30212	**REPAIRS TO STAIRS AND HANDRAILS**								
3021201	**Strengthening handrail and balusters**								
3021201A	including renewing defective balusters	m	1.25	34.75	-	7.34	42.09	46.30	0.590
3021202	**Cutting out defective or worn portion of tread**								
3021202A	piecing in new	Each	0.80	22.24	-	3.05	25.29	27.82	1.190
30213	**TAKE OFF AND RENEW IRONMONGERY**								
3021301	**Take off and renew ironmongery fixed to softwood**								
3021301A	75 mm strong pattern steel butts	Pair	1.33	36.97	-	3.48	40.45	44.50	0.850
3021301B	100 mm strong pattern steel butts	Pair	1.58	43.92	-	5.18	49.10	54.01	0.980
3021301C	76 mm steel washered brass butts	Pair	1.33	36.97	-	6.86	43.83	48.21	1.050
3021301D	102 mm steel washered brass butts	Pair	1.58	43.92	-	9.23	53.15	58.47	1.250
3021301E	76 mm brass rising butts	Pair	1.61	44.76	-	5.98	50.74	55.81	1.050
3021301F	102 mm brass rising butts	Pair	1.86	51.71	-	8.82	60.53	66.58	1.250
3021301G	305 mm steel tee hinges	Pair	1.13	31.41	-	11.68	43.09	47.40	2.140
3021301H	457 mm steel tee hinges	Pair	1.22	33.92	-	15.86	49.78	54.76	2.950
3021301I	rim lock and furniture	Each	1.58	43.92	-	38.67	82.59	90.85	5.740
3021301J	mortice lock and furniture	Each	1.84	51.15	-	44.98	96.13	105.74	5.630
3021301K	Suffolk latch	Each	1.33	36.97	-	7.07	44.04	48.44	1.130
3021301L	150 mm bolt; straight; barrel	Each	0.68	18.90	-	5.75	24.65	27.12	0.650
3021301M	225 mm bolt; straight; barrel	Each	0.78	21.68	-	7.31	28.99	31.89	1.010
3021301N	250 mm casement stay with two pins	Each	0.62	17.24	-	5.53	22.77	25.05	0.300
3021301O	casement fastener; wedge pattern	Each	0.72	20.02	-	5.74	25.76	28.34	0.300
3021301P	sliding sash fastener	Each	1.47	40.87	-	6.32	47.19	51.91	0.340
3021301Q	sash lift	Each	0.47	13.07	-	3.80	16.87	18.56	1.570
30214	**TEMPORARY SHORING**								
3021401	**Erecting temporary dead shoring to form opening using three pairs 150 mm x 150 mm uprights and three 225 mm x 150 mm needles, braces and 225 mm base plates, holing brickwork for needles, all cartage, making good and removing on completion**								
3021401A	volume of timber 0.90 cu.m	Item	34.95	1,700.32	-	119.02	1,819.34	2,001.27	63.190
3021401B	add or deduct for every 0.30 cu.m more or less than 0.90 cu.m	Item	1.00	48.60	-	3.99	52.59	57.85	2.120
3021402	**Erecting temporary raking shoring including rakers, wall plates, needles, holing brickwork, cartage and making good on completion**								
3021402A	volume of timber 0.30 cu.m	Item	15.98	777.28	-	39.67	816.95	898.65	21.060
3021402B	add or deduct for every 0.03 cu.m more or less than 0.30 cu.m	Item	1.50	72.88	-	3.99	76.87	84.56	2.120
3021404	**Erecting temporary flying shoring including horizontal shores, struts, wall plates, posts, needles, holing brickwork, cartage and making good on completion**								
3021404A	volume of timber 0.60 cu.m	Item	39.94	1,943.23	-	79.35	2,022.58	2,224.84	42.130
3021404B	add or deduct for every 0.03 cu.m more or less than 0.60 cu.m	Item	2.00	97.15	-	3.99	101.14	111.25	2.120

Small Works 2011		Unit	Labour Hours	Labour Net £	Plant Net £	Materials Net £	Unit Net £	Unit with 10% £	CO$_2$ Kg
302	**REPAIRS AND ALTERATIONS**								
30214	**TEMPORARY SHORING**								
3021406	**Erecting permanent raking shoring including horizontal shores, struts, wall plates, posts, needles, holing brickwork, cartage, left in position for an indefinite period**								
3021406A	volume of timber 0.30 cu.m	Item	9.99	485.82	-	85.65	571.47	628.62	84.260
3021406B	add or deduct for each 0.30 cu.m more or less than 0.30 cu.m	Item	1.00	48.60	-	8.62	57.22	62.94	8.480
3021407	**Erecting permanent flying shoring including horizontal shores, struts, wall plates, posts, needles, holing brickwork, cartage, left in position for an indefinite period**								
3021407A	volume of timber 0.60 cu.m	Item	26.96	1,311.65	-	171.30	1,482.95	1,631.25	168.510
3021407B	add or deduct for every 0.03 cu.m more or less than 0.60 cu.m	Item	1.35	65.58	-	8.62	74.20	81.62	8.480

Floor, Wall and Ceiling Finishes

Small Works 2011	Unit	Labour Hours	Labour Net £	Plant Net £	Materials Net £	Unit Net £	Unit with 10% £	CO$_2$ Kg
401 **NEW WORK**								
40101 **CARLITE PLASTER**								
4010101 Plaster; 8 mm bonding; 2 mm finish; steel trowelled; internal; 10 mm work; concrete or plasterboard base								
4010101A over 300 mm wide to walls	m²	0.26	12.75	-	2.09	14.84	16.32	1.300
4010101B not exceeding 300 mm wide to walls	m²	0.39	19.15	-	2.09	21.24	23.36	1.300
4010101C over 300 mm wide to ceilings	m²	0.33	15.93	-	2.09	18.02	19.82	1.300
4010101D not exceeding 300 mm wide to ceilings	m²	0.49	23.79	-	2.09	25.88	28.47	1.300
4010102 Plaster; 11 mm browning; 2 mm finish; steel trowelled; internal; 13 mm work; to brick or block base								
4010102A over 300 mm wide to walls	m²	0.27	13.00	-	2.39	15.39	16.93	1.440
4010102B not exceeding 300 mm wide to ceilings	m²	0.40	19.40	-	2.39	21.79	23.97	1.440
4010104 Plaster; 11 mm metal lathing undercoat; 2 mm finish; steel trowelled; internal; 13 mm work; metal lathing base								
4010104A over 300 mm wide to walls	m²	0.27	13.00	-	4.45	17.45	19.20	2.740
4010104B not exceeding 300 mm wide to walls	m²	0.40	19.40	-	4.45	23.85	26.24	2.740
4010104C over 300 mm wide to ceilings	m²	0.34	16.71	-	4.45	21.16	23.28	2.740
4010104D not exceeding 300 mm wide to ceilings	m²	0.51	25.02	-	4.45	29.47	32.42	2.740
40103 **THISTLE PLASTER**								
4010301 Plaster; 11 mm renovating; 2 mm renovating finish; steel trowelled; internal; 13 mm work; to existing concrete, brick or block base								
4010301A over 300 mm wide to walls	m²	0.27	13.00	-	3.49	16.49	18.14	1.870
4010301B not exceeding 300 mm wide to walls	m²	0.40	19.40	-	3.49	22.89	25.18	1.870
4010302 Plaster; Universal one coat; steel trowelled; internal; 10 mm work; to concrete base								
4010302A over 300 mm wide to walls	m²	0.20	9.82	-	3.15	12.97	14.27	2.790
4010302B not exceeding 300 mm wide to walls	m²	0.30	14.71	-	3.15	17.86	19.65	2.790
4010302C over 300 mm wide to ceilings	m²	0.26	12.75	-	3.15	15.90	17.49	2.790
4010302D not exceeding 300 mm wide to ceilings	m²	0.39	18.91	-	3.15	22.06	24.27	2.790
4010303 Plaster; Universal one coat; steel trowelled; internal; 13 mm work; to brick or block base								
4010303A over 300 mm wide to walls	m²	0.21	10.31	-	3.72	14.03	15.43	3.290
4010303B not exceeding 300 mm wide to walls	m²	0.31	15.20	-	3.72	18.92	20.81	3.290
4010304 Plaster; Universal one coat; steel trowelled; internal; 5 mm work; to plasterboard base								
4010304A over 300 mm wide to walls	m²	0.19	9.09	-	1.43	10.52	11.57	1.270
4010304B not exceeding 300 mm wide to walls	m²	0.29	13.97	-	1.43	15.40	16.94	1.270
4010304C over 300 mm wide to ceilings	m²	0.25	12.02	-	1.43	13.45	14.80	1.270
4010304D not exceeding 300 mm wide to ceilings	m²	0.37	18.18	-	1.43	19.61	21.57	1.270
4010305 Plaster; Thistle; 3 mm one coat board finish; steel trowelled; internal; to plasterboard base								
4010305A over 300 mm wide to walls	m²	0.19	9.09	-	0.85	9.94	10.93	0.580
4010305B not exceeding 300 mm wide to walls	m²	0.29	13.97	-	0.85	14.82	16.30	0.580

Small Works 2011		Unit	Labour Hours	Labour Net	Plant Net	Materials Net	Unit Net	Unit with 10%	CO₂
				£	£	£	£	£	Kg
401	**NEW WORK**								
40103	**THISTLE PLASTER**								
4010305	**Plaster; Thistle; 3 mm one coat board finish; steel trowelled; internal; to plasterboard base**								
4010305C	over 300 mm wide to ceilings	m²	0.25	12.02	-	0.85	12.87	14.16	0.580
4010305D	not exceeding 300 mm wide to ceilings	m²	0.37	18.18	-	0.85	19.03	20.93	0.580
4010307	**Plaster; Thistle; 10 mm cement and sand (1:3); 3 mm finish; 13 mm work to concrete, brick or block base**								
4010307A	over 300 mm wide to walls	m²	0.28	13.49	-	2.33	15.82	17.40	5.640
4010307B	not exceeding 300 mm wide to walls	m²	0.42	20.37	-	2.33	22.70	24.97	5.640
4010307C	over 300 mm wide to ceilings	m²	0.36	17.69	-	2.33	20.02	22.02	5.640
4010307D	not exceeding 300 mm wide to ceilings	m²	0.54	26.24	-	2.33	28.57	31.43	5.640
40105	**LABOURS ON PLASTERING**								
4010501	**Rounded internal angle**								
4010501A	not exceeding 10 mm radius	m	0.03	1.47	-	-	1.47	1.62	-
4010501B	over 10 mm radius	m	0.04	1.95	-	-	1.95	2.15	-
4010502	**Rounded external angle**								
4010502A	not exceeding 10 mm radius	m	0.04	1.71	-	-	1.71	1.88	-
4010502B	over 10 mm radius	m	0.05	2.44	-	-	2.44	2.68	-
4010503	**Make good plaster around pipes, angles and the like**								
4010503A	not exceeding 300 mm girth	Each	0.04	1.71	-	-	1.71	1.88	-
4010503B	over 300 mm girth	Each	0.04	1.95	-	-	1.95	2.15	-
40106	**PLASTER BEADS AND THE LIKE**								
4010601	**Catnic galvanised steel beads; fixed with plaster dabs**								
4010601A	standard angle bead	m	0.07	3.42	-	1.94	5.36	5.90	2.540
4010601B	Supasave angle bead	m	0.07	3.42	-	0.91	4.33	4.76	1.840
4010601C	micro mesh angle bead	m	0.07	3.42	-	1.02	4.44	4.88	1.840
4010601D	dry wall angle bead	m	0.07	3.42	-	1.94	5.36	5.90	1.840
4010601E	dry wall stop bead; 3 mm	m	0.07	3.42	-	1.94	5.36	5.90	2.030
4010601F	dry wall stop bead; 6 mm	m	0.07	3.42	-	1.94	5.36	5.90	4.050
4010601G	renderstop	m	0.07	3.42	-	1.55	4.97	5.47	1.840
4010601H	plaster stop; 12 mm	m	0.07	3.42	-	1.94	5.36	5.90	2.213
4010601I	plaster stop; 15 mm	m	0.07	3.42	-	1.94	5.36	5.90	2.766
4010601J	plaster stop; 18 mm	m	0.07	3.42	-	1.94	5.36	5.90	3.319
4010601K	plaster stop; 21 mm	m	0.07	3.42	-	1.94	5.36	5.90	3.872
4010601L	plasterboard edging bead; 9.5 mm	m	0.07	3.42	-	3.67	7.09	7.80	1.752
4010601M	plasterboard edging bead; 12.5 mm	m	0.07	3.42	-	3.67	7.09	7.80	2.305
4010601N	architrave bead; 10 mm	m	0.07	3.42	-	1.62	5.04	5.54	0.310
4010601O	movement bead; 12 mm	m	0.07	3.42	-	6.06	9.48	10.43	0.740
40108	**PORTLAND CEMENT FINISHES**								
4010801	**Render; cement and sand (1:3); 6 mm work; dubbing out; internal; to walls; brick or block base**								
4010801A	over 300 mm wide	m²	0.15	7.13	-	0.74	7.87	8.66	2.530
4010801B	not exceeding 300 mm wide	m²	0.22	10.55	-	0.74	11.29	12.42	2.530
4010802	**Render; cement and sand (1:3); 13 mm work dubbing out; internal; to walls; brick or block base**								
4010802A	over 300 mm wide	m²	0.21	10.31	-	1.85	12.16	13.38	6.330
4010802B	not exceeding 300 mm wide	m²	0.31	15.20	-	1.85	17.05	18.76	6.330

Small Works 2011	Unit	Labour Hours	Labour Net	Plant Net	Materials Net	Unit Net	Unit with 10%	CO₂
			£	£	£	£	£	Kg
401	**NEW WORK**							
40108	**PORTLAND CEMENT FINISHES**							
4010803	**Render; cement and sand (1:3); 19 mm work dubbing out; internal; to walls; brick or block base**							
4010803A	over 300 mm wide	m²	0.27	13.00	-	2.59	15.59	17.15	8.860
4010803B	not exceeding 300 mm wide	m²	0.39	19.15	-	2.59	21.74	23.91	8.860
4010804	**Render; cement and sand (1:3); 25 mm work dubbing out; internal; to walls; brick or block base**							
4010804A	over 300 mm wide	m²	0.30	14.71	-	3.46	18.17	19.99	11.810
4010804B	not exceeding 300 mm wide	m²	0.42	20.62	-	3.46	24.08	26.49	11.810
4010806	**Render; cement and sand (1:3); 13 mm on coat work to walls; wood floated; plain face; internal; to brick or block base**							
4010806A	over 300 mm wide	m²	0.21	10.31	-	1.85	12.16	13.38	6.330
4010806B	not exceeding 300 mm wide	m²	0.31	15.20	-	1.85	17.05	18.76	6.330
4010807	**Render; cement and sand (1:3); 20 mm two coat work to walls; wood floated; plain face; internal; to brick or block base**							
4010807A	over 300 mm wide	m²	0.30	14.71	-	2.72	17.43	19.17	9.280
4010807B	not exceeding 300 mm wide	m²	0.45	22.08	-	2.72	24.80	27.28	9.280
4010807C	curb to gulley	Each	0.43	20.86	-	1.61	22.47	24.72	5.480
4010807D	plinth at back of gulley	Each	0.20	9.82	-	0.99	10.81	11.89	3.370
4010808	**Render; cement and sand (1:3); rough cast face; wood floated; external; 20 mm two coat work to walls; brick or block base**							
4010808A	over 300 mm wide	m²	0.45	22.08	-	2.72	24.80	27.28	9.280
4010808B	not exceeding 300 mm wide	m²	0.60	29.46	-	2.72	32.18	35.40	9.280
4010809	**Render; cement and sand (1:3); pebble dash finish; wood floated; external; 20 mm two coat work to walls; brick or block base**							
4010809A	over 300 mm wide	m²	0.48	23.55	-	2.32	25.87	28.46	7.280
4010809B	not exceeding 300 mm wide	m²	0.63	30.93	-	2.32	33.25	36.58	7.280
4010811	**Render; cement-lime-sand (1:1:6); wood floated; plain face; external; 13 mm one coat work to walls; brick or block base**							
4010811A	over 300 mm wide	m²	0.21	10.31	-	2.04	12.35	13.59	4.840
4010811B	not exceeding 300 mm wide	m²	0.31	15.20	-	2.04	17.24	18.96	4.840
4010812	**Render; cement-lime-sand (1:1:6); wood floated; plain face; external; 20 mm two coat work to walls; brick or block base**							
4010812A	over 300 mm wide	m²	0.30	14.71	-	2.99	17.70	19.47	7.100
4010812B	not exceeding 300 mm wide	m²	0.45	22.08	-	2.99	25.07	27.58	7.100
4010813	**Render; cement-lime-sand (1:1:6); wood floated; rough cast face; external; 20 mm two coat work to walls; brick or block base**							
4010813A	over 300 mm wide	m²	0.45	22.08	-	2.99	25.07	27.58	7.100
4010813B	not exceeding 300 mm wide	m²	0.60	29.46	-	2.99	32.45	35.70	7.100

Small Works 2011		Unit	Labour Hours	Labour Net	Plant Net	Materials Net	Unit Net	Unit with 10%	CO₂
				£	£	£	£	£	Kg
401	**NEW WORK**								
40108	**PORTLAND CEMENT FINISHES**								
4010814	**Render; cement-lime-sand (1:1:6); wood floated; pebbledash finish; external; 20 mm two coat work to walls; brick or block base**								
4010814A	over 300 mm wide	m²	0.48	23.55	-	3.21	26.76	29.44	7.210
4010814B	not exceeding 300 mm wide	m²	0.63	30.93	-	3.21	34.14	37.55	7.210
4010815	**Render; cement-lime-sand (1:1:6); Snowcem; Cullamix Tyrolean finish; external; 16 mm one coat work to walls; brick or block base**								
4010815A	over 300 mm wide	m²	0.39	19.15	-	5.84	24.99	27.49	6.530
4010815B	not exceeding 300 mm wide	m²	0.58	28.49	-	5.84	34.33	37.76	6.530
40109	**LABOURS ON RENDERING**								
4010901	**Rounded internal angle**								
4010901A	not exceeding 10 mm radius	m	0.04	1.95	-	-	1.95	2.15	-
4010901B	over 10 mm radius	m	0.06	2.69	-	-	2.69	2.96	-
4010902	**Rounded external angle**								
4010902A	not exceeding 10 mm radius	m	0.05	2.44	-	-	2.44	2.68	-
4010902B	over 10 mm radius	m	0.06	2.93	-	-	2.93	3.22	-
4010903	**Make good rendering around pipes, angles and the like**								
4010903A	not exceeding 300 mm girth	Each	0.04	1.71	-	-	1.71	1.88	-
4010903B	over 300 mm girth	Each	0.04	1.95	-	-	1.95	2.15	-
40110	**RENDER BEADS AND THE LIKE**								
4011001	**Expamet beads for external use; stainless steel**								
4011001A	angle bead	m	0.07	3.42	-	4.45	7.87	8.66	2.880
4011001B	movement bead	m	0.07	3.42	-	10.00	13.42	14.76	4.110
4011001C	stop bead; 10 mm	m	0.07	3.42	-	3.62	7.04	7.74	1.770
4011001D	stop bead; 13 mm	m	0.07	3.42	-	3.62	7.04	7.74	1.770
4011001E	stop bead; 16 mm	m	0.07	3.42	-	3.62	7.04	7.74	1.770
4011001F	stop bead; 19 mm	m	0.07	3.42	-	3.93	7.35	8.09	2.050
4011001G	external render stop	m	0.07	3.42	-	3.62	7.04	7.74	1.770
40111	**CEMENT SCREEDS**								
4011101	**Screed; cement and sand (1:3); steel trowelled smooth; floors; level and to falls**								
4011101A	25 mm; over 300 mm wide	m²	0.45	22.08	-	3.70	25.78	28.36	12.650
4011101B	25 mm; not exceeding 300 mm wide	m²	0.90	44.17	-	3.70	47.87	52.66	12.650
4011101C	32 mm; over 300 mm wide	m²	0.50	24.53	-	4.57	29.10	32.01	15.600
4011101D	32 mm; not exceeding 300 mm wide	m²	1.00	49.06	-	4.57	53.63	58.99	15.600
4011101E	38 mm; over 300 mm wide	m²	0.55	26.97	-	5.56	32.53	35.78	18.980
4011101F	38 mm; not exceeding 300 mm wide	m²	1.11	53.99	-	5.56	59.55	65.51	18.980
4011101G	50 mm; over 300 mm wide	m²	0.65	31.91	-	7.16	39.07	42.98	24.460
4011101H	50 mm; not exceeding 300 mm wide	m²	1.31	63.81	-	7.16	70.97	78.07	24.460
4011102	**Skirtings; cement and sand (1:3); 150 mm high; fair edge; ends and the like**								
4011102A	straight	m	0.28	13.49	-	0.49	13.98	15.38	1.690
4011102B	curved	m	0.43	20.86	-	0.49	21.35	23.49	1.690
4011103	**Make good paving to**								
4011103A	floor channel	m	0.13	6.16	-	-	6.16	6.78	-
4011103B	rainwater, soil and ventilation pipes	Each	0.20	9.82	-	-	9.82	10.80	-
4011103C	yard gulley	Each	0.25	12.26	-	-	12.26	13.49	-
4011103D	manhole cover frame	Each	0.50	24.53	-	-	24.53	26.98	-

Floor, Wall and Ceiling Finishes

		Unit	Labour Hours	Labour Net £	Plant Net £	Materials Net £	Unit Net £	Unit with 10% £	CO₂ Kg
401	**NEW WORK**								
40112	**GRANOLITHIC**								
4011201	**Granolithic; cement and granite chippings (2:5); steel trowelled smooth floors; level and to falls**								
4011201A	25 mm; over 300 mm wide	m²	0.23	11.29	-	1.98	13.27	14.60	11.230
4011201B	25 mm; not exceeding 300 mm wide	m²	0.34	16.71	-	1.98	18.69	20.56	11.230
4011201C	32 mm; over 300 mm wide	m²	0.25	12.26	-	2.45	14.71	16.18	13.850
4011201D	32 mm; not exceeding 300 mm wide	m²	0.38	18.66	-	2.45	21.11	23.22	13.850
4011201E	38 mm; over 300 mm wide	m²	0.27	13.24	-	2.97	16.21	17.83	16.850
4011201F	38 mm; not exceeding 300 mm wide	m²	0.41	20.13	-	2.97	23.10	25.41	16.850
4011201G	50 mm; over 300 mm wide	m²	0.29	14.22	-	3.83	18.05	19.86	21.720
4011201H	50 mm; not exceeding 300 mm wide	m²	0.43	21.11	-	3.83	24.94	27.43	21.720
4011202	**Lining to channels; to falls; rounded arrises; coved junction; ends, angles and the like; 150 mm girth**								
4011202A	25 mm	m	0.26	12.75	-	0.26	13.01	14.31	1.500
4011202B	32 mm	m	0.28	13.49	-	0.33	13.82	15.20	1.870
4011202C	38 mm	m	0.46	22.33	-	0.40	22.73	25.00	2.250
4011202D	50 mm	m	0.48	23.55	-	0.53	24.08	26.49	3.000
4011203	**Treads; rounded nosing; ends, angles and the like; 275 mm wide**								
4011203A	25 mm	m	0.21	10.07	-	0.46	10.53	11.58	2.620
4011203B	32 mm	m	0.24	11.53	-	0.66	12.19	13.41	3.740
4011203C	38 mm	m	0.27	13.00	-	0.79	13.79	15.17	4.490
4011203D	50 mm	m	0.30	14.46	-	0.99	15.45	17.00	5.620
4011204	**Risers; coved junction to tread; undercut; 150 mm high**								
4011204A	13 mm	m	0.16	7.87	-	0.13	8.00	8.80	0.750
4011204B	19 mm	m	0.19	9.09	-	0.20	9.29	10.22	1.120
4011205	**Strings or aprons; rounded top edge; ends, angles and the like; 275 mm wide**								
4011205A	13 mm	m	0.30	14.46	-	0.26	14.72	16.19	1.500
4011205B	19 mm	m	0.39	19.15	-	0.40	19.55	21.51	2.250
4011206	**Skirtings; rounded top edge; coved junction to paving; ends, angles and the like; 150 mm high**								
4011206A	13 mm	m	0.26	12.75	-	0.13	12.88	14.17	0.750
4011206B	19 mm	m	0.36	17.69	-	0.20	17.89	19.68	1.120
4011207	**Carborundum surface dressing**								
4011207A	1 Kg per sq.m	m²	0.06	2.93	-	1.23	4.16	4.58	0.080
4011208	**Fair joint to flush edge**								
4011208A	of existing finishes	m	0.07	3.42	-	-	3.42	3.76	-
4011209	**Making good around pipes and the like; not exceeding 300 mm girth**								
4011209A	25 mm	Each	0.06	2.93	-	-	2.93	3.22	-
4011209B	32 mm	Each	0.06	2.93	-	-	2.93	3.22	-
4011209C	38 mm	Each	0.07	3.42	-	-	3.42	3.76	-
4011209D	50 mm	Each	0.07	3.42	-	-	3.42	3.76	-
40114	**METAL LATHING**								
4011401	**Expamet; 9 mm galvanised expanded metal lathing; BB263; 0.500 mm thick; to walls**								
4011401A	over 300 mm wide; fixed to softwood with galvanised nails	m²	0.10	4.89	-	7.45	12.34	13.57	3.920
4011401B	not exceeding 300 mm wide; fixed to softwood with galvanised nails	m²	0.16	7.62	-	7.45	15.07	16.58	3.920

Small Works 2011		Unit	Labour Hours	Labour Net	Plant Net	Materials Net	Unit Net	Unit with 10%	CO$_2$
				£	£	£	£	£	Kg
401	**NEW WORK**								
40114	**METAL LATHING**								
4011401	**Expamet; 9 mm galvanised expanded metal lathing; BB263; 0.500 mm thick; to walls**								
4011401C	over 300 mm wide; fixed to steel with tying wire	m^2	0.13	6.16	-	7.45	13.61	14.97	3.920
4011401D	not exceeding 300 mm wide; fixed to steel with tying wire	m^2	0.18	8.84	-	7.45	16.29	17.92	3.920
4011402	**Expamet; 9 mm galvanised expanded metal lathing; BB263; 0.500 mm thick; to ceilings**								
4011402A	over 300 mm wide; fixed to softwood with galvanised nails	m^2	0.12	5.91	-	7.45	13.36	14.70	3.920
4011402B	not exceeding 300 mm wide; fixed to softwood with galvanised nails	m^2	0.18	8.84	-	7.45	16.29	17.92	3.920
4011402C	over 300 mm wide; fixed to steel with tying wire	m^2	0.15	7.13	-	7.45	14.58	16.04	3.920
4011402D	not exceeding 300 mm wide; fixed to steel with tying wire	m^2	0.21	10.07	-	7.45	17.52	19.27	3.920
4011403	**Expamet; 9 mm galvanised expanded metal lathing; BB263; 0.500 mm thick; to beams, sides, soffits and tops**								
4011403A	over 300 mm wide; fixed to steel with tying wire	m^2	0.18	8.60	-	7.45	16.05	17.66	3.920
4011403B	not exceeding 300 mm wide; fixed to steel with tying wire	m^2	0.25	12.26	-	7.45	19.71	21.68	3.920
4011403C	raking cutting	m	0.06	2.93	-	-	2.93	3.22	-
4011403D	curved cutting	m	0.09	4.40	-	-	4.40	4.84	-
4011404	**Expamet; 9 mm galvanised expanded metal lathing; BB264; 0.725 mm thick; to walls**								
4011404A	over 300 mm wide; fixed to softwood with galvanised nails	m^2	0.12	5.67	-	7.45	13.12	14.43	3.810
4011404B	not exceeding 300 mm wide; fixed to softwood with galvanised nails	m^2	0.17	8.36	-	7.45	15.81	17.39	3.810
4011404C	over 300 mm wide; fixed to steel with tying wire	m^2	0.14	6.89	-	7.45	14.34	15.77	3.810
4011404D	not exceeding 300 mm wide; fixed to steel with tying wire	m^2	0.20	9.58	-	7.45	17.03	18.73	3.810
4011405	**Expamet; 9 mm galvanised expanded metal lathing; BB264; 0.725 mm thick; to ceilings**								
4011405A	over 300 mm wide; fixed to softwood with galvanised nails	m^2	0.13	6.40	-	7.45	13.85	15.24	3.810
4011405B	not exceeding 300 mm wide; fixed to softwood with galvanised nails	m^2	0.19	9.33	-	7.45	16.78	18.46	3.810
4011405C	over 300 mm wide; fixed to steel with tying wire	m^2	0.16	7.62	-	7.45	15.07	16.58	3.810
4011405D	not exceeding 300 mm wide; fixed to steel with tying wire	m^2	0.22	10.55	-	7.45	18.00	19.80	3.810
4011406	**Expamet; 9 mm galvanised expanded metal lathing; BB264; 0.725 mm thick; to beams, sides, soffits and tops**								
4011406A	over 300 mm wide; fixed to steel with tying wire	m^2	0.19	9.09	-	7.45	16.54	18.19	3.810
4011406B	not exceeding 300 mm wide; fixed to steel with tying wire	m^2	0.27	13.00	-	7.45	20.45	22.50	3.810
4011406C	raking cutting	m	0.07	3.18	-	-	3.18	3.50	-
4011406D	curved cutting	m	0.10	4.64	-	-	4.64	5.10	-

Small Works 2011		Unit	Labour Hours	Labour Net	Plant Net	Materials Net	Unit Net	Unit with 10%	CO$_2$
				£	£	£	£	£	Kg
401	**NEW WORK**								
40116	**DRY LININGS AND PARTITIONS**								
4011601	**Thistle baseboard; 9.5 mm work; fixed to timber base with galvanised nails; taped butt joints**								
4011601A	over 300 mm wide; to walls	m^2	0.16	7.62	-	3.57	11.19	12.31	4.600
4011601B	not exceeding 300 mm wide; to walls	m^2	0.24	11.78	-	3.57	15.35	16.89	4.600
4011601C	over 300 mm wide; to ceilings	m^2	0.19	9.09	-	3.57	12.66	13.93	4.600
4011601D	not exceeding 300 mm wide; to ceilings	m^2	0.28	13.49	-	3.57	17.06	18.77	4.600
4011603	**Gyproc square edge wallboard; 9.5 mm work; fixed to timber base with galvanised nails; taped butt joints**								
4011603A	over 300 mm wide; to walls	m^2	0.13	6.40	-	3.57	9.97	10.97	4.600
4011603B	not exceeding 300 mm wide; to walls	m^2	0.20	9.82	-	3.57	13.39	14.73	4.600
4011603C	over 300 mm wide; to ceilings	m^2	0.16	7.62	-	3.57	11.19	12.31	4.600
4011603D	not exceeding 300 mm wide; to ceilings	m^2	0.24	11.53	-	3.57	15.10	16.61	4.600
4011604	**Gyproc square edge wallboard; 12.5 mm work; fixed to timber base with galvanised nails; taped butt joints**								
4011604A	over 300 mm wide; to walls	m^2	0.16	7.62	-	3.57	11.19	12.31	6.050
4011604B	not exceeding 300 mm wide; to walls	m^2	0.24	11.78	-	3.57	15.35	16.89	6.050
4011604C	over 300 mm wide; to ceilings	m^2	0.19	9.09	-	3.57	12.66	13.93	6.050
4011604D	not exceeding 300 mm wide; to ceilings	m^2	0.28	13.73	-	3.57	17.30	19.03	6.050
4011606	**Gyproc taper edge thermal board; 25 mm work; fixed to timber base with galvanised nails; taped butt joints**								
4011606A	over 300 mm wide; to walls	m^2	0.19	9.09	-	14.33	23.42	25.76	12.090
4011606B	not exceeding 300 mm wide; to walls	m^2	0.27	13.24	-	14.33	27.57	30.33	12.090
4011606C	over 300 mm wide; to ceilings	m^2	0.22	10.55	-	14.33	24.88	27.37	12.090
4011606D	not exceeding 300 mm wide; to ceilings	m^2	0.31	14.95	-	14.33	29.28	32.21	12.090
4011608	**Gyproc taper edge thermal board; 40 mm work; fixed to timber base with galvanised nails; taped butt joints**								
4011608A	over 300 mm wide; to walls	m^2	0.22	10.55	-	18.08	28.63	31.49	19.340
4011608B	not exceeding 300 mm wide; to walls	m^2	0.30	14.71	-	18.08	32.79	36.07	19.340
4011608C	over 300 mm wide; to ceilings	m^2	0.25	12.02	-	18.08	30.10	33.11	19.340
4011608D	not exceeding 300 mm wide; to ceilings	m^2	0.34	16.42	-	18.08	34.50	37.95	19.340
4011610	**Gyproc taper edge vapour check thermal board; 25 mm work; fixed to timber base with galvanised nails; taped butt joints**								
4011610A	over 300 mm wide; to walls	m^2	0.19	9.09	-	14.77	23.86	26.25	12.090
4011610B	not exceeding 300 mm wide; to walls	m^2	0.27	13.24	-	14.77	28.01	30.81	12.090
4011610C	over 300 mm wide; to ceilings	m^2	0.22	10.55	-	14.77	25.32	27.85	12.090
4011610D	not exceeding 300 mm wide; to ceilings	m^2	0.31	14.95	-	14.77	29.72	32.69	12.090
4011612	**Gyproc taper edge vapour check thermal board; 40 mm work; fixed to timber base with galvanised nails; taped butt joints**								
4011612A	over 300 mm wide; to walls	m^2	0.22	10.55	-	21.01	31.56	34.72	19.340

Small Works 2011		Unit	Labour Hours	Labour Net	Plant Net	Materials Net	Unit Net	Unit with 10%	CO$_2$
				£	£	£	£	£	Kg
401	**NEW WORK**								
40116	**DRY LININGS AND PARTITIONS**								
4011612	**Gyproc taper edge vapour check thermal board; 40 mm work; fixed to timber base with galvanised nails; taped butt joints**								
4011612B	not exceeding 300 mm wide; to walls	m²	0.30	14.71	-	21.01	35.72	39.29	19.340
4011612C	over 300 mm wide; to ceilings	m²	0.25	12.02	-	21.01	33.03	36.33	19.340
4011612D	not exceeding 300 mm wide; to ceilings	m²	0.34	16.42	-	21.01	37.43	41.17	19.340
4011614	**Paramount dry partition; cardboard egg crate core; faced both sides with plasterboard; 30 mm x 37 mm vertical jointing battens; grey faced with square butt joints for plastering**								
4011614C	57 mm; over 300 mm wide	m²	0.43	20.86	-	14.58	35.44	38.98	12.630
4011614D	57 mm; not exceeding 300 mm wide	m²	0.64	31.42	-	14.58	46.00	50.60	12.630
4011614E	63 mm; over 300 mm wide	m²	0.45	22.08	-	16.39	38.47	42.32	30.380
4011614F	63 mm; not exceeding 300 mm wide	m²	0.68	33.13	-	16.39	49.52	54.47	30.380
4011616	**Extra for taped joints**								
4011616A	filled; one coat Gyproc drywall top coat to plasterboard; (both sides measured)	m²	0.09	4.40	-	1.56	5.96	6.56	1.740
4011620	**Perimeter fixing; battens for 57 mm or 63 mm partitions**								
4011620A	37 mm x 19 mm	m	0.07	3.18	-	0.72	3.90	4.29	0.230
4011620B	37 mm x 19 mm; plugged to concrete of brickwork	m	0.23	11.29	-	0.79	12.08	13.29	0.400
4011624	**Angle junction fixings; battens for 57 mm partitions**								
4011624A	37 mm x 19 mm and 37 mm x 37 mm	m	0.22	10.55	-	1.10	11.65	12.82	0.720
4011626	**Angle junction fixings; battens for 63 mm partitions**								
4011626A	37 mm x 19 mm and 37 mm x 37 mm	m	0.23	11.04	-	1.10	12.14	13.35	0.720
4011630	**Tee junction fixings; battens for 57 mm partitions**								
4011630A	37 mm x 19 mm and 37 mm x 37 mm	m	0.17	8.36	-	1.10	9.46	10.41	0.720
4011632	**Tee junction fixings; battens for 63 mm partitions**								
4011632A	37 mm x 19 mm and 37 mm x 37 mm	m	0.18	8.60	-	1.10	9.70	10.67	0.720
4011636	**Gyproc metal stud partition; 75 mm; comprising 50 mm metal stud framing, clad both sides with one layer of 12.5 mm Gyproc wallboard**								
4011636A	over 300 mm wide	m²	0.65	31.91	-	17.06	48.97	53.87	53.780
4011636B	not exceeding 300 mm wide	m²	1.63	79.74	-	17.06	96.80	106.48	53.780
4011638	**Gyproc metal stud partition; 95 mm; comprising 70 mm metal stud framing clad both sides with one layer of 12.5 mm Gyproc wallboard**								
4011638A	over 300 mm wide	m²	0.65	31.91	-	15.84	47.75	52.53	64.840
4011638B	not exceeding 300 mm wide	m²	1.63	79.74	-	15.84	95.58	105.14	64.840
4011639	**Tape and fill joints**								
4011639A	with mechanical jointer	m	0.13	6.16	-	0.28	6.44	7.08	0.640

Small Works 2011	Unit	Labour Hours	Labour Net	Plant Net	Materials Net	Unit Net	Unit with 10%	CO$_2$
			£	£	£	£	£	Kg
401	**NEW WORK**							
40116	**DRY LININGS AND PARTITIONS**							
4011643	**Gyproc DriLyner system; Gyproc square edge wallboard; fixed with adhesive dab to masonry walls; taped butt joints; 9. mm work**							
4011643A	over 300 mm wide	m^2	0.21	10.07	-	4.58	14.65	16.12	8.550
4011643B	not exceeding 300 mm wide	m^2	0.32	15.44	-	4.58	20.02	22.02	8.550
4011645	**Gyproc DriLyner system; Gyproc square edge wallboard; fixed with adhesive dab to masonry walls; taped butt joints; 12.5 mm work**							
4011645A	over 300 mm wide	m^2	0.25	12.02	-	4.42	16.44	18.08	9.780
4011645B	not exceeding 300 mm wide	m^2	0.38	18.66	-	4.58	23.24	25.56	10.070
4011647	**Gyproc DriLyner system; taper edge thermal board; fixed with adhesive dabs to masonry walls; taped butt joints; 25 mm work**							
4011647A	over 300 mm wide	m^2	0.29	14.22	-	15.22	29.44	32.38	15.810
4011647B	not exceeding 300 mm wide	m^2	0.43	20.86	-	15.90	36.76	40.44	16.380
4011649	**Gyproc DriLyner system; taper edge wallboard; fixed with adhesive dabs to masonry walls; taped butt joints; 40 mm work**							
4011649A	over 300 mm wide	m^2	0.34	16.71	-	18.94	35.65	39.22	23.040
4011649B	not exceeding 300 mm wide	m^2	0.48	23.31	-	19.79	43.10	47.41	23.960
4011651	**Gyproc DriLyner system; 30 mm Tri-line laminate board; fixed with adhesive dab on masonry walls; taped butt joints**							
4011651A	over 300 mm wide	m^2	0.29	14.22	-	36.24	50.46	55.51	19.180
4011651B	not exceeding 300 mm wide	m^2	0.43	20.86	-	37.93	58.79	64.67	19.920
4011653	**Gyproc DriLyner system; 40 mm Tri-line laminate board; fixed with adhesive dab masonry walls; taped butt joints**							
4011653A	over 300 mm wide	m^2	0.34	16.71	-	38.73	55.44	60.98	23.040
4011653B	not exceeding 300 mm wide	m^2	0.48	23.31	-	40.53	63.84	70.22	23.960
4011655	**Gyproc DriLyner system; 50 mm Tri-line laminate board; fixed with adhesive dab to masonry walls; taped butt joints**							
4011655A	over 300 mm wide	m^2	0.43	20.86	-	46.73	67.59	74.35	27.860
4011655B	not exceeding 300 mm wide	m^2	0.59	28.97	-	48.91	77.88	85.67	29.010
40118	**FIBROUS PLASTER**							
4011802	**Ventilator; louvred; fixing to plastered wall with adhesive**							
4011802A	225 mm x 75 mm	Each	0.08	3.66	-	2.84	6.50	7.15	0.230
4011802B	225 mm x 150 mm	Each	0.10	4.89	-	3.40	8.29	9.12	0.450
4011802C	225 mm x 225 mm	Each	0.13	6.16	-	5.58	11.74	12.91	5.980
4011804	**Ventilator; louvred; perforated zinc flyscreen; fixing to plastered wall with adhesive**							
4011804A	225 mm x 75 mm	Each	0.10	4.89	-	2.84	7.73	8.50	0.230
4011804B	225 mm x 150 mm	Each	0.13	6.16	-	3.40	9.56	10.52	0.450
4011804C	225 mm x 225 mm	Each	0.15	7.38	-	5.58	12.96	14.26	5.980
4011806	**Gyproc plaster core cornice cove; with mitres and ends; fixed with adhesive**							
4011806A	100 mm girth	m	0.20	9.82	-	2.26	12.08	13.29	1.030

Small Works 2011		Unit	Labour Hours	Labour Net	Plant Net	Materials Net	Unit Net	Unit with 10%	CO₂
				£	£	£	£	£	Kg
401	**NEW WORK**								
40118	**FIBROUS PLASTER**								
4011806	**Gyproc plaster core cornice cove; with mitres and ends; fixed with adhesive**								
4011806B	127 mm girth	m	0.22	10.80	-	2.26	13.06	14.37	1.120
40120	**BEDS AND BACKINGS PORTLAND CEMENT**								
4012001	**Cement and sand (1:3); floated bed; laid level and to falls on concrete**								
4012001A	19 mm; over 300 mm wide	m²	0.30	14.71	-	2.58	17.29	19.02	9.280
4012001B	19 mm; not exceeding 300 mm wide	m²	0.60	29.46	-	2.58	32.04	35.24	9.280
4012001C	25 mm; over 300 mm wide	m²	0.35	17.20	-	3.51	20.71	22.78	12.650
4012001D	25 mm; not exceeding 300 mm wide	m²	0.70	34.35	-	4.33	38.68	42.55	15.600
4012001E	32 mm; over 300 mm wide	m²	0.40	19.64	-	4.33	23.97	26.37	15.600
4012001F	32 mm; not exceeding 300 mm wide	m²	0.80	39.28	-	5.27	44.55	49.01	18.980
4012001G	38 mm; over 300 mm wide	m²	0.45	22.08	-	5.27	27.35	30.09	18.980
4012001H	38 mm; not exceeding 300 mm wide	m²	0.90	44.17	-	5.27	49.44	54.38	18.980
4012001I	50 mm; over 300 mm wide	m²	0.55	26.97	-	6.79	33.76	37.14	24.460
4012001J	50 mm; not exceeding 300 mm wide	m²	1.11	53.99	-	6.79	60.78	66.86	24.460
4012002	**Cement and sand (1:3) trowelled paving; laid level and to falls on concrete**								
4012002A	19 mm; over 300 mm wide	m²	0.40	19.64	-	2.58	22.22	24.44	9.280
4012002B	19 mm; not exceeding 300 mm wide	m²	0.80	39.28	-	2.58	41.86	46.05	9.280
4012002C	25 mm; over 300 mm wide	m²	0.45	22.08	-	3.51	25.59	28.15	12.650
4012002D	25 mm; not exceeding 300 mm wide	m²	0.90	44.17	-	3.51	47.68	52.45	12.650
4012002E	32 mm; over 300 mm wide	m²	0.50	24.53	-	4.33	28.86	31.75	15.600
4012002F	32 mm; not exceeding 300 mm wide	m²	1.00	49.06	-	4.33	53.39	58.73	15.600
4012002G	38 mm; over 300 mm wide	m²	0.55	26.97	-	5.27	32.24	35.46	18.980
4012002H	38 mm; not exceeding 300 mm wide	m²	1.11	53.99	-	5.27	59.26	65.19	18.980
4012002I	50 mm; over 300 mm wide	m²	0.65	31.91	-	6.79	38.70	42.57	24.460
4012002J	50 mm; not exceeding 300 mm wide	m²	1.31	63.81	-	6.79	70.60	77.66	24.460
4012006	**Cement and sand (1:3); screeded backings; to walls**								
4012006A	13 mm work over 300 mm wide	m²	0.27	13.24	-	1.85	15.09	16.60	6.330
4012006B	13 mm work not exceeding 300 mm wide	m²	0.54	26.48	-	1.85	28.33	31.16	6.330
4012008	**Cement and sand (1:3); trowelled backings; to walls**								
4012008A	13 mm work over 300 mm wide	m²	0.37	18.18	-	1.76	19.94	21.93	6.330
4012008B	13 mm work not exceeding 300 mm wide	m²	0.74	36.30	-	1.76	38.06	41.87	6.330
40122	**LATEX SCREEDS**								
4012201	**Latex cement; screeded bed; laid level and to falls on existing concrete**								
4012201A	3 mm; over 300 mm wide	m²	0.10	4.89	-	5.07	9.96	10.96	7.370
4012201B	3 mm; not exceeding 300 mm wide	m²	0.20	9.82	-	5.07	14.89	16.38	7.370
4012201C	5 mm; over 300 mm wide	m²	0.13	6.40	-	8.55	14.95	16.45	12.440
4012201D	5 mm; not exceeding 300 mm wide	m²	0.26	12.75	-	8.55	21.30	23.43	12.440

Floor, Wall and Ceiling Finishes

Small Works 2011		Unit	Labour Hours	Labour Net	Plant Net	Materials Net	Unit Net	Unit with 10%	CO$_2$
				£	£	£	£	£	Kg
401	**NEW WORK**								
40124	**INSULATING SCREEDS**								
4012401	**Lightweight concrete screed; cement and vermiculite aggregate (1:8) on 13 mm cement and sand (1:4) screeded bed; laid level and to falls**								
4012401A	25 mm; over 300 mm wide	m²	0.13	6.16	-	3.98	10.14	11.15	9.030
4012401B	25 mm; not exceeding 300 mm wide	m²	0.25	12.26	-	3.98	16.24	17.86	9.030
4012401C	38 mm; over 300 mm wide	m²	0.15	7.38	-	6.97	14.35	15.79	13.340
4012401D	38 mm; not exceeding 300 mm wide	m²	0.30	14.71	-	6.97	21.68	23.85	13.340
4012401E	50 mm; over 300 mm wide	m²	0.18	8.60	-	9.40	18.00	19.80	16.840
4012401F	50 mm; not exceeding 300 mm wide	m²	0.35	17.20	-	9.40	26.60	29.26	16.840
4012401G	75 mm; over 300 mm wide	m²	0.23	11.04	-	14.82	25.86	28.45	24.650
4012401H	75 mm; not exceeding 300 mm wide	m²	0.45	22.08	-	14.82	36.90	40.59	24.650
40126	**SCREED REINFORCEMENT**								
4012601	**Galvanised wire netting reinforcement; 150 mm laps; placing in floors**								
4012601A	25 mm mesh; 20 gauge wire	m²	0.06	2.93	-	3.27	6.20	6.82	2.080
4012601B	38 mm mesh; 19 gauge wire	m²	0.06	2.93	-	2.72	5.65	6.22	1.930
4012601C	50 mm mesh; 19 gauge wire	m²	0.06	2.93	-	0.52	3.45	3.80	1.890
40128	**GLAZED CERAMIC WALL TILING**								
4012801	**Glazed ceramic wall tiles; fixed with adhesive; butt joints; straight both ways; flush pointing with white grout; to plastered backings; to walls**								
4012801A	102 mm x 102 mm x 6.5 mm (Group G); over 300 mm wide	m²	1.18	57.41	-	42.02	99.43	109.37	13.660
4012801B	102 mm x 102 mm x 6.5 mm (Group G); not exceeding 300 mm wide	m²	2.35	114.82	-	42.02	156.84	172.52	13.660
4012801C	152 mm x 152 mm x 5.5 mm (Group A); over 300 mm wide	m²	0.81	39.77	-	20.14	59.91	65.90	11.940
4012801D	152 mm x 152 mm x 5.5 mm (Group A); not exceeding 300 mm wide	m²	1.63	79.50	-	20.14	99.64	109.60	11.940
4012801E	152 mm x 152 mm x 5.5 mm (Group C); over 300 mm wide	m²	0.81	39.77	-	30.90	70.67	77.74	11.940
4012801F	152 mm x 152 mm x 5.5 mm (Group C); not exceeding 300 mm wide	m²	1.63	79.50	-	30.90	110.40	121.44	11.940
4012801G	200 mm x 100 mm x 6.5 mm (Group A); over 300 mm wide	m²	0.87	42.70	-	30.51	73.21	80.53	13.520
4012801H	200 mm x 100 mm x 6.5 mm (Group A); not exceeding 300 mm wide	m²	1.75	85.41	-	30.51	115.92	127.51	13.520
4012801I	straight cutting	m	0.03	1.47	-	-	1.47	1.62	-
4012801J	raking cutting	m	0.06	2.93	-	-	2.93	3.22	-
4012801K	curved cutting	m	0.12	5.91	-	-	5.91	6.50	-
4012801L	cut and fit tiling around small pipe	Each	0.11	5.42	-	-	5.42	5.96	-
4012801M	cut and fit tiling around large pipe	Each	0.18	8.60	-	-	8.60	9.46	-
40132	**CLAY FLOOR TILING**								
4013203	**Heather brown tiles to BS 1286; bedded and jointed in cement mortar (1:3); but joints both ways; flush pointed with grout; to cement and sand backing**								
4013203A	194 mm x 194 mm x 12.5 mm; to floors over 300 mm wide	m²	0.60	29.46	-	25.18	54.64	60.10	20.200
4013203B	194 mm x 194 mm x 12.5 mm; to floors not exceeding 300 mm wide	m²	1.21	58.88	-	25.00	83.88	92.27	19.500

Small Works 2011		Unit	Labour Hours	Labour Net	Plant Net	Materials Net	Unit Net	Unit with 10%	CO$_2$
				£	£	£	£	£	Kg
401	**NEW WORK**								
40132	**CLAY FLOOR TILING**								
4013203	**Heather brown tiles to BS 1286; bedded and jointed in cement mortar (1:3); but joints both ways; flush pointed with grout; to cement and sand backing**								
4013203C	150 mm x 150 mm x 19 mm; to floors; over 300 mm wide	m²	0.78	38.26	-	34.81	73.07	80.38	28.950
4013203D	150 mm x 150 mm x 19 mm; to floors; not exceeding 300 mm wide	m²	1.57	76.56	-	34.81	111.37	122.51	28.950
4013204	**Coved skirtings; rounded top edge**								
4013204A	194 mm x 112.5 mm x 12.5 mm	m	0.27	13.24	-	5.76	19.00	20.90	4.520
4013204B	150 mm x 150 mm x 12.5 mm	m	0.24	11.78	-	6.57	18.35	20.19	3.880
4013204C	150 mm x 112.5 mm x 12.5 mm	m	0.24	11.78	-	6.57	18.35	20.19	3.880
4013205	**Red tiles to BS 1286; bedded and jointed in cement mortar (1:3); butt joints both ways; flush pointed with grout; to cement and sand backing**								
4013205A	200 mm x 200 mm x 19 mm; to floors; over 300 mm wide	m²	0.58	28.24	-	46.20	74.44	81.88	27.790
4013205B	200 mm x 200 mm x 19 mm; to floors; not exceeding 300 mm wide	m²	1.16	56.43	-	46.20	102.63	112.89	27.790
4013205C	150 mm x 150 mm x 20 mm; to floors; over 300 mm wide	m²	0.78	38.26	-	34.81	73.07	80.38	28.950
4013205D	150 mm x 150 mm x 20 mm; to floors; not exceeding 300 mm wide	m²	1.57	76.56	-	34.81	111.37	122.51	28.950
4013206	**Coved skirtings; rounded top edge**								
4013206A	194 mm x 112.5 mm x 12.5 mm	m	0.27	13.24	-	5.76	19.00	20.90	4.520
4013206B	150 mm x 150 mm x 12.5 mm	m	0.24	11.78	-	6.44	18.22	20.04	3.590
4013206C	150 mm x 112.5 mm x 12.5 mm	m	0.24	11.78	-	6.44	18.22	20.04	3.590
4013210	**Labours on tiling**								
4013210A	straight cutting	m	0.03	1.47	-	-	1.47	1.62	-
4013210B	raking cutting	m	0.08	3.91	-	-	3.91	4.30	-
4013210C	curved cutting	m	0.16	7.87	-	-	7.87	8.66	-
4013210D	cut and fit tiling around small pipe	Each	0.25	12.26	-	-	12.26	13.49	-
4013210E	cut and fit tiling around large pipe	Each	0.35	17.20	-	-	17.20	18.92	-
4013210F	cut and fit tiling around pedestal of W.C. or lavatory basin	Each	0.50	24.53	-	-	24.53	26.98	-
40134	**HARDWOOD FLOORING BY SPECIALISTS**								
4013401	**Supplying and laying 25 mm x 75 mm nominal tongued and grooved and end matched flooring, kiln dried and secret nailed to joists or battens provided by contractor. Filled, sanded and sealed by either wax finish or lacquer and then polished**								
4013401A	Prime Canadian Maple	m²	1.30	36.14	-	39.38	75.52	83.07	10.360
4013401B	Iroko	m²	1.25	34.75	-	43.50	78.25	86.08	10.360
4013401C	American White Oak Prime	m²	1.35	37.53	-	40.95	78.48	86.33	10.360
4013401D	European Oak	m²	1.30	36.14	-	54.72	90.86	99.95	10.360
4013401E	Merbau	m²	1.20	33.36	-	28.35	61.71	67.88	10.360

Small Works 2011		Unit	Labour Hours	Labour Net	Plant Net	Materials Net	Unit Net	Unit with 10%	CO₂
				£	£	£	£	£	Kg
401	**NEW WORK**								
40134	**HARDWOOD FLOORING BY SPECIALISTS**								
4013402	**Supplying and laying 22 mm x 75 mm x 225 mm solid tongued and grooved hardwood blocks in mastic composition on cement floated level concrete surfacing provided by contractor and wax polishing or sealing on completion herring-bone pattern with two-block border**								
4013402A	Merbau	m²	1.20	33.36	-	44.95	78.31	86.14	11.240
4013402B	Iroko	m²	1.30	36.14	-	41.55	77.69	85.46	13.170
4013402C	American Oak Prime	m²	1.40	38.92	-	59.12	98.04	107.84	11.240
4013402D	Rhodesian Teak	m²	1.35	37.53	-	45.99	83.52	91.87	11.460
4013402E	European Oak Prime 10 mm	m²	1.48	41.14	-	40.60	81.74	89.91	7.190
4013403	**8 mm felt backed mosaic flooring; laid basket pattern; sanded off, preparing and wax polishing or sealing on completion**								
4013403A	Iroko	m²	0.85	23.63	-	13.84	37.47	41.22	3.380
4013403B	Merbau	m²	0.85	23.63	-	13.58	37.21	40.93	3.380
4013403C	Teak	m²	0.85	23.63	-	15.93	39.56	43.52	3.380
4013403D	European Oak Prime	m²	0.85	23.63	-	24.24	47.87	52.66	3.380
4013404	**8 mm paper faced mosaic flooring; laid basket pattern; sanded off, preparing and wax polishing or sealing on completion**								
4013404A	Iroko	m²	0.85	23.63	-	13.31	36.94	40.63	3.380
4013404B	Jatoba	m²	0.85	23.63	-	13.31	36.94	40.63	3.380
4013404C	Teak	m²	0.85	23.63	-	25.50	49.13	54.04	3.380
40136	**FLOOR TILING AND COVERINGS BY SPECIALISTS**								
4013601	**Econoflex tiles 300 mm x 300 mm x 2 mm**								
4013601A	series 1/2	m²	0.25	7.00	-	8.93	15.93	17.52	7.640
4013601B	series 4	m²	0.25	7.00	-	8.93	15.93	17.52	7.640
4013602	**Marleyflex International Series 700/800 floor tiles**								
4013602A	300 mm x 300 mm x 2 mm	m²	0.28	7.84	-	8.93	16.77	18.45	7.640
4013602B	300 mm x 300 mm x 2.5 mm	m²	0.31	8.68	-	8.93	17.61	19.37	9.370
4013603	**Travertine tiles**								
4013603A	2.5 mm	m²	0.31	8.68	-	9.16	17.84	19.62	9.610
4013604	**Marley Vylon vinyl tiles**								
4013604A	300 mm x 300 mm x 2 mm	m²	0.28	7.84	-	9.16	17.00	18.70	7.870
4013605	**Marley HD series 2 vinyl tiles**								
4013605A	300 mm x 300 mm x 2 mm	m²	0.28	7.84	-	9.16	17.00	18.70	7.870
4013606	**Marley HD series 2 vinyl sheet**								
4013606A	2 mm thick	m²	0.28	7.84	-	10.64	18.48	20.33	7.870
4013607	**Marley HD Acoustic foam backed vinyl sheeting**								
4013607A	3 mm thick	m²	0.42	11.76	-	10.76	22.52	24.77	7.870
4013608	**Marley HD format extra contract quality vinyl sheet**								
4013608A	2 mm thick	m²	0.42	11.76	-	22.88	34.64	38.10	12.030
4013609	**Marley Vynatred vinyl sheeting**								
4013609A	felt backed	m²	0.40	11.20	-	17.46	28.66	31.53	9.510

Small Works 2011		Unit	Labour Hours	Labour Net	Plant Net	Materials Net	Unit Net	Unit with 10%	CO₂
				£	£	£	£	£	Kg
401	**NEW WORK**								
40136	**FLOOR TILING AND COVERINGS BY SPECIALISTS**								
4013610	**Marley Safetred Universal**								
4013610A	sheet	m²	0.40	11.20	-	18.26	29.46	32.41	9.510
4013611	**Marleytex heavy contract cord carpet**								
4013611A	needleloom CT	m²	0.40	11.20	-	18.26	29.46	32.41	7.810
4013612	**Gradus PVC-u skirting**								
4013612A	70 mm	m²	0.15	4.20	-	1.68	5.88	6.47	1.490
4013612B	100 mm	m²	0.12	3.36	-	4.88	8.24	9.06	4.950
4013612C	100 mm, set in	m²	0.23	6.44	-	2.86	9.30	10.23	3.610
40138	**CARPETING**								
4013801	**Take up loose carpet; set aside**								
4013801A	loose lay	m²	0.02	0.73	-	-	0.73	0.80	-
4013801B	gripper battens	m²	0.02	0.98	-	-	0.98	1.08	-
4013801C	stuck around edge	m²	0.03	1.22	-	-	1.22	1.34	-
4013801D	stuck direct	m²	0.05	2.44	-	-	2.44	2.68	-
4013802	**Lay only carpet**								
4013802A	loose lay	m²	0.02	0.73	-	-	0.73	0.80	-
4013802B	gripper battens	m²	0.03	1.22	-	-	1.22	1.34	-
4013802C	stuck around edge	m²	0.04	1.71	-	0.09	1.80	1.98	0.010
4013802D	stuck direct	m²	0.07	3.18	-	1.27	4.45	4.90	0.180
4013804	**Fitted carpeting; domestic grade; to floors over 300 mm wide**								
4013804A	loose lay	m²	0.15	7.38	-	76.76	84.14	92.55	13.040
4013804B	gripper battens	m²	0.18	8.60	-	76.76	85.36	93.90	13.040
4013804C	stuck around edge	m²	0.20	9.82	-	76.85	86.67	95.34	13.050
4013804D	stuck direct	m²	0.30	14.71	-	77.55	92.26	101.49	13.150
4013805	**Fitted carpeting; domestic grade; to floors not exceeding 300 mm wide**								
4013805A	loose lay	m²	0.18	8.60	-	76.76	85.36	93.90	13.040
4013805B	gripper battens	m²	0.20	9.82	-	76.76	86.58	95.24	13.040
4013805C	stuck around edge	m²	0.23	11.04	-	76.85	87.89	96.68	13.050
4013805D	stuck direct	m²	0.33	15.93	-	76.83	92.76	102.04	13.050
4013806	**Fitted carpeting; domestic grade; to treads and risers over 300 mm wide**								
4013806A	gripper battens	m²	0.70	34.35	-	76.76	111.11	122.22	13.040
4013808	**Underlay to carpeting; to floors**								
4013808A	over 300 mm wide	m²	0.09	4.40	-	6.86	11.26	12.39	0.770
4013808B	not exceeding 300 mm wide	m²	0.10	4.89	-	6.86	11.75	12.93	0.770
4013809	**Tackless wood gripper; fixing carpet**								
4013809A	to perimeter of floor	m	0.05	2.44	-	-	2.44	2.68	-
4013810	**Cutting carpet**								
4013810A	raking cutting	m	0.05	2.44	-	-	2.44	2.68	-
4013810B	curved cutting	m	0.08	3.66	-	-	3.66	4.03	-
4013812	**Aluminium cover strip**								
4013812A	to openings	m	0.08	3.66	-	2.91	6.57	7.23	3.710

Small Works 2011		Unit	Labour Hours	Labour Net	Plant Net	Materials Net	Unit Net	Unit with 10%	CO₂
				£	£	£	£	£	Kg
402	**REPAIRS AND ALTERATIONS**								
40201	**REMOVE SURFACE FINISHES**								
4020101	**Floors**								
4020101A	linoleum sheeting	m²	0.12	2.50	-	-	2.50	2.75	-
4020101B	carpet and underlay	m²	0.13	2.71	-	-	2.71	2.98	-
4020101C	screed	m²	0.50	10.43	-	-	10.43	11.47	-
4020101D	granolithic and screed	m²	0.67	13.97	-	-	13.97	15.37	-
4020101E	terrazzo or ceramic tiles; screed	m²	1.10	22.94	-	-	22.94	25.23	-
4020102	**Walls**								
4020102A	plasterboard	m²	0.45	9.38	-	-	9.38	10.32	-
4020102B	plaster	m²	0.22	4.59	-	-	4.59	5.05	-
4020102C	cement rendering; pebbledashing	m²	0.45	9.38	-	-	9.38	10.32	-
4020102D	tiling and screed	m²	0.55	11.47	-	-	11.47	12.62	-
4020103	**Ceilings**								
4020103A	plasterboard and skim including withdrawing nails	m²	0.33	6.88	-	-	6.88	7.57	-
4020103B	wood lath and plaster including withdrawing nails	m²	0.55	11.47	-	-	11.47	12.62	-
4020103C	suspended	m²	0.83	17.31	-	-	17.31	19.04	-
4020103D	plaster moulded cornice; per 25 mm girth	m	0.17	3.54	-	-	3.54	3.89	-
40202	**PREPARE SURFACES**								
4020201	**Prepare surface to be sound and clean, apply Unibond universal pva adhesive and sealer to receive plaster or cement rendering**								
4020201A	walls; existing cement and sand base over 300 mm wide	m²	0.15	7.38	-	0.84	8.22	9.04	0.640
4020201B	walls; existing glazed tile base over 300 mm wide	m²	0.12	5.91	-	0.56	6.47	7.12	0.430
4020201C	walls; existing painted base over 300 mm wide	m²	0.14	6.89	-	0.65	7.54	8.29	0.500
4020201D	walls; existing concrete base over 300 mm wide	m²	0.15	7.38	-	0.70	8.08	8.89	0.530
4020201E	ceilings; existing cement and sand base over 300 mm wide	m²	0.19	9.09	-	0.84	9.93	10.92	0.640
4020201F	ceilings; existing painted base over 300 mm wide	m²	0.17	8.36	-	0.65	9.01	9.91	0.500
4020201G	ceilings; existing concrete base over 300 mm wide	m²	0.19	9.09	-	0.70	9.79	10.77	0.530
4020202	**Hack down defective ceiling plaster and laths**								
4020202A	clean out old nails ready for new plaster	m²	0.43	20.86	-	-	20.86	22.95	-
4020204	**Take down temporary boarded linings and clean joists**								
4020204A	to ceilings	m²	0.40	8.34	-	-	8.34	9.17	-
40204	**CEILING REPAIRS**								
4020401	**Expanded metal lathing and 13 mm Carlite plaster to**								
4020401A	ceiling joists	m²	0.85	41.73	-	11.83	53.56	58.92	6.910
4020403	**Thistle baseboard, scrim and 3 mm Thistle finish**								
4020403A	to ceilings	m²	0.50	24.53	-	6.20	30.73	33.80	6.350
4020404	**Hack down defective ceiling plaster and fix Thistle baseboard, scrim and 3 mm Thistle finish including jointing to existing**								
4020404A	area not exceeding 1 sq.m	m²	1.00	49.06	-	6.20	55.26	60.79	6.350
4020404B	area 1 - 4 sq.m	m²	0.70	34.35	-	6.20	40.55	44.61	6.350

Small Works 2011		Unit	Labour Hours	Labour Net	Plant Net	Materials Net	Unit Net	Unit with 10%	CO$_2$
				£	£	£	£	£	Kg
402	**REPAIRS AND ALTERATIONS**								
40206	**PLASTERWORK TO WALLS; REPAIRS**								
4020601	**Make good at intersection of wall and ceiling plaster after replastering**								
4020601A	wall or ceiling	m	0.28	13.49	-	0.27	13.76	15.14	0.140
4020602	**Make good cracks in**								
4020602A	ceiling plaster	m	0.23	11.04	-	0.27	11.31	12.44	0.140
4020603	**Hack brick, stone or concrete walls to form key for**								
4020603A	plaster	m^2	0.75	15.64	-	-	15.64	17.20	-
4020604	**Hack off wall plaster and rake out brick joints to form key for**								
4020604A	new plaster	m^2	0.75	15.64	-	-	15.64	17.20	-
4020605	**Rake out joints of brickwork to**								
4020605A	form key	m^2	0.40	8.34	-	-	8.34	9.17	-
4020606	**Dub out uneven walls to receive**								
4020606A	new plaster	m^2	0.20	9.82	-	1.90	11.72	12.89	7.360
4020607	**13 mm Thistle plaster on**								
4020607A	brick or breeze walls	m^2	0.43	20.86	-	3.15	24.01	26.41	2.790
4020610	**Hack down defective wall plaster in small quantities; apply 13 mm Thistle plaster including jointing to existing**								
4020610A	area not exceeding 1 sq.m	m^2	0.88	42.95	-	3.15	46.10	50.71	2.790
4020610B	area 1 - 4 sq.m	m^2	0.45	22.08	-	3.15	25.23	27.75	2.790
4020611	**13 mm Thistle plaster to brick walls including**								
4020611A	jointing new to old and a small quantity of dubbing out	m^2	0.55	26.97	-	3.24	30.21	33.23	1.730
4020612	**Make good cracks in plaster**								
4020612A	walls	m	0.23	11.04	-	0.24	11.28	12.41	0.140
4020612B	moulded cornice, per 25 mm girth of cornice	m	0.13	6.16	-	0.24	6.40	7.04	0.140
4020612C	around door and window frames and repoint	m	0.20	9.82	-	0.24	10.06	11.07	0.140
4020613	**Hack down and re-run plaster cornices per 25 mm girth of cornice**								
4020613A	coved	m	0.13	6.16	-	0.24	6.40	7.04	0.140
4020613B	moulded	m	0.17	8.11	-	0.24	8.35	9.19	0.140
4020614	**Make good plaster around pipes**								
4020614A	small pipes	Each	0.15	7.38	-	0.24	7.62	8.38	0.140
4020614B	large pipes	Each	0.17	8.11	-	0.24	8.35	9.19	0.140
40208	**CERAMIC TILING; REPAIRS**								
4020801	**Glazed ceramic wall tiles; fixed with adhesive, pointed in white cement grout in small quantities in repairs**								
4020801A	102 mm x 102 mm x 6.5 mm; Group G	m^2	2.35	114.82	-	39.54	154.36	169.80	13.340
4020801B	152 mm x 152 mm x 5.5 mm; Group B	m^2	1.63	79.50	-	22.28	101.78	111.96	11.840
4020804	**Hack off glazed tiles to wall in**								
4020804A	detached areas 2.0 - 5.0 sq.m	m^2	1.00	20.85	-	-	20.85	22.94	-
4020804B	patches 0.5 - 2.0 sq.m	Each	2.50	52.13	-	-	52.13	57.34	-
4020804C	single tiles in patches up to 0.5 sq.m	Each	0.30	6.25	-	-	6.25	6.88	-

Small Works 2011		Unit	Labour Hours	Labour Net	Plant Net	Materials Net	Unit Net	Unit with 10%	CO₂
				£	£	£	£	£	Kg
402	**REPAIRS AND ALTERATIONS**								
40208	**CERAMIC TILING; REPAIRS**								
4020805	**Take out broken angle beads horizontal or vertical and renew**								
4020805A	150 mm x 25 mm	Each	0.09	4.40	-	0.58	4.98	5.48	0.100
4020805B	150 mm x 50 mm moulded cappings	Each	0.10	4.89	-	0.52	5.41	5.95	0.340
4020806	**Holes through wall tiling, any colour, and make good**								
4020806A	for small pipes	Each	0.28	5.84	-	-	5.84	6.42	-
4020806B	for large pipes	Each	0.38	7.92	-	-	7.92	8.71	-
4020807	**Stripping loose tiles and cleaning**								
4020807A	for reuse	m²	0.40	8.34	-	-	8.34	9.17	-
4020808	**Refixing only salvaged tiles**								
4020808A	with adhesive	m²	1.13	55.21	-	1.15	56.36	62.00	2.150
40209	**RENDERING; REPAIRS**								
4020901	**Hack off defective rendering to concreted areas; grout and render in cement mortar**								
4020901A	19 mm thick	m²	0.50	24.53	-	2.17	26.70	29.37	8.410
4020902	**Hack off and renew cement rendered plinth**								
4020902A	225 mm high including joints new to old	m	0.15	7.38	-	0.47	7.85	8.64	1.690
4020903	**Cut out cracks in Snowcrete or rough cast rendering**								
4020903A	make good to existing	m	0.40	19.64	-	0.48	20.12	22.13	0.430
4020903B	make good to existing to match adjacent work around reset window and door frames	m	0.24	11.78	-	0.16	11.94	13.13	0.140
4020905	**Hack off defective rendering, prepare for and re-render in cement and sand (1:3); plain face**								
4020905A	to walls	m²	0.50	24.53	-	2.26	26.79	29.47	8.760
4020907	**Hack off broken cement rendering and renew rendering to**								
4020907A	three-sided curb to gulley	Each	0.45	22.08	-	2.59	24.67	27.14	8.860
4020908	**Hack off all loose rendering, hack back brick (or concrete) to form key and re-render with cement and sand (1:3), plain face including reproducing all profiles and ruled joints**								
4020908A	to match existing	m²	1.00	49.06	-	2.26	51.32	56.45	8.760
4020908B	to match existing in patches not exceeding 1 sq.m	Each	1.26	61.32	-	2.26	63.58	69.94	8.760

Plumbing and Heating

Small Works 2011		Unit	Labour Hours	Labour Net	Plant Net	Materials Net	Unit Net	Unit with 10%	CO₂
				£	£	£	£	£	Kg
501	**NEW WORK**								
50120	**GUTTERWORK AND FITTINGS**								
5012001	**PVC-u Osma Mini-Fit 3/2 System; fixing with standard brackets**								
5012001A	75 mm	m	0.15	9.40	-	5.81	15.21	16.73	4.220
5012001B	Extra for stopend outlet	Each	0.09	5.67	-	6.59	12.26	13.49	0.240
5012001C	Extra for stopend; external	Each	0.08	4.92	-	2.29	7.21	7.93	0.120
5012001D	Extra for running outlet	Each	0.15	9.40	-	6.70	16.10	17.71	0.250
5012001E	Extra for angle	Each	0.15	9.40	-	6.59	15.99	17.59	0.230
5012002	**PVC-u Osma RoundLine 4"/112mm 1/2 System; fixing with standard brackets**								
5012002A	112 mm	m	0.16	10.15	-	6.93	17.08	18.79	5.670
5012002B	Extra for swivelock running outlet; straight	Each	0.16	10.15	-	7.29	17.44	19.18	0.480
5012002C	Extra for stopend; external	Each	0.09	5.67	-	4.48	10.15	11.17	0.290
5012002D	Extra for angle	Each	0.16	10.15	-	8.42	18.57	20.43	0.680
5012002F	Extra for connector to cast iron half round gutter	Each	0.18	10.90	-	7.03	17.93	19.72	0.320
5012002G	Extra for connector to cast iron ogee gutter	Each	0.18	10.90	-	11.14	22.04	24.24	0.320
5012003	**PVC-u Osma SuperLine 5"/125mm System; fixing with standard brackets**								
5012003A	125 mm	m	0.16	10.15	-	8.25	18.40	20.24	2.340
5012003B	Extra for stopend; external	Each	0.09	5.67	-	5.27	10.94	12.03	0.380
5012003D	Extra for running outlet	Each	0.16	10.15	-	9.13	19.28	21.21	1.210
5012003E	Extra for angle	Each	0.16	10.15	-	9.96	20.11	22.12	0.980
5012004	**PVC-u Osma RoofLine 6"/150mm System; fixing with standard brackets**								
5012004A	150 mm	m	0.19	11.71	-	20.14	31.85	35.04	10.380
5012004B	Extra for stopend; external	Each	0.10	6.41	-	10.85	17.26	18.99	0.360
5012004C	Extra for running outlet	Each	0.18	10.90	-	21.87	32.77	36.05	1.590
5012004D	Extra for angle	Each	0.18	10.90	-	30.26	41.16	45.28	1.360
5012005	**PVC-u Osma Squareline 4"/100mm System; fixing with standard brackets**								
5012005A	100 mm	m	0.16	10.15	-	7.52	17.67	19.44	1.870
5012005B	Extra for stopend; external	Each	0.09	5.67	-	2.59	8.26	9.09	0.320
5012005C	Extra for running outlet	Each	0.16	10.15	-	9.35	19.50	21.45	0.920
5012005D	Extra for angle	Each	0.16	10.15	-	10.33	20.48	22.53	0.670
5012006	**Cast iron; half round; fixing with standard brackets**								
5012006A	100 mm	m	0.22	13.58	-	21.71	35.29	38.82	16.550
5012006B	Extra for stopend	Each	0.12	7.16	-	4.25	11.41	12.55	0.970
5012006C	Extra for stopend outlet	Each	0.13	7.91	-	9.23	17.14	18.85	0.970
5012006D	Extra for running outlet	Each	0.22	13.58	-	15.72	29.30	32.23	2.790
5012006E	Extra for angle	Each	0.22	13.58	-	16.05	29.63	32.59	2.920
5012007	**Cast iron; half round; fixing with standard brackets**								
5012007A	115 mm	m	0.22	13.58	-	22.44	36.02	39.62	19.850
5012007B	Extra for stopend	Each	0.12	7.16	-	5.51	12.67	13.94	0.970
5012007C	Extra for stopend outlet	Each	0.13	7.91	-	13.60	21.51	23.66	3.400
5012007D	Extra for running outlet	Each	0.22	13.58	-	16.84	30.42	33.46	4.370
5012007E	Extra for angle	Each	0.22	13.58	-	16.42	30.00	33.00	4.130
5012008	**Cast iron; half round; fixing with standard brackets**								
5012008A	125 mm	m	0.25	15.45	-	25.67	41.12	45.23	22.150
5012008B	Extra for stopend	Each	0.15	9.03	-	8.94	17.97	19.77	2.190
5012008C	Extra for stopend outlet	Each	0.16	9.78	-	17.08	26.86	29.55	3.640
5012008D	Extra for running outlet	Each	0.25	15.45	-	18.77	34.22	37.64	4.370
5012008E	Extra for angle	Each	0.25	15.45	-	18.77	34.22	37.64	4.370
5012009	**Cast iron; half round; fixing with standard brackets**								
5012009A	150 mm	m	0.28	17.31	-	42.38	59.69	65.66	27.500
5012009B	Extra for stopend	Each	0.18	10.90	-	11.68	22.58	24.84	2.430
5012009C	Extra for stopend outlet	Each	0.19	11.71	-	30.41	42.12	46.33	5.340
5012009D	Extra for running outlet	Each	0.28	17.31	-	30.85	48.16	52.98	5.590
5012009E	Extra for angle	Each	0.28	17.31	-	32.31	49.62	54.58	5.830

Small Works 2011		Unit	Labour Hours	Labour Net £	Plant Net £	Materials Net £	Unit Net £	Unit with 10% £	CO₂ Kg
501	**NEW WORK**								
50120	**GUTTERWORK AND FITTINGS**								
5012012	**Cast iron; ogee; fixing with standard brackets**								
5012012A	100 mm	m	0.23	14.32	-	23.75	38.07	41.88	23.930
5012012B	Extra for stopend	Each	0.13	7.91	-	7.56	15.47	17.02	2.190
5012012C	Extra for stopend outlet	Each	0.14	8.66	-	13.62	22.28	24.51	2.790
5012012D	Extra for running outlet	Each	0.23	14.32	-	16.69	31.01	34.11	2.920
5012012E	Extra for angle	Each	0.23	14.32	-	16.69	31.01	34.11	3.400
5012013	**Cast iron; ogee; fixing with standard brackets**								
5012013A	115 mm	m	0.23	14.32	-	26.18	40.50	44.55	27.760
5012013B	Extra for stopend	Each	0.13	7.91	-	8.51	16.42	18.06	2.190
5012013C	Extra for stopend outlet	Each	0.14	8.66	-	13.47	22.13	24.34	3.040
5012013D	Extra for running outlet	Each	0.23	14.32	-	17.69	32.01	35.21	4.620
5012013E	Extra for angle	Each	0.23	14.32	-	17.69	32.01	35.21	4.620
5012014	**Cast iron; ogee; fixing with standard brackets**								
5012014A	125 mm	m	0.26	16.19	-	27.78	43.97	48.37	33.100
5012014B	Extra for stopend	Each	0.16	9.78	-	9.39	19.17	21.09	2.670
5012014C	Extra for stopend outlet	Each	0.17	10.53	-	16.21	26.74	29.41	4.860
5012014D	Extra for running outlet	Each	0.26	16.19	-	19.89	36.08	39.69	5.830
5012014E	Extra for angle	Each	0.26	16.19	-	19.89	36.08	39.69	5.830
50122	**RAINWATER PIPEWORK**								
5012201	**PVC-u; Osma Mini-Fit 32 System; fixing with standard brackets**								
5012201A	55 mm	m	0.13	7.91	-	9.31	17.22	18.94	2.010
5012201B	Extra for offset bend	Each	0.09	5.67	-	4.07	9.74	10.71	0.180
5012201C	Extra for bend	Each	0.09	5.67	-	5.51	11.18	12.30	0.180
5012201E	hopper head adaptor	Each	0.08	4.92	-	5.52	10.44	11.48	0.250
5012201F	hopper head	Each	0.33	20.74	-	16.57	37.31	41.04	0.250
5012201G	connection to back inlet gulley; cement mortar (1:3)	Each	0.09	5.67	-	0.37	6.04	6.64	1.270
5012202	**PVC-u; Osma RoundLine 2½"/68mm System; fixing with standard brackets**								
5012202A	68 mm	m	0.16	9.78	-	7.04	16.82	18.50	4.180
5012202B	Extra for offset bend	Each	0.10	6.04	-	4.21	10.25	11.28	0.590
5012202D	Extra for shoe	Each	0.19	11.71	-	4.44	16.15	17.77	0.230
5012202E	Extra for branch	Each	0.13	7.91	-	13.41	21.32	23.45	0.490
5012202F	Extra for access pipe; bolted access door	Each	0.13	7.91	-	20.53	28.44	31.28	0.450
5012202G	hopper head	Each	0.28	17.31	-	17.02	34.33	37.76	1.910
5012202H	connection to back inlet gulley; cement mortar (1:3)	Each	0.10	6.04	-	0.37	6.41	7.05	1.270
5012202I	connector; to 63 mm cast iron	Each	0.12	7.16	-	6.74	13.90	15.29	0.250
5012202J	connector; to 82 mm PVC-u drain socket	Each	0.07	4.17	-	9.41	13.58	14.94	0.250
5012202K	universal connector to 110 mm PVC-u drain	Each	0.07	4.17	-	6.93	11.10	12.21	0.250
5012203	**PVC-u; Osma SquareLine 2¼"/61mm System; fixing with standard brackets**								
5012203A	61 mm	m	0.16	9.78	-	7.32	17.10	18.81	2.040
5012203B	Extra for offset bend	Each	0.10	6.04	-	4.43	10.47	11.52	0.590
5012203D	Extra for shoe	Each	0.19	11.71	-	6.19	17.90	19.69	0.100
5012203E	Extra for branch	Each	0.13	7.91	-	14.98	22.89	25.18	0.480
5012203F	adaptor; square to round	Each	0.07	4.17	-	5.93	10.10	11.11	0.560
5012203G	hopper head	Each	0.25	15.45	-	18.88	34.33	37.76	1.910
5012203H	connection to back inlet gulley; cement mortar (1:3)	Each	0.10	6.04	-	0.37	6.41	7.05	1.270
5012203I	connector; to 82 mm PVC-u drain socket	Each	0.13	7.91	-	9.41	17.32	19.05	0.250
5012203J	universal connector to 110 mm PVC-u drain	Each	0.13	7.91	-	5.79	13.70	15.07	0.250
5012203K	Access pipe bolted access door	Each	0.13	7.91	-	20.54	28.45	31.30	0.590
5012205	**Cast iron; round; fixing with standard holderbats**								
5012205A	65 mm	m	0.18	10.90	-	46.82	57.72	63.49	16.000
5012205B	Extra for bend	Each	0.12	7.16	-	17.59	24.75	27.23	1.970
5012205C	Extra for branch	Each	0.15	9.03	-	37.40	46.43	51.07	5.470
5012205F	Extra for offset; 150 mm projection	Each	0.15	9.03	-	26.92	35.95	39.55	4.370

Small Works 2011		Unit	Labour Hours	Labour Net	Plant Net	Materials Net	Unit Net	Unit with 10%	CO$_2$
				£	£	£	£	£	Kg
501	**NEW WORK**								
50122	**RAINWATER PIPEWORK**								
5012205	**Cast iron; round; fixing with standard holderbats**								
5012205G	Extra for offset; 230 mm projection	Each	0.15	9.03	-	31.35	40.38	44.42	4.810
5012205H	Extra for shoe	Each	0.21	12.83	-	28.73	41.56	45.72	4.590
5012205J	hopper head; flat back	Each	0.25	15.45	-	15.49	30.94	34.03	7.770
5012205L	connection to back inlet gulley; cement mortar (1:3)	Each	0.10	6.04	-	0.37	6.41	7.05	1.270
5012206	**Cast iron; round; fixing with standard holderbats**								
5012206A	75 mm	m	0.22	13.58	-	46.82	60.40	66.44	18.830
5012206B	Extra for bend	Each	0.16	9.78	-	19.41	29.19	32.11	2.190
5012206C	Extra for branch	Each	0.19	11.71	-	37.40	49.11	54.02	6.070
5012206F	Extra for offset; 150 mm projection	Each	0.19	11.71	-	26.92	38.63	42.49	4.860
5012206G	Extra for offset; 230 mm projection	Each	0.19	11.71	-	31.35	43.06	47.37	5.340
5012206H	Extra for shoe	Each	0.25	15.45	-	24.91	40.36	44.40	5.100
5012206J	hopper head; flat back	Each	0.25	15.45	-	22.44	37.89	41.68	9.720
5012206L	connection to back inlet gulley; cement mortar (1:3)	Each	0.11	6.79	-	0.37	7.16	7.88	1.270
5012207	**Cast iron; round; fixing with standard holderbats**								
5012207A	100 mm	m	0.25	15.45	-	63.71	79.16	87.08	24.840
5012207B	Extra for bend	Each	0.19	11.71	-	30.17	41.88	46.07	3.890
5012207C	Extra for branch	Each	0.22	13.58	-	44.44	58.02	63.82	6.560
5012207F	Extra for offset; 150 mm projection	Each	0.22	13.58	-	50.79	64.37	70.81	7.050
5012207G	Extra for offset; 230 mm projection	Each	0.22	13.58	-	61.51	75.09	82.60	7.530
5012207H	Extra for shoe	Each	0.28	17.31	-	33.59	50.90	55.99	9.230
5012207J	hopper head; flat back	Each	0.25	15.45	-	56.53	71.98	79.18	15.060
5012207L	connection to back inlet gulley; cement mortar (1:3)	Each	0.13	7.91	-	0.62	8.53	9.38	2.110
50124	**RAINWATER ANCILLARIES**								
5012402	**Balloon guards; plastic coated wire**								
5012402A	50 mm	Each	0.09	5.29	-	3.37	8.66	9.53	0.810
5012402B	65 mm	Each	0.10	6.04	-	3.37	9.41	10.35	1.130
5012402C	75 mm	Each	0.11	6.79	-	3.46	10.25	11.28	1.450
5012402D	100 mm	Each	0.13	7.91	-	3.68	11.59	12.75	1.610
5012402E	150 mm	Each	0.15	9.03	-	8.66	17.69	19.46	2.090
50126	**SOIL AND VENT PIPEWORK**								
5012601	**PVC-u; OsmaSoil ring seal; fixing with standard brackets**								
5012601A	82 mm	m	0.21	12.83	-	17.89	30.72	33.79	4.260
5012601B	Extra for bend	Each	0.19	11.71	-	19.17	30.88	33.97	0.930
5012601C	Extra for offset bend	Each	0.19	11.71	-	14.91	26.62	29.28	0.570
5012601D	Extra for branch	Each	0.22	13.58	-	27.62	41.20	45.32	1.800
5012601E	Extra for bossed pipe	Each	0.16	9.78	-	13.69	23.47	25.82	0.810
5012601F	Extra for access pipe; bolted access door	Each	0.22	13.58	-	32.73	46.31	50.94	1.430
5012601G	connection to drain; connector ring	Each	0.16	9.78	-	0.49	10.27	11.30	1.690
5012602	**PVC-u; OsmaSoil ring seal; fixing with standard brackets**								
5012602A	110 mm	m	0.23	14.32	-	16.21	30.53	33.58	5.830
5012602B	Extra for bend	Each	0.21	13.20	-	19.17	32.37	35.61	2.070
5012602C	Extra for offset bend	Each	0.21	13.20	-	21.37	34.57	38.03	3.980
5012602D	Extra for branch	Each	0.24	15.07	-	28.21	43.28	47.61	2.450
5012602E	Extra for bossed pipe	Each	0.21	13.20	-	16.70	29.90	32.89	5.580
5012602F	Extra for access pipe; bossed; screwed	Each	0.21	13.20	-	31.30	44.50	48.95	3.150
5012602G	Extra for w.c. connecting bend	Each	0.18	11.27	-	16.61	27.88	30.67	1.090
5012602H	w.c. connector	Each	0.18	11.27	-	14.14	25.41	27.95	1.090
5012602I	connection to drain; connector ring	Each	0.18	11.27	-	10.37	21.64	23.80	0.250
5012603	**Cast iron; Timesaver System; flexible joints; fixing with holderbats**								
5012603A	50 mm	m	0.25	15.45	-	32.53	47.98	52.78	8.390

Plumbing and Heating

Small Works 2011		Unit	Labour Hours	Labour Net £	Plant Net £	Materials Net £	Unit Net £	Unit with 10% £	CO$_2$ Kg
501	**NEW WORK**								
50126	**SOIL AND VENT PIPEWORK**								
5012603	**Cast iron; Timesaver System; flexible joints; fixing with holderbats**								
5012603B	Extra for bend	Each	0.19	11.71	-	18.63	30.34	33.37	9.840
5012603C	Extra for access bend	Each	0.19	11.71	-	45.93	57.64	63.40	9.840
5012603D	Extra for branch; single	Each	0.22	13.58	-	28.02	41.60	45.76	9.480
5012603F	Extra for access pipe; oval door	Each	0.19	11.71	-	44.84	56.55	62.21	11.780
5012603J	roof connector; for asphalt	Each	0.25	15.45	-	84.64	100.09	110.10	5.100
5012603M	connection to stoneware drain; cement mortar (1:3) joint	Each	0.10	6.04	-	0.37	6.41	7.05	1.270
5012604	**Cast iron; Timesaver System; flexible joints; fixing with holderbats**								
5012604A	75 mm	m	0.28	17.31	-	32.50	49.81	54.79	42.360
5012604B	Extra for bend	Each	0.22	13.58	-	18.63	32.21	35.43	9.230
5012604C	Extra for access bend	Each	0.22	13.58	-	45.93	59.51	65.46	14.090
5012604D	Extra for branch; single	Each	0.25	15.45	-	28.02	43.47	47.82	20.650
5012604E	Extra for branch; double	Each	0.28	17.31	-	47.18	64.49	70.94	25.150
5012604F	Extra for access pipe; round door	Each	0.22	13.58	-	44.84	58.42	64.26	20.170
5012604H	Extra for offset; 150 mm projection	Each	0.25	15.45	-	22.97	38.42	42.26	8.500
5012604I	Extra for offset; 300 mm projection	Each	0.28	17.31	-	22.97	40.28	44.31	13.360
5012604K	roof connector; for asphalt	Each	0.28	17.31	-	51.06	68.37	75.21	4.130
5012604M	roof outlet; circular; flat grate	Each	0.31	19.18	-	123.04	142.22	156.44	49.560
5012604N	connection to stoneware drain; cement mortar (1:3) joint	Each	0.11	6.79	-	0.49	7.28	8.01	1.690
5012605	**Cast iron; Timesaver System; flexible joints; fixing with holderbats**								
5012605A	100 mm	m	0.34	21.11	-	38.61	59.72	65.69	53.290
5012605B	Extra for bend	Each	0.28	17.31	-	25.80	43.11	47.42	21.380
5012605C	Extra for access bend	Each	0.28	17.31	-	54.56	71.87	79.06	26.240
5012605D	Extra for branch; single	Each	0.31	19.18	-	39.88	59.06	64.97	18.950
5012605E	Extra for branch; double	Each	0.34	21.11	-	49.33	70.44	77.48	28.180
5012605F	Extra for access pipe; round door	Each	0.28	17.31	-	47.18	64.49	70.94	45.430
5012605H	Extra for offset; 150 mm projection	Each	0.31	19.18	-	32.35	51.53	56.68	10.690
5012605I	Extra for offset; 300 mm projection	Each	0.34	21.11	-	41.80	62.91	69.20	14.820
5012605K	w.c. connecting pipe	Each	0.31	19.18	-	28.06	47.24	51.96	7.050
5012605L	roof connector; for asphalt	Each	0.34	21.11	-	45.00	66.11	72.72	5.100
5012605M	roof connector; for felt	Each	0.34	21.11	-	141.17	162.28	178.51	10.200
5012605N	roof outlet; circular; flat grate	Each	0.37	22.98	-	148.62	171.60	188.76	49.560
5012605O	connection to stoneware drain; cement mortar (1:3) joint	Each	0.13	7.91	-	0.62	8.53	9.38	2.110
50128	**WASTE PIPEWORK**								
5012801	**ABS; OsmaWeld System; solvent welded joints; fixing with clips or brackets**								
5012801A	32 mm	m	0.15	9.40	-	3.26	12.66	13.93	0.870
5012801C	bend	Each	0.14	8.66	-	4.95	13.61	14.97	0.080
5012801F	tee	Each	0.16	9.78	-	3.10	12.88	14.17	0.100
5012801H	straight tank connector	Each	0.15	9.40	-	3.91	13.31	14.64	0.170
5012801I	bottle trap; 38 mm seal	Each	0.16	9.78	-	6.49	16.27	17.90	0.100
5012801J	bottle trap; 76 mm seal	Each	0.16	9.78	-	8.08	17.86	19.65	0.100
5012801K	tubular P trap; 76 mm seal	Each	0.17	10.53	-	6.12	16.65	18.32	0.100
5012801L	tubular S trap; 76 mm seal	Each	0.17	10.53	-	7.49	18.02	19.82	0.100
5012802	**ABS; OsmaWeld System; solvent welded joints; fixing with clips or brackets**								
5012802A	40 mm	m	0.17	10.53	-	3.84	14.37	15.81	1.090
5012802C	bend	Each	0.15	9.40	-	2.33	11.73	12.90	0.090
5012802F	tee	Each	0.18	10.90	-	3.38	14.28	15.71	0.140
5012802H	straight tank connector	Each	0.16	10.15	-	4.30	14.45	15.90	0.200
5012802I	bottle trap; 38 mm seal	Each	0.19	11.71	-	7.94	19.65	21.62	0.140
5012802J	bottle trap; 76 mm seal	Each	0.19	11.71	-	9.88	21.59	23.75	0.140
5012802K	tubular P trap; 76 mm seal	Each	0.20	12.46	-	7.34	19.80	21.78	0.140
5012802L	tubular S trap; 76 mm seal	Each	0.20	12.46	-	10.09	22.55	24.81	0.140
5012802N	bath trap; 76 mm seal	Each	0.21	12.83	-	10.42	23.25	25.58	0.140
5012802P	washing machine half trap; 76 mm seal	Each	0.25	15.45	-	11.12	26.57	29.23	0.200

Small Works 2011		Unit	Labour Hours	Labour Net	Plant Net	Materials Net	Unit Net	Unit with 10%	CO$_2$
				£	£	£	£	£	Kg
501	**NEW WORK**								
50128	**WASTE PIPEWORK**								
5012803	**ABS; OsmaWeld System; solvent welded joints; fixing with clips or brackets**								
5012803A	50 mm	m	0.19	11.71	-	9.48	21.19	23.31	1.450
5012803B	bend	Each	0.16	10.15	-	3.56	13.71	15.08	0.230
5012803E	tee	Each	0.19	11.71	-	4.90	16.61	18.27	0.230
5012804	**Polypropylene; Osma ClearBore System; ring seal socket joints; fixing with clips or brackets**								
5012804A	32 mm	m	0.13	8.28	-	2.31	10.59	11.65	0.720
5012804C	bend	Each	0.12	7.54	-	2.86	10.40	11.44	0.180
5012804E	tee	Each	0.14	8.66	-	4.10	12.76	14.04	0.180
5012804F	straight tank connector	Each	0.16	9.78	-	4.07	13.85	15.24	0.170
5012804G	bottle trap; 38 mm seal	Each	0.16	9.78	-	5.34	15.12	16.63	0.080
5012804H	bottle trap; 76 mm seal	Each	0.16	9.78	-	6.14	15.92	17.51	0.080
5012804I	tubular P trap; 76 mm seal	Each	0.17	10.53	-	5.67	16.20	17.82	0.080
5012804J	tubular S trap; 76 mm seal	Each	0.17	10.53	-	6.81	17.34	19.07	0.080
5012805	**Polypropylene; Osma ClearBore System; ring seal socket joints; fixing with clips or brackets**								
5012805A	40 mm	m	0.15	9.40	-	2.88	12.28	13.51	0.910
5012805D	bend	Each	0.13	8.28	-	3.21	11.49	12.64	0.160
5012805E	tee	Each	0.16	9.78	-	4.73	14.51	15.96	0.160
5012805F	straight tank connector	Each	0.18	11.27	-	4.44	15.71	17.28	0.200
5012805G	bottle trap; 38 mm seal	Each	0.19	11.71	-	6.60	18.31	20.14	0.200
5012805H	bottle trap; 76 mm seal	Each	0.19	11.71	-	7.30	19.01	20.91	0.200
5012805I	tubular P trap; 76 mm seal	Each	0.20	12.46	-	6.83	19.29	21.22	0.200
5012805J	tubular S trap; 76 mm seal	Each	0.20	12.46	-	8.27	20.73	22.80	0.200
5012805L	bath trap; 76 mm seal	Each	0.21	12.83	-	7.67	20.50	22.55	0.200
5012805N	washing machine half trap; 76 mm seal	Each	0.25	15.45	-	12.44	27.89	30.68	0.240
5012806	**Polypropylene; Osma ClearBore System; ring seal socket joints; fixing with clips or brackets**								
5012806A	50 mm	m	0.17	10.53	-	3.83	14.36	15.80	1.240
5012806B	bend	Each	0.15	9.03	-	5.63	14.66	16.13	0.330
5012806D	tee	Each	0.17	10.53	-	6.92	17.45	19.20	0.330
50130	**OVERFLOW PIPEWORK**								
5013001	**ABS; OsmaWeld System; solvent welded joints; fixing with clips or brackets**								
5013001A	19 mm	m	0.12	7.54	-	1.75	9.29	10.22	0.270
5013001B	bend	Each	0.11	6.79	-	1.55	8.34	9.17	0.030
5013001C	tee	Each	0.13	7.91	-	1.69	9.60	10.56	0.030
5013001D	tank connector; straight	Each	0.13	7.91	-	2.01	9.92	10.91	0.060
5013001E	tank connector; bent	Each	0.13	7.91	-	2.28	10.19	11.21	0.060
5013002	**Polypropylene; Osma ClearBore System; ring seal socket joints; fixing with clips or brackets**								
5013002A	19 mm	m	0.12	7.54	-	1.41	8.95	9.85	0.070
5013002B	bend	Each	0.11	6.79	-	1.55	8.34	9.17	0.030
5013002C	tee	Each	0.13	7.91	-	1.69	9.60	10.56	0.060
5013002D	tank connector; bent	Each	0.13	7.91	-	2.16	10.07	11.08	0.060
50132	**WATER MAINS**								
5013201	**Form stopcock pit with 100 mm concrete base and with one length 102 mm clayware pipe set vertically and surrounded with concrete with 125 mm x 125 mm x 100 mm cast iron stopcock box with flanged hinged lid provide stopcock key**								
5013201A	650 mm deep	Each	0.73	56.04	-	26.23	82.27	90.50	31.980
5013201B	650 mm deep with half brick sides	Each	1.10	84.02	-	32.50	116.52	128.17	86.450

Small Works 2011		Unit	Labour Hours	Labour Net £	Plant Net £	Materials Net £	Unit Net £	Unit with 10% £	CO$_2$ Kg
501	**NEW WORK**								
50132	**WATER MAINS**								
5013202	**Stopcock, jointing to MDPE pipe**								
5013202A	20 mm	Each	0.14	8.66	-	11.88	20.54	22.59	0.200
5013202B	25 mm	Each	0.16	9.78	-	20.72	30.50	33.55	0.250
5013203	**Excavate trench 750 mm deep for and supply and lay Blue MDPE pressure water service pipe with push fit joints; refill and consolidate trench**								
5013203A	20 mm	m	1.13	86.31	-	10.06	96.37	106.01	0.460
5013203B	25 mm	m	1.14	86.85	-	10.52	97.37	107.11	0.580
50134	**SERVICE PIPEWORK COPPER**								
5013401	**Pipes; Table Y; laid in trench**								
5013401A	15 mm	m	0.09	5.67	-	7.81	13.48	14.83	0.710
5013401B	22 mm	m	0.10	6.04	-	13.86	19.90	21.89	1.530
5013402	**Pipes; Table X; fixing with pipe clips plugged and screwed to walls**								
5013402A	15 mm	m	0.18	11.27	-	3.94	15.21	16.73	0.720
5013402B	15 mm in short lengths	m	0.19	12.08	-	3.94	16.02	17.62	0.720
5013402C	22 mm	m	0.19	11.71	-	7.70	19.41	21.35	1.540
5013402D	22 mm in short lengths	m	0.20	12.46	-	7.70	20.16	22.18	1.540
5013402E	28 mm	m	0.21	13.20	-	10.92	24.12	26.53	2.480
5013403	**Made bends**								
5013403A	15 mm	Each	0.11	6.79	-	-	6.79	7.47	-
5013403B	22 mm	Each	0.15	9.03	-	-	9.03	9.93	-
5013403C	28 mm	Each	0.18	11.27	-	-	11.27	12.40	-
5013404	**Made offsets**								
5013404A	15 mm	Each	0.29	18.06	-	-	18.06	19.87	-
5013404B	22 mm	Each	0.33	20.37	-	-	20.37	22.41	-
5013404C	28 mm	Each	0.36	22.61	-	-	22.61	24.87	-
5013405	**Pipes; Table Z; fixing with pipe clips plugged and screwed to walls**								
5013405A	15 mm	m	0.18	11.27	-	4.01	15.28	16.81	0.720
5013405B	15 mm in short lengths	m	0.19	12.08	-	4.02	16.10	17.71	0.720
5013405C	22 mm	m	0.19	11.71	-	7.46	19.17	21.09	1.540
5013405D	22 mm in short lengths	m	0.20	12.46	-	7.46	19.92	21.91	1.540
5013405E	28 mm	m	0.21	13.20	-	9.95	23.15	25.47	2.490
5013406	**Capillary fittings; straight union couplings**								
5013406A	15 mm	Each	0.12	7.54	-	0.50	8.04	8.84	0.290
5013406B	22 mm	Each	0.16	9.78	-	1.12	10.90	11.99	0.630
5013406C	28 mm	Each	0.21	12.83	-	2.35	15.18	16.70	1.010
5013408	**Capillary fittings; elbows**								
5013408A	15 mm	Each	0.12	7.54	-	1.12	8.66	9.53	0.290
5013408B	22 mm	Each	0.16	9.78	-	2.32	12.10	13.31	0.630
5013408C	28 mm	Each	0.21	12.83	-	4.36	17.19	18.91	1.010
5013409	**Capillary fittings; equal tees**								
5013409A	15 mm	Each	0.18	11.27	-	2.12	13.39	14.73	0.290
5013409B	22 mm	Each	0.24	15.07	-	4.46	19.53	21.48	0.630
5013409C	28 mm	Each	0.30	18.43	-	10.11	28.54	31.39	1.010
5013410	**Capillary fittings; straight tap connectors**								
5013410A	15 mm	Each	0.10	6.04	-	3.57	9.61	10.57	0.380
5013410B	22 mm	Each	0.12	7.54	-	18.41	25.95	28.55	0.810
5013411	**Capillary fittings; straight tank connectors; backnut**								
5013411A	15 mm	Each	0.18	11.27	-	8.81	20.08	22.09	0.380
5013411B	22 mm	Each	0.24	15.07	-	13.04	28.11	30.92	0.810
5013411C	28 mm	Each	0.30	18.43	-	15.28	33.71	37.08	0.140
5013414	**Compression fittings; straight couplings**								
5013414A	15 mm	Each	0.11	6.79	-	2.65	9.44	10.38	0.290
5013414B	22 mm	Each	0.15	9.03	-	4.41	13.44	14.78	0.620
5013414C	28 mm	Each	0.18	11.27	-	10.80	22.07	24.28	1.000

Small Works 2011		Unit	Labour Hours	Labour Net	Plant Net	Materials Net	Unit Net	Unit with 10%	CO$_2$
				£	£	£	£	£	Kg
501	**NEW WORK**								
50134	**SERVICE PIPEWORK COPPER**								
5013415	**Compression fittings; elbows**								
5013415A	15 mm	Each	0.11	6.79	-	1.12	7.91	8.70	0.290
5013415B	22 mm	Each	0.15	9.03	-	2.32	11.35	12.49	0.630
5013415C	28 mm	Each	0.18	11.27	-	4.36	15.63	17.19	1.010
5013416	**Compression fittings; equal tees**								
5013416A	15 mm	Each	0.16	9.78	-	2.12	11.90	13.09	0.290
5013416B	22 mm	Each	0.22	13.58	-	4.46	18.04	19.84	0.630
5013416C	28 mm	Each	0.27	16.57	-	10.11	26.68	29.35	1.010
5013418	**Compression fittings; straight swivel tap adaptors**								
5013418A	15 mm	Each	0.09	5.29	-	5.34	10.63	11.69	0.440
5013418B	22 mm	Each	0.12	7.16	-	10.30	17.46	19.21	0.860
5013420	**Compression fittings; tank couplings; flange and locknut**								
5013420A	15 mm	Each	0.16	9.78	-	5.42	15.20	16.72	0.270
5013420B	22 mm	Each	0.22	13.58	-	5.42	19.00	20.90	0.550
5013420C	28 mm	Each	0.27	16.57	-	15.28	31.85	35.04	0.140
50136	**SERVICE PIPEWORK GALVANISED STEEL**								
5013601	**Pipes; medium grade; screwed and socketed joints; fixing with galvanised steel clips plugged and screwed to walls**								
5013601A	15 mm	m	0.22	13.58	-	6.91	20.49	22.54	1.900
5013601B	20 mm	m	0.23	14.32	-	8.61	22.93	25.22	6.120
5013601C	25 mm	m	0.26	16.19	-	12.33	28.52	31.37	9.050
5013601D	32 mm	m	0.30	18.81	-	15.59	34.40	37.84	12.290
5013602	**Pipes; heavy grade; screwed and socketed joints; laying in trench**								
5013602A	15 mm	m	0.11	6.79	-	7.88	14.67	16.14	5.420
5013602B	20 mm	m	0.12	7.16	-	9.59	16.75	18.43	9.150
5013602C	25 mm	m	0.13	8.28	-	13.70	21.98	24.18	13.530
5013604	**Fittings; elbows**								
5013604A	15 mm	Each	0.18	11.27	-	3.64	14.91	16.40	4.360
5013604B	20 mm	Each	0.24	15.07	-	4.63	19.70	21.67	5.800
5013604C	25 mm	Each	0.30	18.81	-	7.24	26.05	28.66	8.590
5013604D	32 mm	Each	0.36	22.61	-	11.64	34.25	37.68	11.680
5013605	**Fittings; bends**								
5013605A	15 mm	Each	0.18	11.27	-	5.33	16.60	18.26	4.360
5013605B	20 mm	Each	0.24	15.07	-	7.43	22.50	24.75	5.800
5013605C	25 mm	Each	0.30	18.81	-	10.57	29.38	32.32	8.590
5013605D	32 mm	Each	0.36	22.61	-	14.92	37.53	41.28	11.680
5013606	**Fittings; equal tees**								
5013606A	15 mm	Each	0.27	16.57	-	4.66	21.23	23.35	4.360
5013606B	20 mm	Each	0.34	21.11	-	6.31	27.42	30.16	5.800
5013606C	25 mm	Each	0.41	25.60	-	8.59	34.19	37.61	8.590
5013606D	32 mm	Each	0.48	30.14	-	13.67	43.81	48.19	11.680
5013607	**Fittings; longscrews complete with backnut**								
5013607A	15 mm	Each	0.27	16.57	-	10.23	26.80	29.48	0.020
5013607B	20 mm	Each	0.34	21.11	-	11.75	32.86	36.15	0.020
5013607C	25 mm	Each	0.41	25.60	-	16.76	42.36	46.60	0.020
5013607D	32 mm	Each	0.48	30.14	-	20.78	50.92	56.01	0.020
50138	**SERVICE PIPEWORK POLYTHENE**								
5013802	**Pipes; medium density; black; fixing with galvanised clips plugged and screwed to walls**								
5013802A	20 mm	m	0.18	11.27	-	3.63	14.90	16.39	0.240
5013802B	20 mm in short lengths	m	0.19	12.08	-	4.40	16.48	18.13	0.290
5013802C	25 mm	m	0.21	12.83	-	4.38	17.21	18.93	0.310
5013802D	25 mm in short lengths	m	0.22	13.58	-	5.31	18.89	20.78	0.370
5013802E	32 mm	m	0.23	14.32	-	8.39	22.71	24.98	0.550

Plumbing and Heating

	Unit	Labour Hours	Labour Net £	Plant Net £	Materials Net £	Unit Net £	Unit with 10% £	CO₂ Kg

	Unit	Labour Hours	Labour Net £	Plant Net £	Materials Net £	Unit Net £	Unit with 10% £	CO₂ Kg
501 **NEW WORK**								
50138 **SERVICE PIPEWORK POLYTHENE**								
5013804 **Compression fittings; straight couplings**								
5013804A 20 mm	Each	0.15	9.03	-	6.46	15.49	17.04	0.480
5013804B 25 mm	Each	0.18	11.27	-	7.75	19.02	20.92	0.540
5013804C 32 mm	Each	0.22	13.58	-	17.58	31.16	34.28	1.140
5013805 **Compression fittings; elbows**								
5013805A 20 mm	Each	0.15	9.03	-	8.45	17.48	19.23	1.300
5013805B 25 mm	Each	0.18	11.27	-	12.43	23.70	26.07	1.750
5013805C 32 mm	Each	0.22	13.58	-	21.29	34.87	38.36	3.820
5013806 **Compression fittings; equal tees**								
5013806A 20 mm	Each	0.22	13.58	-	12.22	25.80	28.38	2.230
5013806B 25 mm	Each	0.27	16.57	-	18.52	35.09	38.60	2.620
5013806C 32 mm	Each	0.30	18.81	-	26.38	45.19	49.71	4.960
50140 **ANCILLARIES, SCREWED JOINTS AND FITTINGS**								
5014001 **Bib tap; brass**								
5014001A 13 mm	Each	0.11	6.79	-	14.54	21.33	23.46	0.710
5014001B 19 mm	Each	0.15	9.03	-	19.46	28.49	31.34	0.770
5014002 **Bib tap; chromium plated; cross top**								
5014002A 13 mm	Each	0.19	11.71	-	28.80	40.51	44.56	1.140
5014002B 19 mm	Each	0.22	13.58	-	43.76	57.34	63.07	1.240
5014003 **Bib tap; brass; hose union**								
5014003A 13 mm	Each	0.11	6.79	-	16.57	23.36	25.70	0.710
5014003B 19 mm	Each	0.15	9.03	-	28.31	37.34	41.07	0.770
5014004 **Pillar tap; basin and bath; chromium plated; cross top**								
5014004A 13 mm	Each	0.19	11.71	-	29.32	41.03	45.13	3.780
5014004B 19 mm	Each	0.22	13.58	-	39.22	52.80	58.08	3.870
5014005 **Mixer tap; sink; chromium plated; deck pattern; swivel spout**								
5014005A 13 mm	Each	0.24	15.07	-	92.72	107.79	118.57	1.240
5014006 **Mixer tap; basin; chromium plated; monobloc pop-up waste; fixed spout**								
5014006A 13 mm	Each	0.30	18.81	-	112.74	131.55	144.71	1.240
5014007 **Mixer tap; bath; chromium plated; deck pattern; hose and handspray; fixed spout**								
5014007A 19 mm	Each	0.42	26.34	-	100.21	126.55	139.21	1.490
5014008 **Servicing valve; brass; compression joint for copper**								
5014008A 13 mm	Each	0.13	8.28	-	5.86	14.14	15.55	0.260
5014008B 19 mm	Each	0.18	10.90	-	25.67	36.57	40.23	0.520
5014009 **Drain cock; brass**								
5014009A 13 mm	Each	0.07	4.55	-	6.40	10.95	12.05	0.280
5014010 **Spring safety valve; brass**								
5014010A 13 mm	Each	0.19	11.71	-	8.09	19.80	21.78	0.210
5014010B 19 mm	Each	0.22	13.58	-	8.84	22.42	24.66	0.310
5014011 **Main gas cock; brass**								
5014011A 13 mm	Each	0.12	7.54	-	20.82	28.36	31.20	1.540
5014011B 19 mm	Each	0.15	9.40	-	27.83	37.23	40.95	2.310
5014012 **High pressure ball valve; brass; with plastic float**								
5014012A 13 mm	Each	0.18	11.27	-	12.61	23.88	26.27	0.870
5014012B 19 mm	Each	0.22	13.58	-	20.47	34.05	37.46	1.260
5014012C 25 mm	Each	0.25	15.82	-	42.50	58.32	64.15	1.570
5014013 **Gate valve; brass; wheelhead**								
5014013A 13 mm	Each	0.13	8.28	-	10.88	19.16	21.08	0.620
5014013B 19 mm	Each	0.18	10.90	-	13.14	24.04	26.44	0.920

Small Works 2011		Unit	Labour Hours	Labour Net	Plant Net	Materials Net	Unit Net	Unit with 10%	CO$_2$
				£	£	£	£	£	Kg
501	**NEW WORK**								
50140	**ANCILLARIES, SCREWED JOINTS AND FITTINGS**								
5014013	**Gate valve; brass; wheelhead**								
5014013C	25 mm	Each	0.22	13.58	-	19.04	32.62	35.88	1.230
5014014	**Gunmetal stopcock**								
5014014A	15 mm	Each	0.15	9.03	-	9.04	18.07	19.88	0.890
5014014B	22 mm	Each	0.19	12.08	-	15.82	27.90	30.69	1.080
5014014C	28 mm	Each	0.25	15.45	-	38.30	53.75	59.13	1.230
50142	**EQUIPMENT**								
5014201	**Plastic water storage cistern; 13 mm ball valve; holes for pipes; hoisting and placing in position; complete with lid; capacity**								
5014201A	18 litre	Each	0.70	43.28	-	26.62	69.90	76.89	4.860
5014201B	114 litre	Each	0.77	48.20	-	110.56	158.76	174.64	26.180
5014201C	227 litre	Each	0.94	58.36	-	209.52	267.88	294.67	51.270
5014202	**Galvanised steel open top water storage cistern; 13 mm ball valve; holes for pipes; hoisting and placing in position; capacity**								
5014202A	227 litre	Each	1.08	67.39	-	215.85	283.24	311.56	113.440
5014202B	327 litre	Each	1.13	70.44	-	253.08	323.52	355.87	158.470
5014203	**Galvanised steel hot water tank; Grade A; bolted hand hole cover; holes for pipes; hoisting and placing in position; capacity**								
5014203A	95 litre	Each	0.86	53.50	-	269.83	323.33	355.66	51.780
5014203B	123 litre	Each	1.06	65.89	-	288.16	354.05	389.46	54.030
5014204	**Galvanised steel; direct cylinder; Grade A with five screwed bosses; immersion heater boss; hoisting and placing in position; capacity**								
5014204A	100 litre	Each	0.64	39.55	-	458.85	498.40	548.24	54.030
5014204B	136 litre	Each	0.79	49.33	-	492.49	541.82	596.00	63.040
5014205	**Galvanised steel indirect cylinder; Grade B; with five screwed bosses; immersion heater boss; hoisting and placing in position; capacity**								
5014205A	109 litre	Each	0.64	39.55	-	685.44	724.99	797.49	56.290
5014205B	136 litre	Each	0.79	49.33	-	730.17	779.50	857.45	65.290
5014206	**Copper direct cylinder; Grade 3; with four bosses; immersion heater boss; hoisting and placing in position; capacity**								
5014206A	96 litre	Each	0.67	41.42	-	234.87	276.29	303.92	91.890
5014206B	120 litre	Each	0.70	43.28	-	276.62	319.90	351.89	99.550
5014206C	166 litre	Each	0.86	53.50	-	328.52	382.02	420.22	134.010
5014207	**Copper indirect cylinder; Grade 3; with four bosses; immersion heater boss; hoisting and placing in position; capacity**								
5014207A	114 litre	Each	0.70	43.28	-	301.13	344.41	378.85	99.550
5014207B	140 litre	Each	0.77	48.20	-	336.48	384.68	423.15	107.200
5014207C	162 litre	Each	0.86	53.50	-	429.77	483.27	531.60	134.010
5014208	**Copper combination hot water storage units; direct pattern; insulation; four connections; immersion heater boss; drain boss; hoisting and placing in position; capacity**								
5014208A	115 litre hot; 25 litre cold	Each	0.91	56.49	-	396.27	452.76	498.04	114.860
5014208B	115 litre hot; 45 litre cold	Each	0.94	58.73	-	421.86	480.59	528.65	114.860

Plumbing and Heating

		Unit	Labour Hours	Labour Net	Plant Net	Materials Net	Unit Net	Unit with 10%	CO$_2$
				£	£	£	£	£	Kg
501	**NEW WORK**								
50142	**EQUIPMENT**								
5014208	**Copper combination hot water storage units; direct pattern; insulation; four connections; immersion heater boss; drain boss; hoisting and placing in position; capacity**								
5014208C	115 litre hot; 115 litre cold	Each	0.98	61.03	-	639.42	700.45	770.50	114.860
5014209	**Copper combination hot water storage units; indirect pattern; insulation; four connections; immersion heater boss drain boss; hoisting and placing in position; capacity**								
5014209A	115 litre hot; 25 litre cold	Each	0.91	56.49	-	491.34	547.83	602.61	114.860
5014209B	115 litre hot; 45 litre cold	Each	0.94	58.73	-	516.56	575.29	632.82	114.860
5014209C	115 litre hot; 115 litre cold	Each	0.98	61.03	-	711.47	772.50	849.75	114.860
5014213	**Solid fuel boiler for domestic central heating and indirect hot water; white stove enamelled casing; thermostat; conventional flue; placing in position; capacity**								
5014213A	45000 Btu/h	Each	3.99	248.56	-	2,324.75	2,573.31	2,830.64	554.900
5014213B	60000 Btu/h	Each	3.99	248.56	-	2,705.37	2,953.93	3,249.32	578.020
5014214	**Oil fired boiler for domestic central heating and indirect hot water; white stove enamelled casing; fully automatic; conventional flue; placing in position; capacity**								
5014214A	70000 Btu/h	Each	3.19	198.86	-	1,864.62	2,063.48	2,269.83	584.330
5014214B	90000 Btu/h	Each	3.19	198.86	-	2,182.69	2,381.55	2,619.71	612.700
5014216	**Gas fired boiler for domestic central heating and indirect hot water; white stove enamelled casing; floor standing; conventional flue; placing in position; capacity**								
5014216A	output 30 - 40000 Btu/h	Each	2.79	174.01	-	999.64	1,173.65	1,291.02	368.750
5014216B	output 45 - 60000 Btu/h	Each	2.79	174.01	-	1,113.08	1,287.09	1,415.80	382.940
5014217	**Gas fired boiler for domestic central heating and indirect hot water; white stove enamelled casing; floor standing; balanced flue; placing in position; capacity**								
5014217A	output 40 - 50000 Btu/h	Each	3.40	211.69	-	1,281.76	1,493.45	1,642.80	397.120
5014217B	output 45 - 60000 Btu/h	Each	3.40	211.69	-	1,444.10	1,655.79	1,821.37	419.810
5014218	**Circulator pump; domestic type**								
5014218A	all connections	Each	0.72	44.84	-	255.01	299.85	329.84	21.270
5014219	**Programming control**								
5014219A	domestic type; combined heating and hot water system; all connections	Each	0.80	49.70	-	127.76	177.46	195.21	6.200
5014220	**Oil storage tank 12 gauge mild steel; rectangular; primed finish; fill and vent holes; screwed sockets for fill, vent, sludge and draw-off; capacity**								
5014220A	1364 litre	Each	0.92	57.24	-	406.10	463.34	509.67	337.910
5014220B	1818 litre	Each	1.08	67.39	-	464.56	531.95	585.15	579.270
5014220C	2727 litre	Each	1.24	77.23	-	581.51	658.74	724.61	675.810

Small Works 2011		Unit	Labour Hours	Labour Net	Plant Net	Materials Net	Unit Net	Unit with 10%	CO₂
				£	£	£	£	£	Kg
501	**NEW WORK**								
50143	**RADIATORS**								
5014301	**Radiators; steel single panel 600 mm high; 3 mm chromium plated air valve; 15 mm chromium plated easy clean straight valve with union; 15 mm chromium plated lockshield valve with union; concealed brackets plugged and screwed to wall length**								
5014301A	640 mm	Each	1.51	94.17	-	106.38	200.55	220.61	41.410
5014301B	800 mm	Each	1.51	94.17	-	120.39	214.56	236.02	50.860
5014301C	1280 mm	Each	1.66	103.57	-	162.00	265.57	292.13	61.760
5014301D	1760 mm	Each	1.66	103.57	-	201.82	305.39	335.93	83.560
50144	**SANITARY FITTINGS**								
5014401	**Sink; stainless steel; waste; overflow with chain and plastic plug; fixing to top of standard sink unit (excluding taps and trap)**								
5014401A	single bowl with single drainer; 1000 mm x 500 mm (PC £140 per Nr)	Each	2.24	139.32	-	149.07	288.39	317.23	38.120
5014401B	single bowl with double drainer; 1500 mm x 500 mm (PC £155 per Nr)	Each	2.40	149.16	-	164.07	313.23	344.55	56.220
5014402	**Sink; fireclay; Belfast pattern; white glazed; waste; chain and plastic plug; wall mounted on pair brackets screwed to wall (excluding taps and trap)**								
5014402A	610 mm x 455 mm x 255 mm (PC £210 per Nr)	Each	1.95	121.63	-	228.89	350.52	385.57	34.580
5014402B	760 mm x 455 mm x 255 mm (PC £300 per Nr)	Each	1.95	121.63	-	318.89	440.52	484.57	39.020
5014403	**Bath; white reinforced acrylic; rectangular; with cradle feet; waste; overflow with chain and plastic plug (excluding taps and trap)**								
5014403A	1700 mm long (PC £180 per Nr)	Each	2.60	161.93	-	185.04	346.97	381.67	66.780
5014404	**Bath; cast iron; white porcelain enamelled; rectangular; with cradle feet; waste; overflow with chain and plastic plug (excluding taps or trap)**								
5014404A	1700 mm long (PC £360 per Nr)	Each	3.00	186.78	-	365.04	551.82	607.00	229.140
5014405	**Bath panel; enamelled hardboard; cutting to required size; fixed with chromium plated dome headed screws to timber frame**								
5014405A	end panel	Each	0.28	17.31	-	11.77	29.08	31.99	6.170
5014405B	side panel	Each	0.44	27.47	-	25.45	52.92	58.21	22.160
5014406	**Bath panel angle strip; polished aluminium; cut to length**								
5014406A	fixing with chromium plated dome headed screws	Each	0.16	9.78	-	3.45	13.23	14.55	11.000
5014407	**Basin; white vitreous china; 560 mm x 405 mm; waste; overflow with chain and plastic plug**								
5014407A	wall mounted on pair of brackets screwed to wall, (excluding taps or traps) (PC £110 per Nr)	Each	2.07	129.17	-	123.45	252.62	277.88	27.080
5014407B	bowl screwed to wall and bedded in mastic on pedestal mounting screwed to floor, (excluding taps or trap) (PC £150 per Nr)	Each	2.52	156.70	-	153.63	310.33	341.36	56.570

Plumbing and Heating

Small Works 2011		Unit	Labour Hours	Labour Net	Plant Net	Materials Net	Unit Net	Unit with 10%	CO₂
				£	£	£	£	£	Kg
501	**NEW WORK**								
50144	**SANITARY FITTINGS**								
5014408	**W.C. suite; white vitreous china; trapped pan screwed to floor; plastic seat and cover; plastic cistern with brackets screwed to wall; ball valve and fittings; connection to cistern and pan**								
5014408A	high level; plastic flush pipe with clips to wall; (PC £180 per Nr)	Each	2.58	160.43	–	180.00	340.43	374.47	41.440
5014408B	low level; flush bend connected (PC £140 per Nr)	Each	2.66	165.73	–	140.00	305.73	336.30	37.000
5014408C	close-coupled; washdown; flush bend (PC £240 per Nr)	Each	1.91	119.02	–	240.00	359.02	394.92	44.400
5014408D	close-coupled; syphonic; flush bend (PC £390 per Nr)	Each	2.00	124.31	–	390.00	514.31	565.74	56.240
5014409	**Urinal; white vitreous china; white vitreous chine automatic cistern on wall hangers screwed to wall; stainless steel flush pipe with spreader; domed outlet grating**								
5014409A	single bowl (PC £300 per Nr)	Each	1.79	111.48	–	300.00	411.48	452.63	50.320
5014409B	single stall 610 mm x 1065 mm high (PC £600 per Nr)	Each	3.04	189.08	–	600.00	789.08	867.99	66.600
50146	**INSULATION**								
5014601	**Hardboard casing comprising; 3 mm hardboard sides; bottom and loose lid; on and including 50 mm x 38 mm softwood framing; 50 mm space packed with Micafil; to cold water storage tank**								
5014601A	182 litre	Each	0.81	61.62	–	30.39	92.01	101.21	38.860
5014601B	273 litre	Each	1.03	78.44	–	38.40	116.84	128.52	49.740
5014601C	455 litre	Each	1.21	92.43	–	48.76	141.19	155.31	66.980
5014602	**Matchboard casing comprising; 19 mm matchboard sides; bottom and loose lid; on and including 50 mm x 38 mm softwood framing; 50 mm space packed with Micafil; to cold water storage tank**								
5014602A	182 litre	Each	1.47	112.08	–	61.24	173.32	190.65	45.970
5014602B	273 litre	Each	1.65	126.07	–	78.07	204.14	224.55	58.880
5014602C	455 litre	Each	1.83	140.06	–	103.16	243.22	267.54	79.510
5014603	**50 mm fibreglass jacket in one piece; fixed complete with hoop iron bands; to enclose tank**								
5014603A	182 litre	Each	0.28	21.02	–	20.72	41.74	45.91	24.620
5014603B	273 litre	Each	0.37	27.98	–	22.41	50.39	55.43	30.150
5014603C	455 litre	Each	0.46	35.01	–	26.89	61.90	68.09	38.950
5014604	**Hair felt pipe sheath around pipes; external dia**								
5014604A	13 mm	m	0.07	5.58	–	0.59	6.17	6.79	0.840
5014604B	19 mm	m	0.08	6.19	–	0.59	6.78	7.46	0.840
5014604C	25 mm	m	0.09	7.03	–	0.59	7.62	8.38	0.840
5014604D	38 mm	m	0.12	9.25	–	0.59	9.84	10.82	0.840
5014605	**Flexible foam pipe lagging around pipes; external dia**								
5014605A	13 mm	m	0.04	2.83	–	1.16	3.99	4.39	0.970
5014605B	19 mm	m	0.04	3.36	–	1.52	4.88	5.37	1.420
5014605C	25 mm	m	0.05	3.90	–	2.24	6.14	6.75	1.860
5014605D	38 mm	m	0.06	4.74	–	3.77	8.51	9.36	2.830

Small Works 2011		Unit	Labour Hours	Labour Net	Plant Net	Materials Net	Unit Net	Unit with 10%	CO$_2$
				£	£	£	£	£	Kg
501	**NEW WORK**								
50156	**BUILDERS WORK**								
5015601	**Cut holes for pipes or the like; not exceeding 55 mm dia; make good**								
5015601A	100 mm concrete	Each	0.22	16.82	-	0.37	17.19	18.91	1.270
5015601B	150 mm concrete	Each	0.37	27.98	-	0.37	28.35	31.19	1.270
5015601C	100 mm reinforced concrete	Each	0.29	22.40	-	0.37	22.77	25.05	1.270
5015601D	150 mm reinforced concrete	Each	0.39	29.43	-	0.37	29.80	32.78	1.270
5015601E	75 mm blockwork	Each	0.12	9.25	-	0.37	9.62	10.58	1.270
5015601F	100 mm blockwork	Each	0.12	9.25	-	0.37	9.62	10.58	1.270
5015601G	102 mm brickwork	Each	0.17	12.61	-	0.37	12.98	14.28	1.270
5015601H	215 mm brickwork	Each	0.29	22.40	-	0.37	22.77	25.05	1.270
5015601I	softwood floor boarding	Each	0.06	4.20	-	-	4.20	4.62	-
5015601J	softwood floor boarding and plaster board soffit under	Each	0.13	9.79	-	0.43	10.22	11.24	0.290
5015602	**Cut holes for pipes or the like; 55 mm - 110 mm dia; make good**								
5015602A	100 mm concrete	Each	0.31	23.78	-	0.62	24.40	26.84	2.110
5015602B	150 mm concrete	Each	0.46	35.01	-	0.62	35.63	39.19	2.110
5015602C	100 mm reinforced concrete	Each	0.37	27.98	-	0.62	28.60	31.46	2.110
5015602D	150 mm reinforced concrete	Each	0.51	39.22	-	0.62	39.84	43.82	2.110
5015602E	75 mm blockwork	Each	0.17	12.61	-	0.62	13.23	14.55	2.110
5015602F	100 mm blockwork	Each	0.17	12.61	-	0.62	13.23	14.55	2.110
5015602G	102 mm brickwork	Each	0.22	16.82	-	0.62	17.44	19.18	2.110
5015602H	215 mm brickwork	Each	0.40	30.81	-	0.62	31.43	34.57	2.110
5015602I	softwood floor boarding	Each	0.07	5.58	-	-	5.58	6.14	-
5015602J	softwood floor boarding and plaster board soffit under	Each	0.18	13.99	-	0.57	14.56	16.02	0.510
5015603	**Framing; sawn softwood; 38 mm x 50 mm; for bath panel**								
5015603A	end panel	Each	0.13	10.09	-	6.27	16.36	18.00	1.670
5015603B	side panel	Each	0.26	20.18	-	12.31	32.49	35.74	3.290
5015604	**Take up existing softwood floor boarding; 25 mm thick; one board wide; cut holes or notches for pipes and refix boards**								
5015604A	service cables	m	0.33	25.23	-	-	25.23	27.75	-
5015604B	pipes not exceeding 55 mm dia	m	0.40	30.81	-	-	30.81	33.89	-
5015604C	pipes 55 mm - 110 mm dia	m	0.48	36.39	-	-	36.39	40.03	-
5015605	**Tank bearers nailed to ceiling joists**								
5015605A	75 mm x 50 mm	m	0.04	3.36	-	1.60	4.96	5.46	1.240
5015605B	100 mm x 50 mm	m	0.06	4.51	-	2.00	6.51	7.16	1.650
5015606	**Boarded platform; softwood nailed to bearers**								
5015606A	for tank or cistern	m^2	0.57	43.42	-	17.56	60.98	67.08	7.270

Small Works 2011	Unit	Labour Hours	Labour Net	Plant Net	Materials Net	Unit Net	Unit with 10%	CO$_2$
			£	£	£	£	£	Kg
502	**REPAIRS AND ALTERATIONS**							
50201	**REMOVE GUTTERWORK AND PIPEWORK**							
5020101	**Gutterwork and supports**							
5020101A	asbestos-free cement	m	0.21	13.20	-	-	13.20	14.52	-
5020101B	PVC-u	m	0.23	14.32	-	-	14.32	15.75	-
5020101C	cast iron	m	0.27	16.94	-	-	16.94	18.63	-
5020102	**Rainwater pipework and supports**							
5020102A	asbestos-free cement	m	0.18	11.27	-	-	11.27	12.40	-
5020102B	PVC-u	m	0.20	12.46	-	-	12.46	13.71	-
5020102C	cast iron	m	0.24	15.07	-	-	15.07	16.58	-
5020103	**Rainwater shoe**							
5020103A	PVC-u	Each	0.04	2.62	-	-	2.62	2.88	-
5020103B	cast iron	Each	0.06	3.80	-	-	3.80	4.18	-
5020104	**Rainwater head and support**							
5020104A	PVC-u	Each	0.22	13.95	-	-	13.95	15.35	-
5020104B	cast iron	Each	0.27	16.94	-	-	16.94	18.63	-
5020105	**Soil and ventilation pipework and supports**							
5020105A	PVC-u	m	0.36	22.61	-	-	22.61	24.87	-
5020105B	cast iron	m	0.41	25.22	-	-	25.22	27.74	-
5020105C	lead	m	0.45	28.28	-	-	28.28	31.11	-
5020106	**Service, waste and overflow pipework and supports**							
5020106A	PVC-u	m	0.08	4.92	-	-	4.92	5.41	-
5020106B	copper	m	0.10	6.41	-	-	6.41	7.05	-
5020106C	lead	m	0.10	6.41	-	-	6.41	7.05	-
5020106D	galvanised steel	m	0.10	6.41	-	-	6.41	7.05	-
5020107	**Remove sanitary fittings including taps and trap**							
5020107A	w.c. suite	Each	0.25	15.82	-	-	15.82	17.40	-
5020107B	wash hand basin	Each	0.22	13.95	-	-	13.95	15.35	-
5020107C	bath	Each	0.32	19.62	-	-	19.62	21.58	-
5020107D	sink unit	Each	0.22	13.95	-	-	13.95	15.35	-
5020107E	shower	Each	0.09	5.67	-	-	5.67	6.24	-
5020108	**Remove sanitary fittings including taps, trap and service and waste pipes not exceeding 3.00 m girth**							
5020108A	w.c. suite	Each	0.32	19.62	-	-	19.62	21.58	-
5020108B	wash hand basin	Each	0.25	15.82	-	-	15.82	17.40	-
5020108C	bath	Each	0.38	23.36	-	-	23.36	25.70	-
5020108D	sink unit	Each	0.25	15.82	-	-	15.82	17.40	-
5020108E	shower	Each	0.13	8.28	-	-	8.28	9.11	-
5020109	**Remove bathroom toilet fittings**							
5020109A	toilet roll holder	Each	0.03	1.87	-	-	1.87	2.06	-
5020109B	soap dispenser	Each	0.03	1.87	-	-	1.87	2.06	-
5020109C	towel rail	Each	0.05	2.99	-	-	2.99	3.29	-
5020109D	towel holder	Each	0.10	6.41	-	-	6.41	7.05	-
5020109E	mirror	Each	0.10	6.41	-	-	6.41	7.05	-
5020110	**Remove equipment; excluding any necessary draining down of system**							
5020110A	cold water tank	Each	1.60	99.83	-	-	99.83	109.81	-
5020110B	hot water cylinder	Each	0.80	50.07	-	-	50.07	55.08	-
5020110C	gas water heater	Each	2.66	165.73	-	-	165.73	182.30	-
5020110D	gas fire	Each	1.33	82.83	-	-	82.83	91.11	-
5020110E	expansion tank	Each	1.21	75.30	-	-	75.30	82.83	-
50202	**REPAIRS TO PIPEWORK AND GUTTERWORK**							
5020201	**Cleaning out eaves or parapet gutters, removing rubbish**							
5020201A	any height or position	m	0.08	4.92	-	-	4.92	5.41	-
5020202	**Cleaning out rainwater pipes, stack pipes etc, removing rubbish**							
5020202A	any height or position	m	0.08	4.92	-	-	4.92	5.41	-

Small Works 2011		Unit	Labour Hours	Labour Net	Plant Net	Materials Net	Unit Net	Unit with 10%	CO₂
				£	£	£	£	£	Kg
502	**REPAIRS AND ALTERATIONS**								
50202	**REPAIRS TO PIPEWORK AND GUTTERWORK**								
5020203	**Take down existing gutters, clean and refix to fascia or on brackets**								
5020203A	seal joints with red lead putty and set to proper falls	m	0.42	26.34	-	0.48	26.82	29.50	1.930
5020204	**Take down and remove existing 100 mm iron gutters and provide and fix new gutters**								
5020204A	half-round	m	0.67	41.42	-	21.71	63.13	69.44	16.550
5020204B	ogee	m	0.67	41.42	-	23.75	65.17	71.69	23.930
5020205	**Take down existing rainwater pipes and refix to walls**								
5020205A	50 mm, 63 mm, or 75 mm	m	0.45	28.28	-	-	28.28	31.11	-
5020206	**Take down and remove existing iron rain water pipes and provide and fix new**								
5020206A	63 mm and 75 mm pipes	m	0.67	41.42	-	37.04	78.46	86.31	11.780
5020206B	rainwater shoe (not extra over)	Each	0.30	18.81	-	28.47	47.28	52.01	5.830
5020207	**Cut out and reform caulked lead joints in cast-iron soil, vent or waste pipes**								
5020207A	50 mm	Each	0.42	26.34	-	-	26.34	28.97	-
5020207B	75 mm	Each	0.48	30.14	-	-	30.14	33.15	-
5020207C	100 mm	Each	0.70	43.28	-	-	43.28	47.61	-
5020208	**Cut and adapt existing 100 mm iron soil pipe for a new w.c. by inserting branch and bend (or long junction), connect to pan trap and make good to**								
5020208A	wall	Each	2.90	180.80	-	93.73	274.53	301.98	47.380
5020208B	Extra for access door	Each	-	-	-	47.18	47.18	51.90	45.430
50206	**REPAIRS TO PIPEWORK AND PLUMBING**								
5020601	**Renew broken stopcock box with hinged lid**								
5020601A	127 mm x 127 mm x 76 mm	Each	0.30	18.81	-	13.77	32.58	35.84	12.340
5020601B	152 mm x 152 mm x 76 mm	Each	0.33	20.74	-	15.18	35.92	39.51	14.690
5020604	**Cutting existing iron pipe and inserting new tees**								
5020604A	15 mm	Each	0.42	26.34	-	4.66	31.00	34.10	4.360
5020604B	20 mm	Each	0.51	32.01	-	6.31	38.32	42.15	5.800
5020604C	25 mm	Each	0.61	37.68	-	8.59	46.27	50.90	8.590
5020607	**Cutting existing copper pipes and inserting new capillary tees**								
5020607A	15 mm	Each	0.61	37.68	-	2.12	39.80	43.78	0.290
5020607B	22 mm	Each	0.73	45.22	-	4.46	49.68	54.65	0.630
5020607C	28 mm	Each	0.91	56.49	-	10.11	66.60	73.26	1.010
5020609	**Cutting existing polythene pipes and inserting new compression tees**								
5020609A	20 mm	Each	0.91	56.49	-	12.22	68.71	75.58	2.230
5020609B	25 mm	Each	1.03	64.02	-	18.52	82.54	90.79	2.620
5020609C	32 mm	Each	1.21	75.30	-	26.38	101.68	111.85	4.960
5020610	**Covering iron or copper pipes with hair felt and twine in any position**								
5020610A	up to 25 mm dia	m	0.42	26.34	-	0.59	26.93	29.62	0.840
5020612	**Take off existing bib valves and prepare iron or copper pipes and provide and fix new bib valve**								
5020612A	13 mm	Each	0.61	37.68	-	14.54	52.22	57.44	0.710

Plumbing and Heating

Small Works 2011		Unit	Labour Hours	Labour Net	Plant Net	Materials Net	Unit Net	Unit with 10%	CO$_2$
				£	£	£	£	£	Kg
502	**REPAIRS AND ALTERATIONS**								
50206	**REPAIRS TO PIPEWORK AND PLUMBING**								
5020612	**Take off existing bib valves and prepare iron or copper pipes and provide and fix new bib valve**								
5020612B	19 mm	Each	0.73	45.22	-	19.46	64.68	71.15	0.770
5020614	**Cut into iron or copper pipes and fit new stopcock**								
5020614A	13 mm	Each	0.79	48.95	-	8.62	57.57	63.33	0.770
5020614B	19 mm	Each	0.91	56.49	-	13.67	70.16	77.18	1.020
5020616	**Rewasher ball valve, tap or indoor stopcock**								
5020616A	13 mm	Each	0.30	18.81	-	0.37	19.18	21.10	0.010
5020616B	19 mm	Each	0.36	22.61	-	0.37	22.98	25.28	0.010
5020618	**Take off existing copper trap to bath, basin or sink and provide and fit new plastic trap**								
5020618A	32 mm	Each	0.73	45.22	-	3.63	48.85	53.74	4.770
5020618B	38 mm	Each	0.79	48.95	-	9.07	58.02	63.82	1.910
5020620	**Take off stopcock to iron or copper pipe both ends and provide and fit new stopcock**								
5020620A	13 mm	Each	0.39	24.48	-	8.62	33.10	36.41	0.770
5020620B	19 mm	Each	0.51	32.01	-	13.67	45.68	50.25	1.020
5020620C	25 mm	Each	0.64	39.55	-	35.03	74.58	82.04	1.170
5020622	**Take off ball valve to iron or copper pipes and provide and fit new ball valve and ball float complete**								
5020622A	13 mm	Each	0.30	18.81	-	12.61	31.42	34.56	0.870
5020622C	19 mm	Each	0.39	24.48	-	20.47	44.95	49.45	1.260
50208	**REPAIRS TO SANITARYWARE AND FITTINGS**								
5020801	**Supply w.c. suite complete (PC £180 per Nr) and connect to existing services**								
5020801A	copper or iron	Each	3.51	218.42	-	180.00	398.42	438.26	41.440
5020802	**Supply low level w.c. suite (PC £140 per Nr) complete and connect to existing services**								
5020802A	copper or iron	Each	3.81	237.29	-	140.00	377.29	415.02	37.000
5020803	**Remove defective w.c. pan and fix new; make good all connections**								
5020803A	(PC £90 per Nr)	Each	2.36	146.86	-	90.00	236.86	260.55	29.600
5020804	**Take off defective seat to pedestal pan and supply and fix new plastic seat**								
5020804A	single	Each	0.45	28.28	-	17.83	46.11	50.72	2.400
5020804B	double	Each	0.54	33.88	-	24.97	58.85	64.74	4.800
5020805	**Take off w.c. seat, renew joints to flush pipe including closet and outlet connection and pan**								
5020805A	refix seat	Each	0.70	43.28	-	2.65	45.93	50.52	0.190
5020806	**Disconnect and remove 9 litres of water waste preventer, supply and fix new complete with ball valve and brackets and joint to existing overflow and service pipe**								
5020806A	copper or iron	Each	1.94	120.51	-	112.61	233.12	256.43	1.730

Small Works 2011		Unit	Labour Hours	Labour Net	Plant Net	Materials Net	Unit Net	Unit with 10%	CO$_2$
				£	£	£	£	£	Kg
502	**REPAIRS AND ALTERATIONS**								
50208	**REPAIRS TO SANITARYWARE AND FITTINGS**								
5020807	**Disconnect ball valve to water waste preventer or storage tank**								
5020807A	re-washer and clean out	Each	0.88	54.62	-	0.37	54.99	60.49	0.010
5020807B	unscrew ball valve and supply and fit new ball	Each	0.18	11.27	-	4.54	15.81	17.39	3.220
5020808	**Supply and fix flat back basin (PC £90 per Nr) including taps, traps and wall brackets, connect to existing services**								
5020808A	iron or copper	Each	3.51	218.42	-	90.00	308.42	339.26	29.600
5020809	**Supply and fix pedestal basin (PC £150 per Nr) including taps, traps and wall brackets, connect to existing services**								
5020809A	iron or copper	Each	3.51	218.42	-	150.00	368.42	405.26	28.650
5020812	**Supply and fix cast iron; white porcelain enamelled; rectangular; 1700 mm long bath complete with taps and trap, connect to existing services**								
5020812A	iron or copper	Each	3.51	218.42	-	475.85	694.27	763.70	224.390
5020814	**Clear blockage and flush out; to**								
5020814A	w.c. pans and traps	Each	0.76	47.08	-	-	47.08	51.79	-
5020814B	traps and waste pipes of baths, sinks, lavatory basins etc	Each	0.61	37.68	-	-	37.68	41.45	-
5020816	**Disconnect all pipework, take out and remove galvanised steel hot water tank, provide and install copper indirect cylinder, allow for cutting holes, tank connectors, make up and connections to existing pipework**								
5020816A	114 litre	Each	1.81	112.98	-	333.34	446.32	490.95	102.760
5020818	**Empty water storage system and disconnect back boiler and supply and connect**								
5020818A	new back boiler and test (PC £180 per Nr)	Each	2.42	150.66	-	180.00	330.66	363.73	77.900
5020819	**Clean and scale back boiler and ends of pipe**								
5020819A	reconnect and recirculate water	Each	4.23	263.63	-	-	263.63	289.99	-
5020820	**Turn off water supply, disconnect all pipework, take out and remove galvanised steel cold water storage tank, provide and install plastic tank complete with ball valve, lid and insulation and allow for cutting holes, tank connectors, make up and connections to existing pipework**								
5020820A	182 litre	Each	3.81	237.29	-	172.19	409.48	450.43	26.110
5020821	**Cleaning and scouring out open-top storage tanks**								
5020821A	generally	Each	4.48	278.70	-	-	278.70	306.57	-

Glazing, Painting and Decorating

Small Works 2011		Unit	Labour Hours	Labour Net	Plant Net	Materials Net	Unit Net	Unit with 10%	CO$_2$
				£	£	£	£	£	Kg
601	**NEW WORK**								
60101	**GLASS IN OPENINGS**								
6010101	**2 mm Clear sheet glass and glazing to wood with putty; in panes**								
6010101A	not exceeding 0.10 sq.m	m²	1.20	33.61	-	32.73	66.34	72.97	13.120
6010101B	0.10 - 0.50 sq.m	m²	0.90	25.21	-	32.32	57.53	63.28	9.580
6010101C	0.50 - 1.0 sq.m	m²	0.45	12.60	-	32.32	44.92	49.41	9.580
6010102	**3 mm Clear sheet glass and glazing to wood with putty; in panes**								
6010102A	not exceeding 0.10 sq.m	m²	1.20	33.61	-	44.66	78.27	86.10	12.420
6010102B	0.10 - 0.50 sq.m	m²	0.90	25.21	-	44.66	69.87	76.86	12.420
6010102C	0.50 - 1.0 sq.m	m²	0.45	12.60	-	44.66	57.26	62.99	12.420
6010102D	exceeding 1.0 sq.m	m²	0.35	9.80	-	44.66	54.46	59.91	12.420
6010103	**4 mm Clear sheet glass and glazing to wood with putty; in panes**								
6010103A	0.10 - 0.50 sq.m	m²	1.00	28.01	-	50.53	78.54	86.39	15.250
6010103B	0.50 - 1.0 sq.m	m²	0.50	14.01	-	50.94	64.95	71.45	18.800
6010103C	exceeding 1.0 sq.m	m²	0.40	11.20	-	50.94	62.14	68.35	18.800
6010104	**2 mm Clear sheet glass and glazing to metal with putty; in panes**								
6010104A	not exceeding 0.10 sq.m	m²	1.75	49.02	-	33.85	82.87	91.16	20.570
6010104B	0.10 - 0.50 sq.m	m²	1.35	37.81	-	33.38	71.19	78.31	17.020
6010104C	0.50 - 1.0 sq.m	m²	0.70	19.61	-	32.86	52.47	57.72	13.120
6010105	**3 mm Clear sheet glass and glazing to metal with putty; in panes**								
6010105A	not exceeding 0.10 sq.m	m²	1.75	49.02	-	45.72	94.74	104.21	19.860
6010105B	0.10 - 0.50 sq.m	m²	1.35	37.81	-	45.20	83.01	91.31	15.960
6010105C	0.50 - 1.0 sq.m	m²	0.70	19.61	-	44.73	64.34	70.77	12.420
6010105D	exceeding 1.0 sq.m	m²	0.55	15.41	-	44.73	60.14	66.15	12.420
6010106	**4 mm Clear sheet glass and glazing to metal with putty; in panes**								
6010106A	0.10 - 0.50 sq.m	m²	1.50	42.02	-	51.06	93.08	102.39	18.800
6010106B	0.50 - 1.0 sq.m	m²	0.80	22.41	-	50.59	73.00	80.30	15.250
6010106C	exceeding 1.0 sq.m	m²	0.65	18.21	-	50.59	68.80	75.68	15.250
6010107	**Figured, Rolled or Cathedral glass and glazing to wood with putty; in panes**								
6010107A	not exceeding 0.10 sq.m	m²	1.20	33.61	-	76.25	109.86	120.85	24.410
6010107B	0.10 - 0.50 sq.m	m²	0.90	25.21	-	76.25	101.46	111.61	24.410
6010107C	0.50 - 1.0 sq.m	m²	0.45	12.60	-	76.70	89.30	98.23	28.310
6010107D	exceeding 1.0 sq.m	m²	0.35	9.80	-	75.84	85.64	94.20	20.860
6010108	**Figured, Rolled or Cathedral glass and glazing to metal with putty; in panes**								
6010108A	not exceeding 0.10 sq.m	m²	1.75	49.02	-	77.36	126.38	139.02	31.860
6010108B	0.10 - 0.50 sq.m	m²	1.35	37.81	-	76.37	114.18	125.60	24.410
6010108C	0.50 - 1.0 sq.m	m²	0.70	19.61	-	75.90	95.51	105.06	20.860
6010108D	exceeding 1.0 sq.m	m²	0.50	14.01	-	76.37	90.38	99.42	24.410
6010109	**6 mm Wired cast glass and glazing to wood with putty; in panes**								
6010109A	not exceeding 0.10 sq.m	m²	1.40	39.21	-	44.61	83.82	92.20	31.860
6010109B	0.10 - 0.50 sq.m	m²	1.20	33.61	-	44.19	77.80	85.58	28.310
6010109C	0.50 - 1.0 sq.m	m²	0.60	16.81	-	43.33	60.14	66.15	20.860
6010109D	exceeding 1.0 sq.m	m²	0.50	14.01	-	43.74	57.75	63.53	24.410
6010110	**6 mm Wired cast glass and glazing to metal with putty; in panes**								
6010110A	not exceeding 0.10 sq.m	m²	2.10	58.82	-	43.86	102.68	112.95	24.410
6010110B	0.10 - 0.50 sq.m	m²	1.65	46.22	-	44.86	91.08	100.19	31.860

Small Works 2011		Unit	Labour Hours	Labour Net	Plant Net	Materials Net	Unit Net	Unit with 10%	CO$_2$
				£	£	£	£	£	Kg
601	**NEW WORK**								
60101	**GLASS IN OPENINGS**								
6010110	**6 mm Wired cast glass and glazing to metal with putty; in panes**								
6010110C	0.50 - 1.0 sq.m	m^2	0.85	23.81	-	43.86	67.67	74.44	24.410
6010110D	exceeding 1.0 sq.m	m^2	0.75	21.01	-	43.39	64.40	70.84	20.860
6010111	**6 mm Wired glass and glazing to wood with putty, roof lights, lantern lights, skylights etc; in panes**								
6010111A	0.10 - 0.50 sq.m	m^2	2.20	61.62	-	43.74	105.36	115.90	24.410
6010111B	0.50 - 1.0 sq.m	m^2	1.10	30.81	-	43.33	74.14	81.55	20.860
6010111C	exceeding 1.0 sq.m	m^2	0.90	25.21	-	43.74	68.95	75.85	24.410
6010112	**6 mm Wired glass glazing to metal with putty; in panes**								
6010112A	0.10 - 0.50 sq.m	m^2	3.00	84.03	-	43.39	127.42	140.16	20.860
6010112B	0.50 - 1.0 sq.m	m^2	1.70	47.62	-	43.86	91.48	100.63	24.410
6010112C	exceeding 1.0 sq.m	m^2	1.50	42.02	-	44.15	86.17	94.79	26.540
6010113	**6 mm Single glaze quality float glass, bedding in wash-leather and beads, both measured separately; in panes**								
6010113A	not exceeding 4.0 sq.m	m^2	3.30	92.43	-	80.53	172.96	190.26	40.340
6010114	**Bed edges of glass in**								
6010114A	wash leather	m	0.07	1.96	-	0.65	2.61	2.87	3.220
6010114B	velvet	m	0.06	1.68	-	0.84	2.52	2.77	4.020
6010114C	fix only beads	m	0.07	1.96	-	-	1.96	2.16	-
6010114D	fix only beads (if screwed)	m	0.09	2.52	-	-	2.52	2.77	-
6010115	**Curved cutting, including risk, on the following**								
6010115A	sheet glass	m	0.25	7.00	-	-	7.00	7.70	-
6010115B	obscure glass	m	0.33	9.24	-	-	9.24	10.16	-
6010115C	wire cast glass	m	0.60	16.81	-	-	16.81	18.49	-
6010115D	6 mm single glaze quality float glass	m	0.40	11.20	-	-	11.20	12.32	-
60103	**DOUBLE GLAZING UNITS**								
6010301	**Hermetically sealed in two panes of 4 mm clear float glass to wood or metal with non-setting compound and screwed or clipped beads**								
6010301B	1.00 - 2.00 sq.m	m^2	2.00	56.02	-	36.37	92.39	101.63	25.500
6010301C	0.75 - 1.00 sq.m	m^2	2.50	70.03	-	42.79	112.82	124.10	25.500
6010301D	0.50 - 0.75 sq.m	m^2	3.00	84.03	-	51.98	136.01	149.61	25.500
6010301E	0.35 - 0.50 sq.m	m^2	3.50	98.04	-	60.20	158.24	174.06	25.500
6010301F	0.25 - 0.35 sq.m	m^2	4.00	112.04	-	79.63	191.67	210.84	25.500
6010301G	not exceeding 0.25 sq.m	m^2	4.50	126.05	-	79.63	205.68	226.25	25.500
6010302	**Hermetically sealed one pane of 4 mm clear float glass and one pane of 4 mm white patterned glass with non-setting compound and screwed or clipped beads**								
6010302B	1.00 - 2.00 sq.m	m^2	2.00	56.02	-	41.36	97.38	107.12	38.100
6010302C	0.75 - 1.00 sq.m	m^2	2.50	70.03	-	47.80	117.83	129.61	38.100
6010302D	0.50 - 0.75 sq.m	m^2	3.00	84.03	-	56.96	140.99	155.09	38.100
6010302E	0.35 - 0.50 sq.m	m^2	3.50	98.04	-	65.23	163.27	179.60	38.100
6010302F	0.25 - 0.35 sq.m	m^2	4.00	112.04	-	84.64	196.68	216.35	38.100
6010302G	not exceeding 0.25 sq.m	m^2	4.50	126.05	-	84.64	210.69	231.76	38.100
60106	**PAINTING AND DECORATING INTERNALLY**								
6010601	**Limewhite**								
6010601A	one coat brick walls	m^2	0.15	4.20	-	0.11	4.31	4.74	0.360
6010601B	two coat brick walls	m^2	0.25	7.00	-	0.20	7.20	7.92	0.640
6010601C	two coat plaster walls	m^2	0.20	5.60	-	0.04	5.64	6.20	0.130

Glazing, Painting and Decorating

	Unit	Labour Hours	Labour Net £	Plant Net £	Materials Net £	Unit Net £	Unit with 10% £	CO$_2$ Kg
601	**NEW WORK**							
60106	**PAINTING AND DECORATING INTERNALLY**							
6010601	**Limewhite**							
6010601D	two coat plaster ceilings	m^2	0.22	6.16	-	0.04	6.20	6.82	0.130
6010602	**Primer, two coats matt or silk emulsion paint**							
6010602A	concrete walls	m^2	0.41	11.48	-	3.28	14.76	16.24	1.580
6010602B	concrete walls to stairwell	m^2	0.50	14.01	-	3.28	17.29	19.02	1.580
6010602C	concrete ceilings	m^2	0.53	14.85	-	3.28	18.13	19.94	1.580
6010602D	concrete ceilings to stairwell	m^2	0.59	16.53	-	3.28	19.81	21.79	1.580
6010602E	brick walls	m^2	0.50	14.01	-	4.21	18.22	20.04	2.030
6010602F	brick walls to stairwell	m^2	0.56	15.69	-	4.21	19.90	21.89	2.030
6010602G	block walls	m^2	0.62	17.37	-	4.21	21.58	23.74	2.030
6010602H	block walls to stairwell	m^2	0.68	19.05	-	4.21	23.26	25.59	2.030
6010602I	plastered walls	m^2	0.38	10.64	-	2.83	13.47	14.82	1.370
6010602J	plastered walls to stairwell	m^2	0.44	12.32	-	2.83	15.15	16.67	1.370
6010602K	plastered ceilings	m^2	0.50	14.01	-	2.83	16.84	18.52	1.370
6010602L	plastered ceilings to stairwell	m^2	0.53	14.85	-	2.83	17.68	19.45	1.370
6010602M	embossed papered or textured walls	m^2	0.41	11.48	-	3.28	14.76	16.24	1.580
6010602N	embossed papered or textured walls to stairwell	m^2	0.50	14.01	-	3.28	17.29	19.02	1.580
6010602O	embossed papered or textured ceilings	m^2	0.53	14.85	-	3.28	18.13	19.94	1.580
6010602P	embossed papered or textured ceilings to stairwell	m^2	0.59	16.53	-	3.28	19.81	21.79	1.580
6010603	**Primer, two coats eggshell paint**							
6010603A	concrete walls	m^2	0.46	12.88	-	3.56	16.44	18.08	1.580
6010603B	concrete walls to stairwell	m^2	0.55	15.41	-	3.56	18.97	20.87	1.580
6010603C	concrete ceilings	m^2	0.58	16.25	-	3.56	19.81	21.79	1.580
6010603D	concrete ceilings to stairwell	m^2	0.64	17.93	-	3.56	21.49	23.64	1.580
6010603E	brick walls	m^2	0.54	15.13	-	4.09	19.22	21.14	1.820
6010603F	brick walls to stairwell	m^2	0.60	16.81	-	4.09	20.90	22.99	1.820
6010603G	block walls	m^2	0.66	18.49	-	5.10	23.59	25.95	2.260
6010603H	block walls to stairwell	m^2	0.72	20.17	-	5.10	25.27	27.80	2.260
6010603I	plastered walls	m^2	0.43	12.04	-	3.08	15.12	16.63	1.370
6010603J	plastered walls to stairwell	m^2	0.50	14.01	-	3.08	17.09	18.80	1.370
6010603K	plastered ceilings	m^2	0.55	15.41	-	3.08	18.49	20.34	1.370
6010603L	plastered ceilings to stairwell	m^2	0.59	16.53	-	3.08	19.61	21.57	1.370
6010603M	embossed papered or textured walls	m^2	0.47	13.16	-	3.56	16.72	18.39	1.580
6010603N	embossed papered or textured walls to stairwell	m^2	0.56	15.69	-	3.56	19.25	21.18	1.580
6010603O	embossed papered or textured ceiling	m^2	0.59	16.53	-	3.56	20.09	22.10	1.580
6010603P	embossed papered or textured ceilings to stairwell	m^2	0.66	18.49	-	3.56	22.05	24.26	1.580
6010604	**Primer, one undercoat, one coat gloss finishing paint**							
6010604A	concrete walls	m^2	0.46	12.88	-	2.43	15.31	16.84	1.350
6010604B	concrete walls to stairwell	m^2	0.55	15.41	-	2.43	17.84	19.62	1.350
6010604C	concrete ceilings	m^2	0.58	16.25	-	2.43	18.68	20.55	1.350
6010604D	concrete ceilings to stairwell	m^2	0.64	17.93	-	2.43	20.36	22.40	1.350
6010604E	brick walls	m^2	0.54	15.13	-	3.31	18.44	20.28	1.820
6010604F	brick walls to stairwell	m^2	0.60	16.81	-	3.31	20.12	22.13	1.820
6010604G	block walls	m^2	0.66	18.49	-	3.71	22.20	24.42	2.050
6010604H	block walls to stairwell	m^2	0.72	20.17	-	3.71	23.88	26.27	2.050
6010604I	plastered walls	m^2	0.43	12.04	-	2.43	14.47	15.92	1.350
6010604J	plastered walls to stairwell	m^2	0.50	14.01	-	2.43	16.44	18.08	1.350
6010604K	plastered ceilings	m^2	0.55	15.41	-	2.43	17.84	19.62	1.350
6010604L	plastered ceilings to stairwell	m^2	0.59	16.53	-	2.43	18.96	20.86	1.350
6010604M	embossed papered or textured walls	m^2	0.47	13.16	-	2.43	15.59	17.15	1.350
6010604N	embossed papered or textured walls to stairwell	m^2	0.56	15.69	-	2.43	18.12	19.93	1.350
6010604O	embossed papered or textured ceilings	m^2	0.59	16.53	-	2.43	18.96	20.86	1.350
6010604P	embossed papered or textured ceilings to stairwell	m^2	0.66	18.49	-	2.43	20.92	23.01	1.350

Small Works 2011		Unit	Labour Hours	Labour Net	Plant Net	Materials Net	Unit Net	Unit with 10%	CO$_2$
				£	£	£	£	£	Kg
601	**NEW WORK**								
60106	**PAINTING AND DECORATING INTERNALLY**								
6010604	**Primer, one undercoat, one coat gloss finishing paint**								
6010604Q	dado line 25 mm wide including cutting in both edges	m	0.30	8.40	-	0.12	8.52	9.37	0.060
6010605	**Primer, two undercoats, one coat gloss finishing paint**								
6010605A	concrete walls	m^2	0.58	16.25	-	4.01	20.26	22.29	2.260
6010605B	concrete walls to stairwell	m^2	0.70	19.61	-	4.01	23.62	25.98	2.260
6010605C	concrete ceilings	m^2	0.74	20.73	-	4.01	24.74	27.21	2.260
6010605D	concrete ceilings to stairwell	m^2	0.82	22.97	-	4.01	26.98	29.68	2.260
6010605E	brick walls	m^2	0.69	19.33	-	4.07	23.40	25.74	2.260
6010605F	brick walls to stairwell	m^2	0.77	21.57	-	4.07	25.64	28.20	2.260
6010605G	block walls	m^2	0.85	23.81	-	4.88	28.69	31.56	2.730
6010605H	block walls to stairwell	m^2	0.93	26.05	-	4.88	30.93	34.02	2.730
6010605I	plastered walls	m^2	0.54	15.13	-	2.84	17.97	19.77	1.580
6010605J	plastered walls to stairwell	m^2	0.63	17.65	-	2.84	20.49	22.54	1.580
6010605K	plastered ceilings	m^2	0.70	19.61	-	2.84	22.45	24.70	1.580
6010605L	plastered ceilings to stairwell	m^2	0.75	21.01	-	2.84	23.85	26.24	1.580
6010605M	embossed papered or textured walls	m^2	0.59	16.53	-	3.20	19.73	21.70	1.790
6010605N	embossed papered or textured walls to stairwell	m^2	0.71	19.89	-	3.20	23.09	25.40	1.790
6010605O	embossed papered or textured ceilings	m^2	0.75	21.01	-	3.20	24.21	26.63	1.790
6010605P	embossed papered or textured ceilings to stairwell	m^2	0.84	23.53	-	3.20	26.73	29.40	1.790
6010605Q	dado line 25 mm wide included cutting in both edges	m	0.40	11.20	-	0.15	11.35	12.49	0.090
6010606	**Knot, stop, prime, one undercoat, one gloss finishing coat oil paint on woodwork**								
6010606A	general surfaces not exceeding 150 mm girth	m	0.32	8.96	-	0.27	9.23	10.15	0.150
6010606B	general surfaces 150 - 300 mm girth	m	0.41	11.48	-	0.61	12.09	13.30	0.340
6010606C	general surfaces over 300 mm girth	m^2	0.75	21.01	-	2.15	23.16	25.48	1.200
6010606G	windows, glazed doors, screens in small panes	m^2	1.66	46.50	-	1.77	48.27	53.10	0.980
6010606H	windows, glazed doors, screens in medium panes	m^2	1.45	40.61	-	1.53	42.14	46.35	0.850
6010606I	windows, glazed doors, screens in large panes	m^2	1.23	34.45	-	1.38	35.83	39.41	0.770
6010606J	windows, glazed doors, screens in extra large panes	m^2	1.01	28.29	-	1.07	29.36	32.30	0.600
6010606K	frames and sashes (measure over glass)	m^2	1.11	31.09	-	1.38	32.47	35.72	0.770
6010606L	open balustrade to staircase (measured flat both sides overall)	m^2	0.78	21.85	-	1.92	23.77	26.15	1.070
6010608	**Knot, stop, prime, two undercoats, one finishing coat gloss oil paint on woodwork**								
6010608A	general surfaces not exceeding 150 mm girth	m	0.41	11.48	-	0.38	11.86	13.05	0.210
6010608B	general surfaces 150 - 300 mm girth	m	0.52	14.57	-	0.83	15.40	16.94	0.470
6010608C	general surfaces over 300 mm girth	m^2	0.97	27.17	-	2.77	29.94	32.93	1.560
6010608G	windows, glazed doors, screens in small panes	m^2	2.16	60.50	-	2.28	62.78	69.06	1.280
6010608H	windows, glazed doors, screens in medium panes	m^2	1.88	52.66	-	1.94	54.60	60.06	1.090
6010608I	windows, glazed doors, screens in large panes	m^2	1.60	44.82	-	1.71	46.53	51.18	0.960
6010608J	windows, glazed doors, screens in extra large panes	m^2	1.31	36.69	-	1.40	38.09	41.90	0.790
6010608K	frames and sashes (measure over glass)	m^2	1.44	40.33	-	1.71	42.04	46.24	0.960
6010608L	open balustrade to staircase (measured flat both sides overall)	m^2	1.02	28.57	-	2.50	31.07	34.18	1.410

Glazing, Painting and Decorating

Small Works 2011		Unit	Labour Hours	Labour Net £	Plant Net £	Materials Net £	Unit Net £	Unit with 10% £	CO₂ Kg
601	**NEW WORK**								
60106	**PAINTING AND DECORATING INTERNALLY**								
6010609	**Primer, one undercoat, one finishing coat gloss oil paint on metalwork**								
6010609A	general surfaces not exceeding 150 mm girth	m	0.30	8.40	-	0.27	8.67	9.54	0.150
6010609B	general surfaces 150 - 300 mm girth	m	0.39	10.92	-	0.62	11.54	12.69	0.340
6010609C	general surfaces over 300 mm girth	m²	0.69	19.33	-	2.15	21.48	23.63	1.200
6010609D	windows, glazed doors, screens in small panes	m²	1.66	46.50	-	1.77	48.27	53.10	0.980
6010609E	windows, glazed doors, screens in medium panes	m²	1.45	40.61	-	1.54	42.15	46.37	0.850
6010609F	windows, glazed doors, screens in large panes	m²	1.23	34.45	-	1.38	35.83	39.41	0.770
6010609G	windows, glazed doors, screens in extra large panes	m²	1.01	28.29	-	1.07	29.36	32.30	0.600
6010609H	corrugated surfaces over 300 mm girth	m²	0.75	21.01	-	2.42	23.43	25.77	1.350
6010609I	structural steelwork over 300 mm girth	m²	0.84	23.53	-	2.15	25.68	28.25	1.200
6010609J	radiators over 300 mm girth	m²	0.69	19.33	-	2.15	21.48	23.63	1.200
6010609K	pipes, ducts etc. not exceeding 150 mm girth	m	0.25	7.00	-	0.27	7.27	8.00	0.150
6010609L	pipes, ducts etc. 150 mm - 300 mm girth	m	0.35	9.80	-	0.62	10.42	11.46	0.340
6010609M	pipes, ducts etc. over 300 mm girth	m²	0.68	19.05	-	2.15	21.20	23.32	1.200
6010609O	sundry fittings - casement stays etc	Each	0.15	4.20	-	0.15	4.35	4.79	0.090
6010610	**Primer, two undercoats, one finishing coat gloss oil paint on metalwork**								
6010610A	general surfaces not exceeding 150 mm girth	m	0.38	10.64	-	0.38	11.02	12.12	0.210
6010610B	general surfaces 150 - 300 mm girth	m	0.50	14.01	-	0.84	14.85	16.34	0.470
6010610C	general surfaces over 300 mm girth	m²	0.90	25.21	-	2.77	27.98	30.78	1.560
6010610D	windows, glazed doors, screens in small panes	m²	2.16	60.50	-	2.28	62.78	69.06	1.280
6010610E	windows, glazed doors, screens in medium panes	m²	1.88	52.66	-	1.94	54.60	60.06	1.090
6010610F	windows, glazed doors, screens in large panes	m²	1.60	44.82	-	1.71	46.53	51.18	0.960
6010610G	windows, glazed doors, screens in extra large panes	m²	1.31	36.69	-	1.40	38.09	41.90	0.790
6010610H	corrugated surfaces over 300 mm girth	m²	0.98	27.45	-	3.12	30.57	33.63	1.750
6010610I	structural steelwork over 300 mm girth	m²	1.10	30.81	-	2.77	33.58	36.94	1.560
6010610J	radiators over 300 mm girth	m²	0.90	25.21	-	2.77	27.98	30.78	1.560
6010610K	pipes, ducts etc. not exceeding 150 mm girth	m	0.33	9.24	-	0.38	9.62	10.58	0.210
6010610L	pipes, ducts etc. 150 mm - 300 mm girth	m	0.46	12.88	-	0.84	13.72	15.09	0.470
6010610M	pipes, ducts etc. over 300 mm girth	m²	0.89	24.93	-	2.77	27.70	30.47	1.560
6010610O	sundry fittings - casement stays etc	Each	0.20	5.60	-	0.23	5.83	6.41	0.130
6010620	**One coat Cuprinol clear preserver on wrought timber**								
6010620A	General surfaces not exceeding 150 mm girth	m	0.09	2.52	-	0.06	2.58	2.84	0.040
6010620B	General surfaces 150 mm - 300 mm girth	m	0.14	3.92	-	0.15	4.07	4.48	0.110
6010620C	General surfaces over 300 mm girth	m²	0.19	5.32	-	0.48	5.80	6.38	0.340
6010621	**Two coats Cuprinol clear preserver on wrought timber**								
6010621A	General surfaces not exceeding 150 mm girth	m	0.18	5.04	-	0.15	5.19	5.71	0.110
6010621B	General surfaces 150 mm - 300 mm girth	m	0.25	7.00	-	0.30	7.30	8.03	0.210

Small Works 2011		Unit	Labour Hours	Labour Net	Plant Net	Materials Net	Unit Net	Unit with 10%	CO$_2$
				£	£	£	£	£	Kg

601   **NEW WORK**

60106   **PAINTING AND DECORATING INTERNALLY**

		Unit	Labour Hours	Labour Net	Plant Net	Materials Net	Unit Net	Unit with 10%	CO$_2$
6010621	**Two coats Cuprinol clear preserver on wrought timber**								
6010621C	General surfaces over 300 mm girth	m²	0.37	10.36	-	1.00	11.36	12.50	0.700
6010622	**One coat Cuprinol oak preserver on wrought timber**								
6010622A	General surfaces not exceeding 150 mm girth	m	0.08	2.24	-	0.06	2.30	2.53	0.040
6010622B	General surfaces 150 mm - 300 mm girth	m	0.12	3.36	-	0.15	3.51	3.86	0.110
6010622C	General surfaces over 300 mm girth	m²	0.18	5.04	-	0.51	5.55	6.11	0.360
6010623	**Two coats Cuprinol oak preserver wrought timber**								
6010623A	General surfaces not exceeding 150 mm girth	m	0.16	4.48	-	0.15	4.63	5.09	0.110
6010623B	General surfaces 150 mm - 300 mm girth	m	0.23	6.44	-	0.30	6.74	7.41	0.210
6010623C	General surfaces over 300 mm girth	m²	0.36	10.08	-	1.00	11.08	12.19	0.700
6010624	**Two coats clear polyurethane on woodwork**								
6010624A	General surfaces not exceeding 150 mm girth	m	0.16	4.48	-	0.32	4.80	5.28	0.090
6010624B	General surfaces 150 mm - 300 mm girth	m	0.24	6.72	-	0.64	7.36	8.10	0.170
6010624C	General surfaces over 300 mm girth	m²	0.36	10.08	-	2.11	12.19	13.41	0.570
6010624G	windows, glazed doors, screens in small panes	m²	0.80	22.41	-	1.67	24.08	26.49	0.450
6010624H	windows, glazed doors, screens in medium panes	m²	0.72	20.17	-	1.47	21.64	23.80	0.400
6010624I	windows, glazed doors, screens in large panes	m²	0.64	17.93	-	1.27	19.20	21.12	0.340
6010624J	windows, glazed doors, screens in extra large panes	m²	0.56	15.69	-	1.07	16.76	18.44	0.290
6010625	**Three coats clear polyurethane on woodwork**								
6010625A	General surfaces not exceeding 150 mm girth	m	0.26	7.28	-	0.48	7.76	8.54	0.130
6010625B	General surfaces 150 mm - 300 mm girth	m	0.32	8.96	-	0.95	9.91	10.90	0.260
6010625C	General surfaces over 300 mm girth	m²	0.54	15.13	-	3.18	18.31	20.14	0.850
6010625G	windows, glazed doors, screens in small panes	m²	1.10	30.81	-	2.54	33.35	36.69	0.680
6010625H	windows, glazed doors, screens in medium panes	m²	1.02	28.57	-	2.23	30.80	33.88	0.600
6010625I	windows, glazed doors, screens in large panes	m²	0.94	26.33	-	1.91	28.24	31.06	0.510
6010625J	windows, glazed doors, screens in extra large panes	m²	0.86	24.09	-	1.59	25.68	28.25	0.430
6010626	**Two coats coloured polyurethane on woodwork**								
6010626A	General surfaces not exceeding 150 mm girth	m	0.16	4.48	-	0.64	5.12	5.63	0.170
6010626B	General surfaces 150 mm - 300 mm girth	m	0.24	6.72	-	1.27	7.99	8.79	0.340
6010626C	General surfaces over 300 mm girth	m²	0.36	10.08	-	4.21	14.29	15.72	1.130
6010626G	windows, glazed doors, screens in small panes	m²	0.80	22.41	-	3.34	25.75	28.33	0.900
6010626H	windows, glazed doors, screens in medium panes	m²	0.72	20.17	-	2.94	23.11	25.42	0.790
6010626I	windows, glazed doors, screens in large panes	m²	0.64	17.93	-	2.54	20.47	22.52	0.680
6010626J	windows, glazed doors, screens in extra large panes	m²	0.56	15.69	-	2.15	17.84	19.62	0.580
6010627	**Three coats coloured polyurethane on woodwork**								
6010627A	General surfaces not exceeding 150 mm girth	m	0.26	7.28	-	0.95	8.23	9.05	0.260

Glazing, Painting and Decorating

	Unit	Labour Hours	Labour Net £	Plant Net £	Materials Net £	Unit Net £	Unit with 10% £	CO₂ Kg
601	**NEW WORK**							
60106	**PAINTING AND DECORATING INTERNALLY**							
6010627	**Three coats coloured polyurethane on woodwork**							
6010627B	General surfaces 150 mm - 300 mm girth	m	0.32	8.96	-	1.91	10.87	11.96	0.510
6010627C	General surfaces over 300 mm girth	m²	0.54	15.13	-	6.36	21.49	23.64	1.710
6010627G	windows, glazed doors, screens in small panes	m²	1.10	30.81	-	5.09	35.90	39.49	1.370
6010627H	windows, glazed doors, screens in medium panes	m²	1.02	28.57	-	4.45	33.02	36.32	1.200
6010627I	windows, glazed doors, screens in large panes	m²	0.94	26.33	-	3.82	30.15	33.17	1.030
6010627J	windows, glazed doors, screens in extra large panes	m²	0.86	24.09	-	3.18	27.27	30.00	0.850
6010628	**Two coats raw or boiled linseed oil on woodwork**							
6010628A	General surfaces not exceeding 150 mm girth	m	0.12	3.36	-	0.18	3.54	3.89	0.070
6010628B	General surfaces 150 mm - 300 mm girth	m	0.16	4.48	-	0.33	4.81	5.29	0.130
6010628C	General surfaces over 300 mm girth	m²	0.30	8.40	-	1.12	9.52	10.47	0.440
6010630	**Seal and wax polish woodwork**							
6010630A	General surfaces not exceeding 150 mm girth	m	0.09	2.52	-	0.26	2.78	3.06	0.220
6010630B	General surfaces 150 mm - 300 mm girth	m	0.13	3.64	-	0.54	4.18	4.60	0.460
6010630C	General surfaces over 300 mm girth	m²	0.20	5.60	-	2.01	7.61	8.37	1.690
6010630G	windows, glazed doors, screens in small panes	m²	0.60	16.81	-	1.50	18.31	20.14	1.260
6010630H	windows, glazed doors, screens in medium panes	m²	0.50	14.01	-	1.23	15.24	16.76	1.030
6010630I	windows, glazed doors, screens in large panes	m²	0.40	11.20	-	1.01	12.21	13.43	0.850
6010630J	windows, glazed doors, screens in extra large panes	m²	0.30	8.40	-	0.60	9.00	9.90	0.500
6010640	**One coat Artex sealer, one coat Artex standard compound with stipple finish**							
6010640A	Concrete walls	m²	0.42	11.76	-	1.42	13.18	14.50	6.020
6010640B	Concrete walls to stairwell	m²	0.44	12.32	-	1.42	13.74	15.11	6.020
6010640C	Brick walls	m²	0.42	11.76	-	1.64	13.40	14.74	6.960
6010640D	Brick walls to stairwell	m²	0.44	12.32	-	1.64	13.96	15.36	6.960
6010640E	Block walls	m²	0.42	11.76	-	1.86	13.62	14.98	7.900
6010640F	Block walls to stairwell	m²	0.44	12.32	-	1.86	14.18	15.60	7.900
6010640G	Plastered walls	m²	0.37	10.36	-	1.42	11.78	12.96	6.020
6010640H	Plastered walls to stairwell	m²	0.39	10.92	-	1.42	12.34	13.57	6.020
6010640I	Plastered ceilings	m²	0.41	11.48	-	1.42	12.90	14.19	6.020
6010640J	Plastered ceilings to stairwell	m²	0.43	12.04	-	1.42	13.46	14.81	6.020
6010640K	Plasterboard walls	m²	0.37	10.36	-	1.42	11.78	12.96	6.020
6010640L	Plasterboard walls to stairwell	m²	0.39	10.92	-	1.42	12.34	13.57	6.020
6010640M	Plasterboard ceiling	m²	0.41	11.48	-	1.42	12.90	14.19	6.020
6010640N	Plasterboard ceiling to stairwell	m²	0.43	12.04	-	1.42	13.46	14.81	6.020
60108	**PAINTING AND DECORATING EXTERNALLY**							
6010802	**Two coats Snowcem on walls**							
6010802A	Concrete	m²	0.45	12.60	-	0.61	13.21	14.53	1.170
6010802B	Brick	m²	0.48	13.44	-	0.61	14.05	15.46	1.170
6010802C	Block	m²	0.54	15.13	-	0.61	15.74	17.31	1.170
6010802D	Cement rendered	m²	0.42	11.76	-	0.61	12.37	13.61	1.170
6010802E	Rough cast	m²	0.57	15.97	-	1.77	17.74	19.51	3.420
6010803	**Stabilising solution, two coats Sandtex matt on walls**							
6010803A	Concrete	m²	0.57	15.97	-	3.56	19.53	21.48	2.180
6010803B	Brick	m²	0.60	16.81	-	4.19	21.00	23.10	2.560
6010803C	Block	m²	0.66	18.49	-	5.18	23.67	26.04	3.160

Small Works 2011		Unit	Labour Hours	Labour Net	Plant Net	Materials Net	Unit Net	Unit with 10%	CO$_2$
				£	£	£	£	£	Kg
601	**NEW WORK**								
60108	**PAINTING AND DECORATING EXTERNALLY**								
6010803	**Stabilising solution, two coats Sandtex matt on walls**								
6010803D	Cement rendered	m^2	0.54	15.13	-	3.56	18.69	20.56	2.180
6010803E	Rough cast	m^2	0.69	19.33	-	7.39	26.72	29.39	4.530
6010804	**Two coats Weathershield masonry paint on walls**								
6010804A	Concrete	m^2	0.50	14.01	-	1.61	15.62	17.18	1.280
6010804B	Brick	m^2	0.61	17.09	-	1.91	19.00	20.90	1.520
6010804C	Block	m^2	0.69	19.33	-	2.29	21.62	23.78	1.820
6010804D	Cement rendered	m^2	0.53	14.85	-	1.91	16.76	18.44	1.520
6010804E	Rough cast	m^2	0.72	20.17	-	2.85	23.02	25.32	2.260
6010810	**Prime only woodwork**								
6010810A	General surfaces not exceeding 150 mm girth	m	0.13	3.64	-	0.11	3.75	4.13	0.060
6010810B	General surfaces 150 mm - 300 mm girth	m	0.17	4.76	-	0.22	4.98	5.48	0.130
6010810C	General surfaces over 300 mm girth	m^2	0.26	7.28	-	0.80	8.08	8.89	0.470
6010810G	Windows, glazed doors, screens in small panes	m^2	0.66	18.49	-	0.65	19.14	21.05	0.380
6010810H	Windows, glazed doors, screens in medium panes	m^2	0.58	16.25	-	0.58	16.83	18.51	0.340
6010810I	Windows, glazed doors, screens in large panes	m^2	0.50	14.01	-	0.51	14.52	15.97	0.300
6010810J	Windows, glazed doors, screens in extra large panes	m^2	0.42	11.76	-	0.44	12.20	13.42	0.260
6010810K	Frames and sashes (measured over glass)	m^2	0.44	12.32	-	0.51	12.83	14.11	0.300
6010820	**Knot, stop, prime, one undercoat one gloss finishing coat oil paint on woodwork**								
6010820A	General surfaces not exceeding 150 mm girth	m	0.39	10.92	-	0.27	11.19	12.31	0.150
6010820B	General surfaces 150 mm - 300 mm girth	m	0.51	14.29	-	0.61	14.90	16.39	0.340
6010820C	General surfaces over 300 mm girth	m^2	0.78	21.85	-	2.15	24.00	26.40	1.200
6010820G	Windows, glazed doors, screens in small panes	m^2	1.98	55.46	-	1.77	57.23	62.95	0.980
6010820H	Windows, glazed doors, screens in medium panes	m^2	1.74	48.74	-	1.53	50.27	55.30	0.850
6010820I	Windows, glazed doors, screens in large panes	m^2	1.50	42.02	-	1.38	43.40	47.74	0.770
6010820J	Windows, glazed doors, screens in extra large panes	m^2	1.20	33.61	-	1.07	34.68	38.15	0.600
6010820K	Frames and sashes (measured over glass)	m^2	1.32	36.97	-	1.38	38.35	42.19	0.770
6010820L	Open balustrade to staircase (measured flat both sides)	m^2	0.87	24.37	-	1.92	26.29	28.92	1.070
6010821	**Knot, stop, prime, two undercoats, one gloss finishing coat oil paint on woodwork**								
6010821A	General surfaces not exceeding 150 mm girth	m	0.52	14.57	-	0.38	14.95	16.45	0.210
6010821B	General surfaces 150 mm - 300 mm girth	m	0.68	19.05	-	0.83	19.88	21.87	0.470
6010821C	General surfaces over 300 mm girth	m^2	1.04	29.13	-	2.77	31.90	35.09	1.560
6010821G	Windows, glazed doors, screens in small panes	m^2	2.64	73.95	-	2.28	76.23	83.85	1.280
6010821H	Windows, glazed doors, screens in medium panes	m^2	2.32	64.98	-	1.94	66.92	73.61	1.090
6010821I	Windows, glazed doors, screens in large panes	m^2	2.00	56.02	-	1.71	57.73	63.50	0.960
6010821J	Windows, glazed doors, screens in extra large panes	m^2	1.60	44.82	-	1.40	46.22	50.84	0.790
6010821K	Frames and sashes (measured over glass)	m^2	1.76	49.30	-	1.71	51.01	56.11	0.960
6010821L	Open balustrade to staircase (measured flat both sides)	m^2	1.16	32.49	-	3.19	35.68	39.25	1.750

Small Works 2011		Unit	Labour Hours	Labour Net	Plant Net	Materials Net	Unit Net	Unit with 10%	CO$_2$
				£	£	£	£	£	Kg
601	**NEW WORK**								
60108	**PAINTING AND DECORATING EXTERNALLY**								
6010830	**Prime only metalwork**								
6010830A	General surfaces not exceeding 150 mm girth	m	0.13	3.64	-	0.11	3.75	4.13	0.060
6010830B	General surfaces 150 mm - 300 mm girth	m	0.17	4.76	-	0.22	4.98	5.48	0.130
6010830C	General surfaces over 300 mm girth	m^2	0.26	7.28	-	0.80	8.08	8.89	0.470
6010830D	Windows, glazed doors, screens in small panes	m^2	0.66	18.49	-	0.66	19.15	21.07	0.380
6010830E	Windows, glazed doors, screens in medium panes	m^2	0.58	16.25	-	0.58	16.83	18.51	0.340
6010830F	Windows, glazed doors, screens in large panes	m^2	0.50	14.01	-	0.51	14.52	15.97	0.300
6010830G	Windows, glazed doors, screens in extra large panes	m^2	0.42	11.76	-	0.44	12.20	13.42	0.260
6010830H	Stairs (measured overall)	m^2	0.28	7.84	-	0.69	8.53	9.38	0.410
6010830I	Corrugated surfaces over 300 mm girth	m^2	0.29	8.12	-	0.91	9.03	9.93	0.530
6010830J	Structural steelwork over 300 mm girth	m^2	0.32	8.96	-	0.80	9.76	10.74	0.470
6010830K	Railings, balustrades (measured flat both sides overall)	m^2	0.29	8.12	-	0.69	8.81	9.69	0.410
6010830L	Eaves gutters inside and out not exceeding 150 mm girth	m	0.15	4.20	-	0.11	4.31	4.74	0.060
6010830M	Eaves gutters inside and out 150 mm - 300 mm girth	m	0.17	4.76	-	0.22	4.98	5.48	0.130
6010830N	Eaves gutters inside and out over 300 mm girth	m^2	0.27	7.56	-	0.80	8.36	9.20	0.470
6010830O	Pipes, ducts etc not exceeding 150 m girth	m	0.15	4.20	-	0.11	4.31	4.74	0.060
6010830P	Pipes, ducts etc 150 mm - 300 mm girth	m	0.19	5.32	-	0.22	5.54	6.09	0.130
6010830Q	Pipes, ducts etc over 300 mm girth	m^2	0.26	7.28	-	0.80	8.08	8.89	0.470
6010830R	Rainwater heads inside and out	Each	0.08	2.24	-	0.11	2.35	2.59	0.060
6010831	**Primer, one undercoat, one gloss finishing coat oil paint on metalwork**								
6010831A	General surfaces not exceeding 150 mm girth	m	0.39	10.92	-	0.27	11.19	12.31	0.150
6010831B	General surfaces 150 mm - 300 mm girth	m	0.51	14.29	-	0.62	14.91	16.40	0.340
6010831C	General surfaces over 300 mm girth	m^2	0.78	21.85	-	2.15	24.00	26.40	1.200
6010831D	Windows, glazed doors, screens in small panes	m^2	1.98	55.46	-	1.77	57.23	62.95	0.980
6010831E	Windows, glazed doors, screens in medium panes	m^2	1.74	48.74	-	1.54	50.28	55.31	0.850
6010831F	Windows, glazed doors, screens in large panes	m^2	1.50	42.02	-	1.38	43.40	47.74	0.770
6010831G	Windows, glazed doors, screens in extra large panes	m^2	1.20	33.61	-	1.07	34.68	38.15	0.600
6010831H	Stairs (measured overall)	m^2	0.84	23.53	-	1.88	25.41	27.95	1.050
6010831I	Corrugated surfaces over 300 mm girth	m^2	0.87	24.37	-	2.42	26.79	29.47	1.350
6010831J	Structural steelwork over 300 mm girth	m^2	0.96	26.89	-	2.15	29.04	31.94	1.200
6010831K	Railings, balustrades (measured flat both sides overall)	m^2	0.87	24.37	-	1.64	26.01	28.61	0.920
6010831L	Eaves gutters inside and out not exceeding 150 mm girth	m	0.45	12.60	-	0.27	12.87	14.16	0.150
6010831M	Eaves gutters inside and out 150 mm - 300 mm girth	m	0.51	14.29	-	0.62	14.91	16.40	0.340
6010831N	Eaves gutters inside and out over 300 mm girth	m^2	0.81	22.69	-	2.15	24.84	27.32	1.200
6010831O	Pipes, ducts etc not exceeding 150 m girth	m	0.45	12.60	-	0.27	12.87	14.16	0.150
6010831P	Pipes, ducts etc 150 mm - 300 mm girth	m	0.51	14.29	-	0.62	14.91	16.40	0.340
6010831Q	Pipes, ducts etc. over 300 mm girth	m^2	0.78	21.85	-	2.15	24.00	26.40	1.200
6010831R	Rainwater heads inside and out	Each	0.24	6.72	-	0.27	6.99	7.69	0.150

Small Works 2011		Unit	Labour Hours	Labour Net	Plant Net	Materials Net	Unit Net	Unit with 10%	CO₂
				£	£	£	£	£	Kg
601	**NEW WORK**								
60108	**PAINTING AND DECORATING EXTERNALLY**								
6010832	**Primer, two undercoats, one gloss coat oil finishing paint on metalwork**								
6010832A	General surfaces not exceeding 150 mm girth	m	0.52	14.57	-	0.38	14.95	16.45	0.210
6010832B	General surfaces 150 mm - 300 mm girth	m	0.68	19.05	-	0.84	19.89	21.88	0.470
6010832C	General surfaces over 300 mm girth	m²	1.04	29.13	-	2.77	31.90	35.09	1.560
6010832D	Windows, glazed doors, screens in small panes	m²	2.64	73.95	-	2.28	76.23	83.85	1.280
6010832E	Windows, glazed doors, screens in medium panes	m²	2.32	64.98	-	1.94	66.92	73.61	1.090
6010832F	Windows, glazed doors, screens in large panes	m²	2.00	56.02	-	1.71	57.73	63.50	0.960
6010832G	Windows, glazed doors, screens in extra large panes	m²	1.60	44.82	-	1.40	46.22	50.84	0.790
6010832H	Stairs (measured overall)	m²	1.12	31.37	-	2.40	33.77	37.15	1.350
6010832I	Corrugated surfaces over 300 mm girth	m²	1.16	32.49	-	3.12	35.61	39.17	1.750
6010832J	Structural steelwork over 300 mm girth	m²	1.28	35.85	-	2.77	38.62	42.48	1.560
6010832K	Railings, balustrades (measured flat both sides overall)	m²	1.16	32.49	-	2.05	34.54	37.99	1.150
6010832L	Eaves gutters inside and out not exceeding 150 mm girth	m	0.60	16.81	-	0.38	17.19	18.91	0.210
6010832M	Eaves gutters inside and out 150 mm - 300 mm girth	m	0.68	19.05	-	0.84	19.89	21.88	0.470
6010832N	Eaves gutters inside and out over 300 mm girth	m²	1.08	30.25	-	2.77	33.02	36.32	1.560
6010832O	Pipes, ducts etc not exceeding 150 m girth	m	0.60	16.81	-	0.38	17.19	18.91	0.210
6010832P	Pipes, ducts etc 150 mm - 300 mm girth	m	0.68	19.05	-	0.84	19.89	21.88	0.470
6010832Q	Pipes, ducts etc over 300 mm girth	m²	1.04	29.13	-	2.77	31.90	35.09	1.560
6010832R	Rainwater heads inside and out	Each	0.32	8.96	-	0.38	9.34	10.27	0.210
6010840	**One coat bituminous paint on metalwork**								
6010840A	Water storage cistern, tanks, inside and out	m²	0.40	11.20	-	0.18	11.38	12.52	0.170
6010840B	Gutters (inside surfaces)	m	0.10	2.80	-	0.07	2.87	3.16	0.060
6010841	**Two coat bituminous paint on metalwork**								
6010841A	Water storage cistern, tanks, inside and out	m²	0.80	22.41	-	0.39	22.80	25.08	0.360
6010841B	Corrugated surfaces over 300 mm girth	m²	1.00	28.01	-	0.39	28.40	31.24	0.360
6010841C	Gutters (inside surfaces)	m	0.18	5.04	-	0.12	5.16	5.68	0.110
6010841D	Pipes not exceeding 150 mm girth	m	0.13	3.64	-	0.07	3.71	4.08	0.060
6010841E	Pipes 150 mm - 300 mm girth	m	0.24	6.72	-	0.12	6.84	7.52	0.110
6010841F	Pipes over 300 mm girth	m²	0.34	9.52	-	0.39	9.91	10.90	0.360
6010842	**Two coats timber preserver on wrought timber**								
6010842A	General surfaces not exceeding 150 m girth	m	0.20	5.60	-	0.13	5.73	6.30	0.190
6010842B	General surfaces 150 mm - 300 mm girth	m	0.26	7.28	-	0.25	7.53	8.28	0.360
6010842C	General surfaces over 300 mm girth	m²	0.38	10.64	-	0.89	11.53	12.68	1.260
6010843	**Two coats timber preserver on sawn timber**								
6010843A	General surfaces not exceeding 150 m girth	m	0.21	5.88	-	0.25	6.13	6.74	0.360
6010843B	General surfaces 150 mm - 300 mm girth	m	0.27	7.56	-	0.48	8.04	8.84	0.680
6010843C	General surfaces over 300 mm girth	m²	0.40	11.20	-	1.14	12.34	13.57	1.620

Glazing, Painting and Decorating

Small Works 2011		Unit	Labour Hours	Labour Net	Plant Net	Materials Net	Unit Net	Unit with 10%	CO$_2$
				£	£	£	£	£	Kg
601	**NEW WORK**								
60108	**PAINTING AND DECORATING EXTERNALLY**								
6010850	**Two coats Solignum on wrought timber**								
6010850A	General surfaces not exceeding 150 mm girth	m	0.19	5.32	-	0.22	5.54	6.09	0.130
6010850B	General surfaces 150 mm - 300 mm girth	m	0.25	7.00	-	0.43	7.43	8.17	0.250
6010850C	General surfaces over 300 mm girth	m²	0.36	10.08	-	1.41	11.49	12.64	0.820
6010851	**Two coats Solignum on sawn timber**								
6010851A	General surfaces not exceeding 150 mm girth	m	0.20	5.60	-	0.29	5.89	6.48	0.170
6010851B	General surfaces 150 mm - 300 mm girth	m	0.26	7.28	-	0.65	7.93	8.72	0.380
6010851C	General surfaces over 300 mm girth	m²	0.38	10.64	-	2.10	12.74	14.01	1.220
6010855	**Two coats Cuprinol preserver on wrought timber (green)**								
6010855A	General surfaces not exceeding 150 mm girth	m	0.20	5.60	-	0.24	5.84	6.42	0.170
6010855B	General surfaces 150 mm - 300 mm girth	m	0.26	7.28	-	0.48	7.76	8.54	0.340
6010855C	General surfaces over 300 mm girth	m²	0.38	10.64	-	1.60	12.24	13.46	1.130
6010856	**Two coats Cuprinol preserver on sawn timber (green)**								
6010856A	General surfaces not exceeding 150 mm girth	m	0.21	5.88	-	0.33	6.21	6.83	0.230
6010856B	General surfaces 150 mm - 300 mm girth	m	0.27	7.56	-	0.63	8.19	9.01	0.450
6010856C	General surfaces over 300 mm girth	m²	0.40	11.20	-	2.14	13.34	14.67	1.520
6010857	**Two coats Cuprinol preserver on wrought timber (clear)**								
6010857A	General surfaces not exceeding 150 mm girth	m	0.20	5.60	-	0.24	5.84	6.42	0.170
6010857B	General surfaces 150 mm - 300 mm girth	m	0.26	7.28	-	0.48	7.76	8.54	0.340
6010857C	General surfaces over 300 mm girth	m²	0.38	10.64	-	1.60	12.24	13.46	1.130
6010858	**Two coats Cuprinol preserver on sawn timber (clear)**								
6010858A	General surfaces not exceeding 150 mm girth	m	0.21	5.88	-	0.33	6.21	6.83	0.230
6010858B	General surfaces 150 mm - 300 mm girth	m	0.27	7.56	-	0.63	8.19	9.01	0.450
6010858C	General surfaces over 300 mm girth	m²	0.40	11.20	-	2.14	13.34	14.67	1.520
6010859	**Two coats raw or boiled linseed oil on woodwork**								
6010859A	General surfaces not exceeding 150 mm girth	m	0.14	3.92	-	0.40	4.32	4.75	0.150
6010859B	General surfaces 150 mm - 300 mm girth	m	0.18	5.04	-	0.78	5.82	6.40	0.300
6010859C	General surfaces over 300 mm girth	m²	0.32	8.96	-	2.62	11.58	12.74	1.020
6010860	**Two coats clear polyurethane on woodwork**								
6010860A	General surfaces not exceeding 150 mm girth	m	0.20	5.60	-	0.32	5.92	6.51	0.090
6010860B	General surfaces 150 mm - 300 mm girth	m	0.26	7.28	-	0.68	7.96	8.76	0.180
6010860C	General surfaces over 300 mm girth	m²	0.38	10.64	-	2.23	12.87	14.16	0.600
6010860G	Windows, glazed doors, screens in small panes	m²	0.84	23.53	-	1.67	25.20	27.72	0.450
6010860H	Windows, glazed doors, screens medium panes	m²	0.76	21.29	-	1.43	22.72	24.99	0.380
6010860I	Windows, glazed doors, screens large panes	m²	0.68	19.05	-	1.15	20.20	22.22	0.310

Small Works 2011		Unit	Labour Hours	Labour Net	Plant Net	Materials Net	Unit Net	Unit with 10%	CO$_2$
				£	£	£	£	£	Kg
601	**NEW WORK**								
60108	**PAINTING AND DECORATING EXTERNALLY**								
6010860	**Two coats clear polyurethane on woodwork**								
6010860J	Windows, glazed doors, screens extra large panes	m^2	0.60	16.81	-	0.68	17.49	19.24	0.180
6010861	**Three coats clear polyurethane on woodwork**								
6010861A	General surfaces not exceeding 150 mm girth	m	0.28	7.84	-	0.52	8.36	9.20	0.140
6010861B	General surfaces 150 mm - 300 mm girth	m	0.34	9.52	-	0.99	10.51	11.56	0.270
6010861C	General surfaces over 300 mm girth	m^2	0.56	15.69	-	3.38	19.07	20.98	0.910
6010861G	Windows, glazed doors, screens in small panes	m^2	1.14	31.93	-	2.54	34.47	37.92	0.680
6010861H	Windows, glazed doors, screens medium panes	m^2	1.06	29.69	-	2.15	31.84	35.02	0.580
6010861I	Windows, glazed doors, screens large panes	m^2	0.98	27.45	-	1.67	29.12	32.03	0.450
6010861J	Windows, glazed doors, screens extra large panes	m^2	0.90	25.21	-	0.99	26.20	28.82	0.270
60109	**SIGNWRITING**								
6010901	**Gloss oil paint, per coat, per 25 mm high**								
6010901A	Capital letters	Each	0.14	3.92	-	0.09	4.01	4.41	0.040
6010901B	Lower case letters	Each	0.16	4.48	-	0.04	4.52	4.97	0.020
6010901C	Numerals	Each	0.16	4.48	-	0.09	4.57	5.03	0.040
6010901D	Stops, commas and hyphens	Each	0.05	1.40	-	0.04	1.44	1.58	0.020
6010902	**Gilt or gold leaf, per 25 mm high**								
6010902A	Capital letters	Each	0.16	4.48	-	0.38	4.86	5.35	0.020
6010902B	Lower case letters	Each	0.14	3.92	-	0.28	4.20	4.62	0.020
6010902C	Numerals	Each	0.16	4.48	-	0.38	4.86	5.35	0.020
60110	**PRESSURE SPRAY PAINTING**								
6011001	**One coat emulsion paint**								
6011001A	Brick	m^2	0.07	3.32	-	0.93	4.25	4.68	0.450
6011001B	Block	m^2	0.08	4.10	-	1.20	5.30	5.83	0.580
6011001C	Concrete	m^2	0.05	2.59	-	0.93	3.52	3.87	0.450
6011001D	Plaster	m^2	0.05	2.59	-	0.80	3.39	3.73	0.380
6011002	**One coat oil colour**								
6011002B	Brick	m^2	0.10	4.64	-	0.90	5.54	6.09	0.450
6011002C	Block	m^2	0.12	5.91	-	1.15	7.06	7.77	0.580
6011002D	Concrete	m^2	0.12	5.91	-	0.90	6.81	7.49	0.450
6011002E	Plaster	m^2	0.08	3.86	-	0.77	4.63	5.09	0.380
6011003	**One basecoat by brush; one coat multicolour**								
6011003A	Brick	m^2	0.18	8.70	-	5.55	14.25	15.68	1.580
6011003C	Block	m^2	0.18	8.70	-	5.55	14.25	15.68	1.580
6011003D	Concrete	m^2	0.18	8.70	-	5.55	14.25	15.68	1.580
6011003E	Plaster	m^2	0.16	7.67	-	5.55	13.22	14.54	1.580
60111	**PAPERHANGING**								
6011101	**Strip off one layer woodchip paper, stop cracks and rub down**								
6011101A	Walls	m^2	0.18	5.04	-	0.09	5.13	5.64	0.060
6011101B	Walls to stairwell	m^2	0.20	5.60	-	0.09	5.69	6.26	0.060
6011101C	Ceilings	m^2	0.22	6.16	-	0.09	6.25	6.88	0.060
6011101D	Ceilings to stairwell	m^2	0.24	6.72	-	0.09	6.81	7.49	0.060
6011102	**Strip off one layer of standard patterned or ready pasted paper, stop cracks and rub down**								
6011102A	Walls	m^2	0.21	5.88	-	0.09	5.97	6.57	0.060
6011102B	Walls to stairwell	m^2	0.23	6.44	-	0.09	6.53	7.18	0.060

Glazing, Painting and Decorating

Small Works 2011		Unit	Labour Hours	Labour Net	Plant Net	Materials Net	Unit Net	Unit with 10%	CO$_2$
				£	£	£	£	£	Kg
601	**NEW WORK**								
60111	**PAPERHANGING**								
6011102	**Strip off one layer of standard patterned or ready pasted paper, stop cracks and rub down**								
6011102C	Ceilings	m^2	0.25	7.00	-	0.09	7.09	7.80	0.060
6011102D	Ceilings to stairwell	m^2	0.27	7.56	-	0.09	7.65	8.42	0.060
6011103	**Strip off one layer of vinyl paper, stop cracks and rub down**								
6011103A	Walls	m^2	0.23	6.44	-	0.09	6.53	7.18	0.060
6011103B	Walls to stairwell	m^2	0.25	7.00	-	0.09	7.09	7.80	0.060
6011103C	Ceilings	m^2	0.27	7.56	-	0.09	7.65	8.42	0.060
6011103D	Ceilings to stairwell	m^2	0.29	8.12	-	0.09	8.21	9.03	0.060
6011104	**Strip off one layer of embossed paper, stop cracks and rub down**								
6011104A	Walls	m^2	0.23	6.44	-	0.09	6.53	7.18	0.060
6011104B	Walls to stairwell	m^2	0.25	7.00	-	0.09	7.09	7.80	0.060
6011104C	Ceilings	m^2	0.27	7.56	-	0.09	7.65	8.42	0.060
6011104D	Ceilings to stairwell	m^2	0.29	8.12	-	0.09	8.21	9.03	0.060
6011105	**Strip off one layer of lincrusta or anaglypta paper, stop cracks and rub down**								
6011105A	Walls	m^2	0.28	7.84	-	0.09	7.93	8.72	0.060
6011105B	Walls to stairwell	m^2	0.30	8.40	-	0.09	8.49	9.34	0.060
6011105C	Ceilings	m^2	0.33	9.24	-	0.09	9.33	10.26	0.060
6011105D	Ceilings to stairwell	m^2	0.38	10.64	-	0.09	10.73	11.80	0.060
6011106	**Strip off two layers of woodchip paper, stop cracks and rub down**								
6011106A	Walls	m^2	0.28	7.84	-	0.09	7.93	8.72	0.060
6011106B	Walls to stairwell	m^2	0.30	8.40	-	0.09	8.49	9.34	0.060
6011106C	Ceilings	m^2	0.35	9.80	-	0.09	9.89	10.88	0.060
6011106D	Ceilings to stairwell	m^2	0.38	10.64	-	0.09	10.73	11.80	0.060
6011107	**Strip off two layers of standard patterned or ready pasted paper, stop cracks and rub down**								
6011107A	Walls	m^2	0.32	8.96	-	0.09	9.05	9.96	0.060
6011107B	Walls to stairwell	m^2	0.35	9.80	-	0.09	9.89	10.88	0.060
6011107C	Ceilings	m^2	0.38	10.64	-	0.09	10.73	11.80	0.060
6011107D	Ceilings to stairwell	m^2	0.42	11.76	-	0.09	11.85	13.04	0.060
6011108	**Strip off two layers of vinyl paper, stop cracks and rub down**								
6011108A	Walls	m^2	0.35	9.80	-	0.09	9.89	10.88	0.060
6011108B	Walls to stairwell	m^2	0.38	10.64	-	0.09	10.73	11.80	0.060
6011108C	Ceilings	m^2	0.40	11.20	-	0.09	11.29	12.42	0.060
6011108D	Ceilings to stairwell	m^2	0.45	12.60	-	0.09	12.69	13.96	0.060
6011109	**Strip off two layers of embossed paper, stop cracks and rub down**								
6011109A	Walls	m^2	0.34	9.52	-	0.09	9.61	10.57	0.060
6011109B	Walls to stairwell	m^2	0.37	10.36	-	0.09	10.45	11.50	0.060
6011109C	Ceilings	m^2	0.42	11.76	-	0.09	11.85	13.04	0.060
6011109D	Ceilings to stairwell	m^2	0.45	12.60	-	0.09	12.69	13.96	0.060
6011110	**Strip off two layers of lincrusta or anaglypta paper, stop cracks and rub down**								
6011110A	Walls	m^2	0.38	10.64	-	0.09	10.73	11.80	0.060
6011110B	Walls to stairwell	m^2	0.42	11.76	-	0.09	11.85	13.04	0.060
6011110C	Ceilings	m^2	0.50	14.01	-	0.09	14.10	15.51	0.060
6011110D	Ceilings to stairwell	m^2	0.53	14.85	-	0.09	14.94	16.43	0.060

Small Works 2011		Unit	Labour Hours	Labour Net	Plant Net	Materials Net	Unit Net	Unit with 10%	CO₂
				£	£	£	£	£	Kg
601	**NEW WORK**								
60111	**PAPERHANGING**								
6011111	**Prepare and hang lining paper**								
6011111A	Walls	m²	0.25	7.00	-	0.55	7.55	8.31	0.310
6011111B	Walls to stairwell	m²	0.28	7.84	-	0.55	8.39	9.23	0.310
6011111C	Ceilings	m²	0.30	8.40	-	0.55	8.95	9.85	0.310
6011111D	Ceilings to stairwell	m²	0.32	8.96	-	0.55	9.51	10.46	0.310
6011112	**Prepare and hang woodchip paper**								
6011112A	Walls	m²	0.26	7.28	-	0.50	7.78	8.56	0.190
6011112B	Walls to stairwell	m²	0.29	8.12	-	0.50	8.62	9.48	0.190
6011112C	Ceilings	m²	0.31	8.68	-	0.50	9.18	10.10	0.190
6011112D	Ceilings to stairwell	m²	0.33	9.24	-	0.50	9.74	10.71	0.190
6011113	**Prepare and hang ready pasted paper**								
6011113A	Walls	m²	0.26	7.28	-	2.73	10.01	11.01	1.230
6011113B	Walls to stairwell	m²	0.29	8.12	-	2.73	10.85	11.94	1.230
6011113C	Ceilings	m²	0.31	8.68	-	2.73	11.41	12.55	1.230
6011113D	Ceilings to stairwell	m²	0.33	9.24	-	2.73	11.97	13.17	1.230
6011114	**Prepare and hang standard patterned paper**								
6011114A	Walls	m²	0.26	7.28	-	3.11	10.39	11.43	1.230
6011114B	Walls to stairwell	m²	0.29	8.12	-	3.11	11.23	12.35	1.230
6011114C	Ceilings	m²	0.31	8.68	-	3.11	11.79	12.97	1.230
6011114D	Ceilings to stairwell	m²	0.33	9.24	-	3.11	12.35	13.59	1.230
6011115	**Prepare and hang vinyl surface paper**								
6011115A	Walls	m²	0.26	7.28	-	2.98	10.26	11.29	1.230
6011115B	Walls to stairwell	m²	0.29	8.12	-	2.98	11.10	12.21	1.230
6011115C	Ceilings	m²	0.31	8.68	-	2.98	11.66	12.83	1.230
6011115D	Ceilings to stairwell	m²	0.33	9.24	-	2.98	12.22	13.44	1.230
6011116	**Prepare and hang anaglypta paper**								
6011116A	Walls	m²	0.27	7.56	-	1.13	8.69	9.56	1.230
6011116B	Walls to stairwell	m²	0.30	8.40	-	1.13	9.53	10.48	1.230
6011116C	Ceilings	m²	0.32	8.96	-	1.13	10.09	11.10	1.230
6011116D	Ceilings to stairwell	m²	0.33	9.24	-	1.13	10.37	11.41	1.230
6011117	**Prepare and hang flock paper**								
6011117A	Walls	m²	0.27	7.56	-	3.48	11.04	12.14	1.230
6011117B	Walls to stairwell	m²	0.30	8.40	-	3.48	11.88	13.07	1.230
6011117C	Ceilings	m²	0.32	8.96	-	3.48	12.44	13.68	1.230
6011117D	Ceilings to stairwell	m²	0.33	9.24	-	3.48	12.72	13.99	1.230
6011118	**Cut and hang standard border strip**								
6011118A	75 mm - 150 mm wide	m	0.09	2.52	-	0.20	2.72	2.99	1.240
60112	**POLISHING BY SPECIALIST**								
6011201	**Body in and polish**								
6011201A	General surfaces	m²	1.05	29.41	-	1.93	31.34	34.47	1.070
6011201B	General surfaces in narrow widths; not exceeding 150 mm	m	0.25	7.00	-	0.29	7.29	8.02	0.160
6011201C	General surfaces in narrow widths; 150 mm - 300 mm	m	0.40	11.20	-	0.58	11.78	12.96	0.320
6011202	**Seal and wax polish**								
6011202A	General surfaces	m²	0.45	12.60	-	1.06	13.66	15.03	0.850
6011202B	General surfaces in narrow widths; not exceeding 150 mm	m	0.11	3.08	-	0.16	3.24	3.56	0.130
6011202C	General surfaces in narrow widths; 150 mm - 300 mm	m	0.18	5.04	-	0.32	5.36	5.90	0.260
6011203	**Body in and wax polish**								
6011203A	General surfaces	m²	0.68	19.05	-	1.06	20.11	22.12	0.850
6011203B	General surfaces in narrow widths; not exceeding 150 mm	m	0.17	4.76	-	0.16	4.92	5.41	0.130
6011203C	General surfaces in narrow widths; 150 mm - 300 mm	m	0.27	7.56	-	0.32	7.88	8.67	0.260

Glazing, Painting and Decorating

	Unit	Labour Hours	Labour Net £	Plant Net £	Materials Net £	Unit Net £	Unit with 10% £	CO$_2$ Kg
601	**NEW WORK**							
60112	**POLISHING BY SPECIALIST**							
6011204	**Set and dry shine**							
6011204A	General surfaces	m^2	0.60	16.81	-	-	16.81	18.49	-
6011204B	General surfaces in narrow widths; not exceeding 150 mm	m	0.15	4.20	-	-	4.20	4.62	-
6011204C	General surfaces in narrow widths; 150 mm - 300 mm	m	0.20	5.60	-	-	5.60	6.16	
6011205	**Body in with polish and two coats yacht varnish**							
6011205A	General surfaces	m^2	1.11	31.09	-	2.14	33.23	36.55	1.490
6011205B	General surfaces in narrow widths; not exceeding 150 mm	m	0.26	7.28	-	0.32	7.60	8.36	0.220
6011205C	General surfaces in narrow widths; 150 mm - 300 mm	m	0.42	11.76	-	0.64	12.40	13.64	0.450
6011206	**Grain fill, body in and spirit off piano type finish**							
6011206A	General surfaces	m^2	2.75	77.03	-	2.55	79.58	87.54	2.050
6011206B	General surfaces in narrow widths; not exceeding 150 mm	m	0.65	18.21	-	0.36	18.57	20.43	0.300
6011206C	General surfaces in narrow widths; 150 mm - 300 mm	m	1.05	29.41	-	0.79	30.20	33.22	0.640
60113	**FIRE RETARDANT CLEAR FINISHES**							
6011301	**Quelfire**							
6011301A	Class 1	m^2	0.50	14.01	-	22.43	36.44	40.08	5.340
6011301B	Class O	m^2	0.65	18.21	-	28.71	46.92	51.61	6.840
6011302	**Nullifire**							
6011302A	Class 1	m^2	0.60	16.81	-	27.34	44.15	48.57	7.050
6011302B	Class O	m^2	0.70	19.61	-	33.14	52.75	58.03	8.540
6011303	**Albi**							
6011303A	Class 1	m^2	0.60	16.81	-	13.43	30.24	33.26	3.840
6011304	**Envirograf**							
6011304A	Class 0	m^2	0.60	16.81	-	23.90	40.71	44.78	5.770
6011304B	Class 1	m^2	0.45	12.60	-	18.59	31.19	34.31	4.490
60114	**LACQUERS AND POLYURETHANE BY SPECIALIST**							
6011401	**Prepare and seal**							
6011401A	General surfaces	m^2	0.24	6.72	-	1.64	8.36	9.20	0.700
6011401B	General surfaces in narrow widths; not exceeding 150 mm girth	m	0.06	1.68	-	0.26	1.94	2.13	0.120
6011401C	General surfaces in narrow widths; 150 mm - 300 mm girth	m	0.08	2.24	-	0.51	2.75	3.03	0.230
6011402	**Each additional coat of lacquer**							
6011402A	General surfaces	m^2	0.20	5.60	-	1.64	7.24	7.96	0.700
6011402B	General surfaces in narrow widths; not exceeding 150 mm girth	m	0.05	1.40	-	0.26	1.66	1.83	0.120
6011402C	General surfaces in narrow widths; 150 mm - 300 mm girth	m	0.07	1.96	-	0.51	2.47	2.72	0.230
6011403	**Wire wool and burnish with wax**							
6011403A	General surfaces	m^2	0.55	15.41	-	2.51	17.92	19.71	0.580
6011403B	General surfaces in narrow widths; not exceeding 150 mm girth	m	0.15	4.20	-	0.40	4.60	5.06	0.090
6011403C	General surfaces in narrow widths; 150 mm - 300 mm girth	m	0.20	5.60	-	0.78	6.38	7.02	0.180

Small Works 2011		Unit	Labour Hours	Labour Net	Plant Net	Materials Net	Unit Net	Unit with 10%	CO₂
				£	£	£	£	£	Kg
601	**NEW WORK**								
60115	**PREPARE EXISTING WORK BY SPECIALIST**								
6011501	**Wash down to degrease and repolish**								
6011501A	General surfaces	m²	0.60	16.81	-	2.51	19.32	21.25	0.580
6011501B	General surfaces in narrow widths; not exceeding 150 mm girth	m	0.15	4.20	-	0.40	4.60	5.06	0.090
6011501C	General surfaces in narrow widths; 150 mm - 300 mm girth	m	0.20	5.60	-	0.78	6.38	7.02	0.180
6011502	**Wash down, degrease and clean to revive**								
6011502A	General surfaces	m²	0.55	15.41	-	-	15.41	16.95	-
6011502B	General surfaces in narrow widths; not exceeding 150 mm girth	m	0.14	3.92	-	-	3.92	4.31	-
6011502C	General surfaces in narrow widths; 150 mm - 300 mm girth	m	0.18	5.04	-	-	5.04	5.54	-
6011503	**Wash down to degrease and rewax**								
6011503A	General surfaces	m²	0.46	12.88	-	2.13	15.01	16.51	0.450
6011503B	General surfaces in narrow widths; not exceeding 150 mm girth	m	0.12	3.36	-	0.32	3.68	4.05	0.070
6011503C	General surfaces in narrow widths; 150 mm - 300 mm girth	m	0.16	4.48	-	0.64	5.12	5.63	0.130
6011504	**Strip off chemically, standard bleach and neutralise**								
6011504A	General surfaces	m²	0.75	21.01	-	2.96	23.97	26.37	1.200
6011504B	General surfaces in narrow widths; not exceeding 150 mm girth	m	0.19	5.32	-	0.44	5.76	6.34	0.180
6011504C	General surfaces in narrow widths; 150 mm - 300 mm girth	m	0.23	6.44	-	0.89	7.33	8.06	0.360

Small Works 2011	Unit	Labour Hours	Labour Net	Plant Net	Materials Net	Unit Net	Unit with 10%	CO₂
			£	£	£	£	£	Kg
602	**REPAIRS AND ALTERATIONS**							
60201	**GLAZING**							
6020101	**Hack out**							
6020101A	broken glass other than plate	m²	2.34	65.54	-	-	65.54	72.09	-
6020101B	plate glass	m²	3.55	99.44	-	-	99.44	109.38	-
6020102	**Carefully take out**							
6020102A	all types of glass other than plate and set aside for re-use	m²	3.23	90.47	-	-	90.47	99.52	-
6020102B	plate glass and set aside for re-use	m²	4.68	131.09	-	-	131.09	144.20	-
6020103	**Remove old putty**							
6020103A	paint rebate one coat oil colour ready to receive new glass	m	0.16	4.48	-	0.40	4.88	5.37	0.230
6020104	**Glaze, sprig and putty to wood**							
6020104A	sashes; average 0.40 sq.m 3 mm sheet	m²	1.10	30.81	-	44.66	75.47	83.02	12.420
6020104B	sashes; average 0.40 sq.m obscured	m²	1.10	30.81	-	50.54	81.35	89.49	20.860
6020104C	sashes; average 0.40 sq.m wired cast	m²	1.20	33.61	-	43.33	76.94	84.63	20.860
6020105	**Glaze, putty and sprig to metal**							
6020105A	sashes extra over foregoing	m²	0.40	11.20	-	-	11.20	12.32	-
6020106	**Wired cast glass in rooflights**							
6020106A	panes up to 0.70 sq.m	m²	0.90	25.21	-	43.33	68.54	75.39	20.860
6020106B	panes exceeding 0.70 sq.m	m²	1.00	28.01	-	43.33	71.34	78.47	20.860
6020107	**S.G. quality float glass**							
6020107A	6 mm	m²	3.50	98.04	-	79.25	177.29	195.02	29.340
6020108	**Bed edge of glass**							
6020108A	in chamois leather	m	0.23	6.44	-	0.65	7.09	7.80	3.220
6020108B	in velvet	m	0.17	4.76	-	0.84	5.60	6.16	4.020
6020109	**Remove temporary coverings to sashes**							
6020109A	stopping up nail holes etc.	m²	1.10	30.81	-	-	30.81	33.89	-
60202	**INTERNAL DECORATING**							
6020201	**Brush down and apply two coats lime white on brick walls, plaster walls and ceilings**							
6020201A	new work	m²	0.33	9.24	-	0.15	9.39	10.33	0.470
6020201B	old work	m²	0.38	10.64	-	0.15	10.79	11.87	0.470
6020202	**Brush down and apply two coats emulsion to plaster**							
6020202A	new work	m²	0.46	12.88	-	1.59	14.47	15.92	0.770
6020202B	old work	m²	0.51	14.29	-	1.59	15.88	17.47	0.770
6020203	**Brush down and apply two coats emulsion paint on brick walls**							
6020203A	new work	m²	0.58	16.25	-	2.97	19.22	21.14	1.430
6020203B	old work	m²	0.63	17.65	-	2.97	20.62	22.68	1.430
6020204	**Wash down plaster surfaces, fill cracks nail holes etc with filler**							
6020204A	bring forward for new decoration	m²	0.20	5.60	-	0.38	5.98	6.58	0.240
6020205	**Prepare and apply oil colour on plaster ceilings**							
6020205A	one coat	m²	0.27	7.56	-	0.87	8.43	9.27	0.380
6020205B	two coats	m²	0.55	15.41	-	1.73	17.14	18.85	0.770
6020206	**Prepare and apply oil colour on walls**							
6020206A	plaster walls; one coat	m²	0.21	5.88	-	0.87	6.75	7.43	0.380
6020206B	plaster walls; two coats	m²	0.43	12.04	-	1.73	13.77	15.15	0.770
6020206C	brick walls; one coat	m²	0.27	7.56	-	1.73	9.29	10.22	0.770

Small Works 2011		Unit	Labour Hours	Labour Net	Plant Net	Materials Net	Unit Net	Unit with 10%	CO$_2$
				£	£	£	£	£	Kg
602	**REPAIRS AND ALTERATIONS**								
60202	**INTERNAL DECORATING**								
6020206	**Prepare and apply oil colour on walls**								
6020206D	brick walls; two coats	m^2	0.54	15.13	-	3.46	18.59	20.45	1.540
6020207	**Wash down, touch up and two coats oil**								
6020207A	general surfaces of wood	m^2	0.65	18.21	-	0.92	19.13	21.04	0.530
6020207B	add for each extra coat applied or deduct for one coat	m^2	0.24	6.72	-	0.48	7.20	7.92	0.280
6020207C	general surfaces of windows frames and sashes (measured over glass)	m^2	1.00	28.01	-	1.39	29.40	32.34	0.810
6020207D	add for each extra coat applied or deduct for one coat	m^2	0.40	11.20	-	0.70	11.90	13.09	0.410
6020207E	on surfaces exceeding 150 mm girth	m	0.14	3.92	-	0.18	4.10	4.51	0.110
6020207F	on surfaces 150 mm - 300 mm girth	m	0.24	6.72	-	0.40	7.12	7.83	0.230
6020207G	add for each extra coat applied or deduct for one coat, not exceeding 150 mm girth	m	0.07	1.96	-	0.11	2.07	2.28	0.060
6020207H	add for extra coat applied or deduct for one coat, 150 mm - 300 mm girth	m	0.11	3.08	-	0.18	3.26	3.59	0.110
6020208	**Clean down and apply two coats oil colour to metal frames and sashes, bring forward bare patches**								
6020208A	measured over glass	m^2	1.11	31.09	-	1.39	32.48	35.73	0.810
6020208B	general surfaces over 300 mm girth	m^2	0.69	19.33	-	1.32	20.65	22.72	0.770
6020208C	general surfaces not exceeding 150 m girth	m	0.30	8.40	-	0.37	8.77	9.65	0.210
6020208D	general surfaces 150 mm - 300 mm girth	m	0.39	10.92	-	0.70	11.62	12.78	0.410
6020209	**Clean down and one coat gloss oil paint**								
6020209A	to fireplace jambs, stoves, mantel registers and the like	Each	1.00	28.01	-	1.15	29.16	32.08	0.580
6020210	**Prepare and two coats oil paint**								
6020210A	to water waste preventer and backboard	Each	0.55	15.41	-	0.40	15.81	17.39	0.230
6020210B	add to last if including overflow pipes	Each	0.45	12.60	-	0.26	12.86	14.15	0.150
6020211	**Clean and apply one coat gloss paint**								
6020211A	on casement stays, fasteners, bolts, rimlocks and sundry fittings	Each	0.20	5.60	-	0.13	5.73	6.30	0.060
6020212	**Prepare and repolish existing wood surfaces**								
6020212A	general surfaces	m^2	2.10	58.82	-	0.64	59.46	65.41	0.140
6020212B	handrails	m	0.60	16.81	-	0.25	17.06	18.77	0.050
6020213	**Strip, body in and repolish wood surfaces**								
6020213A	general surfaces	m^2	4.70	131.65	-	0.88	132.53	145.78	0.180
6020213B	handrails	m	1.10	30.81	-	0.26	31.07	34.18	0.050
6020214	**Prepare and wax polish floors**								
6020214A	general surfaces	m^2	0.50	14.01	-	0.70	14.71	16.18	0.150
6020216	**Strip paper from walls or ceilings**								
6020216A	stop, size ready for new paper; first layer	m^2	0.30	8.40	-	0.20	8.60	9.46	0.510
6020216B	add for each extra layer stripped	m^2	0.12	3.36	-	-	3.36	3.70	-
6020217	**Strip varnished paper from walls or ceilings**								
6020217A	stop, size ready for new paper; first layer	m^2	0.60	16.81	-	0.20	17.01	18.71	0.510

Glazing, Painting and Decorating

Small Works 2011		Unit	Labour Hours	Labour Net	Plant Net	Materials Net	Unit Net	Unit with 10%	CO₂
				£	£	£	£	£	Kg
602	**REPAIRS AND ALTERATIONS**								
60202	**INTERNAL DECORATING**								
6020217	**Strip varnished paper from walls or ceilings**								
6020217B	add for each extra layer stripped	m²	0.22	6.16	-	-	6.16	6.78	-
6020218	**Cut, trim and hang paper to walls**								
6020218A	woodchip	m²	0.26	7.28	-	0.63	7.91	8.70	0.210
6020218B	standard	m²	0.26	7.28	-	3.24	10.52	11.57	1.260
6020219	**Cut, trim and hang paper to ceilings**								
6020219A	lining	m²	0.30	8.40	-	0.69	9.09	10.00	0.330
60203	**EXTERNAL DECORATING**								
6020301	**Wash down and apply two coats of masonry paint on**								
6020301A	rendered walls	m²	0.53	14.85	-	1.78	16.63	18.29	1.410
6020302	**Wash down and apply two coats Sandtex Matt masonry paint on**								
6020302A	rendered walls	m²	0.54	15.13	-	2.34	17.47	19.22	1.410
6020303	**Wash down and apply two coats Snowcem masonry paint on**								
6020303A	rendered walls	m²	0.42	11.76	-	1.05	12.81	14.09	2.030
6020305	**Wash down, touch up and two coats oil**								
6020305A	General surfaces wood	m²	0.68	19.05	-	1.32	20.37	22.41	0.770
6020305B	Add for each extra coat applied	m²	0.27	7.56	-	0.66	8.22	9.04	0.380
6020305C	Window frames and sashes (over glass)	m²	1.21	33.89	-	1.39	35.28	38.81	0.810
6020305D	Add for each extra coat applied	m²	0.43	12.04	-	0.70	12.74	14.01	0.410
6020306	**Burn off paint to woodwork general surfaces;**								
6020306A	and prepare for priming	m²	0.80	22.41	-	-	22.41	24.65	-
6020307	**Strip paint to wood with paint remover**								
6020307A	and prepare for priming	m²	0.50	14.01	-	0.17	14.18	15.60	0.070
6020308	**Prime and two coats oil paint to putties**								
6020308A	after reglazing	m	0.18	5.04	-	0.13	5.17	5.69	0.060
6020313	**Clean down wire brush metal surfaces an bring forward bare patches and apply oil colour on previously painted surfaces;**								
6020313A	general surfaces; over 300 mm girth	m²	0.78	21.85	-	0.99	22.84	25.12	0.580
6020313B	general surfaces; not exceeding 150 mm girth	m	0.39	10.92	-	0.29	11.21	12.33	0.170
6020313C	general surfaces 150 mm - 300 mm girth	m	0.51	14.29	-	0.62	14.91	16.40	0.360
6020313D	corrugated iron surfaces; (measured flat)	m²	0.87	24.37	-	1.10	25.47	28.02	0.640
6020313E	structural steelwork	m²	0.96	26.89	-	0.99	27.88	30.67	0.580
6020313G	railings, balustrades; (measured flat overall)	m²	0.87	24.37	-	0.84	25.21	27.73	0.490
6020313I	stairs; (measured overall)	m²	0.84	23.53	-	0.70	24.23	26.65	0.410
6020313J	windows, glazed doors in small panes	m²	1.98	55.46	-	0.70	56.16	61.78	0.410
6020313K	windows, glazed doors in medium panes	m²	1.74	48.74	-	0.62	49.36	54.30	0.360
6020313L	windows, glazed doors in large panes	m²	1.50	42.02	-	0.55	42.57	46.83	0.320
6020313M	eaves gutters (inside and outside)	m	0.51	14.29	-	0.37	14.66	16.13	0.210
6020313N	rainwater pipes, soil pipes etc	m	0.51	14.29	-	0.15	14.44	15.88	0.090

Small Works 2011		Unit	Labour Hours	Labour Net	Plant Net	Materials Net	Unit Net	Unit with 10%	CO_2
				£	£	£	£	£	Kg
602	**REPAIRS AND ALTERATIONS**								
60203	**EXTERNAL DECORATING**								
6020313	**Clean down wire brush metal surfaces an bring forward bare patches and apply oil colour on previously painted surfaces;**								
6020313O	pipes, bars, straps, etc up to 150 mm girth	m	0.45	12.60	-	0.15	12.75	14.03	0.090
60204	**WOOD PRESERVATIVES**								
6020401	**Two coats timber preserver**								
6020401A	sawn surfaces	m²	0.40	11.20	-	1.14	12.34	13.57	1.620
6020401B	wrought surfaces	m²	0.38	10.64	-	0.89	11.53	12.68	1.260
6020402	**Two coats Cuprinol clear preserver**								
6020402A	sawn surfaces	m²	0.40	11.20	-	1.60	12.80	14.08	1.130
6020402B	wrought surfaces	m²	0.38	10.64	-	1.27	11.91	13.10	0.900
6020403	**Two coats Solignum**								
6020403A	sawn surfaces	m²	0.38	10.64	-	1.92	12.56	13.82	1.120
6020403B	wrought surfaces	m²	0.36	10.08	-	1.52	11.60	12.76	0.890

Masonry

Masonry

	Unit	Labour Hours	Labour Net £	Plant Net £	Materials Net £	Unit Net £	Unit with 10% £	CO₂ Kg

		Labour Hours	Labour Net £	Plant Net £	Materials Net £	Unit Net £	Unit with 10% £	CO₂ Kg
701	**NEW WORK**							
70101	**RECONSTRUCTED STONE BY SPECIALIST**							
7010101	**Plain cladding**							
7010101A	50 mm	m²	2.26	109.95	-	123.32	233.27	256.60	11.450
7010101B	75 mm	m²	2.51	122.16	-	34.50	156.66	172.33	16.850
7010102	**Plain face ashlar**							
7010102A	100 mm	m²	2.76	134.37	-	41.88	176.25	193.88	22.580
7010103	**Plain string**							
7010103A	100 mm x 300 mm	m	0.75	36.49	-	41.88	78.37	86.21	8.360
7010104	**Plain cills, jambs and heads**							
7010104A	150 mm x 75 mm	m	0.55	26.76	-	16.30	43.06	47.37	4.540
7010104B	200 mm x 75 mm	m	0.60	29.19	-	23.67	52.86	58.15	3.370
7010104C	280 mm x 100 mm	m	0.85	41.35	-	38.34	79.69	87.66	6.010
7010105	**Coping**							
7010105A	300 mm x 75 mm	m	0.85	41.35	-	30.83	72.18	79.40	4.900
7010105B	325 mm x 100 mm	m	1.20	58.38	-	44.48	102.86	113.15	6.930
7010105C	400 mm x 125 mm	m	1.70	82.70	-	68.35	151.05	166.16	10.480
7010106	**Chimney cap; weathered and throated all round**							
7010106A	940 mm x 600 mm x 100 mm holed for two 225 mm x 225 mm flues	Each	2.25	109.46	-	126.94	236.40	260.04	11.560
7010107	**Pier cap; weathered and throated all round**							
7010107A	525 mm x 100 mm	Each	0.60	29.19	-	61.85	91.04	100.14	5.660
7010108	**Boot lintel**							
7010108A	325 mm x 150 mm consisting of 225 mm x 100 mm reinforced concrete main section with 100 mm x 75 mm projecting toe in reconstructed stone	m	1.25	60.81	-	47.88	108.69	119.56	10.230
70102	**SOFT STONE BY SPECIALIST**							
7010201	**Cut out to a depth of approximately 25 mm, properly key, dowel and reinforce as necessary with non-ferrous metal and make good in plastic artificial stone to match existing**							
7010201A	ashlar	m²	9.75	474.34	-	217.18	691.52	760.67	105.060
7010201B	moulding 75 mm girth	m	3.25	158.11	-	50.64	208.75	229.63	27.170
7010201C	moulding 75 mm girth increasing per 25 mm of girth	m	0.60	29.19	-	44.75	73.94	81.33	54.690
7010201D	plain or weathered coping, 300 mm wide	m	4.40	214.06	-	69.75	283.81	312.19	33.260
7010201E	plain or weathered coping 300 mm wide increasing per 25 mm of width	m	1.25	60.81	-	8.00	68.81	75.69	3.790
7010201F	tracery	m²	18.00	875.70	-	238.56	1,114.26	1,225.69	114.620
7010201G	mullion front from glazing, 150 mm wide	m	4.75	231.09	-	69.75	300.84	330.92	33.260
7010201H	circular labels or hoods to 225 mm girth	m	6.60	321.09	-	104.68	425.77	468.35	49.920
7010201I	circular columns, plain	m	10.00	486.50	-	229.26	715.76	787.34	111.740
7010201J	circular columns, fluted	m	18.00	875.70	-	229.26	1,104.96	1,215.46	111.740
7010201K	stooling to jambs or mullions, moulded	Each	2.65	128.92	-	24.87	153.79	169.17	11.960
7010201L	stooling to jambs or mullions, plain	Each	1.40	68.11	-	24.36	92.47	101.72	11.680

Small Works 2011		Unit	Labour Hours	Labour Net £	Plant Net £	Materials Net £	Unit Net £	Unit with 10% £	CO$_2$ Kg
701	**NEW WORK**								
70103	**PORTLAND STONE BY SPECIALIST**								
7010301	**Cut out to a depth of approximately 25 mm, properly key, dowel and reinforce as necessary with non-ferrous metal and make good in plastic artificial stone to match existing**								
7010301A	ashlar	m^2	12.50	608.13	-	217.18	825.31	907.84	105.060
7010301B	moulding 75 mm girth	m	4.15	201.90	-	50.64	252.54	277.79	27.170
7010301C	moulding 75 mm girth increasing per 25 mm of girth	m	0.83	40.38	-	46.43	86.81	95.49	55.300
7010301D	plain or weathered coping 300 mm wide	m	5.50	267.57	-	69.75	337.32	371.05	33.260
7010301E	plain or weathered coping 300 mm wide per 25 mm of width	m	1.50	72.97	-	8.00	80.97	89.07	3.790
7010301F	tracery	m^2	22.25	1,082.46	-	238.56	1,321.02	1,453.12	114.620
7010301G	mullion front from glazing, 150 mm wide	m	5.95	289.47	-	69.75	359.22	395.14	33.260
7010301H	circular labels or hoods to 225 mm girth	m	8.25	401.36	-	104.68	506.04	556.64	49.920
7010301I	circular columns, plain	m	12.85	625.15	-	229.26	854.41	939.85	111.740
7010301J	circular columns, fluted	m	22.50	1,094.63	-	229.26	1,323.89	1,456.28	111.740
7010301K	stooling to jambs or mullions, moulded	Each	3.35	162.98	-	24.87	187.85	206.64	11.960
7010301L	stooling to jambs or mullions, plain	Each	1.75	85.14	-	24.87	110.01	121.01	11.960
70104	**YORK STONE BY SPECIALIST**								
7010401	**Cut out to a depth of approximately 25 mm, properly key, dowel and reinforce as necessary with non-ferrous metal and make good in plastic artificial stone to match existing**								
7010401A	ashlar	m^2	13.75	668.94	-	217.18	886.12	974.73	105.060
7010401B	moulding 75 mm girth	m	4.65	226.22	-	50.64	276.86	304.55	27.170
7010401C	moulding 75 mm girth increasing per 25 mm of girth	m	1.00	48.65	-	46.43	95.08	104.59	55.300
7010401D	plain or weathered coping 300 mm wide	m	6.20	301.63	-	69.75	371.38	408.52	33.260
7010401E	plain or weathered coping 300 mm wide increasing per 25 mm of width	m	1.70	82.70	-	8.00	90.70	99.77	3.790
7010401F	tracery	m^2	25.00	1,216.25	-	238.56	1,454.81	1,600.29	114.620
7010401G	mullion front from glazing, 150 mm wide	m	6.65	323.52	-	69.75	393.27	432.60	33.260
7010401H	circular labels or hoods to 225 mm girth	m	9.25	450.01	-	104.68	554.69	610.16	49.920
7010401I	circular columns, plain	m	14.50	705.42	-	229.26	934.68	1,028.15	111.740
7010401J	circular columns, fluted	m	25.00	1,216.25	-	229.26	1,445.51	1,590.06	111.740
7010401K	stooling to jambs or mullions, moulded	Each	3.65	177.57	-	24.87	202.44	222.68	11.960
7010401L	stooling to jambs or mullions, plain	Each	1.95	94.87	-	24.87	119.74	131.71	11.960
70105	**CLEANING STONEWORK OR BRICKWORK BY SPECIALIST**								
7010501	**Cleaning by nebulous cold water**								
7010501A	spray process assisted by suitable graded brushes	m^2	0.43	20.68	17.63	-	38.31	42.14	20.730
7010502	**Dry cleaning**								
7010502A	by the use of silica free abrasive grit under regulated air pressure	m^2	0.37	17.76	15.14	0.41	33.31	36.64	17.880
7010502B	by the use of spinning carborundum pads	m^2	0.65	31.62	11.06	-	42.68	46.95	3.630
7010503	**Cleaning by chemicals**								
7010503A	and high pressure water process	m^2	0.16	7.78	6.64	0.18	14.60	16.06	7.910

Masonry

	Unit	Labour Hours	Labour Net £	Plant Net £	Materials Net £	Unit Net £	Unit with 10% £	CO₂ Kg
701	**NEW WORK**							
70106	**REPOINTING BY SPECIALIST**							
7010601	**Rake out and repoint**							
7010601A	rubble walling	m²	0.67	51.30	-	1.70	53.00	58.30	3.400
7010601B	flint walling	m²	2.26	173.08	-	2.84	175.92	193.51	5.660
7010601C	ashlar walling	m²	0.50	38.45	-	0.99	39.44	43.38	1.980
70107	**STONE FIXING BY SPECIALIST**							
7010701	**Labours on stonework**							
7010701A	fixing only natural or reconstructed stonework	m³	40.25	3,076.73	-	3.55	3,080.28	3,388.31	7.080
7010701B	cutting out and piecing into existing work	m³	125.77	9,614.81	-	1.70	9,616.51	10,578.16	3.400
7010701C	fixing only rubble walling average 125 mm thick faced one side only	m²	4.11	314.13	-	1.84	315.97	347.57	3.680
7010701D	fixing only flint walling	m²	9.64	737.13	-	1.84	738.97	812.87	3.680
7010701E	laying paving stones	m²	1.21	92.28	-	0.71	92.99	102.29	1.420
70110	**BRADSTONE CAST STONEWORK**							
7011001	**Walling blocks 100 mm thick in Cotswold limestone colour in gauged mortar 1:1:6 flush pointed on exposed faces as the work proceeds; walls and skins of hollow walls**							
7011001A	tooled finish	m²	1.38	105.12	-	46.04	151.16	166.28	21.520
7011001B	rough hewn finish	m²	1.38	105.12	-	46.95	152.07	167.28	21.590
7011001C	squared course rubble finish	m²	1.38	105.12	-	47.40	152.52	167.77	21.780
7011001D	masonry finish	m²	1.38	105.12	-	46.95	152.07	167.28	21.590
7011002	**Extra for quoin blocks**							
7011002A	masonry finish	m	0.55	42.35	-	67.81	110.16	121.18	16.590
7011002B	tooled finish	m	0.55	42.35	-	67.81	110.16	121.18	16.590
7011003	**Fair returns 100 mm wide**							
7011003A	masonry finish; masonry ends	m	0.18	13.38	-	-	13.38	14.72	-
7011003B	masonry finish; dressed ends	m	0.18	13.38	-	3.53	16.91	18.60	1.550
7011003C	squared course rubble finish	m	0.35	26.68	-	-	26.68	29.35	-
7011003D	rough hewn finish	m	0.38	28.97	-	-	28.97	31.87	-
7011004	**Lintel dressings in Cotswold limestone colour; bedded, jointed and pointed in cement mortar (1:6); in stock lengths**							
7011004A	102 mm x 152 mm; 762 mm - 1219 mm	m	0.27	20.57	-	13.21	33.78	37.16	3.600
7011004B	102 mm x 152 mm; 1373 mm - 1676 mm	m	0.34	25.61	-	18.43	44.04	48.44	5.030
7011004C	102 mm x 152 mm; 1829 mm - 1981 mm	m	0.47	35.93	-	22.03	57.96	63.76	6.000
7011004D	102 mm x 229 mm; 914 mm - 1524 mm	m	0.40	30.73	-	20.76	51.49	56.64	6.890
7011004E	102 mm x 229 mm; 1676 mm - 1981 mm	m	0.47	35.93	-	34.32	70.25	77.28	9.040
7011004F	102 mm x 229 mm; 2134 mm - 2438 mm	m	0.54	41.05	-	46.57	87.62	96.38	11.080
7011004G	102 mm x 229 mm; 2591 mm - 2896 mm	m	0.60	46.18	-	54.59	100.77	110.85	13.110
7011005	**Cill dressings including stooling in Cotswold limestone colour; bedded, jointed and pointed in cement mortar 1:6; in stock lengths**							
7011005A	197 mm x 67 mm; 673 mm - 2623 mm	m	0.20	15.37	-	22.69	38.06	41.87	7.550
7011006	**Coping dressings in Cotswold limestone colour; bedded, jointed and pointed in cement mortar 1:6**							
7011006A	178 mm x 64 mm x 38 mm; twice weathered and rebated	m	0.13	10.24	-	13.41	23.65	26.02	3.050

Small Works 2011		Unit	Labour Hours	Labour Net	Plant Net	Materials Net	Unit Net	Unit with 10%	CO₂
				£	£	£	£	£	Kg
701	**NEW WORK**								
70110	**BRADSTONE CAST STONEWORK**								
7011006	**Coping dressings in Cotswold limestone colour; bedded, jointed and pointed in cement mortar 1:6**								
7011006B	191 mm x 76 mm x 63 mm; once weathered	m	0.17	12.84	-	14.10	26.94	29.63	4.070
7011006C	305 mm x 76 mm x 51 mm; twice weathered	m	0.24	17.97	-	22.65	40.62	44.68	5.330
7011007	**Traditional window surround components for non-standard windows**								
7011007A	146 mm x 143 mm; head	m	0.27	20.57	-	32.96	53.53	58.88	5.730
7011007B	146 mm x 143 mm; continuous jamb	m	0.27	20.57	-	35.43	56.00	61.60	5.730
7011007C	146 mm x 143 mm; cill	m	0.27	20.57	-	32.62	53.19	58.51	5.730
7011007D	146 mm x 108 mm; mullion	m	0.27	20.57	-	45.84	66.41	73.05	4.740
7011007E	162 mm x 102 mm; label mould	m	0.27	20.57	-	30.04	50.61	55.67	4.880
7011007F	162 mm x 102 mm; kneeler	Each	0.10	7.72	-	17.36	25.08	27.59	4.880
7011008	**Traditional door surround; continuous jambs; to suit 839 mm x 1982 mm door in 102 mm x 63 mm frame**								
7011008A	without label mould	Each	1.01	76.91	-	441.85	518.76	570.64	12.900
7011008B	with label mould	Each	1.11	84.63	-	450.03	534.66	588.13	12.900
70112	**NATURAL STONE RUBBLE WORK**								
7011201	**Random walling in Yorkshire limestone (PC £330 per m³); in mortar; unfaced; average thickness**								
7011201A	300 mm	m²	1.17	89.75	-	120.27	210.02	231.02	75.320
7011201B	450 mm	m²	1.76	134.63	-	181.22	315.85	347.44	114.910
7011201C	600 mm	m²	2.35	179.50	-	240.54	420.04	462.04	150.640
7011201D	Extra for one fair face	m²	0.34	25.61	-	-	25.61	28.17	-
7011201E	Extra for two fair faces	m²	0.64	48.70	-	-	48.70	53.57	-
7011202	**Square rubble walling in Yorkshire limestone (PC £330 per m³); average thickness**								
7011202A	300 mm	m²	1.68	128.21	-	118.91	247.12	271.83	72.090
7011202B	450 mm	m²	2.55	194.87	-	178.23	373.10	410.41	107.810
7011202C	600 mm	m²	3.35	256.41	-	237.69	494.10	543.51	143.860
7011202D	Extra for one fair face	m²	0.34	25.61	-	-	25.61	28.17	-
7011202E	Extra for two fair faces	m²	0.64	48.70	-	-	48.70	53.57	-
70120	**NATURAL FLINTWORK**								
7012010	**Random flintwork; in cement/lime mortar (1:2:9); face pointed one side; to backing blockwork (measured separately); thickness**								
7012010A	100 mm	m²	0.92	70.49	-	47.09	117.58	129.34	44.160
7012010B	215 mm	m²	1.76	134.63	-	85.73	220.36	242.40	71.730

Masonry

Small Works 2011	Unit	Labour Hours	Labour Net £	Plant Net £	Materials Net £	Unit Net £	Unit with 10% £	CO₂ Kg
702	**REPAIRS AND ALTERATIONS**							
70201	**LABOURS**							
7020101	**Take down masonry, clean and set aside**							
7020101A	ashlar walling	m²	1.01	76.91	-	-	76.91	84.60	-
7020101B	cornices etc.	m	0.40	30.73	-	-	30.73	33.80	-
7020101C	arches	Each	0.27	20.57	-	-	20.57	22.63	-
7020101D	steps, cills etc.	m	0.50	38.45	-	-	38.45	42.30	-
7020102	**Take down masonry, clean and reset**							
7020102A	ashlar walling	m²	2.60	198.69	-	12.22	210.91	232.00	29.050
7020102B	cornices etc.	m	1.11	84.63	-	2.85	87.48	96.23	6.780
7020102C	arches	Each	0.74	56.42	-	5.03	61.45	67.60	11.940
7020102D	steps, cills etc.	m	0.67	51.30	-	3.67	54.97	60.47	8.710
7020103	**Cut out decayed Portland (or similar) stone in**							
7020103A	facings of wall built in lime mortar in adjacent stones. Prepare for and supply and fix new stones, average 50 mm thick, point and clean down on completion	m²	1.01	76.91	-	148.83	225.74	248.31	18.950
7020103B	facings of wall built in lime mortar in separate stones. Prepare for and supply and fix new stones, average 50 mm thick, point and clean down on completion.	m²	1.21	92.28	-	156.03	248.31	273.14	36.060
7020104	**Rake out joints of**							
7020104A	ashlar stonework and repoint	m²	0.47	35.93	-	0.95	36.88	40.57	2.260
7020104B	squared rubble and repoint	m²	0.54	41.05	-	0.95	42.00	46.20	2.260
7020105	**Redress face of walling where decayed**							
7020105A	with picked face and repoint	m²	2.68	205.12	-	0.54	205.66	226.23	1.290
7020106	**Take up and reset 50 mm thick Yorkstone slabs, any size, in landings, hearths, cover stones, pavings etc in**							
7020106A	lime mortar	m²	0.67	51.30	-	3.67	54.97	60.47	8.710
7020106B	cement mortar	m²	0.81	61.54	-	3.33	64.87	71.36	11.390
7020107	**Cut and form toothing in old masonry for**							
7020107A	new brick or stone	m²	0.67	51.30	-	-	51.30	56.43	-
7020108	**Take down and reset blocking courses, cornices, strings, plinths, apexes, kneelers etc in**							
7020108A	lime mortar	m	0.40	30.73	-	0.54	31.27	34.40	1.290
7020108B	cement mortar	m	0.47	35.93	-	0.49	36.42	40.06	1.690
7020109	**Take down and reset window cills, steps etc including cutting away and making good**							
7020109A	lime mortar	m	0.67	51.30	-	0.27	51.57	56.73	0.650
7020109B	cement mortar	m	0.74	56.42	-	0.25	56.67	62.34	0.840
7020110	**Repair with granite chippings concrete, including cutting out to a depth of at least 19 mm, finish concrete fair and flush with original surface**							
7020110A	treads	m²	0.87	66.66	-	6.88	73.54	80.89	14.450
7020110B	landing	m²	0.54	41.05	-	6.88	47.93	52.72	14.450

Roofing

FROM INCEPTION TO COMPLETION AND BEYOND

At Franklin + Andrews we provide contract and business advisory services dedicated to the construction industry. Today there is a broader than ever range of procurement options matched by an equally wide range of standard form contracts. The complexity of the procurement choices and the sophistication of today's projects, makes specialist contract, procurement and dispute management advice invaluable.

Our aim is to help our clients maximise, through the contract, the efficiency and bottom line performance of their business. This is achieved through the provision of proactive, pragmatic, innovative and value for money advice on all matters relating to the construction process.

For more information please contact Steve Jackson:
T   +44 (0)20 7633 9966
E   contractadvisory@franklinandrews.com

Franklin + Andrews is part of the Mott MacDonald Group

Franklin+Andrews

www.franklinandrews.com

Small Works 2011		Unit	Labour Hours	Labour Net	Plant Net	Materials Net	Unit Net	Unit with 10%	CO$_2$
				£	£	£	£	£	Kg
801	**SLATE ROOFING**								
80101	**WELSH SLATES**								
8010101	**Welsh slates; size 610 mm x 305 mm; 75 mm lap; 50 x 25 mm treated sawn softwood battens; reinforced slaters underlining felt type 1F**								
8010101A	sloping	m^2	0.12	8.94	-	95.28	104.22	114.64	8.570
8010101B	vertical or mansard	m^2	0.19	14.14	-	95.28	109.42	120.36	8.570
8010101C	Extra for double eaves course	m	0.13	10.24	-	12.96	23.20	25.52	0.270
8010101D	Extra for mitred hips; both sides measured	m	0.81	61.54	-	19.44	80.98	89.08	0.400
8010101E	Extra for cutting to valleys; both sides measured	m	0.49	37.15	-	12.96	50.11	55.12	0.270
8010101F	hole for small pipe	Each	0.20	15.37	-	-	15.37	16.91	-
8010101G	hole for large pipe	Each	0.27	20.49	-	-	20.49	22.54	-
8010101H	fix only lead soakers	Each	0.02	1.30	-	-	1.30	1.43	-
8010101I	fix only hip irons	Each	0.08	6.42	-	-	6.42	7.06	-
8010102	**Welsh slates; size 510 mm x 255 mm; 75 mm lap; 50 mm x 25 mm treated sawn softwood battens; reinforced slaters underlining felt type 1F**								
8010102A	sloping	m^2	0.17	12.84	-	75.36	88.20	97.02	9.000
8010102B	vertical or mansard	m^2	0.27	20.49	-	75.36	95.85	105.44	9.000
8010102C	Extra for double eaves course	m	0.15	11.54	-	7.02	18.56	20.42	0.190
8010102D	Extra for mitred hips; both sides measured	m	0.91	69.26	-	10.53	79.79	87.77	0.280
8010102E	Extra for cutting to valleys; both sides measured	m	0.59	44.88	-	9.82	54.70	60.17	0.240
8010102F	hole for small pipe	Each	0.20	15.37	-	-	15.37	16.91	-
8010102G	hole for large pipe	Each	0.27	20.49	-	-	20.49	22.54	-
8010102H	fix only lead soakers	Each	0.02	1.30	-	-	1.30	1.43	-
8010102I	fix only hip irons	Each	0.08	6.42	-	-	6.42	7.06	-
8010103	**Welsh slates; size 405 mm x 205 mm; 75 mm lap; 50 mm x 25 mm treated sawn softwood battens; reinforced slaters underlining felt type 1F**								
8010103A	sloping	m^2	0.29	21.79	-	87.02	108.81	119.69	9.710
8010103B	vertical or mansard	m^2	0.42	32.03	-	87.02	119.05	130.96	9.710
8010103C	Extra for double eaves course	m	0.20	15.37	-	7.36	22.73	25.00	0.180
8010103D	Extra for mitred hips; both sides measured	m	1.17	89.75	-	9.82	99.57	109.53	0.240
8010103E	Extra for cutting to valleys; both sides measured	m	0.67	51.30	-	7.36	58.66	64.53	0.180
8010103F	hole for small pipe	Each	0.20	15.37	-	-	15.37	16.91	-
8010103G	hole for large pipe	Each	0.27	20.49	-	-	20.49	22.54	-
8010103H	fix only lead soakers	Each	0.02	1.30	-	-	1.30	1.43	-
8010103I	fix only hip irons	Each	0.08	6.42	-	-	6.42	7.06	-
80102	**ARTIFICIAL SLATES**								
8010201	**Asbestos-free artificial slates; blue / black; Eternit 2000 or the like; size 600 mm x 300 mm; 75 mm lap; 50 mm x 25 mm treated sawn softwood battens; reinforced slaters underlining felt type 1F**								
8010201A	sloping	m^2	0.17	12.84	-	24.17	37.01	40.71	26.290
8010201B	vertical or mansard	m^2	0.22	16.67	-	24.17	40.84	44.92	26.290
8010201C	Extra for double eaves course	m	0.13	10.24	-	4.20	14.44	15.88	4.200
8010201D	Extra for mitred hips or cutting to valleys; both sides measured	m	0.49	37.15	-	4.20	41.35	45.49	4.200
80103	**HARDROW SLATES**								
8010301	**Hardrow slates; size 457 x 305 mm; 75 mm lap; 38 x 25 mm treated softwood battens; reinforced slaters underlining felt type 1F**								
8010301A	sloping	m^2	0.17	12.84	-	31.19	44.03	48.43	9.530
8010301B	vertical or mansard	m^2	0.22	16.67	-	31.19	47.86	52.65	9.530
8010301C	Extra for eaves course	m	0.07	5.12	-	4.00	9.12	10.03	0.310
8010301D	Extra for ridge slates	m	0.10	7.72	-	21.32	29.04	31.94	2.250

Roofing

Small Works 2011		Unit	Labour Hours	Labour Net	Plant Net	Materials Net	Unit Net	Unit with 10%	CO₂
				£	£	£	£	£	Kg
801	**SLATE ROOFING**								
80103	**HARDROW SLATES**								
8010301	**Hardrow slates; size 457 x 305 mm; 75 mm lap; 38 x 25 mm treated softwood battens; reinforced slaters underlining felt type 1F**								
8010301E	Extra for mitred hips or cutting to valleys; both sides measured	m	0.49	37.15	-	6.67	43.82	48.20	0.520

Small Works 2011		Unit	Labour Hours	Labour Net	Plant Net	Materials Net	Unit Net	Unit with 10%	CO₂
				£	£	£	£	£	Kg
802	**TILE ROOFING**								
80201	**PLAIN TILES**								
8020101	**Clay plain tiles; machine made; smooth red; size 265 mm x 165 mm; 64 mm lap; 19 mm x 38 mm treated sawn softwood battens; reinforced slaters felt type 1F**								
8020101A	sloping	m²	0.47	35.93	-	54.46	90.39	99.43	37.560
8020101B	vertical or mansard	m²	0.54	41.05	-	54.46	95.51	105.06	37.560
8020101C	Extra for verges	m	0.07	5.12	-	1.48	6.60	7.26	5.060
8020101D	Extra for double eaves course	m	0.07	5.12	-	4.22	9.34	10.27	2.750
8020101E	Extra for half round ridge tiles	m	0.29	21.79	-	22.79	44.58	49.04	1.920
8020101F	Extra for half round hip tiles; cutting both sides	m	0.34	25.61	-	26.14	51.75	56.93	1.920
8020101G	Extra for angle ridge tiles	m	0.29	21.79	-	22.79	44.58	49.04	2.330
8020101H	Extra for bonnet hip tiles; cutting both sides	m	0.34	25.61	-	80.13	105.74	116.31	7.800
8020101I	Extra for valley tiles; cutting both sides	m	0.34	25.61	-	80.13	105.74	116.31	7.800
8020101J	Extra for intersection of ridge and hip	Each	0.24	17.97	-	-	17.97	19.77	-
8020103	**Clay plain tiles; hand made; sand faced size 265 mm x 165 mm; 64 mm lap; 19 mm x 38 mm treated sawn softwood battens; reinforced slaters underlining felt type 1F**								
8020103A	sloping	m²	0.47	35.93	-	119.27	155.20	170.72	37.560
8020103B	vertical or mansard	m²	0.54	41.05	-	119.27	160.32	176.35	37.560
8020103C	Extra for verges	m	0.07	5.12	-	1.48	6.60	7.26	5.060
8020103D	Extra for double eaves course	m	0.07	5.12	-	11.80	16.92	18.61	3.210
8020103E	Extra for half round ridge tiles	m	0.29	21.79	-	27.89	49.68	54.65	1.920
8020103F	Extra for hip tiles; cutting both sides	m	0.34	25.61	-	32.72	58.33	64.16	2.330
8020103G	Extra for angle ridge tiles	m	0.29	21.79	-	27.89	49.68	54.65	1.920
8020103H	Extra for bonnet hip tiles; cutting both sides	m	0.34	25.61	-	100.22	125.83	138.41	7.800
8020103I	Extra for valley tiles; cutting both sides	m	0.34	25.61	-	100.22	125.83	138.41	7.800
8020103J	Extra for intersection of ridge and hip	Each	0.24	17.97	-	-	17.97	19.77	-
8020105	**Concrete plain tiles; BS473 and 550 group A; size 265 mm x 165 mm; 64 mm lap; 19 mm x 38 mm treated sawn softwood battens; reinforced slaters felt type 1F**								
8020105A	sloping	m²	0.47	35.93	-	51.63	87.56	96.32	24.510
8020105B	vertical or mansard	m²	0.54	41.05	-	51.63	92.68	101.95	24.510
8020105C	Extra for verges	m	0.06	4.36	-	1.48	5.84	6.42	5.060
8020105D	Extra for double eaves course	m	0.07	5.12	-	3.96	9.08	9.99	1.570
8020105E	Extra for segmental ridge tiles	m	0.29	21.79	-	10.97	32.76	36.04	0.710
8020105F	Extra for segmental hip tiles; cutting both sides	m	0.34	25.61	-	13.58	39.19	43.11	0.740
8020105G	Extra for bonnet hip tiles; cutting both sides	m	0.34	25.61	-	39.09	64.70	71.17	5.100
8020105H	Extra for valley tiles; cutting both sides	m	0.34	25.61	-	39.09	64.70	71.17	5.100
8020105I	Extra for intersection of ridge and hip	Each	0.24	17.97	-	-	17.97	19.77	-
80202	**INTERLOCKING TILES**								
8020201	**Concrete interlocking tiles; smooth finish; size 381 mm x 229 mm; 75 mm lap 22 mm x 38 mm treated sawn softwood battens; reinforced underlining felt type 1F**								
8020201A	sloping	m²	0.11	8.49	-	19.69	28.18	31.00	10.580
8020201B	vertical or mansard	m²	0.15	11.54	-	19.69	31.23	34.35	10.580
8020201C	Extra for verges; 150 mm fibre reinforced cement strip undercloak	m	0.12	8.94	-	4.38	13.32	14.65	7.860
8020201D	Extra for ridge tiles	m	0.22	16.44	-	10.97	27.41	30.15	0.710

Roofing

		Unit	Labour Hours	Labour Net £	Plant Net £	Materials Net £	Unit Net £	Unit with 10% £	CO₂ Kg
802	**TILE ROOFING**								
80202	**INTERLOCKING TILES**								
8020201	**Concrete interlocking tiles; smooth finish; size 381 mm x 229 mm; 75 mm lap 22 mm x 38 mm treated sawn softwood battens; reinforced underlining felt type 1F**								
8020201E	Extra for hip tiles; cutting both sides	m	0.28	21.25	-	13.58	34.83	38.31	0.740
8020201F	Extra for valley trough tiles; cutting both sides	m	0.23	17.66	-	95.36	113.02	124.32	4.150
8020203	**Concrete interlocking tiles; granular finish; granular finish; size 418 mm x 330 mm; 75 mm lap; 22 mm x 38 mm treated sawn softwood battens; reinforced slaters underlining felt type 1F**								
8020203A	sloping	m²	0.07	5.66	-	20.18	25.84	28.42	8.710
8020203B	vertical or mansard	m²	0.10	7.72	-	20.18	27.90	30.69	8.710
8020203C	Extra for verges; 150 mm fibre reinforced cement strip undercloak	m	0.12	8.94	-	4.38	13.32	14.65	7.860
8020203D	Extra for ridge tiles	m	0.22	16.44	-	10.97	27.41	30.15	0.710
8020203E	Extra for hip tiles; cutting both sides	m	0.28	21.25	-	13.58	34.83	38.31	0.740
8020203F	Extra for valley trough tiles; cutting both sides	m	0.23	17.66	-	85.46	103.12	113.43	3.720

Small Works 2011		Unit	Labour Hours	Labour Net	Plant Net	Materials Net	Unit Net	Unit with 10%	CO$_2$
				£	£	£	£	£	Kg
803	**COUNTER-BATTENS AND UNDERFELT**								
80301	**COUNTER-BATTENS**								
8030101	**Treated sawn softwood counter-battens; fixed with galvanised nails to softwood**								
8030101A	19 mm x 38 mm; 450 mm centres	m^2	0.03	2.06	-	1.30	3.36	3.70	0.510
8030101B	19 mm x 38 mm; 600 mm centres	m^2	0.02	1.83	-	0.98	2.81	3.09	0.380
8030101C	19 mm x 38 mm; 750 mm centres	m^2	0.02	1.53	-	0.78	2.31	2.54	0.300
8030101D	25 mm x 38 mm; 450 mm centres	m^2	0.03	2.60	-	0.96	3.56	3.92	0.660
8030101E	25 mm x 38 mm; 600 mm centres	m^2	0.03	2.29	-	0.72	3.01	3.31	0.500
8030101F	25 mm x 38 mm; 750 mm centres	m^2	0.03	2.06	-	0.58	2.64	2.90	0.400
8030101G	38 mm x 38 mm; 450 mm centres	m^2	0.05	3.59	-	1.41	5.00	5.50	1.010
8030101H	38 mm x 38 mm; 600 mm centres	m^2	0.04	3.06	-	1.06	4.12	4.53	0.760
8030101I	38 mm x 38 mm; 750 mm centres	m^2	0.03	2.60	-	0.85	3.45	3.80	0.600
8030101J	38 mm x 50 mm; 450 mm centres	m^2	0.05	4.13	-	1.86	5.99	6.59	1.330
8030101K	38 mm x 50 mm; 600 mm centres	m^2	0.04	3.36	-	1.40	4.76	5.24	1.000
8030101L	38 mm x 50 mm; 750 mm centres	m^2	0.04	2.83	-	1.12	3.95	4.35	0.800
80303	**UNDERFELT**								
8030301	**Reinforced slaters underlining felt; BS747; type 1F; 150 mm laps; secured with galvanised felt nails**								
8030301A	standard	m^2	0.02	1.83	-	2.14	3.97	4.37	5.000
8030301B	aluminium foil faced	m^2	0.02	1.83	-	3.90	5.73	6.30	5.950

Small Works 2011	Unit	Labour Hours	Labour Net £	Plant Net £	Materials Net £	Unit Net £	Unit with 10% £	CO₂ Kg
804	**ASPHALT BITUMEN FELT**							
80401	**MASTIC ASPHALT TO BS 988**							
8040101	**20 mm two coat coverings; felt isolating membrane**							
8040101A	over 300 mm wide	m²	0.27	20.49	1.56	17.83	39.88	43.87	4.050
8040101B	not exceeding 150 mm wide	m	0.10	7.42	1.02	2.68	11.12	12.23	1.170
8040101C	150 mm - 300 mm wide	m	0.13	9.71	1.69	5.35	16.75	18.43	2.100
8040102	**Extra over two coat coverings for**							
8040102A	turning nibs into grooves	m	0.07	5.50	-	-	5.50	6.05	-
8040102B	working to metal flashings	m	0.10	7.49	-	-	7.49	8.24	-
8040102C	working into outlets	Each	0.68	52.06	-	-	52.06	57.27	-
8040103	**13 mm two coat skirtings; internal angle fillet; top edge turned into groove**							
8040103A	150 mm high	m	0.26	19.72	1.35	1.57	22.64	24.90	1.250
8040103B	250 mm high	m	0.32	24.39	1.08	2.61	28.08	30.89	1.230
8040104	**13 mm two coat aprons; undercut drip edge and rounded arris; including angles**							
8040104A	75 mm high	m	0.24	17.97	1.08	0.78	19.83	21.81	0.920
8040104B	100 mm high	m	0.30	23.09	0.47	1.04	24.60	27.06	0.520
8040105	**13 mm two coat linings to gutter; two rounded arrises; two internal angle fillets; including angles and intersections**							
8040105A	300 mm	m	0.65	50.00	1.22	2.94	54.16	59.58	1.350
8040105B	Extra for ends	Each	0.24	18.58	-	-	18.58	20.44	-
8040105C	Extra for outlets	Each	0.67	51.30	-	-	51.30	56.43	-
8040107	**13 mm two coat collar; 100 mm high; internal angle fillet at junction with covering; fair edge and arris**							
8040107A	small pipes and the like	Each	0.31	23.70	1.02	0.54	25.26	27.79	0.830
8040107B	large pipes and the like	Each	0.46	35.24	1.69	0.99	37.92	41.71	1.400
8040108	**Accessories for asphalt roofing**							
8040108A	aluminium edge trims; 50 mm x 65 mm; including butt straps and working asphalt to trim	m	0.17	12.84	-	5.36	18.20	20.02	0.460
8040108B	Extra for right angle corner pieces	Each	0.29	21.79	-	5.52	27.31	30.04	0.430
8040108C	aluminium edge trims; 75 mm x 65 mm; including butt straps and working asphalt to trim	m	0.17	12.84	-	11.40	24.24	26.66	0.680
8040108D	Extra for right angle corner pieces	Each	0.29	21.79	-	5.22	27.01	29.71	0.650
8040108E	aluminium pressure release ventilators including asphalt collars	Each	0.40	30.81	-	20.02	50.83	55.91	12.360
80402	**BITUMEN FELT ROOFING TO BS 747**							
8040201	**Glassfibre felt coverings; stone chippings surfacing**							
8040201A	two layer; flat coverings; over 300 mm wide	m²	0.20	15.37	-	10.37	25.74	28.31	9.680
8040201B	Extra for working into outlets	Each	0.34	25.61	-	-	25.61	28.17	-
8040201C	three layer; flat coverings; over 300 mm wide	m²	0.27	20.49	-	15.40	35.89	39.48	14.500
8040201D	Extra for working into outlets	Each	0.34	25.61	-	-	25.61	28.17	-
8040203	**Asbex glassfibre felt mineral surface coverings**							
8040203A	two layer; sloping coverings; over 300 mm wide	m²	0.27	20.49	-	8.67	29.16	32.08	9.640
8040203B	Extra for working into outlets	Each	0.34	25.61	-	-	25.61	28.17	-
8040203C	three layer; sloping coverings; over 300 mm wide	m²	0.34	25.61	-	13.00	38.61	42.47	14.460
8040203D	Extra for working into outlets	Each	0.34	25.61	-	-	25.61	28.17	-

Small Works 2011		Unit	Labour Hours	Labour Net	Plant Net	Materials Net	Unit Net	Unit with 10%	CO$_2$
				£	£	£	£	£	Kg
804	**ASPHALT BITUMEN FELT**								
80402	**BITUMEN FELT ROOFING TO BS 747**								
8040203	**Asbex glassfibre felt mineral surface coverings**								
8040203E	75 mm wide aprons; fair drip edge at eaves or verges	m	0.12	9.48	-	0.33	9.81	10.79	0.360
8040203F	150 mm wide aprons; fair drip edge at eaves or verges	m	0.18	13.91	-	0.65	14.56	16.02	0.730
8040203G	150 mm girth skirtings; dressed over angle fillet	m	0.14	10.93	-	0.65	11.58	12.74	0.730
8040203H	300 mm girth skirtings; dressed over angle fillet	m	0.18	13.99	-	1.44	15.43	16.97	1.610
8040203I	200 mm three coat linings to gutters dressed over two angle fillets	m	0.14	10.40	-	2.60	13.00	14.30	2.890
8040203J	Extra for ends	Each	0.25	19.42	-	-	19.42	21.36	-
8040203K	Extra for outlets	Each	0.34	25.61	-	-	25.61	28.17	-
8040203L	300 mm three coat linings to gutters dressed over two angle fillets	m	0.20	15.60	-	3.90	19.50	21.45	4.340
8040203M	Extra for ends	Each	0.25	19.27	-	-	19.27	21.20	-
8040203N	Extra for outlets	Each	0.34	25.61	-	-	25.61	28.17	-
8040203O	collars around small pipes	Each	0.50	38.45	-	-	38.45	42.30	-
8040203P	collars around large pipes	Each	0.67	51.30	-	-	51.30	56.43	-
8040204	**Fibre insulation board; bedded in hot bitumen**								
8040204A	19 mm thick	m^2	0.15	11.77	-	5.52	17.29	19.02	5.500
8040204B	Extra for forming holes for pipes	Each	0.10	7.42	-	-	7.42	8.16	-
8040205	**Resin bonded glassfibre slabs; bedded in hot bitumen**								
8040205A	25 mm thick	m^2	0.38	29.28	-	22.60	51.88	57.07	1.450
8040205B	Extra for forming holes for pipes	Each	0.10	7.57	-	-	7.57	8.33	-
8040206	**Vapour barrier; bedded in hot bitumen**								
8040206A	felt	m^2	0.15	11.54	-	2.29	13.83	15.21	6.010
8040208	**Accessories for felt roofing**								
8040208A	aluminium edge trims; 40 mm x 65 mm; including butt straps; working feltwork to trim	m	0.11	8.72	-	4.04	12.76	14.04	6.132
8040208B	Extra for right angle corner pieces	Each	0.22	16.51	-	4.79	21.30	23.43	0.350
8040208C	aluminium edge trims; 75 mm x 65 mm; including butt straps; working feltwork to trim	m	0.07	5.20	-	10.86	16.06	17.67	0.650
8040208D	Extra for right angle corner pieces	Each	0.20	15.37	-	5.22	20.59	22.65	0.650

Roofing

Small Works 2011	Unit	Labour Hours	Labour Net £	Plant Net £	Materials Net £	Unit Net £	Unit with 10% £	CO₂ Kg
805	**CORRUGATED SHEETING**							
80501	**REINFORCED CEMENT**							
8050101	Coverings; horizontal; 750 mm nominal width; 76 mm corrugations; 100 mm side and 152 mm end laps; straight cutting and waste							
8050101A	fixed to wood with galvanised drive screws and washers	m²	0.17	12.84	-	40.25	53.09	58.40	44.182
8050101B	fixed to steel purlins with hook bolts	m²	0.24	17.97	-	40.08	58.05	63.86	44.046
8050102	Coverings; mansard and vertical; 750 mm nominal width; 76 mm corrugations; 100 mm side and 152 mm end laps; straight cutting and waste							
8050102A	fixed to wood with galvanised drive screws and washers	m²	0.24	17.97	-	41.03	59.00	64.90	44.315
8050102B	fixed to steel framing with hook bolts	m²	0.34	25.61	-	40.81	66.42	73.06	44.315
8050103	Extra over cement sheets for vinyl translucent sheets							
8050103A	762 mm wide	m²	-	-	-	-7.74	-7.74	-8.51	-35.065
8050104	Sundry labours and finishings							
8050104A	raking cutting	m	0.12	8.94	-	-	8.94	9.83	-
8050104B	barge boards	m	0.12	8.94	-	21.16	30.10	33.11	13.080
8050104C	two piece close fitting ridge	m	0.19	14.14	-	24.05	38.19	42.01	21.250
8050104D	ridge finials	Each	0.37	28.21	-	21.28	49.49	54.44	5.880
8050104E	eaves filler pieces	m	0.12	8.94	-	16.12	25.06	27.57	10.790
8050104F	apron flashings	m	0.12	8.94	-	15.68	24.62	27.08	10.460
80502	**GALVANISED STEEL**							
8050201	22 gauge galvanised corrugated steel sheeting; including one corrugation side lap and 150 mm end lap							
8050201A	to wood purlins with drive screws and washers	m²	0.12	8.94	-	35.57	44.51	48.96	64.550
8050201B	to steel purlins with hook bolts	m²	0.17	12.84	-	35.41	48.25	53.08	64.390
8050202	Sundry labours and finishings							
8050202A	raking cutting	m	0.24	17.97	-	-	17.97	19.77	-
8050202B	26 gauge corrugated steel ridge; 375 mm girth	m	0.10	7.72	-	5.88	13.60	14.96	29.420

Small Works 2011		Unit	Labour Hours	Labour Net	Plant Net	Materials Net	Unit Net	Unit with 10%	CO$_2$
				£	£	£	£	£	Kg
806	**NURALITE THATCH**								
80601	**NURALITE SHEET; D12C JOINTING STRIP SYSTEM**								
8060102	**Nuralite FX roof coverings**								
8060102A	flat	m^2	0.15	11.54	-	31.49	43.03	47.33	3.850
8060102B	sloping	m^2	0.20	15.37	-	31.49	46.86	51.55	3.850
8060102C	dormer cheeks	m^2	0.19	14.14	-	31.49	45.63	50.19	3.850
8060102D	gutters	m^2	0.27	20.49	-	31.49	51.98	57.18	3.850
8060102E	flashings; wedging into groove	m	0.24	17.97	-	5.06	23.03	25.33	0.580
8060102F	stepped flashings; wedging into groove	m	0.25	19.27	-	6.18	25.45	28.00	0.690
8060102G	raking cutting	m	0.06	4.36	-	-	4.36	4.80	-
8060102H	curved cutting	m	0.07	5.12	-	-	5.12	5.63	-
80602	**THATCHING BY SPECIALIST**								
8060201	**Thatching to a thickness of about 300 mm fixed with iron hooks and finished with a block cut and patterned and saddled ridge**								
8060201A	best quality water reed	m^2	2.50	121.67	-	32.16	153.83	169.21	0.400
8060201B	best quality combed wheat straw	m^2	2.25	109.51	-	29.91	139.42	153.36	0.400
8060201C	best quality long straw	m^2	2.00	97.30	-	26.88	124.18	136.60	0.330
8060202	**Ridge**								
8060202A	block cut, patterned and saddled	m	5.25	255.46	-	21.37	276.83	304.51	0.300
8060202B	flush	m	3.13	152.08	-	-	152.08	167.29	-
8060203	**Wiring over to thatch with netting**								
8060203A	1200 mm x 19 mm x 20 G galvanised netting	m^2	0.13	6.08	-	0.49	6.57	7.23	1.780
8060210	**Firestopping**								
8060210A	Magma TAS Firestop	m^2	0.10	4.87	-	3.23	8.10	8.91	0.960
8060210B	IMW 435	m^2	0.10	4.87	-	6.82	11.69	12.86	2.030

Small Works 2011		Unit	Labour Hours	Labour Net £	Plant Net £	Materials Net £	Unit Net £	Unit with 10% £	CO$_2$ Kg
808	**SHEET METAL: ROOF DECKING**								
80801	**COVERINGS (CODE 4) LEAD 1.80 mm**								
8080101	**Coverings**								
8080101A	flat roof	m^2	2.32	112.82	-	40.17	152.99	168.29	36.250
8080101B	gutters, valleys, dormer roofs and cheeks	m^2	2.90	141.04	-	40.17	181.21	199.33	36.250
8080101C	aprons; cappings to ridges or hips	m^2	3.00	146.14	-	40.17	186.31	204.94	36.250
8080101D	damp proof course	m^2	1.16	56.43	-	40.17	96.60	106.26	36.250
8080102	**Flashings; wedging into groove**								
8080102A	150 mm girth	m	0.23	11.29	-	6.03	17.32	19.05	5.440
8080102B	200 mm girth	m	0.32	15.37	-	8.05	23.42	25.76	7.260
8080102C	300 mm girth	m	0.46	22.57	-	12.06	34.63	38.09	10.880
8080103	**Stepped flashings; wedging into groove**								
8080103A	150 mm girth	m	0.29	14.11	-	6.03	20.14	22.15	5.440
8080103B	200 mm girth	m	0.50	24.08	-	8.05	32.13	35.34	7.260
8080103C	300 mm girth	m	0.61	29.73	-	12.06	41.79	45.97	10.880
8080104	**Soakers and hand to roofer**								
8080104A	200 mm x 200 mm	Each	0.17	8.47	-	1.62	10.09	11.10	1.470
8080104B	300 mm x 300 mm	Each	0.20	9.73	-	3.61	13.34	14.67	3.260
8080105	**Slate; 400 mm x 400 mm with collar 200 mm high around pipe**								
8080105A	100 mm dia	Each	0.87	42.33	-	9.28	51.61	56.77	8.370
8080105B	150 mm dia	Each	0.88	42.81	-	10.43	53.24	58.56	9.410
8080106	**Slate; dressed through 225 mm wall into rainwater head**								
8080106A	600 mm x 450 mm	Each	1.32	64.12	-	11.26	75.38	82.92	10.160
80802	**COVERINGS (CODE 5) LEAD 2.24 mm**								
8080201	**Coverings**								
8080201A	flat roof	m^2	2.44	118.46	-	50.00	168.46	185.31	45.300
8080201B	gutters, valleys, dormer roofs and cheeks	m^2	3.05	148.19	-	50.00	198.19	218.01	45.300
8080201C	aprons; cappings to ridges or hips	m^2	3.15	153.34	-	50.00	203.34	223.67	45.300
8080201D	damp proof course	m^2	1.22	59.21	-	50.00	109.21	120.13	45.300
8080202	**Flashings; wedging into groove**								
8080202A	150 mm girth	m	0.26	12.55	-	7.50	20.05	22.06	6.800
8080202B	200 mm girth	m	0.35	16.93	-	10.02	26.95	29.65	9.080
8080202C	300 mm girth	m	0.48	23.35	-	15.01	38.36	42.20	13.590
8080203	**Stepped flashings; wedging into groove**								
8080203A	150 mm girth	m	0.32	15.67	-	7.50	23.17	25.49	6.800
8080203B	200 mm girth	m	0.52	25.40	-	10.02	35.42	38.96	9.080
8080203C	300 mm girth	m	0.64	31.04	-	15.01	46.05	50.66	13.590
8080204	**Soakers and hand to roofer**								
8080204A	200 mm x 200 mm	Each	0.23	11.04	-	19.99	31.03	34.13	18.110
8080204B	300 mm x 300 mm	Each	0.25	12.31	-	4.49	16.80	18.48	4.070
8080205	**Slate; 400 mm x 400 mm with collar 200 mm high around pipe**								
8080205A	100 mm dia	Each	0.93	45.15	-	11.55	56.70	62.37	10.460
8080205B	200 mm dia	Each	1.04	50.79	-	12.98	63.77	70.15	11.760
8080206	**Slate; dressed through 225 mm wall into rainwater head**								
8080206A	600 mm x 450 mm	Each	1.37	66.65	-	14.02	80.67	88.74	12.700
80803	**SUNDRIES LEAD SHEET COVERINGS**								
8080301	**Coverings**								
8080301A	beaded edges	m	0.32	15.37	-	-	15.37	16.91	-

Small Works 2011		Unit	Labour Hours	Labour Net	Plant Net	Materials Net	Unit Net	Unit with 10%	CO₂
				£	£	£	£	£	Kg
808	**SHEET METAL: ROOF DECKING**								
80803	**SUNDRIES LEAD SHEET COVERINGS**								
8080301	**Coverings**								
8080301B	soldered seam	m	1.58	76.92	-	7.86	84.78	93.26	7.120
8080301C	soldered dots with brass screws	Each	0.53	25.64	-	0.11	25.75	28.33	0.030
8080301D	bossed ends to rolls	Each	0.63	30.75	-	-	30.75	33.83	-
8080301E	bossed angles to rolls	Each	0.79	38.48	-	-	38.48	42.33	-
8080301F	bossed intersections to rolls	Each	0.92	44.86	-	-	44.86	49.35	-
80804	**COPPER SHEET COVERINGS (24 SWG) 0.55 mm**								
8080401	**Coverings**								
8080401A	flat roof covering; rolls and laps	m²	1.86	90.25	-	58.71	148.96	163.86	19.010
8080401B	gutters, valleys, dormer roofs and cheeks	m²	2.32	112.82	-	58.71	171.53	188.68	19.010
8080401C	aprons; cappings to ridges or hips	m²	2.42	117.93	-	58.71	176.64	194.30	19.010
8080402	**Flashings; wedging into groove**								
8080402A	150 mm girth	m	0.29	14.11	-	8.81	22.92	25.21	2.850
8080402B	200 mm girth	m	0.35	16.93	-	11.76	28.69	31.56	3.810
8080402C	300 mm girth	m	0.52	25.40	-	17.62	43.02	47.32	5.710
8080403	**Stepped flashings; wedging into groove**								
8080403A	150 mm girth	m	0.35	16.93	-	8.81	25.74	28.31	2.850
8080403B	200 mm girth	m	0.41	19.75	-	11.76	31.51	34.66	3.810
8080403C	300 mm girth	m	0.58	28.22	-	17.62	45.84	50.42	5.710
80805	**ZINC SHEET COVERINGS (12.G) 0.64 mm**								
8080501	**Coverings**								
8080501A	flat roof covering; rolls and laps	m²	1.74	84.60	-	25.60	110.20	121.22	19.810
8080501B	gutters, valleys, dormer roofs and cheeks	m²	2.18	105.91	-	25.60	131.51	144.66	19.810
8080501C	aprons; cappings to ridges or hips	m²	2.28	111.02	-	25.60	136.62	150.28	19.810
8080502	**Flashings; wedging to groove**								
8080502A	150 mm girth	m	0.23	11.29	-	3.84	15.13	16.64	2.970
8080502B	200 mm girth	m	0.29	14.11	-	5.13	19.24	21.16	3.970
8080502C	300 mm girth	m	0.46	22.57	-	7.68	30.25	33.28	5.940
8080503	**Stepped flashings; wedging into groove**								
8080503A	150 mm girth	m	0.29	14.11	-	3.84	17.95	19.75	2.970
8080503B	200 mm girth	m	0.35	16.93	-	5.13	22.06	24.27	3.970
8080503C	300 mm girth	m	0.52	25.40	-	7.68	33.08	36.39	5.940
80806	**ZINC SHEET COVERINGS (14.G) 0.79 mm**								
8080601	**Coverings**								
8080601A	flat roof covering; rolls and laps	m²	1.74	84.60	-	31.47	116.07	127.68	24.450
8080601B	gutters, valleys, dormer roofs and cheeks	m²	2.18	105.91	-	31.47	137.38	151.12	24.450
8080601C	aprons; cappings to ridges or hips	m²	2.28	111.02	-	31.47	142.49	156.74	24.450
8080602	**Flashings; wedging to groove**								
8080602A	150 mm girth	m	0.23	11.29	-	4.72	16.01	17.61	3.670
8080602B	200 mm girth	m	0.29	14.11	-	6.30	20.41	22.45	4.900
8080602C	300 mm girth	m	0.46	22.57	-	9.44	32.01	35.21	7.340
8080603	**Stepped flashings; wedging into groove**								
8080603A	150 mm girth	m	0.29	14.11	-	4.72	18.83	20.71	3.670
8080603B	200 mm girth	m	0.35	16.93	-	6.30	23.23	25.55	4.900
8080603C	300 mm girth	m	0.52	25.40	-	9.44	34.84	38.32	7.340

Roofing

		Unit	Labour Hours	Labour Net	Plant Net	Materials Net	Unit Net	Unit with 10%	CO$_2$
				£	£	£	£	£	Kg
808	**SHEET METAL: ROOF DECKING**								
80808	**ALUMINIUM SHEET COVERINGS (21.G) 0.99 mm COMMERCIAL GRADE**								
8080801	**Coverings**								
8080801A	flat roof covering; rolls and laps	m^2	1.86	90.25	-	11.45	101.70	111.87	26.740
8080801B	gutters, valleys, dormer roofs and cheeks	m^2	2.32	112.82	-	11.45	124.27	136.70	26.740
8080801C	aprons; cappings to ridges or hips	m^2	2.42	117.93	-	11.45	129.38	142.32	26.740
8080802	**Flashings; wedging to groove**								
8080802A	150 mm girth	m	0.29	14.11	-	1.72	15.83	17.41	4.010
8080802B	200 mm girth	m	0.35	16.93	-	2.29	19.22	21.14	5.360
8080802C	300 mm girth	m	0.52	25.40	-	3.43	28.83	31.71	8.030
8080803	**Stepped flashings; wedging into groove**								
8080803A	150 mm girth	m	0.35	16.93	-	1.72	18.65	20.52	4.010
8080803B	200 mm girth	m	0.41	19.75	-	2.29	22.04	24.24	5.360
8080803C	300 mm girth	m	0.58	28.22	-	3.43	31.65	34.82	8.030
80809	**ROOF DECKING**								
8080901	**Woodwool unreinforced slabs; BS 1105; type SB; fixing to timber with galvanised nails**								
8080901A	50 mm	m^2	0.25	12.31	-	12.55	24.86	27.35	13.090
8080901B	75 mm	m^2	0.29	13.87	-	15.92	29.79	32.77	19.630
8080901C	100 mm	m^2	0.32	15.37	-	20.96	36.33	39.96	26.180
8080903	**Mineral fibre insulating decking slabs**								
8080903A	50 mm	m^2	0.20	9.73	-	35.54	45.27	49.80	29.810
8080905	**Laminated polyurethane insulation standard roof boarding**								
8080905A	26 mm	m^2	0.13	6.42	-	12.66	19.08	20.99	3.130
8080905B	35 mm	m^2	0.13	6.42	-	13.17	19.59	21.55	4.210
8080905C	50 mm	m^2	0.20	9.73	-	17.22	26.95	29.65	6.010
8080907	**Purldek combined deck insulation board**								
8080907A	50 mm; fixing to timber with galvanised nails	m^2	0.36	17.42	-	52.17	69.59	76.55	1.490
8080907B	raking cutting	m	0.19	9.24	-	-	9.24	10.16	-
8080907C	curved cutting	m	0.32	15.37	-	-	15.37	16.91	-

Small Works 2011		Unit	Labour Hours	Labour Net	Plant Net	Materials Net	Unit Net	Unit with 10%	CO₂
				£	£	£	£	£	Kg
809	**REPAIRS AND ALTERATIONS**								
80901	**REMOVE COVERINGS AND LOAD INTO SKIP**								
8090101	**Roof coverings**								
8090101A	slates	m²	0.55	11.47	-	-	11.47	12.62	-
8090101B	nibbed tiles	m²	0.45	9.38	-	-	9.38	10.32	-
8090101C	corrugated metal sheeting	m²	0.45	9.38	-	-	9.38	10.32	-
8090101D	underfelt and nails	m²	0.07	1.46	-	-	1.46	1.61	-
8090101E	three layers felt	m²	0.28	5.84	-	-	5.84	6.42	-
8090101F	sheet metal	m²	0.55	11.47	-	-	11.47	12.62	-
8090102	**Metal finishings**								
8090102A	horizontal	m	0.22	4.59	-	-	4.59	5.05	-
8090102B	stepped	m	0.28	5.84	-	-	5.84	6.42	-
8090103	**Battens including withdrawing nails**								
8090103A	tile or slate	m²	0.10	2.09	-	-	2.09	2.30	-
8090104	**Remove coverings, carefully handling and disposing of by an approved method toxic or other special waste**								
8090104A	asbestos cement sheeting	m²	0.74	56.42	2.54	-	58.96	64.86	-
8090105	**Stripping, cleaning and setting aside sound slates or tiles for re-use**								
8090105A	slates	m²	0.40	8.34	-	-	8.34	9.17	-
8090105B	tiles	m²	0.30	6.25	-	-	6.25	6.88	-
8090105C	cement slates	m²	0.40	8.34	-	-	8.34	9.17	-
8090106	**Stripping, cleaning and setting aside for removal**								
8090106A	slates	m²	0.30	6.25	-	-	6.25	6.88	-
8090106B	tiles	m²	0.24	5.00	-	-	5.00	5.50	-
8090106C	cement slates	m²	0.30	6.25	-	-	6.25	6.88	-
80902	**RENEWALS**								
8090201	**Tile battens to 100 mm gauge**								
8090201A	area not exceeding 8.5 sq.m	m²	0.11	8.72	-	4.80	13.52	14.87	3.320
8090201B	area exceeding 8.5 sq.m	m²	0.09	6.65	-	4.80	11.45	12.60	3.320
8090202	**Slate battens to 205 mm gauge**								
8090202A	area not exceeding 8.5 sq.m	m²	0.09	6.65	-	2.79	9.44	10.38	1.970
8090202B	area exceeding 8.5 sq.m	m²	0.06	4.36	-	2.79	7.15	7.87	1.970
8090203	**Roofing felt**								
8090203A	per sq.m	m²	0.05	3.59	-	2.24	5.83	6.41	5.220
8090204	**Single slates with clips, including taking off; first slate**								
8090204A	405 mm x 205 mm	Each	0.18	13.61	-	1.65	15.26	16.79	0.060
8090204B	510 mm x 255 mm	Each	0.19	14.37	-	3.41	17.78	19.56	0.100
8090204C	610 mm x 305 mm	Each	0.20	14.91	-	5.88	20.79	22.87	0.140
8090205	**Single slates with clips, including taking off; second and subsequent slate up to 30 no**								
8090205A	405 mm x 205 mm	Each	0.07	5.66	-	1.65	7.31	8.04	0.060
8090205B	510 mm x 255 mm	Each	0.08	5.89	-	3.41	9.30	10.23	0.100
8090205C	610 mm x 305 mm	Each	0.08	6.19	-	5.88	12.07	13.28	0.140
8090206	**Single tiles, including taking off; first tile**								
8090206A	clay	Each	0.12	9.25	-	0.70	9.95	10.95	0.460
8090206B	concrete	Each	0.12	9.25	-	0.66	9.91	10.90	0.260
8090207	**Single tiles, including taking off; second and subsequent tiles up to 50 no**								
8090207A	clay	Each	0.07	5.66	-	0.70	6.36	7.00	0.460
8090207B	concrete	Each	0.07	5.66	-	0.66	6.32	6.95	0.260

Roofing

Small Works 2011	Unit	Labour Hours	Labour Net £	Plant Net £	Materials Net £	Unit Net £	Unit with 10% £	CO₂ Kg
809 **REPAIRS AND ALTERATIONS**								
80902 **RENEWALS**								
8090208 **Single blue asbestos slates, including taking off; first slate**								
8090208A 610 mm x 305 mm	Each	0.12	9.48	-	2.15	11.63	12.79	0.830
8090209 **Single blue asbestos slates, second and subsequent slates up to 30 no**								
8090209A 610 mm x 305 mm	Each	0.07	5.66	-	2.15	7.81	8.59	0.830
8090210 **Cement mortar (1:3) angle fillet to slate, tile or asbestos roof at abutment to**								
8090210A walls or chimney stacks	m	0.13	10.24	-	0.37	10.61	11.67	1.270
8090211 **Strip roof slating, sort slates and reslate roof using 50% salvaged slates**								
8090211A 405 mm x 205 mm	m²	0.39	29.51	-	24.70	54.21	59.63	0.920
8090211B 510 mm x 255 mm	m²	0.27	20.49	-	31.63	52.12	57.33	0.890
8090211C 610 mm x 305 mm	m²	0.17	12.84	-	36.89	49.73	54.70	0.860
8090212 **Strip 267 mm x 165 mm plain roof tiles and retile using 50% salvaged tiles**								
8090212A clay	m²	0.57	43.58	-	23.20	66.78	73.46	15.130
8090212B concrete	m²	0.57	43.58	-	21.79	65.37	71.91	8.610
80903 **REPAIRS TO SHEET METAL**								
8090301 **Take up old lead; any position or weight**								
8090301A and set aside	m²	0.21	10.27	-	-	10.27	11.30	-
8090301B and relay to boarded flats including dressing over rolls and drips, with new bossed ends etc.	m²	2.27	110.24	-	-	110.24	121.26	-
8090302 **Redress lead flashings**								
8090302A and rewedge and repoint	m	0.42	20.53	-	-	20.53	22.58	-
8090303 **Take up old zinc; in any position**								
8090303A and remove from site	m²	0.53	25.64	-	-	25.64	28.20	-
8090304 **Take up existing zinc and supply and lay new zinc including rolls, laps etc**								
8090304A 0.50 mm thick	m²	2.11	102.55	-	13.97	116.52	128.17	15.470
8090304B 0.65 mm thick	m²	2.37	115.40	-	25.60	141.00	155.10	19.810
8090304C 0.80 mm thick	m²	2.64	128.19	-	31.47	159.66	175.63	24.450
8090305 **Prepare zinc roofs and supply and lay bitumenised fabric**								
8090305A bedded in bitumen, apply two coats of bitumen emulsion	m²	1.00	48.70	-	1.58	50.28	55.31	1.820
8090306 **Seal crack in holes in zinc or asphalt flats**								
8090306A and apply two coats of bitumen waterproofer	m²	0.47	23.06	-	1.22	24.28	26.71	0.570
8090307 **Clean and treat defective sheet zinc with**								
8090307A Rito, Matex or similar compound	m²	0.58	28.22	-	1.41	29.63	32.59	0.950
8090308 **Remove slates, take out defective box gutter linings or valleys and**								
8090308A renew wood linings and line with 12 G zinc and replace slates	m²	4.22	205.11	-	409.16	614.27	675.70	48.480
80904 **PROVISION OF LADDERS**								
8090401 **Labour and transport up to 5 miles each way and setting up and removing ladders up to**								
8090401A two storeys high	Each	4.65	97.02	5.35	-	102.37	112.61	8.000
8090401B four storeys high	Each	2.50	52.13	5.35	-	57.48	63.23	8.000

Small Works 2011		Unit	Labour Hours	Labour Net	Plant Net	Materials Net	Unit Net	Unit with 10%	CO$_2$
				£	£	£	£	£	Kg
809	**REPAIRS AND ALTERATIONS**								
80904	**PROVISION OF LADDERS**								
8090401	**Labour and transport up to 5 miles each way and setting up and removing ladders up to**								
8090401C	extra over last two items if access is difficult e.g. one house in a terrace where there is no side entrance	Each	2.00	41.70	5.35	-	47.05	51.76	8.000
80905	**REMOVAL OF ASPHALT**								
8090501	**Remove waterproofing finishes and load into skip**								
8090501A	asphalt paving	m^2	0.67	13.97	2.41	-	16.38	18.02	-
8090501B	asphalt roofing	m^2	1.10	22.94	1.66	-	24.60	27.06	-
8090501C	asphalt skirting	m	0.17	3.54	0.38	-	3.92	4.31	-
80906	**ROOF TREATMENTS BY SPECIALISTS**								
8090601	**Clean, prepare and apply DC500 flexible roofing compound**								
8090601A	to sound surfaces; asbestos, asphalt, concrete, felt, slate or tile	m^2	0.55	11.47	-	6.88	18.35	20.19	0.600
8090601B	and fungicide solution to surfaces likely to support fungal or algae growth; asbestos, asphalt, concrete, felt, slate or tile	m^2	0.60	12.51	-	7.89	20.40	22.44	1.670

Sundries

Sundries

Small Works 2011		Unit	Labour Hours	Labour Net £	Plant Net £	Materials Net £	Unit Net £	Unit with 10% £	CO₂ Kg

901	**STEELWORK AND METALWORK**								
90101	**UNFRAMED STEELWORK**								
9010101	**Rolled joist beams**								
9010101A	127 mm x 76 mm x 13 kg	m	0.15	7.35	-	12.06	19.41	21.35	32.040
9010101B	152 mm x 89 mm x 18 kg	m	0.21	10.02	-	16.07	26.09	28.70	42.720
9010101C	178 mm x 102 mm x 21 kg	m	0.24	11.72	-	20.54	32.26	35.49	49.130
9010101D	203 mm x 102 mm x 25 kg	m	0.29	14.16	-	23.31	37.47	41.22	61.940
9010102	**Universal beams**								
9010102A	203 mm x 133 mm x 25 kg	m	0.29	14.16	-	29.30	43.46	47.81	59.810
9010102B	203 mm x 133 mm x 30 kg	m	0.35	16.88	-	18.68	35.56	39.12	70.490
9010102C	254 mm x 146 mm x 31 kg	m	0.36	17.37	-	37.87	55.24	60.76	74.760
9010102D	254 mm x 146 mm x 37 kg	m	0.43	20.77	-	44.36	65.13	71.64	87.580
9010102E	254 mm x 146 mm x 43 kg	m	0.50	24.18	-	28.17	52.35	57.59	102.530
9010102F	305 mm x 165 mm x 40 kg	m	0.46	22.48	-	48.68	71.16	78.28	96.120
9010102G	305 mm x 165 mm x 46 kg	m	0.53	25.88	-	55.17	81.05	89.16	108.940
9010102H	305 mm x 165 mm x 54 kg	m	0.62	30.31	-	35.22	65.53	72.08	128.160
9010102I	254 mm x 102 mm x 25 kg	m	0.29	14.16	-	35.23	49.39	54.33	59.810
9010102J	305 mm x 102 mm x 33 kg	m	0.38	18.58	-	41.77	60.35	66.39	79.030
9010102K	356 mm x 171 mm x 51 kg	m	0.59	28.61	-	63.01	91.62	100.78	121.750
90102	**METALWORK**								
9010201	**Mild steel flats and plates**								
9010201A	50 mm x 6 mm	m	0.14	6.86	-	5.04	11.90	13.09	5.530
9010201B	80 mm x 6 mm	m	0.20	9.78	-	7.27	17.05	18.76	8.850
9010201C	80 mm x 12 mm	m	0.20	9.78	-	13.73	23.51	25.86	17.700
9010201D	100 mm x 6 mm	m	0.24	11.72	-	9.44	21.16	23.28	11.060
9010201E	100 mm x 12 mm	m	0.24	11.72	-	18.03	29.75	32.73	22.130
9010201F	125 mm x 6 mm	m	0.29	14.16	-	11.55	25.71	28.28	14.380
9010201G	150 mm x 6 mm	m	0.34	16.64	-	13.73	30.37	33.41	16.590
9010201H	150 mm x 12 mm	m	0.34	16.64	-	26.71	43.35	47.69	33.190
9010201I	200 mm x 6 mm	m	0.44	21.50	-	18.03	39.53	43.48	22.130
9010201J	254 mm x 6 mm	m	0.55	26.85	-	22.40	49.25	54.18	27.660
9010201K	254 mm x 12 mm	m	0.55	26.85	-	43.98	70.83	77.91	55.320
90103	**CATNIC; GALVANISED STEEL LINTELS**								
9010301	**CN7; combined lintel; for standard 50 mm cavity wall; 143 mm high; length**								
9010301A	750 mm	Each	0.12	9.25	-	35.23	44.48	48.93	16.720
9010301B	900 mm	Each	0.13	9.71	-	42.42	52.13	57.34	20.060
9010301C	1050 mm	Each	0.13	10.24	-	49.38	59.62	65.58	23.400
9010301D	1200 mm	Each	0.14	10.78	-	56.32	67.10	73.81	26.750
9010301E	1350 mm	Each	0.15	11.24	-	63.36	74.60	82.06	30.090
9010302	**CN7; combined lintel; for standard 50 mm cavity wall; 143 mm high; length**								
9010302A	1500 mm	Each	0.15	11.77	-	73.18	84.95	93.45	33.430
9010302B	1650 mm	Each	0.16	12.31	-	82.29	94.60	104.06	36.780
9010302C	1800 mm	Each	0.17	12.84	-	89.61	102.45	112.70	40.120
9010302E	1950 mm	Each	0.18	13.38	-	98.07	111.45	122.60	43.460
9010302F	2100 mm	Each	0.18	13.84	-	104.47	118.31	130.14	46.810
9010302G	2250 mm	Each	0.19	14.37	-	118.66	133.03	146.33	50.150
9010302H	2400 mm	Each	0.20	14.91	-	126.55	141.46	155.61	53.490
9010302I	2550 mm	Each	0.20	15.37	-	131.91	147.28	162.01	56.840
9010302J	2700 mm	Each	0.21	15.90	-	139.60	155.50	171.05	60.180
9010303	**CN8; combined lintel; for standard 50 mm cavity wall; 219 mm high; length**								
9010303A	2250 mm	Each	0.19	14.37	-	128.36	142.73	157.00	76.490
9010303B	2400 mm	Each	0.20	14.91	-	137.94	152.85	168.14	81.590
9010303C	2550 mm	Each	0.20	15.37	-	147.72	163.09	179.40	91.790
9010303D	2700 mm	Each	0.21	15.90	-	155.64	171.54	188.69	91.790
9010303E	2850 mm	Each	0.22	16.44	-	178.77	195.21	214.73	96.890
9010303F	3000 mm	Each	0.22	16.90	-	189.80	206.70	227.37	101.990
9010303G	3300 mm	Each	0.23	17.43	-	211.28	228.71	251.58	112.190
9010303H	3600 mm	Each	0.24	17.97	-	231.35	249.32	274.25	122.390
9010303I	3900 mm	Each	0.24	18.42	-	308.12	326.54	359.19	132.590
9010303J	4200 mm	Each	0.25	18.96	-	331.67	350.63	385.69	142.790
9010303K	4575 mm	Each	0.26	19.49	-	385.91	405.40	445.94	155.540
9010303L	4800 mm	Each	0.26	20.03	-	406.63	426.66	469.33	163.180

Small Works 2011		Unit	Labour Hours	Labour Net	Plant Net	Materials Net	Unit Net	Unit with 10%	CO$_2$
				£	£	£	£	£	Kg
901	**STEELWORK AND METALWORK**								
90103	**CATNIC; GALVANISED STEEL LINTELS**								
9010304	**CN71; single lintel for external solid walls; 143 mm high; length**								
9010304A	750 mm	Each	0.11	8.72	-	52.65	61.37	67.51	15.700
9010304B	900 mm	Each	0.12	9.25	-	63.23	72.48	79.73	18.840
9010304C	1050 mm	Each	0.13	9.71	-	73.64	83.35	91.69	21.990
9010304D	1200 mm	Each	0.13	10.24	-	81.65	91.89	101.08	25.130
9010304E	1350 mm	Each	0.14	10.78	-	94.47	105.25	115.78	31.410
9010304F	1500 mm	Each	0.15	11.24	-	106.95	118.19	130.01	34.550
9010304G	1650 mm	Each	0.15	11.77	-	118.02	129.79	142.77	34.550
9010304H	1800 mm	Each	0.16	12.31	-	129.10	141.41	155.55	37.690
9010304I	1950 mm	Each	0.17	12.84	-	132.99	145.83	160.41	40.830
9010304J	2100 mm	Each	0.18	13.38	-	150.44	163.82	180.20	43.970
9010304K	2250 mm	Each	0.18	13.84	-	176.17	190.01	209.01	47.110
9010304L	2400 mm	Each	0.19	14.37	-	187.37	201.74	221.91	50.250
9010304M	2550 mm	Each	0.20	14.91	-	193.66	208.57	229.43	53.390
9010304N	2700 mm	Each	0.20	15.37	-	204.98	220.35	242.39	56.530
9010305	**CN92; single lintel; for 75 mm internal partitions and non-loadbearing walls; 23 mm high; length**								
9010305A	900 mm	Each	0.13	9.71	-	8.69	18.40	20.24	2.430
9010305B	1050 mm	Each	0.13	10.24	-	8.69	18.93	20.82	2.840
9010305C	1200 mm	Each	0.14	10.78	-	9.82	20.60	22.66	3.240
9010306	**CN102; single lintel; for 100 mm internal partitions and non-loadbearing walls; 25 mm high; length**								
9010306A	900 mm	Each	0.13	9.71	-	7.59	17.30	19.03	3.650
9010306B	1050 mm	Each	0.13	10.24	-	10.99	21.23	23.35	4.250
9010306C	1200 mm	Each	0.14	10.78	-	12.12	22.90	25.19	4.860
90104	**STRUCTURAL STEELWORK BY SPECIALISTS**								
9010401	**Portal framework where members are in the range of**								
9010401A	18 - 30 kg per linear metre	Tonne	14.56	708.49	-	1,047.76	1,756.25	1,931.88	1,780.000
9010401B	30 - 45 kg per linear metre	Tonne	12.68	616.88	-	1,047.76	1,664.64	1,831.10	1,780.000
9010401C	45 - 70 kg per linear metre	Tonne	11.93	580.20	-	1,125.37	1,705.57	1,876.13	1,780.000
9010401D	70 - 100 kg per linear metre	Tonne	11.30	549.70	-	1,164.17	1,713.87	1,885.26	1,780.000
9010401E	exceeding 100 kg per linear metre	Tonne	10.67	519.14	-	1,202.98	1,722.12	1,894.33	1,780.000
9010401F	purlins	Tonne	13.56	659.60	-	1,028.99	1,688.59	1,857.45	1,780.000
9010402	**Beam and post work with rigid connection where members are in the range of**								
9010402A	18 - 30 kg per linear metre	Tonne	13.81	671.81	-	1,047.76	1,719.57	1,891.53	1,780.000
9010402B	30 - 45 kg per linear metre	Tonne	13.06	635.17	-	1,086.56	1,721.73	1,893.90	1,780.000
9010402C	45 - 70 kg per linear metre	Tonne	12.55	610.75	-	1,125.37	1,736.12	1,909.73	1,780.000
9010402D	70 - 100 kg per linear metre	Tonne	11.05	537.49	-	1,164.17	1,701.66	1,871.83	1,780.000
9010402E	exceeding 100 kg per linear metre	Tonne	9.54	464.17	-	1,202.98	1,667.15	1,833.87	1,780.000
9010403	**Beam and post work with simple web cleated connections where members are in the range of**								
9010403A	18 - 30 kg per linear metre	Tonne	12.68	616.88	-	1,047.76	1,664.64	1,831.10	1,780.000
9010403B	30 - 45 kg per linear metre	Tonne	12.94	629.48	-	1,086.56	1,716.04	1,887.64	1,780.000
9010403C	45 - 70 kg per linear metre	Tonne	10.04	488.59	-	1,125.37	1,613.96	1,775.36	1,780.000
9010403D	70 - 100 kg per linear metre	Tonne	9.54	464.17	-	1,164.17	1,628.34	1,791.17	1,780.000
9010403E	exceeding 100 kg per linear metre	Tonne	8.54	415.33	-	1,202.98	1,618.31	1,780.14	1,780.000
9010404	**Staircase, catwalks, parapets and the like in**								
9010404A	steel	Tonne	17.58	855.07	-	1,997.12	2,852.19	3,137.41	1,780.000
9010406	**Tubular constructions**								
9010406A	light	Tonne	11.93	580.20	-	1,672.02	2,252.22	2,477.44	1,780.000
9010406B	heavy	Tonne	11.17	543.57	-	1,370.12	1,913.69	2,105.06	1,780.000

Sundries

Small Works 2011		Unit	Labour Hours	Labour Net £	Plant Net £	Materials Net £	Unit Net £	Unit with 10% £	CO₂ Kg
902	**METAL WINDOWS AND DOORS**								
90201	**STANDARD GALVANISED STEEL WINDOWS**								
9020101 9020101A	**Type NG1** 508 mm x 292 mm	Each	0.25	18.73	-	69.17	87.90	96.69	14.030
9020102 9020102A	**Type NH1** 508 mm x 457 mm	Each	0.30	22.86	-	81.42	104.28	114.71	17.370
9020103 9020103A	**Type NE6F** 279 mm x 628 mm	Each	0.35	26.38	-	75.29	101.67	111.84	19.380
9020104 9020104A	**Type NE5** 508 mm x 628 mm	Each	0.35	26.38	-	32.98	59.36	65.30	23.590
9020105 9020105A	**Type NES1** 508 mm x 628 mm	Each	0.35	26.38	-	94.34	120.72	132.79	26.940
9020106 9020106A	**Type NC6F** 279 mm x 923 mm	Each	0.40	30.27	-	80.06	110.33	121.36	23.510
9020107 9020107A	**Type NC5** 508 mm x 923 mm	Each	0.40	30.27	-	38.40	68.67	75.54	26.710
9020108 9020108A	**Type NC1** 508 mm x 923 mm	Each	0.40	30.27	-	102.01	132.28	145.51	30.060
9020109 9020109A	**Type NC5F** 508 mm x 923 mm	Each	0.40	30.27	-	89.05	119.32	131.25	28.380
9020110 9020110A	**Type NC05** 508 mm x 1067 mm	Each	0.44	33.87	-	42.79	76.66	84.33	29.730
9020111 9020111A	**Type NC01** 508 mm x 1067 mm	Each	0.44	33.87	-	107.93	141.80	155.98	33.080
9020112 9020112A	**Type NC05F** 508 mm x 1067 mm	Each	0.44	33.87	-	91.77	125.64	138.20	31.400
9020113 9020113A	**Type ND5** 508 mm x 1218 mm	Each	0.50	37.92	-	43.85	81.77	89.95	31.840
9020114 9020114A	**Type ND1** 508 mm x 1218 mm	Each	0.50	37.92	-	116.08	154.00	169.40	35.190
9020115 9020115A	**Type ND5F** 508 mm x 1218 mm	Each	0.50	37.92	-	94.69	132.61	145.87	33.520
90202	**STANDARD GALVANISED STEEL DOORS**								
9020201 9020201A	**Type NA15** 761 mm x 2056 mm	Each	1.29	98.47	-	578.21	676.68	744.35	176.270
9020202 9020202A	**Type NA2** 997 mm x 2056 mm	Each	1.39	106.11	-	868.39	974.50	1,071.95	215.440
9020203 9020203A	**Type NA25** 1143 mm x 2056 mm	Each	1.47	112.31	-	885.55	997.86	1,097.65	238.380
90203	**STANDARD GALVANISED STEEL WINDOWS; WHITE POLYESTER POWDER COATING FINISH**								
9020301 9020301A	**Type NG1** 508 mm x 292 mm	Each	0.24	18.35	-	113.26	131.61	144.77	13.400
9020302 9020302A	**Type NH1** 508 mm x 457 mm	Each	0.30	22.86	-	134.09	156.95	172.65	16.630
9020303 9020303A	**Type NE6F** 279mm x 628mm	Each	0.35	26.38	-	128.60	154.98	170.48	18.730
9020304 9020304A	**Type NE5** 502 mm x 628 mm	Each	0.35	26.38	-	60.33	86.71	95.38	22.720
9020305 9020305A	**Type NES1** 508 mm x 628 mm	Each	0.35	26.38	-	154.73	181.11	199.22	26.070

Small Works 2011		Unit	Labour Hours	Labour Net	Plant Net	Materials Net	Unit Net	Unit with 10%	CO$_2$
				£	£	£	£	£	Kg
902	**METAL WINDOWS AND DOORS**								
90203	**STANDARD GALVANISED STEEL WINDOWS; WHITE POLYESTER POWDER COATING FINISH**								
9020306 9020306A	**Type NC6F** 279 mm x 923 mm	Each	0.40	30.27	-	137.96	168.23	185.05	22.640
9020307 9020307A	**Type NC5** 508 mm x 923 mm	Each	0.40	30.27	-	70.49	100.76	110.84	25.680
9020308 9020308A	**Type NC1** 508 mm x 923 mm	Each	0.40	30.27	-	168.02	198.29	218.12	29.030
9020309 9020309A	**Type NC5F** 508 mm x 923 mm	Each	0.40	30.27	-	158.06	188.33	207.16	27.350
9020310 9020310A	**Type NC05** 508 mm x 1067 mm	Each	0.44	33.87	-	78.97	112.84	124.12	28.550
9020311 9020311A	**Type NC01** 508 mm x 1067 mm	Each	0.44	33.87	-	180.09	213.96	235.36	31.890
9020312 9020312A	**Type NC05F** 508 mm x 1067 mm	Each	0.44	33.87	-	162.97	196.84	216.52	30.220
9020313 9020313A	**Type ND5** 508 mm x 1218 mm	Each	0.50	37.92	-	80.91	118.83	130.71	30.550
9020314 9020314A	**Type ND1** 508 mm x 1218 mm	Each	0.50	37.92	-	192.01	229.93	252.92	33.900
9020315 9020315A	**Type ND5F** 508 mm x 1218 mm	Each	0.50	37.92	-	168.91	206.83	227.51	32.220
90204	**STANDARD GALVANISED STEEL DOORS; WHITE POLYESTER POWDER COATING FINISH**								
9020401 9020401A	**Type NA15** 761 mm x 2056 mm	Each	1.29	98.47	-	889.66	988.13	1,086.94	163.770
9020402 9020402A	**Type NA2** 997 mm x 2056 mm	Each	1.39	106.11	-	1,348.41	1,454.52	1,599.97	200.160
9020403 9020403A	**Type NA25** 1143 mm x 2056 mm	Each	1.47	112.31	-	1,374.73	1,487.04	1,635.74	221.470
90205	**STANDARD GALVANISED STEEL SIDELIGHTS**								
9020501 9020501A	**Type NA6** 279 mm x 2056 mm	Each	0.56	43.12	-	108.21	151.33	166.46	36.300
9020502 9020502A	**Type NA5** 508 mm x 2056 mm	Each	0.68	52.29	-	131.52	183.81	202.19	66.090
9020503 9020503A	**Type NA13F** 997 mm x 2056 mm	Each	0.81	61.54	-	224.97	286.51	315.16	129.710
90206	**STANDARD GALVANISED STEEL SIDELIGHTS; WHITE POLYESTER POWDER COATING FINISH**								
9020601 9020601A	**Type NA6** 279 mm x 2056 mm	Each	0.56	43.12	-	177.08	220.20	242.22	40.050
9020602 9020602A	**Type NA5** 508 mm x 2056 mm	Each	0.68	52.29	-	211.08	263.37	289.71	72.920
9020603 9020603A	**Type NA13F** 997 mm x 2056 mm	Each	0.81	61.54	-	375.43	436.97	480.67	143.110

Small Works 2011		Unit	Labour Hours	Labour Net £	Plant Net £	Materials Net £	Unit Net £	Unit with 10% £	CO$_2$ Kg
903	**ASPHALT WORK**								
90301	**MASTIC ASPHALT TANKING; BS 6925**								
9030101	**13 mm One coat horizontal covering on concrete**								
9030101A	over 300 mm wide	m^2	0.22	16.67	1.45	8.70	26.82	29.50	2.830
9030101B	not exceeding 150 mm wide	m	0.08	5.96	0.54	1.30	7.80	8.58	0.660
9030101C	150 mm - 300 mm wide	m	0.11	8.49	0.71	2.61	11.81	12.99	1.050
9030102	**20 mm Two coat horizontal covering on concrete**								
9030102A	over 300 mm wide	m^2	0.24	18.50	1.56	13.39	33.45	36.80	3.860
9030102B	not exceeding 150 mm wide	m	0.09	7.11	0.68	2.01	9.80	10.78	0.900
9030102C	150 mm - 300 mm wide	m	0.13	9.79	0.88	4.02	14.69	16.16	1.460
9030103	**30 mm Three coat horizontal covering on concrete**								
9030103A	over 300 mm wide	m^2	0.44	33.56	3.14	20.08	56.78	62.46	6.370
9030103B	not exceeding 150 mm wide	m	0.16	12.31	1.12	3.01	16.44	18.08	1.420
9030103C	150 mm - 300 mm wide	m	0.23	17.66	1.56	6.02	25.24	27.76	2.360
9030104	**13 mm Two coat vertical covering on brickwork**								
9030104A	over 300 mm wide	m^2	0.80	60.78	5.42	8.70	74.90	82.39	5.700
9030104B	not exceeding 150 mm wide	m	0.24	18.20	1.69	1.30	21.19	23.31	1.490
9030104C	150 mm - 300 mm wide	m	0.36	27.45	2.64	2.61	32.70	35.97	2.450
9030105	**20 mm Three coat vertical covering on brickwork**								
9030105A	over 300 mm wide	m^2	1.02	78.21	7.45	13.39	99.05	108.96	8.130
9030105B	not exceeding 150 mm wide	m	0.31	23.85	2.30	2.01	28.16	30.98	2.080
9030105C	150 mm - 300 mm wide	m	0.47	35.63	3.39	4.02	43.04	47.34	3.270
9030106	**Labours**								
9030106A	internal angle fillets	m	0.14	10.55	-	-	10.55	11.61	-
9030106B	turning nibs into grooves	m	0.08	5.96	-	-	5.96	6.56	-
9030106C	working into outlets	Each	0.82	62.84	-	-	62.84	69.12	-
9030106D	collars and internal angle fillets around small pipes	Each	0.67	51.07	-	-	51.07	56.18	-
9030106E	collars and internal angle fillets around large pipes	Each	0.98	74.62	-	-	74.62	82.08	-
90302	**MASTIC ASPHALT TANKING; BS 6577**								
9030201	**13 mm One coat horizontal covering on concrete**								
9030201A	over 300 mm wide	m^2	0.38	28.75	2.71	10.44	41.90	46.09	3.740
9030201B	not exceeding 150 mm wide	m	0.13	9.71	0.81	1.57	12.09	13.30	0.860
9030201C	150 mm - 300 mm wide	m	0.19	14.14	1.22	3.13	18.49	20.34	1.420
9030202	**20 mm Two coat horizontal covering on concrete**								
9030202A	over 300 mm wide	m^2	0.43	32.49	2.98	16.06	51.53	56.68	4.890
9030202B	not exceeding 150 mm wide	m	0.15	11.31	1.02	2.41	14.74	16.21	1.150
9030202C	150 mm - 300 mm wide	m	0.21	16.13	1.49	4.82	22.44	24.68	1.900
9030203	**30 mm Three coat horizontal covering on concrete**								
9030203A	over 300 mm wide	m^2	0.72	55.12	5.22	24.09	84.43	92.87	7.870
9030203B	not exceeding 150 mm wide	m	0.22	16.67	1.56	3.61	21.84	24.02	1.740
9030203C	150 mm - 300 mm wide	m	0.36	27.29	2.57	7.23	37.09	40.80	3.090
9030204	**13 mm Two coat vertical covering on brickwork**								
9030204A	over 300 mm wide	m^2	0.99	75.61	7.25	10.44	93.30	102.63	7.030
9030204B	not exceeding 150 mm wide	m	0.30	22.86	2.17	1.57	26.60	29.26	1.840
9030204C	150 mm - 300 mm wide	m	0.45	34.17	3.28	3.13	40.58	44.64	2.910
9030205	**20 mm Three coat vertical covering on brickwork**								
9030205A	over 300 mm wide	m^2	1.28	97.70	9.41	16.06	123.17	135.49	9.550
9030205B	not exceeding 150 mm wide	m	0.39	29.97	2.88	2.41	35.26	38.79	2.500
9030205C	150 mm - 300 mm wide	m	0.58	44.65	4.30	4.82	53.77	59.15	3.940
9030206	**Labours**								
9030206A	internal angle fillets	m	0.14	10.63	-	-	10.63	11.69	-
9030206B	turning nibs into grooves	m	0.08	5.96	-	-	5.96	6.56	-
9030206C	working into outlets	Each	0.82	62.84	-	-	62.84	69.12	-

Small Works 2011		Unit	Labour Hours	Labour Net	Plant Net	Materials Net	Unit Net	Unit with 10%	CO₂
				£	£	£	£	£	Kg
903	**ASPHALT WORK**								
90302	**MASTIC ASPHALT TANKING; BS 6577**								
9030206	**Labours**								
9030206D	collars and internal angle fillets around small pipes	Each	0.67	51.15	-	-	51.15	56.27	-
9030206E	collars and internal angle fillets around large pipes	Each	0.98	74.62	-	-	74.62	82.08	-
90303	**MASTIC ASPHALT FLOORING; BS 6925**								
9030301	**15 mm One coat light duty flooring on and including isolating membrane**								
9030301A	over 300 mm wide	m²	0.27	20.49	1.56	11.81	33.86	37.25	3.370
9030301B	not exceeding 150 mm wide	m	0.10	7.42	0.64	1.77	9.83	10.81	0.800
9030301C	150 mm - 300 mm wide	m	0.13	10.24	1.08	3.54	14.86	16.35	1.460
9030302	**20 mm One coat medium duty flooring on and including isolating membrane**								
9030302A	over 300 mm wide	m²	0.27	20.49	1.56	15.15	37.20	40.92	4.050
9030302B	not exceeding 150 mm wide	m	0.10	7.42	1.02	2.54	10.98	12.08	1.200
9030302C	150 mm - 300 mm wide	m	0.13	9.71	1.69	4.55	15.95	17.55	2.100
9030303	**30 mm One coat medium duty flooring on and including isolating membrane**								
9030303A	over 300 mm wide	m²	0.34	25.61	1.76	21.84	49.21	54.13	5.560
9030303B	not exceeding 150 mm wide	m	0.12	9.33	1.86	3.28	14.47	15.92	1.990
9030303C	150 mm - 300 mm wide	m	0.17	12.69	2.01	6.55	21.25	23.38	2.740
9030304	**Labours**								
9030304A	working against metal frames	m	0.04	2.83	-	-	2.83	3.11	-
9030304B	Extra for working into recessed covers; not exceeding 1.00 m²	Each	0.30	23.09	-	-	23.09	25.40	-
9030305	**Skirtings; 13 mm two coat; fair edge, angles, coved angle fillet and nib turned into groove**								
9030305A	150 mm high	m	0.26	19.72	1.35	1.30	22.37	24.61	1.250
90304	**COLOURED MASTIC ASPHALT FLOORING; BS 6925**								
9030401	**15 mm One coat light duty brown flooring on and including isolating membrane**								
9030401A	over 300 mm wide	m²	0.34	25.99	2.24	13.42	41.65	45.82	3.860
9030401B	not exceeding 150 mm wide	m	0.12	8.94	0.85	2.01	11.80	12.98	0.950
9030401C	150 mm - 300 mm wide	m	0.17	12.84	1.22	4.03	18.09	19.90	1.550
9030402	**Labours**								
9030402A	working against metal frames	m	0.04	2.83	-	-	2.83	3.11	-
9030402B	Extra for working into recessed covers; not exceeding 1.00 m²	Each	0.30	23.09	-	-	23.09	25.40	-
9030403	**Skirtings; 13 mm two coat; brown with fair edge, angles, coved angle fillet and nib turned into groove**								
9030403A	150 mm high	m	0.28	21.18	1.69	1.51	24.38	26.82	1.490

Small Works 2011		Unit	Labour Hours	Labour Net	Plant Net	Materials Net	Unit Net	Unit with 10%	CO₂
				£	£	£	£	£	Kg
904	**ELECTRICAL WORK**								
90401	**LIGHTING POINTS**								
9040101	**P.V.C. insulated and sheathed cables in houses or flats, installed in floor cavities or roof voids, protected by steel or P.V.C. channel in walls**								
9040101A	lighting point controlled by 1 switch	Each	1.32	41.98	-	18.94	60.92	67.01	5.370
9040101B	lighting point controlled by 2 switches	Each	1.58	50.38	-	31.46	81.84	90.02	9.890
9040101C	lighting point controlled by 3 switches	Each	1.73	55.12	-	49.40	104.52	114.97	15.290
9040101D	2 lighting points controlled by 1 switch	Each	1.24	39.38	-	46.19	85.57	94.13	11.500
9040102	**P.V.C. insulated cables contained in black enamelled screwed, welded conduit in commercial property**								
9040102A	lighting point controlled by 1 switch	Each	1.58	50.38	-	37.02	87.40	96.14	14.810
9040102B	lighting point controlled by 2 switches	Each	1.58	50.38	-	37.02	87.40	96.14	14.810
9040102C	lighting point controlled by 3 switches	Each	1.98	62.97	-	94.82	157.79	173.57	38.670
9040102D	2 lighting points controlled by 1 switch	Each	1.49	47.23	-	76.45	123.68	136.05	27.160
9040103	**P.V.C. insulated cables contained in galvanised screwed, welded conduit in industrial property**								
9040103A	lighting point controlled by 1 switch	Each	1.85	58.81	-	44.52	103.33	113.66	14.130
9040103B	lighting point controlled by 2 switches	Each	2.03	64.44	-	82.62	147.06	161.77	27.420
9040103C	lighting point controlled by 3 switches	Each	2.06	65.57	-	114.51	180.08	198.09	36.640
9040103D	2 lighting points controlled by 1 switch	Each	1.73	55.12	-	89.93	145.05	159.56	25.810
9040104	**M.I.C.S. cables in commercial property**								
9040104A	lighting point controlled by 1 switch	Each	1.58	50.38	-	31.64	82.02	90.22	14.810
9040104B	lighting point controlled by 2 switches	Each	1.58	50.38	-	31.64	82.02	90.22	14.810
9040104C	lighting point controlled by 3 switches	Each	1.98	62.97	-	78.17	141.14	155.25	37.030
9040104D	2 lighting points controlled by 3 switches	Each	1.98	62.97	-	97.84	160.81	176.89	45.960
9040105	**M.I.C.S. cables in industrial property**								
9040105A	lighting point controlled by 1 switch	Each	1.85	58.81	-	44.52	103.33	113.66	14.130
9040105B	lighting point controlled by 2 switches	Each	2.03	64.44	-	82.62	147.06	161.77	27.420
9040105C	lighting point controlled by 3 switches	Each	2.06	65.57	-	114.51	180.08	198.09	36.640
9040105D	2 lighting points controlled by 1 switch	Each	1.24	39.38	-	77.76	117.14	128.85	22.810
90402	**SWITCHED SOCKET OUTLETS**								
9040201	**P.V.C. insulated and sheathed cable in houses or flats, installed**								
9040201A	13 amp single switch socket outlet	Each	1.36	43.32	-	31.18	74.50	81.95	9.730
9040201B	1 - 13 amp dual switch socket outlet	Each	1.36	43.32	-	34.84	78.16	85.98	9.730
9040202	**P.V.C. insulated cables contained in black enamelled screwed welded conduit in commercial property**								
9040202A	1 - 13 amp single switch socket outlet	Each	1.44	45.89	-	38.54	84.43	92.87	17.610

Small Works 2011		Unit	Labour Hours	Labour Net	Plant Net	Materials Net	Unit Net	Unit with 10%	CO$_2$
				£	£	£	£	£	Kg
904	**ELECTRICAL WORK**								
90402	**SWITCHED SOCKET OUTLETS**								
9040202	**P.V.C. insulated cables contained in black enamelled screwed welded conduit in commercial property**								
9040202B	13 amp dual switch socket outlet	Each	1.44	45.89	-	42.20	88.09	96.90	17.610
9040203	**P.V.C. insulated cables contained in galvanised screwed welded conduit in industrial property**								
9040203A	1 - 13 amp single switch socket outlet	Each	1.73	55.12	-	46.05	101.17	111.29	16.930
9040203B	1 - 13 amp dual switch socket outlet	Each	1.86	59.06	-	49.71	108.77	119.65	16.930
9040204	**M.I.C.S. cables in commercial property**								
9040204A	1 - 13 amp single switch socket outlet	Each	1.24	39.38	-	45.52	84.90	93.39	14.710
9040204B	1 - 13 amp dual switch socket outlet	Each	1.49	47.23	-	49.18	96.41	106.05	14.710
90404	**COOKER POINTS**								
9040401	**P.V.C. insulated and sheathed cable in houses or flats, installed**								
9040401A	cooker point 30 amp with cooker panel	Each	1.61	51.21	-	66.34	117.55	129.31	12.120
9040401B	cooker point 45 amp with cooker panel	Each	1.61	51.21	-	56.61	107.82	118.60	6.330
9040402	**P.V.C. insulated cables contained in enamelled screwed welded conduit in commercial property**								
9040402A	cooker point 30 amp with cooker panel	Each	1.73	55.12	-	56.53	111.65	122.82	15.210
9040402B	cooker point 45 amp with cooker panel	Each	1.73	55.12	-	155.51	210.63	231.69	36.800
9040403	**M.I.C.S. cables in commercial properties**								
9040403A	cooker point 30 amp with cooker panel	Each	1.86	59.06	-	56.53	115.59	127.15	15.210
9040403B	cooker point 45 amp with cooker panel	Each	1.86	59.06	-	67.24	126.30	138.93	15.800
90406	**IMMERSION HEATER POINTS**								
9040601	**Immersion heater point with control switch (excluding heater)**								
9040601A	P.V.C. insulated cables in P.V.C. conduit (domestic)	Each	1.49	47.23	-	40.10	87.33	96.06	11.090
9040601B	in enamelled steel welded conduit etc	Each	1.86	59.06	-	51.35	110.41	121.45	20.560
9040602	**M.I.C.S. cables in commercial property**								
9040602A	immersion heater point with control switch (excluding heater)	Each	1.65	52.54	-	57.47	110.01	121.01	24.370
9040602B	supply and connect 3 kw immersion heater complete with fixed thermostat to new cylinder	Each	1.36	43.32	-	26.12	69.44	76.38	13.290
90408	**INFRA RED HEATER POINTS**								
9040801	**P.V.C. insulated and sheathed cables installed in houses and flats**								
9040801A	infra red heater with control switch (excluding heater and earth bonding)	Each	1.36	43.32	-	40.00	83.32	91.65	11.080

Sundries

Small Works 2011		Unit	Labour Hours	Labour Net	Plant Net	Materials Net	Unit Net	Unit with 10%	CO₂
				£	£	£	£	£	Kg
904	**ELECTRICAL WORK**								
90408	**INFRA RED HEATER POINTS**								
9040802	**P.V.C. insulated cables in black enamelled screwed conduit in commercial property**								
9040802A	infra red heater point with control switch (excluding heater and earth bonding)	Each	1.36	43.32	-	51.29	94.61	104.07	22.520
9040803	**M.I.C.S. cables in commercial property**								
9040803A	infra red heater point with control switch (excluding heater and earth bonding)	Each	1.36	43.32	-	51.23	94.55	104.01	17.390
9040803B	supply and fix 750 w infra red heater	Each	0.50	15.74	-	49.10	64.84	71.32	11.110
9040803C	supply and fix 1000 w infra red heater	Each	0.50	15.74	-	48.05	63.79	70.17	12.810
90409	**BELL INSTALLATIONS**								
9040901	**P.V.C. insulated cable in houses or flats**								
9040901A	bell controlled by front door push including transformer	Each	1.26	38.69	-	63.05	101.74	111.91	30.070
9040901B	bell and buzzer controlled by front door push and back door push including transformer	Each	1.61	51.21	-	75.27	126.48	139.13	31.430
9040901C	Hi-Low chimes controlled by front door push and back door push including transformer	Each	1.36	43.32	-	88.05	131.37	144.51	15.990
9040902	**P.V.C. insulated cables contained in black enamelled screwed welded conduit in commercial property**								
9040902A	bell controlled by front door push including transformer	Each	1.49	47.23	-	82.23	129.46	142.41	44.370
9040902B	bell and buzzer controlled by front door push and back door push including transformer	Each	1.73	55.12	-	118.16	173.28	190.61	74.370
9040902C	Hi-Low chimes controlled by front door push and back door push including transformer	Each	1.98	62.97	-	135.27	198.24	218.06	39.870
9040903	**M.I.C.S. cables in commercial property**								
9040903A	bell controlled by front door push including transformer	Each	1.49	47.23	-	94.21	141.44	155.58	43.020
9040903B	bell and buzzer controlled by front door push and back door push including transformer	Each	1.61	51.21	-	136.32	187.53	206.28	73.030
9040903C	Hi-Low chimes controlled by front door push and back door push including transformer	Each	1.73	55.12	-	117.12	172.24	189.46	41.220
90410	**T.V. OUTLETS**								
9041001	**Low loss coaxial cable in houses or flats protected by P.V.C. conduit in walls, terminating with a single T.V. outlet and allowing 3 metres of cable in roof void**								
9041001A	for connection to aerial by others	Each	1.73	55.12	-	10.16	65.28	71.81	4.080
90412	**ELECTRICAL SHAVER POINT**								
9041201	**P.V.C. insulated and sheathed cable in houses and flats**								
9041201A	dual voltage type, isolated for bathrooms etc	Each	1.11	35.43	-	71.32	106.75	117.43	6.670
9041202	**P.V.C. insulated cables contained in black enamelled screwed and welded conduit in commercial property**								
9041202A	dual voltage type, isolated for bathrooms etc	Each	1.11	35.43	-	80.77	116.20	127.82	14.450

Small Works 2011		Unit	Labour Hours	Labour Net	Plant Net	Materials Net	Unit Net	Unit with 10%	CO$_2$
				£	£	£	£	£	Kg

904   **ELECTRICAL WORK**

90414   **STORAGE HEATING**

9041401   **P.V.C. insulated and sheathed cable in houses and flats**

9041401A	3 kw heater point controlled by switch adjacent to heater position (from independent fuse)	Each	1.44	45.89	-	33.33	79.22	87.14	8.280

9041402   **P.V.C. insulated cables contained in black enamelled screwed and welded conduit in commercial property**

9041402A	3 kw heater point controlled by switch adjacent to heater position (from independent fuse)	Each	1.73	55.12	-	42.84	97.96	107.76	16.080

90416   **LIGHTING FITTINGS**

9041602   **Fluorescent fitting, single, complete with tube, ceiling mounted**

9041602A	609 mm	Each	0.50	15.74	-	28.06	43.80	48.18	2.030
9041602B	1219 mm	Each	0.50	15.74	-	37.09	52.83	58.11	3.040
9041602C	1524 mm	Each	0.50	15.74	-	41.95	57.69	63.46	4.060
9041602D	1828 mm	Each	0.62	19.68	-	50.68	70.36	77.40	4.560
9041602E	2438 mm	Each	0.62	19.68	-	69.32	89.00	97.90	6.080

9041603   **Fluorescent fitting, single, opal diffuser, complete with tube, ceiling mounted**

9041603A	609 mm	Each	0.50	15.74	-	46.49	62.23	68.45	5.770
9041603B	1219 mm	Each	0.50	15.74	-	57.20	72.94	80.23	10.520
9041603C	1524 mm	Each	0.50	15.74	-	65.41	81.15	89.27	13.410
9041603D	1828 mm	Each	0.62	19.68	-	79.45	99.13	109.04	15.780
9041603E	2438 mm	Each	0.62	19.68	-	105.08	124.76	137.24	21.050

90418   **REWIRING**

9041801   **To an average dwelling house containing**

9041801A	15 no. 13 amp twin power points and 14 no. 5 amp lighting points, 3 no. two-way lighting points complete with switches, lamp holders, all in two circuits and immersion heater and cooker feed complete and 1 no. outside light including consumer unit with MCBs	Each	45.47	1,446.26	-	1,061.13	2,507.39	2,758.13	304.890

Sundries

		Unit	Labour Hours	Labour Net	Plant Net	Materials Net	Unit Net	Unit with 10%	CO$_2$
				£	£	£	£	£	Kg
905	**DAMP-PROOFING**								
90501	**GENERALLY**								
9050101	**Chase out mortar joint in brickwork with mechanical saw, insert flexible membrane of lead, zinc, copper, bituminous material or low density polythene and force in new mortar (material cost of membrane not included)**								
9050101A	to half brick walls	m	0.52	39.98	1.28	0.14	41.40	45.54	1.720
9050101B	to one brick walls	m	1.05	79.97	2.56	0.27	82.80	91.08	3.440
9050101C	to one and a half brick walls	m	1.57	120.03	3.84	0.41	124.28	136.71	5.160
9050101D	Extra over last for material cost of membrane in one brick wall in 26SWG (0.45 mm) copper	m	-	-	-	10.30	10.30	11.33	3.220
9050101E	Extra over for material cost of membrane in one brick wall in 26SWG Code 4 (1.80 mm) lead	m	-	-	-	8.12	8.12	8.93	7.330
9050101F	Extra over for 2000 gauge low density polythene	m	-	-	-	2.44	2.44	2.68	1.190
9050102	**Drill brickwork and provide Vandex damp proof course to**								
9050102A	half brick walls	m	0.08	5.73	-	1.78	7.51	8.26	1.410
9050102B	one brick walls	m	0.14	10.86	-	2.97	13.83	15.21	2.350
9050102C	one and half brick wall	m	0.20	15.37	-	4.86	20.23	22.25	3.840
9050103	**Drill brickwork and provide chemical damp-proof course injected under pressure to**								
9050103A	half brick wall	m	0.07	5.20	-	4.18	9.38	10.32	0.190
9050103B	one brick wall	m	0.13	9.79	-	8.36	18.15	19.97	0.380
9050103C	one and half brick wall	m	0.19	14.22	-	12.54	26.76	29.44	0.580
9050104	**Hack off existing plastering or rendering to a height of one metre above the damp-proof course and later replace with**								
9050104A	two coats of Premix DR5 and a setting coat	m^2	1.08	31.57	-	3.39	34.96	38.46	7.450
9050105	**Cerinol tanking**								
9050105A	five coat	m^2	1.50	31.28	-	17.38	48.66	53.53	11.210
9050106	**Clean, prepare and apply DC500 flexible roofing compound to**								
9050106A	sound surfaces, asbestos, asphalt, concrete, felt, slate or tile	m^2	0.55	11.47	-	6.88	18.35	20.19	0.600
9050107	**Clean, prepare and apply DC500 flexible roofing compound and fungicide solution to**								
9050107A	surfaces likely to support fungal or algae growth, asbestos, asphalt, concrete, felt, slate or tile	m^2	0.60	12.51	-	7.32	19.83	21.81	1.070

Small Works 2011		Unit	Labour Hours	Labour Net £	Plant Net £	Materials Net £	Unit Net £	Unit with 10% £	CO₂ Kg
906	**UNDERPINNING**								
90601	**GENERALLY**								
9060101	**Break up concrete paving and hardcore under, level and ram hardcore on completion, 150 mm concrete paving with screeded finish**								
9060101A	150 mm concrete paving	m²	2.60	54.21	-	19.39	73.60	80.96	48.380
9060102	**Excavate for access trench, part backfill**								
9060102A	dispose of surplus in skip	m³	7.00	145.95	-	-	145.95	160.55	-
9060103	**Excavate under existing wall or foundation**								
9060103A	and get out	m³	5.40	112.59	-	-	112.59	123.85	-
9060104	**Hire of skip; delivery to site; removing when full; dispose of contents; payment of tipping charges**								
9060104A	skip size; 4.5 m³	m³	-	-	33.60	-	33.60	36.96	-
9060106	**Break out existing foundations in short lengths and get out**								
9060106A	concrete	m³	32.00	667.20	-	-	667.20	733.92	-
9060106B	brickwork	m³	27.00	562.95	-	-	562.95	619.25	-
9060107	**Concrete underpinning in short lengths including necessary formwork; mix**								
9060107A	1:2:4	m³	13.00	271.05	-	132.68	403.73	444.10	423.160
9060107B	1:3:6	m³	13.00	271.05	-	126.20	397.25	436.98	314.910
9060108	**Concrete in projecting pier bases including necessary formwork; mix**								
9060108A	1:2:4	m³	15.50	323.18	-	132.68	455.86	501.45	423.160
9060108B	1:3:6	m³	15.50	323.18	-	126.20	449.38	494.32	314.910
9060109	**Reinforced concrete in ground beams including one 13 mm mild steel bar for each 0.02 sq.m sectional area of beam; including necessary formwork; mix**								
9060109A	1:2:4	m³	4.93	376.90	-	178.19	555.09	610.60	529.490
9060110	**Brickwork one brick thick in short lengths in underpinning**								
9060110A	engineering bricks	m²	2.68	205.12	-	59.58	264.70	291.17	248.110
9060110B	common bricks	m²	2.68	205.12	-	45.03	250.15	275.17	116.100
9060111	**Wedge and pin up new brickwork to underside of existing with slates; thickness**								
9060111A	215 mm	m	0.34	25.61	-	12.73	38.34	42.17	0.470
9060111B	327 mm	m	0.47	35.93	-	19.01	54.94	60.43	0.710
9060112	**Timber in dwarf, dead and sundry shoring**								
9060112A	generally	m³	26.83	2,051.15	-	133.10	2,184.25	2,402.68	67.410

House Renovation Grants, Repairs and Alterations

Small Works 2011		Unit	Labour Hours	Labour Net	Plant Net	Materials Net	Unit Net	Unit with 10%	CO$_2$
				£	£	£	£	£	Kg
A01	**GRANTWORK**								
A0101	**HOUSE RENOVATION**								
A010101	**Take up old wood flooring in basement including joists and plates, excavate for, breaking up any obstructions, lay 150 mm hardcore and 100 mm concrete and thermoplastic tile floor on screed base**								
A010101A	take up flooring and excavate to required depth	m^2	6.00	125.10	-	-	125.10	137.61	-
A010101B	lay 150 mm hardcore	m^2	0.30	6.25	-	3.82	10.07	11.08	2.370
A010101C	lay 100 mm concrete	m^2	1.00	20.85	-	12.52	33.37	36.71	31.240
A010101D	lay screed for tiles	m^2	0.60	16.81	-	2.72	19.53	21.48	10.510
A010101E	inclusive cost for preparing	m^2	7.90	169.01	-	18.39	187.40	206.14	43.720
A010101F	Marleyflex tile flooring	m^2	0.28	7.84	-	8.93	16.77	18.45	7.640
A010101G	total cost	m^2	8.18	176.85	-	27.98	204.83	225.31	51.770
A010102	**Break up existing concrete area paving; excavate over site 150 mm deep, prepare subsoil and lay new concrete paving**								
A010102A	break up concrete paving	m^2	2.25	46.91	-	-	46.91	51.60	-
A010102B	excavate over site	m^2	0.42	8.76	-	-	8.76	9.64	-
A010102C	lay 100 mm concrete	m^2	1.00	20.85	-	12.52	33.37	36.71	31.240
A010102D	total cost	m^2	3.67	76.52	-	12.52	89.04	97.94	31.240
A010103	**Build concrete block and cavity lining to existing external and party walls including plastering and two coats emulsion paint**								
A010103A	100 mm concrete block walling with four ties per sq.m	m^2	0.40	30.73	-	15.47	46.20	50.82	9.490
A010103B	render and set walls	m^2	0.43	20.86	-	2.14	23.00	25.30	1.300
A010103C	emulsion paint	m^2	0.32	8.96	-	1.68	10.64	11.70	0.810
A010103D	total cost	m^2	1.15	60.56	-	19.29	79.85	87.84	11.600
A010104	**Rake out existing brickwork joints to form key, plaster walls and emulsion paint**								
A010104A	rake out brickwork	m^2	0.13	10.24	-	-	10.24	11.26	-
A010104B	render and set walls	m^2	0.43	20.86	-	2.14	23.00	25.30	1.300
A010104C	emulsion paint	m^2	0.32	8.96	-	1.68	10.64	11.70	0.810
A010104D	total cost	m^2	0.88	40.07	-	3.82	43.89	48.28	2.110
A010105	**Build 100 mm concrete block partition walls off site concrete, plastered and emulsion painted both sides, including tying into existing walls and pinning to soffit**								
A010105A	100 mm concrete block walling including tying in	m^2	0.40	30.73	-	18.64	49.37	54.31	12.170
A010105B	render and set both sides	m^2	0.85	41.73	-	2.14	43.87	48.26	1.300
A010105C	emulsion paint both sides	m^2	0.84	23.53	-	3.37	26.90	29.59	1.620
A010105D	total cost	m^2	2.10	95.99	-	24.15	120.14	132.15	15.090
A010106	**Take out and remove kitchen range and mantel-shelf; build up half brick thick wall across opening flush with existing walls and render and set**								
A010106A	take out range and remove	Each	6.00	125.10	-	-	125.10	137.61	-
A010106B	take out and remove mantel-shelf	Each	0.80	16.68	-	-	16.68	18.35	-
A010106C	half-brick wall including tying (3 sq.m)	Each	2.35	179.50	-	91.11	270.61	297.67	219.870
A010106D	render and set including jointing to existing (3 sq.m)	Each	1.51	73.63	-	6.86	80.49	88.54	4.180
A010106E	total cost	Each	9.56	437.31	-	97.97	535.28	588.81	224.040

Small Works 2011	Unit	Labour Hours	Labour Net	Plant Net	Materials Net	Unit Net	Unit with 10%	CO$_2$
			£	£	£	£	£	Kg

A01   **GRANTWORK**

A0101   **HOUSE RENOVATION**

A010108   Take out existing window frame, size 1.2 m x 1.0 m. Cut away stone cill and one brick apron below, about 1.2 m x 0.45 m. Reform brick jambs and build in brick-on-edge cill. Provide and fix new standard casement window size 1.2 m x 1.35 m. Glaze, paint both sides and make good all plaster. No alteration work to lintel or arch over

A010108A	take out window cill	Each	1.60	33.36	-	-	33.36	36.70	-
A010108B	cut away brickwork (0.5 sq.m)	Each	1.90	39.62	-	-	39.62	43.58	-
A010108C	reform jambs (1 lin.m)	Each	0.84	64.14	-	6.37	70.51	77.56	15.360
A010108D	brick cill (1 lin.m)	Each	0.44	33.33	-	7.62	40.95	45.05	26.100
A010108E	window casement	Each	0.60	46.18	-	117.26	163.44	179.78	45.740
A010108F	glazing (1.5 sq.m)	Each	1.65	46.22	-	118.69	164.91	181.40	42.080
A010108G	paint window casement (3.5 sq.m)	Each	3.50	98.04	-	3.02	101.06	111.17	1.620
A010108H	make good plaster	Each	0.45	22.08	-	0.94	23.02	25.32	0.580
A010108I	total cost	Each	10.98	382.88	-	253.76	636.64	700.30	131.150

A010109   Take out old door frame and wing light 1.8 m x 2.0 m (extreme). Build up one brick wall in old door opening up to cill level, take out old stone cill and build up new brick cill. Provide and fix new purpose made window frame 1.8 m x 1.0 m. Glaze, paint both sides and make good all plaster

A010109A	take out existing frame	Each	1.85	38.57	-	-	38.57	42.43	-
A010109B	take out old cill	Each	0.40	8.34	-	-	8.34	9.17	-
A010109C	build up one-brick wall in old opening 0.75 m x 0.9 m	Each	1.26	96.17	-	42.11	138.28	152.11	153.930
A010109D	build new brick cill (2 lin.m)	Each	0.87	66.66	-	18.64	85.30	93.83	68.290
A010109E	window frame and sashes	Each	3.69	282.02	-	80.71	362.73	399.00	31.480
A010109F	glass in window frame and sashes (1.6 sq.m)	Each	5.20	145.65	-	126.76	272.41	299.65	46.390
A010109G	painting window frame and sashes (4.0 sq.m)	Each	5.20	145.65	-	2.46	148.11	162.92	1.320
A010109H	make good wall plaster	Each	0.45	22.08	-	1.89	23.97	26.37	1.150
A010109I	total cost	Each	18.92	805.16	-	272.31	1,077.47	1,185.22	301.430

A010110   Make and fix cupboard front and return end to form linen cupboard, internal size 750 mm x 750 mm, full height floor to ceiling 2.40 m. Return wall and over door wall to be 75 mm x 50 mm fir stud covered both sides with expanded metal lathing and plastered. Hardboard flush door hung on 75 mm light steel hinges, fitted with bow handle and Bales catch. Standard door lining with 50 mm x 18 mm architrave outside. Four open slat shelves, comprising 50 mm x 25 mm in softwood slats spaced 25 mm apart and including bearers full width and depth of cupboard. New wall plaster and existing plaster inside cupboard to be painted in two coats emulsion. Door, lining and architrave to be primed and painted two coats of oil colour

A010110A	stud partition wall with expanded metal lathing and plaster both sides 3 sq.m	Each	10.00	278.00	-	93.41	371.41	408.55	55.640
A010110B	shelving 2.5 sq.m including bearers	Each	5.00	139.00	-	56.81	195.81	215.39	13.650
A010110C	door lining	Each	0.75	20.85	-	24.73	45.58	50.14	6.820
A010110D	door	Each	0.75	20.85	-	45.72	66.57	73.23	23.780
A010110E	architrave 5 lin.m	Each	0.75	20.85	-	8.49	29.34	32.27	2.090
A010110F	hinges	Each	0.45	12.51	-	3.41	15.92	17.51	0.620
A010110G	handle	Each	0.30	8.34	-	8.60	16.94	18.63	0.560

House Renovation Grants, Repairs and Alterations

Small Works 2011		Unit	Labour Hours	Labour Net	Plant Net	Materials Net	Unit Net	Unit with 10%	CO₂
				£	£	£	£	£	Kg
A01	**GRANTWORK**								
A0101	**HOUSE RENOVATION**								
A010110	Make and fix cupboard front and return end to form linen cupboard, internal size 750 mm x 750 mm, full height floor to ceiling 2.40 m. Return wall and over door wall to be 75 mm x 50 mm fir stud covered both sides with expanded metal lathing and plastered. Hardboard flush door hung on 75 mm light steel hinges, fitted with bow handle and Bales catch. Standard door lining with 50 mm x 18 mm architrave outside. Four open slat shelves, comprising 50 mm x 25 mm in softwood slats spaced 25 mm apart and including bearers full width and depth of cupboard. New wall plaster and existing plaster inside cupboard to be painted in two coats emulsion. Door, lining and architrave to be primed and painted two coats of oil colour								
A010110H	catch	Each	0.60	16.68	-	3.57	20.25	22.28	0.020
A010110I	emulsion paint 8 sq.m	Each	2.60	72.83	-	10.94	83.77	92.15	5.280
A010110J	painting 4 sq.m	Each	2.75	77.03	-	5.32	82.35	90.59	2.860
A010110K	total cost	Each	23.95	666.93	-	260.99	927.92	1,020.71	111.330
A010112	Take out old door frame, provide and fix new 50 mm standard softwood entrance door and frame, including cylinder night latch and letter plate, and decorate								
A010112A	take out door and frame	Each	1.50	31.28	-	-	31.28	34.41	-
A010112B	new door and frame	Each	3.00	83.40	-	175.89	259.29	285.22	68.610
A010112C	cylinder latch	Each	1.60	44.48	-	41.57	86.05	94.66	3.970
A010112D	letter plate	Each	1.75	48.65	-	11.91	60.56	66.62	3.940
A010112E	painting 3.5 sq.m	Each	3.00	84.03	-	3.26	87.29	96.02	1.750
A010112F	total cost	Each	10.85	291.83	-	232.62	524.45	576.90	78.270
A010113	Take down old timber stair flight and remove, fill over stair opening with 150 mm x 50 mm joists and board over to form extension to upper floor. Plaster baseboard and set soffit and emulsion paint. Make good wall plaster of spandrel and emulsion paint on wall								
A010113A	take out stairs	Each	9.40	195.99	-	-	195.99	215.59	-
A010113B	floor joists and boarding over 2.25 sq.m	Each	3.25	90.35	-	98.36	188.71	207.58	69.590
A010113C	ceiling plaster 2.6 sq.m	Each	1.21	58.88	-	3.83	62.71	68.98	2.590
A010113D	emulsion paint 2.6 sq.m	Each	1.05	29.41	-	1.55	30.96	34.06	0.750
A010113E	wall plaster 3.5 sq.m	Each	1.71	83.40	-	8.31	91.71	100.88	5.040
A010113F	emulsion paint 3.5 sq.m	Each	1.12	31.37	-	5.98	37.35	41.09	2.880
A010113G	total cost	Each	17.73	489.45	-	118.02	607.47	668.22	80.850
A010114	Take down existing door and lining and set aside and fix in new partition wall including architraves both sides. Oil and adjust lock and decorate woodwork								
A010114A	take out door and lining	Each	1.50	31.28	-	-	31.28	34.41	-
A010114B	reset door and lining in new opening	Each	3.75	104.25	-	-	104.25	114.68	-
A010114C	architrave 10 lin.m	Each	1.80	50.04	-	9.57	59.61	65.57	3.210
A010114D	painting 3.5 sq.m	Each	3.30	92.43	-	4.84	97.27	107.00	2.610
A010114E	oil and adjust lock	Each	0.25	6.95	-	-	6.95	7.65	-
A010114F	total cost	Each	10.60	284.95	-	14.41	299.36	329.30	5.820

Small Works 2011		Unit	Labour Hours	Labour Net	Plant Net	Materials Net	Unit Net	Unit with 10%	CO$_2$
				£	£	£	£	£	Kg
A01	**GRANTWORK**								
A0101	**HOUSE RENOVATION**								
A010115	**Excavate over site 225 mm deep to annexe building for bathroom and WC or kitchen and deposit soil over adjacent garden**								
A010115A	excavate and deposit soil	m^2	1.00	20.85	-	-	20.85	22.94	-
A010116	**Excavate foundation trench 450 mm x 600 mm deep. Lay concrete foundation 450 mm x 300 mm thick. New 275 mm cavity brickwork 450 mm high up to and including dampcourse**								
A010116A	trench excavation	m	1.20	25.02	-	-	25.02	27.52	-
A010116B	foundation concrete	m	1.00	20.85	-	17.51	38.36	42.20	43.680
A010116C	brickwork	m	0.57	43.58	-	21.45	65.03	71.53	55.310
A010116D	slate dampcourse	m	0.08	5.89	-	11.98	17.87	19.66	0.440
A010116E	total cost	m	2.85	95.33	-	50.94	146.27	160.90	99.440
A010118	**Lay 100 mm hardcore and 100 mm concrete over site and wood flooring on and including 150 mm x 50 mm joists (no sleeper walls)**								
A010118A	hardcore	m^2	0.25	5.21	-	2.54	7.75	8.53	1.580
A010118B	concrete	m^2	1.00	20.85	-	12.96	33.81	37.19	32.350
A010118C	flooring and joists	m^2	1.10	30.58	-	37.44	68.02	74.82	23.690
A010118D	total cost	m^2	2.35	56.64	-	52.95	109.59	120.55	57.610
A010119	**Build 275 mm cavity brick wall in common bricks with fletton facings externally, plastered and emulsion paint internally**								
A010119A	cavity wall	m^2	1.43	109.02	-	50.76	159.78	175.76	156.800
A010119B	wall plaster	m^2	0.43	20.86	-	2.14	23.00	25.30	1.300
A010119C	emulsion paint	m^2	0.32	8.96	-	1.55	10.51	11.56	0.750
A010119D	total cost	m^2	2.17	138.84	-	54.45	193.29	212.62	158.850
A010120	**Form lean-to roof of concrete tiles on battens including felt, 125 mm x 50 mm rafters and 100 mm x 75 mm plate**								
A010120A	plates and rafters	m^2	0.80	22.24	-	12.78	35.02	38.52	10.210
A010120B	battens and tiles	m^2	0.47	35.93	-	17.97	53.90	59.29	5.510
A010120C	felt	m^2	0.04	3.36	-	2.24	5.60	6.16	5.220
A010120D	total cost	m^2	1.31	61.46	-	32.98	94.44	103.88	20.940
A010121	**150 mm x 25 mm fascia and painting and PVC-u half round gutter**								
A010121A	fascia board	m	0.25	6.95	-	4.52	11.47	12.62	1.270
A010121B	paint fascia boards	m	0.30	8.40	-	0.38	8.78	9.66	0.210
A010121C	PVC-u gutter including stop ends and outlets	m	0.30	18.81	-	10.25	29.06	31.97	5.980
A010121D	total cost	m	0.85	34.16	-	15.15	49.31	54.24	7.460
A010122	**PVC-u downpipe including swanneck and shoe**								
A010122A	63 mm PVC-u downpipe 3 lin.m	Each	0.91	56.49	-	31.01	87.50	96.25	13.030
A010122B	swanneck comprising two bends	Each	0.30	18.81	-	8.84	27.65	30.42	1.230
A010122C	shoe	Each	0.20	12.46	-	4.66	17.12	18.83	0.240
A010122D	total cost	Each	1.41	87.75	-	44.52	132.27	145.50	14.500
A010123	**Renew ceiling joists and plasterboard and emulsion paint ceiling**								
A010123A	joists 100 mm x 50 mm	m^2	0.20	5.56	-	5.01	10.57	11.63	4.130
A010123B	plasterboard and set ceiling	m^2	0.45	22.08	-	4.97	27.05	29.76	5.590
A010123C	emulsion paint plasterboard and ceiling	m^2	0.40	11.20	-	1.82	13.02	14.32	0.880
A010123D	total cost	m^2	1.05	38.85	-	11.80	50.65	55.72	10.600

Small Works 2011		Unit	Labour Hours	Labour Net £	Plant Net £	Materials Net £	Unit Net £	Unit with 10% £	CO_2 Kg
A01	**GRANTWORK**								
A0101	**HOUSE RENOVATION**								
A010124	**Provide and fix standard casement window size 630 mm x 1050 mm including lintel, brick cill, glazing and painting**								
A010124A	steel lintel for external solid wall 143 mm high, 1050 mm long	Each	0.85	17.72	-	52.92	70.64	77.70	24.930
A010124B	brick cill	Each	0.44	33.33	-	5.80	39.13	43.04	19.120
A010124C	casement window	Each	1.20	33.36	-	164.47	197.83	217.61	64.150
A010124D	glazing 0.6 sq.m	Each	0.80	22.41	-	47.59	70.00	77.00	17.150
A010124E	paint both sides 1.3 sq.m	Each	2.00	56.02	-	1.32	57.34	63.07	0.730
A010124F	total cost	Each	5.29	162.84	-	271.97	434.81	478.29	125.750
A010125	**Cut through one brick external wall for new door opening including lintel over. Provide and fix new door and frame size 825 mm x 2025 mm overall**								
A010125A	cut opening through one brick wall 2 sq.m	Each	7.50	156.38	-	-	156.38	172.02	-
A010125B	steel lintel for external solid wall 143 mm high, 1200 mm long	Each	1.00	20.85	-	82.74	103.59	113.95	27.710
A010125C	door frame	Each	1.10	30.58	-	164.47	195.05	214.56	64.150
A010125D	door 762 mm x 1981 mm including lock hinges etc.	Each	4.00	111.20	-	223.30	334.50	367.95	73.240
A010125E	paint door and frame overall both sides 4 sq.m	Each	3.60	100.84	-	6.50	107.34	118.07	3.590
A010125F	make good wall plaster	Each	0.50	24.53	-	4.28	28.81	31.69	2.590
A010125G	total cost	Each	17.70	444.37	-	396.77	841.14	925.25	138.320
A010126	**Break up concrete paving, excavate drain trench, average 0.60 m deep. Lay 3.0 lin.m of 100 mm clayware pipe including hole through existing manhole and make good. Drain bend and vertical pipe set in concrete floor to receive W.C. pan. Trench refilled and paving reinstated on completion**								
A010126A	break up concrete paving 0.60m wide 3 lin.m long	Each	3.00	62.55	-	-	62.55	68.81	-
A010126B	excavate trench 3 lin.m	Each	2.80	58.38	-	-	58.38	64.22	-
A010126C	drain 100 mm 3 lin.m long	Each	1.65	34.40	-	31.45	65.85	72.44	16.770
A010126D	reinstate concrete paving 3 lin.m	Each	3.60	75.06	-	31.69	106.75	117.43	79.070
A010126E	end of drain into side of manhole and reform channel benching	Each	1.80	50.04	-	18.99	69.03	75.93	7.060
A010126F	drain bend and vertical pipe	Each	3.60	75.06	-	60.41	135.47	149.02	83.820
A010126G	total cost	Each	16.45	355.49	-	142.55	498.04	547.84	186.720
A010128	**Break up concrete paving, excavate drain trench, average 0.60 m deep. Lay 3.0 lin.m of 100 mm clayware pipe including hole through existing manhole and make good. Drain for surface and/or disposal waste pipes, 100 mm clayware gully trap in paving with gully surround**								
A010128A	break up concrete paving 0.60 wide, 3 lin.m long	Each	3.00	62.55	-	-	62.55	68.81	-
A010128B	excavate trench 3 lin.m long	Each	2.80	58.38	-	-	58.38	64.22	-
A010128C	drain 100 mm 3 lin.m long	Each	1.65	34.40	-	31.45	65.85	72.44	16.770
A010128D	reinstate concrete paving 3 lin.m	Each	3.60	75.06	-	31.69	106.75	117.43	79.070
A010128E	end of drain into side of manhole and reform channel benching	Each	1.80	50.04	-	18.99	69.03	75.93	7.060
A010128F	clayware gully and curb	Each	1.10	22.94	-	59.42	82.36	90.60	19.630
A010128G	total cost	Each	13.95	303.37	-	141.55	444.92	489.41	122.530

Small Works 2011		Unit	Labour Hours	Labour Net	Plant Net	Materials Net	Unit Net	Unit with 10%	CO₂
				£	£	£	£	£	Kg
A01	**GRANTWORK**								
A0101	**HOUSE RENOVATION**								
A010130	**Take down existing partition wall 2.4 m high (brick, clinker concrete or stud) and clear away. Make good ceiling plaster along top of wall and make good wood flooring at base of wall**								
A010130A	take down and clear away wall	m	0.70	14.60	-	-	14.60	16.06	-
A010130B	make good ceiling plaster and emulsion paint 0.3 m wide	m	0.25	12.26	-	0.47	12.73	14.00	0.250
A010130C	make good wood flooring and emulsion paint 0.3 m wide	m	0.65	18.07	-	5.40	23.47	25.82	2.230
A010130D	total cost	m	1.60	44.93	-	5.87	50.80	55.88	2.490
A010132	**Make good existing wall plaster 2.4 m high after removal of partition wall. Piece in skirting and picture rail and paint**								
A010132A	make good wall plaster 450 mm wide and joint to existing 3 lin.m	Each	0.95	46.61	-	3.59	50.20	55.22	2.160
A010132B	piece in 200 mm wood skirting about 300 mm long and paint	Each	1.10	30.58	-	0.74	31.32	34.45	0.280
A010132C	piece in wood picture rail about 300 mm long and paint	Each	0.50	13.90	-	0.55	14.45	15.90	0.210
A010132D	total cost	Each	2.55	91.09	-	4.80	95.89	105.48	2.610
A010133	**Build half brick partition 2.4 m high, both sides plastered and emulsion painted. Fix 150 mm softwood skirting and decorate both sides**								
A010133A	half brick wall 2.4 m high	m	2.01	153.82	-	56.81	210.63	231.69	137.310
A010133B	plaster both sides half brick wall 2.4 m high	m	2.13	104.27	-	12.27	116.54	128.19	7.490
A010133C	emulsion paint both sides	m	1.53	42.86	-	6.95	49.81	54.79	3.350
A010133D	skirting both sides	m	0.70	19.46	-	9.80	29.26	32.19	2.480
A010133E	paint skirting both sides	m	0.40	11.20	-	1.75	12.95	14.25	0.980
A010133F	total cost	m	6.78	331.60	-	87.59	419.19	461.11	151.620
A010134	**Build 100 mm concrete block wall 2.4 m high, both sides plastered and emulsion painted. Fix 150 mm softwood skirting both sides and paint**								
A010134A	concrete block wall 100 mm	m	1.01	76.91	-	40.56	117.47	129.22	47.820
A010134B	plaster both sides	m	2.13	104.27	-	12.27	116.54	128.19	7.490
A010134C	emulsion paint both sides	m	1.53	42.86	-	6.95	49.81	54.79	3.350
A010134D	skirting both sides	m	0.70	19.46	-	9.80	29.26	32.19	2.480
A010134E	paint both sides	m	0.40	11.20	-	1.75	12.95	14.25	0.980
A010134F	total cost	m	5.77	254.70	-	71.33	326.03	358.63	62.130
A010135	**Construct stud partition 2.4 m high of 100 mm x 50 mm studs clad both sides with plasterboard set in plaster and emulsion painted. Fix 150 mm wood skirting both sides and paint**								
A010135A	stud partition 100 mm x 50 mm - 2.4 m high	m	0.50	24.28	-	20.99	45.27	49.80	17.320
A010135B	plasterboard and set both sides	m	2.18	106.71	-	22.82	129.53	142.48	26.060
A010135C	emulsion paint both sides	m	1.53	42.86	-	6.95	49.81	54.79	3.350
A010135D	skirting both sides	m	0.70	19.46	-	9.80	29.26	32.19	2.480
A010135E	paint both sides	m	0.40	11.20	-	1.75	12.95	14.25	0.980
A010135F	total cost	m	5.31	204.51	-	61.48	265.99	292.59	50.200
A010138	**Take down door and frame and set aside. Fill opening with half brick walling and plaster both sides, including jointing to existing. Emulsion paint both sides. Fix 150 mm skirting both sides and paint**								
A010138A	take down door and frame	Each	1.50	31.28	-	-	31.28	34.41	-
A010138B	half brick wall (2 sq.m)	Each	1.61	123.08	-	45.93	169.01	185.91	111.010
A010138C	plaster both sides (4 sq.m)	Each	2.13	104.27	-	5.22	109.49	120.44	3.170

Small Works 2011		Unit	Labour Hours	Labour Net	Plant Net	Materials Net	Unit Net	Unit with 10%	CO$_2$
				£	£	£	£	£	Kg

A01   GRANTWORK

A0101   HOUSE RENOVATION

A010138   Take down door and frame and set aside. Fill opening with half brick walling and plaster both sides, including jointing to existing. Emulsion paint both sides. Fix 150 mm skirting both sides and paint

A010138D	emulsion paint both sides (4 sq.m)	Each	1.28	35.85	-	5.76	41.61	45.77	2.780
A010138E	skirting (2 lin.m)	Each	0.70	19.46	-	9.80	29.26	32.19	2.480
A010138F	paint (2 lin.m)	Each	0.40	11.20	-	1.75	12.95	14.25	0.980
A010138G	total cost	Each	7.62	325.14	-	68.46	393.60	432.96	120.410

A010140   Take down door and frame and set aside. Fill opening with 50 mm x 100 mm studs clad both sides with plaster baseboard and set in plaster, including making good to existing, emulsion paint both sides. Fix 150 mm skirting both sides and paint

A010140A	stud partition in opening (2 sq.m)	Each	2.00	55.60	-	22.90	78.50	86.35	18.900
A010140B	plaster baseboard and set both sides (4 sq.m)	Each	1.71	83.40	-	21.92	105.32	115.85	23.370
A010140C	emulsion paint both sides (4 sq.m)	Each	1.28	35.85	-	5.76	41.61	45.77	2.780
A010140D	take down door and frame	Each	1.50	31.28	-	-	31.28	34.41	-
A010140E	skirting (2 lin.m)	Each	0.70	19.46	-	9.80	29.26	32.19	2.480
A010140F	paint (2 lin.m)	Each	0.40	11.20	-	1.75	12.95	14.25	0.980
A010140G	total cost	Each	7.59	236.80	-	62.12	298.92	328.81	48.510

A010142   Existing door frame and door re-used in door opening in new partition. Fix new architraves both sides. Paint door frame and architrave both sides

A010142A	Fix existing door frame in new opening	Each	1.20	33.36	-	-	33.36	36.70	-
A010142B	architraves (10 lin.m)	Each	1.50	41.70	-	23.11	64.81	71.29	6.280
A010142C	rehang door	Each	0.50	13.90	-	-	13.90	15.29	-
A010142D	paint door and frame overall sides (4 sq.m)	Each	3.75	105.04	-	6.50	111.54	122.69	3.590
A010142E	total cost	Each	6.95	194.00	-	29.60	223.60	245.96	9.870

A010143   Provide and hang 762 mm x 1981 mm x 35 mm standard hardboard flush door and lining with new architraves both sides in new door opening. Door to be hung on 75 mm butt hinges and fitted with mortice lock, all to be primed and painted two coats oil colour

A010143A	door lining	Each	0.68	18.90	-	31.88	50.78	55.86	8.280
A010143B	door	Each	0.75	20.85	-	46.36	67.21	73.93	26.410
A010143C	architraves (10 lin.m)	Each	1.50	41.70	-	23.11	64.81	71.29	6.280
A010143D	butt hinges 75 mm	Each	0.80	22.24	-	2.16	24.40	26.84	0.400
A010143E	mortice lock and furniture	Each	2.00	55.60	-	44.98	100.58	110.64	5.630
A010143F	painting (4 sq.m)	Each	3.75	105.04	-	6.50	111.54	122.69	3.590
A010143G	total cost	Each	9.48	264.33	-	154.98	419.31	461.24	50.580

Small Works 2011	Unit	Labour Hours	Labour Net	Plant Net	Materials Net	Unit Net	Unit with 10%	CO₂
			£	£	£	£	£	Kg

A01   **GRANTWORK**

A0101   **HOUSE RENOVATION**

A010144   **Cut opening through one brick wall for window frame, 1200 mm x 1200 mm. Build in steel lintel and roofing tile cill and reform brick jambs. Provide and fix new casement window and frame. Glaze and paint both sides. Plaster reveals inside and make good internal wall plaster. Fix 100 mm softwood window board and paint**

A010144A	cut opening through one-brick wall for window 1200 mm x 1200 mm and lintel over (1.5 sq.m)	Each	7.20	150.12	-	-	150.12	165.13	-
A010144B	steel lintel for solid wall 143 mm high 1500 mm long	Each	1.50	31.28	-	109.97	141.25	155.38	44.920
A010144C	roofing tile cill 1.5 m long	Each	0.90	18.77	-	11.65	30.42	33.46	6.760
A010144D	reform brick jambs to opening (3 lin.m)	Each	7.50	208.50	-	13.33	221.83	244.01	40.440
A010144E	casement window and frame	Each	1.80	50.04	-	232.24	282.28	310.51	90.590
A010144F	glazing window and frame (1 sq.m) small squares	Each	1.20	33.61	-	79.19	112.80	124.08	27.890
A010144G	painting window sashes and both side (3.5 sq.m)	Each	4.50	126.05	-	4.53	130.58	143.64	2.500
A010144H	plaster reveals and make good around opening	Each	0.20	9.82	-	3.59	13.41	14.75	2.160
A010144I	window board 1.2 m long including painting	Each	0.50	13.90	-	10.24	24.14	26.55	2.500
A010144J	total cost	Each	25.30	640.88	-	464.86	1,105.74	1,216.31	218.070

A010146   **Take off tiles or slates and form opening in roof size 1200 mm x 1200 mm for dormer window size 1200 mm x 900 mm frame and board dormer flat and cheeks. Provide and fix standard window and glaze and paint. Internally plasterboard and set to soffit and dormer cheeks and make good existing plaster**

A010146A	strip tiles or slates and battens (1.7 sq.m)	Each	1.30	27.11	-	-	27.11	29.82	-
A010146B	trim opening	Each	0.45	12.51	-	30.15	42.66	46.93	18.720
A010146C	carcassing timber 100 mm x 50 mm to sides and roof of dormer (1.5 lin.m)	Each	3.60	100.08	-	28.11	128.19	141.01	23.200
A010146D	boarding to cheeks and roof of dormer (2.5 sq.m)	Each	4.35	120.93	-	41.82	162.75	179.03	17.320
A010146E	2.27 kg lead covering to roof and cheeks (3 sq.m)	Each	10.34	644.04	-	142.87	786.91	865.60	129.420
A010146F	casement window and frame	Each	1.55	43.09	-	200.26	243.35	267.69	78.110
A010146G	glazing window and frame, 1 sq.m (medium squares)	Each	1.10	30.81	-	79.16	109.97	120.97	27.700
A010146H	painting window sashes and frame both sides (3.5 sq.m)	Each	4.50	126.05	-	0.62	126.67	139.34	0.340
A010146I	plasterboard and set to soffit and cheeks (3.5 sq.m)	Each	1.71	83.40	-	17.17	100.57	110.63	18.440
A010146J	make good new plaster to existing	Each	0.25	12.26	-	1.64	13.90	15.29	1.010
A010146K	emulsion paint new plastering (3.5 sq.m)	Each	1.13	31.65	-	6.24	37.89	41.68	3.010
A010146L	total cost	Each	30.28	1,230.51	-	548.02	1,778.53	1,956.38	317.260

House Renovation Grants, Repairs and Alterations

Small Works 2011		Unit	Labour Hours	Labour Net	Plant Net	Materials Net	Unit Net	Unit with 10%	CO$_2$
				£	£	£	£	£	Kg
A01	**GRANTWORK**								
A0101	**HOUSE RENOVATION**								
A010147	**Take down length of stair handrail and balustrade to stair flights 3 m long x 2.4 m high. Fill in triangular stair spandrel between stair tread and soffit with stud partition, covered with expanded metal lathing and plastered both sides. 25 mm x 225 mm cut wall string to be fitted over tread risers 63 mm. Mopstick hand rail to be fixed full length of wall**								
A010147A	Take down and remove handrail and balustrade	Each	3.50	72.98	-	-	72.98	80.28	-
A010147B	triangular stud spandrel wall with expanded metal lathing and plaster both sides (average 4 sq. m)	Each	7.19	349.79	-	97.57	447.36	492.10	61.220
A010147C	emulsion paint wall both sides (8 sq. m)	Each	2.56	71.71	-	6.82	78.53	86.38	3.290
A010147D	225 mm x 25 mm cut wall string planted on (3.6 lin. m) and painting	Each	4.30	119.54	-	25.54	145.08	159.59	7.590
A010147E	mopstick handrail (3.6 lin. m)	Each	2.60	72.28	-	24.27	96.55	106.21	7.690
A010147F	total cost	Each	20.15	686.29	-	154.20	840.49	924.54	79.790
A010148	**Take down length of stair handrail and balustrade to stair flights 3 m long x 2.4 m high. Fill in triangular stair spandrel between stair tread and soffit with stud partition, covered with expanded metal lathing and plastered both sides. 25 mm x 225 mm cut wall string to be fitted over tread risers. 63 mm mopstick hand rail to be fixed full length of wall**								
A010148A	take down handrail and balustrade	Each	3.50	72.98	-	-	72.98	80.28	-
A010148B	spandrel wall as last described but with parallel raking sides (7.5 sq. m)	Each	28.20	783.96	-	183.63	967.59	1,064.35	115.400
A010148C	emulsion paint wall both sides (15 sq. m)	Each	4.80	134.45	-	12.75	147.20	161.92	6.150
A010148D	225 mm x 25 mm cut wall string planted on (3.6 lin. m) and painting	Each	4.30	119.54	-	25.54	145.08	159.59	7.590
A010148E	mopstick handrail (3.5 lin. m)	Each	3.10	86.18	-	24.27	110.45	121.50	7.690
A010148F	total cost	Each	43.90	1,197.10	-	246.20	1,443.30	1,587.63	136.830
A010149	**Take down and remove handrail and balustrade to landing. Form new wall 2.4 m high in studwork covered with metal lath and plastered both sides. Provide and fix 25 mm x 150 mm skirting one side, decorate wall and skirting.**								
A010149A	take down handrail and balustrade	m	1.00	20.85	-	-	20.85	22.94	-
A010149B	stud partition wall as described	m	7.85	218.23	-	80.55	298.78	328.66	50.450
A010149C	emulsion paint wall both sides	m	1.53	42.86	-	3.81	46.67	51.34	1.840
A010149D	skirting one side 150 mm x 25 mm	m	0.35	9.73	-	4.90	14.63	16.09	1.240
A010149E	painting skirting one side 150 mm x 25 mm	m	0.20	5.60	-	0.62	6.22	6.84	0.340
A010149F	total cost	m	10.93	297.27	-	89.88	387.15	425.87	53.870

Small Works 2011		Unit	Labour Hours	Labour Net	Plant Net	Materials Net	Unit Net	Unit with 10%	CO$_2$
				£	£	£	£	£	Kg
A01	**GRANTWORK**								
A0101	**HOUSE RENOVATION**								
A010150	**Make and fix cupboard front in 38 mm softwood framing and plywood panelling including 750 mm x 1950 mm door across recess 1.2 m x 2.4 m high to form food store. Supply and fit three shelves 200 mm x 25 mm and one shelf 300 mm x 25 mm. Cut hole in back wall and fit two 225 mm x 225 mm air bricks with perforated zinc panels inside**								
A010150A	cupboard front 38 mm 1.2 m x 2.4 mm	Each	20.00	556.00	-	93.05	649.05	713.96	29.020
A010150B	Extra over for hanging door on 75 mm butt hinges with bales catch and bow handle	Each	2.00	55.60	-	14.34	69.94	76.93	0.980
A010150C	set of three 200 mm x 25 mm shelves and one 300 mm x 25 mm shelf	Each	3.20	88.96	-	61.64	150.60	165.66	13.990
A010150D	cut hole in wall for two 225 mm x 225 mm air bricks and build in	Each	0.42	32.03	-	29.60	61.63	67.79	3.880
A010150E	two perforated zinc panels	Each	0.30	8.34	-	6.02	14.36	15.80	1.480
A010150F	painting cupboard front both sides 5.75 sq.m	Each	4.60	128.85	-	8.26	137.11	150.82	4.440
A010150G	total cost	Each	30.52	869.78	-	212.90	1,082.68	1,190.95	53.780
A010152	**Stainless steel sink complete with single drainer fixed complete on brackets built into wall. Waste trap fitted and connected to waste pipe and discharging into external hopper head or gully. Mixer tap with swivel spout, service pipes measured separately**								
A010152A	steel sink and drainer (PC £140 per Nr) and fixing	Each	2.48	154.39	-	140.00	294.39	323.83	36.210
A010152B	plastic waste trap 40 mm	Each	0.54	33.88	-	10.09	43.97	48.37	0.140
A010152C	plastic waste pipe 40 mm (2.7 lin. m) long	Each	0.91	56.49	-	10.28	66.77	73.45	2.840
A010152D	hole through wall for plastic waste pipe 40 mm (2.7 lin. m) long and make good	Each	0.26	19.65	-	0.37	20.02	22.02	1.270
A010152E	mixer tap swivel spout	Each	0.24	15.07	-	46.04	61.11	67.22	15.040
A010152F	total cost	Each	4.43	279.54	-	206.78	486.32	534.95	55.500
A010157	**1.7 m enamelled iron panelled bath complete with mixer tap, fixed spout, plug and chain, side panel and fixing. Waste trap fitted and connected, waste pipe discharging into external hopper head or gully. Service pipes measured separately**								
A010157A	bath (PC £360 per Nr) and fixing	Each	3.87	241.02	-	360.00	601.02	661.12	222.700
A010157B	plastic waste trap 40 mm	Each	0.54	33.88	-	10.09	43.97	48.37	0.140
A010157C	plastic waste pipe 40 mm dia x 2.7 m long	Each	0.91	56.49	-	10.28	66.77	73.45	2.840
A010157D	hole through wall for plastic waste pipe 40 mm dia x 2.7 m long and make good	Each	0.26	19.65	-	0.37	20.02	22.02	1.270
A010157E	plastic overflow pipe 19 mm dia x 0.6 m long	Each	0.39	24.48	-	1.64	26.12	28.73	0.290
A010157F	hole through wall for plastic overflow pipe 19 mm dia x 0.6 m long and make good	Each	0.26	19.65	-	0.37	20.02	22.02	1.270
A010157G	total cost	Each	6.23	395.15	-	441.87	837.02	920.72	252.370

Small Works 2011		Unit	Labour Hours	Labour Net £	Plant Net £	Materials Net £	Unit Net £	Unit with 10% £	CO$_2$ Kg
A01	**GRANTWORK**								
A0101	**HOUSE RENOVATION**								
A010158	**550 mm x 400 mm white vitreous china lavatory basin complete with pair of taps, plug and chain. Waste trap fitted and connected to waste pipe discharging into external hopper-head or gully. Service pipes measured separately**								
A010158A	lavatory basin (PC £110 per Nr) and fixing	Each	2.90	180.80	-	110.00	290.80	319.88	22.200
A010158B	plastic waste trap 32 mm	Each	0.39	24.48	-	7.49	31.97	35.17	0.100
A010158C	plastic waste pipe 32 mm dia x 2.7 m long	Each	0.76	47.08	-	8.75	55.83	61.41	2.270
A010158D	hole through wall for plastic waste pipe 32 mm dia x 2.7 m long and make good	Each	0.26	19.65	-	0.37	20.02	22.02	1.270
A010158E	total cost	Each	4.31	272.01	-	173.44	445.45	490.00	42.890
A010159	**Extra over waste pipe in last three items for cutting and fitting end of waste pipe into existing 100 mm cast iron soil stack pipe, including cutting in and jointing 100 mm cast iron boss pipe connector**								
A010159A	labour and material	Each	3.27	203.41	-	45.37	248.78	273.66	27.450
A010160	**W.C. suite low level complete and fixing at upper floor level including 100 mm cast-iron bend, long arm and junction to existing stack pipe. Service pipes measured separately**								
A010160A	W.C. suite complete and fixing	Each	3.27	203.41	-	151.68	355.09	390.60	38.570
A010160B	cast-iron bend 100 mm	Each	0.61	37.68	-	25.80	63.48	69.83	21.380
A010160C	cast-iron bend junction 100 mm	Each	1.21	75.30	-	39.88	115.18	126.70	18.950
A010160D	cut 100 mm cast-iron soil pipe to receive cast-iron bend junction	Each	2.06	128.05	-	-	128.05	140.86	-
A010160E	cut hole through one brick wall for 100 mm pipe and make good	Each	0.40	30.81	-	0.74	31.55	34.71	2.530
A010160F	plastic overflow pipe 19 mm x 1.0 m long	Each	0.45	28.28	-	2.58	30.86	33.95	0.480
A010160G	cut hole through one brick wall for small pipe and make good	Each	0.26	19.65	-	0.37	20.02	22.02	1.270
A010160H	total cost	Each	8.25	523.10	-	226.31	749.41	824.35	84.290
A010161	**W.C. suite low level complete and fixing at ground level including jointing to clayware drain bend (measured separately). Service pipes measured separately**								
A010161A	W.C. suite complete and fixing	Each	3.27	203.41	-	151.68	355.09	390.60	38.570
A010161B	plastic overflow pipe 19 mm dia x 1.0 m long	Each	0.45	28.28	-	2.58	30.86	33.95	0.480
A010161C	cut hole through one brick wall for small pipe and make good	Each	0.26	19.65	-	0.37	20.02	22.02	1.270
A010161D	total cost	Each	3.98	251.27	-	159.78	411.05	452.16	41.010
A010162	**227 litre plastic cold water cistern in loft space, including 13 mm ball valve 19 mm overflow pipe, tank bearers and hardboard tank casing. Service pipes measured separately**								
A010162A	cistern 227 litre ball valve and float	Each	2.09	129.92	-	196.92	326.84	359.52	50.410
A010162B	plastic overflow pipe 19 mm dia x average 3.0 m long	Each	1.36	84.76	-	7.75	92.51	101.76	1.440
A010162C	cut hole through wall for plastic overflow pipe 19 mm dia x average 3.0 m long and make good	Each	0.26	19.65	-	0.37	20.02	22.02	1.270
A010162D	pair tank bearers 100 mm x 50 mm each 1.8 m long	Each	0.12	3.34	-	6.87	10.21	11.23	5.670
A010162E	hardboard tank casing	Each	2.15	59.77	-	18.59	78.36	86.20	28.870
A010162F	total cost	Each	5.97	297.43	-	230.50	527.93	580.72	87.640

Small Works 2011		Unit	Labour Hours	Labour Net	Plant Net	Materials Net	Unit Net	Unit with 10%	CO$_2$
				£	£	£	£	£	Kg
A01	**GRANTWORK**								
A0101	**HOUSE RENOVATION**								
A010163	**Cut through existing ceiling and trim joists to form opening for 750 mm x 750 mm trap door. Softwood lining with planted stop and architraves. Trap door comprises plywood face on 75 mm x 25 mm framed backing, hinged to lining and fitted with bow handle. All exposed woodwork painted**								
A010163A	cut opening and trim joists	Each	0.60	16.68	-	15.40	32.08	35.29	9.630
A010163B	trap door and lining 150 mm x 25 mm x 3.0 m long	Each	2.00	55.60	-	26.18	81.78	89.96	6.980
A010163C	architrave x 3.5 m	Each	0.45	12.51	-	7.02	19.53	21.48	1.910
A010163D	bow handle	Each	0.25	6.95	-	8.60	15.55	17.11	0.560
A010163E	painting (0.85 m^2)	Each	0.80	22.41	-	1.54	23.95	26.35	0.850
A010163F	make good plaster	Each	0.18	8.60	-	0.64	9.24	10.16	0.430
A010163G	total cost	Each	4.28	122.75	-	59.38	182.13	200.34	20.370
A010166	**The following rates for water service pipes including bends, sockets and an average allowance of one tee (or junction) for every four linear metres of pipe. Holes through walls for pipes and making good plaster included, one hole for every four linear metres of pipe**								
A010166A	galvanised steel water pipe 15 mm dia including extra cost of tees and holes and through partition walls etc, all as described	m	0.67	41.42	-	9.77	51.19	56.31	4.620
A010166B	galvanised steel water pipe 20 mm dia including extra cost of tees and holes and through partition walls etc, all as described	m	0.73	45.22	-	12.39	57.61	63.37	9.610
A010166C	copper water pipe 15 mm dia including extra cost of tees and holes and through partition walls etc, all as described	m	0.54	33.88	-	9.26	43.14	47.45	1.200
A010166D	copper water pipe 22 mm dia including extra cost of tees and holes and through partition walls etc, all as described	m	0.58	35.81	-	9.73	45.54	50.09	2.080
A010166E	polythene normal gauge water pipe 20 mm dia including extra cost of tees and holes through partition walls etc, all as described	m	0.76	47.08	-	7.76	54.84	60.32	1.470
A010166F	polythene normal gauge water pipe 25 mm dia including extra cost of tees and holes through partition walls etc, all as described	m	0.97	60.29	-	11.53	71.82	79.00	1.780

Small Works 2011		Unit	Labour Hours	Labour Net	Plant Net	Materials Net	Unit Net	Unit with 10%	CO$_2$
				£	£	£	£	£	Kg
A02	**REPAIRS AND ALTERATIONS**								
A0201	**EXCAVATION**								
A020101	**Excavate by hand over site area, wheel 18 m, deposit in skip**								
A020101A	average 300 mm deep	m^2	1.86	38.78	-	-	38.78	42.66	-
A020102	**Excavate by hand for trenches to receive foundations, wheel 18 m, deposit in skip**								
A020102A	not exceeding 1.0 m deep	m^3	6.52	135.94	-	-	135.94	149.53	-
A020102B	exceeding 1.0 m deep and not exceeding 2.0 deep	m^3	8.02	167.22	-	-	167.22	183.94	-
A020103	**Excavate by hand for basement, wheel 18 m, deposit in skip**								
A020103A	not exceeding 1.0 m deep	m^3	6.00	125.10	-	-	125.10	137.61	-
A020103B	exceeding 1.0 m deep and not exceeding 2.0 deep	m^3	6.72	140.11	-	-	140.11	154.12	-
A020104	**Excavated material as filling to excavations, deposited and compacted by hand**								
A020104A	in 250 mm layers	m^3	2.00	41.70	-	-	41.70	45.87	-
A020105	**Extra over excavation for breaking up brickwork by hand**								
A020105A	in old foundations	m^3	7.09	147.83	-	-	147.83	162.61	-
A020106	**Hire of skip, delivery to site, removing when full, disposal of contents, payment of tipping charges**								
A020106A	size 4.5 m^3	m^3	-	-	33.60	-	33.60	36.96	-
A0202	**EARTHWORK SUPPORT AND HARDCORE**								
A020201	**In firm ground to opposing faces not exceeding 2.00 m apart; maximum depth not exceeding**								
A020201A	1.00 m	m^2	0.85	17.72	-	3.27	20.99	23.09	1.660
A020201B	2.00 m	m^2	0.93	19.39	-	3.60	22.99	25.29	1.830
A020202	**In loose ground to opposing faces not exceeding 2.00 m apart; maximum depth not exceeding**								
A020202A	1.00 m	m^2	6.62	138.03	-	25.82	163.85	180.24	13.070
A020202B	2.00 m	m^2	6.62	138.03	-	25.82	163.85	180.24	13.070
A020203	**Imported hardcore compacted to receive concrete to finished thickness**								
A020203A	100 mm	m^2	0.48	10.01	0.66	2.48	13.15	14.47	2.380
A020203B	150 mm	m^2	0.72	15.01	0.80	3.82	19.63	21.59	3.380
A020203C	225 mm	m^2	1.08	22.52	0.93	5.72	29.17	32.09	4.730
A0203	**CONCRETE**								
A020301	**Portland cement concrete in foundations**								
A020301A	1:2:4 mix	m^3	6.00	125.10	-	135.82	260.92	287.01	360.994
A020301B	1:3:6 mix	m^3	6.00	125.10	-	129.19	254.29	279.72	268.646
A020302	**Concrete 1:3:6 oversite; thickness**								
A020302A	100 mm	m^3	9.00	187.65	-	129.19	316.84	348.52	268.646
A020302B	150 mm	m^3	8.50	177.23	-	129.19	306.42	337.06	268.646

Small Works 2011		Unit	Labour Hours	Labour Net	Plant Net	Materials Net	Unit Net	Unit with 10%	CO$_2$
				£	£	£	£	£	Kg
A02	**REPAIRS AND ALTERATIONS**								
A0203	**CONCRETE**								
A020303	**Concrete 1:3:6 oversite; in patches not exceeding 4 sq.m in area, including jointing to existing, thickness**								
A020303A	100 mm	m^3	14.00	291.90	-	129.19	421.09	463.20	268.646
A020303B	150 mm	m^3	13.50	281.48	-	129.19	410.67	451.74	268.646
A020304	**Extra over site concrete for**								
A020304A	preparing to receive asphalt, tiling etc including extra cement	m^2	0.45	9.38	-	2.08	11.46	12.61	4.640
A020304B	trowelling to smooth surface	m^2	0.55	11.47	-	-	11.47	12.62	-
A020305	**Sprinkling surface with coarse carborundum at**								
A020305A	1 kg per sq. m and lightly trowelling	m^2	0.55	11.47	-	1.30	12.77	14.05	0.090
A020306	**Clean existing concrete or rendered floors**								
A020306A	treat with application of silicate of soda solution	m^2	0.30	6.25	-	0.42	6.67	7.34	0.010
A0204	**PRECAST CONCRETE**								
A020401	**Reinforced concrete lintels cast in situ including reinforcement and formwork**								
A020401A	113 mm x 150 mm	m	0.25	19.19	-	5.52	24.71	27.18	15.640
A020401B	113 mm x 225 mm	m	0.30	23.09	-	6.69	29.78	32.76	19.350
A020401C	225 mm x 150 mm	m	0.44	33.33	-	9.33	42.66	46.93	26.800
A020401D	225 mm x 225 mm	m	0.49	37.15	-	11.66	48.81	53.69	34.230
A020402	**Precast concrete lintels including bedding**								
A020402A	113 mm x 150 mm	m	0.15	11.54	-	8.12	19.66	21.63	9.650
A020402B	113 mm x 225 mm	m	0.22	16.67	-	8.43	25.10	27.61	14.470
A020402C	225 mm x 150 mm	m	0.29	21.79	-	12.65	34.44	37.88	20.740
A020402D	225 mm x 225 mm	m	0.37	28.21	-	16.13	44.34	48.77	5.310
A020403	**Needle through 225 mm brickwork with 150 mm x 100 mm shore with one pair Acrow or other adjustable struts to every linear metre or part thereof (maximum span 2.70 m). Cut out and remove defective lintel. Supply, hoist and build in precast reinforced concrete lintel and make good all brickwork and plaster disturbed**								
A020403A	225 mm x 150 mm lintel	m	1.63	124.38	5.26	12.65	142.29	156.52	20.740
A020403B	225 mm x 225 mm lintel	m	1.71	130.81	5.26	16.13	152.20	167.42	5.310
A020404	**Cut away triangular area of brickwork above lintel. Cut out and remove defective lintel. Supply, hoist and build in precast reinforced concrete lintel, rebuild brickwork over, including facing bricks to match existing, and make good internal plaster**								
A020404A	225 mm x 225 mm lintel	m	3.42	261.54	-	18.74	280.28	308.31	92.450
A020404B	225 mm x 338 mm lintel	m	4.86	371.78	-	29.85	401.63	441.79	138.770
A020405	**Take out stone or concrete cill. Supply and build in cast concrete cill including all making good**								
A020405A	225 mm x 75 mm	m	0.37	28.21	-	10.01	38.22	42.04	13.440
A020406	**Pier caps**								
A020406A	300 mm x 300 mm x 75 mm for 225 mm piers	Each	0.34	25.61	-	8.70	34.31	37.74	8.200
A020406B	400 mm x 400 mm x 75 mm for 338 mm piers	Each	0.44	33.33	-	12.30	45.63	50.19	13.970

Small Works 2011		Unit	Labour Hours	Labour Net £	Plant Net £	Materials Net £	Unit Net £	Unit with 10% £	CO₂ Kg
A02	**REPAIRS AND ALTERATIONS**								
A0205	**BREAKING UP CONCRETE STEPS AND FLOORS**								
A020501	**Break up and remove old concrete steps**								
A020501A	form new steps in concrete 1:3:6 including wrought formwork to risers and ends, surfaces of treads trowelled smooth	m³	19.00	396.15	-	160.80	556.95	612.65	355.210
A020502	**Break up and remove concrete floors, paving etc at ground level and load into skip**								
A020502A	not exceeding 150 mm	m²	2.25	46.91	-	-	46.91	51.60	-
A020502B	150 mm - 225 mm	m²	4.00	83.40	-	-	83.40	91.74	-
A020502C	225 mm - 300 mm	m²	6.00	125.10	-	-	125.10	137.61	-
A020503	**Break up and remove reinforced concrete floors, pavings etc at ground level and load into skip**								
A020503A	not exceeding 150 mm	m²	3.40	70.89	-	-	70.89	77.98	-
A020503B	150 mm - 225 mm	m²	6.00	125.10	-	-	125.10	137.61	-
A020503C	225 mm - 300 mm	m²	9.00	187.65	-	-	187.65	206.42	-
A020504	**Break up concrete paving 750 mm wide and 100 mm thick for new wall and remove. Excavate trench and part return, fill in and ram and remove remainder**								
A020504A	Make good concrete paving. (Foundation concrete measured separately.)	m	2.85	59.42	-	9.75	69.17	76.09	24.330
A020505	**Hack up broken or sunken areas of concrete paving, spread and consolidate hardcore 150 mm, lay new concrete to falls, joint to existing including trowelling to form smooth surface**								
A020505A	100 mm	m²	2.15	44.83	-	17.38	62.21	68.43	35.200
A020505B	150 mm	m²	2.45	51.08	-	23.81	74.89	82.38	51.230
A0206	**PAVINGS**								
A020601	**Hack surface of existing paving of floors and grout and render in**								
A020601A	19 mm cement mortar 1:2:5	m²	0.50	24.53	-	3.00	27.53	30.28	8.540
A020602	**Hack off defective cement rendering to steps (treads and risers) and make out in**								
A020602A	25 mm cement and sand 1:3 trowelled including nosings and arises	m²	1.26	61.32	-	3.70	65.02	71.52	12.650
A020603	**Clean and hack existing concrete surface to form key for**								
A020603A	granolithic paving	m²	0.40	8.34	-	-	8.34	9.17	-
A020604	**Roughen and grout edge of existing concrete paving to new**								
A020604A	100 mm	m	0.40	8.34	-	-	8.34	9.17	-
A020604B	150 mm	m	0.50	10.43	-	-	10.43	11.47	-
A0207	**BREAKING OUT REINFORCED CONCRETE**								
A020701	**Breaking up reinforced concrete**								
A020701A	walls, columns, beams, suspended floors or roofs and loading into skip	m³	27.00	562.95	-	-	562.95	619.25	-

Small Works 2011		Unit	Labour Hours	Labour Net	Plant Net	Materials Net	Unit Net	Unit with 10%	CO₂
				£	£	£	£	£	Kg
A02	**REPAIRS AND ALTERATIONS**								
A0207	**BREAKING OUT REINFORCED CONCRETE**								
A020702	**Cutting holes through concrete for pipes, bars etc, per 25 mm depth of cut and making good**								
A020702A	area not exceeding 0.003 sq.m	Each	0.20	4.17	-	0.74	4.91	5.40	2.530
A020702B	0.003 - 0.023 sq.m	Each	0.40	8.34	-	0.99	9.33	10.26	3.370
A020703	**Cutting holes through reinforced concrete for pipes, bars etc, per 25 mm depth of cut and making good**								
A020703A	area not exceeding 0.003 sq.m	Each	0.30	6.25	-	0.74	6.99	7.69	2.530
A020703B	0.003 - 0.023 sq.m	Each	0.60	12.51	-	0.99	13.50	14.85	3.370
A0208	**CONCRETE CURBS AND CHANNELS**								
A020801	**Forming concrete 1:2:4 curbs and channels including all necessary formwork but excluding excavation**								
A020801A	average 0.047 sq.m sectional area	m	0.50	24.42	-	6.41	30.83	33.91	20.430
A0209	**WORKS TO CHIMNEYS**								
A020901	**Demolishing brickwork, any height, cleaning sound whole bricks to**								
A020901A	reuse and remove remainder	m³	3.19	243.57	-	-	243.57	267.93	-
A020902	**Collect, clean and stack bricks for reuse; in**								
A020902A	lime mortar	1000	4.70	358.93	-	-	358.93	394.82	-
A020902B	compo mortar	1000	5.70	435.84	-	-	435.84	479.42	-
A020902C	cement mortar	1000	7.38	564.05	-	-	564.05	620.46	-
A020903	**Pulling down chimney stacks, clean sound whole bricks for reuse and remove; up to 9 m high or two storeys**								
A020903A	lime mortar	m³	9.39	717.94	-	-	717.94	789.73	-
A020903B	cement mortar	m³	12.07	923.06	-	-	923.06	1,015.37	-
A020904	**Extra over last for each additional 3 m or storey height**								
A020904A	lime mortar	m³	2.35	179.50	-	-	179.50	197.45	-
A020904B	cement mortar	m³	3.02	230.73	-	-	230.73	253.80	-
A020905	**Rebuild single flue chimney in common bricks (PC £300 per 1000), in cement mortar 1:3, including building in 185 m dia socketed and rebated clay flue liners, BS 1181; up to 9 m or two storeys high; overall plan dimensions**								
A020905A	450 x 450 mm	m	0.95	72.78	-	64.87	137.65	151.42	164.050
A020905B	675 x 675 mm	m	2.37	181.26	-	121.45	302.71	332.98	403.040
A020907	**Rebuild double flue chimney in common bricks (PC £300 per 1000), in cement mortar 1:3, including building in 185 m dia socketed and rebated clay flue liners, BS 1181; up to 9 m or two storeys high; overall plan dimensions**								
A020907A	450 x 750 mm	m	1.69	129.51	-	121.87	251.38	276.52	291.680
A020907B	675 x 975 mm	m	3.47	265.05	-	193.76	458.81	504.69	589.930
A020909	**Take off loose chimney pot and reset including flaunching**								
A020909A	up to two storeys or 9 m high	Each	0.67	51.30	-	0.68	51.98	57.18	1.610

House Renovation Grants, Repairs and Alterations

Small Works 2011		Unit	Labour Hours	Labour Net	Plant Net	Materials Net	Unit Net	Unit with 10%	CO₂
				£	£	£	£	£	Kg
A02	**REPAIRS AND ALTERATIONS**								
A0209	**WORKS TO CHIMNEYS**								
A020910	**Take down and remove chimney pot, supply, set and flaunch new pot; up to two storeys or 9 m high**								
A020910A	300 mm pot	Each	0.84	64.14	-	35.11	99.25	109.18	4.170
A020910B	450 mm pot	Each	0.87	66.66	-	42.90	109.56	120.52	6.060
A020910C	600 mm pot	Each	0.91	69.26	-	62.36	131.62	144.78	6.750
A020911	**Add to the foregoing for each additional storey or 3 m high**								
A020911A	300 mm pot	Each	0.09	6.96	-	-	6.96	7.66	-
A020911B	450 mm pot	Each	0.13	9.71	-	-	9.71	10.68	-
A020911C	600 mm pot	Each	0.17	12.84	-	-	12.84	14.12	-
A0212	**BRICKWORK REPAIRS DPCs SUNDRIES**								
A021201	**Treating brick walls with silicone, or similar, damp-proof liquid**								
A021201A	external	m²	0.07	5.66	-	0.88	6.54	7.19	0.080
A021202	**Cut out defective brickwork and reface with new facing bricks (PC £390 per 1000)**								
A021202A	cement mortar	m²	1.91	146.17	-	27.82	173.99	191.39	104.430
A021202B	lime mortar	m²	1.68	128.21	-	28.86	157.07	172.78	103.790
A021203	**Cut out defective brickwork and reface with single facing bricks (PC £390 per 1000)**								
A021203A	cement mortar	Each	0.17	12.84	-	0.53	13.37	14.71	1.780
A021203B	lime mortar	Each	0.12	8.94	-	0.53	9.47	10.42	1.780
A021204	**Rake out mortar and repoint**								
A021204A	perished mortar	m²	0.29	22.09	-	0.54	22.63	24.89	1.290
A021204B	sound mortar	m²	0.72	55.12	-	0.54	55.66	61.23	1.290
A021205	**Cut out fractures in brickwork and build in new brickwork approximately 405 mm wide, 225 thick**								
A021205A	cement mortar	m	1.21	92.28	-	18.49	110.77	121.85	45.190
A021205B	lime mortar	m	0.79	60.24	-	18.53	78.77	86.65	44.890
A021206	**Take down segmental arch and rebuild in facings (PC £390 per 1000) 225 mm high on face including centering**								
A021206A	113 mm wide soffit	m	2.01	153.82	-	12.36	166.18	182.80	37.590
A021206B	225 mm wide soffit	m	2.62	199.99	-	13.60	213.59	234.95	48.320
A021207	**Cut opening through brick walls in cement mortar for doors, windows etc including all necessary shoring and making good**								
A021207A	half brick walls	m²	0.92	42.46	0.41	15.07	57.94	63.73	55.580
A021207B	one brick walls	m²	1.84	84.99	0.83	27.49	113.31	124.64	88.260
A021207C	one and a half brick walls	m²	2.76	127.45	1.14	40.04	168.63	185.49	121.360
A021207D	two brick walls	m²	3.68	169.91	1.50	52.15	223.56	245.92	153.300
A021208	**Brickwork in common bricks (PC £300 per 1000) in gauged mortar in small areas, bonding to existing**								
A021208A	half brick	m²	0.82	62.84	-	23.87	86.71	95.38	106.050
A021208B	one brick	m²	1.51	115.36	-	48.40	163.76	180.14	212.900
A021208C	one and a half brick	m²	2.26	173.08	-	74.76	247.84	272.62	180.550
A021209	**Damp-proof course in short lengths in existing walls including cutting out brickwork and building in with new bricks**								
A021209A	half brick wide - two course slate	m	0.62	47.48	-	10.34	57.82	63.60	4.680

Small Works 2011		Unit	Labour Hours	Labour Net	Plant Net	Materials Net	Unit Net	Unit with 10%	CO$_2$
				£	£	£	£	£	Kg
A02	**REPAIRS AND ALTERATIONS**								
A0212	**BRICKWORK REPAIRS DPCs SUNDRIES**								
A021209	**Damp-proof course in short lengths in existing walls including cutting out brickwork and building in with new bricks**								
A021209B	half brick wide - bitumen felt	m	0.52	39.75	-	4.79	44.54	48.99	4.960
A021209C	one brick wide and over - two course slate	m^2	2.18	166.66	-	104.95	271.61	298.77	45.950
A021209D	one brick wide and over - bitumen felt	m^2	1.79	137.15	-	45.96	183.11	201.42	48.590
A021210	**Cut, tooth and bond new brickwork to existing**								
A021210A	half brick	m	0.19	14.14	-	2.56	16.70	18.37	6.180
A021210B	one brick	m	0.34	25.61	-	5.29	30.90	33.99	12.780
A021210C	one and a half brick	m	0.47	35.93	-	7.84	43.77	48.15	18.960
A021211	**Cut hole for pipes, brackets, fittings etc, through clinker concrete walls per 25 mm in depth of cut and make good**								
A021211A	area n.e. 0.003 sq.m	Each	0.04	3.06	-	0.25	3.31	3.64	0.840
A021211B	exceeding 0.003 sq.m, n.e. 0.03 sq.m	Each	0.06	4.59	-	0.37	4.96	5.46	1.270
A021211C	exceeding 0.03 sq.m, n.e. 0.06 sq.m	Each	0.08	6.42	-	0.49	6.91	7.60	1.690
A021212	**Cut hole for pipes, brackets, fittings etc, through brickwork in lime mortar and make good**								
A021212A	area n.e. 0.003 sq.m	Each	0.07	5.12	-	0.27	5.39	5.93	0.650
A021212B	exceeding 0.003 sq.m, n.e. 0.03 sq.m	Each	0.10	7.72	-	0.41	8.13	8.94	0.970
A021212C	exceeding 0.03 sq.m, n.e. 0.06 sq.m	Each	0.13	10.24	-	0.54	10.78	11.86	1.290
A021213	**Cut hole for pipes, brackets, fittings etc, through brickwork in cement mortar and make good**								
A021213A	area n.e. 0.003 sq.m	Each	0.09	7.19	-	0.25	7.44	8.18	0.840
A021213B	exceeding 0.003 sq.m, n.e. 0.03 sq.m	Each	0.16	12.31	-	0.37	12.68	13.95	1.270
A021213C	exceeding 0.03 sq.m, n.e. 0.06 sq.m	Each	0.21	16.13	-	0.49	16.62	18.28	1.690
A021214	**Cut horizontal chase in brickwork 112 mm deep for concrete floor or landing; chase width**								
A021214A	100 mm	m	0.67	51.30	-	-	51.30	56.43	-
A021214B	125 mm	m	0.74	56.42	-	-	56.42	62.06	-
A021214C	150 mm	m	0.84	64.14	-	-	64.14	70.55	-
A021214D	200 mm	m	1.01	76.91	-	-	76.91	84.60	-
A021215	**Cut horizontal chase in fair faced brickwork 112 mm deep for concrete floor or landing; chase width**								
A021215A	100 mm	m	1.01	76.91	-	-	76.91	84.60	-
A021215B	125 mm	m	1.11	84.63	-	-	84.63	93.09	-
A021215C	150 mm	m	1.26	96.17	-	-	96.17	105.79	-
A021215D	200 mm	m	1.51	115.36	-	-	115.36	126.90	-
A021216	**Reform brick jambs after cutting new opening in existing brickwork, in common bricks (PC £300 per 1000)**								
A021216A	half brick	m	0.67	51.30	-	2.89	54.19	59.61	13.370
A021216B	one brick	m	0.84	64.14	-	5.79	69.93	76.92	26.740
A021216C	one and a half brick	m	1.01	76.91	-	8.93	85.84	94.42	40.950

House Renovation Grants, Repairs and Alterations

Small Works 2011		Unit	Labour Hours	Labour Net	Plant Net	Materials Net	Unit Net	Unit with 10%	CO$_2$
				£	£	£	£	£	Kg
A02	**REPAIRS AND ALTERATIONS**								
A0212	**BRICKWORK REPAIRS DPCs SUNDRIES**								
A021217	**Reform brick jambs after cutting new opening in existing brickwork, in facing bricks (PC £390 per 1000)**								
A021217A	half brick	m	0.91	69.26	-	3.66	72.92	80.21	12.970
A021217B	one brick	m	1.04	79.51	-	7.33	86.84	95.52	25.940
A021217C	one and a half brick	m	1.17	89.75	-	11.26	101.01	111.11	39.560
A021219	**Take out and rebed door or window frame**								
A021219A	point externally and make good internally	m	0.19	14.14	-	0.41	14.55	16.01	0.970
A021220	**Rake out defective pointing around door or window frame and repoint in**								
A021220A	cement mortar	m	0.15	11.54	-	0.41	11.95	13.15	0.970
A021220B	cement mortar but using mastic	m	0.20	15.37	-	0.66	16.03	17.63	1.390
A021222	**Take out existing fireplace including surround and hearth**								
A021222A	small iron	Each	1.34	102.60	-	-	102.60	112.86	-
A021222B	large tiled	Each	1.73	132.03	-	-	132.03	145.23	-
A021222C	free standing	Each	1.07	82.03	-	-	82.03	90.23	-
A021223	**Take out and reset existing fireplace including surround and hearth**								
A021223A	small iron	Each	3.35	256.41	-	3.58	259.99	285.99	12.230
A021223B	large tiled	Each	4.11	314.13	-	5.06	319.19	351.11	17.290
A021223C	free standing	Each	2.75	210.24	-	1.36	211.60	232.76	4.640
A021224	**Fix only new fireplace including surround and hearth**								
A021224A	small iron	Each	2.85	217.96	-	3.58	221.54	243.69	12.230
A021224B	large tiled	Each	3.57	273.08	-	5.06	278.14	305.95	17.290
A021224C	free standing	Each	1.58	120.49	-	1.36	121.85	134.04	4.640
A021225	**Take out existing fireplace and fix only solid brick back with fine concrete behind**								
A021225A	fix tiled surround and tiled hearth (cost of interior, surround, hearth tiles and fret not included)	Each	4.36	333.32	-	2.99	336.31	369.94	7.460
A021226	**Remove small kitchen range, adapt opening for and supply and set**								
A021226A	400 mm fire back and basket fire and fret, fill in and point	Each	3.02	230.73	-	109.50	340.23	374.25	68.260
A021227	**Remove existing basket or other low fire and supply and fix to hearth**								
A021227A	new 400 mm Allnight basket fire with enamelled front. Seal edges and make good all round	Each	2.68	205.12	-	109.23	314.35	345.79	67.620
A021228	**Galvanised iron air bricks built into wall as work proceeds**								
A021228A	225 mm x 75 mm	Each	0.07	5.66	-	5.81	11.47	12.62	0.400
A021228B	225 mm x 150 mm	Each	0.10	7.72	-	10.68	18.40	20.24	0.800
A021229	**Terracotta air bricks built into wall as work proceeds**								
A021229A	225 mm x 75 mm	Each	0.07	5.66	-	3.91	9.57	10.53	0.540
A021229B	225 mm x 150 mm	Each	0.10	7.72	-	5.18	12.90	14.19	1.080
A021229C	225 mm x 225 mm	Each	0.11	8.49	-	14.67	23.16	25.48	1.620
A021230	**Plaster louvre type air bricks into wall as work proceeds**								
A021230A	225 mm x 75 mm	Each	0.07	5.12	-	2.84	7.96	8.76	0.230
A021230B	225 mm x 150 mm	Each	0.08	6.42	-	3.40	9.82	10.80	0.450
A021230C	225 mm x 225 mm	Each	0.10	7.72	-	5.58	13.30	14.63	5.980

Small Works 2011		Unit	Labour Hours	Labour Net	Plant Net	Materials Net	Unit Net	Unit with 10%	CO$_2$
				£	£	£	£	£	Kg
A02	**REPAIRS AND ALTERATIONS**								
A0212	**BRICKWORK REPAIRS DPCs SUNDRIES**								
A021231	**Add to the foregoing air brick items for cutting through existing brick wall (any thickness), building in and make good**								
A021231A	225 mm x 75 mm	Each	0.09	7.19	-	0.41	7.60	8.36	0.970
A021231B	225 mm x 150 mm	Each	0.10	7.72	-	0.54	8.26	9.09	1.290
A021231C	225 mm x 225 mm	Each	0.12	8.94	-	0.68	9.62	10.58	1.610
A021232	**Add to the foregoing for cutting out and removing existing**								
A021232A	225 mm x 75 mm	Each	0.03	2.60	-	-	2.60	2.86	-
A021232B	225 mm x 150 mm	Each	0.04	3.06	-	-	3.06	3.37	-
A021232C	225 mm x 225 mm	Each	0.05	3.82	-	-	3.82	4.20	-
A0214	**DENSE AGGREGATE CONCRETE BLOCK WALLS**								
A021401	**Dense aggregate concrete blocks in walls etc in composition mortar**								
A021401A	rough both sides 100 mm slabs	m^2	0.42	32.03	-	17.30	49.33	54.26	25.870
A021401B	fair face one side	m^2	0.62	47.48	-	17.30	64.78	71.26	25.870
A021401C	fair face both sides	m^2	0.67	51.30	-	17.30	68.60	75.46	25.870
A0216	**WOODWORK REPAIRS AND REMOVALS**								
A021601	**Remove timber and load into skip**								
A021601A	roof timbers complete, including rafters, purlins, ceiling joists, plates and the like (measured flat on plan)	m^2	0.37	7.71	-	-	7.71	8.48	-
A021601B	floor construction; ground floor level	m^2	0.28	5.84	-	-	5.84	6.42	-
A021601C	floor construction; first floor level	m^2	0.55	11.47	-	-	11.47	12.62	-
A021601D	floor construction; roof level	m^2	0.77	16.05	-	-	16.05	17.66	-
A021601E	individual floor or roof members	m	0.30	6.25	-	-	6.25	6.88	-
A021601F	Extra for cutting off ends flush with wall	Each	0.50	10.43	-	-	10.43	11.47	-
A021601G	decayed or infected floor plates	m	0.40	8.34	-	-	8.34	9.17	-
A021601H	tilting fillet or roll	m	0.17	3.54	-	-	3.54	3.89	-
A021601I	fascia or barge board	m	0.65	13.55	-	-	13.55	14.91	-
A021602	**Remove boarding, including withdrawing nails, and load into skip**								
A021602A	softwood flooring; at ground floor level	m^2	0.42	8.76	-	-	8.76	9.64	-
A021602B	softwood flooring; at first floor level	m^2	0.68	14.18	-	-	14.18	15.60	-
A021602C	softwood flooring; at roof level	m^2	0.80	16.68	-	-	16.68	18.35	-
A021602D	softwood flooring; at gutter level	m^2	0.88	18.35	-	-	18.35	20.19	-
A021602E	chipboard flooring; at ground floor level	m^2	0.17	3.54	-	-	3.54	3.89	-
A021602F	chipboard flooring; at first floor level	m^2	0.42	8.76	-	-	8.76	9.64	-
A021602G	plywood flooring; at ground level	m^2	0.25	5.21	-	-	5.21	5.73	-
A021602H	plywood flooring; at first floor level	m^2	0.48	10.01	-	-	10.01	11.01	-
A021603	**Remove stud partition, softwood, including finishings both sides, and load into skip**								
A021603A	solid	m^2	0.50	10.43	-	-	10.43	11.47	-
A021603B	glazed, including removal of glass	m^2	0.67	13.97	-	-	13.97	15.37	-
A021604	**Remove wall linings, including battening behind, and load into skip**								
A021604A	plain sheeting	m^2	0.33	6.88	-	-	6.88	7.57	-
A021604B	matchboarding	m^2	0.45	9.38	-	-	9.38	10.32	-

Small Works 2011		Unit	Labour Hours	Labour Net £	Plant Net £	Materials Net £	Unit Net £	Unit with 10% £	CO$_2$ Kg
A02	**REPAIRS AND ALTERATIONS**								
A0216	**WOODWORK REPAIRS AND REMOVALS**								
A021605	**Remove ceiling linings, including battening behind, and load into skip**								
A021605A	plain sheeting	m²	0.50	10.43	-	-	10.43	11.47	-
A021605B	matchboarding	m²	0.67	13.97	-	-	13.97	15.37	-
A021606	**Remove mouldings and load into skip**								
A021606A	skirtings, picture rails, dado rails, architraves and the like	m	0.12	2.50	-	-	2.50	2.75	-
A021606B	shelves, window boards and the like	m	0.35	7.30	-	-	7.30	8.03	-
A021607	**Remove door and load into skip**								
A021607A	single	Each	0.45	9.38	-	-	9.38	10.32	-
A021607B	single with frame or lining	Each	0.88	18.35	-	-	18.35	20.19	-
A021607C	pair	Each	0.77	16.05	-	-	16.05	17.66	-
A021607D	pair with frame or lining	Each	1.32	27.52	-	-	27.52	30.27	-
A021607E	Extra for taking out spring box	Each	0.83	17.31	-	-	17.31	19.04	-
A021608	**Remove window and load into skip**								
A021608A	casement; with frame	Each	1.32	27.52	-	-	27.52	30.27	-
A021608B	double hung sash; with frame	Each	1.77	36.90	-	-	36.90	40.59	-
A021608C	pair; french with frame	Pair	4.40	91.74	-	-	91.74	100.91	-
A021609	**Remove staircase balustrade and load into skip**								
A021609A	single straight flight	Each	3.85	80.27	-	-	80.27	88.30	-
A021609B	dogleg flight	Each	5.50	114.68	-	-	114.68	126.15	-
A021609C	handrail and brackets	m	0.12	2.50	-	-	2.50	2.75	-
A021610	**Remove bath panels and load into skip**								
A021610A	frame	Each	0.45	9.38	-	-	9.38	10.32	-
A021611	**Remove kitchen fittings and load into skip**								
A021611A	wall units	Each	0.50	10.43	-	-	10.43	11.47	-
A021611B	floor units	Each	0.33	6.88	-	-	6.88	7.57	-
A021611C	larder units	Each	0.45	9.38	-	-	9.38	10.32	-
A021611D	built-in cupboards	Each	1.55	32.32	-	-	32.32	35.55	-
A021611E	pipe casings	m	0.33	6.88	-	-	6.88	7.57	-
A021613	**Erect temporary hoarding comprising second-hand timber posts, rails and struts and covered with second-hand close boarding or corrugated iron sheets and dismantle on completion**								
A021613A	1.8 m high	m	1.37	66.80	-	14.24	81.04	89.14	9.180
A021613B	Extra for 0.75 m wide door	Each	0.33	15.81	-	2.44	18.25	20.08	1.550
A021613C	Extra for pair of gates approximately 2.4 m wide overall	Each	1.05	51.03	-	7.28	58.31	64.14	4.620
A021614	**Enclose frontage to site with chestnut fencing with posts at 1.8 m intervals and dismantle on completion**								
A021614A	1.2 m high	m	0.14	6.81	-	6.43	13.24	14.56	8.910
A021616	**Take up defective gutter boards and bearers, supply and fix**								
A021616A	new	m²	1.85	89.86	-	22.46	112.32	123.55	9.810
A021617	**Take off defective rounded wood rolls to flats, supply and fix**								
A021617A	new	m	0.11	5.35	-	2.28	7.63	8.39	1.270
A021618	**Renew roof timbers**								
A021618A	100 mm x 50 mm	m	0.08	3.65	-	2.05	5.70	6.27	1.690
A021618B	125 mm x 50 mm	m	0.10	4.87	-	2.57	7.44	8.18	2.110
A021618C	150 mm x 50 mm	m	0.13	6.08	-	3.06	9.14	10.05	2.540

Small Works 2011		Unit	Labour Hours	Labour Net	Plant Net	Materials Net	Unit Net	Unit with 10%	CO₂
				£	£	£	£	£	Kg
A02	**REPAIRS AND ALTERATIONS**								
A0216	**WOODWORK REPAIRS AND REMOVALS**								
A021619	**Take down defective timber, supply and fix new**								
A021619A	175 mm x 31 mm hips and ridges	m	0.20	9.73	-	2.60	12.33	13.56	1.890
A021619B	150 mm x 25 mm fascia	m	0.20	9.73	-	4.52	14.25	15.68	1.270
A021619C	225 mm x 19 mm soffit and bearers	m	0.30	14.59	-	7.05	21.64	23.80	2.770
A021620	**Take off front gate, remove defective 150 mm x 150 mm timber posts; grub up concrete, supply new post approximately 1.5 m long, set in new concrete and rehang gate**								
A021620A	creosoted fir post	Each	1.50	72.88	-	30.54	103.42	113.76	50.670
A021620B	oak post	Each	1.62	78.96	-	103.86	182.82	201.10	54.420
A021621	**Excavate for and bolt to wood gate post**								
A021621A	a concrete or oak spur set in concrete	Each	1.00	48.60	-	35.88	84.48	92.93	44.410
A021623	**Take down and remove all temporary weatherproofing, e.g. polythene sheet, hardboard, chipboard and the like, together with all associated timber work to windows and doors**								
A021623A	make good all existing joinery work including withdrawing all nails	m²	0.60	29.14	-		29.14	32.05	-
A021624	**Take down and remove all galvanised iron sheet (or corrugated asbestos) covering**								
A021624A	including all timber backings and make good	m²	0.85	41.30	-	-	41.30	45.43	-
A021626	**Temporary screens comprising**								
A021626A	100 mm x 50 mm framing lined both sides with building paper	m²	0.13	6.32	-	6.98	13.30	14.63	8.930
A021626B	100 mm x 50 mm framing lined one side with 19 mm matchboard	m²	0.30	14.59	-	21.21	35.80	39.38	12.580
A021626C	50 mm x 50 mm framing lined one side with hardboard	m²	0.23	10.95	-	5.51	16.46	18.11	5.930
A021628	**Strut up ceiling floor to ceiling and remove struts on completion**								
A021628A	average 2.6 m	m	0.55	26.71	2.63	-	29.34	32.27	-
A021630	**Strut and support window openings; area of window**								
A021630A	1.0 sq.m	Each	0.23	10.95	-	1.58	12.53	13.78	1.300
A021630B	1.5 sq.m	Each	0.25	12.16	-	1.84	14.00	15.40	1.520
A021630C	2.0 sq.m	Each	0.28	13.38	-	2.05	15.43	16.97	1.690
A021631	**Remove all grease and dirt from existing flooring, remove all projecting lino nails or tacks, punch down all floor brads, resecure any loose boards, plane off and leave smooth**								
A021631A	generally	m²	0.43	20.68	-	-	20.68	22.75	-
A021631B	in areas less than 1 sq.m	m²	0.55	26.71	-	-	26.71	29.38	-
A021632	**Take up loose floor blocks and relay in mastic**								
A021632A	single block	Each	0.18	8.51	-	0.20	8.71	9.58	0.460
A021632B	in patches up to six blocks	Each	0.11	5.35	-	0.41	5.76	6.34	0.960
A021633	**Smooth hardwood floor**								
A021633A	with electric sanding machine	m²	0.50	24.28	-	-	24.28	26.71	-

House Renovation Grants, Repairs and Alterations

Small Works 2011		Unit	Labour Hours	Labour Net	Plant Net	Materials Net	Unit Net	Unit with 10%	CO₂
				£	£	£	£	£	Kg
A02	**REPAIRS AND ALTERATIONS**								
A0216	**WOODWORK REPAIRS AND REMOVALS**								
A021634	**Take off existing skirting**								
A021634A	replug grounds and refix skirting	m	0.18	8.76	-	-	8.76	9.64	-
A021635	**Take off existing softwood skirting, supply and fix new**								
A021635A	25 mm x 150 mm	m	0.25	12.16	-	8.04	20.20	22.22	1.270
A021639	**Take up existing shrunk or worn flooring, any thickness, drawing all nails, relaying, cramping up, making up width or length with extra boarding of same thickness and cleaning off on completion. Areas exceeding 0.5 sq.m**								
A021639A	plain edge	m²	0.45	21.84	-	2.10	23.94	26.33	0.760
A021639B	tongued and grooved	m²	0.55	26.71	-	1.85	28.56	31.42	0.760
A021640	**Remove damaged 25 mm softwood floor boards; clean joists and renew**								
A021640A	plain edge	m²	0.43	20.68	-	22.30	42.98	47.28	8.660
A021640B	tongued and grooved	m²	0.50	24.28	-	19.52	43.80	48.18	8.660
A021640C	plain edge in small detached areas not exceeding 1.0 sq.m	m²	1.10	53.42	-	22.30	75.72	83.29	8.660
A021640D	tongued and grooved in detached area not exceeding 1.0 sq.m	m²	1.35	65.58	-	19.52	85.10	93.61	8.660
A021640E	plain edge exceeding 1.0 sq.m, not exceeding 2.5 sq.m	m²	1.00	48.60	-	22.30	70.90	77.99	8.660
A021640F	tongued and grooved exceeding 1.0 sq.m, not exceeding 2.5 sq.m	m²	1.25	60.72	-	19.52	80.24	88.26	8.660
A021642	**New joists and softwood floor boarding, treating joists and underside of boards with creosote or other preservative**								
A021642A	100 mm x 50 mm floor joists and 25 mm plain edge flooring	m²	1.00	27.80	-	28.18	55.98	61.58	14.190
A021644	**Oak strip flooring pinned and glued to existing softwood floor; clean and wax polish**								
A021644A	13 mm	m²	0.90	25.02	-	63.52	88.54	97.39	5.970
A021646	**Take down door, cut 13 mm off bottom edge and rehang**								
A021646A	rehang	Each	0.80	39.11	-	-	39.11	43.02	-
A021647	**Take down architraves and reduce length by 13 mm and refix**								
A021647A	one side	Set	0.28	13.43	-	-	13.43	14.77	-
A021647B	reduce length without removal	Set	0.25	12.21	-	-	12.21	13.43	-
A021648	**Take off skirting and refix**								
A021648A	at higher level	m	0.15	7.35	-	-	7.35	8.09	-
A021649	**Hardwood border to hearth**								
A021649A	mitred	Each	0.30	14.64	-	4.09	18.73	20.60	0.940
A021649B	add if sheet metal inner lining	Each	0.20	9.78	-	4.84	14.62	16.08	14.730
A021650	**Take down door, take out lining or frame, realign and refix**								
A021650A	ease, adjust and rehang door; refix existing architraves and make good work disturbed	Each	2.51	122.16	-	-	122.16	134.38	-
A021652	**Take down door**								
A021652A	ease and rehang	Each	0.90	43.98	-	-	43.98	48.38	-

Small Works 2011		Unit	Labour Hours	Labour Net	Plant Net	Materials Net	Unit Net	Unit with 10%	CO$_2$
				£	£	£	£	£	Kg
A02	**REPAIRS AND ALTERATIONS**								
A0216	**WOODWORK REPAIRS AND REMOVALS**								
A021653	**Take down door, ease and rehang on new butt hinges; remove lock and furniture, supply and fit new lock and furniture**								
A021653A	rim lock	Each	1.51	73.32	-	38.67	111.99	123.19	5.740
A021653B	mortice lock	Each	1.76	85.53	-	44.98	130.51	143.56	5.630
A021654	**Take down door, take apart and fit new panel or rail**								
A021654A	rehang	Each	2.41	117.25	-	5.90	123.15	135.47	1.620
A021655	**Renew weatherboard**								
A021655A	to external softwood door	Each	0.50	24.42	-	5.94	30.36	33.40	1.180
A021656	**Take down, ease and adjust and rehang**								
A021656A	casement sash	Each	0.60	29.34	-	-	29.34	32.27	-
A021657	**Take off defective staff and parting beads**								
A021657A	to double hung sash window and renew	Each	0.40	19.56	-	3.28	22.84	25.12	0.300
A021658	**Take out double hung sashes**								
A021658A	ease, adjust and rehang, including new cords	Each	0.68	32.98	-	1.02	34.00	37.40	0.310
A021659	**Cut out defective glazing bars to skylights, windows, doors or greenhouses**								
A021659A	renew	m	0.45	21.99	-	0.66	22.65	24.92	0.070
A021660	**Strengthening handrail and balusters including**								
A021660A	renewing defective balusters	m	0.63	30.55	-	7.30	37.85	41.64	0.590
A021661	**Cutting out defective and worn portion of tread**								
A021661A	piecing in new	Each	0.40	19.56	-	1.44	21.00	23.10	2.600
A021662	**Take off and renew ironmongery fixed to softwood**								
A021662A	strong pattern steel butts 75 mm	Pair	0.67	32.50	-	2.96	35.46	39.01	0.400
A021662B	strong pattern steel butts 100 mm	Pair	0.79	38.58	-	4.67	43.25	47.58	0.530
A021662C	steel washered brass butts 76 mm	Pair	0.67	32.50	-	6.35	38.85	42.74	0.600
A021662D	steel washered brass butts 102 mm	Pair	0.79	38.58	-	8.71	47.29	52.02	0.800
A021662E	brass rising butts 76 mm	Pair	0.81	39.36	-	5.47	44.83	49.31	0.600
A021662F	brass rising butts 102 mm	Pair	0.93	45.44	-	8.31	53.75	59.13	0.800
A021662G	steel tee hinges 305 mm	Pair	0.57	27.58	-	6.16	33.74	37.11	1.070
A021662H	steel tee hinges 457 mm	Pair	0.61	29.82	-	13.80	43.62	47.98	1.610
A021662I	rim lock and furniture	Each	0.79	38.58	-	38.67	77.25	84.98	5.740
A021662J	mortice lock and furniture	Each	0.92	44.95	-	44.98	89.93	98.92	5.630
A021662K	suffolk latch	Each	0.67	32.50	-	7.07	39.57	43.53	1.130
A021662L	bolt; straight; barrel 150 mm	Each	0.34	16.64	-	5.75	22.39	24.63	0.650
A021662M	bolt; straight; barrel 225 mm	Each	0.39	19.07	-	7.31	26.38	29.02	1.010
A021662N	casement stay with two pins 250 mm	Each	0.31	15.13	-	5.53	20.66	22.73	0.300
A021662O	casement fastener; wedge pattern	Each	0.36	17.61	-	5.74	23.35	25.69	0.300
A021662P	sliding sash fastener	Each	0.74	35.90	-	6.32	42.22	46.44	0.340
A021662Q	sash lift	Each	0.24	11.48	-	3.80	15.28	16.81	1.570

Small Works 2011		Unit	Labour Hours	Labour Net	Plant Net	Materials Net	Unit Net	Unit with 10%	CO$_2$
				£	£	£	£	£	Kg
A02	**REPAIRS AND ALTERATIONS**								
A0217	**SHORING**								
A021701	**Erecting temporary DEAD shoring to form opening using three pairs 150 mm x 150 mm uprights and three 225 mm x 150 mm needles, braces and 225 mm x 225 mm base plates, holing brickwork for needles, all cartage, making good and removing on completion**								
A021701A	assumed volume of timber - 0.09 cu. m	Item	34.95	1,700.32	-	85.31	1,785.63	1,964.19	32.670
A021701B	add to or deduct for every 0.03 cu. m more or less than 0.09 cu. m	Item	1.00	48.60	-	3.10	51.70	56.87	1.190
A021702	**Erecting temporary RAKING shoring including rakers, wall plate, needles, holing brickwork, cartage and making good on completion**								
A021702A	assumed volume of timber 0.30 cu. m	Item	15.98	777.28	-	27.92	805.20	885.72	10.690
A021702B	add to or deduct for every 0.03 cu. m	Item	1.50	72.88	-	3.10	75.98	83.58	1.190
A021703	**Erecting temporary FLYING shoring including horizontal shores, struts, wall plates, posts, needles, holing brickwork, cartage and making good on completion**								
A021703A	assumed volume of timber 0.60 cu. m	Item	39.94	1,943.23	-	55.84	1,999.07	2,198.98	21.380
A021703B	add to or deduct for every 0.03 cu. m more or less than 0.60 cu. m	Item	2.00	97.15	-	58.94	156.09	171.70	22.570
A021704	**Erecting permanent RAKING shoring as described above but left in position for an indefinite period**								
A021704A	0.30 cu. m	Item	9.99	485.82	-	58.94	544.76	599.24	22.570
A021704B	add to or deduct for each 0.03 cu. m or timber more or less than 0.30 cu. m	Item	1.00	48.60	-	6.20	54.80	60.28	2.380
A021705	**Erecting permanent FLYING shoring as described above but left in position for an indefinite period**								
A021705A	0.60 cu. m	Item	26.96	1,311.65	-	119.43	1,431.08	1,574.19	45.740
A021705B	add to or deduct for every 0.03 cu. m more or less than 0.60 cu. m	Item	1.35	65.58	-	11.63	77.21	84.93	4.460
A0219	**FINISHES, REPAIRS AND RENEWALS**								
A021901	**Remove surface finishes. Floor**								
A021901A	carpet and underlay	m^2	0.13	2.71	-	-	2.71	2.98	-
A021901B	linoleum sheeting	m^2	0.12	2.50	-	-	2.50	2.75	-
A021901C	screed	m^2	0.50	10.43	-	-	10.43	11.47	-
A021901D	granolithic and screed	m^2	0.67	13.97	-	-	13.97	15.37	-
A021901E	terrazzo or ceramic tiles; screed	m^2	1.10	22.94	-	-	22.94	25.23	-
A021902	**Remove surface finishes. Wall**								
A021902A	plasterboard	m^2	0.45	9.38	-	-	9.38	10.32	-
A021902B	plaster	m^2	0.22	4.59	-	-	4.59	5.05	-
A021902C	cement rendering; pebbledashing	m^2	0.45	9.38	-	-	9.38	10.32	-
A021902D	tiling and screed	m^2	0.55	11.47	-	-	11.47	12.62	-
A021903	**Remove surface finishes. Ceiling**								
A021903A	plasterboard and skim including withdrawing nails	m^2	0.33	6.88	-	-	6.88	7.57	-

Small Works 2011		Unit	Labour Hours	Labour Net	Plant Net	Materials Net	Unit Net	Unit with 10%	CO₂
				£	£	£	£	£	Kg
A02	**REPAIRS AND ALTERATIONS**								
A0219	**FINISHES, REPAIRS AND RENEWALS**								
A021903	**Remove surface finishes. Ceiling**								
A021903B	wood lath and plaster including withdrawing nails	m²	0.55	11.47	-	-	11.47	12.62	-
A021903C	suspended	m²	0.83	17.31	-	-	17.31	19.04	-
A021903D	plaster moulded cornice; per 25 mm girth	m	0.17	3.54	-	-	3.54	3.89	-
A021904	**Prepare surface to be sound and clean; apply two coats Unibond universal pva adhesive and sealer to receive plaster or cement rendering**								
A021904A	walls; existing cement and sand base over 300 mm wide	m²	0.15	7.38	-	1.17	8.55	9.41	0.890
A021904B	walls; existing glazed tile base over 300 mm wide	m²	0.12	5.91	-	0.79	6.70	7.37	0.600
A021904C	walls; existing painted base over 300 mm wide	m²	0.14	6.89	-	0.89	7.78	8.56	0.670
A021904D	walls; existing concrete base over 300 mm wide	m²	0.15	7.38	-	0.98	8.36	9.20	0.740
A021904E	ceilings; existing cement and sand base over 300 mm wide	m²	0.19	9.09	-	1.17	10.26	11.29	0.890
A021904F	ceilings; existing painted base over 300 mm wide	m²	0.17	8.36	-	0.89	9.25	10.18	0.670
A021904G	ceilings; existing concrete base over 300 mm wide	m²	0.19	9.09	-	0.98	10.07	11.08	0.740
A021905	**Hack down defective ceiling plaster and laths. Clean out old nails ready for**								
A021905A	new laths or plasterboard	m²	0.43	20.86	-	-	20.86	22.95	-
A021906	**Hack down defective ceiling plaster and clean laths ready for**								
A021906A	new plaster	m²	0.30	14.71	-	-	14.71	16.18	-
A021907	**Take down temporary boarded linings to ceilings**								
A021907A	clean joists	m²	0.40	8.34	-	-	8.34	9.17	-
A021908	**Expanded metal lathing to ceiling joists and render**								
A021908A	float and set	m²	0.85	41.73	-	12.09	53.82	59.20	6.700
A021909	**Plaster and set on**								
A021909A	existing laths	m²	0.63	30.68	-	4.28	34.96	38.46	2.590
A021910	**Plaster baseboard, scrim and set ceilings with**								
A021910A	patent plaster	m²	0.50	24.53	-	4.79	29.32	32.25	5.450
A021912	**Hack down defective ceiling plaster and fix plaster baseboard, scrim and set with patent plaster including jointing to existing**								
A021912A	area n.e. 1 sq.m	m²	1.00	49.06	-	4.79	53.85	59.24	5.450
A021912B	area 1 - 4 sq.m	m²	0.70	34.35	-	4.79	39.14	43.05	5.450
A021913	**Make good at intersection of wall and ceiling plaster after replastering**								
A021913A	wall or ceiling	m	0.28	13.49	-	0.21	13.70	15.07	0.140
A021913B	make good cracks in ceiling plaster	m	0.23	11.04	-	0.21	11.25	12.38	0.140
A021914	**Hack brick, stone or concrete walls to form key**								
A021914A	for plaster	m²	0.75	15.64	-	-	15.64	17.20	-
A021916	**Hack off wall plaster and rake out brick joints to form key**								
A021916A	for new plaster	m²	0.75	15.64	-	-	15.64	17.20	-

Small Works 2011		Unit	Labour Hours	Labour Net	Plant Net	Materials Net	Unit Net	Unit with 10%	CO₂
				£	£	£	£	£	Kg
A02	**REPAIRS AND ALTERATIONS**								
A0219	**FINISHES, REPAIRS AND RENEWALS**								
A021918	**Rake out joints of brickwork**								
A021918A	to form key	m²	0.40	8.34	-	-	8.34	9.17	-
A021919	**Dub out uneven walls to receive**								
A021919A	new plaster	m²	0.20	9.82	-	1.45	11.27	12.40	5.610
A021920	**Render and set**								
A021920A	brick or block walls	m²	0.43	20.86	-	3.18	24.04	26.44	7.520
A021921	**Hack down defective wall plaster in small quantities; plaster and set including jointing to existing**								
A021921A	area n.e. 1 sq.m	m²	0.88	42.95	-	4.40	47.35	52.09	2.590
A021921B	area 1 - 4 sq.m	m²	0.45	22.08	-	4.40	26.48	29.13	2.590
A021924	**Render and set brick walls**								
A021924A	including jointing new to old and a small quantity of dubbing out	m²	0.55	26.97	-	5.65	32.62	35.88	3.310
A021926	**Make good cracks**								
A021926A	in wall plaster	m	0.23	11.04	-	0.21	11.25	12.38	0.140
A021926B	in moulded cornice, per 25 mm girth of cornice	m	0.13	6.16	-	0.43	6.59	7.25	0.290
A021926C	around door and window frames and repoint	m	0.20	9.82	-	0.21	10.03	11.03	0.140
A021928	**Hack down and re-run plaster cornices per 25 mm girth of cornice**								
A021928A	coved	m	0.13	6.16	-	0.43	6.59	7.25	0.290
A021928B	moulded	m	0.17	8.11	-	0.26	8.37	9.21	0.140
A021930	**Make good plaster around pipes**								
A021930A	small pipes	Each	0.15	7.38	-	0.43	7.81	8.59	0.290
A021930B	large pipes	Each	0.17	8.11	-	0.43	8.54	9.39	0.290
A021932	**White glazed wall tiles fixed with adhesive, pointed in white cement grout to wall in small quantities in repairs**								
A021932A	108 mm x 108 mm x 4 mm	m²	1.38	67.48	-	41.93	109.41	120.35	14.080
A021932B	152 mm x 152 mm x 5.5 mm	m²	1.20	58.39	-	30.98	89.37	98.31	12.510
A021934	**White glazed wall tiles bedded in cement mortar, pointed in white cement in small quantities in repairs**								
A021934A	108 mm x 108 mm x 4 mm	m²	2.83	138.13	-	43.82	181.95	200.15	23.890
A021934B	152 mm x 152 mm x 5.5 mm	m²	2.51	122.69	-	32.87	155.56	171.12	22.310
A021936	**Coloured glazed wall tiles fixed with adhesive, pointed in white cement grout to wall in small quantities in repairs**								
A021936A	108 mm x 108 mm x 4 mm	m²	1.38	67.48	-	20.21	87.69	96.46	12.510
A021936B	152 mm x 152 mm x 5.5 mm	m²	1.20	58.39	-	30.59	88.98	97.88	14.080
A021938	**Hack off glazed tiles to wall**								
A021938A	in detached areas 2 - 5 sq.m	m²	1.00	20.85	-	-	20.85	22.94	-
A021938B	in patches 0.5 - 2 sq.m	Each	2.50	52.13	-	-	52.13	57.34	-
A021938C	in single tiles in patches up to 0.5 sq.m	Each	0.30	6.25	-	-	6.25	6.88	-
A021940	**Take out broken cappings horizontal or vertical and renew**								
A021940A	12 mm x 150 mm x 75 mm angle	Each	0.09	4.40	-	6.34	10.74	11.81	0.790
A021941	**Take out broken moulded cappings and renew**								
A021941A	12 mm x 150 mm x 75 mm	Each	0.10	4.89	-	1.06	5.95	6.55	0.430

Small Works 2011		Unit	Labour Hours	Labour Net	Plant Net	Materials Net	Unit Net	Unit with 10%	CO₂
				£	£	£	£	£	Kg
A02	**REPAIRS AND ALTERATIONS**								
A0219	**FINISHES, REPAIRS AND RENEWALS**								
A021942	**Holes through wall tiling, any colour, for pipes, brackets etc and make good**								
A021942A	small pipe	Each	0.28	5.84	-	-	5.84	6.42	-
A021942B	large pipe	Each	0.38	7.92	-	-	7.92	8.71	-
A021944	**Stripping loose tiles and cleaning**								
A021944A	for reuse	m²	0.40	8.34	-	-	8.34	9.17	-
A021945	**Refixing only salvaged tiles with**								
A021945A	adhesive	m²	1.13	55.21	-	1.16	56.37	62.01	2.160
A021948	**Provide and fix wall tiles with adhesive**								
A021948A	150 mm x 150 mm x 6 mm	m²	1.13	55.21	-	31.19	86.40	95.04	12.870
A021949	**Hack off defective rendering to concreted areas; grout and render in cement mortar**								
A021949A	19 mm thick	m²	0.50	24.53	-	0.18	24.71	27.18	0.700
A021950	**Hack off and renew cement rendered plinth including joints new to old**								
A021950A	225 mm high	m	0.15	7.38	-	0.63	8.01	8.81	2.450
A021952	**Cut out cracks in rendering and make good to existing**								
A021952A	Snowcrete or rough cast	m	0.40	19.64	-	0.64	20.28	22.31	1.940
A021952B	make good to Snowcrete or rough cast to match adjacent work around reset window and door frames	m	0.24	11.78	-	0.44	12.22	13.44	1.370
A021954	**Hack off defective rendering to walls, prepare for and cement render**								
A021954A	two coats (plain face)	m²	0.50	24.53	-	2.45	26.98	29.68	9.460
A021956	**Cement wash walls**								
A021956A	one coat	m²	0.15	7.38	-	0.57	7.95	8.75	0.340
A021956B	two coats	m²	0.27	13.24	-	0.75	13.99	15.39	0.450
A021958	**Hack off broken cement rendering and renew rendering to**								
A021958A	three-sided curb to gully	Each	0.45	22.08	-	0.45	22.53	24.78	1.750
A021960	**Hack off all loose stucco rendering, hack back brick or concrete to form key and render with cement mortar, trowelled smooth including reproducing all profiles and ruled joints**								
A021960A	to match existing	m²	1.00	49.06	-	2.17	51.23	56.35	8.410
A021960B	in patches not exceeding 1 sq.m	m²	1.26	61.32	-	2.17	63.49	69.84	8.410
A0229	**PLUMBING REPAIRS AND RENEWALS**								
A022901	**Remove gutterwork and pipework; gutterwork and supports**								
A022901A	asbestos-free cement	m	0.21	13.20	-	-	13.20	14.52	-
A022901B	PVC-u	m	0.23	14.32	-	-	14.32	15.75	-
A022901C	cast iron	m	0.27	16.94	-	-	16.94	18.63	-
A022902	**Remove gutterwork and pipework; rainwater pipework and supports**								
A022902A	asbestos-free cement	m	0.18	11.27	-	-	11.27	12.40	-
A022902B	PVC-u	m	0.20	12.46	-	-	12.46	13.71	-
A022902C	cast iron	m	0.24	15.07	-	-	15.07	16.58	-

Small Works 2011		Unit	Labour Hours	Labour Net £	Plant Net £	Materials Net £	Unit Net £	Unit with 10% £	CO₂ Kg
A02	**REPAIRS AND ALTERATIONS**								
A0229	**PLUMBING REPAIRS AND RENEWALS**								
A022903	**Remove gutterwork and pipework; rainwater shoe**								
A022903A	PVC-u	Each	0.04	2.62	-	-	2.62	2.88	-
A022903B	cast iron	Each	0.06	3.80	-	-	3.80	4.18	-
A022904	**Remove gutterwork and pipework; rainwater head and support**								
A022904A	PVC-u	Each	0.22	13.95	-	-	13.95	15.35	-
A022904B	cast iron	Each	0.27	16.94	-	-	16.94	18.63	-
A022905	**Remove gutterwork and pipework; soil and ventilation pipework and supports**								
A022905A	PVC-u	m	0.36	22.61	-	-	22.61	24.87	-
A022905B	cast iron	m	0.41	25.22	-	-	25.22	27.74	-
A022905C	lead	m	0.45	28.28	-	-	28.28	31.11	-
A022906	**Remove gutterwork and pipework; service, waste and overflow pipework and supports**								
A022906A	PVC-u	m	0.08	4.92	-	-	4.92	5.41	-
A022906B	copper	m	0.10	6.41	-	-	6.41	7.05	-
A022906C	lead	m	0.10	6.41	-	-	6.41	7.05	-
A022906D	galvanised steel	m	0.10	6.41	-	-	6.41	7.05	-
A022908	**Remove sanitary fittings including taps and trap**								
A022908A	W.C. suite	Each	0.25	15.82	-	-	15.82	17.40	-
A022908B	wash hand basin	Each	0.22	13.95	-	-	13.95	15.35	-
A022908C	bath	Each	0.32	19.62	-	-	19.62	21.58	-
A022908D	sink unit	Each	0.22	13.95	-	-	13.95	15.35	-
A022908E	shower	Each	0.09	5.67	-	-	5.67	6.24	-
A022910	**Remove sanitary fittings including taps, trap and service and waste pipes not exceeding 3.00 m girth**								
A022910A	W.C. suite	Each	0.32	19.62	-	-	19.62	21.58	-
A022910B	wash hand basin	Each	0.25	15.82	-	-	15.82	17.40	-
A022910C	bath	Each	0.38	23.36	-	-	23.36	25.70	-
A022910D	sink unit	Each	0.25	15.82	-	-	15.82	17.40	-
A022910E	shower	Each	0.13	8.28	-	-	8.28	9.11	-
A022911	**Remove bathroom toilet fittings**								
A022911A	toilet roll holder	Each	0.03	1.87	-	-	1.87	2.06	-
A022911B	soap dispenser	Each	0.03	1.87	-	-	1.87	2.06	-
A022911C	towel rail	Each	0.05	2.99	-	-	2.99	3.29	-
A022911D	towel holder	Each	0.10	6.41	-	-	6.41	7.05	-
A022911E	mirror	Each	0.10	6.41	-	-	6.41	7.05	-
A022912	**Remove equipment excluding any necessary draining down of system**								
A022912A	cold water tank	Each	1.60	99.83	-	-	99.83	109.81	-
A022912B	hot water cylinder	Each	0.80	50.07	-	-	50.07	55.08	-
A022912C	gas water heater	Each	2.66	165.73	-	-	165.73	182.30	-
A022912D	gas fire	Each	1.33	82.83	-	-	82.83	91.11	-
A022912E	expansion tank	Each	1.21	75.30	-	-	75.30	82.83	-
A022914	**Cleaning out eaves and parapet gutters, removing rubbish**								
A022914A	any height or position	m	0.08	4.92	-	-	4.92	5.41	-
A022916	**Cleaning out rain-water pipes, stack pipes, etc**								
A022916A	any height or position	m	0.08	4.92	-	-	4.92	5.41	-
A022917	**Take down existing gutters, clean and refix to fascia or on brackets, seal joints with red lead putty**								
A022917A	set to proper falls	m	0.42	26.34	-	3.70	30.04	33.04	1.470

Small Works 2011		Unit	Labour Hours	Labour Net	Plant Net	Materials Net	Unit Net	Unit with 10%	CO$_2$
				£	£	£	£	£	Kg
A02	**REPAIRS AND ALTERATIONS**								
A0229	**PLUMBING REPAIRS AND RENEWALS**								
A022918	Take down and remove existing 100 mm cast iron gutters, provide and fix new gutters								
A022918A	half-round	m	0.67	41.42	-	25.34	66.76	73.44	17.250
A022918B	ogee	m	0.67	41.42	-	27.34	68.76	75.64	24.710
A022919	Take down existing rainwater pipes and refix to walls								
A022919A	50 mm, 63 mm, or 75 mm	m	0.45	28.28	-	0.23	28.51	31.36	0.080
A022920	Take down and remove existing cast iron rain-water pipes and provide and fix new pipes								
A022920A	63 mm and 75 mm	m	0.67	41.42	-	47.48	88.90	97.79	16.120
A022920B	rainwater shoe (not extra over)	Each	0.30	18.81	-	28.73	47.54	52.29	4.590
A022922	Cut out and reform caulked lead joints in cast-iron soil, vent or waste pipes								
A022922A	50 mm	Each	0.42	26.34	-	2.81	29.15	32.07	2.050
A022922B	75 mm	Each	0.48	30.14	-	4.21	34.35	37.79	3.070
A022922C	100 mm	Each	0.70	43.28	-	5.11	48.39	53.23	3.720
A022924	Cut and adapt existing iron soil pipe for a new W.C. by inserting a branch and bend or long junction, connect to pan trap and make good to wall								
A022924A	100 mm	Each	2.90	180.80	-	65.67	246.47	271.12	40.330
A022924B	Extra for access door	Each	-	-	-	51.40	51.40	56.54	7.258
A022942	Renew broken stopcock box with hinged lid								
A022942A	127 mm x 127 mm x 76 mm	Each	0.30	18.81	-	11.18	29.99	32.99	3.480
A022942B	152 mm x 152 mm x 76 mm	Each	0.33	20.74	-	12.34	33.08	36.39	4.990
A022944	Galvanised water tube including bends, sockets etc (tees excepted), in repairs to existing work; heavy weight								
A022944A	15 mm	m	0.40	24.85	-	7.87	32.72	35.99	5.420
A022944B	20 mm	m	0.45	28.28	-	9.43	37.71	41.48	9.150
A022944C	25 mm	m	0.48	30.14	-	13.70	43.84	48.22	13.530
A022946	Galvanised water tube including bends, sockets etc (tees excepted), in repairs to existing work; medium weight								
A022946A	15 mm	m	0.40	24.85	-	6.78	31.63	34.79	1.900
A022946B	20 mm	m	0.45	28.28	-	8.02	36.30	39.93	6.100
A022946C	25 mm	m	0.48	30.14	-	11.51	41.65	45.82	9.020
A022948	Cutting existing iron pipe for and inserting new tees								
A022948A	15 mm	Each	0.42	26.34	-	4.66	31.00	34.10	4.360
A022948B	20 mm	Each	0.51	32.01	-	6.31	38.32	42.15	5.800
A022948C	25 mm	Each	0.61	37.68	-	8.59	46.27	50.90	8.590
A022950	Copper tubing including capillary bends etc (tees excepted), in repairs to existing work								
A022950A	15 mm	m	0.36	22.61	-	4.02	26.63	29.29	0.710
A022950B	22 mm	m	0.42	26.34	-	7.96	34.30	37.73	1.530
A022950C	28 mm	m	0.48	30.14	-	11.48	41.62	45.78	2.480
A022952	Cutting existing copper pipes and inserting new capillary tees								
A022952A	15 mm	Each	0.61	37.68	-	2.12	39.80	43.78	0.290
A022952B	22 mm	Each	0.73	45.22	-	4.46	49.68	54.65	0.630
A022952C	28 mm	Each	0.91	56.49	-	10.11	66.60	73.26	1.010

Small Works 2011		Unit	Labour Hours	Labour Net	Plant Net	Materials Net	Unit Net	Unit with 10%	CO₂
				£	£	£	£	£	Kg
A02	**REPAIRS AND ALTERATIONS**								
A0229	**PLUMBING REPAIRS AND RENEWALS**								
A022954	**Polythene tubing including compression bends etc (tees excepted), in repairs to existing work**								
A022954A	20 mm	m	0.73	45.22	-	4.62	49.84	54.82	0.560
A022954B	25 mm	m	0.85	52.75	-	6.58	59.33	65.26	0.780
A022954C	32 mm	m	1.03	64.02	-	11.00	75.02	82.52	1.610
A022956	**Cutting existing polythene pipes and inserting new compression tees**								
A022956A	20 mm	Each	0.91	56.49	-	12.22	68.71	75.58	2.230
A022956B	25 mm	Each	1.03	64.02	-	18.52	82.54	90.79	2.620
A022956C	32 mm	Each	1.21	75.30	-	26.38	101.68	111.85	4.960
A022958	**Covering iron or copper pipes with hair felt and twine; in any position**								
A022958A	up to 25 mm dia	m	0.42	26.34	-	0.59	26.93	29.62	0.840
A022960	**Take off existing bib valve, prepare iron or copper pipes and provide and fit new bib valve**								
A022960A	13 mm	Each	0.61	37.68	-	14.54	52.22	57.44	0.710
A022960B	19 mm	Each	0.73	45.22	-	19.46	64.68	71.15	0.770
A022961	**Cut into iron or copper pipes and fit new stopcock**								
A022961A	13 mm	Each	0.79	48.95	-	8.62	57.57	63.33	0.770
A022961B	19 mm	Each	0.91	56.49	-	13.67	70.16	77.18	1.020
A022962	**Rewasher ball valve, tap or indoor stopcock**								
A022962A	13 mm	Each	0.30	18.81	-	0.39	19.20	21.12	0.010
A022962B	19 mm	Each	0.36	22.61	-	0.39	23.00	25.30	0.010
A022964	**Take off existing copper trap to bath, basin or sink and provide and fit new plastic trap**								
A022964A	32 mm	Each	0.73	45.22	-	8.08	53.30	58.63	0.100
A022964B	38 mm	Each	0.79	48.95	-	9.88	58.83	64.71	0.140
A022966	**Take off stopcock to iron or copper pipes both ends and provide and fit new stopcock**								
A022966A	13 mm	Each	0.39	24.48	-	8.62	33.10	36.41	0.770
A022966B	19 mm	Each	0.51	32.01	-	13.67	45.68	50.25	1.020
A022966C	25 mm	Each	0.64	39.55	-	35.03	74.58	82.04	1.170
A022968	**Take off ball valve to iron or copper pipes and provide and fit new ball valve and ball float complete**								
A022968A	13 mm	Each	0.30	18.81	-	12.61	31.42	34.56	0.870
A022968B	19 mm	Each	0.39	24.48	-	20.47	44.95	49.45	1.260
A022970	**Supply W.C. suite complete (PC £240 per Nr) and connect to existing services**								
A022970A	copper or iron	Each	3.51	218.42	-	240.00	458.42	504.26	44.400
A022971	**Supply low level W.C. suite (PC £140 per Nr) and connect to existing services**								
A022971A	copper or iron	Each	3.81	237.29	-	140.00	377.29	415.02	37.000
A022972	**Remove defective W.C. pan and fix new (PC £60 per Nr)**								
A022972A	make good all connections	Each	2.36	146.86	-	60.00	206.86	227.55	29.600
A022974	**Take off defective seat to pedestal pan and supply and fix new plastic seat**								
A022974A	single	Each	0.45	28.28	-	16.82	45.10	49.61	2.260
A022974B	double	Each	0.54	33.88	-	23.56	57.44	63.18	4.520

Small Works 2011		Unit	Labour Hours	Labour Net	Plant Net	Materials Net	Unit Net	Unit with 10%	CO$_2$
				£	£	£	£	£	Kg
A02	**REPAIRS AND ALTERATIONS**								
A0229	**PLUMBING REPAIRS AND RENEWALS**								
A022976	**Take off W.C. seat, renew joints to flush pipe including closet and outlet connection and pan**								
A022976A	refix seat	Each	0.70	43.28	-	2.65	45.93	50.52	0.190
A022978	**Disconnect and remove 9 litre water waste preventer. Supply and fix new complete with ball valve and brackets (PC £100 per Nr) and joint to existing overflow and service pipes**								
A022978A	copper or iron	Each	1.94	120.51	-	100.00	220.51	242.56	19.100
A022980	**Disconnect ball valve to water waste preventer or storage tank**								
A022980A	re-washer and clean out	Each	0.88	54.62	-	0.39	55.01	60.51	0.010
A022981	**Unscrew ball to valve, supply and fit**								
A022981A	new ball	Each	0.18	11.27	-	4.54	15.81	17.39	3.220
A022982	**Supply and fix flat back basin (PC £100 per Nr) including taps, traps and wall brackets, connect to existing services**								
A022982A	iron or copper	Each	3.51	218.42	-	100.00	318.42	350.26	19.100
A022984	**Supply and fix pedestal basin (PC £150 per Nr) including taps, traps and wall brackets, connecting to existing services**								
A022984A	iron or copper	Each	3.51	218.42	-	150.00	368.42	405.26	28.650
A022986	**Supply and fix cast iron white porcelain enamelled, rectangular 1700 mm long bath (PC £360 per Nr) complete with taps and trap; connect to existing services**								
A022986A	iron or copper	Each	3.51	218.42	-	360.00	578.42	636.26	222.700
A022988	**Clear blockage; flush out to**								
A022988A	W.C. pans and traps	Each	0.76	47.08	-	-	47.08	51.79	-
A022988B	traps and waste pipes of baths, sinks, lavatory basins etc	Each	0.61	37.68	-	-	37.68	41.45	-
A022990	**Disconnect all pipework; take out and remove galvanised steel hot water tank; provide and install 114 litre copper indirect cylinder allow for cutting holes; tank connectors; make up and connections to existing pipework**								
A022990A	complete	Each	1.81	112.98	-	340.72	453.70	499.07	103.340
A022992	**Empty water storage system and disconnect back boiler, supply and connect new boiler and test**								
A022992A	back boiler (PC £180 per Nr)	Each	2.42	150.66	-	180.00	330.66	363.73	77.900
A022994	**Clean and scale back boiler and ends of pipe**								
A022994A	reconnect and recirculate water	Each	4.23	263.63	-	-	263.63	289.99	-

Small Works 2011		Unit	Labour Hours	Labour Net	Plant Net	Materials Net	Unit Net	Unit with 10%	CO$_2$
				£	£	£	£	£	Kg
A02	**REPAIRS AND ALTERATIONS**								
A0229	**PLUMBING REPAIRS AND RENEWALS**								
A022996	**Turn off water supply, disconnect all pipework, take out and remove galvanised steel cold water storage tank, provide and install plastic tank complete with ball valve, lid and insulation and allow for cutting holes, tank connectors, making up and all connections to existing pipework**								
A022996A	182 litre	Each	3.81	237.29	-	188.36	425.65	468.22	26.050
A022998	**Cleaning and scouring out open-top storage tanks**								
A022998A	any size and position	Each	4.48	278.70	-	-	278.70	306.57	-
A0239	**GLAZING REPAIRS AND RENEWALS**								
A023901	**Hack out all types of broken glass**								
A023901A	except plate glass	m^2	2.34	65.54	-	-	65.54	72.09	-
A023901B	plate glass	m^2	3.55	99.44	-	-	99.44	109.38	-
A023902	**Carefully take out all types of glass and set aside for re-use**								
A023902A	except plate glass	m^2	3.23	90.47	-	-	90.47	99.52	-
A023902B	plate glass	m^2	4.68	131.09	-	-	131.09	144.20	-
A023904	**Remove old putty, paint rebate one coat oil colour ready to receive**								
A023904A	new glass	m	0.16	4.48	-	0.15	4.63	5.09	0.090
A023905	**Glaze, sprig and putty to wood sashes; average 0.40 sq.m**								
A023905A	sheet	m^2	1.10	30.81	-	44.33	75.14	82.65	9.580
A023905B	obscured	m^2	1.10	30.81	-	50.21	81.02	89.12	18.030
A023905C	wired cast	m^2	1.20	33.61	-	43.00	76.61	84.27	18.030
A023905D	add for glazing to metal sashes	m^2	0.40	11.20	-	0.11	11.31	12.44	0.710
A023908	**Wired cast glass in roof lights in panes**								
A023908A	up to 0.70 sq.m	m^2	0.90	25.21	-	43.00	68.21	75.03	18.030
A023908B	exceeding 0.70 sq.m	m^2	1.00	28.01	-	43.00	71.01	78.11	18.030
A023910	**S.g. quality Float glass**								
A023910A	6 mm	m^2	3.50	98.04	-	78.92	176.96	194.66	26.510
A023911	**Bed edge of glass in**								
A023911A	chamois leather	m	0.23	6.44	-	0.65	7.09	7.80	3.220
A023911B	velvet	m	0.17	4.76	-	0.84	5.60	6.16	4.020
A023912	**Remove temporary coverings to sashes**								
A023912A	stopping nail holes etc	m^2	1.10	30.81	-	-	30.81	33.89	-
A0241	**PAINTING AND DECORATING**								
A024101	**Brush down brick walls, plaster walls, or ceilings and apply two coats lime white on brick walls**								
A024101A	new work	m^2	0.33	9.24	-	0.15	9.39	10.33	0.470
A024101B	old work	m^2	0.38	10.64	-	0.15	10.79	11.87	0.470
A024102	**Brush down brick walls, plaster walls, or ceilings and apply two coats emulsion paint on plaster**								
A024102A	new work	m^2	0.46	12.88	-	1.59	14.47	15.92	0.770
A024102B	old work	m^2	0.51	14.29	-	1.59	15.88	17.47	0.770

Small Works 2011		Unit	Labour Hours	Labour Net	Plant Net	Materials Net	Unit Net	Unit with 10%	CO₂
				£	£	£	£	£	Kg
A02	**REPAIRS AND ALTERATIONS**								
A0241	**PAINTING AND DECORATING**								
A024103	**Brush down brick walls, plaster walls, or ceiling and apply two coats emulsion paint on brick walls**								
A024103A	new work	m²	0.58	16.25	-	2.39	18.64	20.50	1.150
A024103B	old work	m²	0.63	17.65	-	2.39	20.04	22.04	1.150
A024104	**Wash down plaster surfaces, fill in minor cracks, nail holes etc with filler, bring forward paint as necessary ready for**								
A024104A	new decoration	m²	0.20	5.60	-	0.38	5.98	6.58	0.240
A024106	**Prepare and apply oil colour on ceilings**								
A024106A	one coat	m²	0.27	7.56	-	0.67	8.23	9.05	0.300
A024106B	two coats	m²	0.55	15.41	-	1.40	16.81	18.49	0.620
A024108	**Prepare and apply oil colour on plaster walls**								
A024108A	one coat	m²	0.21	5.88	-	0.67	6.55	7.21	0.300
A024108B	two coats	m²	0.43	12.04	-	1.40	13.44	14.78	0.620
A024110	**Prepare and apply oil colour on brick walls**								
A024110A	one coat	m²	0.27	7.56	-	1.06	8.62	9.48	0.470
A024110B	two coats	m²	0.54	15.13	-	2.17	17.30	19.03	0.960
A024111	**Wash down, touch up and apply two coats of oil colour to**								
A024111A	general wood surfaces	m²	0.65	18.21	-	1.35	19.56	21.52	0.730
A024111B	add for each extra coat applied or deduct for one coat	m²	0.24	6.72	-	0.62	7.34	8.07	0.360
A024111C	window frames and sashes (measured over glass)	m²	1.00	28.01	-	0.95	28.96	31.86	0.510
A024111D	add for each extra coat applied or deduct for one coat on window frames and sashes	m²	0.40	11.20	-	0.44	11.64	12.80	0.260
A024114	**Wash down, touch up and apply two coats of oil colour on surfaces**								
A024114A	n.e. 150 mm girth	m	0.14	3.92	-	0.16	4.08	4.49	0.090
A024114B	150 mm - 300 mm girth	m	0.24	6.72	-	0.40	7.12	7.83	0.210
A024114C	add for each extra cost applied or deduct for one coat n.e. 150 mm girt	m	0.07	1.96	-	0.07	2.03	2.23	0.040
A024114D	add for each extra cost applied or deduct for one coat 150 mm - 300 mm girth	m	0.11	3.08	-	0.18	3.26	3.59	0.110
A024116	**Clean down and bring forward all bare patches and apply oil colour to metal**								
A024116A	frames and sashes (measured over glass)	m²	1.11	31.09	-	1.35	32.44	35.68	0.730
A024116B	general surfaces over 300 mm girth	m²	0.69	19.33	-	0.95	20.28	22.31	0.510
A024116C	not exceeding 150 mm girth	m	0.30	8.40	-	0.16	8.56	9.42	0.090
A024116D	150 mm - 300 mm girth	m	0.39	10.92	-	0.40	11.32	12.45	0.210
A024118	**Clean down and apply gloss oil to fireplace jambs, stoves, mantel registers and similar**								
A024118A	one coat	Each	1.00	28.01	-	2.74	30.75	33.83	1.370
A024120	**Prepare and apply oil colour on water waste preventer and backboard**								
A024120A	two coats	Each	0.55	15.41	-	0.40	15.81	17.39	0.230
A024120B	add if including overflow pipes	Each	0.45	12.60	-	0.40	13.00	14.30	0.230

House Renovation Grants, Repairs and Alterations

Small Works 2011		Unit	Labour Hours	Labour Net	Plant Net	Materials Net	Unit Net	Unit with 10%	CO₂
				£	£	£	£	£	Kg
A02	**REPAIRS AND ALTERATIONS**								
A0241	**PAINTING AND DECORATING**								
A024122	**Clean and apply gloss oil on casement stays, fasteners, bolts, rim locks and sundry similar fittings**								
A024122A	one coat	Each	0.20	5.60	-	0.09	5.69	6.26	0.040
A024124	**Prepare polished wood surfaces and repolish**								
A024124A	existing	m²	2.10	58.82	-	0.64	59.46	65.41	0.140
A024124B	handrails	m	0.60	16.81	-	0.21	17.02	18.72	0.040
A024126	**Strip, body in and repolish**								
A024126A	wood surfaces	m²	4.70	131.65	-	1.08	132.73	146.00	0.230
A024126B	handrail	m	1.10	30.81	-	0.27	31.08	34.19	0.060
A024128	**Prepare and wax polish**								
A024128A	flooring	m²	0.50	14.01	-	0.64	14.65	16.12	0.140
A024132	**Strip paper from walls or ceilings, stop, size ready for new paper**								
A024132A	first layer	m²	0.30	8.40	-	0.08	8.48	9.33	0.340
A024132B	each extra layer	m²	0.12	3.36	-	0.08	3.44	3.78	0.340
A024132C	first layer varnished paper	m²	0.60	16.81	-	0.08	16.89	18.58	0.340
A024132D	each extra layer varnished paper	m²	0.22	6.16	-	0.08	6.24	6.86	0.340
A024134	**Cut, trim and hang paper to**								
A024134A	walls; woodchip	m²	0.26	7.28	-	0.65	7.93	8.72	0.230
A024134B	walls; standard	m²	0.26	7.28	-	3.52	10.80	11.88	1.370
A024134C	ceilings; lining	m²	0.30	8.40	-	0.60	9.00	9.90	0.290
A024136	**Wash down and apply masonry paint on external rendered walls**								
A024136A	two coats	m²	0.53	14.85	-	0.86	15.71	17.28	0.680
A024138	**Wash down, and apply two coats of masonry paint on external rendered walls**								
A024138A	Sandtex Matt	m²	0.54	15.13	-	3.51	18.64	20.50	2.110
A024138B	Snowcem Matt	m²	0.42	11.76	-	0.61	12.37	13.61	1.170
A024144	**Wash down, touch up and apply oil colour externally to general wood surfaces**								
A024144A	two coats external	m²	0.68	19.05	-	1.51	20.56	22.62	0.810
A024144B	add for each extra coat applied external	m²	0.27	7.56	-	0.70	8.26	9.09	0.410
A024146	**Wash down, touch up and apply oil colour on window frames and sashes (measured over glass)**								
A024146A	two coats external	m²	1.21	33.89	-	0.95	34.84	38.32	0.510
A024146B	add for each extra coat applied	m²	0.43	12.04	-	0.44	12.48	13.73	0.260
A024150	**Burn off paint to woodwork and prepare for priming**								
A024150A	general surfaces	m²	0.80	22.41	-	-	22.41	24.65	-
A024151	**Strip paint with**								
A024151A	paint remover	m²	0.50	14.01	-	0.15	14.16	15.58	0.060
A024152	**Prime and apply oil colour to putties after reglazing**								
A024152A	two coats	m	0.18	5.04	-	0.21	5.25	5.78	0.110
A024162	**Clean down, wire brush and bring forward all bare patches and apply oil colour on previously painted metalwork**								
A024162A	general surfaces; over 300 mm girth	m²	0.78	21.85	-	1.51	23.36	25.70	0.810
A024162B	general surfaces; n.e. 150 mm girth	m	0.39	10.92	-	0.24	11.16	12.28	0.130

Small Works 2011		Unit	Labour Hours	Labour Net	Plant Net	Materials Net	Unit Net	Unit with 10%	CO2
				£	£	£	£	£	Kg
A02	**REPAIRS AND ALTERATIONS**								
A0241	**PAINTING AND DECORATING**								
A024162	**Clean down, wire brush and bring forward all bare patches and apply oil colour on previously painted metalwork**								
A024162C	general surfaces; 150 mm - 300 mm girth	m	0.51	14.29	-	0.48	14.77	16.25	0.260
A024162D	corrugated surfaces (measured flat)	m²	0.87	24.37	-	1.75	26.12	28.73	0.940
A024162E	structural steelwork	m²	0.96	26.89	-	1.51	28.40	31.24	0.810
A024162F	railings, balusters etc (measured flat overall)	m²	0.87	24.37	-	1.51	25.88	28.47	0.810
A024162G	stairs (measured overall)	m²	0.84	23.53	-	1.51	25.04	27.54	0.810
A024162H	windows glazed doors in small panes	m²	1.98	55.46	-	1.03	56.49	62.14	0.560
A024162I	windows glazed doors in medium panes	m²	1.74	48.74	-	0.95	49.69	54.66	0.510
A024162J	windows glazed doors in large panes	m²	1.50	42.02	-	0.79	42.81	47.09	0.430
A024162K	eaves gutters (inside and outside)	m	0.51	14.29	-	1.03	15.32	16.85	0.560
A024162L	rainwater pipes, soil pipes etc	m	0.51	14.29	-	0.56	14.85	16.34	0.300
A024162M	pipes bars, straps etc, up to 150 mm girth	m	0.45	12.60	-	0.24	12.84	14.12	0.130
A024166	**Treating wood surfaces with two coats preservative**								
A024166A	sawn surfaces; creosote substitute	m²	0.40	11.20	-	0.80	12.00	13.20	1.140
A024166B	wrought surfaces; creosote substitute	m²	0.38	10.64	-	0.54	11.18	12.30	0.770
A024166C	sawn surfaces; Cuprinol clear	m²	0.40	11.20	-	1.60	12.80	14.08	1.130
A024166D	wrought surfaces; Cuprinol clear	m²	0.38	10.64	-	1.06	11.70	12.87	0.750
A024166E	sawn surfaces; Solignum	m²	0.38	10.64	-	1.92	12.56	13.82	1.120
A024166F	wrought surfaces; Solignum	m²	0.36	10.08	-	1.27	11.35	12.49	0.740
A0244	**MASONRY REPAIRS AND RENEWALS**								
A024401	**Take down masonry, clean and set aside**								
A024401A	ashlar walling	m²	1.01	76.91	-	-	76.91	84.60	-
A024401B	cornices etc	m	0.40	30.73	-	-	30.73	33.80	-
A024401C	arches	Each	0.27	20.57	-	-	20.57	22.63	-
A024401D	steps, cills etc	m	0.50	38.45	-	-	38.45	42.30	-
A024402	**Take down masonry, clean and reset**								
A024402A	ashlar walling	m²	2.60	198.69	-	11.55	210.24	231.26	27.430
A024402B	cornices etc	m	1.11	84.63	-	2.98	87.61	96.37	5.950
A024402C	arches	Each	0.74	56.42	-	5.25	61.67	67.84	10.480
A024402D	steps, cills etc	m	0.67	51.30	-	4.26	55.56	61.12	8.490
A024403	**Cut out decayed Portland (or similar) stone in facings of wall built in lime mortar in adjacent stones. Prepare for, supply and fix new stones**								
A024403A	average 50 mm thick, point and clean down on completion	m²	1.01	76.91	-	153.47	230.38	253.42	16.580
A024403B	in separate stones	m²	1.21	92.28	-	169.66	261.94	288.13	18.920
A024404	**Rake out joints and repoint**								
A024404A	ashlar stonework	m²	0.47	35.93	-	0.71	36.64	40.30	1.420
A024404B	squared rubble	m²	0.54	41.05	-	0.71	41.76	45.94	1.420
A024405	**Redress face of walling, where decayed, with picked face and repoint**								
A024405A	generally	m²	2.68	205.12	-	0.99	206.11	226.72	1.980
A024408	**Take up and reset 50 mm thick Yorkstone slabs, any size, in landings, hearths, cover stones, paving, etc**								
A024408A	in lime mortar	m²	0.67	51.30	-	3.67	54.97	60.47	8.710
A024408B	in cement mortar	m²	0.81	61.54	-	3.33	64.87	71.36	11.390

House Renovation Grants, Repairs and Alterations

	Unit	Labour Hours	Labour Net	Plant Net	Materials Net	Unit Net	Unit with 10%	CO$_2$
			£	£	£	£	£	Kg
A02	**REPAIRS AND ALTERATIONS**							
A0244	**MASONRY REPAIRS AND RENEWALS**							
A024410	**Cut and form toothing in old masonry for**							
A024410A	new brick or stone	m^2	0.67	51.30	-	-	51.30	56.43	-
A024411	**Take down and reset blocking courses, cornices, strings, plinths, apexes, kneelers etc**							
A024411A	in lime mortar	m	0.40	30.73	-	0.68	31.41	34.55	1.610
A024411B	in cement mortar	m	0.47	35.93	-	0.62	36.55	40.21	2.110
A024414	**Take down and reset window cills, steps etc including cutting away and making good**							
A024414A	in lime mortar	m	0.67	51.30	-	0.41	51.71	56.88	0.970
A024414B	in cement mortar	m	0.74	56.42	-	0.37	56.79	62.47	1.270
A024415	**Repair with granite chipping concrete including cutting out to depth of at least 19 mm finish concrete fair and flush with original surface**							
A024415A	treads	m^2	0.87	66.66	-	6.59	73.25	80.58	13.840
A024415B	landings	m^2	0.54	41.05	-	6.59	47.64	52.40	13.840
A0246	**ROOFING REPAIRS AND RENEWALS**							
A024601	**Remove coverings and load into skip; roof coverings**							
A024601A	slates	m^2	0.55	11.47	-	-	11.47	12.62	-
A024601B	nibbed tiles	m^2	0.45	9.38	-	-	9.38	10.32	-
A024601C	corrugated metal sheeting	m^2	0.45	9.38	-	-	9.38	10.32	-
A024601D	underfelt and nails	m^2	0.07	1.46	-	-	1.46	1.61	-
A024601E	three layers felt	m^2	0.28	5.84	-	-	5.84	6.42	-
A024601F	sheet metal	m^2	0.55	11.47	-	-	11.47	12.62	-
A024601G	metal flashings; horizontal	m	0.22	4.59	-	-	4.59	5.05	-
A024601H	metal flashings; stepped	m	0.28	5.84	-	-	5.84	6.42	-
A024601I	tile or slate battens, including withdrawing nails	m^2	0.10	2.09	-	-	2.09	2.30	
A024602	**Remove coverings, carefully handling and disposing by an approved method toxic or other special waste**							
A024602A	asbestos cement sheeting	m^2	0.74	56.42	-	-	56.42	62.06	-
A024603	**Stripping, cleaning and setting aside sound slates or tiles for re-use**							
A024603A	slates	m^2	0.40	8.34	-	-	8.34	9.17	-
A024603B	tiles	m^2	0.30	6.25	-	-	6.25	6.88	-
A024603C	cement slates	m^2	0.40	8.34	-	-	8.34	9.17	-
A024604	**Stripping, cleaning and setting aside for removal**							
A024604A	slates	m^2	0.30	6.25	-	-	6.25	6.88	-
A024604B	tiles	m^2	0.24	5.00	-	-	5.00	5.50	-
A024604C	cement slates	m^2	0.30	6.25	-	-	6.25	6.88	-
A024606	**Renew tile battens to 100 mm gauge**							
A024606A	area n.e. 8.5 sq.m	m^2	0.11	8.72	-	5.73	14.45	15.90	3.230
A024606B	exceeding 8.5 sq.m	m^2	0.09	6.65	-	5.73	12.38	13.62	3.230
A024608	**Renew slate battens to 205 mm gauge**							
A024608A	area n.e. 8.5 sq.m	m^2	0.09	6.65	-	3.12	9.77	10.75	2.250
A024608B	exceeding 8.5 sq.m	m^2	0.06	4.36	-	3.12	7.48	8.23	2.250
A024610	**Renew roofing felt**							
A024610A	generally	m^2	0.05	3.59	-	3.18	6.77	7.45	5.410

Small Works 2011		Unit	Labour Hours	Labour Net	Plant Net	Materials Net	Unit Net	Unit with 10%	CO$_2$
				£	£	£	£	£	Kg
A02	**REPAIRS AND ALTERATIONS**								
A0246	**ROOFING REPAIRS AND RENEWALS**								
A024612	**Taking off and renewing single slates including clips; first slate**								
A024612A	405 mm x 205 mm	Each	0.18	13.61	-	27.00	40.61	44.67	0.660
A024612B	510 mm x 255 mm	Each	0.19	14.37	-	38.62	52.99	58.29	1.040
A024612C	610 mm x 305 mm	Each	0.20	14.91	-	71.27	86.18	94.80	1.460
A024614	**Taking off and renewing second and subsequent slates; up to 30 no**								
A024614A	405 mm x 205 mm	Each	0.07	5.66	-	27.00	32.66	35.93	0.660
A024614B	510 mm x 255 mm	Each	0.08	5.89	-	38.62	44.51	48.96	1.040
A024614C	610 mm x 305 mm	Each	0.08	6.19	-	71.27	77.46	85.21	1.460
A024616	**Taking off and renewing single tiles; first tile**								
A024616A	clay	Each	0.12	9.25	-	0.70	9.95	10.95	0.460
A024616B	concrete	Each	0.12	9.25	-	0.66	9.91	10.90	0.260
A024618	**Taking off and renewing second and subsequent tiles; up to 50 no**								
A024618A	clay	Each	0.07	5.66	-	0.70	6.36	7.00	0.460
A024618B	concrete	Each	0.07	5.66	-	0.66	6.32	6.95	0.260
A024619	**Taking off and renewing single blue asbestos slates; first slate**								
A024619A	610 mm x 305 mm	Each	0.12	9.48	-	2.15	11.63	12.79	0.830
A024620	**Taking off and renewing second and subsequent slates; up to 30 no**								
A024620A	610 mm x 305 mm	Each	0.07	5.66	-	0.20	5.86	6.45	0.080
A024621	**Cement mortar angle fillet to slate, tile or asbestos roof at abutment to walls or chimney stacks**								
A024621A	1 - 3 no	m	0.13	10.24	-	0.37	10.61	11.67	1.270
A024622	**Strip roof slating, sort slates and reslate roof using 50% existing slates**								
A024622A	405 mm x 205 mm	m^2	0.39	29.51	-	407.49	437.00	480.70	10.000
A024622B	510 mm x 255 mm	m^2	0.27	20.49	-	358.13	378.62	416.48	9.630
A024622C	610 mm x 305 mm	m^2	0.17	12.84	-	447.04	459.88	505.87	9.160
A024624	**Strip 267 mm x 165 mm plain roof tiles and retile using 50% existing tiles**								
A024624A	clay	m^2	0.57	43.58	-	24.61	68.19	75.01	16.050
A024624B	concrete	m^2	0.57	43.58	-	23.11	66.69	73.36	9.130
A024626	**Take up old lead, any position or weight**								
A024626A	set aside	m^2	0.24	15.07	-	-	15.07	16.58	-
A024628	**Take up and relay lead to boarded flats**								
A024628A	including dressing over rolls and drips with new bossed ends etc	m^2	2.60	161.93	-	-	161.93	178.12	-
A024629	**Redress lead flashings**								
A024629A	rewedge and repoint	m	0.48	30.14	-	-	30.14	33.15	-
A024630	**Take up old zinc and remove from site**								
A024630A	in any position	m^2	0.61	37.68	-	-	37.68	41.45	-
A024632	**Take up existing zinc and supply and lay new zinc including rolls, laps etc**								
A024632A	0.50 mm thick	m^2	2.42	150.66	-	13.97	164.63	181.09	15.470
A024632B	0.65 mm thick	m^2	2.72	169.46	-	25.60	195.06	214.57	19.810
A024632C	0.80 mm thick	m^2	3.02	188.33	-	31.47	219.80	241.78	24.450

Small Works 2011	Unit	Labour Hours	Labour Net £	Plant Net £	Materials Net £	Unit Net £	Unit with 10% £	CO$_2$ Kg
A02	**REPAIRS AND ALTERATIONS**							
A0246	**ROOFING REPAIRS AND RENEWALS**							
A024634	**Prepare zinc roofs for and supply and lay bitumenised fabric bedded in bitumen and apply bitumen emulsion**							
A024634A	two coats	m^2	0.64	48.70	-	1.67	50.37	55.41	1.760
A024636	**Seal crack in holes in zinc or asphalt flats and apply bitumen waterproofer**							
A024636A	two coats	m^2	0.30	23.09	-	0.45	23.54	25.89	0.210
A024638	**Clean and treat defective sheet zinc**							
A024638A	Rito, Matex or similar compound	m^2	0.37	28.21	-	1.55	29.76	32.74	1.050
A024639	**Remove slates, take out defective box gutter linings or valleys and renew wood linings and line with zinc and replace slates**							
A024639A	12 G	m^2	4.84	301.31	-	51.52	352.83	388.11	37.370
A024640	**Labour and transport up to 5 miles each way, setting up and removing ladders**							
A024640A	up to two storeys high	Job	2.00	41.70	5.77	-	47.47	52.22	8.620
A024640B	up to four storeys high	Job	2.50	52.13	5.77	-	57.90	63.69	8.620
A024640C	Extra over last two items if access is difficult e.g. one house in a terrace where there is no side entrance	Job	2.00	41.70	5.77	-	47.47	52.22	8.620
A024642	**Remove waterproofing finishes and load into skip**							
A024642A	asphalt paving	m^2	0.67	13.97	-	-	13.97	15.37	-
A024642B	asphalt roofing	m^2	1.10	22.94	-	-	22.94	25.23	-
A024642C	asphalt skirting	m	0.17	3.54	-	-	3.54	3.89	-
A0250	**ROOFING REPAIRS BY SPECIALISTS**							
A025001	**Clean, prepare and apply DC500 roofing compound to**							
A025001A	sound surfaces, asbestos, asphalt, concrete, felt, slate or tile	m^2	0.55	11.47	-	6.88	18.35	20.19	0.600
A025002	**Clean, prepare and apply DC500 flexible roofing compound and fungicide solution**							
A025002A	to surfaces likely to support fungal or algae growth, asbestos, asphalt, concrete, felt, slate or tile	m^2	0.60	12.51	-	7.32	19.83	21.81	1.070
A0252	**DRAINAGE REPAIRS AND RENEWALS**							
A025201	**Break up 100 mm concrete paving and hardcore for excavation drain trench**							
A025201A	not exceeding 600 mm wide	m	1.10	22.94	-	-	22.94	25.23	-
A025202	**Hand excavate trench for 100 mm drain including backfilling and carting away remainder including necessary earthwork support**							
A025202A	average 0.5 m deep	m	1.44	30.02	-	-	30.02	33.02	-
A025202B	average 1.0 m deep	m	2.90	60.47	-	-	60.47	66.52	-
A025202C	average 1.5 m deep	m	5.16	107.59	-	-	107.59	118.35	-
A025203	**100 mm concrete bed and haunch to**							
A025203A	pipe	m	1.10	22.94	-	21.05	43.99	48.39	52.530

Small Works 2011		Unit	Labour Hours	Labour Net	Plant Net	Materials Net	Unit Net	Unit with 10%	CO₂
				£	£	£	£	£	Kg
A02	**REPAIRS AND ALTERATIONS**								
A0252	**DRAINAGE REPAIRS AND RENEWALS**								
A025204	**HepSeal clayware pipes, laid and jointed in short lengths**								
A025204A	100 mm	m	0.25	12.21	-	10.48	22.69	24.96	5.590
A025205	**Make good 100 mm concrete paving and hardcore under, after drainwork**								
A025205A	average 600 mm wide	m	1.30	27.11	-	7.76	34.87	38.36	19.350
A025206	**Cutting into brick side of exposed manhole and concrete benching for new branch drain and three quarter section channel, make good brickwork and benching**								
A025206A	100 mm	Each	1.51	73.32	-	42.51	115.83	127.41	6.240
A025207	**Glazed clayware gully and grid 150 mm x 150 mm x 100 mm with 100 mm outlet join to drain**								
A025207A	including necessary excavation and concrete bed	Each	1.21	58.62	-	57.64	116.26	127.89	15.210
A025208	**Concrete curb 100 mm outlet joint to drain**								
A025208A	including necessary formwork	Each	0.63	30.55	-	7.09	37.64	41.40	17.690
A025209	**Demolish curb, disconnect and remove gully, supply and connect new gully and grid including work to concrete bed, new grid, rendering three sides and remake connection after rodding**								
A025209A	150 mm x 150 mm x 100 mm	Each	3.01	146.58	-	60.98	207.56	228.32	26.590
A025210	**Break up defective curb-surround to manhole and reform in**								
A025210A	fine concrete splayed and rendered	Each	0.78	37.85	-	3.28	41.13	45.24	8.740
A025212	**Cut through external 225 mm brick wall and 150 mm concrete floor and connect to trap of pan at one end and existing pipe at the other end**								
A025212A	102 mm bend	Each	3.77	183.22	-	44.06	227.28	250.01	63.570
A025214	**Form new manhole on line of existing drain with 150 mm concrete base, 225 mm brick walls, cover and frame. Cut away existing drain within manhole to form channel, provide and set two three-quarter section channels and form concrete benching and cement render walls**								
A025214A	0.9 m deep	Each	18.08	879.49	-	220.53	1,100.02	1,210.02	642.320
A025214B	add for every extra 300 mm depth in excess of 0.9 m	Each	4.52	219.85	-	44.83	264.68	291.15	186.800
A025215	**Take up existing manhole cover and frame and provide, bed and seal new cover and frame 610 mm x 457 mm**								
A025215A	25 kg	Each	0.55	26.85	-	37.56	64.41	70.85	56.290
A025215B	38 kg	Each	0.65	31.77	-	58.32	90.09	99.10	49.530
A025216	**Excavate for stoppage in 100 mm drain, cut out and renew two lengths of pipe, fill in and test. Reform paving**								
A025216A	assumed depth 0.9 m	Each	5.02	244.32	-	56.66	300.98	331.08	78.690

Small Works 2011		Unit	Labour Hours	Labour Net	Plant Net	Materials Net	Unit Net	Unit with 10%	CO₂
				£	£	£	£	£	Kg
A02	**REPAIRS AND ALTERATIONS**								
A0252	**DRAINAGE REPAIRS AND RENEWALS**								
A025218	**Unstop gullies**								
A025218A	remove silt, clean and flush with disinfectant	Each	0.58	28.12	-	-	28.12	30.93	-
A025220	**Clear soil drains, rod and flush in sections**								
A025220A	average length 25 m	Each	2.89	140.45	-	-	140.45	154.50	-
A025221	**Unstop and smoke test**								
A025221A	cast iron soil pipe	Each	2.11	102.60	-	-	102.60	112.86	-
A025222	**Take up manhole cover, clean and sand out and rebed in grease**								
A025222A	frame channels	Each	0.55	26.85	-	-	26.85	29.54	-
A025224	**Clayware channel to gully set in concrete with brick curb rendered in cement mortar**								
A025224A	450 mm long	Each	1.00	48.84	-	12.71	61.55	67.71	18.150
A025224B	supply and fit new gully grid	Each	0.13	6.13	-	5.15	11.28	12.41	1.530
A025226	**Open up manhole, break out brickwork and benching to main channel, provide for and insert one three quarter channel bend and join to existing channel, reform benching, make good all work disturbed and refix manhole cover**								
A025226A	100 mm	Each	5.02	244.32	-	27.84	272.16	299.38	13.940
A025228	**Open up manhole 0.9 m x 0.9 m inside on plan and 1.27 m deep. Break out all channels and branches. Break out one brick side of manhole at one end and extend manhole**								
A025228A	by 150 mm x 0.9 m inside with 150 mm concrete at bottom, one brick side in stock bricks and 150 mm concrete cover. Build in two pipes 150 mm and one pipe 100 mm, provide and insert straight main channel 150 mm and six half branch channel bends 100 mm and reform benching. Make good all work disturbed and refix manhole cover	Each	12.05	586.33	-	350.37	936.70	1,030.37	428.740
A025228B	Extra over excavation for breaking out brick manhole 0.8 m x 0.7 m inside on plan and 0.9 m deep to invert	Each	1.51	73.32	-	-	73.32	80.65	-
A025228C	add or deduct for every 300 mm more or less than 0.9 m deep to invert	Each	0.50	24.42	-	-	24.42	26.86	-
A025230	**Seal open ends of disused clayware pipes with concrete plugs 300 mm long**								
A025230A	100 mm dia	Each	0.30	14.64	-	0.33	14.97	16.47	0.830
A025230B	150 mm dia	Each	0.40	19.56	-	0.78	20.34	22.37	1.940
A025230C	225 mm dia	Each	0.55	26.85	-	2.66	29.51	32.46	6.640

Drainage, Sewerage
and Public Works

Small Works 2011		Unit	Labour Hours	Labour Net	Plant Net	Materials Net	Unit Net	Unit with 10%	CO$_2$
				£	£	£	£	£	Kg
B01	**DRAINAGE AND SEWERAGE**								
B0101	**EXCAVATING TRENCHES**								
B010101	**Excavate trenches in firm clay; 450 mm wide; earthwork support; grade bottom; backfill; compact; dispose of surplus; hand labour; average depth**								
B010101A	0.50 m	m	1.31	27.31	-	0.42	27.73	30.50	0.210
B010101B	0.75 m	m	1.97	41.07	-	0.58	41.65	45.82	0.290
B010101C	1.00 m	m	2.63	54.84	-	0.75	55.59	61.15	0.380
B010101D	1.25 m	m	3.92	81.73	-	0.94	82.67	90.94	0.480
B010101E	1.50 m	m	4.69	97.79	-	1.16	98.95	108.85	0.590
B010101F	1.75 m	m	5.48	114.26	-	1.33	115.59	127.15	0.670
B010101G	2.00 m	m	6.26	130.52	-	1.50	132.02	145.22	0.760
B010101H	2.25 m	m	8.52	177.64	-	1.66	179.30	197.23	0.840
B010101I	2.50 m	m	9.46	197.24	-	1.94	199.18	219.10	0.980
B010101J	2.75 m	m	10.42	217.26	-	2.08	219.34	241.27	1.050
B010101K	3.00 m	m	11.35	236.65	-	2.22	238.87	262.76	1.120
B010102	**Excavate trenches in firm soil; 600 mm wide earthwork support; grade bottom; compact; dispose of surplus; hand labour; average depth**								
B010102A	0.50 m	m	1.75	36.49	-	0.47	36.96	40.66	0.240
B010102B	0.75 m	m	2.63	54.84	-	0.75	55.59	61.15	0.380
B010102C	1.00 m	m	3.50	72.98	-	1.00	73.98	81.38	0.510
B010102D	1.25 m	m	5.22	108.84	-	1.28	110.12	121.13	0.650
B010102E	1.50 m	m	6.26	130.52	-	1.50	132.02	145.22	0.760
B010102F	1.75 m	m	7.30	152.21	-	1.75	153.96	169.36	0.880
B010102G	2.00 m	m	8.34	173.89	-	2.00	175.89	193.48	1.010
B010102H	2.25 m	m	11.35	236.65	-	2.22	238.87	262.76	1.120
B010102I	2.50 m	m	12.62	263.13	-	2.50	265.63	292.19	1.260
B010102J	2.75 m	m	13.88	289.40	-	2.75	292.15	321.37	1.390
B010102K	3.00 m	m	15.14	315.67	-	3.02	318.69	350.56	1.530
B010103	**Excavate trenches in firm soil; 750 mm wide earthwork support; grade bottom; compact; dispose of surplus; hand labour; average depth**								
B010103A	0.50 m	m	2.18	45.45	-	0.67	46.12	50.73	0.340
B010103B	0.75 m	m	3.29	68.60	-	0.94	69.54	76.49	0.480
B010103C	1.00 m	m	4.37	91.11	-	1.28	92.39	101.63	0.650
B010103D	1.25 m	m	6.54	136.36	-	1.61	137.97	151.77	0.810
B010103E	1.50 m	m	7.82	163.05	-	1.94	164.99	181.49	0.980
B010103F	1.75 m	m	9.13	190.36	-	2.16	192.52	211.77	1.100
B010103G	2.00 m	m	10.44	217.67	-	2.50	220.17	242.19	1.260
B010103H	2.25 m	m	14.21	296.28	-	2.83	299.11	329.02	1.430
B010103I	2.50 m	m	15.78	329.01	-	3.16	332.17	365.39	1.600
B010103J	2.75 m	m	17.35	361.75	-	3.41	365.16	401.68	1.730
B010103K	3.00 m	m	18.94	394.90	-	3.74	398.64	438.50	1.900
B010104	**Excavate trenches in firm soil; 450 mm wide earthwork support; grade bottom; compact; dispose of surplus; machine excavation; average depth**								
B010104A	0.50 m	m	0.17	3.54	4.93	0.30	8.77	9.65	4.860
B010104B	0.75 m	m	0.24	5.00	6.97	0.80	12.77	14.05	7.070
B010104C	1.00 m	m	0.34	7.09	9.85	0.54	17.48	19.23	9.690
B010104D	1.25 m	m	0.47	9.80	13.64	0.30	23.74	26.11	13.200
B010104E	1.50 m	m	0.55	11.47	15.97	0.61	28.05	30.86	15.580
B010104F	1.75 m	m	0.65	13.55	18.89	0.42	32.86	36.15	18.270
B010104G	2.00 m	m	0.74	15.43	21.48	0.37	37.28	41.01	20.730
B010104H	2.25 m	m	0.97	20.22	25.27	0.75	46.24	50.86	24.540
B010104I	2.50 m	m	1.07	22.31	29.03	0.58	51.92	57.11	28.060
B010104J	2.75 m	m	1.18	24.60	31.36	0.78	56.74	62.41	30.380
B010104K	3.00 m	m	1.28	26.69	34.28	0.57	61.54	67.69	33.070
B010105	**Excavate trenches in firm soil; 600 mm wide earthwork support; grade bottom; compact; dispose of surplus; machine excavation; average depth**								
B010105A	0.50 m	m	0.23	4.80	6.67	0.29	11.76	12.94	6.530
B010105B	0.75 m	m	0.34	7.09	9.85	0.54	17.48	19.23	9.690

Drainage, Sewerage and Public Works

Small Works 2011		Unit	Labour Hours	Labour Net	Plant Net	Materials Net	Unit Net	Unit with 10%	CO₂
				£	£	£	£	£	Kg
B01	**DRAINAGE AND SEWERAGE**								
B0101	**EXCAVATING TRENCHES**								
B010105	**Excavate trenches in firm soil; 600 mm wide earthwork support; grade bottom; compact; dispose of surplus; machine excavation; average depth**								
B010105C	1.00 m	m	0.44	9.17	12.77	1.08	23.02	25.32	12.760
B010105D	1.25 m	m	0.62	12.93	18.01	0.37	31.31	34.44	17.410
B010105E	1.50 m	m	0.74	15.43	21.48	0.37	37.28	41.01	20.730
B010105F	1.75 m	m	0.88	18.35	24.10	1.11	43.56	47.92	23.610
B010105G	2.00 m	m	1.00	20.85	27.60	1.14	49.59	54.55	26.970
B010105H	2.25 m	m	1.28	26.69	34.28	0.57	61.54	67.69	33.070
B010105I	2.50 m	m	1.43	29.82	38.62	0.58	69.02	75.92	37.230
B010105J	2.75 m	m	1.57	32.73	42.12	0.61	75.46	83.01	40.580
B010105K	3.00 m	m	1.70	35.45	46.46	0.58	82.49	90.74	44.720
B010106	**Excavate trenches in firm soil; 750 mm wide earthwork support; grade bottom; compact; dispose of surplus; machine excavation; average depth**								
B010106A	0.50 m	m	0.26	5.42	7.55	0.40	13.37	14.71	7.420
B010106B	0.75 m	m	0.40	8.34	11.63	0.67	20.64	22.70	11.460
B010106C	1.00 m	m	0.53	11.05	15.39	1.19	27.63	30.39	15.320
B010106D	1.25 m	m	0.74	15.43	21.48	0.51	37.42	41.16	20.800
B010106E	1.50 m	m	0.90	18.77	26.14	0.32	45.23	49.75	25.160
B010106F	1.75 m	m	1.04	21.68	30.20	1.14	53.02	58.32	29.450
B010106G	2.00 m	m	1.19	24.81	34.54	1.22	60.57	66.63	33.650
B010106H	2.25 m	m	1.55	32.32	42.12	0.69	75.13	82.64	40.630
B010106I	2.50 m	m	1.72	35.86	46.46	0.75	83.07	91.38	44.810
B010106J	2.75 m	m	1.88	39.20	50.83	1.37	91.40	100.54	49.300
B010106K	3.00 m	m	2.05	42.74	56.63	0.30	99.67	109.64	54.310
B0102	**PIPE BEDS AND COVERINGS**								
B010201	**Sand; 50 mm beds; width**								
B010201A	450 mm	m	0.11	2.29	-	1.07	3.36	3.70	0.250
B010201B	525 mm	m	0.12	2.50	-	1.35	3.85	4.24	0.320
B010201C	600 mm	m	0.12	2.50	-	1.35	3.85	4.24	0.320
B010201D	750 mm	m	0.17	3.54	-	1.88	5.42	5.96	0.440
B010202	**Granular material; DTp grade 1; 50 mm beds; width**								
B010202A	450 mm	m	0.11	2.29	-	0.61	2.90	3.19	0.280
B010202B	525 mm	m	0.12	2.50	-	0.94	3.44	3.78	0.430
B010202C	600 mm	m	0.12	2.50	-	0.94	3.44	3.78	0.430
B010202D	750 mm	m	0.17	3.54	-	1.23	4.77	5.25	0.560
B010203	**Granular material; DTp grade 1; 100 mm beds; width**								
B010203A	450 mm	m	0.20	4.17	-	1.55	5.72	6.29	0.710
B010203B	525 mm	m	0.24	5.00	-	1.55	6.55	7.21	0.710
B010203C	600 mm	m	0.28	5.84	-	1.87	7.71	8.48	0.860
B010203D	750 mm	m	0.35	7.30	-	2.49	9.79	10.77	1.140
B010204	**Granular material; DTp grade 1; 150 mm beds; width**								
B010204A	450 mm	m	0.31	6.46	-	2.16	8.62	9.48	0.990
B010204B	525 mm	m	0.36	7.51	-	2.49	10.00	11.00	1.140
B010204C	600 mm	m	0.42	8.76	-	2.78	11.54	12.69	1.280
B010204D	750 mm	m	0.53	11.05	-	3.42	14.47	15.92	1.570
B010205	**Granular material; DTp grade 1; 100 mm beds; filling to half height of pipe; width**								
B010205A	450 mm to 100 mm pipe	m	0.32	6.67	-	1.87	8.54	9.39	0.860
B010205B	525 mm to 150 mm pipe	m	0.42	8.76	-	2.49	11.25	12.38	1.140
B010205C	600 mm to 225 mm pipe	m	0.53	11.05	-	3.10	14.15	15.57	1.420
B010205D	750 mm to 300 mm pipe	m	0.73	15.22	-	4.33	19.55	21.51	1.990
B010206	**Granular material; DTp grade 1; 150 mm beds; filling to half height of pipe; width**								
B010206A	450 mm to 100 mm pipe	m	0.43	8.97	-	2.78	11.75	12.93	1.280
B010206B	525 mm to 150 mm pipe	m	0.54	11.26	-	3.42	14.68	16.15	1.570
B010206C	600 mm to 225mm pipe	m	0.66	13.76	-	4.04	17.80	19.58	1.850
B010206D	750 mm to 300 mm pipe	m	0.91	18.97	-	5.59	24.56	27.02	2.570

Small Works 2011		Unit	Labour Hours	Labour Net	Plant Net	Materials Net	Unit Net	Unit with 10%	CO₂
				£	£	£	£	£	Kg
B01	**DRAINAGE AND SEWERAGE**								
B0102	**PIPE BEDS AND COVERINGS**								
B010207	**Granular material; DTp grade 1; bed and covering; thickness**								
B010207A	450 mm x 350 mm thick to 100 mm pipe	m	0.70	14.60	-	4.65	19.25	21.18	2.140
B010207B	450 mm x 450 mm thick to 100 mm pipe	m	0.90	18.77	-	6.20	24.97	27.47	2.850
B010207C	525 mm x 400 mm thick to 150 mm pipe	m	0.89	18.56	-	6.20	24.76	27.24	2.850
B010207D	525 mm x 500 mm thick to 150 mm pipe	m	1.14	23.77	-	7.75	31.52	34.67	3.560
B010207E	600 mm x 475 mm thick to 225 mm pipe	m	1.14	23.77	-	7.75	31.52	34.67	3.560
B010207F	600 mm x 575 mm thick to 225 mm pipe	m	1.42	29.61	-	9.62	39.23	43.15	4.420
B010207G	750 mm x 550 mm thick to 300 mm pipe	m	1.58	32.94	-	10.85	43.79	48.17	4.990
B010207H	750 mm x 650 mm thick to 300 mm pipe	m	1.91	39.82	-	13.01	52.83	58.11	5.980
B010209	**Plain concrete mix 1:3:6 - 40 mm aggregate; 100 mm beds; width**								
B010209A	450 mm	m	0.29	6.05	-	5.87	11.92	13.11	14.650
B010209B	525 mm	m	0.34	7.09	-	6.76	13.85	15.24	16.870
B010209C	600 mm	m	0.38	7.92	-	7.76	15.68	17.25	19.350
B010209D	750 mm	m	0.48	10.01	-	9.75	19.76	21.74	24.330
B010210	**Plain concrete mix 1:3:6 - 40 mm aggregate; 150 mm beds; width**								
B010210A	450 mm	m	0.43	8.97	-	8.64	17.61	19.37	21.570
B010210B	525 mm	m	0.50	10.43	-	10.19	20.62	22.68	25.440
B010210C	600 mm	m	0.58	12.09	-	11.63	23.72	26.09	29.030
B010210D	750 mm	m	0.72	15.01	-	14.51	29.52	32.47	36.220
B010211	**Plain concrete mix 1:3:6 - 40 mm aggregate; 100 mm beds; filling to half height of pipe; width**								
B010211A	450 mm to 100 mm pipe	m	0.44	9.17	-	8.64	17.81	19.59	21.570
B010211B	525 mm to 150 mm pipe	m	0.56	11.68	-	11.19	22.87	25.16	27.920
B010211C	600 mm to 225 mm pipe	m	0.72	15.01	-	11.19	26.20	28.82	27.920
B010211D	750 mm to 300 mm pipe	m	1.01	21.06	-	14.29	35.35	38.89	35.670
B010212	**Plain concrete mix 1:3:6 - 40 mm aggregate; 150 mm beds; filling to half height of pipe; width**								
B010212A	450 mm to 100 mm pipe	m	0.59	12.30	-	9.20	21.50	23.65	22.950
B010212B	525 mm to 150 mm pipe	m	0.74	15.43	-	10.86	26.29	28.92	27.100
B010212C	600 mm to 225 mm pipe	m	0.91	18.97	-	14.96	33.93	37.32	37.320
B010212D	750 mm to 300 mm pipe	m	1.25	26.06	-	19.61	45.67	50.24	48.940
B010213	**Plain concrete mix 1:3:6 - 40 mm aggregate; bed and covering; 450 mm wide**								
B010213A	350 mm thick to 100 mm pipe	m	0.96	20.02	-	20.28	40.30	44.33	50.600
B010213B	450 mm thick to 100 mm pipe	m	1.24	25.85	-	26.15	52.00	57.20	65.250
B010214	**Plain concrete mix 1:3:6 - 40 mm aggregate; bed and covering; 525 mm wide**								
B010214A	400 mm thick to 150 mm pipe	m	1.22	25.44	-	27.03	52.47	57.72	67.460
B010214B	500 mm thick to 150 mm pipe	m	1.56	32.53	-	33.90	66.43	73.07	84.600
B010215	**Plain concrete mix 1:3:6 - 40 mm aggregate; bed and covering; 600 mm wide**								
B010215A	475 mm thick to 225 mm pipe	m	1.56	32.53	-	34.01	66.54	73.19	84.880
B010215B	575 mm thick to 225 mm pipe	m	1.94	40.45	-	42.32	82.77	91.05	105.620
B010216	**Plain concrete mix 1:3:6 - 40 mm aggregate; bed and covering; 750 mm wide**								
B010216A	550 mm thick to 300 mm pipe	m	2.17	45.24	-	48.20	93.44	102.78	120.270
B010216B	650 mm thick to 300 mm pipe	m	2.62	54.63	-	57.50	112.13	123.34	143.490

Small Works 2011		Unit	Labour Hours	Labour Net	Plant Net	Materials Net	Unit Net	Unit with 10%	CO$_2$
				£	£	£	£	£	Kg
B01	**DRAINAGE AND SEWERAGE**								
B0104	**BREAKING UP PAVED SURFACES**								
B010401	**Break up paving with compressed air equipment for trenches 600 mm wide; average thickness**								
B010401A	75 mm tarmacadam	m	0.43	8.97	1.59	-	10.56	11.62	1.530
B010401B	150 mm plain concrete	m	1.35	28.15	4.94	-	33.09	36.40	4.720
B010401C	150 mm reinforced concrete	m	1.83	38.16	9.79	-	47.95	52.75	9.370
B0105	**REINSTATE PAVED SURFACES**								
B010501	**Reinstate paving; average 600 mm wide; 100 mm hardcore bed; paving average thickness**								
B010501A	75 mm tarmacadam	m^2	0.42	8.76	-	7.55	16.31	17.94	1.730
B010501B	150 mm concrete	m^2	0.85	17.72	-	37.51	55.23	60.75	8.590
B0106	**SUPERSLEVE DRAIN PIPES AND FITTINGS**								
B010601	**Push-fit polypropylene flexible couplings; for underground drainage; in trenches; 100 mm nominal size pipes**								
B010601A	in runs exceeding 3.00 m long	m	0.11	5.40	-	10.48	15.88	17.47	5.590
B010601B	in runs not exceeding 3.00 m long	m	0.14	6.86	-	10.48	17.34	19.07	5.590
B010601C	Extra for; bend	Each	0.15	7.35	-	13.05	20.40	22.44	1.280
B010601E	Extra for; junction	Each	0.13	6.13	-	59.30	65.43	71.97	2.040
B010602	**Push-fit polypropylene flexible couplings; for underground drainage; in trenches; 150 mm nominal size pipes**								
B010602A	in runs exceeding 3.00 m long	m	0.14	6.86	-	20.74	27.60	30.36	10.530
B010602B	in runs not exceeding 3.00 m long	m	0.19	9.29	-	20.74	30.03	33.03	10.530
B010602C	Extra for; bend	Each	0.17	8.08	-	17.44	25.52	28.07	2.750
B010602E	Extra for; junction	Each	0.15	7.35	-	23.34	30.69	33.76	4.120
B0107	**SUPERSLEVE ACCESSORIES**								
B010701	**Jointing to drains; excavation and concrete surrounds**								
B010701A	square gulley; trapped; square grid; 100 mm outlet	Each	0.75	36.63	-	63.06	99.69	109.66	12.270
B010701B	square gulley; trapped; horizontal back inlet to small waste pipe; square grid; 100 mm outlet	Each	0.90	43.98	-	53.88	97.86	107.65	5.810
B010701C	square gulley; trapped; horizontal back inlet to large waste pipe; square grid; 100 mm outlet	Each	0.90	43.98	-	36.81	80.79	88.87	12.990
B010701D	square hopper; integral vertical back inlet; trapped; square sealing plate; 100 mm outlet	Each	0.90	43.98	-	53.88	97.86	107.65	5.810
B010701E	square hopper; integral vertical back inlet; untrapped; square sealing plate; 100 mm outlet	Each	0.90	43.98	-	57.69	101.67	111.84	10.180
B010701F	access gulley; integral vertical back inlet; rodding eye; stopper; plastic grid; hinged grate and frame	Each	0.90	43.98	-	57.69	101.67	111.84	10.180
B010701G	inspection chamber; vitrified clay; 225 mm dia; 600 mm deep; comprising straight through base with junction for 100 mm pipes; raising piece with cover and frame; couplings to sleeve and pipes	Each	1.00	48.84	-	205.09	253.93	279.32	10.410
B010701H	inspection chamber; PPIC polypropylene; 475 mm dia; 585 mm deep; five 100 mm stoppered inlets; base; ductile iron cover and frame	Each	1.00	48.84	-	285.84	334.68	368.15	50.970

Small Works 2011		Unit	Labour Hours	Labour Net	Plant Net	Materials Net	Unit Net	Unit with 10%	CO₂
				£	£	£	£	£	Kg
B01	**DRAINAGE AND SEWERAGE**								
B0107	**SUPERSLEVE ACCESSORIES**								
B010701	**Jointing to drains; excavation and concrete surrounds**								
B010701I	inspection chamber; PICC polypropylene; 930 mm deep; five 100 mm inlets; base; Ductile iron cover and frame	Each	1.00	48.84	-	388.36	437.20	480.92	79.300
B010701J	inspection chamber; PPIC polypropylene; 930 mm deep; three 150 mm inlets (two stoppered); base; ductile iron cover and frame	Each	1.11	53.76	-	388.36	442.12	486.33	79.300
B0108	**HEPSEAL DRAIN PIPES AND FITTINGS**								
B010801	**Push-fit flexible socket joints; for drainage; in trenches; 100 mm nominal size pipes**								
B010801A	in runs exceeding 3.00 m long	m	0.13	6.13	-	10.48	16.61	18.27	5.590
B010801B	in runs not exceeding 3.00 m long	m	0.17	8.08	-	10.48	18.56	20.42	5.590
B010801C	Extra for; bend	Each	0.15	7.35	-	13.05	20.40	22.44	1.280
B010801E	Extra for; junction	Each	0.13	6.13	-	59.30	65.43	71.97	2.040
B010802	**Push-fit flexible socket joints; for drainage; in trenches; 150 mm nominal size pipes**								
B010802A	in runs exceeding 3.00 m long	m	0.18	8.56	-	20.74	29.30	32.23	10.530
B010802B	in runs not exceeding 3.00 m long	m	0.23	10.99	-	20.74	31.73	34.90	10.530
B010802C	Extra for; bend	Each	0.24	11.48	-	41.75	53.23	58.55	2.750
B010802E	Extra for; junction	Each	0.15	7.35	-	48.32	55.67	61.24	4.120
B010803	**Push-fit flexible socket joints; for drainage; in trenches; 225 mm nominal size pipes**								
B010803A	in runs exceeding 3.00 m long	m	0.20	9.78	-	43.39	53.17	58.49	20.030
B010803B	in runs not exceeding 3.00 m long	m	0.25	12.21	-	43.39	55.60	61.16	20.030
B010803C	Extra for; bend	Each	0.25	12.21	-	97.83	110.04	121.04	7.790
B010803E	Extra for; junction	Each	0.22	10.75	-	136.55	147.30	162.03	11.330
B010804	**Push-fit flexible socket joints; for drainage; in trenches; 300 mm nominal size pipes**								
B010804A	in runs exceeding 3.00 m long	m	0.31	15.13	-	62.81	77.94	85.73	43.870
B010804B	in runs not exceeding 3.00 m long	m	0.39	19.07	-	62.81	81.88	90.07	43.870
B010804C	Extra for; bend	Each	0.39	19.07	-	168.92	187.99	206.79	21.110
B010804E	Extra for; junction	Each	0.37	18.10	-	265.87	283.97	312.37	25.330
B0110	**PLASTIDRAIN PVC-u UNDERGROUND DRAINAGE PIPES AND FITTINGS**								
B011001	**Seal ring jointing; in trenches; 110 mm nominal size pipes**								
B011001A	in runs exceeding 3.00 m long	m	0.12	5.89	-	8.27	14.16	15.58	5.570
B011001B	in runs not exceeding 3.00 m long	m	0.14	6.86	-	8.27	15.13	16.64	5.570
B011001C	Extra for; bend	Each	0.14	6.86	-	20.76	27.62	30.38	1.150
B011001E	Extra for; junction	Each	0.12	5.89	-	27.58	33.47	36.82	1.230
B011002	**Seal ring jointing; in trenches; 160 mm nominal size pipe**								
B011002A	in runs exceeding 3.00 m long	m	0.15	7.10	-	19.01	26.11	28.72	10.210
B011002B	in runs not exceeding 3.00 m long	m	0.17	8.08	-	19.01	27.09	29.80	10.210
B011002C	Extra for; short radius bend	Each	0.18	8.56	-	52.98	61.54	67.69	2.660
B011002E	Extra for; junction	Each	0.17	8.08	-	90.02	98.10	107.91	6.800
B011003	**Plastidrain PVC-u accessories; jointing to drains; excavation and concrete surrounds**								
B011003A	Rodding eye; sealed; 110 mm rodding point	Each	0.36	17.61	-	65.36	82.97	91.27	1.790

Drainage, Sewerage and Public Works

Small Works 2011		Unit	Labour Hours	Labour Net	Plant Net	Materials Net	Unit Net	Unit with 10%	CO$_2$
				£	£	£	£	£	Kg
B01	**DRAINAGE AND SEWERAGE**								
B0110	**PLASTIDRAIN PVC-u UNDERGROUND DRAINAGE PIPES AND FITTINGS**								
B011003	**Plastidrain PVC-u accessories; jointing to drains; excavation and concrete surrounds**								
B011003C	Access gulley; round; sealing rings; grid and access plug; 110 mm outlet	Each	0.60	29.34	–	41.17	70.51	77.56	7.760
B011003D	Inspection chamber; 315 mm dia; 600 mm deep; concrete cover and plastic frame; stoppered inlets; lifting handle; 110 mm outlet	Each	1.04	50.60	–	257.01	307.61	338.37	32.490
B0112	**CAST IRON DRAIN PIPES AND FITTINGS**								
B011201	**Spigot and socket caulked lead joints; in trenches; 100 mm pipes**								
B011201A	laid straight	m	0.56	34.63	–	36.24	70.87	77.96	23.690
B011201B	in runs not exceeding 3.00 m long	m	0.76	47.08	–	36.03	83.11	91.42	23.540
B011201C	Extra for; bend; short radius	Each	0.56	34.63	–	34.45	69.08	75.99	17.810
B011201D	Extra for; bend; long radius	Each	0.56	34.63	–	52.65	87.28	96.01	35.790
B011201E	Extra for; branch; single	Each	0.76	47.08	–	50.48	97.56	107.32	31.170
B011201F	Extra for; branch; double	Each	0.94	58.36	–	64.67	123.03	135.33	35.620
B011201G	Extra for; drain connector; large socket for clayware; 305 mm long	Each	0.56	34.63	–	32.69	67.32	74.05	5.100
B011201H	Extra for; drain connector; large socket for WC; 300 mm long	Each	0.42	25.97	–	29.98	55.95	61.55	7.050
B011202	**Spigot and socket caulked lead joints; in trenches; 150 mm pipes**								
B011202A	laid straight	m	0.70	43.28	–	73.75	117.03	128.73	34.130
B011202B	in runs not exceeding 3.00 m long	m	0.94	58.36	–	73.75	132.11	145.32	34.130
B011202C	Extra for; bend; short radius	Each	0.70	43.28	–	60.10	103.38	113.72	32.300
B011202D	Extra for; bend; long radius	Each	0.70	43.28	–	111.30	154.58	170.04	66.310
B011202E	Extra for; branch; single	Each	0.94	58.36	–	120.14	178.50	196.35	42.990
B011202F	Extra for; branch; double	Each	1.18	73.43	–	166.94	240.37	264.41	49.540
B011202G	Extra for; drain connector; large socket for clayware; 305 mm long	Each	0.70	43.28	–	57.29	100.57	110.63	6.800
B011203	**Rainwater shoes; horizontal or vertical inlet; setting on and bedding in site mixed concrete 1:3:6**								
B011203A	100 mm	Each	0.52	32.39	–	50.38	82.77	91.05	60.180
B011203B	150 mm	Each	0.59	36.93	–	90.62	127.55	140.31	80.860
B011204	**Yard gulley; bedding on and setting in site mixed concrete 1:3:6**								
B011204A	Deans; trapped; galvanised sediment pan; 267 mm round heavy grating; 100 mm outlet	Each	2.24	139.32	–	441.80	581.12	639.23	139.370
B011204B	Garage; trapless; galvanised sediment pan; 267 mm round heavy grating; 100 mm outlet	Each	2.09	129.92	–	901.45	1,031.37	1,134.51	174.360
B011204C	Garage; trapped; rodding eye; galvanised perforated sediment pan; stopper; 267 mm round heavy grating; 100 mm outlet	Each	2.78	173.26	–	952.33	1,125.59	1,238.15	206.780
B011204D	Square top; trapped; galvanised sediment pan; 255 x 255 mm square grating; 100 mm outlet	Each	2.75	171.33	–	372.00	543.33	597.66	124.790

Small Works 2011		Unit	Labour Hours	Labour Net	Plant Net	Materials Net	Unit Net	Unit with 10%	CO₂
				£	£	£	£	£	Kg
B01	**DRAINAGE AND SEWERAGE**								
B0114	**CAST IRON TIMESAVER PIPES AND FITTINGS**								
B011401	**Drainage Castings Timesaver System; mechanical coupling joints; in trenches; 100 mm pipes**								
B011401A	laid straight	m	0.35	21.86	-	37.16	59.02	64.92	22.820
B011401B	in runs not exceeding 3.00 m long	m	0.47	29.40	-	37.16	66.56	73.22	22.820
B011401C	Extra for; bend; medium radius	Each	0.42	25.97	-	50.66	76.63	84.29	17.490
B011401D	Extra for; bend; long radius	Each	0.42	25.97	-	50.66	76.63	84.29	17.490
B011401E	Extra for; branch; single - plain 100 x 100 mm	Each	0.52	32.39	-	74.68	107.07	117.78	16.030
B011401G	Extra for; branch double - plain 100 x 100 mm	Each	0.67	41.42	-	108.78	150.20	165.22	20.410
B011401I	Extra for; transitional pipe; socket for WC	Each	0.35	21.86	-	32.69	54.55	60.01	5.100
B011401J	Extra for; transitional pipe; socket for clayware	Each	0.24	15.07	-	11.05	26.12	28.73	3.400
B011402	**Drainage Castings Timesaver System; mechanical coupling joints; in trenches 150 mm pipes**								
B011402A	laid straight	m	0.42	25.97	-	66.59	92.56	101.82	29.850
B011402B	in runs not exceeding 3.00 m long	m	0.57	35.38	-	66.59	101.97	112.17	29.850
B011402C	Extra for; bend; medium radius	Each	0.49	30.52	-	91.16	121.68	133.85	26.720
B011402D	Extra for; bend; long radius	Each	0.49	30.52	-	66.59	97.11	106.82	29.850
B011402E	Extra for; branch; single	Each	0.59	36.93	-	118.80	155.73	171.30	14.820
B011402H	Extra for; transitional pipe; socket for clayware	Each	0.56	34.63	-	31.89	66.52	73.17	20.650
B011402I	Extra for; isolated Timesaver joint	Each	0.29	18.06	-	11.05	29.11	32.02	3.400
B011403	**Rainwater shoes; horizontal or vertical inlet; setting on and bedding in site mixed concrete 1:3:6**								
B011403A	100 mm	Each	0.35	21.86	-	48.79	70.65	77.72	41.060
B011403B	150 mm	Each	0.59	36.93	-	87.86	124.79	137.27	64.990
B011404	**Yard gulley; bedding on and setting in site mixed concrete 1:3:6**								
B011404A	Deans; trapped; galvanised sediment pan; 267 mm round heavy grating; 100 mm outlet	Each	2.03	126.18	-	436.22	562.40	618.64	110.300
B011404B	Garage; trapless; galvanised sediment pan; 267 mm round heavy grating; 100 mm outlet	Each	1.88	116.78	-	895.87	1,012.65	1,113.92	145.290
B011404C	Garage; trapped; rodding eye; galvanised perforated sediment pan; stopper; 267 mm round heavy grating; 100 mm outlet	Each	2.09	129.92	-	950.41	1,080.33	1,188.36	186.830
B011404D	Square top; trapped; galvanised sediment pan; 255 x 255 mm square grating; 100 mm outlet	Each	2.06	128.05	-	366.43	494.48	543.93	95.720
B011405	**Inspection chambers; bolted flat cover; bedding in cement mortar 1:3**								
B011405A	100 x 100 mm; one branch either side	Each	0.73	45.22	-	224.24	269.46	296.41	18.090
B011405B	100 x 100 mm; one branch each side	Each	0.73	45.22	-	224.24	269.46	296.41	18.570
B011405C	100 x 100 mm; two branches either side	Each	1.18	73.43	-	439.71	513.14	564.45	25.960
B011405D	150 x 100 mm; one branch either side	Each	1.00	62.16	-	290.50	352.66	387.93	26.210
B011405E	150 x 100 mm; one branch each side	Each	1.00	62.16	-	585.88	648.04	712.84	29.260
B011405F	150 x 100 mm; two branches either side	Each	1.54	96.04	-	442.54	538.58	592.44	36.650

Small Works 2011	Unit	Labour Hours	Labour Net	Plant Net	Materials Net	Unit Net	Unit with 10%	CO₂
			£	£	£	£	£	Kg
B01	**DRAINAGE AND SEWERAGE**							
B0116	**HEPWORTH DRAIN PIPES AND FITTINGS**							
B011601	**Butt jointed; in trenches; 75 mm nominal size pipes**							
B011601A	in runs exceeding 3.00 m long	m	0.25	5.21	-	3.71	8.92	9.81	2.720
B011601B	in runs not exceeding 3.00 m long	m	0.30	6.25	-	3.71	9.96	10.96	2.720
B011601C	Extra for; junction	Each	0.23	4.80	-	17.31	22.11	24.32	1.710
B011602	**Butt jointed; in trenches; 100 mm nominal size pipes**							
B011602A	in runs exceeding 3.00 m long	m	0.29	6.05	-	6.60	12.65	13.92	3.630
B011602B	in runs not exceeding 3.00 m long	m	0.34	7.09	-	6.60	13.69	15.06	3.630
B011602C	Extra for; junction	Each	0.24	5.00	-	22.97	27.97	30.77	2.010
B011603	**Butt jointed; in trenches; 150 mm nominal size pipes**							
B011603A	in runs exceeding 3.00 m long	m	0.37	7.71	-	13.32	21.03	23.13	6.850
B011603B	in runs not exceeding 3.00 m long	m	0.42	8.76	-	13.32	22.08	24.29	6.850
B011603C	Extra for; junction	Each	0.29	6.05	-	28.29	34.34	37.77	4.750
B011604	**Butt jointed; in trenches; 225 mm nominal size pipes**							
B011604A	in runs exceeding 3.00 m long	m	0.57	11.88	-	34.02	45.90	50.49	14.560
B011604B	in runs not exceeding 3.00 m long							
		m	0.62	12.93	-	34.02	46.95	51.65	14.560
B011604C	Extra for; junction	Each	0.43	8.97	-	28.29	37.26	40.99	7.760
B0118	**HEPLINE PERFORATED PIPES AND FITTINGS**							
B011801	**Dry push-fit flexible integral polyethylene sleeve joints; in trenches 100 mm nominal size pipes**							
B011801A	in runs exceeding 3.00 m long	m	0.21	4.38	-	11.05	15.43	16.97	5.560
B011801B	in runs not exceeding 3.00 m long	m	0.26	5.42	-	11.05	16.47	18.12	5.560
B011801C	Extra for; bends	Each	0.29	6.05	-	13.05	19.10	21.01	2.450
B011801D	Extra for; junctions	Each	0.24	5.00	-	27.53	32.53	35.78	4.520
B011802	**Dry push-fit flexible integral polyethylene sleeve joints; in trenches 150 mm nominal size pipes**							
B011802A	in runs exceeding 3.00 m long	m	0.28	5.84	-	20.07	25.91	28.50	10.480
B011802B	in runs not exceeding 3.00 m long	m	0.38	7.92	-	20.07	27.99	30.79	10.480
B011802C	Extra for; bends	Each	0.32	6.67	-	17.44	24.11	26.52	3.890
B011802D	Extra for; junctions	Each	0.29	6.05	-	54.56	60.61	66.67	5.570
B011803	**Dry push-fit flexible integral polyethylene sleeve joints; in trenches 225 mm nominal size pipes**							
B011803A	in runs exceeding 3.00 m long	m	0.45	9.38	-	40.47	49.85	54.84	20.330
B011803B	in runs not exceeding 3.00 m long	m	0.51	10.63	-	40.47	51.10	56.21	20.330
B011803C	Extra for; bends	Each	0.50	10.43	-	119.49	129.92	142.91	7.790
B011803D	Extra for; junctions	Each	0.40	8.34	-	136.55	144.89	159.38	11.330
B0120	**PVC-u PERFORATED FLEXIBLE CORRUGATED DRAIN PIPES AND FITTINGS**							
B012002	**Polythene joints; in trenches; 82 mm nominal size pipes**							
B012002A	in runs exceeding 3.00 m long	m	0.15	3.13	-	6.58	9.71	10.68	4.140
B012002B	in runs not exceeding 3.00 m long	m	0.20	4.17	-	6.58	10.75	11.83	4.140
B012002C	Extra for; end cap	Each	0.10	2.09	-	1.06	3.15	3.47	1.190
B012002D	Extra for; junction	Each	0.18	3.75	-	31.81	35.56	39.12	1.800
B012003	**Polythene joints; in trenches; 110 mm nominal size pipes**							
B012003A	in runs exceeding 3.00 m long	m	0.20	4.17	-	23.75	27.92	30.71	5.580
B012003B	in runs not exceeding 3.00 m long	m	0.25	5.21	-	23.75	28.96	31.86	5.580

Small Works 2011		Unit	Labour Hours	Labour Net	Plant Net	Materials Net	Unit Net	Unit with 10%	CO$_2$
				£	£	£	£	£	Kg
B01	**DRAINAGE AND SEWERAGE**								
B0120	**PVC-u PERFORATED FLEXIBLE CORRUGATED DRAIN PIPES AND FITTINGS**								
B012003	**Polythene joints; in trenches; 110 mm nominal size pipes**								
B012003C	Extra for; end cap	Each	0.10	2.09	-	1.77	3.86	4.25	1.450
B012003D	Extra for; junction	Each	0.22	4.59	-	27.58	32.17	35.39	1.230
B0122	**POROUS CONCRETE DRAIN PIPES**								
B012202	**Ogee joints; in trenches; 150 mm nominal size pipes**								
B012202A	in runs exceeding 3.00 m long	m	0.53	11.05	-	8.41	19.46	21.41	13.780
B012202B	in runs not exceeding 3.00 m long	m	0.56	11.68	-	8.41	20.09	22.10	13.780
B012203	**Ogee joints; in trenches; 225 mm nominal size pipes**								
B012203A	in runs exceeding 3.00 m long	m	0.80	16.68	-	15.29	31.97	35.17	17.800
B012203B	in runs not exceeding 3.00 m long	m	0.83	17.31	-	15.29	32.60	35.86	17.800
B0124	**MANHOLES ETC**								
B012401	**Excavate for manholes and soakaways; dispose of surplus; hand labour; maximum depth not exceeding**								
B012401A	1.00 m	m^3	5.45	113.63	-	-	113.63	124.99	-
B012401B	2.00 m	m^3	6.58	137.19	-	-	137.19	150.91	-
B012402	**Excavated material; part backfill**								
B012402A	remainder wheel and deposit	m^3	2.50	52.13	-	-	52.13	57.34	-
B012403	**Fill hardcore**								
B012403A	into soakaways	m^3	0.50	10.43	-	20.03	30.46	33.51	12.470
B012404	**Earthwork support to sides of excavation**								
B012404A	firm ground; depth n.e. 1.00 m	m^2	0.64	13.34	-	2.61	15.95	17.55	1.320
B012404B	firm ground; depth n.e. 2.00 m	m^2	0.70	14.60	-	2.91	17.51	19.26	1.470
B012404C	loose ground; depth n.e. 1.00 m	m^2	4.98	103.83	-	20.66	124.49	136.94	10.460
B012404D	loose ground; depth n.e. 2.00 m	m^2	4.98	103.83	-	20.66	124.49	136.94	10.460
B012405	**Hire of skip; delivery to site; removing when full; disposal of contents; payment of tipping charges; size of skip**								
B012405A	4.5 m^3	m^3	-	-	33.60	-	33.60	36.96	-
B012406	**Base; concrete 1:3:6**								
B012406A	100 mm thick	m^3	0.75	15.64	-	129.19	144.83	159.31	322.380
B012406B	150 mm thick	m^3	1.15	23.98	-	129.19	153.17	168.49	322.380
B012407	**Benching; concrete 1:3:6 to steep slopes to channels and branches; finished with 13 mm cement mortar 1:3 trowelled smooth; average thickness**								
B012407A	225 mm	m^2	2.65	55.25	-	27.44	82.69	90.96	72.110
B012407B	300 mm	m^2	3.31	69.01	-	36.86	105.87	116.46	95.610
B012408	**Fine concrete splayed curb around manhole frame**								
B012408A	600 mm x 450 mm	Each	1.40	29.19	-	2.33	31.52	34.67	5.810
B012409	**Reinforced suspended cover slab; including fabric reinforcement**								
B012409A	100 mm - 150 mm thick	m^3	7.76	161.80	-	131.74	293.54	322.89	329.440

Small Works 2011		Unit	Labour Hours	Labour Net £	Plant Net £	Materials Net £	Unit Net £	Unit with 10% £	CO$_2$ Kg
B01	**DRAINAGE AND SEWERAGE**								
B0124	**MANHOLES ETC**								
B012410	**Common bricks in cement mortar 1:3 manhole walls**								
B012410A	half brick	m^2	1.00	48.60	-	23.11	71.71	78.88	58.840
B012410B	one brick	m^2	1.63	79.40	-	47.27	126.67	139.34	121.570
B012411	**Extra over common brickwork for fair face and flush pointing as the work proceeds**								
B012411A	stretcher bond	m^2	0.28	13.67	-	-	13.67	15.04	-
B012411B	Flemish bond	m^2	0.30	14.64	-	-	14.64	16.10	-
B012412	**Oversail common brickwork at top of manhole**								
B012412A	one course	m	0.20	9.78	-	-	9.78	10.76	-
B012412B	two courses	m	0.40	19.56	-	-	19.56	21.52	-
B012412C	three courses	m	0.60	29.34	-	-	29.34	32.27	-
B012413	**Building in end of pipe to half brick wall; common bricks**								
B012413A	100 mm pipe	Each	0.09	4.14	-	-	4.14	4.55	-
B012413B	150 mm pipe	Each	0.10	4.87	-	-	4.87	5.36	-
B012413C	225 mm pipe	Each	0.11	5.40	-	-	5.40	5.94	-
B012415	**Building in end of pipe to one brick wall; common bricks**								
B012415A	100 mm pipe	Each	0.10	7.42	-	-	7.42	8.16	-
B012415B	150 mm pipe	Each	0.12	8.94	-	-	8.94	9.83	-
B012415C	225 mm pipe	Each	0.13	9.71	-	-	9.71	10.68	-
B012416	**Class B engineering bricks in cement mortar 1:3 manhole walls**								
B012416A	half brick	m^2	1.03	50.30	-	29.95	80.25	88.28	123.660
B012416B	one brick	m^2	1.76	85.53	-	60.71	146.24	160.86	249.780
B012417	**Extra over engineering brickwork for fair face and flush pointing as the work proceeds**								
B012417A	stretcher bond	m^2	0.28	13.67	-	-	13.67	15.04	-
B012417B	Flemish bond	m^2	0.30	14.64	-	-	14.64	16.10	-
B012418	**Oversail engineering brickwork at top of manhole**								
B012418A	one course	m	0.20	9.78	-	-	9.78	10.76	-
B012418B	two courses	m	0.40	19.56	-	-	19.56	21.52	-
B012418C	three courses	m	0.60	29.34	-	-	29.34	32.27	-
B012419	**Building in end of pipe to half brick wall; engineering bricks**								
B012419A	100 mm pipe	Each	0.10	4.87	-	-	4.87	5.36	-
B012419B	150 mm pipe	Each	0.12	5.64	-	-	5.64	6.20	-
B012419C	225 mm pipe	Each	0.12	5.89	-	-	5.89	6.48	-
B012420	**Building in end of pipe to one brick wall; engineering bricks**								
B012420A	100 mm pipe	Each	0.16	7.59	-	-	7.59	8.35	-
B012420B	150 mm pipe	Each	0.19	9.05	-	-	9.05	9.96	-
B012420C	225 mm pipe	Each	0.21	10.27	-	-	10.27	11.30	-
B012421	**Step irons; galvanised general purpose pattern; building into brickwork**								
B012421A	115 mm tails	Each	0.06	2.68	-	6.53	9.21	10.13	2.790
B012421B	230 mm tails	Each	0.07	3.16	-	8.32	11.48	12.63	3.040
B012422	**Vitrified clay channel; set and jointed in cement mortar 1:3**								
B012422A	100 mm half round straight main channel 600 mm long	Each	0.20	9.78	-	8.28	18.06	19.87	6.340
B012422B	150 mm half round straight main channel 600 mm long	Each	0.28	13.43	-	13.58	27.01	29.71	10.910
B012422C	100 mm half round main channel bend	Each	0.21	10.27	-	8.61	18.88	20.77	6.870
B012422D	150 mm half round main channel bend	Each	0.30	14.64	-	14.46	29.10	32.01	10.200

Small Works 2011		Unit	Labour Hours	Labour Net	Plant Net	Materials Net	Unit Net	Unit with 10%	CO₂
				£	£	£	£	£	Kg
B01	**DRAINAGE AND SEWERAGE**								
B0124	**MANHOLES ETC**								
B012422	**Vitrified clay channel; set and jointed in cement mortar 1:3**								
B012422E	150 mm - 100 mm half round straight taper main channel	Each	0.30	14.64	-	34.67	49.31	54.24	10.650
B012422F	150 mm - 100 mm half round taper main channel bend	Each	0.30	14.64	-	44.40	59.04	64.94	10.820
B012422G	100 mm half section branch channel bend	Each	0.21	10.27	-	22.45	32.72	35.99	6.310
B012422H	150 mm half section branch channel bend	Each	0.29	14.16	-	36.51	50.67	55.74	10.290
B012422I	100 mm three quarter section branch channel bend	Each	0.21	10.27	-	24.59	34.86	38.35	6.710
B012422J	150 mm three quarter section branch channel bend	Each	0.29	14.16	-	40.94	55.10	60.61	10.670
B012423	**Covers and frames; bedded and flaunched in cement mortar 1:3; cover sealed in grease and sand**								
B012423A	Grade B class 2; 600 mm x 450 mm	Each	0.57	27.58	-	169.13	196.71	216.38	149.720
B012423B	Grade C double seal; 600 mm x 450 mm	Each	0.33	16.10	-	38.80	54.90	60.39	38.270
B012424	**Intercepting trap; vitrified clay; with stopper; cement joints to channel and pipe; bedding and surrounding with 150 mm concrete 1:3:6**								
B012424A	100 mm	Each	0.53	25.88	-	132.74	158.62	174.48	38.120
B012424B	150 mm	Each	0.73	35.42	-	189.19	224.61	247.07	51.710
B012424C	225 mm	Each	1.00	48.84	-	347.21	396.05	435.66	85.890
B012425	**Sewer connection; hand excavation; searching for existing 225 mm vitrified clay live sewer pipe; breaking into; inserting and connecting new 100 mm vitrified clay saddle junction; make good; backfill; consolidate; depth**								
B012425A	2.00 m	Each	10.81	526.00	-	17.96	543.96	598.36	1.020
B012425B	3.00 m	Each	13.47	655.46	-	17.96	673.42	740.76	1.020
B012426	**Inspection chamber; 0.60 m x 0.45 m x 0.90 m deep. All excavation work; concrete base 150 mm; one brick walls in common bricks in cement mortar, rendered internally; one straight channel and two branch channels with concrete benching; building in ends of 100 mm drain pipes; manhole cover and frame**								
B012426A	0.60 m x 0.45 m x 38 kg	Each	14.56	708.49	-	280.44	988.93	1,087.82	473.200
B012426B	Extra; Class B engineering bricks in lieu of commons	Each	0.45	21.99	-	39.99	61.98	68.18	362.780
B012426C	add or deduct for each 150 mm depth in excess of or less than 0.9 m in the foregoing inspection chamber if built in common bricks	Each	1.76	85.53	-	44.91	130.44	143.48	109.610
B012426D	add or deduct for each 150 mm depth in excess of or less than 0.9 m in the foregoing inspection chamber if built in class B engineering bricks	Each	2.01	97.74	-	57.90	155.64	171.20	227.510
B012427	**Rendering; 13 mm cement and sand**								
B012427A	to brick walls; internally	m²	0.40	19.56	-	1.98	21.54	23.69	6.750

Small Works 2011		Unit	Labour Hours	Labour Net £	Plant Net £	Materials Net £	Unit Net £	Unit with 10% £	CO$_2$ Kg
B01	**DRAINAGE AND SEWERAGE**								
B0124	**MANHOLES ETC**								
B012428	**Interceptor chamber; 0.75 m x 0.60 m x 1.20 m deep. All excavation work; concrete base 150 mm; one brick walls in common bricks in cement mortar, rendered internally; one straight channel and concrete benching; 100 mm interceptor trap and one end of 100 mm drain pipe built in; brickwork at top corbelled over for, and fitted with, manhole cover and frame**								
B012428A	0.60 m x 0.45 m x 38 kg	Each	22.10	1,074.92	-	384.25	1,459.17	1,605.09	636.680
B012428B	Extra; Class B engineering bricks in lieu of commons	Each	0.75	36.63	-	63.09	99.72	109.69	476.984
B012428C	add or deduct for each 150 mm depth in excess of or less than 1.20 m in the foregoing interceptor chamber built in common bricks	Each	2.11	102.60	-	53.74	156.34	171.97	128.090
B012428D	add or deduct for each 150 mm depth in excess of or less than 1.20 m in the foregoing interceptor chamber built in class B engineering bricks	Each	2.41	117.25	-	69.51	186.76	205.44	271.180
B0126	**INSPECTION CHAMBERS**								
B012601	**Shallow inspection chamber; 250 mm dia; placing in excavation; invert depth**								
B012601A	600 mm	Each	0.83	40.57	-	111.57	152.14	167.35	3.190
B012602	**Single seal circular cast iron cover and frame**								
B012602A	Grade C	Each	0.29	14.16	-	102.45	116.61	128.27	35.420
B012603	**Universal inspection chamber; 450 mm dia; placing in excavation; invert depth**								
B012603A	500 mm	Each	0.88	42.76	-	194.25	237.01	260.71	42.650
B012603B	730 mm	Each	1.05	50.84	-	280.99	331.83	365.01	48.720
B012603C	960 mm	Each	1.21	58.62	-	296.77	355.39	390.93	70.970
B012604	**Single seal circular cast iron cover and frame**								
B012604A	Grade C	Each	0.33	16.10	-	102.45	118.55	130.41	35.420
B012610	**Inspection chamber; bolted flat cover; bedding in cement mortar 1:3**								
B012610A	100 x 100 mm; one branch either side	Each	1.15	71.56	-	221.65	293.21	322.53	9.230
B012610B	150 x 100 mm; one branch either side	Each	1.33	82.83	-	287.17	370.00	407.00	14.820
B012610C	150 x 150 mm; one branch either side	Each	1.39	86.63	-	583.29	669.92	736.91	20.410
B0128	**PIPE TRENCHES IN SOFT SOIL**								
B012801	**Excavate trenches; by machine; grade bottoms; backfill; compact; dispose of surplus excavated material; earthwork support measured separately**								
B012801A	0.60 m width x 0.90 m depth	m	1.45	30.23	2.91	-	33.14	36.45	2.790
B012801B	0.60 m width x 1.20 m depth	m	1.80	37.53	3.79	-	41.32	45.45	3.620
B012801C	0.60 m width x 1.50 m depth	m	2.30	47.95	4.66	-	52.61	57.87	4.460
B012801D	0.75 m width x 0.90 m depth	m	1.65	34.40	3.47	-	37.87	41.66	3.320
B012801E	0.75 m width x 1.20 m depth	m	2.30	47.95	4.66	-	52.61	57.87	4.460
B012801F	0.75 m width x 1.50 m depth	m	2.70	56.30	5.80	-	62.10	68.31	5.550
B012801G	0.75 m width x 1.80 m depth	m	3.50	72.98	6.97	-	79.95	87.95	6.660
B012801H	0.75 m width x 2.10 m depth	m	3.65	76.10	8.42	-	84.52	92.97	8.060
B012801I	0.75 m width x 2.40 m depth	m	4.40	91.74	9.30	-	101.04	111.14	8.890
B012801J	0.75 m width x 2.70 m depth	m	5.00	104.25	11.31	-	115.56	127.12	10.810

Small Works 2011		Unit	Labour Hours	Labour Net	Plant Net	Materials Net	Unit Net	Unit with 10%	CO$_2$
				£	£	£	£	£	Kg
B01	**DRAINAGE AND SEWERAGE**								
B0128	**PIPE TRENCHES IN SOFT SOIL**								
B012801	**Excavate trenches; by machine; grade bottoms; backfill; compact; dispose of surplus excavated material; earthwork support measured separately**								
B012801K	0.75 m width x 3.00 m depth	m	5.90	123.02	11.31	-	134.33	147.76	10.810
B012801L	0.90 m width x 1.80 m depth	m	3.65	76.10	8.42	-	84.52	92.97	8.060
B012801M	0.90 m width x 2.10 m depth	m	4.00	83.40	9.85	-	93.25	102.58	9.420
B012801N	0.90 m width x 2.40 m depth	m	5.00	104.25	11.31	-	115.56	127.12	10.810
B012801O	0.90 m width x 2.70 m depth	m	5.40	112.59	12.50	-	125.09	137.60	11.960
B012801P	0.90 m width x 3.00 m depth	m	6.70	139.70	13.93	-	153.63	168.99	13.320
B0129	**PIPE TRENCHES IN CLAY OR COMPACT GRAVEL**								
B012901	**Excavate trenches; by machine; grade bottoms; backfill; compact; dispose of surplus excavated material; earthwork support measured separately**								
B012901A	0.60 m width x 0.90 m depth	m	1.55	32.32	3.47	-	35.79	39.37	3.320
B012901B	0.60 m width x 1.20 m depth	m	1.90	39.62	4.66	-	44.28	48.71	4.460
B012901C	0.60 m width x 1.50 m depth	m	2.40	50.04	5.80	-	55.84	61.42	5.550
B012901D	0.75 m width x 0.90 m depth	m	1.75	36.49	3.79	-	40.28	44.31	3.620
B012901E	0.75 m width x 1.20 m depth	m	2.40	50.04	5.51	-	55.55	61.11	5.270
B012901F	0.75 m width x 1.50 m depth	m	2.80	58.38	6.97	-	65.35	71.89	6.660
B012901G	0.75 m width x 1.80 m depth	m	3.40	70.89	8.42	-	79.31	87.24	8.060
B012901H	0.75 m width x 2.10 m depth	m	3.80	79.23	9.85	-	89.08	97.99	9.420
B012901I	0.75 m width x 2.40 m depth	m	4.60	95.91	11.31	-	107.22	117.94	10.810
B012901J	0.75 m width x 2.70 m depth	m	5.30	110.51	12.50	-	123.01	135.31	11.960
B012901K	0.75 m width x 3.00 m depth	m	6.50	135.53	13.64	-	149.17	164.09	13.040
B012901L	0.90 m width x 1.80 m depth	m	3.80	79.23	9.85	-	89.08	97.99	9.420
B012901M	0.90 m width x 2.10 m depth	m	4.15	86.53	11.92	-	98.45	108.30	11.400
B012901N	0.90 m width x 2.40 m depth	m	5.30	110.51	13.38	-	123.89	136.28	12.790
B012901O	0.90 m width x 2.70 m depth	m	5.60	116.76	15.10	-	131.86	145.05	14.440
B012901P	0.90 m width x 3.00 m depth	m	7.25	151.16	16.85	-	168.01	184.81	16.110
B0130	**PIPE TRENCHES IN CHALK**								
B013001	**Excavate trenches; by machine; grade bottoms; backfill; compact; dispose of surplus excavated material; earthwork support measured separately**								
B013001A	0.60 m width x 0.90 m depth	m	1.80	37.53	4.05	-	41.58	45.74	3.870
B013001B	0.60 m width x 1.20 m depth	m	2.75	57.34	5.25	-	62.59	68.85	5.020
B013001C	0.60 m width x 1.50 m depth	m	3.20	66.72	6.67	-	73.39	80.73	6.380
B013001D	0.75 m width x 0.90 m depth	m	2.10	43.79	4.93	-	48.72	53.59	4.710
B013001E	0.75 m width x 1.20 m depth	m	3.20	66.72	6.67	-	73.39	80.73	6.380
B013001F	0.75 m width x 1.50 m depth	m	4.35	90.70	7.84	-	98.54	108.39	7.500
B013001G	0.75 m width x 1.80 m depth	m	4.80	100.08	9.85	-	109.93	120.92	9.420
B013001H	0.75 m width x 2.10 m depth	m	5.10	106.33	11.63	-	117.96	129.76	11.120
B013001I	0.75 m width x 2.40 m depth	m	5.90	123.02	13.06	-	136.08	149.69	12.490
B013001J	0.75 m width x 2.70 m depth	m	7.00	145.95	14.51	-	160.46	176.51	13.880
B013001K	0.75 m width x 3.00 m depth	m	8.70	181.40	15.97	-	197.37	217.11	15.270
B013001L	0.90 m width x 1.80 m depth	m	5.10	106.33	11.63	-	117.96	129.76	11.120
B013001M	0.90 m width x 2.10 m depth	m	5.90	123.02	13.93	-	136.95	150.65	13.320
B013001N	0.90 m width x 2.40 m depth	m	7.00	145.95	15.68	-	161.63	177.79	15.000
B013001O	0.90 m width x 2.70 m depth	m	7.75	161.59	17.43	-	179.02	196.92	16.670
B013001P	0.90 m width x 3.00 m depth	m	9.00	187.65	19.44	-	207.09	227.80	18.590
B0132	**BREAK UP PAVED SURFACES**								
B013201	**Extra over trench excavation for breaking up with compressed air equipment**								
B013201A	75 mm tarmacadam	m^2	0.43	8.97	-	-	8.97	9.87	-
B013201B	150 mm plain concrete	m^2	1.35	28.15	4.94	-	33.09	36.40	4.720
B013201C	150 mm reinforced concrete	m^2	1.83	38.16	6.68	-	44.84	49.32	6.390

Small Works 2011		Unit	Labour Hours	Labour Net	Plant Net	Materials Net	Unit Net	Unit with 10%	CO$_2$
				£	£	£	£	£	Kg
B01	**DRAINAGE AND SEWERAGE**								
B0133	**REINSTATE PAVED SURFACES**								
B013301	**Reinstate paving; 100 mm hardcore bed**								
B013301A	75 mm tarmacadam	m^2	0.42	8.76	-	28.32	37.08	40.79	7.860
B013302	**Reinstate paving; 150 mm hardcore bed**								
B013302A	150 mm plain concrete	m^2	0.85	17.72	-	24.37	42.09	46.30	51.600
B0134	**OPEN EARTHWORK SUPPORT**								
B013401	**Both sides of trench measured; average depth of trench**								
B013401A	0.90 m	m	0.22	4.59	-	3.11	7.70	8.47	1.570
B013401B	1.20 m	m	0.30	6.25	-	3.97	10.22	11.24	2.010
B013401C	1.50 m	m	0.40	8.34	-	4.91	13.25	14.58	2.490
B013401D	1.80 m	m	0.45	9.38	-	5.77	15.15	16.67	2.920
B013401E	2.10 m	m	0.55	11.47	-	7.13	18.60	20.46	3.610
B013401F	2.40 m	m	0.70	14.60	-	8.04	22.64	24.90	4.070
B013401G	2.70 m	m	0.85	17.72	-	8.87	26.59	29.25	4.490
B013401H	3.00 m	m	1.00	20.85	-	9.79	30.64	33.70	4.960
B0136	**CLOSE EARTHWORK SUPPORT**								
B013601	**Both sides of trench measured; average depth of trench**								
B013601A	0.90 m	m	1.65	34.40	-	9.29	43.69	48.06	4.700
B013601B	1.20 m	m	2.20	45.87	-	12.01	57.88	63.67	6.080
B013601C	1.50 m	m	2.90	60.47	-	14.64	75.11	82.62	7.410
B013601D	1.80 m	m	3.50	72.98	-	17.36	90.34	99.37	8.790
B013601E	2.10 m	m	4.10	85.48	-	21.38	106.86	117.55	10.830
B013601F	2.40 m	m	5.20	108.42	-	24.79	133.21	146.53	12.550
B013601G	2.70 m	m	6.20	129.27	-	26.70	155.97	171.57	13.520
B013601H	3.00 m	m	7.25	151.16	-	29.28	180.44	198.48	14.830
B0138	**PIPE BEDS AND COVERINGS**								
B013801	**Plain concrete mix 1:3:6; 150 mm bed; width**								
B013801A	400 mm	m	0.43	8.97	-	7.42	16.39	18.03	18.520
B013801B	450 mm	m	0.50	10.43	-	8.31	18.74	20.61	20.740
B013801C	525 mm	m	0.58	12.09	-	9.75	21.84	24.02	24.330
B013801D	600 mm	m	0.72	15.01	-	11.08	26.09	28.70	27.650
B013801E	675 mm	m	0.85	17.72	-	12.41	30.13	33.14	30.970
B013801F	750 mm	m	1.00	20.85	-	13.85	34.70	38.17	34.560
B013801G	825 mm	m	1.14	23.77	-	15.29	39.06	42.97	38.150
B013801H	900 mm	m	1.28	26.69	-	16.73	43.42	47.76	41.750
B013802	**Plain concrete mix 1:3:6; 150 mm bed and filling to half height of pipe; width**								
B013802A	400 mm to 100 mm pipe	m	0.59	12.30	-	9.31	21.61	23.77	23.220
B013802B	450 mm to 150 mm pipe	m	0.74	15.43	-	11.30	26.73	29.40	28.200
B013802C	525 mm to 225 mm pipe	m	0.91	18.97	-	13.41	32.38	35.62	33.450
B013802D	600 mm to 300 mm pipe	m	1.25	26.06	-	17.06	43.12	47.43	42.580
B013802E	675 mm to 375 mm pipe	m	1.37	28.56	-	20.16	48.72	53.59	50.320
B013802F	750 mm to 450 mm pipe	m	1.63	33.99	-	23.49	57.48	63.23	58.610
B013802G	825 mm to 525 mm pipe	m	1.90	39.62	-	27.15	66.77	73.45	67.740
B013802H	900 mm to 600 mm pipe	m	2.06	42.95	-	30.69	73.64	81.00	76.580
B013804	**Plain concrete mix 1:3:6; 150 mm bed and covering; width**								
B013804A	400 mm to 100 mm pipe	m	1.24	25.85	-	18.39	44.24	48.66	45.900
B013804B	450 mm to 150 mm pipe	m	1.56	32.53	-	22.38	54.91	60.40	55.850
B013804C	525 mm to 225 mm pipe	m	1.94	40.45	-	26.70	67.15	73.87	66.630
B013804D	600 mm to 300 mm pipe	m	2.62	54.63	-	33.90	88.53	97.38	84.600
B013804E	675 mm to 375 mm pipe	m	3.44	71.72	-	40.33	112.05	123.26	100.640
B013804F	750 mm to 450 mm pipe	m	5.00	104.25	-	46.98	151.23	166.35	117.230
B013804G	825 mm to 525 mm pipe	m	7.58	158.04	-	54.40	212.44	233.68	135.750
B013804H	900 mm to 600 mm pipe	m	9.77	203.70	-	61.16	264.86	291.35	152.620

Small Works 2011		Unit	Labour Hours	Labour Net	Plant Net	Materials Net	Unit Net	Unit with 10%	CO₂
				£	£	£	£	£	Kg
B01	**DRAINAGE AND SEWERAGE**								
B0140	**SOLID WALL CONCENTRIC EXTERNAL RIB REINFORCED PVC-u**								
B014001	**For sewers; in trenches; 150 mm nominal size pipes**								
B014001A	in runs exceeding 3.00 m long	m	0.25	5.21	-	10.07	15.28	16.81	7.800
B014001B	Extra for; bends	Each	0.22	4.59	-	23.65	28.24	31.06	2.320
B014001C	Extra for; junctions	Each	0.29	6.05	-	48.68	54.73	60.20	2.640
B014001D	Extra for; adaptor to clay	Each	0.13	2.71	-	92.36	95.07	104.58	1.760
B014002	**For sewers; in trenches; 225 mm nominal size pipes**								
B014002A	in runs exceeding 3.00 m long	m	0.29	6.05	-	24.96	31.01	34.11	16.340
B014002B	Extra for; bends	Each	0.26	5.42	-	100.81	106.23	116.85	7.540
B014002C	Extra for; junctions	Each	0.35	7.30	-	132.56	139.86	153.85	14.740
B014002D	Extra for; adaptor to clay	Each	0.17	3.54	-	115.07	118.61	130.47	2.310
B014003	**For sewers; in trenches; 300 mm nominal size pipes**								
B014003A	in runs exceeding 3.00 m long	m	0.42	8.76	-	38.44	47.20	51.92	24.270
B014003B	Extra for; bends	Each	0.37	7.71	-	201.34	209.05	229.96	14.630
B014003C	Extra for; junctions	Each	0.48	10.01	-	270.96	280.97	309.07	27.030
B014003D	Extra for; adaptor to clay	Each	0.18	3.75	-	302.66	306.41	337.05	3.240
B0142	**HEPSEAL DRAIN PIPES AND FITTINGS**								
B014201	**Push-fit flexible socket joints; for sewerage; in trenches; 100 mm nominal size pipes**								
B014201A	in runs exceeding 3.00 m long	m	0.13	6.13	-	10.48	16.61	18.27	5.590
B014201B	in runs not exceeding 3.00 m long	m	0.17	8.08	-	10.48	18.56	20.42	5.590
B014201C	Extra for; bend	Each	0.15	7.35	-	13.05	20.40	22.44	1.280
B014201E	Extra for; junction	Each	0.13	6.13	-	59.30	65.43	71.97	2.040
B014202	**Push-fit flexible socket joints; for sewerage; in trenches; 150 mm nominal size pipes**								
B014202A	in runs exceeding 3.00 m long	m	0.18	8.56	-	20.74	29.30	32.23	10.530
B014202B	in runs not exceeding 3.00 m long	m	0.23	10.99	-	20.74	31.73	34.90	10.530
B014202C	Extra for; bend	Each	0.24	11.48	-	41.75	53.23	58.55	2.750
B014202E	Extra for; junction	Each	0.15	7.35	-	48.32	55.67	61.24	4.120
B014203	**Push-fit flexible socket joints; for sewerage; in trenches; 225 mm nominal size pipes**								
B014203A	in runs exceeding 3.00 m long	m	0.20	9.78	-	43.39	53.17	58.49	20.030
B014203B	in runs not exceeding 3.00 m long	m	0.25	12.21	-	43.39	55.60	61.16	20.030
B014203C	Extra for; bend	Each	0.25	12.21	-	97.83	110.04	121.04	7.790
B014203E	Extra for; junction	Each	0.22	10.75	-	136.55	147.30	162.03	11.330
B014204	**Push-fit flexible socket joints; for sewerage; in trenches; 300 mm nominal size pipes**								
B014204A	in runs exceeding 3.00 m long	m	0.31	15.13	-	62.81	77.94	85.73	43.870
B014204B	in runs not exceeding 3.00 m long	m	0.39	19.07	-	62.81	81.88	90.07	43.870
B014204C	Extra for; bend	each	0.39	19.07	-	168.92	187.99	206.79	21.110
B014204E	Extra for; junction	each	0.37	18.10	-	265.87	283.97	312.37	25.330
B014205	**Push-fit flexible socket joints; for sewerage; in trenches; 400 mm nominal size pipes**								
B014205A	in runs exceeding 3.00 m long	m	0.37	18.10	-	98.02	116.12	127.73	110.090
B014205B	in runs not exceeding 3.00 m long	m	0.43	20.77	-	98.99	119.76	131.74	111.190
B014205C	Extra for; bend	each	0.17	8.32	-	570.12	578.44	636.28	57.570
B014205D	Extra for; junction	each	0.12	5.64	-	570.12	575.76	633.34	57.570
B014206	**Push-fit flexible socket joints; for sewerage; in trenches; 450 mm nominal size pipes**								
B014206A	in runs exceeding 3.00 m long	m	0.42	20.53	-	128.58	149.11	164.02	134.330
B014206B	in runs not exceeding 3.00 m long	m	0.48	23.45	-	128.58	152.03	167.23	134.330
B014206C	Extra for; bend	each	0.20	9.78	-	572.30	582.08	640.29	70.360

Small Works 2011		Unit	Labour Hours	Labour Net	Plant Net	Materials Net	Unit Net	Unit with 10%	CO₂
				£	£	£	£	£	Kg
B01	**DRAINAGE AND SEWERAGE**								
B0142	**HEPSEAL DRAIN PIPES AND FITTINGS**								
B014206	**Push-fit flexible socket joints; for sewerage; in trenches; 450 mm nominal size pipes**								
B014206D	Extra for; junction	each	0.13	6.37	-	570.12	576.49	634.14	57.570
B014207	**Push-fit flexible socket joints; for sewerage; in trenches; 500 mm nominal size pipes**								
B014207A	in runs exceeding 3.00 m long	m	0.47	22.72	-	143.31	166.03	182.63	170.490
B014207B	in runs not exceeding 3.00 m long	m	0.53	25.88	-	143.31	169.19	186.11	170.490
B014207C	Extra for; bend	each	0.23	10.99	-	710.45	721.44	793.58	77.230
B014207D	Extra for; junction	each	0.15	7.10	-	742.42	749.52	824.47	113.080
B0144	**CONCRETE CYLINDRICAL CLASS L DRAIN PIPES AND FITTINGS**								
B014401	**Flexible joints; for drainage and sewerage; in trenches; 150 mm nominal size pipes**								
B014401A	in runs exceeding 3.00 m long	m	0.25	12.21	-	8.03	20.24	22.26	12.200
B014401B	in runs not exceeding 3.00 m long	m	0.31	15.13	-	8.03	23.16	25.48	12.200
B014401C	Extra for; bend	each	0.13	6.13	-	76.50	82.63	90.89	11.170
B014401D	Extra for; junction 150 mm	each	0.09	4.14	-	53.55	57.69	63.46	29.540
B014402	**Flexible joints; for drainage and sewerage; in trenches; 225 mm nominal size pipes**								
B014402A	in runs exceeding 3.00 m long	m	0.38	18.34	-	12.05	30.39	33.43	27.460
B014402B	in runs not exceeding 3.00 m long	m	0.50	24.18	-	12.05	36.23	39.85	27.460
B014402C	Extra for; bend	each	0.17	8.08	-	114.76	122.84	135.12	25.130
B014402D	Extra for; junction 150 mm	each	0.11	5.16	-	80.33	85.49	94.04	66.470
B014403	**Flexible joints; for drainage and sewerage; in trenches; 300 mm nominal size pipes**								
B014403A	in runs exceeding 3.00 m long	m	0.44	21.50	-	16.07	37.57	41.33	48.820
B014403B	in runs not exceeding 3.00 m long	m	0.55	26.85	-	16.07	42.92	47.21	48.820
B014403C	Extra for; bend	each	0.21	10.27	-	153.01	163.28	179.61	44.670
B014403D	Extra for; junction 150 mm	each	0.11	5.16	-	107.10	112.26	123.49	118.170
B014404	**Flexible joints; for drainage and sewerage; in trenches; 375 mm nominal size pipes**								
B014404A	in runs exceeding 3.00 m long	m	0.53	25.64	-	19.82	45.46	50.01	58.010
B014404B	in runs not exceeding 3.00 m long	m	0.62	30.31	-	19.82	50.13	55.14	58.010
B014404C	Extra for; bend	each	0.23	11.24	-	188.78	200.02	220.02	54.010
B014404D	Extra for; junction 150 mm	each	0.11	5.16	-	132.15	137.31	151.04	140.200
B014405	**Flexible joints; for drainage and sewerage; in trenches; 450 mm nominal size pipes**								
B014405A	in runs exceeding 3.00 m long	m	0.67	32.50	-	23.89	56.39	62.03	81.550
B014405B	in runs not exceeding 3.00 m long	m	0.75	36.63	-	23.89	60.52	66.57	81.550
B014405C	Extra for; bend	each	0.39	18.83	-	227.52	246.35	270.99	75.720
B014405D	Extra for; junction 150 mm	each	0.11	5.16	-	159.27	164.43	180.87	198.960
B014406	**Flexible joints; for drainage and sewerage; in trenches; 525 mm nominal size pipes**								
B014406A	in runs exceeding 3.00 m long	m	0.75	36.63	-	30.47	67.10	73.81	126.880
B014406B	in runs not exceeding 3.00 m long	m	0.85	41.55	-	30.47	72.02	79.22	126.880
B014406C	Extra for; bend	each	0.42	20.29	-	290.12	310.41	341.45	90.580
B014406D	Extra for; junction 150 mm	each	0.11	5.16	-	203.09	208.25	229.08	265.000
B014407	**Flexible joints; for drainage and sewerage; in trenches; 600 mm nominal size pipes**								
B014407A	in runs exceeding 3.00 m long	m	0.83	40.57	-	38.60	79.17	87.09	139.560

Small Works 2011		Unit	Labour Hours	Labour Net	Plant Net	Materials Net	Unit Net	Unit with 10%	CO$_2$
				£	£	£	£	£	Kg
B01	**DRAINAGE AND SEWERAGE**								
B0144	**CONCRETE CYLINDRICAL CLASS L DRAIN PIPES AND FITTINGS**								
B014407	**Flexible joints; for drainage and sewerage; in trenches; 600 mm nominal size pipes**								
B014407B	in runs not exceeding 3.00 m long	m	0.94	45.93	-	38.60	84.53	92.98	139.560
B014407C	Extra for; bend	each	0.49	23.69	-	367.61	391.30	430.43	118.040
B014407D	Extra for; junction 150 mm	each	0.11	5.16	-	257.33	262.49	288.74	338.850
B0148	**HEPWORTH PRECAST CONCRETE CIRCULAR MANHOLE RINGS AND ACCESSORIES**								
B014801	**Bedding, jointing and pointing in cement mortar (1:3) on prepared bed; ring dia**								
B014801B	900 mm	m	4.02	195.43	-	44.77	240.20	264.22	134.010
B014801C	1050 mm	m	5.40	262.61	-	47.32	309.93	340.92	176.120
B014801D	1200 mm	m	6.78	329.80	-	57.97	387.77	426.55	233.000
B014802	**Cover slabs; heavy duty; reinforced; 600 mm access opening; ring dia**								
B014802B	900 mm	each	1.56	75.75	-	58.75	134.50	147.95	38.260
B014802C	1050 mm	each	1.81	87.96	-	62.99	150.95	166.05	52.070
B014802D	1200 mm	each	2.06	100.17	-	78.42	178.59	196.45	68.010
B014803	**Reducing slab; heavy duty; reinforced**								
B014803A	1200 - 900 mm dia	each	0.63	30.55	-	105.55	136.10	149.71	183.510
B0150	**ROAD GULLIES, GRATINGS, COVERS AND FRAMES**								
B015001	**Vitrified clay road gullies including excavation, 150 mm concrete bed and surround and jointing to drain**								
B015001A	300 mm x 600 mm deep; 100 mm outlet	each	2.18	106.25	-	157.35	263.60	289.96	92.210
B015001B	450 mm x 900 mm deep; 150 mm outlet	each	4.32	210.12	-	261.91	472.03	519.23	222.900
B015002	**Cast iron hinged roadway gratings and frames; bedding on one course of brickwork built brick-on-edge**								
B015002A	400 mm x 350 mm x 58 kg	each	1.06	51.33	-	212.58	263.91	290.30	23.010
B015002B	500 mm x 350 mm x 66 kg	each	1.11	53.76	-	223.02	276.78	304.46	180.890
B015003	**Access cover and frame; Grade B; medium duty; circular single seal solid top; bedding frame in cement and sand 1:3 and the cover in grease and sand**								
B015003A	600 mm dia	each	1.26	61.06	-	98.08	159.14	175.05	31.390
B015004	**Access cover and frame; grade A; heavy duty; double triangular solid top; bedding frame in cement and sand 1:3 an the cover in grease and sand**								
B015004A	600 mm x 600 mm	each	1.26	61.06	-	153.67	214.73	236.20	48.700

Small Works 2011		Unit	Labour Hours	Labour Net	Plant Net	Materials Net	Unit Net	Unit with 10%	CO$_2$
				£	£	£	£	£	Kg
B02	**DRAINAGE AND SEWERAGE REPAIRS AND ALTERATIONS**								
B0201	**REPAIRS**								
B020101	**Break up concrete paving and hardcore under 600 mm wide for excavation drain trench**								
B020101A	100 mm thick	m	1.10	22.94	-	-	22.94	25.23	-
B020102	**Hand excavate trench for 100 mm drain including backfilling, carting away remainder, including necessary earthwork support**								
B020102A	average 0.5 m deep	m	1.44	30.02	-	4.30	34.32	37.75	2.180
B020102B	average 1.0 m deep	m	2.90	60.47	-	8.60	69.07	75.98	4.350
B020102C	average 1.5 m deep	m	5.16	107.59	-	12.89	120.48	132.53	6.530
B020102D	100 mm concrete bed and haunch to pipe	m	1.10	22.94	-	9.20	32.14	35.35	22.950
B020104	**HepSeal clayware pipes, laid and jointed in short lengths**								
B020104A	100 mm	m	0.25	12.21	-	10.48	22.69	24.96	5.590
B020105	**Make good 100 mm concrete paving and hardcore under, after drainwork**								
B020105A	average 600 mm wide	m	1.30	27.11	-	7.76	34.87	38.36	19.350
B020106	**Cutting into brick side of exposed manhole and concrete benching for new branch drain and three quarter section channel, make good brickwork and benching**								
B020106A	100 mm	each	1.51	73.32	-	48.53	121.85	134.04	50.400
B020108	**Glazed clayware gully and grid with 100 mm outlet joint to drain, including necessary excavation and concrete bed**								
B020108A	150 mm x 150 mm x 100 mm	each	1.21	58.62	-	55.09	113.71	125.08	8.850
B020109	**Concrete curb around glazed clayware gully including necessary formwork**								
B020109A	100 mm	each	0.63	30.55	-	6.43	36.98	40.68	16.040
B020110	**Demolish curb, disconnect and remove gully, supply and connect new gully and grid including work to concrete bed, new curb, rendering three sides and remake connection after rodding**								
B020110A	150 mm x 150 mm x 100 mm	each	3.01	146.58	-	59.18	205.76	226.34	19.960
B020111	**Break up defective curb surround to manhole and reform in**								
B020111A	fine concrete splayed and rendered	each	0.78	37.85	-	7.41	45.26	49.79	19.410
B020112	**Cut through external brick wall and 150 mm concrete floor and connect 102 mm bend to trap of pan at one end and existing pipe at the other end**								
B020112A	225 mm brick wall	each	3.77	183.22	-	21.38	204.60	225.06	21.890

Small Works 2011		Unit	Labour Hours	Labour Net	Plant Net	Materials Net	Unit Net	Unit with 10%	CO₂
				£	£	£	£	£	Kg
B02	**DRAINAGE AND SEWERAGE REPAIRS AND ALTERATIONS**								
B0201	**REPAIRS**								
B020114	**Form new manhole on line of existing drain with 150 mm concrete base, 225 mm brick walls, cover and frame. Cut away existing drain within manhole to form channel, provide and set 2 no. three-quarter section channels, form concrete benching and cement render walls**								
B020114A	0.9 m deep	each	18.08	879.49	-	263.28	1,142.77	1,257.05	473.100
B020114B	add for every extra 300 mm depth in excess depth in excess of 0.9 m	each	4.52	219.85	-	38.73	258.58	284.44	100.000
B020116	**Take up existing manhole cover and frame and provide, bed and seal new cover and frame 610 mm x 457 mm**								
B020116A	25 kg	each	0.55	26.85	-	37.93	64.78	71.26	57.550
B020116B	38 kg	each	0.65	31.77	-	58.69	90.46	99.51	50.800
B020118	**Excavate for stoppage in 100 mm drain, cut out and renew two lengths of pipe, fill in and test. Reform paving**								
B020118A	assumed depth 0.9 m	each	5.02	244.32	-	38.59	282.91	311.20	55.140
B020119	**Unstop gullies, remove silt**								
B020119A	clean and flush with disinfectant	each	0.58	28.12	-	-	28.12	30.93	-
B020121	**Clear drains, rod and flush in sections**								
B020121A	average length 25 m	each	2.89	140.45	-	-	140.45	154.50	-
B020122	**Unstop and smoke test soil pipe**								
B020122A	cast iron	each	2.11	102.60	-	-	102.60	112.86	-
B020123	**Take up manhole cover, clean and sand out frame channels**								
B020123A	rebed in grease	each	0.55	26.85	-	-	26.85	29.54	-
B020124	**Clayware channel to gully set in concrete with brick curb rendered in cement mortar**								
B020124A	450 mm long	each	1.00	48.84	-	10.16	59.00	64.90	8.930
B020124B	supply and fit new gully grid	each	0.13	6.13	-	5.15	11.28	12.41	1.530
B020126	**Open up manhole, break out brickwork and benching to main channel, provide for and insert one three quarter channel bend 100 mm and join to existing channel, reform benching**								
B020126A	make good all work disturbed and refix manhole cover	each	5.02	244.32	-	33.48	277.80	305.58	37.070

Small Works 2011		Unit	Labour Hours	Labour Net	Plant Net	Materials Net	Unit Net	Unit with 10%	CO₂
				£	£	£	£	£	Kg
B02	**DRAINAGE AND SEWERAGE REPAIRS AND ALTERATIONS**								
B0201	**REPAIRS**								
B020128	**Open up manhole, 0.9 m x 0.9 m inside on plan. Break out all channels and branches. Break out one brick side of manhole at one end and extend manhole by 150 mm x 0.9 m inside with 150 mm concrete at bottom, one brick side in stock bricks and 150 mm concrete cover. Build in two pipes 150 mm and one pipe 100 mm provide and insert straight main channel 150 mm and six half branch channel bends 100 mm and reform benching. Make good all work disturbed and refix manhole cover**								
B020128A	1.27 m deep	each	12.05	586.33	-	350.37	936.70	1,030.37	428.740
B020128B	Extra over excavation for breaking out brick manhole 0.8 m x 0.7 m inside on plan and 0.9 m deep to invert	each	1.51	73.32	-	-	73.32	80.65	-
B020128C	add or deduct for every 300 mm more or less than 0.9 m deep to invert	each	0.50	24.42	-	-	24.42	26.86	-
B020130	**Seal open ends of disused clayware pipes with concrete plugs 300 mm long**								
B020130A	100 mm dia	each	0.30	14.64	-	0.33	14.97	16.47	0.830
B020130B	150 mm dia	each	0.40	19.56	-	0.78	20.34	22.37	1.940
B020130C	225 mm dia	each	0.55	26.85	-	2.66	29.51	32.46	6.640

Small Works 2011		Unit	Labour Hours	Labour Net	Plant Net	Materials Net	Unit Net	Unit with 10%	CO₂
				£	£	£	£	£	Kg
B03	ROADS AND FOOTWAYS, KERBS ETC WATER MAINS CABLE LAYING PILING								
B0301	ROADS								
B030101	Cut up turves, wheel away and stack								
B030101A	not exceeding 100 mm	m²	0.40	8.34	-	-	8.34	9.17	-
B030102	Take turves off stack, re-lay, level an well roll								
B030102A	not exceeding 100 m	m²	0.55	11.47	-	-	11.47	12.62	-
B030103	Excavate over site average 150 mm deep and wheel and deposit								
B030103A	by hand	m²	0.38	7.92	-	-	7.92	8.71	-
B030103B	by machine	m²	-	-	0.58	-	0.58	0.64	0.560
B030104	Hand excavation to reduce levels average 150 mm deep; remove excavated material by dumper 100 m; spread and level								
B030104A	loose soil	m²	0.55	11.47	0.24	-	11.71	12.88	1.570
B030104B	firm soil; sand	m²	0.66	13.76	0.24	-	14.00	15.40	1.570
B030104C	light clay; compact soil; gravel	m²	0.69	14.39	0.24	-	14.63	16.09	1.570
B030104D	stiff heavy clay	m²	0.92	19.18	0.24	-	19.42	21.36	1.570
B030104E	soft chalk	m²	1.38	28.77	0.24	-	29.01	31.91	1.570
B030105	Hand excavation to reduce levels average 225 mm deep; remove excavated material by dumper 100 m; and deposit								
B030105A	loose soil	m²	0.65	13.55	0.41	-	13.96	15.36	2.610
B030105B	firm soil; sand	m²	0.78	16.26	0.41	-	16.67	18.34	2.610
B030105C	light clay; compact soil; gravel	m²	0.81	16.89	0.41	-	17.30	19.03	2.610
B030105D	stiff heavy clay	m²	1.08	22.52	0.41	-	22.93	25.22	2.610
B030105E	soft chalk	m²	1.63	33.99	0.41	-	34.40	37.84	2.610
B030106	Machine excavation to reduce level; load excavated material into								
B030106A	lorries	m³	1.00	20.85	7.55	-	28.40	31.24	7.220
B030107	Hand excavation to reduce levels; remove excavated material by dumper 400 m and deposit								
B030107A	loose soil	m³	3.00	62.55	6.50	-	69.05	75.96	32.039
B030107B	firm soil; sand	m³	3.60	75.06	6.50	-	81.56	89.72	32.039
B030107C	light clay; compact soil; gravel	m³	3.75	78.19	6.50	-	84.69	93.16	32.039
B030107D	stiff heavy clay	m³	5.00	104.25	6.50	-	110.75	121.83	32.039
B030107E	soft chalk	m³	7.50	156.38	6.50	-	162.88	179.17	32.039
B030108	Consolidate								
B030108A	formation	m²	0.10	2.09	-	Net	2.09	2.30	-
B030109	Roll formation								
B030109B	8 Tonne roller	m²	0.10	2.09	0.30	-	2.39	2.63	1.020
B030110	Break up 100 mm tarmacadam paving								
B030110A	by hand	m²	1.30	27.11	-	-	27.11	29.82	-
B030110B	by two tool compressor	m²	0.20	4.17	1.86	-	6.03	6.63	15.620
B030111	Break up 100 mm tarmacadam paving and hardcore bed								
B030111A	by hand	m²	1.50	31.28	-	-	31.28	34.41	-
B030111B	by two tool compressor	m²	0.30	6.25	2.61	-	8.86	9.75	21.890
B030113	Break up 150 mm surface concrete								
B030113A	by hand	m²	2.50	52.13	-	-	52.13	57.34	-
B030113B	by two tool compressor	m²	0.40	8.34	2.76	-	11.10	12.21	23.080

Small Works 2011		Unit	Labour Hours	Labour Net	Plant Net	Materials Net	Unit Net	Unit with 10%	CO$_2$
				£	£	£	£	£	Kg
B03	**ROADS AND FOOTWAYS, KERBS ETC WATER MAINS CABLE LAYING PILING**								
B0301	**ROADS**								
B030114	**Break up 150 mm surface concrete and 100 mm hardcore bed**								
B030114A	by hand	m^2	3.00	62.55	-	-	62.55	68.81	-
B030114B	by two tool compressor	m^2	0.50	10.43	4.70	-	15.13	16.64	39.380
B030115	**Break up 225 mm surface concrete**								
B030115A	by hand	m^2	4.00	83.40	-	-	83.40	91.74	-
B030115B	by two tool compressor	m^2	0.60	12.51	6.79	-	19.30	21.23	56.880
B030116	**Break up 300 mm surface concrete**								
B030116A	by hand	m^2	6.00	125.10	-	-	125.10	137.61	-
B030116B	by two tool compressor	m^2	1.00	20.85	7.83	-	28.68	31.55	65.600
B030118	**Break up 150 mm reinforced surface concrete**								
B030118A	by hand	m^2	3.75	78.19	-	-	78.19	86.01	-
B030118B	by two tool compressor	m^2	0.60	12.51	6.79	-	19.30	21.23	56.880
B030120	**Break up 225 mm reinforced surface concrete**								
B030120A	by hand	m^2	6.00	125.10	-	-	125.10	137.61	-
B030120B	by two tool compressor	m^2	0.90	18.77	10.15	-	28.92	31.81	84.970
B030121	**Break up 300 mm reinforced surface concrete**								
B030121A	by hand	m^2	9.00	187.65	-	-	187.65	206.42	-
B030121B	by two tool compressor	m^2	1.50	31.28	13.51	-	44.79	49.27	113.130
B030122	**Levelling off slightly uneven areas by bulldozer and remove arisings; distance**								
B030122A	20 m	m^2	0.25	5.21	1.46	-	6.67	7.34	1.390
B030124	**Take up granite sets**								
B030124A	set aside for reuse	m^2	0.60	12.51	-	-	12.51	13.76	-
B030125	**Clean granite sets; relay on**								
B030125A	25 mm cement and sand bed and grout joints	m^2	2.70	56.30	-	5.19	61.49	67.64	17.710
B030126	**Hand packed boulder stone pitching blinded with ashes or fine ballast and rolled with heavy roller**								
B030126A	225 mm thick	m^2	1.15	23.98	1.91	6.37	32.26	35.49	10.700
B030128	**Furnace clinker hardcore spread levelled and rolled; thickness**								
B030128A	100 mm	m^2	0.20	4.17	-	2.54	6.71	7.38	1.580
B030128B	150 mm	m^2	0.25	5.21	-	3.82	9.03	9.93	2.370
B030129	**Brick hardcore bed spread levelled and rolled; thickness**								
B030129A	100 mm	m^2	0.36	7.51	-	2.54	10.05	11.06	1.580
B030129B	150 mm	m^2	0.54	11.26	-	3.82	15.08	16.59	2.370
B030129C	225 mm	m^2	0.81	16.89	-	5.71	22.60	24.86	3.550
B030130	**Blind hardcore with**								
B030130A	ashes	m^2	0.16	3.34	-	1.17	4.51	4.96	1.150
B030132	**Bitumen macadam 100 mm work to roads in two coats; 70 mm thick base course; 30 mm thick wearing course of 10 mm graded limestone aggregate; grit sprayed on**								
B030132A	generally	m^2	0.60	12.51	-	50.01	62.52	68.77	11.450

Small Works 2011		Unit	Labour Hours	Labour Net	Plant Net	Materials Net	Unit Net	Unit with 10%	CO$_2$
				£	£	£	£	£	Kg
B03	**ROADS AND FOOTWAYS, KERBS ETC WATER MAINS CABLE LAYING PILING**								
B0301	**ROADS**								
B030134	**Polythene building sheets; medium grade laying on**								
B030134A	hardcore or ashes including laps	m²	0.05	1.04	-	1.17	2.21	2.43	6.140
B030136	**Blinding layer**								
B030136A	50 mm concrete 1:3:6	m²	0.35	7.30	-	6.76	14.06	15.47	16.870
B030138	**Surface concrete 1:2:4 spread and levelled to falls and cambers; tamped around reinforcement (measured separately); thickness**								
B030138A	125 mm	m²	0.75	15.64	-	17.01	32.65	35.92	54.240
B030138B	150 mm	m²	0.85	17.72	-	19.45	37.17	40.89	62.040
B030138C	175 mm	m²	1.00	20.85	-	22.71	43.56	47.92	72.450
B030138D	225 mm	m²	1.15	23.98	-	29.12	53.10	58.41	92.880
B030139	**Fabric reinforcement lapped in surface concrete; ref**								
B030139A	C283 weighing 2.61 kg/m²	m²	0.06	2.92	-	2.38	5.30	5.83	6.170
B030139B	C385 weighing 3.41 kg/m²	m²	0.08	3.65	-	3.07	6.72	7.39	8.060
B030139C	C503 weighing 4.34 kg/m²	m²	0.10	4.87	-	3.79	8.66	9.53	10.260
B030139D	C636 weighing 5.55 kg/m²	m²	0.13	6.13	-	8.25	14.38	15.82	13.120
B030140	**Expansion joint**								
B030140A	13 mm x 175 mm high including formwork	m	0.25	5.21	-	2.39	7.60	8.36	3.680
B030141	**Running top edge of expansion joint with**								
B030141A	bitumen	m	0.18	3.75	-	0.19	3.94	4.33	0.090
B030142	**Extra over surface concrete for forming channel**								
B030142A	300 mm wide including formwork	m	0.25	5.21	-	0.95	6.16	6.78	0.350
B030144	**Treating surface of concrete with silicate of soda**								
B030144A	two coats	m²	0.12	2.50	-	0.55	3.05	3.36	0.020
B030144B	three coats	m²	0.20	4.17	-	0.83	5.00	5.50	0.020
B030146	**Formwork to edge of surface concrete; straight; height not exceeding**								
B030146A	125 mm	m	0.19	5.28	-	0.32	5.60	6.16	0.350
B030146B	150 mm	m	0.23	6.39	-	0.38	6.77	7.45	0.420
B030146C	175 mm	m	0.27	7.51	-	0.44	7.95	8.75	0.480
B030146D	225 mm	m	0.34	9.45	-	0.50	9.95	10.95	0.550
B030147	**Formwork to edge of surface concrete; curved; height not exceeding**								
B030147B	125 mm	m	0.38	10.56	-	0.65	11.21	12.33	0.720
B030147B	150 mm	m	0.46	12.79	-	0.76	13.55	14.91	0.830
B030147C	175 mm	m	0.54	15.01	-	0.78	15.79	17.37	0.860
B030147D	225 mm	m	0.68	18.90	-	1.19	20.09	22.10	1.330
B0304	**FOOTWAYS**								
B030401	**Take up precast concrete paving slabs; rebed in**								
B030401A	lime mortar 1:4, grout in cement mortar 1:3	m²	1.20	25.02	-	5.80	30.82	33.90	15.590
B030402	**Precast concrete paving slabs 50 mm thick; bedding in**								
B030402A	lime mortar 1:4, grout in cement mortar 1:3	m²	0.65	13.55	-	12.42	25.97	28.57	49.160
B030403	**Cutting on paving slabs**								
B030403A	raking	m	0.63	13.14	-	1.35	14.49	15.94	6.810
B030403B	curved	m	1.10	22.94	-	2.25	25.19	27.71	11.330

Small Works 2011	Unit	Labour Hours	Labour Net	Plant Net	Materials Net	Unit Net	Unit with 10%	CO₂
			£	£	£	£	£	Kg
B03	**ROADS AND FOOTWAYS, KERBS ETC WATER MAINS CABLE LAYING PILING**							
B0304	**FOOTWAYS**							
B030404	**Gravel paving; two coats; rolled; thickness**							
B030404A	50 mm	m²	0.30	6.25	1.02	1.55	8.82	9.70	2.310
B030404B	63 mm	m²	0.35	7.30	1.27	2.02	10.59	11.65	2.920
B030405	**Fine clinker ash bed; 75 mm thick**							
B030405A	spread, levelled and rolled	m²	0.30	6.25	-	2.14	8.39	9.23	2.100
B030406	**Sand bed; 25 mm thick**							
B030406A	spread, levelled and rolled	m²	0.10	2.09	0.51	0.89	3.49	3.84	1.010
B030408	**Bitumen macadam; 65 mm work to footway**							
B030408A	two coats; 45 mm base course; 20 mm wearing course of 6 mm medium graded limestone aggregate; 14 mm chippings sprinkled and rolled into wearing course	m²	0.85	17.72	1.91	37.51	57.14	62.85	15.090
B030410	**Concrete 1:2:4 paving; thickness**							
B030410A	100 mm	m²	0.60	12.51	-	12.93	25.44	27.98	41.240
B030410B	150 mm	m²	0.85	17.72	-	19.45	37.17	40.89	62.040
B030411	**Extra for marking out**							
B030411A	concrete paving in panels	m²	0.30	6.25	-	-	6.25	6.88	-
B030412	**Precast concrete edging; bedded and pointed in cement mortar 1:3 on and including 150 mm x 75 mm concrete foundation and haunching**							
B030412A	38 mm x 125 mm	m	0.40	8.34	-	6.08	14.42	15.86	9.120
B030412B	50 mm x 150 mm	m	0.40	8.34	-	6.06	14.40	15.84	11.970
B030413	**Creosoted softwood edging 150 mm x 38 mm staked at**							
B030413A	1050 mm centres	m	0.30	6.25	-	2.94	9.19	10.11	2.100
B0305	**KERBS**							
B030501	**Hand excavation; 300 mm x 300 mm foundation trench**							
B030501A	consolidate	m	0.20	4.17	-	-	4.17	4.59	-
B030502	**Concrete 1:3:6 bed and haunching to kerb**							
B030502A	300 mm high overall	m	0.33	6.88	-	5.87	12.75	14.03	14.650
B030503	**Precast concrete kerb 152 mm x 305 mm; bedded, jointed and pointed in cement mortar 1:3, haunched both sides with concrete**							
B030503A	straight	m	0.35	17.12	-	13.33	30.45	33.50	27.230
B030503B	curved	m	0.70	34.20	-	13.33	47.53	52.28	27.230
B030504	**Precast concrete channel 127 mm x 254 mm; bedded, jointed and pointed in cement mortar 1:3, haunched both sides with concrete**							
B030504A	straight	m	0.25	12.21	-	10.99	23.20	25.52	18.310
B030504B	curved	m	0.50	24.42	-	10.99	35.41	38.95	18.310
B030505	**Precast concrete quadrant; bedded, jointed and pointed in cement mortar 1:3, haunched with concrete**							
B030505A	300 mm radius x 250 mm deep	each	0.28	13.43	-	9.71	23.14	25.45	6.830
B030505B	450 mm radius x 250 mm deep	each	0.33	15.86	-	12.78	28.64	31.50	31.460

Small Works 2011		Unit	Labour Hours	Labour Net	Plant Net	Materials Net	Unit Net	Unit with 10%	CO_2
				£	£	£	£	£	Kg
B03	**ROADS AND FOOTWAYS, KERBS ETC WATER MAINS CABLE LAYING PILING**								
B0306	**WATER MAINS**								
B030601	**Excavation of trenches to receive pipes 0.60 m wide x 1.00 m deep; grading bottom; earthwork support; backfilling; compacting; disposal of surplus excavated material; by hand**								
B030601B	firm soil	m	2.63	54.84	-	-	54.84	60.32	-
B030602	**Excavation of trenches to receive pipes 0.60 m wide x 1.00 m deep; grading bottom; earthwork support; backfilling compacting; disposal of surplus excavated material; by machine**								
B030602B	firm soil	m	0.34	7.09	11.05	-	18.14	19.95	10.560
B030604	**Extra over excavating tarmacadam road surfacing**								
B030604A	replacing with existing consolidated broken tarmacadam as temporary surfacing	m	0.70	14.60	-	-	14.60	16.06	-
B030604B	removing existing tarmacadam and reinstating with new tarmacadam	m	1.10	22.94	4.34	32.55	59.83	65.81	11.600
B030606	**Break up concrete paving by drill; replacing with existing broken concrete; consolidate as temporary surfacing**								
B030606A	150 mm	m	1.00	20.85	-	-	20.85	22.94	-
B030610	**Hand excavation for hydrant pit beyond extent of pipe trench**								
B030610A	part backfill and dispose of surplus excavated material	each	1.50	31.28	-	-	31.28	34.41	-
B030611	**Class B engineering bricks; walls of hydrant pit; half brick thick**								
B030611A	laid dry	each	1.00	48.84	-	38.06	86.90	95.59	159.450
B030611B	cement mortar 1:3	each	2.51	122.16	-	42.01	164.17	180.59	172.950
B030612	**Concrete surround to surface box**								
B030612A	01:03:06	each	0.45	9.38	-	9.42	18.80	20.68	23.500
B030614	**Surface box; cast iron opening size 380 mm x 230 mm; 100 mm deep with drop-in lid and chain; bedded and flaunched in cement mortar 1:3**								
B030614A	420 mm x 255 mm overall	each	0.50	24.42	-	53.21	77.63	85.39	11.310
B030614B	temporary reinstatement	each	1.00	20.85	-	2.99	23.84	26.22	7.460
B030614C	cost per pit complete	each	5.96	208.09	-	107.51	315.60	347.16	214.940
B0307	**CABLE LAYING FOR ELECTRICITY AUTHORITIES**								
B030701	**Excavation of trenches to receive cables; grading bottom; compacting; part backfill and dispose of surplus excavated material; by hand**								
B030701A	300 mm wide x 525 mm deep	m	0.75	15.64	-	-	15.64	17.20	-
B030701B	373 mm wide x 675 mm deep	m	1.30	27.11	-	-	27.11	29.82	-

Small Works 2011		Unit	Labour Hours	Labour Net £	Plant Net £	Materials Net £	Unit Net £	Unit with 10% £	CO$_2$ Kg
B03	**ROADS AND FOOTWAYS, KERBS ETC WATER MAINS CABLE LAYING PILING**								
B0307	**CABLE LAYING FOR ELECTRICITY AUTHORITIES**								
B030702	**Excavation of trenches to receive cables; grading bottom; compacting; part backfill and dispose of surplus excavated material; by machine**								
B030702A	300 mm wide x 525 mm deep	m	0.40	8.34	1.14	-	9.48	10.43	1.090
B030702B	373 mm wide x 675 mm deep	m	0.70	14.60	1.75	-	16.35	17.99	1.670
B030703	**Break up 50 mm tarmacadam paving and 75 mm hardcore bed**								
B030703A	450 mm wide	m	0.60	12.51	1.08	-	13.59	14.95	1.040
B030704	**Temporarily re-lay paving with existing broken tarmacadam and consolidate**								
B030704A	450 mm wide	m	0.30	6.25	6.88	-	13.13	14.44	23.440
B030705	**Take up paving slabs and ash bed**								
B030705A	450 mm wide	m	0.40	8.34	-	-	8.34	9.17	-
B030706	**Temporarily re-lay paving with**								
B030706A	existing slabs on ash bed	m	0.45	9.38	-	6.65	16.03	17.63	6.510
B030708	**Take up granite sett paving**								
B030708A	450 mm wide	m	0.55	11.47	-	-	11.47	12.62	-
B030709	**Temporarily re-lay paving with existing setts**								
B030709A	450 mm wide	m	0.40	8.34	-	-	8.34	9.17	-
B030710	**Break up 75 mm tarmacadam road and 100 mm hardcore bed**								
B030710A	450 mm wide	m	0.70	14.60	1.53	-	16.13	17.74	1.460
B030712	**Temporarily re-lay paving with existing broken tarmacadam and consolidate**								
B030712A	450 mm wide	m	0.40	8.34	9.56	-	17.90	19.69	32.560
B030713	**Break up 150 mm concrete paving and 150 mm hardcore bed**								
B030713A	450 mm wide	m	1.00	20.85	8.34	-	29.19	32.11	7.990
B030714	**Temporarily re-lay paving with existing broken concrete and consolidate**								
B030714A	450 mm wide	m	0.60	12.51	6.88	-	19.39	21.33	23.440
B030716	**Labour unwinding and laying cable direct in trench**								
B030716A	25 mm	m	0.10	2.09	-	-	2.09	2.30	-
B030716B	31 mm - 50 mm	m	0.12	2.50	-	-	2.50	2.75	-
B030716C	50 mm - 63 mm	m	0.14	2.92	-	-	2.92	3.21	-
B030716D	63 mm - 75 mm	m	0.20	4.17	-	-	4.17	4.59	-
B030718	**Labour unwinding and drawing cable through ducts in trench**								
B030718A	25 mm	m	0.22	4.59	-	-	4.59	5.05	-
B030718B	31 mm - 50 mm	m	0.25	5.21	-	-	5.21	5.73	-
B030718C	50 mm - 63 mm	m	0.30	6.25	-	-	6.25	6.88	-
B030718D	63 mm - 75 mm	m	0.40	8.34	-	-	8.34	9.17	-
B030719	**Labour laying tile cable covers**								
B030719A	300 mm x 100 mm	m	0.30	6.25	-	-	6.25	6.88	-
B030719B	225 mm x 150 mm	m	0.35	7.30	-	-	7.30	8.03	-

Small Works 2011		Unit	Labour Hours	Labour Net	Plant Net	Materials Net	Unit Net	Unit with 10%	CO$_2$
				£	£	£	£	£	Kg
B03	**ROADS AND FOOTWAYS, KERBS ETC WATER MAINS CABLE LAYING PILING**								
B0307	**CABLE LAYING FOR ELECTRICITY AUTHORITIES**								
B030720	**Labour laying concrete cable covers**								
B030720A	900 mm x 175 mm	m	0.40	8.34	-	-	8.34	9.17	-
B030720B	900 mm x 225 mm	m	0.50	10.43	-	-	10.43	11.47	-
B030721	**Labour laying stoneware ducts**								
B030721A	100 mm	m	0.25	5.21	-	-	5.21	5.73	-
B0309	**PILING BY SPECIALISTS**								
B030901	**Driven mini-shell piles 340 mm dia**								
B030901A	maximum load 400 kN	m	0.11	10.95	35.74	33.52	80.21	88.23	89.710
B030901B	Extra per metre over 250 m length	m	0.04	3.65	11.91	33.52	49.08	53.99	75.080
B030902	**Driven shell piles 400 mm dia**								
B030902A	maximum load 600 kN	m	0.09	9.38	30.64	44.41	84.43	92.87	115.030
B030902B	Extra per metre over 250 m length	m	0.02	2.09	6.81	44.41	53.31	58.64	100.400
B030903	**Driven shell piles 440 mm dia**								
B030903A	maximum load 700 kN	m	0.08	8.34	27.23	53.28	88.85	97.74	137.490
B030903B	Extra per metre over 250 m length	m	0.02	1.88	5.96	53.28	61.12	67.23	124.420
B030904	**Driven shell piles 530 mm dia**								
B030904A	maximum load 1000 kN	m	0.05	5.21	17.02	75.09	97.32	107.05	193.180
B030904B	Extra per metre over 250 m length	m	0.01	1.36	4.25	75.09	80.70	88.77	185.340
B030905	**Driven Hardrive piles 270 mm x 270 mm**								
B030905A	maximum load 1200 kN	m	0.11	11.47	37.44	37.89	86.80	95.48	67.230
B030905B	Extra per metre over 250 mm length	m	0.03	2.61	8.51	37.89	49.01	53.91	49.460

Landscaping

Landscaping

Small Works 2011		Unit	Labour Hours	Labour Net £	Plant Net £	Materials Net £	Unit Net £	Unit with 10% £	CO$_2$ Kg
C01	**SEEDING, TURFING AND PLANTING**								
C0101	**PREPARATORY ITEMS**								
C010101	**Temporarily enclose site with chestnut fencing; up to twenty times used**								
C010101A	1.35 m high	m	0.25	5.21	-	0.71	5.92	6.51	1.230
C010102	**Cut down hedge; grub up roots; burn or deposit in skip; height**								
C010102A	600 mm	m	1.97	41.07	-	-	41.07	45.18	-
C010102B	900 mm	m	2.63	54.84	-	-	54.84	60.32	-
C010102C	1200 mm	m	3.12	65.05	-	-	65.05	71.56	-
C010102D	1500 mm	m	4.27	89.03	-	-	89.03	97.93	-
C010102E	1800 mm	m	5.74	119.68	-	-	119.68	131.65	-
C010103	**Cut down tree; lop off branches; grub up roots; burn or deposit in skip; fill hole with excavated material; girth and dia**								
C010103A	450 mm girth; 140 mm dia	each	16.00	333.60	-	-	333.60	366.96	-
C010103B	900 mm girth; 290 mm dia	each	28.00	583.80	-	-	583.80	642.18	-
C010103C	1350 mm girth; 430 mm dia	each	42.00	875.70	-	-	875.70	963.27	-
C010103D	1800 mm girth; 570 mm dia	each	56.00	1,167.60	-	-	1,167.60	1,284.36	-
C010103E	2250 mm girth; 720 mm dia	each	69.00	1,438.65	-	-	1,438.65	1,582.52	-
C010103F	2700 mm girth; 860 mm dia	each	81.00	1,688.85	-	-	1,688.85	1,857.74	-
C010103G	3150 mm girth; 1000 mm dia	each	92.00	1,918.20	-	-	1,918.20	2,110.02	-
C010103H	3600 mm girth; 1150 mm dia	each	102.00	2,126.70	-	-	2,126.70	2,339.37	-
C010104	**Clear site of bushes, scrub and undergrowth; cutting down small trees; grub up roots; burn or deposit in skip; average height**								
C010104A	1.50 m	m^2	0.30	6.25	0.87	-	7.12	7.83	-
C0102	**SEEDING**								
C010201	**Ground preparation**								
C010201A	clear site of rubbish	m^2	0.08	1.67	-	-	1.67	1.84	-
C010201B	strip site of surface vegetation	m^2	0.07	1.46	-	-	1.46	1.61	-
C010201C	cultivate 150 mm deep; remove stones and vegetable matter	m^2	0.12	2.50	-	-	2.50	2.75	-
C010201D	fill into barrows; wheel up to 20 m; deposit in skip	m^2	0.17	3.54	-	-	3.54	3.89	-
C010201E	hire of 4.5 m^3 skip; delivery to site; removing when full; disposal of contents; payment of tipping charges	m^2	-	-	12.78	-	12.78	14.06	-
C010201F	grade	m^2	0.08	1.67	-	-	1.67	1.84	-
C010201G	imported standard loam 150 mm deep; spread and levelled	m^2	0.41	8.55	-	4.03	12.58	13.84	7.700
C010201H	fork and rake	m^2	0.06	1.25	-	-	1.25	1.38	-
C010201I	dress with bonemeal lightly raked in	m^2	0.02	0.42	-	0.22	0.64	0.70	0.630
C010202	**Sowing and maintenance**								
C010202A	seed with seed mixture	m^2	0.10	2.09	-	0.19	2.28	2.51	-
C010202B	twice roll	m^2	0.07	1.46	-	-	1.46	1.61	-
C010202C	scythe to top	m^2	0.01	0.21	-	-	0.21	0.23	-
C010202D	scythe to reduce	m^2	0.01	0.21	-	-	0.21	0.23	-
C010202E	keep grass mown to height of 50 mm during contract	m^2	0.07	1.46	-	-	1.46	1.61	-
C010202F	keep area free of stones exceeding 12 mm	m^2	0.07	1.46	-	-	1.46	1.61	-
C010202G	roll in two directions (maintenance)	m^2	0.06	1.25	-	-	1.25	1.38	-
C010202H	scythe to top (maintenance)	m^2	0.06	1.25	-	-	1.25	1.38	-
C010202I	scythe to reduce (maintenance)	m^2	0.06	1.25	-	-	1.25	1.38	-
C010202J	twice box mow (maintenance)	m^2	0.08	1.67	-	-	1.67	1.84	-
C010202K	dress with fish manure (maintenance)	m^2	0.01	0.21	-	0.08	0.29	0.32	0.450
C010202L	water as necessary (maintenance)	m^2	0.06	1.25	-	-	1.25	1.38	-

Landscaping

Small Works 2011		Unit	Labour Hours	Labour Net £	Plant Net £	Materials Net £	Unit Net £	Unit with 10% £	CO₂ Kg
C01	**SEEDING, TURFING AND PLANTING**								
C0103	**TURFING**								
C010301	**Ground preparation**								
C010301A	clear site of rubbish	m²	0.08	1.67	-	-	1.67	1.84	-
C010301B	strip site of surface vegetation	m²	0.07	1.46	-	-	1.46	1.61	-
C010301C	cultivate 150 mm deep; remove stones and vegetable matter	m²	0.12	2.50	-	-	2.50	2.75	-
C010301D	fill into barrows; wheel up to 20 m deposit in skip	m²	0.17	3.54	-	-	3.54	3.89	-
C010301E	hire of 4.5 m³ skip; delivery to site; removing when full; disposal of contents; payment of tipping charges	m²	-	-	12.78	-	12.78	14.06	-
C010301F	grade	m²	0.08	1.67	-	-	1.67	1.84	-
C010301G	imported standard loam 100 mm deep; spread and levelled	m²	0.27	5.63	-	2.68	8.31	9.14	5.120
C010301H	fork and rake	m²	0.06	1.25	-	-	1.25	1.38	-
C010301I	dress with bonemeal lightly raked in	m²	0.02	0.42	-	0.16	0.58	0.64	0.450
C010302	**Laying and maintenance**								
C010302A	25 mm turves and laying	m²	0.33	6.88	-	2.67	9.55	10.51	-
C010302B	twice roll	m²	0.07	1.46	-	-	1.46	1.61	-
C010302C	scythe to top	m²	0.01	0.21	-	-	0.21	0.23	-
C010302D	scythe to reduce	m²	0.01	0.21	-	-	0.21	0.23	-
C010302E	keep grass mown to height of 50 mm during contract	m²	0.07	1.46	-	-	1.46	1.61	-
C010302F	roll in two directions	m²	0.06	1.25	-	-	1.25	1.38	-
C010302G	scythe to top (maintenance)	m²	0.06	1.25	-	-	1.25	1.38	-
C010302H	scythe to reduce (maintenance)	m²	0.06	1.25	-	-	1.25	1.38	-
C010302I	twice box mow (maintenance)	m²	0.08	1.67	-	-	1.67	1.84	-
C010302J	top dress with fine sifted soil brushed into joints (maintenance)	m²	0.06	1.25	-	0.44	1.69	1.86	0.850
C010302K	dress with fish manure (maintenance)	m²	0.01	0.21	-	0.08	0.29	0.32	0.450
C010302L	water as necessary (maintenance)	m²	0.06	1.25	-	-	1.25	1.38	-
C0104	**SHRUB PLANTING**								
C010401	**Preparation**								
C010401A	clear site of rubbish	m²	0.08	1.67	-	-	1.67	1.84	-
C010401B	excavation to reduce levels 300 mm deep	m²	1.08	22.52	-	-	22.52	24.77	-
C010401C	fill into barrows; wheel up to 20 m; deposit in skip	m²	0.33	6.88	-	-	6.88	7.57	-
C010401D	hire of 4.5 m³ skip; delivery to site; removing when full; disposal of contents; payment of tipping charges	m²	-	-	20.17	-	20.17	22.19	-
C010401E	cultivate 150 mm deep; remove stones and vegetable matter	m²	0.08	1.67	-	-	1.67	1.84	-
C010401F	manure 100 mm deep worked into subsoil	m²	0.17	3.54	-	4.02	7.56	8.32	10.530
C010401G	imported fibrous loam 375 mm deep	m²	1.00	20.85	-	9.18	30.03	33.03	17.530
C010401H	spread topsoil to even levels and camber where necessary	m²	0.05	1.04	-	-	1.04	1.14	-
C010402	**Preparation to existing areas**								
C010402A	clear beds of rubbish; debris; vegetation	m²	0.08	1.67	-	-	1.67	1.84	-
C010402B	cultivate 150 mm deep; remove stones and vegetable matter	m²	0.08	1.67	-	-	1.67	1.84	-
C010402C	raking to even levels and camber where necessary	m²	0.05	1.04	-	-	1.04	1.14	-
C010403	**Planting operations**								
C010403A	clear weed growth and rubbish before planting	m²	0.08	1.67	-	-	1.67	1.84	-
C010403B	peat 50 mm deep forked into upper 200 mm of topsoil	m²	0.25	5.21	-	2.74	7.95	8.75	-
C010403C	bulb planting in beds	each	0.04	0.83	-	0.25	1.08	1.19	-
C010403D	bulb planting in grassed areas with dibber; topped up with loose topsoil	each	0.09	1.88	-	0.25	2.13	2.34	-
C010403E	ground cover shrubs	each	0.22	4.59	-	10.00	14.59	16.05	-

Landscaping

		Unit	Labour Hours	Labour Net £	Plant Net £	Materials Net £	Unit Net £	Unit with 10% £	CO₂ Kg
C01	**SEEDING, TURFING AND PLANTING**								
C0104	**SHRUB PLANTING**								
C010403	**Planting operations**								
C010403F	hedging plants	each	0.27	5.63	-	3.90	9.53	10.48	-
C010403G	plants; open ground grown	each	0.28	5.84	-	10.00	15.84	17.42	-
C010403H	plants; container grown	each	0.30	6.25	-	14.00	20.25	22.28	-
C010403I	water at time of planting	m²	0.15	3.13	-	-	3.13	3.44	-
C010403J	fertiliser; John Innes based	m²	0.02	0.42	-	0.27	0.69	0.76	0.360
C010403K	cultivation, lightly, after planting	m²	0.08	1.67	-	-	1.67	1.84	
C010404	**Maintenance**								
C010404A	remove weed growth and rubbish; light cultivation; per visit	m²	0.17	3.54	-	-	3.54	3.89	-
C010404B	water; per visit	m²	0.05	1.04	-	-	1.04	1.14	-
C010404C	mulching; spent mushroom compost; spread over area 80 mm deep; per visit	m²	0.13	2.71	-	2.32	5.03	5.53	8.370
C010404D	prune shrubs; per visit	each	0.07	1.46	-	-	1.46	1.61	-
C010404E	prune roses; per visit	each	0.12	2.50	-	-	2.50	2.75	-
C0105	**CLIMBER PLANTING**								
C010501	**Preparation**								
C010501A	clear rubbish, debris and vegetation from position	each	0.08	1.67	-	-	1.67	1.84	-
C010501B	excavate position 900 x 230 x 450 mm deep	each	0.47	9.80	-	-	9.80	10.78	
C010501C	fill into barrows; wheel up to 20 m; deposit in skip	each	0.19	3.96	-	-	3.96	4.36	
C010501D	hire of 4.5 m³ skip; delivery to site; removing when full; disposal of contents; payment of tipping charges	each	-	-	8.06	-	8.06	8.87	-
C010501E	cultivate bottom of position to depth of 150 mm	each	0.03	0.63	-	-	0.63	0.69	-
C010501F	manure in bottom of position 100 mm deep	each	0.17	3.54	-	1.44	4.98	5.48	3.780
C010501G	imported fibrous loam 475 mm deep	each	0.71	14.80	-	1.76	16.56	18.22	4.710
C010501H	spread topsoil to even levels and camber	each	0.03	0.63	-	-	0.63	0.69	-
C010502	**Planting operations**								
C010502A	clear weed growth and rubbish before planting	each	0.05	1.04	-	-	1.04	1.14	-
C010502B	peat 50 mm deep forked into upper 200 mm of topsoil	each	0.22	4.59	-	0.92	5.51	6.06	-
C010502C	climber plant; open ground grown	each	0.28	5.84	-	-	5.84	6.42	-
C010502D	climber plant; container grown	each	0.30	6.25	-	-	6.25	6.88	-
C010502E	water at time of planting	each	0.05	1.04	-	-	1.04	1.14	-
C010502F	fertiliser; John Innes based	each	0.02	0.42	-	0.07	0.49	0.54	0.090
C010502G	cultivation; lightly; after planting	each	0.05	1.04	-	-	1.04	1.14	-
C010502H	climber guards; semi-circular section; secured to wall at 6 no points	each	1.75	36.49	-	17.40	53.89	59.28	5.980
C010503	**Maintenance**								
C010503A	remove weed growth and rubbish; light cultivation; per visit	each	0.10	2.09	-	-	2.09	2.30	-
C010503B	water; per visit	each	0.01	0.21	-	-	0.21	0.23	-
C010503C	mulching; spent mushroom compost; spread over area 80 mm deep; per visit	each	0.07	1.46	-	2.12	3.58	3.94	7.650
C010503D	prune climber; per visit	each	0.10	2.09	-	-	2.09	2.30	-
C0106	**TREE PLANTING**								
C010602	**Preparation**								
C010602A	clear rubbish, debris and vegetation from position; size 300 x 300 x 300 mm; for transplants, whips and feathered trees	each	0.01	0.21	-	-	0.21	0.23	-
C010602B	clear rubbish; debris and vegetation from position size 900 x 900 x 600 mm for light standard and selected standard trees	each	0.07	1.46	-	-	1.46	1.61	-

Small Works 2011		Unit	Labour Hours	Labour Net	Plant Net	Materials Net	Unit Net	Unit with 10%	CO$_2$
				£	£	£	£	£	Kg
C01	**SEEDING, TURFING AND PLANTING**								
C0106	**TREE PLANTING**								
C010602	**Preparation**								
C010602C	clear rubbish; debris and vegetation from position size 1200 x 1200 x 1000 mm for heavy and extra heavy standard trees	each	0.12	2.50	-	-	2.50	2.75	-
C010602D	excavate to form tree pit size 300 x 300 x 300 mm	each	0.14	2.92	-	-	2.92	3.21	-
C010602E	excavate to form tree pit size 900 x 900 x 600 mm	each	2.43	50.67	-	-	50.67	55.74	-
C010602F	excavate to form tree pit size 1200 x 1200 x 1000 mm	each	7.20	150.12	-	-	150.12	165.13	-
C010602G	fill into barrows; wheel up to 20 m; deposit in skip; tree pit size 300 x 300 x 300 mm	each	0.03	0.63	-	-	0.63	0.69	-
C010602H	fill into barrows; wheel up to 20 m; deposit in skip; tree pit size 900 x 900 x 600 mm	each	0.54	11.26	-	-	11.26	12.39	-
C010602I	fill into barrows; wheel up to 20 m; deposit in skip; tree pit size 1200 x 1200 x 1000 mm	each	1.58	32.94	-	-	32.94	36.23	-
C010602J	hire of 4.5 m^3 skip; delivery to site; removing when full; disposal of contents; payment of tipping charges; 300 x 300 x 300 mm	each	-	-	2.36	-	2.36	2.60	-
C010602K	hire of 4.5 m^3 skip; delivery to site; removing when full; disposal of contents; payment of tipping charges; 900 x 900 x 600 mm	each	-	-	42.03	-	42.03	46.23	-
C010602L	hire of 4.5 m^3 skip; delivery to site; removing when full; disposal of contents; payment of tipping charges; 1200 x 1200 x 1000 mm	each	-	-	48.38	-	48.38	53.22	-
C010602M	cultivate 150 mm deep to bottom of pit size 300 x 300 mm	each	0.01	0.21	-	-	0.21	0.23	-
C010602N	cultivate 150 mm deep to bottom of pit size 900 x 900 mm	each	0.07	1.46	-	-	1.46	1.61	-
C010602O	cultivate 150 mm deep to bottom of pit size 1200 x 1200 mm	each	0.12	2.50	-	-	2.50	2.75	-
C010602P	manure 100 mm deep to bottom of pit size 300 x 300 mm	each	0.02	0.42	-	0.55	0.97	1.07	1.440
C010602Q	manure 100 mm deep to bottom of pit size 900 x 900 mm	each	0.13	2.71	-	4.91	7.62	8.38	12.870
C010602R	manure 100 mm deep to bottom of pit size 1200 x 1200 mm	each	0.23	4.80	-	8.73	13.53	14.88	22.860
C010602S	imported fibrous loam to pit size 300 x 300 mm	each	0.07	1.46	-	0.48	1.94	2.13	1.290
C010602T	imported fibrous loam to pit size 900 x 900 x 600 mm	each	1.26	26.27	-	7.80	34.07	37.48	20.910
C010602U	imported fibrous loam to pit size 1200 x 1200 x 1000 mm	each	3.73	77.77	-	22.93	100.70	110.77	61.490
C010602V	finish soil to even levels to pit size 300 x 300 mm	each	0.01	0.21	-	-	0.21	0.23	-
C010602W	finish soil to even levels to pit size 900 x 900 mm	each	0.03	0.63	-	-	0.63	0.69	-
C010602X	finish soil to even levels to pit size 1200 x 1200 mm	each	0.04	0.83	-	-	0.83	0.91	-
C010604	**Planting operations**								
C010604A	clear weed growth and rubbish before planting to pit size 300 mm x 300 m	each	0.01	0.21	-	-	0.21	0.23	-
C010604B	clear weed growth and rubbish before planting to pit size 900 mm x 900 m	each	0.09	1.88	-	-	1.88	2.07	-
C010604C	clear weed growth and rubbish before planting to pit size 1200 mm x 1200 mm	each	0.16	3.34	-	-	3.34	3.67	-
C010604D	peat 50 mm deep forked into upper 200 mm of topsoil to pit size 300 mm x 300 mm	each	0.02	0.42	-	0.31	0.73	0.80	-
C010604E	peat 50 mm deep forked into upper 200 mm of topsoil to pit size 900 mm x 900 mm	each	0.16	3.34	-	2.74	6.08	6.69	-

Landscaping

		Unit	Labour Hours	Labour Net £	Plant Net £	Materials Net £	Unit Net £	Unit with 10% £	CO$_2$ Kg
C01	**SEEDING, TURFING AND PLANTING**								
C0106	**TREE PLANTING**								
C010604	**Planting operations**								
C010604F	peat 50 mm deep forked into upper 200 mm of topsoil to pit size 1200 mm x 1200 mm	each	0.29	6.05	-	4.26	10.31	11.34	-
C010604G	tree planting; transplants	each	0.10	2.09	-	0.60	2.69	2.96	-
C010604H	tree planting; whips	each	0.12	2.50	-	4.95	7.45	8.20	-
C010604I	tree planting; feathered	each	0.15	3.13	-	18.63	21.76	23.94	-
C010604J	tree planting; light standard	each	0.19	3.96	-	43.49	47.45	52.20	-
C010604K	tree planting; standard	each	0.19	3.96	-	43.49	47.45	52.20	-
C010604L	tree planting; selected standard	each	0.22	4.59	-	43.49	48.08	52.89	-
C010604M	tree planting; heavy standard	each	0.24	5.00	-	49.00	54.00	59.40	-
C010604N	tree planting; extra heavy standard	each	0.27	5.63	-	173.97	179.60	197.56	-
C010604O	water at time of planting to pit size 300 mm x 300 mm	each	0.01	0.21	-	-	0.21	0.23	-
C010604P	water at time of planting to pit size 900 mm x 900 mm	each	0.05	1.04	-	-	1.04	1.14	-
C010604Q	water at time of planting to pit size 1200 mm x 1200 mm	each	0.08	1.67	-	-	1.67	1.84	-
C010604R	fertiliser; John Innes based to pit size 300 mm x 300 mm	each	0.01	0.21	-	0.13	0.34	0.37	0.180
C010604S	fertiliser; John Innes based to pit size 900 mm x 900 mm	each	0.01	0.21	-	1.01	1.22	1.34	1.350
C010604T	fertiliser; John Innes based to pit size 1200 mm x 1200 mm	each	0.02	0.42	-	1.69	2.11	2.32	2.250
C010604U	lightly cultivate after planting to pit size; 300 mm x 300 mm	each	0.01	0.21	-	-	0.21	0.23	-
C010604V	lightly cultivate after planting to pit size; 900 mm x 900 mm	each	0.03	0.63	-	-	0.63	0.69	-
C010604W	lightly cultivate after planting to pit size; 1200 mm x 1200 mm	each	0.04	0.83	-	-	0.83	0.91	-
C010604X	turf around tree position after planting to form opening 600 x 600mm to pit size 900 mm x 900 mm	each	0.25	5.21	-	1.27	6.48	7.13	-
C010604Y	turf around tree position after planting to form opening 600 mm x 600 mm to pit size 1200 mm x 1200 m	each	0.45	9.38	-	2.42	11.80	12.98	-
C010605	**Maintenance**								
C010605A	remove weed growth and rubbish; light cultivation; per visit; to pit size 300 mm x 300 mm	each	0.01	0.21	-	-	0.21	0.23	-
C010605B	remove weed growth and rubbish; light cultivation; per visit; to pit size 900 mm x 900 mm	each	0.06	1.25	-	-	1.25	1.38	-
C010605C	remove weed growth and rubbish; light cultivation; per visit; to pit size 1200 mm x 1200 mm	each	0.11	2.29	-	-	2.29	2.52	-
C010605D	watering; per visit; to pit size 300 mm x 300 mm	each	0.01	0.21	-	-	0.21	0.23	-
C010605E	watering; per visit; to pit size 900 mm x 900 mm	each	0.04	0.83	-	-	0.83	0.91	-
C010605F	watering; per visit; to pit size 1200 mm x 1200 mm	each	0.07	1.46	-	-	1.46	1.61	-
C010605G	mulching; spent mushroom compost; spread 80 mm deep; per visit; over pit size 300 mm x 300 mm	each	0.01	0.21	-	0.67	0.88	0.97	2.430
C010605H	mulching; spent mushroom compost; spread 80 mm deep; per visit; over pit size 900 mm x 900 mm	each	0.10	2.09	-	3.57	5.66	6.23	12.870
C010605I	mulching; spent mushroom compost; spread 80 mm deep; per visit; over pit size 1200 mm x 1200 mm	each	0.17	3.54	-	6.35	9.89	10.88	22.860
C010605J	prune trees; per visit	each	0.17	3.54	-	-	3.54	3.89	-
C010606	**Sundry items**								
C010606A	spiral tree guards for protection against rabbit damage	each	0.03	0.63	-	1.25	1.88	2.07	0.110
C010606B	tree spats	each	0.08	1.67	-	1.23	2.90	3.19	0.770
C010606E	tree stake	each	0.33	6.88	-	0.95	7.83	8.61	1.180
C010606F	tree stake ties (3 no.)	each	0.15	3.13	-	2.14	5.27	5.80	0.230
C010606G	tree guard	each	1.58	32.94	-	29.83	62.77	69.05	10.760

Small Works 2011		Unit	Labour Hours	Labour Net	Plant Net	Materials Net	Unit Net	Unit with 10%	CO₂
				£	£	£	£	£	Kg

C02   **PATHS AND WALLS**

C0201   **PATHS**

C020101	**Surface excavation**								
C020101A	150 mm deep, remove soil up to 18 m; deposit; trim and consolidate new surface	m²	0.50	10.43	-	-	10.43	11.47	-
C020101B	fill into barrows; wheel up to 20 m deposit in skip	m²	0.15	3.13	-	-	3.13	3.44	-
C020101C	hire of 4.5 m³ skip; delivery to site; removing when full; disposal of contents; payment of tipping charges	m²	-	-	12.78	-	12.78	14.06	-
C020102	**Ash or fine clinker; spread, levelled and rolled**								
C020102A	50 mm thick	m²	0.25	5.21	-	1.17	6.38	7.02	1.150
C020102B	75 mm thick	m²	0.30	6.25	-	1.78	8.03	8.83	1.740
C020103	**Brick hardcore 100 mm; spread, levelled watered, rammed, blinded with ashes and rolled; cambered surface**								
C020103A	finished to receive surfacing material	m²	0.35	7.30	-	3.27	10.57	11.63	2.570
C020104	**Brick hardcore 75 mm; spread, levelled, watered, rammed and blinded with ashes; 100 mm concrete paving**								
C020104A	to falls; in bays; formwork; expansion joints; spade finish to falls	m²	1.20	25.02	-	20.94	45.96	50.56	36.990
C020105	**Crazy paving; broken precast concrete slabs; mortar bed; pointing**								
C020105A	50 mm	m²	0.29	21.79	-	8.44	30.23	33.25	30.100
C020106	**Precast concrete slabs 50 mm; natural finish; mortar bed; pointing**								
C020106A	600 mm x 600 mm	m²	0.33	15.86	-	11.84	27.70	30.47	45.380
C020106B	600 mm x 750 mm	m²	0.28	13.43	-	11.57	25.00	27.50	46.440
C020106C	600 mm x 900 mm	m²	0.25	12.21	-	10.45	22.66	24.93	46.650
C020107	**Precast concrete slabs 50 mm; 25 mm sand bed**								
C020107A	spread; levelled; consolidated 600 mm x 600 mm	m²	0.60	29.34	-	8.81	38.15	41.97	33.130
C020107B	75 mm fine clinker; spread; levelled consolidated 600 x 600 mm	m²	0.75	36.63	-	10.59	47.22	51.94	34.880
C020108	**Precast concrete edging to paths; bedding; pointing in cement mortar; haunched with concrete**								
C020108A	50 mm x 150 mm; flat top	m	0.20	9.78	-	9.52	19.30	21.23	20.770
C020108B	50 mm x 150 mm; round top	m	0.20	9.78	-	9.52	19.30	21.23	20.770
C020109	**Concrete (1:3:6) path; slightly cambered; formwork; trowelled smooth**								
C020109A	75 mm	m²	0.45	21.99	-	12.64	34.63	38.09	24.880
C020109B	100 mm	m²	0.55	26.85	-	16.81	43.66	48.03	33.090
C020109C	Extra for marking out concrete in square or crazy pattern	m²	0.15	7.35	-	-	7.35	8.09	-
C020110	**Formwork to edge of path**								
C020110A	75 mm high	m	0.10	2.78	-	0.46	3.24	3.56	0.210
C020110B	100 mm high	m	0.11	3.06	-	0.58	3.64	4.00	0.260
C020110C	150 mm high	m	0.14	3.89	-	0.72	4.61	5.07	0.320
C020110D	75 mm high, left in	m	0.10	2.78	-	2.10	4.88	5.37	0.750
C020110E	100 mm high, left in	m	0.11	3.06	-	2.54	5.60	6.16	0.930
C020110F	150 mm high, left in	m	0.14	3.89	-	2.47	6.36	7.00	1.010

Landscaping

		Unit	Labour Hours	Labour Net	Plant Net	Materials Net	Unit Net	Unit with 10%	CO₂
				£	£	£	£	£	Kg
C02	**PATHS AND WALLS**								
C0201	**PATHS**								
C020111	**Paving; paviors laid to flats, falls, cross falls, slopes not exceeding 15 deg from horizontal**								
C020111A	brick paviors; (PC £1135 per 1000) 75 mm thick; bedding and jointing in cement mortar (1:3); laid stretcher bond	m²	1.39	67.43	-	52.51	119.94	131.93	75.440
C020111B	brick paviors; (PC £1135 per 1000); 75 mm thick; bedding and jointing in cement mortar (1:3); laid in herringbone bond	m²	1.50	72.78	-	52.51	125.29	137.82	75.440
C020111C	Keyblok concrete block paviors; 200 mm x 100 mm; 65 mm thick; red colour; laid on 50 mm screeded bed; compacting and vibrating with hand operated vibrating plate; laid flat in herringbone bond	m²	0.75	36.63	4.43	15.92	56.98	62.68	42.170
C020111D	Keyblok concrete block paviors; 200 mm x 100 mm; 80 mm thick; red colour; laid on 50 mm screeded bed; compacting and vibrating with hand operated vibrating plate; laid flat in herringbone bond	m²	0.85	41.55	4.43	15.92	61.90	68.09	42.170
C020112	**Kerb; brick on flat; brick paviors; (PC £1135 per 1000); bedding and jointing; flush pointing; straight**								
C020112A	102.5 mm wide x 75 mm high	m	0.14	6.86	-	6.29	13.15	14.47	9.410
C020112B	215 mm wide x 75 mm high	m	0.25	12.21	-	12.71	24.92	27.41	19.240
C020113	**Creosoted sawn timber edging, nailed to and including 50 mm x 50 mm creosoted and pointed stakes driven in at 1.50 m centres (one side only measured)**								
C020113A	150 mm x 25 mm or 100 mm x 31 mm	m	0.15	7.35	-	2.79	10.14	11.15	2.070
C0202	**WALLS**								
C020201	**Excavate trench; garden wall foundations; part backfill; part wheel and disposal by skip**								
C020201A	375 mm x 300 mm deep	m	0.56	11.68	4.65	-	16.33	17.96	-
C020201B	375 mm x 450 mm deep	m	0.80	16.68	6.95	-	23.63	25.99	-
C020202	**Concrete (1:3:6) in trench**								
C020202A	375 mm wide x 150 mm thick	m	0.60	12.51	-	8.82	21.33	23.46	18.250
C020203	**Brick wall in common bricks**								
C020203A	half brick thick; pointed both sides; brick-on-edge coping	m²	1.31	63.54	-	22.58	86.12	94.73	54.620
C020203B	one brick thick; pointed both sides; brick-on-edge coping	m²	2.26	109.95	-	47.16	157.11	172.82	113.990
C020203C	half brick thick; joints raked out; rendered in cement mortar both sides	m²	1.96	95.26	-	26.65	121.91	134.10	70.390
C020203D	one brick thick; joints raked out; rendered in cement mortar both sides	m²	2.81	136.80	-	51.23	188.03	206.83	129.760
C020204	**Brick wall in second hand stocks; (PC £780 per 1000); brick-on-edge coping**								
C020204A	one brick thick; pointed both sides	m²	2.26	109.95	-	108.29	218.24	240.06	205.800
C020204B	one brick thick; rendered in cement mortar both sides	m²	2.81	136.80	-	113.18	249.98	274.98	223.510

Small Works 2011		Unit	Labour Hours	Labour Net	Plant Net	Materials Net	Unit Net	Unit with 10%	CO$_2$
				£	£	£	£	£	Kg
C02	**PATHS AND WALLS**								
C0202	**WALLS**								
C020205	**Brick wall in facing bricks; (PC £390 per 1000); brick-on-edge coping**								
C020205A	half brick thick; pointed both sides	m^2	1.31	63.54	-	28.05	91.59	100.75	101.860
C020205B	one brick thick; pointed both sides	m^2	2.26	109.95	-	58.02	167.97	184.77	207.740
C020206	**Double course tile creasing**								
C020206A	brick-on-flat coping; cement mortar fillets	m	0.58	28.12	-	14.20	42.32	46.55	19.410
C020207	**Coping flat; twice throated; precast concrete**								
C020207A	600 mm x 300 mm x 50 mm	m	0.60	29.34	-	11.40	40.74	44.81	8.800
C020208	**Metal coping**								
C020208A	angle iron at ends	each	0.04	1.95	-	3.80	5.75	6.33	3.010
C020209	**Excavate pit; part backfill; part wheel and disposal by skip**								
C020209A	525 mm x 525 mm x 300 mm deep for 225 mm x 225 mm brick pier	each	0.68	14.18	3.46	-	17.64	19.40	-
C020209B	650 mm x 650 mm x 300 mm deep for 338 mm x 338 mm brick pier	each	0.93	19.39	5.50	-	24.89	27.38	-
C020210	**Concrete (1:3:6) in pits**								
C020210A	525 mm x 525 mm x 150 mm	each	0.30	6.25	-	6.42	12.67	13.94	13.270
C020210B	650 mm x 650 mm x 150 mm	each	0.40	8.34	-	9.89	18.23	20.05	20.460
C020211	**Brick piers; 225 mm x 225 mm; pointed o all faces**								
C020211A	common bricks	m	0.90	43.98	-	10.84	54.82	60.30	26.210
C020211B	facing bricks; (PC £390 per 1000)	m	1.06	51.33	-	13.33	64.66	71.13	47.680
C020212	**Pier cap; weathered four ways; precast concrete**								
C020212A	305 mm x 305 mm	each	0.50	24.42	-	5.52	29.94	32.93	3.600
C020214	**Brick piers; 338 mm x 338 mm; pointed on all faces**								
C020214A	common bricks	m	1.51	73.32	-	22.47	95.79	105.37	54.250
C020214B	facing bricks; (PC £390 per 1000)	m	1.76	85.53	-	29.94	115.47	127.02	102.610
C020215	**Pier cap; weathered four ways; precast concrete**								
C020215A	420 mm x 420 mm	each	0.65	31.77	-	10.18	41.95	46.15	5.690
C020216	**Flint stone (PC £215 per m^3) walling built in cement lime mortar and pointed both sides**								
C020216A	225 mm thick	m^2	3.14	152.71	-	85.47	238.18	262.00	73.390
C020217	**Flint stone (PC £215 per m^3) cavity walling comprising 100 mm flint facework to backing of**								
C020217A	half brick inner skin in cement lime mortar and pointed one side	m^2	2.47	119.97	-	69.22	189.19	208.11	100.430
C020218	**Marshalls Superscreen walling; 90 mm precast concrete blocks; type Porto, Virgo or Fargo; bedded in gauged mortar (1:1:6); jointing with flush joints both sides**								
C020218A	290 mm x 290 mm open	m^2	1.11	53.76	-	26.73	80.49	88.54	13.770
C020218B	290 mm x 290 mm solid	m^2	1.11	53.76	-	32.30	86.06	94.67	16.850
C020218C	pilaster; 190 mm x 194 mm x 194 mm; pointed all round	m	1.11	53.76	-	18.37	72.13	79.34	6.960

Landscaping

	Unit	Labour Hours	Labour Net £	Plant Net £	Materials Net £	Unit Net £	Unit with 10% £	CO₂ Kg

		Labour Hours	Labour Net	Plant Net	Materials Net	Unit Net	Unit with 10%	CO₂
	Unit		£	£	£	£	£	Kg
C02 **PATHS AND WALLS**								
C0202 **WALLS**								
C020218 Marshalls Superscreen walling; 90 mm precast concrete blocks; type Porto, Virgo or Fargo; bedded in gauged mortar (1:1:6); jointing with flush joints both sides								
C020218D add for reinforcing pilasters over three courses high; 4 No. - 12 mm dia mild steel reinforcing rods set in concrete foundations (measured separately); placing pilaster blocks over rods; filling centre void with cement mortar packed around rods	m	0.55	26.85	-	6.09	32.94	36.23	19.420
C020218E pilaster cap 194 mm x 194 mm x 51 mm	each	0.28	13.67	-	1.75	15.42	16.96	1.390
C020220 Marshalite reconstructed Yorkstone walling; pitched faced stones and jumpers; 100 mm bedded and pointed in cement mortar (1:3)								
C020220A natural	m²	1.21	58.62	-	44.19	102.81	113.09	28.180
C020220B red or buff	m²	1.21	58.62	-	47.83	106.45	117.10	28.180
C020222 Marshalite reconstructed Yorkstone walling; rustic faced stones and jumpers; 100 mm bedded and pointed in cement mortar (1:3)								
C020222A natural	m²	1.21	58.62	-	44.19	102.81	113.09	28.180
C020222B red or buff	m²	1.21	58.62	-	47.83	106.45	117.10	28.180
C020224 Marshalite reconstructed Yorkstone coping; Saxon textured split faced stone; 600 mm x 1:3:6 mm x 50 mm bedded and pointed in cement mortar (1:3)								
C020224A natural	m	2.00	97.49	-	10.09	107.58	118.34	2.270
C020224B red or buff	m	2.00	97.49	-	7.38	104.87	115.36	2.270
C020226 Marshalite reconstructed Yorkstone attached pier; pitched faced stone and jumpers; 300 mm x 300 mm; bedded and pointed in cement mortar (1:3)								
C020226A natural	m	1.51	73.32	-	32.76	106.08	116.69	13.680
C020226B red or buff	m	1.51	73.32	-	35.67	108.99	119.89	13.680
C020228 Marshalite reconstructed Yorkstone attached pier; pitched faced stone and jumpers; 400 mm x 400 mm; bedded and pointed in cement mortar (1:3)								
C020228A natural	m	2.01	97.74	-	49.07	146.81	161.49	20.310
C020228B red or buff	m	2.01	97.74	-	53.44	151.18	166.30	20.310
C020230 Marshalite reconstructed Yorkstone pillar cap; pitched faced stone; 350 mm x 350 mm x 50 mm; bedded and pointed in cement mortar (1:3)								
C020230A natural	each	0.50	24.42	-	9.42	33.84	37.22	2.170
C020230B red or buff	each	0.50	24.42	-	10.49	34.91	38.40	2.170
C020232 Marshalite reconstructed Yorkstone pillar cap; pitched faced stone; 450 mm x 450 mm x 50 mm; bedded and pointed in cement mortar (1:3)								
C020232A natural	each	0.75	36.63	-	10.39	47.02	51.72	3.180
C020232B red or buff	each	0.75	36.63	-	11.13	47.76	52.54	4.070

Small Works 2011		Unit	Labour Hours	Labour Net £	Plant Net £	Materials Net £	Unit Net £	Unit with 10% £	CO₂ Kg

C03 FENCING AND GATES

C0301 PANEL FENCING

C030101 Lapped panels; 1800 mm wide; natural waney edged timber; overlapped; weathered capping strip; waney edged timber sandwiched between five pairs planed battens; timber posts; treated; including excavating holes, setting posts, backfilling with concrete; height

C030101A	900 mm	m	0.57	27.58	-	41.31	68.89	75.78	69.170
C030101B	1200 mm	m	0.64	31.04	-	43.46	74.50	81.95	77.520
C030101C	1500 mm	m	0.71	34.44	-	46.48	80.92	89.01	86.390
C030101D	1800 mm	m	0.78	37.85	-	54.79	92.64	101.90	98.500

C030102 Lapped panels; 1800 mm wide; natural waney edged timber; overlapped; weathered capping strip; waney edged timber sandwiched between five pairs planed battens treated; concrete gravel board; H section posts; including excavating holes, setting posts, backfilling; height

C030102A	1350 mm	m	0.50	24.42	-	66.67	91.09	100.20	86.990
C030102B	1650 mm	m	0.53	25.88	-	60.27	86.15	94.77	96.540
C030102C	1950 mm	m	0.57	27.58	-	62.70	90.28	99.31	106.100

C030105 Featherboard panels; 1800 mm wide; three horizontal rails; weathered; clad with 100 mm featherboard pales; timber posts; treated; chamfered post cap; timber gravel board including excavating, setting post and backfilling with concrete; height

C030105B	1200 mm	m	0.68	33.23	-	53.89	87.12	95.83	78.600
C030105C	1500 mm	m	0.76	36.88	-	58.15	95.03	104.53	87.460
C030105D	1800 mm	m	0.83	40.33	-	66.77	107.10	117.81	96.330

C030106 Featherboard panels; 1800 mm wide; three horizontal rails; weathered; clad with 100 mm featherboard pales; treated concrete gravel board; concrete H section posts; including excavating, setting posts and backfilling with concrete; height

C030106B	1200 mm	m	0.52	25.15	-	72.97	98.12	107.93	83.860
C030106C	1500 mm	m	0.56	27.10	-	67.80	94.90	104.39	93.420
C030106D	1800 mm	m	0.60	29.09	-	75.88	104.97	115.47	102.970

C030107 Trellis panels; square top 1800 mm wide 38 mm x 19 mm softwood framing; weathered capping; 19 mm x 19 mm softwood horizontal and vertical infill at 150 mm centres; timber posts; chamfered post cap; timber gravel board; treated; height

| C030107A | 1350 mm | m | 0.41 | 20.04 | - | 49.90 | 69.94 | 76.93 | 74.320 |
| C030107B | 1650 mm | m | 0.55 | 26.85 | - | 61.93 | 88.78 | 97.66 | 81.210 |

Landscaping

		Unit	Labour Hours	Labour Net	Plant Net	Materials Net	Unit Net	Unit with 10%	CO2
				£	£	£	£	£	Kg
C03	**FENCING AND GATES**								
C0301	**PANEL FENCING**								
C030109	**Trellis panels; square top; 1800 mm wide; 38 mm x 19 mm softwood framing; weathered capping; 19 mm x 19 mm softwood horizontal and vertical infill at 150 mm centres; treated; concrete gravel board; concrete H section posts; height**								
C030109A	1350 mm	m	0.50	24.18	-	59.56	83.74	92.11	80.270
C030109B	1650 mm	m	0.64	31.04	-	70.17	101.21	111.33	87.320
C0303	**GATES**								
C030301	**Lapped panel gate; 900 mm wide; galvanised ring latch; heavy hinges; hanging**								
C030301A	fence height 900 mm; gate height 850 mm	each	0.13	6.13	-	87.88	94.01	103.41	21.360
C030301B	fence height 1200 mm; gate height 1150 mm	each	0.25	12.21	-	90.36	102.57	112.83	25.540
C030301C	fence height 1500 mm; gate height 1450 mm	each	0.38	18.34	-	92.84	111.18	122.30	29.710
C030301D	fence height 1800 mm; gate height 1750 mm	each	0.48	23.21	-	95.31	118.52	130.37	33.880
C030303	**Featherboard panel gate; 1000 mm wide; galvanised ring latch; heavy hinges; hanging**								
C030303A	fence height 1200 mm; gate height 1150 mm	each	0.38	18.34	-	95.31	113.65	125.02	27.310
C030303B	fence height 1500 mm; gate height 1450 mm	each	0.50	24.42	-	97.79	122.21	134.43	31.950
C030303C	fence height 1800 mm; gate height 1750 mm	each	0.60	29.34	-	100.28	129.62	142.58	36.590
C030305	**Trellis panel gate; square top; 900 mm wide; galvanised fittings; hanging**								
C030305A	1750 mm high	each	0.48	23.21	-	90.36	113.57	124.93	27.800
C0305	**WOOD PRESERVATIVES**								
C030501	**One coat timber preservative on wrought timber**								
C030501A	general surfaces not exceeding 150 mm girth	m	0.04	1.11	-	0.05	1.16	1.28	0.070
C030501B	150 - 300 mm girth	m	0.09	2.50	-	0.12	2.62	2.88	0.170
C030501C	over 300 mm girth	m²	0.19	5.28	-	0.37	5.65	6.22	0.530
C030502	**One coat timber preservative on sawn timber**								
C030502A	general surfaces not exceeding 150 mm girth	m	0.05	1.39	-	0.14	1.53	1.68	0.210
C030502B	150 - 300 mm girth	m	0.10	2.78	-	0.29	3.07	3.38	0.410
C030502C	over 300 mm girth	m²	0.20	5.56	-	0.96	6.52	7.17	1.370
C030503	**One coat Solignum preservative on wrought timber**								
C030503A	general surfaces not exceeding 150 mm girth	m	0.04	1.11	-	0.07	1.18	1.30	0.040
C030503B	150 - 300 mm girth	m	0.07	1.95	-	0.14	2.09	2.30	0.080
C030503C	over 300 mm girth	m²	0.18	5.00	-	0.40	5.40	5.94	0.230
C030504	**One coat Solignum preservative on sawn timber**								
C030504A	general surfaces not exceeding 150 mm girth	m	0.05	1.39	-	0.11	1.50	1.65	0.060
C030504B	150 - 300 mm girth	m	0.08	2.22	-	0.18	2.40	2.64	0.110
C030504C	over 300 mm girth	m²	0.19	5.28	-	0.62	5.90	6.49	0.360
C030505	**One coat Cuprinol preservative on wrought timber**								
C030505A	general surfaces not exceeding 150 mm girth	m	0.04	1.11	-	0.22	1.33	1.46	0.060

Small Works 2011		Unit	Labour Hours	Labour Net	Plant Net	Materials Net	Unit Net	Unit with 10%	CO₂
				£	£	£	£	£	Kg
C03	**FENCING AND GATES**								
C0305	**WOOD PRESERVATIVES**								
C030505	**One coat Cuprinol preservative on wrought timber**								
C030505B	150 - 300 mm girth	m	0.08	2.22	-	0.37	2.59	2.85	0.110
C030505C	over 300 mm girth	m²	0.19	5.28	-	1.25	6.53	7.18	0.360
C030506	**One coat Cuprinol preservative on sawn timber**								
C030506A	general surfaces not exceeding 150 mm girth	m	0.05	1.39	-	0.37	1.76	1.94	0.110
C030506B	150 - 300 mm girth	m	0.09	2.50	-	0.74	3.24	3.56	0.210
C030506C	over 300 mm girth	m²	0.20	5.56	-	2.07	7.63	8.39	0.590

Landscaping

		Unit	Labour Hours	Labour Net £	Plant Net £	Materials Net £	Unit Net £	Unit with 10% £	CO₂ Kg

C04	**GENERAL FENCING**								
C0401	**POST AND WIRE FENCING**								
C040101	**Fencing of five 4 mm line wires and 125 mm x 125 mm to 75 mm x 75 mm x 1670 mm reinforced concrete tapered posts at 3000 mm centres set 600 mm deep into ground in concrete**								
C040101A	height; 1000 mm	m	0.28	13.67	-	4.42	18.09	19.90	2.610
C040101B	Extra for 125 mm x 125 mm end straining posts with 100 mm x 75 mm strut set in concrete	each	0.44	21.50	-	40.23	61.73	67.90	44.250
C040101C	Extra for corner straining posts with two struts set in concrete	each	0.66	32.25	-	45.81	78.06	85.87	42.890
C040102	**Fencing of seven 4 mm line wires and 125 mm x 125 mm to 75 mm x 2070 mm reinforced concrete tapered posts at centres set 600 mm deep into ground**								
C040102A	height; 1400 mm	m	0.31	14.84	-	9.21	24.05	26.46	12.490
C040102B	Extra for 125 mm x 125 mm end straining posts with 100 mm x 75 mm strut set in concrete	each	0.22	10.75	-	40.23	50.98	56.08	44.250
C040102C	Extra for corner straining posts with two struts set in concrete	each	0.44	21.50	-	45.81	67.31	74.04	42.890
C0402	**GALVANISED CHAIN-LINK FENCING**								
C040201	**Fencing of 50 mm mesh x 3 mm chain link two 3 mm line wires and 40 mm x 40 mm x 1500 mm steel angle posts at 3000 mm centres set 600 mm deep into ground in concrete**								
C040201A	height; 900 mm	m	0.32	15.62	-	6.59	22.21	24.43	13.880
C040201B	Extra for 50 mm x 50 mm angle end straining posts with 40 mm x 40 mm steel angle strut, each bent over at bottom and set in concrete	each	0.49	23.94	-	19.16	43.10	47.41	52.310
C040201C	Extra for corner straining posts with two struts set in concrete	each	0.74	35.90	-	21.46	57.36	63.10	60.300
C040202	**Fencing of 50 mm mesh x 3 mm chain link three 3.55 mm line wires and 45 mm x 45 mm x 2000 mm steel angle posts at 3000 mm centres set 600 mm deep into ground in concrete**								
C040202A	height; 1400 mm	m	0.38	18.34	-	8.38	26.72	29.39	16.320
C040202B	Extra for 50 mm x 50 mm angle end straining posts with 45 mm x 45 mm steel angle strut, each bent over at bottom and set in concrete	each	0.58	28.12	-	17.27	45.39	49.93	52.140
C040202C	Extra for corner straining posts with two struts set in concrete	each	0.86	42.03	-	22.32	64.35	70.79	68.300
C040203	**Fencing of 50 mm mesh x 3 mm chain link, three 3.55 mm line wires and 45 mm x 45 mm x 2600 mm steel angle posts at 3000 mm centres set 760 mm deep into ground in concrete**								
C040203A	height; 1800 mm	m	0.48	23.45	-	9.70	33.15	36.47	18.320
C040203B	Extra for 60 mm x 60 mm angle end straining posts with 45 mm x 45 mm steel angle strut, each bent over at bottom and set in concrete	each	0.74	36.15	-	21.52	57.67	63.44	65.630
C040203C	Extra for corner straining posts with two struts set in concrete	each	1.11	54.00	-	22.23	76.23	83.85	71.130

Small Works 2011		Unit	Labour Hours	Labour Net	Plant Net	Materials Net	Unit Net	Unit with 10%	CO₂
				£	£	£	£	£	Kg
C04	**GENERAL FENCING**								
C0402	**GALVANISED CHAIN-LINK FENCING**								
C040204	**Fencing of 50 mm mesh x 3 mm chain link, two 3 mm line wires and 120 mm x 120 mm to 75 mm x 75 mm x 1600 mm reinforced concrete tapered posts at 3000 mm centres set 600 mm deep into ground in concrete**								
C040204A	height; 900 mm	m	0.30	14.64	-	21.63	36.27	39.90	41.730
C040204B	Extra for 125 mm x 125 mm end straining posts with 100 mm x 75 mm strut set in concrete	each	0.60	29.34	-	54.07	83.41	91.75	88.630
C040204C	Extra for corner, straining posts with two struts set in concrete	each	0.90	43.98	-	78.32	122.30	134.53	129.060
C040205	**Fencing of 50 mm mesh x 3 mm chain link, three 3.55 mm line wires and 125 mm x 125 mm to 75 x 75 mm x 2070 mm reinforced concrete tapered posts at 3000 mm centres set 600 mm deep into ground in concrete**								
C040205A	height; 1400 mm	m	0.38	18.34	-	23.23	41.57	45.73	41.690
C040205B	Extra for 125 mm x 125 mm end straining posts with 100 mm x 75 mm strut set in concrete	each	0.71	34.44	-	60.43	94.87	104.36	92.230
C040205C	Extra for corner, straining posts with two struts set in concrete	each	1.07	52.06	-	87.61	139.67	153.64	133.930
C040206	**Fencing of 50 mm mesh x 3 mm chain link, three 3.55 mm line wires and 125 mm x 125 mm to 75 mm x 75 mm x 2630 mm reinforced concrete tapered posts at 3000 mm centres set 760 mm deep into ground in concrete**								
C040206A	height; 1800 mm	m	0.47	22.96	-	14.48	37.44	41.18	13.690
C040206B	Extra for 125 mm x 125 mm end straining posts with 100 mm x 75 mm strut set in concrete	each	0.88	43.01	-	59.52	102.53	112.78	69.360
C040206C	Extra for corner straining posts with two struts set in concrete	each	1.33	64.51	-	75.10	139.61	153.57	76.090
C040207	**Security fencing of 50 mm mesh x 3 mm chain link, three 3.55 mm line wires, three rows of barbed wire and 125 mm x 125 mm to 75 mm x 75 mm x 3000 mm reinforced concrete tapered posts, with cranked top, at 3000 mm centres set 760 mm deep into ground in concrete**								
C040207A	height; 1820 mm	m	0.48	23.45	-	14.97	38.42	42.26	13.960
C040207B	Extra for 125 mm x 125 mm end straining posts with 100 mm x 75 mm strut set in concrete	each	0.88	43.01	-	59.52	102.53	112.78	69.360
C040207C	Extra for corner straining posts with two struts set in concrete	each	1.33	64.51	-	68.49	133.00	146.30	91.750
C0404	**CLEFT-PALE FENCING**								
C040401	**Fencing of chestnut pales 75 mm apart, two lines of binding wire and 63 mm approximate dia x 1670 mm chestnut posts at 2280 mm centres driven 600 mm into ground**								
C040401A	height; 1060 mm	m	0.32	15.62	-	6.66	22.28	24.51	2.130
C040401B	Extra for 75 mm to 85 mm approximate dia straining posts with strut spiked to post	each	0.50	24.42	-	4.08	28.50	31.35	4.730
C040401C	Extra for corner straining posts with two struts spiked to post	each	0.75	36.63	-	6.06	42.69	46.96	6.970

Landscaping

	Unit	Labour Hours	Labour Net	Plant Net	Materials Net	Unit Net	Unit with 10%	CO₂
			£	£	£	£	£	Kg
C04	**GENERAL FENCING**							
C0406	**GALVANISED STEEL PALISADE FENCING**							
C040601	Fencing of triple pointed corrugated pales (1.9 Kg/m) fixed with 6 mm Avelok rivets to two 50 mm x 40 mm x 6 mm horizontal angle rails, bottom rail fitted with two support feet per bay set into ground in concrete and with 102 mm x 44 mm RSJ posts at 2750 mm centres set 760 mm deep into concrete							
C040601A	height; 1800 mm	m	0.67	32.50	-	31.56	64.06	70.47	49.200
C040601B	height; 2400 mm	m	0.75	36.63	-	40.13	76.76	84.44	59.850
C040602	Fencing of triple pointed corrugated pales (2.42 Kg/m) fixed with 8 mm Avelok rivets to two 50 mm x 40 mm x 6 mm horizontal angle rails, bottom rail fitted with two support feet per bay set into ground in concrete and with 102 mm x 44 mm RSJ posts at 2750 mm centres set 760 mm deep into ground in concrete							
C040602A	height; 1800 mm	m	0.75	36.63	-	37.96	74.59	82.05	59.070
C040602B	height; 2400 mm	m	0.88	42.76	-	44.95	87.71	96.48	68.030
C0408	**TREATED SOFTWOOD CLOSE-BOARDED FENCING**							
C040801	Fencing of 14 mm to 7 mm x 100 mm feather edged boarding, two 75 mm x 75 mm arris rails, 100 mm x 100 mm x 1600 mm sawn posts at 3000 mm centres set 600 mm deep into ground in concrete, 32 mm x 200 mm gravel board with 50 mm x 50 mm centre stumps driven 600 mm into ground, 25 mm x 65 mm counter rail and 38 mm x 65 mm weather capping							
C040801A	height; 1000 mm	m	0.73	35.42	-	21.33	56.75	62.43	69.760
C040802	Fencing of 14 mm to 7 mm x 100 mm feather edged boarding, three 75 mm x 75 mm arris rails, 100 mm x 125 mm x 2350 mm sawn posts at 3000 mm centres set 760 mm deep into ground in concrete, 32 mm x 200 mm gravel board with 50 mm x 50 mm centre stumps driven 600 mm into ground, 25 mm x 65 mm counter rail and 38 mm x 65 mm weather capping							
C040802A	height; 1600 mm	m	1.03	50.06	-	28.36	78.42	86.26	103.350
C040803	Fencing of 1830 mm x 910 mm interwoven panels, of 6 mm x 75 mm woven slats, 19 mm x 38 mm framing and weathered capping, nailed between 75 mm x 75 mm x 1520 mm capped posts at 1900 mm centres set 600 mm deep into ground in concrete							
C040803A	height; 910 mm	m	0.45	21.99	-	18.40	40.39	44.43	29.980

Small Works 2011		Unit	Labour Hours	Labour Net £	Plant Net £	Materials Net £	Unit Net £	Unit with 10% £	CO$_2$ Kg
C04	**GENERAL FENCING**								
C0408	**TREATED SOFTWOOD CLOSE-BOARDED FENCING**								
C040804	**Fencing of 1830 mm x 1830 mm interwoven panels, of 6 mm x 75 mm woven slats, 19 mm x 38 mm framing and weathered capping, nailed between 75 mm x 75 mm x 2590 mm capped posts at 1900 mm centres set 760 mm deep into ground in concrete**								
C040804A	height; 1830 mm	m	0.60	29.34	-	20.88	50.22	55.24	42.750
C040805	**Fencing of 1830 mm x 910 mm waney edged panels, of 5 mm x 100 mm to 125 mm waney edged slats, 16 mm x 38 mm framing and weathered capping, nailed between 75 mm x 75 mm x 1520 mm capped posts at 1900 mm centres set 600 mm into ground set in concrete**								
C040805A	height; 910 mm	m	0.45	21.99	-	17.60	39.59	43.55	29.980
C040806	**Fencing of 1830 mm x 1830 mm waney edge panels, of 5 mm x 100 mm to 125 mm waney edged slats, 16 mm x 38 mm framing and weathered capping, nailed between 75 mm x 75 mm x 2590 mm capped posts at 1900 mm centres set 760 mm into ground set in concrete**								
C040806A	height; 1830 mm	m	0.60	29.34	-	20.73	50.07	55.08	42.750
C0409	**GATES**								
C040901	**42 mm (outside dia) primed tubular steel single leaf gates filled in with chain link and with two 150 mm x 150 mm reinforced concrete gate posts each with strut and set of fittings including setting posts and struts in concrete and hanging gates**								
C040901A	1000 mm x 900 mm	each	2.39	116.03	-	195.69	311.72	342.89	293.030
C040901B	1000 mm x 1400 mm	each	2.51	122.16	-	227.75	349.91	384.90	369.660
C040901C	1000 mm x 1800 mm	each	2.64	128.24	-	263.85	392.09	431.30	437.800
C040902	**48 mm (outside dia) primed tubular steel single leaf gates filled in with chain link and with two 150 mm x 150 mm reinforced concrete gate posts each with strut and set of fittings including setting posts and struts in concrete and hanging gates**								
C040902A	3000 mm x 900 mm	pair	3.77	183.22	-	367.11	550.33	605.36	544.340
C040902B	3000 mm x 1400 mm	pair	4.02	195.43	-	448.55	643.98	708.38	735.030
C040903	**Galvanised steel single leaf gates, to match corrugated pale (1.9 Kg/m) fencing, with two 127 mm x 76 mm RSJ gate posts including setting posts in concrete and hanging gates**								
C040903A	1000 mm x 1800 mm	each	3.77	183.22	-	278.50	461.72	507.89	297.480
C040903B	1000 mm x 2400 mm	each	4.14	201.56	-	335.26	536.82	590.50	364.470

Landscaping

		Unit	Labour Hours	Labour Net	Plant Net	Materials Net	Unit Net	Unit with 10%	CO$_2$
				£	£	£	£	£	Kg
C04	**GENERAL FENCING**								
C0409	**GATES**								
C040904	**Galvanised steel double leaf gates, to match corrugated pale (1.9 Kg/m) fencing, with two 125 mm x 125 mm SHS gate posts including setting posts in concrete and hanging gates**								
C040904A	3000 mm x 1800 mm	pair	9.04	439.75	-	717.13	1,156.88	1,272.57	592.820
C040905	**Treated sawn softwood close-boarded gates, to match close-boarded fencing, complete with all necessary hanging and closing fittings including hanging gates**								
C040905A	3000 mm x 1800 mm	each	2.76	134.37	-	234.53	368.90	405.79	197.200

HUTCHINS'
MAJOR WORKS

Existing Site, Buildings, Services

CITADEL OFFICE, MOOR HOUSE, LONDON

MAKING YOUR BUSINESS OUR PRIORITY

In today's constantly shifting global business climate our customers' operations are constantly expanding and diversifying into new services and markets. Combine this with the ever growing complexity of projects and the application of expert project management becomes vital.

It's not only the quality of personnel that is vital for delivering an excellent service, it is just as important that they're supported by advanced systems, reliable and accurate data and innovative management techniques.

Mott MacDonald fully understands the ever-changing commercial environment of our clients and develops and delivers solutions that best meet the needs of their business and culture.

To find out more please contact Charles Blane:
T   +44 (0)20 7593 9700
E   charles.blane@mottmac.com

Mott MacDonald

www.mottmac.com

Major Works 2011		Unit	Labour Hours	Labour Net	Plant Net	Materials Net	Unit Net	Unit with 10%	CO₂
				£	£	£	£	£	Kg
C11	**C11: GROUND INVESTIGATION**								
C1101	**Machine excavation of trial holes**								
C110102	**Excavate trial holes; backfill with excavated material, compacted in 250 mm layers; maximum depth not exceeding**								
C110102A	0.25 m	m³	0.30	3.81	9.78	-	13.59	14.95	8.777
C110102B	1.00 m	m³	0.30	3.81	8.92	-	12.73	14.00	8.037
C110102C	2.00 m	m³	0.30	3.81	9.49	-	13.30	14.63	8.589
C110102D	4.00 m	m³	0.35	4.44	10.49	-	14.93	16.42	9.501
C110102E	6.00 m	m³	0.35	4.44	11.95	-	16.39	18.03	10.814
C1105	**Hand excavation of trial holes**								
C110511	**Excavate trial holes; backfill with excavated material, compacted in 250 mm layers; maximum depth not exceeding**								
C110511A	0.25 m	m³	3.15	40.00	0.51	-	40.51	44.56	0.643
C110511B	1.00 m	m³	3.30	41.91	0.51	-	42.42	46.66	0.643
C110511C	2.00 m	m³	3.75	47.63	0.51	-	48.14	52.95	0.643
C110511D	4.00 m	m³	4.80	60.96	0.60	-	61.56	67.72	0.750
C110511E	6.00 m	m³	5.95	75.56	0.60	-	76.16	83.78	0.750
C1111	**Extra over trial hole excavation and filling for removal of excavated material from site, filling with imported materials; by machine**								
C111104	**Filling with**								
C111104A	sand	m³	-	-	20.83	23.59	44.42	48.86	17.350
C111104B	hardcore	m³	-	-	20.83	24.67	45.50	50.05	20.150
C111104C	hoggin	m³	-	-	20.83	24.15	44.98	49.48	17.910
C1112	**Extra over trial hole excavation and filling for removal of excavated material from site and filling with imported materials; by hand**								
C111213	**Filling with**								
C111213A	sand	m³	1.25	15.88	22.37	23.59	61.84	68.02	14.000
C111213B	hardcore	m³	1.25	15.88	22.37	24.67	62.92	69.21	16.800
C111213C	hoggin	m³	1.25	15.88	22.37	24.15	62.40	68.64	14.560

Existing Site, Buildings, Services

		Unit	Labour Hours	Labour Net £	Plant Net £	Materials Net £	Unit Net £	Unit with 10% £	CO₂ Kg
C20	**C20: DEMOLITION**								
C2003	**Demolition of concrete structural elements**								
C200343	**Reinforced concrete walls and attached columns**								
C200343A	not exceeding 150 mm thick	m³	12.00	152.40	101.76	-	254.16	279.58	353.760
C200343B	150 - 300 mm thick	m³	14.00	177.80	118.72	-	296.52	326.17	412.720
C200343C	over 300 mm thick	m³	18.00	228.60	152.64	-	381.24	419.36	530.640
C200344	**Reinforced concrete ground slabs**								
C200344A	not exceeding 150 mm thick	m³	6.00	76.20	50.88	-	127.08	139.79	176.880
C200344B	150 - 300 mm thick	m³	8.00	101.60	67.84	-	169.44	186.38	235.840
C200344C	over 300 mm thick	m³	10.00	127.00	84.80	-	211.80	232.98	294.800
C200345	**Reinforced concrete suspended slab and attached beams**								
C200345A	not exceeding 150 mm thick	m³	10.00	127.00	84.80	-	211.80	232.98	294.800
C200345B	150 - 300 mm thick	m³	16.00	203.20	135.68	-	338.88	372.77	471.680
C200345C	over 300 mm thick	m³	19.00	241.30	161.12	-	402.42	442.66	560.120
C200346	**Reinforced concrete isolated beams**								
C200346A	not exceeding 0.1 m² sectional area	m³	12.00	152.40	101.76	-	254.16	279.58	353.760
C200346B	0.1 - 0.25 m² sectional area	m³	14.00	177.80	118.72	-	296.52	326.17	412.720
C200346C	over 0.25 m² sectional area	m³	19.00	241.30	161.12	-	402.42	442.66	560.120
C200347	**Reinforced concrete isolated columns**								
C200347A	not exceeding 0.1 m² sectional area	m³	10.00	127.00	84.80	-	211.80	232.98	294.800
C200347B	0.1 - 0.25 m² sectional area	m³	13.00	165.10	73.84	-	238.94	262.83	348.400
C200347C	over 0.25 m² sectional area	m³	18.00	228.60	102.24	-	330.84	363.92	482.400
C2005	**Demolition of masonry structural elements**								
C200548	**Brick walls**								
C200548A	half brick thick	m²	0.80	10.16	0.94	-	11.10	12.21	0.344
C200548B	one brick thick	m²	1.40	17.78	1.65	-	19.43	21.37	0.602
C200548C	one and a half brick thick	m²	2.10	26.67	2.48	-	29.15	32.07	0.903
C200548D	two brick thick	m²	2.70	34.29	3.19	-	37.48	41.23	1.161
C200549	**Block walls**								
C200549A	50 mm thick	m²	0.50	6.35	-	-	6.35	6.99	-
C200549B	75 mm thick	m²	0.55	6.99	-	-	6.99	7.69	-
C200549C	100 mm thick	m²	0.60	7.62	0.71	-	8.33	9.16	0.258
C200549D	125 mm thick	m²	0.65	8.25	0.78	-	9.03	9.93	0.284
C200549E	150 mm thick	m²	0.70	8.89	0.83	-	9.72	10.69	0.301
C200549F	200 mm thick	m²	0.80	10.16	0.94	-	11.10	12.21	0.344
C200549G	225 mm thick	m²	1.10	13.97	1.30	-	15.27	16.80	0.473
C200553	**Attached chimney breasts**								
C200553A	half brick common brickwork	m²	0.90	11.43	1.06	-	12.49	13.74	0.387
C200553B	one brick common brickwork	m²	1.60	20.32	1.89	-	22.21	24.43	0.688
C200553C	one and a half brick common brickwork	m²	2.30	29.21	2.71	-	31.92	35.11	0.989
C200553D	two brick common brickwork	m²	2.80	35.56	3.30	-	38.86	42.75	1.204
C200553E	100 mm blockwork	m²	0.70	8.89	0.83	-	9.72	10.69	0.301
C200553F	200 mm blockwork	m²	0.90	11.43	1.06	-	12.49	13.74	0.387
C200553G	300 mm blockwork	m²	1.40	17.78	1.65	-	19.43	21.37	0.602
C200553H	400 mm blockwork	m²	1.60	20.32	1.89	-	22.21	24.43	0.688
C200554	**Isolated chimney stacks**								
C200554A	common brickwork; within building	m³	9.60	121.92	5.66	-	127.58	140.34	2.064
C200554B	common brickwork; above roof slope	m³	8.40	106.68	4.96	-	111.64	122.80	1.806
C200554C	facing brickwork; above roof slope	m³	8.70	110.49	5.19	-	115.68	127.25	1.892
C200554D	rendered blockwork; within building	m³	7.50	95.25	8.97	-	104.22	114.64	3.268

Major Works 2011		Unit	Labour Hours	Labour Net	Plant Net	Materials Net	Unit Net	Unit with 10%	CO₂
				£	£	£	£	£	Kg
C20	**C20: DEMOLITION**								
C2005	**Demolition of masonry structural elements**								
C200554	**Isolated chimney stacks**								
C200554E	rendered blockwork; above roof slope	m^3	6.30	80.01	7.55	–	87.56	96.32	2.752
C2007	**Removal of roofs, ceilings and timber suspended floors**								
C200750	**Pitched roofs; placing debris in rubbish skips**								
C200750A	tiles or slates on battens and underfelt; 50 x 150 mm softwood rafters at 400 mm centres; 50 x 200 mm softwood purlin at midspan; 50 x 100 mm softwood wall plate, binders, hangers and collars	m^2	0.37	4.70	–	–	4.70	5.17	–
C200750B	50 x 100 mm ceiling joists; fibreglass insulation laid between joists; plasterboard ceiling	m^2	0.15	1.90	–	–	1.90	2.09	–
C200751	**Flat roofs; placing debris in rubbish skips**								
C200751A	three layer built up felt roofing on ply or chipboard decking; 50 x 200 mm ceiling joists at 400 mm centres with fibreglass laid between; 50 x 100 mm wall plate; plasterboard ceiling	m^2	0.45	5.71	–	–	5.71	6.28	–
C200752	**Timber suspended floors; placing debris in rubbish skips**								
C200752A	softwood boarding on 50 x 200 mm softwood floor joists at 400 mm centres; plasterboard ceiling	m^2	0.30	3.81	–	–	3.81	4.19	–
C200752B	chipboard flooring on 50 x 150 mm softwood floor joists at 400 mm centres; plasterboard ceiling	m^2	0.25	3.17	–	–	3.17	3.49	–
C2010	**Removal of internal partitions**								
C201001	**Take down stud partitions, faced both sides; place debris in rubbish skip**								
C201001A	lath and plaster finish	m^2	0.65	8.25	2.24	–	10.49	11.54	–
C201001B	plasterboard finish	m^2	0.60	7.62	2.24	–	9.86	10.85	–
C201001C	softwood board finish	m^2	0.55	6.99	1.68	–	8.67	9.54	–
C2035	**Taking down, cleaning and setting aside materials for re-use**								
C203571	**Facing brickwork; placing debris in rubbish skips**								
C203571A	half brick wall	m^2	1.20	15.24	–	–	15.24	16.76	–
C203571B	one brick wall	m^2	2.10	26.67	–	–	26.67	29.34	–
C203571C	one and a half brick wall	m^2	3.15	40.00	–	–	40.00	44.00	–
C203581	**Roof coverings; placing debris in rubbish skips**								
C203581A	roof slating	m^2	0.25	3.17	–	–	3.17	3.49	–
C203581B	roof tiling	m^2	0.20	2.54	–	–	2.54	2.79	–
C2095	**Temporary roofs**								
C209599	**Temporary roofs; corrugated sheeting laid to slope on and including 50 x 150 mm softwood framing**								
C209599A	fibre cement sheets	m^2	0.48	8.15	–	34.77	42.92	47.21	73.748
C209599B	galvanised sheets	m^2	0.48	8.15	–	30.86	39.01	42.91	59.910
C209599C	translucent PVC-u sheets	m^2	0.48	8.15	–	28.29	36.44	40.08	15.062
C209599D	extra for 50 x 150 mm softwood posts	m^2	0.35	5.94	–	0.49	6.43	7.07	1.949

Existing Site, Buildings, Services

Major Works 2011		Unit	Labour Hours	Labour Net	Plant Net	Materials Net	Unit Net	Unit with 10%	CO₂
				£	£	£	£	£	Kg
C20	**C20: DEMOLITION**								
C2097	**Temporary screens**								
C209792	**Temporary dustproof screens; 1200 gauge polythene sheeting on 50 x 100 mm sawn softwood framing; joints sealed with self adhesive PVC-u tape**								
C209792A	vertical screens	m²	0.35	5.94	-	1.99	7.93	8.72	9.172
C209792B	extra for sealing perimeters with self adhesive PVC-u tape	m²	0.05	0.85	-	0.04	0.89	0.98	0.443
C209792C	extra for access door	m²	1.50	25.47	-	4.49	29.96	32.96	22.297

Major Works 2011		Unit	Labour Hours	Labour Net	Plant Net	Materials Net	Unit Net	Unit with 10%	CO_2
				£	£	£	£	£	Kg
C41	**C41: REPAIRING, RENOVATING, CONSERVING MASONRY**								
C4131	**Cutting out decayed and defective work and replacing with new**								
C413111	**Cut out damaged or decayed common brickwork; cut, tooth and bond new commons to existing in gauged mortar (1:1:6); half brick thick**								
C413111A	stretcher bond; single brick	Nr	0.25	7.45	-	0.37	7.82	8.60	0.889
C413111B	stretcher bond; in areas not exceeding 0.50 m²	Nr	1.25	37.22	-	10.20	47.42	52.16	24.611
C413111C	stretcher bond; in areas 0.50 - 1.00 m²	Nr	2.41	71.47	-	20.40	91.87	101.06	49.223
C413111D	stretcher bond; crack repair average 225 mm wide	m	1.15	34.25	-	4.15	38.40	42.24	10.030
C413111E	stretcher bond; crack repair average 450 mm wide	m	1.66	49.15	-	8.30	57.45	63.20	20.061
C413111F	English or Flemish bond (snapped headers); single brick	Nr	0.23	6.86	-	0.37	7.23	7.95	0.889
C413111G	English or Flemish bond (snapped headers); in areas not exceeding 0.50 m²	Nr	1.46	43.18	-	12.44	55.62	61.18	30.030
C413111H	English or Flemish bond (snapped headers); in areas 0.50 - 1.00 m²	Nr	2.66	78.92	-	25.62	104.54	114.99	61.839
C413111I	English or Flemish bond (snapped headers); crack repair average 225 m wide	m	1.36	40.22	-	6.51	46.73	51.40	15.718
C413111J	English or Flemish bond (snapped headers); crack repair average 450 m wide	m	1.86	55.09	-	11.22	66.31	72.94	27.093
C413113	**Cut out damaged or decayed facing brickwork; cut, tooth and bond new facings to existing in gauged mortar (1:1:6); half brick thick**								
C413113A	stretcher bond; single brick	Nr	0.30	8.93	-	0.41	9.34	10.27	1.729
C413113B	stretcher bond; in areas not exceeding 0.50 m²	Nr	1.66	49.15	-	11.56	60.71	66.78	50.644
C413113C	stretcher bond; in areas 0.50 - 1.00 m²	Nr	2.91	86.37	-	23.13	109.50	120.45	101.288
C413113D	stretcher bond; crack repair average 225 mm wide	m	1.56	46.15	-	5.07	51.22	56.34	23.247
C413113E	stretcher bond; crack repair average 450 mm wide	m	2.01	59.57	-	10.13	69.70	76.67	46.494
C413113F	English or Flemish bond (snapped headers); single brick	Nr	0.26	7.75	-	0.41	8.16	8.98	1.729
C413113G	English or Flemish bond (snapped headers); in areas not exceeding 0.50 m²	Nr	1.86	55.09	-	14.12	69.21	76.13	61.941
C413113H	English or Flemish bond (snapped headers); in areas 0.50 - 1.00 m²	Nr	3.16	93.82	-	29.06	122.88	135.17	127.340
C413113I	English or Flemish bond (snapped headers); crack repair average 225 m wide	m	1.86	55.09	-	7.73	62.82	69.10	34.813
C413113J	English or Flemish bond (snapped headers); crack repair average 450 m wide	m	2.21	65.50	-	15.46	80.96	89.06	69.626
C4141	**Repointing brickwork**								
C414111	**Rake out joints of brick walls and repoint in gauged mortar (1:1:6)**								
C414111A	flush pointing; stretcher bond	m²	0.50	14.90	-	0.45	15.35	16.89	1.076
C414111B	flush pointing; Flemish bond	m²	0.75	22.35	-	0.68	23.03	25.33	1.614
C414111C	flush pointing; English bond	m²	0.95	28.29	-	0.91	29.20	32.12	2.152
C414111D	tooled pointing; stretcher bond	m²	0.55	16.38	-	0.45	16.83	18.51	1.076
C414111E	tooled pointing; Flemish bond	m²	0.80	23.83	-	0.68	24.51	26.96	1.614
C414111F	tooled pointing; English bond	m²	1.00	29.77	-	0.91	30.68	33.75	2.152

Major Works 2011		Unit	Labour Hours	Labour Net	Plant Net	Materials Net	Unit Net	Unit with 10%	CO₂
				£	£	£	£	£	Kg
C45	**C45: DAMP PROOF COURSE RENEWAL AND INSERTION**								
C4501	**Chemical damp proof course injection**								
C450190	**Silicone injection damp proof coursing**								
C450190A	half brick walls	m	0.70	11.89	-	11.72	23.61	25.97	0.651
C450190B	one brick walls	m	0.75	12.73	-	23.44	36.17	39.79	1.302
C450190C	one and a half brick walls	m	0.75	12.73	-	35.16	47.89	52.68	1.953
C450190D	two brick walls	m	0.80	13.58	-	46.88	60.46	66.51	2.604
C4522	**Removal of existing joinery and wall finishes**								
C452201	**Timber mouldings; setting aside for reuse**								
C452201A	architraves	m	0.08	0.95	-	-	0.95	1.05	-
C452201B	dado rails	m	0.10	1.27	-	-	1.27	1.40	-
C452201C	skirtings	m	0.13	1.59	-	-	1.59	1.75	-
C452211	**Wall finishes; placing debris in rubbish skips**								
C452211A	plaster	m²	0.60	7.62	0.67	-	8.29	9.12	-
C452211B	render	m²	0.85	10.80	0.67	-	11.47	12.62	-
C452211C	plasterboard and battens	m²	0.45	5.71	1.01	-	6.72	7.39	-
C452211D	plaster, lath and battens	m²	0.50	6.35	1.23	-	7.58	8.34	-
C452211E	asphalt	m²	0.65	8.25	0.56	-	8.81	9.69	-
C452211F	ceramic tiles	m²	0.45	5.71	0.56	-	6.27	6.90	-
C452211G	softwood matching and battens	m²	0.55	6.99	0.78	-	7.77	8.55	-
C4531	**Reinstatement of plaster finishes and refixing of salvaged joinery**								
C453101	**Refixing salvaged timber mouldings**								
C453101A	architraves	m	0.25	4.25	-	-	4.25	4.68	-
C453101B	dado rails	m	0.45	7.64	-	-	7.64	8.40	-
C453101C	skirtings	m	0.55	9.34	-	-	9.34	10.27	-
C453178	**Making good after damp course works in Carlite lightweight plaster; 2 mm finish on undercoat; jointing and finishing flush to existing; average 1.0 m high**								
C453178A	13 mm two coat work to masonry walls browning undercoat	m	1.51	44.67		2.15	46.82	51.50	1.320
C453179	**Dubbing out with Carlite undercoat; average 1.0 m high**								
C453179A	6 mm browning to walls	m	0.35	10.42	-	1.05	11.47	12.62	0.600
C453179B	12 mm browning to walls	m	0.50	14.90	-	1.88	16.78	18.46	1.080
C453179C	15 mm browning to walls	m	0.60	17.87	-	2.51	20.38	22.42	1.440
C453179D	20 mm browning to walls	m	0.75	22.35	-	3.14	25.49	28.04	1.800
C453179E	6 mm bonding to walls	m	0.35	10.42	-	1.22	11.64	12.80	0.720
C453179F	12 mm bonding to walls	m	0.50	14.90	-	2.44	17.34	19.07	1.440
C453179G	15 mm bonding to walls	m	0.60	17.87	-	3.05	20.92	23.01	1.800
C453179H	20 mm bonding to walls	m	0.75	22.35	-	4.06	26.41	29.05	2.400
C4539	**Cutting in physical damp course**								
C453989	**Cut out 1 metre alternate lengths of existing brick wall one course high; lay Hyload pitch polymer damp proof course and make good wall with bricks to match existing in cement mortar (1:3)**								
C453989A	half brick wall in commons	m	1.15	34.25	-	2.62	36.87	40.56	4.660
C453989B	one brick wall in commons	m	2.26	67.02	-	5.33	72.35	79.59	9.363
C453989C	half brick wall in facings	m	1.36	40.22	-	2.84	43.06	47.37	8.859
C453989D	one brick wall in facings	m	2.66	78.92	-	5.77	84.69	93.16	17.760

Major Works 2011		Unit	Labour Hours	Labour Net	Plant Net	Materials Net	Unit Net	Unit with 10%	CO₂
				£	£	£	£	£	Kg
C90	**C90: ALTERATIONS - SPOT ITEMS**								
C9011	**Removal of building fabric fittings and fixtures**								
C901101	**Timber mouldings**								
C901101A	architraves	m	0.08	0.95	-	-	0.95	1.05	-
C901101B	picture and dado rails	m	0.10	1.27	-	-	1.27	1.40	-
C901101C	skirtings	m	0.13	1.59	-	-	1.59	1.75	-
C901114	**Straight flight timber staircase; placing debris in rubbish skips**								
C901114A	600 mm wide x 2600 mm rise	Nr	2.00	25.40	8.95	-	34.35	37.79	-
C901114B	900 mm wide x 2600 mm rise	Nr	2.20	27.94	11.19	-	39.13	43.04	-
C901114C	1200 mm wide x 2600 mm rise	Nr	2.60	33.02	15.66	-	48.68	53.55	-
C901115	**Two flight timber staircase with landing; placing debris in rubbish skips**								
C901115A	600 mm wide x 2600 mm rise	Nr	3.00	38.10	8.95	-	47.05	51.76	-
C901115B	900 mm wide x 2600 mm rise	Nr	3.20	40.64	11.19	-	51.83	57.01	-
C901115C	1200 mm wide x 2600 mm rise	Nr	3.50	44.45	15.66	-	60.11	66.12	-
C901116	**Timber balustrading; placing debris in rubbish skips**								
C901116A	horizontal	m	0.25	3.17	2.01	-	5.18	5.70	-
C901116B	raking	m	0.35	4.44	2.01	-	6.45	7.10	-
C9012	**Removal of general fittings and fixtures and placing in rubbish skips**								
C901203	**Fire surround and hearth not exceeding 2 m² area**								
C901203A	masonry	Nr	1.25	15.88	4.47	-	20.35	22.39	-
C901203B	cast iron	Nr	0.50	6.35	2.24	-	8.59	9.45	-
C901203C	tiled concrete	Nr	0.75	9.52	4.47	-	13.99	15.39	-
C901203D	plaster	Nr	0.50	6.35	2.24	-	8.59	9.45	-
C901203E	timber	Nr	0.25	3.17	2.24	-	5.41	5.95	-
C901204	**Wall units**								
C901204A	600 x 300 x 300 mm	Nr	0.25	3.17	1.12	-	4.29	4.72	-
C901204B	300 x 300 x 600 mm	Nr	0.25	3.17	1.12	-	4.29	4.72	-
C901204C	600 x 300 x 600 mm	Nr	0.25	3.17	2.24	-	5.41	5.95	-
C901204D	1000 x 300 x 600 mm	Nr	0.30	3.81	3.36	-	7.17	7.89	-
C901204E	1200 x 300 x 600 mm	Nr	0.30	3.81	3.36	-	7.17	7.89	-
C901204F	300 x 300 x 900 mm	Nr	0.25	3.17	1.12	-	4.29	4.72	-
C901204G	600 x 300 x 900 mm	Nr	0.25	3.17	1.79	-	4.96	5.46	-
C901204H	1000 x 300 x 900 mm	Nr	0.30	3.81	2.91	-	6.72	7.39	-
C901204I	1200 x 300 x 900 mm	Nr	0.30	3.81	3.80	-	7.61	8.37	-
C901205	**Base units**								
C901205A	300 x 600 x 900 mm	Nr	0.18	2.29	1.79	-	4.08	4.49	-
C901205B	600 x 600 x 900 mm	Nr	0.18	2.29	3.58	-	5.87	6.46	-
C901205C	1000 x 600 x 900 mm	Nr	0.25	3.17	6.04	-	9.21	10.13	-
C901205D	1200 x 600 x 900 mm	Nr	0.25	3.17	7.16	-	10.33	11.36	-
C901206	**Sink base units**								
C901206A	1000 x 600 x 900 mm	Nr	0.25	3.17	6.04	-	9.21	10.13	-
C901206B	1200 x 600 x 900 mm	Nr	0.25	3.17	7.16	-	10.33	11.36	-
C901206C	1500 x 600 x 900 mm	Nr	0.30	3.81	8.95	-	12.76	14.04	-
C901207	**Corner base units**								
C901207A	800 x 600 x 900 mm	Nr	0.18	2.29	8.95	-	11.24	12.36	-
C901207B	900 x 600 x 900 mm	Nr	0.18	2.29	8.95	-	11.24	12.36	-
C901207C	1000 x 600 x 900 mm	Nr	0.25	3.17	6.04	-	9.21	10.13	-
C901207D	1200 x 600 x 900 mm	Nr	0.25	3.17	7.16	-	10.33	11.36	-
C901208	**Appliance housing units**								
C901208A	1200 x 600 x 900 mm	Nr	0.25	3.17	7.16	-	10.33	11.36	-
C901208B	600 x 600 x 1950 mm	Nr	0.30	3.81	7.83	-	11.64	12.80	-
C901208C	600 x 600 x 900 mm	Nr	0.25	3.17	7.16	-	10.33	11.36	-
C901209	**Store units**								
C901209A	600 x 600 x 300 mm	Nr	0.25	3.17	2.46	-	5.63	6.19	-
C901209B	600 x 600 x 1950 mm	Nr	0.30	3.81	7.83	-	11.64	12.80	-
C901210	**Worktops**								
C901210A	500 mm wide	m	0.25	3.17	1.12	-	4.29	4.72	-
C901210B	600 mm wide	m	0.25	3.17	1.34	-	4.51	4.96	-

Major Works 2011		Unit	Labour Hours	Labour Net	Plant Net	Materials Net	Unit Net	Unit with 10%	CO₂
				£	£	£	£	£	Kg
C90	**C90: ALTERATIONS - SPOT ITEMS**								
C9012	**Removal of general fittings and fixtures and placing in rubbish skips**								
C901211	**Draining boards**								
C901211A	500 x 400 mm	Nr	0.15	1.90	0.22	-	2.12	2.33	-
C901211B	800 x 600 mm	Nr	0.18	2.29	0.45	-	2.74	3.01	-
C901212	**Shelving units**								
C901212A	1500 x 300 x 1000 mm	Nr	0.25	3.17	6.71	-	9.88	10.87	-
C901212B	2000 x 300 x 1500 mm	Nr	0.30	3.81	6.71	-	10.52	11.57	-
C901213	**Shelving**								
C901213A	not exceeding 300 mm wide	m	0.13	1.65	0.22	-	1.87	2.06	-
C901213B	300 - 600 mm wide	m	0.20	2.54	0.22	-	2.76	3.04	-
C9015	**Removal of windows, doors and frames**								
C901572	**Timber doors, frames and linings; removing ironmongery and piecing out; placing debris in rubbish skips**								
C901572A	timber doors	Nr	1.00	16.98	-	1.47	18.45	20.30	0.422
C901572B	timber door frames, linings and architraves	Nr	0.50	8.49	-	0.90	9.39	10.33	0.232
C901575	**Timber window frames and linings; removing ironmongery and piecing out; placing debris in rubbish skips**								
C901575A	timber window frames and linings; not exceeding 0.50 m²	Nr	0.75	12.73	-	0.90	13.63	14.99	0.232
C901575B	timber window frames and linings; 0.50 - 1.00 m²	Nr	1.00	16.98	-	1.05	18.03	19.83	0.268
C901575C	timber window frames and linings; 1.00 - 2.00 m²	Nr	1.25	21.23	-	1.19	22.42	24.66	0.303
C901575D	timber window frames and linings; 2.00 - 3.00 m²	Nr	1.50	25.47	-	6.78	32.25	35.48	2.101
C9023	**Removal of plumbing and engineering installations; fixtures and fittings**								
C902320	**Plumbing and heating installations; fixtures and fittings; placing debris in rubbish skips**								
C902320A	back boiler	Nr	0.50	8.20	2.68	-	10.88	11.97	-
C902320B	boiler and flue pipe	Nr	0.80	13.12	4.47	-	17.59	19.35	-
C902320C	feed and expansion tank	Nr	0.50	8.20	2.24	-	10.44	11.48	-
C902320D	cold water storage tank	Nr	0.80	13.12	8.05	-	21.17	23.29	-
C902320E	hot water cylinder	Nr	1.00	16.40	4.03	-	20.43	22.47	-
C902320F	oil tank and supply pipe	Nr	2.00	32.80	15.66	-	48.46	53.31	-
C902320G	radiators	Nr	0.50	8.20	1.12	-	9.32	10.25	-
C902320H	circulating pump	Nr	0.50	8.20	-	-	8.20	9.02	-
C902320I	pipework to fittings not exceeding 5 m run	Nr	0.50	8.20	0.02	-	8.22	9.04	-
C902320J	pipework to fittings 5 - 10 m run	Nr	0.80	13.12	0.07	-	13.19	14.51	-
C902320K	drain down domestic hot and cold water system	Nr	1.00	16.40	-	-	16.40	18.04	-
C902320L	drain down central heating system not exceeding 10 radiators	Nr	1.00	16.40	-	-	16.40	18.04	-
C902320M	disconnect and make safe mains water supply	Nr	0.50	8.20	-	2.56	10.76	11.84	0.048
C902321	**Sanitary fittings, complete with taps and traps; placing debris in rubbish skips**								
C902321A	w.c. suite	Nr	0.50	8.20	2.24	-	10.44	11.48	-
C902321B	bidet	Nr	0.50	8.20	2.24	-	10.44	11.48	-
C902321C	bath	Nr	0.75	12.30	11.19	-	23.49	25.84	-
C902321D	shower tray	Nr	0.30	4.92	5.59	-	10.51	11.56	-
C902321E	hand basin	Nr	0.50	8.20	2.24	-	10.44	11.48	-
C902321F	sink	Nr	0.50	8.20	3.36	-	11.56	12.72	-
C902321G	w.c. or shower cubicle partition	Nr	0.30	3.81	1.12	-	4.93	5.42	-

Major Works 2011		Unit	Labour Hours	Labour Net £	Plant Net £	Materials Net £	Unit Net £	Unit with 10% £	CO₂ Kg
C90	**C90: ALTERATIONS - SPOT ITEMS**								
C9023	**Removal of plumbing and engineering installations; fixtures and fittings**								
C902321	**Sanitary fittings, complete with taps and traps; placing debris in rubbish skips**								
C902321H	service and waste pipes to fittings not exceeding 5 m run	Nr	0.50	8.20	0.02	-	8.22	9.04	-
C902321I	service and waste pipes to fittings 5 - 10 m run	Nr	0.80	13.12	0.07	-	13.19	14.51	-
C9024	**Removal of electrical installations; fixtures and fittings**								
C902430	**Electrical fixtures and fittings; placing debris in rubbish skips**								
C902430A	distribution and switch boards	Nr	0.50	8.70	0.67	-	9.37	10.31	-
C902430B	meters	Nr	0.30	5.22	0.22	-	5.44	5.98	-
C902430C	light fittings	Nr	0.15	2.61	-	-	2.61	2.87	-
C902430D	flush power sockets	Nr	0.20	3.48	-	-	3.48	3.83	-
C902430E	surface mounted power sockets	Nr	0.15	2.61	-	-	2.61	2.87	-
C902430F	flush switch boxes	Nr	0.20	3.48	-	-	3.48	3.83	-
C902430G	surface mounted switch boxes	Nr	0.15	2.61	-	-	2.61	2.87	-
C902430H	flush cooker outlets	Nr	0.22	3.83	-	-	3.83	4.21	-
C902430I	surface mounted cooker outlets	Nr	0.17	2.96	-	-	2.96	3.26	-
C902430J	immersion heaters	Nr	0.25	4.35	-	-	4.35	4.79	-
C902430K	night storage heaters	Nr	0.45	7.83	4.47	-	12.30	13.53	-
C902430L	wall mounted extractor fans	Nr	0.30	5.22	-	-	5.22	5.74	-
C902430M	ceiling mounted extractor fans	Nr	0.40	6.96	-	-	6.96	7.66	-
C902430N	window mounted extractor fans	Nr	0.40	6.96	-	-	6.96	7.66	-
C902430O	surface mounted cabling or trunking not exceeding 5 m length	Nr	0.15	2.61	-	-	2.61	2.87	-
C902430P	surface mounted cabling or trunking 5 - 10 m length	Nr	0.30	5.22	-	-	5.22	5.74	-
C902430Q	cap off and make safe buried cables not exceeding 30 Amp	Nr	1.00	21.74	-	5.08	26.82	29.50	1.770
C902430R	disconnect and make safe mains supply	Nr	0.75	16.31	-	2.78	19.09	21.00	1.770
C9031	**Removal of floor, wall and ceiling finishes**								
C903101	**Floor finishes; placing debris in rubbish skips**								
C903101A	sand and cement screed	m²	0.80	10.16	1.68	-	11.84	13.02	-
C903101B	quarry tiles	m²	0.80	10.16	1.12	-	11.28	12.41	-
C903101C	ceramic tiles	m²	0.55	6.99	0.56	-	7.55	8.31	-
C903101D	plastic floor tiles	m²	0.65	8.25	0.56	-	8.81	9.69	-
C903101E	carpeting	m²	0.10	1.27	2.24	-	3.51	3.86	-
C903101F	asphalt	m²	0.75	9.52	1.12	-	10.64	11.70	-
C903101G	linoleum	m²	0.08	1.02	0.45	-	1.47	1.62	-
C903111	**Wall finishes; placing debris in rubbish skips**								
C903111A	plaster	m²	0.60	7.62	0.67	-	8.29	9.12	-
C903111B	render	m²	0.85	10.80	0.67	-	11.47	12.62	-
C903111C	plasterboard	m²	0.35	4.44	0.89	-	5.33	5.86	-
C903111D	lath and plaster	m²	0.45	5.71	1.12	-	6.83	7.51	-
C903111E	asphalt	m²	0.65	8.25	0.56	-	8.81	9.69	-
C903111F	ceramic tiles	m²	0.45	5.71	0.56	-	6.27	6.90	-
C903111G	matching	m²	0.50	6.35	0.67	-	7.02	7.72	-
C903121	**Ceiling finishes; placing debris in rubbish skips**								
C903121A	lath and plaster	m²	0.45	5.71	1.12	-	6.83	7.51	-
C903121B	plasterboard	m²	0.40	5.08	0.89	-	5.97	6.57	-
C903121C	softwood matching	m²	0.50	6.35	0.67	-	7.02	7.72	-
C903121D	rigid sheeting	m²	0.25	3.17	0.56	-	3.73	4.10	-

Major Works 2011		Unit	Labour Hours	Labour Net £	Plant Net £	Materials Net £	Unit Net £	Unit with 10% £	CO$_2$ Kg
C90	**C90: ALTERATIONS - SPOT ITEMS**								
C9041	**Removal of roof coverings**								
C904181	**Slates and tiles; taking off, cleaning and setting aside for re-use; placing debris in rubbish skips**								
C904181A	roof slating	m²	0.25	3.17	-	-	3.17	3.49	-
C904181B	roof tiling	m²	0.20	2.54	-	-	2.54	2.79	-
C9051	**Cutting openings in existing structures**								
C905161	**Cutting openings in load bearing walls; placing debris in rubbish skips**								
C905161A	half brick common brickwork	m²	2.00	25.40	6.68	-	32.08	35.29	0.215
C905161B	one brick common brickwork	m²	2.30	29.21	7.03	-	36.24	39.86	0.344
C905161C	one and a half brick common brickwork	m²	3.00	38.10	8.72	-	46.82	51.50	0.516
C905161D	two brick common brickwork	m²	3.80	48.26	10.24	-	58.50	64.35	0.774
C905161E	half brick engineering brickwork	m²	2.20	27.94	6.92	-	34.86	38.35	0.301
C905161F	one brick engineering brickwork	m²	2.50	31.75	7.27	-	39.02	42.92	0.430
C905161G	one and a half brick engineering brickwork	m²	3.20	40.64	8.96	-	49.60	54.56	0.602
C905161H	two brick engineering brickwork	m²	4.00	50.80	10.48	-	61.28	67.41	0.860
C905161I	half brick facing brickwork	m²	1.90	24.13	6.56	-	30.69	33.76	0.172
C905161J	one brick facing brickwork	m²	2.20	27.94	6.92	-	34.86	38.35	0.301
C905161K	100 or 125 mm blockwork	m²	1.70	21.59	6.33	-	27.92	30.71	0.086
C905161L	150 mm blockwork	m²	1.80	22.86	6.44	-	29.30	32.23	0.129
C905161M	200 mm blockwork	m²	2.20	27.94	7.78	-	35.72	39.29	0.172
C905161N	225 mm blockwork	m²	2.40	30.48	8.59	-	39.07	42.98	0.172
C905161O	250 or 275 mm cavity wall (half facing brick outer, 100 or 125 mm block inner skin)	m²	2.50	31.75	8.13	-	39.88	43.87	0.301
C905161P	300 mm cavity wall (half brick outer 150 mm block inner skin)	m²	2.80	35.56	9.06	-	44.62	49.08	0.344
C905161Q	300 mm cavity wall (half brick outer 100 mm block inner skin)	m²	2.50	31.75	8.13	-	39.88	43.87	0.301
C905161R	100 mm reinforced concrete wall	m²	1.50	19.05	1.77	-	20.82	22.90	0.645
C905161S	150 mm reinforced concrete wall	m²	2.10	26.67	2.48	-	29.15	32.07	0.903
C905161T	200 mm reinforced concrete wall	m²	2.90	36.83	3.42	-	40.25	44.28	1.247
C905161U	250 mm reinforced concrete wall	m²	3.50	44.45	4.13	-	48.58	53.44	1.505
C905161V	300 mm reinforced concrete wall	m²	4.00	50.80	4.72	-	55.52	61.07	1.720
C905162	**Cutting openings in non-load bearing walls; placing debris in rubbish skips**								
C905162A	half brick common brickwork	m²	0.75	9.52	-	-	9.52	10.47	-
C905162B	half brick facing brickwork	m²	0.60	7.62	-	-	7.62	8.38	-
C905162C	50 mm blockwork	m²	0.25	3.17	-	-	3.17	3.49	-
C905162D	75 mm blockwork	m²	0.30	3.81	-	-	3.81	4.19	-
C905162E	100 mm blockwork	m²	0.40	5.08	-	-	5.08	5.59	-
C905163	**Making good to reveals of openings with materials to match existing**								
C905163A	half brick common brickwork	m	0.25	7.45	-	2.31	9.76	10.74	6.100
C905163B	one brick common brickwork	m	0.40	11.90	-	4.77	16.67	18.34	12.469
C905163C	one and a half brick common brickwork	m	0.65	19.35	-	7.07	26.42	29.06	18.569
C905163D	two brick common brickwork	m	0.85	25.32	-	9.27	34.59	38.05	24.318
C905163E	half brick engineering brickwork	m	0.30	8.93	-	2.65	11.58	12.74	10.924
C905163F	one brick engineering brickwork	m	0.45	13.42	-	5.54	18.96	20.86	22.957
C905163G	one and a half brick engineering brickwork	m	0.70	20.84	-	8.18	29.02	31.92	33.881
C905163H	two brick engineering brickwork	m	0.90	26.80	-	10.72	37.52	41.27	44.453
C905163I	half brick facing brickwork	m	0.50	14.90	-	2.33	17.23	18.95	10.759
C905163J	one brick facing brickwork	m	0.90	26.80	-	4.95	31.75	34.93	22.978
C905163K	250 or 275 mm cavity wall (100 or 125 mm inner and outer skins)	m	0.60	17.87	-	3.21	21.08	23.19	1.834
C905163M	250 or 275 mm cavity wall (half brick facings outer, 100 mm block inner skins)	m	0.90	26.80	-	3.75	30.55	33.61	11.604
C905163N	300 mm cavity wall (half brick facing outer, 150 mm block inner skins)	m	1.00	29.77	-	4.51	34.28	37.71	12.161

Major Works 2011		Unit	Labour Hours	Labour Net	Plant Net	Materials Net	Unit Net	Unit with 10%	CO₂
				£	£	£	£	£	Kg
C90	**C90: ALTERATIONS - SPOT ITEMS**								
C9051	**Cutting openings in existing structures**								
C905163	**Making good to reveals of openings with materials to match existing**								
C905163O	300 mm cavity wall (half brick facing outer, 100 mm block inner skins)	m	0.85	25.32	-	3.75	29.07	31.98	11.604
C905163P	50 mm blockwork	m	0.15	4.48	-	0.97	5.45	6.00	0.557
C905163Q	75 mm blockwork	m	0.18	5.37	-	1.09	6.46	7.11	0.701
C905163R	100 mm blockwork	m	0.20	5.97	-	1.42	7.39	8.13	0.845
C905163S	125 mm blockwork	m	0.25	7.45	-	1.79	9.24	10.16	0.989
C905163T	150 mm blockwork	m	0.35	10.42	-	2.18	12.60	13.86	1.402
C905163U	200 mm blockwork	m	0.45	13.42	-	2.84	16.26	17.89	1.690
C905163V	215 mm blockwork	m	0.55	16.38	-	3.12	19.50	21.45	1.776
C905163W	100 mm reinforced concrete wall	m	0.25	7.45	-	0.31	7.76	8.54	1.054
C905163X	150 mm reinforced concrete wall	m	0.30	8.93	-	0.41	9.34	10.27	1.406
C905163Y	300 mm reinforced concrete wall	m	0.40	11.90	-	0.82	12.72	13.99	2.812
C9076	**Filling in openings in existing structures**								
C907601	**Infilling with brickwork in gauged mortar (1:1:6)**								
C907601A	half brick wall in commons	m²	0.75	22.35	-	18.58	40.93	45.02	44.920
C907601B	one brick wall in commons	m²	1.51	44.67	-	38.53	83.20	91.52	93.067
C907601C	one and a half brick wall in commons	m²	2.26	67.02	-	57.37	124.39	136.83	138.607
C907601D	two brick wall in commons	m²	2.91	86.37	-	77.31	163.68	180.05	186.754
C907601E	half brick wall in engineering brick	m²	0.90	26.80	-	23.64	50.44	55.48	95.371
C907601F	one brick wall in engineering bricks	m²	1.66	49.15	-	48.65	97.80	107.58	193.969
C907601G	one and a half brick wall in engineering bricks	m²	2.41	71.47	-	72.64	144.11	158.52	290.801
C907601H	two brick wall in engineering bricks	m²	3.11	92.30	-	97.64	189.94	208.93	389.399
C907601I	half brick wall in facing bricks	m²	1.00	29.77	-	20.98	50.75	55.83	96.178
C907601J	one brick wall in facing bricks	m²	1.81	53.60	-	43.09	96.69	106.36	195.045
C907603	**Infilling with blockwork in gauged mortar (1:1:6)**								
C907603A	50 mm blockwork	m²	0.65	19.35	-	7.81	27.16	29.88	3.327
C907603B	75 mm blockwork	m²	0.70	20.84	-	9.02	29.86	32.85	4.856
C907603C	100 mm blockwork	m²	0.75	22.35	-	11.99	34.34	37.77	6.385
C907603D	125 mm blockwork	m²	0.80	23.83	-	15.38	39.21	43.13	7.914
C907603E	150 mm blockwork	m²	0.85	25.32	-	18.02	43.34	47.67	9.712
C907603F	200 mm blockwork	m²	0.95	28.29	-	23.96	52.25	57.48	12.770
C907603G	215 mm blockwork	m²	1.10	32.77	-	26.76	59.53	65.48	14.332
C907605	**Infilling with composite walling in gauged mortar (1:1:6)**								
C907605A	250 or 275 mm cavity wall (100 or 125 mm block outer and inner skins)	m²	1.66	49.15	-	37.44	86.59	95.25	38.235
C907605B	250 or 275 mm cavity wall (half brick outer and 100 or 125 mm inner skins)	m²	1.91	56.57	-	36.36	92.93	102.22	104.092
C907605C	300 mm cavity wall (half brick facing outer, 150 mm inner skins)	m²	1.96	58.08	-	39.00	97.08	106.79	105.889
C907605D	300 mm cavity wall (half brick facing outer, 100 mm inner skins)	m²	1.86	55.09	-	32.97	88.06	96.87	102.563
C9079	**Cutting, toothing and bonding ends of new walls into existing**								
C907901	**Common brickwork; in alternate courses**								
C907901A	half brick wall	m	0.42	12.50	-	2.31	14.81	16.29	6.100
C907901B	one brick wall	m	0.62	18.46	-	4.77	23.23	25.55	12.469
C907901C	one and a half brick wall	m	0.82	24.43	-	7.07	31.50	34.65	18.569
C907901D	two brick wall	m	1.22	36.33	-	9.27	45.60	50.16	24.318
C907903	**Engineering brickwork; in alternate courses**								
C907903A	half brick wall	m	0.45	13.42	-	2.65	16.07	17.68	10.924
C907903B	one brick wall	m	0.65	19.35	-	5.54	24.89	27.38	22.957
C907903C	one and a half brick wall	m	0.85	25.32	-	8.18	33.50	36.85	33.881

Major Works 2011		Unit	Labour Hours	Labour Net	Plant Net	Materials Net	Unit Net	Unit with 10%	CO₂
				£	£	£	£	£	Kg
C90	**C90: ALTERATIONS - SPOT ITEMS**								
C9079	**Cutting, toothing and bonding ends of new walls into existing**								
C907903	**Engineering brickwork; in alternate courses**								
C907903D	two brick wall	m	1.25	37.22	-	10.72	47.94	52.73	44.453
C907905	**Facing brickwork; in alternate courses**								
C907905A	half brick wall	m	0.60	17.87	-	2.31	20.18	22.20	10.924
C907905B	one brick wall	m	0.85	25.32	-	4.91	30.23	33.25	23.308
C907908	**Blockwork; in alternate courses**								
C907908A	50 mm thick	m	0.25	7.45	-	1.67	9.12	10.03	0.879
C907908B	75 mm thick	m	0.28	8.34	-	1.90	10.24	11.26	1.143
C907908C	100 mm thick	m	0.32	9.53	-	2.50	12.03	13.23	1.407
C907908D	125 mm thick	m	0.35	10.42	-	3.18	13.60	14.96	1.671
C907908E	150 mm thick	m	0.40	11.90	-	3.79	15.69	17.26	2.287
C907908F	200 mm thick	m	0.50	14.90	-	4.99	19.89	21.88	2.815
C907908G	215 mm thick	m	0.55	16.38	-	5.50	21.88	24.07	2.973
C9082	**Making good to floors after alterations in materials to match existing**								
C908201	**Concrete floor slabs; jointing to existing; 100 mm thick**								
C908201A	not exceeding 150 mm wide	m	0.30	3.81	-	2.45	6.26	6.89	5.263
C908201B	150 - 300 mm wide	m	0.40	5.08	-	4.76	9.84	10.82	10.217
C908201C	isolated areas; not exceeding 1.00 m²	Nr	0.50	6.35	-	15.86	22.21	24.43	34.056
C908201D	isolated areas; 1.00 - 2.00 m²	Nr	0.75	9.52	-	31.72	41.24	45.36	68.112
C908203	**Concrete floor slabs; jointing to existing; 150 mm thick**								
C908203A	not exceeding 150 mm wide	m	0.33	4.19	-	3.61	7.80	8.58	7.740
C908203B	150 - 300 mm wide	m	0.43	5.46	-	7.21	12.67	13.94	15.480
C908203C	isolated areas; not exceeding 1.00 m²	Nr	0.55	6.99	-	23.79	30.78	33.86	51.084
C908203D	isolated areas; 1.00 - 2.00 m²	Nr	0.80	10.16	-	47.59	57.75	63.53	102.168
C908208	**Cement and sand (1:3) trowelled screed; jointing to existing**								
C908208A	25 mm thick	m²	0.25	7.45	-	2.88	10.33	11.36	9.841
C908208B	38 mm thick	m²	0.28	8.34	-	4.32	12.66	13.93	14.761
C908208C	50 mm thick	m²	0.32	9.53	-	5.66	15.19	16.71	19.330
C908208D	65 mm thick	m²	0.40	11.90	-	7.41	19.31	21.24	25.304
C908211	**Timber floors; 25 mm thick tongued and grooved softwood boarding on 50 x 150 mm joists at 400 mm centres**								
C908211A	not exceeding 150 mm wide	m	0.50	8.49	-	5.69	14.18	15.60	3.621
C908211B	150 - 300 mm wide	m	0.75	12.73	-	7.70	20.43	22.47	4.565
C908211C	over 300 mm wide	m²	1.00	16.98	-	22.80	39.78	43.76	13.280
C908211D	isolated areas; not exceeding 1.00 m²	Nr	1.50	25.47	-	23.14	48.61	53.47	13.434
C908211E	isolated areas; 1.00 - 2.00 m²	Nr	2.00	33.96	-	30.94	64.90	71.39	20.062
C908213	**Timber floors; 25 mm thick tongued and grooved softwood boarding on 50 x 200 mm joists at 400 mm centres**								
C908213A	not exceeding 150 mm wide	m	0.50	8.49	-	6.54	15.03	16.53	4.333
C908213B	150 - 300 mm wide	m	0.75	12.73	-	8.51	21.24	23.36	5.246
C908213C	over 300 mm wide	m²	1.00	16.98	-	24.74	41.72	45.89	14.905
C908213D	isolated areas; not exceeding 1.00 m²	Nr	1.50	25.47	-	25.09	50.56	55.62	15.059
C908213E	isolated areas; 1.00 - 2.00 m²	Nr	2.00	33.96	-	34.83	68.79	75.67	23.312

Major Works 2011		Unit	Labour Hours	Labour Net	Plant Net	Materials Net	Unit Net	Unit with 10%	CO$_2$
				£	£	£	£	£	Kg
C90	**C90: ALTERATIONS - SPOT ITEMS**								
C9082	**Making good to floors after alterations in materials to match existing**								
C908215	**Timber floors; 22 mm thick tongued and grooved V313 moisture resistant chipboard, BS 5669, on 50 x 150 mm joists at 400 mm centres**								
C908215A	not exceeding 150 mm wide	m	0.35	5.94	-	3.92	9.86	10.85	3.775
C908215B	150 - 300 mm wide	m	0.50	8.49	-	4.58	13.07	14.38	4.799
C908215C	over 300 mm wide	m^2	0.65	11.04	-	11.97	23.01	25.31	12.959
C908215D	isolated areas; not exceeding 1.00 m^2	Nr	0.95	16.13	-	12.16	28.29	31.12	13.242
C908215E	isolated areas; 1.00 - 2.00 m^2	Nr	1.75	29.72	-	23.93	53.65	59.02	25.919
C908217	**Timber floors; 25 mm thick tongued and grooved V313 moisture resistant chipboard, BS 5669, on 50 x 200 mm joists at 400 mm centres**								
C908217A	not exceeding 150 mm wide	m	0.35	5.94	-	4.86	10.80	11.88	4.628
C908217B	150 - 300 mm wide	m	0.50	8.49	-	5.39	13.88	15.27	5.480
C908217C	over 300 mm wide	m^2	0.65	11.04	-	13.91	24.95	27.45	14.584
C908217D	isolated areas; not exceeding 1.00 m^2	Nr	0.95	16.13	-	14.10	30.23	33.25	14.867
C908217E	isolated areas; 1.00 - 2.00 m^2	Nr	1.75	29.72	-	27.82	57.54	63.29	29.169
C9083	**Making good to faces of walls after alterations in materials to match existing**								
C908301	**Common brickwork; in cement mortar (1:3)**								
C908301A	half brick wide	m	0.25	7.45	-	1.54	8.99	9.89	4.239
C908301B	one brick wide	m	0.40	11.90	-	2.72	14.62	16.08	7.506
C908301C	one and a half brick wide	m	0.60	17.87	-	4.26	22.13	24.34	11.745
C908301D	two brick wide	m	0.80	23.83	-	5.79	29.62	32.58	15.984
C908301E	isolated areas; not exceeding 0.01 m^2	Nr	0.10	2.97	-	0.36	3.33	3.66	0.972
C908301F	isolated areas; 0.01 - 0.05 m^2	Nr	0.25	7.45	-	1.08	8.53	9.38	2.916
C908301G	isolated areas; 0.05 - 0.10 m^2	Nr	0.40	11.90	-	2.51	14.41	15.85	6.803
C908303	**Engineering brickwork; in cement mortar (1:3)**								
C908303A	half brick wide	m	0.30	8.93	-	1.60	10.53	11.58	6.544
C908303B	one brick wide	m	0.45	13.42	-	2.75	16.17	17.79	11.275
C908303C	one and a half brick wide	m	0.65	19.35	-	4.35	23.70	26.07	17.819
C908303D	two brick wide	m	0.85	25.32	-	5.95	31.27	34.40	24.363
C908303E	isolated areas; not exceeding 0.01 m^2	Nr	0.13	3.86	-	0.45	4.31	4.74	1.812
C908303F	isolated areas; 0.01 - 0.05 m^2	Nr	0.28	8.34	-	1.25	9.59	10.55	5.083
C908303G	isolated areas; 0.05 - 0.10 m^2	Nr	0.43	12.79	-	2.85	15.64	17.20	11.627
C908305	**Facing brickwork; in cement mortar (1:3)**								
C908305A	half brick wide	m	0.40	11.90	-	1.41	13.31	14.64	6.544
C908305B	one brick wide	m	0.55	16.38	-	2.71	19.09	21.00	12.736
C908305C	one and a half brick wide	m	0.75	22.35	-	4.41	26.76	29.44	20.739
C908305D	two brick wide	m	0.95	28.29	-	5.82	34.11	37.52	27.283
C908305E	isolated areas; not exceeding 0.01 m^2	Nr	0.15	4.48	-	0.40	4.88	5.37	1.812
C908305F	isolated areas; 0.01 - 0.05 m^2	Nr	0.30	8.93	-	1.11	10.04	11.04	5.083
C908305G	isolated areas; 0.05 - 0.10 m^2	Nr	0.45	13.42	-	2.51	15.93	17.52	11.627
C908307	**Blockwork; in cement mortar (1:3)**								
C908307A	50 mm wide	m	0.20	5.97	-	0.96	6.93	7.62	0.639
C908307B	75 mm wide	m	0.23	6.86	-	1.08	7.94	8.73	0.783
C908307C	100 mm wide	m	0.27	8.04	-	1.41	9.45	10.40	0.927
C908307D	125 mm wide	m	0.30	8.93	-	1.78	10.71	11.78	1.071
C908307E	150 mm wide	m	0.35	10.42	-	2.16	12.58	13.84	1.567
C908307F	200 mm wide	m	0.45	13.42	-	2.81	16.23	17.85	1.855
C908307G	215 mm wide	m	0.50	14.90	-	3.10	18.00	19.80	1.941

Major Works 2011		Unit	Labour Hours	Labour Net	Plant Net	Materials Net	Unit Net	Unit with 10%	CO$_2$
				£	£	£	£	£	Kg
C90	**C90: ALTERATIONS - SPOT ITEMS**								
C9083	**Making good to faces of walls after alterations in materials to match existing**								
C908309	**Concrete work; in cement mortar (1:3)**								
C908309A	not exceeding 250 mm wide	m	0.30	8.93	-	0.72	9.65	10.62	2.460
C908309B	250 - 500 mm wide	m	0.55	16.38	-	1.44	17.82	19.60	4.920
C908309C	500 - 1000 mm wide	m	0.90	26.80	-	2.88	29.68	32.65	9.841
C908309D	exceeding 1000 mm wide	m^2	0.75	22.35	-	2.88	25.23	27.75	9.841
C9084	**Making good to roof coverings after alterations in materials to match existing**								
C908401	**600 x 300 mm natural slates on and including 25 x 38 mm treated softwood battens, underfelting and 50 x 150 mm treated sawn softwood infill rafters at 400 mm centres**								
C908401A	areas not exceeding 1.00 m^2	Nr	2.00	49.32	-	86.31	135.63	149.19	12.402
C908401B	areas 1.00 - 2.00 m^2	Nr	2.81	71.85	-	165.09	236.94	260.63	20.169
C908401C	areas 2.00 - 3.00 m^2	Nr	4.01	103.75	-	238.63	342.38	376.62	27.952
C908403	**268 x 165 mm plain concrete tiles on and including 25 x 38 mm treated softwood battens, underfelting and 50 x 150 mm treated sawn softwood infill rafters at 400 mm centres**								
C908403A	areas not exceeding 1.00 m^2	Nr	2.81	73.15	-	46.32	119.47	131.42	17.872
C908403B	areas 1.00 - 2.00 m^2	Nr	4.41	119.52	-	89.10	208.62	229.48	31.000
C908403C	areas 2.00 - 3.00 m^2	Nr	6.22	169.28	-	131.10	300.38	330.42	44.442
C908405	**381 x 227 mm interlocking concrete tiles on and including 25 x 38 mm treated softwood battens, underfelting and 50 x 150 mm treated sawn softwood infill rafters at 400 mm centres**								
C908405A	areas not exceeding 1.00 m^2	Nr	1.90	46.35	-	23.60	69.95	76.95	14.589
C908405B	areas 1.00 - 2.00 m^2	Nr	2.71	68.88	-	44.26	113.14	124.45	24.410
C908405C	areas 2.00 - 3.00 m^2	Nr	3.91	100.78	-	64.42	165.20	181.72	34.169
C908407	**381 x 227 mm secondhand clay pantiles on and including 25 x 38 mm treated softwood battens, underfelting and 50 x 150 mm treated sawn softwood infill rafters at 400 mm centres**								
C908407A	areas not exceeding 1.00 m^2	Nr	2.10	52.29	-	30.61	82.90	91.19	32.876
C908407B	areas 1.00 - 2.00 m^2	Nr	2.91	74.85	-	59.18	134.03	147.43	61.256
C908407C	areas 2.00 - 3.00 m^2	Nr	4.11	106.74	-	85.81	192.55	211.81	87.526
C908411	**Slating or tiling as reclaimed and previously removed and stacked; 75 mm lap with aluminium alloy nails on new 25 x 38 mm treated sawn softwood battens and underfelt; slate and tile costs included**								
C908411A	600 x 300 mm slates	m^2	1.20	35.73	-	74.87	110.60	121.66	7.200
C908411B	268 x 165 mm plain tiles	m^2	2.01	59.57	-	39.02	98.59	108.45	12.605
C908411C	381 x 227 mm interlocking tiles	m^2	1.10	32.77	-	16.50	49.27	54.20	9.146
C908411D	secondhand pantiles	m^2	1.30	38.70	-	21.52	60.22	66.24	22.312

Major Works 2011		Unit	Labour Hours	Labour Net	Plant Net	Materials Net	Unit Net	Unit with 10%	CO₂
				£	£	£	£	£	Kg
C90	**C90: ALTERATIONS - SPOT ITEMS**								
C9084	**Making good to roof coverings after alterations in materials to match existing**								
C908413	**Relaying roof coverings previously removed and stacked; 75 mm lap with aluminium alloy nails on new 25 x 38 mm treated sawn softwood battens and underfelt; allowing 20 per cent new samples**								
C908413A	600 x 300 mm slates	m²	1.20	35.73	-	20.88	56.61	62.27	6.093
C908413B	268 x 165 mm plain tiles	m²	2.01	59.57	-	13.87	73.44	80.78	8.498
C908413C	381 x 227 mm interlocking tiles	m²	1.10	32.77	-	6.21	38.98	42.88	6.103
C908413D	secondhand pantiles	m²	1.30	38.70	-	6.48	45.18	49.70	5.752
C9086	**Making good to wall and ceiling finishes after alterations in materials to match existing**								
C908678	**Carlite lightweight plaster; 2 mm finish on undercoat; jointing and finishing flush to existing; to masonry walls**								
C908678A	13 mm two coat work to masonry walls browning undercoat	m²	1.51	44.67	-	2.15	46.82	51.50	1.320
C908678F	10 mm two coat work to concrete walls; bonding undercoat	m²	1.46	43.18	-	2.10	45.28	49.81	1.320
C908679	**Dubbing out with Carlite undercoat to walls**								
C908679A	6 mm browning to walls	m²	0.35	10.42	-	1.05	11.47	12.62	0.600
C908679B	12 mm browning to walls	m²	0.50	14.90	-	1.88	16.78	18.46	1.080
C908679C	15 mm browning to walls	m²	0.60	17.87	-	2.51	20.38	22.42	1.440
C908679D	20 mm browning to walls	m²	0.75	22.35	-	3.14	25.49	28.04	1.800
C908679E	6 mm bonding to walls	m²	0.35	10.42	-	1.22	11.64	12.80	0.720
C908679F	12 mm bonding to walls	m²	0.50	14.90	-	2.44	17.34	19.07	1.440
C908679G	15 mm bonding to walls	m²	0.60	17.87	-	3.05	20.92	23.01	1.800
C908679H	20 mm bonding to walls	m²	0.75	22.35	-	4.06	26.41	29.05	2.400
C908681	**12.5 mm Gypsum plasterboard and 5 mm Thistle board finish; jointing to existing; to walls**								
C908681A	to woodwork backgrounds	m²	0.75	22.35	-	4.30	26.65	29.32	5.677
C908681D	to masonry backgrounds	m²	0.55	16.38	-	4.31	20.69	22.76	5.744
C908681F	to concrete backgrounds	m²	0.55	16.38	-	4.31	20.69	22.76	5.744
C908688	**Carlite lightweight plaster; 2 mm finish on undercoat; jointing and finishing flush to existing; to concrete ceilings**								
C908688A	10 mm two coat work to concrete ceilings; bonding undercoat	m²	1.66	49.15	-	2.10	51.25	56.38	1.320
C908689	**Dubbing out with Carlite undercoat to ceilings**								
C908689E	6 mm bonding to ceilings	m²	0.45	13.42	-	1.22	14.64	16.10	0.720
C908689F	12 mm bonding to ceilings	m²	0.60	17.87	-	2.44	20.31	22.34	1.440
C908689G	15 mm bonding to ceilings	m²	0.70	20.84	-	3.05	23.89	26.28	1.800
C908689H	20 mm bonding to ceilings	m²	0.85	25.32	-	4.06	29.38	32.32	2.400
C908691	**12.5 mm Gypsum plasterboard and 5 mm Thistle board finish; jointing to existing; to ceilings**								
C908691A	to woodwork backgrounds	m²	0.95	28.29	-	4.30	32.59	35.85	5.677
C908691F	to concrete backgrounds	m²	0.75	22.35	-	4.31	26.66	29.33	5.744

Major Works 2011		Unit	Labour Hours	Labour Net	Plant Net	Materials Net	Unit Net	Unit with 10%	CO$_2$
				£	£	£	£	£	Kg
C90	**C90: ALTERATIONS - SPOT ITEMS**								
C9089	**Making good to timber mouldings after alterations in materials to match existing**								
C908901	**Moulded softwood sections in lengths not exceeding 1000 mm; jointing to existing**								
C908901A	19 x 50 mm	Nr	0.30	5.09	-	0.83	5.92	6.51	0.284
C908901B	19 x 75 mm	Nr	0.32	5.43	-	1.22	6.65	7.32	0.414
C908901C	19 x 100 mm	Nr	0.35	5.94	-	1.59	7.53	8.28	0.542
C908901D	25 x 125 mm	Nr	0.36	6.11	-	3.90	10.01	11.01	0.876
C908901E	25 x 150 mm	Nr	0.38	6.45	-	4.10	10.55	11.61	1.046
C908901F	25 x 175 mm	Nr	0.40	6.79	-	4.85	11.64	12.80	1.217
C9095	**Temporary roofs**								
C909599	**Temporary roofs; corrugated sheeting laid to slope on and including 50 x 150 mm softwood framing**								
C909599A	fibre cement sheets	m^2	0.35	5.94	-	24.90	30.84	33.92	45.621
C909599B	galvanised sheets	m^2	0.35	5.94	-	22.32	28.26	31.09	36.788
C909599C	translucent PVC-u sheets	m^2	0.35	5.94	-	20.70	26.64	29.30	8.463
C909599D	extra for 50 x 150 mm softwood posts	m	0.30	5.09	-	2.44	7.53	8.28	2.098
C9097	**Temporary screens**								
C909792	**Temporary dustproof screens; 1200 gauge polythene sheeting on 50 x 100 mm sawn softwood framing; joints sealed with self adhesive PVC-u tape**								
C909792A	vertical screens	m^2	0.35	5.94	-	3.24	9.18	10.10	6.237
C909792B	extra for sealing perimeters with self adhesive PVC-u tape	m	0.05	0.85	-	0.77	1.62	1.78	0.238
C909792C	extra for access door	Nr	1.50	25.47	-	13.14	38.61	42.47	17.950

Groundwork

Major Works 2011		Unit	Labour Hours	Labour Net	Plant Net	Materials Net	Unit Net	Unit with 10%	CO₂
				£	£	£	£	£	Kg
D20	**D20: EXCAVATING AND FILLING**								
D2011	**Site preparation**								
D201101	**Removing trees; girth**								
D201101A	600 mm - 1.50 m	Nr	4.00	50.80	79.39	-	130.19	143.21	49.207
D201101B	1.50 - 3.00 m	Nr	16.00	203.20	318.50	-	521.70	573.87	196.895
D201101C	3.00 - 4.50 m	Nr	36.00	457.20	715.46	-	1,172.66	1,289.93	442.930
D201101D	4.50 - 6.00 m	Nr	64.00	812.80	1,273.99	-	2,086.79	2,295.47	787.580
D201102	**Removing trees; filling voids with topsoil; girth**								
D201102A	600 mm - 1.50 m	Nr	4.00	50.80	79.58	13.02	143.40	157.74	60.868
D201102B	1.50 - 3.00 m	Nr	16.00	203.20	318.50	52.21	573.91	631.30	243.599
D201102C	3.00 - 4.50 m	Nr	36.00	457.20	715.46	116.94	1,289.60	1,418.56	547.538
D201102D	4.50 - 6.00 m	Nr	64.00	812.80	1,273.99	208.71	2,295.50	2,525.05	974.284
D201103	**Removing trees; filling voids with DTp aggregate; girth**								
D201103A	600 mm - 1.50 m	Nr	4.00	50.80	79.39	18.68	148.87	163.76	60.855
D201103B	1.50 - 3.00 m	Nr	16.00	203.20	318.50	74.89	596.59	656.25	243.599
D201103C	3.00 - 4.50 m	Nr	36.00	457.20	715.46	167.75	1,340.41	1,474.45	547.538
D201103D	4.50 - 6.00 m	Nr	64.00	812.80	1,273.99	299.39	2,386.18	2,624.80	974.284
D201110	**Cut down hedges; grub up roots and remove from site; height**								
D201110A	not exceeding 2.00 m	m	1.33	16.89	49.71	-	66.60	73.26	22.043
D201110B	2.00 - 3.00 m	m	5.33	67.69	193.64	-	261.33	287.46	87.797
D201110C	3.00 - 4.00 m	m	12.00	152.40	447.74	-	600.14	660.15	198.414
D201110D	4.00 - 5.00 m	m	21.70	275.59	813.68	-	1,089.27	1,198.20	354.015
D201111	**Removing tree stumps; filling voids with topsoil; girth**								
D201111A	600 mm - 1.50 m	Nr	1.33	16.89	49.71	13.02	79.62	87.58	33.691
D201111B	1.50 - 3.00 m	Nr	5.33	67.69	193.64	52.21	313.54	344.89	134.501
D201111C	3.00 - 4.50 m	Nr	12.00	152.40	447.74	116.94	717.08	788.79	303.022
D201111D	4.50 - 6.00 m	Nr	21.70	275.59	813.68	208.71	1,297.98	1,427.78	540.719
D201112	**Removing tree stumps; filling voids with DTp type 2 aggregate; girth**								
D201112A	600 mm - 1.50 m	Nr	1.33	16.89	49.71	18.68	85.28	93.81	33.691
D201112B	1.50 - 3.00 m	Nr	5.33	67.69	193.64	74.89	336.22	369.84	134.501
D201112C	3.00 - 4.50 m	Nr	12.00	152.40	447.74	167.75	767.89	844.68	303.022
D201112D	4.50 - 6.00 m	Nr	21.70	275.59	813.68	299.39	1,388.66	1,527.53	540.719
D201120	**Clear site of vegetation, undergrowth, bushes, hedges, trees or the like and remove from site**								
D201120A	generally	m²	0.02	0.19	1.39	-	1.58	1.74	0.654
D201130	**Lifting turf for preservation; by machine**								
D201130A	stacking on site	m²	0.06	0.76	0.23	-	0.99	1.09	0.139
D201140	**Lifting turf for preservation; by hand**								
D201140A	stacking on site	m²	0.25	3.17	-	-	3.17	3.49	-
D2021	**Machine excavation**								
D202102	**Oversite excavation to remove topsoil, average depth**								
D202102A	150 mm	m²	-	-	0.46	-	0.46	0.51	0.402
D202102B	300 mm	m²	-	-	0.57	-	0.57	0.63	0.503
D202103	**Excavation to reduce levels, depth not exceeding**								
D202103A	0.25 m	m³	-	-	1.82	-	1.82	2.00	1.608
D202103B	1.00 m	m³	-	-	1.37	-	1.37	1.51	1.206
D202103C	2.00 m	m³	-	-	2.05	-	2.05	2.26	1.809
D202103D	4.00 m	m³	-	-	2.74	-	2.74	3.01	2.412
D202103E	6.00 m	m³	-	-	3.19	-	3.19	3.51	2.814
D202104	**Excavation in cuttings, depth not exceeding**								
D202104A	0.25 m	m³	0.10	1.27	3.44	-	4.71	5.18	2.010
D202104B	1.00 m	m³	0.08	1.02	2.76	-	3.78	4.16	1.608

Groundwork

Major Works 2011	Unit	Labour Hours	Labour Net £	Plant Net £	Materials Net £	Unit Net £	Unit with 10% £	CO₂ Kg
D20	**D20: EXCAVATING AND FILLING**							
D2021	**Machine excavation**							
D202104	**Excavation in cuttings, depth not exceeding**							
D202104C	2.00 m	m³	0.10	1.27	3.44	-	4.71	5.18	2.010
D202104D	4.00 m	m³	0.12	1.52	4.13	-	5.65	6.22	2.412
D202104E	6.00 m	m³	0.14	1.78	4.82	-	6.60	7.26	2.814
D202105	**Basement excavation, depth not exceeding**							
D202105A	0.25 m	m³	0.12	1.52	4.13	-	5.65	6.22	2.412
D202105B	1.00 m	m³	0.10	1.27	3.44	-	4.71	5.18	2.010
D202105C	2.00 m	m³	0.12	1.52	4.13	-	5.65	6.22	2.412
D202105D	4.00 m	m³	0.14	1.78	4.82	-	6.60	7.26	2.814
D202105E	6.00 m	m³	0.16	2.03	5.51	-	7.54	8.29	3.216
D202106	**Trench excavation to receive foundations, pile caps and ground beams, depth not exceeding**							
D202106A	0.25 m	m³	0.30	3.81	6.84	-	10.65	11.72	6.030
D202106B	1.00 m	m³	0.26	3.30	5.93	-	9.23	10.15	5.226
D202106C	2.00 m	m³	0.30	3.81	6.84	-	10.65	11.72	6.030
D202106D	4.00 m	m³	0.33	4.19	7.53	-	11.72	12.89	6.633
D202106E	6.00 m	m³	0.40	5.08	9.12	-	14.20	15.62	8.040
D202107	**Pit excavation to receive foundation bases (in Nr. 1 - 5), depth not exceeding**							
D202107A	0.25 m	m³	0.35	4.44	7.98	-	12.42	13.66	7.035
D202107B	1.00 m	m³	0.31	3.94	7.07	-	11.01	12.11	6.231
D202107C	2.00 m	m³	0.35	4.44	7.98	-	12.42	13.66	7.035
D202107D	4.00 m	m³	0.40	5.08	9.12	-	14.20	15.62	8.040
D202107E	6.00 m	m³	0.44	5.59	10.04	-	15.63	17.19	8.844
D202108	**Pit excavation to receive foundation bases (in Nr. 6 - 10), depth not exceeding**							
D202108A	0.25 m	m³	0.39	4.95	8.90	-	13.85	15.24	7.839
D202108B	1.00 m	m³	0.34	4.32	7.76	-	12.08	13.29	6.834
D202108C	2.00 m	m³	0.39	4.95	8.90	-	13.85	15.24	7.839
D202108D	4.00 m	m³	0.44	5.59	10.04	-	15.63	17.19	8.844
D202108E	6.00 m	m³	0.48	6.10	10.95	-	17.05	18.76	9.648
D202109	**Pit excavation to receive foundation bases (in Nr. 11 - 20), depth not exceeding**							
D202109A	0.25 m	m³	0.44	5.59	10.04	-	15.63	17.19	8.844
D202109B	1.00 m	m³	0.39	4.95	8.90	-	13.85	15.24	7.839
D202109C	2.00 m	m³	0.44	5.59	10.04	-	15.63	17.19	8.844
D202109D	4.00 m	m³	0.50	6.35	11.40	-	17.75	19.53	10.050
D202109E	6.00 m	m³	0.55	6.99	12.55	-	19.54	21.49	11.055
D202110	**Pit excavation to receive foundation bases (in Nr. 21 or more), depth not exceeding**							
D202110A	0.25 m	m³	0.53	6.73	12.09	-	18.82	20.70	10.653
D202110B	1.00 m	m³	0.45	5.71	10.26	-	15.97	17.57	9.045
D202110C	2.00 m	m³	0.53	6.73	12.09	-	18.82	20.70	10.653
D202110D	4.00 m	m³	0.60	7.62	13.69	-	21.31	23.44	12.060
D202110E	6.00 m	m³	0.66	8.38	15.05	-	23.43	25.77	13.266
D2026	**Hand excavation**							
D202631	**Oversite excavation to remove topsoil, average depth**							
D202631A	150 mm	m²	0.18	2.29	-	-	2.29	2.52	-
D202631B	300 mm	m²	0.32	4.06	-	-	4.06	4.47	-
D202632	**Excavation to reduce levels, depth not exceeding**							
D202632A	0.25 m	m³	1.50	19.05	-	-	19.05	20.96	-
D202632B	1.00 m	m³	2.00	25.40	-	-	25.40	27.94	-

Major Works 2011		Unit	Labour Hours	Labour Net	Plant Net	Materials Net	Unit Net	Unit with 10%	CO$_2$
				£	£	£	£	£	Kg
D20	**D20: EXCAVATING AND FILLING**								
D2026	**Hand excavation**								
D202632	**Excavation to reduce levels, depth not exceeding**								
D202632C	2.00 m	m^3	2.30	29.21	-	-	29.21	32.13	-
D202632D	4.00 m	m^3	2.60	33.02	-	-	33.02	36.32	-
D202632E	6.00 m	m^3	3.20	40.64	-	-	40.64	44.70	-
D202633	**Excavation in cuttings, depth not exceeding**								
D202633A	0.25 m	m^3	1.80	22.86	-	-	22.86	25.15	-
D202633B	1.00 m	m^3	2.20	27.94	-	-	27.94	30.73	-
D202633C	2.00 m	m^3	2.45	31.12	-	-	31.12	34.23	-
D202633D	4.00 m	m^3	3.50	44.45	-	-	44.45	48.90	-
D202633E	6.00 m	m^3	4.30	54.61	-	-	54.61	60.07	-
D202634	**Basement excavations, depth not exceeding**								
D202634A	0.25 m	m^3	2.00	25.40	-	-	25.40	27.94	-
D202634B	1.00 m	m^3	2.40	30.48	-	-	30.48	33.53	-
D202634C	2.00 m	m^3	2.65	33.65	-	-	33.65	37.02	-
D202634D	4.00 m	m^3	3.70	46.99	-	-	46.99	51.69	-
D202634E	6.00 m	m^3	4.50	57.15	-	-	57.15	62.87	-
D202635	**Trench excavation to receive foundations, pile caps and ground beams, depth not exceeding**								
D202635A	0.25 m	m^3	2.30	29.21	-	-	29.21	32.13	-
D202635B	1.00 m	m^3	2.85	36.20	-	-	36.20	39.82	-
D202635C	2.00 m	m^3	3.30	41.91	-	-	41.91	46.10	-
D202635D	4.00 m	m^3	3.80	48.26	-	-	48.26	53.09	-
D202635E	6.00 m	m^3	5.00	63.50	-	-	63.50	69.85	-
D202636	**Pit excavation to receive foundation bases (in Nr. 1 - 5), depth not exceeding**								
D202636A	0.25 m	m^3	2.80	35.56	-	-	35.56	39.12	-
D202636B	1.00 m	m^3	3.45	43.81	-	-	43.81	48.19	-
D202636C	2.00 m	m^3	3.80	48.26	-	-	48.26	53.09	-
D202636D	4.00 m	m^3	4.45	56.52	-	-	56.52	62.17	-
D202636E	6.00 m	m^3	5.50	69.85	-	-	69.85	76.84	-
D202637	**Pit excavation to receive foundation bases (in Nr. 6 - 10), depth not exceeding**								
D202637A	0.25 m	m^3	3.10	39.37	-	-	39.37	43.31	-
D202637B	1.00 m	m^3	3.80	48.26	-	-	48.26	53.09	-
D202637C	2.00 m	m^3	4.20	53.34	-	-	53.34	58.67	-
D202637D	4.00 m	m^3	4.90	62.23	-	-	62.23	68.45	-
D202637E	6.00 m	m^3	6.10	77.47	-	-	77.47	85.22	-
D202638	**Pit excavation to receive foundation bases (in Nr. 10 - 20), depth not exceeding**								
D202638A	0.25 m	m^3	3.50	44.45	-	-	44.45	48.90	-
D202638B	1.00 m	m^3	4.30	54.61	-	-	54.61	60.07	-
D202638C	2.00 m	m^3	4.75	60.32	-	-	60.32	66.35	-
D202638D	4.00 m	m^3	5.60	71.12	-	-	71.12	78.23	-
D202638E	6.00 m	m^3	6.80	86.36	-	-	86.36	95.00	-
D202639	**Pit excavation to receive foundation bases (in Nr. 21 or more), depth not exceeding**								
D202639A	0.25 m	m^3	4.20	53.34	-	-	53.34	58.67	-
D202639B	1.00 m	m^3	5.10	64.77	-	-	64.77	71.25	-
D202639C	2.00 m	m^3	5.70	72.39	-	-	72.39	79.63	-
D202639D	4.00 m	m^3	6.65	84.45	-	-	84.45	92.90	-
D202639E	6.00 m	m^3	8.25	104.77	-	-	104.77	115.25	-

Groundwork

		Unit	Labour Hours	Labour Net	Plant Net	Materials Net	Unit Net	Unit with 10%	CO₂
				£	£	£	£	£	Kg
D20	**D20: EXCAVATING AND FILLING**								
D2041	**Breaking up obstructions with machine driven hammer**								
D204142	**Extra over excavation for breaking out**								
D204142A	soft rock or brickwork	m³	-	-	7.85	-	7.85	8.64	7.504
D204142B	hard rock	m³	-	-	12.33	-	12.33	13.56	11.792
D204142C	plain concrete	m³	-	-	10.09	-	10.09	11.10	9.648
D204142D	reinforced concrete	m³	-	-	14.57	-	14.57	16.03	13.936
D2043	**Breaking up obstructions with hand held mechanical tools**								
D204344	**Extra over excavation for breaking out**								
D204344A	soft rock or brickwork	m³	3.60	45.72	30.53	-	76.25	83.88	106.128
D204344B	hard rock	m³	6.40	81.28	54.27	-	135.55	149.11	188.672
D204344C	plain concrete	m³	5.00	63.50	42.40	-	105.90	116.49	147.400
D204344D	reinforced concrete	m³	7.20	91.44	61.06	-	152.50	167.75	212.256
D2051	**Breaking out pavings with machine driven hammer**								
D205133	**Excavation in tarmac paving**								
D205133A	not exceeding 150 mm thick	m²	-	-	0.67	-	0.67	0.74	0.643
D205133B	150 - 300 mm thick	m²	-	-	1.12	-	1.12	1.23	1.072
D205133C	300 - 450 mm thick	m²	-	-	1.79	-	1.79	1.97	1.715
D205134	**Excavation in plain concrete paving**								
D205134A	not exceeding 150 mm thick	m²	-	-	1.35	-	1.35	1.49	1.286
D205134B	150 - 300 mm thick	m²	-	-	2.24	-	2.24	2.46	2.144
D205134C	300 - 450 mm thick	m²	-	-	3.59	-	3.59	3.95	3.430
D205135	**Excavation in reinforced concrete paving**								
D205135A	not exceeding 150 mm thick	m²	0.08	1.02	2.47	-	3.49	3.84	2.151
D205135B	150 - 300 mm thick	m²	0.08	1.02	3.59	-	4.61	5.07	3.223
D205135C	300 - 450 mm thick	m²	0.08	1.02	4.71	-	5.73	6.30	4.295
D2052	**Breaking out pavings with hand held compressor tools**								
D205237	**Excavation in tarmac paving**								
D205237A	not exceeding 150 mm thick	m²	0.40	5.08	1.70	-	6.78	7.46	5.896
D205237B	150 - 300 mm thick	m²	0.70	8.89	3.39	-	12.28	13.51	11.792
D205237C	300 - 450 mm thick	m²	1.00	12.70	5.09	-	17.79	19.57	17.688
D205238	**Excavation in plain concrete paving**								
D205238A	not exceeding 150 mm thick	m²	0.60	7.62	3.39	-	11.01	12.11	11.792
D205238B	150 - 300 mm thick	m²	0.90	11.43	5.09	-	16.52	18.17	17.688
D205238C	300 - 450 mm thick	m²	0.12	1.52	6.78	-	8.30	9.13	23.584
D205239	**Excavation in reinforced concrete paving**								
D205239A	not exceeding 150 mm thick	m²	0.80	10.16	5.51	-	15.67	17.24	17.701
D205239B	150 - 300 mm thick	m²	1.30	16.51	8.90	-	25.41	27.95	29.493
D205239C	300 - 450 mm thick	m²	2.00	25.40	13.99	-	39.39	43.33	47.181
D2061	**Working space allowance to excavations; by hand**								
D206101	**Excavating for working space, by hand, additional earthwork support, compacting in layers; backfilling with excavated material**								
D206101A	basements	m²	1.59	20.19	0.51	-	20.70	22.77	0.643
D206101B	pits	m²	2.28	28.96	0.51	-	29.47	32.42	0.643
D206101C	trenches	m²	1.98	25.15	0.51	-	25.66	28.23	0.643
D206101D	pile caps and ground beams	m²	1.98	25.15	0.51	-	25.66	28.23	0.643

Major Works 2011		Unit	Labour Hours	Labour Net	Plant Net	Materials Net	Unit Net	Unit with 10%	CO₂
				£	£	£	£	£	Kg
D20	**D20: EXCAVATING AND FILLING**								
D2061	**Working space allowance to excavations; by hand**								
D206111	**Excavating for working space, by hand, disposal, additional earthwork support, compacting in layers; backfilling with hardcore**								
D206111A	basements	m²	2.95	37.46	11.44	14.49	63.39	69.73	9.926
D206111B	pits	m²	3.64	46.23	11.44	14.49	72.16	79.38	9.926
D206111C	trenches	m²	3.34	42.42	11.44	14.49	68.35	75.19	9.926
D206111D	pile caps and ground beams	m²	3.34	42.42	11.44	14.49	68.35	75.19	9.926
D206121	**Excavating for working space, by hand, disposal, additional earthwork support, backfilling with concrete, mix C15P**								
D206121A	basements	m²	2.95	37.46	11.13	47.44	96.03	105.63	206.724
D206121B	pits	m²	3.64	46.23	11.13	47.44	104.80	115.28	206.724
D206121C	trenches	m²	3.34	42.42	11.13	47.44	100.99	111.09	206.724
D206121D	pile caps and ground beams	m²	3.34	42.42	11.13	47.44	100.99	111.09	206.724
D2062	**Working space allowance to excavations; by machine**								
D206201	**Excavating for working space, by machine, additional earthwork support, compacting in layers; backfilling with excavated material**								
D206201A	basements	m²	0.25	3.20	6.21	-	9.41	10.35	4.848
D206201B	pits	m²	0.39	4.95	8.52	-	13.47	14.82	7.622
D206201C	trenches	m²	0.36	4.57	7.84	-	12.41	13.65	7.019
D206201D	pile caps and ground beams	m²	0.36	4.57	7.84	-	12.41	13.65	7.019
D206211	**Excavating for working space, by machine, disposal, additional earthwork support, compacting in layers; backfilling with hardcore**								
D206211A	basements	m²	0.25	3.20	18.98	14.49	36.67	40.34	15.835
D206211B	pits	m²	0.39	4.95	21.29	14.49	40.73	44.80	18.609
D206211C	trenches	m²	0.36	4.57	20.61	14.49	39.67	43.64	18.006
D206211D	pile caps and ground beams	m²	0.36	4.57	20.61	14.49	39.67	43.64	18.006
D206221	**Excavating for working space, by machine, additional earthwork support, backfilling with concrete, mix C15P**								
D206221A	basements	m²	0.61	7.77	14.57	47.44	69.78	76.76	209.015
D206221B	pits	m²	0.75	9.52	16.88	47.44	73.84	81.22	211.789
D206221C	trenches	m²	0.72	9.14	16.19	47.44	72.77	80.05	211.186
D206221D	pile caps and ground beams	m²	0.72	9.14	16.19	47.44	72.77	80.05	211.186
D2070	**Timber earthwork support to firm ground open boarded (risk item)**								
D207003	**To sides of excavation not exceeding 2.00 m apart, depth not exceeding**								
D207003A	1.00 m	m²	0.10	3.79	-	0.91	4.70	5.17	0.461
D207003B	2.00 m	m²	0.12	4.57	-	1.21	5.78	6.36	0.613
D207003C	4.00 m	m²	0.16	6.10	-	1.81	7.91	8.70	0.919
D207003D	6.00 m	m²	0.23	9.15	-	2.42	11.57	12.73	1.225
D207004	**To sides of excavation 2.00 - 4.00 m apart, depth not exceeding**								
D207004A	1.00 m	m	0.14	5.32	-	1.51	6.83	7.51	0.765
D207004B	2.00 m	m²	0.16	6.10	-	1.81	7.91	8.70	0.919
D207004C	4.00 m	m²	0.20	7.62	-	2.42	10.04	11.04	1.225
D207004D	6.00 m	m²	0.27	10.67	-	3.03	13.70	15.07	1.535

Groundwork

		Unit	Labour Hours	Labour Net	Plant Net	Materials Net	Unit Net	Unit with 10%	CO₂
				£	£	£	£	£	Kg
D20	D20: EXCAVATING AND FILLING								
D2070	Timber earthwork support to firm ground open boarded (risk item)								
D207005	To sides of excavation over 4.00 m apart, depth not exceeding								
D207005A	1.00 m	m²	0.12	4.57	-	0.91	5.48	6.03	0.461
D207005B	2.00 m	m²	0.20	7.62	-	1.81	9.43	10.37	0.919
D207005C	4.00 m	m²	0.23	9.15	-	3.02	12.17	13.39	1.532
D207005D	6.00 m	m²	0.31	12.20	-	4.23	16.43	18.07	2.145
D2071	Timber earthwork support to firm ground								
D207103	To sides of excavation not exceeding 2.00 m apart, depth not exceeding								
D207103A	1.00 m	m²	0.33	12.71	-	1.82	14.53	15.98	0.922
D207103B	2.00 m	m²	0.39	15.25	-	2.42	17.67	19.44	1.225
D207103C	4.00 m	m²	0.52	20.33	-	3.63	23.96	26.36	1.838
D207103D	6.00 m	m²	0.78	30.50	-	4.84	35.34	38.87	2.451
D207104	To sides of excavation 2.00 - 4.00 m apart, depth not exceeding								
D207104A	1.00 m	m²	0.46	17.79	-	3.02	20.81	22.89	1.529
D207104B	2.00 m	m²	0.52	20.33	-	3.63	23.96	26.36	1.838
D207104C	4.00 m	m²	0.65	25.42	-	4.84	30.26	33.29	2.451
D207104D	6.00 m	m²	0.91	35.58	-	6.06	41.64	45.80	3.069
D207105	To sides of excavation over 4.00 m apart, depth not exceeding								
D207105A	1.00 m	m²	0.39	15.25	-	1.82	17.07	18.78	0.922
D207105B	2.00 m	m²	0.65	25.42	-	3.63	29.05	31.96	1.838
D207105C	4.00 m	m²	0.78	30.50	-	6.05	36.55	40.21	3.064
D207105D	6.00 m	m²	1.04	40.62	-	8.47	49.09	54.00	4.289
D2072	Timber earthwork support to loose ground								
D207207	To sides of excavation not exceeding 2.00 m apart, depth not exceeding								
D207207A	1.00 m	m²	0.43	16.77	-	8.57	25.34	27.87	3.000
D207207B	2.00 m	m²	0.51	19.82	-	9.17	28.99	31.89	3.303
D207207C	4.00 m	m²	0.62	24.40	-	10.38	34.78	38.26	3.916
D207207D	6.00 m	m²	0.90	35.07	-	11.59	46.66	51.33	4.529
D207208	To sides of excavation 2.00 - 4.00 m apart, depth not exceeding								
D207208A	1.00 m	m²	0.66	25.92	-	9.77	35.69	39.26	3.607
D207208B	2.00 m	m²	0.60	23.38	-	10.38	33.76	37.14	3.916
D207208C	4.00 m	m²	0.75	29.48	-	11.59	41.07	45.18	4.529
D207208D	6.00 m	m²	0.99	38.59	-	12.81	51.40	56.54	5.147
D207209	To sides of excavation over 4.00 m apart, depth not exceeding								
D207209A	1.00 m	m²	0.49	19.32	-	8.57	27.89	30.68	3.000
D207209B	2.00 m	m²	0.74	28.97	-	10.38	39.35	43.29	3.916
D207209C	4.00 m	m²	0.90	35.07	-	12.80	47.87	52.66	5.142
D207209D	6.00 m	m²	1.12	43.67	-	15.22	58.89	64.78	6.367
D2075	Steel trench sheeting to firm ground								
D207511	To sides of excavation not exceeding 2.00 m apart, depth not exceeding								
D207511A	1.00 m	m²	0.20	7.62	5.34	1.20	14.16	15.58	4.024
D207511B	2.00 m	m²	0.20	7.62	5.98	1.20	14.80	16.28	4.828
D207511C	4.00 m	m²	0.20	7.62	6.56	1.20	15.38	16.92	5.230

Major Works 2011		Unit	Labour Hours	Labour Net	Plant Net	Materials Net	Unit Net	Unit with 10%	CO₂
				£	£	£	£	£	Kg

		Unit	Labour Hours	Labour Net	Plant Net	Materials Net	Unit Net	Unit with 10%	CO₂
D20	**D20: EXCAVATING AND FILLING**								
D2075	**Steel trench sheeting to firm ground**								
D207511	**To sides of excavation not exceeding 2.00 m apart, depth not exceeding**								
D207511D	6.00 m	m²	0.33	12.71	5.98	1.20	19.89	21.88	4.828
D207512	**To sides of excavation 2.00 - 4.00 m apart, depth not exceeding**								
D207512A	1.00 m	m²	0.33	12.71	5.34	2.40	20.45	22.50	4.631
D207512B	2.00 m	m²	0.33	12.71	5.98	2.40	21.09	23.20	5.435
D207512C	4.00 m	m²	0.39	15.25	6.56	2.40	24.21	26.63	5.837
D207512D	6.00 m	m²	0.46	17.79	5.98	2.40	26.17	28.79	5.435
D207513	**To sides of excavation over 4.00 m apart, depth not exceeding**								
D207513A	1.00 m	m²	0.20	7.62	5.34	1.20	14.16	15.58	4.024
D207513B	2.00 m	m²	0.26	10.17	5.98	1.42	17.57	19.33	4.939
D207513C	4.00 m	m²	0.33	12.71	6.56	1.74	21.01	23.11	5.506
D207513D	6.00 m	m²	0.39	15.25	5.98	1.96	23.19	25.51	5.215
D2076	**Steel trench sheeting to loose ground**								
D207615	**To sides of excavation not exceeding 2.00 m apart, depth not exceeding**								
D207615A	1.00 m	m²	0.20	7.62	14.21	1.20	23.03	25.33	8.044
D207615B	2.00 m	m²	0.20	7.62	20.12	1.20	28.94	31.83	9.853
D207615C	4.00 m	m²	0.20	7.62	32.81	1.20	41.63	45.79	10.858
D207615D	6.00 m	m²	0.33	12.71	39.37	1.20	53.28	58.61	9.853
D207616	**To sides of excavation 2.00 - 4.00 m apart, depth not exceeding**								
D207616A	1.00 m	m²	0.33	12.71	14.21	2.40	29.32	32.25	8.651
D207616B	2.00 m	m²	0.33	12.71	20.12	2.40	35.23	38.75	10.460
D207616C	4.00 m	m²	0.39	15.25	32.81	2.40	50.46	55.51	11.465
D207616D	6.00 m	m²	0.46	17.79	39.37	2.40	59.56	65.52	10.460
D207617	**To sides of excavation over 4.00 m apart, depth not exceeding**								
D207617A	1.00 m	m²	0.20	7.62	14.21	1.20	23.03	25.33	8.044
D207617B	2.00 m	m²	0.26	10.17	20.12	1.42	31.71	34.88	9.964
D207617C	4.00 m	m²	0.33	12.71	32.81	1.74	47.26	51.99	11.134
D207617D	6.00 m	m²	0.39	15.25	39.37	1.96	56.58	62.24	10.240
D2082	**Off site disposal of material arising from earthworks**								
D208209	**Removed, including providing a suitable tip**								
D208209A	hand loading	m³	1.37	17.40	22.30	-	39.70	43.67	1.340
D208209B	machine loading	m³	-	-	23.90	-	23.90	26.29	2.747
D2084	**On site disposal of material arising from earthworks**								
D208402	**Backfilled into excavation; compacting in 250 mm layers**								
D208402A	by hand	m³	1.30	16.51	0.51	-	17.02	18.72	0.643
D208402B	by machine	m³	0.30	3.81	6.22	-	10.03	11.03	5.668
D208403	**Backfilled in making up levels; by hand; compacting in 250 mm layers; wheeling average**								
D208403A	25 m	m³	1.66	21.08	0.51	-	21.59	23.75	0.801
D208403B	50 m	m³	2.00	25.40	0.51	-	25.91	28.50	0.801
D208403C	75 m	m³	2.33	29.59	0.51	-	30.10	33.11	0.801
D208403D	100 m	m³	2.66	33.78	0.51	-	34.29	37.72	0.801

Groundwork

		Unit	Labour Hours	Labour Net £	Plant Net £	Materials Net £	Unit Net £	Unit with 10% £	CO₂ Kg
D20	**D20: EXCAVATING AND FILLING**								
D2084	**On site disposal of material arising from earthworks**								
D208404	**Backfilled in making up levels; by machine; compacting in 250 mm layers; transporting average**								
D208404A	25 m	m³	0.27	3.43	3.21	-	6.64	7.30	8.037
D208404B	50 m	m³	0.33	4.19	3.59	-	7.78	8.56	10.449
D208404C	75 m	m³	0.40	5.08	4.03	-	9.11	10.02	13.263
D208404D	100 m	m³	0.47	5.97	4.47	-	10.44	11.48	16.077
D208405	**Backfilled oversite to make up levels; by hand; compacting in 250 mm layers; wheeling average**								
D208405A	25 m	m³	1.86	23.62	0.67	-	24.29	26.72	1.048
D208405B	50 m	m³	2.20	27.94	0.67	-	28.61	31.47	1.048
D208405C	75 m	m³	2.53	32.13	0.67	-	32.80	36.08	1.048
D208405D	100 m	m³	2.86	36.32	0.67	-	36.99	40.69	1.048
D208406	**Backfilled oversite to make up levels; by machine; compacting in 250 mm layers; transporting average**								
D208406A	25 m	m³	0.35	4.44	4.76	-	9.20	10.12	10.897
D208406B	50 m	m³	0.41	5.21	5.14	-	10.35	11.39	13.309
D208406C	75 m	m³	0.49	6.22	5.64	-	11.86	13.05	16.525
D208406D	100 m	m³	0.55	6.99	6.02	-	13.01	14.31	18.937
D208407	**Grading backfilled oversite to contours, embankments or the like; by hand**								
D208407A	to falls	m³	0.08	1.02	-	-	1.02	1.12	-
D208407B	to falls and cross-falls	m³	0.14	1.78	-	-	1.78	1.96	-
D208407C	to slopes	m³	0.07	0.89	-	-	0.89	0.98	-
D208408	**Grading backfilled oversite to contours, embankments or the like; by machine**								
D208408A	to falls	m³	0.03	0.38	0.68	-	1.06	1.17	0.603
D208408B	to falls and cross-falls	m³	0.05	0.64	1.14	-	1.78	1.96	1.005
D208408C	to slopes	m³	0.02	0.25	0.46	-	0.71	0.78	0.402
D2091	**Filling to excavations with materials arising from earthworks**								
D209102	**Backfilled into excavation; compacting in 250 mm layers**								
D209102A	by hand	m³	1.30	16.51	0.51	-	17.02	18.72	0.643
D209102B	by machine	m³	0.30	3.81	6.22	-	10.03	11.03	5.668
D209103	**Backfilled in making up levels; by hand; compacting in 250 mm layers; wheeling average**								
D209103A	25 m	m³	1.66	21.08	0.51	-	21.59	23.75	0.801
D209103B	50 m	m³	2.00	25.40	0.51	-	25.91	28.50	0.801
D209103C	75 m	m³	2.33	29.59	0.51	-	30.10	33.11	0.801
D209103D	100 m	m³	2.66	33.78	0.51	-	34.29	37.72	0.801
D209104	**Backfilled in making up levels; by machine; compacting in 250 mm layers; transporting average**								
D209104A	25 m	m³	0.27	3.43	3.21	-	6.64	7.30	8.037
D209104B	50 m	m³	0.33	4.19	3.59	-	7.78	8.56	10.449
D209104C	75 m	m³	0.40	5.08	4.03	-	9.11	10.02	13.263
D209104D	100 m	m³	0.47	5.97	4.47	-	10.44	11.48	16.077
D209105	**Backfilled oversite to make up levels; by hand; compacting in 250 mm layers; wheeling average**								
D209105A	25 m	m³	1.86	23.62	0.67	-	24.29	26.72	1.048

Major Works 2011		Unit	Labour Hours	Labour Net	Plant Net	Materials Net	Unit Net	Unit with 10%	CO$_2$
				£	£	£	£	£	Kg
D20	**D20: EXCAVATING AND FILLING**								
D2091	**Filling to excavations with materials arising from earthworks**								
D209105	**Backfilled oversite to make up levels; by hand; compacting in 250 mm layers; wheeling average**								
D209105B	50 m	m^3	2.20	27.94	0.67	-	28.61	31.47	1.048
D209105C	75 m	m^3	2.53	32.13	0.67	-	32.80	36.08	1.048
D209105D	100 m	m^3	2.86	36.32	0.67	-	36.99	40.69	1.048
D209106	**Backfilled oversite to make up levels; by machine; compacting in 250 mm layers; transporting average**								
D209106A	25 m	m^3	0.35	4.44	4.76	-	9.20	10.12	10.897
D209106B	50 m	m^3	0.41	5.21	5.14	-	10.35	11.39	13.309
D209106C	75 m	m^3	0.49	6.22	5.64	-	11.86	13.05	16.525
D209106D	100 m	m^3	0.55	6.99	6.02	-	13.01	14.31	18.937
D209107	**Grading backfilled oversite to contours, embankments or the like; by hand**								
D209107A	to falls	m^3	0.08	1.02	-	-	1.02	1.12	-
D209107B	to falls and cross-falls	m^3	0.14	1.78	-	-	1.78	1.96	-
D209107C	to slopes	m^3	0.07	0.89	-	-	0.89	0.98	-
D209108	**Grading backfilled oversite to contours, embankments or the like; by machine**								
D209108A	to falls	m^3	0.03	0.38	0.68	-	1.06	1.17	0.603
D209108B	to falls and cross-falls	m^3	0.05	0.64	1.14	-	1.78	1.96	1.005
D209108C	to slopes	m^3	0.02	0.25	0.46	-	0.71	0.78	0.402
D2093	**Filling to excavations with imported materials**								
D209301	**Filled into excavation; by hand compacting in layers**								
D209301A	sand	m^3	0.80	10.16	0.51	23.59	34.26	37.69	14.643
D209301B	hardcore	m^3	1.65	20.95	0.60	24.67	46.22	50.84	17.550
D209301C	hoggin	m^3	0.90	11.43	0.51	24.15	36.09	39.70	15.203
D209301D	DTp type 1	m^3	1.63	20.70	0.56	26.95	48.21	53.03	15.828
D209301E	DTp type 2	m^3	1.63	20.70	0.56	24.25	45.51	50.06	15.828
D209301F	stone rejects	m^3	1.65	20.95	0.60	25.20	46.75	51.43	16.990
D209301G	granite scalpings	m^3	1.65	20.95	0.56	22.32	43.83	48.21	16.388
D209302	**Filled into excavation; by machine; compacting in layers**								
D209302A	sand	m^3	0.30	3.81	5.08	23.59	32.48	35.73	18.663
D209302B	hardcore	m^3	0.35	4.44	8.58	24.67	37.69	41.46	24.585
D209302C	hoggin	m^3	0.30	3.81	7.36	24.15	35.32	38.85	21.233
D209302D	DTp type 1	m^3	0.33	4.19	8.55	26.95	39.69	43.66	22.863
D209302E	DTp type 2	m^3	0.33	4.19	8.55	24.25	36.99	40.69	22.863
D209302F	stone rejects	m^3	0.35	4.44	8.58	25.20	38.22	42.04	24.025
D209302G	granite scalpings	m^3	0.33	4.19	8.55	22.32	35.06	38.57	23.423
D209303	**Filled in making up levels; by hand; compacting in layers**								
D209303A	sand	m^3	0.83	10.54	0.77	23.59	34.90	38.39	16.613
D209303B	hardcore	m^3	1.46	18.54	0.77	24.67	43.98	48.38	19.413
D209303C	hoggin	m^3	0.93	11.81	0.77	24.15	36.73	40.40	17.173
D209303D	DTp type 1	m^3	1.40	17.78	0.77	26.95	45.50	50.05	17.733
D209303E	DTp type 2	m^3	1.40	17.78	0.77	24.25	42.80	47.08	17.733
D209303F	stone rejects	m^3	1.46	18.54	0.77	25.20	44.51	48.96	18.853
D209303G	granite scalpings	m^3	1.46	18.54	0.77	22.32	41.63	45.79	18.293
D209304	**Filled in making up levels; by machine; compacting in layers**								
D209304A	sand	m^3	0.13	1.65	1.91	23.59	27.15	29.87	17.618
D209304B	hardcore	m^3	0.13	1.65	3.05	24.67	29.37	32.31	21.423

Groundwork

Major Works 2011		Unit	Labour Hours	Labour Net £	Plant Net £	Materials Net £	Unit Net £	Unit with 10% £	CO₂ Kg
D20	**D20: EXCAVATING AND FILLING**								
D2093	**Filling to excavations with imported materials**								
D209304	**Filled in making up levels; by machine; compacting in layers**								
D209304C	hoggin	m³	0.13	1.65	2.59	24.15	28.39	31.23	18.781
D209304D	DTp type 1	m³	0.13	1.65	2.59	26.95	31.19	34.31	19.341
D209304E	DTp type 2	m³	0.13	1.65	2.59	24.25	28.49	31.34	19.341
D209304F	stone rejects	m³	0.13	1.65	3.05	25.20	29.90	32.89	20.863
D209304G	granite scalpings	m³	0.13	1.65	3.05	22.32	27.02	29.72	20.303
D209305	**Filled into oversite to make up levels; by hand; compacting in layers; average 150 mm thick**								
D209305A	sand	m³	1.03	13.08	1.00	23.59	37.67	41.44	17.417
D209305B	hardcore	m³	1.66	21.08	1.00	24.67	46.75	51.43	20.217
D209305C	hoggin	m³	1.13	14.35	1.00	24.15	39.50	43.45	17.977
D209305D	DTp type 1	m³	1.60	20.32	1.00	26.95	48.27	53.10	18.537
D209305E	DTp type 2	m³	1.60	20.32	1.00	24.25	45.57	50.13	18.537
D209305F	stone rejects	m³	1.66	21.08	1.00	25.20	47.28	52.01	19.657
D209305G	granite scalpings	m³	1.66	21.08	1.00	22.32	44.40	48.84	19.097
D209306	**Filled into oversite to make up levels; by machine; compacting in layers; average 150 mm thick**								
D209306A	sand	m³	0.17	2.16	3.28	23.59	29.03	31.93	19.427
D209306B	hardcore	m³	0.17	2.16	4.42	24.67	31.25	34.38	23.232
D209306C	hoggin	m³	0.17	2.16	3.97	24.15	30.28	33.31	20.590
D209306D	DTp type 1	m³	0.17	2.16	3.97	26.95	33.08	36.39	21.150
D209306E	DTp type 2	m³	0.17	2.16	3.97	24.25	30.38	33.42	21.150
D209306F	stone rejects	m³	0.17	2.16	4.42	25.20	31.78	34.96	22.672
D209306G	granite scalpings	m³	0.17	2.16	4.42	22.32	28.90	31.79	22.112
D209307	**Grading filled oversite to contours, embankments or the like; by hand**								
D209307A	to falls	m²	0.10	1.27	-	-	1.27	1.40	-
D209307B	to falls and cross-falls	m²	0.17	2.16	-	-	2.16	2.38	-
D209307C	to slopes	m²	0.09	1.14	-	-	1.14	1.25	-
D209308	**Grading filled oversite to contours, embankments or the like; by machine**								
D209308A	to falls	m²	0.03	0.38	0.68	-	1.06	1.17	0.603
D209308B	to falls and cross-falls	m²	0.05	0.64	1.14	-	1.78	1.96	1.005
D209308C	to slopes	m²	0.02	0.25	0.46	-	0.71	0.78	0.402
D209309	**Blinding to hardcore**								
D209309A	25 mm sand	m²	0.04	0.51	-	0.53	1.04	1.14	0.314
D209309B	50 mm sand	m²	0.06	0.70	-	1.04	1.74	1.91	0.616
D2095	**Surface treatment**								
D209520	**Level and compact**								
D209520A	ground	m²	0.05	0.64	0.09	-	0.73	0.80	0.107
D209520B	filling	m²	0.05	0.64	0.09	-	0.73	0.80	0.107
D209520C	bottoms of excavations	m²	0.06	0.70	0.09	-	0.79	0.87	0.118

Major Works 2011		Unit	Labour Hours	Labour Net	Plant Net	Materials Net	Unit Net	Unit with 10%	CO$_2$
				£	£	£	£	£	Kg
D30	**D30: CAST IN PLACE CONCRETE PILING**								
D3020	**Driven shell piles; rotary bored**								
D302010	**Provision of all plant including bringing to site and removal on completion; setting up and subsequent dismantling; general maintenance**								
D302010A	average 100 Nr piles	Item	60.31	3,244.84	8,712.00	–	11,956.84	13,152.52	5,628.000
D302020	**Piles 400 mm dia**								
D302020A	total number of piles	Nr	0.36	19.48	52.27	–	71.75	78.93	33.768
D302020B	total concreted length	m	0.22	12.00	32.23	19.45	63.68	70.05	82.366
D302020F	10 m max bored depth	m	0.26	14.04	37.75	–	51.79	56.97	24.388
D302020G	15 m max bored depth	m	0.29	15.71	42.11	–	57.82	63.60	27.202
D302020H	20 m max bored depth	m	0.32	17.05	45.74	–	62.79	69.07	29.547
D302020M	Extra over for enlarging bases 900 m extreme dia	Nr	0.85	45.95	123.42	26.81	196.18	215.80	178.946
D302030	**Cutting off tops of piles; 400 mm dia**								
D302030C	total length 2.0 m	m	0.60	32.44	2.04	–	34.48	37.93	10.934
D302050	**Pile tests; 400 mm dia**								
D302050A	working piles; maintained loading 500 Kn	Nr	5.28	283.90	204.36	–	488.26	537.09	139.360

Groundwork

		Unit	Labour Hours	Labour Net £	Plant Net £	Materials Net £	Unit Net £	Unit with 10% £	CO$_2$ Kg
D31	**D31: PREFORMED CONCRETE PILES**								
D3120	**Reinforced concrete piles**								
D312010	**Provision of all plant including bringing to site and removal on completion; setting up and subsequent dismantling; general maintenance**								
D312010A	average 100 Nr piles	Item	48.25	2,595.85	6,284.16	-	8,880.01	9,768.01	3,859.200
D312020	**Sectional size; 600 mm dia**								
D312020A	10 m max total driven depth	m	0.26	14.04	34.04	173.32	221.40	243.54	173.508
D312020B	15 m total driven depth	m	0.75	40.57	98.19	173.32	312.08	343.29	212.904
D312020C	20 m total driven depth	m	1.21	64.88	157.10	173.32	395.30	434.83	249.084
D312030	**Cutting off tops of piles; 600 mm dia**								
D312030A	total length 2.0 m	Nr	1.26	67.63	4.25	-	71.88	79.07	22.780
D312050	**Pile tests; 600 mm dia**								
D312050A	working pile; maintained loading 500 Kn	Nr	5.28	283.90	94.32	-	378.22	416.04	64.320

Major Works 2011		Unit	Labour Hours	Labour Net £	Plant Net £	Materials Net £	Unit Net £	Unit with 10% £	CO₂ Kg
D50	**D50: UNDERPINNING**								
D5021	**Machine excavation**								
D502102	**Excavation in preliminary trenches down to the base of the existing foundations, depth not exceeding**								
D502102A	0.25 m	m³	0.30	3.81	6.84	-	10.65	11.72	6.030
D502102B	1.00 m	m³	0.25	3.17	5.70	-	8.87	9.76	5.025
D502102C	2.00 m	m³	0.35	4.44	7.98	-	12.42	13.66	7.035
D502102D	4.00 m	m³	0.45	5.71	10.26	-	15.97	17.57	9.045
D502102E	6.00 m	m³	0.50	6.35	11.40	-	17.75	19.53	10.050
D502103	**Excavation below the base of the existing foundations, depth not exceeding**								
D502103A	1.00 m	m³	0.40	5.08	9.12	-	14.20	15.62	8.040
D502103B	2.00 m	m³	0.70	8.89	15.97	-	24.86	27.35	14.070
D502103C	4.00 m	m³	0.90	11.43	20.53	-	31.96	35.16	18.090
D502103D	6.00 m	m³	1.10	13.97	25.09	-	39.06	42.97	22.110
D5025	**Hand excavation**								
D502501	**Excavation in preliminary trenches down to the base of the existing foundations, depth not exceeding**								
D502501A	0.25 m	m³	4.50	57.15	-	-	57.15	62.87	-
D502501B	1.00 m	m³	4.20	53.34	-	-	53.34	58.67	-
D502501C	2.00 m	m³	4.80	60.96	-	-	60.96	67.06	-
D502501D	4.00 m	m³	5.60	71.12	-	-	71.12	78.23	-
D502501E	6.00 m	m³	6.50	82.55	-	-	82.55	90.81	-
D502502	**Excavation below the base of the existing foundations, depth not exceeding**								
D502502B	1.00 m	m³	5.70	72.39	-	-	72.39	79.63	-
D502502C	2.00 m	m³	6.60	83.82	-	-	83.82	92.20	-
D502502D	4.00 m	m³	7.50	95.25	-	-	95.25	104.78	-
D502502E	6.00 m	m³	9.20	116.84	-	-	116.84	128.52	-
D5031	**Breaking up obstructions with hand held mechanical tools**								
D503144	**Extra over excavation for breaking out**								
D503144A	soft rock or brickwork	m³	3.60	45.72	30.53	-	76.25	83.88	106.128
D503144B	hard rock	m³	6.40	81.28	54.27	-	135.55	149.11	188.672
D503144C	plain concrete	m³	5.00	63.50	42.40	-	105.90	116.49	147.400
D503144D	reinforced concrete	m³	7.20	91.44	61.06	-	152.50	167.75	212.256
D5033	**Breaking out pavings with hand held compressor tools**								
D503337	**Excavation in tarmac paving**								
D503337A	not exceeding 150 mm thick	m²	0.40	5.08	1.70	-	6.78	7.46	5.896
D503337B	150 - 300 mm thick	m²	0.70	8.89	3.39	-	12.28	13.51	11.792
D503337C	300 - 450 mm thick	m²	1.00	12.70	5.09	-	17.79	19.57	17.688
D503338	**Excavation in plain concrete paving**								
D503338A	not exceeding 150 mm thick	m²	0.60	7.62	3.39	-	11.01	12.11	11.792
D503338B	150 - 300 mm thick	m²	0.90	11.43	5.09	-	16.52	18.17	17.688
D503338C	300 - 450 mm thick	m²	0.12	1.52	6.78	-	8.30	9.13	23.584
D503339	**Excavation in reinforced concrete paving**								
D503339A	not exceeding 150 mm thick	m²	0.80	10.16	5.51	-	15.67	17.24	17.701
D503339B	150 - 300 mm thick	m²	1.30	16.51	8.90	-	25.41	27.95	29.493
D503339C	300 - 450 mm thick	m²	2.00	25.40	13.99	-	39.39	43.33	47.181

Groundwork

Major Works 2011	Unit	Labour Hours	Labour Net	Plant Net	Materials Net	Unit Net	Unit with 10%	CO₂
			£	£	£	£	£	Kg
D50	**D50: UNDERPINNING**							
D5041	**Timber earthwork support to firm ground**							
D504103	**To sides of excavation not exceeding 2.00 m apart, depth not exceeding**							
D504103A	1.00 m	m²	0.33	12.71	-	1.82	14.53	15.98	0.922
D504103B	2.00 m	m²	0.39	15.25	-	2.42	17.67	19.44	1.225
D504103C	4.00 m	m²	0.52	20.33	-	3.63	23.96	26.36	1.838
D504103D	6.00 m	m²	0.78	30.50	-	4.84	35.34	38.87	2.451
D504104	**To sides of excavation 2.00 - 4.00 m apart, depth not exceeding**							
D504104A	1.00 m	m²	0.46	17.79	-	3.02	20.81	22.89	1.529
D504104B	2.00 m	m²	0.52	20.33	-	3.63	23.96	26.36	1.838
D504104C	4.00 m	m²	0.65	25.42	-	4.84	30.26	33.29	2.451
D504104D	6.00 m	m²	0.91	35.58	-	6.06	41.64	45.80	3.069
D504105	**To sides of excavation over 4.00 m apart, depth not exceeding**							
D504105A	1.00 m	m²	0.39	15.25	-	1.82	17.07	18.78	0.922
D504105B	2.00 m	m²	0.65	25.42	-	3.63	29.05	31.96	1.838
D504105C	4.00 m	m²	0.78	30.50	-	6.05	36.55	40.21	3.064
D504105D	6.00 m	m²	1.04	40.62	-	8.47	49.09	54.00	4.289
D5042	**Timber earthwork support to loose ground**							
D504207	**To sides of excavation not exceeding 2.00 m apart, depth not exceeding**							
D504207A	1.00 m	m²	0.43	16.77	-	8.57	25.34	27.87	3.000
D504207B	2.00 m	m²	0.51	19.82	-	9.17	28.99	31.89	3.303
D504207C	4.00 m	m²	0.62	24.40	-	10.38	34.78	38.26	3.916
D504207D	6.00 m	m²	0.90	35.07	-	11.59	46.66	51.33	4.529
D504208	**To sides of excavation 2.00 - 4.00 m apart, depth not exceeding**							
D504208A	1.00 m	m²	0.66	25.92	-	9.77	35.69	39.26	3.607
D504208B	2.00 m	m²	0.60	23.38	-	10.38	33.76	37.14	3.916
D504208C	4.00 m	m²	0.75	29.48	-	11.59	41.07	45.18	4.529
D504208D	6.00 m	m²	0.99	38.59	-	12.81	51.40	56.54	5.147
D504209	**To sides of excavation over 4.00 m apart, depth not exceeding**							
D504209A	1.00 m	m²	0.49	19.32	-	8.57	27.89	30.68	3.000
D504209B	2.00 m	m²	0.74	28.97	-	10.38	39.35	43.29	3.916
D504209C	4.00 m	m²	0.90	35.07	-	12.80	47.87	52.66	5.142
D504209D	6.00 m	m²	1.12	43.67	-	15.22	58.89	64.78	6.367
D5045	**Steel trench sheeting to firm ground**							
D504511	**To sides of excavation not exceeding 2.00 m apart, depth not exceeding**							
D504511A	1.00 m	m²	0.20	7.62	5.34	1.20	14.16	15.58	4.024
D504511B	2.00 m	m²	0.20	7.62	5.98	1.20	14.80	16.28	4.828
D504511C	4.00 m	m²	0.20	7.62	6.56	1.20	15.38	16.92	5.230
D504511D	6.00 m	m²	0.33	12.71	5.98	1.20	19.89	21.88	4.828
D504512	**To sides of excavation 2.00 - 4.00 m apart, depth not exceeding**							
D504512A	1.00 m	m²	0.33	12.71	5.34	2.40	20.45	22.50	4.631
D504512B	2.00 m	m²	0.33	12.71	5.98	2.40	21.09	23.20	5.435
D504512C	4.00 m	m²	0.39	15.25	6.56	2.40	24.21	26.63	5.837
D504512D	6.00 m	m²	0.46	17.79	5.98	2.40	26.17	28.79	5.435

Major Works 2011		Unit	Labour Hours	Labour Net	Plant Net	Materials Net	Unit Net	Unit with 10%	CO$_2$
				£	£	£	£	£	Kg
D50	**D50: UNDERPINNING**								
D5045	**Steel trench sheeting to firm ground**								
D504513	**To sides of excavation over 4.00 m apart, depth not exceeding**								
D504513A	1.00 m	m²	0.20	7.62	5.34	1.20	14.16	15.58	4.024
D504513B	2.00 m	m²	0.26	10.17	5.98	1.42	17.57	19.33	4.939
D504513C	4.00 m	m²	0.33	12.71	6.56	1.74	21.01	23.11	5.506
D504513D	6.00 m	m²	0.39	15.25	5.98	1.96	23.19	25.51	5.215
D5046	**Steel trench sheeting to loose ground**								
D504615	**To sides of excavation not exceeding 2.00 m apart; depth not exceeding**								
D504615A	1.00 m	m²	0.20	7.62	14.21	1.20	23.03	25.33	8.044
D504615B	2.00 m	m²	0.20	7.62	20.12	1.20	28.94	31.83	9.853
D504615C	4.00 m	m²	0.20	7.62	32.81	1.20	41.63	45.79	10.858
D504615D	6.00 m	m²	0.33	12.71	39.37	1.20	53.28	58.61	9.853
D504616	**To sides of excavation 2.00 - 4.00 m apart; depth not exceeding**								
D504616A	1.00 m	m²	0.33	12.71	14.21	2.40	29.32	32.25	8.651
D504616B	2.00 m	m²	0.33	12.71	20.12	2.40	35.23	38.75	10.460
D504616C	4.00 m	m²	0.39	15.25	32.81	2.40	50.46	55.51	11.465
D504616D	6.00 m	m²	0.46	17.79	39.37	2.40	59.56	65.52	10.460
D504617	**To sides of excavation over 4.00 m apart; depth not exceeding**								
D504617A	1.00 m	m²	0.20	7.62	14.21	1.20	23.03	25.33	8.044
D504617B	2.00 m	m²	0.26	10.17	20.12	1.42	31.71	34.88	9.964
D504617C	4.00 m	m²	0.33	12.71	32.81	1.74	47.26	51.99	11.134
D504617D	6.00 m	m²	0.39	15.25	39.37	1.96	56.58	62.24	10.240
D5051	**Cutting away projecting foundations**								
D505121	**Brick**								
D505121A	half brick thick, one course	m	0.25	3.17	-	-	3.17	3.49	-
D505121B	half brick thick, two course	m	0.40	5.08	-	-	5.08	5.59	-
D505121C	half brick thick, three course	m	0.20	2.54	0.24	-	2.78	3.06	0.086
D505121D	half brick thick, four course	m	0.30	3.81	0.35	-	4.16	4.58	0.129
D505121E	half brick thick, five course	m	0.50	6.35	0.59	-	6.94	7.63	0.215
D505121F	one brick thick, one course	m	0.25	3.17	0.31	-	3.48	3.83	0.112
D505121G	one brick thick, two course	m	0.35	4.44	0.40	-	4.84	5.32	0.146
D505121H	one brick thick, three course	m	0.45	5.71	0.59	-	6.30	6.93	0.215
D505121I	one brick thick, four course	m	0.60	7.62	0.83	-	8.45	9.30	0.301
D505121J	one brick thick, five course	m	0.75	9.52	0.94	-	10.46	11.51	0.344
D505121K	one and a half brick thick, one course	m	0.30	3.81	0.35	-	4.16	4.58	0.129
D505121L	one and a half brick thick, two course	m	0.45	5.71	0.54	-	6.25	6.88	0.198
D505121M	one and a half brick thick, three course	m	0.55	6.99	0.71	-	7.70	8.47	0.258
D505121N	one and a half brick thick, four course	m	0.35	4.44	0.84	-	5.28	5.81	0.804
D505121O	one and a half brick thick, five course	m	0.40	5.08	1.01	-	6.09	6.70	0.965
D505121P	two brick thick, one course	m	0.40	5.08	0.47	-	5.55	6.11	0.172
D505121Q	two brick thick, two course	m	0.50	6.35	0.59	-	6.94	7.63	0.215
D505121R	two brick thick, three course	m	0.40	5.08	0.84	-	5.92	6.51	0.804
D505121S	two brick thick, four course	m	0.50	6.35	1.12	-	7.47	8.22	1.072
D505121T	two brick thick, five course	m	0.60	7.62	1.40	-	9.02	9.92	1.340
D505122	**Concrete**								
D505122A	not exceeding 150 mm thick, not exceeding 150 mm wide	m	0.45	5.71	0.47	-	6.18	6.80	0.172
D505122B	not exceeding 150 mm thick, 150 - 300 mm wide	m	0.55	6.99	0.47	-	7.46	8.21	0.172
D505122C	not exceeding 150 mm thick, 300 - 450 mm wide	m	0.65	8.25	0.47	-	8.72	9.59	0.172
D505122D	150 - 300 mm thick, not exceeding 150 mm wide	m	0.45	5.71	1.12	-	6.83	7.51	1.072

Groundwork

Major Works 2011		Unit	Labour Hours	Labour Net	Plant Net	Materials Net	Unit Net	Unit with 10%	CO$_2$
				£	£	£	£	£	Kg
D50	**D50: UNDERPINNING**								
D5051	**Cutting away projecting foundations**								
D505122	**Concrete**								
D505122E	150 - 300 mm thick, 150 - 300 mm wide	m	0.55	6.99	1.12	-	8.11	8.92	1.072
D505122F	150 - 300 mm thick, 300 - 450 mm wide	m	0.65	8.25	1.12	-	9.37	10.31	1.072
D505122G	300 - 450 mm thick, not exceeding 150 mm wide	m	0.85	10.80	1.96	-	12.76	14.04	1.876
D505122H	300 - 450 mm thick, 150 - 300 mm wide	m	0.95	12.07	1.96	-	14.03	15.43	1.876
D505122I	300 - 450 mm thick, 300 - 450 mm wide	m	1.10	13.97	1.96	-	15.93	17.52	1.876
D5061	**Wedging and grouting up between new and existing work**								
D506131	**Slates in cement mortar (1:3)**								
D506131A	half brick wide	m	0.75	22.35	-	1.48	23.83	26.21	2.220
D506131B	one brick wide	m	1.25	37.22	-	2.95	40.17	44.19	4.439
D506131C	one and a half brick wide	m	1.51	44.67	-	4.32	48.99	53.89	6.308
D506131D	two brick wide	m	1.76	52.12	-	5.80	57.92	63.71	8.527
D506132	**Neat cement slurry**								
D506132A	not exceeding 150 mm wide	m	0.70	15.73	-	1.35	17.08	18.79	1.894
D506132B	150 - 300 mm wide	m	0.75	17.21	-	1.98	19.19	21.11	3.300
D506132C	300 - 450 mm wide	m	0.90	21.69	-	2.61	24.30	26.73	4.706
D506133	**Epoxy cement non shrinking grout**								
D506133A	not exceeding 150 mm wide	m	0.70	15.73	-	1.91	17.64	19.40	2.557
D506133B	150 - 300 mm wide	m	0.75	17.21	-	3.06	20.27	22.30	4.566
D506133C	300 - 450 mm wide	m	0.90	21.69	-	4.25	25.94	28.53	6.635
D5065	**Off site disposal of material arising from earthworks**								
D506509	**Removed, including providing a suitable tip**								
D506509A	hand loading	m^3	1.37	17.40	18.55	-	35.95	39.55	1.340
D506509B	machine loading	m^3	-	-	20.15	-	20.15	22.17	2.747
D5066	**Filling to excavations with materials arising from earthworks**								
D506602	**Backfilled into excavation; compacting in layers**								
D506602A	by hand	m^3	1.30	16.51	0.51	-	17.02	18.72	0.643
D506603	**Backfilled in making up levels; by hand; compacting in layers; wheeling average**								
D506603A	25 m	m^3	1.66	21.08	0.51	-	21.59	23.75	0.801
D506603B	50 m	m^3	2.00	25.40	0.51	-	25.91	28.50	0.801
D506603C	75 m	m^3	2.33	29.59	0.51	-	30.10	33.11	0.801
D506603D	100 m	m^3	2.66	33.78	0.51	-	34.29	37.72	0.801
D5069	**Filling to excavations with imported materials**								
D506901	**Filled into excavation; by hand; compacting in layers**								
D506901A	sand	m^3	0.80	10.16	0.51	23.59	34.26	37.69	14.643
D506901B	hardcore	m^3	1.65	20.95	0.60	24.67	46.22	50.84	17.550
D506901C	hoggin	m^3	0.90	11.43	0.51	24.15	36.09	39.70	15.203
D506901D	DTp type 1	m^3	1.63	20.70	0.56	26.95	48.21	53.03	15.828
D506901E	DTp type 2	m^3	1.63	20.70	0.56	24.25	45.51	50.06	15.828
D506901F	stone rejects	m^3	1.65	20.95	0.60	25.20	46.75	51.43	16.990
D506901G	granite scalpings	m^3	1.65	20.95	0.56	22.32	43.83	48.21	16.388
D506903	**Filled in making up levels; by hand; compacting in layers**								
D506903A	sand	m^3	0.83	10.54	0.77	23.59	34.90	38.39	16.613
D506903B	hardcore	m^3	1.46	18.54	0.77	24.67	43.98	48.38	19.413
D506903C	hoggin	m^3	0.93	11.81	0.77	24.15	36.73	40.40	17.173

Major Works 2011		Unit	Labour Hours	Labour Net	Plant Net	Materials Net	Unit Net	Unit with 10%	CO₂
				£	£	£	£	£	Kg
D50	**D50: UNDERPINNING**								
D5069	**Filling to excavations with imported materials**								
D506903	**Filled in making up levels; by hand; compacting in layers**								
D506903D	DTp type 1	m³	1.40	17.78	0.77	26.95	45.50	50.05	17.733
D506903E	DTp type 2	m³	1.40	17.78	0.77	24.25	42.80	47.08	17.733
D506903F	stone rejects	m³	1.46	18.54	0.77	25.20	44.51	48.96	18.853
D506903G	granite chippings	m³	1.46	18.54	0.77	22.32	41.63	45.79	18.293
D5071	**Plain in situ concrete; mix C15P**								
D507101	**Foundations; poured on or against earth or unblinded hardcore**								
D507101B	generally	m³	0.90	11.43	-	79.07	90.50	99.55	343.200
D507103	**Isolated foundations; poured on or against earth or unblinded hardcore**								
D507103B	generally	m³	1.90	24.13	-	77.27	101.40	111.54	335.400
D5072	**Plain in situ concrete; mix C20P**								
D507201	**Foundations; poured on or against earth or unblinded hardcore**								
D507201B	generally	m³	0.90	11.43	-	81.64	93.07	102.38	343.200
D507203	**Isolated foundations; poured on or against earth or unblinded hardcore**								
D507203B	generally	m³	1.90	24.13	-	79.79	103.92	114.31	335.400
D5073	**Reinforced in situ concrete; mix C25P**								
D507301	**Foundations**								
D507301B	generally	m³	0.36	13.96	4.61	80.98	99.55	109.51	342.792
D507303	**Isolated foundations**								
D507303B	generally	m³	0.70	27.29	8.93	80.08	116.30	127.93	345.978
D507318	**Walls**								
D507318A	not exceeding 150 mm thick	m³	0.75	29.33	9.50	79.10	117.93	129.72	342.846
D507318B	150 - 450 mm thick	m³	0.67	26.04	8.35	79.10	113.49	124.84	340.998
D507318C	over 450 mm thick	m³	0.46	17.79	5.76	79.10	102.65	112.92	336.840
D507326	**Upstands**								
D507326B	generally	m³	0.89	34.92	11.23	80.98	127.13	139.84	353.418
D5075	**Formwork to general finish**								
D507501	**Sides of foundations**								
D507501A	not exceeding 250 mm high	m	0.76	12.90	-	4.07	16.97	18.67	3.853
D507501B	250 - 500 mm high	m	1.15	19.44	-	7.23	26.67	29.34	6.800
D507501C	500 - 1000 mm high	m	2.04	34.55	-	13.49	48.04	52.84	12.599
D507501D	over 1000 mm high	m²	1.86	31.50	-	13.33	44.83	49.31	12.352
D507504	**Sides of upstands**								
D507504A	not exceeding 250 mm wide	m	0.71	11.97	-	1.98	13.95	15.35	1.770
D507504B	250 - 500 mm wide	m	0.90	15.28	-	3.17	18.45	20.30	2.783
D507504C	500 - 1000 mm wide	m	1.60	27.15	0.67	5.36	33.18	36.50	4.656
D507504D	over 1000 mm wide	m²	1.46	24.76	1.33	6.40	32.49	35.74	5.520
D507526	**Walls**								
D507526A	vertical surfaces	m²	1.78	30.14	1.46	6.30	37.90	41.69	5.416
D507526B	curved surfaces	m²	2.00	33.91	1.46	6.61	41.98	46.18	5.684
D507526C	conical surfaces	m²	2.66	45.22	1.64	7.99	54.85	60.34	6.767
D507526D	spherical surfaces	m²	4.44	75.36	1.82	11.09	88.27	97.10	9.284
D507526E	battering surfaces	m²	2.13	36.10	1.46	6.82	44.38	48.82	5.856
D507563	**Wall ends and steps in walls**								
D507563A	not exceeding 250 mm wide	m	0.50	8.54	-	1.61	10.15	11.17	1.549
D507563B	250 - 500 mm wide	m	0.69	11.68	-	3.04	14.72	16.19	2.681

Groundwork

	Unit	Labour Hours	Labour Net £	Plant Net £	Materials Net £	Unit Net £	Unit with 10% £	CO₂ Kg
D50	**D50: UNDERPINNING**							
D5075	**Formwork to general finish**							
D507563	**Wall ends and steps in walls**							
D507563C	500 - 1000 mm wide	m	0.83	14.01	1.09	5.73	20.83	22.91	4.719
D507563D	over 1000 mm wide	m²	0.75	12.77	1.46	6.25	20.48	22.53	5.138
D507564	**Openings in walls**							
D507564A	not exceeding 250 mm wide	m	0.50	8.54	-	1.61	10.15	11.17	1.549
D507564B	250 - 500 mm wide	m	0.69	11.68	-	3.04	14.72	16.19	2.681
D507564C	500 - 1000 mm wide	m	0.83	14.01	1.09	5.73	20.83	22.91	4.719
D507564D	over 1000 mm wide	m²	0.75	12.77	1.46	6.25	20.48	22.53	5.138
D5081	**Bar reinforcement; high yield steel bars, BS 4449, delivered to site cut, bent and labelled**							
D508105	**Bars, fixing with tying wire**							
D508105A	6 mm	Tonne	72.00	1,065.60	-	876.08	1,941.68	2,135.85	1,782.850
D508105B	8 mm	Tonne	54.00	799.20	-	854.14	1,653.34	1,818.67	1,775.240
D508105C	10 mm	Tonne	44.00	651.20	-	799.18	1,450.38	1,595.42	1,756.960
D508105D	12 mm	Tonne	38.00	562.40	-	762.27	1,324.67	1,457.14	1,744.665
D508105E	16 mm	Tonne	30.00	444.00	-	711.06	1,155.06	1,270.57	1,735.525
D508105F	20 mm	Tonne	26.00	384.80	-	696.28	1,081.08	1,189.19	1,727.590
D508105G	25 mm	Tonne	23.00	340.40	-	673.54	1,013.94	1,115.33	1,722.160
D508105H	32 mm	Tonne	20.00	296.00	-	661.00	957.00	1,052.70	1,720.210
D508105I	40 mm	Tonne	17.00	251.60	-	647.73	899.33	989.26	1,715.430
D5086	**Walls**							
D508602	**Common bricks, BS 3921, in cement mortar (1:3)**							
D508602B	one brick thick	m²	0.99	45.96	-	37.91	83.87	92.26	98.017
D508602C	one and a half brick thick	m²	1.48	68.82	-	56.50	125.32	137.85	145.537
D508602D	two brick thick	m²	1.97	91.92	-	76.07	167.99	184.79	196.654
D508603	**Class A engineering bricks, BS 3921, in cement mortar (1:3)**							
D508603B	one brick thick	m²	1.07	49.74	-	55.30	105.04	115.54	197.929
D508603C	one and a half brick thick	m²	1.60	74.61	-	82.74	157.35	173.09	296.246
D508603D	two brick thick	m²	2.13	99.48	-	111.01	210.49	231.54	397.319
D508604	**Class B engineering bricks, BS 3921, in cement mortar (1:3)**							
D508604B	one brick thick	m²	1.02	47.73	-	48.15	95.88	105.47	197.929
D508604C	one and a half brick thick	m²	1.54	71.86	-	71.96	143.82	158.20	296.246
D508604D	two brick thick	m²	2.05	95.70	-	96.65	192.35	211.59	397.319
D508605	**Facing bricks (PC £300 per 1000), in gauged mortar (1:1:6); flush pointing both sides**							
D508605B	one brick thick; double stretcher bond	m²	1.09	51.00	-	43.09	94.09	103.50	195.045
D508605C	one brick thick; English bond	m²	1.15	53.57	-	43.43	97.00	106.70	195.852
D508605F	one brick thick; Flemish bond	m²	1.18	55.25	-	43.31	98.56	108.42	195.583
D5088	**Extra over general brickwork for fair faced work**							
D508882	**Fair facing and flush pointing**							
D508882A	stretcher bond	m²	0.03	1.40	-	0.21	1.61	1.77	0.703
D508882B	English bond	m²	0.03	1.49	-	0.41	1.90	2.09	1.406
D508882E	Flemish bond	m²	0.03	1.54	-	0.31	1.85	2.04	1.054
D508883	**Fair facing and struck or weather struck pointing**							
D508883A	stretcher bond	m²	0.03	1.45	-	0.21	1.66	1.83	0.703
D508883B	English bond	m²	0.03	1.54	-	0.41	1.95	2.15	1.406
D508883E	Flemish bond	m²	0.04	1.63	-	0.31	1.94	2.13	1.054
D508884	**Fair facing and tooled or keyed pointing**							
D508884A	stretcher bond	m²	0.03	1.54	-	0.21	1.75	1.93	0.703
D508884B	English bond	m²	0.04	1.63	-	0.41	2.04	2.24	1.406
D508884E	Flemish bond	m²	0.04	1.68	-	0.31	1.99	2.19	1.054

Major Works 2011		Unit	Labour Hours	Labour Net	Plant Net	Materials Net	Unit Net	Unit with 10%	CO$_2$
				£	£	£	£	£	Kg
D50	**D50: UNDERPINNING**								
D5091	**Cutting, toothing and bonding ends of new walls into existing**								
D509101	**Common brickwork; in alternate courses**								
D509101B	one brick wall	m	0.84	25.02	-	4.77	29.79	32.77	12.469
D509101C	one and a half brick wall	m	1.11	33.06	-	7.07	40.13	44.14	18.569
D509101D	two brick wall	m	1.66	49.15	-	9.27	58.42	64.26	24.318
D509103	**Engineering brickwork; in alternate courses**								
D509103B	one brick wall	m	0.88	26.15	-	5.54	31.69	34.86	22.957
D509103C	one and a half brick wall	m	1.15	34.25	-	8.18	42.43	46.67	33.881
D509103D	two brick wall	m	1.70	50.34	-	10.72	61.06	67.17	44.453
D509105	**Facing brickwork; in alternate courses**								
D509105B	one brick wall	m	1.15	34.25	-	4.91	39.16	43.08	23.308

In Situ Concrete and
Large Precast Concrete

In Situ Concrete & Large Precast Concrete

Major Works 2011		Unit	Labour Hours	Labour Net	Plant Net	Materials Net	Unit Net	Unit with 10%	CO₂
				£	£	£	£	£	Kg
E10	E10: MIXING, CASTING, CURING IN SITU CONCRETE								
E1001	Plain in situ concrete; mix C10P								
E100101	Foundations; poured on or against earth or unblinded hardcore								
E100101B	generally	m³	0.90	11.43	-	78.25	89.68	98.65	343.200
E100102	Ground beams; poured on or against earth or unblinded hardcore								
E100102B	generally	m³	1.90	24.13	-	76.48	100.61	110.67	335.400
E100103	Isolated foundations; poured on or against earth or unblinded hardcore								
E100103B	generally	m³	1.90	24.13	-	76.48	100.61	110.67	335.400
E100104	Beds; poured on or against earth or unblinded hardcore								
E100104A	not exceeding 150 mm thick	m³	1.05	13.33	-	74.70	88.03	96.83	327.600
E100104B	150 - 450 mm thick	m³	0.70	8.89	-	74.70	83.59	91.95	327.600
E100104C	over 450 mm thick	m³	0.50	6.35	-	74.70	81.05	89.16	327.600
E100106	Filling hollow walls								
E100106A	not exceeding 150 mm thick	m³	2.70	34.29	-	74.70	108.99	119.89	327.600
E1002	Plain in situ concrete; mix C15P								
E100201	Foundations; poured on or against unblinded hardcore								
E100201B	generally	m³	0.90	11.43	-	79.07	90.50	99.55	343.200
E100202	Ground beams; poured on or against earth or unblinded hardcore								
E100202B	generally	m³	1.90	24.13	-	77.27	101.40	111.54	335.400
E100203	Isolated foundations; poured on or against earth or unblinded hardcore								
E100203B	generally	m³	1.90	24.13	-	77.27	101.40	111.54	335.400
E100204	Beds; poured on or against earth or unblinded hardcore								
E100204A	not exceeding 150 mm thick	m³	1.05	13.33	-	75.47	88.80	97.68	327.600
E100204B	150 - 450 mm thick	m³	0.70	8.89	-	75.47	84.36	92.80	327.600
E100204C	over 450 mm thick	m³	0.50	6.35	-	75.47	81.82	90.00	327.600
E100205	Walls								
E100205A	not exceeding 150 mm thick	m³	1.90	24.13	-	75.47	99.60	109.56	327.600
E100205B	150 - 450 mm thick	m³	1.60	20.32	-	75.47	95.79	105.37	327.600
E100205C	over 450 mm thick	m³	1.15	14.60	-	75.47	90.07	99.08	327.600
E100206	Filling hollow walls								
E100206A	not exceeding 150 mm thick	m³	2.70	34.29	-	75.47	109.76	120.74	327.600
E1005	Plain in situ concrete; mix C20P								
E100501	Foundations; poured on or against earth or unblinded hardcore								
E100501B	generally	m³	0.90	11.43	-	81.64	93.07	102.38	343.200
E100502	Ground beams; poured on or against earth or unblinded hardcore								
E100502B	generally	m³	1.90	24.13	-	79.79	103.92	114.31	335.400
E100503	Isolated foundations; poured on or against earth or unblinded hardcore								
E100503B	generally	m³	1.90	24.13	-	79.79	103.92	114.31	335.400

Major Works 2011		Unit	Labour Hours	Labour Net	Plant Net	Materials Net	Unit Net	Unit with 10%	CO$_2$
				£	£	£	£	£	Kg
E10	**E10: MIXING, CASTING, CURING IN SITU CONCRETE**								
E1005	**Plain in situ concrete; mix C20P**								
E100504	**Beds; poured on or against earth or unblinded hardcore**								
E100504A	not exceeding 150 mm thick	m^3	1.05	13.33	-	77.93	91.26	100.39	327.600
E100504B	150 - 450 mm thick	m^3	0.70	8.89	-	77.93	86.82	95.50	327.600
E100504C	over 450 mm thick	m^3	0.50	6.35	-	77.93	84.28	92.71	327.600
E100505	**Walls**								
E100505A	not exceeding 150 mm thick	m^3	1.90	24.13	-	77.93	102.06	112.27	327.600
E100505B	150 - 450 mm thick	m^3	1.60	20.32	-	77.93	98.25	108.08	327.600
E100505C	over 450 mm thick	m^3	1.15	14.60	-	77.93	92.53	101.78	327.600
E100506	**Filling hollow walls**								
E100506A	not exceeding 150 mm thick	m^3	2.70	34.29	-	77.93	112.22	123.44	327.600
E100511	**Columns**								
E100511B	generally	m^3	2.15	27.30	-	79.79	107.09	117.80	335.400
E100512	**Column casings**								
E100512B	generally	m^3	2.47	31.37	-	79.79	111.16	122.28	335.400
E1006	**Plain in situ concrete; mix C25P**								
E100601	**Foundations; poured on or against earth or unblinded hardcore**								
E100601B	generally	m^3	0.90	11.43	-	82.86	94.29	103.72	343.200
E100602	**Ground beams; poured on or against earth or unblinded hardcore**								
E100602B	generally	m^3	1.90	24.13	-	80.98	105.11	115.62	335.400
E100603	**Isolated foundations; poured on or against earth or unblinded hardcore**								
E100603B	generally	m^3	1.90	24.13	-	80.98	105.11	115.62	335.400
E100604	**Beds; poured on or against earth or unblinded hardcore**								
E100604A	not exceeding 150 mm thick	m^3	1.05	13.33	-	79.10	92.43	101.67	327.600
E100604B	150 - 450 mm thick	m^3	0.70	8.89	-	79.10	87.99	96.79	327.600
E100604C	over 450 mm thick	m^3	0.50	6.35	-	79.10	85.45	94.00	327.600
E100605	**Walls**								
E100605A	not exceeding 150 mm thick	m^3	1.90	24.13	-	79.10	103.23	113.55	327.600
E100605B	150 - 450 mm thick	m^3	1.60	20.32	-	79.10	99.42	109.36	327.600
E100605C	over 450 mm thick	m^3	1.15	14.60	-	79.10	93.70	103.07	327.600
E100606	**Filling hollow walls**								
E100606A	not exceeding 150 mm thick	m^3	2.70	34.29	-	79.10	113.39	124.73	327.600
E100611	**Columns**								
E100611B	generally	m^3	2.15	27.30	-	80.98	108.28	119.11	335.400
E100612	**Column casings**								
E100612B	generally	m^3	2.47	31.37	-	80.98	112.35	123.59	335.400
E1011	**Reinforced in situ concrete; mix C20P**								
E101101	**Foundations**								
E101101B	generally	m^3	0.36	13.96	4.61	79.79	98.36	108.20	342.792
E101102	**Ground beams**								
E101102B	generally	m^3	0.70	27.29	8.93	78.90	115.12	126.63	345.978
E101103	**Isolated foundations**								
E101103B	generally	m^3	0.70	27.29	8.93	78.90	115.12	126.63	345.978
E101116	**Beds**								
E101116A	not exceeding 150 mm thick	m^3	0.46	17.79	3.12	77.93	98.84	108.72	335.640

Major Works 2011		Unit	Labour Hours	Labour Net £	Plant Net £	Materials Net £	Unit Net £	Unit with 10% £	CO₂ Kg
E10	**E10: MIXING, CASTING, CURING IN SITU CONCRETE**								
E1011	**Reinforced in situ concrete; mix C20P**								
E101116	**Beds**								
E101116B	150 - 450 mm thick	m³	0.33	12.71	2.18	77.93	92.82	102.10	333.228
E101116C	over 450 mm thick	m³	0.23	8.88	1.56	77.93	88.37	97.21	331.620
E101117	**Slabs**								
E101117A	not exceeding 150 mm thick	m³	0.68	26.67	4.68	77.93	109.28	120.21	339.660
E101117B	150 - 450 mm thick	m³	0.50	19.71	3.43	77.93	101.07	111.18	336.444
E101117C	over 450 mm thick	m³	0.34	13.33	2.34	77.93	93.60	102.96	333.630
E101118	**Walls**								
E101118A	not exceeding 150 mm thick	m³	0.75	29.33	9.50	77.93	116.76	128.44	342.846
E101118B	150 - 450 mm thick	m³	0.67	26.04	8.35	77.93	112.32	123.55	340.998
E101118C	over 450 mm thick	m³	0.46	17.79	5.76	77.93	101.48	111.63	336.840
E101119	**Diaphragm walls**								
E101119A	not exceeding 150 mm thick	m³	0.97	38.08	12.38	77.93	128.39	141.23	347.466
E101119B	150 - 450 mm thick	m³	0.75	29.21	9.50	77.93	116.64	128.30	342.846
E101119C	over 450 mm thick	m³	0.67	26.04	8.35	77.93	112.32	123.55	340.998
E101120	**Beams**								
E101120B	generally	m³	0.91	35.58	11.52	78.90	126.00	138.60	350.136
E101121	**Beam casings**								
E101121B	generally	m³	1.05	40.90	13.25	78.90	133.05	146.36	352.908
E101123	**Columns**								
E101123B	generally	m³	1.30	50.79	16.56	78.90	146.25	160.88	358.221
E101124	**Column casings**								
E101124B	generally	m³	1.49	58.42	19.04	78.90	156.36	172.00	362.194
E101125	**Staircases**								
E101125A	generally	m³	0.91	35.58	11.52	78.90	126.00	138.60	350.136
E101126	**Upstands**								
E101126B	generally	m³	0.89	34.92	11.23	79.79	125.94	138.53	353.418
E1012	**Reinforced in situ concrete; mix C25P**								
E101201	**Foundations**								
E101201B	generally	m³	0.36	13.96	4.61	80.98	99.55	109.51	342.792
E101202	**Ground beams**								
E101202B	generally	m³	0.70	27.29	8.93	80.08	116.30	127.93	345.978
E101203	**Isolated foundations**								
E101203B	generally	m³	0.70	27.29	8.93	80.08	116.30	127.93	345.978
E101216	**Beds**								
E101216A	not exceeding 150 mm thick	m³	0.46	17.79	3.12	79.10	100.01	110.01	335.640
E101216B	150 - 450 mm thick	m³	0.33	12.71	2.18	79.10	93.99	103.39	333.228
E101216C	over 450 mm thick	m³	0.23	8.88	1.56	79.10	89.54	98.49	331.620
E101217	**Slabs**								
E101217A	not exceeding 150 mm thick	m³	0.68	26.67	4.68	79.10	110.45	121.50	339.660
E101217B	150 - 450 mm thick	m³	0.50	19.71	3.43	79.10	102.24	112.46	336.444
E101217C	over 450 mm thick	m³	0.34	13.33	2.34	79.10	94.77	104.25	333.630
E101218	**Walls**								
E101218A	not exceeding 150 mm thick	m³	0.75	29.33	9.50	79.10	117.93	129.72	342.846
E101218B	150 - 450 mm thick	m³	0.67	26.04	8.35	79.10	113.49	124.84	340.998
E101218C	over 450 mm thick	m³	0.46	17.79	5.76	79.10	102.65	112.92	336.840
E101219	**Diaphragm walls**								
E101219A	not exceeding 150 mm thick	m³	0.97	38.08	12.38	79.10	129.56	142.52	347.466
E101219B	150 - 450 mm thick	m³	0.75	29.21	9.50	79.10	117.81	129.59	342.846
E101219C	over 450 mm thick	m³	0.67	26.04	8.35	79.10	113.49	124.84	340.998
E101220	**Beams**								
E101220B	generally	m³	0.91	35.58	11.52	80.08	127.18	139.90	350.136

Major Works 2011		Unit	Labour Hours	Labour Net	Plant Net	Materials Net	Unit Net	Unit with 10%	CO$_2$
				£	£	£	£	£	Kg
E10	**E10: MIXING, CASTING, CURING IN SITU CONCRETE**								
E1012	**Reinforced in situ concrete; mix C25P**								
E101221	**Beam casings**								
E101221B	generally	m^3	1.05	40.90	13.25	80.08	134.23	147.65	352.908
E101223	**Columns**								
E101223B	generally	m^3	1.30	50.79	16.56	80.08	147.43	162.17	358.221
E101224	**Column casings**								
E101224B	generally	m^3	1.49	58.42	19.04	80.08	157.54	173.29	362.194
E101225	**Staircases**								
E101225A	generally	m^3	0.91	35.58	11.52	80.08	127.18	139.90	350.136
E101226	**Upstands**								
E101226B	generally	m^3	0.89	34.92	11.23	80.98	127.13	139.84	353.418
E1013	**Reinforced in situ concrete; mix C30P**								
E101301	**Foundations**								
E101301B	generally	m^3	0.36	13.96	4.61	82.28	100.85	110.94	342.792
E101302	**Ground beams**								
E101302B	generally	m^3	0.70	27.29	8.93	81.36	117.58	129.34	345.978
E101303	**Isolated foundations**								
E101303B	generally	m^3	0.70	27.29	8.93	81.36	117.58	129.34	345.978
E101316	**Beds**								
E101316A	not exceeding 150 mm thick	m^3	0.46	17.79	3.12	80.37	101.28	111.41	335.640
E101316B	150 - 450 mm thick	m^3	0.33	12.71	2.18	80.37	95.26	104.79	333.228
E101316C	over 450 mm thick	m^3	0.23	8.88	1.56	80.37	90.81	99.89	331.620
E101317	**Slabs**								
E101317A	not exceeding 150 mm thick	m^3	0.68	26.67	4.68	80.37	111.72	122.89	339.660
E101317B	150 - 450 mm thick	m^3	0.50	19.71	3.43	80.37	103.51	113.86	336.444
E101317C	over 450 mm thick	m^3	0.34	13.33	2.34	80.37	96.04	105.64	333.630
E101318	**Walls**								
E101318A	not exceeding 150 mm thick	m^3	0.75	29.33	9.50	80.37	119.20	131.12	342.846
E101318B	150 - 450 mm thick	m^3	0.67	26.04	8.35	80.37	114.76	126.24	340.998
E101318C	over 450 mm thick	m^3	0.46	17.79	5.76	80.37	103.92	114.31	336.840
E101319	**Diaphragm walls**								
E101319A	not exceeding 150 mm thick	m^3	0.97	38.08	12.38	80.37	130.83	143.91	347.466
E101319B	150 - 450 mm thick	m^3	0.75	29.21	9.50	80.37	119.08	130.99	342.846
E101319C	over 450 mm thick	m^3	0.67	26.04	8.35	80.37	114.76	126.24	340.998
E101320	**Beams**								
E101320B	generally	m^3	0.91	35.58	11.52	81.36	128.46	141.31	350.136
E101321	**Beam casings**								
E101321B	generally	m^3	1.05	40.90	13.25	81.36	135.51	149.06	352.908
E101323	**Columns**								
E101323B	generally	m^3	1.30	50.79	16.56	81.36	148.71	163.58	358.221
E101324	**Column casings**								
E101324B	generally	m^3	1.49	58.42	19.04	81.36	158.82	174.70	362.194
E101325	**Staircases**								
E101325A	generally	m^3	0.91	35.58	11.52	81.36	128.46	141.31	350.136
E101326	**Upstands**								
E101326B	generally	m^3	0.89	34.92	11.23	82.28	128.43	141.27	353.418
E1014	**Reinforced in situ concrete; mix C35P**								
E101401	**Foundations**								
E101401B	generally	m^3	0.36	13.96	4.61	83.88	102.45	112.70	342.792

Major Works 2011		Unit	Labour Hours	Labour Net	Plant Net	Materials Net	Unit Net	Unit with 10%	CO$_2$
				£	£	£	£	£	Kg
E10	**E10: MIXING, CASTING, CURING IN SITU CONCRETE**								
E1014	**Reinforced in situ concrete; mix C35P**								
E101402	**Ground beams**								
E101402B	generally	m^3	0.70	27.29	8.93	82.95	119.17	131.09	345.978
E101403	**Isolated foundations**								
E101403B	generally	m^3	0.70	27.29	8.93	82.95	119.17	131.09	345.978
E101416	**Beds**								
E101416A	not exceeding 150 mm thick	m^3	0.46	17.79	3.12	81.93	102.84	113.12	335.640
E101416B	150 - 450 mm thick	m^3	0.33	12.71	2.18	81.93	96.82	106.50	333.228
E101416C	over 450 mm thick	m^3	0.23	8.88	1.56	81.93	92.37	101.61	331.620
E101417	**Slabs**								
E101417A	not exceeding 150 mm thick	m^3	0.68	26.67	4.68	81.93	113.28	124.61	339.660
E101417B	150 - 450 mm thick	m^3	0.50	19.71	3.43	81.93	105.07	115.58	336.444
E101417C	over 450 mm thick	m^3	0.34	13.33	2.34	81.93	97.60	107.36	333.630
E101418	**Walls**								
E101418A	not exceeding 150 mm thick	m^3	0.75	29.33	9.50	81.93	120.76	132.84	342.846
E101418B	150 - 450 mm thick	m^3	0.67	26.04	8.35	81.93	116.32	127.95	340.998
E101418C	over 450 mm thick	m^3	0.46	17.79	5.76	81.93	105.48	116.03	336.840
E101419	**Diaphragm walls**								
E101419A	not exceeding 150 mm thick	m^3	0.97	38.08	12.38	81.93	132.39	145.63	347.466
E101419B	150 - 450 mm thick	m^3	0.75	29.21	9.50	81.93	120.64	132.70	342.846
E101419C	over 450 mm thick	m^3	0.67	26.04	8.35	81.93	116.32	127.95	340.998
E101420	**Beams**								
E101420B	generally	m^3	0.91	35.58	11.52	82.95	130.05	143.06	350.136
E101421	**Beam casings**								
E101421B	generally	m^3	1.05	40.90	13.25	82.95	137.10	150.81	352.908
E101423	**Columns**								
E101423B	generally	m^3	1.30	50.79	16.56	82.95	150.30	165.33	358.221
E101424	**Column casings**								
E101424B	generally	m^3	1.49	58.42	19.04	82.95	160.41	176.45	362.194
E101425	**Staircases**								
E101425A	generally	m^3	0.91	35.58	11.52	82.95	130.05	143.06	350.136
E101426	**Upstands**								
E101426B	generally	m^3	0.89	34.92	11.23	83.88	130.03	143.03	353.418
E1015	**Reinforced in situ concrete; mix C40P**								
E101501	**Foundations**								
E101501B	generally	m^3	0.36	13.96	4.61	85.49	104.06	114.47	342.792
E101502	**Ground beams**								
E101502B	generally	m^3	0.70	27.29	8.93	84.54	120.76	132.84	345.978
E101503	**Isolated foundations**								
E101503B	generally	m^3	0.70	27.29	8.93	84.54	120.76	132.84	345.978
E101516	**Beds**								
E101516A	not exceeding 150 mm thick	m^3	0.46	17.79	3.12	83.51	104.42	114.86	335.640
E101516B	150 - 450 mm thick	m^3	0.33	12.71	2.18	83.51	98.40	108.24	333.228
E101516C	over 450 mm thick	m^3	0.23	8.88	1.56	83.51	93.95	103.35	331.620
E101517	**Slabs**								
E101517A	not exceeding 150 mm thick	m^3	0.68	26.67	4.68	83.51	114.86	126.35	339.660
E101517B	150 - 450 mm thick	m^3	0.50	19.71	3.43	83.51	106.65	117.32	336.444
E101517C	over 450 mm thick	m^3	0.34	13.33	2.34	83.51	99.18	109.10	333.630
E101518	**Walls**								
E101518A	not exceeding 150 mm thick	m^3	0.75	29.33	9.50	83.51	122.34	134.57	342.846
E101518B	150 - 450 mm thick	m^3	0.67	26.04	8.35	83.51	117.90	129.69	340.998
E101518C	over 450 mm thick	m^3	0.46	17.79	5.76	83.51	107.06	117.77	336.840

Major Works 2011		Unit	Labour Hours	Labour Net	Plant Net	Materials Net	Unit Net	Unit with 10%	CO$_2$
				£	£	£	£	£	Kg
E10	**E10: MIXING, CASTING, CURING IN SITU CONCRETE**								
E1015	**Reinforced in situ concrete; mix C40P**								
E101519	**Diaphragm walls**								
E101519A	not exceeding 150 mm thick	m^3	0.97	38.08	12.38	83.51	133.97	147.37	347.466
E101519B	150 - 450 mm thick	m^3	0.75	29.21	9.50	83.51	122.22	134.44	342.846
E101519C	over 450 mm thick	m^3	0.67	26.04	8.35	83.51	117.90	129.69	340.998
E101520	**Beams**								
E101520B	generally	m^3	0.91	35.58	11.52	84.54	131.64	144.80	350.136
E101521	**Beam casings**								
E101521B	generally	m^3	1.05	40.90	13.25	84.54	138.69	152.56	352.908
E101523	**Columns**								
E101523B	generally	m^3	1.30	50.79	16.56	84.54	151.89	167.08	358.221
E101524	**Column casings**								
E101524B	generally	m^3	1.49	58.42	19.04	84.54	162.00	178.20	362.194
E101525	**Staircases**								
E101525A	generally	m^3	0.91	35.58	11.52	84.54	131.64	144.80	350.136
E101526	**Upstands**								
E101526B	generally	m^3	0.89	34.92	11.23	85.49	131.64	144.80	353.418
E1021	**Wedging and grouting bases or the like**								
E102101	**Wedging up with steel shims and grouting under bases with cement mortar (1:3); 25 mm thick**								
E102101A	not exceeding 0.10 m^2	Nr	0.20	2.54	-	0.31	2.85	3.14	1.054
E102101B	0.10 - 0.25 m^2	Nr	0.35	4.44	-	0.62	5.06	5.57	2.109
E102101C	0.25 - 0.50 m^2	Nr	0.50	6.35	-	1.34	7.69	8.46	4.569
E102102	**Wedging up with steel shims and grouting under bases with cement mortar (1:3); 50 mm thick**								
E102102D	not exceeding 0.10 m^2	Nr	0.40	5.08	-	0.62	5.70	6.27	2.109
E102102E	0.10 - 0.25 m^2	Nr	0.70	8.89	-	1.34	10.23	11.25	4.569
E102102F	0.25 - 0.50 m^2	Nr	1.00	12.70	-	2.57	15.27	16.80	8.786

Major Works 2011		Unit	Labour Hours	Labour Net	Plant Net	Materials Net	Unit Net	Unit with 10%	CO₂
				£	£	£	£	£	Kg
E20	**E20: FORMWORK FOR IN SITU CONCRETE**								
E2001	**Formwork to general finish**								
E200101	**Sides of foundations**								
E200101A	not exceeding 250 mm high	m	0.76	12.90	-	2.26	15.16	16.68	2.062
E200101B	250 - 500 mm high	m	1.15	19.44	-	3.59	23.03	25.33	3.218
E200101C	500 - 1000 mm high	m	2.04	34.55	-	6.22	40.77	44.85	5.433
E200101D	over 1000 mm high	m²	1.86	31.50	-	6.71	38.21	42.03	5.820
E200102	**Sides of ground beams and edges of beds**								
E200102A	not exceeding 250 mm high	m	0.76	12.90	-	2.26	15.16	16.68	2.062
E200102B	250 - 500 mm high	m	1.15	19.44	-	3.59	23.03	25.33	3.218
E200102C	500 - 1000 mm high	m	2.04	34.55	-	6.22	40.77	44.85	5.430
E200102D	over 1000 mm high	m²	1.86	31.50	-	6.71	38.21	42.03	5.820
E200103	**Edges of suspended slabs**								
E200103A	not exceeding 250 mm wide	m	0.71	11.97	-	1.98	13.95	15.35	1.770
E200103B	250 - 500 mm wide	m	0.90	15.28	-	3.17	18.45	20.30	2.783
E200103C	500 - 1000 mm wide	m	1.60	27.15	0.67	5.36	33.18	36.50	4.656
E200103D	over 1000 mm wide	m²	1.46	24.76	1.33	6.40	32.49	35.74	5.520
E200104	**Sides of upstands**								
E200104A	not exceeding 250 mm wide	m	0.71	11.97	-	1.98	13.95	15.35	1.770
E200104B	250 - 500 mm wide	m	0.90	15.28	-	3.17	18.45	20.30	2.783
E200104C	500 - 1000 mm wide	m	1.60	27.15	0.67	5.36	33.18	36.50	4.656
E200104D	over 1000 mm wide	m²	1.46	24.76	1.33	6.40	32.49	35.74	5.520
E200105	**Steps in top surfaces**								
E200105A	not exceeding 250 mm wide	m	0.71	11.97	-	1.98	13.95	15.35	1.770
E200105B	250 - 500 mm wide	m	0.90	15.28	-	3.17	18.45	20.30	2.783
E200105C	500 - 1000 mm wide	m	1.60	27.15	0.67	5.36	33.18	36.50	4.656
E200105D	over 1000 mm wide	m²	1.46	24.76	1.33	6.40	32.49	35.74	5.520
E200106	**Steps in soffits**								
E200106A	not exceeding 250 mm wide	m	1.24	21.00	0.88	2.34	24.22	26.64	2.049
E200106B	250 - 500 mm wide	m	1.44	24.42	0.88	3.97	29.27	32.20	3.473
E200106C	500 - 1000 mm wide	m	1.77	30.12	1.75	6.23	38.10	41.91	5.120
E200106D	over 1000 mm wide	m²	2.34	39.70	1.46	6.77	47.93	52.72	5.851
E200107	**Machine bases and plinths**								
E200107A	not exceeding 250 mm high	m	0.76	12.90	-	4.07	16.97	18.67	3.853
E200107B	250 - 500 mm high	m	1.15	19.44	-	7.23	26.67	29.34	6.800
E200107C	500 - 1000 mm high	m	2.04	34.55	-	13.49	48.04	52.84	12.599
E200107D	over 1000 mm high	m²	1.86	31.50	-	13.33	44.83	49.31	12.352
E200111	**Soffits; not exceeding 1.5 mm above floor level**								
E200111A	not exceeding 200 mm thick	m²	1.46	24.71	0.56	6.62	31.89	35.08	5.733
E200111B	200 - 300 mm thick	m²	2.04	34.55	0.56	6.62	41.73	45.90	5.733
E200112	**Soffits; 1.5 - 3.0 m above floor level**								
E200112E	not exceeding 200 mm thick	m²	1.79	30.36	0.56	6.62	37.54	41.29	5.733
E200112F	200 - 300 mm thick	m²	2.50	42.45	0.56	6.62	49.63	54.59	5.733
E200113	**Sloping soffits; not exceeding 1.5 m above floor level**								
E200113A	not exceeding 200 mm thick	m²	1.46	24.71	0.56	6.62	31.89	35.08	5.733
E200113B	200 - 300 mm thick	m²	2.04	34.61	0.56	6.62	41.79	45.97	5.733
E200114	**Sloping soffits; 1.5 - 3.0 m above floor level**								
E200114E	not exceeding 200 mm thick	m²	1.79	30.36	0.56	6.62	37.54	41.29	5.733
E200114F	200 - 300 mm thick	m²	2.50	42.45	0.56	6.62	49.63	54.59	5.733
E200125	**Top formwork; over 15 deg from horizontal**								
E200125A	generally	m²	1.86	31.63	-	7.62	39.25	43.18	6.563
E200126	**Walls**								
E200126A	vertical surfaces	m²	1.78	30.14	1.46	6.30	37.90	41.69	5.416
E200126B	curved surfaces	m²	2.00	33.91	1.46	6.61	41.98	46.18	5.684
E200126C	conical surfaces	m²	2.66	45.22	1.64	7.99	54.85	60.34	6.767
E200126D	spherical surfaces	m²	4.44	75.36	1.82	11.09	88.27	97.10	9.284
E200126E	battering surfaces	m²	2.13	36.10	1.46	6.82	44.38	48.82	5.856

Major Works 2011		Unit	Labour Hours	Labour Net	Plant Net	Materials Net	Unit Net	Unit with 10%	CO₂
				£	£	£	£	£	Kg
E20	**E20: FORMWORK FOR IN SITU CONCRETE**								
E2001	**Formwork to general finish**								
E200129	**Sides and soffits of attached beams; height to soffit**								
E200129A	not exceeding 1.50 m	m²	2.08	35.32	1.46	6.72	43.50	47.85	5.815
E200129B	1.51 - 3.00 m	m²	2.03	34.47	1.46	6.70	42.63	46.89	5.792
E200129C	3.01 - 4.50 m	m²	2.08	35.32	1.46	6.70	43.48	47.83	5.792
E200129D	4.51 - 6.00 m	m²	2.25	38.20	1.46	6.69	46.35	50.99	5.786
E200130	**Sides and soffits of isolated beams; height to soffit**								
E200130A	not exceeding 1.50 m	m²	2.25	38.20	2.12	6.70	47.02	51.72	5.792
E200130B	1.51 - 3.00 m	m²	2.20	37.36	2.12	6.70	46.18	50.80	5.792
E200130C	3.01 - 4.50 m	m²	2.32	39.34	2.12	6.71	48.17	52.99	5.799
E200130D	4.51 - 6.00 m	m²	2.43	41.26	2.13	6.62	50.01	55.01	5.733
E200131	**Sides and soffits of sloping attached beams; height to soffit**								
E200131A	not exceeding 1.50 m	m²	2.39	40.58	1.46	6.70	48.74	53.61	5.792
E200131B	1.51 - 3.00 m	m²	2.34	39.73	1.46	6.77	47.96	52.76	5.866
E200131C	3.01 - 4.50 m	m²	2.46	41.77	1.46	6.72	49.95	54.95	5.808
E200131D	4.51 - 6.00 m	m²	2.58	43.81	1.46	6.77	52.04	57.24	5.851
E200132	**Sides and soffits of sloping isolated beams; height to soffit**								
E200132A	not exceeding 1.50 m	m²	2.70	45.85	2.12	6.70	54.67	60.14	5.792
E200132B	1.51 - 3.00 m	m²	2.63	44.66	2.12	6.70	53.48	58.83	5.792
E200132C	3.01 - 4.50 m	m²	2.76	46.86	2.12	6.72	55.70	61.27	5.808
E200132D	4.51 - 6.00 m	m²	2.90	49.24	2.13	6.77	58.14	63.95	5.851
E200135	**Sides and soffits of attached beam casings; height to soffit**								
E200135A	not exceeding 1.50 m	m²	2.08	35.32	0.88	6.70	42.90	47.19	5.792
E200135B	1.51 - 3.00 m	m²	2.03	34.47	0.88	6.70	42.05	46.26	5.792
E200135C	3.01 - 4.50 m	m²	2.13	36.17	0.88	6.64	43.69	48.06	5.753
E200135D	4.51 - 6.00 m	m²	2.24	38.07	0.88	6.62	45.57	50.13	5.733
E200136	**Sides and soffits of isolated beam casings; height to soffit**								
E200136A	not exceeding 1.50 m	m²	2.26	38.37	2.12	6.70	47.19	51.91	5.792
E200136B	1.51 - 3.00 m	m²	2.20	37.36	2.12	6.70	46.18	50.80	5.792
E200136C	3.01 - 4.50 m	m²	2.31	39.22	2.12	6.65	47.99	52.79	5.767
E200136D	4.50 - 6.00 m	m²	2.43	41.26	2.13	6.62	50.01	55.01	5.733
E200137	**Sides of isolated rectangular columns**								
E200137A	not exceeding 250 mm wide	m²	2.26	38.37	1.10	6.70	46.17	50.79	5.792
E200137B	250 - 500 mm wide	m²	2.20	37.36	1.10	6.70	45.16	49.68	5.792
E200137C	500 - 1000 mm wide	m²	2.31	39.22	1.10	6.64	46.96	51.66	5.753
E200137D	over 1000 mm wide	m²	2.43	41.26	1.10	6.63	48.99	53.89	5.747
E200139	**Sides of isolated circular columns**								
E200139A	not exceeding 300 mm dia	m²	1.71	29.04	1.13	15.77	45.94	50.53	5.380
E200139B	300 - 600 mm dia	m²	1.40	23.77	0.57	13.82	38.16	41.98	5.380
E200139C	600 - 900 mm dia	m²	1.25	21.23	0.38	11.84	33.45	36.80	5.380
E200139D	over 900 mm dia	m²	1.18	20.04	0.28	9.86	30.18	33.20	5.380
E200145	**Grooves, throats, rebates, chamfers or the like; sectional area**								
E200145A	2500 - 5000 mm²	m	0.26	4.47	-	0.68	5.15	5.67	0.713
E200145B	5000 - 10000 mm²	m	0.69	11.68	-	1.24	12.92	14.21	1.280
E200145C	10000 - 20000 mm²	m	0.83	14.01	-	4.03	18.04	19.84	3.508
E200163	**Wall ends, soffits and steps in walls**								
E200163A	not exceeding 250 mm wide	m	0.50	8.54	-	1.61	10.15	11.17	1.549
E200163B	250 - 500 mm wide	m	0.69	11.68	-	3.04	14.72	16.19	2.681
E200163C	500 - 1000 mm wide	m	0.83	14.01	1.09	5.73	20.83	22.91	4.719
E200163D	over 1000 mm wide	m²	0.75	12.77	1.46	6.25	20.48	22.53	5.138

In Situ Concrete & Large Precast Concrete

	Unit	Labour Hours	Labour Net	Plant Net	Materials Net	Unit Net	Unit with 10%	CO₂
			£	£	£	£	£	Kg
E20	**E20: FORMWORK FOR IN SITU CONCRETE**							
E2001	**Formwork to general finish**							
E200164	**Openings in walls**							
E200164A	not exceeding 250 mm wide	m	0.50	8.54	-	1.61	10.15	11.17	1.549
E200164B	250 - 500 mm wide	m	0.69	11.68	-	3.04	14.72	16.19	2.681
E200164C	500 - 1000 mm wide	m	0.83	14.01	1.09	5.73	20.83	22.91	4.719
E200164D	over 1000 mm wide	m²	0.75	12.77	1.46	6.25	20.48	22.53	5.138
E200175	**Staircases**							
E200175A	not exceeding 250 mm wide	m	0.41	6.94	-	1.98	8.92	9.81	1.770
E200175B	250 - 500 mm wide	m	0.85	14.37	-	3.55	17.92	19.71	3.368
E200175C	500 - 1000 mm wide	m	1.02	17.23	-	5.37	22.60	24.86	4.686
E200175D	over 1000 mm wide	m²	0.93	15.71	-	6.39	22.10	24.31	5.571
E2016	**Holodeck galvanised steel permanent formwork weighing 14.3 Kg/m²; laid horizontally**							
E201642	**Not exceeding 3.5 m above floor level; strutting and supports at**							
E201642A	2500 - 3000 mm centres	m²	0.30	5.16	0.27	16.96	22.39	24.63	69.427
E201642B	3000 - 3500 mm centres	m²	0.28	4.81	0.22	16.92	21.95	24.15	69.399
E201642C	3500 - 4000 mm centres	m²	0.27	4.60	0.19	16.91	21.70	23.87	69.385
E201643	**3.5 - 5.0 m above floor level; strutting and supports at**							
E201643A	2500 - 3000 mm centres	m²	0.33	5.54	0.32	16.96	22.82	25.10	69.427
E201643B	3000 - 3500 mm centres	m²	0.30	5.11	0.26	16.92	22.29	24.52	69.399
E201643C	3500 - 4000 mm centres	m²	0.39	6.55	0.23	16.91	23.69	26.06	69.385
E2017	**Super Holorib galvanised steel permanent formwork weighing 13.27 Kg/m² (0.9 mm gauge); laid horizontally**							
E201745	**Not exceeding 3.5 m above floor level; strutting and supports at**							
E201745A	2500 - 3000 mm centres	m²	0.29	4.92	0.27	23.68	28.87	31.76	115.619
E201745B	3000 - 3500 mm centres	m²	0.27	4.57	0.22	23.64	28.43	31.27	115.590
E201745C	3500 - 4000 mm centres	m²	0.26	4.36	0.19	23.63	28.18	31.00	115.577
E201746	**3.5 - 5.0 m above floor level; strutting and supports at**							
E201746A	2500 - 3000 mm centres	m²	0.31	5.30	0.32	23.68	29.30	32.23	115.619
E201746B	3000 - 3500 mm centres	m²	0.29	4.87	0.26	23.64	28.77	31.65	115.590
E201746C	3500 - 4000 mm centres	m²	0.27	4.62	0.23	23.63	28.48	31.33	115.577
E2018	**Super Holorib galvanised steel permanent formwork weighing 17.69 Kg/m² (1.2 mm gauge); laid horizontally**							
E201848	**Not exceeding 3.5 m above floor level; strutting and supports at**							
E201848A	2500 - 3000 mm centres	m²	0.35	5.96	0.27	23.68	29.91	32.90	115.619
E201848B	3000 - 3500 mm centres	m²	0.33	5.60	0.22	23.64	29.46	32.41	115.590
E201848C	3500 - 4000 mm centres	m²	0.32	5.40	0.19	23.63	29.22	32.14	115.577
E201849	**3.5 - 5.0 m above floor level; strutting and supports at**							
E201849A	2500 - 3000 mm centres	m²	0.37	6.33	0.32	23.68	30.33	33.36	115.619
E201849B	3000 - 3500 mm centres	m²	0.35	5.91	0.26	23.64	29.81	32.79	115.590
E201849C	3500 - 4000 mm centres	m²	0.33	5.65	0.23	23.63	29.51	32.46	115.577
E2020	**Formwork to provide special finishes**							
E202031	**Extra over formwork to general finish for fair face formed with**							
E202031A	wrought face timber lining	m²	0.17	2.89	-	7.17	10.06	11.07	3.458
E202031B	oil tempered hardboard lining	m²	-	-	-	0.43	0.43	0.47	0.666

Major Works 2011		Unit	Labour Hours	Labour Net £	Plant Net £	Materials Net £	Unit Net £	Unit with 10% £	CO₂ Kg
E20	**E20: FORMWORK FOR IN SITU CONCRETE**								
E2020	**Formwork to provide special finishes**								
E202031	**Extra over formwork to general finish for fair face formed with**								
E202031C	plastic faced plywood lining	m²	-	-	-	1.05	1.05	1.16	0.120
E202031D	application of silver sand and cement mortar to surface imperfections and rubbing down with a carborundum stone	m²	0.11	1.87	-	0.12	1.99	2.19	0.351
E202032	**Extra over formwork to general finish for forming ribbed or fluted finish; planted timber fillets**								
E202032A	38 x 50 mm at 100 mm centres	m²	0.63	10.70	-	13.95	24.65	27.12	10.431
E202032B	50 x 50 mm at 150 mm centres	m²	0.43	7.30	-	10.00	17.30	19.03	7.227
E202032C	75 x 75 mm at 200 mm centres	m²	0.35	5.94	-	11.23	17.17	18.89	6.441
E202032D	50 x 100 mm at 300 mm centres	m²	0.27	4.58	-	6.91	11.49	12.64	4.136
E202033	**Extra over formwork to general finish for exposed aggregate finish**								
E202033A	applying retarding agent to shutter face; brushing off concrete laitance after striking	m²	0.47	7.98	-	0.20	8.18	9.00	0.540

In Situ Concrete & Large Precast Concrete

Major Works 2011		Unit	Labour Hours	Labour Net	Plant Net	Materials Net	Unit Net	Unit with 10%	CO₂
				£	£	£	£	£	Kg
E30	**E30: REINFORCEMENT FOR IN SITU CONCRETE**								
E3010	**Bar reinforcement; mild steel bars, BS 4449, delivered to site cut, bent and labelled**								
E301003	**Bars, fixing with tying wire**								
E301003A	6 mm	Tonne	72.00	1,065.60	-	807.64	1,873.24	2,060.56	1,782.850
E301003B	8 mm	Tonne	54.00	799.20	-	784.18	1,583.38	1,741.72	1,775.240
E301003C	10 mm	Tonne	44.00	651.20	-	733.34	1,384.54	1,522.99	1,756.960
E301003D	12 mm	Tonne	38.00	562.40	-	699.18	1,261.58	1,387.74	1,744.665
E301003E	16 mm	Tonne	30.00	444.00	-	652.08	1,096.08	1,205.69	1,735.525
E301003F	20 mm	Tonne	26.00	384.80	-	637.98	1,022.78	1,125.06	1,727.590
E301003G	25 mm	Tonne	23.00	340.40	-	616.62	957.02	1,052.72	1,722.160
E301003H	32 mm	Tonne	20.00	296.00	-	604.77	900.77	990.85	1,720.210
E301003I	40 mm	Tonne	17.00	251.60	-	592.18	843.78	928.16	1,715.430
E3011	**Bar reinforcement; high yield steel bars, BS 4449, delivered to site cut, bent and labelled**								
E301105	**Bars, fixing with tying wire**								
E301105A	6 mm	Tonne	72.00	1,065.60	-	876.08	1,941.68	2,135.85	1,782.850
E301105B	8 mm	Tonne	54.00	799.20	-	854.14	1,653.34	1,818.67	1,775.240
E301105C	10 mm	Tonne	44.00	651.20	-	799.18	1,450.38	1,595.42	1,756.960
E301105D	12 mm	Tonne	38.00	562.40	-	762.27	1,324.67	1,457.14	1,744.665
E301105E	16 mm	Tonne	30.00	444.00	-	711.06	1,155.06	1,270.57	1,735.525
E301105F	20 mm	Tonne	26.00	384.80	-	696.28	1,081.08	1,189.19	1,727.590
E301105G	25 mm	Tonne	23.00	340.40	-	673.54	1,013.94	1,115.33	1,722.160
E301105H	32 mm	Tonne	20.00	296.00	-	661.00	957.00	1,052.70	1,720.210
E301105I	40 mm	Tonne	17.00	251.60	-	647.73	899.33	989.26	1,715.430
E3012	**Bar reinforcement; stainless steel bars type 316 S66, delivered to site cut, bent and labelled**								
E301207	**Plain bars, fixing with stainless steel tying wire**								
E301207A	10 mm	Tonne	44.00	651.20	-	2,980.73	3,631.93	3,995.12	6,236.800
E301207B	12 mm	Tonne	38.00	562.40	-	2,963.85	3,526.25	3,878.88	6,211.225
E301207C	16 mm	Tonne	30.00	444.00	-	2,901.95	3,345.95	3,680.55	6,192.125
E301207D	20 mm	Tonne	26.00	384.80	-	2,889.27	3,274.07	3,601.48	6,177.550
E301207E	25 mm	Tonne	23.00	340.40	-	3,007.96	3,348.36	3,683.20	6,168.800
E301207F	32 mm	Tonne	20.00	296.00	-	3,003.34	3,299.34	3,629.27	6,166.850
E301208	**Ribbed bars, fixing with stainless steel tying wire**								
E301208A	10 mm	Tonne	44.00	651.20	-	2,980.73	3,631.93	3,995.12	6,236.800
E301208B	12 mm	Tonne	38.00	562.40	-	2,963.85	3,526.25	3,878.88	6,211.225
E301208C	16 mm	Tonne	30.00	444.00	-	2,901.95	3,345.95	3,680.55	6,192.125
E301208D	20 mm	Tonne	26.00	384.80	-	2,889.27	3,274.07	3,601.48	6,177.550
E301208E	25 mm	Tonne	23.00	340.40	-	3,007.96	3,348.36	3,683.20	6,168.800
E301208F	32 mm	Tonne	20.00	296.00	-	3,003.34	3,299.34	3,629.27	6,166.850
E3040	**Steel fabric reinforcement, BS 4483, delivered to site in standard sheets**								
E304022	**Fabric reinforcement, laid horizontally; ref**								
E304022A	A98; 1.54 kg/m²	m²	0.02	0.30	-	1.54	1.84	2.02	3.366
E304022B	A142; 2.22 kg/m²	m²	0.03	0.46	-	1.93	2.39	2.63	4.808
E304022C	A193; 3.02 kg/m²	m²	0.03	0.44	-	2.55	2.99	3.29	6.506
E304022D	A252; 3.95 kg/m²	m²	0.03	0.44	-	3.24	3.68	4.05	8.481
E304022E	A393; 6.16 kg/m²	m²	0.05	0.74	-	5.00	5.74	6.31	13.170
E304022F	B196; 3.05 kg/m²	m²	0.03	0.44	-	4.37	4.81	5.29	6.306
E304022G	B283; 3.73 kg/m²	m²	0.03	0.44	-	3.07	3.51	3.86	7.690
E304022H	B385; 4.53 kg/m²	m²	0.04	0.62	-	3.59	4.21	4.63	9.318
E304022I	B503; 5.93 kg/m²	m²	0.05	0.74	-	4.67	5.41	5.95	12.168
E304022J	B785; 8.14 kg/m²	m²	0.05	0.74	-	6.29	7.03	7.73	16.667
E304022K	B1131; 10.90 kg/m²	m²	0.07	1.04	-	13.19	14.23	15.65	22.284
E304022L	C283; 2.61 kg/m²	m²	0.03	0.44	-	2.37	2.81	3.09	5.637
E304022M	C385; 3.41 kg/m²	m²	0.03	0.44	-	2.99	3.43	3.77	7.335
E304022N	C503; 4.34 kg/m²	m²	0.04	0.62	-	3.64	4.26	4.69	9.308
E304022O	C636; 5.55 kg/m²	m²	0.04	0.59	-	7.64	8.23	9.05	11.876
E304022P	C785; 6.72 kg/m²	m²	0.05	0.74	-	8.42	9.16	10.08	14.358

Major Works 2011		Unit	Labour Hours	Labour Net	Plant Net	Materials Net	Unit Net	Unit with 10%	CO₂
				£	£	£	£	£	Kg
E30	**E30: REINFORCEMENT FOR IN SITU CONCRETE**								
E3040	**Steel fabric reinforcement, BS 4483, delivered to site in standard sheets**								
E304023	**Fabric reinforcement fixed vertically; ref**								
E304023A	A98; 1.54 kg/m²	m²	0.08	1.18	-	1.36	2.54	2.79	3.339
E304023B	A142; 2.22 kg/m²	m²	0.09	1.33	-	1.76	3.09	3.40	4.782
E304023C	A193; 3.02 kg/m²	m²	0.09	1.33	-	2.37	3.70	4.07	6.479
E304023D	A252; 3.95 kg/m²	m²	0.09	1.33	-	3.07	4.40	4.84	8.454
E304023E	A393; 6.16 kg/m²	m²	0.02	0.24	-	4.83	5.07	5.58	13.144
E304023F	B196; 3.05 kg/m²	m²	0.09	1.33	-	4.20	5.53	6.08	6.280
E304023G	B283; 3.73 kg/m²	m²	0.10	1.48	-	2.90	4.38	4.82	7.663
E304023H	B385; 4.53 kg/m²	m²	0.12	1.78	-	3.41	5.19	5.71	9.292
E304023I	B503; 5.93 kg/m²	m²	0.16	2.37	-	4.50	6.87	7.56	12.141
E304023J	B785; 8.14 kg/m²	m²	0.20	2.96	-	6.12	9.08	9.99	16.640
E304023K	B1131; 10.90 kg/m²	m²	0.22	3.26	-	13.02	16.28	17.91	22.258
E304023L	C283; 2.61 kg/m²	m²	0.08	1.18	-	2.19	3.37	3.71	5.610
E304023M	C385; 3.41 kg/m²	m²	0.09	1.33	-	2.81	4.14	4.55	7.308
E304023N	C503; 4.34 kg/m²	m²	0.12	1.78	-	3.46	5.24	5.76	9.282
E304023O	C636; 5.55 kg/m²	m²	0.15	2.22	-	7.47	9.69	10.66	11.850
E304023P	C785; 6.72 kg/m²	m²	0.16	2.37	-	8.25	10.62	11.68	14.332
E304024	**Fabric wrapping to column and beam casings; ref**								
E304024A	D49	m²	0.32	4.74	-	1.01	5.75	6.33	1.536
E304024B	D98	m²	0.32	4.74	-	1.23	5.97	6.57	3.072
E3041	**Expamet Hy-rib self centering reinforcement and permanent formwork with one rib side laps and 150 mm end laps; laid horizontally; ref 2411 weighing 5.71 kg/m²**								
E304132	**Not exceeding 3.5 m above floor level; strutting and supports at**								
E304132A	450 mm centres	m²	0.65	11.04	1.48	14.20	26.72	29.39	19.358
E304132B	600 mm centres	m²	0.60	10.19	1.11	13.97	25.27	27.80	19.166
E304132C	900 mm centres	m²	0.45	7.64	0.74	13.73	22.11	24.32	18.972
E304132D	1200 mm centres	m²	0.38	6.45	0.56	13.61	20.62	22.68	18.875
E304133	**3.5 - 5.0 m above floor level; strutting and supports at**								
E304133A	450 mm centres	m²	0.78	13.24	1.76	14.20	29.20	32.12	19.358
E304133B	600 mm centres	m²	0.71	12.06	1.32	13.97	27.35	30.09	19.166
E304133C	900 mm centres	m²	0.54	9.17	0.88	13.73	23.78	26.16	18.972
E304133D	1200 mm centres	m²	0.45	7.64	0.66	13.61	21.91	24.10	18.875
E3042	**Expamet Hy-rib self centering reinforcement and permanent formwork with one rib side laps and 150 mm end laps; laid horizontally; ref 2611 weighing 4.02 Kg/m²**								
E304235	**Not exceeding 3.5 m above floor level; strutting and supports at**								
E304235A	450 mm centres	m²	0.67	11.38	1.48	12.72	25.58	28.14	19.358
E304235B	600 mm centres	m²	0.62	10.53	1.11	12.48	24.12	26.53	19.166
E304235C	900 mm centres	m²	0.47	7.98	0.74	12.25	20.97	23.07	18.972
E304235D	1200 mm centres	m²	0.40	6.79	0.56	12.13	19.48	21.43	18.875
E304236	**3.5 - 5.0 m above floor level; strutting and supports at**								
E304236A	450 mm centres	m²	0.80	13.58	1.76	12.72	28.06	30.87	19.358
E304236B	600 mm centres	m²	0.64	10.87	1.32	12.48	24.67	27.14	19.166
E304236C	900 mm centres	m²	0.49	8.32	0.88	12.25	21.45	23.60	18.972
E304236D	1200 mm centres	m²	0.42	7.13	0.66	12.13	19.92	21.91	18.875

In Situ Concrete & Large Precast Concrete

Major Works 2011		Unit	Labour Hours	Labour Net	Plant Net	Materials Net	Unit Net	Unit with 10%	CO₂
				£	£	£	£	£	Kg
E40	**E40: DESIGNED JOINTS IN IN SITU CONCRETE**								
E4002	**Plain joints**								
E400223	**Horizontal joints; including 4 uses of formwork materials and zero waste in use**								
E400223B	not exceeding 150 mm high	m	0.72	12.23	-	1.60	13.83	15.21	1.486
E400223E	150 - 300 mm high	m	0.82	13.92	-	3.45	17.37	19.11	3.221
E400224	**Vertical joints; including 4 uses of formwork materials and zero waste in use**								
E400224B	not exceeding 150 mm wide	m	0.45	7.64	-	0.99	8.63	9.49	1.005
E400224E	150 - 300 mm wide	m	0.52	8.83	0.20	1.89	10.92	12.01	1.803
E4003	**Keyed joints**								
E400326	**Horizontal joints; including 4 uses of formwork materials and zero waste in use**								
E400326B	not exceeding 150 mm high	m	0.77	13.07	-	1.84	14.91	16.40	1.680
E400326E	150 - 300 mm high	m	0.82	13.92	-	3.93	17.85	19.64	3.608
E400327	**Vertical joints; including 4 uses of formwork materials and zero waste in use**								
E400327B	not exceeding 150 mm wide	m	0.50	8.49	-	1.26	9.75	10.73	1.233
E400327E	150 - 300 mm wide	m	0.57	9.68	0.20	2.36	12.24	13.46	2.200
E4004	**Movement joints**								
E400429	**Horizontal joints; including formwork; 25 mm mild steel dowel bars 600 mm long debonded for half length, dowel caps with compressible filler; notching formwork for dowels at 300 mm centres**								
E400429B	not exceeding 150 mm high	m	1.09	18.51	-	10.09	28.60	31.46	1.679
E400429E	150 - 300 mm high	m	1.19	20.21	-	11.98	32.19	35.41	3.438
E400430	**Vertical joints; including formwork; 25 mm mild steel dowel bars 600 mm long debonded for half length, dowel caps with compressible filler; notching formwork for dowels at 300 mm centres**								
E400430B	not exceeding 150 mm wide	m	0.82	13.92	-	9.45	23.37	25.71	1.175
E400430E	150 - 300 mm wide	m	0.89	15.11	0.20	10.35	25.66	28.23	1.973
E4010	**Schlegal crack inducer**								
E401032	**Horizontal joints; placing in position**								
E401032A	generally	m	0.25	4.25	-	1.43	5.68	6.25	0.154
E4011	**Serviseal PVC-u waterstops**								
E401142	**Flat dumbell**								
E401142A	100 mm wide	m	0.12	2.04	-	4.47	6.51	7.16	2.619
E401142B	170 mm wide	m	0.13	2.21	-	6.08	8.29	9.12	4.452
E401142C	210 mm wide	m	0.16	2.72	-	8.25	10.97	12.07	5.500
E401142D	250 mm wide	m	0.18	3.06	-	9.88	12.94	14.23	6.548
E401143	**Centre bulb**								
E401143A	160 mm wide	m	0.12	2.04	-	12.89	14.93	16.42	3.929
E401143B	210 mm wide	m	0.13	2.21	-	8.25	10.46	11.51	5.500
E401143C	260 mm wide	m	0.18	3.06	-	9.88	12.94	14.23	6.809
E401143D	325 mm wide	m	0.21	3.57	-	17.09	20.66	22.73	8.512
E401144	**Servi-tite flat dumbell CJ**								
E401144A	150 mm wide	m	0.12	2.04	-	12.89	14.93	16.42	3.929
E401144B	230 mm wide	m	0.15	2.55	-	18.92	21.47	23.62	6.024
E401144C	305 mm wide	m	0.18	3.06	-	31.25	34.31	37.74	7.988
E401145	**Servi-tite centre bulb XJ**								
E401145A	150 mm wide	m	0.12	2.04	-	12.89	14.93	16.42	3.929
E401145B	230 mm wide	m	0.15	2.55	-	18.92	21.47	23.62	6.024
E401145C	305 mm wide	m	0.18	3.06	-	31.25	34.31	37.74	7.988

Major Works 2011		Unit	Labour Hours	Labour Net	Plant Net	Materials Net	Unit Net	Unit with 10%	CO_2
				£	£	£	£	£	Kg
E40	**E40: DESIGNED JOINTS IN IN SITU CONCRETE**								
E4021	**Sinkings, channels or the like**								
E402153	**Form sinkings, channels or the like in face of concrete; including 4 uses of formwork materials with zero waste in use; horizontally**								
E402153A	not exceeding 150 mm girth	m	0.42	7.18	-	1.34	8.52	9.37	1.339
E402153B	150 - 300 mm girth	m	0.85	14.37	-	2.47	16.84	18.52	2.233
E402153C	over 300 mm girth	m²	1.46	24.76	-	6.27	31.03	34.13	5.160
E402154	**Form sinkings, channels or the like in face of concrete; including 4 uses of formwork materials with zero waste in use; vertically**								
E402154A	not exceeding 150 mm girth	m	0.34	5.77	-	1.00	6.77	7.45	1.045
E402154B	150 - 300 mm girth	m	0.60	10.19	-	1.87	12.06	13.27	1.728
E402154C	over 300 mm girth	m²	0.75	12.73	-	6.25	18.98	20.88	5.138
E4041	**Expansion materials**								
E404111	**Flexcell fibreboard compressible joint filler; 10 mm thick**								
E404111A	not exceeding 150 mm wide	m	0.10	1.70	-	1.44	3.14	3.45	1.820
E404111B	150 - 300 mm wide	m	0.18	2.97	-	2.88	5.85	6.44	3.629
E404111C	300 - 450 mm wide	m	0.22	3.74	-	4.32	8.06	8.87	5.449
E404112	**Flexcell fibreboard compressible joint filler; 13 mm thick**								
E404112A	not exceeding 150 mm wide	m	0.11	1.78	-	1.54	3.32	3.65	2.366
E404112B	150 - 300 mm wide	m	0.18	3.06	-	3.06	6.12	6.73	4.717
E404112C	300 - 450 mm wide	m	0.23	3.82	-	4.60	8.42	9.26	7.084
E404113	**Flexcell fibreboard compressible joint filler; 19 mm thick**								
E404113A	not exceeding 150 mm wide	m	0.12	1.95	-	2.82	4.77	5.25	3.458
E404113B	150 - 300 mm wide	m	0.20	3.31	-	5.62	8.93	9.82	6.895
E404113C	300 - 450 mm wide	m	0.23	3.91	-	8.43	12.34	13.57	10.353
E404114	**Flexcell fibreboard compressible joint filler; 25 mm thick**								
E404114A	not exceeding 150 mm wide	m	0.13	2.12	-	2.77	4.89	5.38	4.550
E404114B	150 - 300 mm wide	m	0.20	3.31	-	5.52	8.83	9.71	9.072
E404114C	300 - 450 mm wide	m	0.24	4.08	-	8.28	12.36	13.60	13.622
E4042	**Joint sealants**								
E404234	**Hot poured bituminous rubber compound**								
E404234A	10 x 25 mm	m	0.03	0.42	0.20	1.78	2.40	2.64	4.168
E404234B	13 x 25 mm	m	0.03	0.51	0.22	2.15	2.88	3.17	5.204
E404234C	19 x 25 mm	m	0.04	0.68	0.25	3.33	4.26	4.69	7.616
E404234D	25 x 25 mm	m	0.06	1.02	0.29	4.54	5.85	6.44	10.125
E404235	**Cold poured polysulphide rubber compound**								
E404235A	10 x 25 mm	m	0.03	0.53	-	3.94	4.47	4.92	3.706
E404235B	13 x 25 mm	m	0.03	0.51	-	5.15	5.66	6.23	4.840
E404235C	19 x 25 mm	m	0.04	0.70	-	7.52	8.22	9.04	7.068
E404235D	25 x 25 mm	m	0.06	1.02	-	9.85	10.87	11.96	9.255
E404236	**Cold poured polysulphide epoxy based compound**								
E404236A	10 x 25 mm	m	0.03	0.53	-	0.65	1.18	1.30	0.473
E404236B	13 x 25 mm	m	0.03	0.51	-	0.85	1.36	1.50	0.621
E404236C	19 x 25 mm	m	0.04	0.70	-	1.23	1.93	2.12	0.898
E404236D	25 x 25 mm	m	0.06	1.02	-	2.01	3.03	3.33	1.466
E404237	**Gun grade polysulphide rubber compound**								
E404237A	10 x 10 mm	m	0.04	0.68	-	0.37	1.05	1.16	0.372
E404237B	13 x 13 mm	m	0.06	1.02	-	0.64	1.66	1.83	0.638
E404237C	19 x 19 mm	m	0.13	2.21	-	1.35	3.56	3.92	1.353
E404237D	25 x 25 mm	m	0.23	3.91	-	2.31	6.22	6.84	2.317

In Situ Concrete & Large Precast Concrete

Major Works 2011		Unit	Labour Hours	Labour Net	Plant Net	Materials Net	Unit Net	Unit with 10%	CO₂
				£	£	£	£	£	Kg
E41	**E41: WORKED FINISHES AND CUTTING TO IN SITU CONCRETE**								
E4101	**Surface finishes**								
E410102	**Trowelling surfaces of concrete**								
E410102A	to levels	m²	0.16	2.03	-	-	2.03	2.23	-
E410102B	to falls and crossfalls	m²	0.25	3.17	-	-	3.17	3.49	-
E410103	**Power floating and trowelling concrete surfaces**								
E410103A	to levels	m²	0.15	1.90	0.38	-	2.28	2.51	0.693
E410103B	to falls and crossfalls	m²	0.18	2.29	0.45	-	2.74	3.01	0.832
E410104	**Lithurin surface hardener applied in accordance with manufacturer's instructions to surfaces of concrete; brush applied**								
E410104A	two coats to general surfaces of floors	m²	0.16	2.03	-	2.10	4.13	4.54	0.137
E410105	**Bush hammer treatment to surfaces of concrete**								
E410105A	vertical surfaces	m²	0.50	6.35	2.92	-	9.27	10.20	9.112
E410105B	horizontal upper faces	m²	0.40	5.08	2.33	-	7.41	8.15	7.290
E410105C	horizontal soffits	m²	0.65	8.25	3.79	-	12.04	13.24	11.846

Major Works 2011		Unit	Labour Hours	Labour Net	Plant Net	Materials Net	Unit Net	Unit with 10%	CO_2
				£	£	£	£	£	Kg
E42	E42: ACCESSORIES CAST INTO IN SITU CONCRETE								
E4210	Anchor bolts								
E421010	Steel anchor bolts; indented; with nut; BS 916: 1953; size								
E421010A	M10 100 mm	Nr	0.07	1.04	-	0.64	1.68	1.85	0.105
E421010B	M10 120 mm	Nr	0.08	1.18	-	0.65	1.83	2.01	0.126
E421010C	M10 140 mm	Nr	0.08	1.18	-	0.65	1.83	2.01	0.147
E421010D	M10 160 mm	Nr	0.09	1.33	-	0.66	1.99	2.19	0.168
E421010H	M12 100 mm	Nr	0.09	1.33	-	0.67	2.00	2.20	0.151
E421010I	M12 120 mm	Nr	0.09	1.33	-	0.83	2.16	2.38	0.181
E421010J	M12 140 mm	Nr	0.10	1.48	-	0.83	2.31	2.54	0.211
E421010K	M12 160 mm	Nr	0.11	1.63	-	0.85	2.48	2.73	0.271
E421010L	M12 180 mm	Nr	0.13	1.92	-	0.87	2.79	3.07	0.271
E421010M	M12 200 mm	Nr	0.13	1.92	-	0.94	2.86	3.15	0.302
E421010N	M12 220 mm	Nr	0.14	2.07	-	0.97	3.04	3.34	0.332
E421010O	M12 240 mm	Nr	0.14	2.07	-	0.99	3.06	3.37	0.362
E421010P	M12 260 mm	Nr	0.16	2.37	-	1.01	3.38	3.72	0.392
E421010V	M16 120 mm	Nr	0.17	2.52	-	1.01	3.53	3.88	0.322
E421010W	M16 140 mm	Nr	0.19	2.81	-	1.26	4.07	4.48	0.375

In Situ Concrete & Large Precast Concrete

Major Works 2011		Unit	Labour Hours	Labour Net	Plant Net	Materials Net	Unit Net	Unit with 10%	CO₂
				£	£	£	£	£	Kg
E60	E60: PRECAST AND COMPOSITE CONCRETE DECKING								
E6010	Trent precast concrete block and plank composite flooring system; comprising precast planks at 650 mm centres with precast concrete block infill; cement slurry grouting to joints with (1:3) mix mortar								
E601003	Floors and roofs; suspended with soffit not exceeding 3.50 m above floor level								
E601003A	standard JJ1	m²	0.23	10.83	-	26.94	37.77	41.55	74.046
E601003B	standard RJ1	m²	0.23	10.83	-	30.09	40.92	45.01	74.046
E601003C	Jetplus JP1	m²	0.16	7.28	-	34.36	41.64	45.80	98.728
E601003D	Jetplus RP1	m²	0.16	7.28	-	38.69	45.97	50.57	98.728

Masonry

Major Works 2011		Unit	Labour Hours	Labour Net	Plant Net	Materials Net	Unit Net	Unit with 10%	CO$_2$
				£	£	£	£	£	Kg
F10	**F10: BRICK AND BLOCK WALLING**								
F1001	**Walls**								
F100102	**Common bricks, BS 3921, in cement mortar (1:3)**								
F100102A	half brick thick	m^2	0.37	17.03	-	18.34	35.37	38.91	46.900
F100102B	one brick thick	m^2	0.73	34.06	-	37.91	71.97	79.17	98.017
F100102C	one and a half brick thick	m^2	1.09	51.05	-	56.50	107.55	118.31	145.537
F100102D	two brick thick	m^2	1.46	68.03	-	76.07	144.10	158.51	196.654
F100103	**Class A engineering bricks BS 3921, in cement mortar (1:3)**								
F100103A	half brick thick	m^2	0.40	18.43	-	27.03	45.46	50.01	96.856
F100103B	one brick thick	m^2	0.79	36.86	-	55.30	92.16	101.38	197.929
F100103C	one and a half brick thick	m^2	1.19	55.29	-	82.74	138.03	151.83	296.246
F100103D	two brick thick	m^2	1.58	73.72	-	111.01	184.73	203.20	397.319
F100104	**Class B engineering bricks, BS 3921, in cement mortar (1:3)**								
F100104A	half brick thick	m^2	0.38	17.73	-	23.46	41.19	45.31	96.856
F100104B	one brick thick	m^2	0.76	35.46	-	48.15	83.61	91.97	197.929
F100104C	one and a half brick thick	m^2	1.14	53.15	-	71.96	125.11	137.62	296.246
F100104D	two brick thick	m^2	1.52	70.88	-	96.65	167.53	184.28	397.319
F100105	**Facing bricks (PC £300 per 1000) in gauged mortar (1:1:6); flush pointing both sides**								
F100105A	half brick thick; stretcher bond	m^2	0.43	19.83	-	20.98	40.81	44.89	96.178
F100105B	one brick thick; double stretcher bond	m^2	0.81	37.70	-	43.09	80.79	88.87	195.045
F100105C	one brick thick; English bond	m^2	0.85	39.71	-	43.43	83.14	91.45	195.852
F100105D	one brick thick; English garden wall bond	m^2	0.83	38.49	-	43.43	81.92	90.11	195.852
F100105E	one brick thick; English cross bond	m^2	0.89	41.67	-	44.33	86.00	94.60	200.233
F100105F	one brick thick; Flemish bond	m^2	0.88	40.87	-	43.31	84.18	92.60	195.583
F100105G	one brick thick; Flemish garden wall bond	m^2	0.83	38.87	-	43.31	82.18	90.40	195.583
F100105H	one brick thick; Dutch bond	m^2	0.94	43.67	-	43.91	87.58	96.34	198.503
F100105I	one brick thick; monk bond	m^2	0.87	40.50	-	43.09	83.59	91.95	195.045
F100106	**Precast concrete blocks, BS 6073, strength 3.5 N/mm^2; in cement mortar (1:3)**								
F100106A	100 mm solid blocks	m^2	0.29	13.62	-	13.27	26.89	29.58	16.541
F100106B	140 mm solid blocks	m^2	0.32	15.02	-	18.50	33.52	36.87	23.158
F100106C	150 mm solid blocks	m^2	0.32	15.02	-	21.19	36.21	39.83	24.988
F100106D	200 mm solid blocks	m^2	0.36	16.94	-	29.96	46.90	51.59	33.083
F100106E	215 mm solid blocks	m^2	0.37	17.17	-	31.80	48.97	53.87	35.652
F100106F	100 mm hollow blocks	m^2	0.27	12.50	-	12.77	25.27	27.80	9.501
F100106G	140 mm hollow blocks	m^2	0.30	13.95	-	18.31	32.26	35.49	12.809
F100106H	150 mm hollow blocks	m^2	0.31	14.51	-	18.51	33.02	36.32	14.251
F100106I	200 mm hollow blocks	m^2	0.34	15.63	-	24.48	40.11	44.12	18.650
F100106J	215 mm hollow blocks	m^2	0.34	16.05	-	26.41	42.46	46.71	20.462
F100107	**Precast concrete blocks, BS 6073, strength 7 N/mm^2, in cement mortar (1:3)**								
F100107A	60 mm solid blocks	m^2	0.28	13.20	-	8.28	21.48	23.63	12.344
F100107B	75 mm solid blocks	m^2	0.30	13.81	-	10.41	24.22	26.64	15.518
F100107C	90 mm solid blocks	m^2	0.31	14.32	-	12.39	26.71	29.38	18.692
F100107D	100 mm solid blocks	m^2	0.31	14.32	-	13.47	27.79	30.57	20.573
F100107E	125 mm solid blocks	m^2	0.32	14.93	-	16.85	31.78	34.96	25.629
F100107F	140 mm solid blocks	m^2	0.33	15.58	-	18.91	34.49	37.94	28.803
F100107G	150 mm solid blocks	m^2	0.34	15.82	-	20.29	36.11	39.72	31.036
F100107H	190 mm solid blocks	m^2	0.38	17.82	-	24.72	42.54	46.79	39.265
F100107I	200 mm solid blocks	m^2	0.38	17.82	-	28.07	45.89	50.48	41.147
F100107J	215 mm solid blocks	m^2	0.39	18.10	-	35.84	53.94	59.33	44.320
F100107K	100 mm hollow blocks	m^2	0.28	13.16	-	12.56	25.72	28.29	6.987
F100107L	140 mm hollow blocks	m^2	0.31	14.46	-	17.52	31.98	35.18	9.642
F100107M	215 mm hollow blocks	m^2	0.36	16.56	-	36.05	52.61	57.87	15.058

Masonry

		Unit	Labour Hours	Labour Net £	Plant Net £	Materials Net £	Unit Net £	Unit with 10% £	CO₂ Kg
F10	**F10: BRICK AND BLOCK WALLING**								
F1001	**Walls**								
F100108	**Thermalite blocks in gauged mortar (1:1:6)**								
F100108A	50 mm Shield blocks	m²	0.24	11.01	-	7.81	18.82	20.70	3.327
F100108B	60 mm Shield blocks	m²	0.24	11.01	-	8.15	19.16	21.08	3.831
F100108C	75 mm Shield blocks	m²	0.25	11.48	-	9.02	20.50	22.55	4.856
F100108D	90 mm Shield blocks	m²	0.26	11.94	-	10.83	22.77	25.05	5.881
F100108E	100 mm Shield blocks	m²	0.26	11.94	-	11.99	23.93	26.32	6.385
F100108F	140 mm Shield blocks	m²	0.28	13.16	-	16.78	29.94	32.93	8.939
F100108G	150 mm Shield blocks	m²	0.28	13.16	-	18.02	31.18	34.30	9.712
F100108H	190 mm Shield blocks	m²	0.32	14.84	-	22.81	37.65	41.42	12.266
F100108I	200 mm Shield blocks	m²	0.32	14.84	-	23.96	38.80	42.68	12.770
F100108J	215 mm Shield blocks	m²	0.32	15.07	-	26.53	41.60	45.76	13.794
F100108K	255 mm Trench blocks	m²	0.35	16.14	-	30.85	46.99	51.69	16.348
F100108L	305 mm Trench blocks	m²	0.36	16.75	-	36.95	53.70	59.07	19.675
F100108M	100 mm Turbo blocks	m²	0.26	11.94	-	12.37	24.31	26.74	6.385
F100108N	125 mm Turbo blocks	m²	0.27	12.46	-	15.38	27.84	30.62	7.914
F100108O	150 mm Turbo blocks	m²	0.28	13.16	-	18.43	31.59	34.75	9.443
F100109	**Lignacite blocks in gauged mortar (1:1:6)**								
F100109A	70 mm solid blocks	m²	0.33	15.26	-	8.30	23.56	25.92	10.307
F100109B	100 mm solid blocks	m²	0.34	15.91	-	11.21	27.12	29.83	14.533
F100109C	140 mm solid blocks	m²	0.36	16.56	-	17.23	33.79	37.17	20.077
F100109D	150 mm solid blocks	m²	0.38	17.54	-	17.32	34.86	38.35	21.665
F100109E	190 mm solid blocks	m²	0.42	19.74	-	25.90	45.64	50.20	27.747
F100109F	100 mm cellular blocks	m²	0.26	11.94	-	11.33	23.27	25.60	7.358
F100110	**Durox Supablocs in gauged mortar (1:1:6)**								
F100110A	100 mm 3.5 N/mm² blocks	m²	0.26	11.94	-	11.69	23.63	25.99	5.965
F100110B	125 mm 3.5 N/mm² blocks	m²	0.27	12.46	-	14.47	26.93	29.62	7.410
F100110C	150 mm 3.5 N/mm² blocks	m²	0.28	13.16	-	17.43	30.59	33.65	9.124
F100110D	200 mm 3.5 N/mm² blocks	m²	0.32	14.84	-	23.18	38.02	41.82	12.014
F100110E	100 mm 7 N/mm² blocks	m²	0.26	12.04	-	13.39	25.43	27.97	8.275
F100110F	125 mm 7 N/mm² blocks	m²	0.27	12.55	-	16.17	28.72	31.59	10.308
F100110G	150 mm 7 N/mm² blocks	m²	0.29	13.30	-	19.13	32.43	35.67	12.610
F100110H	200 mm 7 N/mm² blocks	m²	0.32	15.07	-	24.88	39.95	43.95	16.676
F1002	**Sloping walls**								
F100212	**Common bricks, BS 3921, in cement mortar (1:3)**								
F100212A	half brick thick	m²	0.40	18.71	-	18.34	37.05	40.76	46.900
F100212B	one brick thick	m²	0.80	37.47	-	37.91	75.38	82.92	98.017
F100212C	one and a half brick thick	m²	1.20	56.13	-	56.50	112.63	123.89	145.537
F100212D	two brick thick	m²	1.60	74.84	-	76.07	150.91	166.00	196.654
F100213	**Class A engineering bricks, BS 3921, in cement mortar (1:3)**								
F100213A	half brick thick	m²	0.44	20.30	-	27.03	47.33	52.06	96.856
F100213B	one brick thick	m²	0.87	40.55	-	55.30	95.85	105.44	197.929
F100213C	one and a half brick thick	m²	1.30	60.80	-	82.74	143.54	157.89	296.246
F100213D	two brick thick	m²	1.74	81.10	-	111.01	192.11	211.32	397.319
F100214	**Class B engineering bricks, BS 3921, in cement mortar (1:3)**								
F100214A	half brick thick	m²	0.42	19.50	-	23.46	42.96	47.26	96.856
F100214B	one brick thick	m²	0.84	39.01	-	48.15	87.16	95.88	197.929
F100214C	one and a half brick thick	m²	1.25	58.46	-	71.96	130.42	143.46	296.246
F100214D	two brick thick	m²	1.67	77.97	-	96.65	174.62	192.08	397.319
F100215	**Facing bricks (PC £300 per 1000), in gauged mortar (1:1:6); flush pointing both sides**								
F100215A	half brick thick, stretcher bond	m²	0.47	21.84	-	20.98	42.82	47.10	96.178
F100215B	one brick thick, double stretcher bond	m²	0.89	41.48	-	43.09	84.57	93.03	195.045
F100215C	one brick thick, English bond	m²	0.94	43.67	-	43.43	87.10	95.81	195.852

Major Works 2011		Unit	Labour Hours	Labour Net	Plant Net	Materials Net	Unit Net	Unit with 10%	CO$_2$
				£	£	£	£	£	Kg
F10	**F10: BRICK AND BLOCK WALLING**								
F1002	**Sloping walls**								
F100215	**Facing bricks (PC £300 per 1000), in gauged mortar (1:1:6); flush pointing both sides**								
F100215D	one brick thick, English garden wall bond	m^2	0.91	42.37	-	43.43	85.80	94.38	195.852
F100215E	one brick thick, English cross bond	m^2	0.98	45.87	-	44.33	90.20	99.22	200.233
F100215F	one brick thick, Flemish bond	m^2	0.96	44.98	-	43.31	88.29	97.12	195.583
F100215G	one brick thick, Flemish garden wall bond	m^2	0.92	42.79	-	43.31	86.10	94.71	195.583
F100215H	one brick thick, Dutch bond	m^2	1.03	48.01	-	43.91	91.92	101.11	198.503
F100215I	one brick thick, monk bond	m^2	0.96	44.56	-	43.09	87.65	96.42	195.045
F1003	**Battering walls**								
F100317	**Common bricks, BS 3921, in cement mortar (1:3)**								
F100317A	half brick thick	m^2	0.44	20.39	-	18.34	38.73	42.60	46.900
F100317B	one brick thick	m^2	0.88	40.83	-	37.91	78.74	86.61	98.017
F100317C	one and a half brick thick	m^2	1.31	61.26	-	56.50	117.76	129.54	145.537
F100317D	two brick thick	m^2	1.75	81.66	-	76.07	157.73	173.50	196.654
F100318	**Class A engineering bricks, BS 3921, in cement mortar (1:3)**								
F100318A	half brick thick	m^2	0.47	22.12	-	27.03	49.15	54.07	96.856
F100318B	one brick thick	m^2	0.95	44.23	-	55.30	99.53	109.48	197.929
F100318C	one and a half brick thick	m^2	1.42	66.35	-	82.74	149.09	164.00	296.246
F100318D	two brick thick	m^2	1.90	88.47	-	111.01	199.48	219.43	397.319
F100319	**Class B engineering bricks, BS 3921, in cement mortar (1:3)**								
F100319A	half brick thick	m^2	0.46	21.28	-	23.46	44.74	49.21	96.856
F100319B	one brick thick	m^2	0.91	42.51	-	48.15	90.66	99.73	197.929
F100319C	one and a half brick thick	m^2	1.37	63.78	-	71.96	135.74	149.31	296.246
F100319D	two brick thick	m^2	1.82	85.06	-	96.65	181.71	199.88	397.319
F100320	**Facing bricks (PC £300 per 1000), in gauged mortar (1:1:6); flush pointing both sides**								
F100320A	half brick thick, stretcher bond	m^2	0.51	23.80	-	20.98	44.78	49.26	96.178
F100320B	one brick thick, double stretcher bond	m^2	0.97	45.26	-	43.09	88.35	97.19	195.045
F100320C	one brick thick, English bond	m^2	1.02	47.64	-	43.43	91.07	100.18	195.852
F100320D	one brick thick, English garden wall bond	m^2	0.99	46.24	-	43.43	89.67	98.64	195.852
F100320E	one brick thick, English cross bond	m^2	1.07	50.02	-	44.33	94.35	103.79	200.233
F100320F	one brick thick, Flemish bond	m^2	1.05	49.04	-	43.31	92.35	101.59	195.583
F100320G	one brick thick, Flemish garden wall bond	m^2	1.00	46.66	-	43.31	89.97	98.97	195.583
F100320H	one brick thick, Dutch bond	m^2	1.12	52.40	-	43.91	96.31	105.94	198.503
F100320I	one brick thick, monk bond	m^2	1.04	48.57	-	43.09	91.66	100.83	195.045
F1004	**Curved walls**								
F100422	**Common bricks, BS 3921, in cement mortar (1:3)**								
F100422A	half brick thick	m^2	0.55	25.52	-	18.34	43.86	48.25	46.900
F100422B	one brick thick	m^2	1.10	51.09	-	37.91	89.00	97.90	98.017
F100422C	one and a half brick thick	m^2	1.64	76.57	-	56.50	133.07	146.38	145.537
F100422D	two brick thick	m^2	2.19	102.09	-	76.07	178.16	195.98	196.654
F100423	**Class A engineering bricks, BS 3921, in cement mortar (1:3)**								
F100423A	half brick thick	m^2	0.59	27.67	-	27.03	54.70	60.17	96.856
F100423B	one brick thick	m^2	1.19	55.29	-	55.30	110.59	121.65	197.929
F100423C	one and a half brick thick	m^2	1.78	82.96	-	82.74	165.70	182.27	296.246
F100423D	two brick thick	m^2	2.37	110.58	-	111.01	221.59	243.75	397.319

Masonry

		Unit	Labour Hours	Labour Net £	Plant Net £	Materials Net £	Unit Net £	Unit with 10% £	CO₂ Kg
F10	**F10: BRICK AND BLOCK WALLING**								
F1004	**Curved walls**								
F100424	**Class B engineering bricks, BS 3921, in cement mortar (1:3)**								
F100424A	half brick thick	m²	0.57	26.60	-	23.46	50.06	55.07	96.856
F100424B	one brick thick	m²	1.14	53.19	-	48.15	101.34	111.47	197.929
F100424C	one and a half brick thick	m²	1.71	79.74	-	71.96	151.70	166.87	296.246
F100424D	two brick thick	m²	2.28	106.34	-	96.65	202.99	223.29	397.319
F100425	**Facing bricks (PC £300 per 1000), in gauged mortar; flush pointing both sides**								
F100425A	half brick thick, stretcher bond	m²	0.64	29.77	-	20.98	50.75	55.83	96.178
F100425B	one brick thick, double stretcher bond	m²	1.21	56.55	-	43.09	99.64	109.60	195.045
F100425C	one brick thick, English bond	m²	1.28	59.54	-	43.43	102.97	113.27	195.852
F100425D	one brick thick, English garden wall bond	m²	1.24	57.77	-	43.43	101.20	111.32	195.852
F100425E	one brick thick, English cross bond	m²	1.34	62.52	-	44.33	106.85	117.54	200.233
F100425F	one brick thick, Flemish bond	m²	1.31	61.31	-	43.31	104.62	115.08	195.583
F100425G	one brick thick, Flemish garden wall bond	m²	1.25	58.32	-	43.31	101.63	111.79	195.583
F100425H	one brick thick, Dutch bond	m²	1.40	65.51	-	44.21	109.72	120.69	199.964
F100425I	one brick thick, monk bond	m²	1.30	60.75	-	42.55	103.30	113.63	199.335
F100426	**Precast concrete blocks, BS 6073, strength 3.5 N/mm²; in cement mortar (1:3)**								
F100426A	100 mm solid blocks	m²	0.44	20.44	-	13.27	33.71	37.08	16.541
F100426B	140 mm solid blocks	m²	0.48	22.54	-	18.50	41.04	45.14	23.158
F100426C	150 mm solid blocks	m²	0.49	22.86	-	21.19	44.05	48.46	24.988
F100426D	200 mm solid blocks	m²	0.54	25.38	-	29.96	55.34	60.87	33.083
F100426E	215 mm solid blocks	m²	0.55	25.76	-	31.80	57.56	63.32	35.652
F100427	**Precast concrete blocks, BS 6073, strength 7 N/mm²; in cement mortar (1:3)**								
F100427A	100 mm solid blocks	m²	0.46	21.51	-	13.47	34.98	38.48	20.573
F100427B	140 mm solid blocks	m²	0.50	23.38	-	18.90	42.28	46.51	28.803
F100427C	150 mm solid blocks	m²	0.51	23.70	-	20.29	43.99	48.39	31.036
F100427D	200 mm solid blocks	m²	0.57	26.74	-	28.07	54.81	60.29	41.147
F100427E	215 mm solid blocks	m²	0.58	27.11	-	35.84	62.95	69.25	44.320
F1005	**Walls built against other construction**								
F100531	**Common bricks, BS 3921, in cement mortar (1:3)**								
F100531A	half brick thick	m²	0.40	18.71	-	18.95	37.66	41.43	49.008
F100531B	one brick thick	m²	0.80	37.47	-	39.45	76.92	84.61	103.288
F100531C	one and a half brick thick	m²	1.20	56.13	-	58.66	114.79	126.27	152.917
F100531D	two brick thick	m²	1.60	74.84	-	79.16	154.00	169.40	207.197
F100532	**Class A engineering bricks, BS 3921, in cement mortar (1:3)**								
F100532A	half brick thick	m²	0.44	20.30	-	27.55	47.85	52.64	98.613
F100532B	one brick thick	m²	0.87	40.55	-	56.54	97.09	106.80	202.147
F100532C	one and a half brick thick	m²	1.30	60.80	-	84.49	145.29	159.82	302.220
F100532D	two brick thick	m²	1.74	81.10	-	113.48	194.58	214.04	405.754
F100533	**Class B engineering bricks, BS 3921, in cement mortar (1:3)**								
F100533A	half brick thick	m²	0.42	19.50	-	23.97	43.47	47.82	98.613
F100533B	one brick thick	m²	0.84	39.01	-	49.39	88.40	97.24	202.147
F100533C	one and a half brick thick	m²	1.25	58.46	-	73.71	132.17	145.39	302.220
F100533D	two brick thick	m²	1.67	77.97	-	99.12	177.09	194.80	405.754

Major Works 2011		Unit	Labour Hours	Labour Net £	Plant Net £	Materials Net £	Unit Net £	Unit with 10% £	CO$_2$ Kg
F10	**F10: BRICK AND BLOCK WALLING**								
F1005	**Walls built against other construction**								
F100534	**Facing bricks (PC £300 per 1000), in gauged mortar (1:1:6); flush pointing one side**								
F100534A	half brick thick; stretcher bond	m^2	0.47	21.84	-	21.43	43.27	47.60	97.254
F100534B	half brick thick; English bond (snapped headers)	m^2	0.52	24.45	-	23.94	48.39	53.23	109.204
F100534C	half brick thick; Flemish bond (snapped headers)	m^2	0.54	25.10	-	23.94	49.04	53.94	109.204
F100535	**Precast concrete blocks, BS 6073, strength 3.5 N/mm^2; in cement mortar (1:3)**								
F100535A	100 mm solid blocks	m^2	0.32	14.98	-	13.37	28.35	31.19	16.893
F100535B	140 mm solid blocks	m^2	0.35	16.52	-	18.70	35.22	38.74	23.861
F100535C	150 mm solid blocks	m^2	0.35	16.52	-	21.40	37.92	41.71	25.691
F100535D	200 mm solid blocks	m^2	0.40	18.62	-	30.27	48.89	53.78	34.137
F100535E	215 mm solid blocks	m^2	0.41	18.90	-	32.11	51.01	56.11	36.706
F100535F	100 mm hollow blocks	m^2	0.30	13.76	-	12.97	26.73	29.40	10.204
F100536	**Precast concrete blocks, BS 6073, strength 7 N/mm^2; in cement mortar (1:3)**								
F100536A	60 mm solid blocks	m^2	0.31	14.56	-	8.38	22.94	25.23	12.695
F100536B	75 mm solid blocks	m^2	0.33	15.16	-	10.51	25.67	28.24	15.869
F100536C	90 mm solid blocks	m^2	0.34	15.77	-	12.49	28.26	31.09	19.043
F100536D	100 mm solid blocks	m^2	0.34	15.77	-	13.57	29.34	32.27	20.925
F100536E	125 mm solid blocks	m^2	0.35	16.42	-	17.06	33.48	36.83	26.332
F100536F	140 mm solid blocks	m^2	0.37	17.40	-	19.11	36.51	40.16	29.505
F100536G	150 mm solid blocks	m^2	0.37	17.40	-	20.50	37.90	41.69	31.739
F100536H	190 mm solid blocks	m^2	0.42	19.60	-	25.03	44.63	49.09	40.319
F100536I	200 mm solid blocks	m^2	0.42	19.60	-	28.38	47.98	52.78	42.201
F100536J	215 mm solid blocks	m^2	0.43	19.88	-	36.15	56.03	61.63	45.375
F100536K	100 mm hollow blocks	m^2	0.31	14.46	-	12.76	27.22	29.94	7.690
F100536L	140 mm hollow blocks	m^2	0.34	15.91	-	17.72	33.63	36.99	10.345
F100536M	215 mm hollow blocks	m^2	0.39	18.24	-	36.36	54.60	60.06	16.113
F100537	**Thermalite blocks in gauged mortar (1:1:6)**								
F100537A	50 mm Shield blocks	m^2	0.26	12.13	-	7.92	20.05	22.06	3.596
F100537B	60 mm Shield blocks	m^2	0.26	12.13	-	8.26	20.39	22.43	4.100
F100537C	75 mm Shield blocks	m^2	0.27	12.64	-	9.13	21.77	23.95	5.125
F100537D	90 mm Shield blocks	m^2	0.28	13.16	-	10.95	24.11	26.52	6.150
F100537E	100 mm Shield blocks	m^2	0.28	13.16	-	12.10	25.26	27.79	6.654
F100537F	140 mm Shield blocks	m^2	0.31	14.46	-	17.01	31.47	34.62	9.477
F100537G	150 mm Shield blocks	m^2	0.31	14.46	-	18.25	32.71	35.98	10.250
F100537H	190 mm Shield blocks	m^2	0.35	16.28	-	23.15	39.43	43.37	13.072
F100537I	200 mm Shield blocks	m^2	0.35	16.28	-	24.30	40.58	44.64	13.576
F100537J	215 mm Shield blocks	m^2	0.36	16.56	-	26.87	43.43	47.77	14.601
F100537K	255 mm Trench blocks	m^2	0.38	17.78	-	31.19	48.97	53.87	17.155
F100537L	305 mm Trench blocks	m^2	0.40	18.43	-	37.41	55.84	61.42	20.751
F100537M	100 mm Turbo blocks	m^2	0.28	13.16	-	12.48	25.64	28.20	6.654
F100537N	125 mm Turbo blocks	m^2	0.29	13.67	-	15.61	29.28	32.21	8.452
F100537O	150 mm Turbo blocks	m^2	0.31	14.46	-	18.77	33.23	36.55	10.250
F100538	**Lignacite blocks in gauged mortar (1:1:6)**								
F100538A	70 mm solid blocks	m^2	0.36	16.80	-	8.41	25.21	27.73	10.576
F100538B	100 mm solid blocks	m^2	0.38	17.50	-	11.33	28.83	31.71	14.802
F100538C	140 mm solid blocks	m^2	0.39	18.20	-	17.45	35.65	39.22	20.615
F100538D	150 mm solid blocks	m^2	0.41	19.22	-	17.55	36.77	40.45	22.203
F100538E	190 mm solid blocks	m^2	0.47	21.70	-	26.24	47.94	52.73	28.554
F100538F	100 mm cellular blocks	m^2	0.28	13.16	-	11.55	24.71	27.18	7.896
F100539	**Durox Supablocs in gauged mortar (1:1:6)**								
F100539A	100 mm 3.5 N/mm^2 blocks	m^2	0.28	13.16	-	11.80	24.96	27.46	6.234
F100539B	125 mm 3.5 N/mm^2 blocks	m^2	0.29	13.67	-	14.69	28.36	31.20	7.948
F100539C	150 mm 3.5 N/mm^2 blocks	m^2	0.31	14.46	-	17.66	32.12	35.33	9.662
F100539D	200 mm 3.5 N/mm^2 blocks	m^2	0.35	16.28	-	23.52	39.80	43.78	12.820

Masonry

		Unit	Labour Hours	Labour Net £	Plant Net £	Materials Net £	Unit Net £	Unit with 10% £	CO₂ Kg
F10	**F10: BRICK AND BLOCK WALLING**								
F1005	**Walls built against other construction**								
F100539	**Durox Supablocs in gauged mortar (1:1:6)**								
F100539E	100 mm 7 N/mm² blocks	m²	0.28	13.25	–	13.50	26.75	29.43	8.544
F100539F	125 mm 7 N/mm² blocks	m²	0.30	13.81	–	16.39	30.20	33.22	10.846
F100539G	150 mm 7 N/mm² blocks	m²	0.31	14.65	–	19.36	34.01	37.41	13.148
F100539H	200 mm 7 N/mm² blocks	m²	0.36	16.56	–	24.09	40.65	44.72	16.816
F1006	**Cavity walls**								
F100641	**Common bricks, BS 3921, in cement mortar (1:3)**								
F100641A	half brick skins	m²	0.37	17.03	–	18.34	35.37	38.91	46.900
F100641B	one brick skins	m²	0.73	34.06	–	37.91	71.97	79.17	98.017
F100641C	one and a half brick skins	m²	1.09	51.05	–	56.50	107.55	118.31	145.537
F100641D	two brick skins	m²	1.46	68.03	–	76.07	144.10	158.51	196.654
F100642	**Class A engineering bricks, BS 3921, in cement mortar (1:3)**								
F100642A	half brick skins	m²	0.40	18.43	–	27.03	45.46	50.01	96.856
F100642B	one brick skins	m²	0.79	36.86	–	55.30	92.16	101.38	197.929
F100642C	one and a half brick skins	m²	1.19	55.29	–	82.74	138.03	151.83	296.246
F100642D	two brick skins	m²	1.58	73.72	–	111.01	184.73	203.20	397.319
F100643	**Class B engineering bricks, BS 3921, in cement mortar (1:3)**								
F100643A	half brick skins	m²	0.38	17.73	–	23.46	41.19	45.31	96.856
F100643B	one brick skins	m²	0.76	35.46	–	48.15	83.61	91.97	197.929
F100643C	one and a half brick skins	m²	1.14	53.15	–	71.96	125.11	137.62	296.246
F100643D	two brick skins	m²	1.52	70.88	–	96.65	167.53	184.28	397.319
F100644	**Facing bricks (PC £300 per 1000), in gauged mortar (1:1:6); flush pointing one side**								
F100644A	half brick skins; stretcher bond	m²	0.42	19.46	–	20.86	40.32	44.35	95.909
F100644B	half brick skins; English bond (snapped headers)	m²	0.47	21.79	–	23.38	45.17	49.69	107.859
F100644C	half brick skins; Flemish bond (snapped headers)	m²	0.48	22.35	–	23.38	45.73	50.30	107.859
F100645	**Precast concrete blocks, BS 6073, strength 3.5 N/mm² in cement mortar (1:3)**								
F100645A	100 mm solid block skins	m²	0.29	13.62	–	13.37	26.99	29.69	16.893
F100645B	140 mm solid block skins	m²	0.32	15.02	–	18.70	33.72	37.09	23.861
F100645C	150 mm solid block skins	m²	0.32	15.02	–	21.40	36.42	40.06	25.691
F100645D	200 mm solid block skins	m²	0.36	16.94	–	30.27	47.21	51.93	34.137
F100645E	215 mm solid block skins	m²	0.37	17.17	–	32.11	49.28	54.21	36.706
F100645F	100 mm hollow block skins	m²	0.27	12.50	–	12.97	25.47	28.02	10.204
F100646	**Precast concrete blocks, BS 6073, strength 7 N/mm², in cement mortar (1:3)**								
F100646A	60 mm solid block skins	m²	0.28	13.20	–	8.38	21.58	23.74	12.695
F100646B	75 mm solid block skins	m²	0.30	13.81	–	10.51	24.32	26.75	15.869
F100646C	90 mm solid block skins	m²	0.31	14.32	–	12.49	26.81	29.49	19.043
F100646D	100 mm solid block skins	m²	0.31	14.32	–	13.57	27.89	30.68	20.925
F100646E	125 mm solid block skins	m²	0.32	14.93	–	17.06	31.99	35.19	26.332
F100646F	140 mm solid block skins	m²	0.34	15.82	–	19.11	34.93	38.42	29.505
F100646G	150 mm solid block skins	m²	0.34	15.82	–	20.50	36.32	39.95	31.739
F100646H	190 mm solid block skins	m²	0.38	17.82	–	25.03	42.85	47.14	40.319
F100646I	200 mm solid block skins	m²	0.38	17.82	–	28.38	46.20	50.82	42.201
F100646J	215 mm solid block skins	m²	0.39	18.10	–	36.15	54.25	59.68	45.375
F100646K	100 mm hollow block skins	m²	0.28	13.16	–	12.76	25.92	28.51	7.690
F100646L	140 mm hollow block skins	m²	0.31	14.46	–	17.72	32.18	35.40	10.345
F100646M	215 mm hollow block skins	m²	0.36	16.56	–	36.36	52.92	58.21	16.113

Major Works 2011		Unit	Labour Hours	Labour Net £	Plant Net £	Materials Net £	Unit Net £	Unit with 10% £	CO$_2$ Kg
F10	**F10: BRICK AND BLOCK WALLING**								
F1006	**Cavity walls**								
F100647	**Thermalite blocks in gauged mortar (1:1:6)**								
F100647A	50 mm Shield block skins	m^2	0.24	11.01	-	7.92	18.93	20.82	3.596
F100647B	60 mm Shield block skins	m^2	0.24	11.01	-	8.26	19.27	21.20	4.100
F100647C	75 mm Shield block skins	m^2	0.25	11.48	-	9.13	20.61	22.67	5.125
F100647D	90 mm Shield block skins	m^2	0.26	11.94	-	10.95	22.89	25.18	6.150
F100647E	100 mm Shield block skins	m^2	0.26	11.94	-	12.10	24.04	26.44	6.654
F100647F	140 mm Shield block skins	m^2	0.28	13.16	-	17.01	30.17	33.19	9.477
F100647G	150 mm Shield block skins	m^2	0.28	13.16	-	18.25	31.41	34.55	10.250
F100647H	190 mm Shield block skins	m^2	0.32	14.84	-	23.15	37.99	41.79	13.072
F100647I	200 mm Shield block skins	m^2	0.32	14.84	-	24.30	39.14	43.05	13.576
F100647J	215 mm Shield block skins	m^2	0.32	15.07	-	26.87	41.94	46.13	14.601
F100647K	255 mm Trench block skins	m^2	0.35	16.14	-	31.19	47.33	52.06	17.155
F100647L	305 mm Trench block skins	m^2	0.36	16.75	-	37.41	54.16	59.58	20.751
F100647M	100 mm Turbo block skins	m^2	0.26	11.94	-	12.48	24.42	26.86	6.654
F100647N	125 mm Turbo block skins	m^2	0.27	12.46	-	15.61	28.07	30.88	8.452
F100647O	150 mm Turbo block skins	m^2	0.28	13.16	-	18.77	31.93	35.12	10.250
F100648	**Lignacite blocks in gauged mortar (1:1:6)**								
F100648A	70 mm solid block skins	m^2	0.33	15.26	-	8.41	23.67	26.04	10.576
F100648B	100 mm solid block skins	m^2	0.34	15.91	-	11.33	27.24	29.96	14.802
F100648C	140 mm solid block skins	m^2	0.35	16.52	-	17.45	33.97	37.37	20.615
F100648D	150 mm solid block skins	m^2	0.38	17.50	-	17.55	35.05	38.56	22.203
F100648E	190 mm solid block skins	m^2	0.42	19.74	-	26.24	45.98	50.58	28.554
F100648F	100 mm cellular block skins	m^2	0.34	15.91	-	11.55	27.46	30.21	7.896
F100649	**Durox Supablocs in gauged mortar (1:1:6)**								
F100649A	100 mm skins 3.5 N/mm^2 blocks	m^2	0.26	11.94	-	11.80	23.74	26.11	6.234
F100649B	125 mm skins 3.5 N/mm^2 blocks	m^2	0.27	12.46	-	14.69	27.15	29.87	7.948
F100649C	150 mm skins 3.5 N/mm^2 blocks	m^2	0.28	13.16	-	17.66	30.82	33.90	9.662
F100649D	200 mm skins 3.5 N/mm^2 blocks	m^2	0.32	14.84	-	23.52	38.36	42.20	12.820
F100649E	100 mm skins 7 N/mm^2 blocks	m^2	0.26	12.04	-	13.39	25.43	27.97	8.275
F100649F	125 mm skins 7 N/mm^2 blocks	m^2	0.27	12.55	-	16.17	28.72	31.59	10.308
F100649G	150 mm skins 7 N/mm^2 blocks	m^2	0.29	13.30	-	19.13	32.43	35.67	12.610
F100649H	200 mm skins 7 N/mm^2 blocks	m^2	0.32	15.07	-	24.88	39.95	43.95	16.676
F1007	**Isolated piers**								
F100761	**Common bricks, BS 3921, in cement mortar (1:3)**								
F100761A	half brick thick	m^2	0.44	20.39	-	19.62	40.01	44.01	50.002
F100761B	one brick thick	m^2	0.88	40.83	-	40.21	81.04	89.14	103.600
F100761C	one and a half brick thick	m^2	1.31	61.26	-	60.09	121.35	133.49	154.222
F100761D	two brick thick	m^2	1.75	81.66	-	80.94	162.60	178.86	208.441
F100762	**Class A engineering bricks, BS 3921, in cement mortar (1:3)**								
F100762A	half brick thick	m^2	0.47	22.12	-	29.06	51.18	56.30	104.157
F100762B	one brick thick	m^2	0.95	44.23	-	58.96	103.19	113.51	211.071
F100762C	one and a half brick thick	m^2	1.42	66.35	-	88.43	154.78	170.26	316.688
F100762D	two brick thick	m^2	1.90	88.47	-	118.73	207.20	227.92	425.062
F100763	**Class B engineering bricks, BS 3921, in cement mortar (1:3)**								
F100763A	half brick thick	m^2	0.46	21.28	-	25.20	46.48	51.13	104.157
F100763B	one brick thick	m^2	0.91	42.51	-	51.29	93.80	103.18	211.071
F100763C	one and a half brick thick	m^2	1.37	63.78	-	76.84	140.62	154.68	316.688
F100763D	two brick thick	m^2	1.82	85.06	-	103.27	188.33	207.16	425.062
F100764	**Facing bricks (PC £300 per 1000), in gauged mortar (1:1:6); flush pointing all round**								
F100764A	half brick thick; stretcher bond	m^2	0.51	23.80	-	22.48	46.28	50.91	103.479
F100764B	one brick thick; English bond	m^2	1.02	47.64	-	46.13	93.77	103.15	208.994
F100764C	one brick thick; English garden wall bond	m^2	0.99	46.24	-	46.13	92.37	101.61	208.994

Masonry

Major Works 2011		Unit	Labour Hours	Labour Net	Plant Net	Materials Net	Unit Net	Unit with 10%	CO₂
				£	£	£	£	£	Kg
F10	**F10: BRICK AND BLOCK WALLING**								
F1007	**Isolated piers**								
F100764	**Facing bricks (PC £300 per 1000), in gauged mortar (1:1:6); flush pointing all round**								
F100764D	one brick thick; English cross bond	m²	1.07	50.02	-	47.03	97.05	106.76	213.374
F100764E	one brick thick; Flemish bond	m²	1.05	49.04	-	46.01	95.05	104.56	208.725
F100764F	one brick thick; Flemish garden wall bond	m²	1.00	46.66	-	46.01	92.67	101.94	208.725
F100764G	one brick thick; Dutch bond	m²	1.12	52.40	-	46.61	99.01	108.91	211.645
F100764H	one brick thick; monk bond	m²	1.04	48.57	-	45.79	94.36	103.80	208.187
F100765	**Precast concrete blocks, BS 6073, strength 3.5 N/mm²; in cement mortar (1:3)**								
F100765A	100 mm solid blocks	m²	0.35	16.33	-	14.18	30.51	33.56	17.597
F100765B	140 mm solid blocks	m²	0.39	18.06	-	19.77	37.83	41.61	24.636
F100765C	150 mm solid blocks	m²	0.39	18.06	-	22.65	40.71	44.78	26.572
F100765D	200 mm solid blocks	m²	0.44	20.34	-	32.02	52.36	57.60	35.195
F100765E	215 mm solid blocks	m²	0.44	20.62	-	33.99	54.61	60.07	37.922
F100765F	100 mm hollow blocks	m²	0.32	15.02	-	13.63	28.65	31.52	10.029
F100765G	140 mm hollow blocks	m²	0.35	16.47	-	19.56	36.03	39.63	13.548
F100765H	150 mm hollow blocks	m²	0.37	17.08	-	19.77	36.85	40.54	15.043
F100765I	200 mm hollow blocks	m²	0.39	18.38	-	26.15	44.53	48.98	19.706
F100765J	215 mm hollow blocks	m²	0.41	18.90	-	28.20	47.10	51.81	21.597
F100766	**Precast concrete blocks, BS 6073, strength 7 N/mm²; in cement mortar (1:3)**								
F100766A	60 mm solid blocks	m²	0.34	15.86	-	8.85	24.71	27.18	13.150
F100766B	75 mm solid blocks	m²	0.36	16.56	-	11.12	27.68	30.45	16.526
F100766C	90 mm solid blocks	m²	0.37	17.22	-	13.24	30.46	33.51	19.901
F100766D	100 mm solid blocks	m²	0.37	17.22	-	14.40	31.62	34.78	21.917
F100766E	125 mm solid blocks	m²	0.38	17.92	-	18.01	35.93	39.52	27.309
F100766F	140 mm solid blocks	m²	0.41	18.99	-	20.21	39.20	43.12	30.684
F100766G	150 mm solid blocks	m²	0.41	18.99	-	21.68	40.67	44.74	33.052
F100766H	190 mm solid blocks	m²	0.46	21.37	-	26.41	47.78	52.56	41.819
F100766I	200 mm solid blocks	m²	0.46	21.37	-	30.00	51.37	56.51	43.835
F100766J	215 mm solid blocks	m²	0.46	21.60	-	38.32	59.92	65.91	47.210
F100766K	100 mm hollow blocks	m²	0.34	15.82	-	13.41	29.23	32.15	7.335
F100766L	140 mm hollow blocks	m²	0.37	17.36	-	18.71	36.07	39.68	10.130
F100766M	215 mm hollow blocks	m²	0.43	19.88	-	38.53	58.41	64.25	15.808
F100767	**Thermalite blocks in gauged mortar (1:1:6)**								
F100767A	50 mm Shield blocks	m²	0.28	13.20	-	8.34	21.54	23.69	3.507
F100767B	60 mm Shield blocks	m²	0.28	13.20	-	8.71	21.91	24.10	4.047
F100767C	75 mm Shield blocks	m²	0.30	13.76	-	9.63	23.39	25.73	5.126
F100767D	90 mm Shield blocks	m²	0.31	14.32	-	11.57	25.89	28.48	6.205
F100767E	100 mm Shield blocks	m²	0.31	14.32	-	12.81	27.13	29.84	6.745
F100767F	140 mm Shield blocks	m²	0.34	15.82	-	17.93	33.75	37.13	9.443
F100767G	150 mm Shield blocks	m²	0.34	15.82	-	19.24	35.06	38.57	10.252
F100767H	190 mm Shield blocks	m²	0.38	17.78	-	24.36	42.14	46.35	12.950
F100767I	200 mm Shield blocks	m²	0.38	17.78	-	25.49	43.27	47.60	14.315
F100767J	215 mm Shield blocks	m²	0.39	18.10	-	28.34	46.44	51.08	14.568
F100767K	255 mm Trench blocks	m²	0.42	19.41	-	32.95	52.36	57.60	17.266
F100767L	305 mm Trench blocks	m²	0.43	20.11	-	39.46	59.57	65.53	20.773
F100767M	100 mm Turbo blocks	m²	0.31	14.32	-	13.21	27.53	30.28	6.745
F100767N	125 mm Turbo blocks	m²	0.32	14.93	-	16.43	31.36	34.50	8.364
F100767O	150 mm Turbo blocks	m²	0.34	15.82	-	19.69	35.51	39.06	9.983
F100768	**Lignacite blocks in gauged mortar (1:1:6)**								
F100768A	70 mm solid blocks	m²	0.39	18.34	-	8.86	27.20	29.92	10.967
F100768B	100 mm solid blocks	m²	0.41	19.08	-	11.97	31.05	34.16	15.475
F100768C	140 mm solid blocks	m²	0.43	19.97	-	18.41	38.38	42.22	21.396
F100768D	150 mm solid blocks	m²	0.45	21.04	-	18.50	39.54	43.49	23.078
F100768E	190 mm solid blocks	m²	0.51	23.66	-	27.67	51.33	56.46	29.537
F100768F	100 mm cellular blocks	m²	0.41	19.08	-	12.09	31.17	34.29	7.769

Major Works 2011		Unit	Labour Hours	Labour Net	Plant Net	Materials Net	Unit Net	Unit with 10%	CO$_2$
				£	£	£	£	£	Kg

F10 **F10: BRICK AND BLOCK WALLING**

F1007 **Isolated piers**

F100769 **Durox Supablocs in gauged mortar (1:1:6)**

F100769A	100 mm 3.5 N/mm^2 blocks	m^2	0.31	14.32	-	12.48	26.80	29.48	6.295
F100769B	125 mm 3.5 N/mm^2 blocks	m^2	0.32	14.93	-	15.45	30.38	33.42	7.824
F100769C	150 mm 3.5 N/mm^2 blocks	m^2	0.34	15.82	-	18.61	34.43	37.87	9.622
F100769D	200 mm 3.5 N/mm^2 blocks	m^2	0.38	17.78	-	24.76	42.54	46.79	12.680
F100769E	100 mm 7 N/mm^2 blocks	m^2	0.31	14.32	-	14.30	28.62	31.48	8.770
F100769F	125 mm 7 N/mm^2 blocks	m^2	0.32	14.93	-	17.27	32.20	35.42	10.929
F100769G	150 mm 7 N/mm^2 blocks	m^2	0.34	15.82	-	20.44	36.26	39.89	13.357
F100769H	200 mm 7 N/mm^2 blocks	m^2	0.37	17.36	-	26.69	44.05	48.46	17.943

F1008 **Extra over general brickwork for fair faced work**

F100882 **Fair facing and flush pointing**

F100882A	stretcher bond	m^2	0.03	1.40	-	0.21	1.61	1.77	0.703
F100882B	English bond	m^2	0.03	1.49	-	0.41	1.90	2.09	1.406
F100882C	English garden wall bond	m^2	0.03	1.45	-	0.31	1.76	1.94	1.054
F100882D	English cross bond	m^2	0.03	1.54	-	0.41	1.95	2.15	1.406
F100882E	Flemish bond	m^2	0.03	1.54	-	0.31	1.85	2.04	1.054
F100882F	Flemish garden wall bond	m^2	0.03	1.45	-	0.41	1.86	2.05	1.406
F100882G	Dutch bond	m^2	0.04	1.63	-	0.51	2.14	2.35	1.757
F100882H	monk bond	m^2	0.03	1.49	-	0.31	1.80	1.98	1.054

F100883 **Fair facing and struck or weather struck pointing**

F100883A	stretcher bond	m^2	0.03	1.45	-	0.21	1.66	1.83	0.703
F100883B	English bond	m^2	0.03	1.54	-	0.41	1.95	2.15	1.406
F100883C	English garden wall bond	m^2	0.03	1.49	-	0.31	1.80	1.98	1.054
F100883D	English cross bond	m^2	0.04	1.63	-	0.41	2.04	2.24	1.406
F100883E	Flemish bond	m^2	0.04	1.63	-	0.31	1.94	2.13	1.054
F100883F	Flemish Garden wall bond	m^2	0.03	1.54	-	0.41	1.95	2.15	1.406
F100883G	Dutch bond	m^2	0.04	1.73	-	0.51	2.24	2.46	1.757
F100883H	monk bond	m^2	0.03	1.59	-	0.31	1.90	2.09	1.054

F100884 **Fair facing and tooled or keyed pointing**

F100884A	stretcher bond	m^2	0.03	1.54	-	0.21	1.75	1.93	0.703
F100884B	English bond	m^2	0.04	1.63	-	0.41	2.04	2.24	1.406
F100884C	English garden wall bond	m^2	0.03	1.59	-	0.31	1.90	2.09	1.054
F100884D	English cross bond	m^2	0.04	1.73	-	0.41	2.14	2.35	1.406
F100884E	Flemish bond	m^2	0.04	1.68	-	0.31	1.99	2.19	1.054
F100884F	Flemish garden wall bond	m^2	0.04	1.63	-	0.41	2.04	2.24	1.406
F100884G	Dutch bond	m^2	0.04	1.82	-	0.51	2.33	2.56	1.757
F100884H	monk bond	m^2	0.04	1.68	-	0.31	1.99	2.19	1.054

F100887 **Extra over common brickwork in cement mortar (1:3) for facing brickwork (PC £300 per 1000), in gauged mortar (1:1:6); flush pointing one side**

F100887A	stretcher bond	m^2	0.06	2.85	-	2.96	5.81	6.39	52.603
F100887B	English bond	m^2	0.09	4.25	-	4.55	8.80	9.68	79.173
F100887C	English garden wall bond	m^2	0.08	3.55	-	3.78	7.33	8.06	66.308
F100887D	English cross bond	m^2	0.10	4.43	-	4.73	9.16	10.08	82.533
F100887E	Flemish bond	m^2	0.08	3.78	-	4.00	7.78	8.56	70.507
F100887F	Flemish garden wall bond	m^2	0.07	3.22	-	3.58	6.80	7.48	60.699
F100887G	Dutch bond	m^2	0.10	4.67	-	5.11	9.78	10.76	87.840
F100887H	monk bond	m^2	0.09	4.25	-	4.44	8.69	9.56	78.905

F1009 **Extra over general blockwork for fair faced work**

F100986 **Fair facing and flush pointing**

F100986A	precast concrete blocks, BS 6073	m^2	0.01	0.61	-	0.11	0.72	0.79	0.269
F100986B	Thermalite blocks	m^2	0.01	0.61	-	0.11	0.72	0.79	0.269
F100986C	Lignacite blocks	m^2	0.01	0.61	-	0.11	0.72	0.79	0.269
F100986D	Durox Supablocs	m^2	0.01	0.61	-	0.11	0.72	0.79	0.269

Masonry

		Unit	Labour Hours	Labour Net £	Plant Net £	Materials Net £	Unit Net £	Unit with 10% £	CO₂ Kg

F10	**F10: BRICK AND BLOCK WALLING**								
F1009	**Extra over general blockwork for fair faced work**								
F100987	**Extra over blockwork in cement mortar (1:3) for facing brickwork (PC £300 per 1000), in gauged mortar (1:1:6); flush pointing one side**								
F100987A	stretcher bond	m²	0.06	2.85	-	5.87	8.72	9.59	72.252
F100987B	English bond	m²	0.09	4.25	-	8.89	13.14	14.45	108.647
F100987C	English garden wall bond	m²	0.08	3.55	-	7.51	11.06	12.17	91.179
F100987D	English cross bond	m²	0.10	4.43	-	10.09	14.52	15.97	114.487
F100987E	Flemish bond	m²	0.08	3.78	-	7.05	10.83	11.91	95.658
F100987F	Flemish garden wall bond	m²	0.07	3.22	-	5.52	8.74	9.61	81.227
F100987G	Dutch bond	m²	0.10	4.67	-	7.78	12.45	13.70	115.991
F100987H	monk bond	m²	0.09	4.25	-	10.05	14.30	15.73	110.259
F1065	**Cills, bands and features**								
F106511	**Cills and copings; facing bricks (PC £300 per 1000), in gauged mortar (1:1:6); flush pointing all exposed edges**								
F106511A	brick on edge cills; flush; flat top half brick wide (snapped headers)	m	0.13	6.02	-	3.04	9.06	9.97	13.948
F106511B	brick on edge cills; flush; flat top one brick wide	m	0.20	9.29	-	4.88	14.17	15.59	22.056
F106511C	brick on edge cills; 50 mm projection weathered; half brick wide (snapped headers)	m	0.25	11.80	-	4.54	16.34	17.97	21.249
F106511D	brick on edge cills; 50 mm projection weathered; one brick wide	m	0.29	13.30	-	5.48	18.78	20.66	24.976
F106511E	brick on edge copings; one brick wide	m	0.20	9.29	-	4.88	14.17	15.59	22.056
F106511F	brick on end copings; half brick wide	m	0.30	14.09	-	4.88	18.97	20.87	22.056
F106521	**Quoins and reveals; facing bricks (PC £300 per 1000), in gauged mortar (1:1:6); flush pointing all exposed edges**								
F106521M	oversailing reveals; 25 mm projection toothed in three course bands; 161.2 mm average width	m	0.32	14.84	-	4.28	19.12	21.03	19.136
F106521N	oversailing quoins; 25 mm projection toothed in three course bands; 322.5 average girth	m	0.38	17.82	-	5.71	23.53	25.88	25.514
F106521U	receding reveals; 25 mm inset; toothed in three course bands; 161.25 mm average width	m	0.32	14.84	-	3.98	18.82	20.70	17.675
F106521V	receding quoins; 25 mm inset; toothed in three course bands; 322.5 mm average girth	m	0.38	17.82	-	5.11	22.93	25.22	22.594
F106531	**Bands and plain courses; facing bricks (PC £300 per 1000), in gauged mortar (1:1:6); flush pointing all exposed edges**								
F106531G	oversailing plain courses; 25 mm projection; one course	m	0.13	6.02	-	1.84	7.86	8.65	8.108
F106531H	oversailing plain courses; 25 mm projection; two course	m	0.20	9.29	-	3.98	13.27	14.60	17.675
F106531I	oversailing plain courses; 25 mm projection; three course	m	0.25	11.80	-	5.71	17.51	19.26	25.514
F106531J	oversailing brick on end bands; half brick thick	m	0.19	9.05	-	5.48	14.53	15.98	24.976
F106531K	oversailing brick on edge bands; half brick thick (snapped headers)	m	0.19	9.05	-	4.54	13.59	14.95	21.249
F106531L	oversailing brick on edge bands; one brick thick	m	0.30	14.09	-	5.48	19.57	21.53	24.976
F106531O	receding plain courses; 25 mm inset; one course	m	0.13	6.02	-	1.84	7.86	8.65	8.108
F106531P	receding plain course; 25 mm inset; two course	m	0.20	9.29	-	3.38	12.67	13.94	14.755

Major Works 2011		Unit	Labour Hours	Labour Net	Plant Net	Materials Net	Unit Net	Unit with 10%	CO₂
				£	£	£	£	£	Kg
F10	**F10: BRICK AND BLOCK WALLING**								
F1065	**Cills, bands and features**								
F106531	**Bands and plain courses; facing bricks (PC £300 per 1000), in gauged mortar (1:1:6); flush pointing all exposed edges**								
F106531Q	receding plain courses; 25 mm inset; three course	m	0.25	11.80	-	5.11	16.91	18.60	22.594
F106531R	receding brick on end bands; half brick thick	m	0.19	9.05	-	4.88	13.93	15.32	22.056
F106531S	receding brick on edge bands; half brick thick (snapped headers)	m	0.10	4.76	-	4.54	9.30	10.23	21.249
F106531T	receding brick on edge bands; one brick thick	m	0.30	14.09	-	4.88	18.97	20.87	22.056
F1066	**Arches**								
F106621	**Facing bricks (PC £300 per 1000), in gauged mortar (1:1:6); flush pointing all exposed edges**								
F106621A	brick on edge flat arches; half brick wide (snapped headers)	m	0.17	8.03	-	3.04	11.07	12.18	13.948
F106621B	brick on edge flat arches; one brick wide	m	0.25	11.57	-	4.88	16.45	18.10	22.056
F106621C	brick on end flat arches; half brick wide	m	0.36	16.56	-	4.88	21.44	23.58	22.056
F106621D	brick on edge segmental arches; half brick wide (snapped headers)	m	0.21	9.80	-	3.04	12.84	14.12	13.948
F106621E	brick on edge segmental arches; one brick wide; one course	m	0.31	14.32	-	4.88	19.20	21.12	22.056
F106621F	brick on edge segmental arches; one brick wide; two course	m	0.45	20.86	-	9.76	30.62	33.68	44.112
F106621G	brick on end segmental arches; half brick wide	m	0.45	20.86	-	4.88	25.74	28.31	22.056
F106621H	brick on edge semi-circular arches; half brick wide (snapped headers)	m	0.42	19.60	-	3.04	22.64	24.90	13.948
F106621I	brick on edge semi-circular arches; one brick wide; one course	m	0.56	26.13	-	4.88	31.01	34.11	22.056
F106621J	brick on edge semi-circular arches; one brick wide; two course	m	0.89	41.71	-	9.76	51.47	56.62	44.112
F106621K	brick on end semi-circular arches; half brick wide	m	0.89	41.71	-	4.88	46.59	51.25	22.056

Masonry

		Unit	Labour Hours	Labour Net £	Plant Net £	Materials Net £	Unit Net £	Unit with 10% £	CO₂ Kg
F30	**F30: ACCESSORIES AND SUNDRY ITEMS**								
F3001	**Forming cavities**								
F300150	**Form cavity to hollow wall**								
F300150A	25 mm wide	m²	0.01	0.61	-	-	0.61	0.67	-
F300150B	50 mm wide	m²	0.01	0.51	-	-	0.51	0.56	-
F300150C	75 mm wide	m²	0.01	0.47	-	-	0.47	0.52	-
F300150D	100 mm wide	m²	0.01	0.37	-	-	0.37	0.41	-
F300151	**Build in wall ties; 3 per m²**								
F300151A	3 mm galvanised wire butterfly ties, 200 mm long	m²	0.05	2.29	-	0.40	2.69	2.96	0.373
F300151B	3 mm stainless steel wire butterfly ties, 200 mm long	m²	0.05	2.29	-	0.48	2.77	3.05	0.813
F300151C	3 x 19 mm galvanised steel twisted ties, 200 mm long	m²	0.05	2.29	-	0.74	3.03	3.33	0.373
F300151D	3 x 19 mm stainless steel twisted ties 200 mm long	m²	0.05	2.29	-	1.31	3.60	3.96	0.813
F300152	**Build in wall ties; 5 per m²**								
F300152A	3 mm galvanised wire butterfly ties, 200 mm long	m²	0.08	3.78	-	0.67	4.45	4.90	0.622
F300152B	3 mm stainless steel wire butterfly ties, 200 mm long	m²	0.08	3.78	-	0.80	4.58	5.04	1.356
F300152C	3 x 19 mm galvanised steel twisted ties 200 mm long	m²	0.08	3.78	-	1.24	5.02	5.52	0.622
F300152D	3 x 19 mm stainless steel twisted ties 200 mm long	m²	0.08	3.78	-	2.19	5.97	6.57	1.356
F3003	**Closing cavities**								
F300310	**Thermabate insulated cavity closer; hollow PVC-u extrusion with core of polyisocyanate foam; fixed in accordance with manufacturer's instructions; to suit cavity width**								
F300310A	50 - 60 mm; Thermabate 50	m	0.06	2.75	-	5.66	8.41	9.25	36.667
F300310B	65 - 75 mm; Thermabate 65	m	0.07	3.27	-	6.24	9.51	10.46	47.667
F300310C	75 - 85 mm; Thermabate 75	m	0.08	3.50	-	6.84	10.34	11.37	55.000
F300310D	85 - 95 mm; Thermabate 85	m	0.08	3.50	-	7.46	10.96	12.06	62.334
F300310E	90 - 100 mm; Thermabate 90	m	0.08	3.78	-	8.00	11.78	12.96	66.001
F300310F	100 - 110 mm; Thermabate 100	m	0.08	3.78	-	8.60	12.38	13.62	73.334
F3005	**Cavity wall insulation**								
F300508	**Jablite expanded polystyrene cavity wall insulation; fitting between wall ties**								
F300508A	25 mm thick	m²	0.08	3.78	-	2.39	6.17	6.79	6.563
F300508B	50 mm thick	m²	0.09	4.01	-	4.82	8.83	9.71	13.125
F300508C	75 mm thick	m²	0.10	4.53	-	7.64	12.17	13.39	19.688
F300509	**Dritherm fibre glass cavity wall insulation slabs; fitting between wall ties**								
F300509A	50 mm thick	m²	0.09	4.01	-	4.50	8.51	9.36	9.533
F300509B	75 mm thick	m²	0.10	4.53	-	5.37	9.90	10.89	14.299
F3011	**Damp proof courses and cavity trays**								
F301113	**Hyload pitch polymer d.p.c.; horizontal**								
F301113A	not exceeding 225 mm wide	m²	0.12	5.51	-	9.06	14.57	16.03	4.410
F301113C	over 225 mm wide	m²	0.09	4.29	-	9.06	13.35	14.69	4.410
F301115	**Hyload pitch polymer d.p.c.; vertical**								
F301115A	not exceeding 225 mm wide	m²	0.16	7.56	-	9.06	16.62	18.28	4.410
F301115G	over 225 mm wide	m²	0.14	6.30	-	9.06	15.36	16.90	4.410
F301121	**Hyload pitch polymer d.p.c.; forming cavity trays**								
F301121D	over 300 mm wide	m²	0.18	8.31	-	9.06	17.37	19.11	4.410

Major Works 2011		Unit	Labour Hours	Labour Net	Plant Net	Materials Net	Unit Net	Unit with 10%	CO$_2$
				£	£	£	£	£	Kg
F30	**F30: ACCESSORIES AND SUNDRY ITEMS**								
F3030	**Expanded metal reinforcement**								
F303001	**24 gauge galvanised mild steel expanded metal brick reinforcement**								
F303001A	half brick wide	m	0.08	3.78	-	0.59	4.37	4.81	1.408
F303001B	one brick wide	m	0.09	4.29	-	1.01	5.30	5.83	2.508
F303001C	one and a half brick wide	m	0.10	4.76	-	1.59	6.35	6.99	3.915
F303001D	two brick wide	m	0.11	5.27	-	2.04	7.31	8.04	5.037
F303002	**24 gauge stainless steel expanded metal brick reinforcement**								
F303002A	half brick wide	m	0.08	3.78	-	1.41	5.19	5.71	3.070
F303002B	one brick wide	m	0.09	4.29	-	1.30	5.59	6.15	5.469
F303002C	one and a half brick wide	m	0.10	4.76	-	1.99	6.75	7.43	8.539
F303002D	two brick wide	m	0.11	5.27	-	2.58	7.85	8.64	10.985
F3048	**Expansion joints or the like**								
F304811	**19 mm Flexcell compressible joint filler; fixing in place in brickwork or blockwork**								
F304811A	half brick wide	m	0.07	3.27	-	2.07	5.34	5.87	2.539
F304811B	one brick wide	m	0.08	3.78	-	4.12	7.90	8.69	5.056
F304811C	one and a half brick wide	m	0.09	4.29	-	6.19	10.48	11.53	7.595
F304811D	two brick wide	m	0.10	4.76	-	8.24	13.00	14.30	10.112
F304811E	50 mm	m	0.06	2.75	-	0.94	3.69	4.06	1.160
F304811F	60 mm	m	0.06	2.75	-	1.12	3.87	4.26	1.379
F304811G	70 mm	m	0.07	3.03	-	1.32	4.35	4.79	1.620
F304811H	75 mm	m	0.07	3.03	-	1.41	4.44	4.88	1.729
F304811I	90 mm	m	0.07	3.27	-	1.69	4.96	5.46	2.079
F304811J	100 mm	m	0.07	3.27	-	1.87	5.14	5.65	2.298
F304811K	125 mm	m	0.07	3.27	-	2.34	5.61	6.17	2.867
F304811L	140 mm	m	0.08	3.50	-	2.62	6.12	6.73	3.218
F304811M	150 mm	m	0.08	3.50	-	2.82	6.32	6.95	3.458
F304811N	190 mm	m	0.08	3.78	-	3.57	7.35	8.09	4.378
F304811O	200 mm	m	0.08	3.78	-	3.74	7.52	8.27	4.596
F304811P	215 mm	m	0.08	3.78	-	4.03	7.81	8.59	4.947
F304812	**Gun grade polysulphide rubber compound**								
F304812A	19 x 19 mm	m	0.14	2.45	-	1.35	3.80	4.18	1.353
F3055	**Tile cills and creasings**								
F305502	**Cills; 265 x 165 mm plain concrete tiles in gauged mortar (1:1:6); double course breaking joint 50 mm projection; weathered; flush pointing all exposed edges**								
F305502A	152 mm wide	m	0.14	6.30	-	6.77	13.07	14.38	1.606
F305502B	265 mm wide	m	0.14	6.30	-	6.99	13.29	14.62	2.144
F305512	**Creasings; 265 x 165 mm plain concrete tiles in gauged mortar (1:1:6); single course; 50 mm projection one side; flush pointing all exposed edges**								
F305512C	152 mm wide	m	0.12	5.51	-	3.24	8.75	9.63	1.031
F305512D	265 mm wide	m	0.12	5.51	-	3.47	8.98	9.88	1.569
F305515	**Creasings; 265 x 165 mm plain concrete tiles in gauged mortar (1:1:6); single course; 50 mm projection both sides; flush pointing all exposed edges**								
F305515E	202 mm wide	m	0.12	5.51	-	3.24	8.75	9.63	1.031
F305515F	315 mm wide	m	0.15	7.05	-	6.99	14.04	15.44	2.144

Masonry

		Unit	Labour Hours	Labour Net	Plant Net	Materials Net	Unit Net	Unit with 10%	CO₂
				£	£	£	£	£	Kg
F30	**F30: ACCESSORIES AND SUNDRY ITEMS**								
F3055	**Tile cills and creasings**								
F305517	**Creasings; 265 x 165 mm plain concrete tiles in gauged mortar (1:1:6); double course; 50 mm projection one side; flush pointing all exposed edges**								
F305517G	152 mm wide	m	0.21	9.57	-	3.36	12.93	14.22	1.300
F305517H	265 mm wide	m	0.21	9.57	-	7.22	16.79	18.47	2.682
F305519	**Creasings; 265 x 165 mm plain concrete tiles in gauged mortar (1:1:6); double course; 50 mm projection both sides; flush pointing all exposed edges**								
F305519I	202 mm wide	m	0.25	11.80	-	6.99	18.79	20.67	2.144
F305519J	315 mm wide	m	0.33	15.30	-	13.37	28.67	31.54	3.936
F3061	**Flue linings, bends, chimney pots and terminals**								
F306101	**Clay circular section rebated and socketed flue liners; BS 1181; bedded and pointed in cement mortar (1:3); internal dia**								
F306101A	125 mm	m	0.11	5.04	-	27.74	32.78	36.06	13.332
F306101B	150 mm	m	0.12	5.51	-	28.00	33.51	36.86	19.202
F306101C	185 mm	m	0.13	6.02	-	27.79	33.81	37.19	17.961
F306101D	200 mm	m	0.13	6.02	-	44.55	50.57	55.63	25.646
F306101E	225 mm	m	0.14	6.30	-	54.92	61.22	67.34	22.225
F306101F	300 mm	m	0.15	7.05	-	110.03	117.08	128.79	33.551
F306106	**Clay square section rebated and socketed flue liners; BS 1181; bedded and pointed in cement mortar (1:3); internal size**								
F306106A	185 x 185 mm	m	0.13	6.02	-	41.30	47.32	52.05	20.331
F306106B	200 x 200 mm	m	0.13	6.02	-	44.49	50.51	55.56	19.002
F306106C	225 x 225 mm	m	0.14	6.30	-	53.12	59.42	65.36	34.137
F306111	**Clay circular section rebated and socketed flue bends; BS 1181; bedded and pointed in cement mortar (1:3); internal dia**								
F306111A	125 mm	Nr	0.12	5.79	-	26.24	32.03	35.23	4.180
F306111B	150 mm	Nr	0.14	6.30	-	26.24	32.54	35.79	4.180
F306111C	185 mm	Nr	0.15	7.05	-	29.57	36.62	40.28	4.997
F306111D	200 mm	Nr	0.16	7.56	-	37.08	44.64	49.10	8.055
F306111E	225 mm	Nr	0.16	7.56	-	41.74	49.30	54.23	5.925
F306111F	300 mm	Nr	0.27	12.55	-	104.99	117.54	129.29	8.840
F306116	**Clay square section rebated and socketed flue bends; BS 1181; bedded and pointed in cement mortar (1:3); internal size**								
F306116A	185 x 185 mm	Nr	0.14	6.30	-	40.58	46.88	51.57	17.870
F306116B	200 x 200 mm	Nr	0.15	7.05	-	43.87	50.92	56.01	16.894
F306116C	225 x 225 mm	Nr	0.16	7.56	-	52.29	59.85	65.84	31.326
F306121	**Clay chimney pots; set and flaunched in cement mortar (1:3); Cannon head pattern; height**								
F306121A	300 mm	Nr	0.19	8.77	-	31.00	39.77	43.75	10.900
F306121B	450 mm	Nr	0.19	8.77	-	37.42	46.19	50.81	12.459
F306121C	600 mm	Nr	0.20	9.29	-	53.49	62.78	69.06	13.025
F306121D	750 mm	Nr	0.30	13.81	-	68.85	82.66	90.93	14.746
F306131	**Clay flue terminal; dry fitted to flue liner; internal dia**								
F306131A	185 mm	Nr	0.16	7.56	-	35.00	42.56	46.82	3.222
F306131B	225 mm	Nr	0.19	8.77	-	58.53	67.30	74.03	4.112

Major Works 2011		Unit	Labour Hours	Labour Net	Plant Net	Materials Net	Unit Net	Unit with 10%	CO$_2$
				£	£	£	£	£	Kg
F30	**F30: ACCESSORIES AND SUNDRY ITEMS**								
F3082	**Air bricks or the like**								
F308221	**Form opening in wall; build in terracotta air brick; bed and point in cement mortar (1:3)**								
F308221A	225 x 75 mm	Nr	0.07	3.03	-	3.07	6.10	6.71	0.423
F308221B	225 x 150 mm	Nr	0.08	3.78	-	4.07	7.85	8.64	0.846
F308221C	225 x 225 mm	Nr	0.10	4.53	-	11.53	16.06	17.67	1.270
F308222	**Line opening with slates in cement mortar (1:3)**								
F308222A	225 x 75 mm; one brick wall	Nr	0.07	3.03	-	4.09	7.12	7.83	0.100
F308222B	225 x 75 mm; one and a half brick wall	Nr	0.08	3.78	-	6.14	9.92	10.91	0.151
F308222C	225 x 75 mm; two brick wall	Nr	0.10	4.53	-	6.14	10.67	11.74	0.151
F308222D	225 x 75 mm; 250 mm cavity wall	Nr	0.10	4.76	-	4.09	8.85	9.74	0.100
F308222E	225 x 75 mm; 275 mm cavity wall	Nr	0.11	5.04	-	6.14	11.18	12.30	0.151
F308222F	225 x 75 mm; 300 mm cavity wall	Nr	0.12	5.51	-	6.14	11.65	12.82	0.151
F308222G	225 x 150 mm; one brick wall	Nr	0.08	3.50	-	4.09	7.59	8.35	0.100
F308222H	225 x 150 mm; one and a half brick wall	Nr	0.09	4.29	-	8.18	12.47	13.72	0.201
F308222I	225 x 150 mm; two brick wall	Nr	0.11	5.04	-	8.18	13.22	14.54	0.201
F308222J	225 x 150 mm; 250 mm cavity wall	Nr	0.11	5.27	-	8.18	13.45	14.80	0.201
F308222K	225 x 150 mm; 275 mm cavity wall	Nr	0.12	5.51	-	8.18	13.69	15.06	0.201
F308222L	225 x 150 mm; 300 mm cavity wall	Nr	0.12	5.79	-	8.18	13.97	15.37	0.201
F308222M	225 x 225 mm; one brick wall	Nr	0.11	5.04	-	6.14	11.18	12.30	0.151
F308222N	225 x 225 mm; one and a half brick wall	Nr	0.12	5.51	-	10.23	15.74	17.31	0.251
F308222O	225 x 225 mm; two brick wall	Nr	0.13	6.02	-	10.23	16.25	17.88	0.251
F308222P	225 x 225 mm; 250 mm cavity wall	Nr	0.14	6.30	-	10.23	16.53	18.18	0.251
F308222Q	225 x 225 mm; 275 mm cavity wall	Nr	0.14	6.53	-	10.23	16.76	18.44	0.251
F308222R	225 x 225 mm; 300 mm cavity wall	Nr	0.15	6.77	-	10.23	17.00	18.70	0.251
F308223	**Line opening with terracotta cavity wall liner in cement mortar (1:3)**								
F308223A	225 x 75 mm; 250 mm cavity wall	Nr	0.07	3.03	-	4.13	7.16	7.88	1.763
F308223B	225 x 75 mm; 275 mm cavity wall	Nr	0.08	3.50	-	4.24	7.74	8.51	1.940
F308223C	225 x 75 mm; 300 mm cavity wall	Nr	0.09	4.01	-	4.34	8.35	9.19	2.116
F308223D	225 x 150 mm; 250 mm cavity wall	Nr	0.08	3.78	-	4.58	8.36	9.20	3.527
F308223E	225 x 150 mm; 275 mm cavity wall	Nr	0.09	4.29	-	4.79	9.08	9.99	3.880
F308223F	225 x 150 mm; 300 mm cavity wall	Nr	0.10	4.76	-	5.23	9.99	10.99	4.232
F308223G	225 x 225 mm; 250 mm cavity wall	Nr	0.10	4.53	-	12.70	17.23	18.95	5.290
F308223H	225 x 225 mm; 275 mm cavity wall	Nr	0.11	5.04	-	13.28	18.32	20.15	5.819
F308223I	225 x 225 mm; 300 mm cavity wall	Nr	0.12	5.51	-	13.83	19.34	21.27	6.348
F308224	**Plug and screw plastic inner screen with hit and miss vent; to brickwork or blockwork**								
F308224A	225 x 75 mm	Nr	0.30	5.09	-	2.25	7.34	8.07	0.387
F308224B	225 x 150 mm	Nr	0.30	5.09	-	3.56	8.65	9.52	0.667
F308224C	225 x 225 mm	Nr	0.30	5.09	-	4.52	9.61	10.57	0.948
F3085	**Proprietary steel lintels; Catnic galvanised polyester powder coated; insulated; built into brick or block walling**								
F308501	**Open back range; Cougar 50/100; length**								
F308501A	750 mm	Nr	0.03	1.26	-	32.27	33.53	36.88	7.700
F308501B	900 mm	Nr	0.04	1.77	-	39.07	40.84	44.92	9.239
F308501C	1050 mm	Nr	0.05	2.52	-	44.85	47.37	52.11	10.779
F308501D	1200 mm	Nr	0.07	3.03	-	50.63	53.66	59.03	12.319
F308501E	1350 mm	Nr	0.07	3.27	-	58.00	61.27	67.40	13.859
F308501F	1500 mm	Nr	0.08	3.78	-	65.44	69.22	76.14	15.399
F308501G	1650 mm	Nr	0.09	4.29	-	73.37	77.66	85.43	16.939

Masonry

		Unit	Labour Hours	Labour Net £	Plant Net £	Materials Net £	Unit Net £	Unit with 10% £	CO$_2$ Kg
F30	**F30: ACCESSORIES AND SUNDRY ITEMS**								
F3085	**Proprietary steel lintels; Catnic galvanised polyester powder coated; insulated; built into brick or block walling**								
F308501	**Open back range; Cougar 50/100; length**								
F308501H	1800 mm	Nr	0.10	4.53	-	81.35	85.88	94.47	23.258
F308501I	1950 mm	Nr	0.11	5.04	-	88.74	93.78	103.16	25.196
F308501J	2100 mm	Nr	0.11	5.27	-	93.40	98.67	108.54	29.736
F308501K	2250 mm	Nr	0.12	5.51	-	108.78	114.29	125.72	31.860
F308501L	2400 mm	Nr	0.13	6.02	-	114.49	120.51	132.56	36.533
F308501M	2550 mm	Nr	0.14	6.53	-	122.23	128.76	141.64	38.816
F308501N	2700 mm	Nr	0.15	6.77	-	129.95	136.72	150.39	46.834
F308501O	2850 mm	Nr	0.15	7.05	-	162.92	169.97	186.97	49.436
F308501P	3000 mm	Nr	0.16	7.56	-	179.91	187.47	206.22	65.313
F308501Q	3300 mm	Nr	0.17	8.03	-	200.83	208.86	229.75	71.844
F308501R	3600 mm	Nr	0.18	8.54	-	220.38	228.92	251.81	78.376
F308501S	3900 mm	Nr	0.19	9.05	-	286.73	295.78	325.36	84.907
F308505	**Open back range; Cougar 50/125; length**								
F308505A	750 mm	Nr	0.03	1.26	-	31.73	32.99	36.29	8.363
F308505B	900 mm	Nr	0.04	1.77	-	37.90	39.67	43.64	10.036
F308505C	1050 mm	Nr	0.05	2.52	-	44.85	47.37	52.11	10.779
F308505D	1200 mm	Nr	0.07	3.03	-	50.56	53.59	58.95	13.381
F308505E	1350 mm	Nr	0.07	3.27	-	57.77	61.04	67.14	15.054
F308505F	1500 mm	Nr	0.08	3.78	-	64.97	68.75	75.63	20.709
F308505G	1650 mm	Nr	0.09	4.29	-	72.39	76.68	84.35	22.780
F308505H	1800 mm	Nr	0.10	4.53	-	80.70	85.23	93.75	24.851
F308505I	1950 mm	Nr	0.11	5.04	-	88.91	93.95	103.35	24.851
F308505J	2100 mm	Nr	0.11	5.27	-	93.16	98.43	108.27	33.453
F308505K	2250 mm	Nr	0.12	5.51	-	106.64	112.15	123.37	35.843
F308505L	2400 mm	Nr	0.13	6.02	-	113.58	119.60	131.56	38.232
F308505M	2550 mm	Nr	0.14	6.53	-	121.76	128.29	141.12	40.622
F308505N	2700 mm	Nr	0.15	6.77	-	129.95	136.72	150.39	61.649
F308505O	2850 mm	Nr	0.16	7.28	-	162.64	169.92	186.91	65.074
F308505P	3000 mm	Nr	0.17	7.79	-	179.50	187.29	206.02	68.499
F308509	**Open back range; Cougar 70/100; length**								
F308509A	750 mm	Nr	0.03	1.49	-	31.73	33.22	36.54	7.965
F308509B	900 mm	Nr	0.04	2.01	-	37.90	39.91	43.90	9.558
F308509C	1050 mm	Nr	0.06	2.75	-	44.24	46.99	51.69	11.151
F308509D	1200 mm	Nr	0.07	3.27	-	50.56	53.83	59.21	12.744
F308509E	1350 mm	Nr	0.08	3.78	-	56.85	60.63	66.69	14.337
F308509F	1500 mm	Nr	0.09	4.29	-	63.16	67.45	74.20	15.930
F308509G	1650 mm	Nr	0.10	4.53	-	71.11	75.64	83.20	21.904
F308509H	1800 mm	Nr	0.10	4.76	-	79.06	83.82	92.20	23.895
F308509I	1950 mm	Nr	0.11	5.27	-	85.86	91.13	100.24	25.886
F308509J	2100 mm	Nr	0.12	5.51	-	90.42	95.93	105.52	30.108
F308509K	2250 mm	Nr	0.12	5.79	-	101.86	107.65	118.42	32.258
F308509L	2400 mm	Nr	0.14	6.30	-	107.21	113.51	124.86	36.958
F308509M	2550 mm	Nr	0.15	6.77	-	117.44	124.21	136.63	39.267
F308509N	2700 mm	Nr	0.15	7.05	-	123.72	130.77	143.85	47.790
F308509O	2850 mm	Nr	0.16	7.56	-	163.42	170.98	188.08	50.445
F308509P	3000 mm	Nr	0.17	8.03	-	176.06	184.09	202.50	66.375
F308509Q	3300 mm	Nr	0.18	8.54	-	195.38	203.92	224.31	73.013
F308509R	3600 mm	Nr	0.19	9.05	-	213.09	222.14	244.35	79.650
F308509S	3900 mm	Nr	0.20	9.29	-	263.25	272.54	299.79	86.288
F308512	**Open back range; Cougar 70/125; length**								
F308512A	750 mm	Nr	0.03	1.49	-	40.40	41.89	46.08	8.363
F308512B	900 mm	Nr	0.04	2.01	-	48.25	50.26	55.29	10.036
F308512C	1050 mm	Nr	0.06	2.75	-	58.26	61.01	67.11	11.709
F308512D	1200 mm	Nr	0.07	3.27	-	63.41	66.68	73.35	13.381
F308512E	1350 mm	Nr	0.08	3.78	-	74.23	78.01	85.81	19.116
F308512F	1500 mm	Nr	0.09	4.29	-	79.79	84.08	92.49	21.240
F308512G	1650 mm	Nr	0.10	4.76	-	99.42	104.18	114.60	23.364
F308512H	1800 mm	Nr	0.11	5.27	-	109.51	114.78	126.26	25.488
F308512I	1950 mm	Nr	0.12	5.79	-	122.35	128.14	140.95	27.612
F308512J	2100 mm	Nr	0.13	6.02	-	128.96	134.98	148.48	34.196
F308512K	2250 mm	Nr	0.14	6.53	-	161.35	167.88	184.67	36.639
F308512L	2400 mm	Nr	0.15	7.05	-	178.05	185.10	203.61	39.082
F308512M	2550 mm	Nr	0.16	7.28	-	198.49	205.77	226.35	41.524
F308512N	2700 mm	Nr	0.17	7.79	-	209.05	216.84	238.52	62.605
F308512O	2850 mm	Nr	0.18	8.31	-	263.19	271.50	298.65	66.083
F308512P	3000 mm	Nr	0.18	8.54	-	291.08	299.62	329.58	69.561

Major Works 2011		Unit	Labour Hours	Labour Net	Plant Net	Materials Net	Unit Net	Unit with 10%	CO₂
				£	£	£	£	£	Kg

F30	**F30: ACCESSORIES AND SUNDRY ITEMS**								
F3085	**Proprietary steel lintels; Catnic galvanised polyester powder coated; insulated; built into brick or block walling**								
F308515	**Open back range; Cougar 90/100; length**								
F308515A	750 mm	Nr	0.04	1.77	-	33.64	35.41	38.95	8.098
F308515B	900 mm	Nr	0.05	2.29	-	39.41	41.70	45.87	9.717
F308515C	1050 mm	Nr	0.07	3.03	-	45.06	48.09	52.90	11.337
F308515D	1200 mm	Nr	0.08	3.50	-	52.54	56.04	61.64	12.956
F308515E	1350 mm	Nr	0.09	4.01	-	59.13	63.14	69.45	14.576
F308515F	1500 mm	Nr	0.10	4.53	-	65.69	70.22	77.24	16.196
F308515G	1650 mm	Nr	0.11	5.04	-	72.39	77.43	85.17	22.196
F308515H	1800 mm	Nr	0.12	5.51	-	79.06	84.57	93.03	24.214
F308515I	1950 mm	Nr	0.13	6.02	-	88.95	94.97	104.47	28.647
F308515J	2100 mm	Nr	0.14	6.53	-	94.04	100.57	110.63	30.851
F308515K	2250 mm	Nr	0.15	7.05	-	106.82	113.87	125.26	35.444
F308515L	2400 mm	Nr	0.16	7.56	-	113.40	120.96	133.06	37.807
F308515M	2550 mm	Nr	0.17	8.03	-	124.58	132.61	145.87	46.038
F308515N	2700 mm	Nr	0.18	8.54	-	135.78	144.32	158.75	48.746
F308515O	2850 mm	Nr	0.19	8.77	-	162.77	171.54	188.69	65.579
F308515P	3000 mm	Nr	0.19	8.77	-	176.65	185.42	203.96	69.030
F308515Q	3300 mm	Nr	0.20	9.29	-	200.23	209.52	230.47	75.933
F308515R	3600 mm	Nr	0.21	9.80	-	219.73	229.53	252.48	82.836
F308515S	3900 mm	Nr	0.21	9.80	-	283.96	293.76	323.14	89.739
F308519	**Open back range; Cougar 90/125; length**								
F308519A	750 mm	Nr	0.04	2.01	-	44.93	46.94	51.63	8.629
F308519B	900 mm	Nr	0.05	2.52	-	53.92	56.44	62.08	10.355
F308519C	1050 mm	Nr	0.07	3.03	-	62.96	65.99	72.59	12.080
F308519D	1200 mm	Nr	0.08	3.50	-	70.80	74.30	81.73	13.806
F308519E	1350 mm	Nr	0.09	4.01	-	82.16	86.17	94.79	19.355
F308519F	1500 mm	Nr	0.10	4.53	-	88.29	92.82	102.10	21.506
F308519G	1650 mm	Nr	0.11	5.04	-	101.74	106.78	117.46	23.656
F308519H	1800 mm	Nr	0.12	5.51	-	111.71	117.22	128.94	25.807
F308519I	1950 mm	Nr	0.13	6.02	-	131.84	137.86	151.65	27.957
F308519J	2100 mm	Nr	0.14	6.53	-	132.39	138.92	152.81	34.940
F308519K	2250 mm	Nr	0.15	7.05	-	173.82	180.87	198.96	37.436
F308519L	2400 mm	Nr	0.16	7.56	-	187.01	194.57	214.03	39.931
F308519M	2550 mm	Nr	0.17	8.03	-	203.77	211.80	232.98	42.427
F308519N	2700 mm	Nr	0.18	8.54	-	216.39	224.93	247.42	63.561
F308519O	2850 mm	Nr	0.19	9.05	-	308.29	317.34	349.07	67.092
F308519P	3000 mm	Nr	0.21	9.57	-	311.24	320.81	352.89	70.623
F308525	**Combined box lintel range; CN7A; length**								
F308525A	750 mm	Nr	0.03	1.26	-	28.66	29.92	32.91	13.142
F308525B	900 mm	Nr	0.04	1.77	-	34.70	36.47	40.12	15.771
F308525C	1050 mm	Nr	0.05	2.52	-	39.97	42.49	46.74	18.399
F308525D	1200 mm	Nr	0.07	3.03	-	44.97	48.00	52.80	21.028
F308525E	1350 mm	Nr	0.07	3.27	-	51.42	54.69	60.16	23.656
F308525F	1500 mm	Nr	0.08	3.78	-	54.32	58.10	63.91	26.285
F308525G	1650 mm	Nr	0.09	4.29	-	65.20	69.49	76.44	28.913
F308525H	1800 mm	Nr	0.10	4.53	-	70.84	75.37	82.91	31.541
F308525I	1950 mm	Nr	0.11	5.04	-	79.32	84.36	92.80	34.170
F308525J	2100 mm	Nr	0.11	5.04	-	83.69	88.73	97.60	36.798
F308525K	2250 mm	Nr	0.12	5.51	-	97.67	103.18	113.50	39.427
F308525L	2400 mm	Nr	0.13	6.02	-	105.54	111.56	122.72	42.055
F308525M	2550 mm	Nr	0.14	6.53	-	113.52	120.05	132.06	44.684
F308525N	2700 mm	Nr	0.15	6.77	-	119.79	126.56	139.22	47.312
F308527	**Combined box lintel range; CN8C; length**								
F308527A	2250 mm	Nr	0.12	5.51	-	149.50	155.01	170.51	76.464
F308527B	2400 mm	Nr	0.13	6.02	-	156.81	162.83	179.11	81.562
F308527C	2550 mm	Nr	0.14	6.53	-	161.81	168.34	185.17	86.659
F308527D	2700 mm	Nr	0.15	6.77	-	166.37	173.14	190.45	91.757
F308527E	2850 mm	Nr	0.16	7.28	-	176.27	183.55	201.91	96.854
F308527F	3000 mm	Nr	0.16	7.56	-	178.41	185.97	204.57	101.952
F308527G	3300 mm	Nr	0.18	8.31	-	206.68	214.99	236.49	112.147
F308527H	3600 mm	Nr	0.19	9.05	-	222.38	231.43	254.57	122.342
F308527I	3900 mm	Nr	0.21	9.80	-	237.94	247.74	272.51	132.538
F308527J	4200 mm	Nr	0.23	10.55	-	238.07	248.62	273.48	142.733
F308527K	4500 mm	Nr	0.25	11.57	-	275.08	286.65	315.32	155.477
F308527L	4800 mm	Nr	0.27	12.55	-	288.83	301.38	331.52	163.123

Masonry

		Unit	Labour Hours	Labour Net	Plant Net	Materials Net	Unit Net	Unit with 10%	CO₂
				£	£	£	£	£	Kg
F30	**F30: ACCESSORIES AND SUNDRY ITEMS**								
F3085	**Proprietary steel lintels; Catnic galvanised polyester powder coated; insulated; built into brick or block walling**								
F308532	**Combined box lintel range; CN3A; length**								
F308532A	750 mm	Nr	0.03	1.26	-	28.17	29.43	32.37	13.541
F308532B	900 mm	Nr	0.04	1.77	-	33.66	35.43	38.97	16.249
F308532C	1050 mm	Nr	0.05	2.52	-	39.54	42.06	46.27	18.957
F308532D	1200 mm	Nr	0.07	3.03	-	44.87	47.90	52.69	21.665
F308532E	1350 mm	Nr	0.08	3.50	-	51.01	54.51	59.96	24.373
F308532F	1500 mm	Nr	0.08	3.78	-	54.80	58.58	64.44	27.081
F308532G	1650 mm	Nr	0.09	4.29	-	64.57	68.86	75.75	29.789
F308532H	1800 mm	Nr	0.10	4.53	-	70.23	74.76	82.24	32.497
F308532I	1950 mm	Nr	0.10	4.76	-	75.88	80.64	88.70	35.205
F308532J	2100 mm	Nr	0.11	5.04	-	80.33	85.37	93.91	37.913
F308532K	2250 mm	Nr	0.12	5.51	-	90.42	95.93	105.52	40.622
F308532L	2400 mm	Nr	0.14	6.30	-	95.25	101.55	111.71	43.330
F308532M	2550 mm	Nr	0.14	6.53	-	101.70	108.23	119.05	46.038
F308532N	2700 mm	Nr	0.15	6.77	-	108.17	114.94	126.43	48.746
F308533	**Combined box lintel range; CN3C; length**								
F308533A	750 mm	Nr	0.03	1.26	-	48.58	49.84	54.82	21.240
F308533B	900 mm	Nr	0.04	1.77	-	55.68	57.45	63.20	25.488
F308533C	1050 mm	Nr	0.05	2.52	-	67.94	70.46	77.51	29.736
F308533D	1200 mm	Nr	0.07	3.03	-	74.26	77.29	85.02	33.984
F308533E	1350 mm	Nr	0.08	3.50	-	86.53	90.03	99.03	38.232
F308533F	1500 mm	Nr	0.08	3.78	-	92.84	96.62	106.28	42.480
F308533G	1650 mm	Nr	0.09	4.29	-	96.92	101.21	111.33	46.728
F308533H	1800 mm	Nr	0.10	4.53	-	99.02	103.55	113.91	50.976
F308533I	1950 mm	Nr	0.10	4.76	-	115.25	120.01	132.01	55.224
F308534	**Combined box lintel range; CN4B; length**								
F308534A	2100 mm	Nr	0.12	5.51	-	104.43	109.94	120.93	59.844
F308534B	2250 mm	Nr	0.12	5.79	-	114.62	120.41	132.45	64.118
F308534C	2400 mm	Nr	0.13	6.02	-	135.19	141.21	155.33	68.393
F308534D	2550 mm	Nr	0.14	6.53	-	143.61	150.14	165.15	72.667
F308534E	2700 mm	Nr	0.15	6.77	-	145.97	152.74	168.01	76.942
F308534F	3000 mm	Nr	0.16	7.28	-	156.37	163.65	180.02	85.491
F308534G	3300 mm	Nr	0.17	7.79	-	172.01	179.80	197.78	94.040
F308534H	3600 mm	Nr	0.18	8.31	-	187.71	196.02	215.62	102.589
F308535	**Combined box lintel range; CN4C; length**								
F308535A	2100 mm	Nr	0.13	6.02	-	143.88	149.90	164.89	75.827
F308535B	2250 mm	Nr	0.14	6.30	-	146.15	152.45	167.70	81.243
F308535C	2400 mm	Nr	0.15	6.77	-	148.05	154.82	170.30	86.659
F308535D	2550 mm	Nr	0.15	7.05	-	149.89	156.94	172.63	92.075
F308535E	2700 mm	Nr	0.16	7.56	-	156.61	164.17	180.59	97.492
F308535F	3000 mm	Nr	0.17	8.03	-	172.80	180.83	198.91	108.324
F308535G	3300 mm	Nr	0.18	8.31	-	206.56	214.87	236.36	119.156
F308535H	3600 mm	Nr	0.19	8.77	-	222.38	231.15	254.27	129.989
F308535I	3900 mm	Nr	0.19	9.05	-	233.62	242.67	266.94	140.821
F308535J	4200 mm	Nr	0.21	9.57	-	238.07	247.64	272.40	151.654
F308535K	4575 mm	Nr	0.22	10.03	-	254.45	264.48	290.93	165.194
F308535L	4800 mm	Nr	0.22	10.31	-	267.18	277.49	305.24	173.318
F308537	**Combined box lintel range; CN43A; length**								
F308537A	750 mm	Nr	0.03	1.26	-	28.17	29.43	32.37	13.806
F308537B	900 mm	Nr	0.04	1.77	-	33.66	35.43	38.97	16.567
F308537C	1050 mm	Nr	0.05	2.52	-	39.54	42.06	46.27	19.328
F308537D	1200 mm	Nr	0.07	3.03	-	44.89	47.92	52.71	22.090
F308537E	1350 mm	Nr	0.08	3.50	-	51.01	54.51	59.96	24.851
F308537F	1500 mm	Nr	0.08	3.78	-	58.27	62.05	68.26	27.612
F308537G	1650 mm	Nr	0.09	4.29	-	65.79	70.08	77.09	30.373
F308537H	1800 mm	Nr	0.10	4.53	-	71.68	76.21	83.83	33.134
F308537I	1950 mm	Nr	0.10	4.76	-	78.30	83.06	91.37	35.896
F308537J	2100 mm	Nr	0.11	5.04	-	82.76	87.80	96.58	38.657
F308537K	2250 mm	Nr	0.12	5.51	-	94.86	100.37	110.41	41.418
F308537L	2400 mm	Nr	0.14	6.30	-	100.91	107.21	117.93	44.179
F308537M	2550 mm	Nr	0.14	6.53	-	108.98	115.51	127.06	46.940
F308537N	2700 mm	Nr	0.15	6.77	-	115.43	122.20	134.42	49.702

Major Works 2011		Unit	Labour Hours	Labour Net	Plant Net	Materials Net	Unit Net	Unit with 10%	CO$_2$
				£	£	£	£	£	Kg

F30   **F30: ACCESSORIES AND SUNDRY ITEMS**

F3085   **Proprietary steel lintels; Catnic galvanised polyester powder coated; insulated; built into brick or block walling**

F308538   **Combined box lintel range; CN44C; length**

Code	Size	Unit	Labour Hours	Labour Net	Plant Net	Materials Net	Unit Net	Unit with 10%	CO$_2$
F308538A	750 mm	Nr	0.03	1.49	-	51.37	52.86	58.15	26.816
F308538B	900 mm	Nr	0.04	2.01	-	55.68	57.69	63.46	32.179
F308538C	1050 mm	Nr	0.05	2.52	-	67.94	70.46	77.51	37.542
F308538D	1200 mm	Nr	0.07	3.03	-	74.26	77.29	85.02	42.905
F308538E	1350 mm	Nr	0.08	3.50	-	84.86	88.36	97.20	48.268
F308538F	1500 mm	Nr	0.09	4.01	-	90.32	94.33	103.76	53.631
F308538G	1650 mm	Nr	0.10	4.53	-	98.27	102.80	113.08	58.994
F308538H	1800 mm	Nr	0.11	5.04	-	102.37	107.41	118.15	64.357
F308538I	1950 mm	Nr	0.11	5.27	-	114.31	119.58	131.54	69.720
F308538J	2100 mm	Nr	0.12	5.79	-	116.72	122.51	134.76	75.083
F308538K	2250 mm	Nr	0.14	6.30	-	135.00	141.30	155.43	80.447
F308538L	2400 mm	Nr	0.15	6.77	-	143.29	150.06	165.07	85.810
F308538M	2550 mm	Nr	0.16	7.28	-	151.32	158.60	174.46	91.173
F308538N	2700 mm	Nr	0.17	7.79	-	159.44	167.23	183.95	96.536
F308538O	2850 mm	Nr	0.18	8.31	-	166.41	174.72	192.19	101.899
F308538P	3000 mm	Nr	0.19	8.77	-	182.98	191.75	210.93	107.262
F308538Q	3300 mm	Nr	0.19	9.05	-	199.62	208.67	229.54	117.988
F308538R	3600 mm	Nr	0.21	9.57	-	214.80	224.37	246.81	128.714
F308538S	3900 mm	Nr	0.22	10.03	-	226.20	236.23	259.85	139.441
F308538T	4200 mm	Nr	0.23	10.55	-	237.94	248.49	273.34	150.167
F308538U	4575 mm	Nr	0.24	11.06	-	268.20	279.26	307.19	163.575
F308538V	4800 mm	Nr	0.24	11.29	-	336.59	347.88	382.67	171.619

F308539   **Combined box lintel range; CN11A; length**

Code	Size	Unit	Labour Hours	Labour Net	Plant Net	Materials Net	Unit Net	Unit with 10%	CO$_2$
F308539A	750 mm	Nr	0.03	1.26	-	28.17	29.43	32.37	8.363
F308539B	900 mm	Nr	0.04	1.77	-	33.66	35.43	38.97	10.036
F308539C	1050 mm	Nr	0.05	2.52	-	39.54	42.06	46.27	11.709
F308539D	1200 mm	Nr	0.07	3.03	-	44.87	47.90	52.69	13.381
F308539E	1350 mm	Nr	0.08	3.50	-	53.23	56.73	62.40	15.054
F308539F	1500 mm	Nr	0.08	3.78	-	60.50	64.28	70.71	20.709
F308539G	1650 mm	Nr	0.09	4.29	-	70.65	74.94	82.43	22.780
F308539H	1800 mm	Nr	0.10	4.53	-	75.01	79.54	87.49	24.851
F308539I	1950 mm	Nr	0.10	4.76	-	81.65	86.41	95.05	26.922
F308539J	2100 mm	Nr	0.11	5.27	-	88.15	93.42	102.76	33.453
F308539K	2250 mm	Nr	0.12	5.79	-	99.62	105.41	115.95	35.843
F308539L	2400 mm	Nr	0.13	6.02	-	102.03	108.05	118.86	38.232
F308539M	2550 mm	Nr	0.14	6.53	-	117.92	124.45	136.90	40.622
F308539N	2700 mm	Nr	0.15	6.77	-	119.91	126.68	139.35	61.649

F308558   **External solid wall range; CN71A; length**

Code	Size	Unit	Labour Hours	Labour Net	Plant Net	Materials Net	Unit Net	Unit with 10%	CO$_2$
F308558A	750 mm	Nr	0.03	1.26	-	41.39	42.65	46.92	12.346
F308558B	900 mm	Nr	0.04	1.77	-	49.71	51.48	56.63	14.815
F308558C	1050 mm	Nr	0.05	2.52	-	57.89	60.41	66.45	17.284
F308558D	1200 mm	Nr	0.06	2.75	-	64.19	66.94	73.63	19.753
F308558E	1350 mm	Nr	0.07	3.27	-	74.27	77.54	85.29	22.222
F308558F	1500 mm	Nr	0.08	3.78	-	84.08	87.86	96.65	24.692
F308558G	1650 mm	Nr	0.09	4.29	-	92.78	97.07	106.78	27.161
F308558H	1800 mm	Nr	0.10	4.53	-	101.49	106.02	116.62	29.630
F308558I	1950 mm	Nr	0.11	5.04	-	104.55	109.59	120.55	32.099
F308558J	2100 mm	Nr	0.11	5.04	-	118.27	123.31	135.64	34.568
F308558K	2250 mm	Nr	0.12	5.51	-	138.50	144.01	158.41	37.037
F308558L	2400 mm	Nr	0.13	6.02	-	147.30	153.32	168.65	39.506
F308558M	2550 mm	Nr	0.14	6.53	-	152.25	158.78	174.66	41.976
F308558N	2700 mm	Nr	0.15	6.77	-	161.15	167.92	184.71	44.445

F308560   **External solid wall range; CN81C; length**

Code	Size	Unit	Labour Hours	Labour Net	Plant Net	Materials Net	Unit Net	Unit with 10%	CO$_2$
F308560A	2100 mm	Nr	0.11	5.04	-	160.48	165.52	182.07	68.765
F308560B	2250 mm	Nr	0.12	5.51	-	263.91	269.42	296.36	73.676
F308560C	2400 mm	Nr	0.13	6.02	-	270.35	276.37	304.01	78.588
F308560D	2550 mm	Nr	0.14	6.53	-	279.68	286.21	314.83	83.500
F308560E	2700 mm	Nr	0.15	6.77	-	287.10	293.87	323.26	88.412
F308560F	2850 mm	Nr	0.16	7.28	-	310.34	317.62	349.38	93.323
F308560G	3000 mm	Nr	0.17	7.79	-	326.27	334.06	367.47	98.235
F308560H	3300 mm	Nr	0.18	8.31	-	337.65	345.96	380.56	108.059
F308560I	3600 mm	Nr	0.19	8.77	-	366.64	375.41	412.95	117.882
F308560J	3900 mm	Nr	0.20	9.29	-	395.74	405.03	445.53	127.706
F308560K	4200 mm	Nr	0.21	9.80	-	419.93	429.73	472.70	137.529
F308560L	4575 mm	Nr	0.22	10.31	-	440.19	450.50	495.55	149.808
F308560M	4800 mm	Nr	0.23	10.83	-	469.18	480.01	528.01	157.176

Masonry

		Unit	Labour Hours	Labour Net £	Plant Net £	Materials Net £	Unit Net £	Unit with 10% £	CO₂ Kg
F30	**F30: ACCESSORIES AND SUNDRY ITEMS**								
F3085	**Proprietary steel lintels; Catnic galvanised polyester powder coated; insulated; built into brick or block walling**								
F308565	**Internal solid wall range; CN92; length**								
F308565A	900 mm	Nr	0.06	2.75	-	6.83	9.58	10.54	1.912
F308565B	1050 mm	Nr	0.06	2.75	-	6.83	9.58	10.54	2.230
F308565C	1200 mm	Nr	0.07	3.03	-	7.72	10.75	11.83	2.549
F308566	**Internal solid wall range; CN102; length**								
F308566A	900 mm	Nr	0.06	2.75	-	5.97	8.72	9.59	2.867
F308566B	1050 mm	Nr	0.06	2.75	-	8.64	11.39	12.53	3.345
F308566C	1200 mm	Nr	0.07	3.03	-	9.53	12.56	13.82	3.823
F308567	**Internal solid wall range; CN100; length**								
F308567A	1050 mm	Nr	0.06	2.75	-	21.09	23.84	26.22	8.735
F308567B	1200 mm	Nr	0.06	2.75	-	26.21	28.96	31.86	9.983
F308567C	1350 mm	Nr	0.07	3.03	-	30.63	33.66	37.03	14.098
F308567D	1500 mm	Nr	0.07	3.27	-	32.40	35.67	39.24	15.665
F308567E	1800 mm	Nr	0.08	3.50	-	32.82	36.32	39.95	14.974
F308567F	2100 mm	Nr	0.08	3.78	-	38.17	41.95	46.15	17.470
F308568	**Internal solid wall range; CN5XA; length**								
F308568A	900 mm	Nr	0.04	1.77	-	36.33	38.10	41.91	12.107
F308568B	1050 mm	Nr	0.05	2.52	-	39.83	42.35	46.59	14.125
F308568C	1200 mm	Nr	0.07	3.03	-	40.87	43.90	48.29	16.142
F308568D	1350 mm	Nr	0.08	3.50	-	43.37	46.87	51.56	18.160
F308568E	1500 mm	Nr	0.08	3.78	-	45.91	49.69	54.66	20.178
F308568F	1650 mm	Nr	0.09	4.29	-	58.14	62.43	68.67	22.196
F308568G	1800 mm	Nr	0.10	4.53	-	63.60	68.13	74.94	24.214
F308568H	1950 mm	Nr	0.10	4.76	-	69.22	73.98	81.38	26.231
F308568I	2100 mm	Nr	0.11	5.04	-	72.69	77.73	85.50	28.249
F308568J	2250 mm	Nr	0.12	5.51	-	81.77	87.28	96.01	30.267
F308568K	2400 mm	Nr	0.14	6.30	-	87.25	93.55	102.91	32.285
F308568L	2550 mm	Nr	0.14	6.53	-	94.49	101.02	111.12	34.303
F308568M	2700 mm	Nr	0.15	6.77	-	99.95	106.72	117.39	36.320
F308570	**Internal solid wall range; CN6XC; length**								
F308570A	2250 mm	Nr	0.12	5.51	-	188.04	193.55	212.91	62.525
F308570B	2400 mm	Nr	0.14	6.30	-	203.16	209.46	230.41	66.694
F308570C	2550 mm	Nr	0.14	6.53	-	203.89	210.42	231.46	70.862
F308570D	2700 mm	Nr	0.15	6.77	-	206.51	213.28	234.61	75.030
F308570E	2850 mm	Nr	0.16	7.28	-	208.12	215.40	236.94	79.199
F308570F	3000 mm	Nr	0.16	7.56	-	215.65	223.21	245.53	83.367
F308570G	3300 mm	Nr	0.18	8.31	-	218.59	226.90	249.59	91.704
F308570H	3600 mm	Nr	0.19	9.05	-	236.02	245.07	269.58	100.040
F308570I	3900 mm	Nr	0.21	9.80	-	248.10	257.90	283.69	108.377
F308570J	4200 mm	Nr	0.23	10.55	-	266.75	277.30	305.03	116.714
F308570K	4575 mm	Nr	0.25	11.57	-	329.63	341.20	375.32	127.135
F308570L	4800 mm	Nr	0.27	12.55	-	339.34	351.89	387.08	133.387
F308572	**Internal solid wall range; CN56XA; length**								
F308572A	900 mm	Nr	0.04	1.77	-	25.80	27.57	30.33	14.337
F308572B	1050 mm	Nr	0.05	2.52	-	36.33	38.85	42.74	16.727
F308572C	1200 mm	Nr	0.07	3.03	-	43.00	46.03	50.63	19.116
F308572D	1350 mm	Nr	0.08	3.50	-	50.06	53.56	58.92	21.506
F308572E	1500 mm	Nr	0.08	3.78	-	53.71	57.49	63.24	23.895
F308572F	1650 mm	Nr	0.09	4.29	-	64.97	69.26	76.19	26.285
F308572G	1800 mm	Nr	0.10	4.53	-	72.08	76.61	84.27	28.674
F308572H	1950 mm	Nr	0.10	4.76	-	77.90	82.66	90.93	31.064
F308572I	2100 mm	Nr	0.11	5.04	-	84.43	89.47	98.42	33.453
F308572J	2250 mm	Nr	0.12	5.51	-	90.61	96.12	105.73	35.843
F308572K	2400 mm	Nr	0.13	6.02	-	96.71	102.73	113.00	38.232
F308572L	2550 mm	Nr	0.14	6.53	-	102.78	109.31	120.24	40.622
F308572M	2700 mm	Nr	0.15	6.77	-	108.96	115.73	127.30	43.011

Major Works 2011		Unit	Labour Hours	Labour Net £	Plant Net £	Materials Net £	Unit Net £	Unit with 10% £	CO₂ Kg

F30	**F30: ACCESSORIES AND SUNDRY ITEMS**								
F3087	**Proprietary steel lintels; IG galvanised polyester powder coated; insulated; built into brick or block walling**								
F308702	**L1/S 50; standard duty; length**								
F308702A	600 mm	Nr	0.03	1.49	-	23.27	24.76	27.24	5.391
F308702B	750 mm	Nr	0.04	2.01	-	23.27	25.28	27.81	6.739
F308702C	900 mm	Nr	0.05	2.52	-	27.91	30.43	33.47	8.086
F308702D	1050 mm	Nr	0.07	3.03	-	32.44	35.47	39.02	9.434
F308702E	1200 mm	Nr	0.07	3.27	-	36.90	40.17	44.19	10.782
F308702F	1350 mm	Nr	0.08	3.78	-	43.27	47.05	51.76	12.130
F308702G	1500 mm	Nr	0.09	4.29	-	48.16	52.45	57.70	13.477
F308702H	1650 mm	Nr	0.10	4.53	-	54.47	59.00	64.90	14.825
F308702I	1800 mm	Nr	0.10	4.76	-	59.39	64.15	70.57	16.173
F308702J	1950 mm	Nr	0.11	5.27	-	64.89	70.16	77.18	17.520
F308702K	2100 mm	Nr	0.12	5.51	-	69.41	74.92	82.41	18.868
F308702L	2250 mm	Nr	0.12	5.79	-	77.81	83.60	91.96	20.216
F308702M	2400 mm	Nr	0.13	6.02	-	83.07	89.09	98.00	21.564
F308702N	2550 mm	Nr	0.14	6.30	-	96.04	102.34	112.57	22.911
F308702O	2700 mm	Nr	0.14	6.53	-	101.00	107.53	118.28	24.259
F308702P	2850 mm	Nr	0.15	6.77	-	125.36	132.13	145.34	25.607
F308702Q	3000 mm	Nr	0.16	7.28	-	136.07	143.35	157.69	26.955
F308702R	3150 mm	Nr	0.16	7.56	-	161.31	168.87	185.76	28.302
F308702S	3300 mm	Nr	0.17	7.79	-	161.31	169.10	186.01	29.650
F308702T	3450 mm	Nr	0.18	8.31	-	179.49	187.80	206.58	30.998
F308702U	3600 mm	Nr	0.18	8.54	-	179.49	188.03	206.83	32.345
F308702V	3750 mm	Nr	0.19	8.77	-	210.95	219.72	241.69	33.693
F308702W	3900 mm	Nr	0.20	9.29	-	210.95	220.24	242.26	35.041
F308702X	4050 mm	Nr	0.21	9.57	-	245.71	255.28	280.81	36.389
F308702Y	4200 mm	Nr	0.21	9.80	-	245.71	255.51	281.06	37.736
F308705	**L1/S 75; standard duty; length**								
F308705A	600 mm	Nr	0.03	1.49	-	23.27	24.76	27.24	6.200
F308705B	750 mm	Nr	0.04	2.01	-	23.27	25.28	27.81	7.750
F308705C	900 mm	Nr	0.05	2.52	-	27.91	30.43	33.47	9.300
F308705D	1050 mm	Nr	0.07	3.03	-	32.44	35.47	39.02	10.850
F308705E	1200 mm	Nr	0.08	3.50	-	32.44	35.94	39.53	12.400
F308705F	1350 mm	Nr	0.09	4.01	-	43.27	47.28	52.01	13.950
F308705G	1500 mm	Nr	0.10	4.53	-	48.16	52.69	57.96	15.500
F308705H	1650 mm	Nr	0.10	4.76	-	54.47	59.23	65.15	17.050
F308705I	1800 mm	Nr	0.11	5.27	-	59.39	64.66	71.13	18.600
F308705J	1950 mm	Nr	0.12	5.79	-	64.89	70.68	77.75	20.150
F308705K	2100 mm	Nr	0.13	6.02	-	69.41	75.43	82.97	21.700
F308705L	2250 mm	Nr	0.14	6.53	-	77.81	84.34	92.77	23.250
F308705M	2400 mm	Nr	0.15	6.77	-	83.07	89.84	98.82	24.800
F308705N	2550 mm	Nr	0.15	7.05	-	96.04	103.09	113.40	26.350
F308705O	2700 mm	Nr	0.16	7.56	-	101.00	108.56	119.42	27.900
F308705P	2850 mm	Nr	0.17	7.79	-	125.36	133.15	146.47	29.450
F308705Q	3000 mm	Nr	0.18	8.31	-	136.07	144.38	158.82	31.000
F308705R	3150 mm	Nr	0.18	8.54	-	161.31	169.85	186.84	32.550
F308705S	3300 mm	Nr	0.19	9.05	-	161.31	170.36	187.40	34.100
F308705T	3450 mm	Nr	0.20	9.29	-	179.49	188.78	207.66	35.650
F308705U	3600 mm	Nr	0.21	9.80	-	179.49	189.29	208.22	37.200
F308705V	3750 mm	Nr	0.22	10.03	-	210.95	220.98	243.08	38.750
F308705W	3900 mm	Nr	0.22	10.31	-	210.95	221.26	243.39	40.300
F308705X	4050 mm	Nr	0.23	10.55	-	245.71	256.26	281.89	41.850
F308705Y	4200 mm	Nr	0.23	10.83	-	245.71	256.54	282.19	43.400
F308708	**L1/S 100; standard duty; length**								
F308708A	600 mm	Nr	0.03	1.49	-	25.06	26.55	29.21	6.291
F308708B	750 mm	Nr	0.04	2.01	-	25.06	27.07	29.78	7.864
F308708C	900 mm	Nr	0.06	2.75	-	29.61	32.36	35.60	9.437
F308708D	1050 mm	Nr	0.07	3.27	-	34.99	38.26	42.09	11.009
F308708E	1200 mm	Nr	0.08	3.78	-	38.82	42.60	46.86	12.582
F308708F	1350 mm	Nr	0.09	4.29	-	45.16	49.45	54.40	14.155
F308708G	1500 mm	Nr	0.10	4.76	-	48.39	53.15	58.47	15.728
F308708H	1650 mm	Nr	0.11	5.27	-	54.73	60.00	66.00	17.300
F308708I	1800 mm	Nr	0.12	5.51	-	59.69	65.20	71.72	18.873
F308708J	1950 mm	Nr	0.13	6.02	-	68.37	74.39	81.83	20.446
F308708K	2100 mm	Nr	0.14	6.53	-	71.95	78.48	86.33	22.019
F308708L	2250 mm	Nr	0.15	7.05	-	85.60	92.65	101.92	23.592
F308708M	2400 mm	Nr	0.16	7.28	-	91.09	98.37	108.21	25.164
F308708N	2550 mm	Nr	0.17	7.79	-	91.09	98.88	108.77	25.164
F308708O	2700 mm	Nr	0.18	8.31	-	107.69	116.00	127.60	28.310
F308708P	2850 mm	Nr	0.18	8.54	-	124.71	133.25	146.58	29.883
F308708Q	3000 mm	Nr	0.19	9.05	-	134.88	143.93	158.32	31.455
F308708R	3150 mm	Nr	0.20	9.29	-	156.73	166.02	182.62	33.028
F308708S	3300 mm	Nr	0.21	9.80	-	156.73	166.53	183.18	34.601

Masonry

		Unit	Labour Hours	Labour Net £	Plant Net £	Materials Net £	Unit Net £	Unit with 10% £	CO₂ Kg
F30	**F30: ACCESSORIES AND SUNDRY ITEMS**								
F3087	**Proprietary steel lintels; IG galvanised polyester powder coated; insulated; built into brick or block walling**								
F308708	**L1/S 100; standard duty; length**								
F308708T	3450 mm	Nr	0.22	10.31	-	175.35	185.66	204.23	36.174
F308708U	3600 mm	Nr	0.23	10.55	-	175.35	185.90	204.49	37.747
F308708V	3750 mm	Nr	0.24	11.06	-	217.06	228.12	250.93	39.319
F308708W	3900 mm	Nr	0.24	11.29	-	217.06	228.35	251.19	40.892
F308708X	4050 mm	Nr	0.25	11.80	-	230.57	242.37	266.61	42.465
F308708Y	4200 mm	Nr	0.26	12.04	-	230.57	242.61	266.87	44.038

Major Works 2011		Unit	Labour Hours	Labour Net	Plant Net	Materials Net	Unit Net	Unit with 10%	CO₂
				£	£	£	£	£	Kg
F31	**F31: PRECAST CONCRETE CILLS, LINTELS, COPINGS AND FEATURES**								
F3101	**Lintels; 20 N/mm² concrete; bedding and pointing in cement mortar (1:3)**								
F310112	**100 x 150 mm plain rectangular section**								
F310112A	900 mm long	Nr	0.12	5.65	-	5.57	11.22	12.34	6.853
F310112B	1200 mm long	Nr	0.13	5.93	-	7.40	13.33	14.66	9.020
F310112C	1500 mm long	Nr	0.13	6.02	-	9.22	15.24	16.76	11.187
F310112D	1800 mm long	Nr	0.13	6.16	-	11.05	17.21	18.93	13.355
F310113	**100 x 225 mm plain rectangular section**								
F310113A	900 mm long	Nr	0.13	6.02	-	5.78	11.80	12.98	10.104
F310113B	1200 mm long	Nr	0.13	6.16	-	7.67	13.83	15.21	13.355
F310113C	1500 mm long	Nr	0.14	6.30	-	9.57	15.87	17.46	16.605
F310113D	1800 mm long	Nr	0.14	6.39	-	11.46	17.85	19.64	19.856
F310113E	2100 mm long	Nr	0.15	6.77	-	13.35	20.12	22.13	23.107
F3103	**Prestressed lintels; bedding and pointing in cement mortar (1:3); temporary support**								
F310315	**65 x 100 mm rectangular section**								
F310315A	450 mm long	Nr	0.08	3.50	-	1.84	5.34	5.87	1.760
F310315B	600 mm long	Nr	0.08	3.78	-	2.44	6.22	6.84	2.229
F310315C	900 mm long	Nr	0.09	4.01	-	3.57	7.58	8.34	3.168
F310315D	1050 mm long	Nr	0.09	4.29	-	4.15	8.44	9.28	3.638
F310315E	1200 mm long	Nr	0.10	4.53	-	4.72	9.25	10.18	4.107
F310315F	1500 mm long	Nr	0.11	5.04	-	5.85	10.89	11.98	5.047
F310315G	1800 mm long	Nr	0.12	5.51	-	9.98	15.49	17.04	5.986
F310315H	2100 mm long	Nr	0.14	6.30	-	11.61	17.91	19.70	6.925
F310315I	2400 mm long	Nr	0.15	7.05	-	13.28	20.33	22.36	7.864
F310316	**65 x 140 mm rectangular section**								
F310316A	900 mm long	Nr	0.10	4.53	-	4.27	8.80	9.68	4.577
F310316B	1200 mm long	Nr	0.11	5.27	-	5.64	10.91	12.00	5.986
F310316C	1500 mm long	Nr	0.13	6.02	-	7.03	13.05	14.36	7.394
F310316D	1800 mm long	Nr	0.14	6.53	-	13.18	19.71	21.68	8.240
F310316E	2100 mm long	Nr	0.15	7.05	-	15.38	22.43	24.67	9.554
F310316F	2400 mm long	Nr	0.17	7.79	-	17.54	25.33	27.86	10.869
F310317	**65 x 220 mm rectangular section**								
F310317A	900 mm long	Nr	0.11	5.04	-	5.63	10.67	11.74	6.408
F310317B	1200 mm long	Nr	0.12	5.79	-	7.43	13.22	14.54	8.427
F310317C	1500 mm long	Nr	0.14	6.53	-	9.12	15.65	17.22	10.447
F310317D	1800 mm long	Nr	0.16	7.56	-	21.70	29.26	32.19	12.747
F310317E	2100 mm long	Nr	0.18	8.31	-	25.29	33.60	36.96	14.813
F310317F	2400 mm long	Nr	0.19	9.05	-	28.86	37.91	41.70	16.880
F310317G	2700 mm long	Nr	0.21	9.57	-	33.63	43.20	47.52	18.946
F310318	**100 x 140 mm rectangular section**								
F310318A	1200 mm long	Nr	0.14	6.30	-	7.02	13.32	14.65	9.020
F310318B	1500 mm long	Nr	0.15	7.05	-	8.74	15.79	17.37	11.187
F310318C	1800 mm long	Nr	0.17	7.79	-	23.63	31.42	34.56	12.487
F310318D	2100 mm long	Nr	0.19	8.77	-	27.56	36.33	39.96	14.510
F3105	**Padstones; 21 N/mm² concrete; bedding jointing and pointing in cement mortar (1:3)**								
F310522	**Plain rectangular section**								
F310522A	225 x 100 x 225 mm	Nr	0.11	5.04	-	2.48	7.52	8.27	2.789
F310522B	225 x 150 x 225 mm	Nr	0.12	5.51	-	3.66	9.17	10.09	4.008
F310522C	225 x 225 x 225 mm	Nr	0.13	6.02	-	5.45	11.47	12.62	5.837
F310522D	450 x 100 x 450 mm	Nr	0.12	5.51	-	4.85	10.36	11.40	10.103
F310522E	450 x 150 x 450 mm	Nr	0.13	6.02	-	7.23	13.25	14.58	14.980
F310522F	450 x 225 x 450 mm	Nr	0.14	6.53	-	10.79	17.32	19.05	22.294

Masonry

		Unit	Labour Hours	Labour Net £	Plant Net £	Materials Net £	Unit Net £	Unit with 10% £	CO₂ Kg
F31	**F31: PRECAST CONCRETE CILLS, LINTELS, COPINGS AND FEATURES**								
F3106	**Coping units; BS3798; bedding, jointing and pointing in cement mortar (1:3)**								
F310624	**Splayed copings**								
F310624A	75 x 200 mm	m	0.24	11.29	-	7.00	18.29	20.12	8.108
F310624B	100 x 300 mm	m	0.35	16.33	-	12.06	28.39	31.23	15.864
F310625	**Saddleback copings**								
F310625A	75 x 200 mm	m	0.27	12.55	-	8.02	20.57	22.63	8.108
F310625B	100 x 300 mm	m	0.40	18.85	-	16.51	35.36	38.90	15.864
F310626	**Pier caps, weathered four ways**								
F310626A	425 x 425 x 125 mm	Nr	0.16	7.56	-	7.08	14.64	16.10	11.577

Structural and Carcassing

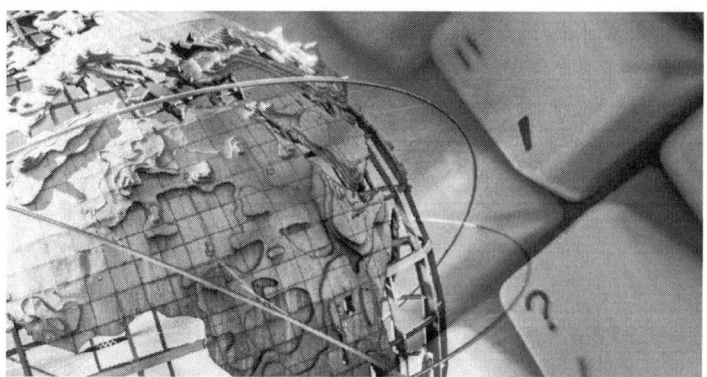

Major Works 2011		Unit	Labour Hours	Labour Net	Plant Net	Materials Net	Unit Net	Unit with 10%	CO$_2$
				£	£	£	£	£	Kg
G10	**G10: STRUCTURAL STEEL FRAMING**								
G1011	**Columns**								
G101111	**Universal columns; BS 4360; shot blasted and primed at works**								
G101111A	356 x 406 mm x 634 Kg/m	Tonne	2.67	169.79	73.30	759.02	1,002.11	1,102.32	1,849.770
G101111B	356 x 406 mm x 235 Kg/m	Tonne	3.47	220.77	95.29	759.02	1,075.08	1,182.59	1,860.021
G101111C	356 x 368 mm x 202 Kg/m	Tonne	3.74	237.70	102.62	759.02	1,099.34	1,209.27	1,863.438
G101111D	305 x 305 mm x 283 Kg/m	Tonne	3.20	203.78	87.96	759.02	1,050.76	1,155.84	1,856.604
G101111E	305 x 305 mm x 96 Kg/m	Tonne	4.00	254.69	109.95	733.73	1,098.37	1,208.21	1,866.855
G101111F	254 x 254 mm x 167 Kg/m	Tonne	4.00	254.69	109.95	733.73	1,098.37	1,208.21	1,866.855
G101111G	203 x 203 mm x 52 Kg/m	Tonne	4.80	305.66	13.14	708.42	1,027.22	1,129.94	1,815.600
G101111H	152 x 152 mm x 37 Kg/m	Tonne	5.34	339.58	14.60	775.89	1,130.07	1,243.08	1,815.600
G101112	**Rectangular hollow sections; BS 4360; shot blasted and primed at works**								
G101112A	450 x 250 x 16.0 mm x 167.0 Kg/m	Tonne	4.00	254.69	109.95	859.00	1,223.64	1,346.00	1,866.855
G101112B	400 x 200 x 16.0 mm x 142.0 Kg/m	Tonne	4.27	271.68	117.28	859.00	1,247.96	1,372.76	1,870.272
G101112C	300 x 200 x 12.5 mm x 92.6 Kg/m	Tonne	4.54	288.67	12.41	831.30	1,132.38	1,245.62	1,815.600
G101112D	250 x 150 x 12.5 mm x 73.0 Kg/m	Tonne	4.80	305.66	13.14	831.30	1,150.10	1,265.11	1,815.600
G101112E	200 x 100 x 10.0 mm x 43.6 Kg/m	Tonne	5.07	322.65	13.87	803.60	1,140.12	1,254.13	1,815.600
G101112F	150 x 100 x 10.0 mm x 35.7 Kg/m	Tonne	5.34	339.58	14.60	803.60	1,157.78	1,273.56	1,815.600
G101112G	120 x 60 x 6.3 mm x 16.4 Kg/m	Tonne	5.60	356.57	15.33	748.19	1,120.09	1,232.10	1,815.600
G101112H	100 x 50 x 5.0 mm x 10.9 Kg/m	Tonne	5.87	373.57	16.06	720.47	1,110.10	1,221.11	1,815.600
G101112I	60 x 40 x 4.0 mm x 5.72 Kg/m	Tonne	6.14	390.56	16.79	706.62	1,113.97	1,225.37	1,815.600
G101112J	50 x 30 x 2.6 mm x 3.03 Kg/m	Tonne	6.40	407.55	17.52	706.62	1,131.69	1,244.86	1,815.600
G101113	**Square hollow sections; BS 4360; shot blasted and primed at works**								
G101113A	400 x 400 x 12.5 mm x 152.0 Kg/m	Tonne	4.00	254.69	109.95	859.00	1,223.64	1,346.00	1,866.855
G101113B	300 x 300 x 12.5 mm x 112.0 Kg/m	Tonne	4.27	271.68	117.28	831.30	1,220.26	1,342.29	1,870.272
G101113C	200 x 200 x 10.0 mm x 59.3 Kg/m	Tonne	4.80	305.66	13.14	803.60	1,122.40	1,234.64	1,815.600
G101113D	150 x 150 x 10.0 mm x 43.6 Kg/m	Tonne	5.07	322.65	13.87	803.60	1,140.12	1,254.13	1,815.600
G101113E	100 x 100 x 8.0 mm x 22.9 Kg/m	Tonne	5.34	339.58	14.60	775.89	1,130.07	1,243.08	1,815.600
G101113F	70 x 70 x 5.0 mm x 10.1 Kg/m	Tonne	5.87	373.57	16.06	720.47	1,110.10	1,221.11	1,815.600
G101113G	50 x 50 x 5.0 mm x 6.97 Kg/m	Tonne	6.14	390.56	16.79	706.62	1,113.97	1,225.37	1,815.600
G101114	**Circular hollow sections; BS 4360; shot blasted and primed at works**								
G101114A	457.0 mm dia x 40.0 mm x 411.0 Kg/m	Tonne	3.47	220.77	95.29	859.00	1,175.06	1,292.57	1,860.021
G101114B	355.6 mm dia x 25.0 mm x 204.0 Kg/m	Tonne	3.74	237.70	102.62	859.00	1,199.32	1,319.25	1,863.438
G101114C	273.0 mm dia x 20.0 mm x 125.0 Kg/m	Tonne	4.00	254.69	109.95	845.16	1,209.80	1,330.78	1,866.855
G101114D	193.7 mm dia x 16.0 mm x 70.1 Kg/m	Tonne	4.80	305.66	13.14	831.30	1,150.10	1,265.11	1,815.600
G101114E	139.7 mm dia x 10.0 mm x 32.0 Kg/m	Tonne	5.34	339.58	14.60	803.60	1,157.78	1,273.56	1,815.600
G101114F	88.9 mm dia x 5.0 mm x 10.3 Kg/m	Tonne	5.87	373.57	16.06	836.03	1,225.66	1,348.23	1,815.600
G101114G	60.3 mm dia x 5.0 mm x 6.82 Kg/m	Tonne	6.14	390.56	16.79	819.95	1,227.30	1,350.03	1,815.600
G101114H	33.7 mm dia x 4.0 mm x 2.93 Kg/m	Tonne	6.40	407.55	17.52	819.95	1,245.02	1,369.52	1,815.600
G1012	**Beams**								
G101206	**Universal beams; BS 4360; shot blasted and primed at works**								
G101206A	914 x 305 mm x 289 Kg/m	Tonne	2.67	169.79	73.30	759.02	1,002.11	1,102.32	1,849.770
G101206B	838 x 292 mm x 226 Kg/m	Tonne	3.47	220.77	95.29	759.02	1,075.08	1,182.59	1,860.021
G101206C	610 x 305 mm x 238 Kg/m	Tonne	3.47	220.77	95.29	534.54	850.60	935.66	1,860.021
G101206D	533 x 210 mm x 122 Kg/m	Tonne	3.74	237.70	10.22	733.73	981.65	1,079.82	1,815.600
G101206E	457 x 191 mm x 98 Kg/m	Tonne	4.00	254.69	10.95	516.72	782.36	860.60	1,815.600
G101206F	406 x 178 mm x 74 Kg/m	Tonne	4.27	271.68	11.68	498.90	782.26	860.49	1,815.600

Major Works 2011		Unit	Labour Hours	Labour Net	Plant Net	Materials Net	Unit Net	Unit with 10%	CO$_2$
				£	£	£	£	£	Kg
G10	**G10: STRUCTURAL STEEL FRAMING**								
G1012	**Beams**								
G101206	**Universal beams; BS 4360; shot blasted and primed at works**								
G101206G	356 x 171 mm x 67 Kg/m	Tonne	4.54	288.67	12.41	708.42	1,009.50	1,110.45	1,815.600
G101206H	305 x 165 mm x 54 Kg/m	Tonne	4.80	305.66	13.14	498.90	817.70	899.47	1,815.600
G101206I	254 x 146 mm x 43 Kg/m	Tonne	5.07	322.65	13.87	498.90	835.42	918.96	1,815.600
G101206J	203 x 133 mm x 30 Kg/m	Tonne	5.34	339.58	14.60	481.08	835.26	918.79	1,815.600
G101207	**Rolled steel joists; BS 4360; shot blasted and primed at works**								
G101207A	254 x 203 mm x 81.85 Kg/m	Tonne	3.20	203.78	8.76	708.42	920.96	1,013.06	1,815.600
G101207B	254 x 114 mm x 37.20 Kg/m	Tonne	4.00	254.69	10.95	708.42	974.06	1,071.47	1,815.600
G101207C	203 x 152 mm x 52.09 Kg/m	Tonne	4.80	305.66	13.14	708.42	1,027.22	1,129.94	1,815.600
G101207D	203 x 102 mm x 25.33 Kg/m	Tonne	6.40	407.55	17.52	683.12	1,108.19	1,219.01	1,815.600
G101207E	152 x 89 mm x 17.09 Kg/m	Tonne	6.40	407.55	17.52	683.12	1,108.19	1,219.01	1,815.600
G101207F	127 x 76 mm x 16.37 Kg/m	Tonne	6.40	407.55	17.52	683.12	1,108.19	1,219.01	1,815.600
G101207G	102 x 102 mm x 23.06 Kg/m	Tonne	6.40	407.55	17.52	683.12	1,108.19	1,219.01	1,815.600
G101207H	89 x 89 mm x 19.35 Kg/m	Tonne	6.40	407.55	17.52	683.12	1,108.19	1,219.01	1,815.600
G101207I	76 x 76 mm x 12.65 Kg/m	Tonne	6.40	407.55	17.52	657.83	1,082.90	1,191.19	1,815.600
G101208	**Rolled steel channels; BS 4360; shot blasted and primed at works**								
G101208A	432 x 102 mm x 65.54 Kg/m	Tonne	4.00	254.69	10.95	771.67	1,037.31	1,141.04	1,815.600
G101208B	305 x 89 mm x 41.69 Kg/m	Tonne	4.80	305.66	13.14	771.67	1,090.47	1,199.52	1,815.600
G101208C	254 x 76 mm x 28.89 Kg/m	Tonne	5.87	373.57	16.06	759.02	1,148.65	1,263.52	1,815.600
G101208D	203 x 89 mm x 29.78 Kg/m	Tonne	5.87	373.57	16.06	759.02	1,148.65	1,263.52	1,815.600
G101208E	178 x 76 mm x 20.84 Kg/m	Tonne	6.40	407.55	17.52	759.02	1,184.09	1,302.50	1,815.600
G101208F	152 x 76 mm x 17.88 Kg/m	Tonne	6.40	407.55	17.52	759.02	1,184.09	1,302.50	1,815.600
G101208G	127 x 64 mm x 14.90 Kg/m	Tonne	6.40	407.55	17.52	759.02	1,184.09	1,302.50	1,815.600
G101208H	76 x 51 mm x 9.34 Kg/m	Tonne	6.40	407.55	17.52	733.73	1,158.80	1,274.68	1,815.600
G101208I	51 x 38 mm x 5.81 Kg/m	Tonne	6.40	407.55	17.52	733.73	1,158.80	1,274.68	1,815.600
G1013	**Support steelwork and bracings**								
G101326	**Equal angles; BS 4360; shot blasted and primed at works**								
G101326A	250 x 250 x 25 mm x 93.60 Kg/m	Tonne	3.74	237.70	10.22	868.17	1,116.09	1,227.70	1,815.600
G101326B	200 x 200 x 16 mm x 48.50 Kg/m	Tonne	4.00	254.69	10.95	868.17	1,133.81	1,247.19	1,815.600
G101326C	150 x 150 x 10 mm x 23.00 Kg/m	Tonne	4.54	288.67	12.41	852.10	1,153.18	1,268.50	1,815.600
G101326D	100 x 100 x 15 mm x 21.90 Kg/m	Tonne	4.80	305.66	13.14	852.10	1,170.90	1,287.99	1,815.600
G101326E	80 x 80 x 10 mm x 11.90 Kg/m	Tonne	6.40	407.55	17.52	836.03	1,261.10	1,387.21	1,815.600
G101326F	50 x 50 x 8 mm x 5.82 Kg/m	Tonne	6.94	441.47	18.98	836.03	1,296.48	1,426.13	1,815.600
G101326G	40 x 40 x 6 mm x 3.52 Kg/m	Tonne	7.47	475.45	20.44	836.03	1,331.92	1,465.11	1,815.600
G101326H	25 x 25 x 5 mm x 1.77 Kg/m	Tonne	8.00	509.37	21.90	836.03	1,367.30	1,504.03	1,815.600
G101327	**Unequal angles; BS 4360; shot blasted and primed at works**								
G101327A	200 x 150 x 18 mm x 47.10 Kg/m	Tonne	4.00	254.69	10.95	868.17	1,133.81	1,247.19	1,815.600
G101327B	200 x 100 x 15 mm x 33.70 Kg/m	Tonne	4.27	271.68	11.68	868.17	1,151.53	1,266.68	1,815.600
G101327C	150 x 75 x 15 mm x 24.80 Kg/m	Tonne	4.54	288.67	12.41	868.17	1,169.25	1,286.18	1,815.600
G101327D	100 x 75 x 12 mm x 15.40 Kg/m	Tonne	5.87	373.57	16.06	868.17	1,257.80	1,383.58	1,815.600
G101327E	75 x 50 x 8 mm x 7.39 Kg/m	Tonne	6.94	441.47	18.98	836.03	1,296.48	1,426.13	1,815.600
G101327F	65 x 50 x 8 mm x 6.75 Kg/m	Tonne	6.94	441.47	18.98	836.03	1,296.48	1,426.13	1,815.600
G101327G	60 x 30 x 6 mm x 3.99 Kg/m	Tonne	7.47	475.45	20.44	836.03	1,331.92	1,465.11	1,815.600
G101327H	40 x 25 x 4 mm x 1.93 Kg/m	Tonne	8.00	509.37	21.90	836.03	1,367.30	1,504.03	1,815.600
G1018	**Framing; erection**								
G101810	**Trial erection**								
G101810A	at shop	Tonne	12.97	356.59	-	-	356.59	392.25	-
G101820	**Permanent erection**								
G101820A	on site	Tonne	10.37	285.29	-	-	285.29	313.82	-
G1021	**Fixings**								
G102151	**Bolts; BS 4190 high strength friction grip (HSFG) black metric hexagon head with nut and washer**								
G102151A	M6 x 25 mm	Nr	0.01	0.83	-	0.10	0.93	1.02	0.011
G102151B	M6 x 50 mm	Nr	0.02	1.02	-	0.22	1.24	1.36	0.021
G102151C	M6 x 75 mm	Nr	0.02	1.21	-	0.29	1.50	1.65	0.033
G102151D	M6 x 100 mm	Nr	0.02	1.34	-	0.43	1.77	1.95	0.044

Major Works 2011		Unit	Labour Hours	Labour Net	Plant Net	Materials Net	Unit Net	Unit with 10%	CO$_2$
				£	£	£	£	£	Kg
G10	**G10: STRUCTURAL STEEL FRAMING**								
G1021	**Fixings**								
G102151	**Bolts; BS 4190 high strength friction grip (HSFG) black metric hexagon head with nut and washer**								
G102151E	M8 x 25 mm	Nr	0.02	1.21	-	0.29	1.50	1.65	0.019
G102151F	M8 x 50 mm	Nr	0.02	1.34	-	0.33	1.67	1.84	0.039
G102151G	M8 x 75 mm	Nr	0.02	1.53	-	0.36	1.89	2.08	0.058
G102151H	M8 x 100 mm	Nr	0.03	1.72	-	0.51	2.23	2.45	0.078
G102151I	M10 x 50 mm	Nr	0.03	1.85	-	0.51	2.36	2.60	0.060
G102151J	M10 x 75 mm	Nr	0.03	2.04	-	0.58	2.62	2.88	0.091
G102151K	M10 x 100 mm	Nr	0.04	2.23	-	0.85	3.08	3.39	0.120
G102151L	M10 x 150 mm	Nr	0.04	2.35	-	1.29	3.64	4.00	0.181
G102151M	M12 x 50 mm	Nr	0.04	2.23	-	0.71	2.94	3.23	0.087
G102151N	M12 x 75 mm	Nr	0.04	2.35	-	0.85	3.20	3.52	0.131
G102151O	M12 x 100 mm	Nr	0.04	2.55	-	0.99	3.54	3.89	0.017
G102151P	M12 x 150 mm	Nr	0.04	2.74	-	1.86	4.60	5.06	0.260
G102151Q	M12 x 200 mm	Nr	0.05	2.86	-	3.14	6.00	6.60	0.347
G102151R	M12 x 300 mm	Nr	0.05	3.37	-	3.67	7.04	7.74	0.520
G102151S	M16 x 100 mm	Nr	0.05	3.05	-	1.71	4.76	5.24	0.308
G102151T	M16 x 150 mm	Nr	0.05	3.25	-	2.85	6.10	6.71	0.463
G102151U	M16 x 200 mm	Nr	0.05	3.37	-	4.27	7.64	8.40	0.617
G102151V	M16 x 300 mm	Nr	0.06	3.88	-	4.97	8.85	9.74	0.925
G102151W	M20 x 100 mm	Nr	0.05	3.37	-	3.43	6.80	7.48	0.481
G102151X	M20 x 150 mm	Nr	0.06	3.56	-	4.63	8.19	9.01	0.723
G102151Y	M20 x 200 mm	Nr	0.06	3.75	-	6.33	10.08	11.09	0.964
G102151Z	M20 x 300 mm	Nr	0.07	4.26	-	7.84	12.10	13.31	1.445
G102152	**Drill steelwork for bolts**								
G102152A	6 mm steel for M6 bolt	Nr	0.05	3.37	-	-	3.37	3.71	-
G102152B	6 mm steel for M8 bolt	Nr	0.06	3.75	-	-	3.75	4.13	-
G102152C	6 mm steel for M10 bolt	Nr	0.06	4.07	-	-	4.07	4.48	-
G102152D	6 mm steel for M12 bolt	Nr	0.08	4.77	-	-	4.77	5.25	-
G102152E	6 mm steel for M16 bolt	Nr	0.09	5.41	-	-	5.41	5.95	-
G102152F	6 mm steel for M20 bolt	Nr	0.11	6.81	-	-	6.81	7.49	-
G102152G	10 mm steel for M6 bolt	Nr	0.06	3.75	-	-	3.75	4.13	-
G102152H	10 mm steel for M8 bolt	Nr	0.07	4.26	-	-	4.26	4.69	-
G102152I	10 mm steel for M10 bolt	Nr	0.07	4.58	-	-	4.58	5.04	-
G102152J	10 mm steel for M12 bolt	Nr	0.09	5.41	-	-	5.41	5.95	-
G102152K	10 mm steel for M16 bolt	Nr	0.10	6.11	-	-	6.11	6.72	-
G102152L	10 mm steel for M20 bolt	Nr	0.12	7.64	-	-	7.64	8.40	-
G102152M	13 mm steel for M6 bolt	Nr	0.07	4.26	-	-	4.26	4.69	-
G102152N	13 mm steel for M8 bolt	Nr	0.08	4.77	-	-	4.77	5.25	-
G102152O	13 mm steel for M10 bolt	Nr	0.08	5.09	-	-	5.09	5.60	-
G102152P	13 mm steel for M12 bolt	Nr	0.10	6.11	-	-	6.11	6.72	-
G102152Q	13 mm steel for M16 bolt	Nr	0.11	6.81	-	-	6.81	7.49	-
G102152R	13 mm steel for M20 bolt	Nr	0.13	8.46	-	-	8.46	9.31	-
G1070	**Surface preparation**								
G107010	**Blast cleaning**								
G107010A	at works	m^2	0.07	1.79	0.45	0.34	2.58	2.84	1.251
G107030	**Wire brushing**								
G107030A	at works	m^2	0.07	1.90	-	-	1.90	2.09	-
G1080	**Surface treatment**								
G108010	**Galvanising**								
G108010A	at works	m^2	0.22	5.94	9.16	-	15.10	16.61	-
G108030	**Protective painting; at works**								
G108030A	zinc chromate primer; one coat	m^2	0.04	1.04	0.14	1.13	2.31	2.54	0.560

Major Works 2011		Unit	Labour Hours	Labour Net	Plant Net	Materials Net	Unit Net	Unit with 10%	CO$_2$
				£	£	£	£	£	Kg
G20	**G20: CARPENTRY, TIMBER FRAMING AND FIRST FIXING**								
G2001	**Trussed rafters; preservative treated and stress graded softwood**								
G200101	**Standard trusses; 450 mm overhang at eaves; 22.5 deg pitch; span**								
G200101A	5.00 m	Nr	0.80	13.58	-	33.18	46.76	51.44	20.250
G200101B	6.00 m	Nr	0.83	14.09	-	36.65	50.74	55.81	22.500
G200101C	7.00 m	Nr	0.85	14.43	-	41.49	55.92	61.51	24.750
G200101D	8.00 m	Nr	0.90	15.28	-	48.41	63.69	70.06	27.000
G200101E	9.00 m	Nr	0.95	16.13	-	57.38	73.51	80.86	29.250
G200101F	10.00 m	Nr	1.00	16.98	-	68.46	85.44	93.98	31.500
G200102	**Standard trusses; 450 mm overhang at eaves; 35 deg pitch; span**								
G200102G	5.00 m	Nr	0.85	14.43	-	35.65	50.08	55.09	20.250
G200102H	6.00 m	Nr	0.88	14.94	-	38.90	53.84	59.22	22.500
G200102I	7.00 m	Nr	0.90	15.28	-	43.43	58.71	64.58	24.750
G200102J	8.00 m	Nr	0.95	16.13	-	49.91	66.04	72.64	27.000
G200102K	9.00 m	Nr	1.00	16.98	-	58.34	75.32	82.85	29.250
G200102L	10.00 m	Nr	1.05	17.83	-	68.73	86.56	95.22	31.500
G200106	**Standard trusses; 450 mm overhang at eaves; 45 deg pitch; span**								
G200106M	5.00 m	Nr	0.90	15.28	-	57.88	73.16	80.48	20.250
G200106N	6.00 m	Nr	0.93	15.79	-	62.55	78.34	86.17	22.500
G200106O	7.00 m	Nr	0.95	16.13	-	69.08	85.21	93.73	24.750
G200106P	8.00 m	Nr	1.00	16.98	-	78.41	95.39	104.93	27.000
G200106Q	9.00 m	Nr	1.05	17.83	-	90.55	108.38	119.22	29.250
G200106R	10.00 m	Nr	1.10	18.68	-	105.49	124.17	136.59	31.500
G200113	**Monopitch trusses; 450 mm overhang at eaves; 22.5 deg pitch; span**								
G200113A	2.00 m	Nr	0.55	9.34	-	38.03	47.37	52.11	15.750
G200113B	3.00 m	Nr	0.58	9.85	-	39.42	49.27	54.20	13.500
G200113C	4.00 m	Nr	0.60	10.19	-	41.49	51.68	56.85	18.000
G200113D	5.00 m	Nr	0.65	11.04	-	42.88	53.92	59.31	20.250
G200113E	6.00 m	Nr	0.70	11.89	-	46.32	58.21	64.03	22.500
G200114	**Monopitch trusses; 450 mm overhang at eaves; 35 deg pitch; span**								
G200114F	2.00 m	Nr	0.60	10.19	-	38.25	48.44	53.28	15.750
G200114G	3.00 m	Nr	0.63	10.70	-	39.86	50.56	55.62	13.500
G200114H	4.00 m	Nr	0.65	11.04	-	41.49	52.53	57.78	18.000
G200114I	5.00 m	Nr	0.70	11.89	-	42.78	54.67	60.14	20.250
G200114J	6.00 m	Nr	0.75	12.73	-	46.03	58.76	64.64	22.500
G200115	**Monopitch trusses; 450 mm overhang at eaves; 45 deg pitch; span**								
G200115K	2.00 m	Nr	0.65	11.04	-	58.82	69.86	76.85	15.750
G200115L	3.00 m	Nr	0.68	11.55	-	61.13	72.68	79.95	13.500
G200115M	4.00 m	Nr	0.70	11.89	-	63.47	75.36	82.90	18.000
G200115N	5.00 m	Nr	0.75	12.73	-	65.35	78.08	85.89	20.250
G200115O	6.00 m	Nr	0.80	13.58	-	70.01	83.59	91.95	22.500
G200121	**Girder trusses; 22.5 deg pitch; span**								
G200121A	5.00 m	Nr	0.75	12.73	-	118.93	131.66	144.83	20.250
G200121B	6.00 m	Nr	0.78	13.24	-	135.52	148.76	163.64	22.500
G200121C	7.00 m	Nr	0.80	13.58	-	146.59	160.17	176.19	24.750
G200121D	8.00 m	Nr	0.85	14.43	-	165.96	180.39	198.43	27.000
G200121E	9.00 m	Nr	0.90	15.28	-	193.62	208.90	229.79	29.250
G200121F	10.00 m	Nr	0.95	16.13	-	221.26	237.39	261.13	31.500
G200122	**Girder trusses; 35 deg pitch; span**								
G200122G	5.00 m	Nr	0.80	13.58	-	116.69	130.27	143.30	20.250
G200122H	6.00 m	Nr	0.83	14.09	-	133.55	147.64	162.40	22.500
G200122I	7.00 m	Nr	0.85	14.43	-	143.93	158.36	174.20	24.750
G200122J	8.00 m	Nr	0.90	15.28	-	163.36	178.64	196.50	27.000
G200122K	9.00 m	Nr	0.95	16.13	-	190.59	206.72	227.39	29.250
G200122L	10.00 m	Nr	1.00	16.98	-	217.81	234.79	258.27	31.500

Major Works 2011		Unit	Labour Hours	Labour Net	Plant Net	Materials Net	Unit Net	Unit with 10%	CO$_2$
				£	£	£	£	£	Kg
G20	**G20: CARPENTRY, TIMBER FRAMING AND FIRST FIXING**								
G2001	**Trussed rafters; preservative treated and stress graded softwood**								
G200123	**Girder trusses; 45 deg pitch; span**								
G200123M	5.00 m	Nr	0.85	14.43	-	182.95	197.38	217.12	20.250
G200123N	6.00 m	Nr	0.88	14.94	-	214.71	229.65	252.62	22.500
G200123O	7.00 m	Nr	0.90	15.28	-	227.76	243.04	267.34	24.750
G200123P	8.00 m	Nr	0.95	16.13	-	257.65	273.78	301.16	27.000
G200123Q	9.00 m	Nr	1.00	16.98	-	302.46	319.44	351.38	29.250
G200123R	10.00 m	Nr	1.05	17.83	-	345.40	363.23	399.55	31.500
G200131	**Hip reducing set; 22.5 deg pitch; span**								
G200131A	5.00 m	Nr	2.00	33.96	-	66.38	100.34	110.37	20.250
G200131B	6.00 m	Nr	2.91	49.41	-	88.51	137.92	151.71	22.500
G200131C	7.00 m	Nr	3.83	65.03	-	96.80	161.83	178.01	24.750
G200131D	8.00 m	Nr	4.05	68.77	-	99.56	168.33	185.16	27.000
G200131E	9.00 m	Nr	5.70	96.79	-	102.33	199.12	219.03	29.250
G200131F	10.00 m	Nr	7.00	118.86	-	105.12	223.98	246.38	31.500
G200132	**Hip reducing set; 35 deg pitch; span**								
G200132G	5.00 m	Nr	2.13	36.17	-	67.43	103.60	113.96	20.250
G200132H	6.00 m	Nr	3.08	52.30	-	88.16	140.46	154.51	22.500
G200132I	7.00 m	Nr	4.05	68.77	-	95.94	164.71	181.18	24.750
G200132J	8.00 m	Nr	5.23	88.81	-	98.55	187.36	206.10	27.000
G200132K	9.00 m	Nr	6.00	101.88	-	103.71	205.59	226.15	29.250
G200132L	10.00 m	Nr	7.35	124.80	-	108.92	233.72	257.09	31.500
G200133	**Hip reducing set; 45 deg pitch; span**								
G200133M	5.00 m	Nr	2.25	38.20	-	112.03	150.23	165.25	20.250
G200133N	6.00 m	Nr	3.26	55.35	-	141.89	197.24	216.96	22.500
G200133O	7.00 m	Nr	4.28	72.67	-	153.09	225.76	248.34	24.750
G200133P	8.00 m	Nr	5.50	93.39	-	156.83	250.22	275.24	27.000
G200133Q	9.00 m	Nr	6.30	106.97	-	164.28	271.25	298.38	29.250
G200133R	10.00 m	Nr	7.70	130.75	-	171.77	302.52	332.77	31.500
G200141	**Gable ladders; length**								
G200141A	2.5 - 3.0 m	Nr	0.75	12.73	-	31.94	44.67	49.14	12.715
G200141B	3.0 - 3.5 m	Nr	0.80	13.58	-	34.54	48.12	52.93	14.965
G200141C	3.5 - 4.0 m	Nr	0.85	14.43	-	37.42	51.85	57.04	17.328
G200141D	4.0 - 4.5 m	Nr	0.90	15.28	-	42.59	57.87	63.66	19.578
G200141E	4.5 - 5.0 m	Nr	0.95	16.13	-	48.06	64.19	70.61	21.941
G200141F	5.0 - 5.5 m	Nr	1.00	16.98	-	53.23	70.21	77.23	24.191
G200141G	5.5 - 6.0 m	Nr	1.10	18.68	-	58.72	77.40	85.14	26.554
G200141H	6.0 - 6.5 m	Nr	1.20	20.38	-	63.89	84.27	92.70	28.804
G2005	**Glued laminated timber beams**								
G200521	**Beams, BS 4169, treated wrought softwood**								
G200521A	65 x 150 mm	m	0.17	2.89	-	11.66	14.55	16.01	3.042
G200521B	65 x 200 mm	m	0.17	2.89	-	15.55	18.44	20.28	4.056
G200521C	65 x 300 mm	m	0.18	3.06	-	23.32	26.38	29.02	6.084
G200521D	90 x 150 mm	m	0.18	3.06	-	16.14	19.20	21.12	4.212
G200521E	90 x 200 mm	m	0.18	3.06	-	21.52	24.58	27.04	5.616
G200521F	90 x 300 mm	m	0.20	3.40	-	32.29	35.69	39.26	8.424
G200521G	90 x 400 mm	m	0.22	3.74	-	43.05	46.79	51.47	11.232
G200521H	90 x 450 mm	m	0.23	3.91	-	48.43	52.34	57.57	12.636
G200521I	115 x 250 mm	m	0.25	4.25	-	34.38	38.63	42.49	8.970
G200521J	115 x 300 mm	m	0.25	4.25	-	41.26	45.51	50.06	10.764
G200521K	115 x 400 mm	m	0.27	4.58	-	55.01	59.59	65.55	14.352
G200521L	115 x 500 mm	m	0.27	4.58	-	68.76	73.34	80.67	17.940
G200521M	140 x 350 mm	m	0.28	4.75	-	58.60	63.35	69.69	15.288
G200521N	140 x 400 mm	m	0.28	4.75	-	66.97	71.72	78.89	17.472
G200521O	140 x 475 mm	m	0.30	5.09	-	79.52	84.61	93.07	20.748
G200521P	165 x 425 mm	m	0.32	5.43	-	83.86	89.29	98.22	21.879
G200521Q	165 x 450 mm	m	0.32	5.43	-	88.79	94.22	103.64	23.166
G200521R	165 x 475 mm	m	0.34	5.77	-	93.72	99.49	109.44	24.453
G200521S	190 x 475 mm	m	0.37	6.28	-	107.92	114.20	125.62	28.158
G2021	**Floors**								
G202102	**Treated sawn softwood; grade SC3; basic sizes**								
G202102A	38 x 100 mm	m	0.12	2.04	-	1.47	3.51	3.86	1.030
G202102B	38 x 150 mm	m	0.13	2.21	-	2.16	4.37	4.81	1.541

Structural & Carcassing

Major Works 2011		Unit	Labour Hours	Labour Net	Plant Net	Materials Net	Unit Net	Unit with 10%	CO₂
				£	£	£	£	£	Kg
G20	**G20: CARPENTRY, TIMBER FRAMING AND FIRST FIXING**								
G2021	**Floors**								
G202102	**Treated sawn softwood; grade SC3; basic sizes**								
G202102C	50 x 100 mm	m	0.13	2.21	-	1.67	3.88	4.27	1.353
G202102D	50 x 150 mm	m	0.14	2.38	-	2.50	4.88	5.37	2.028
G202102E	50 x 200 mm	m	0.15	2.55	-	3.35	5.90	6.49	2.705
G202102F	50 x 225 mm	m	0.15	2.55	-	3.89	6.44	7.08	3.045
G202102H	75 x 150 mm	m	0.15	2.55	-	4.14	6.69	7.36	3.045
G202102I	75 x 200 mm	m	0.19	3.23	-	5.50	8.73	9.60	4.058
G202102J	75 x 225 mm	m	0.22	3.74	-	6.41	10.15	11.17	4.565
G202102M	100 x 200 mm	m	0.26	4.41	-	7.58	11.99	13.19	5.410
G202102N	100 x 225 mm	m	0.29	4.92	-	8.84	13.76	15.14	6.086
G202102O	100 x 300 mm	m	0.39	6.62	-	12.52	19.14	21.05	8.115
G2023	**Walls**								
G202321	**Treated sawn softwood; grade GS; basic sizes**								
G202321A	38 x 75 mm	m	0.10	1.70	-	1.21	2.91	3.20	0.784
G202321B	38 x 100 mm	m	0.12	2.04	-	1.40	3.44	3.78	1.035
G202321C	50 x 50 mm	m	0.10	1.70	-	0.90	2.60	2.86	0.691
G202321D	50 x 75 mm	m	0.12	2.04	-	1.31	3.35	3.69	1.021
G202321E	50 x 100 mm	m	0.15	2.55	-	1.67	4.22	4.64	1.353
G202321G	75 x 100 mm	m	0.17	2.89	-	2.93	5.82	6.40	2.043
G202321H	100 x 100 mm	m	0.20	3.40	-	3.90	7.30	8.03	2.705
G2025	**Plates or the like**								
G202531	**Treated sawn softwood; grade GS; basic sizes**								
G202531A	19 x 38 mm	m	0.08	1.36	-	0.32	1.68	1.85	0.220
G202531B	19 x 50 mm	m	0.08	1.36	-	0.41	1.77	1.95	0.280
G202531C	25 x 50 mm	m	0.09	1.53	-	0.50	2.03	2.23	0.360
G202531D	25 x 75 mm	m	0.09	1.53	-	0.80	2.33	2.56	0.525
G202531E	25 x 100 mm	m	0.10	1.70	-	0.92	2.62	2.88	0.691
G202531F	38 x 38 mm	m	0.08	1.36	-	0.62	1.98	2.18	0.410
G202531G	38 x 50 mm	m	0.09	1.53	-	0.82	2.35	2.59	0.531
G202531H	38 x 100 mm	m	0.10	1.70	-	1.40	3.10	3.41	1.035
G202531I	50 x 50 mm	m	0.09	1.53	-	0.90	2.43	2.67	0.691
G202531J	50 x 75 mm	m	0.09	1.53	-	1.31	2.84	3.12	1.021
G202531K	50 x 100 mm	m	0.10	1.70	-	1.67	3.37	3.71	1.353
G202531L	50 x 150 mm	m	0.12	2.04	-	2.46	4.50	4.95	2.043
G202531M	75 x 100 mm	m	0.14	2.38	-	2.93	5.31	5.84	2.043
G202531N	75 x 150 mm	m	0.16	2.72	-	4.04	6.76	7.44	3.037
G202531O	75 x 200 mm	m	0.22	3.74	-	5.38	9.12	10.03	4.058
G202531P	100 x 100 mm	m	0.15	2.55	-	3.90	6.45	7.10	2.705
G2027	**Flat roofs**								
G202702	**Treated sawn softwood; grade SC3; basic sizes**								
G202702A	38 x 100 mm	m	0.12	2.04	-	1.47	3.51	3.86	1.030
G202702B	38 x 150 mm	m	0.13	2.21	-	2.16	4.37	4.81	1.541
G202702C	50 x 100 mm	m	0.13	2.21	-	1.67	3.88	4.27	1.353
G202702D	50 x 150 mm	m	0.14	2.38	-	2.50	4.88	5.37	2.028
G202702E	50 x 200 mm	m	0.15	2.55	-	3.35	5.90	6.49	2.705
G202702F	50 x 225 mm	m	0.15	2.55	-	3.89	6.44	7.08	3.045
G202702H	75 x 150 mm	m	0.15	2.55	-	4.14	6.69	7.36	3.045
G202702I	75 x 200 mm	m	0.19	3.23	-	5.50	8.73	9.60	4.058
G202702J	75 x 225 mm	m	0.22	3.74	-	6.41	10.15	11.17	4.565
G202702M	100 x 200 mm	m	0.26	4.41	-	7.58	11.99	13.19	5.410
G202702N	100 x 225 mm	m	0.29	4.92	-	8.84	13.76	15.14	6.086
G202702O	100 x 300 mm	m	0.39	6.62	-	12.52	19.14	21.05	8.115
G2029	**Pitched roofs**								
G202911	**Treated sawn softwood; grade SC3; basic sizes**								
G202911A	25 x 100 mm	m	0.12	2.04	-	0.96	3.00	3.30	0.676
G202911B	25 x 150 mm	m	0.14	2.38	-	1.39	3.77	4.15	1.016
G202911C	25 x 175 mm	m	0.16	2.72	-	1.63	4.35	4.79	1.184
G202911D	25 x 200 mm	m	0.17	2.89	-	1.85	4.74	5.21	1.353
G202911E	38 x 100 mm	m	0.14	2.38	-	1.44	3.82	4.20	1.030
G202911F	38 x 150 mm	m	0.19	3.23	-	2.12	5.35	5.89	1.541
G202911G	38 x 200 mm	m	0.22	3.74	-	2.81	6.55	7.21	2.055
G202911H	50 x 50 mm	m	0.12	2.04	-	0.88	2.92	3.21	0.676
G202911I	50 x 100 mm	m	0.14	2.38	-	1.67	4.05	4.46	1.353
G202911J	50 x 150 mm	m	0.16	2.72	-	2.50	5.22	5.74	2.028
G202911K	50 x 200 mm	m	0.17	2.89	-	3.35	6.24	6.86	2.705

Major Works 2011		Unit	Labour Hours	Labour Net	Plant Net	Materials Net	Unit Net	Unit with 10%	CO₂
				£	£	£	£	£	Kg
G20	**G20: CARPENTRY, TIMBER FRAMING AND FIRST FIXING**								
G2029	**Pitched roofs**								
G202911	**Treated sawn softwood; grade SC3; basic sizes**								
G202911L	50 x 225 mm	m	0.19	3.23	-	3.89	7.12	7.83	3.045
G202911M	75 x 100 mm	m	0.23	3.91	-	2.94	6.85	7.54	2.028
G202911N	75 x 150 mm	m	0.25	4.25	-	4.14	8.39	9.23	3.045
G202911O	75 x 200 mm	m	0.28	4.75	-	5.50	10.25	11.28	4.058
G202911P	75 x 250 mm	m	0.32	5.43	-	7.07	12.50	13.75	5.073
G202911Q	75 x 300 mm	m	0.38	6.45	-	8.14	14.59	16.05	6.086
G202911R	100 x 100 mm	m	0.25	4.25	-	4.04	8.29	9.12	2.705
G202911S	100 x 150 mm	m	0.28	4.75	-	6.08	10.83	11.91	4.058
G202911T	100 x 200 mm	m	0.30	5.09	-	7.58	12.67	13.94	5.410
G2031	**Strutting and bridging; treated sawn softwood; grade GS; basic sizes:**								
G203152	**Solid strutting**								
G203152A	50 x 100 mm	m	0.28	4.75	-	2.09	6.84	7.52	1.523
G203152B	50 x 150 mm	m	0.30	5.09	-	2.80	7.89	8.68	2.184
G203152C	50 x 200 mm	m	0.35	5.94	-	3.59	9.53	10.48	2.846
G203152D	50 x 225 mm	m	0.37	6.28	-	4.13	10.41	11.45	3.178
G203152E	50 x 250 mm	m	0.39	6.62	-	4.73	11.35	12.49	3.509
G203153	**Herringbone strutting**								
G203153A	38 x 38 x 100 mm deep	m	0.35	5.94	-	1.14	7.08	7.79	0.756
G203153B	38 x 38 x 150 mm deep	m	0.38	6.45	-	1.17	7.62	8.38	0.781
G203153C	38 x 38 x 200 mm deep	m	0.40	6.79	-	1.23	8.02	8.82	0.817
G203153D	38 x 38 x 225 mm deep	m	0.42	7.13	-	1.26	8.39	9.23	0.835
G203153E	38 x 38 x 250 mm deep	m	0.45	7.64	-	1.29	8.93	9.82	0.856
G203153F	50 x 50 x 100 mm deep	m	0.35	5.94	-	1.64	7.58	8.34	1.270
G203153G	50 x 50 x 125 mm deep	m	0.38	6.45	-	1.67	8.12	8.93	1.288
G203153H	50 x 50 x 150 mm deep	m	0.38	6.45	-	1.70	8.15	8.97	1.313
G203153I	50 x 50 x 200 mm deep	m	0.40	6.79	-	1.78	8.57	9.43	1.375
G203153J	50 x 50 x 225 mm deep	m	0.42	7.13	-	1.82	8.95	9.85	1.406
G2032	**Catnic galvanised mild steel herringbone joist struts; fixing between joists:**								
G203241	**To suit joist size**								
G203241A	38 x 150/175 mm; 400 mm centres	m	0.35	5.94	-	2.68	8.62	9.48	3.730
G203241B	38 x 150/175 mm; 450 mm centres	m	0.30	5.09	-	2.40	7.49	8.24	3.328
G203241C	38 x 150/175 mm; 600 mm centres	m	0.25	4.25	-	1.80	6.05	6.66	2.496
G203241D	50 x 150/175 mm; 400 mm centres	m	0.35	5.94	-	2.68	8.62	9.48	3.730
G203241E	50 x 150/175 mm; 450 mm centres	m	0.30	5.09	-	2.40	7.49	8.24	3.328
G203241F	50 x 150/175 mm; 600 mm centres	m	0.25	4.25	-	1.80	6.05	6.66	2.496
G203241G	63 x 150/175 mm; 400 mm centres	m	0.35	5.94	-	2.68	8.62	9.48	3.730
G203241H	63 x 150/175 mm; 450 mm centres	m	0.30	5.09	-	2.40	7.49	8.24	3.328
G203241I	63 x 150/175 mm; 600 mm centres	m	0.25	4.25	-	1.80	6.05	6.66	2.496
G203241J	38 x 200/225 mm; 400 mm centres	m	0.35	5.94	-	2.68	8.62	9.48	3.730
G203241K	38 x 200/225 mm; 450 mm centres	m	0.30	5.09	-	2.40	7.49	8.24	3.328
G203241L	38 x 200/225 mm; 600 mm centres	m	0.25	4.25	-	1.80	6.05	6.66	2.496
G203241M	50 x 200/225 mm; 400 mm centres	m	0.35	5.94	-	2.68	8.62	9.48	3.730
G203241N	50 x 200/225 mm; 450 mm centres	m	0.30	5.09	-	2.40	7.49	8.24	3.328
G203241O	50 x 200/225 mm; 600 mm centres	m	0.25	4.25	-	1.80	6.05	6.66	2.496
G203241P	63 x 200/225 mm; 400 mm centres	m	0.35	5.94	-	2.68	8.62	9.48	3.730
G203241Q	63 x 200/225 mm; 450 mm centres	m	0.30	5.09	-	2.40	7.49	8.24	3.328
G203241R	63 x 200/225 mm; 600 mm centres	m	0.25	4.25	-	1.80	6.05	6.66	2.496

Structural & Carcassing

		Unit	Labour Hours	Labour Net	Plant Net	Materials Net	Unit Net	Unit with 10%	CO₂
				£	£	£	£	£	Kg
G20	**G20: CARPENTRY, TIMBER FRAMING AND FIRST FIXING**								
G2033	**Supports, kerbs, bearers or the like**								
G203331	**Treated sawn softwood; grade GS; basic sizes**								
G203331A	19 x 38 mm	m	0.08	1.36	-	0.32	1.68	1.85	0.220
G203331B	19 x 50 mm	m	0.08	1.36	-	0.41	1.77	1.95	0.280
G203331C	25 x 50 mm	m	0.09	1.53	-	0.50	2.03	2.23	0.360
G203331D	25 x 75 mm	m	0.09	1.53	-	0.80	2.33	2.56	0.525
G203331E	25 x 100 mm	m	0.10	1.70	-	0.92	2.62	2.88	0.691
G203331F	38 x 38 mm	m	0.08	1.36	-	0.62	1.98	2.18	0.410
G203331G	38 x 50 mm	m	0.09	1.53	-	0.82	2.35	2.59	0.531
G203331H	38 x 100 mm	m	0.10	1.70	-	1.40	3.10	3.41	1.035
G203331I	50 x 50 mm	m	0.09	1.53	-	0.90	2.43	2.67	0.691
G203331J	50 x 75 mm	m	0.09	1.53	-	1.31	2.84	3.12	1.021
G203331K	50 x 100 mm	m	0.10	1.70	-	1.67	3.37	3.71	1.353
G203331L	50 x 150 mm	m	0.12	2.04	-	2.46	4.50	4.95	2.043
G203331M	75 x 100 mm	m	0.14	2.38	-	2.93	5.31	5.84	2.043
G203331N	75 x 150 mm	m	0.16	2.72	-	4.04	6.76	7.44	3.037
G203331O	75 x 200 mm	m	0.22	3.74	-	5.38	9.12	10.03	4.058
G203331P	100 x 100 mm	m	0.15	2.55	-	3.90	6.45	7.10	2.705
G2039	**Fillets and rolls; treated sawn softwood grade GS; basic sizes**								
G203992	**Angle fillets**								
G203992A	ex - 25 x 50 mm	m	0.12	2.04	-	0.38	2.42	2.66	0.353
G203992B	ex - 38 x 38 mm	m	0.13	2.21	-	0.46	2.67	2.94	0.403
G203992C	ex - 38 x 75 mm	m	0.14	2.38	-	0.73	3.11	3.42	0.769
G203992D	ex - 50 x 50 mm	m	0.15	2.55	-	0.56	3.11	3.42	0.678
G203992E	ex - 75 x 75 mm	m	0.17	2.89	-	1.13	4.02	4.42	1.490
G203993	**Rolls**								
G203993A	ex - 50 x 50 mm	m	0.25	4.25	-	1.47	5.72	6.29	0.781
G203993B	ex - 50 x 75 mm	m	0.27	4.58	-	1.92	6.50	7.15	1.106
G2041	**Grounds and battens; treated sawn softwood, grade GS; basic sizes**								
G204102	**Open spaced grounds and battens**								
G204102A	13 x 38 mm; 300 mm centres one way	m²	0.38	6.45	-	0.83	7.28	8.01	0.484
G204102B	13 x 38 mm; 450 centres one way	m²	0.29	4.92	-	0.57	5.49	6.04	0.341
G204102C	13 x 38 mm; 600 centres one way	m²	0.24	4.08	-	0.41	4.49	4.94	0.242
G204102D	13 x 38 mm; 900 centres one way	m²	0.19	3.23	-	0.29	3.52	3.87	0.171
G204102E	13 x 38 mm; 300 mm centres both ways	m²	0.71	12.06	-	1.68	13.74	15.11	0.996
G204102F	13 x 38 mm; 450 mm centres both ways	m²	0.52	8.83	-	1.11	9.94	10.93	0.653
G204102G	13 x 38 mm; 600 mm centres both ways	m²	0.43	7.30	-	0.83	8.13	8.94	0.484
G204102H	13 x 38 mm; 900 mm centres both ways	m²	0.34	5.77	-	0.57	6.34	6.97	0.342
G204102I	25 x 38 mm; 300 mm centres one way	m²	0.45	7.64	-	1.32	8.96	9.86	0.879
G204102J	25 x 38 mm; 450 mm centres one way	m²	0.33	5.60	-	0.90	6.50	7.15	0.604
G204102K	25 x 38 mm; 600 mm centres one way	m²	0.28	4.75	-	0.66	5.41	5.95	0.440
G204102L	25 x 38 mm; 900 mm centres one way	m²	0.22	3.74	-	0.45	4.19	4.61	0.303
G204102M	25 x 38 mm; 300 mm centres both ways	m²	0.85	14.43	-	2.66	17.09	18.80	1.787
G204102N	25 x 38 mm; 450 mm centres both ways	m²	0.62	10.53	-	1.76	12.29	13.52	1.180
G204102O	25 x 38 mm; 600 mm centres both ways	m²	0.50	8.49	-	1.32	9.81	10.79	0.879
G204102P	25 x 38 mm; 900 mm centres both ways	m²	0.38	6.45	-	0.90	7.35	8.09	0.607
G204102Q	38 x 50 mm; 300 mm centres one way	m²	0.49	8.32	-	2.65	10.97	12.07	1.702
G204102R	38 x 50 mm; 450 mm centres one way	m²	0.36	6.11	-	1.78	7.89	8.68	1.152

Major Works 2011		Unit	Labour Hours	Labour Net	Plant Net	Materials Net	Unit Net	Unit with 10%	CO$_2$
				£	£	£	£	£	Kg
G20	**G20: CARPENTRY, TIMBER FRAMING AND FIRST FIXING**								
G2041	**Grounds and battens; treated sawn softwood, grade GS; basic sizes**								
G204102	**Open spaced grounds and battens**								
G204102S	38 x 50 mm; 600 mm centres one way	m^2	0.29	4.92	-	1.32	6.24	6.86	0.851
G204102T	38 x 50 mm; 900 mm centres one way	m^2	0.23	3.91	-	0.89	4.80	5.28	0.578
G204102U	38 x 50 mm; 300 mm centres both ways	m^2	0.92	15.62	-	5.32	20.94	23.03	3.432
G204102V	38 x 50 mm; 450 mm centres both ways	m^2	0.66	11.21	-	3.53	14.74	16.21	2.275
G204102W	38 x 50 mm; 600 mm centres both ways	m^2	0.54	9.17	-	2.65	11.82	13.00	1.702
G204102X	38 x 50 mm; 900 mm centres both ways	m^2	0.41	6.96	-	1.79	8.75	9.63	1.156
G204110	**Individual grounds and battens**								
G204110A	13 x 25 mm	m	0.08	1.36	-	0.17	1.53	1.68	0.113
G204110B	13 x 38 mm	m	0.08	1.36	-	0.26	1.62	1.78	0.156
G204110C	13 x 50 mm	m	0.08	1.36	-	0.31	1.67	1.84	0.197
G204110D	19 x 38 mm	m	0.09	1.53	-	0.31	1.84	2.02	0.216
G204110E	19 x 50 mm	m	0.09	1.53	-	0.41	1.94	2.13	0.275
G204110G	25 x 25 mm	m	0.10	1.70	-	0.31	2.01	2.21	1.302
G204110H	25 x 38 mm	m	0.10	1.70	-	0.41	2.11	2.32	0.275
G204110I	25 x 50 mm	m	0.10	1.70	-	0.49	2.19	2.41	0.354
G204110J	38 x 50 mm	m	0.11	1.87	-	0.81	2.68	2.95	0.522
G204110K	50 x 50 mm	m	0.13	2.21	-	0.88	3.09	3.40	0.678
G2043	**Framework; treated sawn softwood, grade GS; basic sizes**								
G204302	**Framework to receive boarded finish**								
G204302A	19 x 38 mm; 300 mm centres both ways	m^2	0.75	12.73	-	2.03	14.76	16.24	1.395
G204302B	25 x 50 mm; 300 mm centres both ways	m^2	0.83	14.09	-	3.22	17.31	19.04	2.312
G204302C	50 x 50 mm; 300 mm centres both ways	m^2	1.08	18.34	-	5.81	24.15	26.57	4.475
G204302D	50 x 75 mm; 450 mm centres both ways	m^2	0.72	12.23	-	5.69	17.92	19.71	4.419
G204303	**Framework around structural metalwork**								
G204303A	50 x 50 mm horizontally at 450 mm centres and 38 x 38 mm vertically at 600 mm centres	m^2	1.30	22.07	-	2.94	25.01	27.51	2.152
G204303B	50 x 75 mm horizontally at 450 mm centres and 50 x 50 mm vertically at 600 mm centres	m^2	1.36	23.09	-	4.30	27.39	30.13	3.330
G204310	**Framework to receive pipe casings and the like; 25 x 38 mm vertically; 25 x 25 mm horizontally at 450 mm centres**								
G204310A	one sided; not exceeding 150 mm wide	m	0.40	6.79	-	0.94	7.73	8.50	1.015
G204310B	one sided; 150 - 300 mm wide	m	0.43	7.30	-	1.03	8.33	9.16	1.440
G204310C	two sided; 150 - 300 mm girth	m	0.54	9.17	-	1.44	10.61	11.67	1.715
G204310D	two sided; 300 - 450 mm girth	m	0.57	9.68	-	1.57	11.25	12.38	2.180
G204310E	two sided; 450 - 600 mm girth	m	0.61	10.36	-	1.66	12.02	13.22	2.616
G204310F	three sided; 300 - 450 mm girth	m	0.68	11.55	-	1.97	13.52	14.87	2.455
G204310G	three sided; 450 - 600 mm girth	m	0.71	12.06	-	2.07	14.13	15.54	2.891
G204310H	three sided; 600 - 900 mm girth	m	0.78	13.24	-	2.29	15.53	17.08	3.781
G2051	**Eaves, verges, soffits, fascias, barge boards or the like**								
G205181	**Wrought softwood cross-tongued boarding; basic sizes**								
G205181A	16 mm thick; not exceeding 150 mm wide	m	0.11	1.87	-	2.57	4.44	4.88	0.702
G205181B	16 mm thick; 150 - 300 mm wide	m	0.15	2.55	-	4.98	7.53	8.28	1.363
G205181C	16 mm thick; 300 - 450 mm wide	m	0.19	3.23	-	7.55	10.78	11.86	2.065

Major Works 2011		Unit	Labour Hours	Labour Net	Plant Net	Materials Net	Unit Net	Unit with 10%	CO$_2$
				£	£	£	£	£	Kg
G20	**G20: CARPENTRY, TIMBER FRAMING AND FIRST FIXING**								
G2051	**Eaves, verges, soffits, fascias, barge boards or the like**								
G205181	**Wrought softwood cross-tongued boarding; basic sizes**								
G205181D	16 mm thick; 450 - 600 mm wide	m	0.22	3.74	-	9.79	13.53	14.88	2.659
G205181E	19 mm thick; not exceeding 150 mm wide	m	0.12	2.04	-	2.74	4.78	5.26	0.828
G205181F	19 mm thick; 150 - 300 mm wide	m	0.16	2.72	-	5.31	8.03	8.83	1.609
G205181G	19 mm thick; 300 - 450 mm wide	m	0.20	3.40	-	8.05	11.45	12.60	2.436
G205181H	19 mm thick; 450 - 600 mm wide	m	0.23	3.91	-	10.44	14.35	15.79	3.142
G205181I	25 mm thick; not exceeding 150 mm wide	m	0.13	2.21	-	3.08	5.29	5.82	1.080
G205181J	25 mm thick; 150 - 300 mm wide	m	0.17	2.89	-	5.97	8.86	9.75	2.099
G205181K	25 mm thick; 300 - 450 mm wide	m	0.21	3.57	-	9.05	12.62	13.88	3.179
G205181L	25 mm thick; 450 - 600 mm wide	m	0.24	4.08	-	11.74	15.82	17.40	4.107
G205182	**Wrought softwood tongued and grooved and V-jointed one side matchboarding; basic sizes**								
G205182A	13 mm thick; not exceeding 150 mm wide	m	0.15	2.55	-	1.15	3.70	4.07	0.604
G205182B	13 mm thick; 150 - 300 mm wide	m	0.30	5.09	-	2.24	7.33	8.06	1.175
G205182C	13 mm thick; 300 - 450 mm wide	m	0.40	6.79	-	3.39	10.18	11.20	1.779
G205182D	13 mm thick; 450 - 600 mm thick	m	0.55	9.34	-	4.39	13.73	15.10	2.290
G205182E	19 mm thick; not exceeding 150 mm wide	m	0.15	2.55	-	2.00	4.55	5.01	0.856
G205182F	19 mm thick; 150 - 300 mm wide	m	0.30	5.09	-	3.88	8.97	9.87	1.665
G205182G	19 mm thick; 300 - 450 mm wide	m	0.40	6.79	-	5.88	12.67	13.94	2.521
G205182H	19 mm thick; 450 - 600 mm wide	m	0.55	9.34	-	7.63	16.97	18.67	3.255
G205183	**Marine plywood; BS 1088**								
G205183A	12 mm thick; not exceeding 150 mm wide	m	0.11	1.87	-	2.18	4.05	4.46	0.921
G205183B	12 mm thick; 150 - 300 mm wide	m	0.15	2.55	-	4.23	6.78	7.46	1.789
G205183C	12 mm thick; 300 - 450 mm wide	m	0.19	3.23	-	6.41	9.64	10.60	2.709
G205183D	12 mm thick; 450 - 600 mm wide	m	0.22	3.74	-	8.31	12.05	13.26	3.497
G205183I	18 mm thick; not exceeding 150 mm wide	m	0.12	2.04	-	3.19	5.23	5.75	1.367
G205183J	18 mm thick; 150 - 300 mm wide	m	0.16	2.72	-	6.19	8.91	9.80	2.655
G205183K	18 mm thick; 300 - 450 mm wide	m	0.20	3.40	-	9.38	12.78	14.06	4.021
G205183L	18 mm thick; 450 - 600 mm wide	m	0.23	3.91	-	12.17	16.08	17.69	5.202
G205183M	25 mm thick; not exceeding 150 mm wide	m	0.13	2.21	-	4.77	6.98	7.68	1.887
G205183N	25 mm thick; 150 - 300 mm wide	m	0.17	2.89	-	9.26	12.15	13.37	3.665
G205183O	25 mm thick; 300 - 450 mm wide	m	0.21	3.57	-	14.03	17.60	19.36	5.552
G205183P	25 mm thick; 450 - 600 mm wide	m	0.24	4.08	-	18.21	22.29	24.52	7.193
G205186	**Non-asbestos flameproof class 1 boarding; BS 476**								
G205186A	6 mm thick; not exceeding 150 mm wide	m	0.25	4.25	-	2.28	6.53	7.18	0.501
G205186B	6 mm thick; 150 - 300 mm wide	m	0.28	4.75	-	4.31	9.06	9.97	0.868
G205186C	6 mm thick; 300 - 450 mm wide	m	0.35	5.94	-	6.51	12.45	13.70	1.303
G205186D	6 mm thick; 450 - 600 mm wide	m	0.38	6.45	-	8.41	14.86	16.35	1.647
G205186E	9 mm thick; not exceeding 150 mm wide	m	0.25	4.25	-	3.40	7.65	8.42	0.696
G205186F	9 mm thick; 150 - 300 mm wide	m	0.28	4.75	-	6.48	11.23	12.35	1.247
G205186G	9 mm thick; 300 - 450 mm wide	m	0.35	5.94	-	9.80	15.74	17.31	1.877
G205186H	9 mm thick; 450 - 600 mm wide	m	0.38	6.45	-	12.69	19.14	21.05	2.393
G205186I	12 mm thick; not exceeding 150 mm wide	m	0.25	4.25	-	4.46	8.71	9.58	0.891
G205186J	12 mm thick; 150 - 300 mm wide	m	0.28	4.75	-	8.54	13.29	14.62	1.626
G205186K	12 mm thick; 300 - 450 mm wide	m	0.35	5.94	-	12.93	18.87	20.76	2.450
G205186L	12 mm thick; 450 - 600 mm wide	m	0.38	6.45	-	16.76	23.21	25.53	3.139
G2067	**Cleats, sprockets or the like**								
G206741	**Treated sawn softwood; grade GS; basic sizes**								
G206741A	ex - 38 x 100 x 200 mm long	Nr	0.12	2.04	-	0.17	2.21	2.43	0.132
G206741B	ex - 38 x 150 x 300 mm long	Nr	0.16	2.72	-	0.33	3.05	3.36	0.254
G206741C	ex - 50 x 100 x 300 mm long	Nr	0.16	2.72	-	0.27	2.99	3.29	0.226
G206741D	ex - 50 x 150 x 400 mm long	Nr	0.20	3.40	-	0.48	3.88	4.27	0.418
G206741E	ex - 75 x 150 x 300 mm long	Nr	0.20	3.40	-	0.61	4.01	4.41	0.474
G206741F	ex - 75 x 150 x 450 mm long	Nr	0.22	3.74	-	0.90	4.64	5.10	0.697
G206741G	ex - 100 x 200 x 400 mm long	Nr	0.23	3.91	-	1.42	5.33	5.86	1.068
G206741H	ex - 100 x 200 x 600 mm long	Nr	0.25	4.25	-	2.15	6.40	7.04	1.612

Major Works 2011		Unit	Labour Hours	Labour Net	Plant Net	Materials Net	Unit Net	Unit with 10%	CO$_2$
				£	£	£	£	£	Kg
G20	**G20: CARPENTRY, TIMBER FRAMING AND FIRST FIXING**								
G2071	**Finished surfaces on sawn items**								
G207102	**Hand labours**								
G207102A	wrought face; not exceeding 150 mm wide	m	0.08	1.36	-	-	1.36	1.50	-
G207102B	wrought face; 150 - 300 mm wide	m	0.12	2.04	-	-	2.04	2.24	-
G207102C	wrought face; over 300 mm wide	m	0.33	5.60	-	-	5.60	6.16	-
G207102D	rounds	m	0.15	2.55	-	-	2.55	2.81	-
G207102E	rebates	m	0.18	3.06	-	-	3.06	3.37	-
G207102F	tongues	m	0.25	4.25	-	-	4.25	4.68	-
G207102G	grooves	m	0.18	3.06	-	-	3.06	3.37	-
G207102H	chamfers	m	0.13	2.21	-	-	2.21	2.43	-
G207102I	throats	m	0.18	3.06	-	-	3.06	3.37	-
G207102J	mouldings; not exceeding 50 mm girth	m	0.20	3.40	-	-	3.40	3.74	-
G207102K	mouldings; 50 - 100 mm girth	m	0.32	5.43	-	-	5.43	5.97	-
G207102L	mouldings; 100 - 150 mm girth	m	0.45	7.64	-	-	7.64	8.40	-
G2081	**Straps and frame cramps**								
G208107	**Galvanised mild steel fish-tail frame cramps; fixing to woodwork and masonry**								
G208107A	200 x 25 x 2 mm	Nr	0.11	1.87	-	0.58	2.45	2.70	0.300
G208107B	250 x 25 x 2 mm	Nr	0.11	1.87	-	0.61	2.48	2.73	0.358
G208108	**30 x 2.5 mm BAT galvanised mild steel restraint straps; fixing to woodwork**								
G208108A	600 mm long; straight	Nr	0.08	1.36	-	1.43	2.79	3.07	1.043
G208108B	800 mm long; straight	Nr	0.08	1.36	-	1.80	3.16	3.48	1.381
G208108C	1000 mm long; straight	Nr	0.10	1.70	-	1.98	3.68	4.05	1.720
G208108D	1200 mm long; straight	Nr	0.10	1.70	-	2.22	3.92	4.31	2.058
G208108E	1600 mm long; straight	Nr	0.12	2.04	-	3.03	5.07	5.58	2.763
G208108F	600 mm long; straight; once twisted	Nr	0.08	1.36	-	1.10	2.46	2.71	1.043
G208108G	800 mm long; straight; once twisted	Nr	0.08	1.36	-	1.57	2.93	3.22	1.381
G208108H	1000 mm long; straight; once twisted	Nr	0.10	1.70	-	1.96	3.66	4.03	1.720
G208108I	1200 mm long; straight; once twisted	Nr	0.10	1.70	-	2.35	4.05	4.46	2.058
G208108J	1600 mm long; straight; once twisted	Nr	0.12	2.04	-	3.15	5.19	5.71	2.763
G208108K	600 mm long; once bent	Nr	0.08	1.36	-	1.20	2.56	2.82	1.043
G208108L	800 mm long; once bent	Nr	0.08	1.36	-	1.65	3.01	3.31	1.381
G208108M	1000 mm long; once bent	Nr	0.10	1.70	-	2.04	3.74	4.11	1.720
G208108N	1200 mm long; once bent	Nr	0.10	1.70	-	2.40	4.10	4.51	2.058
G208108O	1600 mm long; once bent	Nr	0.12	2.04	-	3.24	5.28	5.81	2.763
G208108P	600 mm long; once bent; once twisted	Nr	0.08	1.36	-	1.29	2.65	2.92	1.043
G208108Q	800 mm long; once bent; once twisted	Nr	0.08	1.36	-	1.74	3.10	3.41	1.381
G208108R	1000 mm long; once bent; once twisted	Nr	0.10	1.70	-	2.11	3.81	4.19	1.720
G208108S	1200 mm long; once bent; once twisted	Nr	0.10	1.70	-	2.47	4.17	4.59	2.058
G208108T	1600 mm long; once bent; once twisted	Nr	0.12	2.04	-	3.35	5.39	5.93	2.763
G208109	**30 x 5 mm BAT galvanised mild steel restraint straps; fixing to woodwork and masonry**								
G208109A	700 mm long; once bent	Nr	0.20	3.40	-	2.63	6.03	6.63	2.837
G208109B	800 mm long; once bent	Nr	0.25	4.25	-	3.03	7.28	8.01	3.214
G208109C	1000 mm long; once bent	Nr	0.30	5.09	-	3.73	8.82	9.70	3.591
G208109D	1200 mm long; once bent	Nr	0.30	5.09	-	4.40	9.49	10.44	4.606
G208109E	1300 mm long; once bent	Nr	0.36	6.11	-	4.42	10.53	11.58	4.983
G208109F	1500 mm long; once bent	Nr	0.36	6.11	-	5.03	11.14	12.25	5.660
G208109G	1700 mm long; once bent	Nr	0.42	7.13	-	5.82	12.95	14.25	6.375
G2083	**BAT SPW galvanised joist hangers; building into masonry**								
G208312	**Type S; joist size**								
G208312A	38 x 100 mm	Nr	0.03	1.26	-	1.60	2.86	3.15	0.629
G208312B	38 x 125 mm	Nr	0.03	1.26	-	1.64	2.90	3.19	0.787

Structural & Carcassing

		Unit	Labour Hours	Labour Net £	Plant Net £	Materials Net £	Unit Net £	Unit with 10% £	CO₂ Kg
G20	**G20: CARPENTRY, TIMBER FRAMING AND FIRST FIXING**								
G2083	**BAT SPW galvanised joist hangers; building into masonry**								
G208312	**Type S; joist size**								
G208312C	38 x 150 mm	Nr	0.03	1.26	-	1.64	2.90	3.19	0.944
G208312D	38 x 175 mm	Nr	0.03	1.26	-	1.76	3.02	3.32	1.102
G208312E	38 x 200 mm	Nr	0.03	1.26	-	1.88	3.14	3.45	1.259
G208312F	38 x 225 mm	Nr	0.03	1.26	-	2.23	3.49	3.84	1.417
G208312G	38 x 250 mm	Nr	0.03	1.26	-	2.36	3.62	3.98	1.573
G208312H	50 x 100 mm	Nr	0.03	1.26	-	1.40	2.66	2.93	0.745
G208312I	50 x 125 mm	Nr	0.03	1.26	-	1.40	2.66	2.93	0.902
G208312J	50 x 150 mm	Nr	0.03	1.26	-	1.53	2.79	3.07	1.060
G208312K	50 x 175 mm	Nr	0.03	1.26	-	1.53	2.79	3.07	1.218
G208312L	50 x 200 mm	Nr	0.03	1.26	-	1.64	2.90	3.19	1.375
G208312M	50 x 225 mm	Nr	0.03	1.26	-	1.88	3.14	3.45	1.532
G208312N	50 x 250 mm	Nr	0.03	1.26	-	2.10	3.36	3.70	1.689
G208312O	63 x 100 mm	Nr	0.03	1.26	-	1.64	2.90	3.19	0.861
G208312P	63 x 125 mm	Nr	0.03	1.26	-	1.71	2.97	3.27	1.018
G208312Q	63 x 150 mm	Nr	0.03	1.26	-	1.88	3.14	3.45	1.176
G208312R	63 x 175 mm	Nr	0.03	1.26	-	2.01	3.27	3.60	1.333
G208312S	63 x 200 mm	Nr	0.03	1.26	-	2.01	3.27	3.60	1.490
G208312T	63 x 225 mm	Nr	0.03	1.26	-	2.10	3.36	3.70	1.647
G208312U	63 x 250 mm	Nr	0.03	1.26	-	2.23	3.49	3.84	1.805
G208312V	75 x 100 mm	Nr	0.03	1.26	-	1.70	2.96	3.26	1.185
G208312W	75 x 125 mm	Nr	0.03	1.26	-	2.01	3.27	3.60	1.301
G208312X	75 x 150 mm	Nr	0.03	1.26	-	2.19	3.45	3.80	1.417
G208312Y	75 x 175 mm	Nr	0.03	1.26	-	2.19	3.45	3.80	1.532
G208312Z	75 x 200 mm	Nr	0.03	1.26	-	2.23	3.49	3.84	1.647
G208313	**Type S; joist size**								
G208313A	75 x 225 mm	Nr	0.03	1.26	-	2.29	3.55	3.91	1.763
G208313B	75 x 250 mm	Nr	0.03	1.26	-	2.40	3.66	4.03	1.879
G208313C	100 x 100 mm	Nr	0.04	2.01	-	2.23	4.24	4.66	1.301
G208313D	100 x 125 mm	Nr	0.04	2.01	-	2.29	4.30	4.73	1.417
G208313E	100 x 150 mm	Nr	0.04	2.01	-	2.36	4.37	4.81	1.532
G208313F	100 x 175 mm	Nr	0.04	2.01	-	2.47	4.48	4.93	1.647
G208313G	100 x 200 mm	Nr	0.04	2.01	-	2.53	4.54	4.99	1.763
G208313H	100 x 225 mm	Nr	0.04	2.01	-	2.64	4.65	5.12	1.879
G208313I	100 x 250 mm	Nr	0.04	2.01	-	2.76	4.77	5.25	1.995
G208314	**Type ST; joist size**								
G208314A	38 x 100 mm	Nr	0.03	1.26	-	3.23	4.49	4.94	2.332
G208314B	38 x 125 mm	Nr	0.03	1.26	-	3.29	4.55	5.01	2.553
G208314C	38 x 150 mm	Nr	0.03	1.26	-	3.29	4.55	5.01	2.775
G208314D	38 x 175 mm	Nr	0.03	1.26	-	3.46	4.72	5.19	2.996
G208314E	38 x 200 mm	Nr	0.03	1.26	-	3.75	5.01	5.51	3.219
G208314F	38 x 225 mm	Nr	0.03	1.26	-	3.99	5.25	5.78	3.440
G208314G	50 x 100 mm	Nr	0.03	1.26	-	3.23	4.49	4.94	2.553
G208314H	50 x 125 mm	Nr	0.03	1.26	-	3.29	4.55	5.01	2.775
G208314I	50 x 150 mm	Nr	0.03	1.26	-	3.29	4.55	5.01	2.996
G208314J	50 x 175 mm	Nr	0.03	1.26	-	3.46	4.72	5.19	3.219
G208314K	50 x 200 mm	Nr	0.03	1.26	-	3.75	5.01	5.51	3.440
G208314L	50 x 225 mm	Nr	0.03	1.26	-	3.99	5.25	5.78	3.661
G208314M	50 x 250 mm	Nr	0.03	1.26	-	4.99	6.25	6.88	3.883
G208314N	63 x 100 mm	Nr	0.03	1.26	-	3.59	4.85	5.34	2.775
G208314O	63 x 125 mm	Nr	0.03	1.26	-	3.65	4.91	5.40	2.775
G208314P	63 x 150 mm	Nr	0.03	1.26	-	3.65	4.91	5.40	2.996
G208314Q	63 x 175 mm	Nr	0.03	1.26	-	3.82	5.08	5.59	3.219
G208314R	63 x 200 mm	Nr	0.03	1.26	-	4.12	5.38	5.92	3.440
G208314S	63 x 225 mm	Nr	0.03	1.26	-	4.35	5.61	6.17	3.661
G208314T	63 x 250 mm	Nr	0.03	1.26	-	5.35	6.61	7.27	3.883
G208314U	75 x 100 mm	Nr	0.03	1.26	-	4.17	5.43	5.97	3.267
G208314V	75 x 125 mm	Nr	0.03	1.26	-	4.23	5.49	6.04	3.488
G208314W	75 x 150 mm	Nr	0.03	1.26	-	4.23	5.49	6.04	3.709
G208314X	75 x 175 mm	Nr	0.03	1.26	-	4.40	5.66	6.23	3.931
G208314Y	75 x 200 mm	Nr	0.03	1.26	-	4.70	5.96	6.56	4.152
G208315	**Type ST; joist size**								
G208315A	75 x 225 mm	Nr	0.03	1.26	-	4.93	6.19	6.81	4.375
G208315B	75 x 250 mm	Nr	0.03	1.26	-	5.81	7.07	7.78	4.596
G208315C	100 x 100 mm	Nr	0.04	2.01	-	4.76	6.77	7.45	3.497
G208315D	100 x 125 mm	Nr	0.04	2.01	-	4.84	6.85	7.54	3.719
G208315E	100 x 150 mm	Nr	0.04	2.01	-	4.84	6.85	7.54	3.941
G208315F	100 x 175 mm	Nr	0.04	2.01	-	4.99	7.00	7.70	4.163
G208315G	100 x 200 mm	Nr	0.04	2.01	-	5.30	7.31	8.04	4.384
G208315H	100 x 225 mm	Nr	0.04	2.01	-	5.52	7.53	8.28	4.605
G208315I	100 x 250 mm	Nr	0.04	2.01	-	6.40	8.41	9.25	4.827

Major Works 2011		Unit	Labour Hours	Labour Net	Plant Net	Materials Net	Unit Net	Unit with 10%	CO$_2$
				£	£	£	£	£	Kg
G20	**G20: CARPENTRY, TIMBER FRAMING AND FIRST FIXING**								
G2083	**BAT SPW galvanised joist hangers; building into masonry**								
G208316	**Type R; joist size**								
G208316A	38 x 100 mm	Nr	0.03	1.26	-	2.40	3.66	4.03	1.021
G208316B	38 x 125 mm	Nr	0.03	1.26	-	2.47	3.73	4.10	1.147
G208316C	38 x 150 mm	Nr	0.03	1.26	-	2.64	3.90	4.29	1.272
G208316D	38 x 175 mm	Nr	0.03	1.26	-	2.64	3.90	4.29	1.397
G208316E	38 x 200 mm	Nr	0.03	1.26	-	2.95	4.21	4.63	1.522
G208316F	38 x 225 mm	Nr	0.03	1.26	-	3.23	4.49	4.94	1.647
G208316G	38 x 250 mm	Nr	0.03	1.26	-	3.40	4.66	5.13	1.773
G208316H	50 x 100 mm	Nr	0.03	1.26	-	2.53	3.79	4.17	1.147
G208316I	50 x 125 mm	Nr	0.03	1.26	-	2.58	3.84	4.22	1.272
G208316J	50 x 150 mm	Nr	0.03	1.26	-	2.82	4.08	4.49	1.431
G208316K	50 x 175 mm	Nr	0.03	1.26	-	2.76	4.02	4.42	1.522
G208316L	50 x 200 mm	Nr	0.03	1.26	-	3.04	4.30	4.73	1.647
G208316M	50 x 225 mm	Nr	0.03	1.26	-	3.34	4.60	5.06	1.773
G208316N	50 x 250 mm	Nr	0.03	1.26	-	3.54	4.80	5.28	1.898
G208316O	63 x 100 mm	Nr	0.03	1.26	-	2.89	4.15	4.57	1.272
G208316P	63 x 125 mm	Nr	0.03	1.26	-	2.95	4.21	4.63	1.397
G208316Q	63 x 150 mm	Nr	0.03	1.26	-	3.12	4.38	4.82	1.522
G208316R	63 x 175 mm	Nr	0.03	1.26	-	3.12	4.38	4.82	1.647
G208316S	63 x 200 mm	Nr	0.03	1.26	-	3.40	4.66	5.13	1.773
G208316T	63 x 225 mm	Nr	0.03	1.26	-	3.69	4.95	5.45	1.898
G208316U	63 x 250 mm	Nr	0.03	1.26	-	3.88	5.14	5.65	2.023
G208316V	75 x 100 mm	Nr	0.03	1.26	-	3.34	4.60	5.06	1.647
G208316W	75 x 125 mm	Nr	0.03	1.26	-	3.40	4.66	5.13	1.773
G208316X	75 x 150 mm	Nr	0.03	1.26	-	3.59	4.85	5.34	1.898
G208316Y	75 x 175 mm	Nr	0.03	1.26	-	3.59	4.85	5.34	2.023
G208316Z	75 x 200 mm	Nr	0.03	1.26	-	3.88	5.14	5.65	2.148
G208317	**Type R; joist size**								
G208317A	75 x 225 mm	Nr	0.03	1.26	-	4.17	5.43	5.97	2.273
G208317B	75 x 250 mm	Nr	0.03	1.26	-	4.35	5.61	6.17	2.400
G208317C	100 x 100 mm	Nr	0.04	2.01	-	3.75	5.76	6.34	1.773
G208317D	100 x 125 mm	Nr	0.04	2.01	-	3.82	5.83	6.41	1.898
G208317E	100 x 150 mm	Nr	0.04	2.01	-	3.99	6.00	6.60	2.023
G208317F	100 x 175 mm	Nr	0.04	2.01	-	4.40	6.41	7.05	2.148
G208317G	100 x 200 mm	Nr	0.04	2.01	-	4.70	6.71	7.38	2.273
G208317H	100 x 225 mm	Nr	0.04	2.01	-	4.84	6.85	7.54	2.400
G208317I	100 x 250 mm	Nr	0.04	2.01	-	4.99	7.00	7.70	2.525
G2084	**BAT SPW joist hangers; fixing to masonry or concrete**								
G208419	**Type FF; joist width**								
G208419A	38 mm	Nr	0.35	5.94	-	1.09	7.03	7.73	0.860
G208419B	50 mm	Nr	0.35	5.94	-	1.09	7.03	7.73	1.093
G208419C	63 mm	Nr	0.35	5.94	-	1.18	7.12	7.83	2.901
G208419D	75 mm	Nr	0.35	5.94	-	1.18	7.12	7.83	2.901
G208419E	100 mm	Nr	0.35	5.94	-	1.24	7.18	7.90	2.901
G2085	**BAT truss clips; fixing to woodwork**								
G208531	**To suit truss width**								
G208531A	38 mm	Nr	0.15	2.55	-	0.67	3.22	3.54	0.198
G208531B	50 mm	Nr	0.15	2.55	-	0.72	3.27	3.60	0.198
G2091	**Dowels, bolts, water bars**								
G209102	**Galvanised mild steel dowels**								
G209102A	8 mm dia	m	0.30	5.09	-	3.12	8.21	9.03	1.116
G209102B	10 mm dia	m	0.30	5.09	-	3.56	8.65	9.52	1.744
G209102C	12 mm dia	m	0.30	5.09	-	3.96	9.05	9.96	2.511
G209102D	16 mm dia	m	0.30	5.09	-	5.23	10.32	11.35	4.464
G209103	**Black hexagon head bolts BS 4190 with nut and washer**								
G209103A	M10 x 50 mm	Nr	0.08	1.36	-	0.26	1.62	1.78	0.054
G209103B	M10 x 75 mm	Nr	0.08	1.36	-	0.30	1.66	1.83	0.081
G209103C	M10 x 100 mm	Nr	0.09	1.53	-	0.45	1.98	2.18	0.108
G209103D	M10 x 150 mm	Nr	0.09	1.53	-	0.95	2.48	2.73	0.162
G209103E	M12 x 100 mm	Nr	0.10	1.70	-	0.58	2.28	2.51	0.156
G209103F	M12 x 150 mm	Nr	0.10	1.70	-	1.03	2.73	3.00	0.233
G209103G	M12 x 200 mm	Nr	0.11	1.87	-	1.61	3.48	3.83	0.311
G209103H	M12 x 250 mm	Nr	0.11	1.87	-	1.84	3.71	4.08	0.388
G209103I	M12 x 300 mm	Nr	0.11	1.87	-	2.00	3.87	4.26	0.466
G209103J	M16 x 100 mm	Nr	0.11	1.87	-	0.94	2.81	3.09	0.276

Structural & Carcassing

Major Works 2011		Unit	Labour Hours	Labour Net	Plant Net	Materials Net	Unit Net	Unit with 10%	CO₂
				£	£	£	£	£	Kg
G20	**G20: CARPENTRY, TIMBER FRAMING AND FIRST FIXING**								
G2091	**Dowels, bolts, water bars**								
G209103	**Black hexagon head bolts BS 4190 with nut and washer**								
G209103K	M16 x 150 mm	Nr	0.12	2.04	-	1.49	3.53	3.88	0.414
G209103L	M16 x 200 mm	Nr	0.13	2.21	-	2.25	4.46	4.91	0.552
G209103M	M16 x 250 mm	Nr	0.13	2.21	-	3.30	5.51	6.06	0.690
G209103N	M16 x 300 mm	Nr	0.13	2.21	-	3.61	5.82	6.40	0.828
G209103O	M20 x 100 mm	Nr	0.13	2.21	-	1.68	3.89	4.28	0.432
G209103P	M20 x 150 mm	Nr	0.14	2.38	-	2.36	4.74	5.21	0.647
G209103Q	M20 x 200 mm	Nr	0.15	2.55	-	3.35	5.90	6.49	0.863
G209103R	M20 x 250 mm	Nr	0.15	2.55	-	3.82	6.37	7.01	1.078
G209103S	M20 x 300 mm	Nr	0.15	2.55	-	4.08	6.63	7.29	1.294
G209104	**Rawlbolt projecting expansion bolt with nut and washer; to masonry**								
G209104A	M10 15	Nr	0.17	2.89	-	2.20	5.09	5.60	0.016
G209104B	M10 30	Nr	0.17	2.89	-	2.31	5.20	5.72	0.032
G209104C	M10 60	Nr	0.17	2.89	-	2.40	5.29	5.82	0.065
G209104D	M12 15	Nr	0.20	3.40	-	3.34	6.74	7.41	0.024
G209104E	M12 30	Nr	0.20	3.40	-	3.58	6.98	7.68	0.046
G209104F	M12 75	Nr	0.20	3.40	-	4.47	7.87	8.66	0.116
G209104G	M16 15	Nr	0.23	3.91	-	7.14	11.05	12.16	0.041
G209104H	M16 35	Nr	0.23	3.91	-	8.55	12.46	13.71	0.097
G209104I	M16 75	Nr	0.23	3.91	-	9.07	12.98	14.28	0.207
G209104J	M20 15	Nr	0.27	4.58	-	12.06	16.64	18.30	0.065
G209104K	M20 30	Nr	0.27	4.58	-	13.02	17.60	19.36	0.130
G209104L	M20 100	Nr	0.27	4.58	-	14.83	19.41	21.35	0.432
G209105	**Rawlbolt loose expansion bolt; to concrete**								
G209105A	M6 10	Nr	0.16	2.72	-	1.49	4.21	4.63	0.004
G209105B	M6 25	Nr	0.16	2.72	-	1.50	4.22	4.64	0.009
G209105C	M6 40	Nr	0.16	2.72	-	1.62	4.34	4.77	0.015
G209105D	M8 10	Nr	0.20	3.40	-	1.69	5.09	5.60	0.007
G209105E	M8 25	Nr	0.20	3.40	-	1.74	5.14	5.65	0.017
G209105F	M8 40	Nr	0.20	3.40	-	1.85	5.25	5.78	0.028
G209105G	M10 10	Nr	0.25	4.25	-	2.19	6.44	7.08	0.010
G209105H	M10 25	Nr	0.25	4.25	-	2.26	6.51	7.16	0.027
G209105I	M10 50	Nr	0.25	4.25	-	2.36	6.61	7.27	0.053
G209105J	M10 75	Nr	0.25	4.25	-	2.45	6.70	7.37	0.081
G209105K	M12 10	Nr	0.30	5.09	-	3.23	8.32	9.15	0.015
G209105L	M12 25	Nr	0.30	5.09	-	3.61	8.70	9.57	0.039
G209105M	M12 40	Nr	0.30	5.09	-	3.74	8.83	9.71	0.061
G209105N	M12 60	Nr	0.30	5.09	-	3.97	9.06	9.97	0.092
G209105O	M16 15	Nr	0.35	5.94	-	7.23	13.17	14.49	0.041
G209105P	M16 30	Nr	0.35	5.94	-	8.47	14.41	15.85	0.082
G209105Q	M16 60	Nr	0.35	5.94	-	8.98	14.92	16.41	0.164
G209105R	M20 60	Nr	0.40	6.79	-	13.21	20.00	22.00	0.256
G209105S	M20 100	Nr	0.40	6.79	-	13.58	20.37	22.41	0.427
G209106	**Galvanised mild steel round toothed-plate connectors; BS 1579 Table 4**								
G209106A	38 mm dia; single sided	Nr	0.02	0.34	-	0.47	0.81	0.89	0.082
G209106B	51 mm dia; single sided	Nr	0.02	0.34	-	0.47	0.81	0.89	0.142
G209106C	64 mm dia; single sided	Nr	0.02	0.34	-	0.70	1.04	1.14	0.233
G209106D	76 mm dia; single sided	Nr	0.02	0.34	-	0.70	1.04	1.14	0.329
G209106E	38 mm dia; double sided	Nr	0.02	0.34	-	0.47	0.81	0.89	0.082
G209106F	51 mm dia; double sided	Nr	0.02	0.34	-	0.48	0.82	0.90	0.142
G209106G	64 mm dia; double sided	Nr	0.02	0.34	-	0.70	1.04	1.14	0.233
G209106H	76 mm dia; double sided	Nr	0.02	0.34	-	0.91	1.25	1.38	0.329
G209107	**Galvanised mild steel fish tailed frame cramps**								
G209107A	200 x 25 x 2 mm	Nr	0.11	1.87	-	0.58	2.45	2.70	0.300
G209107B	250 x 25 x 2 mm	Nr	0.11	1.87	-	0.61	2.48	2.73	0.358
G209108	**30 x 2.5 mm BAT galvanised mild steel restraint straps; fixing to wood work**								
G209108A	600 mm long; straight	Nr	0.08	1.36	-	1.43	2.79	3.07	1.043
G209108B	800 mm long; straight	Nr	0.08	1.36	-	1.80	3.16	3.48	1.381
G209108C	1000 mm long; straight	Nr	0.10	1.70	-	1.98	3.68	4.05	1.720
G209108D	1200 mm long; straight	Nr	0.10	1.70	-	2.22	3.92	4.31	2.058
G209108E	1600 mm long; straight	Nr	0.12	2.04	-	3.03	5.07	5.58	2.763

Major Works 2011		Unit	Labour Hours	Labour Net	Plant Net	Materials Net	Unit Net	Unit with 10%	CO₂
				£	£	£	£	£	Kg
G20	**G20: CARPENTRY, TIMBER FRAMING AND FIRST FIXING**								
G2091	**Dowels, bolts, water bars**								
G209108	**30 x 2.5 mm BAT galvanised mild steel restraint straps; fixing to wood work**								
G209108F	600 mm long; straight; once twisted	Nr	0.08	1.36	-	1.10	2.46	2.71	1.043
G209108G	800 mm long; straight; once twisted	Nr	0.08	1.36	-	1.57	2.93	3.22	1.381
G209108H	1000 mm long; straight; once twisted	Nr	0.10	1.70	-	1.96	3.66	4.03	1.720
G209108I	1200 mm long; straight; once twisted	Nr	0.10	1.70	-	2.35	4.05	4.46	2.058
G209108J	1600 mm long; straight; once twisted	Nr	0.12	2.04	-	3.15	5.19	5.71	2.763
G209108K	600 mm long; once bent	Nr	0.08	1.36	-	1.20	2.56	2.82	1.043
G209108L	800 mm long; once bent	Nr	0.08	1.36	-	1.65	3.01	3.31	1.381
G209108M	1000 mm long; once bent	Nr	0.10	1.70	-	2.04	3.74	4.11	1.720
G209108N	1200 mm long; once bent	Nr	0.10	1.70	-	2.40	4.10	4.51	2.058
G209108O	1600 mm long; once bent	Nr	0.12	2.04	-	3.24	5.28	5.81	2.763
G209108P	600 mm long; once bent; once twisted	Nr	0.08	1.36	-	1.29	2.65	2.92	1.043
G209108Q	800 mm long; once bent; once twisted	Nr	0.08	1.36	-	1.74	3.10	3.41	1.381
G209108R	1000 mm long; once bent; once twisted	Nr	0.10	1.70	-	2.11	3.81	4.19	1.720
G209108S	1200 mm long; once bent; once twisted	Nr	0.10	1.70	-	2.47	4.17	4.59	2.058
G209108T	1600 mm long; once bent; once twisted	Nr	0.12	2.04	-	3.35	5.39	5.93	2.763
G209109	**30 x 5 mm BAT galvanised mild steel restraint straps; fixing to woodwork and masonry**								
G209109A	700 mm long; once bent	Nr	0.20	3.40	-	2.63	6.03	6.63	2.837
G209109B	800 mm long; once bent	Nr	0.25	4.25	-	3.03	7.28	8.01	3.214
G209109C	1000 mm long; once bent	Nr	0.30	5.09	-	3.73	8.82	9.70	3.591
G209109D	1200 mm long; once bent	Nr	0.30	5.09	-	4.40	9.49	10.44	4.606
G209109E	1300 mm long; once bent	Nr	0.36	6.11	-	4.42	10.53	11.58	4.983
G209109F	1500 mm long; once bent	Nr	0.36	6.11	-	5.03	11.14	12.25	5.660
G209109G	1700 mm long; once bent	Nr	0.42	7.13	-	5.82	12.95	14.25	6.375
G209110	**Galvanised mild steel water bars**								
G209110A	25 x 3 mm	m	0.20	3.40	-	5.85	9.25	10.18	1.733
G209110B	40 x 3 mm	m	0.20	3.40	-	6.13	9.53	10.48	2.772
G209110C	40 x 6 mm	m	0.20	3.40	-	9.29	12.69	13.96	5.543
G209110D	50 x 6 mm	m	0.20	3.40	-	12.88	16.28	17.91	6.929
G2097	**Additional fixings for woodwork**								
G209711	**Drilling and plugging concrete; plastic plugs**								
G209711A	No.8; isolated	Nr	0.08	1.36	-	0.01	1.37	1.51	0.004
G209711B	No.8; 300 mm centres	m	0.28	4.75	-	0.03	4.78	5.26	0.013
G209711C	No.8; 450 mm centres	m	0.19	3.23	-	0.02	3.25	3.58	0.009
G209711D	No.8; 600 mm centres	m	0.14	2.38	-	0.02	2.40	2.64	0.009
G209711E	No.8; 750 mm centres	m	0.11	1.87	-	0.01	1.88	2.07	0.004
G209711F	No.8; 1200 mm centres	m	0.07	1.19	-	0.01	1.20	1.32	0.004
G209711G	No.10; isolated	Nr	0.10	1.70	-	0.01	1.71	1.88	0.007
G209711H	No.10; 300 mm centres	m	0.33	5.60	-	0.04	5.64	6.20	0.021
G209711I	No.10; 450 mm centres	m	0.22	3.74	-	0.03	3.77	4.15	0.014
G209711J	No.10; 600 mm centres	m	0.17	2.89	-	0.03	2.92	3.21	0.014
G209711K	No.10; 750 mm centres	m	0.13	2.21	-	0.01	2.22	2.44	0.007
G209711L	No.10; 1200 mm centres	m	0.08	1.36	-	0.01	1.37	1.51	0.007
G209711M	No.12; isolated	Nr	0.11	1.87	-	0.02	1.89	2.08	0.010
G209711N	No.12; 300 mm centres	m	0.38	6.45	-	0.07	6.52	7.17	0.030
G209711O	No.12; 450 mm centres	m	0.26	4.41	-	0.05	4.46	4.91	0.020
G209711P	No.12; 600 mm centres	m	0.19	3.23	-	0.05	3.28	3.61	0.020
G209711Q	No.12; 750 mm centres	m	0.16	2.72	-	0.02	2.74	3.01	0.010
G209711R	No.12; 1200 mm centres	m	0.10	1.70	-	0.02	1.72	1.89	0.010
G209712	**Drilling and plugging masonry; plastic plugs**								
G209712A	No.8; isolated	Nr	0.03	0.51	-	0.01	0.52	0.57	0.004
G209712B	No.8; 300 mm centres	m	0.10	1.70	-	0.03	1.73	1.90	0.013
G209712C	No.8; 450 mm centres	m	0.07	1.19	-	0.02	1.21	1.33	0.009
G209712D	No.8; 600 mm centres	m	0.06	1.02	-	0.02	1.04	1.14	0.009

Major Works 2011		Unit	Labour Hours	Labour Net	Plant Net	Materials Net	Unit Net	Unit with 10%	CO₂
				£	£	£	£	£	Kg
G20	**G20: CARPENTRY, TIMBER FRAMING AND FIRST FIXING**								
G2097	**Additional fixings for woodwork**								
G209712	**Drilling and plugging masonry; plastic plugs**								
G209712E	No.8; 750 mm centres	m	0.04	0.68	-	0.01	0.69	0.76	0.004
G209712F	No.8; 1200 mm centres	m	0.03	0.51	-	0.01	0.52	0.57	0.004
G209712G	No.10; isolated	Nr	0.05	0.85	-	0.01	0.86	0.95	0.007
G209712H	No.10; 300 mm centres	m	0.17	2.89	-	0.04	2.93	3.22	0.021
G209712I	No.10; 450 mm centres	m	0.11	1.87	-	0.03	1.90	2.09	0.014
G209712J	No.10; 600 mm centres	m	0.08	1.36	-	0.03	1.39	1.53	0.014
G209712K	No.10; 750 mm centres	m	0.07	1.19	-	0.01	1.20	1.32	0.007
G209712L	No.10; 1200 mm centres	m	0.04	0.68	-	0.01	0.69	0.76	0.007
G209712M	No.12; isolated	Nr	0.06	1.02	-	0.02	1.04	1.14	0.010
G209712N	No.12; 300 mm centres	m	0.19	3.23	-	0.07	3.30	3.63	0.030
G209712O	No.12; 450 mm centres	m	0.13	2.21	-	0.05	2.26	2.49	0.020
G209712P	No.12; 600 mm centres	m	0.10	1.70	-	0.05	1.75	1.93	0.020
G209712Q	No.12; 750 mm centres	m	0.08	1.36	-	0.02	1.38	1.52	0.010
G209712R	No.12; 1200 mm centres	m	0.05	0.85	-	0.02	0.87	0.96	0.010
G209713	**Fixing with steel countersunk wood screws**								
G209713A	38 mm No.8; isolated	Nr	0.03	0.51	-	0.03	0.54	0.59	0.022
G209713B	38 mm No.8; 300 mm centres	m	0.11	1.87	-	0.08	1.95	2.15	0.067
G209713C	38 mm No.8; 450 mm centres	m	0.07	1.19	-	0.05	1.24	1.36	0.044
G209713D	38 mm No.8; 600 mm centres	m	0.06	1.02	-	0.05	1.07	1.18	0.044
G209713E	38 mm No.8; 750 mm centres	m	0.04	0.68	-	0.03	0.71	0.78	0.022
G209713F	38 mm No.8; 1200 mm centres	m	0.03	0.51	-	0.03	0.54	0.59	0.022
G209713G	50 mm No.8; isolated	Nr	0.03	0.51	-	0.01	0.52	0.57	0.035
G209713H	50 mm No.8; 300 mm centres	m	0.11	1.87	-	0.02	1.89	2.08	0.104
G209713I	50 mm No.8; 450 mm centres	m	0.07	1.19	-	0.01	1.20	1.32	0.069
G209713J	50 mm No.8; 600 mm centres	m	0.06	1.02	-	0.01	1.03	1.13	0.069
G209713K	50 mm No.8; 750 mm centres	m	0.04	0.68	-	0.01	0.69	0.76	0.035
G209713L	50 mm No.8; 1200 mm centres	m	0.03	0.51	-	0.01	0.52	0.57	0.035
G209713M	75 mm No.10; isolated	Nr	0.04	0.68	-	0.05	0.73	0.80	0.044
G209713N	75 mm No.10; 300 mm centres	m	0.13	2.21	-	0.16	2.37	2.61	0.131
G209713O	75 mm No.10; 450 mm centres	m	0.09	1.53	-	0.11	1.64	1.80	0.087
G209713P	75 mm No.10; 600 mm centres	m	0.07	1.19	-	0.11	1.30	1.43	0.087
G209713Q	75 mm No.10; 750 mm centres	m	0.05	0.85	-	0.05	0.90	0.99	0.044
G209713R	75 mm No.10; 1200 mm centres	m	0.03	0.51	-	0.05	0.56	0.62	0.044
G209713S	100 mm No.12; isolated	Nr	0.05	0.85	-	0.08	0.93	1.02	0.065
G209713T	100 mm No.12; 300 mm centres	m	0.17	2.89	-	0.25	3.14	3.45	0.195
G209713U	100 mm No.12; 450 mm centres	m	0.11	1.87	-	0.17	2.04	2.24	0.130
G209713V	100 mm No.12; 600 mm centres	m	0.08	1.36	-	0.17	1.53	1.68	0.130
G209713W	100 mm No.12; 750 mm centres	m	0.07	1.19	-	0.08	1.27	1.40	0.065
G209713X	100 mm No.12; 1200 mm centres	m	0.04	0.68	-	0.08	0.76	0.84	0.065

Cladding and Covering

Major Works 2011		Unit	Labour Hours	Labour Net	Plant Net	Materials Net	Unit Net	Unit with 10%	CO$_2$
				£	£	£	£	£	Kg
H10	**H10: PATENT GLAZING**								
H1010	**Patent glazing; aluminium alloy glazing bars 2400 mm long at 600 mm centres**								
H101010	**In roofing areas; single tier**								
H101010A	7 mm Georgian wired cast glass	m^2	1.69	107.23	-	57.88	165.11	181.62	52.176
H101010B	6 mm Georgian polished plate glass	m^2	1.93	122.51	-	110.00	232.51	255.76	48.843
H101020	**In roofing areas; multi-tier**								
H101020A	7 mm Georgian wired cast glass	m^2	1.69	107.23	-	105.70	212.93	234.22	75.513
H101020B	6 mm Georgian polished plate glass	m^2	1.93	122.51	-	209.94	332.45	365.70	68.845
H101030	**In vertical areas; single tier**								
H101030A	7 mm Georgian wired cast glass	m^2	2.01	127.60	-	57.88	185.48	204.03	52.176
H101030B	6 mm Georgian polished plate glass	m^2	2.25	142.94	-	110.00	252.94	278.23	48.843
H101040	**In vertical areas; multi-tier**								
H101040A	7 mm Georgian wired cast glass	m^2	2.01	127.60	-	105.70	233.30	256.63	75.513
H101040B	6 mm Georgian polished plate glass	m^2	2.25	142.94	-	209.94	352.88	388.17	68.845

Major Works 2011		Unit	Labour Hours	Labour Net	Plant Net	Materials Net	Unit Net	Unit with 10%	CO$_2$
				£	£	£	£	£	Kg
H11	**H11: CURTAIN WALLING**								
H1110	**Curtain walling system; extruded powder coated aluminium; insulated spandrel panels; double glazed vision panels and opening casement lights; fixed to supporting structure**								
H111010	**Flat vertical curtain walling in sections**								
H111010A	185 mm thick	m²	2.17	137.84	-	272.50	410.34	451.37	128.822
H111010B	250 mm thick	m²	3.69	234.83	-	347.75	582.58	640.84	160.908
H111012	**Flat sloping curtain walling in sections**								
H111012A	185 mm thick	m²	3.13	199.13	-	272.50	471.63	518.79	128.822
H111012B	250 mm thick	m²	4.09	260.35	-	347.75	608.10	668.91	160.908
H111013	**Curved vertical curtain walling in sections**								
H111013A	185 mm thick	m²	2.89	183.79	-	435.00	618.79	680.67	128.822
H111013B	250 mm thick	m²	3.69	234.83	-	552.50	787.33	866.06	160.908
H111014	**Curved sloping curtain walling in sections**								
H111014A	185 mm thick	m²	3.45	219.49	-	435.00	654.49	719.94	128.822
H111014B	250 mm thick	m²	4.09	260.35	-	552.50	812.85	894.14	160.908
H111015	**Extra over curtain walling for**								
H111015A	insulated spandrel panels; 185 mm thick	m	0.05	3.05	-	20.75	23.80	26.18	
H111015B	insulated spandrel panels; 250 mm thick	m	0.05	3.05	-	20.75	23.80	26.18	-
H111015E	insulated extruded aluminium channel 75 x 250 mm high	m	0.56	35.77	-	54.34	90.11	99.12	17.304
H111015F	insulated parapet flashing; vertical 600 mm girth	m	0.72	45.95	-	45.94	91.89	101.08	17.304
H111015G	bottom flashing; horizontal; 195 mm	m	0.48	30.61	-	31.50	62.11	68.32	17.304
H111015H	abutment to corner profile panel; vertical	m	0.35	22.46	-	-	22.46	24.71	
H111015K	abutment to metal composite panel cladding; vertical	m	0.35	22.46	-	-	22.46	24.71	-
H111015N	opening light; 1500 x 900 mm; 90 mm thick	Nr	1.04	66.38	-	357.50	423.88	466.27	81.917

Major Works 2011		Unit	Labour Hours	Labour Net £	Plant Net £	Materials Net £	Unit Net £	Unit with 10% £	CO₂ Kg
H20	**H20: RIGID SHEET CLADDING**								
H2021	**Marine plywood square edged boarding; BS1088**								
H202158	**Flat; firring pieces and bearers included**								
H202158A	18 mm thick	m²	0.85	14.43	-	23.73	38.16	41.98	11.704
H202158B	25 mm thick	m²	0.85	14.43	-	33.76	48.19	53.01	15.011
H202159	**Sloping; bearers included**								
H202159A	18 mm thick	m²	0.66	11.21	-	22.18	33.39	36.73	10.146
H202159B	25 mm thick	m²	0.66	11.21	-	32.21	43.42	47.76	13.453
H202160	**Vertical; bearers included**								
H202160A	18 mm thick	m²	0.81	13.75	-	22.01	35.76	39.34	9.791
H202160B	25 mm thick	m²	0.81	13.75	-	32.05	45.80	50.38	13.098
H2031	**Marine plywood tongued and grooved boarding; BS1088**								
H203162	**Flat; firring pieces and bearers included**								
H203162A	18 mm thick	m²	0.95	16.13	-	25.74	41.87	46.06	11.704
H203162B	25 mm thick	m²	0.95	16.13	-	36.78	52.91	58.20	15.011
H203163	**Sloping; bearers included**								
H203163A	18 mm thick	m²	0.76	12.90	-	24.19	37.09	40.80	10.146
H203163B	25 mm thick	m²	0.76	12.90	-	35.23	48.13	52.94	13.453
H203164	**Vertical; bearers included**								
H203164A	18 mm thick	m²	0.91	15.45	-	24.02	39.47	43.42	9.791
H203164B	25 mm thick	m²	0.91	15.45	-	35.06	50.51	55.56	13.098
H2041	**Roofing grade chipboard square edged boarding; BS 5669**								
H204166	**Flat; firring pieces and bearers included**								
H204166A	18 mm thick	m²	0.80	13.58	-	9.40	22.98	25.28	9.447
H204166B	22 mm thick	m²	0.80	13.58	-	8.19	21.77	23.95	10.836
H204167	**Sloping; bearers included**								
H204167A	18 mm thick	m²	0.61	10.36	-	7.85	18.21	20.03	7.889
H204167B	22 mm thick	m²	0.61	10.36	-	6.64	17.00	18.70	9.278
H204168	**Vertical; bearers included**								
H204168A	18 mm thick	m²	0.76	12.90	-	7.68	20.58	22.64	7.534
H204168B	22 mm thick	m²	0.76	12.90	-	6.47	19.37	21.31	8.923
H2051	**Roofing grade chipboard tongued and grooved boarding; BS 5669**								
H205170	**Flat; firring pieces and bearers included**								
H205170A	18 mm thick	m²	0.90	15.28	-	7.34	22.62	24.88	9.447
H205170B	22 mm thick	m²	0.90	15.28	-	8.37	23.65	26.02	10.836
H205171	**Sloping; bearers included**								
H205171A	18 mm thick	m²	0.71	12.06	-	5.78	17.84	19.62	7.889
H205171B	22 mm thick	m²	0.71	12.06	-	6.82	18.88	20.77	9.278
H205172	**Vertical; bearers included**								
H205172A	18 mm thick	m²	0.86	14.60	-	5.62	20.22	22.24	7.534
H205172B	22 mm thick	m²	0.86	14.60	-	6.65	21.25	23.38	8.923

Cladding & Covering

		Unit	Labour Hours	Labour Net £	Plant Net £	Materials Net £	Unit Net £	Unit with 10% £	CO$_2$ Kg
H21	**H21: TIMBER WEATHERBOARDING**								
H2110	**Shiplap boarding; wrought softwood; nominal 125 mm board face; fixing to timber backgrounds**								
H211010	**To walls**								
H211010A	19 mm thick; over 300 mm wide	m²	0.65	11.04	-	22.13	33.17	36.49	5.165
H211010B	19 mm thick; not exceeding 300 mm wide	m	0.24	4.08	-	6.64	10.72	11.79	1.552
H211010C	19 mm thick; in areas not exceeding 1.00 m²	Nr	0.80	13.58	-	22.15	35.73	39.30	5.193
H211010D	25 mm thick; over 300 mm wide	m²	0.70	11.89	-	14.01	25.90	28.49	6.724
H211010E	25 mm thick; not exceeding 300 mm wide	m	0.27	4.50	-	4.21	8.71	9.58	2.020
H211010F	25 mm thick; in areas not exceeding 1.00 m²	Nr	0.88	14.94	-	14.04	28.98	31.88	6.752
H2120	**Feather-edge boarding; sawn softwood; nominal 150 mm board face; fixing to timber backgrounds**								
H212010	**To walls**								
H212010A	14-7 mm thick; over 300 mm wide	m²	0.65	11.04	-	11.33	22.37	24.61	4.473
H212010B	14-7 mm thick; not exceeding 300 mm wide	m	0.24	4.08	-	3.40	7.48	8.23	1.345
H212010C	14-7 mm thick; in areas not exceeding 1.00 m²	Nr	0.80	13.58	-	11.35	24.93	27.42	4.501
H212010D	19-9 mm thick; over 300 mm wide	m²	0.70	11.89	-	18.79	30.68	33.75	5.974
H212010E	19-9 mm thick; not exceeding 300 mm wide	m	0.27	4.58	-	5.64	10.22	11.24	1.795
H212010F	19-9 mm thick; in areas not exceeding 1.00 m²	Nr	0.88	14.94	-	18.82	33.76	37.14	6.003

Major Works 2011		Unit	Labour Hours	Labour Net	Plant Net	Materials Net	Unit Net	Unit with 10%	CO$_2$
				£	£	£	£	£	Kg
H30	**H30: FIBRE CEMENT PROFILED SHEET CLADDING, COVERING AND SIDING**								
H3005	**Roof coverings**								
H300510	**Eternit 2000 asbestos free corrugated sheeting; sloping not exceeding 50 deg; fixing to timber members with drive screws**								
H300510A	Profile 3 natural finish	m^2	0.25	4.25	-	16.50	20.75	22.83	4.302
H300510F	Profile 6R natural finish	m^2	0.28	4.75	-	19.02	23.77	26.15	4.302
H300510G	Profile 6R painted finish	m^2	0.28	4.75	-	22.54	27.29	30.02	4.302
H300510K	Extra for 60 mm glassfibre infill insulation and lining panel	m^2	0.50	8.49	-	36.11	44.60	49.06	14.317
H300520	**Eternit 2000 asbestos free corrugated sheeting; sloping not exceeding 50 deg; fixing to steel members with hook bolts**								
H300520A	Profile 3 natural finish	m^2	0.30	5.09	-	15.44	20.53	22.58	4.150
H300520F	Profile 6R natural finish	m^2	0.35	5.94	-	17.96	23.90	26.29	4.150
H300520G	Profile 6R painted finish	m^2	0.35	5.94	-	21.47	27.41	30.15	4.150
H300520K	Extra for 60 mm glass fibre infill insulation and lining panel	m^2	0.55	9.34	-	36.11	45.45	50.00	14.317
H300525	**Eternit 2000 accessories**								
H300525A	Profile 3 two piece close fitting ridge; natural finish	m	0.20	3.40	-	26.06	29.46	32.41	6.988
H300525B	Profile 3 eaves filler piece; natural finish	m	0.13	2.21	-	18.58	20.79	22.87	6.397
H300525C	Profile 3 eaves corrugation closure piece; natural finish	m	0.19	3.23	-	18.58	21.81	23.99	6.397
H300525D	Profile 3 roll top barge board; natural finish	m	0.19	3.23	-	14.88	18.11	19.92	2.491
H300525J	Profile 6R two piece close fitting ridge; natural finish	m	0.22	3.74	-	22.44	26.18	28.80	5.470
H300525K	Profile 6R eaves filler piece; natural finish	m	0.17	2.89	-	12.66	15.55	17.11	4.127
H300525L	Profile 6R eaves corrugation closure piece; natural finish	m	0.25	4.25	-	12.66	16.91	18.60	4.127
H300525M	Profile 6R roll top barge board; natural finish	m	0.25	4.25	-	14.88	19.13	21.04	2.491
H300525Q	Profile 6R two piece close fitting ridge; painted finish	m	0.22	3.74	-	27.83	31.57	34.73	6.142
H300525R	Profile 6R eaves filler piece; painted finish	m	0.17	2.89	-	15.55	18.44	20.28	4.799
H300525S	Profile 6R eaves corrugation closure piece; painted finish	m	0.25	4.25	-	15.59	19.84	21.82	4.799
H300525T	Profile 6R roll top barge board; painted finish	m	0.25	4.25	-	18.37	22.62	24.88	2.969

Major Works 2011		Unit	Labour Hours	Labour Net	Plant Net	Materials Net	Unit Net	Unit with 10%	CO$_2$
				£	£	£	£	£	Kg
H31	**H31: METAL PROFILED AND FLAT SHEET CLADDING, COVERING AND SIDING**								
H3110	**Aluminium mill finished standing seam roofing; 0.9 mm nominal thickness; 65 m standing seam; mechanically sealed end laps**								
H311010	**Mechanically fixed to structural frame; 15 deg pitch**								
H311010A	over 300 mm wide	m^2	0.22	10.22	-	57.46	67.68	74.45	33.471

Major Works 2011		Unit	Labour Hours	Labour Net	Plant Net	Materials Net	Unit Net	Unit with 10%	CO$_2$
				£	£	£	£	£	Kg
H60	**H60: PLAIN ROOF TILING & H65: SINGLE LAP ROOF TILING**								
H6011	**Sloping coverings**								
H601133	**Clay tile roofing; Redland; alloy nailed every fifth course; 38 x 25 mm tanalised softwood battens; Type 1F underfelt; 65 mm lap**								
H601133A	265 x 165 mm Rosemary Plain, red	m²	1.64	27.85	-	46.75	74.60	82.06	45.597
H601133B	265 x 165 mm Rosemary Plain, red sanded	m²	1.64	27.85	-	46.75	74.60	82.06	45.597
H601133C	265 x 165 mm Rosemary Plain, brindle	m²	1.64	27.85	-	56.97	84.82	93.30	45.597
H601133D	265 x 165 mm Rosemary Plain, russet mix	m²	1.64	27.85	-	46.75	74.60	82.06	45.597
H601133E	265 x 165 mm Rosemary Plain, Cheslyn	m²	1.64	27.85	-	70.81	98.66	108.53	45.597
H601133F	380 x 260 mm Clay Pantile, red	m²	0.56	9.51	-	23.04	32.55	35.81	14.723
H601133G	380 x 260 mm Clay Pantile, brindled	m²	0.56	9.51	-	24.76	34.27	37.70	14.723
H601134	**Clay tile roofing; Sandtoft Goxhill; alloy nailed alternate courses; 38 x 25 mm tanalised softwood battens; Type 1F underfelt**								
H601134A	384 x 267 mm County Pantiles; 58 mm lap; red	m²	0.54	9.17	-	17.60	26.77	29.45	24.542
H601134B	384 x 267 mm County Pantiles; 58 mm lap; mixed russet	m²	0.54	9.17	-	18.59	27.76	30.54	24.542
H601134C	384 x 267 mm County Pantiles; 58 mm lap; brown/antique	m²	0.54	9.17	-	19.43	28.60	31.46	24.542
H601134D	342 x 252 mm Old English Pantiles; 72 mm lap; red	m²	0.56	9.51	-	24.61	34.12	37.53	25.290
H601134E	342 x 252 mm Old English Pantiles; 72 mm lap; mixed russet	m²	0.56	9.51	-	23.23	32.74	36.01	25.290
H601134F	342 x 252 mm Old English Pantiles; 72 mm lap; brown/antique	m²	0.56	9.51	-	24.24	33.75	37.13	25.290
H601134G	342 x 255 mm Gaelic tiles; 75 mm lap red	m²	0.56	9.51	-	23.73	33.24	36.56	25.290
H601134H	342 x 255 mm Gaelic tiles; 75 mm lap mixed russet	m²	0.56	9.51	-	24.91	34.42	37.86	25.290
H601134I	342 x 255 mm Gaelic tiles; 75 mm lap brown/antique	m²	0.56	9.51	-	25.92	35.43	38.97	25.290
H601134J	342 x 253 Greenwood Pantiles; 75 mm lap; red	m²	0.56	9.51	-	23.51	33.02	36.32	26.128
H601134K	342 x 276 mm Provincial Pantiles; 75 mm lap; red	m²	0.56	9.51	-	27.38	36.89	40.58	24.975
H601134L	342 x 267 mm Barrow Bold Roman tiles 75 mm lap; red	m²	0.56	9.51	-	34.41	43.92	48.31	25.300
H601135	**Concrete tile roofing; Redland, laid unfixed; 38 x 25 mm tanalised softwood battens; Type 1F underfelt**								
H601135A	412 x 332 mm Richmond; 112 mm lap	m²	0.44	7.47	-	22.52	29.99	32.99	7.606
H601135B	412 x 332 mm Saxon; 112 mm lap	m²	0.44	7.47	-	26.47	33.94	37.33	6.988
H601135C	430 x 380 mm Stonewold II; 75 mm lap	m²	0.38	6.45	-	19.28	25.73	28.30	6.553
H601135D	418 x 334 mm Mini Stonewold; 75 mm lap	m²	0.40	6.79	-	16.10	22.89	25.18	6.735
H601135E	418 x 334 mm Mini Stonewold; 100 mm lap	m²	0.42	7.13	-	17.47	24.60	27.06	6.940
H601135F	430 x 380 mm Delta; 75 mm lap	m²	0.38	6.45	-	26.03	32.48	35.73	5.660
H601135G	430 x 380 mm Delta and Stonewold combination in equal numbers; 75 mm lap	m²	0.38	6.45	-	24.83	31.28	34.41	6.215
H601135H	418 x 332 mm Regent; 75 mm lap	m²	0.40	6.79	-	14.86	21.65	23.82	8.772
H601135I	418 x 332 mm Regent; 100 mm lap	m²	0.42	7.13	-	16.11	23.24	25.56	9.181
H601135J	418 x 332 mm Grovebury; 75 mm lap	m²	0.40	6.79	-	14.86	21.65	23.82	8.928
H601135K	418 x 332 mm Grovebury; 100 mm lap	m²	0.42	7.13	-	16.11	23.24	25.56	9.352

Cladding & Covering

Major Works 2011		Unit	Labour Hours	Labour Net £	Plant Net £	Materials Net £	Unit Net £	Unit with 10% £	CO₂ Kg

		Unit	Labour Hours	Labour Net £	Plant Net £	Materials Net £	Unit Net £	Unit with 10% £	CO₂ Kg
H60	**H60: PLAIN ROOF TILING & H65: SINGLE LAP ROOF TILING**								
H6011	**Sloping coverings**								
H601135	**Concrete tile roofing; Redland, laid unfixed; 38 x 25 mm tanalised softwood battens; Type 1F underfelt**								
H601135L	418 x 330 mm Redland 50; 75 mm lap	m²	0.40	6.79	-	14.64	21.43	23.57	5.743
H601135M	418 x 330 mm Redland 50; 100 mm lap	m²	0.42	7.13	-	15.86	22.99	25.29	5.848
H601135N	418 x 330 mm Bridgewater; 75 mm lap	m²	0.40	6.79	-	17.99	24.78	27.26	5.743
H601135O	418 x 330 mm Renown; 75 mm lap	m²	0.40	6.79	-	15.54	22.33	24.56	7.327
H601135P	418 x 330 mm Renown; 100 mm lap	m²	0.42	7.13	-	16.85	23.98	26.38	7.592
H601135Q	381 x 227 mm Norfolk Pantile; 75 mm lap	m²	0.52	8.83	-	19.42	28.25	31.08	8.885
H601135R	381 x 227 mm Norfolk Pantile; 100 mm lap	m²	0.56	9.51	-	21.47	30.98	34.08	9.414
H601135S	381 x 227 mm Redland 49; 75 mm lap	m²	0.52	8.83	-	15.68	24.51	26.96	8.919
H601135T	381 x 227 mm Redland 49; 100 mm lap	m²	0.56	9.51	-	17.28	26.79	29.47	9.453
H601135U	268 x 165 mm Downland Plain tile; 65 mm lap	m²	1.64	27.85	-	40.68	68.53	75.38	20.897
H601135V	268 x 165 mm Redland Plain tile; 65 mm lap	m²	1.64	27.85	-	37.70	65.55	72.11	12.378
H601136	**Underslating felt; fixing with battens (measured separately), 150 mm laps all round**								
H601136A	BS 747; Type 1B	m²	0.04	0.68	-	2.40	3.08	3.39	4.080
H601136B	BS 747; Type 1F	m²	0.04	0.68	-	1.84	2.52	2.77	4.284
H601136C	BS 747; Type 1F aluminium foil faced	m²	0.04	0.68	-	3.35	4.03	4.43	5.100
H6021	**Vertical coverings**								
H602158	**Clay plain tile and ornamental tile cladding; Redland Rosemary; two alloy nails per tile; 38 x 25 mm tanalised softwood battens; 35 mm lap**								
H602158A	265 x 165 mm; plain tiles; Red	m²	1.98	33.62	-	40.81	74.43	81.87	36.578
H602158B	265 x 165 mm; ornamental tiles, Bullnose	m²	1.98	33.62	-	60.24	93.86	103.25	36.578
H602158C	265 x 165 mm; alternate courses plain and ornamental, Red and Bullnose	m²	1.98	33.62	-	51.34	84.96	93.46	37.185
H602159	**Concrete plain tile cladding; Redland Plain tile two alloy nails per tile; 38 x 25 mm tanalised softwood battens; 35 mm lap**								
H602159A	265 x 165 mm; plain tiles	m²	1.98	33.62	-	33.29	66.91	73.60	7.700
H602159B	265 x 165 mm; ornamental tiles, Club	m²	1.98	33.62	-	45.23	78.85	86.74	9.287
H602159C	265 x 165 mm; alternate courses plain and ornamental, Club	m²	1.98	33.62	-	39.87	73.49	80.84	8.590
H6031	**Eaves, verges, ridges, hips or the like**								
H603183	**Clay tile roofing; Sandtoft Goxhill; 38 x 25 mm tanalised softwood battens; extra for**								
H603183A	eaves with plastic filler, County pantiles	m	0.20	3.40	-	2.19	5.59	6.15	0.470
H603183B	eaves with undercloak; bed and point in cement mortar (1:3); Old English, Greenwood, Provincial or Barrow	m	0.40	6.79	-	4.59	11.38	12.52	8.467

Major Works 2011		Unit	Labour Hours	Labour Net	Plant Net	Materials Net	Unit Net	Unit with 10%	CO$_2$
				£	£	£	£	£	Kg
H60	**H60: PLAIN ROOF TILING & H65: SINGLE LAP ROOF TILING**								
H6031	**Eaves, verges, ridges, hips or the like**								
H603183	**Clay tile roofing; Sandtoft Goxhill; 38 x 25 mm tanalised softwood battens; extra for**								
H603183C	right hand verge with undercloak; bed and point in cement mortar (1:3); County, Old English, Gaelic, Greenwood, Provincial or Barrow	m	0.80	13.58	-	3.97	17.55	19.31	8.108
H603183D	left hand verge with undercloak; bed and point in cement mortar (1:3); County or Old English; red or mixed russet	m	0.80	13.58	-	22.00	35.58	39.14	18.136
H603183E	left hand verge with undercloak; bed and point in cement mortar (1:3); Old English or County; brown or antique	m	0.80	13.58	-	23.01	36.59	40.25	18.136
H603183F	left hand verge tiles with undercloak bed and point in cement mortar (1:3) Gaelic	m	0.80	13.58	-	3.97	17.55	19.31	8.108
H603183G	left hand verge with undercloak bed and point in cement mortar (1:3); Greenwood; red	m	0.80	13.58	-	23.43	37.01	40.71	19.010
H603183H	left hand verge with undercloak bed and point in cement mortar (1:3); Provincial; red	m	0.80	13.58	-	33.90	47.48	52.23	20.160
H603183I	left hand verge with undercloak; bed and point in cement mortar (1:3); Barrow; red	m	0.80	13.58	-	39.20	52.78	58.06	22.092
H603183J	Goxhill concrete valley trough; battens both sides; red or antique	m	0.40	6.79	-	16.25	23.04	25.34	4.442
H603183K	cutting against valley gutters with undercloak; bed and point in cement mortar (1:3); County red	m	0.30	5.09	0.28	6.09	11.46	12.61	11.395
H603183L	cutting against valley gutters with undercloak; bed and point in cement mortar (1:3); Old English red	m	0.30	5.09	0.28	6.51	11.88	13.07	11.027
H603183M	cutting against valley gutters with undercloak; bed and point in cement mortar (1:3); Gaelic red	m	0.30	5.09	0.28	6.41	11.78	12.96	11.027
H603183N	cutting against valley gutters with undercloak; bed and point in cement mortar (1:3); Greenwood red	m	0.30	5.09	0.28	6.39	11.76	12.94	11.119
H603183O	cutting against valley gutters with undercloak; bed and point in cement mortar (1:3); Provincial red	m	0.30	5.09	0.28	6.98	12.35	13.59	11.119
H603183P	cutting against valley gutters with undercloak; bed and point in cement mortar (1:3); Barrow red	m	0.30	5.09	0.28	7.60	12.97	14.27	11.027
H603183Q	half or third round ridge and hip tiles; bedding and pointing in cement mortar (1:3); double dentil slips both sides; County, Old English, half or third round ridge and hip tiles;	m	0.80	13.58	-	23.09	36.67	40.34	25.043
H603183R	half or third round ridge and hip tiles; bedding and pointing in cement mortar (1:3); double dentil slips both sides; County or Old English half or third round ridge and hip tiles;	m	0.80	13.58	-	23.33	36.91	40.60	25.043
H603183S	half or third round ridge and hip tiles; bedding and pointing in cement mortar (1:3); Gaelic red or russet	m	0.80	13.58	-	16.82	30.40	33.44	12.163
H603183T	half or third round ridge and hip tiles; bedding and pointing in cement mortar (1:3); Gaelic brown or antique	m	0.80	13.58	-	17.06	30.64	33.70	12.163

Cladding & Covering

Major Works 2011		Unit	Labour Hours	Labour Net	Plant Net	Materials Net	Unit Net	Unit with 10%	CO₂
				£	£	£	£	£	Kg
H60	**H60: PLAIN ROOF TILING & H65: SINGLE LAP ROOF TILING**								
H6031	**Eaves, verges, ridges, hips or the like**								
H603183	**Clay tile roofing; Sandtoft Goxhill; 38 x 25 mm tanalised softwood battens; extra for**								
H603183U	half round monopitch ridge; bedding and pointing in cement mortar (1:3); double dentil slips one side; County Old English, Greenwood, Provincial o Barrow; red, russet, brown or antique	m	0.80	13.58	-	40.80	54.38	59.82	18.603
H603183V	half round monopitch ridge; bedding and pointing in cement mortar (1:3); Gaelic; red, russet, brown or antique	m	0.80	13.58	-	37.66	51.24	56.36	12.163
H603184	**Clay plain tile roofing; Redland Rosemary 265 x 165 mm; 38 x 25 mm tanalised softwood battens; extra for**								
H603184A	double course at eaves	m	0.40	6.79	-	4.79	11.58	12.74	1.332
H603184B	verge with undercloak; bed and point cement mortar (1:3)	m	0.80	13.58	-	8.19	21.77	23.95	2.655
H603184C	universal angular valley	m	0.50	8.49	-	93.87	102.36	112.60	23.731
H603184D	universal curved valley	m	0.50	8.49	-	93.87	102.36	112.60	23.731
H603184E	cutting against valley gutters; bed and point in cement mortar (1:3)	m	0.64	10.87	0.28	12.03	23.18	25.50	6.306
H603184F	half round ridge; bed and point in cement mortar (1:3)	m	0.80	13.58	-	32.77	46.35	50.99	12.365
H603184G	plain angle ridge; bed and point in cement mortar (1:3)	m	0.80	13.58	-	24.96	38.54	42.39	12.336
H603184H	hogsback ridge; bed and point in cement mortar (1:3)	m	0.80	13.58	-	32.77	46.35	50.99	12.365
H603184I	baby ridge; bed and point in cement mortar (1:3)	m	0.80	13.58	-	32.77	46.35	50.99	12.365
H603184J	third round hip; bed and point in cement mortar (1:3)	m	1.00	16.98	-	46.72	63.70	70.07	21.085
H603184K	universal bonnet hip	m	0.50	8.49	-	94.04	102.53	112.78	23.787
H603184L	universal arris hip	m	0.50	8.49	-	94.04	102.53	112.78	23.787
H603184M	half round monoridge; bed and point in cement mortar (1:3)	m	0.80	13.58	-	9.00	22.58	24.84	4.790
H603185	**Concrete tile roofing; Redland; 38 x 25 mm tanalised softwood battens; extra for**								
H603185A	eaves; Richmond	m	0.10	1.70	-	12.26	13.96	15.36	1.354
H603185B	eaves; Saxon	m	0.10	1.70	-	12.26	13.96	15.36	1.354
H603185C	eaves; Stonewold II, Mini Stonewold, 50, Bridgewater, Renown, 49	m	0.10	1.70	-	0.44	2.14	2.35	0.274
H603185D	eaves; Delta, Regent, Grovebury, Norfolk	m	0.10	1.70	-	1.19	2.89	3.18	0.465
H603185E	eaves; Downland/Plain	m	0.40	6.79	-	3.70	10.49	11.54	0.596
H603185F	Ambi-dry verges; Richmond	m	0.30	5.09	-	18.28	23.37	25.71	0.856
H603185G	Ambi-dry verges; Saxon	m	0.30	5.09	-	19.12	24.21	26.63	0.805
H603185H	right hand verge with undercloak; bed and point in cement mortar (1:3); Stonewold II	m	0.40	6.79	-	9.33	16.12	17.73	1.835
H603185I	left hand verge with undercloak; bed and point in cement mortar (1:3); Stonewold II	m	0.50	8.49	-	16.21	24.70	27.17	2.117
H603185J	verge with undercloak; bed and point in cement mortar (1:3); Mini, Stonewold, Renown, Norfolk, 49	m	0.40	6.79	-	5.13	11.92	13.11	1.565
H603185K	right hand verge with undercloak; bed and point in cement mortar (1:3); Delta, Regent, Grovebury, 50, Bridgewater	m	0.40	6.79	-	5.00	11.79	12.97	1.553
H603185L	left hand verge with undercloak; bed and point in cement mortar (1:3); Delta	m	0.40	6.79	-	26.93	33.72	37.09	1.978
H603185M	left hand verge with undercloak; bed and point in cement mortar (1:3); Regent	m	0.40	6.79	-	17.08	23.87	26.26	2.984
H603185N	left hand verge with undercloak; bed and point in cement mortar (1:3); Grovebury	m	0.40	6.79	-	17.08	23.87	26.26	3.031

Major Works 2011		Unit	Labour Hours	Labour Net	Plant Net	Materials Net	Unit Net	Unit with 10%	CO$_2$
				£	£	£	£	£	Kg
H60	**H60: PLAIN ROOF TILING & H65: SINGLE LAP ROOF TILING**								
H6031	**Eaves, verges, ridges, hips or the like**								
H603185	**Concrete tile roofing; Redland; 38 x 25 mm tanalised softwood battens; extra for**								
H603185O	left hand verge with undercloak bed and point in cement mortar (1:3); Redland 50	m	0.40	6.79	-	16.12	22.91	25.20	2.075
H603185P	left hand verge with undercloak; bed and point in cement mortar (1:3); Bridgewater	m	0.40	6.79	-	18.23	25.02	27.52	1.879
H603185Q	verge with undercloak; bed and point in cement mortar; plain, Downland	m	0.80	13.58	-	6.34	19.92	21.91	0.738
H603185R	cloaked verge: Regent	m	0.20	3.40	-	14.08	17.48	19.23	1.482
H603185S	cloaked verge; Grovebury	m	0.20	3.40	-	14.08	17.48	19.23	1.528
H603185T	cloaked verge; Redland 50	m	0.20	3.40	-	14.01	17.41	19.15	0.573
H603185U	cloaked verge; Renown	m	0.20	3.40	-	14.28	17.68	19.45	0.966
H603185V	Redland Universal valley troughs; battens both sides	m	0.40	6.79	-	25.74	32.53	35.78	0.839
H603185W	Cutting against valley gutters; bed and point in cement mortar (1:3); Richmond	m	0.24	4.08	0.28	3.61	7.97	8.77	1.484
H603185X	Cutting against valley gutters; bed and point in cement mortar (1:3); Saxon	m	0.24	4.08	0.28	4.27	8.63	9.49	1.381
H603185Y	Cutting against valley gutters; bed and point in cement mortar (1:3); Stonewold II	m	0.30	5.09	0.28	2.20	7.57	8.33	1.249
H603185Z	Cutting against valley gutters; bed and point in cement mortar (1:3); Mini Stonewold	m	0.30	5.09	0.28	3.00	8.37	9.21	1.407
H603186	**Concrete tile roofing; Redland; 38 x 25 mm tanalised softwood battens; extra for**								
H603186A	Cutting against valley gutters; bed and point in cement mortar (1:3); Delta	m	0.32	5.43	0.28	5.50	11.21	12.33	1.209
H603186B	Cutting against valley gutters; bed and point in cement mortar (1:3); Regent	m	0.32	5.43	0.28	2.75	8.46	9.31	1.815
H603186C	Cutting against valley gutters; bed and point in cement mortar (1:3); Grovebury	m	0.32	5.43	0.28	2.75	8.46	9.31	1.846
H603186D	Cutting against valley gutters; bed and point in cement mortar (1:3); 50	m	0.32	5.43	0.48	2.71	8.62	9.48	1.215
H603186E	Cutting against valley gutters; bed and point in cement mortar (1:3); Bridgewater	m	0.32	5.43	0.48	3.38	9.29	10.22	1.215
H603186F	Cutting against valley gutters; bed and point in cement mortar (1:3); Renown	m	0.30	5.09	0.48	2.89	8.46	9.31	1.532
H603186G	Cutting against valley gutters; bed and point in cement mortar (1:3); Norfolk	m	0.30	5.09	0.48	2.31	7.88	8.67	1.528
H603186H	Cutting against valley gutters; bed and point in cement mortar (1:3); 49	m	0.30	5.09	0.48	1.87	7.44	8.18	1.532
H603186I	Cutting against valley gutters; bed and point in cement mortar (1:3); Downland	m	0.64	10.87	0.48	9.74	21.09	23.20	2.328
H603186J	Cutting against valley gutters; bed and point in cement mortar (1:3); Plain tiles	m	0.64	10.87	0.48	9.36	20.71	22.78	1.246
H603186K	Universal angle dry ridge; Richmond or Saxon	m	0.50	8.49	-	36.05	44.54	48.99	0.324
H603186L	Universal angle dry hip; Richmond or Saxon	m	0.50	8.49	-	22.99	31.48	34.63	0.310
H603186M	Universal angle Dry Mono ridge; Richmond or Saxon	m	0.50	8.49	-	17.31	25.80	28.38	0.456
H603186N	Angular hip and ridge tiles; bedding and pointing in cement mortar (1:3); Stonewold II or Mini-Stonewold	m	0.80	13.58	-	11.54	25.12	27.63	6.210

Cladding & Covering

H60	**H60: PLAIN ROOF TILING & H65: SINGLE LAP ROOF TILING**							
H6031	**Eaves, verges, ridges, hips or the like**							
H603186	**Concrete tile roofing; Redland; 38 x 25 mm tanalised softwood battens; extra for**							
H603186O	Universal angle monoridge; bedding and pointing in cement mortar (1:3); Stonewold II or Mini Stonewold	m	0.80	13.58	-	19.54	33.12	36.43	6.167
H603186P	Delta ridge and hip tiles; bedding and pointing in cement mortar (1:3); Delta	m	0.80	13.58	-	18.03	31.61	34.77	7.326
H603186Q	Delta Mono ridge tiles; bedding and pointing in cement mortar (1:3); Delta	m	0.80	13.58	-	26.60	40.18	44.20	4.146
H603186R	half round ridge and hip tiles; bedding and pointing in cement mortar (1:3); Redland 49 or Renown	m	0.80	13.58	-	9.61	23.19	25.51	3.767
H603186S	half round mono ridge tiles; bedding and pointing in cement mortar (1:3); Redland 49 or Renown	m	0.80	13.58	-	18.52	32.10	35.31	3.036
H603186T	half round ridge and hip tiles; bedding and pointing in cement mortar (1:3); dentil slips; Regent, Grovebury, Redland 50, Bridgewater o Norfolk	m	0.80	13.58	-	12.92	26.50	29.15	4.926
H603186U	half round mono ridge tiles; bedding and pointing in cement mortar (1:3); dentil slips; Regent, Grovebury, Redland 50, Bridgewater or Norfolk	m	0.80	13.58	-	20.18	33.76	37.14	3.615
H603186V	half round ridge and hip tiles; bedding and pointing in cement mortar (1:3); Plain tiles or Downland	m	0.80	13.58	-	21.09	34.67	38.14	9.001
H603186W	half round monoridge; bedding and pointing in cement mortar (1:3); Plain or Downland	m	0.80	13.58	-	23.45	37.03	40.73	3.574
H603186X	bonnet hip tiles; Plain or Downland	m	0.50	8.49	-	53.24	61.73	67.90	3.720
H603186Y	arris hip tiles; Plain or Downland	m	0.50	8.49	-	53.24	61.73	67.90	3.720
H603186Z	valley tiles; Plain or Downland	m	0.50	8.49	-	53.07	61.56	67.72	3.664
H603187	**Clay plain tiles and ornamental tile cladding; Redland Rosemary; 38 x 25 mm tanalised softwood battens; extra for**							
H603187A	double course at eaves	m	0.40	6.79	-	4.79	11.58	12.74	1.332
H603187B	external angle tiles	m	0.50	8.49	-	94.04	102.53	112.78	23.787
H603187C	top edge tiling	m	0.40	6.79	-	4.79	11.58	12.74	1.332
H603188	**Concrete plain tile and ornamental tile cladding; Redland; 38 x 25 mm tanalised softwood battens; extra for**							
H603188A	double course at eaves	m	0.40	6.79	-	3.70	10.49	11.54	0.596
H603188B	external angle tiles	m	0.50	8.49	-	53.24	61.73	67.90	3.720
H603188C	top edge tiling	m	0.40	6.79	-	3.70	10.49	11.54	0.596
H603189	**Redland ventilation systems; extra over tiling for**							
H603189A	Redvent eaves vent	m	0.20	3.40	-	10.50	13.90	15.29	0.088
H603189B	ridge vents; half round or Universal angle concrete	Nr	-	-	-	99.09	99.09	109.00	0.364
H603189C	ridge vents; Delta	Nr	-	-	-	120.84	120.84	132.92	0.364
H603189D	ridge vents; Rosemary half round	Nr	-	-	-	111.40	111.40	122.54	1.191
H603189E	gas flue ridge vent and accessories; half round or universal angle concrete	Nr	-	-	-	130.92	130.92	144.01	0.364
H603189F	gas flue ridge vent; Delta	Nr	-	-	-	152.68	152.68	167.95	0.364
H603189G	Thruvent; Rosemary	Nr	-	-	-	79.98	79.98	87.98	0.887
H603189H	Thruvent; Cambrian	Nr	-	-	-	66.25	66.25	72.88	0.349
H603189I	Thruvent; concrete tiles	Nr	-	-	-	59.06	59.06	64.97	0.280

Major Works 2011		Unit	Labour Hours	Labour Net	Plant Net	Materials Net	Unit Net	Unit with 10%	CO$_2$
				£	£	£	£	£	Kg
H62	**H62: NATURAL SLATING**								
H6211	**Sloping coverings**								
H621130	**Natural blue/grey roofing; 75 mm lap; two aluminium alloy nails per slate; 38 x 25 mm tanalised softwood battens; Type 1F underfelt**								
H621130A	600 x 300 mm	m^2	0.62	10.53	-	68.60	79.13	87.04	6.834
H621130B	500 x 250 mm	m^2	0.86	14.60	-	60.17	74.77	82.25	7.438
H621130C	450 x 225 mm	m^2	1.00	16.98	-	54.13	71.11	78.22	7.404
H621136	**Underslating felt; fixing with battens (measured separately), 150 mm laps all round**								
H621136A	BS 747; Type 1B	m^2	0.04	0.68	-	2.40	3.08	3.39	4.080
H621136B	BS 747; Type 1F	m^2	0.04	0.68	-	1.84	2.52	2.77	4.284
H621136C	BS 747; Type 1F aluminium foil faced	m^2	0.04	0.68	-	3.35	4.03	4.43	5.100
H6231	**Eaves, verges, ridges, hips or the like**								
H623180	**Natural blue/grey slate roofing; 75 mm lap; two aluminium alloy nails per slate; 38 x 25 mm tanalised softwood battens; extra for**								
H623180A	double course at eaves; 600 x 300mm	m	0.28	4.75	-	22.16	26.91	29.60	0.788
H623180B	double course at eaves; 500 x 250mm	m	0.30	5.09	-	12.29	17.38	19.12	0.669
H623180C	double course at eaves; 450 x 225mm	m	0.32	5.43	-	10.83	16.26	17.89	0.608
H623180D	verge with undercloak; bed and point cement mortar (1:3): 600 x 300 mm	m	0.32	5.43	-	11.42	16.85	18.54	2.330
H623180E	verge with undercloak; bed and point cement mortar (1:3); 500 x 250 mm	m	0.34	5.77	-	11.42	17.19	18.91	2.330
H623180F	verge with undercloak; bed and point cement mortar (1:3); 450 x 225 mm	m	0.34	5.77	-	11.42	17.19	18.91	2.330
H623180G	laced valleys; 600 x 300 mm	m	0.50	8.49	-	54.53	63.02	69.32	1.118
H623180H	laced valleys; 500 x 250 mm	m	0.50	8.49	-	37.77	46.26	50.89	0.988
H623180I	laced valleys; 450 x 225 mm	m	0.50	8.49	-	31.49	39.98	43.98	0.887
H623180J	cutting against valley gutters; 600 x 300 mm	m	0.24	4.08	-	10.80	14.88	16.37	0.221
H623180K	cutting against valley gutters; 500 x 250 mm	m	0.28	4.75	-	5.85	10.60	11.66	0.157
H623180L	cutting against valley gutters; 450 x 225 mm	m	0.28	4.75	-	6.14	10.89	11.98	0.151
H623180M	mitred hips; 600 x 300 mm	m	0.50	8.49	-	87.46	95.95	105.55	1.794
H623180N	mitred hips; 500 x 250 mm	m	0.60	10.19	-	56.27	66.46	73.11	1.459
H623180O	mitred hips; 450 x 225 mm	m	0.80	13.58	-	45.47	59.05	64.96	1.328
H623180P	clay angular ridge or hip tiles; bed and point in cement mortar (1:3)	m	0.52	8.83	-	9.74	18.57	20.43	0.880

Cladding & Covering

		Unit	Labour Hours	Labour Net	Plant Net	Materials Net	Unit Net	Unit with 10%	CO₂
				£	£	£	£	£	Kg
H63	**H63: RECONSTRUCTED STONE SLATING AND TILING**								
H6311	**Sloping coverings**								
H631131	**Asbestos free cement slate roofing; Eternit 2000; two copper nails and one copper disc rivet per slate; 38 x 25 mm tanalised softwood battens; Type 1F underfelt**								
H631131A	600 x 300 mm; 100 mm lap	m²	0.66	11.21	-	21.07	32.28	35.51	22.565
H631131B	600 x 300 mm; 110 mm lap	m²	0.68	11.55	-	21.10	32.65	35.92	22.584
H631131C	500 x 250 mm; 80 mm lap	m²	0.84	14.26	-	24.33	38.59	42.45	22.987
H631131D	500 x 250 mm; 100 mm lap	m²	0.88	14.94	-	25.44	40.38	44.42	23.911
H631132	**Reconstituted slate interlocking roofing; Redland Cambrian; two stainless steel ring shank nails and one stainless steel clip per slate; 38 x 25 mm tanalised softwood battens; Type 1F underfelt**								
H631132A	330 x 336 mm; 50 mm lap	m²	0.60	10.19	-	45.26	55.45	61.00	8.468
H631132B	330 x 336 mm; 90 mm lap	m²	0.68	11.55	-	54.51	66.06	72.67	9.327
H631136	**Underslating felt; fixing with battens (measured separately), 150 mm laps all round**								
H631136A	BS 747; Type 1B	m²	0.04	0.68	-	2.40	3.08	3.39	4.080
H631136B	BS 747; Type 1F	m²	0.04	0.68	-	1.84	2.52	2.77	4.284
H631136C	BS 747; Type 1F aluminium foil faced	m²	0.04	0.68	-	3.35	4.03	4.43	5.100
H631136D	Klober Span-Flex Type 1F	m²	0.05	0.85	-	1.84	2.69	2.96	4.284
H631136E	Klober Permo Forte breather membrane	m²	0.05	0.85	-	1.97	2.82	3.10	5.100
H6331	**Eaves, verges, ridges, hips or the like**								
H633181	**Asbestos-free cement slate roofing; Eternit 2000; 38 x 25 mm tanalised softwood battens; extra for**								
H633181A	double course at eaves; 600 x 300 mm	m	0.26	4.41	-	5.44	9.85	10.84	5.188
H633181B	double course at eaves; 500 x 250 mm	m	0.26	4.41	-	4.53	8.94	9.83	3.764
H633181D	verge with undercloak; bed and point cement mortar (1:3); 600 x 300 mm, 90 mm lap	m	0.26	4.41	-	2.95	7.36	8.10	4.439
H633181E	verge with undercloak; bed and point cement mortar (1:3); 600 x 300 mm 11 mm lap	m	0.26	4.41	-	2.95	7.36	8.10	4.439
H633181F	verge with undercloak; bed and point cement mortar (1:3); 500 x 250 mm, 90 mm lap	m	0.28	4.75	-	2.95	7.70	8.47	4.439
H633181G	verge with undercloak; bed and point cement mortar (1:3); 500 x 250 mm 11 mm lap	m	0.28	4.75	-	2.95	7.70	8.47	4.439
H633181J	cutting against valley gutters; 600 x 300 mm	m	0.24	4.08	-	2.33	6.41	7.05	2.331
H633181K	cutting against valley gutters; 500 x 250 mm	m	0.28	4.75	-	1.88	6.63	7.29	1.619
H633181M	mitred hips; 600 x 300 mm, 90 mm lap	m	0.50	8.49	-	23.47	31.96	35.16	23.352
H633181N	mitred hips; 600 x 300 mm, 110 mm lap	m	0.50	8.49	-	23.47	31.96	35.16	23.352
H633181O	mitred hips; 500 x 250 mm, 90 mm lap	m	0.70	11.89	-	23.63	35.52	39.07	20.288
H633181P	mitred hips; 500 x 250 mm, 110 mm lap	m	0.70	11.89	-	23.63	35.52	39.07	20.288
H633181S	half round ridge or hip coverings	m	0.50	8.49	-	29.62	38.11	41.92	4.933
H633181T	roll top angular ridge coverings	m	0.40	6.79	-	36.26	43.05	47.36	4.887
H633181U	internally socketed ridge coverings	m	0.40	6.79	-	33.68	40.47	44.52	4.904
H633181V	externally socketed monopitch ridge coverings	m	0.40	6.79	-	41.25	48.04	52.84	3.002

Major Works 2011		Unit	Labour Hours	Labour Net	Plant Net	Materials Net	Unit Net	Unit with 10%	CO$_2$
				£	£	£	£	£	Kg
H63	**H63: RECONSTRUCTED STONE SLATING AND TILING**								
H6331	**Eaves, verges, ridges, hips or the like**								
H633182	**Reconstituted slate interlocking roofing; Redland Cambrian; 38 x 25 mm tanalised softwood battens; extra for Drytech detailing**								
H633182A	stainless steel clips at eaves	m	0.10	1.70	-	1.13	2.83	3.11	0.329
H633182B	right hand Ambi-dry verges	m	0.30	5.09	-	35.92	41.01	45.11	1.416
H633182C	left hand Ambi-dry verges; special slates	m	0.30	5.09	-	46.29	51.38	56.52	1.693
H633182D	mitred hip	m	0.50	8.49	-	17.83	26.32	28.95	0.148
H633182E	universal angle Dry Hip	m	0.50	8.49	-	36.05	44.54	48.99	0.324
H633182F	universal angle Dry Ridge	m	0.50	8.49	-	22.99	31.48	34.63	0.310
H633182G	universal angle Dry Mono ridge	m	0.50	8.49	-	18.15	26.64	29.30	0.464
H633182H	Redland GRP valley; battens both sides	m	0.40	6.79	-	10.59	17.38	19.12	4.839
H633182I	cutting against valley gutters	m	0.24	4.08	0.28	53.19	57.55	63.31	1.708

Cladding & Covering

Major Works 2011		Unit	Labour Hours	Labour Net	Plant Net	Materials Net	Unit Net	Unit with 10%	CO$_2$
				£	£	£	£	£	Kg
H71	**H71: LEAD SHEET COVERINGS AND FLASHINGS**								
H7101	**Flat coverings**								
H710103	**Sheet lead roofing; BS 1178; waterproof building paper underlay; wood cored roll joints in direction of falls; welted joints across falls**								
H710103B	Code 4	m²	3.50	59.43	-	48.17	107.60	118.36	44.184
H710103C	Code 5	m²	3.80	64.52	-	56.34	120.86	132.95	51.825
H710103D	Code 6	m²	4.10	69.62	-	60.58	130.20	143.22	58.648
H710103E	Code 7	m²	4.40	74.71	-	75.87	150.58	165.64	69.280
H7111	**Sloping coverings**								
H711122	**Sheet lead roofing; BS 1178; waterproof building paper underlay; wood cored roll joints in direction of falls; welted joints across falls**								
H711122B	Code 4	m²	3.80	64.52	-	48.17	112.69	123.96	44.184
H711122C	Code 5	m²	4.10	69.62	-	56.34	125.96	138.56	51.825
H711122D	Code 6	m²	4.40	74.71	-	62.29	137.00	150.70	60.261
H711122E	Code 7	m²	4.70	79.81	-	75.87	155.68	171.25	69.280
H7121	**Vertical coverings**								
H712152	**Sheet lead roofing; BS 1178; waterproof building paper underlay; wood cored roll joints vertically; welted joints horizontally**								
H712152B	Code 4	m²	4.00	67.92	-	46.78	114.70	126.17	42.702
H712152C	Code 5	m²	4.30	73.01	-	56.08	129.09	142.00	51.320
H712152D	Code 6	m²	4.60	78.11	-	59.72	137.83	151.61	57.580
H7141	**Eaves, ridges, skirtings, fascias, flashings, aprons or the like**								
H714172	**Sheet lead; BS 1178; working over fillets, slating or tiling**								
H714172A	Code 3 flashings, aprons, soakers or the like; wedging into grooves with lead wedges; not exceeding 150 mm girth	m	0.35	5.94	-	3.55	9.49	10.44	3.385
H714172B	Code 3 lead flashings, aprons, soakers or the like; wedging into grooves with lead wedges; 150 - 300 mm girth	m	0.60	10.19	-	6.90	17.09	18.80	6.570
H714172C	Code 4 lead flashings, aprons, soakers or the like; wedging into grooves with lead wedges; not exceeding 150 mm girth	m	0.40	6.79	-	5.11	11.90	13.09	4.615
H714172D	Code 4 lead flashings, aprons, soakers or the like; wedging into grooves with lead wedges; 150 - 300 mm girth	m	0.69	11.72	-	9.93	21.65	23.82	8.958
H714172E	Code 4 stepped flashings; wedging into grooves with lead wedges; 150 - 300 mm girth	m	0.92	15.62	-	9.93	25.55	28.11	8.958
H714172F	Code 4 stepped flashings; wedging into grooves with lead wedges; 300 - 450 mm girth	m	1.25	21.23	-	15.04	36.27	39.90	13.573
H714172G	Code 4 cappings to ridges and hips, valley gutters or the like; 300 - 450 mm girth	m	1.03	17.49	-	15.04	32.53	35.78	13.573
H714172H	Code 4 cappings to ridges and hips, valley gutters or the like; working over fillets, slating or tiling; 450 - 600 mm girth	m	1.38	23.43	-	19.85	43.28	47.61	17.916
H714172I	Code 5 flashings, aprons or the like wedging into grooves with lead wedges; not exceeding 150 mm girth	m	0.43	7.30	-	6.36	13.66	15.03	5.766
H714172J	Code 5 flashings, aprons or the like wedging into grooves with lead wedges; 150 - 300 mm girth	m	0.74	12.57	-	12.36	24.93	27.42	11.192

Major Works 2011		Unit	Labour Hours	Labour Net	Plant Net	Materials Net	Unit Net	Unit with 10%	CO$_2$
				£	£	£	£	£	Kg
H71	**H71: LEAD SHEET COVERINGS AND FLASHINGS**								
H7141	**Eaves, ridges, skirtings, fascias, flashings, aprons or the like**								
H714172	**Sheet lead; BS 1178; working over fillets, slating or tiling**								
H714172K	Code 5 stepped flashings; wedging into grooves with lead wedges; 150 - 300 mm girth	m	1.00	16.98	-	12.36	29.34	32.27	11.192
H714172L	Code 5 stepped flashings; wedging into grooves with lead wedges; 300 - 450 mm girth	m	1.34	22.75	-	18.72	41.47	45.62	16.958
H714172M	Code 5 cappings to ridges and hips, valley gutters or the like; 300 - 450 mm girth	m	1.10	18.68	-	18.72	37.40	41.14	16.958
H714172N	Code 5 cappings to ridges and hips, valley gutters or the like; 450 - 600 mm girth	m	1.48	25.13	-	24.71	49.84	54.82	22.384
H714172O	Code 6 flashings, aprons or the like wedging into grooves with lead wedges; not exceeding 150 mm girth	m	0.48	8.15	-	7.11	15.26	16.79	6.794
H714172P	Code 6 flashings, aprons or the like wedging into grooves with lead wedges; 150 - 300 mm girth	m	0.80	13.58	-	13.79	27.37	30.11	13.189
H714172Q	Code 6 stepped flashings; wedging into grooves with lead wedges; 150 - 300 mm girth	m	1.10	18.68	-	13.79	32.47	35.72	13.189
H714172R	Code 6 stepped flashings; wedging into grooves with lead wedges; 300 - 450 mm girth	m	1.45	24.62	-	20.90	45.52	50.07	19.984
H714172S	Code 6 cappings to ridges and hips, valley gutters or the like; 300 - 450 mm girth	m	1.18	20.04	-	20.90	40.94	45.03	19.984
H714172T	Code 6 cappings to ridges and hips, valley gutters or the like; 450 - 600 mm girth	m	1.59	27.00	-	27.59	54.59	60.05	26.378
H7191	**Soaker collars**								
H719197	**Sheet lead soaker collars; fixing around pipes, standards or the like; dressing over roof coverings; mastic joint at top; 300 mm high**								
H719197A	Code 3; not exceeding 150 mm girth	Nr	0.18	3.06	-	1.24	4.30	4.73	1.196
H719197B	Code 3; 150 - 300 mm girth	Nr	0.30	5.09	-	2.49	7.58	8.34	2.393
H719197C	Code 3; 300 - 450 mm girth	Nr	0.50	8.49	-	3.73	12.22	13.44	3.589
H719197D	Code 3; 450 - 600 mm girth	Nr	0.65	11.04	-	4.97	16.01	17.61	4.786
H719197E	Code 4; not exceeding 150 mm girth	Nr	0.28	4.75	-	1.70	6.45	7.10	1.558
H719197F	Code 4; 150 - 300 mm girth	Nr	0.50	8.49	-	3.40	11.89	13.08	3.116
H719197G	Code 4; 300 - 450 mm girth	Nr	0.75	12.73	-	5.11	17.84	19.62	4.675
H719197H	Code 4; 450 - 600 mm girth	Nr	0.90	15.28	-	6.81	22.09	24.30	6.233

Major Works 2011		Unit	Labour Hours	Labour Net	Plant Net	Materials Net	Unit Net	Unit with 10%	CO₂
				£	£	£	£	£	Kg
H73	**H73: COPPER STRIP AND SHEET COVERINGS AND FLASHINGS**								
H7301	**Flat coverings**								
H730105	**Sheet copper roofing; BS 2870; waterproof inodorous felt No.1 underlay; wood cored roll joints in direction of falls; double lock cross welts across falls**								
H730105A	0.45 mm thick	m²	4.00	67.92	-	68.58	136.50	150.15	24.875
H730105B	0.60 mm thick	m²	4.30	73.01	-	80.09	153.10	168.41	29.353
H730105C	0.70 mm thick	m²	4.50	76.41	-	93.30	169.71	186.68	33.368
H7311	**Sloping coverings**								
H731124	**Sheet copper roofing; BS 2870; inodorous felt No.1 underlay; wood cored roll joints in direction of falls; double lock cross welts across falls**								
H731124A	0.45 mm thick	m²	4.50	76.41	-	68.58	144.99	159.49	24.875
H731124B	0.60 mm thick	m²	4.80	81.50	-	80.09	161.59	177.75	29.353
H731124C	0.70 mm thick	m²	5.00	84.90	-	93.30	178.20	196.02	33.368
H7321	**Vertical coverings**								
H732154	**Sheet copper roofing; BS 2870; inodorous felt No.1 underlay; wood cored roll joints in direction of falls; double lock cross welts across falls**								
H732154A	0.45 mm thick	m²	5.00	84.90	-	68.58	153.48	168.83	24.875
H732154B	0.60 mm thick	m²	5.30	89.99	-	80.09	170.08	187.09	29.353
H732154C	0.70 mm thick	m²	5.50	93.39	-	93.30	186.69	205.36	33.368
H7341	**Eaves, ridges, skirtings, fascias, flashings, aprons or the like**								
H734174	**Sheet copper; BS 2870; working over fillets and into grooves as necessary**								
H734174A	0.45 mm flashings, aprons, soakers or the like; not exceeding 150 mm girth	m	0.48	8.15	-	6.34	14.49	15.94	1.980
H734174B	0.45 mm flashings, aprons, soakers or the like; 150 - 300 mm girth	m	0.91	15.45	-	12.31	27.76	30.54	3.844
H734174C	0.45 mm stepped flashings; 150 - 300 mm girth	m	1.20	20.38	-	12.31	32.69	35.96	3.844
H734174D	0.45 mm stepped flashings; 300 - 450 mm girth	m	1.60	27.17	-	18.66	45.83	50.41	5.825
H734174E	0.45 mm cappings to ridges and hips, valley gutters or the like; 300 - 450 mm girth	m	1.35	22.92	-	18.66	41.58	45.74	5.825
H734174F	0.45 mm cappings to ridges and hips, valley gutters or the like; 450 - 600 mm girth	m	1.80	30.56	-	29.01	59.57	65.53	9.396
H734174G	0.60 mm flashings, aprons, soakers or the like; not exceeding 150 mm girth	m	0.50	8.49	-	7.47	15.96	17.56	2.420
H734174H	0.60 mm flashings, aprons, soakers or the like; 150 - 300 mm girth	m	0.95	16.13	-	14.51	30.64	33.70	4.698
H734174I	0.60 mm stepped flashings; 150 - 300 mm girth	m	1.25	21.23	-	14.51	35.74	39.31	4.698
H734174J	0.60 mm stepped flashings; 300 - 450 mm girth	m	1.70	28.87	-	21.98	50.85	55.94	7.119
H734174K	0.60 mm cappings to ridges and hips, valley gutters or the like; 300 - 450 mm girth	m	1.45	24.62	-	21.98	46.60	51.26	7.119
H734174L	0.60 mm cappings to ridges and hips, valley gutters or the like; 450 - 600 mm girth	m	1.90	32.26	-	29.01	61.27	67.40	9.396

Major Works 2011		Unit	Labour Hours	Labour Net £	Plant Net £	Materials Net £	Unit Net £	Unit with 10% £	CO₂ Kg
H73	**H73: COPPER STRIP AND SHEET COVERINGS AND FLASHINGS**								
H7341	**Eaves, ridges, skirtings, fascias, flashings, aprons or the like**								
H734174	**Sheet copper; BS 2870; working over fillets and into grooves as necessary**								
H734174M	0.70 mm flashings, aprons, soakers or the like; not exceeding 150 mm girth	m	0.53	9.00	-	9.59	18.59	20.45	3.080
H734174N	0.70 mm flashings, aprons, soakers or the like; 150 - 300 mm girth	m	1.05	17.83	-	18.62	36.45	40.10	5.980
H734174O	0.70 mm stepped flashing; 150 - 300 mm girth	m	1.30	22.07	-	18.62	40.69	44.76	5.980
H734174P	0.70 mm stepped flashing; 300 - 450 mm girth	m	1.75	29.72	-	28.20	57.92	63.71	9.060
H734174Q	0.70 mm cappings to ridges and hips valley gutters or the like; 300 - 450 mm girth	m	1.55	26.32	-	28.20	54.52	59.97	9.060
H734174R	0.70 mm cappings to ridges and hips valley gutters or the like; 450 - 600 mm girth	m	2.00	33.96	-	37.23	71.19	78.31	11.959

Cladding & Covering

		Unit	Labour Hours	Labour Net	Plant Net	Materials Net	Unit Net	Unit with 10%	CO$_2$
				£	£	£	£	£	Kg
H74	**H74: ZINC STRIP AND SHEET COVERINGS AND FLASHINGS**								
H7401	**Flat coverings**								
H740104	**Sheet zinc roofing; BS 849; waterproof building paper underlay; wood cored roll joints in direction of falls; beaded drip joints across falls**								
H740104A	0.80 mm thick	m^2	4.00	67.92	-	37.12	105.04	115.54	26.920
H740104B	1.00 mm thick	m^2	4.40	74.71	-	42.06	116.77	128.45	33.396
H7411	**Sloping coverings**								
H741123	**Sheet zinc roofing; BS 849; waterproof building paper underlay; wood cored roll joints in direction of falls; welted joints across falls**								
H741123A	0.80 mm thick	m^2	4.50	76.41	-	36.68	113.09	124.40	26.577
H741123B	1.00 mm thick	m^2	4.90	83.20	-	41.57	124.77	137.25	32.955
H7421	**Vertical coverings**								
H742153	**Sheet zinc roofing; BS 849; waterproof building paper underlay; welted joints vertically and horizontally**								
H742153A	0.80 mm thick	m^2	4.80	81.50	-	32.52	114.02	125.42	26.492
H742153B	1.00 mm thick	m^2	5.20	88.30	-	36.87	125.17	137.69	32.916
H7441	**Eaves, ridges, skirtings, fascias, flashings, aprons or the like**								
H744173	**Sheet zinc; BS 849; working over fillets and into grooves as necessary**								
H744173A	0.80 mm flashings, aprons, soakers or the like; not exceeding 150 mm girth	m	0.45	7.64	-	4.01	11.65	12.82	3.112
H744173B	0.80 mm flashings, aprons, soakers or the like; 150 - 300 mm girth	m	0.87	14.77	-	7.77	22.54	24.79	6.040
H744173C	0.80 mm stepped flashings; 150 - 300 mm girth	m	1.15	19.53	-	7.77	27.30	30.03	6.040
H744173D	0.80 mm stepped flashings; 300 - 450 mm girth	m	1.55	26.32	-	11.78	38.10	41.91	9.152
H744173E	0.80 mm cappings to ridges and hips, valley gutters or the like; 300 - 450 mm girth	m	1.30	22.07	-	11.78	33.85	37.24	9.152
H744173F	0.80 mm cappings to ridges and hips, valley gutters or the like; 450 - 600 mm girth	m	1.75	29.72	-	15.55	45.27	49.80	12.081
H744173G	1.00 mm flashings, aprons, soakers or the like; not exceeding 150 mm girth	m	0.50	8.49	-	4.56	13.05	14.36	3.939
H744173H	1.00 mm flashings, aprons, soakers or the like; 150 - 300 mm girth	m	1.00	16.98	-	8.86	25.84	28.42	7.646
H744173I	1.00 mm stepped flashings; 150 - 300 mm girth	m	1.25	21.23	-	8.86	30.09	33.10	7.646
H744173J	1.00 mm stepped flashings; 300 - 450 mm girth	m	1.65	28.02	-	13.43	41.45	45.60	11.585
H744173K	1.00 mm cappings to ridges and hips, valley gutters or the like; 300 - 450 mm girth	m	1.45	24.62	-	13.43	38.05	41.86	11.585
H744173L	1.00 mm cappings to ridges and hips, valley gutters or the like; 450 - 600 mm girth	m	1.90	32.26	-	17.72	49.98	54.98	15.292

Major Works 2011		Unit	Labour Hours	Labour Net	Plant Net	Materials Net	Unit Net	Unit with 10%	CO$_2$
				£	£	£	£	£	Kg
H92	**H92: RAINSCREEN CLADDING**								
H9210	**Rainscreen cladding to walls**								
H921010	**7.5 mm Eternit Glasal cladding rivet fixed with Eternit Astro rivet system on and including Eternit Ventisol aluminium support framework on 80 mm stand-off brackets to form 100 mm void; fixing to substrate with mechanical fixings**								
H921010A	over 300 mm wide	m^2	1.20	76.56	-	80.00	156.56	172.22	50.625
H9220	**Rainscreen cladding to soffits**								
H922010	**7.5 mm Eternit Glasal cladding; rivet fixed with Eternit Astro rivet system on and including Eternit Omega and Zed 40 mm aluminium support framework; fixing to substrate with screws**								
H922010A	over 300 mm wide	m^2	1.12	71.47	-	72.50	143.97	158.37	50.625
H922020	**4 mm Eternit Alucomat aluminium composite cladding; rivet fixed with Alucomat matched rivets on and including Eternit Omega and Zed 40 mm aluminium support framework; fixing to substrate with screws**								
H922020A	over 300 mm wide	m^2	1.36	86.80	-	117.50	204.30	224.73	94.925
H9230	**Rainscreen cladding to fascias**								
H923010	**7.5 mm Eternit Glasal cladding; secret fixed with Eternit Sikatack structural adhesive system on and including Eternit Omega and Zed 40 mm aluminium support framework; fixing to substrate with screws**								
H923010A	not exceeding 300 mm wide	m	0.72	45.95	-	31.75	77.70	85.47	16.200
H9250	**Rainscreen accessories**								
H925010	**Cladding profiles**								
H925010A	horizontal joint profile	m	0.06	4.07	-	4.80	8.87	9.76	17.304
H925010B	universal corner profile	m	0.11	7.13	-	8.14	15.27	16.80	17.304
H925010C	50 mm perforated vent profile	m	0.07	4.52	-	2.54	7.06	7.77	17.304
H925010D	100 mm perforated vent profile	m	0.13	8.15	-	4.76	12.91	14.20	17.304

Waterproofing

Waterproofing

Major Works 2011		Unit	Labour Hours	Labour Net	Plant Net	Materials Net	Unit Net	Unit with 10%	CO₂
				£	£	£	£	£	Kg
J20	**J20: MASTIC ASPHALT TANKING AND DAMP PROOFING**								
J2011	**Flat coverings**								
J201108	**Mastic asphalt tanking; BS 1097; limestone aggregate**								
J201108A	20 mm two coat work	m²	0.25	10.62	-	11.13	21.75	23.93	2.271
J201108B	30 mm three coat work	m²	0.35	14.89	-	16.70	31.59	34.75	3.406
J2013	**Sloping coverings**								
J201327	**Mastic asphalt tanking; BS 1097; limestone aggregate**								
J201327A	20 mm two coat work	m²	0.33	13.79	-	11.13	24.92	27.41	2.271
J201327B	30 mm three coat work	m²	0.46	19.33	-	16.70	36.03	39.63	3.406
J2015	**Vertical coverings**								
J201557	**Mastic asphalt tanking; BS 1097; limestone aggregate**								
J201557A	20 mm two coat work	m²	0.41	17.43	-	11.13	28.56	31.42	2.271
J201557B	30 mm three coat work	m²	0.57	24.20	-	16.70	40.90	44.99	3.406
J2061	**Skirtings, upstands or the like**								
J206177	**Mastic asphalt tanking; BS 1097; limestone aggregate; skirtings, upstand or the like; rounded arrises and internal angle fillet; turning nib into groove**								
J206177A	20 mm two coat work; not exceeding 150 mm high	m	0.13	5.33	-	2.23	7.56	8.32	0.454
J206177B	20 mm two coat work; 150 - 300 mm high	m	0.20	8.50	-	3.90	12.40	13.64	0.795
J206177E	30 mm three coat work; not exceeding 150 mm high	m	0.18	7.44	-	3.34	10.78	11.86	0.681
J206177F	30 mm three coat work; 150 - 300 mm high	m	0.28	11.67	-	5.84	17.51	19.26	1.192

Major Works 2011		Unit	Labour Hours	Labour Net	Plant Net	Materials Net	Unit Net	Unit with 10%	CO₂
				£	£	£	£	£	Kg
J21	**J21: MASTIC ASPHALT ROOFING, INSULATION AND FINISHES**								
J2131	**Flat coverings**								
J213106	**Mastic asphalt roofing; BS 988; limestone aggregate; sheathing felt underlay; BS 747; rubbing surface with fine sand**								
J213106A	20 mm two coat work	m²	0.25	10.62	-	13.07	23.69	26.06	5.926
J213107	**Mastic asphalt roofing; BS 1162; natural rock aggregate; sheathing felt underlay; BS 747; rubbing surface with fine sand**								
J213107A	20 mm two coat work	m²	0.25	10.62	-	15.38	26.00	28.60	5.926
J2133	**Sloping coverings**								
J213325	**Mastic asphalt roofing; BS 988; limestone aggregate; sheathing felt underlay; BS 747; rubbing surface with fine sand**								
J213325A	20 mm two coat work	m²	0.33	13.79	-	13.07	26.86	29.55	5.926
J213326	**Mastic asphalt roofing; BS 1162; natural rock aggregate; sheathing felt underlay; BS 747; rubbing surface with fine sand**								
J213326A	20 mm two coat work	m²	0.33	13.79	-	15.38	29.17	32.09	5.926
J2135	**Vertical coverings**								
J213555	**Mastic asphalt roofing; BS 988; limestone aggregate; sheathing felt underlay; BS 747; rubbing with fine sand**								
J213555A	20 mm two coat work	m²	0.41	17.43	-	13.07	30.50	33.55	5.926
J213556	**Mastic asphalt roofing; BS 1162; natural rock aggregate; sheathing felt underlay; BS 747; rubbing surface with fine sand**								
J213556A	20 mm two coat work	m²	0.41	17.43	-	15.38	32.81	36.09	5.926
J2161	**Skirtings, upstands or the like**								
J216175	**Mastic asphalt; BS 988; limestone aggregate; sheathing felt underlay; BS 747; rubbing surface with fine sand; 20 mm two coat skirtings, upstands or the like; rounded arrises and internal angle fillet; turning nib into groove**								
J216175A	not exceeding 150 mm high	m	0.13	5.33	-	2.57	7.90	8.69	1.053
J216175B	150 - 300 mm high	m	0.20	8.50	-	4.53	13.03	14.33	1.950
J216176	**Mastic asphalt; BS 1162; natural rock aggregate; sheathing felt underlay BS 747; rubbing surface with fine sand; 20 mm two coat skirtings, upstands or the like; rounded arrises and internal angle fillet; turning nib into groove**								
J216176A	not exceeding 150 mm high	m	0.13	5.33	-	3.03	8.36	9.20	1.053
J216176B	150 - 300 mm high	m	0.20	8.50	-	5.34	13.84	15.22	1.950

Waterproofing

		Unit	Labour Hours	Labour Net	Plant Net	Materials Net	Unit Net	Unit with 10%	CO$_2$
				£	£	£	£	£	Kg
J30	**J30: LIQUID APPLIED TANKING AND DAMP PROOFING**								
J3011	**Membranes and compounds**								
J301103	**RIW liquid asphaltic composition; two coats on concrete surfaces**								
J301103A	horizontal; not exceeding 150 mm wide	m	0.02	0.19	-	1.79	1.98	2.18	1.050
J301103B	horizontal; 150 - 300 mm wide	m	0.03	0.32	-	3.58	3.90	4.29	2.100
J301103C	horizontal; over 300 mm wide	m^2	0.08	0.95	-	12.01	12.96	14.26	7.056
J301103D	vertical; not exceeding 150 mm high	m	0.02	0.25	-	1.79	2.04	2.24	1.050
J301103E	vertical; 150 - 300 mm high	m	0.03	0.38	-	3.58	3.96	4.36	2.100
J301103F	vertical; over 300 mm high	m^2	0.09	1.08	-	12.01	13.09	14.40	7.056
J301104	**RIW liquid asphaltic composition; three coats on masonry surfaces**								
J301104A	vertical; not exceeding 150 mm high	m	0.03	0.32	-	1.72	2.04	2.24	1.008
J301104B	vertical; 150 - 300 mm high	m	0.04	0.44	-	3.43	3.87	4.26	2.016
J301104C	vertical; over 300 mm high	m^2	0.10	1.27	-	11.37	12.64	13.90	6.678
J301105	**Synthaprufe waterproofing compound; two coats on concrete surfaces; final coat dusted with sharp sand**								
J301105A	horizontal; not exceeding 150 mm wide	m	0.02	0.23	-	1.00	1.23	1.35	1.061
J301105B	horizontal; 150 - 300 mm wide	m	0.03	0.36	-	2.00	2.36	2.60	2.122
J301105C	horizontal; over 300 mm wide	m^2	0.09	1.12	-	6.72	7.84	8.62	7.123
J301105D	vertical; not exceeding 150 mm high	m	0.02	0.29	-	1.00	1.29	1.42	1.061
J301105E	vertical; 150 - 300 mm high	m	0.03	0.42	-	2.00	2.42	2.66	2.122
J301105F	vertical; over 300 mm high	m^2	0.10	1.24	-	6.72	7.96	8.76	7.123
J301106	**Synthaprufe waterproofing compound; three coats on concrete surfaces; final coat dusted with sharp sand**								
J301106A	horizontal; not exceeding 150 mm wide	m	0.03	0.33	-	1.51	1.84	2.02	1.607
J301106B	horizontal; 150 - 300 mm wide	m	0.04	0.46	-	3.02	3.48	3.83	3.214
J301106C	horizontal; over 300 mm wide	m^2	0.11	1.40	-	10.02	11.42	12.56	10.651
J301106D	vertical; not exceeding 150 mm high	m	0.03	0.36	-	1.51	1.87	2.06	1.607
J301106E	vertical; 150 - 300 mm high	m	0.04	0.48	-	3.02	3.50	3.85	3.214
J301106F	vertical; over 300 mm high	m^2	0.11	1.44	-	10.02	11.46	12.61	10.651
J301107	**Synthaprufe waterproofing compound; three coats on masonry surfaces; final coat dusted with sharp sand**								
J301107A	vertical; not exceeding 150 mm high	m	0.03	0.36	-	0.94	1.30	1.43	1.008
J301107B	vertical; 150 - 300 mm high	m	0.04	0.48	-	1.89	2.37	2.61	2.016
J301107C	vertical; over 300 mm high	m^2	0.11	1.44	-	6.25	7.69	8.46	6.678

Major Works 2011		Unit	Labour Hours	Labour Net	Plant Net	Materials Net	Unit Net	Unit with 10%	CO₂
				£	£	£	£	£	Kg

J40   **J40: FLEXIBLE SHEET TANKING AND DAMP PROOFING**

J4011   **Membranes**

J401101   **1200 gauge polythene sheeting; 150 mm side and end laps**

J401101A	horizontal; over 300 mm wide	m²	0.04	0.51	-	0.88	1.39	1.53	4.620
J401101B	vertical; not exceeding 150 mm high	m	0.01	0.06	-	0.14	0.20	0.22	0.714
J401101C	vertical; 150 - 300 mm high	m	0.01	0.13	-	0.26	0.39	0.43	1.386
J401101D	vertical; over 300 mm high	m²	0.05	0.64	-	0.88	1.52	1.67	4.620

J401102   **500 gauge polythene sheeting; 150 mm side and end laps**

J401102A	horizontal; over 300 mm wide	m²	0.04	0.51	-	0.66	1.17	1.29	4.620
J401102B	vertical; not exceeding 150 mm high	m	0.01	0.06	-	0.10	0.16	0.18	0.714
J401102C	vertical; 150 - 300 mm high	m	0.01	0.13	-	0.20	0.33	0.36	1.386
J401102D	vertical; over 300 mm high	m²	0.05	0.64	-	0.66	1.30	1.43	4.620

J401108   **Bituthene bitumen coated 1000 gauge polythene sheeting; sticking to concrete surfaces primed with bituthene primer**

J401108A	horizontal; not exceeding 150 mm wide	m	0.02	0.19	-	1.73	1.92	2.11	0.856
J401108B	horizontal; 150 - 300 mm wide	m	0.03	0.38	-	3.55	3.93	4.32	1.755
J401108C	horizontal; over 300 mm wide	m²	0.10	1.27	-	11.78	13.05	14.36	5.833
J401108D	vertical; not exceeding 150 mm high	m	0.02	0.24	-	1.83	2.07	2.28	0.928
J401108E	vertical; 150 - 300 mm high	m	0.04	0.48	-	3.81	4.29	4.72	1.933
J401108F	vertical; over 300 mm high	m²	0.13	1.59	-	12.56	14.15	15.57	6.367

J401109   **Bituthene bitumen coated 1000 gauge polythene sheeting; sticking to masonry surfaces primed with bituthene primer**

J401109A	horizontal; not exceeding 150 mm wide	m	0.02	0.19	-	1.83	2.02	2.22	0.928
J401109B	horizontal; 150 - 300 mm wide	m	0.03	0.38	-	3.81	4.19	4.61	1.933
J401109C	horizontal; over 300 mm wide	m²	0.10	1.27	-	12.56	13.83	15.21	6.367
J401109D	vertical; not exceeding 150 mm high	m	0.02	0.24	-	1.73	1.97	2.17	0.856
J401109E	vertical; 150 - 300 mm high	m	0.04	0.48	-	3.55	4.03	4.43	1.755
J401109F	vertical; over 300 mm high	m²	0.13	1.59	-	11.78	13.37	14.71	5.833

J401110   **Bituthene bitumen coated 500 gauge polythene sheeting; sticking to concrete surfaces primed with bituthene primer**

J401110A	horizontal; not exceeding 150 mm wide	m	0.02	0.25	-	1.55	1.80	1.98	0.856
J401110B	horizontal; 150 - 300 mm wide	m	0.03	0.34	-	3.18	3.52	3.87	1.755
J401110C	horizontal; over 300 mm wide	m²	0.09	1.14	-	10.56	11.70	12.87	5.833
J401110D	vertical; not exceeding 150 mm high	m	0.02	0.23	-	1.65	1.88	2.07	0.928
J401110E	vertical; 150 - 300 mm high	m	0.04	0.44	-	3.44	3.88	4.27	1.933
J401110F	vertical; over 300 mm high	m²	0.12	1.46	-	11.35	12.81	14.09	6.367

J401111   **Bituthene bitumen coated 500 gauge polythene sheeting; sticking to masonry surfaces primed with bituthene primer**

J401111A	horizontal; not exceeding 150 mm wide	m	0.02	0.25	-	1.65	1.90	2.09	0.928
J401111B	horizontal; 150 - 300 mm wide	m	0.03	0.34	-	3.44	3.78	4.16	1.933
J401111C	horizontal; over 300 mm wide	m²	0.09	1.14	-	11.35	12.49	13.74	6.367
J401111D	vertical; not exceeding 150 mm high	m	0.02	0.23	-	1.55	1.78	1.96	0.856
J401111E	vertical; 150 - 300 mm high	m	0.04	0.44	-	3.18	3.62	3.98	1.755
J401111F	vertical; over 300 mm high	m²	0.12	1.46	-	10.56	12.02	13.22	5.833

J401112   **Waterproof building paper; BS 1521**

J401112A	horizontal; over 300 mm wide	m²	0.03	0.42	-	1.19	1.61	1.77	2.297

Waterproofing

		Unit	Labour Hours	Labour Net	Plant Net	Materials Net	Unit Net	Unit with 10%	CO₂
				£	£	£	£	£	Kg
J40	**J40: FLEXIBLE SHEET TANKING AND DAMP PROOFING**								
J4011	**Membranes**								
J401112	**Waterproof building paper; BS 1521**								
J401112B	vertical; over 300 mm high; fixing with staples	m²	0.04	0.65	-	1.19	1.84	2.02	2.297
J401113	**Hyload pitch polymer d.p.c.; horizontal**								
J401113A	not exceeding 150 mm wide	m	0.02	0.84	-	1.38	2.22	2.44	0.672
J401113B	150 - 300 mm wide	m	0.03	1.26	-	2.76	4.02	4.42	1.344
J401113C	over 300 mm wide	m²	0.08	3.78	-	9.06	12.84	14.12	4.410
J401114	**Hyload pitch polymer d.p.c.; forming cavity trays**								
J401114D	over 300 mm girth	m²	0.18	8.31	-	9.06	17.37	19.11	4.410
J401115	**Hyload pitch polymer d.p.c.; vertical**								
J401115E	not exceeding 150 mm high	m	0.03	1.26	-	1.38	2.64	2.90	0.672
J401115F	150 - 300 mm high	m	0.05	2.29	-	2.76	5.05	5.56	1.344
J401115G	over 300 mm high	m²	0.14	6.30	-	9.06	15.36	16.90	4.410
J4016	**Newtonite lathing to concrete or masonry backgrounds**								
J401651	**To walls, returns, reveals of openings or recesses, attached and unattached columns**								
J401651A	lathing	m²	0.06	2.80	-	12.99	15.79	17.37	3.637

Major Works 2011		Unit	Labour Hours	Labour Net	Plant Net	Materials Net	Unit Net	Unit with 10%	CO$_2$
				£	£	£	£	£	Kg
J41	**J41: BUILT UP FELT ROOF COVERINGS**								
J4121	**Flat coverings**								
J412102	**Built up bituminous felt roofing; BS 747; bedding in hot bitumen; laying on timber or screeded backings**								
J412102A	Type 1B; one layer	m²	0.08	3.50	0.61	3.67	7.78	8.56	4.869
J412102B	Type 1B; two layers	m²	0.14	6.58	0.61	6.11	13.30	14.63	8.977
J412102C	Type 1B; three layers	m²	0.20	9.38	1.23	9.79	20.40	22.44	13.846
J412102D	Type 2B; one layer	m²	0.08	3.73	0.61	6.06	10.40	11.44	5.379
J412102E	Type 2B; two layers	m²	0.15	6.81	0.61	10.89	18.31	20.14	9.997
J412102F	Type 2B; three layers	m²	0.21	9.61	1.23	16.95	27.79	30.57	15.376
J412102G	Type 3B; one layer	m²	0.09	3.97	0.61	7.33	11.91	13.10	5.889
J412102H	Type 3B; two layers	m²	0.15	7.05	0.61	13.43	21.09	23.20	11.017
J412102I	Type 3B; three layers	m²	0.21	9.85	1.23	20.77	31.85	35.04	16.906
J412102J	Type 1E; one layer	m²	0.10	4.71	0.61	4.47	9.79	10.77	6.501
J412102K	Type 2E; one layer	m²	0.11	4.95	0.61	6.84	12.40	13.64	6.705
J412102L	Type 3E; one layer	m²	0.11	5.18	0.61	8.45	14.24	15.66	6.909
J412102M	Limestone chippings in cold gritting compound; 6 mm thick	m²	0.09	3.97	-	2.69	6.66	7.33	0.410
J412102N	Limestone chippings in cold gritting compound; 13 mm thick	m²	0.11	5.18	-	4.01	9.19	10.11	0.580
J4131	**Sloping coverings**								
J413121	**Built up bituminous felt roofing; BS 747; bedding in hot bitumen; laying on timber or screeded backings**								
J413121A	Type 1B; one layer	m²	0.10	4.71	0.61	3.67	8.99	9.89	4.869
J413121B	Type 1B; two layers	m²	0.19	8.68	0.61	6.11	15.40	16.94	8.977
J413121C	Type 1B; three layers	m²	0.27	12.41	1.23	9.79	23.43	25.77	13.846
J413121D	Type 2B; one layer	m²	0.11	4.95	0.61	6.06	11.62	12.78	5.379
J413121E	Type 2B; two layers	m²	0.20	9.15	0.61	10.89	20.65	22.72	9.997
J413121F	Type 2B; three layers	m²	0.28	12.88	1.23	16.95	31.06	34.17	15.376
J413121G	Type 3B; one layer	m²	0.12	5.41	0.61	7.33	13.35	14.69	5.889
J413121H	Type 3B; two layers	m²	0.20	9.38	0.61	13.43	23.42	25.76	11.017
J413121I	Type 3B; three layers	m²	0.28	13.11	1.23	20.77	35.11	38.62	16.906
J413121J	Type 1E; one layer	m²	0.14	6.35	0.61	4.47	11.43	12.57	6.501
J413121K	Type 2E; one layer	m²	0.14	6.58	0.61	6.88	14.07	15.48	6.733
J413121L	Type 3E; one layer	m²	0.15	6.81	1.23	8.49	16.53	18.18	7.126
J4141	**Vertical coverings**								
J414151	**Built up bituminous felt roofing; BS 747; bedding in hot bitumen; laying on timber or screeded backings**								
J414151A	Type 1B; one layer	m²	0.13	5.88	0.61	3.67	10.16	11.18	4.869
J414151B	Type 1B; two layers	m²	0.23	10.78	0.61	6.11	17.50	19.25	8.977
J414151C	Type 1B; three layers	m²	0.33	15.49	1.23	9.79	26.51	29.16	13.846
J414151D	Type 2B; one layer	m²	0.13	6.11	0.61	6.06	12.78	14.06	5.379
J414151E	Type 2B; two layers	m²	0.25	11.48	0.61	10.89	22.98	25.28	9.997
J414151F	Type 2B; three layers	m²	0.35	16.19	1.23	16.95	34.37	37.81	15.376
J414151G	Type 3B; one layer	m²	0.15	6.81	0.61	7.33	14.75	16.23	5.889
J414151H	Type 3B; two layers	m²	0.25	11.71	0.61	13.43	25.75	28.33	11.017
J414151I	Type 3B; three layers	m²	0.35	16.42	1.23	20.77	38.42	42.26	16.906
J414151J	Type 1E; one layer	m²	0.17	7.98	0.61	4.47	13.06	14.37	6.501
J414151K	Type 2E; one layer	m²	0.18	8.21	0.61	6.84	15.66	17.23	6.705
J414151L	Type 3E; one layer	m²	0.18	8.45	1.23	8.45	18.13	19.94	7.098
J4161	**Skirtings, upstands, downstands or the like**								
J416171	**Mineral surfaced bituminous felt skirtings, upstands or downstands; BS 747; bedding in hot bitumen on timber, screeded or masonry backings**								
J416171A	Type 1E plain skirting; not exceeding 150 mm high	m	0.05	2.33	0.25	0.67	3.25	3.58	1.024
J416171B	Type 1E plain skirting; 150 - 300 mm high	m	0.08	3.50	0.37	1.35	5.22	5.74	2.009

Waterproofing

		Unit	Labour Hours	Labour Net £	Plant Net £	Materials Net £	Unit Net £	Unit with 10% £	CO$_2$ Kg
J41	**J41: BUILT UP FELT ROOF COVERINGS**								
J4161	**Skirtings, upstands, downstands or the like**								
J416171	**Mineral surfaced bituminous felt skirtings, upstands or downstands; BS 747; bedding in hot bitumen on timber, screeded or masonry backings**								
J416171C	Type 1E upstand; working over fillet and into groove; not exceeding 150 m girth	m	0.09	3.97	0.25	0.89	5.11	5.62	1.338
J416171D	Type 1E upstand; working over fillet and into groove; 150 - 300 mm girth	m	0.11	5.18	0.37	1.57	7.12	7.83	2.324
J416171E	Type 1E downstand; working over fillets and with welted drip; not exceeding 150 mm girth	m	0.13	5.88	0.37	1.19	7.44	8.18	1.746
J416171F	Type 1E downstand; working over fillets and with welted drip; 150 - 300 mm girth	m	0.18	8.21	0.49	1.86	10.56	11.62	2.732
J416171G	Type 2E plain skirting; not exceeding 150 mm high	m	0.05	2.33	0.25	1.03	3.61	3.97	1.054
J416171H	Type 2E plain skirting; 150 - 300 mm high	m	0.08	3.50	0.37	2.06	5.93	6.52	2.070
J416171I	Type 2E upstand; working over fillet and into groove; not exceeding 150 m girth	m	0.09	4.20	0.25	1.37	5.82	6.40	1.379
J416171J	Type 2E upstand; working over fillet and into groove; 150 - 300 mm girth	m	0.12	5.41	0.37	2.40	8.18	9.00	2.395
J416171K	Type 2E downstand; working over fillets and with welted drip; not exceeding 150 mm girth	m	0.13	6.11	0.37	1.78	8.26	9.09	1.797
J416171L	Type 2E downstand; working over fillets and with welted drip; 150 - 300 mm girth	m	0.18	8.45	0.49	2.81	11.75	12.93	2.814
J416171M	Type 3E plain skirting; not exceeding 150 mm girth	m	0.06	2.57	0.25	1.27	4.09	4.50	1.085
J416171N	Type 3E plain skirting; 150 - 300 mm girth	m	0.08	3.73	0.37	2.54	6.64	7.30	2.132
J416171O	Type 3E upstand; working over fillet and into groove; not exceeding 150 m girth	m	0.10	4.43	0.25	1.69	6.37	7.01	1.420
J416171P	Type 3E upstand; working over fillet and into groove; 150 - 300 mm girth	m	0.12	5.65	0.37	2.96	8.98	9.88	2.466
J416171Q	Type 3E downstand; working over fillets and with welted drip; not exceeding 150 mm girth	m	0.14	6.35	0.37	2.18	8.90	9.79	1.848
J416171R	Type 3E downstand; working over fillets and with welted drip; 150 - 300 mm girth	m	0.19	8.68	0.49	3.45	12.62	13.88	2.895

Major Works 2011		Unit	Labour Hours	Labour Net	Plant Net	Materials Net	Unit Net	Unit with 10%	CO₂
				£	£	£	£	£	Kg
J42	**J42: SINGLE LAYER POLYMERIC ROOF COVERINGS**								
J4210	**Flat coverings**								
J421010	**Sarnafil membrane G410-EL adhesive fixed to insulation board substrate (measured separately); on vapour barrier; to concrete base**								
J421010A	horizontal; over 300 mm wide	m²	0.55	25.52	-	15.19	40.71	44.78	7.519
J421010B	horizontal; not exceeding 300 mm wide	m²	0.35	16.14	-	4.74	20.88	22.97	2.350

Linings, Sheathings
and Dry Partitioning

Major Works 2011		Unit	Labour Hours	Labour Net	Plant Net	Materials Net	Unit Net	Unit with 10%	CO$_2$
				£	£	£	£	£	Kg
K10	**K10: PLASTERBOARD DRY LINING, PARTITION AND CEILINGS**								
K1001	**Proprietary partition; Gyproc metal stud partitions and walls**								
K100110	**GypWall Robust system; Gypframe 70 mm Gyproc C studs at 600 mm centres; 13 mm DuraLine each side; joints filled and taped to receive direct decoration**								
K100110A	not exceeding 1200 mm high	m	0.83	38.91	-	38.60	77.51	85.26	15.038
K100110B	1200 - 1500 mm high	m	0.89	41.48	-	46.66	88.14	96.95	18.432
K100110C	1500 - 1800 mm high	m	0.95	44.33	-	55.31	99.64	109.60	21.935
K100110D	1800 - 2100 mm high	m	1.10	51.09	-	64.15	115.24	126.76	25.683
K100110E	2100 - 2400 mm high	m	1.25	58.37	-	72.67	131.04	144.14	29.044
K100110F	2400 - 2700 mm high	m	1.44	67.05	-	81.20	148.25	163.08	32.534
K100110G	2700 - 3000 mm high	m	1.61	75.03	-	89.87	164.90	181.39	36.054
K100115	**Glasroc FireWall system; Gypframe 92 mm Gyproc I studs at 600 mm centres; 15 mm FireLine board outer layer over 25 mm Glasroc board inner layer; 40 mm and 50 mm Rock mineral wool batts to void; joints filled and taped to receive direct decoration**								
K100115A	not exceeding 1200 mm high	m	1.57	73.35	-	127.51	200.86	220.95	62.265
K100115B	1200 - 1500 mm high	m	1.96	91.41	-	157.49	248.90	273.79	77.465
K100115C	1500 - 1800 mm high	m	2.35	109.46	-	187.65	297.11	326.82	92.837
K100115D	1800 - 2100 mm high	m	2.75	128.22	-	218.23	346.45	381.10	108.377
K100115E	2100 - 2400 mm high	m	3.14	146.28	-	248.29	394.57	434.03	123.647
K100115F	2400 - 2700 mm high	m	3.53	164.80	-	278.23	443.03	487.33	138.907
K100115G	2700 - 3000 mm high	m	3.92	182.81	-	308.10	490.91	540.00	153.985
K1011	**Gyproc linings; 9.5 mm wallboard to woodwork backgrounds**								
K101101	**Linings to walls**								
K101101A	not exceeding 1200 mm high	m	0.08	3.73	-	3.34	7.07	7.78	4.357
K101101B	1200 - 1500 mm high	m	0.10	4.43	-	4.17	8.60	9.46	5.447
K101101C	1500 - 1800 mm high	m	0.11	5.09	-	4.99	10.08	11.09	6.527
K101101D	1800 - 2100 mm high	m	0.13	5.93	-	5.83	11.76	12.94	7.616
K101101E	2100 - 2400 mm high	m	0.15	6.77	-	6.66	13.43	14.77	8.706
K101101F	2400 - 2700 mm high	m	0.16	7.61	-	7.49	15.10	16.61	9.795
K101101G	2700 - 3000 mm high	m	0.18	8.45	-	8.33	16.78	18.46	10.884
K101111	**Linings to beams; 3 Nr faces**								
K101111A	not exceeding 600 mm girth	m	0.07	3.03	-	1.67	4.70	5.17	2.179
K101111B	600 - 1200 mm girth	m	0.13	5.88	-	3.34	9.22	10.14	4.357
K101111C	1200 - 1800 mm girth	m	0.19	8.91	-	5.00	13.91	15.30	6.536
K101121	**Linings to columns; 4 Nr faces**								
K101121A	not exceeding 600 mm girth	m	0.06	2.80	-	1.67	4.47	4.92	2.179
K101121B	600 - 1200 mm girth	m	0.12	5.41	-	3.34	8.75	9.63	4.357
K101121C	1200 - 1800 mm girth	m	0.20	9.15	-	5.00	14.15	15.57	6.536
K101131	**Linings to reveals and soffits**								
K101131A	not exceeding 300 mm wide	m	0.05	2.33	-	0.83	3.16	3.48	1.089
K101131B	300 - 600 mm wide	m	0.06	2.80	-	1.67	4.47	4.92	2.179
K101141	**Linings to ceilings**								
K101141A	over 300 mm wide	m^2	0.08	3.50	-	2.78	6.28	6.91	3.628
K101141B	over 300 mm wide; in staircase areas	m^2	0.08	3.87	-	2.78	6.65	7.32	3.628
K1012	**Gyproc linings; 9.5 mm Duplex wallboard to woodwork backgrounds**								
K101201	**Linings to walls**								
K101201A	not exceeding 1200 mm high	m	0.08	3.73	-	4.97	8.70	9.57	4.357
K101201B	1200 - 1500 mm high	m	0.10	4.43	-	6.22	10.65	11.72	5.447
K101201C	1500 - 1800 mm high	m	0.11	5.09	-	7.45	12.54	13.79	6.527
K101201D	1800 - 2100 mm high	m	0.13	5.93	-	8.69	14.62	16.08	7.616
K101201E	2100 - 2400 mm high	m	0.15	6.77	-	9.94	16.71	18.38	8.706
K101201F	2400 - 2700 mm high	m	0.16	7.61	-	11.18	18.79	20.67	9.795
K101201G	2700 - 3000 mm high	m	0.18	8.45	-	12.42	20.87	22.96	10.884

Major Works 2011		Unit	Labour Hours	Labour Net	Plant Net	Materials Net	Unit Net	Unit with 10%	CO$_2$
				£	£	£	£	£	Kg
K10	**K10: PLASTERBOARD DRY LINING, PARTITION AND CEILINGS**								
K1012	**Gyproc linings; 9.5 mm Duplex wallboard to woodwork backgrounds**								
K101211	**Linings to beams; 3 Nr faces**								
K101211A	not exceeding 600 mm girth	m	0.07	3.03	-	2.49	5.52	6.07	2.179
K101211B	600 - 1200 mm girth	m	0.13	5.88	-	4.97	10.85	11.94	4.357
K101211C	1200 - 1800 mm girth	m	0.19	8.91	-	7.46	16.37	18.01	6.536
K101221	**Linings to columns; 4 Nr faces**								
K101221A	not exceeding 600 mm girth	m	0.06	2.80	-	2.49	5.29	5.82	2.179
K101221B	600 - 1200 mm girth	m	0.12	5.41	-	4.97	10.38	11.42	4.357
K101221C	1200 - 1800 mm girth	m	0.20	9.15	-	7.46	16.61	18.27	6.536
K101231	**Linings to reveals and soffits**								
K101231A	not exceeding 300 mm wide	m	0.05	2.33	-	1.24	3.57	3.93	1.089
K101231B	300 - 600 mm wide	m	0.06	2.80	-	2.49	5.29	5.82	2.179
K101241	**Linings to ceilings**								
K101241A	over 300 mm wide	m^2	0.08	3.50	-	4.14	7.64	8.40	3.628
K101241B	over 300 mm wide; in staircase areas	m^2	0.08	3.87	-	4.14	8.01	8.81	3.628
K1013	**Gyproc linings; 9.5 mm plaster lath to woodwork backgrounds**								
K101301	**Linings to walls**								
K101301A	not exceeding 1200 mm high	m	0.08	3.73	-	5.30	9.03	9.93	4.357
K101301B	1200 - 1500 mm high	m	0.10	4.43	-	6.63	11.06	12.17	5.447
K101301C	1500 - 1800 mm high	m	0.11	5.09	-	7.94	13.03	14.33	6.527
K101301D	1800 - 2100 mm high	m	0.13	5.93	-	9.27	15.20	16.72	7.616
K101301E	2100 - 2400 mm high	m	0.15	6.77	-	10.59	17.36	19.10	8.706
K101301F	2400 - 2700 mm high	m	0.16	7.61	-	11.92	19.53	21.48	9.795
K101301G	2700 - 3000 mm high	m	0.18	8.45	-	13.24	21.69	23.86	10.884
K101311	**Linings to beams; 3 Nr faces**								
K101311A	not exceeding 600 mm girth	m	0.07	3.03	-	2.65	5.68	6.25	2.179
K101311B	600 - 1200 mm girth	m	0.13	5.88	-	5.30	11.18	12.30	4.357
K101311C	1200 - 1800 mm girth	m	0.19	8.91	-	7.95	16.86	18.55	6.536
K101321	**Linings to columns; 4 Nr faces**								
K101321A	not exceeding 600 mm girth	m	0.06	2.80	-	2.65	5.45	6.00	2.179
K101321B	600 - 1200 mm girth	m	0.12	5.41	-	5.30	10.71	11.78	4.357
K101321C	1200 - 1800 mm girth	m	0.20	9.15	-	7.95	17.10	18.81	6.536
K101331	**Linings to reveals and soffits**								
K101331A	not exceeding 300 mm wide	m	0.05	2.33	-	1.33	3.66	4.03	1.089
K101331B	300 - 600 mm wide	m	0.06	2.80	-	2.65	5.45	6.00	2.179
K101341	**Linings to ceilings**								
K101341A	over 300 mm wide	m^2	0.08	3.50	-	4.41	7.91	8.70	3.628
K101341B	over 300 mm wide; in staircase areas	m^2	0.08	3.87	-	4.41	8.28	9.11	3.628
K1014	**Gyproc linings; 12.5 mm wallboard to woodwork backgrounds**								
K101401	**Linings to walls**								
K101401A	not exceeding 1200 mm high	m	0.09	4.39	-	3.34	7.73	8.50	5.722
K101401B	1200 - 1500 mm high	m	0.11	5.23	-	4.17	9.40	10.34	7.152
K101401C	1500 - 1800 mm high	m	0.13	5.93	-	4.99	10.92	12.01	8.574
K101401D	1800 - 2100 mm high	m	0.15	6.91	-	5.83	12.74	14.01	10.004
K101401E	2100 - 2400 mm high	m	0.17	7.89	-	6.66	14.55	16.01	11.435
K101401F	2400 - 2700 mm high	m	0.19	8.87	-	7.49	16.36	18.00	12.865
K101401G	2700 - 3000 mm high	m	0.21	9.85	-	8.33	18.18	20.00	14.296
K101411	**Linings to beams; 3 Nr faces**								
K101411A	not exceeding 600 mm girth	m	0.08	3.55	-	1.67	5.22	5.74	2.861
K101411B	600 - 1200 mm girth	m	0.15	6.86	-	3.34	10.20	11.22	5.722
K101411C	1200 - 1800 mm girth	m	0.22	10.41	-	5.00	15.41	16.95	8.583
K101421	**Linings to columns; 4 Nr faces**								
K101421A	not exceeding 600 mm girth	m	0.07	3.27	-	1.67	4.94	5.43	2.861
K101421B	600 - 1200 mm girth	m	0.14	6.30	-	3.34	9.64	10.60	5.722
K101421C	1200 - 1800 mm girth	m	0.23	10.69	-	5.00	15.69	17.26	8.583

Linings, Sheathing & Dry Partitioning

Major Works 2011		Unit	Labour Hours	Labour Net	Plant Net	Materials Net	Unit Net	Unit with 10%	CO$_2$
				£	£	£	£	£	Kg
K10	**K10: PLASTERBOARD DRY LINING, PARTITION AND CEILINGS**								
K1014	**Gyproc linings; 12.5 mm wallboard to woodwork backgrounds**								
K101431	**Linings to reveals and soffits**								
K101431A	not exceeding 300 mm wide	m	0.06	2.75	-	0.83	3.58	3.94	1.430
K101431B	300 - 600 mm wide	m	0.07	3.27	-	1.67	4.94	5.43	2.861
K101441	**Linings to ceilings**								
K101441A	over 300 mm wide	m^2	0.09	3.97	-	2.78	6.75	7.43	4.765
K101441B	over 300 mm wide; in staircase areas	m^2	0.09	4.39	-	2.78	7.17	7.89	4.765
K1015	**Gyproc linings; 12.5 mm Duplex wallboard to woodwork backgrounds**								
K101501	**Linings to walls**								
K101501A	not exceeding 1200 mm high	m	0.09	4.39	-	4.91	9.30	10.23	5.722
K101501B	1200 - 1500 mm high	m	0.11	5.23	-	6.14	11.37	12.51	7.152
K101501C	1500 - 1800 mm high	m	0.13	5.93	-	7.35	13.28	14.61	8.574
K101501D	1800 - 2100 mm high	m	0.15	6.91	-	8.58	15.49	17.04	10.004
K101501E	2100 - 2400 mm high	m	0.17	7.89	-	9.81	17.70	19.47	11.435
K101501F	2400 - 2700 mm high	m	0.19	8.87	-	11.04	19.91	21.90	12.865
K101501G	2700 - 3000 mm high	m	0.21	9.85	-	12.27	22.12	24.33	14.296
K101511	**Linings to beams; 3 Nr faces**								
K101511A	not exceeding 600 mm girth	m	0.08	3.55	-	2.46	6.01	6.61	2.861
K101511B	600 - 1200 mm girth	m	0.15	6.86	-	4.91	11.77	12.95	5.722
K101511C	1200 - 1800 mm girth	m	0.22	10.41	-	7.37	17.78	19.56	8.583
K101521	**Linings to columns; 4 Nr faces**								
K101521A	not exceeding 600 mm girth	m	0.07	3.27	-	2.46	5.73	6.30	2.861
K101521B	600 - 1200 mm girth	m	0.14	6.30	-	4.91	11.21	12.33	5.722
K101521C	1200 - 1800 mm girth	m	0.23	10.69	-	7.37	18.06	19.87	8.583
K101531	**Linings to reveals and soffits**								
K101531A	not exceeding 300 mm wide	m	0.06	2.75	-	1.23	3.98	4.38	1.430
K101531B	300 - 600 mm wide	m	0.07	3.27	-	2.46	5.73	6.30	2.861
K101541	**Linings to ceilings**								
K101541A	over 300 mm wide	m^2	0.09	3.97	-	4.09	8.06	8.87	4.765
K101541B	over 300 mm wide; in staircase areas	m^2	0.09	4.39	-	4.09	8.48	9.33	4.765
K1016	**Gyproc linings; 12.5 mm plaster lath to woodwork backgrounds**								
K101601	**Linings to walls**								
K101601A	not exceeding 1200 mm high	m	0.09	4.39	-	6.62	11.01	12.11	4.357
K101601B	1200 - 1500 mm high	m	0.11	5.23	-	8.28	13.51	14.86	5.447
K101601C	1500 - 1800 mm high	m	0.13	5.93	-	9.93	15.86	17.45	6.527
K101601D	1800 - 2100 mm high	m	0.15	6.91	-	11.58	18.49	20.34	7.616
K101601E	2100 - 2400 mm high	m	0.17	7.89	-	13.24	21.13	23.24	8.706
K101601F	2400 - 2700 mm high	m	0.19	8.87	-	14.89	23.76	26.14	9.795
K101601G	2700 - 3000 mm high	m	0.21	9.85	-	16.55	26.40	29.04	10.884
K101611	**Linings to beams; 3 Nr faces**								
K101611A	not exceeding 600 mm girth	m	0.08	3.55	-	3.31	6.86	7.55	2.179
K101611B	600 - 1200 mm girth	m	0.15	6.86	-	6.62	13.48	14.83	4.357
K101611C	1200 - 1800 mm girth	m	0.22	10.41	-	9.94	20.35	22.39	6.536
K101621	**Linings to columns; 4 Nr faces**								
K101621A	not exceeding 600 mm girth	m	0.07	3.27	-	3.31	6.58	7.24	2.179
K101621B	600 - 1200 mm girth	m	0.14	6.30	-	6.62	12.92	14.21	4.357
K101621C	1200 - 1800 mm girth	m	0.23	10.69	-	9.94	20.63	22.69	6.536
K101631	**Linings to reveals and soffits**								
K101631A	not exceeding 300 mm wide	m	0.06	2.75	-	1.66	4.41	4.85	1.089
K101631B	300 - 600 mm wide	m	0.07	3.27	-	3.31	6.58	7.24	2.179
K101641	**Linings to ceilings**								
K101641A	over 300 mm wide	m^2	0.09	3.97	-	5.52	9.49	10.44	3.628
K101641B	over 300 mm wide; in staircase areas	m^2	0.09	4.39	-	5.52	9.91	10.90	3.628

Major Works 2011		Unit	Labour Hours	Labour Net	Plant Net	Materials Net	Unit Net	Unit with 10%	CO$_2$
				£	£	£	£	£	Kg
K10	**K10: PLASTERBOARD DRY LINING, PARTITION AND CEILINGS**								
K1017	**Gyproc linings; 12.5 mm Fireline board to woodwork backgrounds**								
K101701	**Linings to walls**								
K101701A	not exceeding 1200 mm high	m	0.09	4.39	–	4.13	8.52	9.37	5.722
K101701B	1200 - 1500 mm high	m	0.11	5.23	–	5.16	10.39	11.43	7.152
K101701C	1500 - 1800 mm high	m	0.13	5.93	–	6.18	12.11	13.32	8.574
K101701D	1800 - 2100 mm high	m	0.15	6.91	–	7.22	14.13	15.54	10.004
K101701E	2100 - 2400 mm high	m	0.17	7.89	–	8.25	16.14	17.75	11.435
K101701F	2400 - 2700 mm high	m	0.19	8.87	–	9.28	18.15	19.97	12.865
K101701G	2700 - 3000 mm high	m	0.21	9.85	–	10.31	20.16	22.18	14.296
K101711	**Linings to beams; 3 Nr faces**								
K101711A	not exceeding 600 mm girth	m	0.08	3.55	–	2.07	5.62	6.18	2.861
K101711B	600 - 1200 mm girth	m	0.15	6.86	–	4.13	10.99	12.09	5.722
K101711C	1200 - 1800 mm girth	m	0.22	10.41	–	6.20	16.61	18.27	8.583
K101721	**Linings to columns; 4 Nr faces**								
K101721A	not exceeding 600 mm girth	m	0.07	3.27	–	2.07	5.34	5.87	2.861
K101721B	600 - 1200 mm girth	m	0.14	6.30	–	4.13	10.43	11.47	5.722
K101721C	1200 - 1800 mm girth	m	0.23	10.69	–	6.20	16.89	18.58	8.583
K101731	**Linings to reveals and soffits**								
K101731A	not exceeding 300 mm wide	m	0.06	2.75	–	1.03	3.78	4.16	1.430
K101731B	300 - 600 mm wide	m	0.07	3.27	–	2.07	5.34	5.87	2.861
K101741	**Linings to ceilings**								
K101741A	over 300 mm wide	m^2	0.09	3.97	–	3.44	7.41	8.15	4.765
K101741B	over 300 mm wide; in staircase areas	m^2	0.09	4.39	–	3.44	7.83	8.61	4.765
K1021	**Gyproc linings; 9.5 mm tapered edge wallboard to woodwork backgrounds**								
K102101	**Linings to walls**								
K102101A	not exceeding 1200 mm high	m	0.08	3.73	–	3.70	7.43	8.17	4.764
K102101B	1200 - 1500 mm high	m	0.10	4.43	–	4.64	9.07	9.98	5.969
K102101C	1500 - 1800 mm high	m	0.11	5.09	–	5.56	10.65	11.72	7.155
K102101D	1800 - 2100 mm high	m	0.13	5.93	–	6.42	12.35	13.59	8.271
K102101E	2100 - 2400 mm high	m	0.15	6.77	–	7.40	14.17	15.59	9.529
K102101F	2400 - 2700 mm high	m	0.16	7.61	–	8.34	15.95	17.55	10.733
K102101G	2700 - 3000 mm high	m	0.18	8.45	–	9.26	17.71	19.48	11.920
K102111	**Linings to beams; 3 Nr faces**								
K102111A	not exceeding 600 mm girth	m	0.07	3.03	–	1.86	4.89	5.38	2.391
K102111B	600 - 1200 mm girth	m	0.13	5.88	–	3.70	9.58	10.54	4.764
K102111C	1200 - 1800 mm girth	m	0.19	8.91	–	5.56	14.47	15.92	7.155
K102121	**Linings to columns; 4 Nr faces**								
K102121A	not exceeding 600 mm girth	m	0.06	2.80	–	1.86	4.66	5.13	2.391
K102121B	600 - 1200 mm girth	m	0.12	5.41	–	3.70	9.11	10.02	4.764
K102121C	1200 - 1800 mm girth	m	0.20	9.15	–	5.56	14.71	16.18	7.155
K102131	**Linings to reveals and soffits**								
K102131A	not exceeding 300 mm wide	m	0.05	2.33	–	0.92	3.25	3.58	1.187
K102131B	300 - 600 mm wide	m	0.06	2.80	–	1.86	4.66	5.13	2.391
K102141	**Linings to ceilings**								
K102141A	over 300 mm wide	m^2	0.08	3.50	–	3.07	6.57	7.23	3.956
K102141B	over 300 mm wide; in staircase areas	m^2	0.08	3.87	–	3.07	6.94	7.63	3.956
K1022	**Gyproc linings; 9.5 mm tapered edge Duplex wallboard to woodwork backgrounds**								
K102201	**Linings to walls**								
K102201A	not exceeding 1200 mm high	m	0.08	3.73	–	5.34	9.07	9.98	4.764
K102201B	1200 - 1500 mm high	m	0.10	4.43	–	6.69	11.12	12.23	5.969
K102201C	1500 - 1800 mm high	m	0.11	5.09	–	8.02	13.11	14.42	7.155
K102201D	1800 - 2100 mm high	m	0.13	5.93	–	9.28	15.21	16.73	8.271
K102201E	2100 - 2400 mm high	m	0.15	6.77	–	10.68	17.45	19.20	9.529
K102201F	2400 - 2700 mm high	m	0.16	7.61	–	12.03	19.64	21.60	10.733
K102201G	2700 - 3000 mm high	m	0.18	8.45	–	13.36	21.81	23.99	11.920

Major Works 2011		Unit	Labour Hours	Labour Net £	Plant Net £	Materials Net £	Unit Net £	Unit with 10% £	CO₂ Kg
K10	**K10: PLASTERBOARD DRY LINING, PARTITION AND CEILINGS**								
K1022	**Gyproc linings; 9.5 mm tapered edge Duplex wallboard to woodwork backgrounds**								
K102211	**Linings to beams; 3 Nr faces**								
K102211A	not exceeding 600 mm girth	m	0.07	3.03	-	2.68	5.71	6.28	2.391
K102211B	600 - 1200 mm girth	m	0.13	5.88	-	5.34	11.22	12.34	4.764
K102211C	1200 - 1800 mm girth	m	0.19	8.91	-	8.02	16.93	18.62	7.155
K102221	**Linings to columns; 4 Nr faces**								
K102221A	not exceeding 600 mm girth	m	0.06	2.80	-	2.68	5.48	6.03	2.391
K102221B	600 - 1200 mm girth	m	0.12	5.41	-	5.34	10.75	11.83	4.764
K102221C	1200 - 1800 mm girth	m	0.20	9.15	-	8.02	17.17	18.89	7.155
K102231	**Linings to reveals and soffits**								
K102231A	not exceeding 300 mm wide	m	0.05	2.33	-	1.33	3.66	4.03	1.187
K102231B	300 - 600 mm wide	m	0.06	2.80	-	2.68	5.48	6.03	2.391
K102241	**Linings to ceilings**								
K102241A	over 300 mm wide	m²	0.08	3.50	-	4.44	7.94	8.73	3.956
K102241B	over 300 mm wide; in staircase areas	m²	0.08	3.87	-	4.44	8.31	9.14	3.956
K1023	**Gyproc linings; 12.5 mm tapered edge wallboard to woodwork backgrounds**								
K102301	**Linings to walls**								
K102301A	not exceeding 1200 mm high	m	0.09	4.39	-	3.70	8.09	8.90	6.129
K102301B	1200 - 1500 mm high	m	0.11	5.23	-	4.64	9.87	10.86	7.674
K102301C	1500 - 1800 mm high	m	0.13	5.93	-	5.56	11.49	12.64	9.202
K102301D	1800 - 2100 mm high	m	0.15	6.91	-	6.48	13.39	14.73	10.730
K102301E	2100 - 2400 mm high	m	0.17	7.89	-	7.40	15.29	16.82	12.258
K102301F	2400 - 2700 mm high	m	0.19	8.87	-	8.34	17.21	18.93	13.803
K102301G	2700 - 3000 mm high	m	0.21	9.85	-	9.26	19.11	21.02	15.331
K102311	**Linings to beams; 3 Nr faces**								
K102311A	not exceeding 600 mm girth	m	0.08	3.55	-	1.86	5.41	5.95	3.073
K102311B	600 - 1200 mm girth	m	0.15	6.86	-	3.70	10.56	11.62	6.129
K102311C	1200 - 1800 mm girth	m	0.22	10.41	-	5.56	15.97	17.57	9.202
K102321	**Linings to columns; 4 Nr faces**								
K102321A	not exceeding 600 mm girth	m	0.07	3.27	-	1.86	5.13	5.64	3.073
K102321B	600 - 1200 mm girth	m	0.14	6.30	-	3.70	10.00	11.00	6.129
K102321C	1200 - 1800 mm girth	m	0.23	10.69	-	5.56	16.25	17.88	9.202
K102331	**Linings to reveals and soffits**								
K102331A	not exceeding 300 mm wide	m	0.06	2.75	-	0.92	3.67	4.04	1.528
K102331B	300 - 600 mm wide	m	0.07	3.27	-	1.86	5.13	5.64	3.073
K102341	**Linings to ceilings**								
K102341A	over 300 mm wide	m²	0.09	3.97	-	3.07	7.04	7.74	5.093
K102341B	over 300 mm wide; in staircase areas	m²	0.09	4.39	-	3.07	7.46	8.21	5.093
K1024	**Gyproc linings; 12.5 mm tapered edge Duplex wallboard to woodwork backgrounds**								
K102401	**Linings to walls**								
K102401A	not exceeding 1200 mm high	m	0.09	4.39	-	5.28	9.67	10.64	6.129
K102401B	1200 - 1500 mm high	m	0.11	5.23	-	6.61	11.84	13.02	7.674
K102401C	1500 - 1800 mm high	m	0.13	5.93	-	7.92	13.85	15.24	9.202
K102401D	1800 - 2100 mm high	m	0.15	6.91	-	9.24	16.15	17.77	10.730
K102401E	2100 - 2400 mm high	m	0.17	7.89	-	10.55	18.44	20.28	12.258
K102401F	2400 - 2700 mm high	m	0.19	8.87	-	11.89	20.76	22.84	13.803
K102401G	2700 - 3000 mm high	m	0.21	9.85	-	13.20	23.05	25.36	15.331
K102411	**Linings to beams; 3 Nr faces**								
K102411A	not exceeding 600 mm girth	m	0.08	3.55	-	2.65	6.20	6.82	3.073
K102411B	600 - 1200 mm girth	m	0.15	6.86	-	5.28	12.14	13.35	6.129
K102411C	1200 - 1800 mm girth	m	0.22	10.41	-	7.92	18.33	20.16	9.202
K102421	**Linings to columns; 4 Nr faces**								
K102421A	not exceeding 600 mm girth	m	0.07	3.27	-	2.65	5.92	6.51	3.073
K102421B	600 - 1200 mm girth	m	0.14	6.30	-	5.28	11.58	12.74	6.129

Major Works 2011		Unit	Labour Hours	Labour Net	Plant Net	Materials Net	Unit Net	Unit with 10%	CO$_2$
				£	£	£	£	£	Kg
K10	**K10: PLASTERBOARD DRY LINING, PARTITION AND CEILINGS**								
K1024	**Gyproc linings; 12.5 mm tapered edge Duplex wallboard to woodwork backgrounds**								
K102421	**Linings to columns; 4 Nr faces**								
K102421C	1200 - 1800 mm girth	m	0.23	10.69	-	7.92	18.61	20.47	9.202
K102431	**Linings to reveals and soffits**								
K102431A	not exceeding 300 mm wide	m	0.06	2.75	-	1.32	4.07	4.48	1.528
K102431B	300 - 600 mm wide	m	0.07	3.27	-	2.65	5.92	6.51	3.073
K102441	**Linings to ceilings**								
K102441A	over 300 mm wide	m^2	0.09	3.97	-	4.38	8.35	9.19	5.093
K102441B	over 300 mm wide; in staircase areas	m^2	0.09	4.39	-	4.38	8.77	9.65	5.093
K1025	**Gyproc linings; 12.5 mm tapered edge Fireline wallboard to woodwork backgrounds**								
K102501	**Linings to walls**								
K102501A	not exceeding 1200 mm high	m	0.09	4.39	-	4.50	8.89	9.78	6.129
K102501B	1200 - 1500 mm high	m	0.11	5.23	-	5.63	10.86	11.95	7.674
K102501C	1500 - 1800 mm high	m	0.13	5.93	-	6.75	12.68	13.95	9.202
K102501D	1800 - 2100 mm high	m	0.15	6.91	-	7.87	14.78	16.26	10.730
K102501E	2100 - 2400 mm high	m	0.17	7.89	-	8.99	16.88	18.57	12.258
K102501F	2400 - 2700 mm high	m	0.19	8.87	-	10.13	19.00	20.90	13.803
K102501G	2700 - 3000 mm high	m	0.21	9.85	-	11.25	21.10	23.21	15.331
K102511	**Linings to beams; 3 Nr faces**								
K102511A	not exceeding 600 mm girth	m	0.08	3.55	-	2.26	5.81	6.39	3.073
K102511B	600 - 1200 mm girth	m	0.15	6.86	-	4.50	11.36	12.50	6.129
K102511C	1200 - 1800 mm girth	m	0.22	10.41	-	6.75	17.16	18.88	9.202
K102521	**Linings to columns; 4 Nr faces**								
K102521A	not exceeding 600 mm girth	m	0.07	3.27	-	2.26	5.53	6.08	3.073
K102521B	600 - 1200 mm girth	m	0.14	6.30	-	4.50	10.80	11.88	6.129
K102521C	1200 - 1800 mm girth	m	0.23	10.69	-	6.75	17.44	19.18	9.202
K102531	**Linings to reveals and soffits**								
K102531A	not exceeding 300 mm wide	m	0.06	2.75	-	1.12	3.87	4.26	1.528
K102531B	300 - 600 mm wide	m	0.07	3.27	-	2.26	5.53	6.08	3.073
K102541	**Linings to ceilings**								
K102541A	over 300 mm wide	m^2	0.09	3.97	-	3.73	7.70	8.47	5.093
K102541B	over 300 mm wide; in staircase areas	m^2	0.09	4.39	-	3.73	8.12	8.93	5.093
K1026	**Gyproc linings; 15.0 mm tapered edge wallboard to woodwork backgrounds**								
K102601	**Linings to walls**								
K102601A	not exceeding 1200 mm high	m	0.12	5.65	-	4.38	10.03	11.03	7.265
K102601B	1200 - 1500 mm high	m	0.14	6.67	-	5.49	12.16	13.38	9.095
K102601C	1500 - 1800 mm high	m	0.16	7.61	-	6.58	14.19	15.61	10.907
K102601D	1800 - 2100 mm high	m	0.19	8.87	-	7.67	16.54	18.19	12.719
K102601E	2100 - 2400 mm high	m	0.22	10.13	-	8.77	18.90	20.79	14.531
K102601F	2400 - 2700 mm high	m	0.24	11.39	-	9.87	21.26	23.39	16.360
K102601G	2700 - 3000 mm high	m	0.27	12.64	-	10.96	23.60	25.96	18.172
K102611	**Linings to beams; 3 Nr faces**								
K102611A	not exceeding 600 mm girth	m	0.10	4.57	-	2.20	6.77	7.45	3.642
K102611B	600 - 1200 mm girth	m	0.19	8.82	-	4.38	13.20	14.52	7.265
K102611C	1200 - 1800 mm girth	m	0.29	13.34	-	6.58	19.92	21.91	10.907
K102621	**Linings to columns; 4 Nr faces**								
K102621A	not exceeding 600 mm girth	m	0.09	4.20	-	2.20	6.40	7.04	3.642
K102621B	600 - 1200 mm girth	m	0.17	8.07	-	4.38	12.45	13.70	7.265
K102621C	1200 - 1800 mm girth	m	0.29	13.72	-	6.58	20.30	22.33	10.907
K102631	**Linings to reveals and soffits**								
K102631A	not exceeding 300 mm wide	m	0.08	3.50	-	1.09	4.59	5.05	1.812
K102631B	300 - 600 mm wide	m	0.09	4.20	-	2.20	6.40	7.04	3.642

Linings, Sheathing & Dry Partitioning

		Unit	Labour Hours	Labour Net	Plant Net	Materials Net	Unit Net	Unit with 10%	CO₂
				£	£	£	£	£	Kg
K10	**K10: PLASTERBOARD DRY LINING, PARTITION AND CEILINGS**								
K1026	**Gyproc linings; 15.0 mm tapered edge wallboard to woodwork backgrounds**								
K102641	**Linings to ceilings**								
K102641A	over 300 mm wide	m²	0.11	4.95	-	3.64	8.59	9.45	6.040
K102641B	over 300 mm wide; in staircase areas	m²	0.12	5.41	-	3.64	9.05	9.96	6.040
K1027	**Gyproc linings; 15.0 mm tapered edge Duplex wallboard to woodwork backgrounds**								
K102701	**Linings to walls**								
K102701A	not exceeding 1200 mm high	m	0.12	5.65	-	9.81	15.46	17.01	7.265
K102701B	1200 - 1500 mm high	m	0.14	6.67	-	12.28	18.95	20.85	9.095
K102701C	1500 - 1800 mm high	m	0.16	7.61	-	14.73	22.34	24.57	10.907
K102701D	1800 - 2100 mm high	m	0.19	8.87	-	17.18	26.05	28.66	12.719
K102701E	2100 - 2400 mm high	m	0.22	10.13	-	19.63	29.76	32.74	14.531
K102701F	2400 - 2700 mm high	m	0.24	11.39	-	22.09	33.48	36.83	16.360
K102701G	2700 - 3000 mm high	m	0.27	12.64	-	24.54	37.18	40.90	18.172
K102711	**Linings to beams; 3 Nr faces**								
K102711A	not exceeding 600 mm girth	m	0.10	4.57	-	4.91	9.48	10.43	3.642
K102711B	600 - 1200 mm girth	m	0.19	8.82	-	9.81	18.63	20.49	7.265
K102711C	1200 - 1800 mm girth	m	0.29	13.34	-	14.73	28.07	30.88	10.907
K102721	**Linings to columns; 4 Nr faces**								
K102721A	not exceeding 600 mm girth	m	0.09	4.20	-	4.91	9.11	10.02	3.642
K102721B	600 - 1200 mm girth	m	0.17	8.07	-	9.81	17.88	19.67	7.265
K102721C	1200 - 1800 mm girth	m	0.29	13.72	-	14.73	28.45	31.30	10.907
K102731	**Linings to reveals and soffits**								
K102731A	not exceeding 300 mm wide	m	0.08	3.50	-	2.45	5.95	6.55	1.812
K102731B	300 - 600 mm wide	m	0.09	4.20	-	4.91	9.11	10.02	3.642
K102741	**Linings to ceilings**								
K102741A	over 300 mm wide	m²	0.11	4.95	-	8.16	13.11	14.42	6.040
K102741B	over 300 mm wide; in staircase areas	m²	0.12	5.41	-	8.16	13.57	14.93	6.040
K1028	**Gyproc linings; 15.0 mm tapered edge Fireline wallboard to woodwork backgrounds**								
K102801	**Linings to walls**								
K102801A	not exceeding 1200 mm high	m	0.12	5.65	-	9.88	15.53	17.08	7.265
K102801B	1200 - 1500 mm high	m	0.14	6.67	-	12.36	19.03	20.93	9.095
K102801C	1500 - 1800 mm high	m	0.16	7.61	-	14.82	22.43	24.67	10.907
K102801D	1800 - 2100 mm high	m	0.19	8.87	-	17.29	26.16	28.78	12.719
K102801E	2100 - 2400 mm high	m	0.22	10.13	-	19.75	29.88	32.87	14.531
K102801F	2400 - 2700 mm high	m	0.24	11.39	-	22.23	33.62	36.98	16.360
K102801G	2700 - 3000 mm high	m	0.27	12.64	-	24.70	37.34	41.07	18.172
K102811	**Linings to beams; 3 Nr faces**								
K102811A	not exceeding 600 mm girth	m	0.10	4.57	-	4.95	9.52	10.47	3.642
K102811B	600 - 1200 mm girth	m	0.19	8.82	-	9.88	18.70	20.57	7.265
K102811C	1200 - 1800 mm girth	m	0.29	13.34	-	14.82	28.16	30.98	10.907
K102821	**Linings to columns; 4 Nr faces**								
K102821A	not exceeding 600 mm girth	m	0.09	4.20	-	4.95	9.15	10.07	3.642
K102821B	600 - 1200 mm girth	m	0.17	8.07	-	9.88	17.95	19.75	7.265
K102821C	1200 - 1800 mm girth	m	0.29	13.72	-	14.82	28.54	31.39	10.907
K102831	**Linings to reveals and soffits**								
K102831A	not exceeding 300 mm wide	m	0.08	3.50	-	2.46	5.96	6.56	1.812
K102831B	300 - 600 mm wide	m	0.09	4.20	-	4.95	9.15	10.07	3.642
K102841	**Linings to ceilings**								
K102841A	over 300 mm wide	m²	0.11	4.95	-	8.22	13.17	14.49	6.040
K102841B	over 300 mm wide; in staircase areas	m²	0.12	5.41	-	8.22	13.63	14.99	6.040

Major Works 2011		Unit	Labour Hours	Labour Net	Plant Net	Materials Net	Unit Net	Unit with 10%	CO2
				£	£	£	£	£	Kg
K10	**K10: PLASTERBOARD DRY LINING, PARTITION AND CEILINGS**								
K1029	**Gyproc linings; 19.0 mm tapered edge plank to woodwork backgrounds**								
K102901	**Linings to walls**								
K102901A	not exceeding 1200 mm high	m	0.14	6.58	-	10.12	16.70	18.37	9.085
K102901B	1200 - 1500 mm high	m	0.17	7.79	-	12.66	20.45	22.50	11.369
K102901C	1500 - 1800 mm high	m	0.19	8.87	-	15.18	24.05	26.46	13.636
K102901D	1800 - 2100 mm high	m	0.22	10.36	-	17.71	28.07	30.88	15.903
K102901E	2100 - 2400 mm high	m	0.25	11.80	-	20.23	32.03	35.23	18.170
K102901F	2400 - 2700 mm high	m	0.29	13.30	-	22.77	36.07	39.68	20.454
K102901G	2700 - 3000 mm high	m	0.32	14.79	-	25.30	40.09	44.10	22.721
K102911	**Linings to beams; 3 Nr faces**								
K102911A	not exceeding 600 mm girth	m	0.12	5.37	-	5.07	10.44	11.48	4.551
K102911B	600 - 1200 mm girth	m	0.22	10.31	-	10.12	20.43	22.47	9.085
K102911C	1200 - 1800 mm girth	m	0.33	15.58	-	15.18	30.76	33.84	13.636
K102921	**Linings to columns; 4 Nr faces**								
K102921A	not exceeding 600 mm girth	m	0.11	4.95	-	5.07	10.02	11.02	4.551
K102921B	600 - 1200 mm girth	m	0.20	9.47	-	10.12	19.59	21.55	9.085
K102921C	1200 - 1800 mm girth	m	0.34	16.00	-	15.18	31.18	34.30	13.636
K102931	**Linings to reveals and soffits**								
K102931A	not exceeding 300 mm wide	m	0.09	4.11	-	2.52	6.63	7.29	2.267
K102931B	300 - 600 mm wide	m	0.11	4.95	-	5.07	10.02	11.02	4.551
K102941	**Linings to ceilings**								
K102941A	over 300 mm wide	m²	0.12	5.65	-	8.42	14.07	15.48	7.556
K102941B	over 300 mm wide; in staircase areas	m²	0.13	6.21	-	8.42	14.63	16.09	7.556
K1065	**Gyproc linings; 12.5 mm tapered edge wallboard to woodwork backgrounds; fixing with screws; joints flush filled, taped and finished for direct decoration**								
K106501	**Linings to walls; height**								
K106501A	not exceeding 1200 mm high	m	0.13	6.07	-	5.41	11.48	12.63	7.873
K106501B	1200 - 1500 mm high	m	0.16	7.33	-	5.72	13.05	14.36	9.804
K106501C	1500 - 1800 mm high	m	0.18	8.45	-	6.86	15.31	16.84	11.758
K106501D	1800 - 2100 mm high	m	0.21	9.85	-	8.00	17.85	19.64	13.712
K106501E	2100 - 2400 mm high	m	0.24	11.25	-	9.14	20.39	22.43	15.666
K106501F	2400 - 2700 mm high	m	0.27	12.64	-	10.29	22.93	25.22	17.637
K106501G	2700 - 3000 mm high	m	0.30	14.04	-	11.43	25.47	28.02	19.591
K106511	**Linings to beams; 3 Nr faces; girth**								
K106511A	not exceeding 600 mm girth	m	0.10	4.62	-	3.20	7.82	8.60	3.997
K106511B	600 - 1200 mm girth	m	0.18	8.54	-	5.42	13.96	15.36	7.950
K106511C	1200 - 1800 mm girth	m	0.28	12.92	-	7.64	20.56	22.62	11.798
K106521	**Linings to columns; 4 Nr faces; girth**								
K106521A	not exceeding 600 mm girth	m	0.09	4.11	-	3.68	7.79	8.57	4.009
K106521B	600 - 1200 mm girth	m	0.17	7.98	-	5.90	13.88	15.27	7.963
K106521C	1200 - 1800 mm girth	m	0.28	13.20	-	8.13	21.33	23.46	11.934
K106531	**Linings to reveals and soffits; width**								
K106531A	not exceeding 300 mm wide	m	0.07	3.27	-	1.64	4.91	5.40	2.043
K106531B	300 - 600 mm wide	m	0.09	4.11	-	2.73	6.84	7.52	4.014
K106541	**Linings to ceilings**								
K106541A	over 300 mm wide	m²	0.12	5.41	-	3.65	9.06	9.97	6.509
K106541B	over 300 mm wide; in staircase areas	m²	0.13	5.88	-	3.65	9.53	10.48	6.509

Major Works 2011		Unit	Labour Hours	Labour Net £	Plant Net £	Materials Net £	Unit Net £	Unit with 10% £	CO₂ Kg
K10	**K10: PLASTERBOARD DRY LINING, PARTITION AND CEILINGS**								
K1066	**Gyproc linings; 9.5 mm wallboard to masonry or concrete walls; fixing by Thistlebond system; joints flush filled, taped and finished for direct decoration**								
K106601	**Linings to walls; height**								
K106601A	not exceeding 1200 mm	m	0.14	6.49	-	4.95	11.44	12.58	10.409
K106601B	1200 - 1500 mm	m	0.17	8.07	-	6.21	14.28	15.71	13.020
K106601C	1500 - 1800 mm	m	0.21	9.71	-	7.43	17.14	18.85	15.613
K106601D	1800 - 2100 mm	m	0.24	11.34	-	8.68	20.02	22.02	18.225
K106601E	2100 - 2400 mm	m	0.28	12.92	-	9.91	22.83	25.11	20.818
K106601F	2400 - 2700 mm	m	0.31	14.56	-	11.16	25.72	28.29	23.429
K106601G	2700 - 3000 mm	m	0.35	16.19	-	12.38	28.57	31.43	26.022
K106611	**Linings to beams; 3 Nr faces; girth**								
K106611A	not exceeding 600 mm	m	0.08	3.50	-	3.37	6.87	7.56	5.328
K106611B	600 - 1200 mm	m	0.15	7.05	-	5.77	12.82	14.10	10.631
K106611C	1200 - 1800 mm	m	0.23	10.55	-	8.17	18.72	20.59	15.875
K106621	**Linings to columns; 4 Nr faces; girth**								
K106621A	not exceeding 600 mm	m	0.08	3.50	-	3.85	7.35	8.09	5.341
K106621B	600 - 1200 mm	m	0.15	7.05	-	6.25	13.30	14.63	10.644
K106621C	1200 - 1800 mm	m	0.23	10.55	-	8.65	19.20	21.12	15.888
K106631	**Linings to reveals and soffits; width**								
K106631A	not exceeding 300 mm	m	0.06	2.57	-	1.70	4.27	4.70	2.629
K106631B	300 - 600 mm	m	0.08	3.50	-	2.88	6.38	7.02	5.315
K1067	**Gyproc linings; 12.5 mm wallboard to masonry or concrete walls; fixing by Thistlebond system; joints flush filled, taped and finished for direct decoration**								
K106701	**Linings to walls; height**								
K106701A	not exceeding 1200 mm	m	0.15	7.05	-	4.95	12.00	13.20	11.774
K106701B	1200 - 1500 mm	m	0.19	8.77	-	6.21	14.98	16.48	14.726
K106701C	1500 - 1800 mm	m	0.23	10.55	-	7.43	17.98	19.78	17.660
K106701D	1800 - 2100 mm	m	0.26	12.32	-	8.22	20.54	22.59	19.801
K106701E	2100 - 2400 mm	m	0.30	14.04	-	9.91	23.95	26.35	23.547
K106701F	2400 - 2700 mm	m	0.34	15.82	-	11.16	26.98	29.68	26.500
K106701G	2700 - 3000 mm	m	0.38	17.59	-	12.38	29.97	32.97	29.434
K106711	**Linings to beams; 3 Nr faces; girth**								
K106711A	not exceeding 600 mm	m	0.08	3.50	-	3.37	6.87	7.56	6.010
K106711B	600 - 1200 mm	m	0.15	7.05	-	5.77	12.82	14.10	11.996
K106711C	1200 - 1800 mm	m	0.23	10.55	-	8.17	18.72	20.59	17.922
K106721	**Linings to columns; 4 Nr faces; girth**								
K106721A	not exceeding 600 mm	m	0.08	3.50	-	3.85	7.35	8.09	6.023
K106721B	600 - 1200 mm	m	0.15	7.05	-	6.25	13.30	14.63	12.008
K106721C	1200 - 1800 mm	m	0.23	10.55	-	8.65	19.20	21.12	17.934
K106731	**Linings to reveals and soffits; width**								
K106731A	not exceeding 300 mm	m	0.06	2.57	-	1.70	4.27	4.70	2.970
K106731B	300 - 600 mm	m	0.08	3.50	-	2.88	6.38	7.02	5.998
K1068	**Gyproc linings; 12.5 mm Fireline board to masonry or concrete walls; fixing by Thistlebond system; joints flush filled, taped and finished for direct decoration**								
K106801	**Linings to walls; height**								
K106801A	not exceeding 1200 mm	m	0.15	7.05	-	5.75	12.80	14.08	11.774
K106801B	1200 - 1500 mm	m	0.19	8.77	-	7.20	15.97	17.57	14.726
K106801C	1500 - 1800 mm	m	0.23	10.55	-	8.62	19.17	21.09	17.660
K106801D	1800 - 2100 mm	m	0.26	12.32	-	9.49	21.81	23.99	19.801
K106801E	2100 - 2400 mm	m	0.30	14.04	-	11.49	25.53	28.08	23.547

Major Works 2011		Unit	Labour Hours	Labour Net	Plant Net	Materials Net	Unit Net	Unit with 10%	CO$_2$
				£	£	£	£	£	Kg
K10	**K10: PLASTERBOARD DRY LINING, PARTITION AND CEILINGS**								
K1068	**Gyproc linings; 12.5 mm Fireline board to masonry or concrete walls; fixing by Thistlebond system; joints flush filled, taped and finished for direct decoration**								
K106801	**Linings to walls; height**								
K106801F	2400 - 2700 mm	m	0.34	15.82	-	12.95	28.77	31.65	26.500
K106801G	2700 - 3000 mm	m	0.38	17.59	-	14.37	31.96	35.16	29.434
K106811	**Linings to beams; 3 Nr faces; girth**								
K106811A	not exceeding 600 mm	m	0.08	3.50	-	3.77	7.27	8.00	6.010
K106811B	600 - 1200 mm	m	0.15	7.05	-	6.57	13.62	14.98	11.996
K106811C	1200 - 1800 mm	m	0.23	10.55	-	9.36	19.91	21.90	17.922
K106821	**Linings to columns; 4 Nr faces; girth**								
K106821A	not exceeding 600 mm	m	0.08	3.50	-	4.25	7.75	8.53	6.023
K106821B	600 - 1200 mm	m	0.15	7.05	-	7.05	14.10	15.51	12.008
K106821C	1200 - 1800 mm	m	0.23	10.55	-	9.84	20.39	22.43	17.934
K106831	**Linings to reveals and soffits; width**								
K106831A	not exceeding 300 mm	m	0.06	2.57	-	1.89	4.46	4.91	2.970
K106831B	300 - 600 mm	m	0.08	3.50	-	3.28	6.78	7.46	5.998
K1069	**Gyproc linings; 25 mm thermal board to masonry or concrete walls; fixing by Thistlebond TL system; joints flush filled, taped and finished for direct decoration**								
K106901	**Linings to walls; height**								
K106901A	not exceeding 1200 mm	m	0.17	7.89	-	17.44	25.33	27.86	17.459
K106901B	1200 - 1500 mm	m	0.21	9.85	-	21.82	31.67	34.84	21.833
K106901C	1500 - 1800 mm	m	0.25	11.80	-	26.16	37.96	41.76	26.188
K106901D	1800 - 2100 mm	m	0.30	13.76	-	30.53	44.29	48.72	30.562
K106901E	2100 - 2400 mm	m	0.34	15.77	-	34.88	50.65	55.72	34.917
K106901F	2400 - 2700 mm	m	0.38	17.73	-	39.25	56.98	62.68	39.291
K106901G	2700 - 3000 mm	m	0.42	19.69	-	43.60	63.29	69.62	43.647
K106911	**Linings to beams; 3 Nr faces; girth**								
K106911A	not exceeding 600 mm	m	0.08	3.50	-	9.60	13.10	14.41	8.764
K106911B	600 - 1200 mm	m	0.15	7.05	-	18.24	25.29	27.82	17.503
K106911C	1200 - 1800 mm	m	0.23	10.55	-	26.86	37.41	41.15	26.183
K106921	**Linings to columns; 4 Nr faces; girth**								
K106921A	not exceeding 600 mm	m	0.08	3.50	-	10.08	13.58	14.94	8.776
K106921B	600 - 1200 mm	m	0.15	7.05	-	18.71	25.76	28.34	17.515
K106921C	1200 - 1800 mm	m	0.23	10.55	-	27.34	37.89	41.68	26.195
K106931	**Linings to reveals and soffits; width**								
K106931A	not exceeding 300 mm	m	0.06	2.57	-	4.82	7.39	8.13	4.392
K106931B	300 - 600 mm	m	0.08	3.50	-	9.17	12.67	13.94	8.840
K1070	**Gyproc linings; 32 mm thermal board to masonry or concrete walls; fixing by Thistlebond TL system; joints flush filled, taped and finished for direct decoration**								
K107001	**Linings to walls; height**								
K107001A	not exceeding 1200 mm	m	0.18	8.45	-	18.84	27.29	30.02	20.643
K107001B	1200 - 1500 mm	m	0.23	10.55	-	23.56	34.11	37.52	25.813
K107001C	1500 - 1800 mm	m	0.27	12.64	-	28.26	40.90	44.99	30.964
K107001D	1800 - 2100 mm	m	0.32	14.79	-	32.98	47.77	52.55	36.134
K107001E	2100 - 2400 mm	m	0.36	16.84	-	37.67	54.51	59.96	41.285
K107001F	2400 - 2700 mm	m	0.41	18.94	-	42.40	61.34	67.47	46.455
K107001G	2700 - 3000 mm	m	0.45	21.09	-	47.09	68.18	75.00	51.607

Major Works 2011		Unit	Labour Hours	Labour Net	Plant Net	Materials Net	Unit Net	Unit with 10%	CO₂
				£	£	£	£	£	Kg
K10	**K10: PLASTERBOARD DRY LINING, PARTITION AND CEILINGS**								
K1070	**Gyproc linings; 32 mm thermal board to masonry or concrete walls; fixing by Thistlebond TL system; joints flush filled, taped and finished for direct decoration**								
K107011	**Linings to beams; 3 Nr faces; girth**								
K107011A	not exceeding 600 mm	m	0.08	3.73	-	10.30	14.03	15.43	10.356
K107011B	600 - 1200 mm	m	0.16	7.51	-	19.63	27.14	29.85	20.687
K107011C	1200 - 1800 mm	m	0.24	11.01	-	28.96	39.97	43.97	30.959
K107021	**Linings to columns; 4 Nr faces; girth**								
K107021A	not exceeding 600 mm	m	0.08	3.73	-	10.78	14.51	15.96	10.368
K107021B	600 - 1200 mm	m	0.16	7.51	-	20.11	27.62	30.38	20.699
K107021C	1200 - 1800 mm	m	0.24	11.01	-	29.44	40.45	44.50	30.971
K107031	**Linings to reveals and soffits; width**								
K107031A	not exceeding 300 mm	m	0.06	2.80	-	5.17	7.97	8.77	5.188
K107031B	300 - 600 mm	m	0.08	3.73	-	9.87	13.60	14.96	10.432
K1071	**Gyproc linings; 40 mm thermal board to masonry or concrete walls; fixing by Thistlebond TL system; joints flush filled, taped and finished for direct decoration**								
K107101	**Linings to walls; height**								
K107101A	not exceeding 1200 mm	m	0.19	9.01	-	20.94	29.95	32.95	24.282
K107101B	1200 - 1500 mm	m	0.24	11.25	-	26.19	37.44	41.18	30.361
K107101C	1500 - 1800 mm	m	0.29	13.48	-	31.41	44.89	49.38	36.422
K107101D	1800 - 2100 mm	m	0.34	15.77	-	36.66	52.43	57.67	42.502
K107101E	2100 - 2400 mm	m	0.39	17.96	-	41.88	59.84	65.82	48.563
K107101F	2400 - 2700 mm	m	0.43	20.25	-	47.13	67.38	74.12	54.643
K107101G	2700 - 3000 mm	m	0.48	22.49	-	52.35	74.84	82.32	60.704
K107111	**Linings to beams; 3 Nr faces; girth**								
K107111A	not exceeding 600 mm	m	0.09	3.97	-	11.35	15.32	16.85	12.175
K107111B	600 - 1200 mm	m	0.17	7.98	-	21.74	29.72	32.69	24.326
K107111C	1200 - 1800 mm	m	0.25	11.48	-	32.12	43.60	47.96	36.417
K107121	**Linings to columns; 4 Nr faces; girth**								
K107121A	not exceeding 600 mm	m	0.09	3.97	-	11.83	15.80	17.38	12.188
K107121B	600 - 1200 mm	m	0.17	7.98	-	22.22	30.20	33.22	24.338
K107121C	1200 - 1800 mm	m	0.25	11.48	-	32.59	44.07	48.48	36.429
K107131	**Linings to reveals and soffits; width**								
K107131A	not exceeding 300 mm	m	0.07	3.03	-	5.69	8.72	9.59	6.097
K107131B	300 - 600 mm	m	0.09	3.97	-	10.92	14.89	16.38	12.252
K1072	**Gyproc linings; 50 mm thermal board to masonry or concrete walls; fixing by Thistlebond TL system; joints flush filled, taped and finished for direct decoration**								
K107201	**Linings to walls; height**								
K107201A	not exceeding 1200 mm	m	0.21	9.57	-	24.52	34.09	37.50	28.830
K107201B	1200 - 1500 mm	m	0.26	11.94	-	30.67	42.61	46.87	36.047
K107201C	1500 - 1800 mm	m	0.31	14.32	-	36.78	51.10	56.21	43.245
K107201D	1800 - 2100 mm	m	0.36	16.75	-	42.93	59.68	65.65	50.462
K107201E	2100 - 2400 mm	m	0.41	19.08	-	49.04	68.12	74.93	57.660
K107201F	2400 - 2700 mm	m	0.46	21.51	-	55.19	76.70	84.37	64.877
K107201G	2700 - 3000 mm	m	0.51	23.89	-	61.30	85.19	93.71	72.075
K107211	**Linings to beams; 3 Nr faces; girth**								
K107211A	not exceeding 600 mm	m	0.09	4.20	-	13.14	17.34	19.07	14.450
K107211B	600 - 1200 mm	m	0.18	8.45	-	25.32	33.77	37.15	28.874
K107211C	1200 - 1800 mm	m	0.26	11.94	-	37.48	49.42	54.36	43.240

Major Works 2011		Unit	Labour Hours	Labour Net	Plant Net	Materials Net	Unit Net	Unit with 10%	CO$_2$
				£	£	£	£	£	Kg
K10	**K10: PLASTERBOARD DRY LINING, PARTITION AND CEILINGS**								
K1072	**Gyproc linings; 50 mm thermal board to masonry or concrete walls; fixing by Thistlebond TL system; joints flush filled, taped and finished for direct decoration**								
K107221	**Linings to columns; 4 Nr faces; girth**								
K107221A	not exceeding 600 mm	m	0.09	4.20	-	13.62	17.82	19.60	14.462
K107221B	600 - 1200 mm	m	0.18	8.45	-	25.79	34.24	37.66	28.887
K107221C	1200 - 1800 mm	m	0.26	11.94	-	37.96	49.90	54.89	43.252
K107231	**Linings to reveals and soffits; width**								
K107231A	not exceeding 300 mm	m	0.07	3.27	-	6.59	9.86	10.85	7.235
K107231B	300 - 600 mm	m	0.09	4.20	-	12.71	16.91	18.60	14.526
K1073	**Gyproc linings; 25 mm vapour check thermal board to masonry or concrete walls; fixing by Thistlebond TL system; joints flush filled, taped and finished for direct decoration**								
K107301	**Linings to walls; height**								
K107301A	not exceeding 1200 mm	m	0.17	7.89	-	17.85	25.74	28.31	17.459
K107301B	1200 - 1500 mm	m	0.21	9.85	-	22.33	32.18	35.40	21.833
K107301C	1500 - 1800 mm	m	0.25	11.80	-	26.78	38.58	42.44	26.188
K107301D	1800 - 2100 mm	m	0.30	13.76	-	31.26	45.02	49.52	30.562
K107301E	2100 - 2400 mm	m	0.34	15.77	-	35.71	51.48	56.63	34.917
K107301F	2400 - 2700 mm	m	0.38	17.73	-	40.19	57.92	63.71	39.291
K107301G	2700 - 3000 mm	m	0.42	19.69	-	44.64	64.33	70.76	43.647
K107311	**Linings to beams; 3 Nr faces; girth**								
K107311A	not exceeding 600 mm	m	0.08	3.50	-	9.81	13.31	14.64	8.764
K107311B	600 - 1200 mm	m	0.15	7.05	-	18.65	25.70	28.27	17.503
K107311C	1200 - 1800 mm	m	0.23	10.55	-	27.49	38.04	41.84	26.183
K107321	**Linings to columns; 4 Nr faces; girth**								
K107321A	not exceeding 600 mm	m	0.08	3.50	-	10.29	13.79	15.17	8.776
K107321B	600 - 1200 mm	m	0.15	7.05	-	19.13	26.18	28.80	17.515
K107321C	1200 - 1800 mm	m	0.23	10.55	-	27.96	38.51	42.36	26.195
K107331	**Linings to reveals and soffits; width**								
K107331A	not exceeding 300 mm	m	0.06	2.57	-	4.92	7.49	8.24	4.392
K107331B	300 - 600 mm	m	0.08	3.50	-	9.38	12.88	14.17	8.840
K1074	**Gyproc linings; 32 mm vapour check thermal board to masonry or concrete walls; fixing by Thistlebond TL system; joints flush filled, taped and finished for direct decoration**								
K107401	**Linings to walls; height**								
K107401A	not exceeding 1200 mm	m	0.18	8.45	-	23.76	32.21	35.43	20.643
K107401B	1200 - 1500 mm	m	0.23	10.55	-	29.72	40.27	44.30	25.813
K107401C	1500 - 1800 mm	m	0.27	12.64	-	35.65	48.29	53.12	30.964
K107401D	1800 - 2100 mm	m	0.32	14.79	-	41.60	56.39	62.03	36.134
K107401E	2100 - 2400 mm	m	0.36	16.84	-	47.53	64.37	70.81	41.285
K107401F	2400 - 2700 mm	m	0.41	18.94	-	53.49	72.43	79.67	46.455
K107401G	2700 - 3000 mm	m	0.45	21.09	-	59.41	80.50	88.55	51.607
K107411	**Linings to beams; 3 Nr faces; girth**								
K107411A	not exceeding 600 mm	m	0.08	3.73	-	12.76	16.49	18.14	10.356
K107411B	600 - 1200 mm	m	0.16	7.51	-	24.56	32.07	35.28	20.687
K107411C	1200 - 1800 mm	m	0.24	11.01	-	36.35	47.36	52.10	30.959
K107421	**Linings to columns; 4 Nr faces; girth**								
K107421A	not exceeding 600 mm	m	0.08	3.73	-	13.24	16.97	18.67	10.368
K107421B	600 - 1200 mm	m	0.16	7.51	-	25.04	32.55	35.81	20.699

Linings, Sheathing & Dry Partitioning

Major Works 2011		Unit	Labour Hours	Labour Net £	Plant Net £	Materials Net £	Unit Net £	Unit with 10% £	CO₂ Kg
K10	**K10: PLASTERBOARD DRY LINING, PARTITION AND CEILINGS**								
K1074	**Gyproc linings; 32 mm vapour check thermal board to masonry or concrete walls; fixing by Thistlebond TL system; joints flush filled, taped and finished for direct decoration**								
K107421	**Linings to columns; 4 Nr faces; girth**								
K107421C	1200 - 1800 mm	m	0.24	11.01	-	36.83	47.84	52.62	30.971
K107431	**Linings to reveals and soffits; width**								
K107431A	not exceeding 300 mm	m	0.06	2.80	-	6.40	9.20	10.12	5.188
K107431B	300 - 600 mm	m	0.08	3.73	-	12.33	16.06	17.67	10.432
K1075	**Gyproc linings; 40 mm vapour check thermal board to masonry or concrete walls; fixing by Thistlebond TL system; joints flush filled, taped and finished for direct decoration**								
K107501	**Linings to walls; height**								
K107501A	not exceeding 1200 mm	m	0.19	9.01	-	23.71	32.72	35.99	24.282
K107501B	1200 - 1500 mm	m	0.24	11.25	-	29.66	40.91	45.00	30.361
K107501C	1500 - 1800 mm	m	0.29	13.48	-	35.57	49.05	53.96	36.422
K107501D	1800 - 2100 mm	m	0.34	15.77	-	41.52	57.29	63.02	42.502
K107501E	2100 - 2400 mm	m	0.39	17.96	-	47.43	65.39	71.93	48.563
K107501F	2400 - 2700 mm	m	0.43	20.25	-	53.37	73.62	80.98	54.643
K107501G	2700 - 3000 mm	m	0.48	22.49	-	59.28	81.77	89.95	60.704
K107511	**Linings to beams; 3 Nr faces; girth**								
K107511A	not exceeding 600 mm	m	0.09	3.97	-	12.74	16.71	18.38	12.175
K107511B	600 - 1200 mm	m	0.17	7.98	-	24.51	32.49	35.74	24.326
K107511C	1200 - 1800 mm	m	0.25	11.48	-	36.27	47.75	52.53	36.417
K107521	**Linings to columns; 4 Nr faces; girth**								
K107521A	not exceeding 600 mm	m	0.09	3.97	-	13.22	17.19	18.91	12.188
K107521B	600 - 1200 mm	m	0.17	7.98	-	24.99	32.97	36.27	24.338
K107521C	1200 - 1800 mm	m	0.25	11.48	-	36.75	48.23	53.05	36.429
K107531	**Linings to reveals and soffits; width**								
K107531A	not exceeding 300 mm	m	0.07	3.03	-	6.39	9.42	10.36	6.097
K107531B	300 - 600 mm	m	0.09	3.97	-	12.31	16.28	17.91	12.252
K1076	**Gyproc linings; 50 mm vapour check thermal board to masonry or concrete walls; fixing by Thistlebond TL system; joints flush filled, taped and finished for direct decoration**								
K107601	**Linings to walls; height**								
K107601A	not exceeding 1200 mm	m	0.21	9.57	-	27.64	37.21	40.93	28.830
K107601B	1200 - 1500 mm	m	0.26	11.94	-	34.57	46.51	51.16	36.047
K107601C	1500 - 1800 mm	m	0.31	14.32	-	41.47	55.79	61.37	43.245
K107601D	1800 - 2100 mm	m	0.36	16.75	-	48.39	65.14	71.65	50.462
K107601E	2100 - 2400 mm	m	0.41	19.08	-	55.29	74.37	81.81	57.660
K107601F	2400 - 2700 mm	m	0.46	21.51	-	62.22	83.73	92.10	64.877
K107601G	2700 - 3000 mm	m	0.51	23.89	-	69.11	93.00	102.30	72.075
K107611	**Linings to beams; 3 Nr faces; girth**								
K107611A	not exceeding 600 mm	m	0.09	4.20	-	14.70	18.90	20.79	14.450
K107611B	600 - 1200 mm	m	0.18	8.45	-	28.44	36.89	40.58	28.874
K107611C	1200 - 1800 mm	m	0.26	11.94	-	42.17	54.11	59.52	43.240
K107621	**Linings to columns; 4 Nr faces; girth**								
K107621A	not exceeding 600 mm	m	0.09	4.20	-	15.18	19.38	21.32	14.462
K107621B	600 - 1200 mm	m	0.18	8.45	-	28.92	37.37	41.11	28.887
K107621C	1200 - 1800 mm	m	0.26	11.94	-	42.65	54.59	60.05	43.252

Major Works 2011		Unit	Labour Hours	Labour Net	Plant Net	Materials Net	Unit Net	Unit with 10%	CO₂
				£	£	£	£	£	Kg
K10	**K10: PLASTERBOARD DRY LINING, PARTITION AND CEILINGS**								
K1076	**Gyproc linings; 50 mm vapour check thermal board to masonry or concrete walls; fixing by Thistlebond TL system; joints flush filled, taped and finished for direct decoration**								
K107631	**Linings to reveals and soffits; width**								
K107631A	not exceeding 300 mm	m	0.07	3.27	-	7.37	10.64	11.70	7.235
K107631B	300 - 600 mm	m	0.09	4.20	-	14.27	18.47	20.32	14.526
K1077	**Gyproc linings; 25 mm urethane laminate board to masonry or concrete walls; fixing by Thistlebond TL system; joints flush filled, taped and finished for direct decoration**								
K107701	**Linings to walls; height**								
K107701A	not exceeding 1200 mm	m	0.17	7.89	-	28.50	36.39	40.03	17.459
K107701B	1200 - 1500 mm	m	0.21	9.85	-	35.64	45.49	50.04	21.833
K107701C	1500 - 1800 mm	m	0.25	11.80	-	42.75	54.55	60.01	26.188
K107701D	1800 - 2100 mm	m	0.30	13.76	-	49.89	63.65	70.02	30.562
K107701E	2100 - 2400 mm	m	0.34	15.77	-	57.00	72.77	80.05	34.917
K107701F	2400 - 2700 mm	m	0.38	17.73	-	64.14	81.87	90.06	39.291
K107701G	2700 - 3000 mm	m	0.42	19.69	-	71.25	90.94	100.03	43.647
K107711	**Linings to beams; 3 Nr faces; girth**								
K107711A	not exceeding 600 mm	m	0.08	3.50	-	15.13	18.63	20.49	8.764
K107711B	600 - 1200 mm	m	0.15	7.05	-	29.30	36.35	39.99	17.503
K107711C	1200 - 1800 mm	m	0.23	10.55	-	43.46	54.01	59.41	26.183
K107721	**Linings to columns; 4 Nr faces; girth**								
K107721A	not exceeding 600 mm	m	0.08	3.50	-	15.61	19.11	21.02	8.776
K107721B	600 - 1200 mm	m	0.15	7.05	-	29.78	36.83	40.51	17.515
K107721C	1200 - 1800 mm	m	0.23	10.55	-	43.93	54.48	59.93	26.195
K107731	**Linings to reveals and soffits; width**								
K107731A	not exceeding 300 mm	m	0.06	2.57	-	7.58	10.15	11.17	4.392
K107731B	300 - 600 mm	m	0.08	3.50	-	14.70	18.20	20.02	8.840
K1078	**Gyproc linings; 32 mm urethane laminate board to masonry or concrete walls; fixing by Thistlebond TL system; joints flush filled, taped and finished for direct decoration**								
K107801	**Linings to walls; height**								
K107801A	not exceeding 1200 mm	m	0.18	8.45	-	30.25	38.70	42.57	20.643
K107801B	1200 - 1500 mm	m	0.23	10.55	-	37.83	48.38	53.22	25.813
K107801C	1500 - 1800 mm	m	0.27	12.64	-	45.38	58.02	63.82	30.964
K107801D	1800 - 2100 mm	m	0.32	14.79	-	52.96	67.75	74.53	36.134
K107801E	2100 - 2400 mm	m	0.36	16.84	-	60.50	77.34	85.07	41.285
K107801F	2400 - 2700 mm	m	0.41	18.94	-	68.09	87.03	95.73	46.455
K107801G	2700 - 3000 mm	m	0.45	21.09	-	75.63	96.72	106.39	51.607
K107811	**Linings to beams; 3 Nr faces; girth**								
K107811A	not exceeding 600 mm	m	0.08	3.73	-	16.01	19.74	21.71	10.356
K107811B	600 - 1200 mm	m	0.16	7.51	-	31.05	38.56	42.42	20.687
K107811C	1200 - 1800 mm	m	0.24	11.01	-	46.08	57.09	62.80	30.959
K107821	**Linings to columns; 4 Nr faces; girth**								
K107821A	not exceeding 600 mm	m	0.08	3.73	-	16.49	20.22	22.24	10.368
K107821B	600 - 1200 mm	m	0.16	7.51	-	31.53	39.04	42.94	20.699
K107821C	1200 - 1800 mm	m	0.24	11.01	-	46.56	57.57	63.33	30.971
K107831	**Linings to reveals and soffits; width**								
K107831A	not exceeding 300 mm	m	0.06	2.80	-	8.02	10.82	11.90	5.188

Linings, Sheathing & Dry Partitioning

Major Works 2011		Unit	Labour Hours	Labour Net	Plant Net	Materials Net	Unit Net	Unit with 10%	CO₂
				£	£	£	£	£	Kg
K10	**K10: PLASTERBOARD DRY LINING, PARTITION AND CEILINGS**								
K1078	**Gyproc linings; 32 mm urethane laminate board to masonry or concrete walls; fixing by Thistlebond TL system; joints flush filled, taped and finished for direct decoration**								
K107831	**Linings to reveals and soffits; width**								
K107831B	300 - 600 mm	m	0.08	3.73	-	15.58	19.31	21.24	10.432
K1079	**Gyproc linings; 40 mm urethane laminate board to masonry or concrete walls; fixing by Thistlebond TL system; joints flush filled, taped and finished for direct decoration**								
K107901	**Linings to walls; height**								
K107901A	not exceeding 1200 mm	m	0.19	9.01	-	32.89	41.90	46.09	24.282
K107901B	1200 - 1500 mm	m	0.24	11.25	-	41.12	52.37	57.61	30.361
K107901C	1500 - 1800 mm	m	0.29	13.48	-	49.33	62.81	69.09	36.422
K107901D	1800 - 2100 mm	m	0.34	15.77	-	57.57	73.34	80.67	42.502
K107901E	2100 - 2400 mm	m	0.39	17.96	-	65.77	83.73	92.10	48.563
K107901F	2400 - 2700 mm	m	0.43	20.25	-	74.01	94.26	103.69	54.643
K107901G	2700 - 3000 mm	m	0.48	22.49	-	82.21	104.70	115.17	60.704
K107911	**Linings to beams; 3 Nr faces; girth**								
K107911A	not exceeding 600 mm	m	0.09	3.97	-	17.33	21.30	23.43	12.175
K107911B	600 - 1200 mm	m	0.17	7.98	-	33.68	41.66	45.83	24.326
K107911C	1200 - 1800 mm	m	0.25	11.48	-	50.03	61.51	67.66	36.417
K107921	**Linings to columns; 4 Nr faces; girth**								
K107921A	not exceeding 600 mm	m	0.09	3.97	-	17.80	21.77	23.95	12.188
K107921B	600 - 1200 mm	m	0.17	7.98	-	34.16	42.14	46.35	24.338
K107921C	1200 - 1800 mm	m	0.25	11.48	-	50.51	61.99	68.19	36.429
K107931	**Linings to reveals and soffits; width**								
K107931A	not exceeding 300 mm	m	0.07	3.03	-	8.68	11.71	12.88	6.097
K107931B	300 - 600 mm	m	0.09	3.97	-	16.89	20.86	22.95	12.252
K1085	**Gyproc linings; 32 mm tapered edge Tri-line laminate board to masonry or concrete walls; fixing by Gyplyner system; joints flush filled, taped and finished for direct decoration**								
K108501	**Linings to walls; height**								
K108501A	not exceeding 1200 mm	m	0.15	6.91	-	37.26	44.17	48.59	25.290
K108501B	1200 - 1500 mm	m	0.23	10.55	-	46.57	57.12	62.83	31.612
K108501C	1500 - 1800 mm	m	0.27	12.60	-	55.88	68.48	75.33	37.935
K108501D	1800 - 2100 mm	m	0.32	14.79	-	65.20	79.99	87.99	44.257
K108501E	2100 - 2400 mm	m	0.36	16.89	-	74.51	91.40	100.54	50.580
K108501F	2400 - 2700 mm	m	0.41	18.94	-	83.82	102.76	113.04	56.902
K108501G	2700 - 3000 mm	m	0.45	21.09	-	93.14	114.23	125.65	63.225
K108511	**Linings to beams; 3 Nr faces; girth**								
K108511A	not exceeding 600 mm	m	0.08	3.50	-	20.19	23.69	26.06	12.890
K108511B	600 - 1200 mm	m	0.15	7.05	-	38.61	45.66	50.23	25.719
K108511C	1200 - 1800 mm	m	0.23	10.55	-	56.96	67.51	74.26	38.471
K108521	**Linings to columns; 4 Nr faces; girth**								
K108521A	not exceeding 600 mm	m	0.08	3.50	-	20.94	24.44	26.88	12.914
K108521B	600 - 1200 mm	m	0.15	7.05	-	39.36	46.41	51.05	25.743
K108521C	1200 - 1800 mm	m	0.23	10.55	-	57.71	68.26	75.09	38.496
K108531	**Linings to reveals and soffits; width**								
K108531A	not exceeding 300 mm	m	0.06	2.57	-	9.96	12.53	13.78	6.439
K108531B	300 - 600 mm	m	0.08	3.50	-	19.16	22.66	24.93	12.853

Major Works 2011		Unit	Labour Hours	Labour Net	Plant Net	Materials Net	Unit Net	Unit with 10%	CO$_2$
				£	£	£	£	£	Kg
K10	**K10: PLASTERBOARD DRY LINING, PARTITION AND CEILINGS**								
K1086	**Gyproc linings; 40 mm tapered edge Tri-line laminate board to masonry or concrete walls; fixing by Gyplyner system; joints flush filled, taped and finished for direct decoration**								
K108601	**Linings to walls; height**								
K108601A	not exceeding 1200 mm	m	0.16	7.51	-	39.62	47.13	51.84	28.929
K108601B	1200 - 1500 mm	m	0.25	11.43	-	49.53	60.96	67.06	36.161
K108601C	1500 - 1800 mm	m	0.29	13.67	-	59.43	73.10	80.41	43.393
K108601D	1800 - 2100 mm	m	0.34	16.00	-	69.34	85.34	93.87	50.625
K108601E	2100 - 2400 mm	m	0.39	18.29	-	79.25	97.54	107.29	57.858
K108601F	2400 - 2700 mm	m	0.44	20.53	-	89.15	109.68	120.65	65.090
K108601G	2700 - 3000 mm	m	0.49	22.86	-	99.06	121.92	134.11	72.322
K108611	**Linings to beams; 3 Nr faces; girth**								
K108611A	not exceeding 600 mm	m	0.08	3.78	-	21.43	25.21	27.73	14.709
K108611B	600 - 1200 mm	m	0.16	7.61	-	41.01	48.62	53.48	29.358
K108611C	1200 - 1800 mm	m	0.25	11.43	-	60.54	71.97	79.17	43.930
K108621	**Linings to columns; 4 Nr faces; girth**								
K108621A	not exceeding 600 mm	m	0.08	3.78	-	22.19	25.97	28.57	14.734
K108621B	600 - 1200 mm	m	0.15	7.05	-	41.78	48.83	53.71	29.382
K108621C	1200 - 1800 mm	m	0.25	11.43	-	61.30	72.73	80.00	43.954
K108631	**Linings to reveals and soffits; width**								
K108631A	not exceeding 300 mm	m	0.06	2.80	-	10.57	13.37	14.71	7.349
K108631B	300 - 600 mm	m	0.08	3.78	-	20.35	24.13	26.54	14.673
K1087	**Gyproc linings; 50 mm tapered edge Tri-line laminate board to masonry or concrete walls; fixing by Gyplyner system; joints flush filled, taped and finished for direct decoration**								
K108701	**Linings to walls; height**								
K108701A	not exceeding 1200 mm	m	0.17	8.07	-	47.17	55.24	60.76	33.477
K108701B	1200 - 1500 mm	m	0.26	12.13	-	58.96	71.09	78.20	41.847
K108701C	1500 - 1800 mm	m	0.31	14.51	-	70.76	85.27	93.80	50.216
K108701D	1800 - 2100 mm	m	0.36	16.98	-	82.55	99.53	109.48	58.585
K108701E	2100 - 2400 mm	m	0.42	19.41	-	94.34	113.75	125.13	66.955
K108701F	2400 - 2700 mm	m	0.47	21.79	-	106.13	127.92	140.71	75.324
K108701G	2700 - 3000 mm	m	0.52	24.26	-	117.93	142.19	156.41	83.694
K108711	**Linings to beams; 3 Nr faces; girth**								
K108711A	not exceeding 600 mm	m	0.09	4.06	-	25.20	29.26	32.19	16.984
K108711B	600 - 1200 mm	m	0.18	8.17	-	48.56	56.73	62.40	33.906
K108711C	1200 - 1800 mm	m	0.26	12.27	-	71.86	84.13	92.54	50.752
K108721	**Linings to columns; 4 Nr faces; girth**								
K108721A	not exceeding 600 mm	m	0.09	4.06	-	25.97	30.03	33.03	17.008
K108721B	600 - 1200 mm	m	0.16	7.61	-	49.33	56.94	62.63	33.931
K108721C	1200 - 1800 mm	m	0.26	12.27	-	72.63	84.90	93.39	50.777
K108731	**Linings to reveals and soffits; width**								
K108731A	not exceeding 300 mm	m	0.06	2.94	-	12.45	15.39	16.93	8.486
K108731B	300 - 600 mm	m	0.09	4.06	-	24.13	28.19	31.01	16.947
K1088	**Gyproc linings; 32 mm tapered edge vapour check Tri-line laminate board to masonry or concrete walls; fixing by Gyplyner system; joints flush filled, taped and finished for direct decoration**								
K108801	**Linings to walls; height**								
K108801A	not exceeding 1200 mm	m	0.15	6.91	-	39.01	45.92	50.51	25.290
K108801B	1200 - 1500 mm	m	0.23	10.55	-	48.76	59.31	65.24	31.612

Major Works 2011		Unit	Labour Hours	Labour Net £	Plant Net £	Materials Net £	Unit Net £	Unit with 10% £	CO₂ Kg

		Unit	Labour Hours	Labour Net £	Plant Net £	Materials Net £	Unit Net £	Unit with 10% £	CO₂ Kg
K10	**K10: PLASTERBOARD DRY LINING, PARTITION AND CEILINGS**								
K1088	**Gyproc linings; 32 mm tapered edge vapour check Tri-line laminate board to masonry or concrete walls; fixing by Gyplyner system; joints flush filled, taped and finished for direct decoration**								
K108801	**Linings to walls; height**								
K108801C	1500 - 1800 mm	m	0.27	12.60	-	58.51	71.11	78.22	37.935
K108801D	1800 - 2100 mm	m	0.32	14.79	-	68.26	83.05	91.36	44.257
K108801E	2100 - 2400 mm	m	0.36	16.89	-	78.01	94.90	104.39	50.580
K108801F	2400 - 2700 mm	m	0.41	18.94	-	87.76	106.70	117.37	56.902
K108801G	2700 - 3000 mm	m	0.45	21.09	-	97.52	118.61	130.47	63.225
K108811	**Linings to beams; 3 Nr faces; girth**								
K108811A	not exceeding 600 mm	m	0.08	3.50	-	21.07	24.57	27.03	12.890
K108811B	600 - 1200 mm	m	0.15	7.05	-	40.36	47.41	52.15	25.719
K108811C	1200 - 1800 mm	m	0.23	10.55	-	59.59	70.14	77.15	38.471
K108821	**Linings to columns; 4 Nr faces; girth**								
K108821A	not exceeding 600 mm	m	0.08	3.50	-	21.82	25.32	27.85	12.914
K108821B	600 - 1200 mm	m	0.15	7.05	-	41.11	48.16	52.98	25.743
K108821C	1200 - 1800 mm	m	0.23	10.55	-	60.34	70.89	77.98	38.496
K108831	**Linings to reveals and soffits; width**								
K108831A	not exceeding 300 mm	m	0.06	2.57	-	10.40	12.97	14.27	6.439
K108831B	300 - 600 mm	m	0.08	3.50	-	20.04	23.54	25.89	12.853
K1089	**Gyproc linings; 40 mm tapered edge vapour check Tri-line laminate board to masonry or concrete walls; fixing by Gyplyner system; joints flush filled, taped and finished for direct decoration**								
K108901	**Linings to walls; height**								
K108901A	not exceeding 1200 mm	m	0.16	7.51	-	41.39	48.90	53.79	28.929
K108901B	1200 - 1500 mm	m	0.25	11.43	-	51.73	63.16	69.48	36.161
K108901C	1500 - 1800 mm	m	0.29	13.67	-	62.08	75.75	83.33	43.393
K108901D	1800 - 2100 mm	m	0.34	16.00	-	72.43	88.43	97.27	50.625
K108901E	2100 - 2400 mm	m	0.39	18.29	-	82.77	101.06	111.17	57.858
K108901F	2400 - 2700 mm	m	0.44	20.53	-	93.12	113.65	125.02	65.090
K108901G	2700 - 3000 mm	m	0.49	22.86	-	103.47	126.33	138.96	72.322
K108911	**Linings to beams; 3 Nr faces; girth**								
K108911A	not exceeding 600 mm	m	0.08	3.78	-	22.31	26.09	28.70	14.709
K108911B	600 - 1200 mm	m	0.16	7.61	-	42.78	50.39	55.43	29.358
K108911C	1200 - 1800 mm	m	0.25	11.43	-	63.18	74.61	82.07	43.930
K108921	**Linings to columns; 4 Nr faces; girth**								
K108921A	not exceeding 600 mm	m	0.08	3.78	-	23.07	26.85	29.54	14.734
K108921B	600 - 1200 mm	m	0.15	7.05	-	43.54	50.59	55.65	29.382
K108921C	1200 - 1800 mm	m	0.25	11.43	-	63.95	75.38	82.92	43.954
K108931	**Linings to reveals and soffits; width**								
K108931A	not exceeding 300 mm	m	0.06	2.80	-	11.01	13.81	15.19	7.349
K108931B	300 - 600 mm	m	0.08	3.78	-	21.24	25.02	27.52	14.673
K1090	**Gyproc linings; 50 mm tapered edge vapour check Tri-line laminate board to masonry or concrete walls; fixing by Gyplyner system; joints flush filled, taped and finished for direct decoration**								
K109001	**Linings to walls; height**								
K109001A	not exceeding 1200 mm	m	0.17	8.07	-	41.30	49.37	54.31	33.477
K109001B	1200 - 1500 mm	m	0.26	12.13	-	51.62	63.75	70.13	41.847
K109001C	1500 - 1800 mm	m	0.31	14.51	-	61.95	76.46	84.11	50.216
K109001D	1800 - 2100 mm	m	0.36	16.98	-	72.27	89.25	98.18	58.585

Major Works 2011		Unit	Labour Hours	Labour Net	Plant Net	Materials Net	Unit Net	Unit with 10%	CO$_2$
				£	£	£	£	£	Kg
K10	**K10: PLASTERBOARD DRY LINING, PARTITION AND CEILINGS**								
K1090	**Gyproc linings; 50 mm tapered edge vapour check Tri-line laminate board to masonry or concrete walls; fixing by Gyplyner system; joints flush filled, taped and finished for direct decoration**								
K109001	**Linings to walls; height**								
K109001E	2100 - 2400 mm	m	0.42	19.41	-	82.60	102.01	112.21	66.955
K109001F	2400 - 2700 mm	m	0.47	21.79	-	92.92	114.71	126.18	75.324
K109001G	2700 - 3000 mm	m	0.52	24.26	-	103.25	127.51	140.26	83.694
K109011	**Linings to beams; 3 Nr faces; girth**								
K109011A	not exceeding 600 mm	m	0.09	4.06	-	22.26	26.32	28.95	16.984
K109011B	600 - 1200 mm	m	0.18	8.17	-	42.69	50.86	55.95	33.906
K109011C	1200 - 1800 mm	m	0.26	12.27	-	63.05	75.32	82.85	50.752
K109021	**Linings to columns; 4 Nr faces; girth**								
K109021A	not exceeding 600 mm	m	0.09	4.06	-	23.03	27.09	29.80	17.008
K109021B	600 - 1200 mm	m	0.16	7.61	-	43.46	51.07	56.18	33.931
K109021C	1200 - 1800 mm	m	0.26	12.27	-	63.82	76.09	83.70	50.777
K109031	**Linings to reveals and soffits; width**								
K109031A	not exceeding 300 mm	m	0.06	2.94	-	10.99	13.93	15.32	8.486
K109031B	300 - 600 mm	m	0.09	4.06	-	21.19	25.25	27.78	16.947
K1094	**Gyproc Drywall topcoat**								
K109401	**One coat Gyproc Drywall topcoat to surfaces of tapered edge boarding including filling, taping and finishing joints flush; ready for direct decoration**								
K109401A	walls, returns, reveals of openings or recesses, attached and unattached columns	m^2	0.09	3.97	-	1.40	5.37	5.91	1.431
K109401B	ceilings, attached and unattached beams and soffits of staircases	m^2	0.11	4.95	-	1.26	6.21	6.83	1.427
K109401C	skirtings, bands, strings, coverings kerbs, mouldings, channels or the like; not exceeding 300 mm wide	m	0.05	2.33	-	0.41	2.74	3.01	0.435
K109440	**One coat Gyproc Drywall topcoat to surfaces of boarding excluding filling, taping and finishing joints; ready for direct decoration**								
K109440A	walls, returns, reveals of openings or recesses, attached and unattached columns	m^2	0.06	2.80	-	0.68	3.48	3.83	0.011
K109440B	ceilings, attached and unattached beams and soffits of staircases	m^2	0.08	3.50	-	0.68	4.18	4.60	0.011
K109440C	skirtings, bands, strings, coverings kerbs, mouldings, channels or the like; not exceeding 300 mm wide	m	0.04	1.63	-	0.23	1.86	2.05	0.004
K1095	**Dry-lining beads, stops, edgings and arches**								
K109504	**Expamet galvanised mild steel plaster beads and stops; fixing in accordance with manufacturer's instructions**								
K109504P	10 mm architrave bead ref 513	m	0.04	0.68	-	1.05	1.73	1.90	0.407
K109504Q	10 mm architrave bead ref 514	m	0.04	0.68	-	1.21	1.89	2.08	0.407
K109504X	dry wall corner bead ref 548	m	0.04	0.68	-	0.98	1.66	1.83	0.444
K109504Y	10 mm edge bead ref 567	m	0.04	0.68	-	1.56	2.24	2.46	0.592
K109504Z	12 mm edge bead ref 568	m	0.04	0.68	-	1.56	2.24	2.46	0.592

Major Works 2011		Unit	Labour Hours	Labour Net	Plant Net	Materials Net	Unit Net	Unit with 10%	CO₂
				£	£	£	£	£	Kg
K10	**K10: PLASTERBOARD DRY LINING, PARTITION AND CEILINGS**								
K1095	**Dry-lining beads, stops, edgings and arches**								
K109511	**Expamet galvanised mild steel dry-lining arch formers; fixing in accordance with manufacturer's instructions**								
K109511A	380 mm radius semi-circle ref DSC 30	Nr	0.18	8.21	-	18.26	26.47	29.12	3.540
K109511B	405 mm radius semi-circle ref DSC 32	Nr	0.18	8.21	-	18.80	27.01	29.71	3.540
K109511C	420 mm radius semi-circle ref DSC 33	Nr	0.18	8.21	-	18.80	27.01	29.71	3.540
K109511D	455 mm radius semi-circle ref DSC 36	Nr	0.18	8.21	-	19.93	28.14	30.95	3.983
K109511E	610 mm radius semi-circle ref DSC 48	Nr	0.18	8.21	-	23.47	31.68	34.85	3.983
K109511F	760 mm radius semi-circle ref DSC 60	Nr	0.18	8.21	-	26.46	34.67	38.14	4.425
K109511G	1520 mm wide elliptical ref DEL 60	Nr	0.18	8.21	-	25.89	34.10	37.51	4.425
K109511H	1830 mm wide elliptical ref DEL 72	Nr	0.25	11.71	-	28.69	40.40	44.44	4.425
K109511I	2130 mm wide elliptical ref DEL 84	Nr	0.25	11.71	-	29.97	41.68	45.85	4.425
K109511J	2440 mm wide elliptical ref DEL 96	Nr	0.25	11.71	-	34.64	46.35	50.99	4.868
K109511L	soffit strip 80 mm wide	m	0.06	2.80	-	2.22	5.02	5.52	0.651
K109511M	dry-lining bead ref 553	m	0.02	0.93	-	1.14	2.07	2.28	0.372

Major Works 2011		Unit	Labour Hours	Labour Net	Plant Net	Materials Net	Unit Net	Unit with 10%	CO$_2$
				£	£	£	£	£	Kg
K11	**K11: RIGID SHEET FLOORING, SHEATHING, LININGS AND CASINGS**								
K1111	**Walls**								
K111101	**Hardboard; 3.2 mm standard**								
K111101A	over 300 mm wide	m^2	0.25	4.25	-	1.66	5.91	6.50	2.571
K111101B	n.e. 300 mm wide	m	0.10	1.70	-	0.52	2.22	2.44	0.811
K111102	**Hardboard; 6.0 mm standard**								
K111102C	over 300 mm wide	m^2	0.30	5.09	-	4.61	9.70	10.67	2.634
K111102D	n.e. 300 mm wide	m	0.12	2.04	-	1.45	3.49	3.84	0.830
K111103	**Hardboard; 3.2 mm perforated**								
K111103E	over 300 mm wide	m^2	0.28	4.75	-	1.72	6.47	7.12	1.419
K111103F	n.e. 300 mm wide	m	0.12	1.95	-	0.54	2.49	2.74	0.448
K111104	**Hardboard; 6.0 mm perforated**								
K111104G	over 300 mm wide	m^2	0.32	5.43	-	3.53	8.96	9.86	2.634
K111104H	n.e. 300 mm wide	m	0.13	2.21	-	1.11	3.32	3.65	0.830
K111105	**Hardboard; 6.0 mm flameproof Class 1**								
K111105I	over 300 mm wide	m^2	0.30	5.09	-	12.67	17.76	19.54	2.634
K111105J	n.e. 300 mm wide	m	0.12	2.04	-	3.98	6.02	6.62	0.830
K111106	**Hardboard; 3.2 mm stove enamelled one side**								
K111106K	over 300 mm wide	m^2	0.28	4.75	-	2.47	7.22	7.94	2.571
K111106L	n.e. 300 mm wide	m	0.12	1.95	-	0.78	2.73	3.00	0.811
K111111	**Insulation board; 6.4 mm Sundeala A**								
K111111A	over 300 mm wide	m^2	0.35	5.94	-	10.96	16.90	18.59	3.133
K111111B	n.e. 300 mm wide	m	0.14	2.43	-	3.45	5.88	6.47	0.987
K111112	**Insulation board; 9.5 mm Sundeala A**								
K111112C	over 300 mm wide	m^2	0.38	6.45	-	14.14	20.59	22.65	4.586
K111112D	n.e. 300 mm wide	m	0.15	2.55	-	4.45	7.00	7.70	1.444
K111113	**Insulation board; 12.5 mm Sundeala A**								
K111113E	over 300 mm wide	m^2	0.40	6.79	-	16.41	23.20	25.52	5.297
K111113F	n.e. 300 mm wide	m	0.16	2.72	-	5.16	7.88	8.67	1.661
K111114	**Insulation board; 6.4 mm Sundeala K**								
K111114G	over 300 mm wide	m^2	0.35	5.94	-	9.72	15.66	17.23	3.133
K111114H	n.e. 300 mm wide	m	0.14	2.38	-	3.06	5.44	5.98	0.987
K111115	**Insulation board; 9.5 mm Sundeala K**								
K111115I	over 300 mm wide	m^2	0.38	6.45	-	14.14	20.59	22.65	4.586
K111115J	n.e. 300 mm wide	m	0.15	2.55	-	4.45	7.00	7.70	1.444
K111116	**Insulation board; 12.5 mm Unitex ivory faced**								
K111116K	over 300 mm wide	m^2	0.45	7.64	-	4.03	11.67	12.84	6.136
K111116L	n.e. 300 mm wide	m	0.18	3.06	-	1.27	4.33	4.76	1.925
K111117	**Insulation board; 12.5 mm Unitex white faced**								
K111117M	over 300 mm wide	m^2	0.45	7.64	-	4.96	12.60	13.86	6.136
K111117N	n.e. 300 mm wide	m	0.18	3.06	-	1.56	4.62	5.08	1.925
K111121	**Chipboard; standard grade; 12 mm**								
K111121A	over 300 mm wide	m^2	0.30	5.09	-	2.41	7.50	8.25	4.105
K111121B	n.e. 300 mm wide	m	0.12	2.04	-	0.76	2.80	3.08	1.292
K111122	**Chipboard; standard grade; 15 mm**								
K111122C	over 300 mm wide	m^2	0.35	5.94	-	3.54	9.48	10.43	5.118
K111122D	n.e. 300 mm wide	m	0.14	2.38	-	1.12	3.50	3.85	1.613
K111123	**Chipboard; standard grade; 18 mm**								
K111123E	over 300 mm wide	m^2	0.40	6.79	-	5.66	12.45	13.70	6.129

Major Works 2011		Unit	Labour Hours	Labour Net	Plant Net	Materials Net	Unit Net	Unit with 10%	CO₂
				£	£	£	£	£	Kg
K11	**K11: RIGID SHEET FLOORING, SHEATHING, LININGS AND CASINGS**								
K1111	**Walls**								
K111123	**Chipboard; standard grade; 18 mm**								
K111123F	n.e. 300 mm wide	m	0.16	2.72	-	1.79	4.51	4.96	1.931
K111124	**Chipboard; standard grade; 25 mm**								
K111124E	over 300 mm wide	m²	0.45	7.64	-	5.55	13.19	14.51	8.491
K111124F	n.e. 300 mm wide	m	0.18	3.06	-	1.75	4.81	5.29	2.674
K111126	**Chipboard; faced one side with 1.5 mm Class 1 laminated plastic covering and balancing veneer other side; 15 mm**								
K111126A	over 300 mm wide	m²	0.50	8.49	-	4.47	12.96	14.26	5.338
K111126B	n.e. 300 mm wide	m	0.20	3.40	-	1.39	4.79	5.27	1.601
K111127	**Chipboard; faced one side with 1.5 mm Class 1 laminated plastic covering and balancing veneer other side; 18 mm**								
K111127C	over 300 mm wide	m²	0.60	10.19	-	4.92	15.11	16.62	6.350
K111127D	n.e. 300 mm wide	m	0.24	4.08	-	1.55	5.63	6.19	2.019
K111131	**Finnish birch faced 5 ply blockboard; grade BB; 12 mm**								
K111131A	over 300 mm wide	m²	0.68	11.46	-	10.99	22.45	24.70	6.778
K111131B	n.e. 300 mm wide	m	0.27	4.58	-	3.46	8.04	8.84	2.154
K111132	**Finnish birch faced 5 ply blockboard; grade BB; 18 mm**								
K111132A	over 300 mm wide	m²	0.75	12.73	-	24.61	37.34	41.07	5.929
K111132B	n.e. 300 mm wide	m	0.30	5.09	-	7.74	12.83	14.11	1.887
K111133	**Finnish birch faced 5 ply blockboard; grade BB; 25 mm**								
K111133C	over 300 mm wide	m²	0.80	13.58	-	32.31	45.89	50.48	7.812
K111133D	n.e. 300 mm wide	m	0.32	5.43	-	10.16	15.59	17.15	2.479
K111135	**Far Eastern hardwood faced MR boarding ply; grade B/BB; 4 mm**								
K111135A	over 300 mm wide	m²	0.38	6.45	-	7.55	14.00	15.40	1.866
K111135B	n.e. 300 mm wide	m	0.15	2.55	-	2.38	4.93	5.42	0.589
K111136	**Far Eastern hardwood faced MR boarding ply; grade B/BB; 6 mm**								
K111136C	over 300 wide	m²	0.42	7.13	-	8.27	15.40	16.94	3.013
K111136D	n.e. 300 mm wide	m	0.17	2.89	-	2.60	5.49	6.04	0.950
K111137	**Far Eastern hardwood faced MR boarding ply; grade B/BB; 9 mm**								
K111137E	over 300 mm wide	m²	0.46	7.81	-	6.31	14.12	15.53	4.162
K111137F	n.e. 300 mm wide	m	0.18	3.06	-	1.99	5.05	5.56	1.311
K111138	**Far Eastern hardwood faced MR boarding ply; grade B/BB; 12 mm**								
K111138G	over 300 mm wide	m²	0.50	8.49	-	8.03	16.52	18.17	5.540
K111138H	n.e. 300 mm wide	m	0.20	3.40	-	8.02	11.42	12.56	5.523
K111139	**Far Eastern hardwood faced MR boarding ply; grade B/BB; 15 mm**								
K111139I	over 300 mm wide	m²	0.56	9.51	-	10.23	19.74	21.71	6.917
K111139J	n.e. 300 mm wide	m	0.23	3.82	-	3.22	7.04	7.74	2.176
K111140	**Far Eastern hardwood faced MR boarding ply; grade B/BB; 18 mm**								
K111140K	over 300 mm wide	m²	0.60	10.19	-	11.69	21.88	24.07	8.295
K111140L	n.e. 300 mm wide	m	0.24	4.08	-	3.67	7.75	8.53	2.609

Major Works 2011		Unit	Labour Hours	Labour Net	Plant Net	Materials Net	Unit Net	Unit with 10%	CO₂
				£	£	£	£	£	Kg
K11	**K11: RIGID SHEET FLOORING, SHEATHING, LININGS AND CASINGS**								
K1111	**Walls**								
K111141	**Far Eastern hardwood faced MR boarding ply; grade B/BB; 22 mm**								
K111141M	over 300 mm wide	m²	0.64	10.87	-	13.99	24.86	27.35	10.132
K111141N	n.e. 300 mm wide	m	0.26	4.35	-	4.40	8.75	9.63	3.187
K111142	**Far Eastern hardwood faced MR boarding ply; grade B/BB; 25 mm**								
K111142O	over 300 mm wide	m²	0.69	11.72	-	16.24	27.96	30.76	11.510
K111142P	n.e. 300 mm wide	m	0.28	4.67	-	5.11	9.78	10.76	3.620
K111145	**Finnish birch faced WBP boarding ply; grade BB; 4 mm**								
K111145A	over 300 mm wide	m²	0.35	5.94	-	6.94	12.88	14.17	1.866
K111145B	n.e. 300 mm wide	m	0.14	2.38	-	2.18	4.56	5.02	0.589
K111146	**Finnish birch faced WBP boarding ply; grade BB; 6 mm**								
K111146C	over 300 mm wide	m²	0.38	6.45	-	10.23	16.68	18.35	2.784
K111146D	n.e. 300 mm wide	m	0.15	2.55	-	3.22	5.77	6.35	0.877
K111147	**Finnish birch faced WBP boarding ply; grade BB; 9 mm**								
K111147E	over 300 mm wide	m²	0.40	6.79	-	12.59	19.38	21.32	4.162
K111147F	n.e. 300 mm wide	m	0.16	2.72	-	3.96	6.68	7.35	1.311
K111148	**Finnish birch faced WBP boarding ply; grade BB; 12 mm**								
K111148G	over 300 mm wide	m²	0.45	7.64	-	14.80	22.44	24.68	5.540
K111148H	n.e. 300 mm wide	m	0.18	3.06	-	4.65	7.71	8.48	1.743
K111149	**Finnish birch faced WBP boarding ply; grade BB; 15 mm**								
K111149I	over 300 mm wide	m²	0.48	8.15	-	19.90	28.05	30.86	6.917
K111149J	n.e. 300 mm wide	m	0.19	3.23	-	6.26	9.49	10.44	2.176
K111150	**Finnish birch faced WBP boarding ply; grade BB; 18 mm**								
K111150K	over 300 mm wide	m²	0.52	8.83	-	23.74	32.57	35.83	8.295
K111150L	n.e. 300 mm wide	m	0.21	3.57	-	7.46	11.03	12.13	2.609
K111151	**Finnish birch faced WBP boarding ply; grade BB; 22 mm**								
K111151M	over 300 mm wide	m²	0.56	9.51	-	28.10	37.61	41.37	10.132
K111151N	n.e. 300 mm wide	m	0.23	3.82	-	8.83	12.65	13.92	3.187
K111152	**Finnish birch faced WBP boarding ply; grade BB; 25 mm**								
K111152O	over 300 mm wide	m²	0.60	10.19	-	32.48	42.67	46.94	11.510
K111152P	n.e. 300 mm wide	m	0.24	4.08	-	10.21	14.29	15.72	3.620
K111155	**Non-asbestos, flameproof Class O boards; BS 476; 6 mm**								
K111155A	over 300 mm wide	m²	0.28	4.75	-	10.99	15.74	17.31	1.963
K111155B	n.e. 300 mm wide	m	0.11	1.87	-	3.47	5.34	5.87	0.628
K111156	**Non-asbestos, flameproof Class O boards; BS 476; 9 mm**								
K111156C	over 300 mm wide	m²	0.30	5.09	-	28.88	33.97	37.37	2.879
K111156D	n.e. 300 mm wide	m	0.12	2.04	-	9.09	11.13	12.24	0.916
K111157	**Non-asbestos, flameproof Class O boards; BS 476; 12 mm**								
K111157E	over 300 mm wide	m²	0.35	5.94	-	43.52	49.46	54.41	3.838
K111157F	n.e. 300 mm wide	m	0.14	2.38	-	13.70	16.08	17.69	1.221

Linings, Sheathing & Dry Partitioning

Major Works 2011		Unit	Labour Hours	Labour Net	Plant Net	Materials Net	Unit Net	Unit with 10%	CO$_2$
				£	£	£	£	£	Kg
K11	**K11: RIGID SHEET FLOORING, SHEATHING, LININGS AND CASINGS**								
K1111	**Walls**								
K111158	**Non-asbestos, flameproof Class O boards; BS 476; 15 mm**								
K111158G	over 300 mm wide	m^2	0.40	6.79	-	54.53	61.32	67.45	4.754
K111158H	n.e. 300 mm wide	m	0.16	2.72	-	17.15	19.87	21.86	1.509
K111161	**Medium density fibreboard; MDF; 9 mm**								
K111161A	over 300 mm wide	m^2	0.32	5.43	-	4.23	9.66	10.63	4.443
K111161B	n.e. 300 mm wide	m	0.19	3.23	-	1.30	4.53	4.98	1.371
K111162	**Medium density fibreboard; MDF; 12 mm**								
K111162A	over 300 mm wide	m^2	0.33	5.60	-	4.87	10.47	11.52	5.876
K111162B	n.e. 300 mm wide	m	0.20	3.40	-	1.50	4.90	5.39	1.809
K111163	**Medium density fibreboard; MDF; 15 mm**								
K111163A	over 300 mm wide	m^2	0.34	5.77	-	4.90	10.67	11.74	7.311
K111163B	n.e. 300 mm wide	m	0.21	3.57	-	1.51	5.08	5.59	2.247
K111164	**Medium density fibreboard; MDF; 18 mm**								
K111164A	over 300 mm wide	m^2	0.36	6.11	-	6.79	12.90	14.19	8.800
K111164B	n.e. 300 mm wide	m	0.22	3.74	-	2.09	5.83	6.41	2.713
K111165	**Medium density fibreboard; MDF; 25 mm**								
K111165A	over 300 mm wide	m^2	0.38	6.45	-	9.82	16.27	17.90	12.146
K111165B	n.e. 300 mm wide	m	0.23	3.91	-	3.02	6.93	7.62	3.736
K1113	**Floors**								
K111304	**Marine plywood square edged boarding; BS1088**								
K111304A	12 mm thick; over 300 mm wide	m^2	0.35	5.94	-	13.53	19.47	21.42	5.677
K111304B	12 mm thick; n.e. 300 mm wide	m	0.14	2.38	-	4.30	6.68	7.35	1.809
K111304C	18 mm thick; over 300 mm wide	m^2	0.35	5.94	-	19.83	25.77	28.35	8.459
K111304D	18 mm thick; n.e. 300 mm wide	m	0.14	2.38	-	6.29	8.67	9.54	2.691
K111304E	25 mm thick; over 300 mm wide	m^2	0.35	5.94	-	29.68	35.62	39.18	11.704
K111304F	25 mm thick; n.e. 300 mm wide	m	0.14	2.38	-	9.42	11.80	12.98	3.719
K111305	**Marine plywood tongued and grooved boarding; BS1088**								
K111305A	12 mm thick; over 300 mm wide	m^2	0.45	7.64	-	14.88	22.52	24.77	5.677
K111305B	12 mm thick; n.e. 300 mm wide	m	0.18	3.06	-	4.72	7.78	8.56	1.809
K111305C	18 mm thick; over 300 mm wide	m^2	0.45	7.64	-	21.80	29.44	32.38	8.459
K111305D	18 mm thick; n.e. 300 mm wide	m	0.18	3.06	-	6.92	9.98	10.98	2.691
K111305E	25 mm thick; over 300 mm wide	m^2	0.45	7.64	-	32.63	40.27	44.30	11.704
K111305F	25 mm thick; n.e. 300 mm wide	m	0.18	3.06	-	10.35	13.41	14.75	3.719
K111306	**WBP bonding plywood square edged boarding; grade BB**								
K111306A	12 mm thick; over 300 mm wide	m^2	0.35	5.94	-	8.90	14.84	16.32	5.677
K111306B	12 mm thick; n.e. 300 mm wide	m	0.14	2.38	-	2.83	5.21	5.73	1.809
K111306C	18 mm thick; over 300 mm wide	m^2	0.35	5.94	-	12.95	18.89	20.78	8.459
K111306D	18 mm thick; n.e. 300 mm wide	m	0.14	2.38	-	4.11	6.49	7.14	2.691
K111306E	25 mm thick; over 300 mm wide	m^2	0.35	5.94	-	18.48	24.42	26.86	11.704
K111306F	25 mm thick; n.e. 300 mm wide	m	0.14	2.38	-	5.87	8.25	9.08	3.719
K111307	**V313 moisture resistant chipboard square edged boarding; BS5669**								
K111307A	18 mm thick; over 300 mm wide	m^2	0.30	5.09	-	4.35	9.44	10.38	6.243
K111307B	18 mm thick; n.e. 300 mm wide	m	0.12	2.04	-	1.39	3.43	3.77	1.988
K111307C	22 mm thick; over 300 mm wide	m^2	0.30	5.09	-	5.19	10.28	11.31	7.606
K111307D	22 mm thick; n.e. 300 mm wide	m	0.12	2.04	-	1.65	3.69	4.06	2.420
K111308	**V313 moisture resistant tongued and grooved chipboard boarding; BS5669**								
K111308A	18 mm thick; over 300 mm wide	m^2	0.40	6.79	-	4.38	11.17	12.29	6.243
K111308B	18 mm thick; n.e. 300 mm wide	m	0.16	2.72	-	1.40	4.12	4.53	1.988
K111308C	22 mm thick; over 300 mm wide	m^2	0.40	6.79	-	5.19	11.98	13.18	7.606

Major Works 2011		Unit	Labour Hours	Labour Net	Plant Net	Materials Net	Unit Net	Unit with 10%	CO$_2$
				£	£	£	£	£	Kg
K11	**K11: RIGID SHEET FLOORING, SHEATHING, LININGS AND CASINGS**								
K1113	**Floors**								
K111308	**V313 moisture resistant tongued and grooved chipboard boarding; BS5669**								
K111308D	22 mm thick; n.e. 300 mm wide	m	0.16	2.72	-	1.65	4.37	4.81	2.420
K1115	**Ceilings**								
K111501	**Hardboard; 3.2 mm standard**								
K111501A	over 300 mm wide	m^2	0.30	5.09	-	1.66	6.75	7.43	2.571
K111501B	n.e. 300 mm wide	m	0.12	2.04	-	0.52	2.56	2.82	0.811
K111502	**Hardboard; 6.0 mm standard**								
K111502C	over 300 mm wide	m^2	0.35	5.94	-	4.61	10.55	11.61	2.634
K111502D	n.e. 300 mm wide	m	0.14	2.38	-	1.45	3.83	4.21	0.830
K111503	**Hardboard; 6.0 mm flameproof Class 1**								
K111503E	over 300 mm wide	m^2	0.35	5.94	-	12.67	18.61	20.47	2.634
K111503F	n.e. 300 mm wide	m	0.14	2.38	-	3.98	6.36	7.00	0.830
K111511	**Insulation board; 6.4 mm Sundeala A**								
K111511A	over 300 mm wide	m^2	0.40	6.79	-	10.96	17.75	19.53	3.133
K111511B	n.e. 300 mm wide	m	0.16	2.72	-	3.46	6.18	6.80	0.996
K111512	**Insulation board; 9.5 mm Sundeala A**								
K111512C	over 300 mm wide	m^2	0.43	7.30	-	14.14	21.44	23.58	4.586
K111512D	n.e. 300 mm wide	m	0.17	2.89	-	4.46	7.35	8.09	1.453
K111513	**Insulation board; 12.5 mm Sundeala A**								
K111513E	over 300 mm wide	m^2	0.45	7.64	-	16.41	24.05	26.46	5.297
K111513F	n.e. 300 mm wide	m	0.18	3.06	-	5.16	8.22	9.04	1.689
K111514	**Insulation board; 6.4 mm Sundeala K**								
K111514G	over 300 mm wide	m^2	0.40	6.79	-	9.72	16.51	18.16	3.133
K111514H	n.e. 300 mm wide	m	0.16	2.72	-	3.07	5.79	6.37	0.996
K111515	**Insulation board; 9.5 mm Sundeala K**								
K111515I	over 300 mm wide	m^2	0.43	7.30	-	14.14	21.44	23.58	4.586
K111515J	n.e. 300 mm wide	m	0.17	2.89	-	4.46	7.35	8.09	1.453
K111516	**Insulation board; 12.5 mm ivory faced**								
K111516K	over 300 mm wide	m^2	0.50	8.49	-	4.03	12.52	13.77	6.136
K111516L	n.e. 300 mm wide	m	0.20	3.40	-	1.27	4.67	5.14	1.952
K111517	**Insulation board; 12.5 mm white faced**								
K111517M	over 300 mm wide	m^2	0.50	8.49	-	4.96	13.45	14.80	6.136
K111517N	n.e. 300 mm wide	m	0.20	3.40	-	1.56	4.96	5.46	1.952
K111521	**Non-asbestos flameproof Class O boards; BS 476; 6 mm**								
K111521A	over 300 mm wide	m^2	0.33	5.60	-	11.04	16.64	18.30	2.008
K111521B	300 mm wide	m	0.13	2.21	-	3.49	5.70	6.27	0.646
K111522	**Non-asbestos flameproof Class O boards; BS 476; 9 mm**								
K111522C	over 300 mm wide	m^2	0.35	5.94	-	28.93	34.87	38.36	2.923
K111522D	n.e. 300 mm wide	m	0.14	2.38	-	9.11	11.49	12.64	0.934
K111523	**Non-asbestos flameproof Class O boards; BS 476; 12 mm**								
K111523E	over 300 mm wide	m^2	0.40	6.79	-	43.57	50.36	55.40	3.882
K111523F	n.e. 300 mm wide	m	0.16	2.72	-	13.72	16.44	18.08	1.239

Linings, Sheathing & Dry Partitioning

Major Works 2011		Unit	Labour Hours	Labour Net	Plant Net	Materials Net	Unit Net	Unit with 10%	CO₂
				£	£	£	£	£	Kg
K11	**K11: RIGID SHEET FLOORING, SHEATHING, LININGS AND CASINGS**								
K1115	**Ceilings**								
K111524	**Non-asbestos flameproof Class O boards; BS 476; 15 mm**								
K111524G	over 300 mm wide	m²	0.45	7.64	-	54.58	62.22	68.44	4.798
K111524H	n.e. 300 mm wide	m	0.18	3.06	-	17.17	20.23	22.25	1.527
K1120	**Isolated beams**								
K112001	**Hardboard; 3.2 mm standard**								
K112001A	not exceeding 600 mm girth	m²	0.45	7.64	-	1.74	9.38	10.32	2.693
K112001B	600 - 1200 mm girth	m²	0.36	6.11	-	1.70	7.81	8.59	2.632
K112001C	1200 - 1800 mm girth	m²	0.30	5.09	-	1.66	6.75	7.43	2.571
K112002	**Hardboard; 6.0 mm standard**								
K112002A	not exceeding 600 mm girth	m²	0.53	8.91	-	4.83	13.74	15.11	2.759
K112002B	600 - 1200 mm girth	m²	0.42	7.13	-	4.72	11.85	13.04	2.696
K112002C	1200 - 1800 mm girth	m²	0.35	5.94	-	4.61	10.55	11.61	2.634
K112003	**Hardboard; 6.0 mm flameproof Class 1**								
K112003A	not exceeding 600 mm girth	m²	0.53	8.91	-	13.27	22.18	24.40	2.759
K112003B	600 - 1200 mm girth	m²	0.42	7.13	-	12.97	20.10	22.11	2.696
K112003C	1200 - 1800 mm girth	m²	0.35	5.94	-	12.67	18.61	20.47	2.634
K112011	**Insulation board; 6.4 mm Sundeala A**								
K112011A	not exceeding 600 mm girth	m²	0.60	10.19	-	11.47	21.66	23.83	3.276
K112011B	600 - 1200 mm girth	m²	0.48	8.15	-	11.21	19.36	21.30	3.204
K112011C	1200 - 1800 mm girth	m²	0.40	6.79	-	10.96	17.75	19.53	3.133
K112012	**Insulation board; 9.5 mm Sundeala A**								
K112012A	not exceeding 600 mm girth	m²	0.65	10.95	-	14.80	25.75	28.33	4.798
K112012B	600 - 1200 mm girth	m²	0.52	8.83	-	14.47	23.30	25.63	4.692
K112012C	1200 - 1800 mm girth	m²	0.43	7.30	-	14.14	21.44	23.58	4.586
K112013	**Insulation board; 12.5 mm Sundeala A**								
K112013A	not exceeding 600 mm girth	m²	0.68	11.46	-	17.19	28.65	31.52	5.537
K112013B	600 - 1200 mm girth	m²	0.54	9.17	-	16.80	25.97	28.57	5.417
K112013C	1200 - 1800 mm girth	m²	0.45	7.64	-	16.41	24.05	26.46	5.297
K112014	**Insulation board; 6.4 mm Sundeala K**								
K112014A	not exceeding 600 mm girth	m²	0.60	10.19	-	10.17	20.36	22.40	3.276
K112014B	600 - 1200 mm girth	m²	0.48	8.15	-	9.94	18.09	19.90	3.204
K112014C	1200 - 1800 mm girth	m²	0.40	6.79	-	9.72	16.51	18.16	3.133
K112015	**Insulation board; 9.5 mm Sundeala K**								
K112015A	not exceeding 600 mm girth	m²	0.65	10.95	-	14.80	25.75	28.33	4.798
K112015B	600 - 1200 mm girth	m²	0.52	8.83	-	14.47	23.30	25.63	4.692
K112015C	1200 - 1800 mm girth	m²	0.43	7.30	-	14.14	21.44	23.58	4.586
K112016	**Insulation board; 12.5 mm Pilkington ivory faced**								
K112016A	not exceeding 600 mm girth	m²	0.75	12.73	-	4.22	16.95	18.65	6.415
K112016B	600 - 1200 mm girth	m²	0.60	10.19	-	4.13	14.32	15.75	6.276
K112016C	1200 - 1800 mm girth	m²	0.50	8.49	-	4.03	12.52	13.77	6.136
K112017	**Insulation board; 12.5 mm Unitex white faced**								
K112017A	not exceeding 600 mm girth	m²	0.75	12.73	-	5.19	17.92	19.71	6.415
K112017B	600 - 1200 mm girth	m²	0.60	10.19	-	5.07	15.26	16.79	6.276
K112017C	1200 - 1800 mm girth	m²	0.50	8.49	-	4.96	13.45	14.80	6.136
K112021	**Non-asbestos flameproof Class O boards; BS 476; 6 mm**								
K112021A	not exceeding 600 mm girth	m²	0.50	8.41	-	11.55	19.96	21.96	2.095
K112021B	600 - 1200 mm girth	m²	0.40	6.79	-	11.29	18.08	19.89	2.051
K112021C	1200 - 1800 mm girth	m²	0.33	5.60	-	11.04	16.64	18.30	2.008

Major Works 2011		Unit	Labour Hours	Labour Net	Plant Net	Materials Net	Unit Net	Unit with 10%	CO2
				£	£	£	£	£	Kg
K11	**K11: RIGID SHEET FLOORING, SHEATHING, LININGS AND CASINGS**								
K1120	**Isolated beams**								
K112022	**Non-asbestos flameproof Class O boards; BS 476; 9 mm**								
K112022A	not exceeding 600 mm girth	m²	0.53	8.91	-	30.30	39.21	43.13	3.054
K112022B	600 - 1200 mm girth	m²	0.42	7.13	-	29.61	36.74	40.41	2.989
K112022C	1200 - 1800 mm girth	m²	0.35	5.94	-	28.93	34.87	38.36	2.923
K112023	**Non-asbestos flameproof Class O boards; BS 476; 12 mm**								
K112023A	not exceeding 600 mm girth	m²	0.60	10.19	-	45.64	55.83	61.41	4.057
K112023B	600 - 1200 mm girth	m²	0.48	8.15	-	44.61	52.76	58.04	3.969
K112023C	1200 - 1800 mm girth	m²	0.40	6.79	-	43.57	50.36	55.40	3.882
K112024	**Non-asbestos flameproof Class O boards; BS 476; 15 mm**								
K112024A	not exceeding 600 mm girth	m²	0.68	11.46	-	57.17	68.63	75.49	5.016
K112024B	600 - 1200 mm girth	m²	0.54	9.17	-	55.87	65.04	71.54	4.907
K112024C	1200 - 1800 mm girth	m²	0.45	7.64	-	54.58	62.22	68.44	4.798
K1121	**Isolated columns**								
K112101	**Hardboard; 3.2 mm standard**								
K112101A	not exceeding 600 mm girth	m²	0.38	6.37	-	1.74	8.11	8.92	2.693
K112101B	600 - 1200 mm girth	m²	0.30	5.09	-	1.70	6.79	7.47	2.632
K112101C	1200 - 1800 mm girth	m²	0.25	4.25	-	1.66	5.91	6.50	2.571
K112102	**Hardboard; 6.0 mm standard**								
K112102A	not exceeding 600 mm girth	m²	0.45	7.64	-	4.83	12.47	13.72	2.759
K112102B	600 - 1200 mm girth	m²	0.36	6.11	-	4.72	10.83	11.91	2.696
K112102C	1200 - 1800 mm girth	m²	0.30	5.09	-	4.61	9.70	10.67	2.634
K112103	**Hardboard; 3.2 mm perforated**								
K112103A	not exceeding 600 mm girth	m²	0.42	7.13	-	1.80	8.93	9.82	1.485
K112103B	600 - 1200 mm girth	m²	0.34	5.71	-	1.76	7.47	8.22	1.452
K112103C	1200 - 1800 mm girth	m²	0.28	4.75	-	1.72	6.47	7.12	1.419
K112104	**Hardboard; 6.0 mm perforated**								
K112104A	not exceeding 600 mm girth	m²	0.48	8.15	-	3.70	11.85	13.04	2.759
K112104B	600 - 1200 mm girth	m²	0.38	6.52	-	3.62	10.14	11.15	2.696
K112104C	1200 - 1800 mm girth	m²	0.32	5.43	-	3.53	8.96	9.86	2.634
K112105	**Hardboard; 6.0 mm flameproof Class 1**								
K112105A	not exceeding 600 mm girth	m²	0.45	7.64	-	13.27	20.91	23.00	2.759
K112105B	600 - 1200 mm girth	m²	0.36	6.11	-	12.97	19.08	20.99	2.696
K112105C	1200 - 1800 mm girth	m²	0.30	5.09	-	12.67	17.76	19.54	2.634
K112106	**Hardboard; 3.2 mm stove enamelled one side**								
K112106A	not exceeding 600 mm girth	m²	0.42	7.13	-	2.59	9.72	10.69	2.693
K112106B	600 - 1200 mm girth	m²	0.34	5.71	-	2.53	8.24	9.06	2.632
K112106C	1200 - 1800 mm girth	m²	0.28	4.75	-	2.47	7.22	7.94	2.571
K112111	**Insulation board; 6.4 mm Sundeala A**								
K112111A	not exceeding 600 mm girth	m²	0.53	8.91	-	11.47	20.38	22.42	3.276
K112111B	600 - 1200 mm girth	m²	0.42	7.13	-	11.21	18.34	20.17	3.204
K112111C	1200 - 1800 mm girth	m²	0.35	5.94	-	10.96	16.90	18.59	3.133
K112112	**Insulation board; 9.5 mm Sundeala A**								
K112112A	not exceeding 600 mm girth	m²	0.57	9.68	-	14.80	24.48	26.93	4.798
K112112B	600 - 1200 mm girth	m²	0.46	7.74	-	14.47	22.21	24.43	4.692
K112112C	1200 - 1800 mm girth	m²	0.38	6.45	-	14.14	20.59	22.65	4.586
K112113	**Insulation board; 12.5 mm Sundeala A**								
K112113A	not exceeding 600 mm girth	m²	0.60	10.19	-	17.19	27.38	30.12	5.537
K112113B	600 - 1200 mm girth	m²	0.48	8.15	-	16.80	24.95	27.45	5.417
K112113C	1200 - 1800 mm girth	m²	0.40	6.79	-	16.41	23.20	25.52	5.297

Major Works 2011		Unit	Labour Hours	Labour Net £	Plant Net £	Materials Net £	Unit Net £	Unit with 10% £	CO₂ Kg
K11	**K11: RIGID SHEET FLOORING, SHEATHING, LININGS AND CASINGS**								
K1121	**Isolated columns**								
K112114	**Insulation board; 6.4 mm Sundeala K**								
K112114A	not exceeding 600 mm girth	m²	0.53	8.91	-	10.17	19.08	20.99	3.276
K112114B	600 - 1200 mm girth	m²	0.42	7.13	-	9.94	17.07	18.78	3.204
K112114C	1200 - 1800 mm girth	m²	0.35	5.94	-	9.72	15.66	17.23	3.133
K112115	**Insulation board; 9.5 mm Sundeala K**								
K112115A	not exceeding 600 mm girth	m²	0.57	9.68	-	14.80	24.48	26.93	4.798
K112115B	600 - 1200 mm girth	m²	0.46	7.74	-	14.47	22.21	24.43	4.692
K112115C	1200 - 1800 mm girth	m²	0.38	6.45	-	14.14	20.59	22.65	4.586
K112116	**Insulation board; 12.5 mm Pilkington ivory faced**								
K112116A	not exceeding 600 mm girth	m²	0.68	11.46	-	4.22	15.68	17.25	6.415
K112116B	600 - 1200 mm girth	m²	0.54	9.17	-	4.13	13.30	14.63	6.276
K112116C	1200 - 1800 mm girth	m²	0.45	7.64	-	4.03	11.67	12.84	6.136
K112117	**Insulation board; 12.5 mm Unitex ivory faced**								
K112117A	not exceeding 600 mm girth	m²	0.68	11.46	-	5.19	16.65	18.32	6.415
K112117B	600 - 1200 mm girth	m²	0.54	9.17	-	5.07	14.24	15.66	6.276
K112117C	1200 - 1800 mm girth	m²	0.45	7.64	-	4.96	12.60	13.86	6.136
K112121	**Chipboard; 12 mm**								
K112121A	not exceeding 600 mm girth	m²	0.45	7.64	-	2.52	10.16	11.18	4.298
K112121B	600 - 1200 mm girth	m²	0.36	6.11	-	2.47	8.58	9.44	4.202
K112121C	1200 - 1800 mm girth	m²	0.30	5.09	-	2.41	7.50	8.25	4.105
K112122	**Chipboard; 15 mm**								
K112122A	not exceeding 600 mm girth	m²	0.53	8.91	-	3.71	12.62	13.88	5.359
K112122B	600 - 1200 mm girth	m²	0.42	7.13	-	3.63	10.76	11.84	5.238
K112122C	1200 - 1800 mm girth	m²	0.35	5.94	-	3.54	9.48	10.43	5.118
K112123	**Chipboard; 18 mm**								
K112123A	not exceeding 600 mm girth	m²	0.60	10.19	-	5.93	16.12	17.73	6.418
K112123B	600 - 1200 mm girth	m²	0.48	8.15	-	5.80	13.95	15.35	6.273
K112123C	1200 - 1800 mm girth	m²	0.40	6.79	-	5.66	12.45	13.70	6.129
K112127	**Chipboard faced one side with 1.5 mm Class 1 laminated plastic covering and balancing veneer other side; 15 mm**								
K112127A	not exceeding 600 mm girth	m²	0.75	12.73	-	4.68	17.41	19.15	5.579
K112127B	600 - 1200 mm girth	m²	0.60	10.19	-	4.58	14.77	16.25	5.459
K112127C	1200 - 1800 mm girth	m²	0.50	8.49	-	4.47	12.96	14.26	5.338
K112128	**Chipboard faced one side with 1.5 mm Class 1 laminated plastic covering and balancing veneer other side; 18 mm**								
K112128A	not exceeding 600 mm girth	m²	0.90	15.28	-	5.15	20.43	22.47	6.639
K112128B	600 - 1200 mm girth	m²	0.72	12.23	-	5.03	17.26	18.99	6.494
K112128C	1200 - 1800 mm girth	m²	0.60	10.19	-	4.92	15.11	16.62	6.350
K112131	**Finnish birch faced 5 ply blockboard; grade BB; 18 mm**								
K112131A	not exceeding 600 mm girth	m²	1.13	19.10	-	25.78	44.88	49.37	6.198
K112131B	600 - 1200 mm girth	m²	0.90	15.28	-	25.20	40.48	44.53	6.063
K112131C	1200 - 1800 mm girth	m²	0.75	12.73	-	24.61	37.34	41.07	5.929
K112132	**Finnish birch faced 5 ply blockboard; grade BB; 25 mm**								
K112132A	not exceeding 600 mm wide	m²	1.20	20.38	-	33.85	54.23	59.65	8.171
K112132B	600 - 1200 mm wide	m²	0.96	16.30	-	33.08	49.38	54.32	7.992
K112132C	1200 - 1800 mm wide	m²	0.80	13.58	-	32.31	45.89	50.48	7.812

Major Works 2011		Unit	Labour Hours	Labour Net	Plant Net	Materials Net	Unit Net	Unit with 10%	CO$_2$
				£	£	£	£	£	Kg
K11	**K11: RIGID SHEET FLOORING, SHEATHING, LININGS AND CASINGS**								
K1121	**Isolated columns**								
K112136	**Far Eastern hardwood faced MR boarding ply; grade B/BB; 4 mm**								
K112136A	not exceeding 600 mm girth	m²	0.57	9.68	-	7.91	17.59	19.35	1.953
K112136B	600 - 1200 mm girth	m²	0.46	7.74	-	7.73	15.47	17.02	1.910
K112136C	1200 - 1800 mm girth	m²	0.38	6.45	-	7.55	14.00	15.40	1.866
K112137	**Far Eastern hardwood faced MR boarding ply; grade B/BB; 6 mm**								
K112137A	not exceeding 600 mm girth	m²	0.63	10.70	-	8.66	19.36	21.30	3.156
K112137B	600 - 1200 mm girth	m²	0.50	8.49	-	8.46	16.95	18.65	3.085
K112137C	1200 - 1800 mm girth	m²	0.42	7.13	-	8.27	15.40	16.94	3.013
K112138	**Far Eastern hardwood faced MR boarding ply; grade B/BB; 9 mm**								
K112138A	not exceeding 600 mm girth	m²	0.69	11.72	-	6.61	18.33	20.16	4.359
K112138B	600 - 1200 mm girth	m²	0.55	9.34	-	6.46	15.80	17.38	4.261
K112138C	1200 - 1800 mm girth	m²	0.46	7.81	-	6.31	14.12	15.53	4.162
K112139	**Far Eastern hardwood faced MR boarding ply; grade B/BB; 12 mm**								
K112139A	not exceeding 600 mm girth	m²	0.75	12.73	-	8.42	21.15	23.27	5.802
K112139B	600 - 1200 mm girth	m²	0.60	10.19	-	8.23	18.42	20.26	5.671
K112139C	1200 - 1800 mm girth	m²	0.50	8.49	-	8.03	16.52	18.17	5.540
K112140	**Far Eastern hardwood faced MR boarding ply; grade B/BB; 15 mm**								
K112140A	not exceeding 600 mm girth	m²	0.84	14.26	-	10.71	24.97	27.47	7.245
K112140B	600 - 1200 mm girth	m²	0.67	11.38	-	10.47	21.85	24.04	7.081
K112140C	1200 - 1800 mm girth	m²	0.56	9.51	-	10.23	19.74	21.71	6.917
K112141	**Far Eastern hardwood faced MR boarding ply; grade B/BB; 18 mm**								
K112141A	not exceeding 600 mm girth	m²	0.90	15.28	-	12.24	27.52	30.27	8.689
K112141B	600 - 1200 mm girth	m²	0.72	12.23	-	11.96	24.19	26.61	8.492
K112141C	1200 - 1800 mm girth	m²	0.60	10.19	-	11.69	21.88	24.07	8.295
K112142	**Far Eastern hardwood faced MR boarding ply; grade B/BB; 22 mm**								
K112142A	not exceeding 600 mm girth	m²	0.96	16.30	-	14.65	30.95	34.05	10.614
K112142B	600 - 1200 mm girth	m²	0.77	13.07	-	14.32	27.39	30.13	10.373
K112142C	1200 - 1800 mm girth	m²	0.64	10.87	-	13.99	24.86	27.35	10.132
K112143	**Far Eastern hardwood faced MR boarding ply; grade B/BB; 25 mm**								
K112143A	not exceeding 600 mm girth	m²	1.04	17.57	-	17.02	34.59	38.05	12.057
K112143B	600 - 1200 mm girth	m²	0.83	14.09	-	16.63	30.72	33.79	11.783
K112143C	1200 - 1800 mm girth	m²	0.69	11.72	-	16.24	27.96	30.76	11.510
K112150	**Finnish birch faced WBP boarding ply; grade BB; 4 mm**								
K112150A	not exceeding 600 mm girth	m²	0.53	8.91	-	7.27	16.18	17.80	1.953
K112150B	600 - 1200 mm girth	m²	0.42	7.13	-	7.11	14.24	15.66	1.910
K112150C	1200 - 1800 mm girth	m²	0.35	5.94	-	6.94	12.88	14.17	1.866
K112151	**Finnish birch faced WBP boarding ply; grade BB; 6 mm**								
K112151A	not exceeding 600 mm girth	m²	0.57	9.68	-	10.72	20.40	22.44	2.915
K112151B	600 - 1200 mm girth	m²	0.46	7.74	-	10.47	18.21	20.03	2.849
K112151C	1200 - 1800 mm girth	m²	0.38	6.45	-	10.23	16.68	18.35	2.784
K112152	**Finnish birch faced WBP boarding ply; grade BB; 9 mm**								
K112152A	not exceeding 600 mm girth	m²	0.60	10.19	-	13.19	23.38	25.72	4.359

Major Works 2011		Unit	Labour Hours	Labour Net £	Plant Net £	Materials Net £	Unit Net £	Unit with 10% £	CO₂ Kg
K11	**K11: RIGID SHEET FLOORING, SHEATHING, LININGS AND CASINGS**								
K1121	**Isolated columns**								
K112152	**Finnish birch faced WBP boarding ply; grade BB; 9 mm**								
K112152B	600 - 1200 mm girth	m²	0.48	8.15	-	12.89	21.04	23.14	4.261
K112152C	1200 - 1800 mm girth	m²	0.40	6.79	-	12.59	19.38	21.32	4.162
K112153	**Finnish birch faced WBP boarding ply; grade BB; 12 mm**								
K112153A	not exceeding 600 mm girth	m²	0.68	11.46	-	15.50	26.96	29.66	5.802
K112153B	600 - 1200 mm girth	m²	0.54	9.17	-	15.15	24.32	26.75	5.671
K112153C	1200 - 1800 mm girth	m²	0.45	7.64	-	14.80	22.44	24.68	5.540
K112154	**Finnish birch faced WBP boarding ply; grade BB; 15 mm**								
K112154A	not exceeding 600 mm girth	m²	0.72	12.23	-	20.85	33.08	36.39	7.245
K112154B	600 - 1200 mm girth	m²	0.58	9.85	-	20.37	30.22	33.24	7.081
K112154C	1200 - 1800 mm girth	m²	0.48	8.15	-	19.90	28.05	30.86	6.917
K112155	**Finnish birch faced WBP boarding ply; grade BB; 18 mm**								
K112155A	not exceeding 600 mm girth	m²	0.78	13.24	-	24.87	38.11	41.92	8.689
K112155B	600 - 1200 mm girth	m²	0.63	10.61	-	24.30	34.91	38.40	8.492
K112155C	1200 - 1800 mm girth	m²	0.52	8.83	-	23.74	32.57	35.83	8.295
K112156	**Finnish birch faced WBP boarding ply; grade BB; 22 mm**								
K112156A	not exceeding 600 mm girth	m²	0.84	14.26	-	29.43	43.69	48.06	10.614
K112156B	600 - 1200 mm girth	m²	0.67	11.38	-	28.77	40.15	44.17	10.373
K112156C	1200 - 1800 mm girth	m²	0.56	9.51	-	28.10	37.61	41.37	10.132
K112157	**Finnish birch faced WBP boarding ply; grade BB; 25 mm**								
K112157A	not exceeding 600 mm girth	m²	0.90	15.28	-	34.02	49.30	54.23	12.057
K112157B	600 - 1200 mm girth	m²	0.72	12.23	-	33.25	45.48	50.03	11.783
K112157C	1200 - 1800 mm girth	m²	0.60	10.19	-	32.48	42.67	46.94	11.510
K112161	**Non-asbestos, flameproof Class O boards; BS 476; 6 mm**								
K112161A	not exceeding 600 mm girth	m²	0.42	7.13	-	11.50	18.63	20.49	2.051
K112161B	600 - 1200 mm girth	m²	0.34	5.71	-	11.24	16.95	18.65	2.007
K112161C	1200 - 1800 mm girth	m²	0.28	4.75	-	10.99	15.74	17.31	1.963
K112162	**Non-asbestos, flameproof Class O boards; BS 476; 9 mm**								
K112162A	not exceeding 600 mm girth	m²	0.45	7.64	-	30.25	37.89	41.68	3.010
K112162B	600 - 1200 mm girth	m²	0.36	6.11	-	29.56	35.67	39.24	2.944
K112162C	1200 - 1800 mm girth	m²	0.30	5.09	-	28.88	33.97	37.37	2.879
K112163	**Non-asbestos, flameproof Class O boards; BS 476; 12 mm**								
K112163A	not exceeding 600 mm girth	m²	0.53	8.91	-	45.59	54.50	59.95	4.012
K112163B	600 - 1200 mm girth	m²	0.42	7.13	-	44.56	51.69	56.86	3.925
K112163C	1200 - 1800 mm girth	m²	0.35	5.94	-	43.52	49.46	54.41	3.838
K112164	**Non-asbestos, flameproof Class O boards; BS 476; 15 mm**								
K112164A	not exceeding 600 mm girth	m²	0.60	10.19	-	57.11	67.30	74.03	4.971
K112164B	600 - 1200 mm girth	m²	0.48	8.15	-	55.82	63.97	70.37	4.862
K112164C	1200 - 1800 mm girth	m²	0.40	6.79	-	54.53	61.32	67.45	4.754

Major Works 2011		Unit	Labour Hours	Labour Net	Plant Net	Materials Net	Unit Net	Unit with 10%	CO$_2$
				£	£	£	£	£	Kg
K13	**K13: RIGID SHEET FINE LININGS AND PANELLING**								
K1311	**Walls**								
K131101	**Hardboard; 3.2 mm standard**								
K131101A	over 300 mm wide	m^2	0.25	4.25	-	1.74	5.99	6.59	2.693
K131101B	n.e. 300 mm wide	m	0.10	1.71	-	0.52	2.23	2.45	0.808
K131101C	areas n.e. 1.0 m^2	Nr	0.19	3.19	-	0.83	4.02	4.42	1.286
K131102	**Hardboard; 6.0 mm standard**								
K131102A	over 300 mm wide	m^2	0.30	5.09	-	4.83	9.92	10.91	2.759
K131102B	n.e. 300 mm wide	m	0.12	2.07	-	1.45	3.52	3.87	0.828
K131102C	areas n.e. 1.0 m^2	Nr	0.23	3.82	-	2.31	6.13	6.74	1.317
K131103	**Hardboard; 3.2 mm perforated**								
K131103A	over 300 mm wide	m^2	0.28	4.75	-	1.80	6.55	7.21	1.485
K131103B	n.e. 300 mm wide	m	0.11	1.92	-	0.54	2.46	2.71	0.445
K131103C	areas n.e. 1.0 m^2	Nr	0.21	3.57	-	0.86	4.43	4.87	0.709
K131104	**Hardboard; 6.0 mm perforated**								
K131104A	over 300 mm wide	m^2	0.32	5.43	-	3.70	9.13	10.04	2.759
K131104B	n.e. 300 mm wide	m	0.13	2.21	-	1.11	3.32	3.65	0.828
K131104C	areas n.e. 1.0 m^2	Nr	0.24	4.08	-	1.77	5.85	6.44	1.317
K131105	**Hardboard; 6.0 mm flameproof Class 1**								
K131105A	over 300 mm wide	m^2	0.30	5.09	-	13.27	18.36	20.20	2.759
K131105B	n.e. 300 mm wide	m	0.12	2.07	-	3.98	6.05	6.66	0.828
K131105C	areas n.e. 1.0 m^2	Nr	0.23	3.82	-	6.33	10.15	11.17	1.317
K131106	**Hardboard; 3.2 mm stove enamelled one side**								
K131106A	over 300 mm wide	m^2	0.28	4.75	-	2.59	7.34	8.07	2.693
K131106B	n.e. 300 mm wide	m	0.11	1.92	-	0.78	2.70	2.97	0.808
K131106C	areas n.e. 1.0 m^2	Nr	0.21	3.57	-	1.23	4.80	5.28	1.286
K131111	**Insulation board; 6.4 mm Sundeala A**								
K131111A	over 300 mm wide	m^2	0.35	5.94	-	11.47	17.41	19.15	3.276
K131111B	n.e. 300 mm wide	m	0.14	2.41	-	3.44	5.85	6.44	0.983
K131111C	areas n.e. 1.0 m^2	Nr	0.26	4.47	-	5.48	9.95	10.95	1.567
K131112	**Insulation board; 9.5 mm Sundeala A**								
K131112A	over 300 mm wide	m^2	0.38	6.45	-	14.80	21.25	23.38	4.798
K131112B	n.e. 300 mm wide	m	0.15	2.61	-	4.44	7.05	7.76	1.439
K131112C	areas n.e. 1.0 m^2	Nr	0.29	4.84	-	7.07	11.91	13.10	2.293
K131113	**Insulation board; 12.5 mm Sundeala A**								
K131113A	over 300 mm wide	m^2	0.40	6.79	-	17.19	23.98	26.38	5.537
K131113B	n.e. 300 mm wide	m	0.16	2.75	-	5.16	7.91	8.70	1.661
K131113C	areas n.e. 1.0 m^2	Nr	0.30	5.09	-	8.21	13.30	14.63	2.649
K131114	**Insulation board; 6.4 mm Sundeala K**								
K131114A	over 300 mm wide	m^2	0.35	5.94	-	10.17	16.11	17.72	3.276
K131114B	n.e. 300 mm wide	m	0.14	2.41	-	3.05	5.46	6.01	0.983
K131114C	areas n.e. 1.0 m^2	Nr	0.26	4.47	-	4.86	9.33	10.26	1.567
K131115	**Insulation board; 9.5 mm Sundeala K**								
K131115A	over 300 mm wide	m^2	0.38	6.45	-	14.80	21.25	23.38	4.798
K131115B	n.e. 300 mm wide	m	0.15	2.61	-	4.44	7.05	7.76	1.439
K131115C	areas n.e. 1.0 m^2	Nr	0.29	4.84	-	7.07	11.91	13.10	2.293
K131116	**Insulation board; 12.5 mm Pilkington ivory faced**								
K131116A	over 300 mm wide	m^2	0.45	7.64	-	4.22	11.86	13.05	6.415
K131116B	n.e. 300 mm wide	m	0.18	3.09	-	1.27	4.36	4.80	1.925
K131116C	areas n.e. 1.0 m^2	Nr	0.34	5.74	-	2.02	7.76	8.54	3.068
K131117	**Insulation board; 12.5 mm Unitex ivory faced**								
K131117A	over 300 mm wide	m^2	0.45	7.64	-	5.19	12.83	14.11	6.415
K131117B	n.e. 300 mm wide	m	0.18	3.09	-	1.56	4.65	5.12	1.925
K131117C	areas n.e. 1.0 m^2	Nr	0.34	5.74	-	2.48	8.22	9.04	3.068

Major Works 2011		Unit	Labour Hours	Labour Net	Plant Net	Materials Net	Unit Net	Unit with 10%	CO₂
				£	£	£	£	£	Kg
K13	**K13: RIGID SHEET FINE LININGS AND PANELLING**								
K1311	**Walls**								
K131121	**Chipboard; 12 mm**								
K131121A	over 300 mm wide	m²	0.30	5.09	-	2.52	7.61	8.37	4.298
K131121B	n.e. 300 mm wide	m	0.12	2.07	-	0.76	2.83	3.11	1.289
K131121C	areas n.e. 1.0 m²	Nr	0.23	3.82	-	1.20	5.02	5.52	2.053
K131122	**Chipboard; 15 mm**								
K131122A	over 300 mm wide	m²	0.35	5.94	-	3.71	9.65	10.62	5.359
K131122B	n.e. 300 mm wide	m	0.14	2.41	-	1.11	3.52	3.87	1.608
K131122C	areas n.e. 1.0 m²	Nr	0.26	4.47	-	1.77	6.24	6.86	2.559
K131123	**Chipboard; 18 mm**								
K131123A	over 300 mm wide	m²	0.40	6.79	-	5.93	12.72	13.99	6.418
K131123B	n.e. 300 mm wide	m	0.16	2.75	-	1.78	4.53	4.98	1.925
K131123C	areas n.e. 1.0 m²	Nr	0.30	5.09	-	2.83	7.92	8.71	3.064
K131127	**Chipboard faced one side with 1.5 mm Class 1 laminated plastic covering and balancing veneer other side; 15 mm**								
K131127A	over 300 mm wide	m²	0.50	8.49	-	4.68	13.17	14.49	5.579
K131127B	n.e. 300 mm wide	m	0.20	3.45	-	1.41	4.86	5.35	1.674
K131127C	areas n.e. 1.0 m²	Nr	0.38	6.37	-	2.24	8.61	9.47	2.669
K131128	**Chipboard faced one side with 1.5 mm Class 1 laminated plastic covering and balancing veneer other side; 18 mm**								
K131128A	over 300 mm wide	m²	0.60	10.19	-	5.15	15.34	16.87	6.639
K131128B	n.e. 300 mm wide	m	0.24	4.13	-	1.54	5.67	6.24	1.992
K131128C	areas n.e. 1.0 m²	Nr	0.45	7.64	-	2.46	10.10	11.11	3.175
K131131	**Finnish birch faced 5-ply blockboard; grade BB; 18 mm**								
K131131A	over 300 mm wide	m²	0.75	12.73	-	25.78	38.51	42.36	6.198
K131131B	n.e. 300 mm wide	m	0.30	5.16	-	7.73	12.89	14.18	1.859
K131131C	areas n.e. 1.0 m²	Nr	0.56	9.56	-	12.31	21.87	24.06	2.964
K131132	**Finnish birch faced 5-ply blockboard; grade BB; 25 mm**								
K131132A	over 300 mm wide	m²	0.80	13.58	-	33.85	47.43	52.17	8.171
K131132B	n.e. 300 mm wide	m	0.32	5.50	-	10.15	15.65	17.22	2.451
K131132C	areas n.e. 1.0 m²	Nr	0.60	10.19	-	16.15	26.34	28.97	3.906
K131136	**Far Eastern hardwood faced MR boarding ply; grade B/BB; 4 mm**								
K131136A	over 300 mm wide	m²	0.38	6.45	-	7.91	14.36	15.80	1.953
K131136B	n.e. 300 mm wide	m	0.15	2.61	-	2.37	4.98	5.48	0.586
K131136C	areas n.e. 1.0 m²	Nr	0.29	4.84	-	3.78	8.62	9.48	0.933
K131137	**Far Eastern hardwood faced MR boarding ply; grade B/BB; 6 mm**								
K131137A	over 300 mm wide	m²	0.42	7.13	-	8.66	15.79	17.37	3.156
K131137B	n.e. 300 mm wide	m	0.17	2.89	-	2.60	5.49	6.04	0.947
K131137C	areas n.e. 1.0 m²	Nr	0.32	5.35	-	4.13	9.48	10.43	1.507
K131138	**Far Eastern hardwood faced MR boarding ply; grade B/BB; 9 mm**								
K131138A	over 300 mm wide	m²	0.46	7.81	-	6.61	14.42	15.86	4.359
K131138B	n.e. 300 mm wide	m	0.19	3.16	-	1.98	5.14	5.65	1.308
K131138C	areas n.e. 1.0 m²	Nr	0.35	5.86	-	3.16	9.02	9.92	2.081
K131139	**Far Eastern hardwood faced MR boarding ply; grade B/BB; 12 mm**								
K131139A	over 300 mm wide	m²	0.50	8.49	-	8.42	16.91	18.60	5.802
K131139B	n.e. 300 mm wide	m	0.20	3.45	-	2.52	5.97	6.57	1.741
K131139C	areas n.e. 1.0 m²	Nr	0.38	6.37	-	4.02	10.39	11.43	2.770

Major Works 2011		Unit	Labour Hours	Labour Net	Plant Net	Materials Net	Unit Net	Unit with 10%	CO₂
				£	£	£	£	£	Kg
K13	**K13: RIGID SHEET FINE LININGS AND PANELLING**								
K1311	**Walls**								
K131140	**Far Eastern hardwood faced MR boarding ply; grade B/BB; 15 mm**								
K131140A	over 300 mm wide	m²	0.56	9.51	-	10.71	20.22	22.24	7.245
K131140B	n.e. 300 mm wide	m	0.23	3.85	-	3.21	7.06	7.77	2.174
K131140C	areas n.e. 1.0 m²	Nr	0.42	7.13	-	5.11	12.24	13.46	3.459
K131141	**Far Eastern hardwood faced MR boarding ply; grade B/BB; 18 mm**								
K131141A	over 300 mm wide	m²	0.60	10.19	-	12.24	22.43	24.67	8.689
K131141B	n.e. 300 mm wide	m	0.24	4.13	-	3.67	7.80	8.58	2.607
K131141C	areas n.e. 1.0 m²	Nr	0.45	7.64	-	5.84	13.48	14.83	4.147
K131142	**Far Eastern hardwood faced MR boarding ply; grade B/BB; 22 mm**								
K131142A	over 300 mm wide	m²	0.64	10.87	-	14.65	25.52	28.07	10.614
K131142B	n.e. 300 mm wide	m	0.48	8.15	-	4.40	12.55	13.81	3.184
K131142C	areas n.e. 1.0 m²	Nr	0.48	8.15	-	6.99	15.14	16.65	5.066
K131143	**Far Eastern hardwood faced MR boarding ply; grade B/BB; 25 mm**								
K131143A	over 300 mm wide	m²	0.69	11.72	-	17.02	28.74	31.61	12.057
K131143B	n.e. 300 mm wide	m	0.28	4.74	-	5.10	9.84	10.82	3.617
K131143C	areas n.e. 1.0 m²	Nr	0.52	8.83	-	8.12	16.95	18.65	5.755
K131150	**Finnish birch faced WBP boarding ply; grade BB; 4 mm**								
K131150A	over 300 mm wide	m²	0.35	5.94	-	7.27	13.21	14.53	1.953
K131150B	n.e. 300 mm wide	m	0.14	2.41	-	2.18	4.59	5.05	0.586
K131150C	areas n.e. 1.0 m²	Nr	0.26	4.47	-	3.47	7.94	8.73	0.933
K131151	**Finnish birch faced WBP boarding ply; grade BB; 6 mm**								
K131151A	over 300 mm wide	m²	0.38	6.45	-	10.72	17.17	18.89	2.915
K131151B	n.e. 300 mm wide	m	0.15	2.61	-	3.22	5.83	6.41	0.874
K131151C	areas n.e. 1.0 m²	Nr	0.29	4.84	-	5.12	9.96	10.96	1.392
K131152	**Finnish birch faced WBP boarding ply; grade BB; 9 mm**								
K131152A	over 300 mm wide	m²	0.40	6.79	-	13.19	19.98	21.98	4.359
K131152B	n.e. 300 mm wide	m	0.16	2.75	-	3.96	6.71	7.38	1.308
K131152C	areas n.e. 1.0 m²	Nr	0.30	5.09	-	6.30	11.39	12.53	2.081
K131153	**Finnish birch faced WBP boarding ply; grade BB; 12 mm**								
K131153A	over 300 mm wide	m²	0.45	7.64	-	15.50	23.14	25.45	5.802
K131153B	n.e. 300 mm wide	m	0.18	3.09	-	4.65	7.74	8.51	1.741
K131153C	areas n.e. 1.0 m²	Nr	0.34	5.74	-	7.40	13.14	14.45	2.770
K131154	**Finnish birch faced WBP boarding ply; grade BB; 15 mm**								
K131154A	over 300 mm wide	m²	0.48	8.15	-	20.85	29.00	31.90	7.245
K131154B	n.e. 300 mm wide	m	0.19	3.29	-	6.25	9.54	10.49	2.174
K131154C	areas n.e. 1.0 m²	Nr	0.36	6.11	-	9.95	16.06	17.67	3.459
K131155	**Finnish birch faced WBP boarding ply; grade BB; 18 mm**								
K131155A	over 300 mm wide	m²	0.52	8.83	-	24.87	33.70	37.07	8.689
K131155B	n.e. 300 mm wide	m	0.21	3.58	-	7.46	11.04	12.14	2.607
K131155C	areas n.e. 1.0 m²	Nr	0.39	6.62	-	11.87	18.49	20.34	4.147
K131156	**Finnish birch faced WBP boarding ply; grade BB; 22 mm**								
K131156A	over 300 mm wide	m²	0.56	9.51	-	29.43	38.94	42.83	10.614
K131156B	n.e. 300 mm wide	m	0.23	3.85	-	8.83	12.68	13.95	3.184
K131156C	areas n.e. 1.0 m²	Nr	0.42	7.13	-	14.05	21.18	23.30	5.066

Major Works 2011		Unit	Labour Hours	Labour Net	Plant Net	Materials Net	Unit Net	Unit with 10%	CO$_2$
				£	£	£	£	£	Kg
K13	**K13: RIGID SHEET FINE LININGS AND PANELLING**								
K1311	**Walls**								
K131157	**Finnish birch faced WBP boarding ply; grade BB; 25 mm**								
K131157A	over 300 mm wide	m^2	0.60	10.19	-	34.02	44.21	48.63	12.057
K131157B	n.e. 300 mm wide	m	0.24	4.13	-	10.21	14.34	15.77	3.617
K131157C	areas n.e. 1.0 m^2	Nr	0.45	7.64	-	16.24	23.88	26.27	5.755
K131161	**Non-asbestos, flameproof Class O boards; BS 476; 6 mm**								
K131161A	over 300 mm wide	m^2	0.28	4.75	-	11.50	16.25	17.88	2.051
K131161B	n.e. 300 mm wide	m	0.11	1.92	-	3.45	5.37	5.91	0.615
K131161C	areas n.e. 1.0 m^2	Nr	0.21	3.57	-	5.49	9.06	9.97	0.982
K131162	**Non-asbestos, flameproof Class O boards; BS 476; 9 mm**								
K131162A	over 300 mm wide	m^2	0.30	5.09	-	30.25	35.34	38.87	3.010
K131162B	n.e. 300 mm wide	m	0.12	2.07	-	9.07	11.14	12.25	0.903
K131162C	areas n.e. 1.0 m^2	Nr	0.23	3.82	-	14.44	18.26	20.09	1.439
K131163	**Non-asbestos, flameproof Class O boards; BS 476; 12 mm**								
K131163A	over 300 mm wide	m^2	0.35	5.94	-	45.59	51.53	56.68	4.012
K131163B	n.e. 300 mm wide	m	0.14	2.41	-	13.68	16.09	17.70	1.204
K131163C	areas n.e. 1.0 m^2	Nr	0.26	4.47	-	21.76	26.23	28.85	1.919
K131164	**Non-asbestos, flameproof Class O boards; BS 476; 15 mm**								
K131164A	over 300 mm wide	m^2	0.40	6.79	-	57.11	63.90	70.29	4.971
K131164B	n.e. 300 mm wide	m	0.16	2.75	-	17.13	19.88	21.87	1.491
K131164C	areas n.e. 1.0 m^2	Nr	0.30	5.09	-	27.26	32.35	35.59	2.377
K131171	**MDF board; 12 mm**								
K131171A	over 300 mm wide	m^2	0.40	6.79	-	4.90	11.69	12.86	5.898
K131171B	n.e. 300 mm wide	m	0.16	2.75	-	1.47	4.22	4.64	1.769
K131171C	areas n.e. 1.0 m^2	Nr	0.30	5.09	-	2.34	7.43	8.17	2.816
K131172	**MDF board; 15 mm**								
K131172A	over 300 mm wide	m^2	0.45	7.64	-	4.93	12.57	13.83	7.358
K131172B	n.e. 300 mm wide	m	0.18	3.11	-	1.48	4.59	5.05	2.208
K131172C	areas n.e. 1.0 m^2	Nr	0.34	5.74	-	2.35	8.09	8.90	3.513
K131173	**MDF board; 18 mm**								
K131173A	over 300 mm wide	m^2	0.50	8.49	-	6.81	15.30	16.83	8.818
K131173B	n.e. 300 mm wide	m	0.20	3.45	-	2.04	5.49	6.04	2.645
K131173C	areas n.e. 1.0 m^2	Nr	0.38	6.37	-	3.25	9.62	10.58	4.210
K1315	**Ceilings**								
K131501	**Hardboard; 3.2 mm standard**								
K131501A	over 300 mm wide	m^2	0.28	4.75	-	1.74	6.49	7.14	2.693
K131501B	n.e. 300 mm wide	m	0.11	1.94	-	0.52	2.46	2.71	0.808
K131501C	areas n.e. 1.0 m^2	Nr	0.21	3.58	-	0.83	4.41	4.85	1.286
K131502	**Hardboard; 6.0 mm standard**								
K131502A	over 300 mm wide	m^2	0.34	5.74	-	4.83	10.57	11.63	2.759
K131502B	n.e. 300 mm wide	m	0.14	2.33	-	1.45	3.78	4.16	0.828
K131502C	areas n.e. 1.0 m^2	Nr	0.25	4.31	-	2.31	6.62	7.28	1.317
K131503	**Hardboard; 3.2 mm perforated**								
K131503A	over 300 mm wide	m^2	0.32	5.35	-	1.80	7.15	7.87	1.485
K131503B	n.e. 300 mm wide	m	0.13	2.17	-	0.54	2.71	2.98	0.445
K131503C	areas n.e. 1.0 m^2	Nr	0.24	4.01	-	0.86	4.87	5.36	0.709
K131504	**Hardboard; 6.0 mm perforated**								
K131504A	over 300 mm wide	m^2	0.36	6.11	-	3.70	9.81	10.79	2.759
K131504B	n.e. 300 mm wide	m	0.15	2.48	-	1.11	3.59	3.95	0.828
K131504C	areas n.e. 1.0 m^2	Nr	0.27	4.58	-	1.77	6.35	6.99	1.317
K131505	**Hardboard; 6.0 mm flameproof Class 1**								
K131505A	over 300 mm wide	m^2	0.34	5.74	-	13.27	19.01	20.91	2.759
K131505B	n.e. 300 mm wide	m	0.14	2.33	-	3.98	6.31	6.94	0.828

Major Works 2011		Unit	Labour Hours	Labour Net	Plant Net	Materials Net	Unit Net	Unit with 10%	CO$_2$
				£	£	£	£	£	Kg
K13	**K13: RIGID SHEET FINE LININGS AND PANELLING**								
K1315	**Ceilings**								
K131505	**Hardboard; 6.0 mm flameproof Class 1**								
K131505C	areas n.e. 1.0 m^2	Nr	0.25	4.31	–	6.33	10.64	11.70	1.317
K131506	**Hardboard; 3.2 mm stove enamelled one side**								
K131506A	over 300 mm wide	m^2	0.32	5.35	–	2.59	7.94	8.73	2.693
K131506B	n.e. 300 mm wide	m	0.13	2.17	–	0.78	2.95	3.25	0.808
K131506C	areas n.e. 1.0 m^2	Nr	0.24	4.01	–	1.23	5.24	5.76	1.286
K131511	**Insulation board; 6.4 mm Sundeala A**								
K131511A	over 300 mm wide	m^2	0.39	6.69	–	11.47	18.16	19.98	3.276
K131511B	n.e. 300 mm wide	m	0.16	2.70	–	3.44	6.14	6.75	0.983
K131511C	areas n.e. 1.0 m^2	Nr	0.30	5.03	–	5.48	10.51	11.56	1.567
K131512	**Insulation board; 9.5 mm Sundeala A**								
K131512A	over 300 mm wide	m^2	0.43	7.27	–	14.80	22.07	24.28	4.798
K131512B	n.e. 300 mm wide	m	0.17	2.94	–	4.44	7.38	8.12	1.439
K131512C	areas n.e. 1.0 m^2	Nr	0.32	5.45	–	7.07	12.52	13.77	2.293
K131513	**Insulation board; 12.5 mm Sundeala A**								
K131513A	over 300 mm wide	m^2	0.45	7.64	–	17.19	24.83	27.31	5.537
K131513B	n.e. 300 mm wide	m	0.18	3.09	–	5.16	8.25	9.08	1.661
K131513C	areas n.e. 1.0 m^2	Nr	0.34	5.74	–	8.21	13.95	15.35	2.649
K131514	**Insulation board; 6.4 mm Sundeala K**								
K131514A	over 300 mm wide	m^2	0.39	6.69	–	10.17	16.86	18.55	3.276
K131514B	n.e. 300 mm wide	m	0.16	2.70	–	3.05	5.75	6.33	0.983
K131514C	areas n.e. 1.0 m^2	Nr	0.30	5.03	–	4.86	9.89	10.88	1.567
K131515	**Insulation board; 9.5 mm Sundeala K**								
K131515A	over 300 mm wide	m^2	0.43	7.27	–	14.80	22.07	24.28	4.798
K131515B	n.e. 300 mm wide	m	0.17	2.94	–	4.44	7.38	8.12	1.439
K131515C	areas n.e. 1.0 m^2	Nr	0.32	5.45	–	7.07	12.52	13.77	2.293
K131516	**Insulation board; 12.5 mm Pilkington ivory faced**								
K131516A	over 300 mm wide	m^2	0.51	8.59	–	4.22	12.81	14.09	6.415
K131516B	n.e. 300 mm wide	m	0.21	3.48	–	1.27	4.75	5.23	1.925
K131516C	areas n.e. 1.0 m^2	Nr	0.38	6.45	–	2.02	8.47	9.32	3.068
K131517	**Insulation board; 12.5 mm Unitex ivory faced**								
K131517A	over 300 mm wide	m^2	0.51	8.59	–	5.19	13.78	15.16	6.415
K131517B	n.e. 300 mm wide	m	0.21	3.48	–	1.56	5.04	5.54	1.925
K131517C	areas n.e. 1.0 m^2	Nr	0.38	6.45	–	2.48	8.93	9.82	3.068
K131521	**Chipboard; 12 mm**								
K131521A	over 300 mm wide	m^2	0.34	5.74	–	2.52	8.26	9.09	4.298
K131521B	n.e. 300 mm wide	m	0.14	2.33	–	0.76	3.09	3.40	1.289
K131521C	areas n.e. 1.0 m^2	Nr	0.25	4.31	–	1.20	5.51	6.06	2.053
K131522	**Chipboard; 15 mm**								
K131522A	over 300 mm wide	m^2	0.39	6.69	–	3.71	10.40	11.44	5.359
K131522B	n.e. 300 mm wide	m	0.16	2.70	–	1.11	3.81	4.19	1.608
K131522C	areas n.e. 1.0 m^2	Nr	0.30	5.03	–	1.77	6.80	7.48	2.559
K131523	**Chipboard; 18 mm**								
K131523A	over 300 mm wide	m^2	0.45	7.64	–	5.93	13.57	14.93	6.418
K131523B	n.e. 300 mm wide	m	0.18	3.09	–	1.78	4.87	5.36	1.925
K131523C	areas n.e. 1.0 m^2	Nr	0.34	5.74	–	2.83	8.57	9.43	3.064
K131527	**Chipboard faced one side with 1.5 mm Class 1 laminated plastic covering and balancing veneer other side; 15 mm**								
K131527A	over 300 mm wide	m^2	0.56	9.56	–	4.68	14.24	15.66	5.579
K131527B	n.e. 300 mm wide	m	0.23	3.87	–	1.41	5.28	5.81	1.674

Linings, Sheathing & Dry Partitioning

Major Works 2011		Unit	Labour Hours	Labour Net	Plant Net	Materials Net	Unit Net	Unit with 10%	CO₂
				£	£	£	£	£	Kg
K13	**K13: RIGID SHEET FINE LININGS AND PANELLING**								
K1315	**Ceilings**								
K131527	**Chipboard faced one side with 1.5 mm Class 1 laminated plastic covering and balancing veneer other side; 15 mm**								
K131527C	areas n.e. 1.0 m²	Nr	0.42	7.17	-	2.24	9.41	10.35	2.669
K131528	**Chipboard faced one side with 1.5 mm Class 1 laminated plastic covering and balancing veneer other side; 18 mm**								
K131528A	over 300 mm wide	m²	0.68	11.46	-	5.15	16.61	18.27	6.639
K131528B	n.e. 300 mm wide	m	0.27	4.64	-	1.54	6.18	6.80	1.992
K131528C	areas n.e. 1.0 m²	Nr	0.51	8.59	-	2.46	11.05	12.16	3.175
K131531	**Finnish birch faced 5-ply blockboard; grade BB; 18 mm**								
K131531A	over 300 mm wide	m²	0.84	14.33	-	25.78	40.11	44.12	6.198
K131531B	n.e. 300 mm wide	m	0.34	5.81	-	7.73	13.54	14.89	1.859
K131531C	areas n.e. 1.0 m²	Nr	0.63	10.75	-	12.31	23.06	25.37	2.964
K131532	**Finnish birch faced 5-ply blockboard; grade BB; 25 mm**								
K131532A	over 300 mm wide	m²	0.90	15.28	-	33.85	49.13	54.04	8.171
K131532B	n.e. 300 mm wide	m	0.37	6.20	-	10.15	16.35	17.99	2.451
K131532C	areas n.e. 1.0 m²	Nr	0.68	11.46	-	16.15	27.61	30.37	3.906
K131536	**Far Eastern hardwood faced MR boarding ply; grade B/BB; 4 mm**								
K131536A	over 300 mm wide	m²	0.43	7.27	-	7.91	15.18	16.70	1.953
K131536B	n.e. 300 mm wide	m	0.17	2.94	-	2.37	5.31	5.84	0.586
K131536C	areas n.e. 1.0 m²	Nr	0.32	5.45	-	3.78	9.23	10.15	0.933
K131537	**Far Eastern hardwood faced MR boarding ply; grade B/BB; 6 mm**								
K131537A	over 300 mm wide	m²	0.47	8.03	-	8.66	16.69	18.36	3.156
K131537B	n.e. 300 mm wide	m	0.19	3.24	-	2.60	5.84	6.42	0.947
K131537C	areas n.e. 1.0 m²	Nr	0.36	6.03	-	4.13	10.16	11.18	1.507
K131538	**Far Eastern hardwood faced MR boarding ply; grade B/BB; 9 mm**								
K131538A	over 300 mm wide	m²	0.52	8.80	-	6.61	15.41	16.95	4.359
K131538B	n.e. 300 mm wide	m	0.21	3.57	-	1.98	5.55	6.11	1.308
K131538C	areas n.e. 1.0 m²	Nr	0.39	6.61	-	3.16	9.77	10.75	2.081
K131539	**Far Eastern hardwood faced MR boarding ply; grade B/BB; 12 mm**								
K131539A	over 300 mm wide	m²	0.56	9.56	-	8.42	17.98	19.78	5.802
K131539B	n.e. 300 mm wide	m	0.23	3.87	-	2.52	6.39	7.03	1.741
K131539C	areas n.e. 1.0 m²	Nr	0.42	7.17	-	4.02	11.19	12.31	2.770
K131540	**Far Eastern hardwood faced MR boarding ply; grade B/BB; 15 mm**								
K131540A	over 300 mm wide	m²	0.63	10.70	-	10.71	21.41	23.55	7.245
K131540B	n.e. 300 mm wide	m	0.26	4.33	-	3.21	7.54	8.29	2.174
K131540C	areas n.e. 1.0 m²	Nr	0.47	8.03	-	5.11	13.14	14.45	3.459
K131541	**Far Eastern hardwood faced MR boarding ply; grade B/BB; 18 mm**								
K131541A	over 300 mm wide	m²	0.68	11.46	-	12.24	23.70	26.07	8.689
K131541B	n.e. 300 mm wide	m	0.27	4.64	-	3.67	8.31	9.14	2.607
K131541C	areas n.e. 1.0 m²	Nr	0.51	8.59	-	5.84	14.43	15.87	4.147
K131542	**Far Eastern hardwood faced MR boarding ply; grade B/BB; 22 mm**								
K131542A	over 300 mm wide	m²	0.72	12.23	-	14.65	26.88	29.57	10.614

Major Works 2011		Unit	Labour Hours	Labour Net	Plant Net	Materials Net	Unit Net	Unit with 10%	CO$_2$
				£	£	£	£	£	Kg
K13	**K13: RIGID SHEET FINE LININGS AND PANELLING**								
K1315	**Ceilings**								
K131542	**Far Eastern hardwood faced MR boarding ply; grade B/BB; 22 mm**								
K131542B	n.e. 300 mm wide	m	0.29	4.96	-	4.40	9.36	10.30	3.184
K131542C	areas n.e. 1.0 m^2	Nr	0.54	9.17	-	6.99	16.16	17.78	5.066
K131543	**Far Eastern hardwood faced MR boarding ply; grade B/BB; 25 mm**								
K131543A	over 300 mm wide	m^2	0.78	13.18	-	17.02	30.20	33.22	12.057
K131543B	n.e. 300 mm wide	m	0.31	5.33	-	5.10	10.43	11.47	3.617
K131543C	areas n.e. 1.0 m^2	Nr	0.58	9.88	-	8.12	18.00	19.80	5.755
K131550	**Finnish birch faced WBP boarding ply; grade BB; 4 mm**								
K131550A	over 300 mm wide	m^2	0.39	6.69	-	7.27	13.96	15.36	1.953
K131550B	n.e. 300 mm wide	m	0.16	2.70	-	2.18	4.88	5.37	0.586
K131550C	areas n.e. 1.0 m^2	Nr	0.30	5.03	-	3.47	8.50	9.35	0.933
K131551	**Finnish birch faced WBP boarding ply; grade BB; 6 mm**								
K131551A	over 300 mm wide	m^2	0.43	7.27	-	10.72	17.99	19.79	2.915
K131551B	n.e. 300 mm wide	m	0.17	2.94	-	3.22	6.16	6.78	0.874
K131551C	areas n.e. 1.0 m^2	Nr	0.32	5.45	-	5.12	10.57	11.63	1.392
K131552	**Finnish birch faced WBP boarding ply; grade BB; 9 mm**								
K131552A	over 300 mm wide	m^2	0.45	7.64	-	13.19	20.83	22.91	4.359
K131552B	n.e. 300 mm wide	m	0.18	3.09	-	3.96	7.05	7.76	1.308
K131552C	areas n.e. 1.0 m^2	Nr	0.34	5.74	-	6.30	12.04	13.24	2.081
K131553	**Finnish birch faced WBP boarding ply; grade BB; 12 mm**								
K131553A	over 300 mm wide	m^2	0.51	8.59	-	15.50	24.09	26.50	5.802
K131553B	n.e. 300 mm wide	m	0.21	3.48	-	4.65	8.13	8.94	1.741
K131553C	areas n.e. 1.0 m^2	Nr	0.38	6.45	-	7.40	13.85	15.24	2.770
K131554	**Finnish birch faced WBP boarding ply; grade BB; 15 mm**								
K131554A	over 300 mm wide	m^2	0.54	9.17	-	20.85	30.02	33.02	7.245
K131554B	n.e. 300 mm wide	m	0.22	3.72	-	6.25	9.97	10.97	2.174
K131554C	areas n.e. 1.0 m^2	Nr	0.41	6.88	-	9.95	16.83	18.51	3.459
K131555	**Finnish birch faced WBP boarding ply; grade BB; 18 mm**								
K131555A	over 300 mm wide	m^2	0.59	9.93	-	24.87	34.80	38.28	8.689
K131555B	n.e. 300 mm wide	m	0.24	4.02	-	7.46	11.48	12.63	2.607
K131555C	areas n.e. 1.0 m^2	Nr	0.44	7.45	-	11.87	19.32	21.25	4.147
K131556	**Finnish birch faced WBP boarding ply; grade BB; 22 mm**								
K131556A	over 300 mm wide	m^2	0.63	10.70	-	29.43	40.13	44.14	10.614
K131556B	n.e. 300 mm wide	m	0.26	4.33	-	8.83	13.16	14.48	3.184
K131556C	areas n.e. 1.0 m^2	Nr	0.47	8.03	-	14.05	22.08	24.29	5.066
K131557	**Finnish birch faced WBP boarding ply; grade BB; 25 mm**								
K131557A	over 300 mm wide	m^2	0.68	11.46	-	34.02	45.48	50.03	12.057
K131557B	n.e. 300 mm wide	m	0.27	4.64	-	10.21	14.85	16.34	3.617
K131557C	areas n.e. 1.0 m^2	Nr	0.51	8.59	-	16.24	24.83	27.31	5.755
K131561	**Non-asbestos, flameproof Class O boards; BS 476; 6 mm**								
K131561A	over 300 mm wide	m^2	0.32	5.35	-	11.50	16.85	18.54	2.051
K131561B	n.e. 300 mm wide	m	0.13	2.17	-	3.45	5.62	6.18	0.615
K131561C	areas n.e. 1.0 m^2	Nr	0.24	4.01	-	5.49	9.50	10.45	0.982

Major Works 2011		Unit	Labour Hours	Labour Net	Plant Net	Materials Net	Unit Net	Unit with 10%	CO$_2$
				£	£	£	£	£	Kg
K13	**K13: RIGID SHEET FINE LININGS AND PANELLING**								
K1315	**Ceilings**								
K131562	**Non-asbestos, flameproof Class O boards; BS 476; 9 mm**								
K131562A	over 300 mm wide	m^2	0.34	5.74	-	30.25	35.99	39.59	3.010
K131562B	n.e. 300 mm wide	m	0.14	2.33	-	9.07	11.40	12.54	0.903
K131562C	areas n.e. 1.0 m^2	Nr	0.25	4.31	-	14.44	18.75	20.63	1.439
K131563	**Non-asbestos, flameproof Class O boards; BS 476; 12 mm**								
K131563A	over 300 mm wide	m^2	0.39	6.69	-	45.59	52.28	57.51	4.012
K131563B	n.e. 300 mm wide	m	0.16	2.70	-	13.68	16.38	18.02	1.204
K131563C	areas n.e. 1.0 m^2	Nr	0.30	5.03	-	21.76	26.79	29.47	1.919
K131564	**Non-asbestos, flameproof Class O boards; BS 476; 15 mm**								
K131564A	over 300 mm wide	m^2	0.45	7.64	-	57.11	64.75	71.23	4.971
K131564B	n.e. 300 mm wide	m	0.18	3.09	-	17.13	20.22	22.24	1.491
K131564C	areas n.e. 1.0 m^2	Nr	0.34	5.74	-	27.26	33.00	36.30	2.377
K131571	**MDF board; 12 mm**								
K131571A	over 300 mm wide	m^2	0.45	7.64	-	4.90	12.54	13.79	5.898
K131571B	n.e. 300 mm wide	m	0.18	3.09	-	1.47	4.56	5.02	1.769
K131571C	areas n.e. 1.0 m^2	Nr	0.34	5.74	-	2.34	8.08	8.89	2.816
K131572	**MDF board; 15 mm**								
K131572A	over 300 mm wide	m^2	0.51	8.59	-	4.93	13.52	14.87	7.358
K131572B	n.e. 300 mm wide	m	0.21	3.48	-	1.48	4.96	5.46	2.208
K131572C	areas n.e. 1.0 m^2	Nr	0.38	6.45	-	2.35	8.80	9.68	3.513
K131573	**MDF board; 18 mm**								
K131573A	over 300 mm wide	m^2	0.56	9.56	-	6.81	16.37	18.01	8.818
K131573B	n.e. 300 mm wide	m	0.23	3.87	-	2.04	5.91	6.50	2.645
K131573C	areas n.e. 1.0 m^2	Nr	0.42	7.17	-	3.25	10.42	11.46	4.210
K1319	**Isolated beams**								
K131901	**Hardboard; 3.2 mm standard**								
K131901A	not exceeding 600 mm girth	m^2	0.42	7.13	-	1.74	8.87	9.76	2.693
K131901B	600 - 1200 mm girth	m^2	0.34	5.74	-	1.70	7.44	8.18	2.632
K131901C	1200 - 1800 mm girth	m^2	0.28	4.75	-	1.66	6.41	7.05	2.571
K131902	**Hardboard; 6.0 mm standard**								
K131902A	not exceeding 600 mm girth	m^2	0.51	8.59	-	4.83	13.42	14.76	2.759
K131902B	600 - 1200 mm girth	m^2	0.41	6.88	-	4.72	11.60	12.76	2.696
K131902C	1200 - 1800 mm girth	m^2	0.34	5.74	-	4.61	10.35	11.39	2.634
K131903	**Hardboard; 3.2 mm perforated**								
K131903A	not exceeding 600 mm girth	m^2	0.47	8.03	-	1.80	9.83	10.81	1.485
K131903B	600 - 1200 mm girth	m^2	0.38	6.45	-	1.76	8.21	9.03	1.452
K131903C	1200 - 1800 mm girth	m^2	0.32	5.35	-	1.72	7.07	7.78	1.419
K131904	**Hardboard; 6.0 mm perforated**								
K131904A	not exceeding 600 mm girth	m^2	0.54	9.17	-	3.70	12.87	14.16	2.759
K131904B	600 - 1200 mm girth	m^2	0.43	7.34	-	3.62	10.96	12.06	2.696
K131904C	1200 - 1800 mm girth	m^2	0.36	6.11	-	3.53	9.64	10.60	2.634
K131905	**Hardboard; 6.0 mm flameproof Class 1**								
K131905A	not exceeding 600 mm girth	m^2	0.51	8.59	-	13.27	21.86	24.05	2.759
K131905B	600 - 1200 mm girth	m^2	0.41	6.88	-	12.97	19.85	21.84	2.696
K131905C	1200 - 1800 mm girth	m^2	0.34	5.74	-	12.67	18.41	20.25	2.634
K131906	**Hardboard; 3.2 mm stove enamelled one side**								
K131906A	not exceeding 600 mm girth	m^2	0.47	8.03	-	2.59	10.62	11.68	2.693
K131906B	600 - 1200 mm girth	m^2	0.38	6.45	-	2.53	8.98	9.88	2.632
K131906C	1200 - 1800 mm girth	m^2	0.32	5.35	-	2.47	7.82	8.60	2.571
K131911	**Insulation board; 6.4 mm Sundeala A**								
K131911A	not exceeding 600 mm girth	m^2	0.59	10.02	-	11.47	21.49	23.64	3.276

Major Works 2011		Unit	Labour Hours	Labour Net	Plant Net	Materials Net	Unit Net	Unit with 10%	CO$_2$
				£	£	£	£	£	Kg
K13	**K13: RIGID SHEET FINE LININGS AND PANELLING**								
K1319	**Isolated beams**								
K131911	**Insulation board; 6.4 mm Sundeala A**								
K131911B	600 - 1200 mm girth	m^2	0.47	8.03	-	11.21	19.24	21.16	3.204
K131911C	1200 - 1800 mm girth	m^2	0.39	6.69	-	10.96	17.65	19.42	3.133
K131912	**Insulation board; 9.5 mm Sundeala A**								
K131912A	not exceeding 600 mm girth	m^2	0.64	10.87	-	14.80	25.67	28.24	4.798
K131912B	600 - 1200 mm girth	m^2	0.51	8.71	-	14.47	23.18	25.50	4.692
K131912C	1200 - 1800 mm girth	m^2	0.43	7.30	-	14.14	21.44	23.58	4.586
K131913	**Insulation board; 12.5 mm Sundeala A**								
K131913A	not exceeding 600 mm girth	m^2	0.68	11.46	-	17.19	28.65	31.52	5.537
K131913B	600 - 1200 mm girth	m^2	0.54	9.17	-	16.80	25.97	28.57	5.417
K131913C	1200 - 1800 mm girth	m^2	0.45	7.64	-	16.41	24.05	26.46	5.297
K131914	**Insulation board; 6.4 mm Sundeala K**								
K131914A	not exceeding 600 mm girth	m^2	0.59	10.02	-	10.17	20.19	22.21	3.276
K131914B	600 - 1200 mm girth	m^2	0.47	8.03	-	9.94	17.97	19.77	3.204
K131914C	1200 - 1800 mm girth	m^2	0.39	6.69	-	9.72	16.41	18.05	3.133
K131915	**Insulation board; 9.5 mm Sundeala K**								
K131915A	not exceeding 600 mm girth	m^2	0.64	10.87	-	14.80	25.67	28.24	4.798
K131915B	600 - 1200 mm girth	m^2	0.51	8.71	-	14.47	23.18	25.50	4.692
K131915C	1200 - 1800 mm girth	m^2	0.43	7.30	-	14.14	21.44	23.58	4.586
K131916	**Insulation board; 12.5 mm Pilkington ivory faced**								
K131916A	not exceeding 600 mm girth	m^2	0.76	12.90	-	4.22	17.12	18.83	6.415
K131916B	600 - 1200 mm girth	m^2	0.61	10.32	-	4.13	14.45	15.90	6.276
K131916C	1200 - 1800 mm girth	m^2	0.51	8.59	-	4.03	12.62	13.88	6.136
K131917	**Insulation board; 12.5 mm Unitex ivory faced**								
K131917A	not exceeding 600 mm girth	m^2	0.76	12.90	-	5.19	18.09	19.90	6.415
K131917B	600 - 1200 mm girth	m^2	0.61	10.32	-	5.07	15.39	16.93	6.276
K131917C	1200 - 1800 mm girth	m^2	0.51	8.59	-	4.96	13.55	14.91	6.136
K131921	**Chipboard; 12 mm**								
K131921A	not exceeding 600 mm girth	m^2	0.51	8.59	-	2.52	11.11	12.22	4.298
K131921B	600 - 1200 mm girth	m^2	0.41	6.88	-	2.47	9.35	10.29	4.202
K131921C	1200 - 1800 mm girth	m^2	0.34	5.74	-	2.41	8.15	8.97	4.105
K131922	**Chipboard; 15 mm**								
K131922A	not exceeding 600 mm girth	m^2	0.59	10.02	-	3.71	13.73	15.10	5.359
K131922B	600 - 1200 mm girth	m^2	0.47	8.03	-	3.63	11.66	12.83	5.238
K131922C	1200 - 1800 mm girth	m^2	0.39	6.69	-	3.54	10.23	11.25	5.118
K131923	**Chipboard; 18 mm**								
K131923A	not exceeding 600 mm girth	m^2	0.68	11.46	-	5.93	17.39	19.13	6.418
K131923B	600 - 1200 mm girth	m^2	0.54	9.17	-	5.80	14.97	16.47	6.273
K131923C	1200 - 1800 mm girth	m^2	0.45	7.64	-	5.66	13.30	14.63	6.129
K131927	**Chipboard faced one side with 1.5 mm Class 1 laminated plastic covering and balancing veneer other side; 15 mm**								
K131927A	not exceeding 600 mm girth	m^2	0.84	14.33	-	4.68	19.01	20.91	5.579
K131927B	600 - 1200 mm girth	m^2	0.68	11.46	-	4.58	16.04	17.64	5.459
K131927C	1200 - 1800 mm girth	m^2	0.56	9.56	-	4.47	14.03	15.43	5.338
K131928	**Chipboard faced one side with 1.5 mm Class 1 laminated plastic covering and balancing veneer other side; 18 mm**								
K131928A	not exceeding 600 mm girth	m^2	1.01	17.20	-	5.15	22.35	24.59	6.639
K131928B	600 - 1200 mm girth	m^2	0.81	13.75	-	5.03	18.78	20.66	6.494

Major Works 2011		Unit	Labour Hours	Labour Net	Plant Net	Materials Net	Unit Net	Unit with 10%	CO₂
				£	£	£	£	£	Kg
K13	**K13: RIGID SHEET FINE LININGS AND PANELLING**								
K1319	**Isolated beams**								
K131928	**Chipboard faced one side with 1.5 mm Class 1 laminated plastic covering and balancing veneer other side; 18 mm**								
K131928C	1200 - 1800 mm girth	m²	0.68	11.46	-	4.92	16.38	18.02	6.350
K131931	**Finnish birch faced 5-ply blockboard; grade BB; 18 mm**								
K131931A	not exceeding 600 mm girth	m²	1.27	21.50	-	25.78	47.28	52.01	6.198
K131931B	600 - 1200 mm girth	m²	1.01	17.20	-	25.20	42.40	46.64	6.063
K131931C	1200 - 1800 mm girth	m²	0.84	14.33	-	24.61	38.94	42.83	5.929
K131932	**Finnish birch faced 5-ply blockboard; grade BB; 25 mm**								
K131932A	not exceeding 600 mm girth	m²	1.35	22.92	-	33.85	56.77	62.45	8.171
K131932B	600 - 1200 mm girth	m²	1.08	18.34	-	33.08	51.42	56.56	7.992
K131932C	1200 - 1800 mm girth	m²	0.90	15.28	-	32.31	47.59	52.35	7.812
K131936	**Far Eastern hardwood faced MR boarding ply; grade B/BB; 4 mm**								
K131936A	not exceeding 600 mm girth	m²	0.64	10.87	-	7.91	18.78	20.66	1.953
K131936B	600 - 1200 mm girth	m²	0.51	8.71	-	7.73	16.44	18.08	1.910
K131936C	1200 - 1800 mm girth	m²	0.43	7.27	-	7.55	14.82	16.30	1.866
K131937	**Far Eastern hardwood faced MR boarding ply; grade B/BB; 6 mm**								
K131937A	not exceeding 600 mm girth	m²	0.71	12.04	-	8.66	20.70	22.77	3.156
K131937B	600 - 1200 mm girth	m²	0.56	9.56	-	8.46	18.02	19.82	3.085
K131937C	1200 - 1800 mm girth	m²	0.47	8.03	-	8.27	16.30	17.93	3.013
K131938	**Far Eastern hardwood faced MR boarding ply; grade B/BB; 9 mm**								
K131938A	not exceeding 600 mm girth	m²	0.78	13.18	-	6.61	19.79	21.77	4.359
K131938B	600 - 1200 mm girth	m²	0.62	10.51	-	6.46	16.97	18.67	4.261
K131938C	1200 - 1800 mm girth	m²	0.52	8.80	-	6.31	15.11	16.62	4.162
K131939	**Far Eastern hardwood faced MR boarding ply; grade B/BB; 12 mm**								
K131939A	not exceeding 600 mm girth	m²	0.84	14.33	-	8.42	22.75	25.03	5.802
K131939B	600 - 1200 mm girth	m²	0.68	11.46	-	8.23	19.69	21.66	5.671
K131939C	1200 - 1800 mm girth	m²	0.56	9.56	-	8.03	17.59	19.35	5.540
K131940	**Far Eastern hardwood faced MR boarding ply; grade B/BB; 15 mm**								
K131940A	not exceeding 600 mm girth	m²	0.95	16.05	-	10.71	26.76	29.44	7.245
K131940B	600 - 1200 mm girth	m²	0.75	12.80	-	10.47	23.27	25.60	7.081
K131940C	1200 - 1800 mm girth	m²	0.63	10.70	-	10.23	20.93	23.02	6.917
K131941	**Far Eastern hardwood faced MR boarding ply; grade B/BB; 18 mm**								
K131941A	not exceeding 600 mm girth	m²	1.01	17.20	-	12.24	29.44	32.38	8.689
K131941B	600 - 1200 mm girth	m²	0.81	13.75	-	11.96	25.71	28.28	8.492
K131941C	1200 - 1800 mm girth	m²	0.68	11.46	-	11.69	23.15	25.47	8.295
K131942	**Far Eastern hardwood faced MR boarding ply; grade B/BB; 22 mm**								
K131942A	not exceeding 600 mm girth	m²	1.08	18.34	-	14.65	32.99	36.29	10.614
K131942B	600 - 1200 mm girth	m²	0.87	14.70	-	14.32	29.02	31.92	10.373
K131942C	1200 - 1800 mm girth	m²	0.72	12.23	-	13.99	26.22	28.84	10.132
K131943	**Far Eastern hardwood faced MR boarding ply; grade B/BB; 25 mm**								
K131943A	not exceeding 600 mm girth	m²	1.16	19.76	-	17.02	36.78	40.46	12.057
K131943B	600 - 1200 mm girth	m²	0.93	15.86	-	16.63	32.49	35.74	11.783

Major Works 2011		Unit	Labour Hours	Labour Net	Plant Net	Materials Net	Unit Net	Unit with 10%	CO₂
				£	£	£	£	£	Kg
K13	**K13: RIGID SHEET FINE LININGS AND PANELLING**								
K1319	**Isolated beams**								
K131943	**Far Eastern hardwood faced MR boarding ply; grade B/BB; 25 mm**								
K131943C	1200 - 1800 mm girth	m₂	0.78	13.18	-	16.24	29.42	32.36	11.510
K131950	**Finnish birch faced WBP boarding ply; grade BB; 4 mm**								
K131950A	not exceeding 600 mm girth	m²	0.59	10.02	-	7.27	17.29	19.02	1.953
K131950B	600 - 1200 mm girth	m²	0.47	8.03	-	7.11	15.14	16.65	1.910
K131950C	1200 - 1800 mm girth	m²	0.39	6.69	-	6.94	13.63	14.99	1.866
K131951	**Finnish birch faced WBP boarding ply; grade BB; 6 mm**								
K131951A	not exceeding 600 mm girth	m²	0.64	10.87	-	10.72	21.59	23.75	2.915
K131951B	600 - 1200 mm girth	m²	0.51	8.71	-	10.47	19.18	21.10	2.849
K131951C	1200 - 1800 mm girth	m²	0.43	7.27	-	10.23	17.50	19.25	2.784
K131952	**Finnish birch faced WBP boarding ply; grade BB; 9 mm**								
K131952A	not exceeding 600 mm girth	m²	0.68	11.46	-	13.19	24.65	27.12	4.359
K131952B	600 - 1200 mm girth	m²	0.54	9.17	-	12.89	22.06	24.27	4.261
K131952C	1200 - 1800 mm girth	m²	0.45	7.64	-	12.59	20.23	22.25	4.162
K131953	**Finnish birch faced WBP boarding ply; grade BB; 12 mm**								
K131953A	not exceeding 600 mm girth	m²	0.76	12.90	-	15.50	28.40	31.24	5.802
K131953B	600 - 1200 mm girth	m²	0.61	10.32	-	15.15	25.47	28.02	5.671
K131953C	1200 - 1800 mm girth	m²	1.19	20.21	-	14.80	35.01	38.51	5.540
K131954	**Finnish birch faced WBP boarding ply; grade BB; 15 mm**								
K131954A	not exceeding 600 mm girth	m²	0.81	13.75	-	20.85	34.60	38.06	7.245
K131954B	600 - 1200 mm girth	m²	0.65	11.09	-	20.37	31.46	34.61	7.081
K131954C	1200 - 1800 mm girth	m²	0.54	9.17	-	19.90	29.07	31.98	6.917
K131955	**Finnish birch faced WBP boarding ply; grade BB; 18 mm**								
K131955A	not exceeding 600 mm girth	m²	0.88	14.91	-	24.87	39.78	43.76	8.689
K131955B	600 - 1200 mm girth	m²	0.70	11.94	-	24.30	36.24	39.86	8.492
K131955C	1200 - 1800 mm girth	m²	0.59	9.93	-	23.74	33.67	37.04	8.295
K131956	**Finnish birch faced WBP boarding ply; grade BB; 22 mm**								
K131956A	not exceeding 600 mm girth	m²	0.95	16.05	-	29.43	45.48	50.03	10.614
K131956B	600 - 1200 mm girth	m²	0.75	12.80	-	28.77	41.57	45.73	10.373
K131956C	1200 - 1800 mm girth	m²	0.63	10.70	-	28.10	38.80	42.68	10.132
K131957	**Finnish birch faced WBP boarding ply; grade BB; 25 mm**								
K131957A	not exceeding 600 mm girth	m²	1.01	17.20	-	34.02	51.22	56.34	12.057
K131957B	600 - 1200 mm girth	m²	0.81	13.75	-	33.25	47.00	51.70	11.783
K131957C	1200 - 1800 mm girth	m²	0.68	11.46	-	32.48	43.94	48.33	11.510
K131961	**Non-asbestos, flameproof Class O boards; BS 476; 6 mm**								
K131961A	not exceeding 600 mm girth	m²	0.47	8.03	-	11.50	19.53	21.48	2.051
K131961B	600 - 1200 mm girth	m²	0.38	6.42	-	11.24	17.66	19.43	2.007
K131961C	1200 - 1800 mm girth	m²	0.32	5.35	-	10.99	16.34	17.97	1.963
K131962	**Non-asbestos, flameproof Class O boards; BS 476; 9 mm**								
K131962A	not exceeding 600 mm girth	m²	0.51	8.59	-	30.25	38.84	42.72	3.010
K131962B	600 - 1200 mm girth	m²	0.41	6.88	-	29.56	36.44	40.08	2.944
K131962C	1200 - 1800 mm girth	m²	0.34	5.74	-	28.88	34.62	38.08	2.879

Linings, Sheathing & Dry Partitioning

		Unit	Labour Hours	Labour Net	Plant Net	Materials Net	Unit Net	Unit with 10%	CO₂
				£	£	£	£	£	Kg
K13	**K13: RIGID SHEET FINE LININGS AND PANELLING**								
K1319	**Isolated beams**								
K131963	**Non-asbestos, flameproof Class O boards; BS 476; 12 mm**								
K131963A	not exceeding 600 mm girth	m²	0.59	10.02	-	45.59	55.61	61.17	4.012
K131963B	600 - 1200 mm girth	m²	0.47	8.03	-	44.56	52.59	57.85	3.925
K131963C	1200 - 1800 mm girth	m²	0.39	6.69	-	43.52	50.21	55.23	3.838
K131964	**Non-asbestos, flameproof Class O boards; BS 476; 15 mm**								
K131964A	not exceeding 600 mm girth	m²	0.68	11.46	-	57.11	68.57	75.43	4.971
K131964B	600 - 1200 mm girth	m²	0.54	9.17	-	55.82	64.99	71.49	4.862
K131964C	1200 - 1800 mm girth	m²	0.45	7.64	-	54.53	62.17	68.39	4.754
K131971	**MDF board; 12 mm**								
K131971A	not exceeding 600 mm girth	m²	0.68	11.46	-	4.90	16.36	18.00	5.898
K131971B	600 - 1200 mm girth	m²	0.54	9.17	-	4.79	13.96	15.36	5.765
K131971C	1200 - 1800 mm girth	m²	0.45	7.64	-	4.68	12.32	13.55	5.632
K131972	**MDF board; 15 mm**								
K131972A	not exceeding 600 mm girth	m²	0.76	12.90	-	4.93	17.83	19.61	7.358
K131972B	600 - 1200 mm girth	m²	0.61	10.32	-	4.82	15.14	16.65	7.192
K131972C	1200 - 1800 mm girth	m²	0.51	8.59	-	4.71	13.30	14.63	7.027
K131973	**MDF board; 18 mm**								
K131973A	not exceeding 600 mm girth	m²	0.84	14.33	-	6.81	21.14	23.25	8.818
K131973B	600 - 1200 mm girth	m²	0.68	11.46	-	6.66	18.12	19.93	8.619
K131973C	1200 - 1800 mm girth	m²	0.56	9.56	-	6.50	16.06	17.67	8.420
K1321	**Isolated columns**								
K132101	**Hardboard; 3.2 mm standard**								
K132101A	not exceeding 600 mm girth	m²	0.38	6.37	-	1.74	8.11	8.92	2.693
K132101B	600 - 1200 mm girth	m²	0.30	5.09	-	1.70	6.79	7.47	2.632
K132101C	1200 - 1800 mm girth	m²	0.25	4.25	-	1.66	5.91	6.50	2.571
K132102	**Hardboard; 6.0 mm standard**								
K132102A	not exceeding 600 mm girth	m²	0.45	7.64	-	4.83	12.47	13.72	2.759
K132102B	600 - 1200 mm girth	m²	0.36	6.11	-	4.72	10.83	11.91	2.696
K132102C	1200 - 1800 mm girth	m²	0.30	5.09	-	4.61	9.70	10.67	2.634
K132103	**Hardboard; 3.2 mm perforated**								
K132103A	not exceeding 600 mm girth	m²	0.42	7.13	-	1.80	8.93	9.82	1.485
K132103B	600 - 1200 mm girth	m²	0.34	5.71	-	1.76	7.47	8.22	1.452
K132103C	1200 - 1800 mm girth	m²	0.28	4.75	-	1.72	6.47	7.12	1.419
K132104	**Hardboard; 6.0 mm perforated**								
K132104A	not exceeding 600 mm girth	m²	0.48	8.15	-	3.70	11.85	13.04	2.759
K132104B	600 - 1200 mm girth	m²	0.38	6.52	-	3.62	10.14	11.15	2.696
K132104C	1200 - 1800 mm girth	m²	0.32	5.43	-	3.53	8.96	9.86	2.634
K132105	**Hardboard; 6.0 mm flameproof Class 1**								
K132105A	not exceeding 600 mm girth	m²	0.45	7.64	-	13.27	20.91	23.00	2.759
K132105B	600 - 1200 mm girth	m²	0.36	6.11	-	12.97	19.08	20.99	2.696
K132105C	1200 - 1800 mm girth	m²	0.30	5.09	-	12.67	17.76	19.54	2.634
K132106	**Hardboard; 3.2 mm stove enamelled one side**								
K132106A	not exceeding 600 mm girth	m²	0.42	7.13	-	2.59	9.72	10.69	2.693
K132106B	600 - 1200 mm girth	m²	0.34	5.71	-	2.53	8.24	9.06	2.632
K132106C	1200 - 1800 mm girth	m²	0.28	4.75	-	2.47	7.22	7.94	2.571
K132111	**Insulation board; 6.4 mm Sundeala A**								
K132111A	not exceeding 600 mm girth	m²	0.53	8.91	-	11.47	20.38	22.42	3.276
K132111B	600 - 1200 mm girth	m²	0.42	7.13	-	11.21	18.34	20.17	3.204
K132111C	1200 - 1800 mm girth	m²	0.35	5.94	-	10.96	16.90	18.59	3.133
K132112	**Insulation board; 9.5 mm Sundeala A**								
K132112A	not exceeding 600 mm girth	m²	0.57	9.68	-	14.80	24.48	26.93	4.798

Major Works 2011		Unit	Labour Hours	Labour Net	Plant Net	Materials Net	Unit Net	Unit with 10%	CO₂
				£	£	£	£	£	Kg
K13	**K13: RIGID SHEET FINE LININGS AND PANELLING**								
K1321	**Isolated columns**								
K132112	**Insulation board; 9.5 mm Sundeala A**								
K132112B	600 - 1200 mm girth	m²	0.46	7.74	-	14.47	22.21	24.43	4.692
K132112C	1200 - 1800 mm girth	m²	0.38	6.45	-	14.14	20.59	22.65	4.586
K132113	**Insulation board; 12.5 mm Sundeala A**								
K132113A	not exceeding 600 mm girth	m²	0.60	10.19	-	17.19	27.38	30.12	5.537
K132113B	600 - 1200 mm girth	m²	0.48	8.15	-	16.80	24.95	27.45	5.417
K132113C	1200 - 1800 mm girth	m²	0.40	6.79	-	16.41	23.20	25.52	5.297
K132114	**Insulation board; 6.4 mm Sundeala K**								
K132114A	not exceeding 600 mm girth	m²	0.53	8.91	-	10.17	19.08	20.99	3.276
K132114B	600 - 1200 mm girth	m²	0.42	7.13	-	9.94	17.07	18.78	3.204
K132114C	1200 - 1800 mm girth	m²	0.35	5.94	-	9.72	15.66	17.23	3.133
K132115	**Insulation board; 9.5 mm Sundeala K**								
K132115A	not exceeding 600 mm girth	m²	0.57	9.68	-	14.80	24.48	26.93	4.798
K132115B	600 - 1200 mm girth	m²	0.46	7.74	-	14.47	22.21	24.43	4.692
K132115C	1200 - 1800 mm girth	m²	0.38	6.45	-	14.14	20.59	22.65	4.586
K132116	**Insulation board; 12.5 mm Pilkington ivory faced**								
K132116A	not exceeding 600 mm girth	m²	0.68	11.46	-	4.22	15.68	17.25	6.415
K132116B	600 - 1200 mm girth	m²	0.54	9.17	-	4.13	13.30	14.63	6.276
K132116C	1200 - 1800 mm girth	m²	0.45	7.64	-	4.03	11.67	12.84	6.136
K132117	**Insulation board; 12.5 mm Unitex ivory faced**								
K132117A	not exceeding 600 mm girth	m²	0.68	11.46	-	5.19	16.65	18.32	6.415
K132117B	600 - 1200 mm girth	m²	0.54	9.17	-	5.07	14.24	15.66	6.276
K132117C	1200 - 1800 mm girth	m²	0.45	7.64	-	4.96	12.60	13.86	6.136
K132121	**Chipboard; 12 mm**								
K132121A	not exceeding 600 mm girth	m²	0.45	7.64	-	2.52	10.16	11.18	4.298
K132121B	600 - 1200 mm girth	m²	0.36	6.11	-	2.47	8.58	9.44	4.202
K132121C	1200 - 1800 mm girth	m²	0.30	5.09	-	2.41	7.50	8.25	4.105
K132122	**Chipboard; 15 mm**								
K132122A	not exceeding 600 mm girth	m²	0.53	8.91	-	3.71	12.62	13.88	5.359
K132122B	600 - 1200 mm girth	m²	0.42	7.13	-	3.63	10.76	11.84	5.238
K132122C	1200 - 1800 mm girth	m²	0.35	5.94	-	3.54	9.48	10.43	5.118
K132123	**Chipboard; 18 mm**								
K132123A	not exceeding 600 mm girth	m²	0.60	10.19	-	5.93	16.12	17.73	6.418
K132123B	600 - 1200 mm girth	m²	0.48	8.15	-	5.80	13.95	15.35	6.273
K132123C	1200 - 1800 mm girth	m²	0.40	6.79	-	5.66	12.45	13.70	6.129
K132127	**Chipboard faced one side with 1.5 mm Class 1 laminated plastic covering and balancing veneer other side; 15 mm**								
K132127A	not exceeding 600 mm girth	m²	0.75	12.73	-	4.68	17.41	19.15	5.579
K132127B	600 - 1200 mm girth	m²	0.60	10.19	-	4.58	14.77	16.25	5.459
K132127C	1200 - 1800 mm girth	m²	0.50	8.49	-	4.47	12.96	14.26	5.338
K132128	**Chipboard faced one side with 1.5 mm Class 1 laminated plastic covering and balancing veneer other side; 18 mm**								
K132128A	not exceeding 600 mm girth	m²	0.90	15.28	-	5.15	20.43	22.47	6.639
K132128B	600 - 1200 mm girth	m²	0.72	12.23	-	5.03	17.26	18.99	6.494
K132128C	1200 - 1800 mm girth	m²	0.60	10.19	-	4.92	15.11	16.62	6.350
K132131	**Finnish birch faced 5-ply blockboard; grade BB; 18 mm**								
K132131A	not exceeding 600 mm girth	m²	1.13	19.10	-	25.78	44.88	49.37	6.198
K132131B	600 - 1200 mm girth	m²	0.90	15.28	-	25.20	40.48	44.53	6.063

Major Works 2011		Unit	Labour Hours	Labour Net £	Plant Net £	Materials Net £	Unit Net £	Unit with 10% £	CO$_2$ Kg
K13	**K13: RIGID SHEET FINE LININGS AND PANELLING**								
K1321	**Isolated columns**								
K132131	**Finnish birch faced 5-ply blockboard; grade BB; 18 mm**								
K132131C	1200 - 1800 mm girth	m²	0.75	12.73	-	24.61	37.34	41.07	5.929
K132132	**Finnish birch faced 5-ply blockboard; grade BB; 25 mm**								
K132132A	not exceeding 600 mm girth	m²	1.20	20.38	-	33.85	54.23	59.65	8.171
K132132B	600 - 1200 mm girth	m²	0.96	16.30	-	33.08	49.38	54.32	7.992
K132132C	1200 - 1800 mm girth	m²	0.80	13.58	-	32.31	45.89	50.48	7.812
K132136	**Far Eastern hardwood faced MR boarding ply; grade B/BB; 4 mm**								
K132136A	not exceeding 600 mm girth	m²	0.57	9.68	-	7.91	17.59	19.35	1.953
K132136B	600 - 1200 mm girth	m²	0.46	7.74	-	7.73	15.47	17.02	1.910
K132136C	1200 - 1800 mm girth	m²	0.38	6.45	-	7.55	14.00	15.40	1.866
K132137	**Far Eastern hardwood faced MR boarding ply; grade B/BB; 6 mm**								
K132137A	not exceeding 600 mm girth	m²	0.63	10.70	-	8.66	19.36	21.30	3.156
K132137B	600 - 1200 mm girth	m²	0.50	8.49	-	8.46	16.95	18.65	3.085
K132137C	1200 - 1800 mm girth	m²	0.42	7.13	-	8.27	15.40	16.94	3.013
K132138	**Far Eastern hardwood faced MR boarding ply; grade B/BB; 9 mm**								
K132138A	not exceeding 600 mm girth	m²	0.69	11.72	-	6.61	18.33	20.16	4.359
K132138B	600 - 1200 mm girth	m²	0.55	9.34	-	6.46	15.80	17.38	4.261
K132138C	1200 - 1800 mm girth	m²	0.46	7.81	-	6.31	14.12	15.53	4.162
K132139	**Far Eastern hardwood faced MR boarding ply; grade B/BB; 12 mm**								
K132139A	not exceeding 600 mm girth	m²	0.75	12.73	-	8.42	21.15	23.27	5.802
K132139B	600 - 1200 mm girth	m²	0.60	10.19	-	8.23	18.42	20.26	5.671
K132139C	1200 - 1800 mm girth	m²	0.50	8.49	-	8.03	16.52	18.17	5.540
K132140	**Far Eastern hardwood faced MR boarding ply; grade B/BB; 15 mm**								
K132140A	not exceeding 600 mm girth	m²	0.84	14.26	-	10.71	24.97	27.47	7.245
K132140B	600 - 1200 mm girth	m²	0.67	11.38	-	10.47	21.85	24.04	7.081
K132140C	1200 - 1800 mm girth	m²	0.56	9.51	-	10.23	19.74	21.71	6.917
K132141	**Far Eastern hardwood faced MR boarding ply; grade B/BB; 18 mm**								
K132141A	not exceeding 600 mm girth	m²	0.90	15.28	-	12.24	27.52	30.27	8.689
K132141B	600 - 1200 mm girth	m²	0.72	12.23	-	11.96	24.19	26.61	8.492
K132141C	1200 - 1800 mm girth	m²	0.60	10.19	-	11.69	21.88	24.07	8.295
K132142	**Far Eastern hardwood faced MR boarding ply; grade B/BB; 22 mm**								
K132142A	not exceeding 600 mm girth	m²	0.96	16.30	-	14.65	30.95	34.05	10.614
K132142B	600 - 1200 mm girth	m²	0.77	13.07	-	14.32	27.39	30.13	10.373
K132142C	1200 - 1800 mm girth	m²	0.64	10.87	-	13.99	24.86	27.35	10.132
K132143	**Far Eastern hardwood faced MR boarding ply; grade B/BB; 25 mm**								
K132143A	not exceeding 600 mm girth	m²	1.04	17.57	-	17.02	34.59	38.05	12.057
K132143B	600 - 1200 mm girth	m²	0.83	14.09	-	16.63	30.72	33.79	11.783
K132143C	1200 - 1800 mm girth	m²	0.69	11.72	-	16.24	27.96	30.76	11.510
K132150	**Finnish birch faced WBP boarding ply; grade BB; 4 mm**								
K132150A	not exceeding 600 mm girth	m²	0.53	8.91	-	7.27	16.18	17.80	1.953
K132150B	600 - 1200 mm girth	m²	0.42	7.13	-	7.11	14.24	15.66	1.910
K132150C	1200 - 1800 mm girth	m²	0.35	5.94	-	6.94	12.88	14.17	1.866

Major Works 2011		Unit	Labour Hours	Labour Net	Plant Net	Materials Net	Unit Net	Unit with 10%	CO₂
				£	£	£	£	£	Kg

K13 **K13: RIGID SHEET FINE LININGS AND PANELLING**

K1321 **Isolated columns**

K132151	**Finnish birch faced WBP boarding ply; grade BB; 6 mm**								
K132151A	not exceeding 600 mm girth	m²	0.57	9.68	-	10.72	20.40	22.44	2.915
K132151B	600 - 1200 mm girth	m²	0.46	7.74	-	10.47	18.21	20.03	2.849
K132151C	1200 - 1800 mm girth	m²	0.38	6.45	-	10.23	16.68	18.35	2.784
K132152	**Finnish birch faced WBP boarding ply; grade BB; 9 mm**								
K132152A	not exceeding 600 mm girth	m²	0.60	10.19	-	13.19	23.38	25.72	4.359
K132152B	600 - 1200 mm girth	m²	0.48	8.15	-	12.89	21.04	23.14	4.261
K132152C	1200 - 1800 mm girth	m²	0.40	6.79	-	12.59	19.38	21.32	4.162
K132153	**Finnish birch faced WBP boarding ply; grade BB; 12 mm**								
K132153A	not exceeding 600 mm girth	m²	0.68	11.46	-	15.50	26.96	29.66	5.802
K132153B	600 - 1200 mm girth	m²	0.54	9.17	-	15.15	24.32	26.75	5.671
K132153C	1200 - 1800 mm girth	m²	0.45	7.64	-	14.80	22.44	24.68	5.540
K132154	**Finnish birch faced WBP boarding ply; grade BB; 15 mm**								
K132154A	not exceeding 600 mm girth	m²	0.72	12.23	-	20.85	33.08	36.39	7.245
K132154B	600 - 1200 mm girth	m²	0.58	9.85	-	20.37	30.22	33.24	7.081
K132154C	1200 - 1800 mm girth	m²	0.48	8.15	-	19.90	28.05	30.86	6.917
K132155	**Finnish birch faced WBP boarding ply; grade BB; 18 mm**								
K132155A	not exceeding 600 mm girth	m²	0.78	13.24	-	24.87	38.11	41.92	8.689
K132155B	600 - 1200 mm girth	m²	0.63	10.61	-	24.30	34.91	38.40	8.492
K132155C	1200 - 1800 mm girth	m²	0.52	8.83	-	23.74	32.57	35.83	8.295
K132156	**Finnish birch faced WBP boarding ply; grade BB; 22 mm**								
K132156A	not exceeding 600 mm girth	m²	0.84	14.26	-	29.43	43.69	48.06	10.614
K132156B	600 - 1200 mm girth	m²	0.67	11.38	-	28.77	40.15	44.17	10.373
K132156C	1200 - 1800 mm girth	m²	0.56	9.51	-	28.10	37.61	41.37	10.132
K132157	**Finnish birch faced WBP boarding ply; grade BB; 25 mm**								
K132157A	not exceeding 600 mm girth	m²	0.90	15.28	-	34.02	49.30	54.23	12.057
K132157B	600 - 1200 mm girth	m²	0.72	12.23	-	33.25	45.48	50.03	11.783
K132157C	1200 - 1800 mm girth	m²	0.60	10.19	-	32.48	42.67	46.94	11.510
K132161	**Non-asbestos, flameproof Class O boards; BS 476; 6 mm**								
K132161A	not exceeding 600 mm girth	m²	0.42	7.13	-	11.50	18.63	20.49	2.051
K132161B	600 - 1200 mm girth	m²	0.34	5.71	-	11.24	16.95	18.65	2.007
K132161C	1200 - 1800 mm girth	m²	0.28	4.75	-	10.99	15.74	17.31	1.963
K132162	**Non-asbestos, flameproof Class O boards; BS 476; 9 mm**								
K132162A	not exceeding 600 mm girth	m²	0.45	7.64	-	30.25	37.89	41.68	3.010
K132162B	600 - 1200 mm girth	m²	0.36	6.11	-	29.56	35.67	39.24	2.944
K132162C	1200 - 1800 mm girth	m²	0.30	5.09	-	28.88	33.97	37.37	2.879
K132163	**Non-asbestos, flameproof Class O boards; BS 476; 12 mm**								
K132163A	not exceeding 600 mm girth	m²	0.53	8.91	-	45.59	54.50	59.95	4.012
K132163B	600 - 1200 mm girth	m²	0.42	7.13	-	44.56	51.69	56.86	3.925
K132163C	1200 - 1800 mm girth	m²	0.35	5.94	-	43.52	49.46	54.41	3.838
K132164	**Non-asbestos, flameproof Class O boards; BS 476; 15 mm**								
K132164A	not exceeding 600 mm girth	m²	0.60	10.19	-	57.11	67.30	74.03	4.971
K132164B	600 - 1200 mm girth	m²	0.48	8.15	-	55.82	63.97	70.37	4.862
K132164C	1200 - 1800 mm girth	m²	0.40	6.79	-	54.53	61.32	67.45	4.754

Major Works 2011		Unit	Labour Hours	Labour Net	Plant Net	Materials Net	Unit Net	Unit with 10%	CO$_2$
				£	£	£	£	£	Kg
K13	**K13: RIGID SHEET FINE LININGS AND PANELLING**								
K1321	**Isolated columns**								
K132171	**MDF board; 12 mm**								
K132171A	not exceeding 600 mm girth	m^2	0.52	8.86	-	4.90	13.76	15.14	5.898
K132171B	600 - 1200 mm girth	m^2	0.42	7.13	-	4.79	11.92	13.11	5.765
K132171C	1200 - 1800 mm girth	m^2	0.35	5.94	-	4.68	10.62	11.68	5.632
K132172	**MDF board; 15 mm**								
K132172A	not exceeding 600 mm girth	m^2	0.60	10.19	-	4.93	15.12	16.63	7.358
K132172B	600 - 1200 mm girth	m^2	0.48	8.15	-	4.82	12.97	14.27	7.192
K132172C	1200 - 1800 mm girth	m^2	0.40	6.79	-	4.71	11.50	12.65	7.027
K132173	**MDF board; 18 mm**								
K132173A	not exceeding 600 mm girth	m^2	0.67	11.38	-	6.81	18.19	20.01	8.818
K132173B	600 - 1200 mm girth	m^2	0.54	9.17	-	6.66	15.83	17.41	8.619
K132173C	1200 - 1800 mm girth	m^2	0.45	7.64	-	6.50	14.14	15.55	8.420

Major Works 2011		Unit	Labour Hours	Labour Net	Plant Net	Materials Net	Unit Net	Unit with 10%	CO₂
				£	£	£	£	£	Kg
K20	**K20: TIMBER BOARD FLOORING, SHEATHING, LININGS AND CASINGS**								
K2006	**Walls**								
K200601	**Wrought softwood shiplap boarding; basic sizes; 19 mm thick**								
K200601A	over 300 mm wide	m²	0.75	12.73	-	22.44	35.17	38.69	5.325
K200601B	n.e. 300 mm wide	m	0.45	7.64	-	7.41	15.05	16.56	1.759
K200601C	area n.e. 1.0 m²	Nr	1.13	19.10	-	23.27	42.37	46.61	5.513
K200603	**Wrought softwood shiplap boarding; basic sizes; 25 mm thick**								
K200603E	over 300 mm wide	m²	0.75	12.73	-	14.24	26.97	29.67	6.899
K200603F	n.e. 300 mm wide	m	0.45	7.64	-	4.70	12.34	13.57	2.279
K200603G	area n.e. 1.0 m²	Nr	1.13	19.10	-	14.77	33.87	37.26	7.146
K200611	**Wrought softwood tongued and grooved and V-jointed one side matchboarding; basic sizes; 13 mm thick**								
K200611A	over 300 mm wide	m²	0.80	13.58	-	7.17	20.75	22.83	3.751
K200611B	n.e. 300 mm wide	m	0.48	8.15	-	2.37	10.52	11.57	1.240
K200611C	area n.e. 1.0 m²	Nr	1.20	20.38	-	7.43	27.81	30.59	3.879
K200613	**Wrought softwood tongued and grooved and V-jointed one side matchboarding; basic sizes; 19 mm thick**								
K200613E	over 300 mm wide	m²	0.80	13.58	-	12.45	26.03	28.63	5.325
K200613F	n.e. 300 mm wide	m	0.48	8.15	-	4.11	12.26	13.49	1.759
K200613G	area n.e. 1.0 m²	Nr	1.20	20.38	-	12.91	33.29	36.62	5.513
K2011	**Floors**								
K201101	**Wrought softwood square edged boarding; basic sizes; 19 mm thick**								
K201101A	over 300 mm wide	m²	0.55	9.34	-	15.87	25.21	27.73	6.117
K201101B	n.e. 300 mm wide	m	0.33	5.60	-	5.21	10.81	11.89	1.986
K201101C	area n.e. 1.0 m²	Nr	0.83	14.01	-	16.43	30.44	33.48	6.305
K201102	**Wrought softwood square edged boarding; basic sizes; 22 mm thick**								
K201102D	over 300 mm wide	m²	0.55	9.34	-	16.93	26.27	28.90	6.904
K201102E	n.e. 300 mm wide	m	0.33	5.60	-	5.56	11.16	12.28	2.245
K201102F	area n.e. 1.0 m²	Nr	0.83	14.01	-	17.53	31.54	34.69	7.122
K201103	**Wrought softwood square edged boarding; basic sizes; 25 mm thick**								
K201103G	over 300 mm wide	m²	0.55	9.34	-	17.98	27.32	30.05	7.691
K201103H	n.e. 300 mm wide	m	0.33	5.60	-	5.90	11.50	12.65	2.505
K201103I	area n.e. 1.0 m²	Nr	0.83	14.01	-	18.62	32.63	35.89	7.939
K201111	**Wrought softwood tongued and grooved boarding; basic sizes; 19 mm thick**								
K201111A	over 300 mm wide	m²	0.65	11.04	-	13.23	24.27	26.70	6.117
K201111B	n.e. 300 mm wide	m	0.39	6.62	-	4.34	10.96	12.06	1.986
K201111C	area n.e. 1.0 m²	Nr	0.98	16.56	-	13.69	30.25	33.28	6.305
K201112	**Wrought softwood tongued and grooved boarding; basic sizes; 22 mm thick**								
K201112D	over 300 mm wide	m²	0.65	11.04	-	15.02	26.06	28.67	6.904
K201112E	n.e. 300 mm wide	m	0.39	6.62	-	4.93	11.55	12.71	2.245
K201112F	area n.e. 1.0 m²	Nr	0.98	16.56	-	15.55	32.11	35.32	7.122
K201113	**Wrought softwood tongued and grooved boarding; basic sizes; 25 mm thick**								
K201113G	over 300 mm wide	m²	0.65	11.04	-	15.87	26.91	29.60	7.691
K201113H	n.e. 300 mm wide	m	0.39	6.62	-	5.21	11.83	13.01	2.505
K201113I	area n.e. 1.0 m²	Nr	0.98	16.56	-	16.43	32.99	36.29	7.939

Linings, Sheathing & Dry Partitioning

Major Works 2011		Unit	Labour Hours	Labour Net	Plant Net	Materials Net	Unit Net	Unit with 10%	CO₂
				£	£	£	£	£	Kg
K20	**K20: TIMBER BOARD FLOORING, SHEATHING, LININGS AND CASINGS**								
K2016	**Ceilings**								
K201601	**Wrought softwood tongued and grooved and V-jointed one side matchboarding; basic sizes; 13 mm thick**								
K201601A	over 300 mm wide	m²	0.95	16.13	-	7.17	23.30	25.63	3.751
K201601B	n.e. 300 mm wide	m	0.57	9.68	-	2.37	12.05	13.26	1.240
K201601C	area n.e. 1.0 m²	Nr	1.43	24.20	-	7.43	31.63	34.79	3.879
K201631	**Wrought softwood tongued and grooved and V-jointed one side matchboarding; basic sizes; 19 mm thick**								
K201631D	over 300 mm wide	m²	0.95	16.13	-	12.45	28.58	31.44	5.325
K201631E	n.e. 300 mm wide	m	0.57	9.68	-	4.11	13.79	15.17	1.759
K201631F	area n.e. 1.0 m²	Nr	1.43	24.20	-	12.91	37.11	40.82	5.513
K2021	**Roofs**								
K202101	**Wrought softwood square edged boarding; basic sizes; 19 mm thick**								
K202101A	over 300 mm wide	m²	0.60	10.19	-	15.87	26.06	28.67	6.117
K202101B	n.e. 300 mm wide	m	0.35	5.94	-	5.21	11.15	12.27	1.986
K202101C	area n.e. 1.0 m²	Nr	0.90	15.28	-	16.43	31.71	34.88	6.305
K202102	**Wrought softwood square edged boarding; basic sizes; 22 mm thick**								
K202102D	over 300 mm wide	m²	0.60	10.19	-	16.93	27.12	29.83	6.904
K202102E	n.e. 300 mm wide	m	0.35	5.94	-	5.56	11.50	12.65	2.245
K202102F	area n.e. 1.0 m²	Nr	0.90	15.28	-	17.53	32.81	36.09	7.122
K202103	**Wrought softwood square edged boarding; basic sizes; 25 mm thick**								
K202103G	over 300 mm wide	m²	0.60	10.19	-	17.98	28.17	30.99	7.691
K202103H	n.e. 300 mm wide	m	0.35	5.94	-	5.90	11.84	13.02	2.505
K202103I	area n.e. 1.0 m²	Nr	0.90	15.28	-	18.62	33.90	37.29	7.939
K202111	**Wrought softwood tongued and grooved boarding; basic sizes; 19 mm thick**								
K202111A	over 300 mm wide	m²	0.70	11.89	-	13.23	25.12	27.63	6.117
K202111B	n.e. 300 mm wide	m	0.40	6.79	-	4.34	11.13	12.24	1.986
K202111C	area n.e. 1.0 m²	Nr	1.05	17.83	-	13.69	31.52	34.67	6.305
K202112	**Wrought softwood tongued and grooved boarding; basic sizes; 22 mm thick**								
K202112D	over 300 mm wide	m²	0.70	11.89	-	15.02	26.91	29.60	6.904
K202112E	n.e. 300 mm wide	m	0.40	6.79	-	4.93	11.72	12.89	2.245
K202112F	area n.e. 1.0 m²	Nr	1.05	17.83	-	15.55	33.38	36.72	7.122
K202113	**Wrought softwood tongued and grooved boarding; basic sizes; 25 mm thick**								
K202113G	over 300 mm wide	m²	0.70	11.89	-	15.87	27.76	30.54	7.691
K202113H	n.e. 300 mm wide	m	0.40	6.79	-	5.21	12.00	13.20	2.505
K202113I	area n.e. 1.0 m²	Nr	1.05	17.83	-	16.43	34.26	37.69	7.939
K2025	**Tops and cheeks of dormers**								
K202501	**Wrought softwood square edged boarding; basic sizes; firrings and bearers included as necessary; 19 mm thick**								
K202501A	flat; over 300 mm wide	m²	1.05	17.83	-	18.58	36.41	40.05	8.413
K202501B	flat; n.e. 300 mm wide	m	0.58	9.85	-	5.71	15.56	17.12	2.544
K202501C	flat; area n.e. 1.0 m²	Nr	1.58	26.74	-	18.58	45.32	49.85	8.413
K202501D	sloping; over 300 mm wide	m²	0.86	14.60	-	17.10	31.70	34.87	6.940
K202501E	sloping; n.e. 300 mm wide	m	0.50	8.49	-	5.29	13.78	15.16	2.133
K202501F	sloping; area n.e. 1.0 m²	Nr	1.29	21.90	-	17.10	39.00	42.90	6.940
K202501G	vertical; over 300 mm wide	m²	1.04	17.66	-	16.94	34.60	38.06	6.585

Major Works 2011		Unit	Labour Hours	Labour Net	Plant Net	Materials Net	Unit Net	Unit with 10%	CO₂
				£	£	£	£	£	Kg
K20	**K20: TIMBER BOARD FLOORING, SHEATHING, LININGS AND CASINGS**								
K2025	**Tops and cheeks of dormers**								
K202501	**Wrought softwood square edged boarding; basic sizes; firrings and bearers included as necessary; 19 mm thick**								
K202501H	vertical; n.e. 300 mm wide	m	0.57	9.68	-	5.24	14.92	16.41	2.027
K202501I	vertical; area n.e. 1.0 m²	Nr	1.56	26.49	-	16.94	43.43	47.77	6.585
K202502	**Wrought softwood square edged boarding; basic sizes; firrings and bearers included as necessary; 22 mm thick**								
K202502A	flat; over 300 mm wide	m²	1.05	17.83	-	19.64	37.47	41.22	9.199
K202502B	flat; n.e. 300 mm wide	m	0.58	9.85	-	6.04	15.89	17.48	2.789
K202502C	flat; area n.e. 1.0 m²	Nr	1.58	26.74	-	19.64	46.38	51.02	9.199
K202502D	sloping; over 300 mm wide	m²	0.86	14.60	-	18.16	32.76	36.04	7.726
K202502E	sloping; n.e. 300 mm wide	m	0.50	8.49	-	5.62	14.11	15.52	2.378
K202502F	sloping; area n.e. 1.0 m²	Nr	1.29	21.90	-	18.16	40.06	44.07	7.726
K202502G	vertical; over 300 mm wide	m²	1.04	17.66	-	18.00	35.66	39.23	7.371
K202502H	vertical; n.e. 300 mm wide	m	0.57	9.68	-	5.57	15.25	16.78	2.272
K202502I	vertical; area n.e. 1.0 m²	Nr	1.56	26.49	-	18.00	44.49	48.94	7.371
K202503	**Wrought softwood square edged boarding; basic sizes; firrings and bearers included as necessary; 25 mm thick**								
K202503A	flat; over 300 mm wide	m²	1.05	17.83	-	20.69	38.52	42.37	9.987
K202503B	flat; n.e. 300 mm wide	m	0.58	9.85	-	6.39	16.24	17.86	3.063
K202503C	flat; area n.e. 1.0 m²	Nr	1.58	26.74	-	20.69	47.43	52.17	9.987
K202503D	sloping; over 300 mm wide	m²	0.86	14.60	-	19.21	33.81	37.19	8.514
K202503E	sloping; n.e. 300 mm wide	m	0.50	8.49	-	5.95	14.44	15.88	2.623
K202503F	sloping; area n.e. 1.0 m²	Nr	1.29	21.90	-	34.00	55.90	61.49	13.499
K202503G	vertical; over 300 mm wide	m²	1.04	17.66	-	19.05	36.71	40.38	8.159
K202503H	vertical; n.e. 300 mm wide	m	0.57	9.68	-	5.90	15.58	17.14	2.517
K202503I	vertical; area n.e. 1.0 m²	Nr	1.56	26.49	-	19.05	45.54	50.09	8.159
K202521	**Wrought softwood tongued and grooved boarding; basic sizes; firrings and bearers included as necessary; 19 mm thick**								
K202521A	flat; over 300 mm wide	m²	1.15	19.53	-	16.26	35.79	39.37	8.620
K202521B	flat; n.e. 300 mm wide	m	0.64	10.87	-	4.98	15.85	17.44	2.657
K202521C	flat; area n.e. 1.0 m²	Nr	1.73	29.29	-	16.33	45.62	50.18	8.705
K202521D	sloping; over 300 mm wide	m²	0.94	15.96	-	14.81	30.77	33.85	7.175
K202521E	sloping; n.e. 300 mm wide	m	0.55	9.34	-	4.52	13.86	15.25	2.190
K202521F	sloping; area n.e. 1.0 m²	Nr	1.41	23.94	-	14.81	38.75	42.63	7.175
K202521G	vertical; over 300 mm wide	m²	1.14	19.36	-	14.64	34.00	37.40	6.820
K202521H	vertical; n.e. 300 mm wide	m	0.63	10.70	-	4.47	15.17	16.69	2.084
K202521I	vertical; area n.e. 1.0 m²	Nr	1.71	29.04	-	14.64	43.68	48.05	6.820
K202522	**Wrought softwood tongued and grooved boarding; basic sizes; firrings and bearers included as necessary; 22 mm thick**								
K202522A	flat; over 300 mm wide	m²	1.15	19.53	-	18.09	37.62	41.38	9.421
K202522B	flat; n.e. 300 mm wide	m	0.64	10.87	-	5.54	16.41	18.05	2.902
K202522C	flat; area n.e. 1.0 m²	Nr	1.73	29.29	-	18.16	47.45	52.20	9.506
K202522D	sloping; over 300 mm wide	m²	0.94	15.96	-	16.64	32.60	35.86	7.976
K202522E	sloping; n.e. 300 mm wide	m	0.55	9.34	-	5.08	14.42	15.86	2.434
K202522F	sloping; area n.e. 1.0 m²	Nr	1.41	23.94	-	16.64	40.58	44.64	7.976
K202522G	vertical; over 300 mm wide	m²	1.14	19.36	-	16.47	35.83	39.41	7.622
K202522H	vertical; n.e. 300 mm wide	m	0.63	10.70	-	5.03	15.73	17.30	2.329
K202522I	vertical; area n.e. 1.0 m²	Nr	1.71	29.04	-	16.47	45.51	50.06	7.622
K202523	**Wrought softwood tongued and grooved boarding; basic sizes; firrings and bearers included as necessary; 25 mm thick**								
K202523A	flat; over 300 mm wide	m²	1.15	19.53	-	18.95	38.48	42.33	10.224
K202523B	flat; n.e. 300 mm wide	m	0.64	10.87	-	5.80	16.67	18.34	3.147

Major Works 2011		Unit	Labour Hours	Labour Net	Plant Net	Materials Net	Unit Net	Unit with 10%	CO₂
				£	£	£	£	£	Kg
K20	**K20: TIMBER BOARD FLOORING, SHEATHING, LININGS AND CASINGS**								
K2025	**Tops and cheeks of dormers**								
K202523	**Wrought softwood tongued and grooved boarding; basic sizes; firrings and bearers included as necessary; 25 mm thick**								
K202523C	flat; area n.e. 1.0 m²	Nr	1.73	29.29	-	19.02	48.31	53.14	10.309
K202523D	sloping; over 300 mm wide	m²	0.94	15.96	-	17.50	33.46	36.81	8.779
K202523E	sloping; n.e. 300 mm wide	m	0.55	9.34	-	5.34	14.68	16.15	2.680
K202523F	sloping; area n.e. 1.0 m²	Nr	1.41	23.94	-	17.50	41.44	45.58	8.779
K202523G	vertical; over 300 mm wide	m²	1.14	19.36	-	17.33	36.69	40.36	8.424
K202523H	vertical; n.e. 300 mm wide	m	0.63	10.70	-	5.29	15.99	17.59	2.574
K202523I	vertical; area n.e. 1.0 m²	Nr	1.71	29.04	-	17.33	46.37	51.01	8.424
K2066	**Isolated beams**								
K206601	**Wrought softwood tongued and grooved and V-jointed one side matchboarding; basic sizes; 13 mm thick**								
K206601A	not exceeding 600 mm girth	m²	1.43	24.20	-	7.56	31.76	34.94	3.944
K206601B	600 - 1200 mm girth	m²	1.14	19.36	-	7.30	26.66	29.33	3.815
K206601C	1200 - 1800 mm girth	m²	0.95	16.13	-	7.17	23.30	25.63	3.751
K206631	**Wrought softwood tongued and grooved and V-jointed one side matchboarding; basic sizes; 19 mm thick**								
K206631A	not exceeding 600 mm girth	m²	1.43	24.20	-	13.14	37.34	41.07	5.607
K206631B	600 - 1200 mm girth	m²	1.14	19.36	-	12.68	32.04	35.24	5.419
K206631C	1200 - 1800 mm girth	m²	0.95	16.13	-	12.45	28.58	31.44	5.325
K2076	**Isolated columns**								
K207601	**Wrought softwood shiplap boarding; basic sizes; 19 mm thick**								
K207601A	not exceeding 600 mm girth	m²	1.13	19.10	-	23.69	42.79	47.07	5.607
K207601B	600 - 1200 mm girth	m²	0.90	15.28	-	22.86	38.14	41.95	5.419
K207601C	1200 - 1800 mm girth	m²	0.75	12.73	-	22.44	35.17	38.69	5.325
K207603	**Wrought softwood shiplap boarding; basic sizes; 25 mm thick**								
K207603A	not exceeding 600 mm girth	m²	1.13	19.10	-	15.03	34.13	37.54	7.270
K207603B	600 - 1200 mm girth	m²	0.90	15.28	-	14.51	29.79	32.77	7.023
K207603C	1200 - 1800 mm girth	m²	0.75	12.73	-	14.24	26.97	29.67	6.899
K207611	**Wrought softwood tongued and grooved and V-jointed one side matchboarding; basic sizes; 13 mm thick**								
K207611A	not exceeding 600 mm girth	m²	1.20	20.38	-	7.56	27.94	30.73	3.944
K207611B	600 - 1200 mm girth	m²	0.96	16.30	-	7.30	23.60	25.96	3.815
K207611C	1200 - 1800 mm girth	m²	0.80	13.58	-	7.17	20.75	22.83	3.751
K207613	**Wrought softwood tongued and grooved and V-jointed one side matchboarding; basic sizes; 19 mm thick**								
K207613A	not exceeding 600 mm girth	m²	1.20	20.38	-	13.14	33.52	36.87	5.607
K207613B	600 - 1200 mm girth	m²	0.96	16.30	-	12.68	28.98	31.88	5.419
K207613C	1200 - 1800 mm girth	m²	0.80	13.58	-	12.45	26.03	28.63	5.325

Major Works 2011		Unit	Labour Hours	Labour Net	Plant Net	Materials Net	Unit Net	Unit with 10%	CO₂
				£	£	£	£	£	Kg
K21	**K21: TIMBER STRIP AND BOARD FINE FLOORING AND LININGS**								
K2110	**Prime maple strip flooring; 19 mm thick pre-finished; tongued and grooved joint clipped and laid on and including Sylvaform 4 mm thick and 1000 gauge polythene**								
K211010	**To floors**								
K211010A	over 300 mm wide	m²	2.10	35.66	-	63.68	99.34	109.27	12.234
K2115	**Natural oak strip flooring; 19 mm thick pre-finished; tongued and grooved joint clipped and laid on and including Sylvaform 4 mm thick and 1000 gauge polythene**								
K211510	**To floors**								
K211510A	over 300 mm wide	m²	2.00	33.96	-	47.75	81.71	89.88	12.234
K2120	**Ash strip flooring; 19 mm thick; pre-finished; tongued and grooved joint clipped and laid on and including Sylvaform 4 mm thick and 1000 gauge polythene**								
K212010	**To floors**								
K212010A	over 300 mm wide	m²	2.00	33.96	-	45.00	78.96	86.86	12.234

Linings, Sheathing & Dry Partitioning

Major Works 2011		Unit	Labour Hours	Labour Net	Plant Net	Materials Net	Unit Net	Unit with 10%	CO₂
				£	£	£	£	£	Kg
K32	**K32: PANEL CUBICLES**								
K3210	**Cubicles; Twyford Bushboard System One**								
K321010	**DriCor cubicles against walls; 1800 mm deep x 2000 mm high; cubicle up to 900 mm wide; one panel and door in line; to form**								
K321010A	set of one	Set	4.00	67.92	-	334.29	402.21	442.43	25.194
K321010B	set of two	Set	7.00	118.86	-	766.90	885.76	974.34	37.791
K321010D	set of four	Set	12.00	203.76	-	1,363.40	1,567.16	1,723.88	62.985
K321010F	set of six	Set	16.00	271.68	-	1,980.87	2,252.55	2,477.81	88.179
K321020	**DriCor cubicles against walls; disabled panel and door in line; outward opening door; up to 1800 mm deep x 2208 mm wide x 2000 mm high; to form**								
K321020A	set of one	Set	5.00	84.90	-	486.36	571.26	628.39	25.194
K321030	**DriCor cubicles between walls; up to 1800 mm deep x 2000 mm high; one panel and door in line; to form**								
K321030C	set of six	Set	16.00	271.68	-	1,980.87	2,252.55	2,477.81	88.179

Major Works 2011		Unit	Labour Hours	Labour Net	Plant Net	Materials Net	Unit Net	Unit with 10%	CO₂
				£	£	£	£	£	Kg
K40	**K40: DEMOUNTABLE SUSPENDED CEILINGS**								
K4011	**Gyproc M/F metal framed suspended ceilings; boards to receive direct decoration**								
K401102	**Suspended ceilings with 500 mm drop**								
K401102A	12.5 mm wallboard	m²	0.22	6.53	-	14.35	20.88	22.97	15.954
K401102B	12.5 mm Fireline board	m²	0.22	6.53	-	15.01	21.54	23.69	15.954
K401102C	12.5 mm Duplex board	m²	0.22	6.53	-	15.66	22.19	24.41	15.954
K401103	**Suspended ceilings with 1000 mm drop**								
K401103A	12.5 mm wallboard	m²	0.23	6.86	-	14.35	21.21	23.33	15.954
K401103B	12.5 mm Fireline board	m²	0.23	6.86	-	15.01	21.87	24.06	15.954
K401103C	12.5 mm Duplex board	m²	0.23	6.86	-	15.66	22.52	24.77	15.954
K401104	**Suspended ceilings with 1500 mm drop**								
K401104A	12.5 mm wallboard	m²	0.23	6.86	-	14.35	21.21	23.33	15.954
K401104B	12.5 mm Fireline board	m²	0.23	6.86	-	15.01	21.87	24.06	15.954
K401104C	12.5 mm Duplex board	m²	0.23	6.86	-	15.66	22.52	24.77	15.954
K401105	**Sides and soffits of beams or upstands**								
K401105A	12.5 mm wallboard	m²	0.25	7.45	-	14.61	22.06	24.27	16.237
K401105B	12.5 mm Fireline board	m²	0.25	7.45	-	15.27	22.72	24.99	16.237
K401105C	12.5 mm Duplex board	m²	0.25	7.45	-	15.92	23.37	25.71	16.237
K4013	**Armstrong concealed grid suspended ceilings; factory finished lay-in-grid tiles**								
K401311	**Suspended ceilings with 500 mm drop**								
K401311A	Minaboard 600 x 600 mm	m²	0.35	10.42	-	12.07	22.49	24.74	25.027
K401311B	Minaboard 600 x 1200 mm	m²	0.35	10.42	-	10.95	21.37	23.51	25.027
K401311C	Minatone Tegular 600 x 600 mm	m²	0.35	10.42	-	13.15	23.57	25.93	25.027
K401311D	Minatone Tegular 600 x 1200 mm	m²	0.35	10.42	-	12.19	22.61	24.87	25.027
K401311E	ML Second Look 600 x 1200 mm	m²	0.35	10.42	-	20.55	30.97	34.07	25.027
K401312	**Suspended ceilings with 1000 mm drop**								
K401312A	Minaboard 600 x 600 mm	m²	0.35	10.42	-	12.07	22.49	24.74	25.027
K401312B	Minaboard 600 x 1200 mm	m²	0.35	10.42	-	10.95	21.37	23.51	25.027
K401312C	Minatone Tegular 600 x 600 mm	m²	0.35	10.42	-	13.15	23.57	25.93	25.027
K401312D	Minatone Tegular 600 x 1200 mm	m²	0.35	10.42	-	12.19	22.61	24.87	25.027
K401312E	ML Second Look 600 x 1200 mm	m²	0.35	10.42	-	20.55	30.97	34.07	25.027
K401313	**Suspended ceilings with 1500 mm drop**								
K401313A	Minaboard 600 x 600 mm	m²	0.35	10.42	-	12.07	22.49	24.74	25.027
K401313B	Minaboard 600 x 1200 mm	m²	0.35	10.42	-	10.95	21.37	23.51	25.027
K401313C	Minatone Tegular 600 x 600 mm	m²	0.35	10.42	-	13.15	23.57	25.93	25.027
K401313D	Minatone Tegular 600 x 1200 mm	m²	0.35	10.42	-	12.19	22.61	24.87	25.027
K401313E	ML Second Look 600 x 1200 mm	m²	0.35	10.42	-	20.55	30.97	34.07	25.027
K401314	**Sides and soffits of beams or upstands**								
K401314A	Minaboard 600 x 600 mm	m²	0.40	11.90	-	12.94	24.84	27.32	26.219
K401314B	Minaboard 600 x 1200 mm	m²	0.40	11.90	-	11.76	23.66	26.03	26.219
K401314C	Minatone Tegular 600 x 600 mm	m²	0.40	11.90	-	14.06	25.96	28.56	26.219
K401314D	Minatone Tegular 600 x 1200 mm	m²	0.40	11.90	-	13.06	24.96	27.46	26.219
K401314E	ML Second Look 600 x 1200 mm	m²	0.40	11.90	-	21.81	33.71	37.08	26.219

Major Works 2011		Unit	Labour Hours	Labour Net £	Plant Net £	Materials Net £	Unit Net £	Unit with 10% £	CO₂ Kg
K40	**K40: DEMOUNTABLE SUSPENDED CEILINGS**								
K4015	**Treetex Spa Range suspended ceilings; factory finished lay-in-grid tiles**								
K401516	**Suspended ceilings with 500 mm drop**								
K401516A	Leamington Shadow 24	m²	0.35	10.42	-	13.06	23.48	25.83	19.092
K401516B	Leamington Slimtree 15	m²	0.35	10.42	-	13.21	23.63	25.99	19.092
K401516C	Leamington Slimline 15	m²	0.35	10.42	-	13.36	23.78	26.16	19.092
K401516D	Leamington Square edge	m²	0.35	10.42	-	10.69	21.11	23.22	19.092
K401516E	Bath Shadow 24	m²	0.35	10.42	-	13.21	23.63	25.99	19.092
K401516F	Bath Slimtree 15	m²	0.35	10.42	-	13.43	23.85	26.24	19.092
K401516G	Bath Slimline 15	m²	0.35	10.42	-	13.98	24.40	26.84	19.092
K401516H	Bath Square edge	m²	0.35	10.42	-	12.37	22.79	25.07	19.092
K401517	**Suspended ceilings with 1000 mm drop**								
K401517A	Leamington Shadow 24	m²	0.35	10.42	-	13.06	23.48	25.83	19.092
K401517B	Leamington Slimtree 15	m²	0.35	10.42	-	13.21	23.63	25.99	19.092
K401517C	Leamington Slimline 15	m²	0.35	10.42	-	13.36	23.78	26.16	19.092
K401517D	Leamington Square edge	m²	0.35	10.42	-	10.69	21.11	23.22	19.092
K401517E	Bath Shadow 24	m²	0.35	10.42	-	13.21	23.63	25.99	19.092
K401517F	Bath Slimtree 15	m²	0.35	10.42	-	13.43	23.85	26.24	19.092
K401517G	Bath Slimline 15	m²	0.35	10.42	-	13.98	24.40	26.84	19.092
K401517H	Bath Square edge	m²	0.35	10.42	-	12.37	22.79	25.07	19.092
K401518	**Suspended ceilings with 1500 mm drop**								
K401518A	Leamington Shadow 24	m²	0.35	10.42	-	13.06	23.48	25.83	19.092
K401518B	Leamington Slimtree 15	m²	0.35	10.42	-	13.21	23.63	25.99	19.092
K401518C	Leamington Slimline 15	m²	0.35	10.42	-	13.36	23.78	26.16	19.092
K401518D	Leamington Square edge	m²	0.35	10.42	-	10.69	21.11	23.22	19.092
K401518E	Bath Shadow 24	m²	0.35	10.42	-	13.21	23.63	25.99	19.092
K401518F	Bath Slimtree 15	m²	0.35	10.42	-	13.43	23.85	26.24	19.092
K401518G	Bath Slimline 15	m²	0.35	10.42	-	13.98	24.40	26.84	19.092
K401518H	Bath Square edge	m²	0.35	10.42	-	12.37	22.79	25.07	19.092
K401519	**Sides and soffits of beams or upstands**								
K401519A	Leamington Shadow 24	m²	0.40	11.90	-	13.34	25.24	27.76	19.092
K401519B	Leamington Slimtree 15	m²	0.40	11.90	-	13.48	25.38	27.92	19.092
K401519C	Leamington Slimline 15	m²	0.40	11.90	-	13.63	25.53	28.08	19.092
K401519D	Leamington Square edge	m²	0.40	11.90	-	13.71	25.61	28.17	25.175
K401519E	Bath Shadow 24	m²	0.40	11.90	-	13.48	25.38	27.92	19.092
K401519F	Bath Slimtree 15	m²	0.40	11.90	-	13.70	25.60	28.16	19.092
K401519G	Bath Slimline 15	m²	0.40	11.90	-	14.25	26.15	28.77	19.092
K401519H	Bath Square edge	m²	0.40	11.90	-	12.64	24.54	26.99	19.092
K4017	**Hunter Douglas Luxalon cell system suspended ceilings**								
K401721	**Suspended ceilings with 500 mm drop**								
K401721A	Cell module 75; tone white	m²	0.48	14.28	-	77.23	91.51	100.66	29.993
K401721B	Cell module 75; coloured	m²	0.48	14.28	-	88.19	102.47	112.72	29.993
K401721C	Cell module 75; mirror or brushed finish	m²	0.48	14.28	-	99.14	113.42	124.76	29.993
K401721D	Cell module 100; tone white	m²	0.45	13.39	-	55.32	68.71	75.58	24.802
K401721E	Cell module 100; coloured	m²	0.45	13.39	-	66.28	79.67	87.64	24.802
K401721F	Cell module 100; mirror or brushed finish	m²	0.45	13.39	-	77.23	90.62	99.68	24.802
K401721G	Cell module 150; tone white	m²	0.42	12.50	-	38.89	51.39	56.53	19.611
K401721H	Cell module 150; coloured	m²	0.42	12.50	-	39.60	52.10	57.31	19.611
K401721I	Cell module 150; mirror or brushed finish	m²	0.42	12.50	-	60.80	73.30	80.63	19.611
K401722	**Suspended ceilings with 1000 mm drop**								
K401722A	Cell module 75; tone white	m²	0.48	14.28	-	78.32	92.60	101.86	29.993
K401722B	Cell module 75; coloured	m²	0.48	14.28	-	89.28	103.56	113.92	29.993
K401722C	Cell module 75; mirror or brushed finish	m²	0.48	14.28	-	100.23	114.51	125.96	29.993
K401722D	Cell module 100; tone white	m²	0.45	13.39	-	56.42	69.81	76.79	24.802

Major Works 2011		Unit	Labour Hours	Labour Net	Plant Net	Materials Net	Unit Net	Unit with 10%	CO$_2$
				£	£	£	£	£	Kg
K40	**K40: DEMOUNTABLE SUSPENDED CEILINGS**								
K4017	**Hunter Douglas Luxalon cell system suspended ceilings**								
K401722	**Suspended ceilings with 1000 mm drop**								
K401722E	Cell module 100; coloured	m^2	0.45	13.39	-	67.37	80.76	88.84	24.802
K401722F	Cell module 100; mirror or brushed finish	m^2	0.45	13.39	-	78.32	91.71	100.88	24.802
K401722G	Cell module 150; tone white	m^2	0.42	12.50	-	39.98	52.48	57.73	19.611
K401722H	Cell module 150; coloured	m^2	0.42	12.50	-	40.69	53.19	58.51	19.611
K401722I	Cell module 150; mirror or brushed finish	m^2	0.42	12.50	-	61.89	74.39	81.83	19.611
K401723	**Suspended ceilings with 1500 mm drop**								
K401723A	Cell module 75; tone white	m^2	0.48	14.28	-	78.87	93.15	102.47	29.993
K401723B	Cell module 75; coloured	m^2	0.48	14.28	-	89.83	104.11	114.52	29.993
K401723C	Cell module 75; mirror or brushed finish	m^2	0.48	14.28	-	100.78	115.06	126.57	29.993
K401723D	Cell module 100; tone white	m^2	0.45	13.39	-	56.96	70.35	77.39	24.802
K401723E	Cell module 100; coloured	m^2	0.45	13.39	-	67.91	81.30	89.43	24.802
K401723F	Cell module 100; mirror or brushed finish	m^2	0.45	13.39	-	78.87	92.26	101.49	24.802
K401723G	Cell module 150; tone white	m^2	0.42	12.50	-	40.53	53.03	58.33	19.611
K401723H	Cell module 150; coloured	m^2	0.42	12.50	-	41.23	53.73	59.10	19.611
K401723I	Cell module 150; mirror or brushed finish	m^2	0.42	12.50	-	62.43	74.93	82.42	19.611
K401724	**Sides and soffits of beams or upstands**								
K401724A	Cell module 75; tone white	m^2	0.50	14.87	-	79.41	94.28	103.71	30.282
K401724B	Cell module 75; coloured	m^2	0.50	14.87	-	90.37	105.24	115.76	30.282
K401724C	Cell module 75; mirror or brushed finish	m^2	0.50	14.87	-	101.33	116.20	127.82	30.282
K401724D	Cell module 100; tone white	m^2	0.47	13.98	-	57.51	71.49	78.64	25.091
K401724E	Cell module 100; coloured	m^2	0.47	13.98	-	68.46	82.44	90.68	25.091
K401724F	Cell module 100; mirror or brushed finish	m^2	0.47	13.98	-	79.41	93.39	102.73	25.091
K401724G	Cell module 150; tone white	m^2	0.44	13.09	-	41.08	54.17	59.59	19.900
K401724H	Cell module 150; coloured	m^2	0.44	13.09	-	41.78	54.87	60.36	19.900
K401724I	Cell module 150; mirror or brushed finish	m^2	0.44	13.09	-	62.98	76.07	83.68	19.900
K4080	**Metal framed suspended ceiling grids**								
K408002	**Suspended ceilings; drop**								
K408002A	500 mm	m^2	0.22	6.53	-	10.04	16.57	18.23	9.452
K408002B	1000 mm	m^2	0.22	6.53	-	10.51	17.04	18.74	9.895
K408002C	1500 mm	m^2	0.23	6.86	-	10.51	17.37	19.11	9.895
K408005	**Sides and soffits**								
K408005A	beams and upstands	m^2	0.25	7.45	-	10.71	18.16	19.98	10.054
K4081	**Suspended ceiling grid trims**								
K408110	**Gyproc M/F suspended ceiling edge trim**								
K408110A	MF6A	m	0.20	5.94	-	1.20	7.14	7.85	1.952
K408111	**Armstrong suspended ceiling edge trim**								
K408111A	998	m	0.20	5.94	-	2.38	8.32	9.15	8.694
K408112	**Treetex Spa Range suspended ceiling edge trim**								
K408112A	Shadow 24	m	0.20	5.94	-	1.81	7.75	8.53	1.437
K408112B	Slimtree 15	m	0.20	5.94	-	1.81	7.75	8.53	1.437
K408112C	Slimline 15	m	0.20	5.94	-	1.81	7.75	8.53	1.437
K408112D	square edge	m	0.20	5.94	-	1.81	7.75	8.53	1.437
K408113	**Hunter Luxalon suspended ceiling edge trim**								
K408113A	cover strip and edge cover profile	m	0.20	5.94	-	2.27	8.21	9.03	7.397

Windows, Doors and Stairs

Major Works 2011		Unit	Labour Hours	Labour Net	Plant Net	Materials Net	Unit Net	Unit with 10%	CO₂
				£	£	£	£	£	Kg
L10	**L10: WINDOWS, ROOFLIGHTS, SCREENS AND LOUVRES**								
L1000	**Proprietary PVC-u windows**								
L100072	**Side hung casement window; fully welded; fitted 24 mm Low E insulating double glazing units; including ironmongery; size**								
L100072A	1000 x 600 mm high	Nr	1.00	16.98	-	94.31	111.29	122.42	48.288
L100072B	1000 x 900 mm high	Nr	1.15	19.53	-	108.64	128.17	140.99	72.431
L100072C	1000 x 1200 mm high	Nr	1.30	22.07	-	123.79	145.86	160.45	96.575
L100072D	1200 x 600 mm high	Nr	1.25	21.23	-	105.95	127.18	139.90	57.888
L100072E	1200 x 900 mm high	Nr	1.40	23.77	-	117.78	141.55	155.71	86.831
L100072F	1200 x 1200 mm high	Nr	1.55	26.32	-	133.76	160.08	176.09	115.775
L100072G	1500 x 600 mm high	Nr	1.50	25.47	-	117.58	143.05	157.36	72.288
L100072H	1500 x 900 mm high	Nr	1.65	28.02	-	133.57	161.59	177.75	108.431
L100072I	1500 x 1200 mm high	Nr	1.80	30.56	-	146.23	176.79	194.47	144.575
L100072J	1800 x 600 mm high	Nr	1.75	29.72	-	133.37	163.09	179.40	86.688
L100072K	1800 x 900 mm high	Nr	1.90	32.26	-	146.04	178.30	196.13	130.031
L100072L	1800 x 1200 mm high	Nr	2.05	34.81	-	163.68	198.49	218.34	173.375
L100072M	2100 x 600 mm high	Nr	2.00	33.96	-	145.84	179.80	197.78	101.088
L100072N	2100 x 900 mm high	Nr	2.15	36.51	-	163.49	200.00	220.00	151.631
L100072O	2100 x 1200 mm high	Nr	2.30	39.05	-	185.29	224.34	246.77	202.175
L100072P	2400 x 600 mm high	Nr	2.50	42.45	-	163.29	205.74	226.31	115.488
L100072Q	2400 x 900 mm high	Nr	2.65	45.00	-	185.10	230.10	253.11	173.231
L100072R	2400 x 1200 mm high	Nr	2.80	47.54	-	238.49	286.03	314.63	230.975
L100073	**Top hung and side casement window; fully welded; fitted 24 mm Low E double insulating double glazing units; including ironmongery; size**								
L100073A	1000 x 600 mm high	Nr	1.00	16.98	-	122.57	139.55	153.51	51.288
L100073B	1000 x 900 mm high	Nr	1.15	19.53	-	141.05	160.58	176.64	76.931
L100073C	1000 x 1200 mm high	Nr	1.30	22.07	-	155.37	177.44	195.18	102.575
L100073D	1200 x 600 mm high	Nr	1.25	21.23	-	131.71	152.94	168.23	61.488
L100073E	1200 x 900 mm high	Nr	1.40	23.77	-	151.03	174.80	192.28	92.231
L100073F	1200 x 1200 mm high	Nr	1.55	26.32	-	165.35	191.67	210.84	122.975
L100073G	1500 x 600 mm high	Nr	1.50	25.47	-	150.83	176.30	193.93	76.788
L100073H	1500 x 900 mm high	Nr	1.65	28.02	-	165.16	193.18	212.50	115.181
L100073I	1500 x 1200 mm high	Nr	1.80	30.56	-	182.80	213.36	234.70	153.575
L100073J	1800 x 600 mm high	Nr	1.75	29.72	-	164.96	194.68	214.15	92.088
L100073K	1800 x 900 mm high	Nr	1.90	32.26	-	182.61	214.87	236.36	138.131
L100073L	1800 x 1200 mm high	Nr	2.05	34.81	-	199.42	234.23	257.65	184.175
L1011	**Standard softwood windows**								
L101101	**Boulton and Paul softwood windows; Sovereign; casement; plain; fitted with standard cill; complete with ironmongery; size**								
L101101A	630 x 750 mm; W107C	Nr	0.11	5.04	-	116.12	121.16	133.28	3.590
L101101B	630 x 900 mm; W109C	Nr	0.11	5.04	-	117.38	122.42	134.66	3.807
L101101C	630 x 1050 mm; W110C	Nr	0.11	5.04	-	123.43	128.47	141.32	4.023
L101101D	630 x 1200 mm; W112C	Nr	0.11	5.04	-	129.33	134.37	147.81	4.240
L101101E	630 x 1350 mm; W113C	Nr	0.11	5.04	-	140.23	145.27	159.80	4.457
L101101F	1200 x 750 mm; W207C	Nr	0.14	6.30	-	150.23	156.53	172.18	5.368
L101101G	1200 x 900 mm; W209C	Nr	0.14	6.30	-	151.51	157.81	173.59	5.693
L101101H	1200 x 1050 mm; W210C	Nr	0.14	6.30	-	157.83	164.13	180.54	6.019
L101101I	1200 x 1200 mm; W212C	Nr	0.14	6.30	-	165.35	171.65	188.82	6.344
L101101J	1200 x 1350 mm; W213C	Nr	0.14	6.30	-	154.69	160.99	177.09	5.802
L101101K	1200 x 750 mm; W207CC	Nr	0.14	6.30	-	176.86	183.16	201.48	4.501
L101101L	1200 x 900 mm; W209CC	Nr	0.14	6.30	-	185.31	191.61	210.77	4.826
L101101M	1200 x 1050 mm; W210CC	Nr	0.14	6.30	-	193.55	199.85	219.84	5.151
L101101N	1200 x 1200 mm; W212CC	Nr	0.14	6.30	-	201.18	207.48	228.23	5.477
L101101O	1200 x 1350 mm; W213CC	Nr	0.14	6.30	-	257.81	264.11	290.52	6.669
L101101P	1770 x 750 mm; W307CC	Nr	0.16	7.56	-	238.87	246.43	271.07	7.147
L101101Q	1770 x 900 mm; W309CC	Nr	0.16	7.56	-	245.06	252.62	277.88	7.580
L101101R	1770 x 1050 mm; W310CC	Nr	0.16	7.56	-	250.51	258.07	283.88	8.014
L101101S	1770 x 1200 mm; W312CC	Nr	0.16	7.56	-	261.51	269.07	295.98	8.448
L101101T	1770 x 1350 mm; W313CC	Nr	0.16	7.56	-	281.28	288.84	317.72	8.882
L101101W	2339 x 900 mm; W409CMC	Nr	0.19	8.77	-	243.52	252.29	277.52	7.774
L101101X	2339 x 1050 mm; W410CMC	Nr	0.19	8.77	-	253.78	262.55	288.81	8.316
L101101Y	2339 x 1200 mm; W412CMC	Nr	0.19	8.77	-	264.42	273.19	300.51	8.858
L101101Z	2339 x 1350 mm; W413CMC	Nr	0.19	8.77	-	281.17	289.94	318.93	9.401

Major Works 2011		Unit	Labour Hours	Labour Net	Plant Net	Materials Net	Unit Net	Unit with 10%	CO$_2$
				£	£	£	£	£	Kg
L10	**L10: WINDOWS, ROOFLIGHTS, SCREENS AND LOUVRES**								
L1011	**Standard softwood windows**								
L101102	**Boulton and Paul softwood windows; Sovereign; casement; landscape; fitted with standard cill; complete with ironmongery; size**								
L101102A	1770 x 1050 mm; W310C	Nr	0.16	7.56	-	164.51	172.07	189.28	5.975
L101102B	1770 x 1200 mm; W312C	Nr	0.16	7.56	-	169.30	176.86	194.55	6.301
L101102C	1770 x 1350 mm; W313C	Nr	0.16	7.56	-	177.74	185.30	203.83	6.626
L101102D	1770 x 1050 mm; W310WW	Nr	0.16	7.56	-	225.69	233.25	256.58	6.496
L101102E	1770 x 1200 mm; W312WW	Nr	0.16	7.56	-	231.42	238.98	262.88	6.713
L101102F	1770 x 1350 mm; W313WW	Nr	0.16	7.56	-	236.71	244.27	268.70	6.930
L101102G	2339 x 1050 mm; W410CWC	Nr	0.19	8.77	-	253.78	262.55	288.81	8.316
L101102H	2339 x 1200 mm; W412CWC	Nr	0.19	8.77	-	264.42	273.19	300.51	8.858
L101102I	2339 x 1350 mm; W413CWC	Nr	0.19	8.77	-	281.17	289.94	318.93	9.401
L101102N	915 x 900 mm; W2N09W	Nr	0.12	5.79	-	119.60	125.39	137.93	4.425
L101102O	915 x 1050 mm; W2N10W	Nr	0.12	5.79	-	121.24	127.03	139.73	4.642
L101102P	915 x 1200 mm; W2N12W	Nr	0.12	5.79	-	130.68	136.47	150.12	4.858
L101102Q	915 x 1350 mm; W2N13W	Nr	0.12	5.79	-	133.27	139.06	152.97	5.075
L101102R	915 x 1500 mm; W2N15W	Nr	0.12	5.79	-	135.03	140.82	154.90	5.292
L101102S	1200 x 900 mm; W209W	Nr	0.14	6.30	-	141.98	148.28	163.11	5.043
L101102T	1200 x 1050 mm; W210W	Nr	0.14	6.30	-	144.41	150.71	165.78	5.260
L101102U	1200 x 1200 mm; W212W	Nr	0.14	6.30	-	147.13	153.43	168.77	5.477
L101102V	1200 x 1350 mm; W213W	Nr	0.14	6.30	-	150.09	156.39	172.03	5.693
L101102W	1200 x 1500 mm; W215W	Nr	0.14	6.30	-	153.57	159.87	175.86	5.910
L101102X	1770 x 1050 mm; W310CW	Nr	0.16	7.56	-	210.69	218.25	240.08	7.255
L101102Y	1700 x 1200 mm; W312CW	Nr	0.16	7.56	-	216.17	223.73	246.10	7.580
L101102Z	1700 x 1350 mm; W313CW	Nr	0.16	7.56	-	224.61	232.17	255.39	7.906
L101103	**Boulton and Paul softwood windows; Sovereign; casement; with vents; fitted with standard cill; complete with ironmongery; size**								
L101103A	630 x 750 mm; W107V	Nr	0.11	5.04	-	97.99	103.03	113.33	3.134
L101103B	630 x 900 mm; W109V	Nr	0.11	5.04	-	98.31	103.35	113.69	3.351
L101103C	630 x 1050 mm; W110V	Nr	0.11	5.04	-	100.59	105.63	116.19	3.568
L101103D	630 x 1200 mm; W112V	Nr	0.11	5.04	-	108.38	113.42	124.76	3.785
L101103E	630 x 1350 mm; W113V	Nr	0.11	5.04	-	111.41	116.45	128.10	4.002
L101103F	630 x 1500 mm; W115V	Nr	0.11	5.04	-	115.20	120.24	132.26	4.219
L101103G	1200 x 900 mm; W209T	Nr	0.14	6.30	-	167.79	174.09	191.50	4.826
L101103H	1200 x 1050 mm; W210T	Nr	0.14	6.30	-	175.74	182.04	200.24	5.260
L101103I	1200 x 1200 mm; W212T	Nr	0.14	6.30	-	181.40	187.70	206.47	5.477
L101103J	1200 x 1350 mm; W213T	Nr	0.14	6.30	-	186.51	192.81	212.09	5.693
L101103K	1200 x 1500 mm; W215T	Nr	0.14	6.30	-	199.61	205.91	226.50	5.910
L101103L	1200 x 750 mm; W207CV	Nr	0.14	6.30	-	162.13	168.43	185.27	4.501
L101103M	1200 x 900 mm; W209CV	Nr	0.14	6.30	-	163.69	169.99	186.99	4.826
L101103N	1200 x 1050 mm; W210CV	Nr	0.14	6.30	-	163.89	170.19	187.21	5.151
L101103O	1200 x 1200 mm; W212CV	Nr	0.14	6.30	-	169.04	175.34	192.87	5.477
L101103P	1200 x 1350 mm; W213CV	Nr	0.14	6.30	-	187.00	193.30	212.63	5.802
L101103Q	1770 x 900 mm; W309CVC	Nr	0.16	7.56	-	231.42	238.98	262.88	6.301
L101103R	1779 x 1050 mm; W310CVC	Nr	0.16	7.56	-	238.92	246.48	271.13	6.734
L101103S	1770 x 1200 mm; W312CVC	Nr	0.16	7.56	-	247.10	254.66	280.13	7.168
L101103T	1770 x 1350 mm; W313CVC	Nr	0.16	7.56	-	261.45	269.01	295.91	7.602
L101103U	2339 x 1200 mm; W412CVVC	Nr	0.19	8.77	-	306.56	315.33	346.86	9.682
L101103V	2339 x 1350 mm; W413CVVC	Nr	0.19	8.77	-	322.94	331.71	364.88	10.116
L101103W	2339 x 1200 mm; W412TT	Nr	0.19	8.77	-	304.03	312.80	344.08	9.682
L101103X	2339 x 1350 mm; W413TT	Nr	0.19	8.77	-	312.05	320.82	352.90	10.116
L101103Y	1770 x 1050 mm; W310T	Nr	0.16	7.56	-	195.50	203.06	223.37	8.014
L101103Z	1770 x 1200 mm; W312T	Nr	0.16	7.56	-	200.85	208.41	229.25	8.448
L101105	**Boulton and Paul softwood windows; Sovereign; casement; transom; fitted with standard cill; complete with ironmongery; size**								
L101105A	630 x 900 mm; W109T	Nr	0.11	5.04	-	140.13	145.17	159.69	3.807
L101105B	630 x 1050 mm; W110T	Nr	0.11	5.04	-	144.22	149.26	164.19	4.023
L101105C	630 x 1200 mm; W112T	Nr	0.11	5.04	-	148.27	153.31	168.64	4.240
L101105D	630 x 1350 mm; W113T	Nr	0.11	5.04	-	152.35	157.39	173.13	4.457
L101105E	630 x 1500 mm; W115T	Nr	0.11	5.04	-	164.27	169.31	186.24	4.674
L101105F	1200 x 1050 mm; W210TX	Nr	0.14	6.30	-	175.74	182.04	200.24	5.260
L101105G	1200 x 1200 mm; W212TX	Nr	0.14	6.30	-	181.40	187.70	206.47	5.477
L101105H	1200 x 1350 mm; W213TX	Nr	0.14	6.30	-	186.51	192.81	212.09	5.693
L101105I	1200 x 1500 mm; W215TX	Nr	0.14	6.30	-	199.61	205.91	226.50	5.910
L101105J	1770 x 1050 mm; W310TXT	Nr	0.16	7.56	-	273.75	281.31	309.44	6.496
L101105K	1770 x 1200 mm; W312TXT	Nr	0.16	7.56	-	282.29	289.85	318.84	6.713
L101105L	1770 x 1350 mm; W313TXT	Nr	0.16	7.56	-	288.55	296.11	325.72	6.930

Major Works 2011		Unit	Labour Hours	Labour Net	Plant Net	Materials Net	Unit Net	Unit with 10%	CO₂
				£	£	£	£	£	Kg
L10	**L10: WINDOWS, ROOFLIGHTS, SCREENS AND LOUVRES**								
L1011	**Standard softwood windows**								
L101105	**Boulton and Paul softwood windows; Sovereign; casement; transom; fitted with standard cill; complete with ironmongery; size**								
L101105M	1770 x 1500 mm; W315TXT	Nr	0.16	7.56	-	313.13	320.69	352.76	7.147
L101106	**Boulton and Paul softwood windows; Sovereign; casement; narrow module; fitted with standard cill; complete with ironmongery; size**								
L101106A	488 x 750 mm; WN07C	Nr	0.10	4.53	-	87.85	92.38	101.62	3.282
L101106B	488 x 900 mm; WN09C	Nr	0.10	4.53	-	121.14	125.67	138.24	3.146
L101106C	488 x 1050 mm; WN10C	Nr	0.10	4.53	-	126.43	130.96	144.06	3.363
L101106D	488 x 1200 mm; WN12C	Nr	0.10	4.53	-	130.55	135.08	148.59	3.580
L101106E	488 x 1350 mm; WN13C	Nr	0.10	4.53	-	123.98	128.51	141.36	3.796
L101106F	915 x 750 mm; W2N07C	Nr	0.12	5.79	-	156.77	162.56	178.82	4.750
L101106G	915 x 900 mm; W2N09C	Nr	0.12	5.79	-	159.82	165.61	182.17	5.075
L101106H	915 x 1050 mm; W2N10C	Nr	0.12	5.79	-	168.84	174.63	192.09	5.401
L101106I	915 x 1200 mm; W2N12C	Nr	0.12	5.79	-	174.36	180.15	198.17	5.726
L101106J	915 x 1350 mm; W2N13C	Nr	0.12	5.79	-	172.38	178.17	195.99	6.051
L101106K	915 x 750 mm; W2N07CC	Nr	0.12	5.79	-	171.38	177.17	194.89	4.750
L101106L	915 x 900 mm; W2N09CC	Nr	0.12	5.79	-	172.06	177.85	195.64	5.075
L101106M	915 x 1050 mm; W2N10CC	Nr	0.12	5.79	-	179.12	184.91	203.40	5.401
L101106N	915 x 1200 mm; W2N12CC	Nr	0.12	5.79	-	185.87	191.66	210.83	5.726
L101106O	915 x 1350 mm; W2N13CC	Nr	0.12	5.79	-	192.37	198.16	217.98	6.051
L101106P	1342 x 750 mm; W3N07CC	Nr	0.15	7.05	-	243.19	250.24	275.26	6.218
L101106Q	1342 x 900 mm; W3N09CC	Nr	0.15	7.05	-	253.04	260.09	286.10	6.652
L101106R	1342 x 1050 mm; W3N10CC	Nr	0.15	7.05	-	262.07	269.12	296.03	7.086
L101106S	1342 x 1200 mm; W3N12CC	Nr	0.15	7.05	-	271.15	278.20	306.02	7.520
L101106T	1342 x 1350 mm; W3N13CC	Nr	0.15	7.05	-	251.06	258.11	283.92	7.953
L101106U	1770 x 900 mm; W4N09CMC	Nr	0.18	8.31	-	234.99	243.30	267.63	5.650
L101106V	1770 x 1050 mm; W4N10CMC	Nr	0.18	8.31	-	325.57	333.88	367.27	8.773
L101106W	1770 x 1200 mm; W4N12CMC	Nr	0.18	8.31	-	338.08	346.39	381.03	9.315
L101106X	1770 x 1350 mm; W4N13CMC	Nr	0.18	8.31	-	318.79	327.10	359.81	9.857
L101107	**Boulton and Paul softwood windows; Sovereign; casement; narrow module; with vents; fitted with standard cill; complete with ironmongery; size**								
L101107K	488 x 750 mm; WN07V	Nr	0.10	4.53	-	80.87	85.40	93.94	3.282
L101107L	488 x 900 mm; WN09V	Nr	0.10	4.53	-	83.52	88.05	96.86	3.499
L101107M	488 x 1050 mm; WN10V	Nr	0.10	4.53	-	86.09	90.62	99.68	3.716
L101107N	488 x 1200 mm; WN12V	Nr	0.10	4.53	-	89.11	93.64	103.00	3.932
L101107O	915 x 900 mm; W2N09CV	Nr	0.12	5.79	-	165.14	170.93	188.02	5.075
L101107P	915 x 1050 mm; W2N10CV	Nr	0.12	5.79	-	168.61	174.40	191.84	5.401
L101107Q	915 x 1200 mm; W2N12CV	Nr	0.12	5.79	-	174.86	180.65	198.72	5.726
L101108	**Boulton and Paul softwood windows; Sovereign; all bar; fitted 24 mm Low E insulating glass units; fitted with standard cill; complete with ironmongery; size**								
L101108A	630 x 750 mm; LEWB107C	Nr	0.11	5.04	-	183.77	188.81	207.69	9.159
L101108B	630 x 900 mm; LEWB109C	Nr	0.11	5.04	-	207.60	212.64	233.90	10.580
L101108C	630 x 1050 mm; LEWB110C	Nr	0.11	5.04	-	218.57	223.61	245.97	12.002
L101108D	630 x 1200 mm; LEWB112C	Nr	0.11	5.04	-	240.15	245.19	269.71	13.424
L101108E	630 x 1350 mm; LEWB113C	Nr	0.11	5.04	-	269.88	274.92	302.41	14.846
L101108F	1200 x 750 mm; LEWB207C	Nr	0.14	6.30	-	333.06	339.36	373.30	15.976
L101108G	1200 x 900 mm; LEWB209C	Nr	0.14	6.30	-	373.53	379.83	417.81	18.596
L101108H	1200 x 1050 mm; LEWB210C	Nr	0.14	6.30	-	396.98	403.28	443.61	21.216
L101108I	1200 x 1200 mm; LEWB212C	Nr	0.14	6.30	-	418.80	425.10	467.61	23.837
L101108J	1200 x 1350 mm; LEWB213C	Nr	0.14	6.30	-	491.09	497.39	547.13	26.457
L101108K	1770 x 900 mm; LEWB309CC	Nr	0.16	7.56	-	535.27	542.83	597.11	26.611
L101108L	1770 x 1050 mm; LEWB310CC	Nr	0.16	7.56	-	569.89	577.45	635.20	30.430
L101108M	1770 x 1200 mm; LEWB312CC	Nr	0.16	7.56	-	632.12	639.68	703.65	34.249
L101108N	1770 x 1300 mm; LEWB313CC	Nr	0.16	7.56	-	709.18	716.74	788.41	38.068

Major Works 2011		Unit	Labour Hours	Labour Net	Plant Net	Materials Net	Unit Net	Unit with 10%	CO$_2$
				£	£	£	£	£	Kg
L10	**L10: WINDOWS, ROOFLIGHTS, SCREENS AND LOUVRES**								
L1011	**Standard softwood windows**								
L101109	**Boulton and Paul softwood windows; Sovereign; all bar; with vents; fitted 24 mm Low E insulating glazing units; fitted with standard cill; complete with ironmongery; size**								
L101109A	630 x 1050 mm; LEWB110T	Nr	0.11	5.04	-	296.32	301.36	331.50	12.458
L101109B	630 x 1200 mm; LEWB112T	Nr	0.11	5.04	-	332.31	337.35	371.09	13.879
L101109C	630 x 1350 mm; LEWB113T	Nr	0.11	5.04	-	347.08	352.12	387.33	15.301
L101109D	630 x 750 mm; LEWB107V	Nr	0.11	5.04	-	269.82	274.86	302.35	9.614
L101109E	630 x 900 mm; LEWB109V	Nr	0.11	5.04	-	279.71	284.75	313.23	11.036
L101109F	630 x 1050 mm; LEWB110V	Nr	0.11	5.04	-	289.28	294.32	323.75	12.458
L101109G	630 x 1200 mm; LEWB112V	Nr	0.11	5.04	-	317.34	322.38	354.62	13.879
L101109H	630 x 1350 mm; LEWB113V	Nr	0.11	5.04	-	333.32	338.36	372.20	15.301
L101109I	1200 x 750 mm; LEWB207CV	Nr	0.14	6.30	-	416.08	422.38	464.62	16.843
L101109J	1200 x 900 mm; LEWB209CV	Nr	0.14	6.30	-	444.82	451.12	496.23	19.463
L101109K	1200 x 1050 mm; LEWB210CV	Nr	0.14	6.30	-	462.72	469.02	515.92	22.084
L101109L	1200 x 1200 mm; LEWB212CV	Nr	0.14	6.30	-	505.47	511.77	562.95	24.704
L101109M	1200 x 1350 mm; LEWB213CV	Nr	0.14	6.30	-	553.05	559.35	615.29	27.324
L101109N	1770 x 900 mm; LEWB309CVC	Nr	0.16	7.56	-	612.39	619.95	681.95	27.891
L101109O	1770 x 1050 mm; LEWB310CVC	Nr	0.16	7.56	-	648.45	656.01	721.61	31.710
L101109P	1770 x 1200 mm; LEWB312CVC	Nr	0.16	7.56	-	711.90	719.46	791.41	35.529
L101109Q	1770 x 1350 mm; LEWB313CVC	Nr	0.16	7.56	-	771.57	779.13	857.04	39.348
L101110	**Boulton and Paul softwood windows; Sovereign; all bar; transom; fitted wit 24 mm Low E insulating glazing units; fitted with standard cill; complete with ironmongery; size**								
L101110A	1200 x 1350 mm; LEWB213TX	Nr	0.14	6.30	-	618.74	625.04	687.54	27.324
L101110B	1200 x 1500 mm; LEWB215TX	Nr	0.14	6.30	-	714.88	721.18	793.30	29.945
L101110C	1770 x 1350 mm; LEWB313TXT	Nr	0.16	7.56	-	898.87	906.43	997.07	39.348
L101110D	1770 x 1500 mm; LEWB315TXT	Nr	0.16	7.56	-	1,044.05	1,051.61	1,156.77	43.167
L101110E	2339 x 1500 mm; LEWB415TXXT	Nr	0.19	8.77	-	1,373.66	1,382.43	1,520.67	56.367
L101110F	2339 x 1050 mm; LEWB410CVVC	Nr	0.19	8.77	-	895.58	904.35	994.79	25.764
L101110G	2339 x 1200 mm; LEWB412CVVC	Nr	0.19	8.77	-	978.12	986.89	1,085.58	28.867
L101110H	2339 x 1350 mm; LEWB413CVVC	Nr	0.19	8.77	-	1,052.56	1,061.33	1,167.46	31.970
L101111	**Boulton and Paul softwood windows; Sovereign; all bar; narrow module; fitted with 24 mm Low E glazing units; fitted with standard cill; complete with ironmongery; size**								
L101111A	488 x 750 mm; LEWBN07C	Nr	0.10	4.53	-	158.35	162.88	179.17	7.595
L101111B	488 x 900 mm; LEWBN09C	Nr	0.10	4.53	-	168.73	173.26	190.59	8.746
L101111C	488 x 1050 mm; LEWBN10C	Nr	0.10	4.53	-	180.72	185.25	203.78	9.896
L101111D	488 x 1200 mm; LEWBN12C	Nr	0.10	4.53	-	197.86	202.39	222.63	11.046
L101111E	488 x 900 mm; LEWBN09V	Nr	0.10	4.53	-	252.64	257.17	282.89	9.098
L101111F	488 x 1050 mm; LEWBN10V	Nr	0.10	4.53	-	255.24	259.77	285.75	10.249
L101111G	488 x 1200 mm; LEWBN12V	Nr	0.10	4.53	-	271.58	276.11	303.72	11.399
L101111H	915 x 1050 mm; LEWB2N10CV	Nr	0.12	5.79	-	427.33	433.12	476.43	15.575
L101111I	915 x 1200 mm; LEWB2N12CV	Nr	0.12	5.79	-	458.68	464.47	510.92	19.725
L101111J	915 x 1050 mm; LEWB2N10W	Nr	0.12	5.79	-	363.65	369.44	406.38	16.891
L101111K	915 x 1200 mm; LEWB2N12W	Nr	0.12	5.79	-	410.54	416.33	457.96	18.858
L101112	**Boulton and Paul softwood windows; Sovereign; Cottage; plain; fitted with standard cill; complete with ironmongery; size**								
L101112A	630 x 900 mm; WC109C	Nr	0.11	5.04	-	1.56	6.60	7.26	1.000
L101112B	630 x 1050 mm; WC110C	Nr	0.11	5.04	-	134.52	139.56	153.52	3.568
L101112C	630 x 1200 mm; WC112C	Nr	0.11	5.04	-	139.05	144.09	158.50	3.785
L101112D	630 x 1350 mm; WC113C	Nr	0.11	5.04	-	148.06	153.10	168.41	4.002
L101112E	1200 x 900 mm; WC209C	Nr	0.14	6.30	-	182.41	188.71	207.58	4.826
L101112F	1200 x 1050 mm; WC210C	Nr	0.14	6.30	-	189.05	195.35	214.89	5.151
L101112G	1200 x 1200 mm; WC212C	Nr	0.14	6.30	-	195.75	202.05	222.26	5.477

Major Works 2011		Unit	Labour Hours	Labour Net	Plant Net	Materials Net	Unit Net	Unit with 10%	CO$_2$
				£	£	£	£	£	Kg

L10   **L10: WINDOWS, ROOFLIGHTS, SCREENS AND LOUVRES**

L1011   **Standard softwood windows**

L101112   **Boulton and Paul softwood windows; Sovereign; Cottage; plain; fitted with standard cill; complete with ironmongery; size**

Code	Description	Unit	Labour Hours	Labour Net	Plant Net	Materials Net	Unit Net	Unit with 10%	CO$_2$
L101112H	1200 x 1350 mm; WC213C	Nr	0.14	6.30	-	206.40	212.70	233.97	5.802
L101112I	1200 x 900 mm; WC209CC	Nr	0.14	6.30	-	238.24	244.54	268.99	9.401
L101112J	1200 x 1050 mm; WC210CC	Nr	0.14	6.30	-	247.31	253.61	278.97	5.151
L101112K	1200 x 1200 mm; WC212CC	Nr	0.14	6.30	-	256.28	262.58	288.84	5.477
L101112L	1200 x 1350 mm; WC213CC	Nr	0.14	6.30	-	274.42	280.72	308.79	5.802
L101112M	1770 x 900 mm; WC309CC	Nr	0.16	7.56	-	276.01	283.57	311.93	6.301
L101112N	1770 x 1050 mm; WC310CC	Nr	0.16	7.56	-	285.68	293.24	322.56	6.734
L101112O	1770 x 1200 mm; WC312CC	Nr	0.16	7.56	-	295.54	303.10	333.41	7.168
L101112P	1770 x 1350 mm; WC313CC	Nr	0.16	7.56	-	312.98	320.54	352.59	7.602
L101112Q	2339 x 1050 mm; WC410CMC	Nr	0.19	8.77	-	361.57	370.34	407.37	3.568
L101112R	2339 x 1200 mm; WC412CMC	Nr	0.19	8.77	-	374.48	383.25	421.58	8.316
L101112S	2339 x 1350 mm; WC413CMC	Nr	0.19	8.77	-	395.58	404.35	444.79	9.401

L101113   **Boulton and Paul softwood windows; Sovereign; Cottage; divided casement; fitted with standard cill; complete with ironmongery; size**

Code	Description	Unit	Labour Hours	Labour Net	Plant Net	Materials Net	Unit Net	Unit with 10%	CO$_2$
L101113A	630 x 900 mm; WC109D	Nr	0.11	5.04	-	158.93	163.97	180.37	3.807
L101113B	630 x 1050 mm; WC110D	Nr	0.11	5.04	-	163.48	168.52	185.37	4.023
L101113C	630 x 1200 mm; WC112D	Nr	0.11	5.04	-	168.38	173.42	190.76	4.240
L101113D	630 x 1350 mm; WC113D	Nr	0.11	5.04	-	173.07	178.11	195.92	4.457
L101113E	915 x 1050 mm; WC2N10D	Nr	0.12	5.79	-	189.73	195.52	215.07	4.642
L101113F	915 x 1200 mm; WC2N12D	Nr	0.12	5.79	-	194.82	200.61	220.67	4.858
L101113G	915 x 1350 mm; WC2N13D	Nr	0.12	5.79	-	199.58	205.37	225.91	5.075
L101113H	1200 x 900 mm; WC209CD	Nr	0.14	6.30	-	271.39	277.69	305.46	4.425
L101113I	1200 x 1050 mm; WC210CD	Nr	0.14	6.30	-	279.93	286.23	314.85	6.019
L101113J	1200 x 1200 mm; WC212CD	Nr	0.14	6.30	-	290.22	296.52	326.17	6.344
L101113K	1200 x 1350 mm; WC213CD	Nr	0.14	6.30	-	301.02	307.32	338.05	6.669
L101113L	1770 x 900 mm; WC309CDC	Nr	0.16	7.56	-	372.57	380.13	418.14	7.580
L101113M	1770 x 1050 mm; WC310CDC	Nr	0.16	7.56	-	383.72	391.28	430.41	8.014
L101113N	1770 x 1200 mm; WC312CDC	Nr	0.16	7.56	-	398.82	406.38	447.02	8.448
L101113O	1770 x 1350 mm; WC313CDC	Nr	0.16	7.56	-	416.25	423.81	466.19	8.882
L101113P	2339 x 1050 mm; WC410CDDC	Nr	0.19	8.77	-	543.71	552.48	607.73	10.007
L101113Q	2339 x 1200 mm; WC412CDDC	Nr	0.19	8.77	-	563.78	572.55	629.81	10.549
L101113R	2339 x 1350 mm; WC413CDDC	Nr	0.19	8.77	-	584.43	593.20	652.52	11.092

L101114   **Boulton and Paul softwood windows; Sovereign; horizontal bar; plain; fitted with standard cill; complete with ironmongery; size**

Code	Description	Unit	Labour Hours	Labour Net	Plant Net	Materials Net	Unit Net	Unit with 10%	CO$_2$
L101114A	630 x 750 mm; WH107C	Nr	0.11	5.04	-	117.89	122.93	135.22	3.134
L101114B	630 x 900 mm; WH109C	Nr	0.11	5.04	-	122.16	127.20	139.92	3.351
L101114C	630 x 1050 mm; WH110C	Nr	0.11	5.04	-	126.42	131.46	144.61	3.568
L101114D	630 x 1200 mm; WH112C	Nr	0.11	5.04	-	130.95	135.99	149.59	3.785
L101114E	1200 x 1350 mm; WH113C	Nr	0.11	5.04	-	139.76	144.80	159.28	4.002
L101114F	1200 x 750 mm; WH207C	Nr	0.14	6.30	-	159.08	165.38	181.92	4.501
L101114G	1200 x 900 mm; WH209C	Nr	0.14	6.30	-	160.70	167.00	183.70	4.826
L101114H	1200 x 1050 mm; WH210C	Nr	0.14	6.30	-	161.61	167.91	184.70	5.151
L101114I	1200 x 1200 mm; WH212C	Nr	0.14	6.30	-	167.61	173.91	191.30	5.477
L101114J	1200 x 1350 mm; WH213C	Nr	0.14	6.30	-	187.83	194.13	213.54	5.802
L101114K	1770 x 900 mm; WH309CC	Nr	0.16	7.56	-	250.34	257.90	283.69	6.199
L101114L	1770 x 1050 mm; WH310CC	Nr	0.16	7.56	-	258.95	266.51	293.16	6.633
L101114M	1770 x 1200 mm; WH312CC	Nr	0.16	7.56	-	268.03	275.59	303.15	7.067
L101114N	1770 x 1350 mm; WH313CC	Nr	0.16	7.56	-	284.91	292.47	321.72	7.501
L101114O	2339 x 1050 mm; WH410CMC	Nr	0.19	8.77	-	326.07	334.84	368.32	8.316
L101114P	2339 x 1200 mm; WH412CMC	Nr	0.19	8.77	-	337.70	346.47	381.12	8.858
L101114Q	2339 x 1350 mm; WH413CMC	Nr	0.19	8.77	-	357.84	366.61	403.27	9.401

L101115   **Boulton and Paul softwood windows; Sovereign; horizontal bar; narrow module; fitted with standard cill; complete with ironmongery; size**

Code	Description	Unit	Labour Hours	Labour Net	Plant Net	Materials Net	Unit Net	Unit with 10%	CO$_2$
L101115A	488 x 900 mm; WHN09C	Nr	0.10	4.53	-	101.93	106.46	117.11	3.146
L101115B	488 x 1050 mm; WHN10C	Nr	0.10	4.53	-	106.53	111.06	122.17	3.363
L101115C	488 x 1200 mm; WHN12C	Nr	0.10	4.53	-	111.09	115.62	127.18	3.580
L101115D	488 x 1350 mm; WHN13C	Nr	0.10	4.53	-	120.51	125.04	137.54	3.796
L101115E	915 x 900 mm; WH2N09C	Nr	0.12	5.79	-	159.08	164.87	181.36	4.414
L101115F	915 x 1050 mm; WH2N10C	Nr	0.12	5.79	-	165.50	171.29	188.42	4.739

Major Works 2011		Unit	Labour Hours	Labour Net	Plant Net	Materials Net	Unit Net	Unit with 10%	CO$_2$
				£	£	£	£	£	Kg
L10	**L10: WINDOWS, ROOFLIGHTS, SCREENS AND LOUVRES**								
L1011	**Standard softwood windows**								
L101115	**Boulton and Paul softwood windows; Sovereign; horizontal bar; narrow module; fitted with standard cill; complete with ironmongery; size**								
L101115G	915 x 1200 mm; WH2N12C	Nr	0.12	5.79	-	172.06	177.85	195.64	5.064
L101115H	915 x 1350 mm; WH2N13C	Nr	0.12	5.79	-	182.73	188.52	207.37	5.390
L101115I	915 x 900 mm; WH2N09CC	Nr	0.12	5.79	-	211.79	217.58	239.34	4.414
L101115J	915 x 1050 mm; WH2N10CC	Nr	0.12	5.79	-	220.42	226.21	248.83	4.739
L101115K	915 x 1200 mm; WH2N12CC	Nr	0.12	5.79	-	229.10	234.89	258.38	5.064
L101115L	915 x 1350 mm; WH2N13CC	Nr	0.12	5.79	-	244.43	250.22	275.24	5.390
L101115M	1342 x 900 mm; WH3N09CC	Nr	0.15	7.05	-	238.15	245.20	269.72	6.652
L101115N	1342 x 1050 mm; WH3N10CC	Nr	0.15	7.05	-	247.90	254.95	280.45	7.086
L101115O	1342 x 1200 mm; WH3N12CC	Nr	0.15	7.05	-	257.49	264.54	290.99	7.520
L101115P	1342 x 1350 mm; WH3N13CC	Nr	0.15	7.05	-	274.73	281.78	309.96	7.953
L101115Q	1770 x 1050 mm; W4N10CMC	Nr	0.18	8.31	-	314.83	323.14	355.45	8.773
L101115R	1770 x 1200 mm; W4N12CMC	Nr	0.18	8.31	-	326.53	334.84	368.32	9.315
L101115S	1770 x 1350 mm; W4N13CMC	Nr	0.18	8.31	-	347.39	355.70	391.27	9.857
L101116	**Boulton and Paul softwood windows; Sovereign; horizontal bar; divided casement; fitted with standard cill; complete with ironmongery; size**								
L101116B	630 x 900 mm; WH109D	Nr	0.11	5.04	-	151.26	156.30	171.93	3.807
L101116C	630 x 1050 mm; WH110D	Nr	0.11	5.04	-	155.90	160.94	177.03	4.023
L101116D	630 x 1200 mm; WH112D	Nr	0.11	5.04	-	160.43	165.47	182.02	4.240
L101116E	1200 x 1350 mm; WH113D	Nr	0.11	5.04	-	164.60	169.64	186.60	4.457
L101116G	1200 x 900 mm; WH209CD	Nr	0.14	6.30	-	255.66	261.96	288.16	5.693
L101116H	1200 x 1050 mm; WH210CD	Nr	0.14	6.30	-	263.68	269.98	296.98	6.019
L101116I	1200 x 1200 mm; WH212CD	Nr	0.14	6.30	-	273.55	279.85	307.84	6.344
L101116J	1200 x 1350 mm; WH213CD	Nr	0.14	6.30	-	283.70	290.00	319.00	6.669
L101116K	1770 x 900 mm; WH309CDC	Nr	0.16	7.56	-	354.29	361.85	398.04	7.580
L101116L	1770 x 1050 mm; WH310CDC	Nr	0.16	7.56	-	364.91	372.47	409.72	8.014
L101116M	1770 x 1200 mm; WH312CDC	Nr	0.16	7.56	-	379.80	387.36	426.10	8.448
L101116N	1770 x 1350 mm; WH313CDC	Nr	0.16	7.56	-	396.92	404.48	444.93	8.882
L101116O	2339 x 1050 mm; WH4N410CDDC	Nr	0.19	8.77	-	519.65	528.42	581.26	10.007
L101116P	2339 x 1200 mm; WH4N412CDDC	Nr	0.19	8.77	-	538.98	547.75	602.53	10.549
L101116Q	2339 x 1350 mm; WH4N413CDDC	Nr	0.19	8.77	-	559.30	568.07	624.88	11.092
L101117	**Boulton and Paul softwood windows; Sovereign; top hung; fitted with standard cill; complete with ironmongery; size**								
L101117A	630 x 450 mm; W104A	Nr	0.11	5.04	-	101.59	106.63	117.29	2.701
L101117B	630 x 600 mm; W106A	Nr	0.11	5.04	-	106.57	111.61	122.77	2.917
L101117C	630 x 750 mm; W107A	Nr	0.11	5.04	-	111.10	116.14	127.75	3.134
L101117D	630 x 900 mm; W109A	Nr	0.11	5.04	-	114.45	119.49	131.44	3.351
L101117E	630 x 1050 mm; W110A	Nr	0.11	5.04	-	118.90	123.94	136.33	3.568
L101117F	630 x 1200 mm; W112A	Nr	0.11	5.04	-	122.94	127.98	140.78	3.785
L101117G	915 x 450 mm; W2N04A	Nr	0.12	5.79	-	122.94	128.73	141.60	3.113
L101117H	915 x 600 mm; W2N06A	Nr	0.12	5.79	-	127.85	133.64	147.00	3.329
L101117I	915 x 750 mm; W2N07A	Nr	0.12	5.79	-	132.19	137.98	151.78	3.546
L101117J	915 x 900 mm; W2N09A	Nr	0.12	5.79	-	141.47	147.26	161.99	3.763
L101117K	915 x 1050 mm; W2N10A	Nr	0.12	5.79	-	146.44	152.23	167.45	3.980
L101117L	915 x 1200 mm; W2N12A	Nr	0.12	5.79	-	150.48	156.27	171.90	4.197
L101117M	915 x 1350 mm; W2N13AS	Nr	0.14	6.30	-	165.41	171.71	188.88	4.414
L101117N	1200 x 450 mm; W204A	Nr	0.11	5.04	-	131.51	136.55	150.21	3.525
L101117O	1200 x 600 mm; W206A	Nr	0.14	6.30	-	143.48	149.78	164.76	3.742
L101117P	1200 x 750 mm; W207A	Nr	0.14	6.30	-	132.19	138.49	152.34	3.546
L101117Q	1200 x 900 mm; W209A	Nr	0.14	6.30	-	156.65	162.95	179.25	4.175
L101117R	1200 x 1050 mm; W210A	Nr	0.14	6.30	-	161.55	167.85	184.64	4.392
L101117S	1200 x 1200 mm; W212A	Nr	0.14	6.30	-	166.28	172.58	189.84	4.609
L101117T	1200 x 1350 mm; W213AS	Nr	0.14	6.30	-	181.40	187.70	206.47	4.826
L101117U	1770 x 450 mm; W304AE	Nr	0.16	7.56	-	149.58	157.14	172.85	4.674
L101117V	1770 x 600 mm; W306AE	Nr	0.16	7.56	-	167.42	174.98	192.48	4.999
L101117W	1770 x 750 mm; W307AE	Nr	0.16	7.56	-	173.28	180.84	198.92	5.325
L101117X	1770 x 900 mm; W309AE	Nr	0.16	7.56	-	183.08	190.64	209.70	5.650
L101117Y	1770 x 1050 mm; W310AE	Nr	0.16	7.56	-	189.46	197.02	216.72	5.975
L101117Z	1770 x 1200 mm; W312AE	Nr	0.16	7.56	-	195.01	202.57	222.83	6.301

Major Works 2011		Unit	Labour Hours	Labour Net	Plant Net	Materials Net	Unit Net	Unit with 10%	CO$_2$
				£	£	£	£	£	Kg
L10	**L10: WINDOWS, ROOFLIGHTS, SCREENS AND LOUVRES**								
L1011	**Standard softwood windows**								
L101119	**Boulton and Paul softwood windows; Sovereign; direct glazed; fitted with standard cill; size**								
L101119A	630 x 1050 mm; W110DG	Nr	0.11	5.04	-	67.25	72.29	79.52	4.023
L101119B	630 x 1200 mm; W112DG	Nr	0.11	5.04	-	69.28	74.32	81.75	4.240
L101119C	630 x 1350 mm; W113DG	Nr	0.11	5.04	-	74.55	79.59	87.55	4.457
L101119D	1200 x 450 mm; W204DG	Nr	0.14	6.30	-	83.56	89.86	98.85	4.175
L101119E	1200 x 600 mm; W206DG	Nr	0.14	6.30	-	84.57	90.87	99.96	4.609
L101119F	1200 x 750 mm; W207DG	Nr	0.14	6.30	-	86.80	93.10	102.41	5.043
L101119G	1200 x 900 mm; W209DG	Nr	0.14	6.30	-	93.20	99.50	109.45	5.477
L101119H	1200 x 1050 mm; W210DG	Nr	0.14	6.30	-	96.16	102.46	112.71	5.910
L101119I	1200 x 1200 mm; W212DG	Nr	0.14	6.30	-	98.57	104.87	115.36	6.344
L101119J	1200 x 1350 mm; W213DG	Nr	0.14	6.30	-	101.66	107.96	118.76	6.778
L101121	**Boulton and Paul softwood windows; Sovereign; Regency; non-bar; fitted with standard cill; complete with ironmongery; size**								
L101121A	488 x 750 mm; WSRN07	Nr	0.08	3.78	-	166.30	170.08	187.09	3.282
L101121B	488 x 900 mm; WSRN09	Nr	0.08	3.78	-	172.63	176.41	194.05	3.499
L101121C	488 x 1050 mm; WSRN10	Nr	0.08	3.78	-	179.00	182.78	201.06	3.716
L101121D	488 x 1200 mm; WSRN12	Nr	0.08	3.78	-	185.34	189.12	208.03	3.932
L101121E	488 x 1350 mm; WSRN13	Nr	0.08	3.78	-	191.59	195.37	214.91	4.149
L101121F	488 x 1500 mm; WSRN15	Nr	0.08	3.78	-	197.89	201.67	221.84	4.366
L101121G	630 x 750 mm; WSR107	Nr	0.11	5.04	-	173.84	178.88	196.77	3.590
L101121H	630 x 900 mm; WSR109	Nr	0.11	5.04	-	180.18	185.22	203.74	3.807
L101121I	630 x 1050 mm; WSR110	Nr	0.11	5.04	-	186.45	191.49	210.64	4.023
L101121J	630 x 1200 mm; WSR112	Nr	0.11	5.04	-	192.75	197.79	217.57	4.240
L101121K	630 x 1350 mm; WSR113	Nr	0.11	5.04	-	199.02	204.06	224.47	4.457
L101121L	630 x 1500 mm; WSR115	Nr	0.11	5.04	-	205.46	210.50	231.55	4.674
L101121M	630 x 1650 mm; WSR116	Nr	0.11	5.04	-	211.79	216.83	238.51	4.891
L101121N	915 x 750 mm; WSR2N07	Nr	0.14	6.30	-	186.45	192.75	212.03	4.208
L101121O	915 x 900 mm; WSR2N09	Nr	0.14	6.30	-	192.75	199.05	218.96	4.425
L101121P	915 x 1050 mm; WSR2N10	Nr	0.14	6.30	-	199.02	205.32	225.85	4.642
L101121Q	915 x 1200 mm; WSR2N12	Nr	0.14	6.30	-	205.46	211.76	232.94	4.858
L101121R	915 x 1350 mm; WSR2N13	Nr	0.14	6.30	-	211.71	218.01	239.81	5.075
L101121S	915 x 1500 mm; WSR2N15	Nr	0.14	6.30	-	217.40	223.70	246.07	5.292
L101121T	915 x 1650 mm; WSR2N16	Nr	0.14	6.30	-	224.36	230.66	253.73	5.509
L101121U	1200 x 900 mm; WSR209	Nr	0.14	6.30	-	204.16	210.46	231.51	5.043
L101121V	1200 x 1050 mm; WSR210	Nr	0.14	6.30	-	211.71	218.01	239.81	5.260
L101121W	1200 x 1200 mm; WSR212	Nr	0.14	6.30	-	217.85	224.15	246.57	5.477
L101121X	1200 x 1350 mm; WSR213	Nr	0.14	6.30	-	224.29	230.59	253.65	5.693
L101121Y	1200 x 1500 mm; WSR215	Nr	0.14	6.30	-	230.56	236.86	260.55	5.910
L101121Z	1200 x 1650 mm; WSR216	Nr	0.14	6.30	-	237.90	244.20	268.62	6.127
L101122	**Boulton and Paul softwood windows; Sovereign; Regency; non-bar; fitted with standard cill; complete with ironmongery; size**								
L101122B	1200 x 1050 mm; WSR210D	Nr	0.14	6.30	-	366.58	372.88	410.17	5.260
L101122C	1200 x 1200 mm; WSR212D	Nr	0.14	6.30	-	379.29	385.59	424.15	5.477
L101122D	1200 x 1350 mm; WSR213D	Nr	0.14	6.30	-	391.78	398.08	437.89	5.693
L101122E	1200 x 1500 mm; WSR215D	Nr	0.14	6.30	-	404.35	410.65	451.72	5.910
L101122F	1200 x 1650 mm; WSR216D	Nr	0.14	6.30	-	418.77	425.07	467.58	6.127
L101122G	1770 x 1050 mm; WSR4N10	Nr	0.16	7.56	-	391.78	399.34	439.27	6.496
L101122H	1770 x 1200 mm; WSR4N12	Nr	0.16	7.56	-	404.35	411.91	453.10	6.713
L101122I	1770 x 1350 mm; WSR4N13	Nr	0.16	7.56	-	416.85	424.41	466.85	6.930
L101122J	1770 x 1500 mm; WSR4N15	Nr	0.16	7.56	-	429.42	436.98	480.68	7.147
L101123	**Boulton and Paul softwood windows; Sovereign; Regency; vertical bar; fitted with standard cill; complete with ironmongery; size**								
L101123G	630 x 750 mm; WSRV107	Nr	0.11	5.04	-	203.17	208.21	229.03	3.590
L101123H	630 x 900 mm; WSRV109	Nr	0.11	5.04	-	210.36	215.40	236.94	3.807
L101123I	630 x 1050 mm; WSRV110	Nr	0.11	5.04	-	217.42	222.46	244.71	4.023
L101123J	630 x 1200 mm; WSRV112	Nr	0.11	5.04	-	224.59	229.63	252.59	4.240
L101123K	630 x 1350 mm; WSRV113	Nr	0.11	5.04	-	231.94	236.98	260.68	4.457
L101123L	630 x 1500 mm; WSRV115	Nr	0.11	5.04	-	239.02	244.06	268.47	4.674
L101123M	630 x 1650 mm; WSRV116	Nr	0.11	5.04	-	246.17	251.21	276.33	4.891
L101123N	915 x 750 mm; WSRV2N07	Nr	0.14	6.30	-	216.43	222.73	245.00	4.750
L101123O	915 x 900 mm; WSRV2N09	Nr	0.14	6.30	-	223.51	229.81	252.79	5.075
L101123P	915 x 1050 mm; WSRV2N10	Nr	0.14	6.30	-	230.63	236.93	260.62	5.401

Major Works 2011		Unit	Labour Hours	Labour Net	Plant Net	Materials Net	Unit Net	Unit with 10%	CO$_2$
				£	£	£	£	£	Kg
L10	**L10: WINDOWS, ROOFLIGHTS, SCREENS AND LOUVRES**								
L1011	**Standard softwood windows**								
L101123	**Boulton and Paul softwood windows; Sovereign; Regency; vertical bar; fitted with standard cill; complete with ironmongery; size**								
L101123Q	915 x 1200 mm; WSRV2N12	Nr	0.14	6.30	-	237.79	244.09	268.50	5.726
L101123R	915 x 1350 mm; WSRV2N13	Nr	0.14	6.30	-	244.96	251.26	276.39	6.051
L101123S	915 x 1500 mm; WSRV2N15	Nr	0.14	6.30	-	252.00	258.30	284.13	6.377
L101123T	915 x 1650 mm; WSRV2N16	Nr	0.14	6.30	-	259.43	265.73	292.30	6.702
L101123U	1200 x 900 mm; WSRV209	Nr	0.14	6.30	-	237.79	244.09	268.50	5.693
L101123V	1200 x 1050 mm; WSRV210	Nr	0.14	6.30	-	243.67	249.97	274.97	6.019
L101123W	1200 x 1200 mm; WSRV212	Nr	0.14	6.30	-	250.94	257.24	282.96	6.344
L101123X	1200 x 1350 mm; WSRV213	Nr	0.14	6.30	-	258.01	264.31	290.74	6.669
L101123Y	1200 x 1500 mm; WSRV215	Nr	0.14	6.30	-	265.29	271.59	298.75	6.995
L101123Z	1200 x 1650 mm; WSRV216	Nr	0.14	6.30	-	275.92	282.22	310.44	7.320
L101124	**Boulton and Paul softwood windows; Sovereign; Regency; vertical bar; fitted with standard cill; complete with ironmongery; size**								
L101124C	1770 x 1050 mm; WSRV4N10	Nr	0.16	7.56	-	467.75	475.31	522.84	7.255
L101124D	1770 x 1200 mm; WSRV4N12	Nr	0.16	7.56	-	483.35	490.91	540.00	7.580
L101124E	1770 x 1350 mm; WSRV4N13	Nr	0.16	7.56	-	498.67	506.23	556.85	7.906
L101124F	1770 x 1500 mm; WSRV4N15	Nr	0.16	7.56	-	513.64	521.20	573.32	8.231
L101124G	1770 x 1600 mm; WSRV4N16	Nr	0.16	7.56	-	539.61	547.17	601.89	8.556
L101124H	2339 x 1050 mm; WSRV410	Nr	0.19	8.77	-	475.03	483.80	532.18	10.007
L101124I	2339 x 1200 mm; WSRV412	Nr	0.19	8.77	-	490.35	499.12	549.03	10.549
L101124J	2339 x 1350 mm; WSRV413	Nr	0.19	8.77	-	505.66	514.43	565.87	11.092
L101125	**Boulton and Paul softwood windows; Sovereign; designer range; size**								
L101125L	630 x 345 mm; semi-circular; W638C	Nr	0.14	6.30	-	219.41	225.71	248.28	6.074
L101125M	915 x 488 mm; semi-circular; W952D	Nr	0.16	7.56	-	251.57	259.13	285.04	7.411
L101125N	1200 x 630 mm; semi-circular; W1267E	Nr	0.19	8.77	-	257.26	266.03	292.63	9.083
L101125O	630 x 345 mm; semi-circular; W638CRB	Nr	0.14	6.30	-	255.80	262.10	288.31	6.074
L101125P	915 x 488 mm; semi-circular; W952DRB	Nr	0.16	7.56	-	289.05	296.61	326.27	7.411
L101125Q	1200 x 630 mm; semi-circular; W1267ERB	Nr	0.19	8.77	-	295.60	304.37	334.81	9.083
L101125T	600 mm dia; circular; W120BE	Nr	0.16	7.56	-	164.50	172.06	189.27	6.406
L101125U	600 mm dia; circular; W120BP	Nr	0.16	7.56	-	358.43	365.99	402.59	6.406
L101127	**Boulton and Paul softwood windows; sliding sash; non-bar; fitted with standard cill; complete with ironmongery; size**								
L101127A	410 x 1050 mm; TVS0410	Nr	0.50	8.49	-	399.59	408.08	448.89	2.838
L101127B	410 x 1350 mm; TVS0413	Nr	0.50	8.49	-	427.04	435.53	479.08	3.272
L101127C	410 x 1650 mm; TVS0416	Nr	0.50	8.49	-	458.38	466.87	513.56	3.706
L101127D	635 x 1050 mm; TVS0610	Nr	0.60	10.19	-	454.69	464.88	511.37	3.326
L101127E	635 x 1350 mm; TVS0613	Nr	0.60	10.19	-	482.75	492.94	542.23	3.760
L101127F	635 x 1650 mm; TVS0616	Nr	0.60	10.19	-	510.48	520.67	572.74	4.194
L101127G	860 x 1050 mm; TVS0810	Nr	0.70	11.89	-	482.75	494.64	544.10	3.814
L101127H	860 x 1350 mm; TVS0813	Nr	0.70	11.89	-	510.48	522.37	574.61	4.248
L101127I	860 x 1650 mm; TVS0816	Nr	0.70	11.89	-	545.43	557.32	613.05	4.682
L101127J	1085 x 1050 mm; TVS1010	Nr	0.80	13.58	-	510.48	524.06	576.47	4.302
L101127K	1085 x 1350 mm; TVS1013	Nr	0.43	20.11	-	545.43	565.54	622.09	4.736
L101127L	1085 x 1650 mm; TVS1016	Nr	0.80	13.58	-	569.79	583.37	641.71	5.170
L101127M	1699 x 1050 mm; TVS1710	Nr	0.90	15.28	-	917.03	932.31	1,025.54	6.428
L101127N	1699 x 1350 mm; TVS1713	Nr	0.90	15.28	-	981.27	996.55	1,096.21	7.078
L101127O	1699 x 1650 mm; TVS1716	Nr	0.90	15.28	-	1,038.36	1,053.64	1,159.00	7.729
L101127P	1638 x 1050 mm; TVS1610	Nr	0.90	15.28	-	1,010.80	1,026.08	1,128.69	7.089
L101127Q	1638 x 1350 mm; TVS1613	Nr	0.90	15.28	-	1,094.14	1,109.42	1,220.36	7.957
L101127R	1638 x 1650 mm; TVS1616	Nr	0.90	15.28	-	1,181.18	1,196.46	1,316.11	8.824
L101127S	1863 x 1050 mm; TVS1810	Nr	0.90	15.28	-	1,045.49	1,060.77	1,166.85	7.577
L101127T	1863 x 1350 mm; TVS1813	Nr	0.90	15.28	-	1,129.02	1,144.30	1,258.73	8.445
L101127U	1863 x 1650 mm; TVS1816	Nr	0.90	15.28	-	1,212.77	1,228.05	1,350.86	9.312

Windows, Doors & Stairs

	Unit	Labour Hours	Labour Net £	Plant Net £	Materials Net £	Unit Net £	Unit with 10% £	CO₂ Kg

	Unit	Labour Hours	Labour Net £	Plant Net £	Materials Net £	Unit Net £	Unit with 10% £	CO$_2$ Kg
L10	**L10: WINDOWS, ROOFLIGHTS, SCREENS AND LOUVRES**							
L1011	**Standard softwood windows**							
L101128	**Boulton and Paul softwood windows; semi-circular feature for site coupling with sliding sash windows; fitted with standard cill; complete with ironmongery; size**							
L101128A	635 x 343 mm; VSSEM6	Nr	0.25	4.25	-	322.49	326.74	359.41	1.433
L101128B	860 x 458 mm; VSSEM8	Nr	0.30	5.09	-	346.87	351.96	387.16	1.856
L101128C	1085 x 568 mm; VSSEM10	Nr	0.35	5.94	-	379.33	385.27	423.80	2.269
L101128D	635 x 343 mm; VSSEM6B	Nr	0.25	4.25	-	398.43	402.68	442.95	1.929
L101128E	860 x 458 mm; VSSEM8B	Nr	0.30	5.09	-	426.22	431.31	474.44	2.519
L101128F	1085 x 568 mm; VSSEM10B	Nr	0.35	5.94	-	471.29	477.23	524.95	3.090
L101130	**Boulton and Paul softwood square bay assemblies; including softwood joining and make-up kit; extra over cost of frames; ref**							
L101130A	Two return ends; SQ2	Nr	0.70	11.89	-	244.17	256.06	281.67	7.377
L101130B	Two return ends; SQ3	Nr	0.90	15.28	-	244.17	259.45	285.40	8.200
L101130C	Two return ends; SQ4	Nr	1.20	20.38	-	244.17	264.55	291.01	9.024
L101130D	Two return ends; SQ5	Nr	1.50	25.47	-	244.17	269.64	296.60	9.294
L101130E	One return end; SQR2	Nr	0.70	11.89	-	117.15	129.04	141.94	6.488
L101130F	One return end; SQR3	Nr	0.90	15.28	-	117.15	132.43	145.67	7.310
L101130G	One return end; SQR4	Nr	0.65	30.14	-	117.15	147.29	162.02	8.134
L101130H	One return end; SQR5	Nr	1.50	25.47	-	117.15	142.62	156.88	8.405
L101130I	Narrow module; two return ends; SQ2N	Nr	0.70	11.89	-	244.17	256.06	281.67	6.551
L101130J	Narrow module; two return ends; SQ3N	Nr	0.90	15.28	-	244.17	259.45	285.40	7.169
L101130K	Narrow module; two return ends; SQ4N	Nr	1.20	20.38	-	244.17	264.55	291.01	7.786
L101130L	Narrow module; one return end; SQR2N	Nr	0.70	11.89	-	117.15	129.04	141.94	5.869
L101130M	Narrow module; one return end; SQR3N	Nr	0.90	15.28	-	117.15	132.43	145.67	6.486
L101130N	Narrow module; one return end; SQR4N	Nr	1.20	20.38	-	117.15	137.53	151.28	7.104
L101131	**Boulton and Paul softwood splay bay assemblies; including softwood joining and make-up kit; extra over cost of frames; ref**							
L101131B	Two return ends; SP2	Nr	0.90	15.28	-	244.17	259.45	285.40	7.416
L101131C	Two return ends; SP3	Nr	1.20	20.38	-	244.17	264.55	291.01	8.240
L101131D	Two return ends; SP4	Nr	1.50	25.47	-	244.17	269.64	296.60	8.802
L101131F	One return end; SPR2	Nr	0.90	15.28	-	117.15	132.43	145.67	6.511
L101131G	One return end; SPR3	Nr	1.20	20.38	-	117.15	137.53	151.28	7.335
L101131H	One return end; SPR4	Nr	1.50	25.47	-	117.15	142.62	156.88	7.897
L101131I	Narrow module; two return ends; SP2N	Nr	0.90	15.28	-	244.17	259.45	285.40	6.590
L101131J	Narrow module; two return ends; SP3N	Nr	1.20	20.38	-	244.17	264.55	291.01	7.208
L101131K	Narrow module; two return ends; SP4N	Nr	1.50	25.47	-	244.17	269.64	296.60	7.825
L101131L	Narrow module; one return end; SPR2N	Nr	0.90	15.28	-	117.15	132.43	145.67	5.892
L101131M	Narrow module; one return end; SPR3N	Nr	1.20	20.38	-	117.15	137.53	151.28	6.509
L101131N	Narrow module; one return end; SPR4N	Nr	1.50	25.47	-	117.15	142.62	156.88	7.127
L101143	**Boulton and Paul softwood windows; Hi-Profile Combi; bespoke manufacture; complete with all ironmongery**							
L101143A	450 x 900 mm	Nr	0.08	3.78	-	239.46	243.24	267.56	3.660
L101143B	450 x 1050 mm	Nr	0.08	3.78	-	244.94	248.72	273.59	3.877
L101143C	450 x 1200 mm	Nr	0.08	3.78	-	251.09	254.87	280.36	4.094
L101143D	600 x 600 mm	Nr	0.11	5.04	-	225.15	230.19	253.21	3.443
L101143E	600 x 900 mm	Nr	0.11	5.04	-	235.21	240.25	264.28	3.877
L101143F	600 x 1050 mm	Nr	0.11	5.04	-	240.82	245.86	270.45	4.094
L101143G	600 x 1200 mm	Nr	0.11	5.04	-	246.73	251.77	276.95	5.178
L101143H	600 x 1350 mm	Nr	0.11	5.04	-	271.15	276.19	303.81	5.503
L101143I	600 x 1500 mm	Nr	0.11	5.04	-	279.18	284.22	312.64	5.829
L101143J	600 x 1600 mm	Nr	0.11	5.04	-	284.78	289.82	318.80	7.202

Major Works 2011		Unit	Labour Hours	Labour Net	Plant Net	Materials Net	Unit Net	Unit with 10%	CO₂
				£	£	£	£	£	Kg
L10	**L10: WINDOWS, ROOFLIGHTS, SCREENS AND LOUVRES**								
L1011	**Standard softwood windows**								
L101143	**Boulton and Paul softwood windows; Hi-Profile Combi; bespoke manufacture; complete with all ironmongery**								
L101143K	900 x 600 mm	Nr	0.14	6.30	-	246.84	253.14	278.45	3.877
L101143L	900 x 900 mm	Nr	0.14	6.30	-	256.98	263.28	289.61	4.311
L101143M	900 x 1050 mm	Nr	0.14	6.30	-	262.02	268.32	295.15	4.527
L101143N	900 x 1200 mm	Nr	0.14	6.30	-	269.18	275.48	303.03	5.612
L101143O	900 x 1350 mm	Nr	0.14	6.30	-	295.91	302.21	332.43	5.937
L101143P	900 x 1500 mm	Nr	0.14	6.30	-	304.67	310.97	342.07	6.262
L101143Q	900 x 1600 mm	Nr	0.14	6.30	-	310.78	317.08	348.79	6.479
L101143R	1200 x 600 mm	Nr	0.14	6.30	-	269.18	275.48	303.03	4.311
L101143S	1200 x 900 mm	Nr	0.14	6.30	-	278.97	285.27	313.80	4.744
L101143T	1200 x 1050 mm	Nr	0.14	6.30	-	285.58	291.88	321.07	4.961
L101143U	1200 x 1200 mm	Nr	0.14	6.30	-	293.18	299.48	329.43	6.046
L101143V	1200 x 1350 mm	Nr	0.14	6.30	-	322.23	328.53	361.38	6.371
L101143W	1200 x 1500 mm	Nr	0.14	6.30	-	331.89	338.19	372.01	6.696
L101143X	1200 x 1600 mm	Nr	0.14	6.30	-	338.60	344.90	379.39	6.913
L101143Y	1350 x 600 mm	Nr	0.15	6.91	-	275.50	282.41	310.65	5.395
L101143Z	1350 x 900 mm	Nr	0.15	6.91	-	287.14	294.05	323.46	6.262
L101145	**Boulton and Paul softwood windows; Hi-Profile Combi; bespoke manufacture; complete with all ironmongery**								
L101145A	1350 x 1050 mm	Nr	0.15	6.91	-	294.21	301.12	331.23	6.696
L101145B	1350 x 1200 mm	Nr	0.15	6.91	-	303.64	310.55	341.61	7.130
L101145C	1350 x 1350 mm	Nr	0.15	6.91	-	333.86	340.77	374.85	7.564
L101145D	1500 x 600 mm	Nr	0.15	7.14	-	290.28	297.42	327.16	5.612
L101145E	1500 x 900 mm	Nr	0.15	7.14	-	297.88	305.02	335.52	6.479
L101145F	1500 x 1050 mm	Nr	0.15	7.14	-	317.80	324.94	357.43	6.913
L101145G	1500 x 1200 mm	Nr	0.15	7.14	-	328.73	335.87	369.46	7.347
L101145H	1500 x 1350 mm	Nr	0.15	7.14	-	344.24	351.38	386.52	7.781
L101145I	1500 x 1500 mm	Nr	0.15	7.14	-	352.50	359.64	395.60	8.214
L101145J	1800 x 1050 mm	Nr	0.16	7.56	-	343.23	350.79	385.87	7.347
L101145K	1800 x 1200 mm	Nr	0.16	7.56	-	349.35	356.91	392.60	7.781
L101145L	1800 x 1500 mm	Nr	0.16	7.56	-	374.86	382.42	420.66	8.648
L101147	**Boulton and Paul softwood windows; Hi-Profile; single casement and direct glazed; complete with all ironmongery**								
L101147D	R2109D; 2100 x 900 mm	Nr	0.17	8.03	-	334.96	342.99	377.29	7.347
L101147E	R2110D; 2100 x 1050 mm	Nr	0.17	8.03	-	353.18	361.21	397.33	7.781
L101147F	R2112D; 2100 x 1200 mm	Nr	0.17	8.03	-	363.83	371.86	409.05	8.214
L101147G	R2209D; 2250 x 900 mm	Nr	0.17	8.03	-	340.36	348.39	383.23	7.564
L101147H	R2210D; 2250 x 1050 mm	Nr	0.17	8.03	-	358.61	366.64	403.30	7.997
L101147I	R2212D; 2250 x 1200 mm	Nr	0.17	8.03	-	369.27	377.30	415.03	8.431
L101147J	R2409D; 2400 x 900 mm	Nr	0.19	8.77	-	347.58	356.35	391.99	8.431
L101147K	R2410D; 2400 x 1050 mm	Nr	0.19	8.77	-	366.50	375.27	412.80	8.973
L101147L	R2412D; 2400 x 1200 mm	Nr	0.19	8.77	-	377.53	386.30	424.93	8.973
L101147M	R2415D; 2400 x 1500 mm	Nr	0.19	8.77	-	415.68	424.45	466.90	10.600
L101147N	R3015D; 3000 x 1500 mm	Nr	0.20	9.19	-	448.72	457.91	503.70	11.467
L101147O	R3615D; 3600 x 1500 mm	Nr	0.20	9.43	-	481.71	491.14	540.25	12.335
L101149	**Boulton and Paul softwood windows; Hi-Profile; feature windows; complete with all ironmongery**								
L101149A	R04F12; 450 x 2100 mm	Nr	0.11	5.04	-	357.28	362.32	398.55	4.809
L101149B	R06F12; 600 x 2100 mm	Nr	0.12	5.79	-	466.88	472.67	519.94	5.427
L101149C	R09F12; 900 x 2100 mm	Nr	0.12	5.79	-	480.35	486.14	534.75	5.427
L101149D	R12F12; 1200 x 2100 mm	Nr	0.15	6.77	-	542.13	548.90	603.79	6.615
L101149E	R15F12; 1500 x 2100 mm	Nr	0.18	8.17	-	724.92	733.09	806.40	8.269
L101151	**Boulton and Paul softwood windows; Skyview reversible roof windows; complete with ironmongery**								
L101151A	550 x 780 mm; RL508	Nr	0.85	14.43	-	193.15	207.58	228.34	1.923
L101151B	550 x 980 mm; RL510	Nr	0.90	15.28	-	213.84	229.12	252.03	2.212
L101151C	780 x 980 mm; RL810	Nr	1.00	16.98	-	242.93	259.91	285.90	2.545
L101151D	780 x 1180 mm; RL812	Nr	1.30	22.07	-	252.39	274.46	301.91	2.834
L101151E	780 x 1400 mm; RL814FE	Nr	1.50	25.47	-	428.44	453.91	499.30	3.152
L101151F	1140 x 1180 mm; RL1112	Nr	1.50	25.47	-	310.05	335.52	369.07	3.354
L101151G	450 x 550 mm; RL555	Nr	0.85	14.43	-	143.51	157.94	173.73	1.446

Windows, Doors & Stairs

		Unit	Labour Hours	Labour Net £	Plant Net £	Materials Net £	Unit Net £	Unit with 10% £	CO₂ Kg
L10	**L10: WINDOWS, ROOFLIGHTS, SCREENS AND LOUVRES**								
L1012	**Softwood window sundries and accessories**								
L101251	**Boulton and Paul Skyview roof window tile flashing units**								
L101251A	RL508TF	Nr	0.90	15.28	-	57.05	72.33	79.56	1.923
L101251B	RL510TF	Nr	0.95	16.13	-	61.34	77.47	85.22	2.212
L101251C	RL810TF	Nr	1.00	16.98	-	65.85	82.83	91.11	2.545
L101251D	RL812TF	Nr	1.25	21.23	-	73.36	94.59	104.05	2.834
L101251E	RL814TF	Nr	1.25	21.23	-	78.96	100.19	110.21	3.152
L101251F	RL1112TF	Nr	1.55	26.32	-	82.32	108.64	119.50	3.354
L101252	**Boulton and Paul softwood window surround sets; to suit window size**								
L101252A	488 x 450 mm	Set	0.20	3.40	-	59.38	62.78	69.06	4.009
L101252B	488 x 600 mm	Set	0.20	3.40	-	64.21	67.61	74.37	4.525
L101252C	488 x 750 mm	Set	0.20	3.40	-	69.81	73.21	80.53	5.042
L101252D	488 x 900 mm	Set	0.20	3.40	-	74.91	78.31	86.14	5.558
L101252E	488 x 1050 mm	Set	0.20	3.40	-	79.57	82.97	91.27	6.075
L101252F	488 x 1200 mm	Set	0.20	3.40	-	85.33	88.73	97.60	6.591
L101252G	488 x 1350 mm	Set	0.20	3.40	-	90.50	93.90	103.29	7.107
L101252H	488 x 1500 mm	Set	0.20	3.40	-	95.46	98.86	108.75	7.624
L101252I	630 x 450 mm	Set	0.23	3.82	-	61.91	65.73	72.30	4.498
L101252J	630 x 600 mm	Set	0.23	3.82	-	67.01	70.83	77.91	5.014
L101252K	630 x 750 mm	Set	0.23	3.82	-	72.06	75.88	83.47	5.531
L101252L	630 x 900 mm	Set	0.23	3.82	-	77.61	81.43	89.57	6.047
L101252M	630 x 1050 mm	Set	0.23	3.82	-	82.05	85.87	94.46	6.563
L101252N	630 x 1200 mm	Set	0.23	3.82	-	87.95	91.77	100.95	7.080
L101252O	630 x 1350 mm	Set	0.23	3.82	-	93.57	97.39	107.13	7.596
L101252P	630 x 1500 mm	Set	0.23	3.82	-	97.10	100.92	111.01	8.113
L101252Q	915 x 450 mm	Set	0.25	4.25	-	67.01	71.26	78.39	5.479
L101252R	915 x 600 mm	Set	0.25	4.25	-	69.79	74.04	81.44	5.995
L101252S	915 x 750 mm	Set	0.25	4.25	-	77.61	81.86	90.05	6.512
L101252T	915 x 900 mm	Set	0.25	4.25	-	82.05	86.30	94.93	7.028
L101252U	915 x 1050 mm	Set	0.25	4.25	-	87.95	92.20	101.42	7.545
L101252V	915 x 1200 mm	Set	0.25	4.25	-	93.57	97.82	107.60	8.061
L101252W	915 x 1350 mm	Set	0.25	4.25	-	97.10	101.35	111.49	8.577
L101252X	915 x 1500 mm	Set	0.25	4.25	-	107.76	112.01	123.21	9.094
L101252Y	1200 x 450 mm	Set	0.30	5.09	-	72.06	77.15	84.87	6.460
L101252Z	1200 x 600 mm	Set	0.30	5.09	-	77.61	82.70	90.97	6.977
L101253	**Boulton and Paul softwood window surround sets; to suit window size**								
L101253A	1200 x 750 mm	Set	0.30	5.09	-	82.05	87.14	95.85	7.493
L101253B	1200 x 900 mm	Set	0.30	5.09	-	87.95	93.04	102.34	8.009
L101253C	1200 x 1050 mm	Set	0.30	5.09	-	93.45	98.54	108.39	8.526
L101253D	1200 x 1200 mm	Set	0.30	5.09	-	97.10	102.19	112.41	9.042
L101253E	1200 x 1350 mm	Set	0.30	5.09	-	107.76	112.85	124.14	9.558
L101253F	1200 x 1500 mm	Set	0.30	5.09	-	113.13	118.22	130.04	10.075
L101253G	1342 x 450 mm	Set	0.30	5.09	-	75.45	80.54	88.59	6.949
L101253H	1342 x 600 mm	Set	0.30	5.09	-	80.88	85.97	94.57	7.465
L101253I	1342 x 750 mm	Set	0.30	5.09	-	85.85	90.94	100.03	7.982
L101253J	1342 x 900 mm	Set	0.30	5.09	-	88.75	93.84	103.22	8.498
L101253K	1342 x 1050 mm	Set	0.30	5.09	-	98.23	103.32	113.65	9.014
L101253L	1342 x 1200 mm	Set	0.30	5.09	-	102.53	107.62	118.38	9.531
L101253M	1342 x 1350 mm	Set	0.30	5.09	-	111.37	116.46	128.11	10.047
L101253N	1342 x 1500 mm	Set	0.30	5.09	-	116.39	121.48	133.63	10.564
L101253O	1770 x 450 mm	Set	0.35	5.94	-	81.67	87.61	96.37	8.422
L101253P	1770 x 600 mm	Set	0.35	5.94	-	87.95	93.89	103.28	8.939
L101253Q	1770 x 750 mm	Set	0.35	5.94	-	93.57	99.51	109.46	9.455
L101253R	1770 x 900 mm	Set	0.35	5.94	-	100.16	106.10	116.71	9.971
L101253S	1770 x 1050 mm	Set	0.35	5.94	-	107.76	113.70	125.07	10.488
L101253T	1770 x 1200 mm	Set	0.35	5.94	-	113.13	119.07	130.98	11.004
L101253U	1770 x 1350 mm	Set	0.35	5.94	-	118.27	124.21	136.63	11.521
L101253V	1770 x 1500 mm	Set	0.35	5.94	-	123.34	129.28	142.21	12.037
L101253W	2339 x 450 mm	Set	0.40	6.79	-	93.57	100.36	110.40	10.381
L101253X	2339 x 600 mm	Set	0.40	6.79	-	96.99	103.78	114.16	10.898
L101253Y	2339 x 750 mm	Set	0.40	6.79	-	107.76	114.55	126.01	11.414
L101253Z	2339 x 900 mm	Set	0.40	6.79	-	113.13	119.92	131.91	11.930
L101254	**Boulton and Paul softwood window surround sets; to suit window size**								
L101254A	2339 x 1050 mm	Set	0.50	8.49	-	118.30	126.79	139.47	12.447
L101254B	2339 x 1200 mm	Set	0.50	8.49	-	123.52	132.01	145.21	12.963
L101254C	2339 x 1350 mm	Set	0.50	8.49	-	128.24	136.73	150.40	13.479
L101254D	2339 x 1500 mm	Set	0.50	8.49	-	138.51	147.00	161.70	13.996

Major Works 2011		Unit	Labour Hours	Labour Net	Plant Net	Materials Net	Unit Net	Unit with 10%	CO₂
				£	£	£	£	£	Kg
L10	**L10: WINDOWS, ROOFLIGHTS, SCREENS AND LOUVRES**								
L1012	**Softwood window sundries and accessories**								
L101255	**Boulton and Paul softwood cambered heads**								
L101255A	483 mm wide; CAM483	Nr	0.15	2.55	-	10.22	12.77	14.05	0.718
L101255B	626 mm wide; CAM626	Nr	0.15	2.55	-	11.08	13.63	14.99	0.911
L101255C	913 mm wide; CAM913	Nr	0.20	3.40	-	13.42	16.82	18.50	1.297
L101255D	1200 mm wide; CAM1200	Nr	0.25	4.25	-	15.63	19.88	21.87	1.718
L101255E	1343 mm wide; CAM1343	Nr	0.30	5.09	-	17.05	22.14	24.35	1.910
L101255F	1774 mm wide; CAM1774	Nr	0.35	5.94	-	18.39	24.33	26.76	2.489
L101255G	2348 mm wide; CAM2348	Nr	0.40	6.79	-	25.67	32.46	35.71	3.261
L101258	**Boulton and Paul softwood window board; 32 x 225 mm; fixing with ties to masonry backgrounds**								
L101258A	488 mm long	Set	0.60	10.19	-	22.51	32.70	35.97	1.355
L101258B	630 mm long	Set	0.75	12.73	-	26.72	39.45	43.40	1.561
L101258C	915 mm long	Set	0.85	14.43	-	34.74	49.17	54.09	1.974
L101258D	1200 mm long	Set	0.95	16.13	-	42.64	58.77	64.65	2.710
L101258E	1342 mm long	Set	1.15	19.53	-	46.72	66.25	72.88	3.239
L101258F	1770 mm long	Set	1.20	20.38	-	57.94	78.32	86.15	3.860
L101258G	2339 mm long	Set	1.25	21.23	-	71.95	93.18	102.50	4.685
L1013	**Purpose made window frames; treated softwood; casement style**								
L101382	**Casement style frames; rebated moulded sections; frame size not exceeding 1.0 m²**								
L101382X	small pane, not exceeding 0.10 m²	m²	13.54	205.16	-	34.51	239.67	263.64	8.910
L101382Y	medium pane, 0.10 - 0.50 m²	m²	10.72	162.95	-	34.03	196.98	216.68	8.815
L101382Z	large pane, over 0.50 m²	m²	9.71	147.50	-	33.26	180.76	198.84	8.629
L101383	**Casement style frames; rebated moulded sections; frame size 1.0 - 2.0 m²**								
L101383A	small pane, not exceeding 0.10 m²	m²	10.14	154.70	-	61.46	216.16	237.78	15.374
L101383B	medium pane, 0.10 - 0.50 m²	m²	9.32	142.17	-	59.54	201.71	221.88	14.908
L101383C	large pane, over 0.50 m²	m²	8.41	128.21	-	57.48	185.69	204.26	14.413
L101384	**Casement style frames; rebated moulded sections; frame size over 2.0 m²**								
L101384A	small pane, not exceeding 0.10 m²	m²	8.74	133.92	-	92.53	226.45	249.10	22.819
L101384B	medium pane, 0.10 - 0.50 m²	m²	7.92	121.40	-	88.78	210.18	231.20	21.907
L101384C	large pane, over 0.50 m²	m²	7.31	111.89	-	84.19	196.08	215.69	20.792
L1014	**Purpose made window frames; treated softwood; sliding sash style**								
L101486	**Sliding sash style; rebated moulded sections; including spiral spring balances; frame size not exceeding 1.5 m²**								
L101486A	small pane, not exceeding 0.10 m²	m²	20.14	304.17	-	84.11	388.28	427.11	19.478
L101486B	medium pane, 0.10 - 0.50 m²	m²	18.64	281.91	-	81.91	363.82	400.20	18.953
L101486C	large pane, over 0.50 m²	m²	17.14	259.65	-	88.28	347.93	382.72	20.435
L101487	**Sliding sash style; rebated moulded sections; including spiral spring balances; frame size over 1.5 m²**								
L101487A	small pane, not exceeding 0.10 m²	m²	19.14	289.33	-	161.17	450.50	495.55	37.612
L101487B	medium pane, 0.10 - 0.50 m²	m²	17.64	267.07	-	161.17	428.24	471.06	37.612
L101487C	large pane, over 0.50 m²	m²	16.64	252.23	-	150.33	402.56	442.82	35.080

Windows, Doors & Stairs

		Unit	Labour Hours	Labour Net £	Plant Net £	Materials Net £	Unit Net £	Unit with 10% £	CO₂ Kg
L10	**L10: WINDOWS, ROOFLIGHTS, SCREENS AND LOUVRES**								
L1016	**Standard hardwood windows**								
L101630	**Boulton and Paul hardwood windows; Sovereign; casement; plain, transom and landscape; insulating glass units; standard cill; complete with ironmongery; size**								
L101630A	630 x 750 mm; W107CH	Nr	0.20	3.40	-	327.02	330.42	363.46	3.944
L101630B	630 x 900 mm; W109CH	Nr	0.20	3.40	-	345.69	349.09	384.00	4.255
L101630C	630 x 1050 mm; W110CH	Nr	0.20	3.40	-	274.08	277.48	305.23	4.566
L101630D	630 x 1200 mm; W112CH	Nr	0.20	3.40	-	119.93	123.33	135.66	2.860
L101630E	630 x 1350 mm; W113CH	Nr	0.20	3.40	-	306.06	309.46	340.41	5.188
L101630F	1200 x 750 mm; W207CH	Nr	0.25	4.25	-	323.87	328.12	360.93	6.494
L101630G	1200 x 900 mm; W209CH	Nr	0.25	4.25	-	339.95	344.20	378.62	6.960
L101630H	1200 x 1050 mm; W210CH	Nr	0.25	4.25	-	352.24	356.49	392.14	7.426
L101630I	1200 x 1200 mm; W212CH	Nr	0.25	4.25	-	367.12	371.37	408.51	7.893
L101630J	1200 x 1350 mm; W213CH	Nr	0.25	4.25	-	392.06	396.31	435.94	8.359
L101630K	1200 x 900 mm; W209CCH	Nr	0.25	4.25	-	357.92	362.17	398.39	5.716
L101630L	1200 x 1050 mm; W210CCH	Nr	0.25	4.25	-	375.06	379.31	417.24	6.183
L101630M	1200 x 1200 mm; W212CCH	Nr	0.25	4.25	-	390.35	394.60	434.06	6.649
L101630N	1200 x 1350 mm; W213CCH	Nr	0.25	4.25	-	422.66	426.91	469.60	7.115
L101630O	1770 x 750 mm; W307CCH	Nr	0.30	5.09	-	368.48	373.57	410.93	6.431
L101630P	1770 x 900 mm; W309CCH	Nr	0.30	5.09	-	386.43	391.52	430.67	6.898
L101630Q	1770 x 1050 mm; W310CCH	Nr	0.30	5.09	-	401.83	406.92	447.61	7.364
L101630R	1770 x 1200 mm; W312CCH	Nr	0.30	5.09	-	417.63	422.72	464.99	7.831
L101630S	1770 x 1350 mm; W313CCH	Nr	0.30	5.09	-	447.47	452.56	497.82	8.297
L101630T	2339 x 900 mm; W409CMCH	Nr	0.35	5.94	-	649.75	655.69	721.26	12.367
L101630U	2339 x 1050 mm; W410CMCH	Nr	0.35	5.94	-	665.22	671.16	738.28	13.144
L101630V	2339 x 1200 mm; W412CMCH	Nr	0.35	5.94	-	694.74	700.68	770.75	13.921
L101630W	2339 x 1350 mm; W413CMCH	Nr	0.35	5.94	-	740.74	746.68	821.35	14.698
L101630X	630 x 1050 mm; W110TH	Nr	0.20	3.40	-	272.52	275.92	303.51	4.566
L101630Y	630 x 1200 mm; W112TH	Nr	0.20	3.40	-	280.97	284.37	312.81	4.877
L101630Z	915 x 900 mm; W2N09WH	Nr	0.25	4.25	-	234.73	238.98	262.88	5.141
L101631	**Boulton and Paul hardwood windows; Sovereign; casement; landscape; narrow module; casement vents; standard cill; complete with ironmongery; size**								
L101631A	915 x 1050 mm; W2N10WH	Nr	0.25	4.25	-	238.54	242.79	267.07	5.452
L101631B	915 x 1200 mm; W2N12WH	Nr	0.25	4.25	-	244.46	248.71	273.58	5.763
L101631C	915 x 1350 mm; W2N13WH	Nr	0.25	4.25	-	250.01	254.26	279.69	6.074
L101631D	1200 x 900 mm; W209WH	Nr	0.28	4.67	-	267.93	272.60	299.86	6.027
L101631E	1200 x 1050 mm; W210WH	Nr	0.28	4.67	-	273.10	277.77	305.55	6.338
L101631F	1200 x 1200 mm; W212WH	Nr	0.28	4.67	-	278.58	283.25	311.58	6.649
L101631G	1770 x 1050 mm; W310CWH	Nr	0.30	5.09	-	410.29	415.38	456.92	8.110
L101631H	1770 x 1200 mm; W312CWH	Nr	0.30	5.09	-	421.37	426.46	469.11	8.421
L101631I	630 x 750 mm; W107VH	Nr	0.20	3.40	-	181.59	184.99	203.49	4.069
L101631J	630 x 900 mm; W109VH	Nr	0.20	3.40	-	187.96	191.36	210.50	4.535
L101631K	630 x 1050 mm; W110VH	Nr	0.20	3.40	-	192.76	196.16	215.78	5.001
L101631L	630 x 1200 mm; W112VH	Nr	0.20	3.40	-	198.17	201.57	221.73	5.468
L101631M	630 x 1350 mm; W113VH	Nr	0.20	3.40	-	204.68	208.08	228.89	5.934
L101631N	1200 x 900 mm; W209CVH	Nr	0.28	4.67	-	321.90	326.57	359.23	6.960
L101631O	1200 x 1050 mm; W210CVH	Nr	0.28	4.67	-	331.79	336.46	370.11	7.426
L101631P	1200 x 1200 mm; W212CVH	Nr	0.28	4.67	-	343.46	348.13	382.94	7.893
L101631Q	1200 x 1350 mm; W213CVH	Nr	0.28	4.67	-	361.19	365.86	402.45	8.359
L101631R	1770 x 900 mm; W309CVCH	Nr	0.30	5.09	-	452.89	457.98	503.78	9.665
L101631S	1770 x 1050 mm; W310CVCH	Nr	0.30	5.09	-	468.37	473.46	520.81	10.287
L101631T	1770 x 1200 mm; W312CVCH	Nr	0.30	5.09	-	485.40	490.49	539.54	10.908
L101631U	1770 x 1350 mm; W313CVCH	Nr	0.30	5.09	-	515.20	520.29	572.32	11.530
L101631V	2339 x 1200 mm; W412CVVH	Nr	0.35	5.94	-	608.58	614.52	675.97	13.921
L101631W	2339 x 1350 mm; W413CVVCH	Nr	0.35	5.94	-	642.75	648.69	713.56	14.698
L101631X	488 x 750 mm; WN07VH	Nr	0.15	2.55	-	151.84	154.39	169.83	3.503
L101631Y	488 x 900 mm; WN09VH	Nr	0.15	2.55	-	157.42	159.97	175.97	3.814
L101631Z	488 x 1050 mm; WN10VH	Nr	0.15	2.55	-	163.00	165.55	182.11	4.125
L101632	**Boulton and Paul hardwood windows; Sovereign; casement; narrow module; standard cill; complete with ironmongery; size**								
L101632A	488 x 750 mm; WN07CH	Nr	0.15	2.55	-	166.51	169.06	185.97	2.997
L101632B	488 x 900 mm; WN09CH	Nr	0.15	2.55	-	262.71	265.26	291.79	3.308
L101632C	488 x 1050 mm; WN10CH	Nr	0.15	2.55	-	274.08	276.63	304.29	3.619
L101632D	488 x 1200 mm; WN12CH	Nr	0.15	2.55	-	285.34	287.89	316.68	3.930
L101632E	915 x 750 mm; W2N07CH	Nr	0.25	4.25	-	314.05	318.30	350.13	5.608
L101632F	915 x 900 mm; W2N09CH	Nr	0.25	4.25	-	327.89	332.14	365.35	6.074

Major Works 2011		Unit	Labour Hours	Labour Net	Plant Net	Materials Net	Unit Net	Unit with 10%	CO$_2$
				£	£	£	£	£	Kg
L10	**L10: WINDOWS, ROOFLIGHTS, SCREENS AND LOUVRES**								
L1016	**Standard hardwood windows**								
L101632	**Boulton and Paul hardwood windows; Sovereign; casement, narrow module; standard cill; complete with ironmongery; size**								
L101632G	915 x 1050 mm; W2N10CH	Nr	0.25	4.25	-	339.68	343.93	378.32	6.540
L101632H	915 x 1200 mm; W2N12CH	Nr	0.25	4.25	-	352.41	356.66	392.33	7.007
L101632I	915 x 900 mm; W2N09CCH	Nr	0.25	4.25	-	330.35	334.60	368.06	5.126
L101632J	915 x 1050 mm; W2N10CCH	Nr	0.25	4.25	-	344.68	348.93	383.82	5.592
L101632K	915 x 1200 mm; W2N12CCH	Nr	0.25	4.25	-	358.47	362.72	398.99	6.058
L101632L	1342 x 1050 mm; W3N10CCH	Nr	0.29	4.84	-	381.44	386.28	424.91	7.565
L101632M	1342 x 1200 mm; W3N12CCH	Nr	0.29	4.84	-	395.69	400.53	440.58	8.187
L101632N	1770 x 1050 mm; W4N10CMCH	Nr	0.30	5.09	-	725.78	730.87	803.96	11.375
L101632O	1700 x 1200 mm; W4N12CMCH	Nr	0.30	5.09	-	773.67	778.76	856.64	12.152
L101633	**Boulton and Paul hardwood windows; Sovereign; top hung; standard cill; complete with ironmongery; size**								
L101633A	630 x 450 mm; W104AH	Nr	0.28	4.67	-	271.03	275.70	303.27	4.162
L101633B	630 x 600 mm; W106AH	Nr	0.28	4.67	-	280.57	285.24	313.76	4.473
L101633C	630 x 750 mm; W107AH	Nr	0.28	4.67	-	297.80	302.47	332.72	4.784
L101633D	630 x 900 mm; W109AH	Nr	0.28	4.67	-	308.70	313.37	344.71	5.095
L101633E	915 x 450 mm; W2N04AH	Nr	0.28	4.67	-	318.24	322.91	355.20	5.405
L101633F	915 x 600 mm; W2N06AH	Nr	0.25	4.25	-	238.84	243.09	267.40	3.571
L101633G	915 x 750 mm; W2N07AH	Nr	0.25	4.25	-	247.50	251.75	276.93	3.882
L101633H	915 x 900 mm; W2N09AH	Nr	0.25	4.25	-	266.64	270.89	297.98	4.193
L101633I	915 x 1050 mm; W2N10AH	Nr	0.25	4.25	-	277.11	281.36	309.50	4.504
L101633J	915 x 1200 mm; W2N12AH	Nr	0.25	4.25	-	285.69	289.94	318.93	4.815
L101633K	1200 x 450 mm; W204AH	Nr	0.28	4.67	-	246.35	251.02	276.12	3.851
L101633L	1200 x 600 mm; W206AH	Nr	0.28	4.67	-	271.03	275.70	303.27	4.162
L101633M	1200 x 750 mm; W207AH	Nr	0.28	4.67	-	280.57	285.24	313.76	4.473
L101633N	1200 x 900 mm; W209AH	Nr	0.28	4.67	-	297.80	302.47	332.72	4.784
L101633O	1200 x 1050 mm; W210AH	Nr	0.28	4.67	-	308.70	313.37	344.71	5.095
L101633P	1200 x 1200 mm; W212AH	Nr	0.28	4.67	-	318.24	322.91	355.20	5.405
L101634	**Boulton and Paul hardwood square bay assemblies**								
L101634A	two return ends; SQ2H	Nr	0.30	5.09	-	250.26	255.35	280.89	10.388
L101634B	two return ends; SQ3H	Nr	0.45	7.64	-	250.26	257.90	283.69	11.568
L101634C	two return ends; SQ4H	Nr	0.60	10.19	-	250.26	260.45	286.50	12.749
L101634D	one return end; SQR2H	Nr	0.30	5.09	-	120.06	125.15	137.67	9.114
L101634E	one return end; SQR3H	Nr	0.45	7.64	-	120.06	127.70	140.47	10.293
L101634F	one return end; SQR4H	Nr	0.60	10.19	-	120.06	130.25	143.28	11.474
L101634G	narrow module two return ends; SQ2NH	Nr	0.30	5.09	-	250.26	255.35	280.89	9.205
L101634H	narrow module two return ends; SQ3NH	Nr	0.45	7.64	-	250.26	257.90	283.69	10.090
L101634I	narrow module two return ends; SQ4NH	Nr	0.60	10.19	-	250.26	260.45	286.50	10.975
L101634J	narrow module; one return end; SQR2N	Nr	0.30	5.09	-	120.06	125.15	137.67	8.226
L101634K	narrow module; one return end; SQR3N	Nr	0.45	7.64	-	120.06	127.70	140.47	9.111
L101634L	narrow module; one return end; SQR4N	Nr	0.60	10.19	-	120.06	130.25	143.28	9.997
L101635	**Boulton and Paul hardwood splay bay assemblies**								
L101635A	two return ends; SP145H	Nr	0.30	5.09	-	250.26	255.35	280.89	10.388
L101635B	two return ends; SP245H	Nr	0.45	7.64	-	250.26	257.90	283.69	11.568
L101635C	two return ends; SP345H	Nr	0.60	10.19	-	250.26	260.45	286.50	12.749
L101635D	two return ends; SP445H	Nr	0.75	12.73	-	250.26	262.99	289.29	13.137
L101635E	one return end; SPR145H	Nr	0.30	5.09	-	120.06	125.15	137.67	9.114
L101635F	one return end; SPR245H	Nr	0.45	7.64	-	120.06	127.70	140.47	10.293
L101635G	one return end; SPR345H	Nr	0.60	10.19	-	120.06	130.25	143.28	11.474
L101635H	one return end; SPR445H	Nr	0.75	12.73	-	120.06	132.79	146.07	11.862
L101635I	narrow module; two return ends; SP2N45H	Nr	0.45	7.64	-	250.26	257.90	283.69	9.205
L101635J	narrow module; two return ends; SP3N45H	Nr	0.60	10.19	-	250.26	260.45	286.50	10.090
L101635K	narrow module; two return ends; SP4N45H	Nr	0.75	12.73	-	250.26	262.99	289.29	10.975
L101635L	narrow module; one return end; SPR2N45H	Nr	0.45	7.64	-	120.06	127.70	140.47	8.226
L101635M	narrow module; one return end; SPR3N45H	Nr	0.60	10.19	-	120.06	130.25	143.28	9.111

Major Works 2011		Unit	Labour Hours	Labour Net	Plant Net	Materials Net	Unit Net	Unit with 10%	CO$_2$
				£	£	£	£	£	Kg
L10	**L10: WINDOWS, ROOFLIGHTS, SCREENS AND LOUVRES**								
L1016	**Standard hardwood windows**								
L101635	**Boulton and Paul hardwood splay bay assemblies**								
L101635N	narrow module; one return end; SPR4N45H	Nr	0.75	12.73	-	120.06	132.79	146.07	9.997
L101639	**Boulton and Paul hardwood casement windows; horizontal bar; narrow module; standard cill; complete with ironmongery; size**								
L101639A	488 x 1050 mm; WHN10CH	Nr	0.30	5.09	-	274.08	279.17	307.09	3.619
L101639B	488 x 1200 mm; WHN12CH	Nr	0.30	5.09	-	285.34	290.43	319.47	3.930
L101639C	488 x 1350 mm; WHN13CH	Nr	0.30	5.09	-	224.41	229.50	252.45	4.241
L101639D	915 x 1050 mm; WH2N10CH	Nr	0.32	5.43	-	294.06	299.49	329.44	4.504
L101639E	915 x 1200 mm; WH2N12CH	Nr	0.32	5.43	-	305.67	311.10	342.21	4.815
L101639F	915 x 1350 mm; WH2N13CH	Nr	0.32	5.43	-	324.68	330.11	363.12	5.126
L101639G	915 x 1050 mm; WH2N10CCH	Nr	0.33	5.60	-	391.43	397.03	436.73	5.592
L101639H	915 x 1200 mm; WH2N12CCH	Nr	0.33	5.60	-	406.92	412.52	453.77	6.058
L101639I	915 x 1350 mm; WH2N13CCH	Nr	0.33	5.60	-	434.14	439.74	483.71	6.525
L101639J	1342 x 1050 mm; WH3N10CCH	Nr	0.35	5.94	-	440.65	446.59	491.25	7.565
L101639K	1342 x 1200 mm; WH3N12CCH	Nr	0.35	5.94	-	457.42	463.36	509.70	8.187
L101639L	1342 x 1350 mm; WH3N13CCH	Nr	0.35	5.94	-	488.45	494.39	543.83	8.809
L101639M	1770 x 1050 mm; W4N10CMCH	Nr	0.35	5.94	-	544.48	550.42	605.46	9.541
L101639N	1770 x 1200 mm; W4N12CMCH	Nr	0.36	6.11	-	580.40	586.51	645.16	10.318
L101639O	1770 x 1350 mm; W4N13CMCH	Nr	0.38	6.45	-	902.24	908.69	999.56	14.594
L1017	**Hardwood window sundries and accessories**								
L101759	**Boulton and Paul hardwood window surround sets; to suit window size**								
L101759A	488 x 750 mm	Set	0.25	4.25	-	138.48	142.73	157.00	6.634
L101759B	488 x 900 mm	Set	0.25	4.25	-	149.05	153.30	168.63	7.630
L101759C	488 x 1050 mm	Set	0.25	4.25	-	158.41	162.66	178.93	8.370
L101759D	488 x 1200 mm	Set	0.25	4.25	-	169.47	173.72	191.09	9.110
L101759E	488 x 1350 mm	Set	0.25	4.25	-	179.67	183.92	202.31	9.851
L101759F	630 x 750 mm	Set	0.28	4.67	-	143.09	147.76	162.54	7.590
L101759G	630 x 900 mm	Set	0.28	4.67	-	154.15	158.82	174.70	8.331
L101759H	630 x 1050 mm	Set	0.28	4.67	-	162.66	167.33	184.06	9.071
L101759I	630 x 1200 mm	Set	0.28	4.67	-	175.42	180.09	198.10	9.811
L101759J	630 x 1350 mm	Set	0.28	4.67	-	186.48	191.15	210.27	10.551
L101759K	915 x 750 mm	Set	0.30	5.09	-	154.15	159.24	175.16	8.997
L101759L	915 x 900 mm	Set	0.30	5.09	-	162.66	167.75	184.53	9.737
L101759M	915 x 1050 mm	Set	0.30	5.09	-	175.42	180.51	198.56	10.477
L101759N	915 x 1200 mm	Set	0.30	5.09	-	186.48	191.57	210.73	11.218
L101759O	915 x 1350 mm	Set	0.30	5.09	-	193.29	198.38	218.22	11.958
L101759P	1200 x 750 mm	Set	0.33	5.60	-	162.66	168.26	185.09	10.403
L101759Q	1200 x 900 mm	Set	0.33	5.60	-	175.42	181.02	199.12	11.144
L101759R	1200 x 1050 mm	Set	0.33	5.60	-	184.78	190.38	209.42	11.884
L101759S	1200 x 1200 mm	Set	0.33	5.60	-	192.44	198.04	217.84	12.624
L101759T	1200 x 1350 mm	Set	0.33	5.60	-	213.71	219.31	241.24	13.364
L101759U	1342 x 750 mm	Set	0.33	5.60	-	169.47	175.07	192.58	11.104
L101759V	1342 x 900 mm	Set	0.33	5.60	-	176.27	181.87	200.06	11.844
L101759W	1342 x 1050 mm	Set	0.33	5.60	-	194.99	200.59	220.65	12.585
L101759X	1342 x 1200 mm	Set	0.33	5.60	-	203.50	209.10	230.01	13.325
L101759Y	1342 x 1350 mm	Set	0.33	5.60	-	222.21	227.81	250.59	14.065
L101759Z	1770 x 750 mm	Set	0.39	6.54	-	184.78	191.32	210.45	13.216
L101760	**Boulton and Paul hardwood window surround sets; to suit window size**								
L101760A	1770 x 900 mm	Set	0.39	6.54	-	199.24	205.78	226.36	13.956
L101760B	1770 x 1050 mm	Set	0.39	6.54	-	213.71	220.25	242.28	14.697
L101760C	1770 x 1200 mm	Set	0.39	6.54	-	223.92	230.46	253.51	15.437
L101760D	1770 x 1350 mm	Set	0.39	6.54	-	234.12	240.66	264.73	16.177
L101760E	2339 x 750 mm	Set	0.45	7.64	-	213.71	221.35	243.49	16.024
L101760F	2339 x 900 mm	Set	0.45	7.64	-	223.92	231.56	254.72	16.764
L101760G	2339 x 1050 mm	Set	0.45	7.64	-	234.12	241.76	265.94	17.505
L101760H	2339 x 1200 mm	Set	0.45	7.64	-	246.04	253.68	279.05	18.245
L101760I	2339 x 1350 mm	Set	0.45	7.64	-	254.54	262.18	288.40	18.985
L101761	**Proprietary hardwood cambered heads**								
L101761A	483 mm wide; CAM483H	Nr	0.20	3.40	-	25.91	29.31	32.24	1.000
L101761B	626 mm wide; CAM626H	Nr	0.20	3.40	-	28.73	32.13	35.34	1.276
L101761C	913 mm wide; CAM913H	Nr	0.25	4.25	-	33.98	38.23	42.05	1.829

Major Works 2011		Unit	Labour Hours	Labour Net £	Plant Net £	Materials Net £	Unit Net £	Unit with 10% £	CO$_2$ Kg
L10	**L10: WINDOWS, ROOFLIGHTS, SCREENS AND LOUVRES**								
L1017	**Hardwood window sundries and accessories**								
L101761	**Proprietary hardwood cambered heads**								
L101761D	1200 mm wide; CAM1200H	Nr	0.30	5.09	-	40.35	45.44	49.98	2.417
L101761E	1343 mm wide; CAM1343H	Nr	0.35	5.94	-	43.64	49.58	54.54	2.693
L101761F	1774 mm wide; CAM1774H	Nr	0.35	5.94	-	47.32	53.26	58.59	3.524
L101761G	2348 mm wide; CAM2348H	Nr	0.45	7.64	-	63.47	71.11	78.22	4.630
L1018	**Purpose made window frames; hardwood; casement style**								
L101892	**Casement style frames; rebated moulded sections; frame size not exceeding 1.0 m^2**								
L101892A	medium pane, not exceeding 0.50 m^2	m^2	14.14	214.06	-	26.23	240.29	264.32	12.101
L101892B	large pane, over 0.50 m^2	m^2	12.62	191.15	-	25.03	216.18	237.80	11.844
L101893	**Casement style frames; rebated moulded sections; frame size 1.0 - 2.0 m^2**								
L101893A	medium pane, not exceeding 0.50 m^2	m^2	10.14	154.70	-	46.05	200.75	220.83	20.695
L101893B	large pane, over 0.50 m^2	m^2	10.12	154.05	-	36.20	190.25	209.28	17.724
L101894	**Casement style frames; rebated moulded sections; frame size over 2.0 m^2**								
L101894A	medium pane, not exceeding 0.50 m^2	m^2	14.14	214.06	-	26.23	240.29	264.32	12.101
L101894B	large pane, over 0.50 m^2	m^2	12.62	191.15	-	25.03	216.18	237.80	11.844
L1019	**Purpose made window frames; hardwood; sliding sash style**								
L101996	**Sliding sash style frames; rebated moulded sections; including spiral spring balances; frame size not exceeding 1.5 m^2**								
L101996A	medium pane, not exceeding 0.50 m^2	m^2	21.49	324.52	-	118.67	443.19	487.51	25.061
L101996B	large pane, over 0.50 m^2	m^2	19.79	299.30	-	129.03	428.33	471.16	27.206
L101997	**Sliding sash style frames; rebated moulded sections; including spiral spring balances; frame size over 1.5 m^2**								
L101997A	medium pane, not exceeding 0.50 m^2	m^2	20.29	306.72	-	227.86	534.58	588.04	47.530
L101997B	large pane, over 0.50 m^2	m^2	19.29	291.88	-	210.47	502.35	552.59	43.902
L1040	**Rooflights; PVC-u single skin dome lights complete with outer flange, rubber seal and fixings**								
L104093	**Square rooflights; fixing to upstands**								
L104093A	650 x 650 mm	Nr	0.50	8.49	-	102.44	110.93	122.02	6.684
L104093B	800 x 800 mm	Nr	0.50	8.49	-	121.59	130.08	143.09	9.756
L104093C	950 x 950 mm	Nr	0.50	8.49	-	169.60	178.09	195.90	13.403
L104093D	1100 x 1000 mm	Nr	0.50	8.49	-	201.59	210.08	231.09	17.623
L104093E	1250 x 1250 mm	Nr	0.50	8.49	-	342.39	350.88	385.97	22.416
L104093F	1400 x 1400 mm	Nr	0.50	8.49	-	364.79	373.28	410.61	27.784
L104094	**Circular rooflights; fixing to upstands**								
L104094A	800 mm dia	Nr	0.50	8.49	-	140.81	149.30	164.23	7.659
L104094B	950 mm dia	Nr	0.50	8.49	-	182.40	190.89	209.98	10.521

Major Works 2011		Unit	Labour Hours	Labour Net	Plant Net	Materials Net	Unit Net	Unit with 10%	CO₂
				£	£	£	£	£	Kg
L10	**L10: WINDOWS, ROOFLIGHTS, SCREENS AND LOUVRES**								
L1040	**Rooflights; PVC-u single skin dome lights complete with outer flange, rubber seal and fixings**								
L104094	**Circular rooflights; fixing to upstands**								
L104094C	1100 mm dia	Nr	0.50	8.49	-	220.79	229.28	252.21	13.834
L104094D	1250 mm dia	Nr	0.50	8.49	-	342.39	350.88	385.97	17.597
L104094E	1400 mm dia	Nr	0.50	8.49	-	364.79	373.28	410.61	21.810
L104094F	1550 mm dia	Nr	0.50	8.49	-	447.99	456.48	502.13	26.474
L104094G	1700 mm dia	Nr	0.50	8.49	-	531.18	539.67	593.64	31.588
L104095	**Rectangular rooflights; fixing to upstands**								
L104095A	650 x 950 mm	Nr	0.50	8.49	-	143.97	152.46	167.71	9.470
L104095B	650 x 1250 mm	Nr	0.50	8.49	-	211.18	219.67	241.64	12.255
L104095C	800 x 950 mm	Nr	0.50	8.49	-	159.99	168.48	185.33	11.436
L104095D	800 x 1100 mm	Nr	0.50	8.49	-	166.42	174.91	192.40	13.116
L104095E	800 x 1400 mm	Nr	0.50	8.49	-	220.79	229.28	252.21	16.475
L104095F	950 x 1250 mm	Nr	0.50	8.49	-	262.40	270.89	297.98	17.336
L104095G	1100 x 1400 mm	Nr	0.50	8.49	-	281.56	290.05	319.06	22.129
L1041	**Velux roof windows and accessories**								
L104166	**Velux roof windows; type GGL 3073**								
L104166A	C02: 550 x 780 mm	Nr	0.85	14.43	-	166.90	181.33	199.46	6.720
L104166B	C04: 550 x 980 mm	Nr	0.90	15.28	-	185.73	201.01	221.11	8.122
L104166C	F06: 660 x 1180 mm	Nr	1.00	16.98	-	265.58	282.56	310.82	12.891
L104166D	M04: 780 x 980 mm	Nr	1.00	16.98	-	212.07	229.05	251.96	10.996
L104166E	M08: 780 x 1400 mm	Nr	1.30	22.07	-	312.49	334.56	368.02	16.868
L104166F	P10: 940 x 1600 mm	Nr	1.35	22.92	-	313.71	336.63	370.29	20.426
L104166G	S06: 1140 x 1180 mm	Nr	1.25	21.23	-	355.49	376.72	414.39	20.084
L104166H	U04: 1340 x 980 mm	Nr	1.25	21.23	-	294.88	316.11	347.72	17.993
L104166I	U08: 1340 x 1400 mm	Nr	1.40	23.77	-	430.99	454.76	500.24	26.825
L104167	**Velux RNL roller blinds; type GGL**								
L104167A	C02	Nr	0.30	5.09	-	34.77	39.86	43.85	12.478
L104167B	C04	Nr	0.35	5.94	-	35.38	41.32	45.45	13.102
L104167C	F06	Nr	0.42	7.13	-	45.77	52.90	58.19	13.726
L104167D	M04	Nr	0.40	6.79	-	42.71	49.50	54.45	13.414
L104167E	M08	Nr	0.45	7.64	-	51.85	59.49	65.44	13.976
L104167F	P10	Nr	0.50	8.49	-	63.43	71.92	79.11	14.475
L104167G	S06	Nr	0.45	7.64	-	61.63	69.27	76.20	14.101
L104167H	U04	Nr	0.40	6.79	-	62.84	69.63	76.59	14.350
L104167I	U08	Nr	0.50	8.49	-	75.03	83.52	91.87	14.725
L104168	**Velux EDZ flashings; type GGL**								
L104168A	C02	Nr	0.85	14.43	-	30.98	45.41	49.95	17.754
L104168B	C04	Nr	0.90	15.28	-	32.77	48.05	52.86	20.424
L104168C	F06	Nr	1.00	16.98	-	36.35	53.33	58.66	24.562
L104168D	M04	Nr	0.95	16.13	-	35.44	51.57	56.73	23.494
L104168E	M08	Nr	1.20	20.38	-	39.92	60.30	66.33	29.100
L104168F	P10	Nr	1.30	22.07	-	43.50	65.57	72.13	33.906
L104168G	S06	Nr	1.20	20.38	-	42.58	62.96	69.26	30.969
L104168H	U04	Nr	1.25	21.23	-	45.35	66.58	73.24	30.969
L104168I	U08	Nr	1.35	22.92	-	47.72	70.64	77.70	36.576
L1051	**Screens, borrowed lights and frames**								
L105101	**Proprietary softwood exterior screens with hardwood cills**								
L105101A	1530 x 2100 mm	Nr	0.19	8.77	-	326.04	334.81	368.29	8.063
L105101B	2100 x 2100 mm	Nr	0.22	10.03	-	394.44	404.47	444.92	9.299
L105101C	2100 x 2100 mm	Nr	0.22	10.03	-	409.97	420.00	462.00	9.299
L105101D	2100 x 2100 mm	Nr	0.22	10.03	-	409.97	420.00	462.00	9.299
L105101E	2100 x 2100 mm	Nr	0.22	10.03	-	409.97	420.00	462.00	9.299
L105150	**Steel framed glazed screens; 6 mm clear toughened glass; fixing with screws; size**								
L105150A	250 x 1200 mm	Nr	3.00	44.52	-	113.40	157.92	173.71	12.521
L105150D	300 x 2100 mm	Nr	3.00	44.52	-	207.96	252.48	277.73	23.267
L105150G	700 x 2100 mm	Nr	5.00	74.20	-	354.33	428.53	471.38	41.147

Major Works 2011		Unit	Labour Hours	Labour Net	Plant Net	Materials Net	Unit Net	Unit with 10%	CO₂
				£	£	£	£	£	Kg
L10	**L10: WINDOWS, ROOFLIGHTS, SCREENS AND LOUVRES**								
L1051	**Screens, borrowed lights and frames**								
L105150	**Steel framed glazed screens; 6 mm clear toughened glass; fixing with screws; size**								
L105150L	1200 x 2100 mm	Nr	7.00	103.88	-	537.28	641.16	705.28	66.313
L105150P	1400 x 1200 mm	Nr	5.50	81.62	-	376.89	458.51	504.36	47.494
L105151	**Steel framed glazed screens; bullet-proof glass, ballistic rating to G2 requirements; fixing with screws; size**								
L105151D	1200 x 900 mm	Nr	4.50	66.78	-	390.27	457.05	502.76	36.756
L105160	**Brise-soleil; extruded aluminium blades fixed horizontally on brackets; to frame (measured separately); size**								
L105160A	2.5 x 1.0 m	Nr	5.13	326.73	-	498.14	824.87	907.36	111.240
L105160B	5.0 x 1.5 m	Nr	11.55	735.11	-	1,432.05	2,167.16	2,383.88	333.720
L105160C	7.5 x 2.0 m	Nr	24.39	1,551.93	-	2,739.75	4,291.68	4,720.85	667.440
L105160D	10.0 x 2.5 m	Nr	39.79	2,532.11	-	4,357.77	6,889.88	7,578.87	1,112.400
L1096	**Mastic pointing**								
L109699	**Pointing frames one side with mastic sealant**								
L109699A	standard	m	0.05	0.64	-	0.26	0.90	0.99	0.183
L109699B	coloured	m	0.05	0.64	-	0.27	0.91	1.00	0.183

Windows, Doors & Stairs

Major Works 2011		Unit	Labour Hours	Labour Net	Plant Net	Materials Net	Unit Net	Unit with 10%	CO₂
				£	£	£	£	£	Kg
L20	**L20: DOORS, SHUTTERS AND HATCHES**								
L2011	**Standard softwood exterior doors**								
L201120	**John Carr softwood exterior casement and panel doors; 44 mm thick**								
L201120A	762 x 1981 mm; 26E2XGG	Nr	1.15	19.53	-	60.26	79.79	87.77	12.125
L201120B	838 x 1981 mm; 29E2XGG	Nr	1.20	20.38	-	60.30	80.68	88.75	13.335
L201120C	762 x 1981 mm; 26ESA	Nr	1.15	19.53	-	145.80	165.33	181.86	12.125
L201120D	838 x 1981 mm; 29ESA	Nr	1.20	20.38	-	149.86	170.24	187.26	13.335
L201120E	762 x 1981 mm; 26ESC	Nr	1.15	19.53	-	161.69	181.22	199.34	12.125
L201120F	838 x 1981 mm; 29ESC	Nr	1.20	20.38	-	165.37	185.75	204.33	13.335
L201120G	762 x 1981 mm; 26E10	Nr	1.15	19.53	-	88.07	107.60	118.36	12.125
L201120H	838 x 1981 mm; 29E10	Nr	1.20	20.38	-	91.74	112.12	123.33	13.335
L201120I	762 x 1981 mm; 26EKXT	Nr	1.15	19.53	-	171.36	190.89	209.98	12.125
L201120J	838 x 1981 mm; 29EKXT	Nr	1.20	20.38	-	175.46	195.84	215.42	13.335
L201120K	762 x 1981 mm; 26ESCP	Nr	1.15	19.53	-	178.52	198.05	217.86	12.125
L201120L	838 x 1981 mm; 20ESCP	Nr	1.20	20.38	-	182.63	203.01	223.31	13.335
L201120M	762 x 1981 mm; 26E4XPP	Nr	1.15	19.53	-	158.19	177.72	195.49	12.125
L201120N	838 x 1981 mm; 29E4XPP	Nr	1.20	20.38	-	161.49	181.87	200.06	13.335
L201120O	762 x 1981 mm; 26E50	Nr	1.15	19.53	-	104.79	124.32	136.75	12.125
L201120P	838 x 1981 mm; 29E50	Nr	1.20	20.38	-	108.21	128.59	141.45	13.335
L201120Q	762 x 1981 mm; 26E4XG	Nr	1.15	19.53	-	143.31	162.84	179.12	12.125
L201120R	838 x 1981 mm; 29E4XG	Nr	1.20	20.38	-	146.63	167.01	183.71	13.335
L201120S	762 x 1981 mm; 26E2XG	Nr	1.15	19.53	-	107.43	126.96	139.66	12.125
L201120T	838 x 1981 mm; 29E2XG	Nr	1.20	20.38	-	111.70	132.08	145.29	13.335
L201121	**Premdor feature softwood exterior panel doors; mortice and tenon construction; 44 mm thick**								
L201121A	838 x 1981 mm; 3-panel; ref 33124	Nr	1.20	20.38	-	362.18	382.56	420.82	16.763
L201121B	813 x 2032 mm; 3-panel; ref 33129	Nr	1.20	20.38	-	362.18	382.56	420.82	16.682
L201121C	762 x 1981 mm; 3-panel; ref 33121	Nr	1.15	19.53	-	362.18	381.71	419.88	15.243
L201121D	807 x 2000 mm; 3-panel; ref 33128	Nr	1.20	20.38	-	362.18	382.56	420.82	16.298
L201121E	838 x 1981 mm; 4-panel; ref 26024	Nr	1.20	20.38	-	385.96	406.34	446.97	16.298
L201121F	813 x 2032 mm; 4-panel; ref 26029	Nr	1.20	20.38	-	385.96	406.34	446.97	16.682
L201121G	762 x 1981 mm; 4-panel; ref 26021	Nr	1.15	19.53	-	385.96	405.49	446.04	15.243
L201121H	807 x 2000 mm; 4-panel; ref 26028	Nr	1.20	20.38	-	385.96	406.34	446.97	16.298
L201121I	838 x 1981 mm; 6-panel; ref 91514	Nr	1.20	20.38	-	361.26	381.64	419.80	16.763
L201121J	813 x 2032 mm; 6-panel; ref 91539	Nr	1.20	20.38	-	361.26	381.64	419.80	16.682
L201121K	762 x 1981 mm; 6-panel; ref 91511	Nr	1.15	19.53	-	361.26	380.79	418.87	15.243
L201121L	807 x 2000 mm; 6-panel; ref 91548	Nr	1.15	19.53	-	361.26	380.79	418.87	15.243
L201121M	838 x 1981 mm; 6-panel toplight; ref 28324	Nr	1.20	20.38	-	338.40	358.78	394.66	16.763
L201121N	813 x 2032 mm; 6-panel toplight; ref 28329	Nr	1.20	20.38	-	338.40	358.78	394.66	16.682
L201121O	762 x 1981 mm; 6-panel toplight; ref 28321	Nr	1.15	19.53	-	338.40	357.93	393.72	15.243
L201121P	807 x 2000 mm; 6-panel toplight; ref 28328	Nr	1.20	20.38	-	338.40	358.78	394.66	16.298
L201121Q	838 x 1981 mm; 8-panel; ref 28924	Nr	1.20	20.38	-	415.23	435.61	479.17	1.676
L201121R	813 x 2032 mm; 8-panel toplight; ref 28929	Nr	1.20	20.38	-	415.23	435.61	479.17	16.682
L201121S	762 x 1981 mm; 8-panel toplight; ref 28921	Nr	1.15	19.53	-	415.23	434.76	478.24	15.243
L201121T	807 x 2000 mm; 8-panel toplight; ref 28928	Nr	1.20	20.38	-	415.23	435.61	479.17	16.298
L2012	**Standard softwood utility doors and gates**								
L201223	**John Carr softwood preservative treated utility doors and gates; 44 mm thick**								
L201223A	610 x 1981 mm; 20LB; ledged and braced	Nr	0.70	11.89	-	82.19	94.08	103.49	12.203

Major Works 2011		Unit	Labour Hours	Labour Net	Plant Net	Materials Net	Unit Net	Unit with 10%	CO$_2$
				£	£	£	£	£	Kg
L20	**L20: DOORS, SHUTTERS AND HATCHES**								
L2012	**Standard softwood utility doors and gates**								
L201223	**John Carr softwood preservative treated utility doors and gates; 44 mm thick**								
L201223B	686 x 1981 mm; 23LB; ledged and braced	Nr	0.75	12.73	-	82.19	94.92	104.41	13.723
L201223C	762 x 1981 mm; 26LB; ledged and braced	Nr	0.75	12.73	-	82.19	94.92	104.41	15.243
L201223D	838 x 1981 mm; 29LB; ledged and braced	Nr	0.80	13.58	-	88.44	102.02	112.22	16.763
L201223E	813 x 2032 mm; 28LB; ledged and braced	Nr	0.80	13.58	-	88.44	102.02	112.22	13.723
L201223F	686 x 1981 mm; 23FLB; framed, ledged and braced	Nr	0.75	12.73	-	106.34	119.07	130.98	13.723
L201223G	762 x 1981 mm; 26FLB; framed, ledged and braced	Nr	0.75	12.73	-	106.34	119.07	130.98	15.243
L201223H	838 x 1981 mm; 29FLB; framed, ledged and braced	Nr	0.80	13.58	-	111.67	125.25	137.78	16.763
L201223I	813 x 2032 mm; 28FLB; framed, ledged and braced	Nr	0.80	13.58	-	111.67	125.25	137.78	16.682
L201223J	726 x 2040 mm; 726FLB; framed, ledge and braced	Nr	0.75	12.73	-	106.31	119.04	130.94	14.956
L201223K	826 x 2040 mm; 826FLB; framed, ledge and braced	Nr	0.80	13.58	-	106.31	119.89	131.88	17.016
L201223L	807 x 2000 mm; 807FLB; framed, ledge and braced	Nr	0.80	13.58	-	111.67	125.25	137.78	16.298
L201223M	762 x 1981 mm; 26SD; stable door	Nr	1.40	23.77	-	203.68	227.45	250.20	16.682
L201223N	838 x 1981 mm; 29SD; stable door	Nr	1.50	25.47	-	203.68	229.15	252.07	16.763
L201223O	813 x 2032 mm; 28SD; stable door	Nr	1.50	25.47	-	203.68	229.15	252.07	16.682
L201223P	914 x 1981 mm; 3060GS arch top gate	Nr	0.85	14.43	-	138.98	153.41	168.75	18.284
L201223Q	914 x 1041 mm; 30GTE gate	Nr	0.60	10.19	-	73.73	83.92	92.31	9.608
L201223R	1067 x 1041 mm; 36GTE gate	Nr	0.75	12.73	-	83.51	96.24	105.86	11.216
L2013	**Standard timber patio door sets**								
L201326	**John Carr Ledbury patio door sets complete with frames, clear double glazing and all fittings**								
L201326A	1590 x 2073 mm; LED16LE	Nr	5.00	84.90	-	856.64	941.54	1,035.69	42.025
L201326B	1790 x 2073 mm; LED18LE	Nr	6.00	101.88	-	906.62	1,008.50	1,109.35	47.311
L201326C	2090 x 2073 mm; LED21LE	Nr	7.00	118.86	-	1,086.16	1,205.02	1,325.52	55.240
L201326D	2390 x 2073 mm; LED24LE	Nr	8.00	135.84	-	1,171.54	1,307.38	1,438.12	63.169
L2015	**Standard plywood faced external doors**								
L201524	**John Carr plywood faced lipped exterior flush doors; 44 mm thick**								
L201524A	686 x 1981 mm; 23F1X	Nr	0.90	15.28	-	70.91	86.19	94.81	14.755
L201524B	762 x 1981 mm; 26F1X	Nr	0.85	14.43	-	70.33	84.76	93.24	15.282
L201524C	838 x 1981 mm; 29F1X	Nr	0.90	15.28	-	70.91	86.19	94.81	15.809
L201524D	762 x 1981 mm; 26F2X	Nr	0.85	14.43	-	78.77	93.20	102.52	15.282
L201524E	838 x 1981 mm; 29F2X	Nr	0.90	15.28	-	78.77	94.05	103.46	15.809
L201524F	762 x 1981 mm; 26F3X	Nr	0.85	14.43	-	70.33	84.76	93.24	15.282
L201524G	838 x 1981 mm; 29F3X	Nr	0.90	15.28	-	70.33	85.61	94.17	15.809
L201525	**John Carr half hour firecheck plywood faced lipped exterior flush doors; 44 m thick**								
L201525A	762 x 1981 mm; 26F3XBF	Nr	1.10	18.68	-	119.31	137.99	151.79	15.282
L201525B	838 x 1981 mm; 29F3XBF	Nr	1.05	17.83	-	119.31	137.14	150.85	15.809
L201525C	813 x 2032 mm; 28F3XBF	Nr	1.15	19.53	-	119.31	138.84	152.72	15.781
L2018	**Standard hardwood exterior doors**								
L201830	**John Carr hardwood panel doors; 44 mm thick**								
L201830A	762 x 1981 mm; 26H2XGG	Nr	1.25	21.23	-	147.41	168.64	185.50	21.852
L201830B	838 x 1981 mm; 29H2XGG	Nr	1.30	22.07	-	151.36	173.43	190.77	24.031
L201830C	813 x 2032 mm; 28H2XGG	Nr	1.25	21.23	-	151.35	172.58	189.84	23.915

Windows, Doors & Stairs

		Unit	Labour Hours	Labour Net £	Plant Net £	Materials Net £	Unit Net £	Unit with 10% £	CO$_2$ Kg
L20	**L20: DOORS, SHUTTERS AND HATCHES**								
L2018	**Standard hardwood exterior doors**								
L201830	**John Carr hardwood panel doors; 44 mm thick**								
L201830D	807 x 2000 mm; 807H2XGG	Nr	1.25	21.23	-	151.36	172.59	189.85	23.142
L201830E	762 x 1981 mm; 26H10	Nr	1.25	21.23	-	144.61	165.84	182.42	21.852
L201830F	838 x 1981 mm; 29H10	Nr	1.25	21.23	-	148.48	169.71	186.68	24.031
L201830G	813 x 2032 mm; 28H10	Nr	1.25	21.23	-	148.48	169.71	186.68	23.915
L201830H	807 x 2000 mm; 807H10	Nr	1.25	21.23	-	148.48	169.71	186.68	23.364
L201832	**John Carr hardwood feature doors; 44 mm thick**								
L201832A	838 x 1981 mm; N29HART	Nr	1.30	22.07	-	345.72	367.79	404.57	24.031
L201832B	838 x 1981 mm; 29CARL	Nr	1.30	22.07	-	345.72	367.79	404.57	24.031
L201832C	838 x 1981 mm; 29CLAR	Nr	1.30	22.07	-	345.72	367.79	404.57	24.031
L2019	**Standard PVC-u patio door sets**								
L201936	**John Carr Ingleby PVC-u French doors; white polyester paint finish; 24 mm Low E insulating glass units; toughened inner pane, laminated outer pane; complete with all fittings; size**								
L201936A	1184 x 2090 mm; ING12E	Nr	4.50	76.41	-	905.15	981.56	1,079.72	50.987
L201936B	1484 x 2090 mm; ING15E	Nr	4.75	80.66	-	969.69	1,050.35	1,155.39	49.663
L201936C	1784 x 2090 mm; ING18E	Nr	5.25	89.14	-	1,022.73	1,111.87	1,223.06	50.779
L201937	**John Carr Ingleby PVC-u French doors; white polyester paint finish; 24 mm Low E insulating glass units; toughened inner and outer panes; complete with all fittings; size**								
L201937A	1184 x 2090 mm; ING12	Nr	4.50	76.41	-	905.15	981.56	1,079.72	50.987
L201937B	1484 x 2090 mm; ING15	Nr	4.75	80.66	-	1,022.73	1,103.39	1,213.73	50.928
L201937C	1784 x 2090 mm; ING18	Nr	5.25	89.14	-	969.69	1,058.83	1,164.71	50.978
L201940	**John Carr Claydon sliding patio doors white PVC-u finish; 24 mm Low E insulating glass units; toughened inner laminated outer pane; complete with all fittings; size**								
L201940A	1790 x 2090 mm; CLAY18	Nr	5.25	89.14	-	1,188.65	1,277.79	1,405.57	103.935
L201940B	2090 x 2090 mm; CLAY21	Nr	6.00	101.88	-	1,295.11	1,396.99	1,536.69	121.376
L201940C	2390 x 2090 mm; CLAY24	Nr	7.00	118.86	-	1,401.57	1,520.43	1,672.47	137.801
L201941	**John Carr Claydon sliding patio doors white PVC-u finish; 24 mm Low E insulating glass units; toughened inner and outer panes; complete with all fittings; size**								
L201941A	1790 x 2090 mm; CLAY18	Nr	5.25	89.14	-	1,367.00	1,456.14	1,601.75	103.935
L201941B	2090 x 2090 mm; CLAY21	Nr	6.00	101.88	-	1,497.79	1,599.67	1,759.64	121.376
L201941C	2390 x 2090 mm; CLAY24	Nr	7.00	118.86	-	1,631.09	1,749.95	1,924.95	137.801
L201950	**Premdor PVC-u patio door sets; 24 mm Low E sealed toughened insulating double glazing units; complete with locking system and all fittings; size**								
L201950A	1490 x 2090 mm; 60131	Nr	4.75	80.66	-	777.33	857.99	943.79	88.527
L201950B	1790 x 2090 mm; 60132	Nr	5.25	89.14	-	838.47	927.61	1,020.37	104.951
L201950C	2090 x 2090 mm; 60133	Nr	6.00	101.88	-	914.70	1,016.58	1,118.24	121.376
L201950D	2390 x 2090 mm; 60134	Nr	7.00	118.86	-	990.92	1,109.78	1,220.76	137.801
L2023	**Interior doors**								
L202301	**John Carr Premium softwood interior panel doors; 35 mm thick**								
L202301A	686 x 1981 mm; 23ISC	Nr	1.15	19.53	-	144.64	164.17	180.59	11.772
L202301B	762 x 1981 mm; 26ISC	Nr	1.20	20.38	-	145.87	166.25	182.88	13.076

Major Works 2011		Unit	Labour Hours	Labour Net	Plant Net	Materials Net	Unit Net	Unit with 10%	CO$_2$
				£	£	£	£	£	Kg
L20	**L20: DOORS, SHUTTERS AND HATCHES**								
L2023	**Interior doors**								
L202301	**John Carr Premium softwood interior panel doors; 35 mm thick**								
L202301C	838 x 1981 mm; 29ISC	Nr	1.25	21.23	-	151.36	172.59	189.85	14.380
L202301D	686 x 1981 mm; 23ISA	Nr	1.10	18.68	-	136.09	154.77	170.25	11.772
L202301E	762 x 1981 mm; 26ISA	Nr	1.20	20.38	-	137.19	157.57	173.33	13.076
L202302	**John Carr Eskdale veneered panel effect feature doors; 35 mm thick**								
L202302A	762 x 1981 mm; 26ESK2P	Nr	1.20	20.38	-	143.68	164.06	180.47	13.076
L202302B	762 x 1981 mm; 26ESK4P	Nr	1.20	20.38	-	162.04	182.42	200.66	13.076
L202302C	610 x 1981 mm; 20ESK2P	Nr	1.10	18.68	-	142.14	160.82	176.90	10.468
L202302D	686 x 1981 mm; 23ESK2P	Nr	1.15	19.53	-	142.14	161.67	177.84	11.772
L202302E	686 x 1981 mm; 23ESK4P	Nr	1.20	20.38	-	160.46	180.84	198.92	11.772
L202303	**John Carr Newstead oak veneered panel feature doors; 35 mm thick**								
L202303A	686 x 1981 mm; 23NEWS	Nr	1.10	18.68	-	212.81	231.49	254.64	15.648
L202303B	762 x 1981 mm; 26NEWS	Nr	1.10	18.68	-	212.81	231.49	254.64	17.382
L202303C	838 x 1981 mm; 29NEWS	Nr	1.20	20.38	-	223.45	243.83	268.21	19.116
L202304	**John Carr Chateau wood grain moulded panel doors; 35 mm thick**								
L202304A	457 x 1981 mm; 16CLAS	Nr	1.05	17.83	-	63.26	81.09	89.20	10.425
L202304B	533 x 1981 mm; 19CLAS	Nr	1.05	17.83	-	63.26	81.09	89.20	12.158
L202304C	610 x 1981 mm; 20CLAS	Nr	1.05	17.83	-	63.26	81.09	89.20	13.915
L202304D	686 x 1981 mm; 23CLAS	Nr	1.10	18.68	-	63.26	81.94	90.13	15.648
L202304E	762 x 1981 mm; 26CLAS	Nr	1.10	18.68	-	63.54	82.22	90.44	17.382
L202305	**John Carr Cambridge smooth-skin moulded panel doors; 35 mm thick**								
L202305A	457 x 1981 mm; 16CAMB	Nr	1.05	17.83	-	52.79	70.62	77.68	7.842
L202305B	533 x 1981 mm; 19CAMB	Nr	1.05	17.83	-	52.79	70.62	77.68	9.146
L202305C	610 x 1981 mm; 20CAMB	Nr	1.05	17.83	-	52.79	70.62	77.68	10.468
L202305D	686 x 1981 mm; 23CAMB	Nr	1.10	18.68	-	52.79	71.47	78.62	11.772
L202305E	762 x 1981 mm; 26CAMB	Nr	1.10	18.68	-	52.79	71.47	78.62	13.076
L202306	**John Carr Carrwood hardboard faced flush interior door; lipped two edges; 35 mm thick**								
L202306A	457 x 1981 mm; 16HBL	Nr	1.05	17.83	-	48.17	66.00	72.60	12.446
L202306B	533 x 1981 mm; 19HBL	Nr	1.05	17.83	-	48.17	66.00	72.60	14.516
L202306C	610 x 1981 mm; 20HBL	Nr	1.05	17.83	-	48.17	66.00	72.60	16.613
L202306D	686 x 1981 mm; 23HBL	Nr	1.10	18.68	-	48.17	66.85	73.54	18.683
L202306E	762 x 1981 mm; 26HBL	Nr	1.10	18.68	-	48.17	66.85	73.54	20.753
L202306F	838 x 1981 mm; 29HBL	Nr	1.15	19.53	-	50.34	69.87	76.86	22.823
L202306G	813 x 2032 mm; 28HBL	Nr	1.15	19.53	-	50.34	69.87	76.86	22.701
L202307	**John Carr Carrwood hardboard faced interior flush doors; lipped two edges; 40 mm thick**								
L202307A	626 x 2040 mm; 626HBL	Nr	1.05	17.83	-	50.34	68.17	74.99	20.075
L202307B	726 x 2040 mm; 726HBL	Nr	1.10	18.68	-	50.34	69.02	75.92	24.436
L202307C	826 x 2040 mm; 826HBL	Nr	1.15	19.53	-	50.34	69.87	76.86	26.489
L202308	**John Carr Silverwood hardboard faced interior flush doors; unlipped; 35 mm thick**								
L202308A	457 x 1981 mm; 16HB	Nr	1.05	17.83	-	43.79	61.62	67.78	14.516
L202308B	533 x 1981 mm; 19HB	Nr	1.05	17.83	-	43.79	61.62	67.78	16.613
L202308C	610 x 1981 mm; 20HB	Nr	1.05	17.83	-	43.79	61.62	67.78	16.613
L202308D	686 x 1981 mm; 23HB	Nr	1.10	18.68	-	43.79	62.47	68.72	18.683
L202308E	762 x 1981 mm; 26HB	Nr	1.10	18.68	-	43.79	62.47	68.72	20.753
L202308F	838 x 1981 mm; 29HB	Nr	1.15	19.53	-	45.76	65.29	71.82	22.823
L202308G	813 x 2032 mm; 28HB	Nr	1.15	19.53	-	45.76	65.29	71.82	22.142
L202309	**John Carr Silverwood hardboard faced interior flush doors; unlipped; 40 mm thick**								
L202309A	626 x 2040 mm; 626HB	Nr	1.15	19.53	-	45.76	65.29	71.82	20.075
L202309B	726 x 2040 mm; 726HB	Nr	1.20	20.38	-	45.76	66.14	72.75	23.282
L202309C	826 x 2040 mm; 826HB	Nr	1.25	21.23	-	47.64	68.87	75.76	26.489

Major Works 2011		Unit	Labour Hours	Labour Net	Plant Net	Materials Net	Unit Net	Unit with 10%	CO$_2$
				£	£	£	£	£	Kg
L20	**L20: DOORS, SHUTTERS AND HATCHES**								
L2023	**Interior doors**								
L202310	**Proprietary serving hatch in plywood; assembled; rebated meeting tiles; hung on 2 pr nylon hinges; 133 mm rebated softwood linings; 170 mm cill**								
L202310A	648 x 533 mm	Nr	0.75	12.73	-	108.34	121.07	133.18	2.500
L202312	**John Carr factory finished wood veneered interior flush doors; clear lacquer finish; 35 mm thick**								
L202312A	457 x 1981 mm; Sapele 16SDL	Nr	1.10	18.68	-	69.59	88.27	97.10	8.799
L202312B	533 x 1981 mm; Sapele 19SDL	Nr	1.10	18.68	-	69.59	88.27	97.10	10.262
L202312C	610 x 1981 mm; Sapele 20SDL	Nr	1.15	19.53	-	69.59	89.12	98.03	11.744
L202312D	686 x 1981 mm; Sapele 23SDL	Nr	1.15	19.53	-	69.59	89.12	98.03	13.207
L202312E	762 x 1981 mm; Sapele 26SDL	Nr	1.20	20.38	-	69.59	89.97	98.97	14.671
L202312F	838 x 1981 mm; Sapele 29SDL	Nr	1.25	21.23	-	75.23	96.46	106.11	16.134
L202312G	864 x 1981 mm; Sapele 210SDL	Nr	1.25	21.23	-	82.93	104.16	114.58	16.634
L202312H	457 x 1981 mm; Koto 16KOT	Nr	1.25	21.23	-	77.20	98.43	108.27	8.799
L202312I	533 x 1981 mm; Koto 19KOT	Nr	1.10	18.68	-	77.20	95.88	105.47	10.262
L202312J	610 x 1981 mm; Koto 20KOT	Nr	1.10	18.68	-	77.20	95.88	105.47	11.744
L202312K	686 x 1981 mm; Koto 23KOT	Nr	1.15	19.53	-	77.20	96.73	106.40	13.207
L202312L	762 x 1981 mm; Koto 26KOT	Nr	1.15	19.53	-	77.20	96.73	106.40	14.671
L202312M	838 x 1981 mm; Koto 29KOT	Nr	1.20	20.38	-	87.67	108.05	118.86	16.134
L202312N	457 x 1981 mm; Ash 16ASH	Nr	1.25	21.23	-	101.02	122.25	134.48	8.799
L202312O	533 x 1981 mm; Ash 19ASH	Nr	1.10	18.68	-	101.02	119.70	131.67	10.262
L202312P	610 x 1981 mm; Ash 20ASH	Nr	1.10	18.68	-	101.02	119.70	131.67	11.744
L202312Q	686 x 1981 mm; Ash 23ASH	Nr	1.15	19.53	-	101.02	120.55	132.61	13.207
L202312R	762 x 1981 mm; Ash 26ASH	Nr	1.15	19.53	-	101.02	120.55	132.61	14.671
L202312S	838 x 1981 mm; Ash 29ASH	Nr	1.20	20.38	-	106.66	127.04	139.74	16.134
L202312T	457 x 1981 mm; African Maple 16MPL	Nr	1.25	21.23	-	82.93	104.16	114.58	8.799
L202312U	533 x 1981 mm; African Maple 19MPL	Nr	1.10	18.68	-	82.93	101.61	111.77	10.262
L202312V	610 x 1981 mm; African Maple 20MPL	Nr	1.10	18.68	-	82.93	101.61	111.77	11.744
L202312W	686 x 1981 mm; African Maple 23MPL	Nr	1.15	19.53	-	82.93	102.46	112.71	13.207
L202312X	762 x 1981 mm; African Maple 26MPL	Nr	1.15	19.53	-	82.93	102.46	112.71	14.671
L202312Y	838 x 1981 mm; African Maple 29MPL	Nr	1.25	21.23	-	87.67	108.90	119.79	16.134
L202313	**John Carr Sapele factory finished wood veneered interior flush doors; clear lacquer finish; 40 mm thick**								
L202313A	526 x 2040 mm; 526SDL	Nr	1.10	18.68	-	72.45	91.13	100.24	12.361
L202313B	626 x 2040 mm; 626SDL	Nr	1.15	19.53	-	72.45	91.98	101.18	14.712
L202313C	726 x 2040 mm; 726SDL	Nr	1.20	20.38	-	72.45	92.83	102.11	17.062
L202313D	826 x 2040 mm; 826SDL	Nr	1.25	21.23	-	77.20	98.43	108.27	19.412
L202314	**John Carr Silverwood half hour firecheck hardboard faced interior flush doors; unlipped; 44 mm thick**								
L202314A	686 x 1981 mm; 23HBF	Nr	1.15	19.53	-	73.98	93.51	102.86	23.499
L202314B	762 x 1981 mm; 26HBF	Nr	1.20	20.38	-	73.98	94.36	103.80	26.103
L202314C	838 x 1981 mm; 29HBF	Nr	1.25	21.23	-	76.93	98.16	107.98	28.706
L202314D	726 x 2040 mm; 726HBF	Nr	1.20	20.38	-	76.93	97.31	107.04	26.880
L202314E	826 x 2040 mm; 826HBF	Nr	1.25	21.23	-	77.91	99.14	109.05	29.138
L202316	**John Carr half hour firecheck factory finished wood veneered lipped interior flush doors; clear lacquer finish; 44 m thick**								
L202316A	686 x 1981 mm; Sapele 23SDLF	Nr	1.30	22.07	-	98.24	120.31	132.34	19.672
L202316B	762 x 1981 mm; Sapele 26SDLF	Nr	1.35	22.92	-	98.24	121.16	133.28	21.823
L202316C	838 x 1981 mm; Sapele 29SDLF	Nr	1.40	23.77	-	105.95	129.72	142.69	24.031
L202316D	726 x 2040 mm; Sapele 726SDLF	Nr	1.35	22.92	-	101.11	124.03	136.43	21.440
L202316E	826 x 2040 mm; Sapele 826SDLF	Nr	1.40	23.77	-	108.81	132.58	145.84	24.393
L202316F	762 x 1981 mm; Ash 26ASHF	Nr	1.35	22.92	-	128.60	151.52	166.67	21.823

Major Works 2011		Unit	Labour Hours	Labour Net	Plant Net	Materials Net	Unit Net	Unit with 10%	CO₂
				£	£	£	£	£	Kg
L20	**L20: DOORS, SHUTTERS AND HATCHES**								
L2023	**Interior doors**								
L202316	**John Carr half hour firecheck factory finished wood veneered lipped interior flush doors; clear lacquer finish; 44 m thick**								
L202316G	838 x 1981 mm; Ash 29ASHF	Nr	1.40	23.77	-	136.22	159.99	175.99	24.031
L202316H	762 x 1981 mm; African Maple 26MPL	Nr	1.35	22.92	-	111.67	134.59	148.05	21.852
L202316I	838 x 1981 mm; African Maple 29MPL	Nr	1.40	23.77	-	125.20	148.97	163.87	24.031
L202316J	762 x 1981 mm; Koto 26KOTF	Nr	1.35	22.92	-	119.38	142.30	156.53	21.852
L202316K	838 x 1981 mm; Koto 29KOTF	Nr	1.40	23.77	-	114.63	138.40	152.24	24.031
L202317	**John Carr half hour firecheck interior doors with one piece moulded skin both sides; 44 mm thick**								
L202317A	762 x 1981 mm; Chateau 26CLASF	Nr	1.35	22.92	-	167.81	190.73	209.80	26.103
L202317B	838 x 1981 mm; Chateau 29CLASF	Nr	1.40	23.77	-	175.88	199.65	219.62	28.706
L202317C	762 x 1981 mm; Cambridge 26CAMBF	Nr	1.35	22.92	-	119.74	142.66	156.93	26.103
L202317D	838 x 1981 mm; Cambridge 29CAMBF	Nr	1.40	23.77	-	122.69	146.46	161.11	28.706
L2071	**Standard softwood external door frames**								
L207102	**Boulton and Paul softwood exterior door frames; hardwood cills; heavy duty PVC-u waterbar; for 686 x 1981 mm doors**								
L207102A	780 x 2079 mm; FN23M; opening inward weatherstripped	Nr	0.19	8.77	-	96.22	104.99	115.49	14.457
L207102B	780 x 2079 mm; FX23M; opening outward; weatherstripped	Nr	0.19	8.77	-	96.22	104.99	115.49	14.457
L207102C	780 x 2035 mm; F23; opening inward and outward; weatherstripped; no cill	Nr	0.19	8.77	-	65.17	73.94	81.33	14.230
L207102D	780 x 2035 mm; DF23; opening inward and outward; non-weatherstripped; no cill	Nr	0.19	8.77	-	59.32	68.09	74.90	10.056
L207103	**Boulton and Paul softwood exterior door frames; hardwood cills; heavy duty PVC-u waterbar; for 762 x 1981 mm doors**								
L207103A	856 x 2079 mm; FN26M; opening inward weatherstripped	Nr	0.19	8.77	-	99.17	107.94	118.73	14.654
L207103B	856 x 2079 mm; FX26M; opening outward; weatherstripped	Nr	0.19	8.77	-	99.17	107.94	118.73	14.654
L207103C	856 x 2035 mm; F26; opening inward and outward; weatherstripped; no cill	Nr	0.19	8.77	-	58.33	67.10	73.81	14.426
L207103D	856 x 2035 mm; DF26IN; opening inward; non-weatherstripped	Nr	0.19	8.77	-	82.78	91.55	100.71	10.338
L207103E	856 x 2079 mm; DF26OUT; opening outward; non-weatherstripped	Nr	0.19	8.77	-	82.78	91.55	100.71	10.338
L207103F	856 x 2035 mm; DF26; opening inward and outward; non-weatherstripped; no cill	Nr	0.19	8.77	-	60.20	68.97	75.87	10.187
L207104	**Boulton and Paul softwood exterior door frames; hardwood cills; heavy duty PVC-u waterbar; for 838 x 1981 mm doors**								
L207104A	932 x 2079 mm; FN29M; opening inward weatherstripped	Nr	0.19	8.77	-	103.04	111.81	122.99	14.850

Major Works 2011		Unit	Labour Hours	Labour Net £	Plant Net £	Materials Net £	Unit Net £	Unit with 10% £	CO₂ Kg
L20	**L20: DOORS, SHUTTERS AND HATCHES**								
L2071	**Standard softwood external door frames**								
L207104	**Boulton and Paul softwood exterior door frames; hardwood cills; heavy duty PVC-u waterbar; for 838 x 1981 mm doors**								
L207104B	932 x 2079 mm; FX29M; opening outward; weatherstripped	Nr	0.19	8.77	-	103.58	112.35	123.59	14.850
L207104C	932 x 2035 mm; F29; opening inward and outward; weatherstripped; no cill	Nr	0.19	8.77	-	58.77	67.54	74.29	14.623
L207104D	932 x 2079 mm; DF29IN; opening inward; non-weatherstripped	Nr	0.19	8.77	-	85.59	94.36	103.80	10.318
L207104E	932 x 2079 mm; DF29OUT; opening outward; non-weatherstripped	Nr	0.19	8.77	-	85.59	94.36	103.80	10.469
L207104F	932 x 2035 mm; DF29; opening inward and outward; non-weatherstripped; no cill	Nr	0.19	8.77	-	62.84	71.61	78.77	10.469
L207105	**Boulton and Paul softwood exterior door frames; hardwood cills; heavy duty PVC-u waterbar; for 914 x 1981 mm doors**								
L207105A	1008 x 2130 mm; FN30M; opening inward; weatherstripped	Nr	0.19	8.77	-	103.04	111.81	122.99	10.600
L207105B	1008 x 2130 mm; FX30M; opening outward; weatherstripped	Nr	0.19	8.77	-	103.04	111.81	122.99	10.600
L207105C	1008 x 2086 mm; F30; opening inward and outward; weatherstripped; no cill	Nr	0.19	8.77	-	68.75	77.52	85.27	10.449
L207106	**Boulton and Paul softwood exterior door frames; hardwood cills; heavy duty PVC-u waterbar; for 813 x 2032 mm doors**								
L207106A	907 x 2130 mm; FN28M; opening inward weatherstripped	Nr	0.19	8.77	-	103.58	112.35	123.59	15.049
L207106B	907 x 2130 mm; FX28M; opening outward; weatherstripped	Nr	0.19	8.77	-	103.04	111.81	122.99	15.049
L207106C	907 x 2086 mm; F28; opening inward and outward; weatherstripped; no cill	Nr	0.19	8.77	-	58.67	67.44	74.18	14.816
L207106D	907 x 2086 mm; DF28IN; opening inward; non-weatherstripped	Nr	0.19	8.77	-	85.59	94.36	103.80	10.602
L207106E	907 x 2086 mm; DF28OUT; opening outward; non-weatherstripped	Nr	0.19	8.77	-	85.59	94.36	103.80	10.602
L207106F	907 x 2086 mm; DF28; opening inward and outward; non-weatherstripped; no cill	Nr	0.19	8.77	-	62.84	71.61	78.77	10.450
L207110	**Boulton and Paul softwood garage door frames; supplied unassembled; overall frame size**								
L207110A	2271 x 2052 mm; UF7066NS	Nr	0.27	12.55	-	83.51	96.06	105.67	18.733
L207110B	2271 x 2205 mm; UF7070NS	Nr	0.27	12.55	-	107.04	119.59	131.55	19.128
L207110C	2423 x 2052 mm; UF7666NS	Nr	0.27	12.55	-	85.05	97.60	107.36	19.518
L207110D	2423 x 2205 mm; UF7670NS	Nr	0.27	12.55	-	88.97	101.52	111.67	19.913
L207110E	2575 x 2052 mm; UF8066NS	Nr	0.27	12.55	-	95.41	107.96	118.76	20.303
L207110F	2575 x 2205 mm; UF8070NS	Nr	0.27	12.55	-	97.98	110.53	121.58	20.698
L207110G	4404 x 2052 mm; UF14066NS	Nr	0.38	17.59	-	145.34	162.93	179.22	23.675
L207110H	4404 x 2205 mm; UF14070NS	Nr	0.38	17.59	-	147.92	165.51	182.06	24.465

Major Works 2011		Unit	Labour Hours	Labour Net	Plant Net	Materials Net	Unit Net	Unit with 10%	CO$_2$
				£	£	£	£	£	Kg
L20	**L20: DOORS, SHUTTERS AND HATCHES**								
L2072	**Standard softwood external door frames and side lights**								
L207270	**Boulton and Paul softwood exterior door frames; hardwood cills; factory fitted sidelights; for 838 x 1981 mm doors**								
L207270A	1307 x 2079 mm; FE13029; 332 mm wide sidelight; SL3366SHX	Nr	0.19	8.77	-	231.23	240.00	264.00	14.631
L207270B	1532 x 2079 mm; FE1529; 557 mm wide sidelight; SL5566SHX	Nr	0.19	8.77	-	259.06	267.83	294.61	15.344
L207270C	1682 x 2079 mm; FED16829; 332 mm wide sidelight; SL3366SHX	Nr	0.19	8.77	-	268.87	277.64	305.40	15.276
L207270D	2132 x 2079 mm; FED21329; 557 mm wide sidelight; SL5566SHX	Nr	0.19	8.77	-	309.66	318.43	350.27	16.377
L207271	**Boulton and Paul softwood half hour firecheck exterior door frames; fitted with 15 x 4 mm intumescent strip; for 762 x 1981 mm doors**								
L207271A	856 x 2035 mm; DF26FCA2; opening inward and outward; no cill	Nr	0.14	6.30	-	78.15	84.45	92.90	21.199
L207271B	856 x 2035 mm; DF26FCA1; opening inward; standard cill	Nr	0.14	6.30	-	100.92	107.22	117.94	21.480
L207271C	856 x 2035 mm; DF26FCA3; opening inward and outward; flush cill	Nr	0.14	6.30	-	100.92	107.22	117.94	21.480
L207272	**Boulton and Paul softwood half hour fir check door frames; 15 x 4 mm intumescent strip; for 838 x 1981 mm doors**								
L207272A	932 x 2035 mm; DF29FCA2; opening inward and outward; no cill	Nr	0.14	6.30	-	94.30	100.60	110.66	14.876
L207272B	932 x 2035 mm; DF29FCA1; opening inward; standard cill	Nr	0.14	6.30	-	94.30	100.60	110.66	14.876
L207272C	932 x 2035 mm; DF29FCA3; opening inward and outward; flush cill	Nr	0.14	6.30	-	96.22	102.52	112.77	14.457
L207273	**Boulton and Paul softwood half hour fir check exterior door frames; hardwood cills; 15 x 4 mm intumescent strip; for 813 x 2032 mm doors**								
L207273A	906 x 2086 mm; DF28FCA2; opening inward and outward; no cill	Nr	0.14	6.30	-	104.95	111.25	122.38	14.819
L207275	**Boulton and Paul softwood exterior garage door frames**								
L207275I	2427 x 2054 mm; UF7666NS	Nr	0.27	12.55	-	85.05	97.60	107.36	19.518
L207275J	2275 x 2054 mm; UF7066NS	Nr	0.27	12.55	-	83.51	96.06	105.67	18.733
L207275K	2275 x 2207 mm; UF7070NS	Nr	0.27	12.55	-	107.04	119.59	131.55	19.128
L207275L	4408 x 2254 mm; UF14066NS	Nr	0.38	17.59	-	145.34	162.93	179.22	23.675
L207275M	4408 x 2207 mm; UF14070NS	Nr	0.38	17.59	-	147.92	165.51	182.06	24.465
L207276	**Boulton and Paul softwood side lights; fitting to exterior frames (measured separately); to suit imperial doors**								
L207276A	SL3366PX; 332 mm wide	Nr	0.50	8.49	-	97.88	106.37	117.01	3.655
L207276B	SL5566PX; 557 mm wide	Nr	0.55	9.34	-	134.41	143.75	158.13	3.981
L207276C	SL3366RX; 332 mm wide	Nr	0.50	8.49	-	105.06	113.55	124.91	3.655
L207276D	SL5566RX; 557 mm wide	Nr	0.55	9.34	-	156.64	165.98	182.58	3.981
L207276E	SL3366SBX; 332 mm wide	Nr	0.50	8.49	-	102.54	111.03	122.13	3.655
L207276F	SL5566SBX; 557 mm wide	Nr	0.55	9.34	-	116.71	126.05	138.66	3.981
L207276G	SL3366SHX; 332 mm wide	Nr	0.50	8.49	-	96.21	104.70	115.17	3.655
L207276H	SL5566SHX; 557 mm wide	Nr	0.55	9.34	-	117.05	126.39	139.03	3.981
L207276I	SL3366TBX; 332 mm wide	Nr	0.50	8.49	-	336.86	345.35	379.89	3.655
L207276J	SL5566TBX; 557 mm wide	Nr	0.55	9.34	-	336.86	346.20	380.82	3.981
L207276K	SL3366THX; 332 mm wide	Nr	0.50	8.49	-	187.46	195.95	215.55	3.655

Major Works 2011		Unit	Labour Hours	Labour Net £	Plant Net £	Materials Net £	Unit Net £	Unit with 10% £	CO₂ Kg
L20	**L20: DOORS, SHUTTERS AND HATCHES**								
L2072	**Standard softwood external door frames and side lights**								
L207276	**Boulton and Paul softwood side lights; fitting to exterior frames (measured separately); to suit imperial doors**								
L207276L	SL5566THX; 557 mm wide	Nr	0.55	9.34	-	202.80	212.14	233.35	3.981
L207290	**Boulton and Paul softwood interior door frames**								
L207290A	225DF23 or 26	Nr	0.40	6.79	-	32.84	39.63	43.59	12.628
L207290B	25DF23 or 26	Nr	0.40	6.79	-	32.84	39.63	43.59	12.628
L207290C	4DF23 or 26	Nr	0.40	6.79	-	46.66	53.45	58.80	13.847
L207290D	45DF23 or 26	Nr	0.40	6.79	-	53.71	60.50	66.55	14.457
L207290E	225SF23 or 26	Nr	0.40	6.79	-	35.15	41.94	46.13	12.628
L207290F	25SF23 or 26	Nr	0.40	6.79	-	37.53	44.32	48.75	12.628
L207290G	4SF23 or 26	Nr	0.40	6.79	-	55.66	62.45	68.70	14.457
L207290H	45SF23 or 26	Nr	0.40	6.79	-	62.75	69.54	76.49	14.823
L207290I	225FF23 or 26	Nr	0.40	6.79	-	42.98	49.77	54.75	12.628
L207290J	25FF23 or 26	Nr	0.40	6.79	-	45.03	51.82	57.00	12.628
L207290K	4FF23 or 26	Nr	0.40	6.79	-	65.17	71.96	79.16	15.677
L207290L	45FF23 or 26	Nr	0.40	6.79	-	71.89	78.68	86.55	15.677
L207291	**Boulton and Paul softwood interior door lining sets**								
L207291A	94DL8 or 9	Nr	0.40	6.79	-	40.29	47.08	51.79	2.539
L207291B	107DL8 or 9	Nr	0.40	6.79	-	47.40	54.19	59.61	2.652
L207291C	133DL8 or 9	Nr	0.40	6.79	-	53.00	59.79	65.77	2.697
L207291D	94FL8 or 9	Nr	0.40	6.79	-	57.60	64.39	70.83	2.764
L207291E	107FL8 or 9	Nr	0.40	6.79	-	64.92	71.71	78.88	2.989
L207291F	133FL8 or 9	Nr	0.40	6.79	-	69.93	76.72	84.39	2.989
L207291G	4DL23 or 26	Nr	0.40	6.79	-	34.75	41.54	45.69	2.314
L207291H	45DL23 or 26	Nr	0.40	6.79	-	36.51	43.30	47.63	2.314
L207291I	5DL23 or 26	Nr	0.40	6.79	-	39.42	46.21	50.83	2.427
L207291J	55DL23 or 26	Nr	0.40	6.79	-	42.43	49.22	54.14	2.427
L207291K	5FL23 or 26	Nr	0.40	6.79	-	55.52	62.31	68.54	2.764
L207291L	55FL23 or 26	Nr	0.40	6.79	-	59.52	66.31	72.94	2.764
L207291M	45DLR23A or 26A	Nr	0.40	6.79	-	37.84	44.63	49.09	2.539
L207291N	55DLR23A or 26A	Nr	0.40	6.79	-	43.54	50.33	55.36	2.652
L2073	**Softwood jambs, heads, cills, mullions, transoms or the like**								
L207351	**Wrought softwood plain jambs or heads**								
L207351A	25 x 75 mm	m	0.27	4.58	-	2.33	6.91	7.60	0.558
L207351B	25 x 100 mm	m	0.29	4.92	-	2.82	7.74	8.51	0.716
L207351C	25 x 125 mm	m	0.32	5.43	-	3.49	8.92	9.81	0.874
L207351D	25 x 150 mm	m	0.35	5.94	-	4.22	10.16	11.18	1.032
L207351E	32 x 75 mm	m	0.27	4.58	-	2.82	7.40	8.14	0.691
L207351F	32 x 100 mm	m	0.29	4.92	-	3.74	8.66	9.53	0.892
L207351G	32 x 125 mm	m	0.32	5.43	-	4.28	9.71	10.68	1.095
L207351H	32 x 150 mm	m	0.35	5.94	-	5.52	11.46	12.61	1.297
L207351I	50 x 75 mm	m	0.30	5.09	-	4.06	9.15	10.07	1.032
L207351J	50 x 100 mm	m	0.32	5.43	-	5.48	10.91	12.00	1.348
L207351K	50 x 125 mm	m	0.35	5.94	-	6.89	12.83	14.11	1.662
L207351L	50 x 150 mm	m	0.38	6.45	-	8.25	14.70	16.17	1.978
L207352	**Wrought softwood once rebated jambs or heads**								
L207352A	38 x 100 mm	m	0.36	6.11	-	4.64	10.75	11.83	1.031
L207352B	38 x 125 mm	m	0.38	6.45	-	5.65	12.10	13.31	1.271
L207352C	38 x 150 mm	m	0.40	6.79	-	6.67	13.46	14.81	1.511
L207352D	50 x 75 mm	m	0.35	5.94	-	4.40	10.34	11.37	1.055
L207352E	50 x 100 mm	m	0.37	6.28	-	7.45	13.73	15.10	1.371
L207352F	50 x 150 mm	m	0.43	7.30	-	10.93	18.23	20.05	2.001
L207352G	63 x 75 mm	m	0.37	6.28	-	5.35	11.63	12.79	1.344
L207352H	63 x 100 mm	m	0.40	6.79	-	7.08	13.87	15.26	1.742
L207352I	63 x 125 mm	m	0.43	7.30	-	8.76	16.06	17.67	2.139
L207352J	63 x 150 mm	m	0.45	7.64	-	10.47	18.11	19.92	2.538
L207353	**Wrought softwood once rebated and once grooved jambs or heads**								
L207353A	50 x 100 mm	m	0.37	6.28	-	6.05	12.33	13.56	1.371
L207353B	50 x 125 mm	m	0.40	6.79	-	7.47	14.26	15.69	1.685
L207353C	50 x 150 mm	m	0.43	7.30	-	8.84	16.14	17.75	2.001
L207353D	63 x 75 mm	m	0.37	6.28	-	5.60	11.88	13.07	1.344

Major Works 2011		Unit	Labour Hours	Labour Net £	Plant Net £	Materials Net £	Unit Net £	Unit with 10% £	CO$_2$ Kg
L20	**L20: DOORS, SHUTTERS AND HATCHES**								
L2073	**Softwood jambs, heads, cills, mullions, transoms or the like**								
L207353	**Wrought softwood once rebated and once grooved jambs or heads**								
L207353E	63 x 100 mm	m	0.40	6.79	-	7.33	14.12	15.53	1.742
L207353F	63 x 125 mm	m	0.43	7.30	-	9.00	16.30	17.93	2.139
L207353G	63 x 150 mm	m	0.45	7.64	-	10.71	18.35	20.19	2.538
L207354	**Wrought softwood once sunk weathered, once rebated and three times grooved cills**								
L207354A	63 x 75 mm	m	0.35	5.94	-	6.56	12.50	13.75	1.192
L207354B	75 x 150 mm	m	0.48	8.15	-	13.50	21.65	23.82	1.893
L207355	**Wrought softwood mullions or transoms**								
L207355A	32 x 63 mm	m	0.30	5.09	-	2.24	7.33	8.06	0.606
L207355B	32 x 100 mm	m	0.31	5.26	-	3.66	8.92	9.81	0.807
L207355C	32 x 150 mm	m	0.35	5.94	-	5.43	11.37	12.51	1.212
L207356	**Wrought softwood twice rebated mullions or transoms**								
L207356A	38 x 115 mm	m	0.38	6.45	-	5.81	12.26	13.49	1.103
L207356B	38 x 150 mm	m	0.40	6.79	-	6.82	13.61	14.97	1.439
L207356C	50 x 100 mm	m	0.37	6.28	-	5.91	12.19	13.41	1.263
L207356D	63 x 115 mm	m	0.42	7.13	-	8.75	15.88	17.47	1.829
L207356E	63 x 150 mm	m	0.45	7.64	-	10.65	18.29	20.12	2.386
L2076	**Standard hardwood external door frames**								
L207606	**Boulton and Paul hardwood exterior door frames; standard cills; heavy duty PVC-u waterbar; for 762 x 1981 mm doors**								
L207606A	856 x 2079 mm; FN26MH; opening inward; weatherstripped	Nr	0.50	8.49	-	402.29	410.78	451.86	17.723
L207606B	856 x 2035 mm; F26H; opening inward and outward; weatherstripped	Nr	0.50	8.49	-	417.69	426.18	468.80	17.958
L207606C	FE127RH; 1275 x 2100 mm	Nr	0.50	8.49	-	439.64	448.13	492.94	17.723
L207606D	FE135RH; 1350 x 2100 mm	Nr	0.50	8.49	-	458.78	467.27	514.00	17.958
L207606E	FE127FH; 1275 x 2100 mm	Nr	0.50	8.49	-	478.35	486.84	535.52	17.723
L207606F	FE135FH; 1350 x 2100 mm	Nr	0.50	8.49	-	506.52	515.01	566.51	17.958
L207606G	FED165PPH; 1650 x 2100 mm	Nr	0.50	8.49	-	614.13	622.62	684.88	18.898
L207606H	FED180PPH; 1800 x 2100 mm	Nr	0.50	8.49	-	646.50	654.99	720.49	19.367
L207606I	FED165RRH; 1650 x 2100 mm	Nr	0.50	8.49	-	688.84	697.33	767.06	18.898
L207606J	FED180RRH; 1800 x 2100 mm	Nr	0.50	8.49	-	728.69	737.18	810.90	19.367
L207606K	FED165FFH; 1650 x 2100 mm	Nr	0.50	8.49	-	766.20	774.69	852.16	18.898
L207606L	FED180FFH; 1800 x 2100 mm	Nr	0.50	8.49	-	824.20	832.69	915.96	19.367
L207607	**Boulton and Paul hardwood exterior door frames; standard cill; heavy duty PVC-u waterbar; for 838 x 1981 mm doors**								
L207607A	932 x 2079 mm; FN29MH; opening inward; weatherstripped	Nr	0.50	8.49	-	175.90	184.39	202.83	19.270
L207607B	932 x 2079 mm; FX29MH; opening outward; weatherstripped	Nr	0.50	8.49	-	175.90	184.39	202.83	19.270
L207607C	932 x 2079 mm; F29H; opening inward and outward; weatherstripped	Nr	0.50	8.49	-	147.18	155.67	171.24	19.270
L207608	**Boulton and Paul hardwood exterior door frames; standard cills; heavy duty PVC-u waterbar; for 807 x 2000 mm doors**								
L207608A	900 x 2100 mm; FNSH; opening inward; weatherstripped	Nr	0.50	8.49	-	168.77	177.26	194.99	19.307
L207608B	900 x 2100 mm; FXSH; opening outward weatherstripped	Nr	0.50	8.49	-	168.77	177.26	194.99	19.307
L207608C	900 x 2100 mm; FDH; opening inward and outward; weatherstripped	Nr	0.50	8.49	-	147.18	155.67	171.24	18.959

Major Works 2011		Unit	Labour Hours	Labour Net	Plant Net	Materials Net	Unit Net	Unit with 10%	CO₂
				£	£	£	£	£	Kg
L20	**L20: DOORS, SHUTTERS AND HATCHES**								
L2077	**Standard hardwood door frames**								
L207782	**Boulton and Paul hardwood side lights; fitting to exterior frames (measured separately)**								
L207782A	SL25PXH; 257 mm wide	Nr	0.40	6.79	-	162.64	169.43	186.37	17.175
L207782B	SL33PXH; 332 mm wide	Nr	0.45	7.64	-	173.46	181.10	199.21	17.731
L207782C	SL40PXH; 407 mm wide	Nr	0.40	6.79	-	160.39	167.18	183.90	18.286
L207782D	SL48PXH; 482 mm wide	Nr	0.45	7.64	-	203.64	211.28	232.41	18.841
L207782E	SL55PXH; 557 mm wide	Nr	0.40	6.79	-	177.24	184.03	202.43	19.396
L2078	**Hardwood jambs, heads, cills, mullions, transoms or the like**								
L207860	**Wrought hardwood; Sapele; plain jambs or heads**								
L207860A	20 x 68 mm	m	0.30	5.09	-	1.80	6.89	7.58	0.550
L207860B	20 x 93 mm	m	0.32	5.43	-	2.47	7.90	8.69	0.732
L207860C	20 x 118 mm	m	0.35	5.94	-	3.12	9.06	9.97	0.912
L207860D	20 x 143 mm	m	0.38	6.45	-	3.79	10.24	11.26	1.094
L207860E	26 x 56 mm	m	0.33	5.60	-	3.35	8.95	9.85	0.599
L207860F	26 x 93 mm	m	0.35	5.94	-	3.29	9.23	10.15	0.948
L207860G	26 x 118 mm	m	0.38	6.45	-	4.13	10.58	11.64	1.182
L207860H	26 x 143 mm	m	0.42	7.13	-	4.98	12.11	13.32	1.417
L207860I	44 x 56 mm	m	0.42	7.13	-	3.38	10.51	11.56	1.000
L207860J	44 x 68 mm	m	0.45	7.64	-	4.10	11.74	12.91	1.000
L207860K	44 x 93 mm	m	0.47	7.98	-	5.54	13.52	14.87	1.588
L207860L	44 x 118 mm	m	0.52	8.83	-	6.96	15.79	17.37	1.987
L207860M	44 x 143 mm	m	0.55	9.34	-	8.40	17.74	19.51	2.385
L207861	**Wrought hardwood; Sapele; once rebated jambs or heads**								
L207861A	32 x 93 mm	m	0.35	5.94	-	4.19	10.13	11.14	1.149
L207861B	32 x 118 mm	m	0.38	6.45	-	5.25	11.70	12.87	1.438
L207861C	32 x 143 mm	m	0.42	7.13	-	6.30	13.43	14.77	1.729
L207861D	44 x 68 mm	m	0.45	7.64	-	4.29	11.93	13.12	1.190
L207861E	44 x 93 mm	m	0.47	7.98	-	5.73	13.71	15.08	1.588
L207861F	44 x 118 mm	m	0.52	8.83	-	7.15	15.98	17.58	1.987
L207861G	44 x 143 mm	m	0.55	9.34	-	8.61	17.95	19.75	2.385
L207861H	56 x 68 mm	m	0.50	8.49	-	5.27	13.76	15.14	1.530
L207861I	56 x 93 mm	m	0.52	8.83	-	7.11	15.94	17.53	2.036
L207861J	56 x 118 mm	m	0.57	9.68	-	8.95	18.63	20.49	2.543
L207861K	56 x 143 mm	m	0.60	10.19	-	10.77	20.96	23.06	3.050
L207862	**Wrought hardwood; Sapele; once rebated and once grooved jambs or heads**								
L207862A	44 x 93 mm	m	0.47	7.98	-	5.93	13.91	15.30	1.588
L207862B	44 x 118 mm	m	0.52	8.83	-	7.37	16.20	17.82	1.987
L207862C	44 x 143 mm	m	0.55	9.34	-	8.79	18.13	19.94	2.385
L207862D	56 x 68 mm	m	0.50	8.49	-	5.47	13.96	15.36	1.530
L207862E	56 x 93 mm	m	0.52	8.83	-	7.29	16.12	17.73	1.985
L207862F	56 x 118 mm	m	0.57	9.68	-	9.14	18.82	20.70	2.543
L207862G	56 x 143 mm	m	0.60	10.19	-	10.99	21.18	23.30	3.050
L207863	**Wrought hardwood; Sapele; once sunk weathered, once rebated and three times grooved cills**								
L207863A	56 x 168 mm	m	0.60	10.19	-	13.38	23.57	25.93	3.405
L207863B	68 x 143 mm	m	0.65	11.04	-	13.77	24.81	27.29	3.519
L207864	**Wrought hardwood; Sapele; plain mullion or transoms**								
L207864A	26 x 56 mm	m	0.33	5.60	-	3.26	8.86	9.75	0.527
L207864B	26 x 93 mm	m	0.35	5.94	-	3.19	9.13	10.04	0.876
L207864C	26 x 143 mm	m	0.42	7.13	-	4.88	12.01	13.21	1.345
L207865	**Wrought hardwood; Sapele; twice rebated mullions or transoms**								
L207865A	32 x 118 mm	m	0.38	6.45	-	5.36	11.81	12.99	1.366
L207865B	32 x 143 mm	m	0.42	7.13	-	6.40	13.53	14.88	1.657
L207865C	44 x 93 mm	m	0.47	7.98	-	5.79	13.77	15.15	1.481
L207865D	56 x 118 mm	m	0.57	9.68	-	9.08	18.76	20.64	2.391
L207865E	56 x 143 mm	m	0.60	10.19	-	10.93	21.12	23.23	2.899

Major Works 2011		Unit	Labour Hours	Labour Net	Plant Net	Materials Net	Unit Net	Unit with 10%	CO$_2$
				£	£	£	£	£	Kg
L20	**L20: DOORS, SHUTTERS AND HATCHES**								
L2085	**Standard metal garage doors**								
L208541	**Henderson galvanised steel up-and-over garage doors complete with all gear; to suit opening size**								
L208541A	1981 x 1981 mm; Merlin 6666; canopy	Nr	3.00	50.94	-	271.85	322.79	355.07	172.640
L208541B	2134 x 1981 mm; Merlin 7066; canopy	Nr	3.25	55.19	-	255.67	310.86	341.95	185.974
L208541C	2286 x 1981 mm; Merlin 7666; canopy	Nr	3.50	59.43	-	304.22	363.65	400.02	199.221
L208541D	2438 x 1981 mm; Merlin 8066; canopy	Nr	3.75	63.68	-	351.95	415.63	457.19	212.467
L208541E	1981 x 2134 mm; Merlin 6670; canopy	Nr	3.25	55.19	-	281.56	336.75	370.43	185.974
L208541F	2134 x 2134 mm; Merlin 7070; canopy	Nr	3.75	63.68	-	292.89	356.57	392.23	200.338
L208541G	2286 x 2134 mm; Merlin 7670; canopy	Nr	3.75	63.68	-	348.71	412.39	453.63	214.607
L208541H	2438 x 2134 mm; Merlin 8070; canopy	Nr	4.00	67.92	-	360.04	427.96	470.76	228.877
L208541I	1981 x 1981 mm; Regent 6666; canopy	Nr	3.00	50.94	-	312.31	363.25	399.58	172.640
L208541J	2134 x 1981 mm; Regent 7066; canopy	Nr	3.25	55.19	-	311.50	366.69	403.36	185.974
L208541K	2286 x 1981 mm; Regent 7666; canopy	Nr	3.50	59.43	-	339.01	398.44	438.28	199.221
L208541L	2438 x 1981 mm; Regent 8066; canopy	Nr	3.75	63.68	-	402.11	465.79	512.37	212.467
L208541M	1981 x 2134 mm; Regent 6670; canopy	Nr	3.25	55.19	-	313.12	368.31	405.14	185.974
L208541N	2134 x 2134 mm; Regent 7070; canopy	Nr	3.75	63.68	-	323.63	387.31	426.04	200.338
L208541O	2286 x 2134 mm; Regent 7670; canopy	Nr	3.75	63.68	-	381.08	444.76	489.24	214.607
L208541P	2438 x 2134 mm; Regent 8070; canopy	Nr	4.00	67.92	-	460.37	528.29	581.12	228.877
L208541Q	2743 x 2134 mm; Regent 9070; canopy	Nr	4.50	76.41	-	615.71	692.12	761.33	257.510
L208541R	2134 x 1981 mm; Doric 7066; canopy	Nr	3.25	55.19	-	385.12	440.31	484.34	185.974
L208541S	2134 x 2134 mm; Doric 7070; canopy	Nr	3.75	63.68	-	406.16	469.84	516.82	200.338
L208541T	4267 x 1981 mm; Doric 1466; tracked	Nr	5.00	84.90	-	1,127.86	1,212.76	1,334.04	371.861
L208541U	4267 x 2134 mm; Doric 1470; tracked	Nr	5.50	93.39	-	1,127.86	1,221.25	1,343.38	400.581
L208541V	2134 x 1981 mm; Regent Chevron 7066; canopy	Nr	3.25	55.19	-	323.63	378.82	416.70	185.974
L208541W	2134 x 2134 mm; Regent Chevron 7070; canopy	Nr	3.75	63.68	-	341.43	405.11	445.62	200.338
L208541X	4267 x 1981 mm; Regent Chevron 1466; canopy	Nr	5.00	84.90	-	978.18	1,063.08	1,169.39	371.861
L208541Y	4267 x 2134 mm; Regent Chevron 1470; canopy	Nr	5.50	93.39	-	978.18	1,071.57	1,178.73	400.581
L2090	**Standard GRP and plastic coated garage doors**								
L209042	**Henderson GRP up-and-over garage doors complete with all gear; to suit opening size**								
L209042A	4267 x 1981 mm; Consort 1466; tracked	Nr	4.50	76.41	-	1,545.92	1,622.33	1,784.56	1,068.112
L209042B	4267 x 2134 mm; Consort 1470; tracked	Nr	5.00	84.90	-	1,545.92	1,630.82	1,793.90	1,150.606
L209042C	4267 x 1981 mm; Caversham 1466; tracked	Nr	4.50	76.41	-	1,849.29	1,925.70	2,118.27	371.861
L209042D	4267 x 2134 mm; Caversham 1470; tracked	Nr	5.00	84.90	-	1,849.29	1,934.19	2,127.61	400.581
L209042E	2134 x 1981 mm; Consort 7066; tracked	Nr	3.25	55.19	-	767.14	822.33	904.56	534.181
L209042F	2134 x 2134 mm; Consort 7070; tracked	Nr	3.75	63.68	-	767.14	830.82	913.90	575.438
L209042G	2134 x 1981 mm; Caversham 7066; tracked	Nr	3.25	55.19	-	997.37	1,052.56	1,157.82	185.974
L209042H	2134 x 2134 mm; Caversham 7070; tracked	Nr	3.75	63.68	-	997.37	1,061.05	1,167.16	200.338

Major Works 2011		Unit	Labour Hours	Labour Net	Plant Net	Materials Net	Unit Net	Unit with 10%	CO$_2$
				£	£	£	£	£	Kg
L20	**L20: DOORS, SHUTTERS AND HATCHES**								
L2090	**Standard GRP and plastic coated garage doors**								
L209043	**Henderson roller doors complete with all gear; HP 200 High Performance Plastisol finish; curtain width and height**								
L209043A	2185 x 1829 - 2133 mm	Nr	3.00	50.94	-	429.62	480.56	528.62	205.029
L209043B	2490 x 1829 - 2133 mm	Nr	3.10	52.64	-	438.52	491.16	540.28	233.649
L209043C	2800 x 1829 - 2133 mm	Nr	3.25	55.19	-	484.64	539.83	593.81	262.738
L209043D	3400 x 1829 - 2133 mm	Nr	3.50	59.43	-	608.43	667.86	734.65	319.039
L209043E	4370 x 1829 - 2133 mm	Nr	3.75	63.68	-	864.91	928.59	1,021.45	410.059
L209043F	5000 x 1829 - 2133 mm	Nr	4.00	67.92	-	1,046.95	1,114.87	1,226.36	469.175
L209043G	2185 x 2160 - 2440 mm	Nr	3.50	59.43	-	458.75	518.18	570.00	234.539
L209043H	2490 x 2160 - 2440 mm	Nr	3.60	61.13	-	476.55	537.68	591.45	267.278
L209043I	2800 x 2160 - 2440 mm	Nr	3.75	63.68	-	542.89	606.57	667.23	300.553
L209043J	3400 x 2160 - 2440 mm	Nr	4.00	67.92	-	683.68	751.60	826.76	364.958
L209043K	4370 x 2160 - 2440 mm	Nr	4.30	73.01	-	973.33	1,046.34	1,150.97	469.078
L209043L	5000 x 2160 - 2440 mm	Nr	4.60	78.11	-	1,122.20	1,200.31	1,320.34	536.702
L209043M	2185 x 2465 - 2745 mm	Nr	4.00	67.92	-	528.33	596.25	655.88	263.856
L209043N	2490 x 2465 - 2745 mm	Nr	4.15	70.47	-	581.73	652.20	717.42	300.688
L209043O	2800 x 2465 - 2745 mm	Nr	4.25	72.17	-	606.81	678.98	746.88	338.123
L209043P	3400 x 2465 - 2745 mm	Nr	4.55	77.26	-	711.18	788.44	867.28	410.577
L209043Q	4375 x 2465 - 2745 mm	Nr	4.85	82.35	-	1,051.81	1,134.16	1,247.58	527.713
L209043R	5000 x 2465 - 2745 mm	Nr	5.20	88.30	-	1,173.17	1,261.47	1,387.62	603.790
L209043S	2185 x 2770 - 3000 mm	Nr	4.40	74.71	-	560.69	635.40	698.94	288.368
L209043T	2490 x 2770 - 3000 mm	Nr	4.55	77.26	-	597.91	675.17	742.69	328.620
L209043U	2800 x 2770 - 3000 mm	Nr	4.70	79.81	-	656.98	736.79	810.47	369.533
L209043V	3400 x 2770 - 3000 mm	Nr	5.00	84.90	-	801.80	886.70	975.37	448.718
L209043W	4370 x 2770 - 3000 mm	Nr	5.35	90.84	-	1,115.73	1,206.57	1,327.23	576.735
L209043X	5000 x 2770 - 3000 mm	Nr	5.75	97.64	-	1,195.82	1,293.46	1,422.81	659.880
L209044	**Henderson roller shutter garage doors; accessories**								
L209044A	heavy duty remote control	Nr	-	-	-	275.24	275.24	302.76	10.800
L209044B	dual remote control	Nr	-	-	-	335.07	335.07	368.58	12.000
L209044C	external manual release and electric key switch	Nr	-	-	-	35.95	35.95	39.55	1.200
L209044D	two function transmitter	Nr	-	-	-	33.51	33.51	36.86	0.840
L2096	**Mastic pointing**								
L209699	**Pointing frames one side with mastic sealant**								
L209699A	standard	m	0.05	0.64	-	0.26	0.90	0.99	0.183
L209699B	coloured	m	0.05	0.64	-	0.27	0.91	1.00	0.183

Major Works 2011		Unit	Labour Hours	Labour Net	Plant Net	Materials Net	Unit Net	Unit with 10%	CO₂
				£	£	£	£	£	Kg
L30	**L30: STAIRS, WALKWAYS AND BALUSTRADES**								
L3011	**Staircases, handrails and balustrades**								
L301101	**Boulton and Paul standard stock flight staircase; closed riser straight flight unit; 13 riser; 855 mm overall width; total rise 2600 mm; model ref**								
L301101A	STAIR M; Parana Pine strings and treads	Nr	8.00	135.84	-	490.13	625.97	688.57	9.000
L301101B	STAIR WM; whitewood/composite string and treads	Nr	8.00	135.84	-	335.61	471.45	518.60	9.000
L301111	**Boulton and Paul standard staircase; winder design; o/a size 2940 x 1027 mm; newels and raking balustrade; 13 riser; total rise 2600 mm; model ref**								
L301111A	W4DBTW; whitewood	Nr	18.00	305.64	-	1,346.78	1,652.42	1,817.66	29.250
L301111B	W4DBTP; parana pine	Nr	18.00	305.64	-	1,433.46	1,739.10	1,913.01	31.500
L301111C	W4DBTP; hardwood	Nr	27.00	458.46	-	1,858.80	2,317.26	2,548.99	37.600
L301152	**Handrails**								
L301152A	50 mm dia; softwood mopstick	m	0.40	6.79	-	3.09	9.88	10.87	0.741
L301152B	50 mm dia; hardwood mopstick	m	0.40	6.79	-	4.44	11.23	12.35	1.113
L301152C	50 x 75 mm; softwood moulded	m	0.45	7.64	-	6.61	14.25	15.68	1.344
L301152D	50 x 75 mm; hardwood moulded	m	0.45	7.64	-	8.01	15.65	17.22	1.657
L301152E	75 x 100 mm; moulded	m	0.50	8.49	-	9.89	18.38	20.22	1.946
L301153	**Balustrades; stair and landing kits; hemlock spindles and newels; string capping and moulded handrail; newel caps; type**								
L301153A	SMRKIT36 square stair kit	Nr	2.80	47.54	-	39.74	87.28	96.01	5.890
L301153B	SMLKIT24 square landing kit	Nr	2.80	47.54	-	42.99	90.53	99.58	6.341
L301153C	SKGE Georgian stair kit	Nr	3.60	61.13	-	39.74	100.87	110.96	5.890
L301153D	LKGE Georgian landing kit	Nr	3.60	61.13	-	42.99	104.12	114.53	6.341
L301154	**Newels, caps and accessories**								
L301154A	82 x 82 mm newel; turned softwood	Nr	0.50	8.49	-	82.57	91.06	100.17	0.658
L301154B	82 x 82 mm newel; turned hardwood	Nr	0.75	12.73	-	118.74	131.47	144.62	0.859
L301154C	82 x 82 mm newel; square softwood	Nr	0.50	8.49	-	49.60	58.09	63.90	0.658
L301154D	82 x 82 mm newel; square hardwood	Nr	0.75	12.73	-	76.78	89.51	98.46	0.859
L301154E	caps to suit newels; softwood	Nr	0.22	3.74	-	5.41	9.15	10.07	0.463
L301154F	caps to suit newels; hardwood	Nr	0.25	4.25	-	7.58	11.83	13.01	0.664

Major Works 2011		Unit	Labour Hours	Labour Net	Plant Net	Materials Net	Unit Net	Unit with 10%	CO₂
				£	£	£	£	£	Kg
L40	**L40: GENERAL GLAZING**								
L4011	**Plain glazing**								
L401102	**Clear sheet or float glass to wood with putty**								
L401102A	3 mm	m²	0.60	10.19	-	35.23	45.42	49.96	9.649
L401102B	4 mm	m²	0.60	10.19	-	39.83	50.02	55.02	11.880
L401102C	5 mm	m²	0.70	11.89	-	58.35	70.24	77.26	14.111
L401102D	6 mm	m²	0.70	11.89	-	65.58	77.47	85.22	16.343
L401102E	10 mm	m²	0.90	15.28	-	125.17	140.45	154.50	25.268
L401103	**Clear sheet or float glass to wood with beads (beads measured separately)**								
L401103A	3 mm	m²	0.70	11.89	-	34.76	46.65	51.32	6.694
L401103B	4 mm	m²	0.70	11.89	-	39.36	51.25	56.38	8.925
L401103C	5 mm	m²	0.80	13.58	-	57.88	71.46	78.61	11.156
L401103D	6 mm	m²	0.80	13.58	-	65.11	78.69	86.56	13.388
L401103E	10 mm	m²	1.00	16.98	-	124.70	141.68	155.85	22.313
L401104	**Georgian wired glass to wood with putty**								
L401104A	6 mm polished plate	m²	0.70	11.89	-	100.41	112.30	123.53	22.958
L401104B	7 mm cast glass	m²	0.75	12.73	-	48.29	61.02	67.12	26.291
L401105	**Georgian wired glass to wood with beads (beads measured separately)**								
L401105A	6 mm polished plate	m²	0.80	13.58	-	99.94	113.52	124.87	20.003
L401105B	7 mm cast glass	m²	0.85	14.43	-	47.82	62.25	68.48	23.336
L401106	**Toughened safety glass to wood with putty**								
L401106A	4 mm	m²	0.60	10.19	-	65.90	76.09	83.70	16.290
L401106B	5 mm	m²	0.60	10.19	-	75.04	85.23	93.75	19.624
L401106C	6 mm	m²	0.70	11.89	-	82.39	94.28	103.71	22.958
L401106D	10 mm	m²	0.90	15.28	-	156.38	171.66	188.83	36.293
L401107	**Toughened safety glass to wood with beads (beads measured separately)**								
L401107A	4 mm	m²	0.70	11.89	-	65.43	77.32	85.05	13.335
L401107B	5 mm	m²	0.70	11.89	-	74.57	86.46	95.11	16.669
L401107C	6 mm	m²	0.80	13.58	-	81.92	95.50	105.05	20.003
L401107D	10 mm	m²	1.00	16.98	-	155.91	172.89	190.18	33.338
L401108	**Clear laminated safety glass to wood with beads (beads measured separately)**								
L401108A	4.4 mm	m²	0.75	12.73	-	78.62	91.35	100.49	14.669
L401108B	5.4 mm	m²	0.80	13.58	-	66.76	80.34	88.37	18.002
L401108C	6.4 mm	m²	0.90	15.28	-	66.76	82.04	90.24	21.336
L401108D	6.8 mm	m²	0.95	16.13	-	66.76	82.89	91.18	22.670
L401109	**Clear laminated anti-bandit glass to wood with beads (beads measured separately)**								
L401109A	7.5 mm	m²	0.90	15.28	-	178.72	194.00	213.40	25.004
L401109B	9.5 mm	m²	1.00	16.98	-	209.29	226.27	248.90	31.671
L401109C	11.5 mm	m²	1.10	18.68	-	214.36	233.04	256.34	38.339
L401110	**Antisun float glass to wood with putty**								
L401110A	4 mm	m²	0.65	11.04	-	63.97	75.01	82.51	16.290
L401110B	6 mm	m²	0.75	12.73	-	93.41	106.14	116.75	22.958
L401110C	10 mm	m²	0.95	16.13	-	187.52	203.65	224.02	36.293
L401111	**Antisun float glass to wood with beads (beads measured separately)**								
L401111A	4 mm	m²	0.75	12.73	-	63.50	76.23	83.85	13.335
L401111B	6 mm	m²	0.85	14.43	-	92.94	107.37	118.11	20.003
L401111C	10 mm	m²	1.05	17.83	-	187.05	204.88	225.37	33.338

Major Works 2011		Unit	Labour Hours	Labour Net	Plant Net	Materials Net	Unit Net	Unit with 10%	CO₂
				£	£	£	£	£	Kg

L40   **L40: GENERAL GLAZING**

L4011   **Plain glazing**

L401112   **Extra over clear sheet or float glass for**

L401112A	white patterned glass; 4 mm	m²	-	-	-	5.96	5.96	6.56	7.140
L401112B	white patterned glass; 6 mm	m²	-	-	-	13.67	13.67	15.04	10.710
L401112C	tinted patterned glass; 4 mm	m²	-	-	-	22.00	22.00	24.20	7.140
L401112D	tinted patterned glass; 6 mm	m²	-	-	-	10.94	10.94	12.03	10.710

L401113   **Extra over toughened safety glass for**

L401113A	tempered safety glass; 4 mm	m²	-	-	-	13.20	13.20	14.52	2.730
L401113B	tempered safety glass; 6 mm	m²	-	-	-	7.58	7.58	8.34	4.095
L401113C	white patterned safety glass; 4 mm	m²	-	-	-	13.20	13.20	14.52	2.730
L401113D	white patterned safety glass; 6 mm	m²	-	-	-	7.58	7.58	8.34	4.095
L401113E	tinted patterned safety glass; 4 mm	m²	-	-	-	49.40	49.40	54.34	2.730
L401113F	tinted patterned safety glass; 6 mm	m²	-	-	-	52.19	52.19	57.41	4.095

L4031   **Special glazing**

L403121   **Boulton and Paul hermetically sealed annealed double glazing units to wood with beads (beads measured separately); to suit window ref**

L403121A	WN07C/WN07CH	Set	0.55	9.34	-	36.28	45.62	50.18	6.222
L403121B	WN09C/WN09CH	Set	0.66	11.21	-	36.29	47.50	52.25	7.466
L403121C	WN10C/WN10CH	Set	0.76	12.90	-	42.15	55.05	60.56	8.711
L403121D	WN12C/WN12CH	Set	0.88	14.94	-	133.34	148.28	163.11	9.955
L403121E	WN07V/WN07VH	Set	0.55	9.34	-	72.58	81.92	90.11	6.222
L403121F	WN09V/WN09VH	Set	0.66	11.21	-	72.58	83.79	92.17	7.466
L403121G	WN10V/WN10VH	Set	0.77	13.07	-	72.74	85.81	94.39	8.711
L403121H	WN12V	Set	0.88	14.94	-	81.60	96.54	106.19	9.955
L403121I	W107C/W107CH	Set	0.71	12.06	-	41.06	53.12	58.43	8.033
L403121J	W109C/W109CH	Set	0.85	14.43	-	45.83	60.26	66.29	9.639
L403121K	W110C/W110CH	Set	0.99	16.81	-	50.61	67.42	74.16	11.246
L403121L	W112C/W112CH	Set	1.13	19.19	-	55.36	74.55	82.01	12.852
L403121M	W113C/W113CH	Set	1.28	21.73	-	64.84	86.57	95.23	14.459
L403121N	W110T/W110TH	Set	0.99	16.81	-	77.35	94.16	103.58	11.246
L403121O	W112T/W112TH	Set	1.13	19.19	-	82.13	101.32	111.45	12.852
L403121P	W107V/W107VH	Set	0.71	12.06	-	72.58	84.64	93.10	6.222
L403121Q	W109V/W109VH	Set	0.86	14.60	-	78.11	92.71	101.98	7.466
L403121R	W110V/W110VH	Set	0.99	16.81	-	83.75	100.56	110.62	8.711
L403121S	W112V/W112VH	Set	1.13	19.19	-	89.42	108.61	119.47	9.955
L403121T	W113V/W113VH	Set	1.28	21.73	-	95.07	116.80	128.48	14.459
L403121U	W115V	Set	1.42	24.11	-	119.79	143.90	158.29	16.065
L403121V	W2N09W/W2N09WH	Set	1.23	20.89	-	92.45	113.34	124.67	14.000
L403121W	W2N10W/W2N10WH	Set	1.44	24.45	-	101.10	125.55	138.11	16.333
L403121X	W2N12W/W2N12WH	Set	1.65	28.02	-	117.15	145.17	159.69	18.666
L403121Y	W2N13W/W2N13WH	Set	1.85	31.41	-	118.41	149.82	164.80	20.999
L403121Z	W2N15W	Set	2.06	34.98	-	149.04	184.02	202.42	16.065

L403122   **Boulton and Paul hermetically sealed annealed double glazing units to wood with beads (beads measured separately); to suit window ref**

L403122A	W207C/W207CH	Set	1.35	22.92	-	88.51	111.43	122.57	15.300
L403122B	W209C/W209CH	Set	1.62	27.51	-	98.95	126.46	139.11	18.360
L403122C	W210C/W210CH	Set	1.89	32.09	-	109.41	141.50	155.65	21.420
L403122D	W212C/W212CH	Set	2.16	36.68	-	117.27	153.95	169.35	24.480
L403122E	W213C/W213CH	Set	2.43	41.26	-	139.65	180.91	199.00	27.540
L403122F	W207CV	Set	1.35	22.92	-	82.11	105.03	115.53	15.300
L403122G	W209CV/W209CVH	Set	1.62	27.51	-	91.68	119.19	131.11	18.360
L403122H	W210CV/W210CVH	Set	1.89	32.09	-	101.24	133.33	146.66	21.420
L403122I	W212CV/W212CVH	Set	2.16	36.68	-	144.77	181.45	199.60	24.480
L403122J	W213CV/W213CVH	Set	2.43	41.26	-	159.93	201.19	221.31	27.540
L403122K	W204DG	Set	0.81	13.75	-	49.52	63.27	69.60	9.180
L403122L	W206DG	Set	1.08	18.34	-	65.85	84.19	92.61	12.240
L403122M	W207DG	Set	1.35	22.92	-	77.49	100.41	110.45	15.300
L403122N	W210T	Set	1.89	32.09	-	136.14	168.23	185.05	21.420
L403122O	W212T	Set	2.16	36.68	-	151.25	187.93	206.72	24.480
L403122P	W209W/W209WH	Set	1.62	27.51	-	102.15	129.66	142.63	18.360
L403122Q	W210W/W210WH	Set	1.89	32.09	-	113.78	145.87	160.46	21.420
L403122R	W212W/W212WH	Set	2.16	36.68	-	125.40	162.08	178.29	24.480
L403122S	W213W	Set	2.43	41.26	-	141.74	183.00	201.30	27.540

Major Works 2011		Unit	Labour Hours	Labour Net £	Plant Net £	Materials Net £	Unit Net £	Unit with 10% £	CO_2 Kg
L40	**L40: GENERAL GLAZING**								
L4031	**Special glazing**								
L403122	**Boulton and Paul hermetically sealed annealed double glazing units to wood with beads (beads measured separately); to suit window ref**								
L403122T	W215W	Set	2.70	45.85	-	182.95	228.80	251.68	30.600
L403122U	W312C	Set	3.06	51.96	-	172.44	224.40	246.84	36.108
L403122V	W307CC/W307CCH	Set	1.91	32.43	-	129.58	162.01	178.21	22.568
L403122W	W309CC/W309CCH	Set	2.30	39.05	-	144.80	183.85	202.24	27.081
L403122X	W310CC/W310CCH	Set	2.68	45.51	-	160.03	205.54	226.09	31.595
L403122Y	W312CC/W312CCH	Set	3.06	51.96	-	179.87	231.83	255.01	36.108
L403122Z	W313CC/W313CCH	Set	3.44	58.41	-	204.51	262.92	289.21	40.622
L403123	**Boulton and Paul hermetically sealed annealed double glazing units to wood with beads (beads measured separately); to suit window ref**								
L403123A	W309CVC/W309CVCH	Set	2.30	39.05	-	169.79	208.84	229.72	27.081
L403123B	W310CVC/W310CVCH	Set	2.68	45.51	-	185.00	230.51	253.56	31.595
L403123C	W312CVC/W312CVCH	Set	3.06	51.96	-	200.16	252.12	277.33	36.108
L403123D	W313CVC/W313CVCH	Set	3.44	58.41	-	224.78	283.19	311.51	40.622
L403123E	W310CW/W310CWH	Set	2.68	45.51	-	164.40	209.91	230.90	31.595
L403123F	W312CW/W312CWH	Set	3.06	51.96	-	180.76	232.72	255.99	36.108
L403123G	W313CW	Set	3.44	58.41	-	206.60	265.01	291.51	40.622
L403123H	W310WW	Set	2.68	45.51	-	184.74	230.25	253.28	31.595
L403123I	W312WW	Set	3.06	51.96	-	207.07	259.03	284.93	36.108
L403123J	W310T	Set	2.68	45.51	-	182.80	228.31	251.14	31.595
L403123K	W312T	Set	3.06	51.96	-	208.31	260.27	286.30	36.108
L403123L	W313T	Set	3.44	58.41	-	220.36	278.77	306.65	40.622
L403123M	W315T	Set	3.83	65.03	-	290.35	355.38	390.92	45.135
L403123N	W410CMC/W410CMCH	Set	3.68	62.49	-	183.27	245.76	270.34	41.751
L403123O	W412CMC/W412CMCH	Set	4.21	71.49	-	205.51	277.00	304.70	47.716
L403123P	W413CMC/W413CMCH	Set	4.74	80.49	-	213.05	293.54	322.89	53.680
L403123Q	W410CWC	Set	3.68	62.49	-	215.02	277.51	305.26	41.751
L403123R	W412CWC	Set	4.21	71.49	-	236.15	307.64	338.40	47.716
L403123S	W413CWC	Set	4.74	80.49	-	271.45	351.94	387.13	53.680
L403123T	W410TT	Set	3.68	62.49	-	260.16	322.65	354.92	41.751
L403123U	W412TT	Set	4.21	71.49	-	281.36	352.85	388.14	47.716
L403123V	W413TT	Set	4.74	80.49	-	307.25	387.74	426.51	53.680
L403123W	W415TT	Set	5.26	89.31	-	393.23	482.54	530.79	59.645
L403123X	W104A/W104AH	Set	0.43	7.30	-	36.78	44.08	48.49	4.820
L403123Y	W106A/W106AH	Set	0.57	9.68	-	36.28	45.96	50.56	6.426
L403123Z	W107A/W107AH	Set	0.71	12.06	-	41.06	53.12	58.43	8.033
L403124	**Boulton and Paul hermetically sealed annealed double glazing units to wood with beads (beads measured separately); to suit window ref**								
L403124A	W109A/W109AH	Set	0.86	14.60	-	45.84	60.44	66.48	9.639
L403124B	W110A	Set	0.99	16.81	-	50.62	67.43	74.17	11.246
L403124C	W112A	Set	1.13	19.19	-	55.37	74.56	82.02	12.852
L403124D	W2N04A/W2N04AH	Set	0.62	10.53	-	41.00	51.53	56.68	7.000
L403124E	W2N06A/W2N06AH	Set	0.83	14.09	-	41.00	55.09	60.60	9.333
L403124F	W2N07A/W2N07AH	Set	1.03	17.49	-	44.29	61.78	67.96	11.666
L403124G	W2N09A/W2N09AH	Set	1.23	20.89	-	64.53	85.42	93.96	14.000
L403124H	W2N10A/W2N10AH	Set	1.44	24.45	-	72.28	96.73	106.40	16.333
L403124I	W2N12A/W2N12AH	Set	1.65	28.02	-	80.02	108.04	118.84	18.666
L403124J	W2N13AS	Set	1.85	31.41	-	109.36	140.77	154.85	20.999
L403124L	W204A/W204AH	Set	0.81	13.75	-	41.72	55.47	61.02	9.180
L403124M	W206A/W206AH	Set	1.13	19.19	-	52.27	71.46	78.61	12.240
L403124N	W207A/W207AH	Set	1.35	22.92	-	67.73	90.65	99.72	15.300
L403124O	W209A/W209AH	Set	1.62	27.51	-	78.48	105.99	116.59	18.360
L403124P	W210A/W210AH	Set	1.89	32.09	-	89.22	121.31	133.44	21.420
L403124Q	W212A/W212AH	Set	2.16	36.68	-	104.67	141.35	155.49	24.480
L403124R	W213AS	Set	2.43	41.26	-	133.70	174.96	192.46	27.540
L403124S	W215AS	Set	2.70	45.85	-	156.51	202.36	222.60	34.425
L403124X	W310AE	Set	2.68	45.51	-	154.41	199.92	219.91	31.595
L403124Y	W312AE	Set	3.06	51.96	-	170.79	222.75	245.03	36.108
L403125	**Boulton and Paul hermetically sealed annealed double glazing units to wood with beads (beads measured separately); to suit window ref**								
L403125D	WHN09C/WHN09CH	Set	0.65	11.04	-	72.59	83.63	91.99	7.466
L403125E	WHN10C/WHN10CH	Set	0.77	13.07	-	72.59	85.66	94.23	8.711
L403125F	WH109C/WH109CH	Set	0.86	14.60	-	72.59	87.19	95.91	9.639

Major Works 2011		Unit	Labour Hours	Labour Net	Plant Net	Materials Net	Unit Net	Unit with 10%	CO$_2$
				£	£	£	£	£	Kg
L40	**L40: GENERAL GLAZING**								
L4031	**Special glazing**								
L403125	**Boulton and Paul hermetically sealed annealed double glazing units to wood with beads (beads measured separately); to suit window ref**								
L403125G	WH110C/WH110CH	Set	0.99	16.81	-	72.59	89.40	98.34	11.246
L403125H	WH112C/WH112CH	Set	1.13	19.19	-	72.59	91.78	100.96	12.852
L403125I	WH113C/WH113CH	Set	1.28	21.73	-	82.97	104.70	115.17	14.459
L403125J	WH209C/WH209CH	Set	1.62	27.51	-	145.19	172.70	189.97	18.360
L403125K	WH210C/WH210CH	Set	1.89	32.09	-	145.17	177.26	194.99	21.420
L403125L	WH212C/WH212CH	Set	2.16	36.68	-	159.75	196.43	216.07	24.480
L403125M	WH213C/WH213CH	Set	2.43	41.26	-	175.81	217.07	238.78	27.540
L403125N	WH309CC/WH309CCH	Set	2.30	39.05	-	217.74	256.79	282.47	31.595
L403125O	WH310CC/WH310CCH	Set	2.68	45.51	-	217.74	263.25	289.58	36.108
L403125P	WH312CC/WH312CCH	Set	3.06	51.96	-	232.33	284.29	312.72	36.108
L403125Q	WH313CC/WH313CCH	Set	3.44	58.41	-	258.83	317.24	348.96	40.622
L403126	**Boulton and Paul hermetically sealed toughened double glazing units to wood with beads (beads measured separately); to suit window ref**								
L403126A	WN07C/WN07CH	Set	0.55	9.34	-	29.55	38.89	42.78	9.296
L403126B	WN09C/WN09CH	Set	0.66	11.21	-	34.75	45.96	50.56	11.156
L403126C	WN10C/WN10CH	Set	0.76	12.90	-	41.98	54.88	60.37	13.015
L403126D	WN12C/WN12CH	Set	0.88	14.94	-	49.23	64.17	70.59	14.874
L403126E	WN07V/WN07VH	Set	0.55	9.34	-	59.11	68.45	75.30	9.296
L403126F	WN09V/WN09VH	Set	0.66	11.21	-	59.11	70.32	77.35	11.156
L403126G	WN10V/WN10VH	Set	0.77	13.07	-	66.57	79.64	87.60	13.015
L403126H	WN12V	Set	0.88	14.94	-	75.17	90.11	99.12	14.874
L403126I	W107C/W107CH	Set	0.71	12.06	-	39.44	51.50	56.65	9.296
L403126J	W109C/W109CH	Set	0.85	14.43	-	49.80	64.23	70.65	11.156
L403126K	W110C/W110CH	Set	0.99	16.81	-	47.70	64.51	70.96	13.015
L403126L	W112C/W112CH	Set	1.13	19.19	-	55.95	75.14	82.65	14.874
L403126M	W113C/W113CH	Set	1.28	21.73	-	54.37	76.10	83.71	16.734
L403126N	W110T/W110TH	Set	0.99	16.81	-	68.98	85.79	94.37	16.802
L403126O	W112T/W112TH	Set	1.13	19.19	-	79.36	98.55	108.41	19.202
L403126P	W107V/W107VH	Set	0.71	12.06	-	59.11	71.17	78.29	12.002
L403126Q	W109V/W109VH	Set	0.86	14.60	-	68.26	82.86	91.15	14.402
L403126R	W110V/W110VH	Set	0.99	16.81	-	80.07	96.88	106.57	16.802
L403126S	W112V/W112VH	Set	1.13	19.19	-	78.95	98.14	107.95	19.202
L403126T	W113V/W113VH	Set	1.28	21.73	-	79.36	101.09	111.20	21.603
L403126U	W115V	Set	1.42	24.11	-	87.13	111.24	122.36	24.003
L403126V	W2N09W/W2N09WH	Set	1.23	20.89	-	76.62	97.51	107.26	20.917
L403126W	W2N10W/W2N10WH	Set	1.44	24.45	-	81.52	105.97	116.57	24.403
L403126X	W2N12W/W2N12WH	Set	1.65	28.02	-	93.73	121.75	133.93	27.889
L403126Y	W2N13W/W2N13WH	Set	1.85	31.41	-	105.07	136.48	150.13	31.375
L403126Z	W2N15W	Set	2.06	34.98	-	117.10	152.08	167.29	34.862
L403127	**Boulton and Paul hermetically sealed toughened double glazing units to wood with beads (beads measured separately); to suit window ref**								
L403127A	W207C/W207CH	Set	1.35	22.92	-	89.95	112.87	124.16	22.860
L403127B	W209C/W209CH	Set	1.62	27.51	-	99.19	126.70	139.37	27.432
L403127C	W210C/W210CH	Set	1.89	32.09	-	97.49	129.58	142.54	32.004
L403127D	W212C/W212CH	Set	2.16	36.68	-	113.55	150.23	165.25	36.576
L403127E	W213C/W213CH	Set	2.43	41.26	-	119.99	161.25	177.38	41.148
L403127F	W207CV	Set	1.35	22.92	-	98.55	121.47	133.62	22.860
L403127G	W209CV/W209CVH	Set	1.62	27.51	-	118.05	145.56	160.12	27.432
L403127H	W210CV/W210CVH	Set	1.89	32.09	-	127.79	159.88	175.87	32.004
L403127I	W212CV/W212CVH	Set	2.16	36.68	-	134.94	171.62	188.78	36.576
L403127J	W213CV/W213CVH	Set	2.43	41.26	-	133.71	174.97	192.47	41.148
L403127K	W204DG	Set	0.81	13.75	-	44.04	57.79	63.57	13.716
L403127L	W206DG	Set	1.08	18.34	-	53.57	71.91	79.10	18.288
L403127M	W207DG	Set	1.35	22.92	-	70.04	92.96	102.26	22.860
L403127N	W210T	Set	1.89	32.09	-	118.79	150.88	165.97	32.004
L403127O	W212T	Set	2.16	36.68	-	136.92	173.60	190.96	36.576
L403127P	W209W/W209WH	Set	1.62	27.51	-	84.40	111.91	123.10	27.432
L403127Q	W210W/W210WH	Set	1.89	32.09	-	100.88	132.97	146.27	32.004
L403127R	W212W/W212WH	Set	2.16	36.68	-	116.45	153.13	168.44	36.576
L403127S	W213W	Set	2.43	41.26	-	123.84	165.10	181.61	41.148
L403127T	W215W	Set	2.70	45.85	-	138.69	184.54	202.99	45.720
L403127U	W310C	Set	2.68	45.51	-	140.73	186.24	204.86	47.206
L403127V	W312C	Set	3.06	51.96	-	163.85	215.81	237.39	53.950
L403127W	W307CC/W307CCH	Set	1.91	32.43	-	129.38	161.81	177.99	33.719
L403127X	W309CC/W309CCH	Set	2.30	39.05	-	148.98	188.03	206.83	40.462
L403127Y	W310CC/W310CCH	Set	2.68	45.51	-	145.20	190.71	209.78	47.206

Major Works 2011		Unit	Labour Hours	Labour Net	Plant Net	Materials Net	Unit Net	Unit with 10%	CO₂
				£	£	£	£	£	Kg
L40	**L40: GENERAL GLAZING**								
L4031	**Special glazing**								
L403127	**Boulton and Paul hermetically sealed toughened double glazing units to wood with beads (beads measured separately); to suit window ref**								
L403127Z	W312CC/W312CCH	Set	3.06	51.96	-	169.54	221.50	243.65	53.950
L403128	**Boulton and Paul hermetically sealed toughened double glazing units to wood with beads (beads measured separately); to suit window ref**								
L403128A	W313CC/W313CCH	Set	3.44	58.41	-	174.35	232.76	256.04	60.693
L403128B	W309CVC/W309CVCH	Set	2.30	39.05	-	167.85	206.90	227.59	40.462
L403128C	W310CVC/W310CVCH	Set	2.68	45.51	-	175.47	220.98	243.08	47.206
L403128D	W312CVC/W312CVCH	Set	3.06	51.96	-	190.88	242.84	267.12	53.950
L403128E	W313CVC/W313CVCH	Set	3.44	58.41	-	188.09	246.50	271.15	60.693
L403128F	W310CW/W310CWH	Set	2.68	45.51	-	148.59	194.10	213.51	47.206
L403128G	W312CW/W312CWH	Set	3.06	51.96	-	172.42	224.38	246.82	53.950
L403128H	W313CW	Set	3.44	58.41	-	178.21	236.62	260.28	60.693
L403128I	W310WW	Set	2.68	45.51	-	155.17	200.68	220.75	47.206
L403128J	W312WW	Set	3.06	51.96	-	177.40	229.36	252.30	53.950
L403128K	W310T	Set	2.68	45.51	-	161.97	207.48	228.23	47.206
L403128L	W312T	Set	3.06	51.96	-	187.21	239.17	263.09	53.950
L403128M	W313T	Set	3.44	58.41	-	199.88	258.29	284.12	60.693
L403128N	W315T	Set	3.83	65.03	-	223.01	288.04	316.84	67.437
L403128O	W410CMC/W410CMCH	Set	3.68	62.49	-	195.02	257.51	283.26	62.381
L403128P	W412CMC/W412CMCH	Set	4.21	71.49	-	227.14	298.63	328.49	71.293
L403128Q	W413CMC/W413CMCH	Set	4.74	80.49	-	240.00	320.49	352.54	80.204
L403128R	W410CWC	Set	3.68	62.49	-	196.30	258.79	284.67	62.381
L403128S	W412CWC	Set	4.21	71.49	-	228.44	299.93	329.92	71.293
L403128T	W413CWC	Set	4.74	80.49	-	232.61	313.10	344.41	80.204
L403128U	W410TT	Set	3.68	62.49	-	231.00	293.49	322.84	62.381
L403128V	W412TT	Set	4.21	71.49	-	266.56	338.05	371.86	71.293
L403128W	W413TT	Set	4.74	80.49	-	277.16	357.65	393.42	80.204
L403128X	W415TT	Set	5.26	89.31	-	308.57	397.88	437.67	89.116
L403128Y	W104A/W104AH	Set	0.43	7.30	-	29.55	36.85	40.54	7.201
L403128Z	W106A/W106AH	Set	0.57	9.68	-	29.55	39.23	43.15	9.601
L403129	**Boulton and Paul hermetically sealed toughened double glazing units to wood with beads (beads measured separately); to suit window ref**								
L403129A	W107A/W107AH	Set	0.71	12.06	-	38.79	50.85	55.94	12.002
L403129B	W109A/W109AH	Set	0.86	14.60	-	49.23	63.83	70.21	14.402
L403129C	W110A	Set	0.99	16.81	-	47.30	64.11	70.52	16.802
L403129D	W112A	Set	1.13	19.19	-	55.48	74.67	82.14	19.202
L403129E	W2N04A/W2N04AH	Set	0.62	10.53	-	29.55	40.08	44.09	10.458
L403129F	W2N06A/W2N06AH	Set	0.83	14.09	-	44.40	58.49	64.34	13.945
L403129G	W2N07A/W2N07AH	Set	1.03	17.49	-	48.19	65.68	72.25	17.431
L403129H	W2N09A/W2N09AH	Set	1.23	20.89	-	51.80	72.69	79.96	20.917
L403129I	W2N10A/W2N10AH	Set	1.44	24.45	-	62.65	87.10	95.81	24.403
L403129J	W2N12A/W2N12AH	Set	1.65	28.02	-	73.64	101.66	111.83	27.889
L403129K	W2N13AS	Set	1.85	31.41	-	94.50	125.91	138.50	31.375
L403129M	W204A/W204AH	Set	0.81	13.75	-	39.01	52.76	58.04	13.716
L403129N	W206A/W206AH	Set	1.13	19.19	-	48.99	68.18	75.00	18.288
L403129O	W207A/W207AH	Set	1.35	22.92	-	56.59	79.51	87.46	22.860
L403129P	W209A/W209AH	Set	1.62	27.51	-	71.78	99.29	109.22	27.432
L403129Q	W210A/W210AH	Set	1.89	32.09	-	86.09	118.18	130.00	32.004
L403129R	W212A/W212AH	Set	2.16	36.68	-	92.36	129.04	141.94	36.576
L403129S	W213AS	Set	2.43	41.26	-	128.97	170.23	187.25	41.148
L403129T	W215AS	Set	2.70	45.85	-	135.26	181.11	199.22	45.720
L403129Y	W310AE	Set	2.68	45.51	-	138.15	183.66	202.03	47.206
L403129Z	W312AE	Set	3.06	51.96	-	161.19	213.15	234.47	53.950
L403130	**Boulton and Paul hermetically sealed toughened double glazing units to wood with beads (beads measured separately); to suit window ref**								
L403130A	W310AV	Set	2.68	45.51	-	166.16	211.67	232.84	67.437
L403130E	WHN09C/WHN09CH	Set	0.65	11.04	-	59.11	70.15	77.17	11.156
L403130F	WHN10C/WHN10CH	Set	0.77	13.07	-	59.11	72.18	79.40	13.015
L403130G	WHN09C/WHN09CH	Set	0.86	14.60	-	59.11	73.71	81.08	11.156
L403130H	WH110C/WH110CH	Set	0.99	16.81	-	59.11	75.92	83.51	13.015
L403130I	WH112C/WH112CH	Set	1.13	19.19	-	69.21	88.40	97.24	14.874
L403130J	WH113C/WH113CH	Set	1.28	21.73	-	79.68	101.41	111.55	16.734
L403130K	WH209C/WH209CH	Set	1.62	27.51	-	120.31	147.82	162.60	27.432

Major Works 2011		Unit	Labour Hours	Labour Net	Plant Net	Materials Net	Unit Net	Unit with 10%	CO$_2$
				£	£	£	£	£	Kg
L40	**L40: GENERAL GLAZING**								
L4031	**Special glazing**								
L403130	**Boulton and Paul hermetically sealed toughened double glazing units to wood with beads (beads measured separately); to suit window ref**								
L403130L	WH210C/WH210CH	Set	1.89	32.09	-	132.18	164.27	180.70	32.004
L403130M	WH212C/WH212CH	Set	2.16	36.68	-	154.04	190.72	209.79	36.576
L403130N	WH213C/WH213CH	Set	2.43	41.26	-	176.20	217.46	239.21	41.148
L403130O	WH309CC/WH309CCH	Set	2.30	39.05	-	179.41	218.46	240.31	53.470
L403130P	WH310CC/WH310CCH	Set	2.68	45.51	-	191.31	236.82	260.50	62.381
L403130Q	WH312CC/WH312CCH	Set	3.06	51.96	-	223.28	275.24	302.76	71.293
L403130R	WH313CC/WH313CCH	Set	3.44	58.41	-	255.89	314.30	345.73	80.204
L403131	**John Carr sealed toughened double glazing units; to suit door ref**								
L403131A	231SC	Set	1.71	29.04	-	165.18	194.22	213.64	38.100
L403131B	261SC	Set	1.71	29.04	-	168.40	197.44	217.18	35.560
L403131C	291SC	Set	1.85	31.41	-	181.67	213.08	234.39	53.470
L403131D	231SA	Set	1.65	28.02	-	161.13	189.15	208.07	38.100
L403131E	261SA	Set	1.75	29.72	-	169.99	199.71	219.68	35.560
L403131F	26E2XGG	Set	1.38	23.43	-	123.95	147.38	162.12	27.432
L403131G	29E2XGG	Set	1.40	23.77	-	135.80	159.57	175.53	25.400
L403131H	26ESA	Set	2.00	33.96	-	194.47	228.43	251.27	34.290
L403131I	29ESA	Set	2.10	35.66	-	207.04	242.70	266.97	62.381
L403131J	26ESC	Set	2.55	43.30	-	248.16	291.46	320.61	63.500
L403131K	29ESC	Set	2.55	43.30	-	248.16	291.46	320.61	63.500
L403131L	2.6E+11	Set	1.32	22.41	-	128.22	150.63	165.69	27.940
L403131M	2.9E+11	Set	1.45	24.62	-	141.13	165.75	182.33	27.940
L403131N	26EKXT	Set	1.51	25.64	-	145.79	171.43	188.57	27.940
L403131O	29EKXT	Set	1.51	25.64	-	145.79	171.43	188.57	27.940
L403131P	26ESCP	Set	1.82	30.90	-	176.37	207.27	228.00	35.560
L403131Q	29ESCP	Set	1.82	30.90	-	176.39	207.29	228.02	35.560
L403131R	2.60E+51	Set	1.62	27.51	-	159.19	186.70	205.37	29.210
L403131S	2.90E+51	Set	1.72	29.21	-	167.03	196.24	215.86	38.100
L403131T	26E4XG	Set	0.92	15.62	-	88.78	104.40	114.84	20.320
L403131U	29E4XG	Set	1.00	16.98	-	97.82	114.80	126.28	21.590
L403131V	26E2XG	Set	0.85	14.43	-	80.18	94.61	104.07	22.860
L403131W	29E2XG	Set	0.83	14.09	-	80.19	94.28	103.71	20.320
L403131X	26F2X	Set	0.68	11.46	-	64.80	76.26	83.89	19.050
L403131Y	29F2X	Set	0.70	11.89	-	64.80	76.69	84.36	19.050
L403132	**John Carr hermetically sealed toughened double glazing units to wood with beads (beads measured separately); to suit door ref**								
L403132A	26F3X	Set	1.15	19.53	-	64.80	84.33	92.76	19.050
L403132B	29F3X	Set	1.20	20.38	-	64.80	85.18	93.70	19.050
L403132C	26F3XBF	Set	1.15	19.53	-	69.43	88.96	97.86	19.050
L403132D	29F3XBF	Set	1.20	20.38	-	69.43	89.81	98.79	19.050
L403132E	28F3XBF	Set	1.18	20.04	-	69.43	89.47	98.42	19.050
L403132F	26H2XGG	Set	1.75	29.72	-	128.14	157.86	173.65	27.940
L403132G	29H2XGG	Set	1.75	29.72	-	128.15	157.87	173.66	27.940
L403132H	807H2XGG	Set	1.75	29.72	-	128.15	157.87	173.66	27.940
L403132I	26H10	Set	1.60	27.17	-	119.12	146.29	160.92	27.940
L403132J	29H10	Set	1.65	28.02	-	130.90	158.92	174.81	29.210
L403132K	807H10	Set	1.65	28.02	-	130.90	158.92	174.81	29.210
L403132L	29CARL	Set	1.85	31.41	-	184.97	216.38	238.02	31.750
L403132M	29CLAR	Set	2.17	36.85	-	127.72	164.57	181.03	27.940
L403133	**Boulton and Paul factory glazing; 20 mm Low E clear insulating units; to suit sidelights (measured separately); ref**								
L403133A	SL3366PX	Set	0.80	13.58	-	79.58	93.16	102.48	11.050
L403133B	SL5566PX	Set	1.20	20.38	-	109.31	129.69	142.66	17.000
L403133C	SL3366RX	Set	0.80	13.58	-	85.44	99.02	108.92	10.200
L403133D	SL5566RX	Set	1.20	20.38	-	127.39	147.77	162.55	18.700
L403133E	SL3366SBX	Set	0.80	13.58	-	120.23	133.81	147.19	15.300
L403133F	SL5566SBX	Set	1.20	20.38	-	190.62	211.00	232.10	18.700
L403133G	SL3366SHX	Set	0.80	13.58	-	116.16	129.74	142.71	12.750
L403133H	SL5566SHX	Set	1.20	20.38	-	145.88	166.26	182.89	17.000
L403133I	SL3366TBX	Set	0.80	13.58	-	79.58	93.16	102.48	11.050
L403133J	SL5566TBX	Set	1.20	20.38	-	273.96	294.34	323.77	25.500
L403133K	SL3366THX	Set	0.80	13.58	-	152.44	166.02	182.62	21.250
L403133L	SL5566THX	Set	1.20	20.38	-	164.92	185.30	203.83	18.700

Surface Finishes

Surface Finishes

		Unit	Labour Hours	Labour Net	Plant Net	Materials Net	Unit Net	Unit with 10%	CO$_2$
				£	£	£	£	£	Kg
M10	**M10: CEMENT : SAND, CONCRETE SCREEDS AND TOPPINGS**								
M1011	**Cement and sand (1:3); trowelled finish**								
M101103	**To floors and landings**								
M101103A	25 mm thick	m^2	0.13	5.88	-	2.88	8.76	9.64	9.841
M101103B	32 mm thick	m^2	0.14	6.35	-	3.60	9.95	10.95	12.301
M101103C	38 mm thick	m^2	0.15	6.81	-	4.32	11.13	12.24	14.761
M101103D	50 mm thick	m^2	0.16	7.51	-	5.66	13.17	14.49	19.330
M101103E	65 mm thick	m^2	0.18	8.45	-	7.41	15.86	17.45	25.304
M1012	**Cement and sand (1:3); screeded finish**								
M101206	**To floors and landings**								
M101206A	25 mm thick	m^2	0.10	4.43	-	2.88	7.31	8.04	9.841
M101206B	32 mm thick	m^2	0.10	4.71	-	3.60	8.31	9.14	12.301
M101206C	38 mm thick	m^2	0.11	5.18	-	4.32	9.50	10.45	14.761
M101206D	50 mm thick	m^2	0.12	5.65	-	5.66	11.31	12.44	19.330
M101206E	65 mm thick	m^2	0.14	6.35	-	7.41	13.76	15.14	25.304
M1013	**Cement and sand (1:3); floated finish**								
M101309	**To floors and landings**								
M101309A	25 mm thick	m^2	0.12	5.41	-	2.88	8.29	9.12	9.841
M101309B	32 mm thick	m^2	0.12	5.65	-	3.60	9.25	10.18	12.301
M101309C	38 mm thick	m^2	0.13	6.11	-	4.32	10.43	11.47	14.761
M101309D	50 mm thick	m^2	0.15	6.81	-	5.66	12.47	13.72	19.330
M101309E	65 mm thick	m^2	0.16	7.51	-	7.41	14.92	16.41	25.304
M1016	**Granolithic paving (two parts cement to five parts dustless granite chippings); trowelled finish**								
M101602	**To floors and landings**								
M101602A	25 mm thick	m^2	0.15	7.05	-	1.54	8.59	9.45	8.736
M101602B	32 mm thick	m^2	0.16	7.51	-	1.93	9.44	10.38	10.920
M101602C	38 mm thick	m^2	0.17	7.98	-	2.31	10.29	11.32	13.104
M101602D	50 mm thick	m^2	0.19	8.68	-	3.03	11.71	12.88	17.160
M101603	**To staircases, treads, risers and edges of landings**								
M101603A	25 mm thick	m^2	0.44	20.62	-	1.54	22.16	24.38	8.736
M101603B	32 mm thick	m^2	0.47	22.02	-	1.93	23.95	26.35	10.920
M101603C	38 mm thick	m^2	0.50	23.42	-	2.31	25.73	28.30	13.104
M101603D	50 mm thick	m^2	0.55	25.57	-	3.03	28.60	31.46	17.160
M101604	**To skirtings, bands, strings, coverings to kerbs, mouldings, channels or the like; not exceeding 300 mm wide**								
M101604A	25 mm thick	m	0.11	5.18	-	0.44	5.62	6.18	2.496
M101604B	32 mm thick	m	0.12	5.65	-	0.61	6.26	6.89	3.432
M101604C	38 mm thick	m	0.13	5.88	-	0.72	6.60	7.26	4.056
M101604D	50 mm thick	m	0.14	6.35	-	0.94	7.29	8.02	5.304
M101605	**To risers and edges of landings; not exceeding 150 mm wide**								
M101605A	25 mm thick	m	0.08	3.50	-	0.22	3.72	4.09	1.248
M101605B	32 mm thick	m	0.08	3.78	-	0.33	4.11	4.52	1.872
M101605C	38 mm thick	m	0.09	3.97	-	0.39	4.36	4.80	2.184
M101605D	50 mm thick	m	0.09	3.97	-	0.50	4.47	4.92	2.808
M101606	**To risers and edges of landings; 150 - 300 mm wide**								
M101606A	25 mm thick	m	0.13	6.21	-	0.44	6.65	7.32	2.496
M101606B	32 mm thick	m	0.15	6.77	-	0.61	7.38	8.12	3.432
M101606C	38 mm thick	m	0.15	7.05	-	0.72	7.77	8.55	4.056
M101606D	50 mm thick	m	0.16	7.51	-	0.94	8.45	9.30	5.304

Major Works 2011		Unit	Labour Hours	Labour Net	Plant Net	Materials Net	Unit Net	Unit with 10%	CO$_2$
				£	£	£	£	£	Kg
M11	**M11: MASTIC ASPHALT FLOORING AND FLOOR UNDERLAYS**								
M1121	**Flat coverings**								
M112109	**Mastic asphalt paving; BS 1076; limestone aggregate; rubbing surface with fine sand**								
M112109A	20 mm two coat work	m^2	0.25	10.62	-	12.68	23.30	25.63	5.846
M112110	**Mastic asphalt coloured flooring; BS1451; limestone aggregate; rubbing surface with fine sand**								
M112110A	20 mm two coat work	m^2	0.25	10.62	-	14.46	25.08	27.59	5.846
M112110B	15 mm one coat work	m^2	0.15	6.39	-	11.23	17.62	19.38	5.278
M1123	**Sloping coverings**								
M112328	**Mastic asphalt paving; BS 1076; limestone aggregate; rubbing surface with fine sand**								
M112328A	20 mm two coat work	m^2	0.33	13.79	-	12.68	26.47	29.12	5.846
M112329	**Mastic asphalt coloured flooring; BS 1451; limestone aggregate; rubbing surface with fine sand**								
M112329A	20 mm two coat work	m^2	0.33	13.79	-	14.46	28.25	31.08	5.846
M112329B	15 mm one coat work	m^2	0.20	8.50	-	11.23	19.73	21.70	5.278
M1161	**Skirtings, upstands or the like**								
M116179	**Mastic asphalt coloured flooring; BS 1451; limestone aggregate; rubbing surface with fine sand; skirtings, upstands or the like; rounded arrises and internal angle fillet; turning nib into groove; 20 mm two coat work**								
M116179A	not exceeding 150 mm high	m	0.13	5.33	-	2.69	8.02	8.82	0.475
M116179B	150 - 300 mm high	m	0.20	8.50	-	4.70	13.20	14.52	0.828
M116189	**Mastic asphalt coloured flooring; BS 1451; limestone aggregate; rubbing surface with fine sand; skirtings, upstands or the like; rounded arrises and internal angle fillet; turning nib into groove; 15 mm one coat work**								
M116189E	not exceeding 150 mm high	m	0.08	3.17	-	2.02	5.19	5.71	0.358
M116189F	150 - 300 mm high	m	0.13	5.33	-	3.53	8.86	9.75	0.622

Surface Finishes

Major Works 2011		Unit	Labour Hours	Labour Net £	Plant Net £	Materials Net £	Unit Net £	Unit with 10% £	CO$_2$ Kg
M12	**M12: TROWELLED BITUMEN, RESIN AND RUBBER-LATEX FLOORING**								
M1211	**Evostik floor levelling compound, laid in accordance with the manufacturer's instructions**								
M121118	**To floors and landings**								
M121118A	2 mm nominal thickness	m^2	0.07	3.03	-	3.67	6.70	7.37	5.340
M121118B	5 mm nominal thickness	m^2	0.08	3.50	-	9.18	12.68	13.95	13.350

Major Works 2011		Unit	Labour Hours	Labour Net	Plant Net	Materials Net	Unit Net	Unit with 10%	CO$_2$
				£	£	£	£	£	Kg
M20	**M20: PLASTERED, RENDERED AND ROUGHCAST COATINGS**								
M2011	**Cement and sand (1:3); trowelled finish**								
M201104	**To walls; 12 mm thick; one coat work**								
M201104A	over 300 mm wide	m^2	0.10	4.71	-	1.34	6.05	6.66	4.569
M201104B	not exceeding 300 mm wide	m	0.04	1.91	-	0.41	2.32	2.55	1.406
M201105	**To walls; 18 mm thick; two coat work**								
M201105A	over 300 mm wide	m^2	0.15	7.05	-	2.06	9.11	10.02	7.029
M201105B	not exceeding 300 mm wide	m	0.06	2.85	-	0.62	3.47	3.82	2.109
M201114	**To isolated columns; 12 mm thick; one coat work**								
M201114A	over 300 mm wide	m^2	0.10	4.71	-	1.34	6.05	6.66	4.569
M201114B	not exceeding 300 mm wide	m	0.04	1.91	-	0.41	2.32	2.55	1.406
M201115	**To isolated columns; 18 mm thick; two coat work**								
M201115A	over 300 mm wide	m^2	0.15	7.05	-	2.06	9.11	10.02	7.029
M201115B	not exceeding 300 mm wide	m	0.06	2.85	-	0.62	3.47	3.82	2.109
M2012	**Cement and sand (1:3); screeded finish**								
M201201	**To walls; 6 mm thick; one coat work**								
M201201A	over 300 mm wide	m^2	0.07	3.27	-	0.72	3.99	4.39	2.460
M201201B	not exceeding 300 mm wide	m	0.03	1.35	-	0.21	1.56	1.72	0.703
M201202	**To walls; 12 mm thick; one coat work**								
M201202A	over 300 mm wide	m^2	0.09	4.20	-	1.34	5.54	6.09	4.569
M201202B	not exceeding 300 mm wide	m	0.04	1.73	-	0.41	2.14	2.35	1.406
M201203	**To walls; 18 mm thick; two coat work**								
M201203A	over 300 mm wide	m^2	0.14	6.35	-	2.06	8.41	9.25	7.029
M201203C	not exceeding 300 mm wide	m	0.06	2.57	-	0.62	3.19	3.51	2.109
M201207	**To isolated columns; 6 mm thick; one coat work**								
M201207A	over 300 mm wide	m^2	0.07	3.27	-	0.72	3.99	4.39	2.460
M201207B	not exceeding 300 mm wide	m	0.03	1.35	-	0.41	1.76	1.94	1.406
M201208	**To isolated columns; 12 mm thick; one coat work**								
M201208A	over 300 mm wide	m^2	0.09	4.20	-	1.34	5.54	6.09	4.569
M201208B	not exceeding 300 mm wide	m	0.04	1.73	-	0.41	2.14	2.35	1.406
M201209	**To isolated columns; 18 mm thick; two coat work**								
M201209A	over 300 mm wide	m^2	0.14	6.35	-	2.06	8.41	9.25	7.029
M201209C	not exceeding 300 mm wide	m	0.06	2.57	-	0.62	3.19	3.51	2.109
M2013	**Cement and sand (1:3); floated finish**								
M201301	**To walls; 12 mm thick; one coat work**								
M201301A	over 300 mm wide	m^2	0.10	4.43	-	1.34	5.77	6.35	4.569
M201301B	not exceeding 300 mm wide	m	0.04	1.82	-	0.41	2.23	2.45	1.406
M201302	**To walls; 18 mm thick; two coat work**								
M201302A	over 300 mm wide	m^2	0.15	6.81	-	2.06	8.87	9.76	7.029
M201302B	not exceeding 300 mm wide	m	0.06	2.75	-	0.62	3.37	3.71	2.109
M201310	**To isolated columns; 12 mm thick; one coat work**								
M201310A	over 300 mm wide	m^2	0.10	4.43	-	1.34	5.77	6.35	4.569
M201310B	not exceeding 300 mm wide	m	0.04	1.82	-	0.41	2.23	2.45	1.406

Surface Finishes

		Unit	Labour Hours	Labour Net	Plant Net	Materials Net	Unit Net	Unit with 10%	CO$_2$
				£	£	£	£	£	Kg
M20	**M20: PLASTERED, RENDERED AND ROUGHCAST COATINGS**								
M2013	**Cement and sand (1:3); floated finish**								
M201311	**To isolated columns; 18 mm thick; two coat work**								
M201311A	over 300 mm wide	m²	0.15	6.81	-	2.06	8.87	9.76	7.029
M201311B	not exceeding 300 mm wide	m	0.06	2.75	-	0.62	3.37	3.71	2.109
M2014	**Cement and sand (1:4); screeded finish**								
M201412	**To walls; 12 mm thick; one coat work**								
M201412A	over 300 mm wide	m²	0.09	4.20	-	0.98	5.18	5.70	3.797
M201412B	not exceeding 300 mm wide	m	0.04	1.73	-	0.30	2.03	2.23	1.168
M201414	**To walls; 18 mm thick; two coat work**								
M201414A	over 300 mm wide	m²	0.14	6.35	-	1.51	7.86	8.65	5.841
M201414B	not exceeding 300 mm wide	m	0.06	2.57	-	0.45	3.02	3.32	1.752
M201422	**To isolated columns; 12 mm thick; one coat work**								
M201422A	over 300 mm wide	m²	0.09	4.20	-	0.98	5.18	5.70	3.797
M201422B	not exceeding 300 mm wide	m	0.04	1.73	-	0.30	2.03	2.23	1.168
M201424	**To isolated columns; 18 mm thick; two coat work**								
M201424A	over 300 mm wide	m²	0.14	6.35	-	1.51	7.86	8.65	5.841
M201424B	not exceeding 300 mm wide	m	0.06	2.57	-	0.45	3.02	3.32	1.752
M2015	**Cement, lime and sand (1:1:6); screeded finish**								
M201501	**To walls; 12 mm thick; one coat work**								
M201501A	over 300 mm wide	m²	0.09	4.20	-	1.47	5.67	6.24	3.496
M201501B	not exceeding 300 mm wide	m	0.04	1.73	-	0.45	2.18	2.40	1.076
M201502	**To walls; 18 mm thick; two coat work**								
M201502A	over 300 mm wide	m²	0.14	6.35	-	2.26	8.61	9.47	5.379
M201502B	not exceeding 300 mm wide	m	0.06	2.57	-	0.68	3.25	3.58	1.614
M201511	**To isolated columns; 12 mm thick; one coat work**								
M201511A	over 300 mm wide	m²	0.09	4.20	-	1.47	5.67	6.24	3.496
M201511B	not exceeding 300 mm wide	m	0.04	1.73	-	0.45	2.18	2.40	1.076
M201512	**To isolated columns; 18 mm thick; two coat work**								
M201512A	over 300 mm wide	m²	0.14	6.35	-	2.26	8.61	9.47	5.379
M201512B	not exceeding 300 mm wide	m	0.06	2.57	-	0.68	3.25	3.58	1.614
M2016	**Cement, lime and sand (1:1:6); trowelled finish**								
M201601	**To walls; 12 mm thick; one coat work**								
M201601A	over 300 mm wide	m²	0.10	4.71	-	1.47	6.18	6.80	3.496
M201601B	not exceeding 300 mm wide	m	0.04	1.91	-	0.45	2.36	2.60	1.076
M201602	**To walls; 18 mm thick; two coat work**								
M201602A	over 300 mm wide	m²	0.15	7.05	-	2.26	9.31	10.24	5.379
M201602B	not exceeding 300 mm wide	m	0.06	2.85	-	0.68	3.53	3.88	1.614
M201611	**To isolated columns; 12 mm thick; one coat work**								
M201611A	over 300 mm wide	m²	0.10	4.71	-	1.47	6.18	6.80	3.496
M201611B	not exceeding 300 mm wide	m	0.04	1.91	-	0.45	2.36	2.60	1.076
M201612	**To isolated columns; 18 mm thick; two coat work**								
M201612A	over 300 mm wide	m²	0.15	7.05	-	2.26	9.31	10.24	5.379
M201612B	not exceeding 300 mm wide	m	0.06	2.85	-	0.68	3.53	3.88	1.614

Major Works 2011		Unit	Labour Hours	Labour Net	Plant Net	Materials Net	Unit Net	Unit with 10%	CO$_2$
				£	£	£	£	£	Kg
M20	**M20: PLASTERED, RENDERED AND ROUGHCAST COATINGS**								
M2021	**Carlite lightweight plastering with 2 mm Carlite finish plaster**								
M202101	**To walls; 10 mm thick; two coat work; to concrete backgrounds with bonding backings**								
M202101A	over 300 mm wide	m^2	0.15	7.05	-	1.74	8.79	9.67	1.080
M202101B	not exceeding 300 mm wide	m	0.06	2.85	-	0.57	3.42	3.76	0.360
M202102	**To walls; 10 mm thick; two coat work; to plasterboard backgrounds with bonding backings; including scrimming joints**								
M202102A	over 300 mm wide	m^2	0.15	7.05	-	2.04	9.09	10.00	1.098
M202102B	not exceeding 300 mm wide	m	0.06	2.85	-	0.66	3.51	3.86	0.365
M202103	**To walls; 13 mm thick; two coat work; to masonry backgrounds with browning backings**								
M202103A	over 300 mm wide	m^2	0.15	7.05	-	1.99	9.04	9.94	1.200
M202103C	not exceeding 300 mm wide	m	0.06	2.85	-	0.58	3.43	3.77	0.360
M202104	**To walls; 13 mm thick; two coat work; to masonry backgrounds with special browning backings**								
M202104A	over 300 mm wide	m^2	0.15	7.05	-	2.07	9.12	10.03	1.200
M202104D	not exceeding 300 mm wide	m	0.06	2.85	-	0.60	3.45	3.80	0.360
M202105	**To walls; 13 mm thick; two coat work; to masonry backgrounds with browning HSB backings**								
M202105A	over 300 mm wide	m^2	0.15	7.05	-	2.10	9.15	10.07	1.200
M202105E	not exceeding 300 mm wide	m	0.06	2.85	-	0.61	3.46	3.81	0.360
M202106	**To walls; 13 mm thick; three coat work; metal lathing backgrounds with metal lathing backings**								
M202106A	over 300 mm wide	m^2	0.20	9.38	-	3.51	12.89	14.18	2.160
M202106B	not exceeding 300 mm wide	m	0.08	3.78	-	1.16	4.94	5.43	0.720
M202111	**To ceilings; 10 mm thick; two coat work; to concrete backgrounds with bonding backings**								
M202111A	over 300 mm wide	m^2	0.17	7.98	-	1.74	9.72	10.69	1.080
M202111B	not exceeding 300 mm wide	m	0.07	3.22	-	0.57	3.79	4.17	0.360
M202112	**To ceilings; 10 mm thick; two coat work; to plasterboard backgrounds with bonding backings; including scrimming joints**								
M202112A	over 300 mm wide	m^2	0.17	7.98	-	2.04	10.02	11.02	1.098
M202112B	not exceeding 300 mm wide	m	0.07	3.22	-	0.66	3.88	4.27	0.365
M202116	**To ceilings; 13 mm thick; three coat work; to metal lathing backgrounds with metal lathing backings**								
M202116A	over 300 mm wide	m^2	0.23	10.55	-	3.51	14.06	15.47	2.160
M202116B	not exceeding 300 mm wide	m	0.09	4.29	-	1.16	5.45	6.00	0.720
M202121	**To isolated beams; 10 mm thick; two coat work; to concrete backgrounds with bonding backings**								
M202121A	over 300 mm wide	m^2	0.17	7.98	-	1.74	9.72	10.69	1.080
M202121B	not exceeding 300 mm wide	m	0.07	3.22	-	0.57	3.79	4.17	0.360

Surface Finishes

		Unit	Labour Hours	Labour Net £	Plant Net £	Materials Net £	Unit Net £	Unit with 10% £	CO₂ Kg
M20	**M20: PLASTERED, RENDERED AND ROUGHCAST COATINGS**								
M2021	**Carlite lightweight plastering with 2 mm Carlite finish plaster**								
M202122	**To isolated beams; 10 mm thick; two coat work; to plasterboard backgrounds with bonding backings; including scrimming joints**								
M202122A	over 300 mm wide	m²	0.17	7.98	-	2.04	10.02	11.02	1.098
M202122B	not exceeding 300 mm wide	m	0.07	3.22	-	0.66	3.88	4.27	0.365
M202126	**To isolated beams; 13 mm thick; three coat work; to metal lathing backgrounds with metal lathing backings**								
M202126A	over 300 mm wide	m²	0.23	10.55	-	3.51	14.06	15.47	2.160
M202126B	not exceeding 300 mm wide	m	0.09	4.29	-	1.16	5.45	6.00	0.720
M202141	**To isolated columns; 10 mm thick; two coat work; to concrete backgrounds with bonding backings**								
M202141A	over 300 mm wide	m²	0.15	7.05	-	1.74	8.79	9.67	1.080
M202141B	not exceeding 300 mm wide	m	0.06	2.85	-	0.57	3.42	3.76	0.360
M202142	**To isolated columns; 10 mm thick; two coat work; to plasterboard backgrounds with bonding backings; including scrimming joints**								
M202142A	over 300 mm wide	m²	0.15	7.05	-	2.04	9.09	10.00	1.098
M202142B	not exceeding 300 mm wide	m	0.06	2.85	-	0.66	3.51	3.86	0.365
M202143	**To isolated columns; 13 mm thick; two coat work; to masonry backgrounds with browning backings**								
M202143A	over 300 mm wide	m²	0.15	7.05	-	1.99	9.04	9.94	1.200
M202143B	not exceeding 300 mm wide	m	0.06	2.85	-	0.58	3.43	3.77	0.360
M202144	**To isolated columns; 13 mm thick; two coat work; to masonry backgrounds with special browning backings**								
M202144A	over 300 mm wide	m²	0.15	7.05	-	2.07	9.12	10.03	1.200
M202144B	not exceeding 300 mm wide	m	0.06	2.85	-	0.60	3.45	3.80	0.360
M202145	**To isolated columns; 13 mm thick; two coat work; to masonry backgrounds with browning HSB backings**								
M202145A	over 300 mm wide	m²	0.15	7.05	-	2.10	9.15	10.07	1.200
M202145E	not exceeding 300 mm wide	m	0.06	2.85	-	0.61	3.46	3.81	0.360
M202146	**To isolated columns; 13 mm thick; three coat work; metal lathing backgrounds with metal lathing backings**								
M202146A	over 300 mm wide	m²	0.20	9.38	-	3.51	12.89	14.18	2.160
M202146B	not exceeding 300 mm wide	m	0.08	3.78	-	1.16	4.94	5.43	0.720
M202161	**To skirtings, bands, strings, coverings to kerbs, mouldings, channels or the like; 10 mm thick; two coat work; to concrete backgrounds with bonding backings**								
M202161A	not exceeding 300 mm wide	m	0.09	4.20	-	0.57	4.77	5.25	0.360

Major Works 2011		Unit	Labour Hours	Labour Net	Plant Net	Materials Net	Unit Net	Unit with 10%	CO$_2$
				£	£	£	£	£	Kg
M20	**M20: PLASTERED, RENDERED AND ROUGHCAST COATINGS**								
M2021	**Carlite lightweight plastering with 2 mm Carlite finish plaster**								
M202162	**To skirtings, bands, strings, coverings to kerbs, mouldings, channels or the like; 10 mm thick; two coat work; to plasterboard backgrounds with bonding backings; including scrimming joints**								
M202162B	not exceeding 300 mm wide	m	0.09	4.20	-	0.66	4.86	5.35	0.365
M202163	**To skirtings, bands, strings, coverings to kerbs, mouldings, channels or the like; 13 mm thick; two coat work; to masonry backgrounds with browning backings**								
M202163C	not exceeding 300 mm wide	m	0.09	4.20	-	0.79	4.99	5.49	0.480
M202164	**To skirtings, bands, strings, coverings to kerbs, mouldings, channels or the like; 13 mm thick; two coat work; to masonry backgrounds with special browning backings**								
M202164D	not exceeding 300 mm wide	m	0.09	4.20	-	0.82	5.02	5.52	0.480
M202165	**To skirtings, bands, strings, coverings to kerbs, mouldings, channels or the like; 13 mm thick; two coat work; to masonry backgrounds with browning HSB backings**								
M202165E	not exceeding 300 mm wide	m	0.09	4.20	-	0.83	5.03	5.53	0.480
M202166	**To skirtings, bands, strings, coverings to kerbs, mouldings, channels or the like; 13 mm thick; three coat work; to metal lathing backgrounds with metal lathing backings**								
M202166F	not exceeding 300 mm wide	m	0.12	5.65	-	1.16	6.81	7.49	0.720
M2022	**Thistle 2 mm finish on Thistle renovating plaster**								
M202201	**To walls; 13 mm thick; two coat work**								
M202201A	over 300 mm wide	m^2	0.15	7.05	-	2.68	9.73	10.70	1.440
M202201B	not exceeding 300 mm wide	m	0.06	2.85	-	0.89	3.74	4.11	0.480
M202211	**To isolated columns; 13 mm thick; two coat work**								
M202211A	over 300 mm wide	m^2	0.15	7.05	-	2.68	9.73	10.70	1.440
M202211B	not exceeding 300 mm wide	m	0.06	2.85	-	0.89	3.74	4.11	0.480
M202226	**To skirtings, bands, strings, coverings to kerbs, mouldings, channels or the like; 13 mm thick; two coat work**								
M202226A	not exceeding 300 mm wide	m	0.09	4.20	-	0.89	5.09	5.60	0.480
M2023	**Thistle finishing plaster**								
M202301	**To walls; 2 mm thick; one coat work; to plasterboard backgrounds including scrimming joints and filling nail holes; board finish**								
M202301A	over 300 mm wide	m^2	0.07	3.27	-	0.84	4.11	4.52	0.378

Surface Finishes

		Unit	Labour Hours	Labour Net £	Plant Net £	Materials Net £	Unit Net £	Unit with 10% £	CO₂ Kg

		Unit	Labour Hours	Labour Net £	Plant Net £	Materials Net £	Unit Net £	Unit with 10% £	CO$_2$ Kg
M20	**M20: PLASTERED, RENDERED AND ROUGHCAST COATINGS**								
M2023	**Thistle finishing plaster**								
M202301	**To walls; 2 mm thick; one coat work; to plasterboard backgrounds including scrimming joints and filling nail holes; board finish**								
M202301B	not exceeding 300 mm wide	m	0.03	1.35	-	0.27	1.62	1.78	0.125
M202302	**To walls; 5 mm thick; two coat work; to plasterboard backgrounds including scrimming joints and filling nail holes; board finish**								
M202302A	over 300 mm wide	m²	0.10	4.71	-	1.38	6.09	6.70	0.738
M202302B	not exceeding 300 mm wide	m	0.04	1.91	-	0.45	2.36	2.60	0.245
M202303	**To walls; 2 mm thick; one coat work; to sanded backgrounds**								
M202303A	over 300 mm wide	m²	0.04	1.87	-	0.35	2.22	2.44	0.240
M202303B	not exceeding 300 mm wide	m	0.02	0.75	-	0.18	0.93	1.02	0.120
M202313	**To ceilings; 2 mm thick; one coat work; to plasterboard backgrounds including scrimming joints and filling nail holes; board finish**								
M202313A	over 300 mm wide	m²	0.08	3.73	-	0.84	4.57	5.03	0.378
M202313B	not exceeding 300 mm wide	m	0.03	1.54	-	0.27	1.81	1.99	0.125
M202314	**To ceilings; 5 mm thick; two coat work; to plasterboard backgrounds including scrimming joints and filling nail holes; board finish**								
M202314A	over 300 mm wide	m²	0.12	5.41	-	1.38	6.79	7.47	0.738
M202314B	not exceeding 300 mm wide	m	0.05	2.19	-	0.45	2.64	2.90	0.245
M202315	**To ceilings; 2 mm thick; one coat work; to sanded backgrounds**								
M202315A	over 300 mm wide	m²	0.05	2.33	-	0.35	2.68	2.95	0.240
M202315B	not exceeding 300 mm wide	m	0.02	0.98	-	0.18	1.16	1.28	0.120
M202323	**To isolated beams; 2 mm thick; one coat work; to plasterboard backgrounds including scrimming joints and filling nail holes; board finish**								
M202323A	over 300 mm wide	m²	0.08	3.73	-	0.84	4.57	5.03	0.378
M202323B	not exceeding 300 mm wide	m	0.03	1.54	-	0.27	1.81	1.99	0.125
M202324	**To isolated beams; 5 mm thick; two coat work; to plasterboard backgrounds including scrimming joints and filling nail holes; board finish**								
M202324A	over 300 mm wide	m²	0.12	5.41	-	1.38	6.79	7.47	0.738
M202324B	not exceeding 300 mm wide	m	0.05	2.19	-	0.45	2.64	2.90	0.245
M202325	**To isolated beams; 2 mm thick; one coat work; to sanded backgrounds**								
M202325A	over 300 mm wide	m²	0.05	2.33	-	0.35	2.68	2.95	0.240
M202325B	not exceeding 300 mm wide	m	0.02	0.98	-	0.18	1.16	1.28	0.120
M202341	**To isolated columns; 2 mm thick; one coat work; to plasterboard backgrounds including scrimming joints and filling nail holes; board finish**								
M202341A	over 300 mm wide	m²	0.07	3.27	-	0.84	4.11	4.52	0.378
M202341B	not exceeding 300 mm wide	m	0.03	1.35	-	0.27	1.62	1.78	0.125

Major Works 2011		Unit	Labour Hours	Labour Net	Plant Net	Materials Net	Unit Net	Unit with 10%	CO$_2$
				£	£	£	£	£	Kg
M20	**M20: PLASTERED, RENDERED AND ROUGHCAST COATINGS**								
M2023	**Thistle finishing plaster**								
M202342	**To isolated columns; 5 mm thick; two coat work; to plasterboard backgrounds including scrimming joints and filling nail holes; board finish**								
M202342A	over 300 mm wide	m²	0.10	4.71	-	1.38	6.09	6.70	0.738
M202342B	not exceeding 300 mm wide	m	0.04	1.91	-	0.45	2.36	2.60	0.245
M202343	**To isolated columns; 2 mm thick; one coat work; to sanded backgrounds**								
M202343A	over 300 mm wide	m²	0.04	1.87	-	0.35	2.22	2.44	0.240
M202343B	not exceeding 300 mm wide	m	0.02	0.75	-	0.18	0.93	1.02	0.120
M202361	**To skirtings, bands, strings, coverings to kerbs, mouldings, channels or the like; 2 mm thick; one coat work; to plasterboard backgrounds including scrimming joints and filling nail holes; board finish**								
M202361A	not exceeding 300 mm wide	m	0.04	1.87	-	0.27	2.14	2.35	0.125
M202362	**To skirtings, bands, strings, coverings to kerbs, mouldings, channels or the like; 5 mm thick; two coat work; to plasterboard backgrounds including scrimming joints and filling nail holes; board finish**								
M202362B	not exceeding 300 mm wide	m	0.06	2.80	-	0.45	3.25	3.58	0.245
M202363	**To skirtings, bands, strings, coverings to kerbs, mouldings, channels or the like; 2 mm thick; one coat work; to sanded backgrounds**								
M202363C	not exceeding 300 mm wide	m	0.03	1.17	-	0.18	1.35	1.49	0.120
M2024	**Thistle Universal one coat plaster**								
M202401	**To walls; 10 mm thick; to concrete backgrounds**								
M202401A	over 300 mm wide	m²	0.10	4.71	-	1.97	6.68	7.35	1.080
M202401B	not exceeding 300 mm wide	m	0.04	1.91	-	0.66	2.57	2.83	0.360
M202402	**To walls; 5 mm thick; to plasterboard backgrounds including scrimming joints and filling nail holes**								
M202402A	over 300 mm wide	m²	0.08	3.73	-	1.09	4.82	5.30	0.600
M202402B	not exceeding 300 mm wide	m	0.03	1.54	-	0.44	1.98	2.18	0.240
M202403	**To walls; 13 mm thick; to masonry backgrounds**								
M202403A	over 300 mm wide	m²	0.10	4.71	-	2.62	7.33	8.06	1.440
M202403B	not exceeding 300 mm wide	m	0.04	1.91	-	0.87	2.78	3.06	0.480
M202411	**To ceilings; 10 mm thick; to concrete backgrounds**								
M202411A	over 300 mm wide	m²	0.12	5.41	-	1.97	7.38	8.12	1.080
M202411B	not exceeding 300 mm wide	m	0.05	2.19	-	0.66	2.85	3.14	0.360
M202412	**To ceilings; 5 mm thick; to plasterboard backgrounds including scrimming joints and filling nail holes**								
M202412A	over 300 mm wide	m²	0.09	4.20	-	1.09	5.29	5.82	0.600
M202412B	not exceeding 300 mm wide	m	0.04	1.73	-	0.44	2.17	2.39	0.240

Surface Finishes

Major Works 2011		Unit	Labour Hours	Labour Net £	Plant Net £	Materials Net £	Unit Net £	Unit with 10% £	CO_2 Kg
M20	**M20: PLASTERED, RENDERED AND ROUGHCAST COATINGS**								
M2024	**Thistle Universal one coat plaster**								
M202421	**To isolated beams; 10 mm thick; to concrete backgrounds**								
M202421A	over 300 mm wide	m²	0.12	5.41	-	1.97	7.38	8.12	1.080
M202421B	not exceeding 300 mm wide	m	0.05	2.19	-	0.66	2.85	3.14	0.360
M202422	**To isolated beams; 5 mm thick; to plasterboard backgrounds including scrimming joints and filling nail holes**								
M202422A	over 300 mm wide	m²	0.09	4.20	-	1.09	5.29	5.82	0.600
M202422B	not exceeding 300 mm wide	m	0.04	1.73	-	0.44	2.17	2.39	0.240
M202441	**To isolated columns; 10 mm thick; to concrete backgrounds**								
M202441A	over 300 mm wide	m²	0.10	4.71	-	1.97	6.68	7.35	1.080
M202441B	not exceeding 300 mm wide	m	0.04	1.91	-	0.66	2.57	2.83	0.360
M202442	**To isolated columns; 5 mm thick; to plasterboard backgrounds including scrimming joints and filling nail holes**								
M202442A	over 300 mm wide	m²	0.08	3.73	-	1.09	4.82	5.30	0.600
M202442B	not exceeding 300 mm wide	m	0.03	1.54	-	0.44	1.98	2.18	0.240
M202443	**To isolated columns; 13 mm thick; to masonry backgrounds**								
M202443A	over 300 mm wide	m²	0.10	4.71	-	2.62	7.33	8.06	1.440
M202443B	not exceeding 300 mm wide	m	0.04	1.91	-	0.87	2.78	3.06	0.480
M202461	**To skirtings, bands, strings, coverings to kerbs, mouldings, channels or the like; 10 mm thick; to concrete backgrounds**								
M202461A	not exceeding 300 mm wide	m	0.06	2.80	-	0.66	3.46	3.81	0.360
M202462	**To skirtings, bands, strings, coverings to kerbs, mouldings, channels or the like; 5 mm thick; to plasterboard backgrounds including scrimming joints and filling nail holes**								
M202462B	not exceeding 300 mm wide	m	0.05	2.33	-	0.44	2.77	3.05	0.240
M202463	**To skirtings, bands, strings, coverings to kerbs, mouldings, channels or the like; 13 mm thick; to masonry backgrounds**								
M202463C	not exceeding 300 mm wide	m	0.06	2.80	-	0.87	3.67	4.04	0.480
M2025	**Sirapite B finish plaster**								
M202501	**To walls; 3 mm thick; to sanded backgrounds**								
M202501A	over 300 mm wide	m²	0.04	1.87	-	0.81	2.68	2.95	0.480
M202501B	not exceeding 300 mm wide	m	0.02	0.75	-	0.20	0.95	1.05	0.120
M202511	**To ceilings; 3 mm thick; to sanded backgrounds**								
M202511A	over 300 mm wide	m²	0.05	2.33	-	0.81	3.14	3.45	0.480
M202511B	not exceeding 300 mm wide	m	0.02	0.98	-	0.20	1.18	1.30	0.120
M202521	**To isolated beams; 3 mm thick; to sanded backgrounds**								
M202521A	over 300 mm wide	m²	0.05	2.33	-	0.81	3.14	3.45	0.480
M202521B	not exceeding 300 mm wide	m	0.02	0.98	-	0.20	1.18	1.30	0.120

Major Works 2011		Unit	Labour Hours	Labour Net	Plant Net	Materials Net	Unit Net	Unit with 10%	CO₂
				£	£	£	£	£	Kg
M20	**M20: PLASTERED, RENDERED AND ROUGHCAST COATINGS**								
M2025	**Sirapite B finish plaster**								
M202541	**To isolated columns; 3 mm thick; to sanded backgrounds**								
M202541A	over 300 mm wide	m²	0.04	1.87	-	0.81	2.68	2.95	0.480
M202541B	not exceeding 300 mm wide	m	0.02	0.75	-	0.20	0.95	1.05	0.120
M202561	**To skirtings, bands, strings, coverings to kerbs, mouldings, channels or the like; 3 mm thick; to sanded backgrounds**								
M202561A	not exceeding 300 mm wide	m	0.03	1.17	-	0.20	1.37	1.51	0.120
M2026	**Gyproc Drywall topcoat**								
M202601	**To walls; one coat Gyproc Drywall top coat to surfaces of tapered edge boarding including filling, taping and finishing joints flush; ready for direct decoration**								
M202601A	over 300 mm wide	m²	0.09	3.97	-	1.40	5.37	5.91	1.431
M202601B	not exceeding 300 mm wide	m	0.04	1.63	-	0.42	2.05	2.26	0.429
M202611	**To ceilings; one coat Gyproc Drywall top coat to surfaces of tapered edge boarding including filling, taping and finishing joints flush; ready for direct decoration**								
M202611A	over 300 mm wide	m²	0.11	4.95	-	1.26	6.21	6.83	1.427
M202611B	not exceeding 300 mm wide	m	0.04	2.01	-	0.38	2.39	2.63	0.428
M202621	**To isolated beams; one coat Gyproc Drywall top coat to surfaces of tapered edge boarding including filling, taping and finishing joints flush; ready for direct decoration**								
M202621A	over 300 mm wide	m²	0.11	4.95	-	1.26	6.21	6.83	1.427
M202621B	not exceeding 300 mm wide	m	0.04	2.01	-	0.38	2.39	2.63	0.428
M202641	**To isolated columns; one coat Gyproc Drywall top coat to surfaces of tapered edge boarding including filling, taping and finishing joints flush; ready for direct decoration**								
M202641A	over 300 mm wide	m²	0.09	3.97	-	1.40	5.37	5.91	1.431
M202641B	not exceeding 300 mm wide	m	0.04	1.63	-	0.42	2.05	2.26	0.429
M202661	**To skirtings, bands, strings, coverings to kerbs or the like; one coat Gyproc Drywall top coat to surfaces of tapered edge boarding including filling, taping and finishing joints flush; ready for direct decoration**								
M202661C	not exceeding 300 mm wide	m	0.05	2.33	-	0.41	2.74	3.01	0.435
M2031	**Tyrolean 7 mm three coat rendering to sanded backgrounds**								
M203101	**To walls; honeycomb finish**								
M203101A	over 300 mm wide	m²	0.20	9.38	0.14	2.26	11.78	12.96	0.480
M203101B	not exceeding 300 mm wide	m	0.08	3.78	0.06	0.57	4.41	4.85	0.120
M203102	**To walls; rubbed finish**								
M203102A	over 300 mm wide	m²	0.28	12.88	0.20	2.26	15.34	16.87	0.480
M203102B	not exceeding 300 mm wide	m	0.12	5.37	0.08	0.57	6.02	6.62	0.120

Surface Finishes

		Unit	Labour Hours	Labour Net	Plant Net	Materials Net	Unit Net	Unit with 10%	CO₂
				£	£	£	£	£	Kg
M20	**M20: PLASTERED, RENDERED AND ROUGHCAST COATINGS**								
M2031	**Tyrolean 7 mm three coat rendering to sanded backgrounds**								
M203111	**To isolated columns; honeycomb finish**								
M203111A	over 300 mm wide	m²	0.20	9.38	0.14	2.26	11.78	12.96	0.480
M203111B	not exceeding 300 mm wide	m	0.08	3.78	0.06	0.57	4.41	4.85	0.120
M203112	**To isolated columns; rubbed finish**								
M203112A	over 300 mm wide	m²	0.28	12.88	0.20	2.26	15.34	16.87	0.480
M203112B	not exceeding 300 mm wide	m	0.12	5.37	0.08	0.57	6.02	6.62	0.120
M203161	**To skirtings, bands, strings, coverings to kerbs, mouldings, channels or the like; honeycomb finish**								
M203161A	not exceeding 300 mm wide	m	0.10	4.71	0.07	0.57	5.35	5.89	0.120
M203162	**To skirtings, bands, strings, coverings to kerbs, mouldings, channels or the like; rubbed finish**								
M203162B	not exceeding 300 mm wide	m	0.15	7.05	0.11	0.57	7.73	8.50	0.120
M2033	**Roughcast rendering to sanded backgrounds**								
M203301	**To walls**								
M203301A	over 300 mm wide	m²	0.11	5.18	0.08	0.93	6.19	6.81	0.840
M203301B	not exceeding 300 mm wide	m	0.05	2.10	0.03	0.27	2.40	2.64	0.240
M203341	**To isolated columns**								
M203341A	over 300 mm wide	m²	0.11	5.18	0.08	0.93	6.19	6.81	0.840
M203341B	not exceeding 300 mm wide	m	0.05	2.10	0.03	0.27	2.40	2.64	0.240
M203361	**To skirtings, bands, strings, coverings to kerbs, mouldings, channels or the like**								
M203361A	not exceeding 300 mm wide	m	0.07	3.03	0.05	0.93	4.01	4.41	0.840
M2035	**Pebbledash finish to sanded backgrounds**								
M203501	**To walls**								
M203501A	over 300 mm wide	m²	0.15	7.05	0.11	0.54	7.70	8.47	0.055
M203501B	not exceeding 300 mm wide	m	0.06	2.85	0.04	0.15	3.04	3.34	0.015
M203541	**To isolated columns**								
M203541A	over 300 mm wide	m²	0.15	7.05	0.11	0.54	7.70	8.47	0.055
M203541B	not exceeding 300 mm wide	m	0.06	2.85	0.04	0.15	3.04	3.34	0.015
M203561	**To skirtings, bands, strings, coverings to kerbs, mouldings, channels or the like**								
M203561A	not exceeding 300 mm wide	m	0.09	4.20	0.06	0.54	4.80	5.28	0.055
M2074	**Beads, stops, edging strips and arches**								
M207401	**Division strips; embedding in pavings**								
M207401A	5 x 25 mm brass	m	0.03	1.40	-	5.02	6.42	7.06	2.700
M207401B	5 x 25 mm aluminium	m	0.03	1.40	-	2.29	3.69	4.06	2.920
M207402	**Ferodo nosings; plugging and screwing to concrete backgrounds**								
M207402A	type SD1	m	0.30	5.09	-	22.47	27.56	30.32	0.385
M207402B	type SD2	m	0.30	5.09	-	25.52	30.61	33.67	0.274
M207402C	type HD1	m	0.30	5.09	-	22.99	28.08	30.89	0.385
M207402D	type HD2	m	0.30	5.09	-	27.23	32.32	35.55	0.385

Major Works 2011		Unit	Labour Hours	Labour Net	Plant Net	Materials Net	Unit Net	Unit with 10%	CO₂
				£	£	£	£	£	Kg
M20	**M20: PLASTERED, RENDERED AND ROUGHCAST COATINGS**								
M2074	**Beads, stops, edging strips and arches**								
M207403	**Division strips; plugging and screwing to concrete backgrounds**								
M207403A	aluminium; carpet to carpet	m	0.25	4.25	-	2.43	6.68	7.35	2.981
M207403B	aluminium; carpet to stop edge	m	0.25	4.25	-	2.43	6.68	7.35	2.981
M207403C	aluminium; carpet to vinyl flooring	m	0.25	4.25	-	2.43	6.68	7.35	2.981
M207403D	aluminium; carpet to vinyl flooring stop edge	m	0.25	4.25	-	2.43	6.68	7.35	2.981
M207403E	brass anodised aluminium; carpet to carpet	m	0.25	4.25	-	5.44	9.69	10.66	3.064
M207403F	brass anodised aluminium; carpet to carpet stop edge	m	0.25	4.25	-	5.44	9.69	10.66	3.064
M207403G	brass anodised aluminium; carpet to vinyl flooring	m	0.25	4.25	-	5.44	9.69	10.66	3.064
M207403H	brass anodised aluminium; vinyl flooring to stop edge	m	0.25	4.25	-	5.44	9.69	10.66	3.064
M207404	**Expamet galvanised mild steel plaster beads and stops; fixing in accordance with manufacturer's instructions**								
M207404A	angle bead ref 550	m	0.04	0.68	-	1.52	2.20	2.42	0.260
M207404B	maxicon bead ref 558	m	0.04	0.68	-	1.10	1.78	1.96	0.218
M207404C	10 mm plaster stop ref 562	m	0.04	0.68	-	1.10	1.78	1.96	0.285
M207404D	13 mm plaster stop ref 563	m	0.04	0.68	-	1.10	1.78	1.96	0.285
M207404E	16 mm plaster stop ref 565	m	0.04	0.68	-	1.38	2.06	2.27	0.289
M207404F	19 mm plaster stop ref 566	m	0.04	0.68	-	1.38	2.06	2.27	0.275
M207404G	depth gauge bead ref 569	m	0.04	0.68	-	0.89	1.57	1.73	0.275
M207404H	12 mm movement bead ref 588	m	0.04	0.68	-	4.77	5.45	6.00	0.583
M207404I	18 mm movement bead ref 589	m	0.04	0.68	-	4.81	5.49	6.04	0.583
M207404J	21 mm movement bead ref 590	m	0.04	0.68	-	5.41	6.09	6.70	0.583
M207404K	corner movement bead ref 587	m	0.04	0.68	-	4.77	5.45	6.00	0.285
M207404L	13 mm architrave bead ref 580	m	0.04	0.68	-	1.40	2.08	2.29	0.247
M207404M	10 mm architrave bead ref 586	m	0.04	0.68	-	1.27	1.95	2.15	0.247
M207404N	13 mm architrave bead ref 579	m	0.04	0.68	-	1.41	2.09	2.30	0.247
M207404O	10 mm architrave bead ref 585	m	0.04	0.68	-	1.28	1.96	2.16	0.247
M207404P	10 mm architrave bead ref 513	m	0.04	0.68	-	1.05	1.73	1.90	0.407
M207404Q	10 mm architrave bead ref 514	m	0.04	0.68	-	1.21	1.89	2.08	0.407
M207404R	square nose angle bead ref 559	m	0.04	0.68	-	1.21	1.89	2.08	0.407
M207404S	3 mm angle bead ref 553	m	0.04	0.68	-	1.14	1.82	2.00	0.372
M207404T	6 mm angle bead ref 554	m	0.04	0.68	-	1.20	1.88	2.07	0.372
M207404U	3 mm stop bead ref 560	m	0.04	0.68	-	1.22	1.90	2.09	0.372
M207404V	6 mm stop bead ref 561	m	0.04	0.68	-	1.30	1.98	2.18	0.372
M207404W	thin coat angle bead ref 595	m	0.04	0.68	-	3.17	3.85	4.24	0.740
M207404X	dry wall corner bead ref 548	m	0.04	0.68	-	0.98	1.66	1.83	0.444
M207404Y	10 mm edge bead ref 567	m	0.04	0.68	-	1.56	2.24	2.46	0.592
M207404Z	12 mm edge bead ref 568	m	0.04	0.68	-	1.56	2.24	2.46	0.592
M207405	**Expamet galvanised mild steel render beads and stops; fixing in accordance with manufacturer's instructions**								
M207405A	bellmouth stop ref 570	m	0.04	0.68	-	1.11	1.79	1.97	0.592
M207405B	stop bead ref 1222	m	0.04	0.68	-	3.17	3.85	4.24	0.740
M207405C	bellmouth stop ref 1229	m	0.04	0.68	-	3.17	3.85	4.24	0.740
M207405D	angle bead ref 1019	m	0.04	0.68	-	3.86	4.54	4.99	0.740
M207405E	stripmesh ref 584	m	0.04	0.68	-	1.19	1.87	2.06	0.592
M207405F	corner mesh ref 583	m	0.04	0.68	-	1.19	1.87	2.06	0.592
M207406	**Expamet austenitic stainless steel render beads and stops; fixing in accordance with manufacturer's instructions**								
M207406A	angle bead ref 545	m	0.04	0.68	-	3.19	3.87	4.26	1.033
M207406B	19 mm stop bead ref 546	m	0.04	0.68	-	2.85	3.53	3.88	1.033
M207406C	16 mm stop bead ref 526	m	0.04	0.68	-	2.85	3.53	3.88	1.388
M207406D	13 mm stop bead ref 533	m	0.04	0.68	-	2.85	3.53	3.88	1.388
M207406E	10 mm stop bead ref 534	m	0.04	0.68	-	2.85	3.53	3.88	1.388
M207406F	bellmouth stop ref 547	m	0.04	0.68	-	2.85	3.53	3.88	1.388
M207406G	movement joint ref 544	m	0.04	0.68	-	7.86	8.54	9.39	3.229
M207406H	movement joint ref 538	m	0.04	0.68	-	3.02	3.70	4.07	1.615
M207406I	stripmesh ref 522	m	0.04	0.68	-	2.98	3.66	4.03	1.615
M207406J	corner mesh ref 521	m	0.04	0.68	-	3.06	3.74	4.11	1.615

Surface Finishes

		Unit	Labour Hours	Labour Net £	Plant Net £	Materials Net £	Unit Net £	Unit with 10% £	CO₂ Kg
M20	**M20: PLASTERED, RENDERED AND ROUGHCAST COATINGS**								
M2074	**Beads, stops, edging strips and arches**								
M207407	**Expamet galvanised mild steel arch formers; fixing in accordance with manufacturer's instructions**								
M207407A	380 mm radius half semi-circle; ref EAC15	Nr	0.10	4.71	-	17.51	22.22	24.44	4.549
M207407B	460 mm radius half semi-circle; ref EAC18	Nr	0.10	4.71	-	21.24	25.95	28.55	4.549
M207407C	610 mm radius half semi-circle; ref EAC24	Nr	0.10	4.71	-	26.40	31.11	34.22	4.549
M207407D	760 mm radius half semi-circle; ref EAC30	Nr	0.10	4.71	-	37.36	42.07	46.28	5.434
M207407E	380 mm radius full semi-circle; ref ESC30	Nr	0.18	8.21	-	34.46	42.67	46.94	5.558
M207407F	410 mm radius full semi-circle; ref ESC32	Nr	0.18	8.21	-	35.02	43.23	47.55	5.558
M207407G	420 mm radius full semi-circle; ref ESC33	Nr	0.18	8.21	-	36.16	44.37	48.81	5.558
M207407H	460 mm radius full semi-circle; ref ESC36	Nr	0.18	8.21	-	42.45	50.66	55.73	6.443
M207407I	610 mm radius full semi-circle; ref ESC48	Nr	0.18	8.21	-	52.28	60.49	66.54	7.328
M207407J	760 mm radius full semi-circle; ref ESC60	Nr	0.18	8.21	-	73.60	81.81	89.99	9.098
M207407K	230 mm radius full circle; ref BE18	Nr	0.20	9.38	-	43.75	53.13	58.44	6.443
M207407L	1220 mm wide elliptical arch; ref EEL48	Nr	0.25	11.71	-	66.25	77.96	85.76	8.231
M207407M	1370 mm wide elliptical arch; ref EEL54	Nr	0.25	11.71	-	69.40	81.11	89.22	9.116
M207407N	1520 mm wide elliptical arch; ref EEL60	Nr	0.25	11.71	-	73.66	85.37	93.91	9.116
M207407O	1830 mm wide elliptical arch; ref EEL72	Nr	0.34	15.72	-	79.23	94.95	104.45	9.559
M207407P	2130 mm wide elliptical arch; ref EEL84	Nr	0.34	15.72	-	86.84	102.56	112.82	10.001
M207407Q	2440 mm wide elliptical arch; ref EEL96	Nr	0.34	15.72	-	91.11	106.83	117.51	10.355
M207407R	3050 mm wide elliptical arch; ref EEL120	Nr	0.34	15.72	-	92.96	108.68	119.55	10.267
M207407S	760 mm wide spandrel arch; ref ESP30	Nr	0.20	9.38	-	43.81	53.19	58.51	6.461
M207407T	910 mm wide spandrel arch; ref ESP36	Nr	0.20	9.38	-	78.05	87.43	96.17	9.559
M207407U	1220 mm wide spandrel arch; ref ESP4	Nr	0.20	9.38	-	58.65	68.03	74.83	8.762
M207407V	1520 mm wide spandrel arch; ref ESP6	Nr	0.20	9.38	-	65.15	74.53	81.98	9.116
M207407W	1830 mm wide spandrel arch; ref ESP7	Nr	0.20	9.38	-	71.61	80.99	89.09	9.116
M207407X	2130 mm wide spandrel arch; ref ESP8	Nr	0.20	9.38	-	77.94	87.32	96.05	9.559
M207407Y	2440 mm wide spandrel arch; ref ESP9	Nr	0.34	15.72	-	82.57	98.29	108.12	10.001
M207407Z	3050 mm wide spandrel arch; ref ESP120	Nr	0.34	15.72	-	153.09	168.81	185.69	17.081
M207408	**Expamet galvanised mild steel arch formers; fixing in accordance with manufacturer's instructions**								
M207408A	155 mm wide lath soffit strip; ref LSS6	m	0.06	2.80	-	2.56	5.36	5.90	0.531
M207408B	600 mm long extender piece; ref MP24	Nr	0.05	2.33	-	5.19	7.52	8.27	0.885
M207408C	610 mm dia internal liner for circular windows; ref WBE24	Nr	0.08	3.50	-	37.27	40.77	44.85	5.753

Major Works 2011		Unit	Labour Hours	Labour Net	Plant Net	Materials Net	Unit Net	Unit with 10%	CO$_2$
				£	£	£	£	£	Kg
M30	**M30: METAL MESH LATHING AND ANCHORED REINFORCEMENT FOR PLASTERED COATING**								
M3021	**Expamet expanded metal lathing to woodwork backgrounds**								
M302101	**To walls; over 300 mm wide**								
M302101A	ref BB263	m^2	0.05	2.33	-	6.31	8.64	9.50	3.209
M302101B	ref BB264	m^2	0.05	2.33	-	6.31	8.64	9.50	3.116
M302101C	ref 94G	m^2	0.05	2.33	-	9.46	11.79	12.97	4.770
M302101D	rib lath ref 269	m^2	0.05	2.33	-	7.62	9.95	10.95	3.209
M302101E	rib lath ref 271	m^2	0.05	2.33	-	8.68	11.01	12.11	3.581
M302101F	spray lath ref 273	m^2	0.05	2.33	-	10.51	12.84	14.12	3.581
M302101G	red-rib lath ref 274	m^2	0.05	2.33	-	9.51	11.84	13.02	3.581
M302101H	stainless steel rib lath ref 267	m^2	0.05	2.33	-	22.47	24.80	27.28	10.843
M302101I	stainless steel lath ref 95S	m^2	0.05	2.33	-	22.47	24.80	27.28	7.551
M302102	**To walls; not exceeding 300 mm wide**								
M302102A	ref BB263	m	0.02	0.98	-	1.89	2.87	3.16	0.963
M302102B	ref BB264	m	0.02	0.98	-	1.89	2.87	3.16	0.935
M302102C	ref 94G	m	0.02	0.98	-	2.84	3.82	4.20	1.431
M302102D	rib lath ref 269	m	0.02	0.98	-	2.29	3.27	3.60	0.963
M302102E	rib lath ref 271	m	0.02	0.98	-	2.60	3.58	3.94	1.074
M302102F	spray lath ref 273	m	0.02	0.98	-	3.15	4.13	4.54	1.074
M302102G	red-rib lath ref 274	m	0.02	0.98	-	2.85	3.83	4.21	1.074
M302102H	stainless steel rib lath ref 267	m	0.02	0.98	-	6.74	7.72	8.49	3.253
M302102I	stainless steel lath ref 95S	m	0.02	0.98	-	6.74	7.72	8.49	2.265
M302111	**To ceilings; over 300 mm wide**								
M302111A	ref BB263	m^2	0.08	3.50	-	7.14	10.64	11.70	3.439
M302111B	ref BB264	m^2	0.08	3.50	-	7.14	10.64	11.70	3.347
M302111C	ref 94G	m^2	0.08	3.50	-	10.29	13.79	15.17	5.000
M302111D	rib lath ref 269	m^2	0.08	3.50	-	8.45	11.95	13.15	3.439
M302111E	rib lath ref 271	m^2	0.08	3.50	-	9.51	13.01	14.31	3.811
M302111F	spray lath ref 273	m^2	0.08	3.50	-	11.34	14.84	16.32	3.811
M302111G	red-rib lath ref 274	m^2	0.08	3.50	-	10.34	13.84	15.22	3.811
M302111H	stainless steel rib lath ref 267	m^2	0.08	3.50	-	23.96	27.46	30.21	11.073
M302111I	stainless steel lath ref 95S	m^2	0.08	3.50	-	23.96	27.46	30.21	7.781
M302112	**To ceilings; not exceeding 300 mm wide**								
M302112A	ref BB263	m	0.03	1.45	-	2.14	3.59	3.95	1.032
M302112B	ref BB264	m	0.03	1.45	-	2.14	3.59	3.95	1.004
M302112C	ref 94G	m	0.03	1.45	-	3.09	4.54	4.99	1.500
M302112D	rib lath ref 269	m	0.03	1.45	-	2.54	3.99	4.39	1.032
M302112E	rib lath ref 271	m	0.03	1.45	-	2.85	4.30	4.73	1.143
M302112F	spray lath ref 273	m	0.03	1.45	-	3.40	4.85	5.34	1.143
M302112G	red-rib lath ref 274	m	0.03	1.45	-	3.10	4.55	5.01	1.143
M302112H	stainless steel rib lath ref 267	m	0.03	1.45	-	7.19	8.64	9.50	3.322
M302112I	stainless steel lath ref 95S	m	0.03	1.45	-	7.19	8.64	9.50	2.334
M302121	**To isolated beams; over 300 mm wide**								
M302121A	ref BB263	m^2	0.08	3.50	-	7.14	10.64	11.70	3.439
M302121B	ref BB264	m^2	0.08	3.50	-	7.14	10.64	11.70	3.347
M302121C	ref 94G	m^2	0.08	3.50	-	10.29	13.79	15.17	5.000
M302121D	rib lath ref 269	m^2	0.08	3.50	-	8.45	11.95	13.15	3.439
M302121E	rib lath ref 271	m^2	0.08	3.50	-	9.51	13.01	14.31	3.811
M302121F	spray lath ref 273	m^2	0.08	3.50	-	11.34	14.84	16.32	3.811
M302121G	red-rib lath ref 274	m^2	0.08	3.50	-	10.34	13.84	15.22	3.811
M302121H	stainless steel rib lath ref 267	m^2	0.08	3.50	-	23.96	27.46	30.21	11.073
M302121I	stainless steel lath ref 95S	m^2	0.08	3.50	-	23.96	27.46	30.21	7.781
M302122	**To isolated beams; not exceeding 300 mm wide**								
M302122A	ref BB263	m	0.03	1.45	-	2.14	3.59	3.95	1.032
M302122B	ref BB264	m	0.03	1.45	-	2.14	3.59	3.95	1.004
M302122C	ref 94G	m	0.03	1.45	-	3.09	4.54	4.99	1.500
M302122D	rib lath ref 269	m	0.03	1.45	-	2.54	3.99	4.39	1.032
M302122E	rib lath ref 271	m	0.03	1.45	-	2.85	4.30	4.73	1.143
M302122F	spray lath ref 273	m	0.03	1.45	-	3.40	4.85	5.34	1.143
M302122G	red-rib lath ref 274	m	0.03	1.45	-	3.10	4.55	5.01	1.143
M302122H	stainless steel rib lath ref 267	m	0.03	1.45	-	7.19	8.64	9.50	3.322
M302122I	stainless steel lath ref 95S	m	0.03	1.45	-	7.19	8.64	9.50	2.334

Major Works 2011		Unit	Labour Hours	Labour Net	Plant Net	Materials Net	Unit Net	Unit with 10%	CO₂
				£	£	£	£	£	Kg
M30	**M30: METAL MESH LATHING AND ANCHORED REINFORCEMENT FOR PLASTERED COATING**								
M3021	**Expamet expanded metal lathing to woodwork backgrounds**								
M302141	**To isolated columns; over 300 mm wide**								
M302141A	ref BB263	m²	0.05	2.33	-	6.31	8.64	9.50	3.209
M302141B	ref BB264	m²	0.05	2.33	-	6.31	8.64	9.50	3.116
M302141C	ref 94G	m²	0.05	2.33	-	9.46	11.79	12.97	4.770
M302141D	rib lath ref 269	m²	0.05	2.33	-	7.62	9.95	10.95	3.209
M302141E	rib lath ref 271	m²	0.05	2.33	-	8.68	11.01	12.11	3.581
M302141F	spray lath ref 273	m²	0.05	2.33	-	10.51	12.84	14.12	3.581
M302141G	red-rib lath ref 274	m²	0.05	2.33	-	9.51	11.84	13.02	3.581
M302141H	stainless steel rib lath ref 267	m²	0.05	2.33	-	22.47	24.80	27.28	10.843
M302141I	stainless steel lath ref 95S	m²	0.05	2.33	-	22.47	24.80	27.28	7.551
M302142	**To isolated columns; not exceeding 300 mm wide**								
M302142A	ref BB263	m	0.02	0.98	-	1.89	2.87	3.16	0.963
M302142B	ref BB264	m	0.02	0.98	-	1.89	2.87	3.16	0.935
M302142C	ref 94G	m	0.02	0.98	-	2.84	3.82	4.20	1.431
M302142D	rib lath ref 269	m	0.02	0.98	-	2.29	3.27	3.60	0.963
M302142E	rib lath ref 271	m	0.02	0.98	-	2.60	3.58	3.94	1.074
M302142F	spray lath ref 273	m	0.02	0.98	-	3.15	4.13	4.54	1.074
M302142G	red-rib lath ref 274	m	0.02	0.98	-	2.85	3.83	4.21	1.074
M302142H	stainless steel rib lath ref 267	m	0.02	0.98	-	6.74	7.72	8.49	3.253
M302142I	stainless steel lath ref 95S	m	0.02	0.98	-	6.74	7.72	8.49	2.265
M3022	**Expamet expanded metal lathing to metalwork backgrounds with tying wire**								
M302201	**To walls; over 300 mm wide**								
M302201A	ref BB263	m²	0.08	3.50	-	5.86	9.36	10.30	3.085
M302201B	ref BB264	m²	0.08	3.50	-	5.86	9.36	10.30	2.993
M302201C	ref 94G	m²	0.08	3.50	-	9.01	12.51	13.76	4.646
M302201D	rib lath ref 269	m²	0.08	3.50	-	7.17	10.67	11.74	3.085
M302201E	rib lath ref 271	m²	0.08	3.50	-	8.23	11.73	12.90	3.457
M302201F	spray lath ref 273	m²	0.08	3.50	-	10.06	13.56	14.92	3.457
M302201G	red-rib lath ref 274	m²	0.08	3.50	-	9.06	12.56	13.82	3.457
M302201H	stainless steel rib lath ref 267	m²	0.08	3.50	-	21.67	25.17	27.69	10.719
M302201I	stainless steel lath ref 95S	m²	0.08	3.50	-	21.67	25.17	27.69	7.427
M302202	**To walls; not exceeding 300 mm wide**								
M302202A	ref BB263	m	0.03	1.45	-	1.76	3.21	3.53	0.925
M302202B	ref BB264	m	0.03	1.45	-	1.76	3.21	3.53	0.898
M302202C	ref 94G	m	0.03	1.45	-	2.70	4.15	4.57	1.394
M302202D	rib lath ref 269	m	0.03	1.45	-	2.15	3.60	3.96	0.925
M302202E	rib lath ref 271	m	0.03	1.45	-	2.47	3.92	4.31	1.037
M302202F	spray lath ref 273	m	0.03	1.45	-	3.02	4.47	4.92	1.037
M302202G	red-rib lath ref 274	m	0.03	1.45	-	2.72	4.17	4.59	1.037
M302202H	stainless steel rib lath ref 267	m	0.03	1.45	-	6.50	7.95	8.75	3.216
M302202I	stainless steel lath ref 95S	m	0.03	1.45	-	6.50	7.95	8.75	2.228
M302211	**To ceilings; over 300 mm wide**								
M302211A	ref BB263	m²	0.12	5.41	-	5.86	11.27	12.40	3.085
M302211B	ref BB264	m²	0.12	5.41	-	5.86	11.27	12.40	2.993
M302211C	ref 94G	m²	0.12	5.41	-	9.01	14.42	15.86	4.646
M302211D	rib lath ref 269	m²	0.12	5.41	-	7.17	12.58	13.84	3.085
M302211E	rib lath ref 271	m²	0.12	5.41	-	8.23	13.64	15.00	3.457
M302211F	spray lath ref 273	m²	0.12	5.41	-	10.06	15.47	17.02	3.457
M302211G	red-rib lath ref 274	m²	0.12	5.41	-	9.06	14.47	15.92	3.457
M302211H	stainless steel rib lath ref 267	m²	0.12	5.41	-	21.67	27.08	29.79	10.719
M302211I	stainless steel lath ref 95S	m²	0.12	5.41	-	21.67	27.08	29.79	7.427
M302212	**To ceilings; not exceeding 300 mm wide**								
M302212A	ref BB263	m	0.05	2.19	-	1.76	3.95	4.35	0.925
M302212B	ref BB264	m	0.05	2.19	-	1.76	3.95	4.35	0.898
M302212C	ref 94G	m	0.05	2.19	-	2.70	4.89	5.38	1.394
M302212D	rib lath ref 269	m	0.05	2.19	-	2.15	4.34	4.77	0.925
M302212E	rib lath ref 271	m	0.05	2.19	-	2.47	4.66	5.13	1.037

Major Works 2011		Unit	Labour Hours	Labour Net	Plant Net	Materials Net	Unit Net	Unit with 10%	CO₂
				£	£	£	£	£	Kg
M30	**M30: METAL MESH LATHING AND ANCHORED REINFORCEMENT FOR PLASTERED COATING**								
M3022	**Expamet expanded metal lathing to metalwork backgrounds with tying wire**								
M302212	**To ceilings; not exceeding 300 mm wide**								
M302212F	spray lath ref 273	m	0.05	2.19	-	3.02	5.21	5.73	1.037
M302212G	red-rib lath ref 274	m	0.05	2.19	-	2.72	4.91	5.40	1.037
M302212H	stainless steel rib lath ref 267	m	0.05	2.19	-	6.50	8.69	9.56	3.216
M302212I	stainless steel lath ref 95S	m	0.05	2.19	-	6.50	8.69	9.56	2.228
M302221	**To isolated beams; over 300 mm wide**								
M302221A	ref BB263	m²	0.12	5.41	-	5.86	11.27	12.40	3.085
M302221B	ref BB264	m²	0.12	5.41	-	5.86	11.27	12.40	2.993
M302221C	ref 94G	m²	0.12	5.41	-	9.01	14.42	15.86	4.646
M302221D	rib lath ref 269	m²	0.12	5.41	-	7.17	12.58	13.84	3.085
M302221E	rib lath ref 271	m²	0.12	5.41	-	8.23	13.64	15.00	3.457
M302221F	spray lath ref 273	m²	0.12	5.41	-	10.06	15.47	17.02	3.457
M302221G	red-rib lath ref 274	m²	0.12	5.41	-	9.06	14.47	15.92	3.457
M302221H	stainless steel rib lath ref 267	m²	0.12	5.41	-	21.67	27.08	29.79	10.719
M302221I	stainless steel lath ref 95S	m²	0.12	5.41	-	21.67	27.08	29.79	7.427
M302222	**To isolated beams; not exceeding 300 mm wide**								
M302222A	ref BB263	m	0.05	2.19	-	1.76	3.95	4.35	0.925
M302222B	ref BB264	m	0.05	2.19	-	1.76	3.95	4.35	0.898
M302222C	ref 94G	m	0.05	2.19	-	2.70	4.89	5.38	1.394
M302222D	rib lath ref 269	m	0.05	2.19	-	2.15	4.34	4.77	0.925
M302222E	rib lath ref 271	m	0.05	2.19	-	2.47	4.66	5.13	1.037
M302222F	spray lath ref 273	m	0.05	2.19	-	3.02	5.21	5.73	1.037
M302222G	red-rib lath ref 274	m	0.05	2.19	-	2.72	4.91	5.40	1.037
M302222H	stainless steel rib lath ref 267	m	0.05	2.19	-	6.50	8.69	9.56	3.216
M302222I	stainless steel lath ref 95S	m	0.05	2.19	-	6.50	8.69	9.56	2.228
M302241	**To isolated columns; over 300 mm wide**								
M302241A	ref BB263	m²	0.08	3.50	-	5.86	9.36	10.30	3.085
M302241B	ref BB264	m²	0.08	3.50	-	5.86	9.36	10.30	2.993
M302241C	ref 94G	m²	0.08	3.50	-	9.01	12.51	13.76	4.646
M302241D	rib lath ref 269	m²	0.08	3.50	-	7.17	10.67	11.74	3.085
M302241E	rib lath ref 271	m²	0.08	3.50	-	8.23	11.73	12.90	3.457
M302241F	spray lath ref 273	m²	0.08	3.50	-	10.06	13.56	14.92	3.457
M302241G	red-rib lath ref 274	m²	0.08	3.50	-	9.06	12.56	13.82	3.457
M302241H	stainless steel rib lath ref 267	m²	0.08	3.50	-	21.67	25.17	27.69	10.719
M302241I	stainless steel lath ref 95S	m²	0.08	3.50	-	21.67	25.17	27.69	7.427
M302242	**To isolated columns; not exceeding 300 mm wide**								
M302242A	ref BB263	m	0.03	1.45	-	1.76	3.21	3.53	0.925
M302242B	ref BB264	m	0.03	1.45	-	1.76	3.21	3.53	0.898
M302242C	ref 94G	m	0.03	1.45	-	2.70	4.15	4.57	1.394
M302242D	rib lath ref 269	m	0.03	1.45	-	2.15	3.60	3.96	0.925
M302242E	rib lath ref 271	m	0.03	1.45	-	2.47	3.92	4.31	1.037
M302242F	spray lath ref 273	m	0.03	1.45	-	3.02	4.47	4.92	1.037
M302242G	red-rib lath ref 274	m	0.03	1.45	-	2.72	4.17	4.59	1.037
M302242H	stainless steel rib lath ref 267	m	0.03	1.45	-	6.50	7.95	8.75	3.216
M302242I	stainless steel lath ref 95S	m	0.03	1.45	-	6.50	7.95	8.75	2.228
M3023	**Expamet expanded metal lathing to concrete, masonry or metalwork backgrounds with cartridge fired nails**								
M302301	**To walls; over 300 mm wide**								
M302301A	ref BB263	m²	0.05	2.33	0.27	9.46	12.06	13.27	3.445
M302301B	ref BB264	m²	0.05	2.33	0.27	9.46	12.06	13.27	3.353
M302301C	ref 94G	m²	0.05	2.33	0.27	12.61	15.21	16.73	5.006
M302301D	rib lath ref 269	m²	0.05	2.33	0.27	10.77	13.37	14.71	3.445
M302301E	rib lath ref 271	m²	0.05	2.33	0.27	11.83	14.43	15.87	3.817
M302301F	spray lath ref 273	m²	0.05	2.33	0.27	13.66	16.26	17.89	3.817
M302301G	red-rib lath ref 274	m²	0.05	2.33	0.27	12.66	15.26	16.79	3.817
M302301H	stainless steel rib lath ref 267	m²	0.05	2.33	0.27	25.27	27.87	30.66	11.079

Surface Finishes

Major Works 2011		Unit	Labour Hours	Labour Net £	Plant Net £	Materials Net £	Unit Net £	Unit with 10% £	CO₂ Kg
M30	**M30: METAL MESH LATHING AND ANCHORED REINFORCEMENT FOR PLASTERED COATING**								
M3023	**Expamet expanded metal lathing to concrete, masonry or metalwork backgrounds with cartridge fired nails**								
M302301	**To walls; over 300 mm wide**								
M302301I	stainless steel lath ref 95S	m²	0.05	2.33	0.27	25.27	27.87	30.66	7.787
M302302	**To walls; not exceeding 300 mm wide**								
M302302A	ref BB263	m	0.02	0.98	0.11	2.84	3.93	4.32	1.033
M302302B	ref BB264	m	0.02	0.98	0.11	2.84	3.93	4.32	1.006
M302302C	ref 94G	m	0.02	0.98	0.11	3.78	4.87	5.36	1.502
M302302D	rib lath ref 269	m	0.02	0.98	0.11	3.23	4.32	4.75	1.033
M302302E	rib lath ref 271	m	0.02	0.93	0.11	3.55	4.59	5.05	1.145
M302302F	spray lath ref 273	m	0.02	0.98	0.11	4.10	5.19	5.71	1.145
M302302G	red-rib lath ref 274	m	0.02	0.98	0.11	3.80	4.89	5.38	1.145
M302302H	stainless steel rib lath ref 267	m	0.02	0.98	0.11	7.58	8.67	9.54	3.324
M302302I	stainless steel lath ref 95S	m	0.02	0.98	0.11	7.58	8.67	9.54	2.336
M302311	**To ceilings; over 300 mm wide**								
M302311A	ref BB263	m²	0.08	3.50	0.80	16.66	20.96	23.06	4.165
M302311B	ref BB264	m²	0.08	3.50	0.80	16.66	20.96	23.06	4.073
M302311C	ref 94G	m²	0.08	3.50	0.80	19.81	24.11	26.52	5.726
M302311D	rib lath ref 269	m²	0.08	3.50	0.80	17.97	22.27	24.50	4.165
M302311E	rib lath ref 271	m²	0.08	3.50	0.80	19.03	23.33	25.66	4.537
M302311F	spray lath ref 273	m²	0.08	3.50	0.80	20.86	25.16	27.68	4.537
M302311G	red rib lath ref 274	m²	0.08	3.50	0.80	19.86	24.16	26.58	4.537
M302311H	stainless steel rib lath ref 267	m²	0.08	3.50	0.80	32.47	36.77	40.45	11.799
M302311I	stainless steel lath ref 95S	m²	0.08	3.50	0.80	32.47	36.77	40.45	8.507
M302312	**To ceilings; not exceeding 300 mm wide**								
M302312A	ref BB263	m	0.03	1.45	0.24	5.00	6.69	7.36	1.249
M302312B	ref BB264	m	0.03	1.45	0.24	5.00	6.69	7.36	1.222
M302312C	ref 94G	m	0.03	1.45	0.24	5.94	7.63	8.39	1.718
M302312D	rib lath ref 269	m	0.03	1.45	0.24	5.39	7.08	7.79	1.249
M302312E	rib lath ref 271	m	0.03	1.45	0.24	5.71	7.40	8.14	1.361
M302312F	spray lath ref 273	m	0.03	1.45	0.24	6.26	7.95	8.75	1.361
M302312G	red rib lath ref 274	m	0.03	1.45	0.24	5.96	7.65	8.42	1.361
M302312H	stainless steel rib lath ref 267	m	0.03	1.45	0.24	9.74	11.43	12.57	3.540
M302312I	stainless steel lath ref 95S	m	0.03	1.45	0.24	9.74	11.43	12.57	2.552
M302321	**To isolated beams; over 300 mm wide**								
M302321A	ref BB263	m²	0.08	3.50	0.80	16.66	20.96	23.06	4.165
M302321B	ref BB264	m²	0.08	3.50	0.80	16.66	20.96	23.06	4.073
M302321C	ref 94G	m²	0.08	3.50	0.80	19.81	24.11	26.52	5.726
M302321D	rib lath ref 269	m²	0.08	3.50	0.80	17.97	22.27	24.50	4.165
M302321E	rib lath ref 271	m²	0.08	3.50	0.80	19.03	23.33	25.66	4.537
M302321F	spray lath ref 273	m²	0.08	3.50	0.80	20.86	25.16	27.68	4.537
M302321G	red rib lath ref 274	m²	0.08	3.50	0.80	19.86	24.16	26.58	4.537
M302321H	stainless steel rib lath ref 267	m²	0.08	3.50	0.80	32.47	36.77	40.45	11.799
M302321I	stainless steel lath ref 95S	m²	0.08	3.50	0.80	32.47	36.77	40.45	8.507
M302322	**To isolated beams; not exceeding 300 mm wide**								
M302322A	ref BB263	m	0.03	1.45	0.24	5.00	6.69	7.36	1.249
M302322B	ref BB264	m	0.03	1.45	0.24	5.00	6.69	7.36	1.222
M302322C	ref 94G	m	0.03	1.45	0.24	5.94	7.63	8.39	1.718
M302322D	rib lath ref 269	m	0.03	1.45	0.24	5.39	7.08	7.79	1.249
M302322E	rib lath ref 271	m	0.03	1.45	0.24	5.71	7.40	8.14	1.361
M302322F	spray lath ref 273	m	0.03	1.45	0.24	6.26	7.95	8.75	1.361
M302322G	red rib lath ref 274	m	0.03	1.45	0.24	5.96	7.65	8.42	1.361
M302322H	stainless steel rib lath ref 267	m	0.03	1.45	0.24	9.74	11.43	12.57	3.540
M302322I	stainless steel lath ref 95S	m	0.03	1.45	0.24	9.74	11.43	12.57	2.552
M302341	**To isolated columns; over 300 mm wide**								
M302341A	ref BB263	m²	0.05	2.33	0.27	9.46	12.06	13.27	3.445
M302341B	ref BB264	m²	0.05	2.33	0.27	9.46	12.06	13.27	3.353
M302341C	ref 94G	m²	0.05	2.33	0.27	12.61	15.21	16.73	5.006
M302341D	rib lath ref 269	m²	0.05	2.33	0.27	10.77	13.37	14.71	3.445
M302341E	rib lath ref 271	m²	0.05	2.33	0.27	11.83	14.43	15.87	3.817

Major Works 2011		Unit	Labour Hours	Labour Net	Plant Net	Materials Net	Unit Net	Unit with 10%	CO$_2$
				£	£	£	£	£	Kg
M30	**M30: METAL MESH LATHING AND ANCHORED REINFORCEMENT FOR PLASTERED COATING**								
M3023	**Expamet expanded metal lathing to concrete, masonry or metalwork backgrounds with cartridge fired nails**								
M302341	**To isolated columns; over 300 mm wide**								
M302341F	spray lath ref 273	m^2	0.05	2.33	0.27	13.66	16.26	17.89	3.817
M302341G	red-rib lath ref 274	m^2	0.05	2.33	0.27	12.66	15.26	16.79	3.817
M302341H	stainless steel rib lath ref 267	m^2	0.05	2.33	0.27	25.27	27.87	30.66	11.079
M302341I	stainless steel lath ref 95S	m^2	0.05	2.33	0.27	25.27	27.87	30.66	7.787
M302342	**To isolated columns; not exceeding 300 mm wide**								
M302342A	ref BB263	m	0.02	0.98	0.11	2.84	3.93	4.32	1.033
M302342B	ref BB264	m	0.02	0.98	0.11	2.84	3.93	4.32	1.006
M302342C	ref 94G	m	0.02	0.98	0.11	3.78	4.87	5.36	1.502
M302342D	rib lath ref 269	m	0.02	0.98	0.11	3.23	4.32	4.75	1.033
M302342E	rib lath ref 271	m	0.02	0.93	0.11	3.55	4.59	5.05	1.145
M302342F	spray lath ref 273	m	0.02	0.98	0.11	4.10	5.19	5.71	1.145
M302342G	red-rib lath ref 274	m	0.02	0.98	0.11	3.80	4.89	5.38	1.145
M302342H	stainless steel rib lath ref 267	m	0.02	0.98	0.11	7.58	8.67	9.54	3.324
M302342I	stainless steel lath ref 95S	m	0.02	0.98	0.11	7.58	8.67	9.54	2.336

Surface Finishes

		Unit	Labour Hours	Labour Net	Plant Net	Materials Net	Unit Net	Unit with 10%	CO₂
				£	£	£	£	£	Kg
M31	**M31: FIBROUS PLASTER**								
M3111	**Gyproc coving**								
M311161	**Gyproc coving; fixing with adhesive**								
M311161A	100 mm girth	m	0.06	2.80	-	1.76	4.56	5.02	0.728
M311161B	127 mm girth	m	0.07	3.03	-	1.91	4.94	5.43	1.068

Major Works 2011		Unit	Labour Hours	Labour Net	Plant Net	Materials Net	Unit Net	Unit with 10%	CO$_2$
				£	£	£	£	£	Kg
M40	**M40: STONE, CONCRETE, QUARRY AND CERAMIC TILING AND MOSAIC**								
M4011	**Glazed ceramic tiling; BS6431; fixing with tile adhesive, grouting with neat white cement; to floated backings**								
M401101	**To walls; 108 x 108 x 4 mm plain tiles**								
M401101A	over 300 mm wide	m^2	1.63	27.68	-	24.73	52.41	57.65	8.854
M401101B	not exceeding 300 mm wide	m	0.66	11.21	-	7.42	18.63	20.49	2.656
M401102	**To walls; 108 x 108 x 4 mm patterned tiles**								
M401102A	over 300 mm wide	m^2	1.63	27.68	-	24.73	52.41	57.65	8.854
M401102B	not exceeding 300 mm wide	m	0.66	11.21	-	7.42	18.63	20.49	2.656
M401103	**To walls; 152 x 152 x 5.5 mm plain tiles**								
M401103A	over 300 mm wide	m^2	1.22	20.72	-	24.05	44.77	49.25	10.125
M401103B	not exceeding 300 mm wide	m	0.50	8.41	-	7.22	15.63	17.19	3.038
M401104	**To walls; 152 x 152 x 5.5 mm patterned tiles**								
M401104A	over 300 mm wide	m^2	1.22	20.72	-	24.05	44.77	49.25	10.125
M401104B	not exceeding 300 mm wide	m	0.50	8.41	-	7.22	15.63	17.19	3.038
M401141	**To isolated columns; 108 x 108 x 4 mm plain tiles**								
M401141A	over 300 mm wide	m^2	1.63	27.68	-	24.73	52.41	57.65	8.854
M401141B	not exceeding 300 mm wide	m	0.66	11.21	-	7.42	18.63	20.49	2.656
M401142	**To isolated columns; 108 x 108 x 4 mm patterned tiles**								
M401142A	over 300 mm wide	m^2	1.63	27.68	-	24.73	52.41	57.65	8.854
M401142B	not exceeding 300 mm wide	m	0.66	11.21	-	7.42	18.63	20.49	2.656
M401143	**To isolated columns; 152 x 152 x 5.5 mm plain tiles**								
M401143A	over 300 mm wide	m^2	1.22	20.72	-	24.05	44.77	49.25	10.125
M401143B	not exceeding 300 mm wide	m	0.50	8.41	-	7.22	15.63	17.19	3.038
M401144	**To isolated columns; 152 x 152 x 5.5 mm patterned tiles**								
M401144A	over 300 mm wide	m^2	1.22	20.72	-	24.05	44.77	49.25	10.125
M401144B	not exceeding 300 mm wide	m	0.50	8.41	-	7.22	15.63	17.19	3.038
M401161	**To skirtings, bands, strings, coverings to kerbs, mouldings, channels or the like; 108 x 108 x 4 mm plain tiles**								
M401161A	not exceeding 300 mm wide	m	0.52	8.83	-	7.86	16.69	18.36	2.893
M401162	**To skirtings, bands, strings, coverings to kerbs, mouldings, channels or the like; 108 x 108 x 4 mm patterned tiles**								
M401162B	not exceeding 300 mm wide	m	0.52	8.83	-	7.86	16.69	18.36	2.893
M401163	**To skirtings, bands, strings, coverings to kerbs, mouldings, channels or the like; 152 x 152 x 5.5 mm plain tiles**								
M401163C	not exceeding 300 mm wide	m	0.40	6.79	-	7.62	14.41	15.85	3.263
M401164	**To skirtings, bands, strings, coverings to kerbs, mouldings, channels or the like; 152 x 152 x 5.5 mm patterned tiles**								
M401164D	not exceeding 300 mm wide	m	0.40	6.79	-	7.62	14.41	15.85	3.263

Major Works 2011		Unit	Labour Hours	Labour Net	Plant Net	Materials Net	Unit Net	Unit with 10%	CO₂
				£	£	£	£	£	Kg
M40	**M40: STONE, CONCRETE, QUARRY AND CERAMIC TILING AND MOSAIC**								
M4051	**Quarry tiles; BS 6431; bedded, jointed and pointed in cement mortar (1:3)**								
M405101	**To floors; 150 x 150 x 12.5 mm**								
M405101A	over 300 mm wide	m²	1.00	16.98	-	19.89	36.87	40.56	15.689
M405101B	not exceeding 300 mm wide	m	0.41	6.88	-	6.01	12.89	14.18	4.847
M405102	**To floors; 150 x 150 x 20 mm**								
M405102A	over 300 mm wide	m²	1.03	17.49	-	27.46	44.95	49.45	22.571
M405102B	not exceeding 300 mm wide	m	0.42	7.08	-	8.28	15.36	16.90	6.912
M405103	**To floors; 225 x 225 x 25 mm**								
M405103A	over 300 mm wide	m²	1.05	17.83	-	51.07	68.90	75.79	27.511
M405103B	not exceeding 300 mm wide	m	0.43	7.22	-	15.33	22.55	24.81	8.289
M405111	**To treads; 150 x 150 x 12.5 mm**								
M405111B	150 - 300 mm wide	m	0.38	6.52	-	6.28	12.80	14.08	5.011
M405111C	300 - 450 mm wide	m	0.58	9.78	-	9.31	19.09	21.00	7.165
M405112	**To treads; 150 x 150 x 20 mm**								
M405112B	150 - 300 mm wide	m	0.41	6.88	-	8.66	15.54	17.09	7.174
M405112C	300 - 450 mm wide	m	0.61	10.32	-	12.88	23.20	25.52	10.410
M405113	**To treads; 225 x 225 x 25 mm**								
M405113A	150 - 300 mm wide	m	0.42	7.18	-	16.04	23.22	25.54	8.616
M405113C	300 - 450 mm wide	m	0.64	10.78	-	24.06	34.84	38.32	12.924
M405121	**To risers; 150 x 150 x 12.5 mm**								
M405121A	not exceeding 150 mm high	m	0.20	3.31	-	3.14	6.45	7.10	2.506
M405121B	150 - 300 mm high	m	0.38	6.52	-	6.28	12.80	14.08	5.011
M405122	**To risers; 150 x 150 x 20 mm**								
M405122A	not exceeding 150 mm high	m	0.20	3.45	-	4.33	7.78	8.56	3.587
M405122B	150 - 300 mm high	m	0.41	6.88	-	8.66	15.54	17.09	7.174
M405123	**To risers; 225 x 225 x 25 mm**								
M405123A	not exceeding 150 mm high	m	0.21	3.60	-	8.02	11.62	12.78	4.308
M405123C	150 - 300 mm high	m	0.42	7.18	-	16.04	23.22	25.54	8.616
M405161	**To skirtings, bands, strings, coverings to kerbs, mouldings, channels or the like; not exceeding 300 mm wide**								
M405161A	150 x 150 x 12.5 mm	m	0.44	7.47	-	19.96	27.43	30.17	13.423
M405161B	150 x 150 x 20 mm	m	0.48	8.15	-	27.89	36.04	39.64	20.634
M405161C	225 x 225 x 25 mm	m	0.35	5.94	-	52.51	58.45	64.30	25.441
M405171	**To skirtings; rounded top; not exceeding 150 mm wide**								
M405171D	150 x 150 x 12.5 mm	m	0.44	7.47	-	4.97	12.44	13.68	2.539
M405171E	150 x 150 x 20 mm	m	0.48	8.15	-	5.81	13.96	15.36	3.571
M405172	**To skirtings; square top; not exceeding 150 mm wide**								
M405172F	150 x 150 x 12.5 mm	m	0.44	7.47	-	3.72	11.19	12.31	2.539
M405172G	150 x 150 x 20 mm	m	0.48	8.15	-	5.11	13.26	14.59	3.571
M405173	**To skirtings; rounded top cove base; not exceeding 150 mm wide**								
M405173H	150 x 150 x 12.5 mm	m	0.44	7.47	-	5.83	13.30	14.63	2.539
M405173I	150 x 150 x 20 mm	m	0.48	8.15	-	7.62	15.77	17.35	3.571
M405174	**To skirtings; square top cove base; not exceeding 150 mm wide**								
M405174J	150 x 150 x 12.5 mm	m	0.44	7.47	-	5.83	13.30	14.63	2.539
M405174K	150 x 150 x 20 mm	m	0.48	8.15	-	7.62	15.77	17.35	3.571
M405175	**To edgings; twice rounded; not exceeding 150 mm wide**								
M405175L	150 x 150 x 12.5 mm	m	0.23	3.91	-	14.07	17.98	19.78	2.425
M405175M	150 x 150 x 20 mm	m	0.23	3.91	-	14.91	18.82	20.70	3.454

Major Works 2011		Unit	Labour Hours	Labour Net	Plant Net	Materials Net	Unit Net	Unit with 10%	CO$_2$
				£	£	£	£	£	Kg
M40	**M40: STONE, CONCRETE, QUARRY AND CERAMIC TILING AND MOSAIC**								
M4054	**Vitrified ceramic floor tiles; BS 6431; bedded, jointed and pointed in cement mortar (1:3)**								
M405401	**To floors; 150 x 150 x 9 mm**								
M405401A	over 300 mm wide	m^2	0.93	15.79	-	44.63	60.42	66.46	15.368
M405401B	not exceeding 300 mm wide	m	0.38	6.40	-	13.43	19.83	21.81	4.751
M405402	**To floors; 150 x 150 x 12 mm**								
M405402A	over 300 mm wide	m^2	0.98	16.64	-	28.47	45.11	49.62	19.085
M405402B	not exceeding 300 mm wide	m	0.40	6.74	-	8.58	15.32	16.85	5.866
M405403	**To floors; 150 x 75 x 12 mm**								
M405403A	over 300 mm wide	m^2	1.59	27.00	-	36.42	63.42	69.76	19.085
M405403B	not exceeding 300 mm wide	m	0.64	10.94	-	10.97	21.91	24.10	5.866
M405421	**To treads; 150 x 150 x 9 mm**								
M405421A	150 - 300 mm wide	m	0.42	7.13	-	14.05	21.18	23.30	4.910
M405421B	300 - 450 mm wide	m	0.63	10.70	-	20.97	31.67	34.84	7.014
M405422	**To treads; 150 x 150 x 12 mm**								
M405422A	150 - 300 mm wide	m	0.44	7.49	-	8.97	16.46	18.11	6.079
M405422B	300 - 450 mm wide	m	0.66	11.24	-	13.35	24.59	27.05	8.766
M405423	**To treads; 150 x 75 x 12 mm**								
M405423A	150 - 300 mm wide	m	0.72	12.23	-	11.47	23.70	26.07	6.079
M405423B	300 - 450 mm wide	m	1.08	18.34	-	17.10	35.44	38.98	8.766
M405431	**To risers; 150 x 150 x 9 mm**								
M405431A	not exceeding 150 mm high	m	0.21	3.57	-	7.03	10.60	11.66	2.455
M405431B	150 - 300 mm high	m	0.42	7.13	-	14.05	21.18	23.30	4.910
M405432	**To risers; 150 x 150 x 12 mm**								
M405432A	not exceeding 150 mm high	m	0.22	3.75	-	4.49	8.24	9.06	3.039
M405432B	150 - 300 mm high	m	0.44	7.49	-	8.97	16.46	18.11	6.079
M405433	**To risers; 150 x 75 x 12 mm**								
M405433A	not exceeding 150 mm wide	m	0.36	6.11	-	5.73	11.84	13.02	3.039
M405433B	150 - 300 mm wide	m	0.72	12.23	-	11.47	23.70	26.07	6.079
M405461	**To skirtings, bands, strings, coverings to kerbs, mouldings, channels or the like; not exceeding 300 mm wide**								
M405461A	150 x 150 x 9 mm	m	0.42	7.13	-	14.05	21.18	23.30	4.910
M405461B	150 x 150 x 12 mm	m	0.44	7.47	-	8.97	16.44	18.08	6.079
M405461C	150 x 75 x 12 mm	m	0.72	12.23	-	11.26	23.49	25.84	5.376
M405462	**To skirtings; rounded top; not exceeding 150 mm wide**								
M405462D	150 x 150 x 9 mm	m	0.41	6.96	-	4.29	11.25	12.38	2.523
M405462E	150 x 150 x 12 mm	m	0.44	7.47	-	7.26	14.73	16.20	3.081
M405462F	150 x 75 x 12 mm	m	0.71	12.06	-	6.97	19.03	20.93	3.081
M405463	**To skirtings; square top; not exceeding 150 mm wide**								
M405463G	150 x 150 x 9 mm	m	0.41	6.96	-	4.29	11.25	12.38	2.523
M405463H	150 x 150 x 12 mm	m	0.44	7.47	-	7.26	14.73	16.20	3.081
M405463I	150 x 75 x 12 mm	m	0.71	12.06	-	6.97	19.03	20.93	3.081
M405464	**To skirtings; rounded top cove base; not exceeding 150 mm wide**								
M405464J	150 x 150 x 9 mm	m	0.41	6.96	-	5.47	12.43	13.67	2.523
M405464K	150 x 150 x 12 mm	m	0.44	7.47	-	8.43	15.90	17.49	3.081
M405464L	150 x 75 x 12 mm	m	0.71	12.06	-	8.13	20.19	22.21	3.081
M405465	**To skirtings; square top cove base; not exceeding 150 mm wide**								
M405465M	150 x 150 x 9 mm	m	0.41	6.96	-	4.29	11.25	12.38	2.449
M405465N	150 x 150 x 12 mm	m	0.44	7.47	-	7.26	14.73	16.20	3.044
M405465O	150 x 75 x 12 mm	m	0.71	12.06	-	6.97	19.03	20.93	3.044
M405469	**To edgings; twice rounded; not exceeding 150 mm wide**								
M405469P	150 x 150 x 9 mm	m	0.21	3.57	-	7.24	10.81	11.89	1.230

Surface Finishes

Major Works 2011		Unit	Labour Hours	Labour Net	Plant Net	Materials Net	Unit Net	Unit with 10%	CO$_2$
				£	£	£	£	£	Kg
M40	**M40: STONE, CONCRETE, QUARRY AND CERAMIC TILING AND MOSAIC**								
M4054	**Vitrified ceramic floor tiles; BS 6431; bedded, jointed and pointed in cement mortar (1:3)**								
M405469	**To edgings; twice rounded; not exceeding 150 mm wide**								
M405469Q	150 x 150 x 12 mm	m	0.18	3.06	-	56.91	59.97	65.97	4.833
M405469R	150 x 75 x 12 mm	m	0.36	6.11	-	54.95	61.06	67.17	4.833
M4083	**Division strips and nosings**								
M408301	**Division strips; embedding in pavings**								
M408301A	5 x 25 mm brass	m	0.03	1.40	-	5.02	6.42	7.06	2.700
M408301B	5 x 25 mm aluminium	m	0.03	1.40	-	2.29	3.69	4.06	2.920
M408302	**Ferodo nosings; plugging and screwing to concrete backgrounds**								
M408302A	type SD1	m	0.30	5.09	-	22.47	27.56	30.32	0.385
M408302B	type SD2	m	0.30	5.09	-	25.52	30.61	33.67	0.274
M408302C	type HD1	m	0.30	5.09	-	22.99	28.08	30.89	0.385
M408302D	type HD2	m	0.30	5.09	-	27.23	32.32	35.55	0.385

Major Works 2011		Unit	Labour Hours	Labour Net	Plant Net	Materials Net	Unit Net	Unit with 10%	CO₂
				£	£	£	£	£	Kg
M50	**M50: RUBBER, PLASTIC, CORK, LINO AND CARPET TILING AND SHEETING**								
M5051	**Vinyl sheet flooring**								
M505101	**Standard grade; 2 mm thick**								
M505101A	Marleyflor Plus	m²	0.50	8.49	-	9.16	17.65	19.42	6.245
M505101B	Tarkett IQ Granit	m²	0.50	8.49	-	11.82	20.31	22.34	6.245
M505101C	Tarkett IQ Eminent	m²	0.50	8.49	-	15.49	23.98	26.38	7.688
M505102	**Heavy duty grade; 2.5 mm thick**								
M505102A	Safetred Original	m²	0.50	8.49	-	12.13	20.62	22.68	7.688
M505102B	Safetred Dimension	m²	0.50	8.49	-	13.63	22.12	24.33	7.688
M505102C	Safetred Aqua	m²	0.50	8.49	-	17.99	26.48	29.13	7.688
M5053	**Vinyl floor tiling**								
M505301	**Standard grade**								
M505301A	Marleyflor Plus; 610 x 610 mm	m²	0.50	8.49	-	8.91	17.40	19.14	6.135
M505301B	Tarkett IQ Granit; 610 x 610 mm	m²	0.50	8.49	-	12.09	20.58	22.64	7.551
M505301C	Tarkett IQ Eminent; 610 x 610 mm	m²	0.50	8.49	-	15.75	24.24	26.66	7.551
M505302	**Heavy duty grade**								
M505302A	Tarkett Tapiflex 243 Acoustic; 500 x 500 mm	m²	0.50	8.49	-	12.80	21.29	23.42	9.249
M505302B	Tarkett Tapiflex 163 Acoustic; 500 x 500 mm	m²	0.50	8.49	-	15.17	23.66	26.03	10.098
M505302C	Tarkett Tapiflex 164 Acoustic; 500 x 500 mm	m²	0.50	8.49	-	16.05	24.54	26.99	10.522
M5055	**Carpet tiling**								
M505502	**Carpet tiles**								
M505502A	Huega Interloop 700; 500 x 500 mm	m²	0.50	8.49	-	10.67	19.16	21.08	10.448
M505502B	Huega Horizon; 500 x 500 mm	m²	0.50	8.49	-	16.08	24.57	27.03	11.956
M505502C	Huega Le Bistro; 500 x 500 mm	m²	0.50	8.49	-	20.58	29.07	31.98	12.962
M5083	**Division strips and nosings**								
M508301	**Division strips; embedding in pavings**								
M508301A	5 x 25 mm brass	m	0.03	1.40	-	5.02	6.42	7.06	2.700
M508301B	5 x 25 mm aluminium	m	0.03	1.40	-	2.29	3.69	4.06	2.920
M508302	**Ferodo nosings; plugging and screwing to concrete backgrounds**								
M508302A	type SD1	m	0.30	5.09	-	22.47	27.56	30.32	0.385
M508302B	type SD2	m	0.30	5.09	-	25.65	30.74	33.81	0.385
M508302C	type HD1	m	0.30	5.09	-	22.99	28.08	30.89	0.385
M508302D	type HD2	m	0.30	5.09	-	27.23	32.32	35.55	0.385
M508303	**Division strips; plugging and screwing to concrete backgrounds**								
M508303A	aluminium; carpet to carpet	m	0.25	4.25	-	2.43	6.68	7.35	2.981
M508303B	aluminium; carpet to stop edge	m	0.25	4.25	-	2.43	6.68	7.35	2.981
M508303C	aluminium; carpet to vinyl flooring	m	0.25	4.25	-	2.43	6.68	7.35	2.981
M508303D	aluminium; carpet to vinyl flooring stop edge	m	0.25	4.25	-	2.43	6.68	7.35	2.981
M508303E	brass anodised aluminium; carpet to carpet	m	0.25	4.25	-	5.44	9.69	10.66	3.064
M508303F	brass anodised aluminium; carpet to carpet stop edge	m	0.25	4.25	-	5.44	9.69	10.66	3.064
M508303G	brass anodised aluminium; carpet to vinyl flooring	m	0.25	4.25	-	5.44	9.69	10.66	3.064
M508303H	brass anodised aluminium; vinyl flooring to stop edge	m	0.25	4.25	-	5.44	9.69	10.66	3.064

Surface Finishes

		Unit	Labour Hours	Labour Net	Plant Net	Materials Net	Unit Net	Unit with 10%	CO$_2$
				£	£	£	£	£	Kg
M51	**M51: EDGE FIXED CARPETING**								
M5155	**Carpeting**								
M515501	**Carpet**								
M515501A	twist pile; man-made	m^2	0.50	8.49	-	21.27	29.76	32.74	13.876
M515501B	twist pile; Inspiration 80% wool	m^2	0.50	8.49	-	25.40	33.89	37.28	14.696
M515501C	loop pile; Oasis 100% wool	m^2	0.50	8.49	-	29.06	37.55	41.31	15.208

Major Works 2011		Unit	Labour Hours	Labour Net	Plant Net	Materials Net	Unit Net	Unit with 10%	CO$_2$
				£	£	£	£	£	Kg
M52	**M52: DECORATIVE PAPERS AND FABRICS**								
M5212	**Plain or woodchip lining paper**								
M521201	**Walls and columns; stop, rub down, size and hang to plastered backgrounds**								
M521201A	areas over 0.5 m^2	m^2	0.26	4.41	-	0.61	5.02	5.52	0.379
M521201B	areas not exceeding 0.5 m^2	Nr	0.20	3.31	-	0.32	3.63	3.99	0.239
M521202	**Walls and columns; stop, rub down, size and hang to plasterboard backgrounds**								
M521202A	areas over 0.5 m^2	m^2	0.25	4.25	-	0.61	4.86	5.35	0.379
M521202B	areas not exceeding 0.5 m^2	Nr	0.19	3.19	-	0.32	3.51	3.86	0.239
M521211	**Ceilings and beams; stop, rub down, size and hang to plastered backgrounds**								
M521211A	areas over 0.5 m^2	m^2	0.31	5.26	-	0.61	5.87	6.46	0.379
M521211B	areas not exceeding 0.5 m^2	Nr	0.23	3.96	-	0.32	4.28	4.71	0.239
M521212	**Ceilings and beams; stop, rub down, size and hang to plasterboard backgrounds**								
M521212A	areas over 0.5 m^2	m^2	0.30	5.09	-	0.61	5.70	6.27	0.379
M521212B	areas not exceeding 0.5 m^2	Nr	0.23	3.82	-	0.32	4.14	4.55	0.239
M5214	**Decorative wallpaper**								
M521401	**Walls and columns; stop, rub down, size and hang to plastered backgrounds**								
M521401A	areas over 0.5 m^2	m^2	0.30	5.09	-	2.43	7.52	8.27	0.397
M521401B	areas not exceeding 0.5 m^2	Nr	0.23	3.82	-	1.23	5.05	5.56	0.248
M521402	**Walls and columns; stop, rub down, size and hang to plasterboard backgrounds**								
M521402A	areas over 0.5 m^2	m^2	0.31	5.26	-	2.43	7.69	8.46	0.397
M521402B	areas not exceeding 0.5 m^2	Nr	0.23	3.96	-	1.23	5.19	5.71	0.248
M521411	**Ceilings and beams; stop, rub down, size and hang to plastered backgrounds**								
M521411A	areas over 0.5 m^2	m^2	0.35	5.94	-	2.43	8.37	9.21	0.397
M521411B	areas not exceeding 0.5 m^2	Nr	0.26	4.47	-	1.23	5.70	6.27	0.248
M521412	**Ceilings and beams; stop, rub down, size and hang to plasterboard backgrounds**								
M521412A	areas over 0.5 m^2	m^2	0.36	6.11	-	2.43	8.54	9.39	0.397
M521412B	areas not exceeding 0.5 m^2	Nr	0.27	4.58	-	1.23	5.81	6.39	0.248
M5216	**Decorative wallpaper**								
M521601	**Walls and columns; stop, rub down, size and hang to plastered backgrounds**								
M521601A	areas over 0.5 m^2	m^2	0.30	5.09	-	2.08	7.17	7.89	0.397
M521601B	areas not exceeding 0.5 m^2	Nr	0.23	3.82	-	1.06	4.88	5.37	0.248
M521602	**Walls and columns; stop, rub down, size and hang to plasterboard backgrounds**								
M521602A	areas over 0.5 m^2	m^2	0.31	5.26	-	2.08	7.34	8.07	0.397
M521602B	areas not exceeding 0.5 m^2	Nr	0.23	3.96	-	1.06	5.02	5.52	0.248
M521611	**Ceilings and beams; stop, rub down, size and hang to plastered backgrounds**								
M521611A	areas over 0.5 m^2	m^2	0.35	5.94	-	2.08	8.02	8.82	0.397
M521611B	areas not exceeding 0.5 m^2	Nr	0.26	4.47	-	1.06	5.53	6.08	0.248
M521612	**Ceilings and beams; stop, rub down, size and hang to plasterboard backgrounds**								
M521612A	areas over 0.5 m^2	m^2	0.36	6.11	-	2.08	8.19	9.01	0.397

Surface Finishes

Major Works 2011		Unit	Labour Hours	Labour Net	Plant Net	Materials Net	Unit Net	Unit with 10%	CO₂
				£	£	£	£	£	Kg
M52	**M52: DECORATIVE PAPERS AND FABRICS**								
M5216	**Decorative wallpaper**								
M521612	**Ceilings and beams; stop, rub down, size and hang to plasterboard backgrounds**								
M521612B	areas not exceeding 0.5 m²	Nr	0.27	4.58	-	1.06	5.64	6.20	0.248

Major Works 2011		Unit	Labour Hours	Labour Net	Plant Net	Materials Net	Unit Net	Unit with 10%	CO$_2$
				£	£	£	£	£	Kg
M60	**M60: PAINTING AND CLEAR FINISHING**								
M6010	**Emulsion paint**								
M601001	**Prepare, apply one mist coat and two full coats; plaster backgrounds**								
M601001A	walls	m^2	0.18	3.06	–	2.21	5.27	5.80	1.068
M601001B	walls; 3.5 - 5.0 m high	m^2	0.21	3.48	–	2.21	5.69	6.26	1.068
M601001D	walls; n.e. 300 mm girth	m	0.07	1.24	–	0.66	1.90	2.09	0.320
M601001E	walls; areas n.e. 0.5 m^2	Nr	0.14	2.29	–	1.11	3.40	3.74	0.534
M601001F	ceilings	m^2	0.20	3.36	–	2.21	5.57	6.13	1.068
M601001G	ceilings; 3.5 - 5.0 m high	m^2	0.22	3.68	–	2.21	5.89	6.48	1.068
M601001I	ceilings; n.e. 300 mm girth	m	0.08	1.36	–	0.66	2.02	2.22	0.320
M601001J	ceilings; areas n.e. 0.5 m^2	Nr	0.15	2.51	–	1.11	3.62	3.98	0.534
M601002	**Prepare, apply one mist coat and two full coats; plasterboard backgrounds**								
M601002A	walls	m^2	0.18	3.06	–	2.21	5.27	5.80	1.068
M601002B	walls; 3.5 - 5.0 m high	m^2	0.21	3.48	–	2.21	5.69	6.26	1.068
M601002D	walls; n.e. 300 mm girth	m	0.07	1.24	–	0.66	1.90	2.09	0.320
M601002E	walls; areas n.e. 0.5 m^2	Nr	0.14	2.29	–	1.11	3.40	3.74	0.534
M601002F	ceilings	m^2	0.20	3.36	–	2.21	5.57	6.13	1.068
M601002G	ceilings; 3.5 - 5.0 m high	m^2	0.22	3.68	–	2.21	5.89	6.48	1.068
M601002I	ceilings; n.e. 300 mm girth	m	0.08	1.36	–	0.66	2.02	2.22	0.320
M601002J	ceilings; areas n.e. 0.5 m^2	Nr	0.15	2.51	–	1.11	3.62	3.98	0.534
M601003	**Prepare, apply one mist coat and two full coats; lining paper backgrounds**								
M601003A	walls	m^2	0.19	3.14	–	2.40	5.54	6.09	1.157
M601003B	walls; 3.5 - 5.0 m high	m^2	0.21	3.57	–	2.40	5.97	6.57	1.157
M601003D	walls; n.e. 300 mm girth	m	0.08	1.27	–	0.74	2.01	2.21	0.356
M601003E	walls; areas n.e. 0.5 m^2	Nr	0.14	2.36	–	1.22	3.58	3.94	0.587
M601003F	ceilings	m^2	0.20	3.46	–	2.40	5.86	6.45	1.157
M601003G	ceilings; 3.5 - 5.0 m high	m^2	0.23	3.92	–	2.40	6.32	6.95	1.157
M601003I	ceilings; n.e. 300 mm girth	m	0.08	1.41	–	0.74	2.15	2.37	0.356
M601003J	ceilings; areas n.e. 0.5 m^2	Nr	0.15	2.60	–	1.22	3.82	4.20	0.587
M601004	**Prepare, apply one mist coat and two full coats; concrete backgrounds**								
M601004A	walls	m^2	0.20	3.31	–	2.58	5.89	6.48	1.246
M601004B	walls; 3.5 - 5.0 m high	m^2	0.22	3.74	–	2.58	6.32	6.95	1.246
M601004D	walls; n.e. 300 mm girth	m	0.09	1.51	–	0.77	2.28	2.51	0.374
M601004E	walls; areas n.e. 0.5 m^2	Nr	0.17	2.80	–	1.29	4.09	4.50	0.623
M601004F	ceilings	m^2	0.22	3.65	–	2.58	6.23	6.85	1.246
M601004G	ceilings; 3.5 - 5.0 m high	m^2	0.27	4.52	–	2.58	7.10	7.81	1.246
M601004I	ceilings; n.e. 300 mm girth	m	0.10	1.66	–	0.77	2.43	2.67	0.374
M601004J	ceilings; areas n.e. 0.5 m^2	Nr	0.18	3.09	–	1.29	4.38	4.82	0.623
M601005	**Prepare, apply one mist coat and two full coats; brickwork backgrounds**								
M601005A	walls	m^2	0.25	4.25	–	3.32	7.57	8.33	1.602
M601005B	walls; 3.5 - 5.0 m high	m^2	0.27	4.58	–	3.32	7.90	8.69	1.602
M601005D	walls; n.e. 300 mm girth	m	0.10	1.70	–	1.00	2.70	2.97	0.481
M601005E	walls; areas n.e. 0.5 m^2	Nr	0.19	3.23	–	1.66	4.89	5.38	0.801
M601006	**Prepare, apply one mist coat and two full coats; blockwork backgrounds**								
M601006A	walls	m^2	0.27	4.58	–	3.32	7.90	8.69	1.602
M601006B	walls; 3.5 - 5.0 m high	m^2	0.29	4.92	–	3.32	8.24	9.06	1.602
M601006D	walls; n.e. 300 mm girth	m	0.11	1.87	–	1.00	2.87	3.16	0.481
M601006E	walls; areas n.e. 0.5 m^2	Nr	0.20	3.40	–	1.66	5.06	5.57	0.801
M601007	**Prepare, apply one mist coat and two full coats; rendered backgrounds**								
M601007A	walls	m^2	0.27	4.58	–	3.32	7.90	8.69	1.602
M601007B	walls; 3.5 - 5.0 m high	m^2	0.29	4.92	–	3.32	8.24	9.06	1.602
M601007D	walls; n.e. 300 mm girth	m	0.11	1.87	–	1.00	2.87	3.16	0.481
M601007E	walls; areas n.e. 0.5 m^2	Nr	0.20	3.40	–	1.66	5.06	5.57	0.801

Surface Finishes

		Unit	Labour Hours	Labour Net £	Plant Net £	Materials Net £	Unit Net £	Unit with 10% £	CO₂ Kg
M60	**M60: PAINTING AND CLEAR FINISHING**								
M6010	**Emulsion paint**								
M601008	**Prepare, apply one mist coat and two full coats; textured plastic coating backgrounds**								
M601008A	walls	m²	0.25	4.25	-	2.77	7.02	7.72	1.335
M601008B	walls; 3.5 - 5.0 m high	m²	0.27	4.58	-	2.77	7.35	8.09	1.335
M601008D	walls; n.e. 300 mm girth	m	0.10	1.70	-	0.85	2.55	2.81	0.409
M601008E	walls; areas n.e. 0.5 m²	Nr	0.19	3.19	-	1.40	4.59	5.05	0.676
M601008F	ceilings	m²	0.28	4.67	-	2.77	7.44	8.18	1.335
M601008G	ceilings; 3.5 - 5.0 m high	m²	0.30	5.13	-	2.77	7.90	8.69	1.335
M601008I	ceilings; n.e. 300 mm girth	m	0.11	1.87	-	0.85	2.72	2.99	0.409
M601008J	ceilings; areas n.e. 0.5 m²	Nr	0.21	3.50	-	1.40	4.90	5.39	0.676
M6011	**Eggshell paint**								
M601101	**Prepare, apply one undercoat and two full coats; plaster backgrounds**								
M601101A	walls	m²	0.36	6.11	-	1.70	7.81	8.59	0.926
M601101B	walls; 3.5 - 5.0 m high	m²	0.39	6.54	-	1.70	8.24	9.06	0.926
M601101D	walls; n.e. 300 mm girth	m	0.15	2.48	-	0.56	3.04	3.34	0.303
M601101E	walls; areas n.e. 0.5 m²	Nr	0.27	4.58	-	0.79	5.37	5.91	0.427
M601101F	ceilings	m²	0.38	6.42	-	1.70	8.12	8.93	0.926
M601101G	ceilings; 3.5 - 5.0 m high	m²	0.40	6.84	-	1.70	8.54	9.39	0.926
M601101I	ceilings; n.e. 300 mm girth	m	0.15	2.60	-	0.56	3.16	3.48	0.303
M601101J	ceilings; areas n.e. 0.5 m²	Nr	0.28	4.82	-	0.82	5.64	6.20	0.445
M601102	**Prepare, apply one undercoat and two full coats; plasterboard backgrounds**								
M601102A	walls	m²	0.36	6.11	-	1.70	7.81	8.59	0.926
M601102B	walls; 3.5 - 5.0 m high	m²	0.39	6.54	-	1.70	8.24	9.06	0.926
M601102D	walls; n.e. 300 mm girth	m	0.15	2.48	-	0.56	3.04	3.34	0.303
M601102E	walls; areas n.e. 0.5 m²	Nr	0.27	4.58	-	0.79	5.37	5.91	0.427
M601102F	ceilings	m²	0.38	6.42	-	1.70	8.12	8.93	0.926
M601102G	ceilings; 3.5 - 5.0 m high	m²	0.40	6.84	-	1.70	8.54	9.39	0.926
M601102I	ceilings; n.e. 300 mm girth	m	0.15	2.60	-	0.56	3.16	3.48	0.303
M601102J	ceilings; areas n.e. 0.5 m²	Nr	0.28	4.82	-	0.82	5.64	6.20	0.445
M601103	**Prepare, apply one undercoat and two full coats; lining paper backgrounds**								
M601103A	walls	m²	0.37	6.28	-	1.70	7.98	8.78	0.926
M601103B	walls; 3.5 - 5.0 m high	m²	0.40	6.71	-	1.70	8.41	9.25	0.926
M601103D	walls; n.e. 300 mm girth	m	0.15	2.55	-	0.56	3.11	3.42	0.303
M601103E	walls; areas n.e. 0.5 m²	Nr	0.28	4.72	-	0.79	5.51	6.06	0.427
M601103F	ceilings	m²	0.39	6.61	-	1.70	8.31	9.14	0.926
M601103G	ceilings; 3.5 - 5.0 m high	m²	0.41	7.03	-	1.70	8.73	9.60	0.926
M601103I	ceilings; n.e. 300 mm girth	m	0.16	2.67	-	0.56	3.23	3.55	0.303
M601103J	ceilings; areas n.e. 0.5 m²	Nr	0.29	4.94	-	0.82	5.76	6.34	0.445
M601104	**Prepare, apply one undercoat and two full coats; concrete backgrounds**								
M601104A	walls	m²	0.38	6.45	-	1.70	8.15	8.97	0.926
M601104B	walls; 3.5 - 5.0 m high	m²	0.04	0.70	-	1.70	2.40	2.64	0.926
M601104D	walls; n.e. 300 mm girth	m	0.15	2.61	-	0.56	3.17	3.49	0.303
M601104E	walls; areas n.e. 0.5 m²	Nr	0.29	4.84	-	0.79	5.63	6.19	0.427
M601104F	ceilings	m²	0.40	6.78	-	1.70	8.48	9.33	0.926
M601104G	ceilings; 3.5 - 5.0 m high	m²	0.43	7.22	-	1.70	8.92	9.81	0.926
M601104I	ceilings; n.e. 300 mm girth	m	0.16	2.75	-	0.56	3.31	3.64	0.303
M601104J	ceilings; areas n.e. 0.5 m²	Nr	0.30	5.08	-	0.82	5.90	6.49	0.445
M601105	**Prepare, apply one undercoat and two full coats; brickwork backgrounds**								
M601105A	walls	m²	0.50	8.49	-	2.36	10.85	11.94	1.282
M601105B	walls; 3.5 - 5.0 m high	m²	0.53	8.91	-	2.36	11.27	12.40	1.282
M601105D	walls; n.e. 300 mm girth	m	0.20	3.45	-	0.72	4.17	4.59	0.392
M601105E	walls; areas n.e. 0.5 m²	Nr	0.38	6.37	-	1.15	7.52	8.27	0.623

Major Works 2011		Unit	Labour Hours	Labour Net	Plant Net	Materials Net	Unit Net	Unit with 10%	CO$_2$
				£	£	£	£	£	Kg
M60	**M60: PAINTING AND CLEAR FINISHING**								
M6011	**Eggshell paint**								
M601106	**Prepare, apply one undercoat and two full coats; blockwork backgrounds**								
M601106A	walls	m^2	0.60	10.19	-	2.74	12.93	14.22	1.495
M601106B	walls; 3.5 - 5.0 m high	m^2	0.63	10.61	-	2.74	13.35	14.69	1.495
M601106D	walls; n.e. 300 mm girth	m	0.24	4.13	-	0.81	4.94	5.43	0.445
M601106E	walls; areas n.e. 0.5 m^2	Nr	0.45	7.64	-	1.40	9.04	9.94	0.765
M601107	**Prepare, apply one undercoat and two full coats; rendered backgrounds**								
M601107A	walls	m^2	0.47	7.98	-	2.22	10.20	11.22	1.210
M601107B	walls; 3.5 - 5.0 m high	m^2	0.50	8.41	-	2.22	10.63	11.69	1.210
M601107D	walls; n.e. 300 mm girth	m	0.19	3.23	-	0.68	3.91	4.30	0.374
M601107E	walls; areas n.e. 0.5 m^2	Nr	0.35	5.99	-	1.11	7.10	7.81	0.605
M601107F	ceilings	m^2	0.49	8.39	-	2.22	10.61	11.67	1.210
M601107G	ceilings; 3.5 - 5.0 m high	m^2	0.52	8.81	-	2.22	11.03	12.13	1.210
M601107I	ceilings; n.e. 300 mm girth	m	0.20	3.38	-	0.68	4.06	4.47	0.374
M601107J	ceilings; areas n.e. 0.5 m^2	Nr	0.37	6.27	-	1.11	7.38	8.12	0.605
M601108	**Prepare, apply one undercoat and two full coats; textured plastic coating backgrounds**								
M601108A	walls	m^2	0.50	8.49	-	2.22	10.71	11.78	1.210
M601108B	walls; 3.5 - 5.0 m high	m^2	0.53	8.91	-	2.22	11.13	12.24	1.210
M601108D	walls; n.e. 300 mm girth	m	0.20	3.45	-	0.68	4.13	4.54	0.374
M601108E	walls; areas n.e. 0.5 m^2	Nr	0.38	6.37	-	1.11	7.48	8.23	0.605
M601108F	ceilings	m^2	0.53	8.91	-	2.22	11.13	12.24	1.210
M601108G	ceilings; 3.5 - 5.0 m high	m^2	0.55	9.34	-	2.22	11.56	12.72	1.210
M601108I	ceilings; n.e. 300 mm girth	m	0.21	3.62	-	0.68	4.30	4.73	0.374
M601108J	ceilings; areas n.e. 0.5 m^2	Nr	0.39	6.69	-	1.11	7.80	8.58	0.605
M6015	**Flame retardant coatings**								
M601501	**Prepare and apply two coats Timonox vinyl matt emulsion; to plastered, woodwork or intumescent paint backgrounds; general surfaces**								
M601501A	over 300 mm girth	m^2	0.16	2.72	-	3.36	6.08	6.69	1.015
M601501B	n.e. 300 mm girth	m	0.07	1.10	-	1.06	2.16	2.38	0.320
M601501C	areas n.e. 0.5 m^2	Nr	0.12	2.04	-	1.71	3.75	4.13	0.516
M601502	**Prepare and apply two coats Timonox vinyl silk emulsion; to plastered, woodwork or intumescent paint backgrounds; general surfaces**								
M601502A	over 300 mm girth	m^2	0.16	2.72	-	3.89	6.61	7.27	1.175
M601502B	n.e. 300 mm girth	m	0.07	1.10	-	1.18	2.28	2.51	0.356
M601502C	areas n.e. 0.5 m^2	Nr	0.12	2.04	-	1.94	3.98	4.38	0.587
M601503	**Prepare and apply one coat Timonox alkali resisting primer, one coat Timonox undercoat and one coat Timonox gloss; to plastered backgrounds; general surfaces**								
M601503A	over 300 mm girth	m^2	0.36	6.11	-	3.49	9.60	10.56	1.121
M601503B	n.e. 300 mm girth	m	0.15	2.46	-	1.18	3.64	4.00	0.374
M601503C	areas n.e. 0.5 m^2	Nr	0.27	4.58	-	1.79	6.37	7.01	0.570
M601504	**Prepare and apply one coat Timonox alkali resisting primer, two coats Timonox eggshell; to plastered backgrounds; general surfaces**								
M601504A	over 300 mm girth	m^2	0.36	6.11	-	3.25	9.36	10.30	1.104
M601504B	n.e. 300 mm girth	m	0.15	2.48	-	0.99	3.47	3.82	0.338
M601504C	areas n.e. 0.5 m^2	Nr	0.27	4.58	-	1.64	6.22	6.84	0.552

Surface Finishes

		Unit	Labour Hours	Labour Net	Plant Net	Materials Net	Unit Net	Unit with 10%	CO₂
				£	£	£	£	£	Kg
M60	**M60: PAINTING AND CLEAR FINISHING**								
M6015	**Flame retardant coatings**								
M601511	**Prepare and apply one coat Timonox undercoat and one coat Timonox gloss to intumescent painted backgrounds; general surfaces**								
M601511A	over 300 mm girth	m²	0.27	4.58	-	2.03	6.61	7.27	0.534
M601511B	n.e. 300 mm girth	m	0.11	1.85	-	0.68	2.53	2.78	0.178
M601511C	areas n.e. 0.5 m²	Nr	0.20	3.45	-	1.08	4.53	4.98	0.285
M601512	**Prepare and apply one coat Timonox undercoat and one coat Timonox gloss to intumescent painted backgrounds; glazed windows and screens; in panes n.e. 0.10 m²**								
M601512A	over 300 mm girth	m²	0.75	12.70	-	2.03	14.73	16.20	0.534
M601512B	n.e. 300 mm girth	m	0.30	5.14	-	0.68	5.82	6.40	0.178
M601512C	areas n.e. 0.5 m²	Nr	0.56	9.53	-	1.08	10.61	11.67	0.285
M601513	**Prepare and apply one coat Timonox undercoat and one coat Timonox gloss to intumescent painted backgrounds; glazed windows and screens; in panes 0.10 - 0.50 m²**								
M601513A	over 300 mm girth	m²	0.55	9.34	-	2.03	11.37	12.51	0.534
M601513B	n.e. 300 mm girth	m	0.22	3.79	-	0.68	4.47	4.92	0.178
M601513C	areas n.e. 0.5 m²	Nr	0.41	7.01	-	1.08	8.09	8.90	0.285
M601514	**Prepare and apply one coat Timonox undercoat and one coat Timonox gloss to intumescent painted backgrounds; glazed windows and screens; in panes 0.50 - 1.00 m²**								
M601514A	over 300 mm girth	m²	0.48	8.10	-	2.03	10.13	11.14	0.534
M601514B	n.e. 300 mm girth	m	0.19	3.28	-	0.68	3.96	4.36	0.178
M601515	**Prepare and apply one coat Timonox undercoat and one coat Timonox gloss to intumescent painted backgrounds; glazed windows and screens; in panes over 1.00 m²**								
M601515A	over 300 mm girth	m²	0.43	7.35	-	2.03	9.38	10.32	0.534
M601515B	n.e. 300 mm girth	m	0.18	2.97	-	0.68	3.65	4.02	0.178
M601516	**Prepare and apply one coat Timonox undercoat and one coat Timonox gloss to intumescent painted backgrounds; glazed sash windows; in panes n.e. 0.10 m²**								
M601516A	over 300 mm girth	m²	0.82	13.97	-	2.03	16.00	17.60	0.534
M601516B	n.e. 300 mm girth	m	0.33	5.65	-	0.68	6.33	6.96	0.178
M601516C	areas n.e. 0.5 m²	Nr	0.62	10.48	-	1.08	11.56	12.72	0.285
M601517	**Prepare and apply one coat Timonox undercoat and one coat Timonox gloss to intumescent painted backgrounds; glazed sash windows; in panes 0.10 - 0.50 m²**								
M601517A	over 300 mm girth	m²	0.61	10.27	-	2.03	12.30	13.53	0.534
M601517B	n.e. 300 mm girth	m	0.25	4.16	-	0.68	4.84	5.32	0.178
M601517C	areas n.e. 0.5 m²	Nr	0.45	7.71	-	1.08	8.79	9.67	0.285

Major Works 2011		Unit	Labour Hours	Labour Net	Plant Net	Materials Net	Unit Net	Unit with 10%	CO₂
				£	£	£	£	£	Kg
M60	**M60: PAINTING AND CLEAR FINISHING**								
M6015	**Flame retardant coatings**								
M601518	**Prepare and apply one coat Timonox undercoat and one coat Timonox gloss to intumescent painted backgrounds; glazed sash windows; in panes 0.50 - 1.00 m²**								
M601518A	over 300 mm girth	m²	0.53	8.91	-	2.03	10.94	12.03	0.534
M601518B	n.e. 300 mm girth	m	0.21	3.60	-	0.68	4.28	4.71	0.178
M601519	**Prepare and apply one coat Timonox undercoat and one coat Timonox gloss to intumescent painted backgrounds; glazed sash windows; in panes over 1.00 m²**								
M601519A	over 300 mm girth	m²	0.48	8.08	-	2.03	10.11	11.12	0.534
M601519B	n.e. 300 mm girth	m	0.19	3.28	-	0.68	3.96	4.36	0.178
M601520	**Prepare and apply one coat Timonox undercoat and one coat Timonox gloss to intumescent painted backgrounds; glazed doors; in panes n.e. 0.10 m²**								
M601520A	over 300 mm girth	m²	0.75	12.70	-	2.03	14.73	16.20	0.534
M601520B	n.e. 300 mm girth	m	0.30	5.14	-	0.68	5.82	6.40	0.178
M601520C	areas n.e. 0.5 m²	Nr	0.56	9.53	-	1.08	10.61	11.67	0.285
M601521	**Prepare and apply one coat Timonox undercoat and one coat Timonox gloss to intumescent painted backgrounds; glazed doors; in panes 0.10 - 0.50 m²**								
M601521A	over 300 mm girth	m²	0.55	9.34	-	2.03	11.37	12.51	0.534
M601521B	n.e. 300 mm girth	m	0.22	3.79	-	0.68	4.47	4.92	0.178
M601521C	areas n.e. 0.5 m²	Nr	0.41	7.01	-	1.08	8.09	8.90	0.285
M601522	**Prepare and apply one coat Timonox undercoat and one coat Timonox gloss to intumescent painted backgrounds; glazed doors; in panes 0.50 - 1.00 m²**								
M601522A	over 300 mm girth	m²	0.48	8.10	-	2.03	10.13	11.14	0.534
M601522B	n.e. 300 mm girth	m	0.19	3.28	-	0.68	3.96	4.36	0.178
M601523	**Prepare and apply one coat Timonox undercoat and one coat Timonox gloss to intumescent painted backgrounds; glazed doors; in panes over 1.00 m²**								
M601523A	over 300 mm girth	m²	0.43	7.35	-	2.03	9.38	10.32	0.534
M601523B	n.e. 300 mm girth	m	0.18	2.97	-	0.68	3.65	4.02	0.178
M601531	**Prepare and apply two coats Timonox eggshell to intumescent painted backgrounds; general surfaces**								
M601531A	over 300 mm girth	m²	0.27	4.58	-	1.87	6.45	7.10	0.534
M601531B	n.e. 300 mm girth	m	0.11	1.85	-	0.56	2.41	2.65	0.160
M601531C	areas n.e. 0.5 m²	Nr	0.20	3.45	-	0.94	4.39	4.83	0.267
M601532	**Prepare and apply two coats Timonox eggshell to intumescent painted backgrounds; glazed windows and screens; in panes n.e. 0.10 m²**								
M601532A	over 300 mm girth	m²	0.75	12.70	-	1.87	14.57	16.03	0.534
M601532B	n.e. 300 mm girth	m	0.12	2.09	-	0.56	2.65	2.92	0.160

Major Works 2011		Unit	Labour Hours	Labour Net	Plant Net	Materials Net	Unit Net	Unit with 10%	CO₂
				£	£	£	£	£	Kg
M60	**M60: PAINTING AND CLEAR FINISHING**								
M6015	**Flame retardant coatings**								
M601532	**Prepare and apply two coats Timonox eggshell to intumescent painted backgrounds; glazed windows and screens; in panes n.e. 0.10 m²**								
M601532C	areas n.e. 0.5 m²	Nr	0.42	7.15	-	0.94	8.09	8.90	0.267
M601533	**Prepare and apply two coats Timonox eggshell to intumescent painted backgrounds; glazed windows and screens; in panes 0.10 - 0.50 m²**								
M601533A	over 300 mm girth	m²	0.55	9.34	-	1.87	11.21	12.33	0.534
M601533B	n.e. 300 mm girth	m	0.22	3.79	-	0.56	4.35	4.79	0.160
M601533C	areas n.e. 0.5 m²	Nr	0.41	7.01	-	0.94	7.95	8.75	0.267
M601534	**Prepare and apply two coats Timonox eggshell to intumescent painted backgrounds; glazed windows and screens; in panes 0.50 - 1.00 m²**								
M601534A	over 300 mm girth	m²	0.48	8.10	-	1.87	9.97	10.97	0.534
M601534B	n.e. 300 mm girth	m	0.19	3.28	-	0.56	3.84	4.22	0.160
M601535	**Prepare and apply two coats Timonox eggshell to intumescent painted backgrounds; glazed windows and screens; in panes over 1.00 m²**								
M601535A	over 300 mm girth	m²	0.43	7.35	-	1.87	9.22	10.14	0.534
M601535B	n.e. 300 mm girth	m	0.18	2.97	-	0.56	3.53	3.88	0.160
M601536	**Prepare and apply two coats Timonox eggshell to intumescent painted backgrounds; glazed sash windows; in panes n.e. 0.10 m²**								
M601536A	over 300 mm girth	m²	0.82	13.97	-	1.87	15.84	17.42	0.534
M601536B	n.e. 300 mm girth	m	0.14	2.29	-	0.56	2.85	3.14	0.160
M601536C	areas n.e. 0.5 m²	Nr	0.46	7.86	-	0.94	8.80	9.68	0.267
M601537	**Prepare and apply two coats Timonox eggshell to intumescent painted backgrounds; glazed sash windows; in panes 0.10 - 0.50 m²**								
M601537A	over 300 mm girth	m²	0.61	10.27	-	1.87	12.14	13.35	0.534
M601537B	n.e. 300 mm girth	m	0.25	4.16	-	0.56	4.72	5.19	0.160
M601537C	areas n.e. 0.5 m²	Nr	0.45	7.71	-	0.94	8.65	9.52	0.267
M601538	**Prepare and apply two coats Timonox eggshell to intumescent painted backgrounds; glazed sash windows; in panes 0.50 - 1.00 m²**								
M601538A	over 300 mm girth	m²	0.53	8.91	-	1.87	10.78	11.86	0.534
M601538B	n.e. 300 mm girth	m	0.21	3.60	-	0.56	4.16	4.58	0.160
M601539	**Prepare and apply two coats Timonox eggshell to intumescent painted backgrounds; glazed sash windows; in panes over 1.00 m²**								
M601539A	over 300 mm girth	m²	0.48	8.08	-	1.87	9.95	10.95	0.534
M601539B	n.e. 300 mm girth	m	0.19	3.28	-	0.56	3.84	4.22	0.160

Major Works 2011		Unit	Labour Hours	Labour Net	Plant Net	Materials Net	Unit Net	Unit with 10%	CO₂
				£	£	£	£	£	Kg
M60	**M60: PAINTING AND CLEAR FINISHING**								
M6015	**Flame retardant coatings**								
M601540	**Prepare and apply two coats Timonox eggshell to intumescent painted backgrounds; glazed doors; in panes n.e. 0.10 m²**								
M601540A	over 300 mm girth	m²	0.75	12.70	-	1.87	14.57	16.03	0.534
M601540B	n.e. 300 mm girth	m	0.12	2.09	-	0.56	2.65	2.92	0.160
M601540C	areas n.e. 0.5 m²	Nr	0.42	7.15	-	0.94	8.09	8.90	0.267
M601541	**Prepare and apply two coats Timonox eggshell to intumescent painted backgrounds; glazed doors; in panes 0.10 - 0.50 m²**								
M601541A	over 300 mm girth	m²	0.55	9.34	-	1.87	11.21	12.33	0.534
M601541B	n.e. 300 mm girth	m	0.22	3.79	-	0.56	4.35	4.79	0.160
M601541C	areas n.e. 0.5 m²	Nr	0.41	7.01	-	0.94	7.95	8.75	0.267
M601542	**Prepare and apply two coats Timonox eggshell to intumescent painted backgrounds; glazed doors; in panes 0.50 - 1.00 m²**								
M601542A	over 300 mm girth	m²	0.48	8.10	-	1.87	9.97	10.97	0.534
M601542B	n.e. 300 mm girth	m	0.19	3.28	-	0.56	3.84	4.22	0.160
M601543	**Prepare and apply two coats Timonox eggshell to intumescent painted backgrounds; glazed doors; in panes over 1.00 m²**								
M601543A	over 300 mm girth	m²	0.43	7.35	-	1.87	9.22	10.14	0.534
M601543B	n.e. 300 mm girth	m	0.18	2.97	-	0.56	3.53	3.88	0.160
M601581	**Prepare and apply two coats Timonox intumescent paint to woodwork backgrounds; general surfaces**								
M601581A	over 300 mm girth	m²	0.75	12.73	-	6.56	19.29	21.22	1.495
M601581B	n.e. 300 mm girth	m	0.30	5.16	-	1.95	7.11	7.82	0.445
M601581C	areas n.e. 0.5 m²	Nr	0.56	9.56	-	3.28	12.84	14.12	0.748
M601582	**Prepare and apply two coats Timonox intumescent paint to woodwork backgrounds; glazed windows and screens; in panes n.e. 0.10 m²**								
M601582A	over 300 mm girth	m²	2.29	38.80	-	6.56	45.36	49.90	1.495
M601582B	n.e. 300 mm girth	m	0.93	15.71	-	1.95	17.66	19.43	0.445
M601582C	areas n.e. 0.5 m²	Nr	1.71	29.10	-	3.28	32.38	35.62	0.748
M601583	**Prepare and apply two coats Timonox intumescent paint to woodwork backgrounds; glazed windows and screens; in panes 0.10 - 0.50 m²**								
M601583A	over 300 mm girth	m²	1.68	28.53	-	6.56	35.09	38.60	1.495
M601583B	n.e. 300 mm girth	m	0.68	11.55	-	1.95	13.50	14.85	0.445
M601583C	areas n.e. 0.5 m²	Nr	1.26	21.39	-	3.28	24.67	27.14	0.748
M601584	**Prepare and apply two coats Timonox intumescent paint to woodwork backgrounds; glazed windows and screens; in panes 0.50 - 1.00 m²**								
M601584A	over 300 mm girth	m²	1.46	24.74	-	6.56	31.30	34.43	1.495
M601584B	n.e. 300 mm girth	m	0.59	10.02	-	1.95	11.97	13.17	0.445
M601585	**Prepare and apply two coats Timonox intumescent paint to woodwork backgrounds; glazed windows and screens; in panes over 1.00 m²**								
M601585A	over 300 mm girth	m²	1.32	22.46	-	6.56	29.02	31.92	1.495

Surface Finishes

Code	Description	Unit	Labour Hours	Labour Net £	Plant Net £	Materials Net £	Unit Net £	Unit with 10% £	CO₂ Kg
M60	**M60: PAINTING AND CLEAR FINISHING**								
M6015	**Flame retardant coatings**								
M601585	**Prepare and apply two coats Timonox intumescent paint to woodwork backgrounds; glazed windows and screens; in panes over 1.00 m²**								
M601585B	n.e. 300 mm girth	m	0.54	9.10	-	1.95	11.05	12.16	0.445
M601586	**Prepare and apply two coats Timonox intumescent paint to woodwork backgrounds; glazed sash windows; in panes n.e. 0.10 m²**								
M601586A	over 300 mm girth	m²	2.51	42.69	-	6.56	49.25	54.18	1.495
M601586B	n.e. 300 mm girth	m	1.11	18.81	-	1.95	20.76	22.84	0.445
M601586C	areas n.e. 0.5 m²	Nr	1.89	32.01	-	3.28	35.29	38.82	0.748
M601587	**Prepare and apply two coats Timonox intumescent paint to woodwork backgrounds; glazed sash windows; in panes 0.10 - 0.50 m²**								
M601587A	over 300 mm girth	m²	1.85	31.38	-	6.56	37.94	41.73	1.495
M601587B	n.e. 300 mm girth	m	0.75	12.70	-	1.95	14.65	16.12	0.445
M601587C	areas n.e. 0.5 m²	Nr	1.39	23.53	-	3.28	26.81	29.49	0.748
M601588	**Prepare and apply two coats Timonox intumescent paint to woodwork backgrounds; glazed sash windows; in panes 0.50 - 1.00 m²**								
M601588A	over 300 mm girth	m²	1.60	27.22	-	6.56	33.78	37.16	1.495
M601588B	n.e. 300 mm girth	m	0.65	11.02	-	1.95	12.97	14.27	0.445
M601589	**Prepare and apply two coats Timonox intumescent paint to woodwork backgrounds; glazed sash windows; in panes over 1.00 m²**								
M601589A	over 300 mm girth	m²	1.46	24.71	-	6.56	31.27	34.40	1.495
M601589B	n.e. 300 mm girth	m	0.59	10.02	-	1.95	11.97	13.17	0.445
M601590	**Prepare and apply two coats Timonox intumescent paint to woodwork backgrounds; glazed doors; in panes n.e. 0.10 m²**								
M601590A	over 300 mm girth	m²	2.29	38.80	-	6.56	45.36	49.90	1.495
M601590B	n.e. 300 mm girth	m	0.93	15.71	-	1.95	17.66	19.43	0.445
M601590C	areas n.e. 0.5 m²	Nr	1.71	29.10	-	3.28	32.38	35.62	0.748
M601591	**Prepare and apply two coats Timonox intumescent paint to woodwork backgrounds; glazed doors; in panes 0.10 - 0.50 m²**								
M601591A	over 300 mm girth	m²	1.68	28.53	-	6.56	35.09	38.60	1.495
M601591B	n.e. 300 mm girth	m	0.68	11.55	-	1.95	13.50	14.85	0.445
M601591C	areas n.e. 0.5 m²	Nr	1.26	21.39	-	3.28	24.67	27.14	0.748
M601592	**Prepare and apply two coats Timonox intumescent paint to woodwork backgrounds; glazed doors; in panes 0.50 - 1.00 m²**								
M601592A	over 300 mm girth	m²	1.46	24.74	-	6.56	31.30	34.43	1.495
M601592B	n.e. 300 mm girth	m	0.59	10.02	-	1.95	11.97	13.17	0.445
M601593	**Prepare and apply two coats Timonox intumescent paint to woodwork backgrounds; glazed doors; in panes over 1.00 m²**								
M601593A	over 300 mm girth	m²	1.32	22.46	-	6.56	29.02	31.92	1.495
M601593B	n.e. 300 mm girth	m	0.54	9.10	-	1.95	11.05	12.16	0.445

Major Works 2011		Unit	Labour Hours	Labour Net	Plant Net	Materials Net	Unit Net	Unit with 10%	CO$_2$
				£	£	£	£	£	Kg
M60	**M60: PAINTING AND CLEAR FINISHING**								
M6017	**Textured plastic finish**								
M601722	**Prepare, apply one coat Artex sealer and one coat Artex compound textured finish**								
M601722A	ceilings	m^2	0.30	5.09	-	1.11	6.20	6.82	2.937
M601722B	ceilings; 3.5 - 5.0 m high	m^2	0.33	5.52	-	1.22	6.74	7.41	3.231
M601722C	ceilings; n.e. 300 mm girth	m	0.12	2.07	-	0.37	2.44	2.68	0.979
M601722D	ceilings; areas n.e. 0.5 m^2	Nr	0.23	3.82	-	0.63	4.45	4.90	1.664
M6018	**Masonry paint**								
M601801	**Prepare, apply masonry base coat sealer and two coats of masonry paint finish; rendered backgrounds**								
M601801A	walls	m^2	0.27	4.58	-	2.87	7.45	8.20	1.495
M601801B	walls; 3.5 - 5.0 m high	m^2	0.30	5.01	-	2.87	7.88	8.67	1.495
M601801C	walls; n.e. 300 mm girth	m	0.11	1.87	-	3.17	5.04	5.54	1.219
M601801D	walls; areas n.e. 0.5 m^2	Nr	0.20	3.45	-	1.41	4.86	5.35	0.739
M601801F	ceilings	m^2	0.28	4.82	-	2.87	7.69	8.46	1.495
M601801G	ceilings; 3.5 - 5.0 m high	m^2	0.31	5.25	-	2.87	8.12	8.93	1.495
M601801H	ceilings; n.e. 300 mm girth	m	0.12	1.97	-	3.17	5.14	5.65	1.219
M601801I	ceilings; areas n.e. 0.5 m^2	Nr	0.21	3.62	-	1.41	5.03	5.53	0.739
M601802	**Prepare, apply masonry base coat sealer and two coats of masonry paint finish; concrete backgrounds**								
M601802A	walls	m^2	0.25	4.16	-	2.62	6.78	7.46	1.371
M601802B	walls; 3.5 - 5.0 m high	m^2	0.27	4.58	-	2.62	7.20	7.92	1.371
M601802C	walls; n.e. 300 mm girth	m	0.10	1.68	-	0.80	2.48	2.73	0.418
M601802D	walls; areas n.e. 0.5 m^2	Nr	0.18	3.12	-	1.32	4.44	4.88	0.694
M601802F	ceilings	m^2	0.26	4.36	-	2.62	6.98	7.68	1.371
M601802G	ceilings; 3.5 - 5.0 m high	m^2	0.28	4.79	-	2.62	7.41	8.15	1.371
M601802H	ceilings; n.e. 300 mm girth	m	0.08	1.31	-	0.80	2.11	2.32	0.418
M601802I	ceilings; areas n.e. 0.5 m^2	Nr	0.19	3.28	-	1.32	4.60	5.06	0.694
M601803	**Prepare, apply masonry base coat sealer and two coats of masonry paint finish; brickwork backgrounds**								
M601803A	walls	m^2	0.30	5.09	-	3.05	8.14	8.95	1.602
M601803B	walls; 3.5 - 5.0 m high	m^2	0.33	5.52	-	3.05	8.57	9.43	1.602
M601803C	walls; n.e. 300 mm girth	m	0.12	2.07	-	0.92	2.99	3.29	0.481
M601803D	walls; areas n.e. 0.5 m^2	Nr	0.23	3.82	-	1.47	5.29	5.82	0.774
M601804	**Prepare, apply masonry base coat sealer and two coats of masonry paint finish; blockwork backgrounds**								
M601804A	walls	m^2	0.34	5.77	-	3.57	9.34	10.27	1.887
M601804B	walls; 3.5 - 5.0 m high	m^2	0.37	6.20	-	3.57	9.77	10.75	1.887
M601804C	walls; n.e. 300 mm girth	m	0.14	2.34	-	1.06	3.40	3.74	0.561
M601804D	walls; areas n.e. 0.5 m^2	Nr	0.26	4.33	-	1.81	6.14	6.75	0.952
M6019	**Cement paint**								
M601901	**Prepare, apply one coat stabiliser and two coats Sandtex textured finish; rendered backgrounds**								
M601901A	walls	m^2	0.19	3.23	-	1.54	4.77	5.25	0.943
M601901B	walls; 3.5 - 5.0 m high	m^2	0.22	3.65	-	1.54	5.19	5.71	0.943
M601901C	walls; n.e. 300 mm girth	m	0.08	1.31	-	0.44	1.75	1.93	0.267
M601901D	walls; areas n.e. 0.5 m^2	Nr	0.14	2.29	-	0.76	3.05	3.36	0.463
M601901F	ceilings	m^2	0.20	3.40	-	1.54	4.94	5.43	0.943
M601901G	ceilings; 3.5 - 5.0 m high	m^2	0.23	3.82	-	1.54	5.36	5.90	0.943
M601901H	ceilings; n.e. 300 mm girth	m	0.08	1.38	-	0.44	1.82	2.00	0.267
M601901I	ceilings; areas n.e. 0.5 m^2	Nr	0.15	2.55	-	0.76	3.31	3.64	0.463

Surface Finishes

Major Works 2011		Unit	Labour Hours	Labour Net £	Plant Net £	Materials Net £	Unit Net £	Unit with 10% £	CO₂ Kg
M60	**M60: PAINTING AND CLEAR FINISHING**								
M6019	**Cement paint**								
M601902	**Prepare, apply one coat stabiliser and two coats Sandtex textured finish; concrete backgrounds**								
M601902A	walls	m²	0.20	3.40	-	1.19	4.59	5.05	0.730
M601902B	walls; 3.5 - 5.0 m high	m²	0.23	3.82	-	1.19	5.01	5.51	0.730
M601902C	walls; n.e. 300 mm girth	m	0.08	1.38	-	0.35	1.73	1.90	0.214
M601902D	walls; areas n.e. 0.5 m²	Nr	0.15	2.55	-	0.14	2.69	2.96	0.089
M601902F	ceilings	m²	0.21	3.57	-	1.19	4.76	5.24	0.730
M601902G	ceilings; 3.5 - 5.0 m high	m²	0.24	3.99	-	1.19	5.18	5.70	0.730
M601902H	ceilings; n.e. 300 mm girth	m	0.09	1.44	-	0.35	1.79	1.97	0.214
M601902I	ceilings; areas n.e. 0.5 m²	Nr	0.16	2.68	-	0.14	2.82	3.10	0.089
M601903	**Prepare, apply one coat stabiliser and two coats Sandtex textured finish; brickwork backgrounds**								
M601903A	walls	m²	0.24	4.08	-	1.69	5.77	6.35	1.032
M601903B	walls; 3.5 - 5.0 m high	m²	0.27	4.50	-	1.69	6.19	6.81	1.032
M601903C	walls; n.e. 300 mm girth	m	0.10	1.65	-	0.49	2.14	2.35	0.303
M601903D	walls; areas n.e. 0.5 m²	Nr	0.18	3.06	-	0.87	3.93	4.32	0.534
M601904	**Prepare, apply one coat stabiliser and two coats Sandtex textured finish; blockwork backgrounds**								
M601904A	walls	m²	0.27	4.58	-	1.69	6.27	6.90	1.032
M601904B	walls; 3.5 - 5.0 m high	m²	0.30	5.01	-	1.69	6.70	7.37	1.032
M601904C	walls; n.e. 300 mm girth	m	0.11	1.87	-	0.49	2.36	2.60	0.303
M601904D	walls; areas n.e. 0.5 m²	Nr	0.20	3.45	-	0.87	4.32	4.75	0.534
M6021	**Oil paint; woodwork backgrounds; one undercoat, one top coat**								
M602101	**Prepare, knot, prime and stop, apply one undercoat and one top coat gloss paint; general surfaces**								
M602101A	over 300 mm girth	m²	0.33	5.60	-	1.86	7.46	8.21	1.067
M602101B	n.e. 300 mm girth	m	0.14	2.29	-	0.55	2.84	3.12	0.316
M602101C	areas n.e. 0.5 m²	Nr	0.25	4.21	-	0.96	5.17	5.69	0.555
M602102	**Prepare, knot, prime and stop, apply one undercoat and one top coat gloss paint; glazed windows and screens; in panes n.e. 0.10 m²**								
M602102A	over 300 mm girth	m²	1.02	17.32	-	2.87	20.19	22.21	1.642
M602102B	n.e. 300 mm girth	m	0.41	7.01	-	0.86	7.87	8.66	0.499
M602102C	areas n.e. 0.5 m²	Nr	0.77	12.99	-	1.33	14.32	15.75	0.760
M602103	**Prepare, knot, prime and stop, apply one undercoat and one top coat gloss paint; glazed windows and screens; in panes 0.10 - 0.50 m²**								
M602103A	over 300 mm girth	m²	0.75	12.73	-	2.06	14.79	16.27	1.182
M602103B	n.e. 300 mm girth	m	0.31	5.18	-	0.64	5.82	6.40	0.372
M602103C	areas n.e. 0.5 m²	Nr	0.56	9.56	-	1.07	10.63	11.69	0.614
M602104	**Prepare, knot, prime and stop, apply one undercoat and one top coat gloss paint; glazed windows and screens; in panes 0.50 - 1.00 m²**								
M602104A	over 300 mm girth	m²	0.65	11.04	-	1.84	12.88	14.17	1.053
M602104B	n.e. 300 mm girth	m	0.26	4.47	-	0.63	5.10	5.61	0.368

Major Works 2011		Unit	Labour Hours	Labour Net	Plant Net	Materials Net	Unit Net	Unit with 10%	CO$_2$
				£	£	£	£	£	Kg
M60	**M60: PAINTING AND CLEAR FINISHING**								
M6021	**Oil paint; woodwork backgrounds; one undercoat, one top coat**								
M602105	**Prepare, knot, prime and stop, apply one undercoat and one top coat gloss paint; glazed windows and screens; in panes over 1.00 m^2**								
M602105A	over 300 mm girth	m^2	0.59	10.02	-	1.86	11.88	13.07	1.063
M602105B	n.e. 300 mm girth	m	0.24	4.06	-	0.53	4.59	5.05	0.300
M602106	**Prepare, knot, prime and stop, apply one undercoat and one top coat gloss paint; glazed sash windows; in panes n.e. 0.10 m^2**								
M602106A	over 300 mm girth	m^2	1.12	19.05	-	2.87	21.92	24.11	1.642
M602106B	n.e. 300 mm girth	m	0.45	7.71	-	0.86	8.57	9.43	0.499
M602106C	areas n.e. 0.5 m^2	Nr	0.84	14.30	-	1.33	15.63	17.19	0.760
M602107	**Prepare, knot, prime and stop, apply one undercoat and one top coat gloss paint; glazed sash windows; in panes 0.10 - 0.50 m^2**								
M602107A	over 300 mm girth	m^2	0.83	14.01	-	2.06	16.07	17.68	1.182
M602107B	n.e. 300 mm girth	m	0.33	5.67	-	0.64	6.31	6.94	0.372
M602107C	areas n.e. 0.5 m^2	Nr	0.62	10.51	-	1.07	11.58	12.74	0.614
M602108	**Prepare, knot, prime and stop, apply one undercoat and one top coat gloss paint; glazed sash windows; in panes 0.50 - 1.00 m^2**								
M602108A	over 300 mm girth	m^2	0.72	12.14	-	1.84	13.98	15.38	1.053
M602108B	n.e. 300 mm girth	m	0.29	4.92	-	0.63	5.55	6.11	0.368
M602109	**Prepare, knot, prime and stop, apply one undercoat and one top coat gloss paint; glazed sash windows; in panes over 1.00 m^2**								
M602109A	over 300 mm girth	m^2	0.65	11.02	-	1.86	12.88	14.17	1.063
M602109B	n.e. 300 mm girth	m	0.26	4.47	-	0.53	5.00	5.50	0.300
M602110	**Prepare, knot, prime and stop, apply one undercoat and one top coat gloss paint; glazed doors; in panes n.e. 1.00 m^2**								
M602110A	over 300 mm girth	m^2	1.02	17.32	-	2.06	19.38	21.32	1.182
M602110B	n.e. 300 mm girth	m	0.41	7.01	-	0.64	7.65	8.42	0.372
M602110C	areas n.e. 0.5 m^2	Nr	0.77	12.99	-	1.07	14.06	15.47	0.614
M602111	**Prepare, knot, prime and stop, apply one undercoat and one top coat gloss paint; glazed doors; in panes 0.10 - 0.50 m^2**								
M602111A	over 300 mm girth	m^2	0.75	12.73	-	2.06	14.79	16.27	1.182
M602111B	n.e. 300 mm girth	m	0.31	5.18	-	0.64	5.82	6.40	0.372
M602111C	areas n.e. 0.5 m^2	Nr	0.56	9.56	-	1.07	10.63	11.69	0.614
M602112	**Prepare, knot, prime and stop, apply one undercoat and one top coat gloss paint; glazed doors; in panes 0.50 - 1.00 m^2**								
M602112A	over 300 mm girth	m^2	0.65	11.04	-	2.06	13.10	14.41	1.182
M602112B	n.e. 300 mm girth	m	0.26	4.47	-	0.64	5.11	5.62	0.372
M602113	**Prepare, knot, prime and stop, apply one undercoat and one top coat gloss paint; glazed doors; in panes over 1.00 m^2**								
M602113A	over 300 mm girth	m^2	0.59	10.02	-	2.06	12.08	13.29	1.182
M602113B	n.e. 300 mm girth	m	0.24	4.06	-	0.64	4.70	5.17	0.372

Surface Finishes

Major Works 2011		Unit	Labour Hours	Labour Net £	Plant Net £	Materials Net £	Unit Net £	Unit with 10% £	CO₂ Kg
M60	**M60: PAINTING AND CLEAR FINISHING**								
M6023	**Oil paint; woodwork backgrounds; two undercoats, one top coat**								
M602301	**Prepare, knot, prime and stop, apply two undercoats and one top coat gloss paint; general surfaces**								
M602301A	over 300 mm girth	m²	0.44	7.39	-	2.42	9.81	10.79	1.390
M602301B	n.e. 300 mm girth	m	0.18	2.99	-	0.73	3.72	4.09	0.423
M602301C	areas n.e. 0.5 m²	Nr	0.33	5.54	-	1.24	6.78	7.46	0.715
M602302	**Prepare, knot, prime and stop, apply two undercoats and one top coat gloss paint; glazed windows and screens; in panes n.e. 0.10 m²**								
M602302A	over 300 mm girth	m²	1.35	22.84	-	3.66	26.50	29.15	2.105
M602302B	n.e. 300 mm girth	m	0.55	9.25	-	1.14	10.39	11.43	0.659
M602302C	areas n.e. 0.5 m²	Nr	1.01	17.13	-	1.85	18.98	20.88	1.062
M602303	**Prepare, knot, prime and stop, apply two undercoats and one top coat gloss paint; glazed windows and screens; in panes 0.10 - 0.50 m²**								
M602303A	over 300 mm girth	m²	0.96	16.27	-	2.68	18.95	20.85	1.538
M602303B	n.e. 300 mm girth	m	0.39	6.59	-	0.82	7.41	8.15	0.479
M602303C	areas n.e. 0.5 m²	Nr	0.72	12.21	-	1.38	13.59	14.95	0.792
M602304	**Prepare, knot, prime and stop, apply two undercoats and one top coat gloss paint; glazed windows and screens; in panes 0.50 - 1.00 m²**								
M602304A	over 300 mm girth	m²	0.85	14.35	-	2.33	16.68	18.35	1.338
M602304B	n.e. 300 mm girth	m	0.34	5.81	-	0.75	6.56	7.22	0.439
M602305	**Prepare, knot, prime and stop, apply two undercoats and one top coat gloss paint; glazed windows and screens; in panes over 1.00 m²**								
M602305A	over 300 mm girth	m²	0.77	13.01	-	2.67	15.68	17.25	1.537
M602305B	n.e. 300 mm girth	m	0.31	5.26	-	0.82	6.08	6.69	0.479
M602306	**Prepare, knot, prime and stop, apply two undercoats and one top coat gloss paint; glazed sash windows; in panes n.e. 0.10 m²**								
M602306A	over 300 mm girth	m²	1.48	25.13	-	3.66	28.79	31.67	2.105
M602306B	n.e. 300 mm girth	m	0.60	10.19	-	1.14	11.33	12.46	0.659
M602306C	areas n.e. 0.5 m²	Nr	1.11	18.85	-	1.78	20.63	22.69	1.027
M602307	**Prepare, knot, prime and stop, apply two undercoats and one top coat gloss paint; glazed sash windows; in panes 0.10 - 0.50 m²**								
M602307A	over 300 mm girth	m²	1.05	17.90	-	2.68	20.58	22.64	1.538
M602307B	n.e. 300 mm girth	m	0.43	7.25	-	0.82	8.07	8.88	0.479
M602307C	areas n.e. 0.5 m²	Nr	0.79	13.41	-	1.38	14.79	16.27	0.792
M602308	**Prepare, knot, prime and stop, apply two undercoats and one top coat gloss paint; glazed sash windows; in panes 0.50 - 1.00 m²**								
M602308A	over 300 mm girth	m²	0.93	15.79	-	2.33	18.12	19.93	1.338
M602308B	n.e. 300 mm girth	m	0.38	6.40	-	0.75	7.15	7.87	0.439

Major Works 2011		Unit	Labour Hours	Labour Net	Plant Net	Materials Net	Unit Net	Unit with 10%	CO₂
				£	£	£	£	£	Kg
M60	**M60: PAINTING AND CLEAR FINISHING**								
M6023	**Oil paint; woodwork backgrounds; two undercoats, one top coat**								
M602309	**Prepare, knot, prime and stop, apply two undercoats and one top coat gloss paint; glazed sash windows; in panes over 1.00 m²**								
M602309A	over 300 mm girth	m²	0.84	14.30	-	2.68	16.98	18.68	1.538
M602309B	n.e. 300 mm girth	m	0.63	10.73	-	0.82	11.55	12.71	0.479
M602310	**Prepare, knot, prime and stop, apply two undercoats and one top coat gloss paint; glazed doors; in panes n.e. 1.00 m²**								
M602310A	over 300 mm girth	m²	1.33	22.50	-	2.68	25.18	27.70	1.538
M602310B	n.e. 300 mm girth	m	0.54	9.08	-	0.82	9.90	10.89	0.479
M602310C	areas n.e. 0.5 m²	Nr	0.99	16.81	-	1.38	18.19	20.01	0.792
M602311	**Prepare, knot, prime and stop, apply two undercoats and one top coat gloss paint; glazed doors; in panes 0.10 - 0.50 m²**								
M602311A	over 300 mm girth	m²	0.96	16.30	-	2.68	18.98	20.88	1.538
M602311B	n.e. 300 mm girth	m	0.39	6.59	-	0.82	7.41	8.15	0.479
M602311C	areas n.e. 0.5 m²	Nr	0.72	12.23	-	1.38	13.61	14.97	0.792
M602312	**Prepare, knot, prime and stop, apply two undercoats and one top coat gloss paint; glazed doors; in panes 0.50 - 1.00 m²**								
M602312A	over 300 mm girth	m²	0.85	14.35	-	2.68	17.03	18.73	1.538
M602312B	n.e. 300 mm girth	m	0.34	5.81	-	0.82	6.63	7.29	0.479
M602313	**Prepare, knot, prime and stop, apply two undercoats and one top coat gloss paint; glazed doors; in panes over 1.00 m²**								
M602313A	over 300 mm girth	m²	0.77	13.01	-	2.68	15.69	17.26	1.538
M602313B	n.e. 300 mm girth	m	0.31	5.26	-	0.82	6.08	6.69	0.479
M6024	**Oil paint; metalwork backgrounds; two undercoats, one top coat**								
M602401	**Prepare, apply etching primer, two undercoats and one top coat gloss paint; general surfaces**								
M602401A	over 300 mm girth	m²	0.36	6.11	-	2.81	8.92	9.81	1.566
M602401B	n.e. 300 mm girth	m	0.15	2.46	-	0.86	3.32	3.65	0.481
M602401C	areas n.e. 0.5 m²	Nr	0.27	4.58	-	1.40	5.98	6.58	0.783
M602402	**Prepare, apply etching primer, two undercoats and top coat gloss paint; glazed windows and screens; in panes n.e. 0.10 m²**								
M602402A	over 300 mm girth	m²	1.14	19.39	-	2.81	22.20	24.42	1.566
M602402B	n.e. 300 mm girth	m	0.46	7.86	-	0.86	8.72	9.59	0.481
M602402C	areas n.e. 0.5 m²	Nr	0.86	14.55	-	1.40	15.95	17.55	0.783
M602403	**Prepare, apply etching primer, two undercoats and top coat gloss paint; glazed windows and screens; in panes 0.10 - 0.50 m²**								
M602403A	over 300 mm girth	m²	0.84	14.26	-	2.11	16.37	18.01	1.175
M602403B	n.e. 300 mm girth	m	0.34	5.77	-	0.64	6.41	7.05	0.356
M602403C	areas n.e. 0.5 m²	Nr	0.63	10.70	-	1.05	11.75	12.93	0.587

Surface Finishes

		Unit	Labour Hours	Labour Net £	Plant Net £	Materials Net £	Unit Net £	Unit with 10% £	CO₂ Kg
M60	**M60: PAINTING AND CLEAR FINISHING**								
M6024	**Oil paint; metalwork backgrounds; two undercoats, one top coat**								
M602404	**Prepare, apply etching primer, two undercoats and top coat gloss paint; glazed windows and screens; in panes 0.50 - 1.00 m²**								
M602404A	over 300 mm girth	m²	0.73	12.36	-	1.79	14.15	15.57	0.997
M602404B	n.e. 300 mm girth	m	0.30	5.01	-	0.58	5.59	6.15	0.320
M602405	**Prepare, apply etching primer, two undercoats and top coat gloss paint; glazed windows and screens; in panes over 1.0 m²**								
M602405A	over 300 mm girth	m²	0.66	11.22	-	1.66	12.88	14.17	0.926
M602405B	n.e. 300 mm girth	m	0.27	4.55	-	0.44	4.99	5.49	0.249
M602410	**Prepare, apply etching primer, two undercoats and top coat gloss paint; glazed doors; in panes n.e. 0.10 m²**								
M602410A	over 300 mm girth	m²	1.14	19.39	-	2.81	22.20	24.42	1.566
M602410B	n.e. 300 mm girth	m	0.46	7.86	-	0.86	8.72	9.59	0.481
M602410C	areas n.e. 0.5 m²	Nr	0.86	14.55	-	1.40	15.95	17.55	0.783
M602411	**Prepare, apply etching primer, two undercoats and top coat gloss paint; glazed doors; in panes 0.10 - 0.50 m²**								
M602411A	over 300 mm girth	m²	0.84	14.26	-	2.11	16.37	18.01	1.175
M602411B	n.e. 300 mm girth	m	0.34	5.77	-	0.64	6.41	7.05	0.356
M602411C	areas n.e. 0.5 m²	Nr	0.63	10.70	-	1.05	11.75	12.93	0.587
M602412	**Prepare, apply etching primer, two undercoats and top coat gloss paint; glazed doors; in panes 0.50 - 1.00 m²**								
M602412A	over 300 mm girth	m²	0.73	12.36	-	1.79	14.15	15.57	0.997
M602412B	n.e. 300 mm girth	m	0.30	5.01	-	0.58	5.59	6.15	0.320
M602413	**Prepare, apply etching primer, two undercoats and top coat gloss paint; glazed doors; in panes over 1.0 m²**								
M602413A	over 300 mm girth	m²	0.66	11.22	-	1.66	12.88	14.17	0.926
M602413B	n.e. 300 mm girth	m	0.27	4.55	-	0.44	4.99	5.49	0.249
M602415	**Prepare, apply etching primer, two undercoats and top coat gloss paint; structural metalwork**								
M602415A	over 300 mm girth	m²	0.60	10.19	-	2.81	13.00	14.30	1.566
M602415B	n.e. 300 mm girth	m	0.24	4.13	-	0.86	4.99	5.49	0.481
M602415C	areas n.e. 0.5 m²	Nr	0.45	7.64	-	1.40	9.04	9.94	0.783
M602417	**Prepare, apply etching primer, two undercoats and top coat gloss paint; radiators**								
M602417A	over 300 mm girth	m²	0.36	6.11	-	2.81	8.92	9.81	1.566
M602417B	n.e. 300 mm girth	m	0.15	2.48	-	0.86	3.34	3.67	0.481
M602417C	areas n.e. 0.5 m²	Nr	0.27	4.58	-	1.40	5.98	6.58	0.783
M602418	**Prepare, apply etching primer, two undercoats and top coat of gloss paint; railings, fences and gates**								
M602418A	over 300 mm girth	m²	0.60	10.19	-	2.81	13.00	14.30	1.566
M602418B	n.e. 300 mm girth	m	0.24	4.13	-	0.86	4.99	5.49	0.481
M602418C	areas n.e. 0.5 m²	Nr	0.45	7.64	-	1.40	9.04	9.94	0.783

Major Works 2011		Unit	Labour Hours	Labour Net	Plant Net	Materials Net	Unit Net	Unit with 10%	CO$_2$
				£	£	£	£	£	Kg
M60	**M60: PAINTING AND CLEAR FINISHING**								
M6024	**Oil paint; metalwork backgrounds; two undercoats, one top coat**								
M602419	**Prepare, apply etching primer, two undercoats and top coat gloss paint; staircases and balustrades**								
M602419A	over 300 mm girth	m^2	0.51	8.66	-	2.52	11.18	12.30	1.406
M602419B	n.e. 300 mm girth	m	0.21	3.51	-	0.86	4.37	4.81	0.481
M602419C	areas n.e. 0.5 m^2	Nr	0.38	6.50	-	1.40	7.90	8.69	0.783
M602420	**Prepare, apply etching primer, two undercoats and top coat gloss paint; gutters**								
M602420A	over 300 mm girth	m^2	0.55	9.34	-	2.52	11.86	13.05	1.406
M602420B	n.e. 300 mm girth	m	0.22	3.79	-	0.86	4.65	5.12	0.481
M602420C	areas n.e. 0.5 m^2	Nr	0.41	7.01	-	1.40	8.41	9.25	0.783
M602421	**Prepare, apply etching primer, two undercoats and top coat gloss paint; services**								
M602421A	over 300 mm girth	m^2	0.55	9.34	-	2.52	11.86	13.05	1.406
M602421B	n.e. 300 mm girth	m	0.22	3.79	-	0.86	4.65	5.12	0.481
M602421C	areas n.e. 0.5 m^2	Nr	0.41	7.01	-	1.40	8.41	9.25	0.783
M6025	**Preservative stain**								
M602501	**Prepare, apply one coat Sadolins base and two coats Sadolins Classic finish; general surfaces**								
M602501A	over 300 mm girth	m^2	0.51	8.66	-	2.07	10.73	11.80	0.890
M602501B	n.e. 300 mm girth	m	0.21	3.51	-	0.65	4.16	4.58	0.285
M602501C	areas n.e. 0.5 m^2	Nr	0.38	6.45	-	2.07	8.52	9.37	0.890
M602502	**Prepare, apply one coat Sadolins base and two coats Sadolins Classic finish; glazed windows and screens; in panes n.e. 0.10 m^2**								
M602502A	over 300 mm girth	m^2	1.55	26.32	-	2.73	29.05	31.96	1.175
M602502B	n.e. 300 mm girth	m	0.63	10.66	-	0.82	11.48	12.63	0.356
M602502C	areas n.e. 0.5 m^2	Nr	1.16	19.75	-	1.13	20.88	22.97	0.498
M602503	**Prepare, apply one coat Sadolins base and two coats Sadolins Classic finish; glazed windows; in panes 0.10 - 0.50 m^2**								
M602503A	over 300 mm girth	m^2	1.14	19.36	-	2.07	21.43	23.57	0.890
M602503B	n.e. 300 mm girth	m	0.46	7.84	-	0.65	8.49	9.34	0.285
M602503C	areas n.e. 0.5 m^2	Nr	0.86	14.52	-	1.07	15.59	17.15	0.463
M602504	**Prepare, apply one coat Sadolins base and two coats Sadolins Classic finish; glazed windows and screens; in panes 0.50 - 1.00 m^2**								
M602504A	over 300 mm girth	m^2	0.99	16.81	-	1.79	18.60	20.46	0.765
M602504B	n.e. 300 mm girth	m	0.40	6.79	-	0.55	7.34	8.07	0.231
M602505	**Prepare, apply one coat Sadolins base and two coats Sadolins Classic finish; glazed windows and screens; in panes over 1.00 m^2**								
M602505A	over 300 mm girth	m^2	0.90	15.28	-	1.62	16.90	18.59	0.694
M602505B	n.e. 300 mm girth	m	0.37	6.20	-	0.55	6.75	7.43	0.231
M602506	**Prepare, apply one coat Sadolins base and two coats Sadolins Classic finish; glazed sash windows; in panes n.e. 0.10 m^2**								
M602506A	over 300 mm girth	m^2	1.71	28.95	-	2.73	31.68	34.85	1.175

Surface Finishes

		Unit	Labour Hours	Labour Net £	Plant Net £	Materials Net £	Unit Net £	Unit with 10% £	CO_2 Kg
M60	**M60: PAINTING AND CLEAR FINISHING**								
M6025	**Preservative stain**								
M602506	**Prepare, apply one coat Sadolins base and two coats Sadolins Classic finish; glazed sash windows; in panes n.e. 0.10 m^2**								
M602506B	n.e. 300 mm girth	m	0.69	11.73	-	0.82	12.55	13.81	0.356
M602506C	areas n.e. 0.5 m^2	Nr	1.28	21.72	-	1.13	22.85	25.14	0.498
M602507	**Prepare, apply one coat Sadolins base and two coats Sadolins Classic finish; glazed sash windows; in panes 0.10 - 0.50 m^2**								
M602507A	over 300 mm girth	m^2	1.25	21.29	-	2.07	23.36	25.70	0.890
M602507B	n.e. 300 mm girth	m	0.51	8.63	-	0.65	9.28	10.21	0.285
M602507C	areas n.e. 0.5 m^2	Nr	0.94	15.98	-	1.07	17.05	18.76	0.463
M602508	**Prepare, apply one coat Sadolins base and two coats Sadolins Classic finish; glazed sash windows; in panes 0.50 - 1.00 m^2**								
M602508A	over 300 mm girth	m^2	1.09	18.49	-	1.79	20.28	22.31	0.765
M602508B	n.e. 300 mm girth	m	0.44	7.47	-	0.55	8.02	8.82	0.231
M602509	**Prepare, apply one coat Sadolins base and two coats Sadolins Classic finish; glazed sash windows; in panes over 1.00 m^2**								
M602509A	over 300 mm girth	m^2	0.99	16.81	-	1.62	18.43	20.27	0.694
M602509B	n.e. 300 mm girth	m	0.40	6.83	-	0.55	7.38	8.12	0.231
M602510	**Prepare, apply one coat Sadolins base and two coats Sadolins Classic finish; glazed doors; in panes n.e. 0.10 m^2**								
M602510A	over 300 mm girth	m^2	1.55	26.32	-	2.73	29.05	31.96	1.175
M602510B	n.e. 300 mm girth	m	0.63	10.66	-	0.82	11.48	12.63	0.356
M602510C	areas n.e. 0.5 m^2	Nr	1.16	19.75	-	1.13	20.88	22.97	0.498
M602511	**Prepare, apply one coat Sadolins base and two coats Sadolins Classic finish; glazed doors; in panes 0.10 - 0.50 m^2**								
M602511A	over 300 mm girth	m^2	1.14	19.36	-	2.07	21.43	23.57	0.890
M602511B	n.e. 300 mm girth	m	0.46	7.84	-	0.65	8.49	9.34	0.285
M602511C	areas n.e. 0.5 m^2	Nr	0.86	14.52	-	1.07	15.59	17.15	0.463
M602512	**Prepare, apply one coat Sadolins base and two coats Sadolins Classic finish; glazed doors; in panes 0.50 - 1.00 m^2**								
M602512A	over 300 mm girth	m^2	0.99	16.81	-	1.79	18.60	20.46	0.765
M602512B	n.e. 300 mm girth	m	0.40	6.79	-	0.55	7.34	8.07	0.231
M602513	**Prepare, apply one coat Sadolins base and two coats Sadolins Classic finish; glazed doors; in panes over 1.00 m^2**								
M602513A	over 300 mm girth	m^2	0.90	15.28	-	1.62	16.90	18.59	0.694
M602513B	n.e. 300 mm girth	m	0.37	6.20	-	0.55	6.75	7.43	0.231
	Microporous paint								
M6028									
M602801	**Prepare, apply one coat Hicksons base and two coats Hicksons Decor finish; general surfaces**								
M602801A	over 300 mm girth	m^2	0.51	8.66	-	3.64	12.30	13.53	0.890

Major Works 2011		Unit	Labour Hours	Labour Net	Plant Net	Materials Net	Unit Net	Unit with 10%	CO$_2$
				£	£	£	£	£	Kg
M60	**M60: PAINTING AND CLEAR FINISHING**								
M6028	**Microporous paint**								
M602801	**Prepare, apply one coat Hicksons base and two coats Hicksons Decor finish; general surfaces**								
M602801B	n.e. 300 mm girth	m	0.21	3.51	-	1.17	4.68	5.15	0.285
M602801C	areas n.e. 0.5 m^2	Nr	0.38	6.45	-	1.89	8.34	9.17	0.463
M602802	**Prepare, apply one coat Hicksons base and two coats Hicksons Decor finish; glazed windows and screens; in panes n.e. 0.10 m^2**								
M602802A	over 300 mm girth	m^2	1.55	26.32	-	4.81	31.13	34.24	1.175
M602802B	n.e. 300 mm girth	m	0.63	10.66	-	0.82	11.48	12.63	0.356
M602802C	areas n.e. 0.5 m^2	Nr	1.16	19.75	-	1.07	20.82	22.90	0.463
M602803	**Prepare, apply one coat Hicksons base and two coats Hicksons Decor finish; glazed windows and screens; in panes 0.10 - 0.50 m^2**								
M602803A	over 300 mm girth	m^2	1.14	19.36	-	3.64	23.00	25.30	0.890
M602803B	n.e. 300 mm girth	m	0.46	7.84	-	4.37	12.21	13.43	1.068
M602803C	areas n.e. 0.5 m^2	Nr	0.86	14.52	-	1.07	15.59	17.15	0.463
M602804	**Prepare, apply one coat Hicksons base and two coats Hicksons Decor finish; glazed windows and screens; in panes 0.50 - 1.00 m^2**								
M602804A	over 300 mm girth	m^2	0.99	16.81	-	3.13	19.94	21.93	0.765
M602804B	n.e. 300 mm girth	m	0.40	6.79	-	0.95	7.74	8.51	0.231
M602805	**Prepare, apply one coat Hicksons base and two coats Hicksons Decor finish; glazed windows and screens; in panes over 1.00 m^2**								
M602805A	over 300 mm girth	m^2	0.90	15.28	-	2.84	18.12	19.93	0.694
M602805B	n.e. 300 mm girth	m	0.37	6.20	-	0.95	7.15	7.87	0.231
M602806	**Prepare, apply one coat Hicksons base and two coats Hicksons Decor finish; glazed sash windows; in panes n.e. 0.10 m^2**								
M602806A	over 300 mm girth	m^2	1.71	28.95	-	4.81	33.76	37.14	1.175
M602806B	n.e. 300 mm girth	m	0.69	11.73	-	0.82	12.55	13.81	0.356
M602806C	areas n.e. 0.5 m^2	Nr	1.28	21.72	-	1.07	22.79	25.07	0.463
M602807	**Prepare, apply one coat Hicksons base and two coats Hicksons Decor finish; glazed sash windows; in panes 0.10 - 0.50 m^2**								
M602807A	over 300 mm girth	m^2	1.25	21.29	-	3.64	24.93	27.42	0.890
M602807B	n.e. 300 mm girth	m	0.51	8.63	-	4.37	13.00	14.30	1.068
M602807C	areas n.e. 0.5 m^2	Nr	0.94	15.98	-	1.07	17.05	18.76	0.463
M602808	**Prepare, apply one coat Hicksons base and two coats Hicksons Decor finish; glazed sash windows; in panes 0.50 - 1.00 m^2**								
M602808A	over 300 mm girth	m^2	1.09	18.51	-	3.13	21.64	23.80	0.765
M602808B	n.e. 300 mm girth	m	0.44	7.47	-	0.95	8.42	9.26	0.231
M602809	**Prepare, apply one coat Hicksons base and two coats Hicksons Decor finish; glazed sash windows; in panes over 1.00 m^2**								
M602809A	over 300 mm girth	m^2	0.99	16.81	-	2.84	19.65	21.62	0.694
M602809B	n.e. 300 mm girth	m	0.40	6.83	-	0.95	7.78	8.56	0.231

Major Works 2011		Unit	Labour Hours	Labour Net	Plant Net	Materials Net	Unit Net	Unit with 10%	CO₂
				£	£	£	£	£	Kg
M60	**M60: PAINTING AND CLEAR FINISHING**								
M6028	**Microporous paint**								
M602810	**Prepare, apply one coat Hicksons base and two coats Hicksons Decor finish; glazed doors; in panes n.e. 0.10 m²**								
M602810A	over 300 mm girth	m²	1.55	26.32	-	4.81	31.13	34.24	1.175
M602810B	n.e. 300 mm girth	m	0.63	10.66	-	0.82	11.48	12.63	0.356
M602810C	areas n.e. 0.5 m²	Nr	1.16	19.75	-	1.07	20.82	22.90	0.463
M602811	**Prepare, apply one coat Hicksons base and two coats Hicksons Decor finish; glazed doors; in panes 0.10 - 0.50 m²**								
M602811A	over 300 mm girth	m²	1.14	19.36	-	3.64	23.00	25.30	0.890
M602811B	n.e. 300 mm girth	m	0.46	7.84	-	4.37	12.21	13.43	1.068
M602811C	areas n.e. 0.5 m²	Nr	0.86	14.52	-	1.07	15.59	17.15	0.463
M602812	**Prepare, apply one coat Hicksons base and two coats Hicksons Decor finish; glazed doors; in panes 0.50 - 1.00 m²**								
M602812A	over 300 mm girth	m²	0.99	16.81	-	3.13	19.94	21.93	0.765
M602812B	n.e. 300 mm girth	m	0.40	6.79	-	0.95	7.74	8.51	0.231
M602813	**Prepare, apply one coat Hicksons base and two coats Hicksons Decor finish; glazed doors; in panes over 1.00 m²**								
M602813A	over 300 mm girth	m²	0.90	15.28	-	2.84	18.12	19.93	0.694
M602813B	n.e. 300 mm girth	m	0.37	6.20	-	0.95	7.15	7.87	0.231
M6030	**Polyurethane lacquer**								
M603001	**Prepare, apply one thinned coat and two full coats varnish; general surfaces**								
M603001A	over 300 mm girth	m²	0.51	8.66	-	3.75	12.41	13.65	1.546
M603001B	n.e. 300 mm girth	m	0.21	3.51	-	1.15	4.66	5.13	0.489
M603001C	areas n.e. 0.5 m²	Nr	0.38	6.50	-	1.95	8.45	9.30	0.809
M603002	**Prepare, apply one thinned coat and two full coats varnish; glazed windows and screens; in panes n.e. 0.1 m²**								
M603002A	over 300 mm girth	m²	1.28	21.65	-	3.75	25.40	27.94	1.546
M603002B	n.e. 300 mm girth	m	0.52	8.76	-	1.15	9.91	10.90	0.489
M603002C	areas n.e. 0.5 m²	Nr	0.96	16.23	-	1.95	18.18	20.00	0.809
M603003	**Prepare, apply one thinned coat and two full coats varnish; glazed windows and screens; in panes 0.1 - 0.5 m²**								
M603003A	over 300 mm girth	m²	0.94	15.96	-	3.75	19.71	21.68	1.546
M603003B	n.e. 300 mm girth	m	0.38	6.47	-	1.15	7.62	8.38	0.489
M603003C	areas n.e. 0.5 m²	Nr	0.71	11.97	-	1.95	13.92	15.31	0.809
M603004	**Prepare, apply one thinned coat and two full coats varnish; glazed windows and screens; in panes 0.5 - 1.0 m²**								
M603004A	over 300 mm girth	m²	0.82	13.84	-	3.75	17.59	19.35	1.546
M603004B	n.e. 300 mm girth	m	0.33	5.60	-	1.15	6.75	7.43	0.489
M603005	**Prepare, apply one thinned coat and two full coats varnish; glazed windows and screens; in panes over 1.0 m²**								
M603005A	over 300 mm girth	m²	0.74	12.48	-	3.75	16.23	17.85	1.546
M603005B	n.e. 300 mm girth	m	0.30	5.09	-	1.15	6.24	6.86	0.489
M603006	**Prepare, apply one thinned coat and two full coats varnish; glazed doors; in panes n.e. 0.1 m²**								
M603006A	over 300 mm girth	m²	1.28	21.65	-	3.75	25.40	27.94	1.546

Major Works 2011		Unit	Labour Hours	Labour Net	Plant Net	Materials Net	Unit Net	Unit with 10%	CO₂
				£	£	£	£	£	Kg
M60	**M60: PAINTING AND CLEAR FINISHING**								
M6030	**Polyurethane lacquer**								
M603006	**Prepare, apply one thinned coat and two full coats varnish; glazed doors; in panes n.e. 0.1 m²**								
M603006B	n.e. 300 mm girth	m	0.52	8.76	-	1.15	9.91	10.90	0.489
M603006C	areas n.e. 0.5 m²	Nr	0.96	16.23	-	1.95	18.18	20.00	0.809
M603007	**Prepare, apply one thinned coat and two full coats varnish; glazed doors: in panes 0.1 - 0.5 m²**								
M603007A	over 300 mm girth	m²	0.94	15.96	-	3.75	19.71	21.68	1.546
M603007B	n.e. 300 mm girth	m	0.38	6.47	-	1.15	7.62	8.38	0.489
M603007C	areas n.e. 0.5 m²	Nr	0.71	11.97	-	1.95	13.92	15.31	0.809
M603008	**Prepare, apply one thinned coat and two full coats varnish; glazed doors; in panes 0.5 - 1.0 m²**								
M603008A	over 300 mm girth	m²	0.82	13.84	-	3.75	17.59	19.35	1.546
M603008B	n.e. 300 mm girth	m	0.33	5.60	-	1.15	6.75	7.43	0.489
M603009	**Prepare, apply one thinned coat and two full coats varnish; glazed doors; in panes over 1.0 m²**								
M603009A	over 300 mm girth	m²	0.74	12.48	-	3.75	16.23	17.85	1.546
M603009B	n.e. 300 mm girth	m	0.30	5.09	-	1.15	6.24	6.86	0.489
M6041	**Wood preservative treatment**								
M604101	**Prepare for and apply one coat; general surfaces**								
M604101A	over 300 mm girth	m²	0.10	1.70	-	0.66	2.36	2.60	0.940
M604101B	n.e. 300 mm girth	m	0.04	0.70	-	0.20	0.90	0.99	0.285
M604101C	areas n.e. 0.5 m²	Nr	0.08	1.27	-	0.33	1.60	1.76	0.470
M604102	**Prepare for and apply one coat; railings, fences and gates**								
M604102A	over 300 mm girth	m²	0.14	2.38	-	0.66	3.04	3.34	0.940
M604102B	n.e. 300 mm girth	m	0.06	0.97	-	0.20	1.17	1.29	0.285
M604102C	areas n.e. 0.5 m²	Nr	0.11	1.78	-	0.33	2.11	2.32	0.470
M604111	**Prepare for and apply two coats; general surfaces**								
M604111A	over 300 mm girth	m²	0.18	3.06	-	1.21	4.27	4.70	1.723
M604111B	n.e. 300 mm girth	m	0.07	1.24	-	0.37	1.61	1.77	0.527
M604111C	areas n.e. 0.5 m²	Nr	0.14	2.29	-	0.31	2.60	2.86	0.441
M604112	**Prepare for and apply two coats; railings, fences and gates**								
M604112A	over 300 mm girth	m²	0.25	4.25	-	1.21	5.46	6.01	1.723
M604112B	n.e. 300 mm girth	m	0.10	1.75	-	0.37	2.12	2.33	0.527
M604112C	areas n.e. 0.5 m²	Nr	0.19	3.23	-	0.64	3.87	4.26	0.911
M6051	**Intumescent fire protection; woodwork backgrounds**								
M605101	**Prepare and apply three coats Intuclear decorative translucent intumescent varnish to a total loading of 1 litre per 3 m² for Class 1/0 fire protection; general surfaces**								
M605101A	over 300 mm girth	m²	0.51	8.66	-	5.55	14.21	15.63	1.406
M605101B	n.e. 300 mm girth	m	0.21	3.51	-	1.67	5.18	5.70	0.427
M605101C	areas n.e. 0.5 m²	Nr	0.38	6.50	-	2.81	9.31	10.24	0.712

Surface Finishes

Major Works 2011		Unit	Labour Hours	Labour Net £	Plant Net £	Materials Net £	Unit Net £	Unit with 10% £	CO₂ Kg
M60	**M60: PAINTING AND CLEAR FINISHING**								
M6051	**Intumescent fire protection; woodwork backgrounds**								
M605102	**Prepare and apply three coats Intuclear decorative translucent intumescent varnish to a total loading of 1 litre per 3 m² for Class 1/0 fire protection; glazed windows and screens; in panes n.e. 0.1 m²**								
M605102A	over 300 mm girth	m²	1.55	26.25	-	5.55	31.80	34.98	1.406
M605102B	n.e. 300 mm girth	m	0.63	10.63	-	0.16	10.79	11.87	0.053
M605102C	areas n.e. 0.5 m²	Nr	1.16	19.70	-	2.81	22.51	24.76	0.712
M605103	**Prepare and apply three coats Intuclear decorative translucent intumescent varnish to a total loading of 1 litre per 3 m² for Class 1/0 fire protection; glazed windows and screens; in panes 0.1 - 0.5 m²**								
M605103A	over 300 mm girth	m²	1.14	19.36	-	5.55	24.91	27.40	1.406
M605103B	n.e. 300 mm girth	m	0.46	7.84	-	1.67	9.51	10.46	0.427
M605103C	areas n.e. 0.5 m²	Nr	0.86	14.52	-	2.81	17.33	19.06	0.712
M605104	**Prepare and apply three coats Intuclear decorative translucent intumescent varnish to a total loading of 1 litre per 3 m² for Class 1/0 fire protection; glazed windows and screens; in panes 0.5 - 1.0 m²**								
M605104A	over 300 mm girth	m²	0.99	16.73	-	5.55	22.28	24.51	1.406
M605104B	n.e. 300 mm girth	m	0.40	6.79	-	1.67	8.46	9.31	0.427
M605105	**Prepare and apply three coats Intuclear decorative translucent intumescent varnish to a total loading of 1 litre per 3 m² for Class 1/0 fire protection; glazed windows and screens; in panes over 1.0 m²**								
M605105A	over 300 mm girth	m²	0.89	15.11	-	5.55	20.66	22.73	1.406
M605105B	n.e. 300 mm girth	m	0.36	6.11	-	1.67	7.78	8.56	0.427
M605106	**Prepare and apply three coats Intuclear decorative translucent intumescent varnish to a total loading of 1 litre per 3 m² for Class 1/0 fire protection; glazed doors; in panes n.e. 0.1 m²**								
M605106A	over 300 mm girth	m²	1.55	26.25	-	5.55	31.80	34.98	1.406
M605106B	n.e. 300 mm girth	m	0.63	10.63	-	0.16	10.79	11.87	0.053
M605106C	areas n.e. 0.5 m²	Nr	1.16	19.70	-	2.81	22.51	24.76	0.712
M605107	**Prepare and apply three coats Intuclear decorative translucent intumescent varnish to a total loading of 1 litre per 3 m² for Class 1/0 fire protection; glazed doors; in panes 0.1 - 0.5 m²**								
M605107A	over 300 mm girth	m²	1.14	19.36	-	5.55	24.91	27.40	1.406
M605107B	n.e. 300 mm girth	m	0.46	7.84	-	1.67	9.51	10.46	0.427
M605107C	areas n.e. 0.5 m²	Nr	0.86	14.52	-	2.81	17.33	19.06	0.712

Major Works 2011		Unit	Labour Hours	Labour Net	Plant Net	Materials Net	Unit Net	Unit with 10%	CO$_2$
				£	£	£	£	£	Kg
M60	**M60: PAINTING AND CLEAR FINISHING**								
M6051	**Intumescent fire protection; woodwork backgrounds**								
M605108	**Prepare and apply three coats Intuclear decorative translucent intumescent varnish to a total loading of 1 litre per 3 m^2 for Class 1/0 fire protection; glazed doors; in panes 0.5 - 1.0 m^2**								
M605108A	over 300 mm girth	m^2	0.99	16.73	-	5.55	22.28	24.51	1.406
M605108B	n.e. 300 mm girth	m	0.40	6.79	-	1.67	8.46	9.31	0.427
M605109	**Prepare and apply three coats Intuclear decorative translucent intumescent varnish to a total loading of 1 litre per 3 m^2 for Class 1/0 fire protection; glazed doors; in panes over 1.0 m^2**								
M605109A	over 300 mm girth	m^2	0.89	15.11	-	5.55	20.66	22.73	1.406
M605109B	n.e. 300 mm girth	m	0.36	6.11	-	1.67	7.78	8.56	0.427
M605151	**Prepare and apply one coat Intuclear decorative gloss overcoat; to intumescent varnish backgrounds; general surfaces**								
M605151A	over 300 mm girth	m^2	0.15	2.55	-	1.56	4.11	4.52	0.356
M605151B	n.e. 300 mm girth	m	0.06	1.04	-	0.47	1.51	1.66	0.107
M605151C	areas n.e. 0.5 m^2	Nr	0.11	1.92	-	0.78	2.70	2.97	0.178
M605152	**Prepare and apply one coat Intuclear decorative gloss overcoat; to intumescent varnish backgrounds; glazed windows and screens; in panes n.e. 0.1 m^2**								
M605152A	over 300 mm girth	m^2	0.48	8.07	-	1.56	9.63	10.59	0.356
M605152B	n.e. 300 mm girth	m	0.19	3.26	-	0.47	3.73	4.10	0.107
M605152C	areas n.e. 0.5 m^2	Nr	0.36	6.04	-	0.78	6.82	7.50	0.178
M605153	**Prepare and apply one coat Intuclear decorative gloss overcoat; to intumescent varnish backgrounds; glazed windows and screens; in panes 0.1 - 0.5 m^2**								
M605153A	over 300 mm girth	m^2	0.35	5.94	-	1.56	7.50	8.25	0.356
M605153B	n.e. 300 mm girth	m	0.14	2.41	-	0.47	2.88	3.17	0.107
M605153C	areas n.e. 0.5 m^2	Nr	0.26	4.47	-	0.78	5.25	5.78	0.178
M605154	**Prepare and apply one coat Intuclear decorative gloss overcoat; to intumescent varnish backgrounds; glazed windows and screens; in panes 0.5 - 1.0 m^2**								
M605154A	over 300 mm girth	m^2	0.30	5.09	-	1.56	6.65	7.32	0.356
M605154B	n.e. 300 mm girth	m	0.12	2.07	-	0.47	2.54	2.79	0.107
M605155	**Prepare and apply one coat Intuclear decorative gloss overcoat; to intumescent varnish backgrounds; glazed windows and screens; in panes over 1.0 m^2**								
M605155A	over 300 mm girth	m^2	0.27	4.58	-	1.56	6.14	6.75	0.356
M605155B	n.e. 300 mm girth	m	0.11	1.85	-	0.47	2.32	2.55	0.107
M605156	**Prepare and apply one coat Intuclear decorative gloss overcoat; to intumescent varnish backgrounds; glazed doors; in panes n.e. 0.1 m^2**								
M605156A	over 300 mm girth	m^2	0.48	8.07	-	1.56	9.63	10.59	0.356
M605156B	n.e. 300 mm girth	m	0.19	3.26	-	0.47	3.73	4.10	0.107

Surface Finishes

Major Works 2011		Unit	Labour Hours	Labour Net	Plant Net	Materials Net	Unit Net	Unit with 10%	CO$_2$
				£	£	£	£	£	Kg
M60	**M60: PAINTING AND CLEAR FINISHING**								
M6051	**Intumescent fire protection; woodwork backgrounds**								
M605156	**Prepare and apply one coat Intuclear decorative gloss overcoat; to intumescent varnish backgrounds; glazed doors; in panes n.e. 0.1 m^2**								
M605156C	areas n.e. 0.5 m^2	Nr	0.36	6.04	-	0.78	6.82	7.50	0.178
M605157	**Prepare and apply one coat Intuclear decorative gloss overcoat; to intumescent varnish backgrounds; glazed doors; in panes 0.1 - 0.5 m^2**								
M605157A	over 300 mm girth	m^2	0.35	5.94	-	1.56	7.50	8.25	0.356
M605157B	n.e. 300 mm girth	m	0.14	2.41	-	0.47	2.88	3.17	0.107
M605157C	areas n.e. 0.5 m^2	Nr	0.26	4.47	-	0.78	5.25	5.78	0.178
M605158	**Prepare and apply one coat Intuclear decorative gloss overcoat; to intumescent varnish backgrounds; glazed doors; in panes 0.5 - 1.0 m^2**								
M605158A	over 300 mm girth	m^2	0.30	5.09	-	1.56	6.65	7.32	0.356
M605158B	n.e. 300 mm girth	m	0.12	2.07	-	0.47	2.54	2.79	0.107
M605159	**Prepare and apply one coat Intuclear decorative gloss overcoat; to intumescent varnish backgrounds; glazed doors; in panes over 1.0 m^2**								
M605159A	over 300 mm girth	m^2	0.27	4.58	-	1.56	6.14	6.75	0.356
M605159B	n.e. 300 mm girth	m	0.11	1.85	-	0.47	2.32	2.55	0.107

Major Works 2011		Unit	Labour Hours	Labour Net	Plant Net	Materials Net	Unit Net	Unit with 10%	CO$_2$
				£	£	£	£	£	Kg
M61	**M61: INTUMESCENT COATINGS FOR FIRE PROTECTION OF STEELWORK**								
M6161	**Intumescent fire protection; structural steelwork**								
M616101	**Prepare, epoxy zinc phosphate primer, intumescent Interbond FP build coating to required thickness, Intersheen 54 colour coating overseal; steel sections exposed on three sides; half hour fire protection; FP dry film thickness**								
M616101A	525 microns; over 300 mm girth	m^2	1.60	27.17	-	20.22	47.39	52.13	4.308
M616101B	525 microns; n.e. 300 mm girth	m	0.65	11.00	-	6.08	17.08	18.79	1.296
M616101C	525 microns; areas n.e. 0.5 m^2	Nr	1.20	20.38	-	10.13	30.51	33.56	2.157
M616102	**Prepare, epoxy zinc phosphate primer, intumescent Interbond FP build coating to required thickness, Intersheen 54 colour coating overseal; steel sections exposed on three sides; one hour fire protection; FP dry film thickness**								
M616102A	625 microns; over 300 mm girth	m^2	1.60	27.17	-	22.95	50.12	55.13	4.856
M616102B	625 microns; n.e. 300 mm girth	m	0.65	11.04	-	6.90	17.94	19.73	1.460
M616102C	625 microns; areas n.e. 0.5 m^2	Nr	1.20	20.38	-	11.49	31.87	35.06	2.431
M616102D	825 microns; over 300 mm girth	m^2	2.00	33.96	-	28.60	62.56	68.82	5.991
M616102E	825 microns; n.e. 300 mm girth	m	0.81	13.75	-	8.58	22.33	24.56	1.798
M616102F	825 microns; areas n.e. 0.5 m^2	Nr	1.50	25.47	-	14.30	39.77	43.75	2.998
M616102G	1025 microns; over 300 mm girth	m^2	2.40	40.75	-	34.05	74.80	82.28	7.088
M616102H	1025 microns; n.e. 300 mm girth	m	0.97	16.47	-	10.22	26.69	29.36	2.129
M616102I	1025 microns; areas n.e. 0.5 m^2	Nr	1.80	30.56	-	17.03	47.59	52.35	3.546
M616102J	1125 microns; over 300 mm girth	m^2	2.40	40.75	-	36.97	77.72	85.49	7.675
M616102K	1125 microns; n.e. 300 mm girth	m	0.97	16.47	-	11.09	27.56	30.32	2.303
M616102L	1125 microns; areas n.e. 0.5 m^2	Nr	1.80	30.56	-	18.50	49.06	53.97	3.841
M616102M	1225 microns; over 300 mm girth	m^2	2.40	40.75	-	39.69	80.44	88.48	8.224
M616102N	1225 microns; n.e. 300 mm girth	m	0.97	16.50	-	11.92	28.42	31.26	2.471
M616102O	1225 microns; areas n.e. 0.5 m^2	Nr	1.80	30.56	-	19.86	50.42	55.46	4.115
M616102P	1325 microns; over 300 mm girth	m^2	2.80	47.54	-	42.42	89.96	98.96	8.772
M616102Q	1325 microns; n.e. 300 mm girth	m	1.13	19.26	-	12.74	32.00	35.20	2.634
M616102R	1325 microns; areas n.e. 0.5 m^2	Nr	2.10	35.66	-	21.22	56.88	62.57	4.389
M616102S	1625 microns; over 300 mm girth	m^2	3.20	54.34	-	50.79	105.13	115.64	10.456
M616102T	1625 microns; n.e. 300 mm girth	m	1.30	22.01	-	15.25	37.26	40.99	3.140
M616102U	1625 microns; areas n.e. 0.5 m^2	Nr	2.40	40.75	-	25.40	66.15	72.77	5.230
M616103	**Prepare, epoxy zinc phosphate primer, intumescent Interbond FP build coating to required thickness, Intersheen 54 colour coating overseal; steel sections exposed three sides; one and half hour fire protection; FP dry film thickness**								
M616103A	2335 microns; over 300 mm girth	m^2	4.00	67.92	-	64.23	132.15	145.37	13.136
M616103B	2335 microns; n.e. 300 mm girth	m	1.62	27.51	-	21.20	48.71	53.58	4.336
M616103C	2335 microns; areas n.e. 0.5 m^2	Nr	3.00	50.94	-	35.33	86.27	94.90	7.227
M616104	**Prepare, epoxy zinc phosphate primer, intumescent Interbond FP build coating to required thickness, Intersheen 54 colour coating overseal; steel sections exposed four sides; half hour fire protection; FP dry film thickness**								
M616104A	525 microns; over 300 mm girth	m^2	1.60	27.17	-	20.22	47.39	52.13	4.308
M616104B	525 microns; n.e. 300 mm girth	m	0.65	11.00	-	6.08	17.08	18.79	1.296

Furniture and Equipment

Major Works 2011		Unit	Labour Hours	Labour Net	Plant Net	Materials Net	Unit Net	Unit with 10%	CO$_2$
				£	£	£	£	£	Kg
N10	**N10: GENERAL FIXTURES, FURNISHINGS AND EQUIPMENT**								
N1004	**Mirrors**								
N100410	**Mirrors; 6 mm thick safety glass; polished bevelled edges; fixing with brass screws including polyethylene washers and screw caps; size**								
N100410A	450 x 600 mm	Nr	0.75	12.73	-	37.12	49.85	54.84	2.302
N100410C	450 x 900 mm	Nr	0.80	13.58	-	53.40	66.98	73.68	3.450
N100410E	450 x 1200 mm	Nr	0.95	16.13	-	66.38	82.51	90.76	4.597
N100410G	600 x 900 mm	Nr	1.10	18.68	-	69.67	88.35	97.19	4.597
N100410I	600 x 1200 mm	Nr	1.25	21.23	-	92.69	113.92	125.31	6.127
N100410K	600 x 1500 mm	Nr	1.50	25.47	-	112.34	137.81	151.59	7.657
N100410M	750 x 1200 mm	Nr	1.50	25.47	-	115.15	140.62	154.68	7.657
N100410O	750 x 1500 mm	Nr	1.75	29.72	-	139.29	169.01	185.91	9.570
N100410Q	750 x 1800 mm	Nr	2.00	33.96	-	165.67	199.63	219.59	11.482
N1028	**Door mats**								
N102810	**Entrance mats; William Armes Fitzwell; 17 mm thick; laying loose or in matwell frames**								
N102810A	600 x 450 mm	Nr	0.10	1.70	-	8.90	10.60	11.66	2.773
N102810B	750 x 450 mm	Nr	0.10	1.70	-	11.09	12.79	14.07	3.456
N102810C	750 x 600 mm	Nr	0.11	1.87	-	14.82	16.69	18.36	4.618
N102810D	900 x 600 mm	Nr	0.11	1.87	-	17.77	19.64	21.60	5.536
N102810E	1200 x 750 mm	Nr	0.12	2.04	-	29.62	31.66	34.83	9.227
N1029	**Matwell frames; fabricated, welded or brazed construction with lugs**								
N102922	**Galvanised mild steel angle section; 32 x 32 x 6 mm**								
N102922A	600 x 450 mm	Nr	0.80	13.58	-	56.76	70.34	77.37	8.869
N102922B	750 x 450 mm	Nr	0.90	15.28	-	61.78	77.06	84.77	10.136
N102922C	750 x 600 mm	Nr	1.00	16.98	-	66.79	83.77	92.15	11.403
N102922D	900 x 600 mm	Nr	1.10	18.68	-	71.81	90.49	99.54	12.670
N102922E	1200 x 750 mm	Nr	1.20	20.38	-	81.81	102.19	112.41	16.471
N102923	**Polished brass angle section; 32 x 32 x 6 mm**								
N102923A	600 x 450 mm	Nr	1.20	20.38	-	148.70	169.08	185.99	8.294
N102923B	750 x 450 mm	Nr	1.30	22.07	-	166.39	188.46	207.31	9.479
N102923C	750 x 600 mm	Nr	1.40	23.77	-	184.10	207.87	228.66	10.663
N102923D	900 x 600 mm	Nr	1.50	25.47	-	201.81	227.28	250.01	11.848
N102923E	1200 x 750 mm	Nr	1.60	27.17	-	258.91	286.08	314.69	15.403
N102924	**Aluminium angle section; 32 x 32 x 6 mm**								
N102924A	600 x 450 mm	Nr	1.10	18.68	-	76.33	95.01	104.51	8.970
N102924B	750 x 450 mm	Nr	1.20	20.38	-	85.42	105.80	116.38	10.252
N102924C	750 x 600 mm	Nr	1.30	22.07	-	94.51	116.58	128.24	11.533
N102924D	900 x 600 mm	Nr	1.40	23.77	-	103.60	127.37	140.11	12.815
N102924E	1200 x 750 mm	Nr	1.50	25.47	-	118.14	143.61	157.97	16.659
N1060	**Fire extinguishers**								
N106010	**Halon Small Automatics; fixing support bracket to masonry backgrounds**								
N106010A	GTP1000	Nr	0.50	8.49	-	40.67	49.16	54.08	5.316
N106010C	GTP2000	Nr	0.60	10.19	-	55.99	66.18	72.80	6.201

Major Works 2011		Unit	Labour Hours	Labour Net	Plant Net	Materials Net	Unit Net	Unit with 10%	CO₂
				£	£	£	£	£	Kg
N11	**N11: DOMESTIC KITCHEN FITTINGS**								
N1110	**Kitchen units; proprietary standard ready assembled; Jewson range**								
N111001	**Base units**								
N111001A	Flair 1203; 300 x 600 mm drawerline	Nr	0.70	11.89	-	181.80	193.69	213.06	14.734
N111001B	Flair 1204; 400 x 600 mm drawerline	Nr	0.80	13.58	-	198.47	212.05	233.26	16.983
N111001C	Flair 1245; 450 x 600 mm drawerline	Nr	0.85	14.43	-	200.76	215.19	236.71	18.108
N111001D	Flair 1205; 500 x 600 mm drawerline	Nr	0.90	15.28	-	203.22	218.50	240.35	19.232
N111001E	Flair 1206; 600 x 600 mm drawerline	Nr	1.00	16.98	-	220.25	237.23	260.95	21.481
N111001F	Flair 1208; 800 x 600 mm drawerline	Nr	1.20	20.38	-	325.78	346.16	380.78	25.979
N111001G	Flair 1210; 1000 x 600 mm drawerline	Nr	1.40	23.77	-	340.48	364.25	400.68	30.478
N111001H	Flair 1103; 300 x 600 mm highline	Nr	0.70	11.89	-	105.39	117.28	129.01	14.734
N111001I	Flair 1104; 400 x 600 mm highline	Nr	0.80	13.58	-	110.09	123.67	136.04	16.983
N111001J	Flair 1145; 450 x 600 mm highline	Nr	0.85	14.43	-	112.45	126.88	139.57	18.108
N111001K	Flair 1106; 600 x 600 mm highline	Nr	0.90	15.28	-	114.81	130.09	143.10	19.232
N111001L	Flair 1106; 600 x 600 mm highline	Nr	1.00	16.98	-	121.89	138.87	152.76	21.481
N111001M	Flair 1108; 800 x 600 mm highline	Nr	1.20	20.38	-	154.58	174.96	192.46	25.979
N111001N	Flair 1110; 1000 x 600 mm highline	Nr	1.40	23.77	-	166.36	190.13	209.14	30.478
N111011	**Corner base units**								
N111011A	Flair 2508; 800 x 600 mm; 300 mm door; drawerline	Nr	1.20	20.38	-	220.03	240.41	264.45	25.979
N111011B	Flair 3208; 800 x 600 mm; 400 mm door; drawerline	Nr	1.20	20.38	-	220.19	240.57	264.63	25.979
N111011C	Flair 2608; 800 x 600 mm; 500 mm door; drawerline	Nr	1.20	20.38	-	220.03	240.41	264.45	25.979
N111011D	Flair 2710; 1000 x 600 mm; 400 mm door; drawerline	Nr	1.40	23.77	-	231.97	255.74	281.31	30.478
N111011E	Flair 3210; 1000 x 600 mm; 500 mm door; drawerline	Nr	1.40	23.77	-	232.04	255.81	281.39	30.478
N111011F	Flair 2810; 1000 x 600 mm; 600 mm door; drawerline	Nr	1.40	23.77	-	232.53	256.30	281.93	30.478
N111011G	Flair 2908; 800 x 600 mm; 300 mm door; highline	Nr	1.20	20.38	-	135.71	156.09	171.70	25.979
N111011H	Flair 3410; 800 x 600 mm; 400 mm door; highline	Nr	1.20	20.38	-	147.50	167.88	184.67	25.979
N111011I	Flair 3108; 800 x 600 mm; 400 mm door; highline	Nr	1.20	20.38	-	135.69	156.07	171.68	25.979
N111011J	Flair 3110; 1000 x 600 mm; 500 mm door; highline	Nr	1.40	23.77	-	147.50	171.27	188.40	30.478
N111011K	Flair 3008; 800 x 600 mm; 500 mm door; highline	Nr	1.20	20.38	-	135.71	156.09	171.70	25.979
N111011L	Flair 3101; 925 x 600 mm; L-shaped; highline	Nr	1.60	27.17	-	241.84	269.01	295.91	28.791
N111011M	Flair 3310; 1000 x 600 mm; 600 door; highline	Nr	1.40	23.77	-	147.50	171.27	188.40	30.478
N111021	**Sink base units**								
N111021A	Flair 2105; 500 x 600 mm sink unit; drawerline	Nr	0.90	15.28	-	166.69	181.97	200.17	19.232
N111021B	Flair 2106; 600 x 600 mm sink unit	Nr	1.00	16.98	-	183.19	200.17	220.19	21.481
N111021C	Flair 2108; 800 x 600 mm sink unit; drawerline	Nr	1.20	20.38	-	292.27	312.65	343.92	25.979
N111021D	Flair 2110; 1000 x 600 mm sink unit; drawerline	Nr	1.40	23.77	-	276.01	299.78	329.76	30.478
N111031	**Store units**								
N111031A	Flair 5003; 300 x 600 x 2193 mm high medium larder unit	Nr	1.75	29.72	-	251.75	281.47	309.62	32.952
N111031B	Flair 5005; 500 x 600 x 2193 mm high medium larder unit	Nr	1.85	31.41	-	251.75	283.16	311.48	41.498
N111031C	Flair 5006; 600 x 600 x 2193 mm high medium larder unit	Nr	1.95	33.11	-	346.06	379.17	417.09	45.771

Major Works 2011	Unit	Labour Hours	Labour Net	Plant Net	Materials Net	Unit Net	Unit with 10%	CO₂
			£	£	£	£	£	Kg
N11	**N11: DOMESTIC KITCHEN FITTINGS**							
N1110	**Kitchen units; proprietary standard ready assembled; Jewson range**							
N111031	**Store units**							
N111031D	Flair 5205; 500 x 600 x 2193 mm high medium broom cupboard	Nr	1.85	31.41	-	251.75	283.16	311.48	41.498
N111031E	Flair 5203; 300 x 600 x 1485 mm high studio larder unit	Nr	1.35	22.92	-	245.00	267.92	294.71	23.202
N111031F	Flair 4805; 500 x 600 x 1485 mm high studio larder unit	Nr	1.45	24.62	-	245.00	269.62	296.58	29.583
N111031G	Flair 7506; 600 x 600 x 1485 mm high studio larder unit	Nr	1.55	26.32	-	339.33	365.65	402.22	29.583
N111031H	Flair 4705; 500 x 600 x 1485 mm high studio broom cupboard	Nr	1.45	24.62	-	245.00	269.62	296.58	31.855
N111041	**Appliance housings**							
N111041A	Flair 4606; 600 x 600 x 1485 mm high studio appliance housing Type A1	Nr	1.55	26.32	-	341.69	368.01	404.81	32.773
N111041B	Flair 4706; 600 x 600 x 1485 mm high studio appliance housing Type A2	Nr	1.55	26.32	-	412.11	438.43	482.27	32.773
N111041C	Flair 5967; 600 x 600 x 1485 mm high studio appliance housing Type B	Nr	1.55	26.32	-	412.11	438.43	482.27	32.773
N111041D	Flair 5946; 600 x 600 x 1485 mm high studio appliance housing Type C1	Nr	1.55	26.32	-	341.69	368.01	404.81	32.773
N111041E	Flair 7206; 600 x 600 x 1485 mm high studio appliance housing Type E	Nr	1.55	26.32	-	412.93	439.25	483.18	32.773
N111041F	Flair 6016; 600 x 600 x 2193 mm high medium appliance housing Type C1	Nr	1.95	33.11	-	348.44	381.55	419.71	45.771
N111041G	Flair 6026; 600 x 600 x 2193 mm high medium appliance housing Type C2	Nr	1.95	33.11	-	348.44	381.55	419.71	45.771
N111041H	Flair 6606; 600 x 600 x 2193 mm high medium appliance housing Type F	Nr	1.95	33.11	-	364.95	398.06	437.87	45.771
N111051	**Wall units**							
N111051A	Flair 7703; 300 x 284 x 588 mm high; wall unit	Nr	0.90	15.28	-	86.51	101.79	111.97	6.557
N111051B	Flair 7704; 400 x 284 x 588 mm high; wall unit	Nr	0.95	16.13	-	95.94	112.07	123.28	7.892
N111051C	Flair 7745; 450 x 284 x 588 mm high; wall unit	Nr	1.10	18.68	-	98.30	116.98	128.68	8.559
N111051D	Flair 7705; 500 x 284 x 588 mm high; wall unit	Nr	1.15	19.53	-	100.66	120.19	132.21	9.226
N111051E	Flair 7706; 600 x 284 x 588 mm high; wall unit	Nr	1.35	22.92	-	112.45	135.37	148.91	10.560
N111051F	Flair 7708; 800 x 284 x 588 mm high; wall unit	Nr	1.55	26.32	-	149.87	176.19	193.81	13.228
N111051G	Flair 7710; 1000 x 284 x 588 mm high wall unit	Nr	1.80	30.56	-	156.94	187.50	206.25	15.897
N111051H	Flair 8103; 300 x 284 x 735 mm high; wall unit	Nr	1.00	16.98	-	86.51	103.49	113.84	7.871
N111051I	Flair 8104; 400 x 284 x 735 mm high; wall unit	Nr	1.15	19.53	-	95.94	115.47	127.02	9.430
N111051J	Flair 8145; 450 x 284 x 735 mm high; wall unit	Nr	1.20	20.38	-	98.30	118.68	130.55	10.210
N111051K	Flair 8105; 500 x 284 x 735 mm high; wall unit	Nr	1.25	21.23	-	100.66	121.89	134.08	10.989
N111051L	Flair 8106; 600 x 284 x 735 mm high; wall unit	Nr	1.50	25.47	-	112.45	137.92	151.71	12.548
N111051M	Flair 8108; 800 x 284 x 735 mm high; wall unit	Nr	1.70	28.87	-	149.88	178.75	196.63	15.666
N111051N	Flair 8110; 1000 x 284 x 735 mm high wall unit	Nr	2.00	33.96	-	156.94	190.90	209.99	18.784
N111051O	Flair 8103; 300 x 284 x 735 mm high; wall unit	Nr	0.90	15.28	-	86.51	101.79	111.97	7.871
N111061	**Corner wall units**							
N111061A	Flair 8306; 625 x 284 x 735 mm high; L-shaped corner wall unit	Nr	1.80	30.56	-	206.45	237.01	260.71	12.938
N111061B	Flair 8506; 600 x 284 x 735 mm high; closed corner wall unit	Nr	1.70	28.87	-	117.17	146.04	160.64	12.548

Furniture & Equipment

Major Works 2011		Unit	Labour Hours	Labour Net	Plant Net	Materials Net	Unit Net	Unit with 10%	CO₂
				£	£	£	£	£	Kg
N11	**N11: DOMESTIC KITCHEN FITTINGS**								
N1110	**Kitchen units; proprietary standard ready assembled; Jewson range**								
N111081	**Worktops**								
N111081A	600 x 30 mm thick; lipped long edges	m	1.50	25.47	-	23.53	49.00	53.90	8.130
N111081B	600 x 30 mm thick; double roll edge	m	1.50	25.47	-	37.03	62.50	68.75	8.711
N111081C	600 x 40 mm thick; single roll edge	m	1.70	28.87	-	37.03	65.90	72.49	11.034
N111086	**Worktop sundries**								
N111086A	30 mm jointing strip; rolled edge	m	0.60	10.19	-	6.42	16.61	18.27	1.770
N111086B	40 mm jointing strip; rolled edge	m	0.70	11.89	-	6.42	18.31	20.14	1.770
N111086C	30 mm jointing strip; square edge	m	0.55	9.34	-	6.21	15.55	17.11	1.770
N111086D	30 mm end capping; rolled edge	m	0.65	11.04	-	6.21	17.25	18.98	1.770

Major Works 2011		Unit	Labour Hours	Labour Net	Plant Net	Materials Net	Unit Net	Unit with 10%	CO₂
				£	£	£	£	£	Kg
N13	**N13: SANITARY APPLIANCES AND FITTINGS**								
N1301	**Sanitary fittings**								
N130101	**Baths; complete with taps and associated fittings; fixing in position**								
N130101A	pressed steel (PC £200 each)	Nr	3.26	130.41	-	200.00	330.41	363.45	65.490
N130101B	cast iron (PC £350 each)	Nr	3.76	150.47	-	350.00	500.47	550.52	238.750
N130101C	acrylic (PC £175 each)	Nr	3.01	120.36	-	175.00	295.36	324.90	75.900
N130102	**Basins; complete with taps and associated fittings; fixing in position**								
N130102A	enamelled steel (PC £75 each)	Nr	2.00	80.24	-	75.00	155.24	170.76	26.550
N130102B	vitreous china (PC £80 each)	Nr	2.26	90.29	-	80.00	170.29	187.32	22.200
N130102C	acrylic (PC £95 each)	Nr	1.50	60.18	-	95.00	155.18	170.70	43.010
N130112	**Sinks; complete with taps and associated fittings; fixing in position**								
N130112A	glazed fireclay (PC £185 each)	Nr	1.75	70.23	-	185.00	255.23	280.75	4.400
N130112B	stainless steel (PC £145 each)	Nr	1.50	60.18	-	145.00	205.18	225.70	52.275
N130112C	resin (PC £130 each)	Nr	1.50	60.18	-	130.00	190.18	209.20	22.200
N130121	**WC suites; complete with cistern, seat and flap and associated fittings; fixing in position**								
N130121A	high level washdown (PC £200 each)	Nr	2.51	100.30	-	200.00	300.30	330.33	5.500
N130121B	low level washdown (PC £165 each)	Nr	2.00	80.24	-	165.00	245.24	269.76	3.960
N130121C	low level syphonic (PC £325 each)	Nr	2.26	90.29	-	325.00	415.29	456.82	6.600
N130126	**Bidets; complete with taps and associated fittings; fixing in position**								
N130126A	vitreous china (PC £160 each)	Nr	2.00	80.24	-	160.00	240.24	264.26	29.600
N130131	**Shower trays; complete with fittings; fixing in position**								
N130131A	fireclay (PC £75 each)	Nr	1.25	50.17	-	75.00	125.17	137.69	4.400
N130131B	acrylic (PC £115 each)	Nr	0.75	30.11	-	115.00	145.11	159.62	55.660
N130141	**Shower enclosures; complete with fittings; fixing in position**								
N130141A	acrylic, three sided; front or side entry (PC £200 each)	Nr	1.75	70.23	-	200.00	270.23	297.25	63.250
N130141B	acrylic, two sided; corner entry (PC £275 each)	Nr	1.50	60.18	-	275.00	335.18	368.70	63.250
N130141C	plastic curtain and rail, one sided (PC £40 each)	Nr	0.50	20.06	-	40.00	60.06	66.07	37.950
N130143	**Showers; complete with taps and associated fittings; fixing in position**								
N130143A	recessed mechanical valve and spray head (PC £215 each)	Nr	2.00	80.24	-	215.00	295.24	324.76	25.000
N130143B	recessed thermostatic valve and spray head (PC £375 each)	Nr	2.00	80.24	-	375.00	455.24	500.76	30.000
N130143C	surface mounted mechanical valve and spray head (PC £175 each)	Nr	1.00	40.12	-	175.00	215.12	236.63	17.500
N130143D	surface mounted thermostatic valve and spray head (PC £275 each)	Nr	1.00	40.12	-	275.00	315.12	346.63	25.000

Furniture & Equipment

		Unit	Labour Hours	Labour Net	Plant Net	Materials Net	Unit Net	Unit with 10%	CO₂
				£	£	£	£	£	Kg
N15	**N15: SIGNS AND NOTICES**								
N1510	**Internal signage**								
N151010	**Aluminium plate signage; lettered with lacquer finish; drilled and countersunk four times; fixing to timber substrate with screws; size**								
N151010B	150 x 75 mm	Nr	0.40	6.79	-	8.79	15.58	17.14	0.790
N151010D	200 x 100 mm	Nr	0.60	10.19	-	8.79	18.98	20.88	1.374
N151010G	600 x 300 mm	Nr	0.80	13.58	-	17.56	31.14	34.25	12.073

Building Fabric Sundries

Major Works 2011		Unit	Labour Hours	Labour Net	Plant Net	Materials Net	Unit Net	Unit with 10%	CO$_2$
				£	£	£	£	£	Kg
P10	**P10: SUNDRY INSULATION, PROOFING WORK AND FIRE STOPS**								
P1020	**Insulation quilts**								
P102010	**Crown glass fibre insulation quilt; generally; thickness**								
P102010A	horizontal; 60 mm thick	m^2	0.07	1.19	-	2.52	3.71	4.08	11.624
P102010B	horizontal; 80 mm thick	m^2	0.08	1.36	-	3.13	4.49	4.94	15.498
P102010C	horizontal; 100 mm thick	m^2	0.09	1.53	-	2.75	4.28	4.71	19.373
P102010D	horizontal; 150 mm thick	m^2	0.14	2.38	-	6.39	8.77	9.65	29.059
P102010E	vertical; 60 mm thick	m^2	0.12	2.04	-	2.52	4.56	5.02	11.624
P102010F	vertical; 80 mm thick	m^2	0.14	2.38	-	3.13	5.51	6.06	15.498
P102010G	vertical; 100 mm thick	m^2	0.18	3.06	-	2.75	5.81	6.39	19.373
P102010H	vertical; 150 mm thick	m^2	0.25	4.25	-	6.39	10.64	11.70	29.059
P102020	**Crown glass fibre insulation roll; laid horizontally between joists at 400 mm centres; thickness**								
P102020A	60 mm thick	m^2	0.10	1.70	-	2.52	4.22	4.64	11.624
P102020B	80 mm thick	m^2	0.12	2.04	-	3.13	5.17	5.69	15.498
P102020C	100 mm thick	m^2	0.14	2.38	-	2.75	5.13	5.64	19.373
P102020D	150 mm thick	m^2	0.20	3.40	-	6.39	9.79	10.77	29.059
P102020E	170 mm thick	m^2	0.21	3.57	-	6.93	10.50	11.55	32.933
P102020F	200 mm thick	m^2	0.22	3.74	-	8.27	12.01	13.21	38.745
P102022	**Crown glass fibre insulation roll; laid horizontally between joists at 600 mm centres; thickness**								
P102022A	60 mm thick	m^2	0.08	1.36	-	2.52	3.88	4.27	11.624
P102022B	80 mm thick	m^2	0.10	1.70	-	3.13	4.83	5.31	15.498
P102022C	100 mm thick	m^2	0.12	2.04	-	2.75	4.79	5.27	19.373
P102022D	150 mm thick	m^2	0.18	3.06	-	6.39	9.45	10.40	29.059
P102022E	170 mm thick	m^2	0.19	3.23	-	6.93	10.16	11.18	32.933
P102022F	200 mm thick	m^2	0.20	3.40	-	8.27	11.67	12.84	38.745
P102025	**Crown glass fibre insulation roll; laid horizontally over joists; thickness**								
P102025C	100 mm thick	m^2	0.10	1.70	-	2.75	4.45	4.90	19.373
P102025D	150 mm thick	m^2	0.16	2.72	-	6.39	9.11	10.02	29.059
P102025E	170 mm thick	m^2	0.17	2.89	-	6.93	9.82	10.80	32.933
P102025F	200 mm thick	m^2	0.18	3.06	-	8.27	11.33	12.46	38.745
P102030	**DriTherm Cavity Slab glass fibre wall insulation; medium density; fitting between wall ties; securing with retaining clips; thickness**								
P102030A	50 mm thick	m^2	0.09	4.01	-	4.50	8.51	9.36	9.533
P102030B	65 mm thick	m^2	0.09	4.29	-	5.11	9.40	10.34	26.084
P102030C	75 mm thick	m^2	0.10	4.53	-	5.50	10.03	11.03	30.831
P102030D	85 mm thick	m^2	0.10	4.76	-	6.06	10.82	11.90	34.110
P102030E	100 mm thick	m^2	0.11	5.27	-	6.99	12.26	13.49	40.129
P102032	**DriTherm Cavity Slab 32 glassfibre wall insulation; high density; fitting between wall ties; securing with retaining clips; thickness**								
P102032A	50 mm thick	m^2	0.08	3.78	-	8.71	12.49	13.74	20.064
P102032B	65 mm thick	m^2	0.09	4.29	-	10.80	15.09	16.60	26.084
P102032C	75 mm thick	m^2	0.10	4.53	-	12.46	16.99	18.69	30.097
P102032D	85 mm thick	m^2	0.10	4.76	-	14.05	18.81	20.69	34.110
P102032E	100 mm thick	m^2	0.11	5.27	-	16.27	21.54	23.69	40.129
P102034	**DriTherm Cavity Slab 34 glass fibre wall insulation; medium to high density; fitting between wall ties; securing with retaining clips; thickness**								
P102034A	50 mm thick	m^2	0.09	4.01	-	6.97	10.98	12.08	20.064
P102034B	65 mm thick	m^2	0.09	4.29	-	8.16	12.45	13.70	26.084
P102034C	75 mm thick	m^2	0.10	4.53	-	9.44	13.97	15.37	30.097

Building Fabric Sundries

		Unit	Labour Hours	Labour Net	Plant Net	Materials Net	Unit Net	Unit with 10%	CO$_2$
				£	£	£	£	£	Kg
P10	**P10: SUNDRY INSULATION, PROOFING WORK AND FIRE STOPS**								
P1020	**Insulation quilts**								
P102034	**DriTherm Cavity Slab 34 glass fibre wall insulation; medium to high density; fitting between wall ties; securing with retaining clips; thickness**								
P102034D	85 mm thick	m^2	0.10	4.76	-	10.62	15.38	16.92	34.110
P102034E	100 mm thick	m^2	0.11	5.27	-	12.29	17.56	19.32	40.129
P102040	**Actis Tri-Iso pitched roof insulation; fixed to roof timbers by stapling at 500 mm centres; taping with Isodhesif Alu tape at overlapping joints; over or under rafters**								
P102040A	Tri-Iso Super 9	m^2	0.33	5.60	-	11.63	17.23	18.95	105.186
P102040B	Triso-Super 10	m^2	0.33	5.60	-	12.76	18.36	20.20	108.018
P1030	**Insulation boards**								
P103010	**Dow Floormate expanded polystyrene boards; fixed horizontally with wedges to floors; thickness**								
P103010A	25 mm thick	m^2	0.12	2.04	-	2.43	4.47	4.92	6.563
P103010B	50 mm thick	m^2	0.13	2.21	-	4.86	7.07	7.78	13.125
P103010C	70 mm thick	m^2	0.14	2.38	-	7.28	9.66	10.63	18.375
P103010D	100 mm thick	m^2	0.16	2.72	-	9.71	12.43	13.67	26.250
P103015	**VR Jablite Jabfloor 70 polystyrene thermal insulation sheets to concrete slab ground floor construction; laid to floors; thickness**								
P103015A	25 mm	m^2	0.12	2.04	-	2.43	4.47	4.92	6.836
P103015B	40 mm	m^2	0.13	2.21	-	3.87	6.08	6.69	10.937
P103015C	50 mm	m^2	0.13	2.21	-	4.86	7.07	7.78	13.671
P103015D	60 mm	m^2	0.14	2.38	-	5.82	8.20	9.02	16.405
P103015E	75 mm	m^2	0.14	2.38	-	7.28	9.66	10.63	20.507
P103015F	100 mm	m^2	0.15	2.55	-	9.71	12.26	13.49	27.342
P103015G	125 mm	m^2	0.16	2.72	-	12.14	14.86	16.35	34.178
P103015H	30 x 150 mm high edge trim	m	0.05	0.85	-	0.96	1.81	1.99	1.231
P103020	**Glass fibre medium density insulation boards; laid horizontally or fixed vertically; thickness**								
P103020A	horizontal; 25 mm thick	m^2	0.12	2.04	-	6.55	8.59	9.45	7.980
P103020B	horizontal; 50 mm thick	m^2	0.14	2.38	-	8.22	10.60	11.66	15.960
P103020C	horizontal; 75 mm thick	m^2	0.17	2.89	-	12.80	15.69	17.26	23.940
P103020D	vertical; 25 mm thick	m^2	0.18	3.06	-	6.55	9.61	10.57	7.980
P103020E	vertical; 50 mm thick	m^2	0.21	3.57	-	8.22	11.79	12.97	15.960
P103020F	vertical; 75 mm thick	m^2	0.25	4.25	-	12.80	17.05	18.76	23.940
P103030	**Glass fibre medium density insulation board underlay to roofing; bedding in hot bitumen; thickness**								
P103030A	25 mm thick	m^2	0.08	3.50	0.61	7.83	11.94	13.13	8.769
P103030B	50 mm thick	m^2	0.08	3.50	0.61	9.50	13.61	14.97	16.749
P103030C	75 mm thick	m^2	0.08	3.50	0.61	14.07	18.18	20.00	24.729
P103040	**Insulation board underlay to roofing; BS 1142 part 3; bedding in hot bitumen; thickness**								
P103040A	12 mm thick	m^2	0.08	3.50	0.61	4.60	8.71	9.58	7.585
P103050	**Jablite expanded polystyrene cavity wall insulation; fitting between wall ties; securing with retaining clips; thickness**								
P103050A	25 mm thick	m^2	0.08	3.78	-	2.39	6.17	6.79	6.563

Major Works 2011		Unit	Labour Hours	Labour Net	Plant Net	Materials Net	Unit Net	Unit with 10%	CO₂
				£	£	£	£	£	Kg
P10	**P10: SUNDRY INSULATION, PROOFING WORK AND FIRE STOPS**								
P1030	**Insulation boards**								
P103050	**Jablite expanded polystyrene cavity wall insulation; fitting between wall ties; securing with retaining clips; thickness**								
P103050B	50 mm thick	m²	0.09	4.01	-	4.82	8.83	9.71	13.125
P103050C	75 mm thick	m²	0.10	4.53	-	7.64	12.17	13.39	19.688
P103050D	100 mm thick	m²	0.11	5.27	-	9.71	14.98	16.48	26.250
P103060	**Celotex tuff-R rigid polyurethane foam insulation board; foil faced both sides cut and mechanically fixed; aluminium foil self-adhesive taped joints; board thickness**								
P103060A	12 mm	m²	0.23	3.91	-	3.73	7.64	8.40	13.002
P103060B	20 mm	m²	0.25	4.25	-	4.37	8.62	9.48	17.533
P103060C	25 mm	m²	0.26	4.41	-	5.00	9.41	10.35	20.365
P103060D	30 mm	m²	0.31	5.26	-	5.49	10.75	11.83	23.197
P103060E	35 mm	m²	0.36	6.11	-	6.08	12.19	13.41	26.028
P103060F	40 mm	m²	0.40	6.79	-	6.47	13.26	14.59	28.860
P103060G	45 mm	m²	0.45	7.64	-	7.17	14.81	16.29	31.692
P103060H	50 mm	m²	0.48	8.15	-	7.40	15.55	17.11	34.524
P103060I	55 mm	m²	0.52	8.83	-	8.16	16.99	18.69	37.356
P103060J	60 mm	m²	0.58	9.85	-	8.77	18.62	20.48	40.188
P103060K	65 mm	m²	0.62	10.53	-	9.48	20.01	22.01	43.020
P103060L	70 mm	m²	0.65	11.04	-	10.30	21.34	23.47	45.851
P103060M	80 mm	m²	0.68	11.55	-	11.53	23.08	25.39	51.515
P103060N	90 mm	m²	0.71	12.06	-	12.74	24.80	27.28	57.179
P103070	**Kingspan Kooltherm K7 Pitched Roof Board; foil faced both sides; cut and mechanically fixed over, between or under rafters; aluminium foil self adhesive taped joints; thickness**								
P103070A	20 mm	m²	0.25	4.25	-	7.20	11.45	12.60	17.533
P103070B	25 mm	m²	0.26	4.41	-	8.00	12.41	13.65	20.365
P103070C	30 mm	m²	0.31	5.26	-	8.77	14.03	15.43	23.197
P103070D	35 mm	m²	0.36	6.11	-	9.61	15.72	17.29	26.028
P103070E	40 mm	m²	0.40	6.79	-	10.40	17.19	18.91	28.860
P103070F	50 mm	m²	0.48	8.15	-	12.29	20.44	22.48	34.524
P103070G	60 mm	m²	0.58	9.85	-	14.60	24.45	26.90	40.188
P103070H	70 mm	m²	0.65	11.04	-	16.94	27.98	30.78	45.851
P103073	**Kingspan Thermapitch TP10 rigid urethane insulation board; foil faced both sides secured with Helifix In-Skew fixings over, between or under rafters; aluminium foil self-adhesive taped joints; thickness**								
P103073A	17 mm	m²	0.23	3.91	-	5.52	9.43	10.37	16.139
P103073B	20 mm	m²	0.25	4.25	-	6.16	10.41	11.45	17.838
P103073C	25 mm	m²	0.26	4.41	-	6.79	11.20	12.32	20.670
P103073D	30 mm	m²	0.31	5.26	-	7.28	12.54	13.79	23.502
P103073E	35 mm	m²	0.36	6.11	-	7.87	13.98	15.38	26.334
P103073F	40 mm	m²	0.40	6.79	-	8.26	15.05	16.56	29.166
P103073G	45 mm	m²	0.44	7.47	-	8.96	16.43	18.07	31.997
P103073H	50 mm	m²	0.48	8.15	-	9.19	17.34	19.07	34.829
P103073I	60 mm	m²	0.57	9.68	-	10.56	20.24	22.26	40.493
P103073J	70 mm	m²	0.63	10.70	-	12.09	22.79	25.07	46.157
P103073K	75 mm	m²	0.66	11.21	-	12.55	23.76	26.14	48.989
P103073L	80 mm	m²	0.72	12.23	-	13.32	25.55	28.11	51.820
P103073M	90 mm	m²	0.78	13.24	-	14.53	27.77	30.55	57.484
P103073N	100 mm	m²	0.85	14.43	-	15.68	30.11	33.12	63.148

Building Fabric Sundries

Major Works 2011		Unit	Labour Hours	Labour Net	Plant Net	Materials Net	Unit Net	Unit with 10%	CO₂
				£	£	£	£	£	Kg
P10	**P10: SUNDRY INSULATION, PROOFING WORK AND FIRE STOPS**								
P1030	**Insulation boards**								
P103075	**Kingspan Thermawall TW50 rigid urethane insulation board; foil faced both sides partial cavity fill; cutting and fitting around wall ties and retaining disks; thickness**								
P103075A	17 mm	m²	0.15	2.55	-	3.90	6.45	7.10	9.629
P103075B	20 mm	m²	0.15	2.55	-	3.90	6.45	7.10	11.327
P103075C	25 mm	m²	0.15	2.55	-	4.84	7.39	8.13	14.159
P103075D	30 mm	m²	0.16	2.72	-	5.43	8.15	8.97	16.991
P103075E	35 mm	m²	0.16	2.72	-	5.90	8.62	9.48	19.823
P103075F	40 mm	m²	0.17	2.89	-	6.89	9.78	10.76	22.655
P103075G	50 mm	m²	0.18	3.06	-	8.45	11.51	12.66	28.319
P103075H	60 mm	m²	0.19	3.23	-	10.10	13.33	14.66	33.982
P103075I	75 mm	m²	0.20	3.40	-	13.29	16.69	18.36	42.478
P1040	**Insulation loose fill**								
P104010	**Vermiculite bead insulation; loose fill poured between joists at 400 mm centres thickness**								
P104010A	50 mm thick	m²	0.14	2.38	-	5.36	7.74	8.51	14.787
P104010B	75 mm thick	m²	0.20	3.40	-	7.99	11.39	12.53	22.041
P104010C	100 mm thick	m²	0.27	4.58	-	10.63	15.21	16.73	29.295
P104010D	150 mm thick	m²	0.35	5.94	-	15.99	21.93	24.12	44.082
P1060	**Fire barriers**								
P106010	**Rockwool fire barrier; plain faced roll thickness**								
P106010A	60 mm thick	m²	0.17	2.89	-	8.11	11.00	12.10	11.025
P106015	**Rockwool fire barrier; foil faced one side; thickness**								
P106015A	60 mm thick	m²	0.20	3.40	-	14.29	17.69	19.46	13.230
P1080	**Fire stops**								
P108010	**Rockwool fire stops; fitted between top of masonry wall and underside of concrete soffit; size of void**								
P108010A	30 mm deep x 100 mm wide	m	0.06	1.02	-	0.71	1.73	1.90	6.615
P108010B	50 mm deep x 100 mm wide	m	0.07	1.19	-	1.20	2.39	2.63	11.025
P108010C	100 mm deep x 100 mm wide	m	0.09	1.53	-	2.38	3.91	4.30	22.050
P108010D	30 mm deep x 150 mm wide	m	0.07	1.19	-	1.07	2.26	2.49	6.615
P108010E	50 mm deep x 150 mm wide	m	0.08	1.36	-	1.78	3.14	3.45	11.025
P108010F	100 mm deep x 150 mm wide	m	0.10	1.70	-	3.58	5.28	5.81	22.050
P108010G	30 mm deep x 200 mm wide	m	0.08	1.36	-	1.43	2.79	3.07	6.615
P108010H	50 mm deep x 200 mm wide	m	0.10	1.70	-	2.38	4.08	4.49	11.025
P108010I	100 mm deep x 200 mm wide	m	0.12	2.04	-	4.77	6.81	7.49	22.050

Major Works 2011		Unit	Labour Hours	Labour Net	Plant Net	Materials Net	Unit Net	Unit with 10%	CO$_2$
				£	£	£	£	£	Kg
P11	**P11: FOAMED, FIBRE AND BEAD CAVITY WALL INSULATION**								
P1101	**Blown fibre cavity insulation**								
P110101	**Granulated mineral fibre; drilling walls internally or externally and making good on completion; width of cavity**								
P110101A	50 mm	m^2	0.06	2.71	0.41	0.51	3.63	3.99	2.437
P110101B	75 mm	m^2	0.06	2.80	0.42	0.76	3.98	4.38	2.653
P110101C	100 mm	m^2	0.06	2.94	0.44	1.01	4.39	4.83	2.869

Building Fabric Sundries

Major Works 2011	Unit	Labour Hours	Labour Net	Plant Net	Materials Net	Unit Net	Unit with 10%	CO₂
			£	£	£	£	£	Kg
P20	**P20: UNFRAMED ISOLATED TRIMS, SKIRTINGS AND SUNDRY ITEMS**							
P2011	**Architraves, skirtings, picture rails or the like; wrought softwood; basic sizes**							
P201101	**Architraves; bullnosed or chamfered and rounded**							
P201101A	19 x 50 mm	m	0.08	1.36	-	0.76	2.12	2.33	0.275
P201101B	19 x 75 mm	m	0.08	1.36	-	1.13	2.49	2.74	0.399
P201101C	19 x 100 mm	m	0.08	1.36	-	1.48	2.84	3.12	0.522
P201101D	25 x 50 mm	m	0.08	1.36	-	1.00	2.36	2.60	0.353
P201101E	25 x 75 mm	m	0.08	1.36	-	1.48	2.84	3.12	0.516
P201101F	25 x 100 mm	m	0.08	1.36	-	1.96	3.32	3.65	0.678
P201105	**Architraves; moulded**							
P201105G	19 x 50 mm	m	0.10	1.70	-	0.94	2.64	2.90	0.275
P201105H	19 x 75 mm	m	0.10	1.70	-	1.38	3.08	3.39	0.399
P201105I	19 x 100 mm	m	0.10	1.70	-	1.84	3.54	3.89	0.522
P201105J	25 x 50 mm	m	0.12	2.04	-	1.30	3.34	3.67	0.353
P201105K	25 x 75 mm	m	0.12	2.04	-	1.95	3.99	4.39	0.516
P201105L	25 x 100 mm	m	0.12	2.04	-	2.94	4.98	5.48	0.678
P201105M	25 x 125 mm	m	0.14	2.38	-	3.69	6.07	6.68	0.840
P201105N	25 x 150 mm	m	0.14	2.38	-	3.87	6.25	6.88	1.003
P201105O	25 x 175 mm	m	0.14	2.38	-	4.59	6.97	7.67	1.165
P201116	**Skirtings; bullnosed or chamfered and rounded**							
P201116A	19 x 75 mm	m	0.08	1.36	-	1.12	2.48	2.73	0.399
P201116B	19 x 100 mm	m	0.08	1.36	-	1.48	2.84	3.12	0.522
P201117	**Skirtings; dual purpose**							
P201117C	19 x 100 mm	m	0.08	1.36	-	1.84	3.20	3.52	0.522
P201118	**Skirtings; pencil rounded**							
P201118D	25 x 75 mm	m	0.08	1.36	-	1.48	2.84	3.12	0.516
P201118E	25 x 100 mm	m	0.08	1.36	-	1.96	3.32	3.65	0.678
P201118F	25 x 150 mm	m	0.10	1.70	-	2.92	4.62	5.08	1.003
P201119	**Skirtings; moulded**							
P201119G	19 x 125 mm	m	0.12	2.04	-	2.27	4.31	4.74	0.646
P201119H	19 x 175 mm	m	0.14	2.38	-	3.22	5.60	6.16	0.892
P201119I	25 x 100 mm	m	0.12	2.04	-	2.94	4.98	5.48	0.678
P201119J	25 x 125 mm	m	0.14	2.38	-	3.69	6.07	6.68	0.840
P201119K	25 x 150 mm	m	0.14	2.38	-	3.87	6.25	6.88	1.003
P201119L	25 x 175 mm	m	0.14	2.38	-	4.59	6.97	7.67	1.165
P201126	**Picture rails; moulded**							
P201126A	19 x 50 mm	m	0.10	1.70	-	0.93	2.63	2.89	0.275
P201126B	25 x 50 mm	m	0.10	1.70	-	1.22	2.92	3.21	0.353
P201126C	25 x 75 mm	m	0.12	2.04	-	1.53	3.57	3.93	0.516
P201126D	32 x 75 mm	m	0.12	2.04	-	1.96	4.00	4.40	0.652
P201136	**Dado rails; moulded**							
P201136A	13 x 25 mm	m	0.10	1.70	-	0.50	2.20	2.42	0.112
P201136B	19 x 38 mm	m	0.10	1.70	-	0.76	2.46	2.71	0.216
P201136C	25 x 50 mm	m	0.12	2.04	-	1.29	3.33	3.66	0.353
P201136D	25 x 63 mm	m	0.12	2.04	-	1.66	3.70	4.07	0.438
P2016	**Architraves, skirtings or the like; MDF mouldings; basic sizes**							
P201601	**Architraves**							
P201601A	18 x 75 mm Torus	m	0.10	1.70	-	2.85	4.55	5.01	0.673
P201601B	18 x 63 mm Torus	m	0.10	1.70	-	2.44	4.14	4.55	0.570
P201601C	18 x 75 mm Ogee	m	0.10	1.70	-	2.85	4.55	5.01	0.673
P201601D	18 x 63 mm Ogee	m	0.10	1.70	-	2.44	4.14	4.55	0.570
P201601E	14.5 x 50 mm chamfered and rounded	m	0.08	1.36	-	1.70	3.06	3.37	0.375
P201601F	14.5 x 50 mm pencil rounded	m	0.08	1.36	-	1.70	3.06	3.37	0.375
P201602	**Skirtings**							
P201602A	18 x 175 mm Torus	m	0.14	2.38	-	5.98	8.36	9.20	1.647
P201602B	18 x 150 mm Torus	m	0.14	2.38	-	5.15	7.53	8.28	1.432
P201602C	18 x 125 mm Torus	m	0.14	2.38	-	4.33	6.71	7.38	1.217
P201602D	18 x 150 mm Ogee	m	0.14	2.38	-	5.15	7.53	8.28	1.432
P201602E	18 x 125 mm Ogee	m	0.14	2.38	-	4.33	6.71	7.38	1.217
P201602F	14.5 x 100 mm chamfered and rounded	m	0.08	1.36	-	3.28	4.64	5.10	0.750

Major Works 2011		Unit	Labour Hours	Labour Net	Plant Net	Materials Net	Unit Net	Unit with 10%	CO$_2$
				£	£	£	£	£	Kg
P20	**P20: UNFRAMED ISOLATED TRIMS, SKIRTINGS AND SUNDRY ITEMS**								
P2016	**Architraves, skirtings or the like; MDF mouldings; basic sizes**								
P201602	**Skirtings**								
P201602G	14.5 x 75 mm chamfered and rounded	m	0.08	1.36	-	2.48	3.84	4.22	0.576
P201602H	14.5 x 100 mm pencil rounded	m	0.08	1.36	-	3.68	5.04	5.54	0.750
P201602I	14.5 x 75 mm pencil rounded	m	0.08	1.36	-	2.79	4.15	4.57	0.576
P2021	**Cover fillets, trims or the like; wrought softwood; basic sizes**								
P202104	**Cover fillets**								
P202104A	13 x 25 mm	m	0.05	0.85	-	0.58	1.43	1.57	0.113
P202104B	13 x 50 mm	m	0.05	0.85	-	1.11	1.96	2.16	0.197
P202104C	13 x 75 mm	m	0.05	0.85	-	1.50	2.35	2.59	0.281
P2022	**Beads, stops or the like; wrought softwood; basic sizes**								
P202216	**Beads**								
P202216A	6 x 13 mm	m	0.05	0.85	-	0.21	1.06	1.17	0.048
P202216B	6 x 19 mm	m	0.05	0.85	-	0.32	1.17	1.29	0.058
P202216C	6 x 25 mm	m	0.05	0.85	-	0.44	1.29	1.42	0.067
P202216D	13 x 13 mm	m	0.08	1.36	-	0.32	1.68	1.85	0.072
P202216E	13 x 19 mm	m	0.08	1.36	-	0.44	1.80	1.98	0.092
P202216F	13 x 25 mm	m	0.08	1.36	-	0.58	1.94	2.13	0.113
P202216G	13 x 32 mm	m	0.08	1.36	-	0.74	2.10	2.31	0.136
P202216H	19 x 19 mm	m	0.10	1.70	-	0.58	2.28	2.51	0.123
P202216I	19 x 25 mm	m	0.10	1.70	-	0.78	2.48	2.73	0.151
P202216J	19 x 32 mm	m	0.10	1.70	-	0.89	2.59	2.85	0.186
P202217	**Stops**								
P202217A	13 x 25 mm	m	0.05	0.85	-	0.58	1.43	1.57	0.113
P202217B	13 x 38 mm	m	0.05	0.85	-	0.84	1.69	1.86	0.156
P202217C	13 x 50 mm	m	0.05	0.85	-	1.11	1.96	2.16	0.197
P202217D	19 x 25 mm	m	0.08	1.36	-	0.78	2.14	2.35	0.151
P202217E	19 x 38 mm	m	0.08	1.36	-	0.99	2.35	2.59	0.216
P202217F	19 x 50 mm	m	0.08	1.36	-	1.27	2.63	2.89	0.275
P202217G	25 x 25 mm	m	0.10	1.70	-	1.10	2.80	3.08	0.191
P202217H	25 x 38 mm	m	0.10	1.70	-	1.28	2.98	3.28	0.275
P202217I	25 x 50 mm	m	0.10	1.70	-	1.38	3.08	3.39	0.354
P2024	**Edgings, nosings or the like; wrought softwood; basic sizes**								
P202423	**Edgings**								
P202423A	13 mm quadrant	m	0.08	1.36	-	0.29	1.65	1.82	0.063
P202423B	19 mm quadrant	m	0.08	1.36	-	0.59	1.95	2.15	0.102
P202423C	25 mm quadrant	m	0.08	1.36	-	1.13	2.49	2.74	1.028
P202423D	32 mm quadrant	m	0.08	1.36	-	1.28	2.64	2.90	0.237
P202423E	19 mm half round	m	0.08	1.36	-	0.59	1.95	2.15	0.175
P202423F	25 mm half round	m	0.08	1.36	-	1.12	2.48	2.73	2.028
P202423G	38 mm half round	m	0.08	1.36	-	1.47	2.83	3.11	0.617
P202423H	19 mm rebated half round	m	0.10	1.70	-	0.88	2.58	2.84	0.175
P202423I	25 x 25 mm scotia	m	0.10	1.70	-	1.34	3.04	3.34	0.665
P202423J	38 x 38 mm scotia	m	0.12	2.04	-	1.70	3.74	4.11	0.216
P202423K	50 x 50 mm scotia	m	0.12	2.04	-	2.55	4.59	5.05	0.353
P202425	**Nosings**								
P202425A	25 x 50 mm; nosed	m	0.15	2.55	-	1.66	4.21	4.63	0.353
P202425B	32 x 50 mm; nosed	m	0.15	2.55	-	1.78	4.33	4.76	0.444
P202425C	32 x 50 mm; nosed scotia	m	0.15	2.55	-	2.06	4.61	5.07	0.236
P2025	**1.5 mm laminated plastic covering; fixing with adhesive**								
P202531	**Edgings**								
P202531A	9 mm wide	m	0.20	3.40	-	0.65	4.05	4.46	0.067
P202531B	12 mm wide	m	0.20	3.40	-	0.81	4.21	4.63	0.084
P202531C	15 mm wide	m	0.20	3.40	-	1.11	4.51	4.96	0.119
P202531D	18 mm wide	m	0.22	3.74	-	1.30	5.04	5.54	0.134
P202531E	22 mm wide	m	0.22	3.74	-	1.53	5.27	5.80	0.156
P202531F	25 mm wide	m	0.22	3.74	-	1.84	5.58	6.14	0.191

Building Fabric Sundries

		Unit	Labour Hours	Labour Net £	Plant Net £	Materials Net £	Unit Net £	Unit with 10% £	CO₂ Kg
P20	**P20: UNFRAMED ISOLATED TRIMS, SKIRTINGS AND SUNDRY ITEMS**								
P2030	**Shelving; MDF; medium density fibreboard**								
P203001	**Solid shelving; 15 mm thick**								
P203001A	not exceeding 150 mm wide	m	0.21	3.57	-	0.73	4.30	4.73	1.090
P203001B	150 - 300 mm wide	m	0.24	4.08	-	1.44	5.52	6.07	2.152
P203001C	over 300 mm wide	m²	0.83	14.09	-	4.67	18.76	20.64	6.998
P203002	**Solid shelving; 18 mm thick**								
P203002A	not exceeding 150 mm wide	m	0.22	3.74	-	1.00	4.74	5.21	1.303
P203002B	150 - 300 mm wide	m	0.25	4.25	-	1.99	6.24	6.86	2.577
P203002C	over 300 mm wide	m²	0.85	14.43	-	6.47	20.90	22.99	8.392
P203003	**Solid shelving; 25 mm thick**								
P203003D	not exceeding 150 mm wide	m	0.23	3.91	-	1.45	5.36	5.90	1.798
P203003E	150 - 300 mm wide	m	0.26	4.41	-	2.88	7.29	8.02	3.568
P203003F	over 300 mm wide	m²	0.88	14.94	-	9.41	24.35	26.79	11.644
P2031	**Shelving; wrought softwood; basic sizes**								
P203162	**Cross-tongued solid shelving**								
P203162A	19 mm thick; not exceeding 150 mm wide	m	0.22	3.74	-	2.57	6.31	6.94	0.781
P203162B	19 mm thick; 150 - 300 mm wide	m	0.25	4.25	-	5.12	9.37	10.31	1.533
P203162C	19 mm thick; over 300 mm wide	m²	0.85	14.43	-	16.76	31.19	34.31	4.966
P203162D	25 mm thick; not exceeding 150 mm wide	m	0.23	3.91	-	2.89	6.80	7.48	1.018
P203162E	25 mm thick; 150 - 300 mm wide	m	0.26	4.41	-	5.76	10.17	11.19	2.008
P203162F	25 mm thick; over 300 mm wide	m²	0.88	14.94	-	18.86	33.80	37.18	6.526
P203163	**Slatted shelving**								
P203163A	19 x 38 mm at 50 mm centres	m²	1.30	22.07	-	19.75	41.82	46.00	4.353
P203163B	25 x 50 mm at 75 mm centres	m²	0.95	16.13	-	18.35	34.48	37.93	4.736
P203163C	25 x 75 mm at 100 mm centres	m²	0.70	11.89	-	19.34	31.23	34.35	5.183
P203164	**Removable slatted shelving**								
P203164A	19 x 38 mm at 50 mm centres; 19 x 38 mm cross-bearers	m²	1.50	25.47	-	22.67	48.14	52.95	4.945
P203164B	25 x 50 mm at 75 mm centres; 25 x 50 mm cross-bearers	m²	1.10	18.68	-	22.43	41.11	45.22	5.741
P203164C	25 x 75 mm at 100 mm centres; 25 x 50 mm cross-bearers	m²	0.90	15.28	-	18.97	34.25	37.68	4.895
P2032	**Shelving; birch faced SI grade BR bonding blockboard, BS 3444**								
P203201	**Solid shelving; 18 mm thick**								
P203201A	not exceeding 150 mm wide	m	0.22	3.74	-	3.76	7.50	8.25	0.889
P203201B	150 - 300 mm wide	m	0.25	4.25	-	7.51	11.76	12.94	1.751
P203201C	over 300 mm wide	m²	0.85	14.43	-	24.58	39.01	42.91	5.679
P203202	**Solid shelving; 25 mm thick**								
P203202D	not exceeding 150 mm wide	m	0.23	3.91	-	4.94	8.85	9.74	1.176
P203202E	150 - 300 mm wide	m	0.26	4.41	-	9.85	14.26	15.69	2.325
P203202F	over 300 mm wide	m²	0.88	14.94	-	32.28	47.22	51.94	7.563
P2033	**Chipboard; faced all sides with 1.5 mm Class 1 laminated plastic covering**								
P203372	**Solid shelving; 15 mm thick**								
P203372A	not exceeding 150 mm wide	m	0.28	4.75	-	0.75	5.50	6.05	0.838
P203372B	150 - 300 mm wide	m	0.32	5.43	-	1.42	6.85	7.54	1.609
P203372C	over 300 mm wide	m²	1.10	18.68	-	4.47	23.15	25.47	5.105
P2034	**Laminated plastic covering; Class 1; fixing with adhesive**								
P203474	**To shelving; 1.5 mm thick**								
P203474A	not exceeding 150 mm wide	m	0.45	7.64	-	4.61	12.25	13.48	0.963
P203474B	150 - 300 mm wide	m	0.65	11.04	-	9.21	20.25	22.28	1.925
P203474C	over 300 mm wide	m²	1.20	20.38	-	30.11	50.49	55.54	6.300

Major Works 2011		Unit	Labour Hours	Labour Net	Plant Net	Materials Net	Unit Net	Unit with 10%	CO$_2$
				£	£	£	£	£	Kg
P20	**P20: UNFRAMED ISOLATED TRIMS, SKIRTINGS AND SUNDRY ITEMS**								
P2038	**Fittings; worktops, seats or the like**								
P203809	**MDF; medium density fibreboard; 15 mm thick**								
P203809F	15 x 450 mm	m	0.24	4.08	-	2.17	6.25	6.88	3.243
P203809G	15 x 500 mm	m	0.26	4.41	-	2.44	6.85	7.54	3.641
P203809H	15 x 600 mm	m	0.29	4.92	-	2.93	7.85	8.64	4.371
P203809I	15 x 750 mm	m	0.31	5.26	-	3.63	8.89	9.78	5.433
P203809J	15 x 900 mm	m	0.33	5.60	-	4.34	9.94	10.93	6.495
P203810	**MDF; medium density fibreboard; 18 mm thick**								
P203810A	18 x 450 mm	m	0.25	4.25	-	2.99	7.24	7.96	3.880
P203810B	18 x 500 mm	m	0.27	4.58	-	3.36	7.94	8.73	4.358
P203810C	18 x 600 mm	m	0.30	5.09	-	4.04	9.13	10.04	5.234
P203810D	18 x 750 mm	m	0.32	5.43	-	5.02	10.45	11.50	6.508
P203810E	18 x 900 mm	m	0.34	5.77	-	6.00	11.77	12.95	7.783
P203812	**MDF; medium density fibreboard; 25 mm thick**								
P203812F	25 x 450 mm	m	0.25	4.25	-	4.34	8.59	9.45	5.367
P203812G	25 x 500 mm	m	0.27	4.58	-	4.87	9.45	10.40	6.031
P203812H	25 x 600 mm	m	0.30	5.09	-	5.86	10.95	12.05	7.248
P203812I	25 x 750 mm	m	0.32	5.43	-	7.29	12.72	13.99	9.018
P203812J	25 x 900 mm	m	0.34	5.77	-	8.72	14.49	15.94	10.788
P203822	**Wrought softwood cross-tongued boarding; 19 mm thick**								
P203822A	19 x 450 mm	m	0.25	4.25	-	7.70	11.95	13.15	2.314
P203822B	19 x 500 mm	m	0.27	4.58	-	8.65	13.23	14.55	2.596
P203822C	19 x 600 mm	m	0.30	5.09	-	10.41	15.50	17.05	3.114
P203822D	19 x 750 mm	m	0.32	5.43	-	12.96	18.39	20.23	3.866
P203822E	19 x 900 mm	m	0.34	5.77	-	15.51	21.28	23.41	4.619
P203823	**Wrought softwood cross-tongued boarding; 25 mm thick**								
P203823F	25 x 450 mm	m	0.25	4.25	-	8.66	12.91	14.20	3.027
P203823G	25 x 500 mm	m	0.27	4.58	-	9.73	14.31	15.74	3.398
P203823H	25 x 600 mm	m	0.30	5.09	-	11.71	16.80	18.48	4.079
P203823I	25 x 750 mm	m	0.32	5.43	-	14.58	20.01	22.01	5.069
P203823J	25 x 900 mm	m	0.34	5.77	-	17.45	23.22	25.54	6.059
P203843	**Birch faced SI grade, BR bonding blockboard boarding; BS 3444; 18 mm thick**								
P203843A	18 x 450 mm	m	0.25	4.25	-	11.27	15.52	17.07	2.640
P203843B	18 x 500 mm	m	0.27	4.58	-	12.68	17.26	18.99	2.963
P203843C	18 x 600 mm	m	0.30	5.09	-	15.25	20.34	22.37	3.555
P203843D	18 x 750 mm	m	0.32	5.43	-	18.99	24.42	26.86	4.416
P203843E	18 x 900 mm	m	0.34	5.77	-	22.73	28.50	31.35	5.277
P203844	**Birch faced SI grade, BR bonding blockboard boarding; BS 3444; 25 mm thick**								
P203844F	25 x 450 mm	m	0.25	4.25	-	14.79	19.04	20.94	3.501
P203844G	25 x 500 mm	m	0.27	4.58	-	16.63	21.21	23.33	3.932
P203844H	25 x 600 mm	m	0.30	5.09	-	20.01	25.10	27.61	4.721
P203844I	25 x 750 mm	m	0.32	5.43	-	24.93	30.36	33.40	5.869
P203844J	25 x 900 mm	m	0.34	5.77	-	29.84	35.61	39.17	7.017
P203864	**Birch faced grade BB interior quality plywood boarding; BS 1455; 15 mm thick**								
P203864A	15 x 450 mm	m	0.22	3.74	-	6.86	10.60	11.66	3.206
P203864B	15 x 500 mm	m	0.24	4.08	-	7.71	11.79	12.97	3.600
P203864C	15 x 600 mm	m	0.26	4.41	-	9.28	13.69	15.06	4.321
P203864D	15 x 750 mm	m	0.28	4.75	-	11.55	16.30	17.93	5.371
P203864E	15 x 900 mm	m	0.30	5.09	-	13.82	18.91	20.80	6.421
P203865	**Birch faced grade BB interior quality plywood boarding; BS 1455; 18 mm thick**								
P203865F	18 x 450 mm	m	0.22	3.74	-	8.29	12.03	13.23	3.836
P203865G	18 x 500 mm	m	0.24	4.08	-	9.32	13.40	14.74	4.308

Major Works 2011		Unit	Labour Hours	Labour Net	Plant Net	Materials Net	Unit Net	Unit with 10%	CO$_2$
				£	£	£	£	£	Kg
P20	**P20: UNFRAMED ISOLATED TRIMS, SKIRTINGS AND SUNDRY ITEMS**								
P2038	**Fittings; worktops, seats or the like**								
P203865	**Birch faced grade BB interior quality plywood boarding; BS 1455; 18 mm thick**								
P203865H	18 x 600 mm	m	0.26	4.41	-	11.21	15.62	17.18	5.174
P203865I	18 x 750 mm	m	0.28	4.75	-	13.96	18.71	20.58	6.434
P203865J	18 x 900 mm	m	0.30	5.09	-	16.71	21.80	23.98	7.693
P203866	**Birch faced grade BB interior quality plywood boarding; BS 1455; 25 mm thick**								
P203866K	25 x 450 mm	m	0.25	4.25	-	10.93	15.18	16.70	5.305
P203866L	25 x 500 mm	m	0.27	4.58	-	12.29	16.87	18.56	5.962
P203866M	25 x 600 mm	m	0.30	5.09	-	14.78	19.87	21.86	7.164
P203866N	25 x 750 mm	m	0.32	5.43	-	18.41	23.84	26.22	8.914
P203866O	25 x 900 mm	m	0.34	5.77	-	22.04	27.81	30.59	10.664
P2041	**Window boards or the like; wrought softwood; basic sizes**								
P204124	**Window boards; nosed and tongued**								
P204124A	25 x 150 mm	m	0.40	6.79	-	5.43	12.22	13.44	1.102
P204124B	25 x 175 mm	m	0.40	6.79	-	6.10	12.89	14.18	1.335
P204124C	25 x 200 mm	m	0.42	7.13	-	6.02	13.15	14.47	1.404
P204124D	25 x 225 mm	m	0.42	7.13	-	7.37	14.50	15.95	1.660
P204124E	25 x 250 mm	m	0.44	7.47	-	7.97	15.44	16.98	1.822
P2043	**Window boards or the like; MDF mouldings; basic sizes**								
P204301	**Window boards**								
P204301A	25 x 175 mm	m	0.40	6.79	-	7.44	14.23	15.65	2.289
P204301B	25 x 200 mm	m	0.42	7.13	-	8.67	15.80	17.38	2.588
P204301C	25 x 225 mm	m	0.43	7.30	-	9.40	16.70	18.37	2.886
P204301D	25 x 250 mm	m	0.44	7.47	-	10.45	17.92	19.71	3.185
P204301E	25 x 275 mm	m	0.45	7.64	-	11.69	19.33	21.26	3.483
P2071	**Handrails or balustrades; wrought softwood; basic sizes**								
P207101	**Handrails; mopstick**								
P207101A	50 mm dia	m	0.40	6.79	-	3.09	9.88	10.87	0.741
P207152	**Handrails; moulded**								
P207152B	50 x 75 mm; moulded	m	0.40	6.79	-	4.44	11.23	12.35	1.113
P207152C	50 x 100 mm; moulded	m	0.45	7.64	-	6.61	14.25	15.68	1.344
P207152D	63 x 100 mm; moulded	m	0.45	7.64	-	8.01	15.65	17.22	1.657
P207152E	75 x 100 mm; moulded	m	0.50	8.49	-	9.89	18.38	20.22	1.946
P207153	**Balustrades; 25 x 25 mm balusters housed at 100 mm centres; 50 x 75 mm moulded handrail; 25 x 75 mm string capping**								
P207153A	900 mm high; horizontal	m	2.80	47.54	-	39.74	87.28	96.01	5.890
P207153B	1000 mm high; horizontal	m	2.80	47.54	-	42.99	90.53	99.58	6.341
P207153C	900 mm high; raking	m	3.60	61.13	-	39.74	100.87	110.96	5.890
P207153D	1000 mm high; raking	m	3.60	61.13	-	42.99	104.12	114.53	6.341
P207154	**Newels**								
P207154A	75 x 75 mm	m	0.30	5.09	-	41.48	46.57	51.23	1.551
P207154B	100 x 100 mm	m	0.30	5.09	-	49.71	54.80	60.28	2.605

Major Works 2011		Unit	Labour Hours	Labour Net	Plant Net	Materials Net	Unit Net	Unit with 10%	CO$_2$
				£	£	£	£	£	Kg
P21	**P21: IRONMONGERY**								
P2101	**General ironmongery**								
P210101	**Supply and fit ironmongery to woodwork backgrounds; hinges**								
P210101A	75 mm pressed steel butts	Pr	0.15	2.55	-	0.34	2.89	3.18	0.204
P210101B	100 mm pressed steel butts	Pr	0.17	2.89	-	0.66	3.55	3.91	0.460
P210101C	125 mm pressed steel butts	Pr	0.19	3.23	-	0.90	4.13	4.54	0.513
P210101D	75 mm rising butts	Pr	0.25	4.25	-	1.94	6.19	6.81	0.204
P210101E	100 mm rising butts	Pr	0.27	4.58	-	2.75	7.33	8.06	0.460
P210101F	125 mm rising butts	Pr	0.29	4.92	-	3.26	8.18	9.00	0.513
P210101G	75 mm lift off butts	Pr	0.25	4.25	-	5.01	9.26	10.19	0.584
P210101H	100 mm lift off butts	Pr	0.27	4.58	-	9.03	13.61	14.97	0.779
P210101I	125 mm lift off butts	Pr	0.29	4.92	-	11.04	15.96	17.56	0.974
P210101J	100 mm Parliament hinges	Pr	0.50	8.49	-	12.68	21.17	23.29	0.935
P210101K	300 mm tee hinges	Pr	0.30	5.09	-	1.26	6.35	6.99	1.027
P210101L	400 mm tee hinges	Pr	0.40	6.79	-	2.51	9.30	10.23	1.369
P210101M	500 mm tee hinges	Pr	0.50	8.49	-	5.02	13.51	14.86	1.711
P210101N	450 mm hook and band hinges	Pr	0.75	12.73	-	12.39	25.12	27.63	2.071
P210101O	600 mm hook and band hinges	Pr	0.90	15.28	-	17.62	32.90	36.19	2.761
P210101P	750 mm hook and band hinges	Pr	1.05	17.83	-	26.09	43.92	48.31	3.452
P210101Q	900 mm hook and band hinges	Pr	1.20	20.38	-	45.16	65.54	72.09	4.142
P210103	**Supply and fit ironmongery to woodwork backgrounds; locks and latches**								
P210103A	rebated mortice lock	Nr	0.70	11.89	-	14.60	26.49	29.14	2.124
P210103B	deadlocking cylinder night latch	Nr	0.75	12.73	-	32.68	45.41	49.95	2.655
P210103C	escutcheon	Nr	0.05	0.85	-	1.26	2.11	2.32	0.443
P210103R	rim latch	Nr	0.80	13.58	-	7.48	21.06	23.17	0.885
P210103S	mortice latch	Nr	0.55	9.34	-	4.18	13.52	14.87	0.531
P210103T	rebated mortice latch	Nr	0.70	11.89	-	14.60	26.49	29.14	2.213
P210103U	locking mortice latch	Nr	0.65	11.04	-	12.33	23.37	25.71	1.770
P210103V	Norfolk/Suffolk latch	Nr	0.75	12.73	-	5.56	18.29	20.12	0.885
P210103W	automatic gate latch	Nr	0.60	10.19	-	6.38	16.57	18.23	0.885
P210103X	ball catch	Nr	0.30	5.09	-	5.15	10.24	11.26	0.443
P210103Y	rim lock	Nr	0.80	13.58	-	12.48	26.06	28.67	1.328
P210103Z	mortice lock	Nr	0.55	9.34	-	20.43	29.77	32.75	1.770
P210105	**Supply and fit ironmongery to woodwork backgrounds; door closers**								
P210105D	overhead door closer single action	Nr	0.90	15.28	-	88.92	104.20	114.62	3.098
P210105E	overhead door closer double action	Nr	1.10	18.68	-	162.18	180.86	198.95	5.310
P210105F	Perko door closer	Nr	0.60	10.19	-	11.14	21.33	23.46	1.947
P210106	**Supply and fit ironmongery to woodwork backgrounds; door bolts**								
P210106G	100 mm barrel bolt	Nr	0.25	4.25	-	3.46	7.71	8.48	0.354
P210106H	150 mm barrel bolt	Nr	0.30	5.09	-	4.52	9.61	10.57	0.513
P210106I	225 mm barrel bolt	Nr	0.35	5.94	-	5.75	11.69	12.86	0.797
P210106J	300 mm barrel bolt	Nr	0.40	6.79	-	7.76	14.55	16.01	1.062
P210106K	450 mm barrel bolt	Nr	0.50	8.49	-	9.40	17.89	19.68	1.593
P210106L	450 mm monkey tail bolts	Nr	0.60	10.19	-	18.10	28.29	31.12	2.124
P210106M	600 mm monkey tail bolts	Nr	0.75	12.73	-	22.17	34.90	38.39	2.124
P210106N	750 mm monkey tail bolts	Nr	1.00	16.98	-	44.34	61.32	67.45	2.655
P210106O	100 mm flush bolts	Nr	0.50	8.49	-	10.00	18.49	20.34	0.354
P210106P	150 mm flush bolts	Nr	0.60	10.19	-	15.00	25.19	27.71	0.513
P210106Q	225 mm flush bolts	Nr	0.70	11.89	-	20.00	31.89	35.08	0.797
P210106R	300 mm flush bolts	Nr	0.80	13.58	-	25.00	38.58	42.44	1.062
P210106S	WC indicator bolt	Nr	0.50	8.49	-	8.92	17.41	19.15	0.797
P210106T	single door panic bolt	Nr	0.90	15.28	-	48.64	63.92	70.31	3.098
P210106U	double door panic bolt	Nr	1.40	23.77	-	59.13	82.90	91.19	6.195
P210109	**Supply and fit ironmongery to woodwork backgrounds; door furniture**								
P210109A	lever furniture	Set	0.25	4.25	-	14.93	19.18	21.10	2.655
P210109B	knob furniture	Set	0.30	5.09	-	17.92	23.01	25.31	3.186
P210109C	cupboard knobs	Nr	0.20	3.40	-	6.47	9.87	10.86	1.770
P210109Z	escutcheon	Nr	0.05	0.85	-	1.26	2.11	2.32	0.443
P210110	**Supply and fit ironmongery to woodwork backgrounds; handles and plates**								
P210110D	150 mm pull handles	Nr	0.20	3.40	-	6.76	10.16	11.18	0.443
P210110E	225 mm pull handles	Nr	0.25	4.25	-	7.88	12.13	13.34	0.664
P210110F	300 mm pull handles	Nr	0.30	5.09	-	10.17	15.26	16.79	0.885

Building Fabric Sundries

		Unit	Labour Hours	Labour Net	Plant Net	Materials Net	Unit Net	Unit with 10%	CO₂
				£	£	£	£	£	Kg
P21	**P21: IRONMONGERY**								
P2101	**General ironmongery**								
P210110	**Supply and fit ironmongery to woodwork backgrounds; handles and plates**								
P210110G	450 mm pull handles	Nr	0.35	5.94	-	14.67	20.61	22.67	1.328
P210110H	600 mm pull handles	Nr	0.40	6.79	-	12.46	19.25	21.18	1.770
P210110I	200 mm push plates	Nr	0.15	2.55	-	6.37	8.92	9.81	0.664
P210110J	300 mm push plates	Nr	0.20	3.40	-	7.59	10.99	12.09	0.885
P210110K	600 mm push plates	Nr	0.25	4.25	-	8.91	13.16	14.48	1.770
P210110L	600 x 225 mm kick plates	Nr	0.35	5.94	-	6.74	12.68	13.95	2.237
P210110M	750 x 225 mm kick plates	Nr	0.40	6.79	-	7.07	13.86	15.25	2.796
P210110N	900 x 225 mm kick plates	Nr	0.45	7.64	-	8.95	16.59	18.25	3.355
P210111	**Supply and fit ironmongery to woodwork backgrounds; window furniture**								
P210111O	250 mm casement stay	Nr	0.25	4.25	-	4.35	8.60	9.46	0.239
P210111P	450 mm casement stay	Nr	0.30	5.09	-	6.47	11.56	12.72	0.239
P210111Q	casement fastener	Nr	0.15	2.55	-	4.51	7.06	7.77	0.239
P210111R	sash cockspur fastener	Nr	0.15	2.55	-	4.97	7.52	8.27	0.266
P210111S	sash lift	Nr	0.15	2.55	-	2.99	5.54	6.09	1.236
P210111T	sash pulley and cord	Nr	0.75	12.73	-	19.91	32.64	35.90	1.770
P210112	**Supply and fit ironmongery to woodwork backgrounds; door gear sets**								
P210112A	single door sliding door set	Nr	0.90	15.28	-	18.90	34.18	37.60	2.655
P210112B	double door sliding door set	Nr	1.40	23.77	-	26.74	50.51	55.56	2.921
P210112C	triple door sliding door set	Nr	1.90	32.26	-	45.18	77.44	85.18	3.275
P210112D	double door Bi-Fold gear set	Nr	1.50	25.47	-	26.74	52.21	57.43	2.921
P210112E	triple door Bi-Fold gear set	Nr	1.90	32.26	-	45.18	77.44	85.18	3.275
P210112F	quadruple door Bi-Fold gear set	Nr	2.40	40.75	-	49.33	90.08	99.09	3.452
P210114	**Supply and fit ironmongery to woodwork backgrounds; general items**								
P210114A	towel rail	Nr	0.40	6.79	-	8.54	15.33	16.86	5.310
P210114B	letter plate including hole in door	Nr	0.75	12.73	-	9.36	22.09	24.30	3.098
P210114C	toilet roll holder	Nr	0.25	4.25	-	7.63	11.88	13.07	2.213
P210114D	hat and coat hook	Nr	0.10	1.70	-	2.99	4.69	5.16	1.236
P210114E	padlock hasp and staple	Nr	0.25	4.25	-	4.73	8.98	9.88	0.266
P210114F	rubber door stop	Nr	0.10	1.70	-	0.52	2.22	2.44	0.248
P210114G	curtain track	m	0.40	6.79	-	10.59	17.38	19.12	1.992
P210114H	hanging rail	m	0.45	7.64	-	2.34	9.98	10.98	1.328
P210114I	hanging rail end socket	Nr	0.15	2.55	-	1.48	4.03	4.43	0.266
P210114J	hanging rail centre bracket	Nr	0.15	2.55	-	1.48	4.03	4.43	0.266
P210125	**Supply and fit ironmongery to concrete; drilling, plugging and screwing; floor springs**								
P210125A	single action floor springs	Nr	1.75	29.72	-	194.21	223.93	246.32	5.310
P210125B	double action floor springs	Nr	2.00	33.96	-	269.46	303.42	333.76	6.195
P210125C	rubber door stop	Nr	0.30	5.09	-	0.52	5.61	6.17	0.248
P210136	**Supply and fit ironmongery to masonry; drilling, plugging and screwing; general items**								
P210136A	towel rail	Nr	0.50	8.49	-	8.54	17.03	18.73	5.310
P210136B	toilet roll holder	Nr	0.35	5.94	-	7.63	13.57	14.93	2.213
P210136C	hat and coat hook	Nr	0.20	3.40	-	2.99	6.39	7.03	1.236
P210136D	rubber door stop	Nr	0.20	3.40	-	0.52	3.92	4.31	0.248
P210136E	shelf bracket	Nr	0.25	4.25	-	0.79	5.04	5.54	0.266
P210136F	padlock hasp and staple	Nr	0.35	5.94	-	4.73	10.67	11.74	0.266
P210136G	curtain track	m	0.50	8.49	-	10.59	19.08	20.99	1.992
P210136H	hanging rail	m	0.45	7.64	-	2.34	9.98	10.98	1.328
P210136I	hanging rail end socket	Nr	0.25	4.25	-	1.48	5.73	6.30	0.266
P210136J	hanging rail centre bracket	Nr	0.25	4.25	-	1.48	5.73	6.30	0.266
P210191	**Boulton and Paul ironmongery sets; fixing to woodwork backgrounds**								
P210191A	GENTPAK5L	Set	1.20	20.38	-	45.24	65.62	72.18	5.566
P210191B	VENTPAK5L	Set	1.20	20.38	-	45.24	65.62	72.18	5.566
P210191C	LOCPAK5L	Set	1.20	20.38	-	30.05	50.43	55.47	26.450
P210191D	GFPAK	Set	1.50	25.47	-	50.40	75.87	83.46	4.840
P210191E	VENTPAK	Set	1.50	25.47	-	50.34	75.81	83.39	4.800
P210191F	ENTPAK	Set	1.50	25.47	-	30.95	56.42	62.06	23.000
P210191G	GENTPAK	Set	1.20	20.38	-	30.62	51.00	56.10	4.840
P210191H	VBPAK	Set	1.20	20.38	-	29.87	50.25	55.28	4.840
P210191I	LOCPAK	Set	1.20	20.38	-	16.73	37.11	40.82	23.000

Major Works 2011		Unit	Labour Hours	Labour Net	Plant Net	Materials Net	Unit Net	Unit with 10%	CO$_2$
				£	£	£	£	£	Kg
P21	**P21: IRONMONGERY**								
P2101	**General ironmongery**								
P210191	**Boulton and Paul ironmongery sets; fixing to woodwork backgrounds**								
P210191J	REBPAKG	Set	1.80	30.56	-	68.45	99.01	108.91	4.840
P210191K	REBPAKV	Set	1.80	30.56	-	67.71	98.27	108.10	4.840
P210191L	REBPAK	Set	1.80	30.56	-	16.73	47.29	52.02	23.000
P210191M	GINTPAK	Set	1.00	16.98	-	18.18	35.16	38.68	4.840
P210191N	VINTPAK	Set	1.00	16.98	-	15.73	32.71	35.98	4.840
P210191O	LATPAK	Set	1.00	16.98	-	9.21	26.19	28.81	23.000
P210191P	GILPAK	Set	1.20	20.38	-	31.17	51.55	56.71	4.840
P210191Q	VILPAK	Set	1.20	20.38	-	26.16	46.54	51.19	4.840
P210191R	BATPAK	Set	1.00	16.98	-	15.17	32.15	35.37	23.000
P210192	**Boulton and Paul ironmongery packs; fixing to woodwork backgrounds**								
P210192A	DFMS5L	Nr	0.90	15.28	-	34.16	49.44	54.38	3.630
P210192B	DFLPG; including hole through door	Nr	0.75	12.73	-	13.00	25.73	28.30	2.420
P210192C	DFLPV; including hole through door	Nr	0.75	12.73	-	13.40	26.13	28.74	2.420
P210192D	DFLPA; including hole through door	Nr	0.75	12.73	-	6.15	18.88	20.77	11.500
P210192E	DFKG	Nr	0.25	4.25	-	10.58	14.83	16.31	2.420
P210192F	DFKV	Nr	0.25	4.25	-	9.98	14.23	15.65	2.420
P210192G	DFBG	Nr	0.15	2.55	-	5.39	7.94	8.73	2.420
P210192H	DFBV	Nr	0.15	2.55	-	5.32	7.87	8.66	2.420
P210192I	DFSB8	Nr	0.38	6.45	-	10.66	17.11	18.82	2.420
P210192J	DFSB6	Nr	0.35	5.94	-	7.67	13.61	14.97	2.420
P210192K	DFCB	Nr	0.40	6.79	-	2.19	8.98	9.88	0.605
P210192L	DFCC	Nr	0.40	6.79	-	2.48	9.27	10.20	0.605
P210192M	DFBBB4	Nr	0.25	4.25	-	2.16	6.41	7.05	0.605
P210192N	DFNBB4	Nr	0.28	4.67	-	2.07	6.74	7.41	0.605
P210192O	DFNBA4	Nr	0.28	4.67	-	2.11	6.78	7.46	0.605
P210192P	DFBBA4	Nr	0.25	4.25	-	1.99	6.24	6.86	0.605
P210192Q	DFHGB4	Set	0.30	5.09	-	11.16	16.25	17.88	1.089
P210192R	DFHGS4	Set	0.30	5.09	-	3.63	8.72	9.59	0.688
P210192S	DFHGB3	Set	0.15	2.55	-	6.70	9.25	10.18	0.605
P210192T	DFHGS3	Set	0.15	2.55	-	1.62	4.17	4.59	0.688
P210192U	DFDCS	Nr	0.90	15.28	-	48.09	63.37	69.71	3.438
P210192V	ceramic mortice knob sets	Set	0.80	13.58	-	34.84	48.42	53.26	0.423
P210192W	ceramic privacy adaptors	Nr	0.25	4.25	-	24.89	29.14	32.05	0.325
P210192X	ceramic finger plates	Set	0.25	4.25	-	14.93	19.18	21.10	0.130
P2105	**Security fittings**								
P210513	**Supply and fit security ironmongery to woodwork backgrounds**								
P210513A	door chain	Nr	0.40	6.79	-	3.32	10.11	11.12	0.266
P210513B	door viewer	Nr	0.60	10.19	-	7.25	17.44	19.18	0.266
P210513C	window locks	Nr	0.45	7.64	-	12.25	19.89	21.88	0.885
P2106	**Seals and excluders**								
P210601	**Supply and fit fire resisting intumescent strip to woodwork backgrounds**								
P210601A	Palusol; White	m	0.15	2.55	-	3.94	6.49	7.14	0.633
P210601B	Palusol; Copper	m	0.15	2.55	-	3.94	6.49	7.14	0.791
P210601C	Palusol; White Smoke	m	0.15	2.55	-	8.04	10.59	11.65	1.265
P210601D	Palusol; Copper Smoke	m	0.15	2.55	-	8.04	10.59	11.65	1.580
P210615	**Supply and fit draught excluder seal to woodwork backgrounds**								
P210615A	compression excluder aluminium	m	0.15	2.55	-	17.42	19.97	21.97	1.391
P210615B	brush excluder aluminium	m	0.15	2.55	-	6.25	8.80	9.68	1.391
P210615C	self adhesive rubber	m	0.10	1.70	-	5.15	6.85	7.54	0.318

Building Fabric Sundries

		Unit	Labour Hours	Labour Net £	Plant Net £	Materials Net £	Unit Net £	Unit with 10% £	CO₂ Kg
P30	**P30: TRENCHES, PIPEWAYS AND PITS FOR BURIED ENGINEERING SERVICES**								
P3010	**Excavation of trenches by machine for service pipes, cables and the like including filling and on-site disposal**								
P301001	**Trenches to suit pipes not exceeding 200 mm dia; average depth**								
P301001A	0.50 m	m	0.12	1.52	1.93	-	3.45	3.80	1.737
P301001B	0.75 m	m	0.15	1.90	2.61	-	4.51	4.96	2.340
P301001C	1.00 m	m	0.22	2.79	3.36	-	6.15	6.77	3.028
P3011	**Excavation of trenches by machine for service pipes, cables or the like including filling and off-site disposal**								
P301113	**Trenches to suit pipes not exceeding 200 mm dia; average depth**								
P301113A	0.50 m	m	0.12	1.52	4.02	-	5.54	6.09	1.888
P301113B	0.75 m	m	0.15	1.90	5.73	-	7.63	8.39	2.565
P301113C	1.00 m	m	0.22	2.79	7.56	-	10.35	11.39	3.331
P3015	**Excavation of trenches by hand for service pipes, cables or the like, including disposal and filling**								
P301501	**Trenches to suit pipes not exceeding 200 mm dia; average depth**								
P301501A	0.50 m	m	1.32	16.76	0.10	-	16.86	18.55	0.129
P301501B	0.75 m	m	1.78	22.61	0.10	-	22.71	24.98	0.129
P301501C	1.00 m	m	2.23	28.32	0.17	-	28.49	31.34	0.214
P301542	**Trenches to suit pipes exceeding 200 mm dia; average depth**								
P301542A	0.50 m	m	1.76	22.35	0.14	-	22.49	24.74	0.172
P301542B	0.75 m	m	2.37	30.10	0.14	-	30.24	33.26	0.172
P301542C	1.00 m	m	2.97	37.72	0.23	-	37.95	41.75	0.287
P3040	**Beds for service pipes, ducts, cables and the like**								
P304001	**50 mm sand bed to pipes**								
P304001A	not exceeding 200 mm dia	m	0.06	0.76	0.06	0.57	1.39	1.53	0.738
P3041	**Beds for service pipes, ducts, cables and the like**								
P304131	**100 mm sand bed to pipes**								
P304131A	not exceeding 200 mm dia	m	0.09	1.09	0.10	1.06	2.25	2.48	1.270
P3042	**Beds and coverings for service pipes, ducts, cables or the like**								
P304232	**150 mm bed and 150 mm covering of pea shingle to pipes**								
P304232A	not exceeding 200 mm dia	m	0.20	2.55	0.85	5.96	9.36	10.30	8.390
P304233	**150 mm bed and 150 mm covering of C10P concrete to pipes**								
P304233A	not exceeding 200 mm dia	m	0.25	3.16	0.89	17.79	21.84	24.02	83.708
P3050	**Duct pipework**								
P305001	**Vitrified clay pipes; Hepworth Building Products; HepDuct**								
P305001A	90 mm HepDuct	m	0.18	2.29	-	6.79	9.08	9.99	4.397
P305001B	100 mm HepDuct	m	0.20	2.54	-	7.55	10.09	11.10	4.397
P305001C	125 mm HepDuct	m	0.22	2.79	-	11.56	14.35	15.79	9.449
P305001D	150 mm HepDuct	m	0.23	2.92	-	16.43	19.35	21.29	14.502
P305001E	225 mm HepDuct	m	0.29	3.68	-	39.64	43.32	47.65	23.520

Major Works 2011		Unit	Labour Hours	Labour Net	Plant Net	Materials Net	Unit Net	Unit with 10%	CO$_2$
				£	£	£	£	£	Kg
P30	**P30: TRENCHES, PIPEWAYS AND PITS FOR BURIED ENGINEERING SERVICES**								
P3050	**Duct pipework**								
P305016	**Vitrified clay pipes; Hepworth Building Products; SuperSleve**								
P305016A	100 mm SuperSleve	m	0.20	2.54	-	8.24	10.78	11.86	4.394
P305016B	150 mm SuperSleve	m	0.23	2.92	-	16.31	19.23	21.15	8.277
P305016C	225 mm SuperSleve	m	0.29	3.68	-	34.11	37.79	41.57	15.749
P305024	**Vitrified clay pipes; Hepworth Building Products; HepSeal**								
P305024A	100 mm HepSeal	m	0.22	2.79	-	8.24	11.03	12.13	4.394
P305024B	150 mm HepSeal	m	0.27	3.43	-	16.31	19.74	21.71	8.277
P305024C	225 mm HepSeal	m	0.37	4.70	-	34.11	38.81	42.69	15.749
P305046	**Vitrified clay pipes; Hepworth Building Products; HepLine**								
P305046A	150 mm HepLine	m	0.23	2.92	-	15.78	18.70	20.57	8.235
P305046B	225 mm HepLine	m	0.29	3.68	-	31.82	35.50	39.05	15.984
P305046C	300 mm HepLine	m	0.34	4.32	-	61.95	66.27	72.90	32.485
P305061	**PVC-u pipes; OsmaDrain**								
P305061A	82 mm	m	0.18	2.29	-	10.64	12.93	14.22	3.251
P305061B	110 mm	m	0.20	2.54	-	6.50	9.04	9.94	4.382
P305061C	160 mm	m	0.25	3.17	-	14.94	18.11	19.92	8.023
P305076	**Concrete pipes; BS 5911 Pt 1; Class L**								
P305076A	150 mm	m	0.55	6.99	-	6.31	13.30	14.63	9.595
P305076B	225 mm	m	0.65	8.25	-	9.47	17.72	19.49	21.587
P305076C	300 mm	m	0.70	8.89	7.98	12.63	29.50	32.45	45.413
P305091	**Cast iron pipes; Timesaver; bolted joints**								
P305091A	100 mm	m	0.39	15.35	-	26.32	41.67	45.84	17.047
P305091B	150 mm	m	0.57	22.18	-	54.97	77.15	84.87	24.639
P3055	**Duct pipework fittings**								
P305501	**Vitrified clay fittings; Hepworth Building Products; HepDuct**								
P305501A	90 mm bends	Nr	0.18	2.29	-	6.79	9.08	9.99	2.022
P305501B	100 mm bends	Nr	0.20	2.54	-	7.55	10.09	11.10	2.022
P305501C	125 mm bends	Nr	0.22	2.79	-	11.56	14.35	15.79	2.618
P305501D	150 mm bends	Nr	0.23	2.92	-	16.43	19.35	21.29	3.213
P305501E	225 mm bends	Nr	0.29	3.68	-	39.64	43.32	47.65	3.780
P305516	**Vitrified clay fittings; Hepworth Building Products; SuperSleve**								
P305516A	100 mm bends	Nr	0.20	2.54	-	10.77	13.31	14.64	1.053
P305516B	100 mm rest bends	Nr	0.22	2.79	-	16.17	18.96	20.86	3.899
P305516C	100 x 100 mm junctions	Nr	0.25	3.17	-	48.95	52.12	57.33	1.687
P305516D	150 mm bends	Nr	0.20	2.54	-	14.40	16.94	18.63	2.268
P305516E	150 mm rest bends	Nr	0.22	2.79	-	18.50	21.29	23.42	3.899
P305516F	150 x 100 mm junctions	Nr	0.25	3.17	-	19.27	22.44	24.68	3.402
P305516G	150 x 150 mm junctions	Nr	0.25	3.17	-	21.15	24.32	26.75	4.597
P305524	**Vitrified clay fittings; Hepworth Building Products; HepSleve**								
P305524A	225 mm bends	Nr	0.20	2.54	-	73.43	75.97	83.57	6.431
P305524B	225 mm rest bends	Nr	0.22	2.79	-	80.29	83.08	91.39	10.290
P305524C	225 x 100 mm junctions	Nr	0.25	3.17	-	102.50	105.67	116.24	9.518
P305524D	225 x 150 mm junctions	Nr	0.25	3.17	-	102.50	105.67	116.24	9.354
P305531	**Vitrified clay fittings; Hepworth Building Products; HepSeal**								
P305531A	100 mm bends	Nr	0.20	2.54	-	15.15	17.69	19.46	2.268
P305531B	100 mm rest bends	Nr	0.22	2.79	-	16.17	18.96	20.86	3.899
P305531C	100 x 100 mm junctions	Nr	0.25	3.17	-	22.72	25.89	28.48	3.402
P305531D	150 mm bends	Nr	0.20	2.54	-	34.46	37.00	40.70	2.268
P305531E	150 mm rest bends	Nr	0.22	2.79	-	18.50	21.29	23.42	3.899
P305531F	150 x 100 mm junctions	Nr	0.25	3.17	-	39.89	43.06	47.37	3.402
P305531G	150 x 150 mm junctions	Nr	0.25	3.17	-	45.03	48.20	53.02	4.597
P305531H	225 mm bends	Nr	0.22	2.79	-	80.76	83.55	91.91	6.431
P305531I	225 mm rest bends	Nr	0.25	3.17	-	98.64	101.81	111.99	10.290
P305531J	225 x 100 mm junctions	Nr	0.27	3.43	-	112.72	116.15	127.77	9.518
P305531K	225 x 150 mm junctions	Nr	0.27	3.43	-	112.72	116.15	127.77	9.354
P305531L	300 mm bends	Nr	0.35	4.44	-	139.44	143.88	158.27	17.424
P305531M	300 mm rest bends	Nr	0.38	4.83	-	212.24	217.07	238.78	18.008
P305531N	300 x 100 mm junctions	Nr	0.40	5.08	-	219.47	224.55	247.01	20.910

Building Fabric Sundries

Major Works 2011		Unit	Labour Hours	Labour Net £	Plant Net £	Materials Net £	Unit Net £	Unit with 10% £	CO₂ Kg
P30	**P30: TRENCHES, PIPEWAYS AND PITS FOR BURIED ENGINEERING SERVICES**								
P3055	**Duct pipework fittings**								
P305531	**Vitrified clay fittings; Hepworth Building Products; HepSeal**								
P305531O	300 x 150 mm junctions	Nr	0.40	5.08	–	219.47	224.55	247.01	20.910
P305546	**Vitrified clay fittings; Hepworth Building Products; HepLine**								
P305546A	100 mm bends	Nr	0.20	2.54	–	10.77	13.31	14.64	2.022
P305546B	100 x 100 mm junctions	Nr	0.25	3.17	–	22.72	25.89	28.48	3.733
P305546C	150 mm bends	Nr	0.20	2.54	–	14.40	16.94	18.63	3.213
P305546D	150 x 100 mm junctions	Nr	0.25	3.17	–	39.89	43.06	47.37	3.402
P305546E	150 x 150 mm junctions	Nr	0.25	3.17	–	45.03	48.20	53.02	4.597
P305546F	225 mm bends	Nr	0.22	2.79	–	98.64	101.43	111.57	6.431
P305546G	225 x 100 mm junctions	Nr	0.27	3.43	–	112.72	116.15	127.77	9.518
P305546H	225 x 150 mm junctions	Nr	0.27	3.43	–	112.72	116.15	127.77	9.354
P305546I	300 mm bends	Nr	0.35	4.44	–	139.44	143.88	158.27	19.242
P305546J	300 x 100 mm junctions	Nr	0.40	5.08	–	219.47	224.55	247.01	19.058
P305546K	300 x 150 mm junctions	Nr	0.40	5.08	–	219.47	224.55	247.01	21.964
P305561	**PVC-u fittings; OsmaDrain**								
P305561A	82 mm bends	Nr	0.10	1.27	–	18.04	19.31	21.24	0.483
P305561B	82 x 82 mm junctions	Nr	0.15	1.90	–	26.26	28.16	30.98	1.484
P305561C	110 mm bends	Nr	0.13	1.65	–	17.14	18.79	20.67	0.950
P305561D	110 mm rest bends	Nr	0.15	1.90	–	32.84	34.74	38.21	0.950
P305561E	110 x 110 mm junctions	Nr	0.18	2.29	–	22.76	25.05	27.56	1.016
P305561F	160 mm bends	Nr	0.20	2.54	–	43.73	46.27	50.90	2.200
P305561G	160 x 110 mm junctions	Nr	0.25	3.17	–	57.28	60.45	66.50	4.725
P305561H	160 x 160 mm junctions	Nr	0.25	3.17	–	74.31	77.48	85.23	5.615
P305569	**PVC-u fittings; UltraRib**								
P305569A	150 mm bends	Nr	0.28	3.56	–	19.52	23.08	25.39	1.916
P305569B	150 x 150 mm junctions	Nr	0.30	3.81	–	47.20	51.01	56.11	4.778
P305569C	225 mm bends	Nr	0.32	4.06	–	83.21	87.27	96.00	6.221
P305569D	225 x 110 mm junctions	Nr	0.35	4.44	–	109.42	113.86	125.25	12.170
P305569E	225 x 150 mm junctions	Nr	0.35	4.44	–	112.73	117.17	128.89	13.619
P305569F	225 x 225 mm junctions	Nr	0.35	4.44	–	156.65	161.09	177.20	17.351
P305569G	300 mm bends	Nr	0.34	4.32	–	166.20	170.52	187.57	12.075
P305569H	300 x 150 mm junctions	Nr	0.37	4.70	–	223.67	228.37	251.21	22.313
P305569I	300 x 225 mm junctions	Nr	0.37	4.70	–	344.55	349.25	384.18	35.963
P305576	**Concrete fittings, BS 5911 Part 1, Class L**								
P305576A	150 mm bends	Nr	0.40	5.08	–	63.15	68.23	75.05	9.218
P305576B	150 x 150 mm junctions	Nr	0.50	6.35	–	44.21	50.56	55.62	24.387
P305576C	225 mm bends	Nr	0.45	5.71	–	94.73	100.44	110.48	20.741
P305576D	225 x 150 mm junctions	Nr	0.55	6.99	–	66.31	73.30	80.63	54.871
P305576E	300 mm bends	Nr	0.60	7.62	4.56	126.30	138.48	152.33	40.893
P305576F	300 x 150 mm junctions	Nr	0.70	8.89	4.56	88.41	101.86	112.05	101.567
P305591	**Cast iron fittings; Timesaver bolted joints**								
P305591A	100 mm bends	Nr	0.43	17.03	–	33.03	50.06	55.07	16.245
P305591B	100 x 100 mm junction	Nr	0.57	22.18	–	43.84	66.02	72.62	15.643
P305591C	150 mm bends	Nr	0.65	25.59	–	76.02	101.61	111.77	21.860
P305591D	150 x 100 mm junction	Nr	0.74	29.01	–	99.08	128.09	140.90	32.289
P305591E	150 x 150 mm junction	Nr	0.74	29.01	–	108.17	137.18	150.90	38.305
P3080	**Stop cock pits, valve chambers and the like**								
P308010	**Excavating stop cock pit; half brick wall; 100 mm C20 concrete base; hinged cast iron cover and frame bedded in cement mortar (1:3); nominal internal size**								
P308010A	100 x 100 x 750 mm deep	Nr	2.17	46.97	16.44	33.45	96.86	106.55	42.255
P308010B	225 x 225 x 750 mm deep	Nr	3.38	73.65	6.66	40.37	120.68	132.75	60.186
P308010C	450 x 450 x 750 mm deep	Nr	4.95	114.10	9.31	155.26	278.67	306.54	236.419
P308010G	600 x 450 x 1000 mm deep	Nr	7.19	168.68	27.45	125.91	322.04	354.24	203.566

Major Works 2011		Unit	Labour Hours	Labour Net	Plant Net	Materials Net	Unit Net	Unit with 10%	CO₂
				£	£	£	£	£	Kg
P31	**P31: HOLES, CHASES, COVERS AND SUPPORTS FOR SERVICES**								
P3119	**Builder's work; cutting away for and making good after electrical works including mortices, notches, holes, sinkings and chases in structure and finishes**								
P311910	**Concealed installation works**								
P311910A	lighting points	Nr	0.36	4.57	-	-	4.57	5.03	-
P311910B	socket outlet points	Nr	0.60	7.62	-	-	7.62	8.38	-
P311910C	equipment and control gear points	Nr	0.65	8.25	-	-	8.25	9.08	-
P311910D	fitting points	Nr	0.85	10.80	-	-	10.80	11.88	-
P311920	**Exposed installation works**								
P311920A	lighting points	Nr	0.27	3.43	-	-	3.43	3.77	-
P311920B	socket outlet points	Nr	0.42	5.33	-	-	5.33	5.86	-
P311920C	equipment and control gear points	Nr	0.61	7.75	-	-	7.75	8.53	-
P311920D	fitting points	Nr	0.42	5.33	-	-	5.33	5.86	-
P3125	**Builder's work; cutting away for and making good after services installation including mortices, notches, holes, sinkings and chases in structure and finishes**								
P312510	**Cutting chases in brickwork for service pipework; vertical; nominal pipe dia**								
P312510A	not exceeding 55 mm	m	0.35	4.44	-	-	4.44	4.88	-
P312510B	55 - 110 mm	m	0.65	8.25	-	-	8.25	9.08	-
P312515	**Cutting chases in blockwork for service pipework; vertical; nominal pipe dia**								
P312515A	not exceeding 55 mm	m	0.22	2.79	-	-	2.79	3.07	-
P312515B	55 - 110 mm	m	0.40	5.08	-	-	5.08	5.59	-
P312520	**Cutting holes in structure for pipes or the like; not exceeding 55 mm nominal dia**								
P312520A	half brick wall	Nr	0.30	3.81	-	-	3.81	4.19	-
P312520B	one brick wall	Nr	0.58	7.37	-	-	7.37	8.11	-
P312520C	one and a half brick wall	Nr	0.85	10.80	-	-	10.80	11.88	-
P312520D	100 mm blockwork	Nr	0.24	3.05	-	-	3.05	3.36	-
P312520E	125 mm blockwork	Nr	0.28	3.56	-	-	3.56	3.92	-
P312520F	150 mm blockwork	Nr	0.32	4.06	-	-	4.06	4.47	-
P312520G	200 mm blockwork	Nr	0.39	4.95	-	-	4.95	5.45	-
P312525	**Cutting holes in structure for pipes or the like; 55 - 110 mm nominal dia**								
P312525A	half brick wall	Nr	0.36	4.57	-	-	4.57	5.03	-
P312525B	one brick wall	Nr	0.70	8.89	-	-	8.89	9.78	-
P312525C	one and a half brick wall	Nr	1.02	12.95	-	-	12.95	14.25	-
P312525D	100 mm blockwork	Nr	0.29	3.68	-	-	3.68	4.05	-
P312525E	125 mm blockwork	Nr	0.34	4.32	-	-	4.32	4.75	-
P312525F	150 mm blockwork	Nr	0.38	4.83	-	-	4.83	5.31	-
P312525G	200 mm blockwork	Nr	0.47	5.97	-	-	5.97	6.57	-
P312550	**Mortices in brickwork; grouting up with cement mortar (1:3); size**								
P312550A	50 x 50 x 100 mm deep	Nr	0.25	3.17	-	0.21	3.38	3.72	0.703
P312550B	75 x 75 x 100 mm deep	Nr	0.30	3.81	-	0.51	4.32	4.75	1.757
P312550C	75 x 75 x 150 mm deep	Nr	0.38	4.83	-	0.51	5.34	5.87	1.757
P312550D	75 x 75 x 200 mm deep	Nr	0.45	5.71	-	0.62	6.33	6.96	2.109
P312555	**Mortices in brickwork for bars, bolts and the like**								
P312555A	M10 expansion bolt	Nr	0.16	2.03	-	-	2.03	2.23	-
P312555B	M20 bolt; 75 mm deep	Nr	0.15	1.90	-	-	1.90	2.09	-
P312555C	M20 bolt; 125 mm deep	Nr	0.18	2.29	-	-	2.29	2.52	-

Building Fabric Sundries

Major Works 2011		Unit	Labour Hours	Labour Net	Plant Net	Materials Net	Unit Net	Unit with 10%	CO$_2$
P31	**P31: HOLES, CHASES, COVERS AND SUPPORTS FOR SERVICES**								
P3125	**Builder's work; cutting away for and making good after services installation including mortices, notches, holes, sinkings and chases in structure and finishes**								
P312575	**Holes in softwood for cables, small pipes and the like; timber thickness**								
P312575A	12 mm	Nr	0.03	0.38	-	-	0.38	0.42	-
P312575B	25 mm	Nr	0.05	0.64	-	-	0.64	0.70	-
P312575C	50 mm	Nr	0.08	1.02	-	-	1.02	1.12	-
P312575D	75 mm	Nr	0.12	1.52	-	-	1.52	1.67	-
P312575E	100 mm	Nr	0.15	1.90	-	-	1.90	2.09	-

Paving, Planting, Fencing and Site Furniture

Major Works 2011		Unit	Labour Hours	Labour Net	Plant Net	Materials Net	Unit Net	Unit with 10%	CO₂
				£	£	£	£	£	Kg
Q10	**Q10: KERBS, EDGINGS, CHANNELS AND PAVING ACCESSORIES**								
Q1011	**Kerbs and edgings; Marley concrete block paviors**								
Q101151	**Splayed edging units; 100 mm wide; bed and point in cement mortar (1:3); haunching with 10 N/mm^2 concrete**								
Q101151A	65 mm thick	m	0.25	3.17	-	20.30	23.47	25.82	3.730
Q101151B	65 mm thick; curved work	m	0.35	4.44	-	21.28	25.72	28.29	3.865
Q101151C	80 mm thick	m	0.25	3.17	-	28.96	32.13	35.34	4.985
Q101151D	80 mm thick; curved work	m	0.35	4.44	-	30.35	34.79	38.27	5.150
Q1015	**Kerbs and edgings; facing bricks**								
Q101561	**Kerbs, edgings or the like; bedding and pointing in cement mortar (1:3); haunching with 10 N/mm^2 concrete; brick on flat**								
Q101561A	half brick wide	m	0.25	3.17	-	1.67	4.84	5.32	8.940
Q101561B	half brick wide; curved work	m	0.35	4.44	-	1.67	6.11	6.72	8.940
Q101562	**Kerbs, edgings or the like; bedding and pointing in cement mortar (1:3); haunching with 10 N/mm^2 concrete; brick on edge**								
Q101562C	one brick wide	m	0.70	8.89	-	4.54	13.43	14.77	24.423
Q101562D	one brick wide; curved work	m	0.80	10.16	-	4.79	14.95	16.45	25.883
Q1021	**Kerbs or the like; precast concrete, BS 340**								
Q102101	**Kerbs; 125 x 255 mm; bedding and pointing in cement mortar (1:3); haunching with 20 N/mm^2 concrete**								
Q102101A	Fig 2, 5, 7, 8	m	0.37	4.70	0.50	9.02	14.22	15.64	26.936
Q102101B	Fig 2, 5, 7, 8; curved work	m	0.45	5.71	0.50	9.32	15.53	17.08	27.511
Q102101E	Fig 2a, 7a, 8, 9	m	0.37	4.70	0.50	9.02	14.22	15.64	26.936
Q102101F	Fig 2a, 7a, 8, 9; curved work	m	0.45	5.71	0.50	9.32	15.53	17.08	27.511
Q102143	**Kerbs; 150 x 305 mm; bedding and pointing in cement mortar (1:3); haunching with 20 N/mm^2 concrete**								
Q102143C	Fig. 1, 4, 6, 8	m	0.39	4.95	0.50	13.50	18.95	20.85	38.817
Q102143D	Fig. 1, 4, 6, 8; curved work	m	0.47	5.97	0.50	13.97	20.44	22.48	39.726
Q102144	**Extra for**								
Q102144A	droppers; Fig 16; 255 to 155 mm high 125 mm wide	Nr	-	-	-	3.86	3.86	4.25	2.438
Q102144B	droppers; Fig 16; 305 to 205 mm high 150 mm wide	Nr	-	-	-	3.78	3.78	4.16	4.630
Q102144C	quadrants; Fig 14; 450 x 450 x 250 m	Nr	-	-	-	9.46	9.46	10.41	22.994
Q1031	**Edgings or the like; precast concrete, BS 340**								
Q103101	**Edgings; 50 x 150 mm; bedding and pointing in cement mortar (1:3); haunching with 10 N/mm^2 concrete**								
Q103101A	Fig 11, 12, 13	m	0.20	2.54	0.50	3.71	6.75	7.43	11.014
Q103101B	Fig 11, 12, 13; curved work	m	0.25	3.17	0.50	3.85	7.52	8.27	11.194
Q103102	**Edgings; 50 x 200 mm; bedding and pointing in cement mortar (1:3); haunching with 10 N/mm^2 concrete**								
Q103102C	Fig 11, 13	m	0.20	2.54	0.50	5.35	8.39	9.23	15.368
Q103102D	Fig 11, 13; curved work	m	0.25	3.17	0.50	5.53	9.20	10.12	15.609

Major Works 2011		Unit	Labour Hours	Labour Net	Plant Net	Materials Net	Unit Net	Unit with 10%	CO$_2$
				£	£	£	£	£	Kg
Q10	**Q10: KERBS, EDGINGS, CHANNELS AND PAVING ACCESSORIES**								
Q1031	**Edgings or the like; precast concrete, BS 340**								
Q103145	**Edgings; 50 x 250 mm; bedding and pointing in cement mortar (1:3); haunching with 10 N/mm^2 concrete**								
Q103145E	Fig 11, 12	m	0.22	2.79	0.50	6.95	10.24	11.26	20.346
Q103145F	Fig 11, 12; curved work	m	0.27	3.43	0.50	7.17	11.10	12.21	20.647
Q1041	**Channels or the like; precast concrete, BS 340**								
Q104101	**Channels; 125 x 255 mm; bedding and pointing in cement mortar (1:3); haunching with 10 N/mm^2 concrete**								
Q104101A	Fig 2, 8	m	0.33	4.19	0.50	8.79	13.48	14.83	19.176
Q104101B	Fig 2, 8; curved work	m	0.42	5.33	0.50	9.17	15.00	16.50	19.751
Q104102	**Channels; 150 x 305 mm; bedding and pointing in cement mortar (1:3); haunching with 10 N/mm^2 concrete**								
Q104102C	Fig 1, 8	m	0.35	4.44	0.50	10.83	15.77	17.35	27.000
Q104102D	Fig 1, 8; curved work	m	0.44	5.59	0.50	11.30	17.39	19.13	27.909
Q104142	**Channels; 125 x 150 mm; bedding and pointing in cement mortar (1:3); haunching with 10 N/mm^2 concrete**								
Q104142E	Fig 2a, 8a	m	0.34	4.32	0.50	5.33	10.15	11.17	12.345
Q104142F	Fig 2a, 8a; curved work	m	0.43	5.46	0.50	5.55	11.51	12.66	12.604
Q1043	**Drainage kerbs; precast concrete; Charcon Building Products**								
Q104301	**Safeticurb surface water drainage kerbs; 165 x 165 mm Junior Block; bedding and pointing in cement mortar (1:3); haunching with 10 N/mm^2 concrete**								
Q104301A	76 mm bore	m	0.45	5.71	-	25.83	31.54	34.69	16.583
Q104301B	76 mm bore; curved work	m	0.60	7.62	-	27.03	34.65	38.12	17.129
Q104302	**Safeticurb surface water drainage kerbs; 248 x 248 mm DBA/1; bedding and pointing in cement mortar (1:3); haunching with 10 N/mm^2 concrete**								
Q104302E	127 mm bore	m	0.58	7.37	-	25.84	33.21	36.53	35.769
Q104302F	127 mm bore; curved work	m	0.70	8.89	-	26.97	35.86	39.45	36.945
Q104302I	silt box	Nr	1.80	22.86	-	152.94	175.80	193.38	39.308
Q104302J	inspection unit	Nr	0.65	8.25	-	63.29	71.54	78.69	32.036
Q104303	**Safeticurb surface water drainage kerbs; 248 x 321 or 349 mm DBK; bedding and pointing in cement mortar (1:3); haunching with 10 N/mm^2 concrete**								
Q104303K	248 x 321 or 349 mm DBK 127 mm bore	m	0.65	8.25	-	38.73	46.98	51.68	51.882
Q104303L	248 x 321 or 349 mm DBK 127 mm bore; curved work	m	0.78	9.91	-	40.41	50.32	55.35	53.494
Q104303M	DBK to DBA transition unit	Nr	0.45	5.71	-	41.69	47.40	52.14	27.510

Major Works 2011		Unit	Labour Hours	Labour Net	Plant Net	Materials Net	Unit Net	Unit with 10%	CO$_2$
				£	£	£	£	£	Kg
Q10	**Q10: KERBS, EDGINGS, CHANNELS AND PAVING ACCESSORIES**								
Q1043	**Drainage kerbs; precast concrete; Charcon Building Products**								
Q104347	**Safeticurb surface water drainage kerbs; 305 x 305 mm Jumbo DBJ/2; bedding and pointing in cement mortar (1:3); haunching with 10 N/mm^2 concrete**								
Q104347N	159 mm bore	m	0.85	10.80	-	48.76	59.56	65.52	53.084
Q104347O	159 mm bore; curved work	m	1.00	12.70	-	50.95	63.65	70.02	54.846
Q104347R	silt box	Nr	2.20	27.94	-	281.36	309.30	340.23	32.395
Q104347S	inspection unit	Nr	0.85	10.80	-	88.64	99.44	109.38	32.395

Major Works 2011		Unit	Labour Hours	Labour Net	Plant Net	Materials Net	Unit Net	Unit with 10%	CO$_2$
				£	£	£	£	£	Kg
Q20	**Q20: GRANULAR SUB-BASES TO ROADS AND PAVINGS**								
Q2021	**Aggregate base fill**								
Q202101	**Filled into excavation; by hand; compacting in layers**								
Q202101A	sand	m^3	0.80	10.16	0.51	23.59	34.26	37.69	14.643
Q202101B	hardcore	m^3	1.65	20.95	0.60	24.67	46.22	50.84	17.550
Q202101C	hoggin	m^3	0.90	11.43	0.51	24.15	36.09	39.70	15.203
Q202101D	DTp type 1	m^3	1.63	20.70	0.56	26.95	48.21	53.03	15.828
Q202101E	DTp type 2	m^3	1.63	20.70	0.56	24.25	45.51	50.06	15.828
Q202101F	stone rejects	m^3	1.65	20.95	0.60	25.20	46.75	51.43	16.990
Q202101G	granite scalpings	m^3	1.65	20.95	0.56	22.32	43.83	48.21	16.388
Q202102	**Filled into excavation; by machine; compacting in layers**								
Q202102A	sand	m^3	0.30	3.81	5.08	23.59	32.48	35.73	18.663
Q202102B	hardcore	m^3	0.35	4.44	8.58	24.67	37.69	41.46	24.585
Q202102C	hoggin	m^3	0.30	3.81	7.36	24.15	35.32	38.85	21.233
Q202102D	DTp type 1	m^3	0.33	4.19	8.55	26.95	39.69	43.66	22.863
Q202102E	DTp type 2	m^3	0.33	4.19	8.55	24.25	36.99	40.69	22.863
Q202102F	stone rejects	m^3	0.35	4.44	8.58	25.20	38.22	42.04	24.025
Q202102G	granite scalpings	m^3	0.33	4.19	8.55	22.32	35.06	38.57	23.423
Q202103	**Filled in making up levels; by hand; compacting in layers**								
Q202103A	sand	m^3	0.83	10.54	0.77	23.59	34.90	38.39	16.613
Q202103B	hardcore	m^3	1.46	18.54	0.77	24.67	43.98	48.38	19.413
Q202103C	hoggin	m^3	0.93	11.81	0.77	24.15	36.73	40.40	17.173
Q202103D	DTp type 1	m^3	1.40	17.78	0.77	26.95	45.50	50.05	17.733
Q202103E	DTp type 2	m^3	1.40	17.78	0.77	24.25	42.80	47.08	17.733
Q202103F	stone rejects	m^3	1.46	18.54	0.77	25.20	44.51	48.96	18.853
Q202103G	granite scalpings	m^3	1.46	18.54	0.77	22.32	41.63	45.79	18.293
Q202104	**Filled in making up levels; by machine; compacting in layers**								
Q202104A	sand	m^3	0.13	1.65	1.91	23.59	27.15	29.87	17.618
Q202104B	hardcore	m^3	0.13	1.65	3.05	24.67	29.37	32.31	21.423
Q202104C	hoggin	m^3	0.13	1.65	2.59	24.15	28.39	31.23	18.781
Q202104D	DTp type 1	m^3	0.13	1.65	2.59	26.95	31.19	34.31	19.341
Q202104E	DTp type 2	m^3	0.13	1.65	2.59	24.25	28.49	31.34	19.341
Q202104F	stone rejects	m^3	0.13	1.65	3.05	25.20	29.90	32.89	20.863
Q202104G	granite scalpings	m^3	0.13	1.65	3.05	22.32	27.02	29.72	20.303
Q202105	**Filled into oversite; by hand; compacting in layers; average 150 mm thick**								
Q202105A	sand	m^3	1.03	13.08	1.00	23.59	37.67	41.44	17.417
Q202105B	hardcore	m^3	1.66	21.08	1.00	24.67	46.75	51.43	20.217
Q202105C	hoggin	m^3	1.13	14.35	1.00	24.15	39.50	43.45	17.977
Q202105D	DTp type 1	m^3	1.60	20.32	1.00	26.95	48.27	53.10	18.537
Q202105E	DTp type 2	m^3	1.60	20.32	1.00	24.25	45.57	50.13	18.537
Q202105F	stone rejects	m^3	1.66	21.08	1.00	25.20	47.28	52.01	19.657
Q202105G	granite scalpings	m^3	1.66	21.08	1.00	22.32	44.40	48.84	19.097
Q202106	**Filled into oversite; by machine; compacting in layers; average 150 mm thick**								
Q202106A	sand	m^3	0.17	2.16	3.28	23.59	29.03	31.93	19.427
Q202106B	hardcore	m^3	0.17	2.16	4.42	24.67	31.25	34.38	23.232
Q202106C	hoggin	m^3	0.17	2.16	3.97	24.15	30.28	33.31	20.590
Q202106D	DTp type 1	m^3	0.17	2.16	3.97	26.95	33.08	36.39	21.150
Q202106E	DTp type 2	m^3	0.17	2.16	3.97	24.25	30.38	33.42	21.150
Q202106F	stone rejects	m^3	0.17	2.16	4.42	25.20	31.78	34.96	22.672
Q202106G	granite scalpings	m^3	0.17	2.16	4.42	22.32	28.90	31.79	22.112
Q2091	**Contour grading**								
Q209107	**Grading filled oversite to contours, embankments or the like; by hand**								
Q209107A	to falls	m^2	0.10	1.27	-	-	1.27	1.40	-

Major Works 2011		Unit	Labour Hours	Labour Net £	Plant Net £	Materials Net £	Unit Net £	Unit with 10% £	CO$_2$ Kg
Q20	**Q20: GRANULAR SUB-BASES TO ROADS AND PAVINGS**								
Q2091	**Contour grading**								
Q209107	**Grading filled oversite to contours, embankments or the like; by hand**								
Q209107B	to falls and cross-falls	m²	0.17	2.16	-	-	2.16	2.38	-
Q209107C	to slopes	m²	0.09	1.14	-	-	1.14	1.25	-
Q209108	**Grading filled oversite to contours, embankments or the like; by machine**								
Q209108A	to falls	m²	0.03	0.38	0.68	-	1.06	1.17	0.603
Q209108B	to falls and cross-falls	m²	0.05	0.64	1.14	-	1.78	1.96	1.005
Q209108C	to slopes	m²	0.02	0.25	0.46	-	0.71	0.78	0.402
Q2093	**Blinding surfaces**								
Q209309	**Blinding to hardcore**								
Q209309A	25 mm sand	m²	0.04	0.51	-	0.53	1.04	1.14	0.314
Q209309B	50 mm sand	m²	0.06	0.70	-	1.04	1.74	1.91	0.616

Major Works 2011		Unit	Labour Hours	Labour Net £	Plant Net £	Materials Net £	Unit Net £	Unit with 10% £	CO₂ Kg

Q21	**Q21: IN SITU CONCRETE ROADS AND PAVINGS**								
Q2111	**Plain concrete; mix C20P**								
Q211102	**Foundations; combined and isolated bases**								
Q211102A	not exceeding 150 mm thick	m³	1.20	15.24	-	81.64	96.88	106.57	343.200
Q211102B	150 - 300 mm thick	m³	0.90	11.43	-	81.64	93.07	102.38	343.200
Q211102C	over 300 mm thick	m³	0.70	8.89	-	81.64	90.53	99.58	343.200
Q211104	**Blinding**								
Q211104A	not exceeding 150 mm thick	m³	0.90	11.43	-	77.93	89.36	98.30	327.600
Q211104B	150 - 300 mm thick	m³	0.55	6.99	-	77.93	84.92	93.41	327.600
Q211104C	over 300 mm thick	m³	0.40	5.08	-	77.93	83.01	91.31	327.600
Q211105	**Beds, roads and footpaths**								
Q211105A	not exceeding 150 mm thick	m³	1.05	13.33	-	77.93	91.26	100.39	327.600
Q211105B	150 - 300 mm thick	m³	0.70	8.89	-	77.93	86.82	95.50	327.600
Q211105C	over 300 mm thick	m³	0.50	6.35	-	77.93	84.28	92.71	327.600
Q2115	**Reinforced concrete; mix C30P**								
Q211516	**Beds, roads and footpaths**								
Q211516A	not exceeding 150 mm thick	m³	0.46	17.79	3.12	80.37	101.28	111.41	335.640
Q211516B	150 - 300 mm thick	m³	0.33	12.71	2.18	80.37	95.26	104.79	333.228
Q211516C	over 300 mm thick	m³	0.23	8.88	1.56	80.37	90.81	99.89	331.620
Q2121	**Formwork to general finish**								
Q212107	**Sloping upper surfaces over 15 deg from horizontal**								
Q212107A	over 300 mm wide	m²	1.86	31.63	-	7.62	39.25	43.18	6.563
Q212108	**Sides of foundations, bases and ground beams**								
Q212108A	not exceeding 250 mm high	m	0.76	12.90	-	4.07	16.97	18.67	3.853
Q212108B	250 - 500 mm high	m	1.15	19.44	-	7.23	26.67	29.34	6.800
Q212108C	500 - 1000 mm high	m	2.04	34.55	-	13.49	48.04	52.84	12.599
Q212108D	over 1000 mm high	m²	1.86	31.50	-	13.33	44.83	49.31	12.352
Q212119	**Vertical edges of slabs, faces of kerbs, upstands, breaks in upper surfaces or the like**								
Q212119A	not exceeding 250 mm wide	m	0.71	11.97	-	1.98	13.95	15.35	1.770
Q212119B	250 - 500 mm wide	m	0.90	15.28	-	3.17	18.45	20.30	2.783
Q212119C	500 - 1000 mm wide	m	1.60	27.15	0.67	5.36	33.18	36.50	4.656
Q212119D	over 1000 mm wide	m²	1.46	24.76	1.33	6.40	32.49	35.74	5.520
Q212120	**Grooves, throats, rebates, chamfers or the like; sectional area**								
Q212120A	2500 - 5000 mm²	m	0.26	4.47	-	0.68	5.15	5.67	0.713
Q212120B	5000 - 10000 mm²	m	0.69	11.68	-	1.24	12.92	14.21	1.280
Q212120C	10000 - 20000 mm²	m	0.83	14.01	-	4.03	18.04	19.84	3.508
Q2133	**Steel fabric reinforcement, BS 4483; delivered to site in standard sheets**								
Q213301	**Fabric reinforcement, laid horizontally, ref**								
Q213301A	A98	m²	0.02	0.30	-	1.54	1.84	2.02	3.366
Q213301B	A142	m²	0.03	0.46	-	1.93	2.39	2.63	4.808
Q213301C	A193	m²	0.03	0.44	-	2.55	2.99	3.29	6.506
Q213301D	A252	m²	0.03	0.44	-	3.24	3.68	4.05	8.481
Q213301E	A393	m²	0.05	0.74	-	5.00	5.74	6.31	13.170
Q213301F	B196	m²	0.03	0.44	-	4.37	4.81	5.29	6.306
Q213301G	B283	m²	0.03	0.44	-	3.07	3.51	3.86	7.690
Q213301H	B385	m²	0.04	0.62	-	3.59	4.21	4.63	9.318
Q213301I	B503	m²	0.05	0.74	-	4.67	5.41	5.95	12.168
Q213301J	B785	m²	0.05	0.74	-	6.29	7.03	7.73	16.667
Q213301K	B1131	m²	0.07	1.04	-	13.19	14.23	15.65	22.284
Q213301L	C283	m²	0.03	0.44	-	2.37	2.81	3.09	5.637
Q213301M	C385	m²	0.03	0.44	-	2.99	3.43	3.77	7.335
Q213301N	C503	m²	0.04	0.62	-	3.64	4.26	4.69	9.308

Major Works 2011		Unit	Labour Hours	Labour Net	Plant Net	Materials Net	Unit Net	Unit with 10%	CO$_2$
				£	£	£	£	£	Kg
Q21	**Q21: IN SITU CONCRETE ROADS AND PAVINGS**								
Q2133	**Steel fabric reinforcement, BS 4483; delivered to site in standard sheets**								
Q213301	**Fabric reinforcement, laid horizontally, ref**								
Q213301O	C636	m²	0.04	0.59	-	7.64	8.23	9.05	11.876
Q213301P	C785	m²	0.05	0.74	-	8.42	9.16	10.08	14.358
Q213303	**Fabric reinforcement, fixed vertically, ref**								
Q213303A	A98	m²	0.08	1.18	-	1.36	2.54	2.79	3.339
Q213303B	A142	m²	0.09	1.33	-	1.76	3.09	3.40	4.782
Q213303C	A193	m²	0.09	1.33	-	2.37	3.70	4.07	6.479
Q213303D	A252	m²	0.09	1.33	-	3.07	4.40	4.84	8.454
Q213303E	A393	m²	0.02	0.24	-	4.83	5.07	5.58	13.144
Q213303F	B196	m²	0.09	1.33	-	4.20	5.53	6.08	6.280
Q213303G	B283	m²	0.10	1.48	-	2.90	4.38	4.82	7.663
Q213303H	B385	m²	0.12	1.78	-	3.41	5.19	5.71	9.292
Q213303I	B503	m²	0.16	2.37	-	4.50	6.87	7.56	12.141
Q213303J	B785	m²	0.20	2.96	-	6.12	9.08	9.99	16.640
Q213303K	B1131	m²	0.22	3.26	-	13.02	16.28	17.91	22.258
Q213303L	C283	m²	0.08	1.18	-	2.19	3.37	3.71	5.610
Q213303M	C385	m²	0.09	1.33	-	2.81	4.14	4.55	7.308
Q213303N	C503	m²	0.12	1.78	-	3.46	5.24	5.76	9.282
Q213303O	C636	m²	0.15	2.22	-	7.47	9.69	10.66	11.850
Q213303P	C785	m²	0.16	2.37	-	8.25	10.62	11.68	14.332
Q2143	**Movement joints**								
Q214329	**Horizontal joints; 25 mm steel dowel bars 600 mm long, debonded for half length, dowel caps with compressible filler, notching shuttering for dowels 300 mm centres; including formwork**								
Q214329A	100 mm high	m	0.92	15.62	-	9.77	25.39	27.93	1.366
Q214329B	150 mm high	m	1.09	18.51	-	10.09	28.60	31.46	1.679
Q214329C	200 mm high	m	1.11	18.85	-	10.41	29.26	32.19	1.993
Q214329D	250 mm high	m	1.13	19.19	-	11.64	30.83	33.91	3.126
Q214329E	300 mm high	m	1.19	20.21	-	11.98	32.19	35.41	3.438
Q2146	**Expansion materials**								
Q214611	**Flexcell fibreboard compressible joint filler; 10 mm thick**								
Q214611A	not exceeding 150 mm wide	m	0.10	1.70	-	1.44	3.14	3.45	1.820
Q214611B	150 - 300 mm wide	m	0.18	2.97	-	2.88	5.85	6.44	3.629
Q214611C	300 - 450 mm wide	m	0.22	3.74	-	4.32	8.06	8.87	5.449
Q214612	**Flexcell fibreboard compressible joint filler; 13 mm thick**								
Q214612A	not exceeding 150 mm wide	m	0.11	1.78	-	1.54	3.32	3.65	2.366
Q214612B	150 - 300 mm wide	m	0.18	3.06	-	3.06	6.12	6.73	4.717
Q214612C	300 - 450 mm wide	m	0.23	3.82	-	4.60	8.42	9.26	7.084
Q214613	**Flexcell fibreboard compressible joint filler; 19 mm thick**								
Q214613A	not exceeding 150 mm wide	m	0.12	1.95	-	2.82	4.77	5.25	3.458
Q214613B	150 - 300 mm wide	m	0.20	3.31	-	5.62	8.93	9.82	6.895
Q214613C	300 - 450 mm wide	m	0.23	3.91	-	8.43	12.34	13.57	10.353
Q214614	**Flexcell fibreboard compressible joint filler; 25 mm thick**								
Q214614A	not exceeding 150 mm wide	m	0.13	2.12	-	2.77	4.89	5.38	4.550
Q214614B	150 - 300 mm wide	m	0.20	3.31	-	5.52	8.83	9.71	9.072
Q214614C	300 - 450 mm wide	m	0.24	4.08	-	8.28	12.36	13.60	13.622

Major Works 2011		Unit	Labour Hours	Labour Net	Plant Net	Materials Net	Unit Net	Unit with 10%	CO$_2$
				£	£	£	£	£	Kg
Q21	**Q21: IN SITU CONCRETE ROADS AND PAVINGS**								
Q2148	**Joint sealants**								
Q214834	**Hot poured bituminous rubber compound**								
Q214834A	10 x 25 mm	m	0.03	0.42	0.20	1.78	2.40	2.64	4.168
Q214834B	13 x 25 mm	m	0.03	0.51	0.22	2.15	2.88	3.17	5.204
Q214834C	19 x 25 mm	m	0.04	0.68	0.25	3.33	4.26	4.69	7.616
Q214834D	25 x 25 mm	m	0.06	1.02	0.29	4.54	5.85	6.44	10.125
Q214835	**Cold poured polysulphide rubber compound**								
Q214835A	10 x 25 mm	m	0.03	0.53	-	3.94	4.47	4.92	3.706
Q214835B	13 x 25 mm	m	0.03	0.51	-	5.15	5.66	6.23	4.840
Q214835C	19 x 25 mm	m	0.04	0.70	-	7.52	8.22	9.04	7.068
Q214835D	25 x 25 mm	m	0.06	1.02	-	9.85	10.87	11.96	9.255
Q214836	**Cold poured polysulphide epoxy based compound**								
Q214836A	10 x 25 mm	m	0.03	0.53	-	0.65	1.18	1.30	0.473
Q214836B	13 x 25 mm	m	0.03	0.51	-	0.85	1.36	1.50	0.621
Q214836C	19 x 25 mm	m	0.04	0.70	-	1.23	1.93	2.12	0.898
Q214836D	25 x 25 mm	m	0.06	1.02	-	2.01	3.03	3.33	1.466
Q214837	**Gun grade polysulphide rubber compound**								
Q214837A	10 x 10 mm	m	0.04	0.68	-	0.37	1.05	1.16	0.372
Q214837B	13 x 13 mm	m	0.06	1.02	-	0.64	1.66	1.83	0.638
Q214837C	19 x 19 mm	m	0.13	2.21	-	1.35	3.56	3.92	1.353
Q214837D	25 x 25 mm	m	0.23	3.91	-	2.31	6.22	6.84	2.317
Q2151	**Surface finishes**								
Q215102	**Trowelling surfaces of concrete**								
Q215102A	to levels	m^2	0.16	2.03	-	-	2.03	2.23	-
Q215102B	to falls and crossfalls	m^2	0.25	3.17	-	-	3.17	3.49	-
Q215103	**Power floating and trowelling concrete surfaces**								
Q215103A	to levels	m^2	0.15	1.90	0.38	-	2.28	2.51	0.693
Q215103B	to falls and crossfalls	m^2	0.18	2.29	0.45	-	2.74	3.01	0.832
Q215104	**Lithurin surface hardener; brush applied to surfaces in accordance with manufacturer's instructions; two coats**								
Q215104A	general surfaces of floors	m^2	0.16	2.03	-	2.10	4.13	4.54	0.137
Q2153	**Form sinkings, channels or the like in face of concrete**								
Q215353	**Horizontally; including formwork**								
Q215353A	not exceeding 150 mm girth	m	0.42	7.18	-	1.34	8.52	9.37	1.339
Q215353B	150 - 300 mm girth	m	0.85	14.37	-	2.47	16.84	18.52	2.233
Q215353C	over 300 mm girth	m^2	1.46	24.76	-	6.27	31.03	34.13	5.160

Major Works 2011		Unit	Labour Hours	Labour Net	Plant Net	Materials Net	Unit Net	Unit with 10%	CO₂
				£	£	£	£	£	Kg
Q22	**Q22: COATED MACADAM AND ASPHALT ROADS AND PAVINGS**								
Q2201	**Coated macadam BS 4987**								
Q220124	**Hand laid surfacing**								
Q220124B	60 mm thickness of 20 mm aggregate dense base course, 30 mm thickness on 10 mm aggregate close graded wearing course	m²	0.14	5.49	1.50	10.01	17.00	18.70	15.664
Q220124C	50 mm thickness of 20 mm aggregate open graded base course and 20 mm thickness of 6 mm aggregate medium graded wearing course	m²	0.13	5.01	1.50	7.67	14.18	15.60	12.080
Q220124D	50 mm thickness of 20 mm aggregate dense base course, 20 mm thickness of 6 mm aggregate dense wearing course	m²	0.12	4.69	1.50	7.82	14.01	15.41	12.080
Q220124E	45 mm thickness of 20 mm aggregate open graded base course, 15 mm thickness of fine graded wearing course	m²	0.11	4.29	1.50	7.32	13.11	14.42	11.241
Q220125	**Machine laid surfacing**								
Q220125A	50 mm thickness of 20 mm aggregate dense base course	m²	0.05	1.96	2.37	5.06	9.39	10.33	8.980
Q220125B	100 mm thickness of 40 mm aggregate dense base course	m²	0.07	2.93	3.55	11.10	17.58	19.34	17.512
Q220125C	80 mm thickness of 28 mm aggregate dense base course, 40 mm thickness of 14 mm aggregate close graded wearing course	m²	0.09	3.53	4.26	12.16	19.95	21.95	21.060
Q220125D	60 mm thickness of 20 mm aggregate dense base course, 30 mm thickness of 10 mm aggregate close graded wearing course	m²	0.07	2.93	3.55	9.53	16.01	17.61	15.910
Q220125E	45 mm thickness of 20 mm aggregate dense base course, 20 mm thickness of 6 mm aggregate dense wearing course	m²	0.07	2.93	3.55	6.81	13.29	14.62	11.793
Q220125F	surface dress with cut-back bitumen K1-70 emulsion and 10 mm aggregate single dressing	m²	0.02	0.96	1.18	0.91	3.05	3.36	1.656
Q220125G	surface dress with cut-back bitumen K1-70 emulsion and 10 mm aggregate double dressing	m²	0.03	1.36	1.66	1.73	4.75	5.23	2.942
Q220125H	surface dress with cut-back bitumen K1-70 emulsion and 6 mm aggregate single dressing	m²	0.03	1.08	1.33	0.88	3.29	3.62	1.647
Q220125I	surface dress with cut-back bitumen K1-70 emulsion and 6 mm aggregate double dressing	m²	0.04	1.52	1.85	1.20	4.57	5.03	2.302

Major Works 2011		Unit	Labour Hours	Labour Net	Plant Net	Materials Net	Unit Net	Unit with 10%	CO$_2$
				£	£	£	£	£	Kg
Q23	Q23: GRAVEL, HOGGIN AND WOODCHIP ROADS AND PAVINGS								
Q2301	Aggregate base fill								
Q230105	Filled into oversite to level; by hand; compacting; 100 mm thick								
Q230105B	hardcore	m^2	0.34	4.32	1.00	2.47	7.79	8.57	5.097
Q230105C	hoggin	m^2	0.29	3.68	1.00	2.42	7.10	7.81	4.873
Q230105D	DTp type 1	m^2	0.33	4.19	1.00	2.69	7.88	8.67	4.929
Q230105E	DTp type 2	m^2	0.33	4.19	1.00	2.42	7.61	8.37	4.929
Q230105F	stone rejects	m^2	0.34	4.32	1.00	2.52	7.84	8.62	5.041
Q230105G	granite scalpings	m^2	0.34	4.32	1.00	2.23	7.55	8.31	4.985
Q230107	Filled into oversite to level; by hand; compacting; 150 mm thick								
Q230107B	hardcore	m^2	0.40	5.08	1.00	3.70	9.78	10.76	5.937
Q230107C	hoggin	m^2	0.36	4.57	1.00	3.62	9.19	10.11	5.601
Q230107D	DTp type 1	m^2	0.41	5.21	1.00	4.05	10.26	11.29	5.691
Q230107E	DTp type 2	m^2	0.41	5.21	1.00	3.65	9.86	10.85	5.691
Q230107F	stone rejects	m^2	0.43	5.46	1.00	3.79	10.25	11.28	5.859
Q230107G	granite scalpings	m^2	0.41	5.21	1.00	3.35	9.56	10.52	5.769
Q230116	Filled into oversite to levels; by machine; compacting; 100 mm thick								
Q230116B	hardcore	m^2	0.17	2.16	1.46	2.47	6.09	6.70	5.499
Q230116C	hoggin	m^2	0.17	2.16	1.46	2.42	6.04	6.64	5.275
Q230116D	DTp type 1	m^2	0.17	2.16	1.46	2.69	6.31	6.94	5.331
Q230116E	DTp type 2	m^2	0.17	2.16	1.46	2.42	6.04	6.64	5.331
Q230116F	stone rejects	m^2	0.17	2.16	1.46	2.52	6.14	6.75	5.443
Q230116G	granite scalpings	m^2	0.17	2.16	1.46	2.23	5.85	6.44	5.387
Q230118	Filled into oversite to levels; by machine; compacting; 150 mm thick								
Q230118B	hardcore	m^2	0.17	2.16	1.69	3.70	7.55	8.31	6.540
Q230118C	hoggin	m^2	0.17	2.16	1.69	3.62	7.47	8.22	6.204
Q230118D	DTp type 1	m^2	0.17	2.16	1.69	4.05	7.90	8.69	6.294
Q230118E	DTp type 2	m^2	0.17	2.16	1.69	3.65	7.50	8.25	6.294
Q230118F	stone rejects	m^2	0.17	2.16	1.69	3.79	7.64	8.40	6.462
Q230118G	granite scalpings	m^2	0.17	2.16	1.69	3.35	7.20	7.92	6.372
Q2311	Grading bases								
Q231137	Grading bases to slopes, falls and cross-falls; by hand								
Q231137A	to falls	m^2	0.10	1.27	-	-	1.27	1.40	-
Q231137B	to falls and cross-falls	m^2	0.17	2.16	-	-	2.16	2.38	-
Q231137C	to slopes	m^2	0.09	1.14	-	-	1.14	1.25	-
Q231138	Grading bases to slopes, falls and cross-falls; by machine								
Q231138A	to falls	m^2	0.03	0.38	0.68	-	1.06	1.17	0.603
Q231138B	to falls and cross-falls	m^2	0.05	0.64	1.14	-	1.78	1.96	1.005
Q231138C	to slopes	m^2	0.02	0.25	0.46	-	0.71	0.78	0.402
Q2318	Blinding								
Q231849	Blinding to hardcore base								
Q231849A	25 mm sand	m^2	0.04	0.51	-	0.53	1.04	1.14	0.314
Q231849B	50 mm sand	m^2	0.06	0.70	-	1.04	1.74	1.91	0.616
Q2321	Pea shingle dressing								
Q232122	Roads, paths and driveways								
Q232122A	25 mm thick	m^2	0.10	1.27	0.13	0.78	2.18	2.40	1.185
Q232122B	50 mm thick	m^2	0.12	1.52	0.25	1.55	3.32	3.65	2.370

Major Works 2011		Unit	Labour Hours	Labour Net	Plant Net	Materials Net	Unit Net	Unit with 10%	CO$_2$
				£	£	£	£	£	Kg
Q23	**Q23: GRAVEL, HOGGIN AND WOODCHIP ROADS AND PAVINGS**								
Q2331	**Treated sawn softwood edging**								
Q233171	**Road and path edging; 50 x 50 mm pegs at 1.00 m centres**								
Q233171A	25 x 150 mm	m	0.10	1.27	-	1.38	2.65	2.92	1.073
Q233171C	25 x 200 mm	m	0.12	1.52	-	1.96	3.48	3.83	1.430

Major Works 2011	Unit	Labour Hours	Labour Net	Plant Net	Materials Net	Unit Net	Unit with 10%	CO₂
			£	£	£	£	£	Kg
Q25	**Q25: SLAB, BRICK, BLOCK, SETT AND COBBLE PAVINGS**							
Q2521	**Precast concrete flag paving, BS 368**							
Q252111	**Pavings; bed in cement mortar (1:3), point in lime mortar (1:1:6)**							
Q252111M	600 x 450 x 50 mm thick	m²	0.51	6.48	-	13.47	19.95	21.95	46.596
Q252111N	600 x 600 x 50 mm thick	m²	0.43	5.46	-	12.28	17.74	19.51	45.599
Q252111O	600 x 750 x 50 mm thick	m²	0.39	4.95	-	12.07	17.02	18.72	46.430
Q252111P	600 x 900 x 50 mm thick	m²	0.35	4.44	-	11.08	15.52	17.07	46.328
Q252111Q	600 x 450 x 63 mm thick	m²	0.52	6.60	-	15.22	21.82	24.00	53.548
Q252111R	600 x 600 x 63 mm thick	m²	0.44	5.59	-	15.10	20.69	22.76	52.502
Q252111S	600 x 750 x 63 mm thick	m²	0.40	5.08	-	13.84	18.92	20.81	52.945
Q252111T	600 x 900 x 63 mm thick	m²	0.36	4.57	-	13.10	17.67	19.44	52.444
Q2522	**Brick paving**							
Q252215	**Pavings; bed and point in cement mortar (1:3)**							
Q252215A	brick on flat; half bond or 90 deg herringbone	m²	1.07	18.17	-	17.04	35.21	38.73	83.062
Q252215B	brick on flat; parquet bond or 45 deg herringbone	m²	1.12	19.02	0.20	17.79	37.01	40.71	87.674
Q252215C	brick on edge; half bond or 90 deg herringbone	m²	1.39	23.60	-	23.22	46.82	51.50	116.889
Q252215D	brick on edge; parquet bond or 90 deg herringbone	m²	1.44	24.45	0.20	23.97	48.62	53.48	121.500
Q2523	**Marley concrete block paving**							
Q252313	**200 x 100 mm chamfered blocks; laid and vibrator compacted on 50 mm sand bed**							
Q252313A	65 mm thick; half bond or 90 deg herringbone	m²	1.11	18.85	0.14	12.50	31.49	34.64	28.436
Q252313B	65 mm thick; parquet bond or 45 deg herringbone	m²	1.21	20.55	0.34	13.04	33.93	37.32	30.009
Q252313C	80 mm thick; half bond or 90 deg herringbone	m²	1.11	18.85	0.14	16.23	35.22	38.74	34.783
Q252313D	80 mm thick; parquet bond or 45 deg herringbone	m²	1.21	20.55	0.34	16.96	37.85	41.64	36.665
Q2531	**Granite sett paving**							
Q253101	**Granite setts; bedding in cement mortar (1:3) on concrete base (measured separately); laid**							
Q253101A	100 mm thick; level and to falls	m²	0.94	43.95	-	76.93	120.88	132.97	17.783
Q2545	**Cobble paving**							
Q254501	**Cobbles; set and butted on concrete base (measured separately); dry grouted in cement and sand (1:3); wetted and brushed**							
Q254501A	level and to falls; random	m²	1.05	48.99	-	76.51	125.50	138.05	26.783
Q254501B	level and to falls; to pattern	m²	1.14	53.38	-	78.06	131.44	144.58	32.055
Q2590	**Expansion materials**							
Q259011	**Flexcell fibreboard compressible joint filler; 10 mm thick**							
Q259011A	not exceeding 150 mm wide	m	0.10	1.70	-	1.44	3.14	3.45	1.820
Q259011B	150 - 300 mm wide	m	0.18	2.97	-	2.88	5.85	6.44	3.629
Q259011C	300 - 450 mm wide	m	0.22	3.74	-	4.32	8.06	8.87	5.449
Q259012	**Flexcell fibreboard compressible joint filler; 13 mm thick**							
Q259012A	not exceeding 150 mm wide	m	0.11	1.78	-	1.54	3.32	3.65	2.366
Q259012B	150 - 300 mm wide	m	0.18	3.06	-	3.06	6.12	6.73	4.717
Q259012C	300 - 450 mm wide	m	0.23	3.82	-	4.60	8.42	9.26	7.084

Major Works 2011		Unit	Labour Hours	Labour Net	Plant Net	Materials Net	Unit Net	Unit with 10%	CO₂
				£	£	£	£	£	Kg
Q25	**Q25: SLAB, BRICK, BLOCK, SETT AND COBBLE PAVINGS**								
Q2590	**Expansion materials**								
Q259013	**Flexcell fibreboard compressible joint filler; 19 mm thick**								
Q259013A	not exceeding 150 mm wide	m	0.12	1.95	-	2.82	4.77	5.25	3.458
Q259013B	150 - 300 mm wide	m	0.20	3.31	-	5.62	8.93	9.82	6.895
Q259013C	300 - 450 mm wide	m	0.23	3.91	-	8.43	12.34	13.57	10.353
Q259014	**Flexcell fibreboard compressible joint filler; 25 mm thick**								
Q259014A	not exceeding 150 mm wide	m	0.13	2.12	-	2.77	4.89	5.38	4.550
Q259014B	150 - 300 mm wide	m	0.20	3.31	-	5.52	8.83	9.71	9.072
Q259014C	300 - 450 mm wide	m	0.24	4.08	-	8.28	12.36	13.60	13.622
Q2592	**Joint sealants**								
Q259234	**Hot poured bituminous rubber compound**								
Q259234A	10 x 25 mm	m	0.03	0.42	0.20	1.78	2.40	2.64	4.168
Q259234B	13 x 25 mm	m	0.03	0.51	0.22	2.15	2.88	3.17	5.204
Q259234C	19 x 25 mm	m	0.04	0.68	0.25	3.33	4.26	4.69	7.616
Q259234D	25 x 25 mm	m	0.06	1.02	0.29	4.54	5.85	6.44	10.125
Q259235	**Cold poured polysulphide rubber compound**								
Q259235A	10 x 25 mm	m	0.03	0.53	-	3.94	4.47	4.92	3.706
Q259235B	13 x 25 mm	m	0.03	0.51	-	5.15	5.66	6.23	4.840
Q259235C	19 x 25 mm	m	0.04	0.70	-	7.52	8.22	9.04	7.068
Q259235D	25 x 25 mm	m	0.06	1.02	-	9.85	10.87	11.96	9.255
Q259236	**Cold poured polysulphide epoxy based compound**								
Q259236A	10 x 25 mm	m	0.03	0.53	-	0.65	1.18	1.30	0.473
Q259236B	13 x 25 mm	m	0.03	0.51	-	0.85	1.36	1.50	0.621
Q259236C	19 x 25 mm	m	0.04	0.70	-	1.23	1.93	2.12	0.898
Q259236D	25 x 25 mm	m	0.06	1.02	-	2.01	3.03	3.33	1.466
Q259237	**Gun grade polysulphide rubber compound**								
Q259237A	10 x 10 mm	m	0.04	0.68	-	0.37	1.05	1.16	0.372
Q259237B	13 x 13 mm	m	0.06	1.02	-	0.64	1.66	1.83	0.638
Q259237C	19 x 19 mm	m	0.13	2.21	-	1.35	3.56	3.92	1.353
Q259237D	25 x 25 mm	m	0.23	3.91	-	2.31	6.22	6.84	2.317

Major Works 2011		Unit	Labour Hours	Labour Net	Plant Net	Materials Net	Unit Net	Unit with 10%	CO$_2$
				£	£	£	£	£	Kg
Q30	**Q30: SEEDING AND TURFING**								
Q3010	**Cultivating**								
Q301002	**Cultivating; removing weeds, stones and the like**								
Q301002A	hand excavation	m^2	0.25	3.17	-	-	3.17	3.49	-
Q301002B	rotovating	m^2	0.15	1.90	0.49	-	2.39	2.63	0.347
Q3015	**Soiling**								
Q301521	**Soiling with topsoil excavated from temporary spoil heaps on site; transporting not exceeding 100 m**								
Q301521A	150 mm thick	m^2	0.19	2.41	0.25	-	2.66	2.93	1.608
Q301521B	225 mm thick	m^2	0.28	3.56	0.38	-	3.94	4.33	2.412
Q301521C	300 mm thick	m^2	0.38	4.83	0.50	-	5.33	5.86	3.216
Q301522	**Soiling with imported topsoil**								
Q301522A	150 mm thick	m^2	0.13	1.65	-	2.13	3.78	4.16	1.904
Q301522B	225 mm thick	m^2	0.19	2.41	-	3.26	5.67	6.24	2.912
Q301522C	300 mm thick	m^2	0.25	3.17	-	4.38	7.55	8.31	3.920
Q3020	**Surface applications**								
Q302003	**Fertiliser; spreading by hand**								
Q302003A	0.04 Kg per m^2	m^2	0.05	0.64	-	0.03	0.67	0.74	0.001
Q302003B	0.06 Kg per m^2	m^2	0.05	0.64	-	0.04	0.68	0.75	0.001
Q302005	**Weedkiller; by spreader**								
Q302005A	0.03 Kg per m^2	m^2	0.10	1.27	-	0.11	1.38	1.52	0.001
Q3030	**Seeding**								
Q303001	**Seeding, weeding, watering, re-seeding and cutting until established; utility grass seed**								
Q303001A	0.04 Kg per m^2	m^2	0.10	1.27	0.07	0.08	1.42	1.56	0.047
Q303001B	0.06 Kg per m^2	m^2	0.10	1.27	0.07	0.12	1.46	1.61	0.048
Q303003	**Seeding, weeding, watering, re-seeding and cutting until established; no rye grass seed**								
Q303003A	0.04 Kg per m^2	m^2	0.10	1.27	0.07	0.11	1.45	1.60	0.047
Q303003B	0.06 Kg per m^2	m^2	0.10	1.27	0.07	0.16	1.50	1.65	0.048
Q303005	**Seeding, weeding, watering, re-seeding and cutting until established; low maintenance grass seed**								
Q303005A	0.04 Kg per m^2	m^2	0.10	1.27	0.07	0.21	1.55	1.71	0.047
Q303005B	0.06 Kg per m^2	m^2	0.10	1.27	0.07	0.32	1.66	1.83	0.048
Q3040	**Turfing**								
Q304024	**Turfing, weeding, watering, rolling, re-turfing and cutting until established; turf**								
Q304024A	meadow quality (PC £2 per m^2)	m^2	0.26	3.30	-	2.00	5.30	5.83	-

Major Works 2011		Unit	Labour Hours	Labour Net	Plant Net	Materials Net	Unit Net	Unit with 10%	CO₂
				£	£	£	£	£	Kg
Q31	**Q31: PLANTING**								
Q3104	**Provide trees and shrubs; excavation, disposal and backfilling; maintain until established**								
Q310442	**Trees including 50 x 50 mm treated softwood stakes, PVC-u ties and rabbit guards**								
Q310442A	whip	Nr	0.25	3.17	-	6.29	9.46	10.41	1.072
Q310442B	feathered	Nr	0.40	5.08	-	14.79	19.87	21.86	1.072
Q310442C	standard	Nr	0.65	8.25	-	31.31	39.56	43.52	0.988
Q310442D	semi-mature rootballed	Nr	1.00	12.70	2.07	127.25	142.02	156.22	16.050
Q310443	**Shrubs**								
Q310443A	small (PC £4 each)	Nr	0.15	1.90	-	4.00	5.90	6.49	-
Q310443B	medium (PC £12 each)	Nr	0.25	3.17	-	12.00	15.17	16.69	-
Q310443C	large (PC £35 each)	Nr	0.40	5.08	-	35.00	40.08	44.09	-
Q3106	**Provide two year plants; excavation, disposal and backfilling; maintain until established**								
Q310632	**Privet; single row (PC £3.25 per plant)**								
Q310632A	300 mm centres	m	0.18	2.29	-	11.38	13.67	15.04	-
Q310632B	450 mm centres	m	0.12	1.52	-	7.47	8.99	9.89	-
Q310632C	600 mm centres	m	0.09	1.14	-	5.69	6.83	7.51	-
Q310633	**Beech; double row, staggered (PC £1 per plant)**								
Q310633A	300 mm centres	m	0.37	4.70	-	7.00	11.70	12.87	-
Q310633B	450 mm centres	m	0.24	3.05	-	4.60	7.65	8.42	-
Q310633C	600 mm centres	m	0.18	2.29	-	3.50	5.79	6.37	-

Major Works 2011		Unit	Labour Hours	Labour Net	Plant Net	Materials Net	Unit Net	Unit with 10%	CO₂
				£	£	£	£	£	Kg
Q40	**Q40: FENCING**								
Q4010	**Strained wire; BS 1722 Part 3**								
Q401002	**Concrete posts at 3.0 m centres; excavation, disposal and filling**								
Q401002A	0.85 m high 3 wire fence	m	0.37	9.82	0.90	5.14	15.86	17.45	14.084
Q401002B	end post	Nr	0.89	23.36	5.24	30.28	58.88	64.77	68.354
Q401002C	corner post	Nr	1.19	31.31	8.09	34.07	73.47	80.82	50.631
Q401002D	1.00 m high 6 wire fence	m	0.42	10.98	0.90	6.03	17.91	19.70	16.339
Q401002E	end post	Nr	1.09	28.72	5.24	36.00	69.96	76.96	73.531
Q401002F	corner post	Nr	1.27	33.63	8.09	42.69	84.41	92.85	55.620
Q401002G	1.40 m high 8 wire fence	m	0.48	12.62	0.90	6.47	19.99	21.99	18.259
Q401002H	end post	Nr	1.23	32.47	5.24	39.56	77.27	85.00	76.512
Q401002I	corner post	Nr	3.12	82.47	8.09	33.68	124.24	136.66	46.457
Q401003	**Treated softwood posts at 3.0 m centres; driven**								
Q401003A	0.85 m high 3 wire fence	m	0.27	7.02	0.05	1.85	8.92	9.81	3.163
Q401003B	end post	Nr	0.58	15.18	0.11	11.18	26.47	29.12	6.012
Q401003C	corner post	Nr	0.71	18.69	0.17	16.77	35.63	39.19	7.983
Q401003D	1.00 m high 6 wire fence	m	0.27	7.23	0.06	2.14	9.43	10.37	5.340
Q401003E	end post	Nr	0.58	15.42	0.11	13.49	29.02	31.92	7.247
Q401003F	corner post	Nr	0.73	19.17	0.17	25.45	44.79	49.27	10.151
Q401003G	1.40 m high 8 wire fence	m	0.28	7.47	0.06	2.51	10.04	11.04	7.149
Q401003H	end post	Nr	0.59	15.66	0.11	17.16	32.93	36.22	9.369
Q401003I	corner post	Nr	0.73	19.38	0.17	29.11	48.66	53.53	12.050
Q4011	**Chain link; BS 1722 Part 1; 4 mm PVC-u coated mesh**								
Q401105	**Concrete posts at 3.0 m centres; excavation, disposal and filling**								
Q401105A	0.90 m high fence	m	0.43	11.22	0.90	6.59	18.71	20.58	14.982
Q401105B	end post	Nr	0.89	23.36	4.41	30.59	58.36	64.20	69.541
Q401105C	corner post	Nr	1.19	31.31	8.09	34.07	73.47	80.82	50.631
Q401105D	gate post	Nr	0.89	23.36	5.24	30.59	59.19	65.11	69.602
Q401105E	1.20 m high fence	m	0.47	12.38	0.90	6.90	20.18	22.20	8.488
Q401105F	end post	Nr	1.09	28.72	5.24	34.38	68.34	75.17	73.079
Q401105G	corner post	Nr	1.27	33.63	8.09	39.45	81.17	89.29	55.392
Q401105H	gate post	Nr	1.09	28.72	5.24	34.38	68.34	75.17	73.079
Q401105I	1.80 m high fence	m	0.48	12.62	0.90	9.95	23.47	25.82	19.097
Q401105J	end post	Nr	1.23	32.47	4.41	40.19	77.07	84.78	78.526
Q401105K	corner post	Nr	1.35	35.75	8.09	40.39	84.23	92.65	55.258
Q401105L	gate post	Nr	1.09	28.72	5.24	40.19	74.15	81.57	78.587
Q401106	**Galvanised steel posts at 3.0 m centres; excavation, disposal and filling**								
Q401106A	0.90 m high fence	m	0.39	10.27	0.90	6.56	17.73	19.50	20.160
Q401106B	end post	Nr	0.81	21.49	5.24	29.69	56.42	62.06	93.160
Q401106C	corner post	Nr	0.97	25.69	8.09	44.98	78.76	86.64	134.301
Q401106D	gate post	Nr	0.84	22.20	5.24	29.69	57.13	62.84	93.160
Q401106E	1.20 m high fence	m	0.39	10.27	0.90	11.39	22.56	24.82	34.245
Q401106F	end post	Nr	0.81	21.49	5.24	31.14	57.87	63.66	97.806
Q401106G	corner post	Nr	0.97	25.69	8.09	47.88	81.66	89.83	143.593
Q401106H	gate post	Nr	0.84	22.20	5.24	31.14	58.58	64.44	97.806
Q401106I	1.80 m high fence	m	0.39	10.27	0.90	15.73	26.90	29.59	46.915
Q401106J	end post	Nr	0.81	21.49	5.24	38.38	65.11	71.62	118.922
Q401106K	corner post	Nr	0.97	25.69	8.09	58.02	91.80	100.98	173.155
Q401106L	gate post	Nr	0.84	22.20	5.24	38.38	65.82	72.40	118.922
Q4012	**Chain link BS 1722 Part 1; galvanised mesh; 3 rows barbed wire at top**								
Q401208	**Concrete posts with steel extension arms at 3.0 m centres; excavation, disposal and filling**								
Q401208A	1.80 m high fence	m	0.53	14.02	0.90	16.42	31.34	34.47	32.325
Q401208B	end post	Nr	1.28	33.87	5.24	41.89	81.00	89.10	80.519
Q401208C	corner post	Nr	1.40	36.91	7.84	48.68	93.43	102.77	64.984
Q401208D	gate post	Nr	1.28	33.87	5.24	41.89	81.00	89.10	80.519
Q401208E	2.10 m high fence	m	0.56	14.73	0.90	18.65	34.28	37.71	35.274
Q401208F	end post	Nr	1.31	34.58	5.24	47.74	87.56	96.32	85.576
Q401208G	corner post	Nr	1.43	37.62	7.84	56.77	102.23	112.45	72.208
Q401208H	gate post	Nr	1.31	34.58	5.24	47.74	87.56	96.32	85.576

Major Works 2011		Unit	Labour Hours	Labour Net	Plant Net	Materials Net	Unit Net	Unit with 10%	CO₂
				£	£	£	£	£	Kg
Q40	**Q40: FENCING**								
Q4012	**Chain link BS 1722 Part 1; galvanised mesh; 3 rows barbed wire at top**								
Q401209	**Concrete post with cranked tops at 3.0 m centres; excavation, disposal and filling**								
Q401209A	1.80 m high fence	m	0.55	14.49	0.90	13.28	28.67	31.54	29.941
Q401209B	end post	Nr	1.31	34.58	5.24	39.13	78.95	86.85	78.135
Q401209C	corner post	Nr	1.43	37.86	7.84	45.92	91.62	100.78	62.600
Q401209D	gate post	Nr	1.31	34.58	5.24	39.13	78.95	86.85	78.135
Q401209E	2.10 m high fence	m	0.58	15.18	0.90	14.78	30.86	33.95	32.409
Q401209F	end post	Nr	1.34	35.27	5.24	42.78	83.29	91.62	81.747
Q401209G	corner post	Nr	1.46	38.54	7.84	51.81	98.19	108.01	68.379
Q401209H	gate post	Nr	1.34	35.27	5.24	42.78	83.29	91.62	81.747
Q401210	**Galvanised steel posts with cranked tops at 3.0 m centres; excavation, disposal and filling**								
Q401210A	1.80 m high fence	m	0.51	13.54	0.90	16.17	30.61	33.67	39.727
Q401210B	end post	Nr	1.24	32.71	5.24	43.07	81.02	89.12	124.725
Q401210C	corner post	Nr	1.35	35.51	7.84	51.78	95.13	104.64	131.168
Q401210D	gate post	Nr	1.24	32.71	5.24	43.07	81.02	89.12	124.725
Q401210E	2.10 m high fence	m	0.53	14.02	0.90	17.93	32.85	36.14	44.526
Q401210F	end post	Nr	1.28	33.87	5.24	48.15	87.26	95.99	141.617
Q401210G	corner post	Nr	1.38	36.43	7.84	59.76	104.03	114.43	156.506
Q401210H	gate post	Nr	1.28	33.87	5.24	48.15	87.26	95.99	141.617
Q4013	**Chain link for tennis courts; BS 1722 Part 13; PVC-u coated**								
Q401312	**Galvanised steel posts at 3.0 m centres; excavation, disposal and filling**								
Q401312A	2.75 m high fence	m	0.60	15.89	0.90	16.24	33.03	36.33	30.228
Q401312B	end post	Nr	1.33	35.03	5.24	46.29	86.56	95.22	147.680
Q401312C	corner post	Nr	1.45	38.31	7.84	59.76	105.91	116.50	156.506
Q401312D	gate post	Nr	1.33	35.03	5.24	49.61	89.88	98.87	150.064
Q4014	**Wooden post and rail; BS 1722 Part 7; sawn mortice**								
Q401421	**Treated softwood posts and rails; posts at 3.0 m centres; driven**								
Q401421A	1.10 m high 3 rail fence	m	0.59	15.66	0.06	6.66	22.38	24.62	4.591
Q401421B	end post	Nr	0.42	10.98	0.11	15.39	26.48	29.13	9.354
Q401421C	corner post	Nr	0.49	12.86	0.17	22.32	35.35	38.89	13.568
Q401421D	intersection post	Nr	0.42	10.98	0.11	22.32	33.41	36.75	13.489
Q401421E	gate post	Nr	0.44	11.67	0.11	15.39	27.17	29.89	9.354
Q401421F	1.30 m high 4 rail fence	m	0.63	16.58	0.06	8.45	25.09	27.60	5.838
Q401421G	end post	Nr	0.43	11.46	0.11	18.47	30.04	33.04	11.192
Q401421H	corner post	Nr	0.50	13.31	0.17	26.93	40.41	44.45	16.324
Q401421I	intersection post	Nr	0.43	11.46	0.11	26.93	38.50	42.35	16.246
Q401421J	gate post	Nr	0.44	11.67	0.11	16.81	28.59	31.45	10.187
Q401422	**Untreated oak posts and rails; posts at 3.0 m centres; driven**								
Q401422A	1.10 m high 3 rail fence	m	0.89	23.36	0.06	16.65	40.07	44.08	4.826
Q401422B	end post	Nr	0.42	10.98	0.11	24.06	35.15	38.67	7.038
Q401422C	corner post	Nr	0.49	12.86	0.17	34.89	47.92	52.71	10.210
Q401422D	intersection post	Nr	0.42	10.98	0.11	34.89	45.98	50.58	10.131
Q401422E	gate post	Nr	0.44	11.67	0.11	24.06	35.84	39.42	7.038
Q401422F	1.30 m high 4 rail fence	m	0.63	16.58	0.06	21.53	38.17	41.99	6.216
Q401422G	end post	Nr	0.43	11.46	0.11	28.87	40.44	44.48	8.413
Q401422H	corner post	Nr	0.50	13.31	0.17	41.70	55.18	60.70	12.157
Q401422I	intersection post	Nr	0.43	11.46	0.11	42.10	53.67	59.04	12.193
Q401422J	gate post	Nr	0.48	12.62	0.11	28.87	41.60	45.76	8.413
Q4015	**Wooden post and rail; BS 1722, Part 7; nailed**								
Q401524	**Treated softwood posts and rails; posts at 1.8 m centres; driven**								
Q401524A	1.10 m high 3 rail fence	m	0.40	10.51	0.06	5.74	16.31	17.94	4.067
Q401524B	end post	Nr	0.42	10.98	0.11	9.33	20.42	22.46	5.455
Q401524C	corner post	Nr	0.49	12.86	0.17	13.99	27.02	29.72	8.040

Major Works 2011		Unit	Labour Hours	Labour Net	Plant Net	Materials Net	Unit Net	Unit with 10%	CO$_2$
				£	£	£	£	£	Kg
Q40	**Q40: FENCING**								
Q4015	**Wooden post and rail; BS 1722, Part 7; nailed**								
Q401524	**Treated softwood posts and rails; posts at 1.8 m centres; driven**								
Q401524D	intersection post	Nr	0.42	10.98	0.11	13.99	25.08	27.59	7.961
Q401524E	gate post	Nr	0.44	11.67	0.11	13.99	25.77	28.35	7.961
Q401524F	1.30 m high 4 rail fence	m	0.44	11.67	0.06	7.42	19.15	21.07	5.241
Q401524G	end post	Nr	0.43	11.46	0.11	10.82	22.39	24.63	6.569
Q401524H	corner post	Nr	0.50	13.31	0.17	15.49	28.97	31.87	9.432
Q401524I	intersection post	Nr	0.43	11.46	0.11	15.49	27.06	29.77	9.353
Q401524J	gate post	Nr	0.48	12.62	0.11	10.82	23.55	25.91	6.569
Q4016	**Wooden palisade; BS 1722 Part 6; nailed**								
Q401631	**Treated softwood posts and rails; posts at 3.0 m centres; excavation, disposal and filling**								
Q401631A	1.00 m high 3 rail fence	m	0.78	20.57	0.90	18.11	39.58	43.54	27.339
Q401631B	end post	Nr	0.58	15.42	5.24	24.59	45.25	49.78	63.657
Q401631C	corner post	Nr	0.73	19.17	7.84	24.59	51.60	56.76	43.491
Q401631D	gate post	Nr	0.58	15.42	5.24	29.25	49.91	54.90	66.163
Q401631E	1.40 m high 4 rail fence	m	0.81	21.49	0.90	25.57	47.96	52.76	33.801
Q401631F	end post	Nr	0.59	15.66	5.24	24.56	45.46	50.01	65.327
Q401631G	corner post	Nr	0.73	19.38	7.84	24.45	51.67	56.84	45.996
Q401631H	gate post	Nr	0.59	15.66	5.24	24.56	45.46	50.01	65.327
Q401631I	1.80 m high 6 rail fence	m	0.83	21.96	0.90	30.19	53.05	58.36	38.220
Q401631J	end post	Nr	0.60	15.89	5.24	26.06	47.19	51.91	66.998
Q401631K	corner post	Nr	0.75	19.85	7.84	26.78	54.47	59.92	48.503
Q401631L	gate post	Nr	0.60	15.89	5.24	26.06	47.19	51.91	66.998
Q4017	**Chestnut paling; BS 1722 Part 4**								
Q401733	**Treated softwood posts at 3.0 m centres; driven**								
Q401733A	0.90 m high fence	m	0.30	7.95	0.06	10.42	18.43	20.27	14.349
Q401733B	end post	Nr	0.58	15.18	0.11	8.75	24.04	26.44	5.334
Q401733C	corner post	Nr	0.71	18.69	0.17	11.91	30.77	33.85	7.645
Q401733D	1.05 m high fence	m	0.30	7.95	0.06	11.67	19.68	21.65	16.666
Q401733E	end post	Nr	0.58	15.18	0.11	10.71	26.00	28.60	5.891
Q401733F	corner post	Nr	0.71	18.69	0.17	15.37	34.23	37.65	8.480
Q401733G	1.20 m high fence	m	0.30	7.95	0.06	13.66	21.67	23.84	18.980
Q401733H	end post	Nr	0.58	15.18	0.11	10.14	25.43	27.97	6.447
Q401733I	corner post	Nr	0.71	18.69	0.17	14.81	33.67	37.04	9.314
Q401733J	1.35 m high fence	m	0.30	7.95	0.06	18.22	26.23	28.85	21.293
Q401733K	end post	Nr	0.58	15.18	0.11	12.20	27.49	30.24	7.005
Q401733L	corner post	Nr	0.71	18.69	0.17	17.33	36.19	39.81	10.151
Q401733M	1.80 m high fence	m	0.30	7.95	0.06	22.72	30.73	33.80	28.240
Q401733N	end post	Nr	0.58	15.18	0.11	13.58	28.87	31.76	8.675
Q401733O	corner post	Nr	0.71	18.69	0.17	18.79	37.65	41.42	12.656
Q4018	**Treated softwood close boarded; BS 1722 Part 5**								
Q401841	**Morticed concrete posts at 3.0 m centres; excavation, disposal and filling**								
Q401841A	1.00 m high fence	m	0.75	19.85	0.72	14.30	34.87	38.36	17.162
Q401841B	end post	Nr	0.11	2.80	2.17	13.88	18.85	20.74	28.794
Q401841C	corner post	Nr	0.11	2.80	2.17	15.79	20.76	22.84	28.794
Q401841D	gate post	Nr	0.11	2.80	2.17	13.88	18.85	20.74	28.794
Q401841E	1.20 m high fence	m	0.80	21.01	0.72	15.86	37.59	41.35	18.518
Q401841F	end post	Nr	0.13	3.51	2.17	15.05	20.73	22.80	30.263
Q401841G	corner post	Nr	0.13	3.51	2.17	17.11	22.79	25.07	30.263
Q401841H	gate post	Nr	0.13	3.51	2.17	15.05	20.73	22.80	30.263
Q401841I	1.50 m high fence	m	0.93	24.53	0.72	19.81	45.06	49.57	21.819
Q401841J	end post	Nr	0.13	3.51	2.17	15.60	21.28	23.41	31.732
Q401841K	corner post	Nr	0.13	3.51	2.17	18.23	23.91	26.30	31.732
Q401841L	gate post	Nr	0.13	3.51	2.17	15.60	21.28	23.41	31.732
Q401841M	1.80 m high fence	m	1.02	26.88	0.72	21.62	49.22	54.14	23.614
Q401841N	end post	Nr	0.13	3.51	2.17	15.79	21.47	23.62	33.201
Q401841O	corner post	Nr	0.13	3.51	2.17	18.61	24.29	26.72	33.201
Q401841P	gate post	Nr	0.13	3.51	2.17	15.79	21.47	23.62	33.201

Major Works 2011		Unit	Labour Hours	Labour Net	Plant Net	Materials Net	Unit Net	Unit with 10%	CO₂
				£	£	£	£	£	Kg
Q40	**Q40: FENCING**								
Q4018	**Treated softwood close boarded; BS 1722 Part 5**								
Q401842	**Treated sawn softwood posts at 3.0 m centres; excavation, disposal and filling**								
Q401842A	1.00 m high fence	m	0.71	18.69	0.72	13.10	32.51	35.76	15.737
Q401842B	end post	Nr	0.11	2.80	2.17	10.26	15.23	16.75	24.513
Q401842C	corner post	Nr	0.11	2.80	2.17	10.26	15.23	16.75	24.513
Q401842D	gate post	Nr	0.11	2.80	2.17	10.26	15.23	16.75	24.513
Q401842E	1.20 m high fence	m	0.73	19.27	0.72	14.60	34.59	38.05	16.789
Q401842F	gate post	Nr	0.13	3.51	2.17	11.28	16.96	18.66	25.070
Q401842G	corner post	Nr	0.13	3.51	2.17	11.28	16.96	18.66	25.070
Q401842H	gate post	Nr	0.13	3.51	2.17	11.28	16.96	18.66	25.070
Q401842I	1.50 m high fence	m	0.89	23.36	0.72	18.07	42.15	46.37	19.749
Q401842J	end post	Nr	0.13	3.51	2.17	10.51	16.19	17.81	25.627
Q401842K	corner post	Nr	0.13	3.51	2.17	10.51	16.19	17.81	25.627
Q401842L	gate post	Nr	0.13	3.51	2.17	10.51	16.19	17.81	25.627
Q401842M	1.80 m high fence	m	0.89	23.36	0.72	19.99	44.07	48.48	21.241
Q401842N	end post	Nr	0.13	3.51	2.17	11.01	16.69	18.36	26.183
Q401842O	corner post	Nr	0.13	3.51	2.17	11.01	16.69	18.36	26.183
Q401842P	gate post	Nr	0.13	3.51	2.17	11.01	16.69	18.36	26.183
Q4019	**Treated softwood woven panels; BS 1722 Part 11**								
Q401951	**Concrete posts at 1.8 m centres; excavation, disposal and filling**								
Q401951A	0.60 m high fence	m	0.84	22.20	0.72	11.77	34.69	38.16	17.599
Q401951B	end post	Nr	0.24	6.31	2.17	13.00	21.48	23.63	27.229
Q401951C	corner post	Nr	0.27	7.02	2.17	16.58	25.77	28.35	27.229
Q401951D	gate post	Nr	0.24	6.31	2.17	13.00	21.48	23.63	27.229
Q401951E	0.90 m high fence	m	0.89	23.36	0.72	13.33	37.41	41.15	19.629
Q401951F	end post	Nr	0.25	6.55	2.17	13.86	22.58	24.84	28.674
Q401951G	corner post	Nr	0.27	7.23	2.17	17.67	27.07	29.78	28.674
Q401951H	gate post	Nr	0.25	6.55	2.17	13.86	22.58	24.84	28.674
Q401951I	1.20 m high fence	m	0.93	24.53	0.72	14.54	39.79	43.77	21.659
Q401951J	end post	Nr	0.26	6.78	2.17	15.05	24.00	26.40	30.119
Q401951K	corner post	Nr	0.28	7.47	2.17	19.07	28.71	31.58	30.119
Q401951L	gate post	Nr	0.26	6.78	2.17	15.05	24.00	26.40	30.119
Q401951M	1.50 m high fence	m	0.97	25.69	0.72	15.75	42.16	46.38	23.688
Q401951N	end post	Nr	0.27	7.02	2.17	16.13	25.32	27.85	31.564
Q401951O	corner post	Nr	0.29	7.71	2.17	21.11	30.99	34.09	31.564
Q401951P	gate post	Nr	0.27	7.02	2.17	16.13	25.32	27.85	31.564
Q401951Q	1.80 m high fence	m	1.02	26.88	0.72	17.00	44.60	49.06	25.717
Q401951R	end post	Nr	0.27	7.23	2.17	16.50	25.90	28.49	33.008
Q401951S	corner post	Nr	0.30	7.95	2.17	22.66	32.78	36.06	33.008
Q401951T	gate post	Nr	0.27	7.23	2.17	16.50	25.90	28.49	33.008
Q401952	**Treated softwood posts at 1.8 m centres; excavation, disposal and filling**								
Q401952A	0.60 m high fence	m	0.71	18.69	0.72	9.72	29.13	32.04	15.696
Q401952B	end post	Nr	0.20	5.39	2.17	8.29	15.85	17.44	23.678
Q401952C	corner post	Nr	0.23	6.07	2.17	8.29	16.53	18.18	23.678
Q401952D	gate post	Nr	0.20	5.39	2.17	8.29	15.85	17.44	23.678
Q401952E	0.90 m high fence	m	0.73	19.38	0.72	11.99	32.09	35.30	17.077
Q401952F	end post	Nr	0.20	5.39	2.17	9.79	17.35	19.09	23.956
Q401952G	corner post	Nr	0.24	6.31	2.17	9.79	18.27	20.10	23.956
Q401952H	gate post	Nr	0.20	5.39	2.17	9.79	17.35	19.09	23.956
Q401952I	1.20 m high fence	m	0.76	20.09	0.72	13.10	33.91	37.30	18.457
Q401952J	end post	Nr	0.21	5.60	2.17	7.72	15.49	17.04	22.998
Q401952K	corner post	Nr	0.25	6.55	2.17	7.72	16.44	18.08	22.998
Q401952L	gate post	Nr	0.21	5.60	2.17	7.72	15.49	17.04	22.998
Q401952M	1.50 m high fence	m	0.80	21.01	0.72	14.53	36.26	39.89	20.340
Q401952N	end post	Nr	0.21	5.60	2.17	10.34	18.11	19.92	25.348
Q401952O	corner post	Nr	0.26	6.78	2.17	10.34	19.29	21.22	25.348
Q401952P	gate post	Nr	0.21	5.60	2.17	10.34	18.11	19.92	25.348
Q401952Q	1.80 m high fence	m	0.83	21.96	0.72	16.92	39.60	43.56	21.875
Q401952R	end post	Nr	0.22	5.83	2.17	12.58	20.58	22.64	25.905
Q401952S	corner post	Nr	0.27	7.02	2.17	12.58	21.77	23.95	25.905
Q401952T	gate post	Nr	0.22	5.83	2.17	12.58	20.58	22.64	25.905
Q4050	**Field gates; BS 3470 Table 1**								
Q405062	**Treated softwood**								
Q405062A	2.40 x 1.10 m high	Nr	3.10	81.76	-	95.76	177.52	195.27	29.754
Q405062B	2.70 x 1.10 m high	Nr	3.32	87.60	-	98.09	185.69	204.26	32.816
Q405062C	3.00 x 1.10 m high	Nr	3.76	99.29	-	100.42	199.71	219.68	35.879
Q405062D	3.30 x 1.10 m high	Nr	4.12	108.64	-	103.97	212.61	233.87	38.942

Paving, Planting, Fencing & Furniture

Major Works 2011		Unit	Labour Hours	Labour Net	Plant Net	Materials Net	Unit Net	Unit with 10%	CO₂
				£	£	£	£	£	Kg
Q40	**Q40: FENCING**								
Q4050	**Field gates; BS 3470 Table 1**								
Q405062	**Treated softwood**								
Q405062E	3.60 x 1.10 m high	Nr	4.38	115.63	-	107.36	222.99	245.29	42.005
Q405062F	3.90 x 1.10 m high	Nr	4.73	124.98	-	110.96	235.94	259.53	45.068
Q405062G	4.20 x 1.10 m high	Nr	5.09	134.32	-	115.35	249.67	274.64	48.130
Q405063	**Untreated hardwood**								
Q405063A	2.40 x 1.10 m high	Nr	3.19	84.11	-	201.44	285.55	314.11	37.822
Q405063B	2.70 x 1.10 m high	Nr	3.41	89.94	-	210.04	299.98	329.98	41.893
Q405063C	3.00 x 1.10 m high	Nr	3.85	101.61	-	216.14	317.75	349.53	45.965
Q405063D	3.30 x 1.10 m high	Nr	4.20	110.96	-	238.61	349.57	384.53	50.036
Q405063E	3.60 x 1.10 m high	Nr	4.47	117.98	-	246.38	364.36	400.80	54.108
Q405063F	3.90 x 1.10 m high	Nr	4.82	127.30	-	253.87	381.17	419.29	58.179
Q405063H	4.20 x 1.10 m high	Nr	5.18	136.65	-	259.97	396.62	436.28	62.250
Q4051	**Domestic entrance gates; BS 4092 Part 2**								
Q405165	**Treated softwood**								
Q405165A	0.81 x 0.90 m high	Nr	3.54	93.43	-	65.35	158.78	174.66	7.471
Q405165B	1.02 x 0.90 m high	Nr	3.85	101.61	-	66.46	168.07	184.88	9.225
Q405165C	2.13 x 0.90 m high	Nr	4.12	108.64	-	101.96	210.60	231.66	18.497
Q405165D	2.64 x 0.09 m high	Nr	4.38	115.63	-	108.62	224.25	246.68	22.757
Q4052	**Standard softwood gates**								
Q405223	**Boulton and Paul softwood preservative treated gates**								
Q405223H	GTE 30GTE; 914 x 1041 mm	Nr	0.60	10.19	-	73.73	83.92	92.31	9.608
Q405223I	GTE 36GTE; 1067 x 1041 mm	Nr	0.75	12.73	-	83.51	96.24	105.86	11.216
Q405223K	3060GS; 914 x 1981 mm; arch top gate	Nr	0.85	14.43	-	138.98	153.41	168.75	18.284

Disposal Systems

Major Works 2011		Unit	Labour Hours	Labour Net	Plant Net	Materials Net	Unit Net	Unit with 10%	CO$_2$
				£	£	£	£	£	Kg
R10	**R10: RAINWATER PIPEWORK AND GUTTERS**								
R1011	**PVC-u rainwater pipes and fittings; BS 4576**								
R101103	**Pipes; fixing with standard clips to masonry backgrounds**								
R101103A	50 mm dia	m	0.30	12.05	-	4.66	16.71	18.38	3.115
R101103B	68 mm dia	m	0.31	12.45	-	5.55	18.00	19.80	3.137
R101103C	110 mm dia	m	0.33	13.25	-	10.99	24.24	26.66	4.276
R101104	**Fittings**								
R101104A	50 mm shoes	Nr	0.30	12.05	-	3.20	15.25	16.78	0.138
R101104B	50 mm bends	Nr	0.30	12.05	-	4.33	16.38	18.02	0.145
R101104C	50 mm offsets; 150 mm projection	Nr	0.35	14.05	-	9.71	23.76	26.14	0.386
R101104D	50 mm offsets; 300 mm projection	Nr	0.38	15.26	-	10.30	25.56	28.12	0.850
R101104E	50 mm branches	Nr	0.60	24.06	-	19.32	43.38	47.72	0.441
R101104F	68 mm shoes	Nr	0.32	12.85	-	3.49	16.34	17.97	0.183
R101104G	68 mm bends	Nr	0.32	12.85	-	3.31	16.16	17.78	0.460
R101104H	68 mm offsets; 150 mm projection	Nr	0.36	14.45	-	6.92	21.37	23.51	0.920
R101104I	68 mm offsets; 300 mm projection	Nr	0.40	16.06	-	7.56	23.62	25.98	1.384
R101104J	68 mm branches	Nr	0.32	12.85	-	10.54	23.39	25.73	0.385
R101104K	110 mm shoes	Nr	0.34	13.65	-	21.77	35.42	38.96	1.125
R101104L	110 mm bends	Nr	0.34	13.65	-	15.54	29.19	32.11	0.905
R101104M	110 mm offsets; 150 mm projection	Nr	0.39	15.66	-	29.85	45.51	50.06	2.250
R101104N	110 mm offsets; 300 mm projection	Nr	0.43	17.26	-	31.31	48.57	53.43	2.876
R101104O	110 mm branches	Nr	0.34	13.65	-	21.50	35.15	38.67	0.115
R1051	**PVC-u rainwater gutters and fittings; BS 4576**								
R105106	**Gutters; fixing with standard clips to woodwork backgrounds**								
R105106A	76 mm dia	m	0.25	10.05	-	4.48	14.53	15.98	3.151
R105106B	112 mm dia	m	0.27	10.85	-	5.94	16.79	18.47	4.329
R105106C	150 mm dia	m	0.29	11.65	-	18.41	30.06	33.07	7.914
R105107	**Fittings**								
R105107A	76 mm stop ends	Nr	0.16	6.41	-	4.05	10.46	11.51	0.150
R105107B	76 mm stop end outlets	Nr	0.22	8.85	-	5.18	14.03	15.43	0.190
R105107C	76 mm running outlets	Nr	0.22	8.85	-	5.27	14.12	15.53	0.198
R105107D	76 mm angles	Nr	0.22	8.85	-	5.18	14.03	15.43	0.183
R105107E	112 mm stop ends	Nr	0.16	6.41	-	2.28	8.69	9.56	0.150
R105107F	112 mm stop end outlets	Nr	0.22	8.85	-	8.41	17.26	18.99	0.553
R105107G	112 mm running outlets	Nr	0.22	8.85	-	6.97	15.82	17.40	0.453
R105107H	112 mm angles	Nr	0.22	8.85	-	6.62	15.47	17.02	0.536
R105107I	150 mm stop ends	Nr	0.16	6.41	-	8.53	14.94	16.43	0.285
R105107J	150 mm stop end outlets	Nr	0.22	8.85	-	24.38	33.23	36.55	1.608
R105107K	150 mm running outlets	Nr	0.22	8.85	-	21.67	30.52	33.57	1.390
R105107L	150 mm angles	Nr	0.22	8.85	-	23.79	32.64	35.90	1.068

Disposal Systems

		Unit	Labour Hours	Labour Net	Plant Net	Materials Net	Unit Net	Unit with 10%	CO₂
				£	£	£	£	£	Kg
R11	R11: FOUL DRAINAGE ABOVE GROUND								
R1111	PVC-u soil and vent pipes; BS 4514								
R111122	Pipes; fixing with standard clips to masonry backgrounds								
R111122A	82 mm dia	m	0.40	16.06	–	14.01	30.07	33.08	3.268
R111122B	110 mm dia	m	0.42	16.86	–	12.94	29.80	32.78	4.509
R111122C	160 mm dia	m	0.46	18.46	–	34.85	53.31	58.64	6.844
R1113	ABS waste pipes; BS 5255								
R111325	Pipes including fittings; fixing with standard clips to masonry backgrounds								
R111325A	32 mm dia	m	0.26	10.45	–	2.47	12.92	14.21	0.618
R111325B	40 mm dia	m	0.28	11.25	–	2.91	14.16	15.58	0.782
R111325C	50 mm dia	m	0.30	12.05	–	7.75	19.80	21.78	1.098
R1115	PVC-u overflow pipes								
R111527	Pipes including fittings; fixing with standard clips to masonry backgrounds								
R111527A	19 mm dia	m	0.18	7.21	–	1.66	8.87	9.76	0.369
R1120	PVC-u soil and vent pipe fittings; BS 4514								
R112023	Fittings								
R112023A	82 mm WC connectors	Nr	0.30	12.05	–	6.99	19.04	20.94	0.975
R112023B	82 mm bends	Nr	0.36	14.45	–	18.33	32.78	36.06	0.923
R112023C	82 mm branches	Nr	0.45	18.06	–	24.97	43.03	47.33	1.601
R112023D	82 mm double branches	Nr	0.85	34.11	–	49.94	84.05	92.46	3.202
R112023E	82 mm boss connectors	Nr	0.45	18.06	–	14.02	32.08	35.29	0.826
R112023F	82 mm access doors	Nr	0.52	20.86	–	28.53	49.39	54.33	1.378
R112023G	82 mm bird guards	Nr	0.20	8.01	–	3.97	11.98	13.18	0.150
R112023H	110 mm WC connectors	Nr	0.32	12.85	–	6.99	19.84	21.82	1.390
R112023I	110 mm bends	Nr	0.39	15.66	–	18.71	34.37	37.81	1.105
R112023J	110 mm branches	Nr	0.50	20.06	–	25.35	45.41	49.95	2.123
R112023K	110 mm double branches	Nr	0.60	24.06	–	54.43	78.49	86.34	2.115
R112023L	110 mm boss connectors	Nr	0.50	20.06	–	15.67	35.73	39.30	4.381
R112023M	110 mm access doors	Nr	0.87	34.91	–	12.02	46.93	51.62	0.600
R112023N	110 mm bird guards	Nr	0.20	8.01	–	3.46	11.47	12.62	0.225
R112023O	160 mm WC connectors	Nr	0.34	13.65	–	27.14	40.79	44.87	2.820
R112023P	160 mm bends	Nr	0.41	16.46	–	83.85	100.31	110.34	3.253
R112023Q	160 mm branches	Nr	0.54	21.66	–	97.52	119.18	131.10	5.015
R112023R	160 mm double branches	Nr	0.65	26.07	–	145.15	171.22	188.34	4.860
R112023S	160 mm boss connectors	Nr	0.54	21.66	–	74.76	96.42	106.06	3.535
R112023T	160 mm access doors	Nr	0.90	36.12	–	98.07	134.19	147.61	4.690
R112023U	160 mm bird guards	Nr	0.21	8.41	–	11.40	19.81	21.79	0.540
R1121	Polypropylene accessories; BS 5254								
R112132	Valves								
R112132A	110 mm air admittance valve	Nr	0.45	18.06	–	58.84	76.90	84.59	0.500
R112133	Traps								
R112133A	32 mm bottle trap, 38 mm seal	Nr	0.22	8.85	–	5.10	13.95	15.35	0.078
R112133B	32 mm bottle trap, 76 mm seal, anti-syphon	Nr	0.42	16.86	–	34.25	51.11	56.22	0.349
R112133C	32 mm tubular S trap, 76 mm seal	Nr	0.22	8.85	–	5.89	14.74	16.21	0.078
R112133D	40 mm bottle P trap, 38 mm seal	Nr	0.24	9.65	–	6.24	15.89	17.48	0.113
R112133E	40 mm bottle P trap, 76 mm seal, anti-syphon	Nr	0.45	18.06	–	35.89	53.95	59.35	0.419
R112133F	40 mm tubular S trap, 76 mm seal	Nr	0.24	9.65	–	7.93	17.58	19.34	0.113
R112134	Expansion compensators								
R112134A	32 mm	Nr	0.16	6.41	–	2.01	8.42	9.26	0.058
R112134B	40 mm	Nr	0.17	6.81	–	2.06	8.87	9.76	0.080
R112134C	50 mm	Nr	0.19	7.61	–	3.79	11.40	12.54	0.075

Major Works 2011		Unit	Labour Hours	Labour Net	Plant Net	Materials Net	Unit Net	Unit with 10%	CO$_2$
				£	£	£	£	£	Kg
R12	**R12: DRAINAGE BELOW GROUND**								
R1201	**Excavation of trenches; by machine; for drainage pipes or the like, including disposal and filling**								
R120113	**Trenches to suit pipes not exceeding 200 mm dia; average depth**								
R120113A	0.50 m	m	0.12	1.52	1.93	–	3.45	3.80	1.737
R120113B	0.75 m	m	0.15	1.90	2.61	–	4.51	4.96	2.340
R120113C	1.00 m	m	0.22	2.79	3.36	–	6.15	6.77	3.028
R120113D	1.25 m	m	0.29	3.68	4.54	–	8.22	9.04	4.076
R120113E	1.50 m	m	0.36	4.57	5.29	–	9.86	10.85	4.765
R120113F	1.75 m	m	0.42	5.33	6.24	–	11.57	12.73	5.612
R120113G	2.00 m	m	0.49	6.22	6.99	–	13.21	14.53	6.301
R120113H	2.25 m	m	0.57	7.24	8.62	–	15.86	17.45	7.751
R120113I	2.50 m	m	0.65	8.25	9.60	–	17.85	19.64	8.640
R120113J	2.75 m	m	0.73	9.27	10.58	–	19.85	21.84	9.530
R120113K	3.00 m	m	0.82	10.41	11.79	–	22.20	24.42	10.621
R120113L	3.25 m	m	0.91	11.56	13.00	–	24.56	27.02	11.712
R120113M	3.50 m	m	1.00	12.70	14.21	–	26.91	29.60	12.802
R120114	**Trenches to suit 225 mm dia pipes; average depth**								
R120114A	0.50 m	m	0.15	1.91	2.40	–	4.31	4.74	2.160
R120114B	0.75 m	m	0.19	2.41	3.31	–	5.72	6.29	2.964
R120114C	1.00 m	m	0.30	3.81	4.77	–	8.58	9.44	4.277
R120114D	1.25 m	m	0.37	4.70	5.94	–	10.64	11.70	5.325
R120114E	1.50 m	m	0.46	5.84	6.94	–	12.78	14.06	6.236
R120114F	1.75 m	m	0.53	6.73	8.11	–	14.84	16.32	7.284
R120114G	2.00 m	m	0.61	7.75	9.10	–	16.85	18.54	8.174
R120114H	2.25 m	m	0.73	9.27	11.43	–	20.70	22.77	10.248
R120114I	2.50 m	m	0.81	10.29	12.62	–	22.91	25.20	11.318
R120114J	2.75 m	m	0.89	11.30	13.60	–	24.90	27.39	12.207
R120114K	3.00 m	m	0.98	12.45	14.81	–	27.26	29.99	13.298
R120114L	3.25 m	m	1.07	13.59	16.02	–	29.61	32.57	14.389
R120114M	3.50 m	m	1.16	14.73	17.23	–	31.96	35.16	15.480
R120115	**Trenches to suit 300 mm dia pipes; average depth**								
R120115A	0.50 m	m	0.18	2.29	2.87	–	5.16	5.68	2.584
R120115B	0.75 m	m	0.23	2.92	4.01	–	6.93	7.62	3.589
R120115C	1.00 m	m	0.36	4.57	5.92	–	10.49	11.54	5.304
R120115D	1.25 m	m	0.43	5.46	7.10	–	12.56	13.82	6.352
R120115E	1.50 m	m	0.55	6.99	8.57	–	15.56	17.12	7.686
R120115F	1.75 m	m	0.62	7.87	9.75	–	17.62	19.38	8.734
R120115G	2.00 m	m	0.72	9.14	11.18	–	20.32	22.35	10.026
R120115H	2.25 m	m	0.87	11.05	13.99	–	25.04	27.54	12.524
R120115I	2.50 m	m	0.96	12.19	15.41	–	27.60	30.36	13.794
R120115J	2.75 m	m	1.06	13.46	16.84	–	30.30	33.33	15.086
R120115K	3.00 m	m	1.16	14.73	17.83	–	32.56	35.82	15.975
R120115L	3.25 m	m	1.25	15.88	18.81	–	34.69	38.16	16.865
R120115M	3.50 m	m	1.34	17.02	19.79	–	36.81	40.49	17.755
R120116	**Trenches to suit 400 mm dia pipes; average depth**								
R120116A	0.50 m	m	0.21	2.67	3.58	–	6.25	6.88	3.208
R120116B	0.75 m	m	0.27	3.43	4.94	–	8.37	9.21	4.414
R120116C	1.00 m	m	0.39	4.95	6.63	–	11.58	12.74	5.928
R120116D	1.25 m	m	0.50	6.35	8.94	–	15.29	16.82	7.981
R120116E	1.50 m	m	0.64	8.13	10.66	–	18.79	20.67	9.538
R120116F	1.75 m	m	0.72	9.14	12.06	–	21.20	23.32	10.787
R120116G	2.00 m	m	0.83	10.54	13.73	–	24.27	26.70	12.280
R120116H	2.25 m	m	1.01	12.83	17.23	–	30.06	33.07	15.402
R120116I	2.50 m	m	1.11	14.10	18.88	–	32.98	36.28	16.873
R120116J	2.75 m	m	1.23	15.62	20.77	–	36.39	40.03	18.567
R120116K	3.00 m	m	1.34	17.02	22.44	–	39.46	43.41	20.060
R120116L	3.25 m	m	1.43	18.16	23.86	–	42.02	46.22	21.330
R120116M	3.50 m	m	1.52	19.30	25.05	–	44.35	48.79	22.399
R120117	**Trenches to suit 450 mm dia pipes; average depth**								
R120117A	0.50 m	m	0.24	3.05	4.05	–	7.10	7.81	3.631
R120117B	0.75 m	m	0.30	3.81	5.42	–	9.23	10.15	4.837
R120117C	1.00 m	m	0.42	5.33	7.10	–	12.43	13.67	6.352
R120117D	1.25 m	m	0.56	7.11	10.10	–	17.21	18.93	9.007
R120117E	1.50 m	m	0.72	9.14	12.06	–	21.20	23.32	10.787
R120117F	1.75 m	m	0.82	10.41	13.92	–	24.33	26.76	12.438
R120117G	2.00 m	m	0.94	11.94	15.81	–	27.75	30.53	14.132
R120117H	2.25 m	m	1.15	14.61	19.56	–	34.17	37.59	17.476

Disposal Systems

	Unit	Labour Hours	Labour Net £	Plant Net £	Materials Net £	Unit Net £	Unit with 10% £	CO₂ Kg

R12	**R12: DRAINAGE BELOW GROUND**							
R1201	**Excavation of trenches; by machine; for drainage pipes or the like, including disposal and filling**							
R120117	**Trenches to suit 450 mm dia pipes; average depth**							
R120117I	2.50 m	m	1.28	16.26	21.67	-	37.93	41.72	19.350
R120117J	2.75 m	m	1.39	17.65	23.79	-	41.44	45.58	21.244
R120117K	3.00 m	m	1.52	19.30	25.91	-	45.21	49.73	23.139
R120117L	3.25 m	m	1.64	20.83	27.80	-	48.63	53.49	24.833
R120117M	3.50 m	m	1.76	22.35	29.70	-	52.05	57.26	26.527
R120118	**Trenches to suit 525 mm dia pipes; average depth**							
R120118A	0.50 m	m	0.27	3.43	4.75	-	8.18	9.00	4.256
R120118B	0.75 m	m	0.34	4.32	6.35	-	10.67	11.74	5.663
R120118C	1.00 m	m	0.47	5.97	8.26	-	14.23	15.65	7.378
R120118D	1.25 m	m	0.63	8.00	11.71	-	19.71	21.68	10.436
R120118E	1.50 m	m	0.81	10.29	13.92	-	24.21	26.63	12.438
R120118F	1.75 m	m	0.92	11.68	16.01	-	27.69	30.46	14.290
R120118G	2.00 m	m	1.06	13.46	18.15	-	31.61	34.77	16.206
R120118H	2.25 m	m	1.29	16.38	22.35	-	38.73	42.60	19.953
R120118I	2.50 m	m	1.42	18.03	24.69	-	42.72	46.99	22.027
R120118J	2.75 m	m	1.56	19.81	27.04	-	46.85	51.54	24.123
R120118K	3.00 m	m	1.70	21.59	29.38	-	50.97	56.07	26.218
R120118L	3.25 m	m	1.84	23.37	31.73	-	55.10	60.61	28.314
R120118M	3.50 m	m	1.98	25.15	34.08	-	59.23	65.15	30.410
R120119	**Trenches to suit 600 mm dia pipes; average depth**							
R120119A	1.00 m	m	0.53	6.73	9.43	-	16.16	17.78	8.426
R120119B	1.25 m	m	0.71	9.02	13.12	-	22.14	24.35	11.685
R120119C	1.50 m	m	0.90	11.43	15.55	-	26.98	29.68	13.888
R120119D	1.75 m	m	1.03	13.08	17.88	-	30.96	34.06	15.962
R120119E	2.00 m	m	1.18	14.99	20.25	-	35.24	38.76	18.079
R120119F	2.25 m	m	1.43	18.16	25.14	-	43.30	47.63	22.429
R120119G	2.50 m	m	1.57	19.94	27.70	-	47.64	52.40	24.704
R120119H	2.75 m	m	1.74	22.10	30.07	-	52.17	57.39	26.821
R120119I	3.00 m	m	1.89	24.00	32.65	-	56.65	62.32	29.118
R120119L	3.25 m	m	2.04	25.91	35.22	-	61.13	67.24	31.415
R120119M	3.50 m	m	2.19	27.81	37.80	-	65.61	72.17	33.712
R120120	**Trenches to suit 700 mm dia pipes; average depth**							
R120120A	1.00 m	m	0.58	7.37	10.15	-	17.52	19.27	9.072
R120120B	1.25 m	m	0.76	9.65	13.83	-	23.48	25.83	12.331
R120120C	1.50 m	m	0.96	12.19	16.73	-	28.92	31.81	14.936
R120120D	1.75 m	m	1.11	14.10	19.30	-	33.40	36.74	17.232
R120120E	2.00 m	m	1.27	16.13	21.90	-	38.03	41.83	19.551
R120120F	2.25 m	m	1.54	19.56	26.79	-	46.35	50.99	23.900
R120120G	2.50 m	m	1.70	21.59	29.82	-	51.41	56.55	26.599
R120120H	2.75 m	m	1.87	23.75	32.65	-	56.40	62.04	29.118
R120120I	3.00 m	m	2.03	25.78	35.68	-	61.46	67.61	31.817
R120121	**Trenches to suit 800 mm dia pipes; average depth**							
R120121A	1.00 m	m	0.64	8.13	11.32	-	19.45	21.40	10.120
R120121B	1.25 m	m	0.85	10.79	15.48	-	26.27	28.90	13.802
R120121C	1.50 m	m	1.06	13.46	18.37	-	31.83	35.01	16.407
R120121D	1.75 m	m	1.23	15.62	21.20	-	36.82	40.50	18.926
R120121E	2.00 m	m	1.40	17.78	24.02	-	41.80	45.98	21.445
R120121F	2.25 m	m	1.70	21.59	29.61	-	51.20	56.32	26.419
R120121G	2.50 m	m	1.87	23.75	32.65	-	56.40	62.04	29.118
R120121H	2.75 m	m	2.06	26.16	35.94	-	62.10	68.31	32.061
R120121I	3.00 m	m	2.23	28.32	38.98	-	67.30	74.03	34.760
R1202	**Excavation of trenches; by hand; for drainage pipes or the like, including disposal and filling**							
R120242	**Trenches to suit pipes not exceeding 200 mm dia; average depth**							
R120242A	0.50 m	m	1.32	16.76	0.10	-	16.86	18.55	0.129
R120242B	0.75 m	m	1.78	22.61	0.10	-	22.71	24.98	0.129
R120242C	1.00 m	m	2.23	28.32	0.17	-	28.49	31.34	0.214
R120242D	1.25 m	m	2.94	37.34	0.21	-	37.55	41.31	0.257
R120242E	1.50 m	m	3.45	43.81	0.27	-	44.08	48.49	0.343

Major Works 2011		Unit	Labour Hours	Labour Net £	Plant Net £	Materials Net £	Unit Net £	Unit with 10% £	CO$_2$ Kg
R12	**R12: DRAINAGE BELOW GROUND**								
R1202	**Excavation of trenches; by hand; for drainage pipes or the like, including disposal and filling**								
R120242	**Trenches to suit pipes not exceeding 200 mm dia; average depth**								
R120242F	1.75 m	m	3.96	50.29	0.31	-	50.60	55.66	0.386
R120242G	2.00 m	m	4.46	56.64	0.38	-	57.02	62.72	0.472
R120242H	2.25 m	m	5.48	69.60	0.41	-	70.01	77.01	0.515
R120242I	2.50 m	m	6.04	76.71	0.48	-	77.19	84.91	0.600
R120242J	2.75 m	m	6.60	83.82	0.55	-	84.37	92.81	0.686
R120242K	3.00 m	m	7.16	90.93	0.62	-	91.55	100.71	0.772
R120243	**Trenches to suit pipes not exceeding 225 mm dia; average depth**								
R120243A	0.50 m	m	1.76	22.35	0.12	-	22.47	24.72	0.150
R120243B	0.75 m	m	2.36	29.97	0.12	-	30.09	33.10	0.150
R120243C	1.00 m	m	2.97	37.72	0.21	-	37.93	41.72	0.257
R120243D	1.25 m	m	3.92	49.78	0.24	-	50.02	55.02	0.300
R120243E	1.50 m	m	4.59	58.29	0.32	-	58.61	64.47	0.407
R120243F	1.75 m	m	5.27	66.93	0.36	-	67.29	74.02	0.450
R120243G	2.00 m	m	5.94	75.44	0.43	-	75.87	83.46	0.536
R120243H	2.25 m	m	7.29	92.58	0.48	-	93.06	102.37	0.600
R120243I	2.50 m	m	8.04	102.11	0.53	-	102.64	112.90	0.665
R120243J	2.75 m	m	8.79	111.63	0.60	-	112.23	123.45	0.750
R120243K	3.00 m	m	9.54	121.16	0.67	-	121.83	134.01	0.836
R120244	**Trenches to suit pipes not exceeding 300 mm dia; average depth**								
R120244A	0.50 m	m	2.20	27.94	0.14	-	28.08	30.89	0.172
R120244B	0.75 m	m	2.96	37.59	0.14	-	37.73	41.50	0.172
R120244C	1.00 m	m	3.72	47.24	0.22	-	47.46	52.21	0.279
R120244D	1.25 m	m	4.90	62.23	0.26	-	62.49	68.74	0.322
R120244E	1.50 m	m	5.74	72.90	0.36	-	73.26	80.59	0.450
R120244F	1.75 m	m	6.59	83.69	0.39	-	84.08	92.49	0.493
R120244G	2.00 m	m	7.43	94.36	0.46	-	94.82	104.30	0.579
R120244H	2.25 m	m	9.12	115.82	0.53	-	116.35	127.99	0.665
R120244I	2.50 m	m	10.06	127.76	0.58	-	128.34	141.17	0.729
R120244J	2.75 m	m	10.99	139.57	0.65	-	140.22	154.24	0.815
R120244K	3.00 m	m	11.93	151.51	0.72	-	152.23	167.45	0.900
R120245	**Trenches to suit pipes not exceeding 400 mm dia; average depth**								
R120245A	0.50 m	m	3.24	41.15	0.15	-	41.30	45.43	0.193
R120245B	0.75 m	m	3.88	49.28	0.15	-	49.43	54.37	0.193
R120245C	1.00 m	m	4.80	60.96	0.24	-	61.20	67.32	0.300
R120245D	1.25 m	m	6.21	78.87	0.27	-	79.14	87.05	0.343
R120245E	1.50 m	m	7.33	93.09	0.39	-	93.48	102.83	0.493
R120245F	1.75 m	m	8.24	104.65	0.43	-	105.08	115.59	0.536
R120245G	2.00 m	m	9.25	117.47	0.50	-	117.97	129.77	0.622
R120245H	2.25 m	m	11.28	143.26	0.58	-	143.84	158.22	0.729
R120245I	2.50 m	m	12.40	157.48	0.63	-	158.11	173.92	0.793
R120245J	2.75 m	m	13.53	171.83	0.70	-	172.53	189.78	0.879
R120245K	3.00 m	m	14.65	186.06	0.77	-	186.83	205.51	0.965
R120246	**Trenches to suit pipes not exceeding 450 mm dia; average depth**								
R120246A	0.50 m	m	3.73	47.37	0.17	-	47.54	52.29	0.214
R120246B	0.75 m	m	4.47	56.77	0.17	-	56.94	62.63	0.214
R120246C	1.00 m	m	5.44	69.09	0.26	-	69.35	76.29	0.322
R120246D	1.25 m	m	7.05	89.53	0.29	-	89.82	98.80	0.364
R120246E	1.50 m	m	8.19	104.01	0.43	-	104.44	114.88	0.536
R120246F	1.75 m	m	9.32	118.36	0.46	-	118.82	130.70	0.579
R120246G	2.00 m	m	10.46	132.84	0.53	-	133.37	146.71	0.665
R120246H	2.25 m	m	12.78	162.31	0.63	-	162.94	179.23	0.793
R120246I	2.50 m	m	14.05	178.44	0.68	-	179.12	197.03	0.858
R120246J	2.75 m	m	15.31	194.44	0.75	-	195.19	214.71	0.943
R120246K	3.00 m	m	16.58	210.57	0.82	-	211.39	232.53	1.029
R120247	**Trenches to suit pipes not exceeding 525 mm dia; average depth**								
R120247A	0.50 m	m	5.58	70.87	0.19	-	71.06	78.17	0.236
R120247B	0.75 m	m	6.44	81.79	0.19	-	81.98	90.18	0.236

Disposal Systems

Major Works 2011		Unit	Labour Hours	Labour Net £	Plant Net £	Materials Net £	Unit Net £	Unit with 10% £	CO₂ Kg
R12	**R12: DRAINAGE BELOW GROUND**								
R1202	**Excavation of trenches; by hand; for drainage pipes or the like, including disposal and filling**								
R120247	**Trenches to suit pipes not exceeding 525 mm dia; average depth**								
R120247C	1.00 m	m	7.29	92.58	0.27	-	92.85	102.14	0.343
R120247D	1.25 m	m	9.18	116.59	0.31	-	116.90	128.59	0.386
R120247E	1.50 m	m	10.53	133.73	0.46	-	134.19	147.61	0.579
R120247F	1.75 m	m	11.88	150.88	0.50	-	151.38	166.52	0.622
R120247G	2.00 m	m	13.23	168.02	0.58	-	168.60	185.46	0.729
R120247H	2.25 m	m	15.93	202.31	0.68	-	202.99	223.29	0.858
R120247I	2.50 m	m	17.43	221.36	0.74	-	222.10	244.31	0.922
R120247J	2.75 m	m	18.93	240.41	0.80	-	241.21	265.33	1.008
R120247K	3.00 m	m	20.43	259.46	0.87	-	260.33	286.36	1.093
R120248	**Trenches to suit pipes not exceeding 600 mm dia; average depth**								
R120248A	1.00 m	m	8.91	113.16	0.31	-	113.47	124.82	0.386
R120248B	1.25 m	m	10.63	135.00	0.34	-	135.34	148.87	0.429
R120248C	1.50 m	m	12.15	154.31	0.50	-	154.81	170.29	0.622
R120248D	1.75 m	m	13.67	173.61	0.55	-	174.16	191.58	0.686
R120248E	2.00 m	m	15.19	192.91	0.63	-	193.54	212.89	0.793
R120248F	2.25 m	m	18.22	231.39	0.74	-	232.13	255.34	0.922
R120248G	2.50 m	m	19.92	252.98	0.79	-	253.77	279.15	0.986
R120248H	2.75 m	m	21.60	274.32	0.87	-	275.19	302.71	1.093
R120248I	3.00 m	m	23.29	295.78	0.94	-	296.72	326.39	1.179
R120249	**Trenches to suit pipes not exceeding 700 mm dia; average depth**								
R120249A	1.00 m	m	10.36	131.57	0.34	-	131.91	145.10	0.429
R120249B	1.25 m	m	12.27	155.83	0.38	-	156.21	171.83	0.472
R120249C	1.50 m	m	13.96	177.29	0.53	-	177.82	195.60	0.665
R120249D	1.75 m	m	15.64	198.63	0.60	-	199.23	219.15	0.750
R120249E	2.00 m	m	17.33	220.09	0.68	-	220.77	242.85	0.858
R120249F	2.25 m	m	20.71	263.02	0.79	-	263.81	290.19	0.986
R120249G	2.50 m	m	22.58	286.77	0.85	-	287.62	316.38	1.072
R120249H	2.75 m	m	24.46	310.64	0.94	-	311.58	342.74	1.179
R120249I	3.00 m	m	26.33	334.39	1.01	-	335.40	368.94	1.265
R120250	**Trenches to suit pipes not exceeding 800 mm dia; average depth**								
R120250A	1.00 m	m	11.88	150.88	0.38	-	151.26	166.39	0.472
R120250B	1.25 m	m	13.99	177.67	0.43	-	178.10	195.91	0.536
R120250C	1.50 m	m	15.35	194.94	0.58	-	195.52	215.07	0.729
R120250D	1.75 m	m	17.21	218.57	0.67	-	219.24	241.16	0.836
R120250E	2.00 m	m	19.06	242.06	0.75	-	242.81	267.09	0.943
R120250F	2.25 m	m	22.78	289.31	0.87	-	290.18	319.20	1.093
R120250G	2.50 m	m	24.84	315.47	0.94	-	316.41	348.05	1.179
R120250H	2.75 m	m	26.90	341.63	1.04	-	342.67	376.94	1.308
R120250I	3.00 m	m	28.96	367.79	1.11	-	368.90	405.79	1.394
R1221	**Breaking up obstructions with machine driven hammer**								
R122142	**Extra over excavation for breaking out**								
R122142A	soft rock or brickwork	m³	-	-	7.85	-	7.85	8.64	7.504
R122142B	hard rock	m³	-	-	12.33	-	12.33	13.56	11.792
R122142C	plain concrete	m³	-	-	10.09	-	10.09	11.10	9.648
R122142D	reinforced concrete	m³	-	-	14.57	-	14.57	16.03	13.936
R1223	**Breaking up obstructions with hand held mechanical tools**								
R122344	**Extra over excavation for breaking out**								
R122344A	soft rock or brickwork	m³	3.60	45.72	30.53	-	76.25	83.88	106.128
R122344B	hard rock	m³	6.40	81.28	54.27	-	135.55	149.11	188.672
R122344C	plain concrete	m³	5.00	63.50	42.40	-	105.90	116.49	147.400
R122344D	reinforced concrete	m³	7.20	91.44	61.06	-	152.50	167.75	212.256

Major Works 2011		Unit	Labour Hours	Labour Net	Plant Net	Materials Net	Unit Net	Unit with 10%	CO$_2$
				£	£	£	£	£	Kg
R12	R12: DRAINAGE BELOW GROUND								
R1225	Breaking out pavings with machine driven hammer								
R122533	Excavation in tarmac paving								
R122533A	not exceeding 150 mm thick	m^2	-	-	0.67	-	0.67	0.74	0.643
R122533B	150 - 300 mm thick	m^2	-	-	1.12	-	1.12	1.23	1.072
R122533C	300 - 450 mm thick	m^2	-	-	1.79	-	1.79	1.97	1.715
R122534	Excavation in plain concrete paving								
R122534A	not exceeding 150 mm thick	m^2	-	-	1.35	-	1.35	1.49	1.286
R122534B	150 - 300 mm thick	m^2	-	-	2.24	-	2.24	2.46	2.144
R122534C	300 - 450 mm thick	m^2	-	-	3.59	-	3.59	3.95	3.430
R122535	Excavation in reinforced concrete paving								
R122535A	not exceeding 150 mm thick	m^2	0.08	1.02	2.47	-	3.49	3.84	2.151
R122535B	150 - 300 mm thick	m^2	0.08	1.02	3.59	-	4.61	5.07	3.223
R122535C	300 - 450 mm thick	m^2	0.08	1.02	4.71	-	5.73	6.30	4.295
R1227	Breaking out pavings with hand held compressor tools								
R122737	Excavation in tarmac paving								
R122737A	not exceeding 150 mm thick	m^2	0.40	5.08	1.70	-	6.78	7.46	5.896
R122737B	150 - 300 mm thick	m^2	0.70	8.89	3.39	-	12.28	13.51	11.792
R122737C	300 - 450 mm thick	m^2	1.00	12.70	5.09	-	17.79	19.57	17.688
R122738	Excavation in plain concrete paving								
R122738A	not exceeding 150 mm thick	m^2	0.60	7.62	3.39	-	11.01	12.11	11.792
R122738B	150 - 300 mm thick	m^2	0.90	11.43	5.09	-	16.52	18.17	17.688
R122738C	300 - 450 mm thick	m^2	0.12	1.52	6.78	-	8.30	9.13	23.584
R122739	Excavation in reinforced concrete paving								
R122739A	not exceeding 150 mm thick	m^2	0.80	10.16	5.51	-	15.67	17.24	17.701
R122739B	150 - 300 mm thick	m^2	1.30	16.51	8.90	-	25.41	27.95	29.493
R122739C	300 - 450 mm thick	m^2	2.00	25.40	13.99	-	39.39	43.33	47.181
R1244	Beds for drainage pipes								
R124431	50 mm sand bed to pipes								
R124431A	not exceeding 200 mm dia	m	0.06	0.81	0.09	0.53	1.43	1.57	0.876
R124431B	225 mm dia	m	0.07	0.94	0.12	0.72	1.78	1.96	1.189
R124431C	300 mm dia	m	0.08	1.07	0.15	0.89	2.11	2.32	1.491
R124431D	400 mm dia	m	0.09	1.18	0.18	1.06	2.42	2.66	1.753
R124431E	450 mm dia	m	0.11	1.37	0.21	1.25	2.83	3.11	2.066
R124431F	525 mm dia	m	0.13	1.63	0.24	1.42	3.29	3.62	2.368
R124431G	600 mm dia	m	0.14	1.74	0.26	1.59	3.59	3.95	2.629
R124431H	700 mm dia	m	0.15	1.85	0.29	1.72	3.86	4.25	2.868
R124431I	800 mm dia	m	0.15	1.96	0.31	1.83	4.10	4.51	3.056
R1246	Beds and coverings for drainage pipes								
R124632	150 mm bed and 150 mm covering of pea shingle to pipes								
R124632A	not exceeding 200 mm dia	m	0.20	2.55	0.85	5.96	9.36	10.30	8.390
R124632B	225 mm dia	m	0.29	3.64	1.22	8.49	13.35	14.69	11.965
R124632C	300 mm dia	m	0.40	5.02	1.67	11.69	18.38	20.22	16.468
R124632D	400 mm dia	m	0.53	6.67	2.23	15.55	24.45	26.90	21.898
R124632E	450 mm dia	m	0.65	8.31	2.77	19.36	30.44	33.48	27.266
R124632F	525 mm dia	m	0.81	10.22	3.41	23.83	37.46	41.21	33.562
R124632G	600 mm dia	m	0.97	12.32	4.11	28.72	45.15	49.67	40.421
R124632H	700 mm dia	m	1.11	14.08	4.70	32.83	51.61	56.77	46.215
R124632I	800 mm dia	m	1.25	15.90	5.30	37.08	58.28	64.11	52.198
R124633	150 mm bed and 150 mm covering of C10P concrete to pipes								
R124633A	not exceeding 200 mm dia	m	0.25	3.16	0.89	17.79	21.84	24.02	83.708
R124633B	225 mm dia	m	0.35	4.50	1.27	19.21	24.98	27.48	92.360
R124633C	300 mm dia	m	0.49	6.18	1.74	24.90	32.82	36.10	120.376
R124633D	400 mm dia	m	0.65	8.23	2.32	31.30	41.85	46.04	152.154
R124633E	450 mm dia	m	0.81	10.25	2.89	34.15	47.29	52.02	168.292

Disposal Systems

Major Works 2011		Unit	Labour Hours	Labour Net	Plant Net	Materials Net	Unit Net	Unit with 10%	CO₂
				£	£	£	£	£	Kg
R12	R12: DRAINAGE BELOW GROUND								
R1246	Beds and coverings for drainage pipes								
R124633	150 mm bed and 150 mm covering of C10P concrete to pipes								
R124633F	525 mm dia	m	0.99	12.61	3.56	41.26	57.43	63.17	203.753
R124633G	600 mm dia	m	1.20	15.19	4.28	44.82	64.29	70.72	224.017
R124633H	700 mm dia	m	1.37	17.36	4.90	51.93	74.19	81.61	259.156
R124633I	800 mm dia	m	1.54	19.61	5.53	59.05	84.19	92.61	294.416
R1261	Drainage pipes								
R126102	Vitrified clay pipes; Hepworth Building Products								
R126102A	100 mm SuperSleve	m	0.20	2.54	-	8.24	10.78	11.86	4.394
R126102B	150 mm SuperSleve	m	0.23	2.92	-	16.31	19.23	21.15	8.277
R126102C	225 mm SuperSleve	m	0.29	3.68	-	34.11	37.79	41.57	15.749
R126102E	150 mm SuperSeal	m	0.27	3.43	-	16.31	19.74	21.71	8.277
R126102F	225 mm SuperSeal	m	0.37	4.70	-	34.11	38.81	42.69	15.749
R126102G	300 mm HepSeal	m	0.52	6.60	-	49.38	55.98	61.58	34.493
R126102H	400 mm HepSeal	m	0.72	9.14	-	77.83	86.97	95.67	87.414
R126102I	450 mm HepSeal	m	0.80	10.16	9.12	101.08	120.36	132.40	113.642
R126102J	500 mm HepSeal	m	0.88	11.18	10.04	112.67	133.89	147.28	142.878
R126102K	600 mm HepSeal	m	0.95	12.07	10.95	179.39	202.41	222.65	154.851
R126102N	100 mm HepLine	m	0.20	2.54	-	8.68	11.22	12.34	4.371
R126102O	150 mm HepLine	m	0.23	2.92	-	15.78	18.70	20.57	8.235
R126102P	225 mm HepLine	m	0.29	3.68	-	31.82	35.50	39.05	15.984
R126102Q	300 mm HepLine	m	0.34	4.32	-	61.95	66.27	72.90	32.485
R126103	Concrete pipes, BS 5911 Part 1, Class L								
R126103A	150 mm	m	0.55	6.99	-	6.31	13.30	14.63	9.595
R126103B	225 mm	m	0.65	8.25	-	9.47	17.72	19.49	21.587
R126103C	300 mm	m	0.70	8.89	7.98	12.63	29.50	32.45	45.413
R126103D	375 mm	m	0.85	10.80	9.81	15.58	36.19	39.81	54.245
R126103E	450 mm	m	1.05	13.33	12.09	18.78	44.20	48.62	74.766
R126103F	525 mm	m	1.35	17.15	15.51	23.95	56.61	62.27	113.418
R126103G	600 mm	m	1.65	20.95	18.93	30.34	70.22	77.24	126.398
R126104	Cast iron pipes; Timesaver bolted joints								
R126104A	100 mm	m	0.19	7.50	-	37.46	44.96	49.46	22.199
R126104B	150 mm	m	0.23	9.03	-	80.59	89.62	98.58	31.572
R126105	PVC-u pipes; OsmaDrain								
R126105A	82 mm	m	0.18	2.29	-	10.64	12.93	14.22	3.251
R126105B	110 mm	m	0.20	2.54	-	6.50	9.04	9.94	4.382
R126105C	160 mm	m	0.25	3.17	-	14.94	18.11	19.92	8.023
R126105D	200 mm	m	0.24	3.05	-	7.92	10.97	12.07	6.132
R126105E	225 mm	m	0.28	3.56	-	19.62	23.18	25.50	12.848
R126105F	300 mm	m	0.32	4.06	-	30.22	34.28	37.71	19.084
R126105G	110 mm perforated	m	0.20	2.54	-	15.63	18.17	19.99	4.382
R126105H	160 mm perforated	m	0.25	3.17	-	21.83	25.00	27.50	8.023
R1264	Drainage fittings								
R126411	Vitrified clay fittings; Hepworth Building Products; SuperSleve								
R126411A	100 mm bends	Nr	0.20	2.54	-	10.77	13.31	14.64	1.053
R126411B	100 mm rest bends	Nr	0.22	2.79	-	16.17	18.96	20.86	3.899
R126411C	100 x 100 mm junctions	Nr	0.25	3.17	-	48.95	52.12	57.33	1.687
R126411D	150 mm bends	Nr	0.20	2.54	-	14.40	16.94	18.63	2.268
R126411E	150 mm rest bends	Nr	0.22	2.79	-	18.50	21.29	23.42	3.899
R126411F	150 x 100 mm junctions	Nr	0.25	3.17	-	19.27	22.44	24.68	3.402
R126411G	150 x 150 mm junctions	Nr	0.25	3.17	-	21.15	24.32	26.75	4.597
R126412	Vitrified clay fittings; Hepworth Building Products; HepSleve								
R126412A	225 mm bends	Nr	0.20	2.54	-	73.43	75.97	83.57	6.431
R126412B	225 mm rest bends	Nr	0.22	2.79	-	80.29	83.08	91.39	10.290
R126412C	225 x 100 mm junctions	Nr	0.25	3.17	-	102.50	105.67	116.24	9.518
R126412D	225 x 150 mm junctions	Nr	0.25	3.17	-	102.50	105.67	116.24	9.354
R126413	Vitrified clay fittings; Hepworth Building Products; HepSeal								
R126413A	100 mm bends	Nr	0.20	2.54	-	15.15	17.69	19.46	2.268
R126413B	100 mm rest bends	Nr	0.22	2.79	-	16.17	18.96	20.86	3.899
R126413C	100 x 100 mm junctions	Nr	0.25	3.17	-	22.72	25.89	28.48	3.402
R126413D	150 mm bends	Nr	0.20	2.54	-	34.46	37.00	40.70	2.268

Major Works 2011		Unit	Labour Hours	Labour Net	Plant Net	Materials Net	Unit Net	Unit with 10%	CO$_2$
				£	£	£	£	£	Kg
R12	**R12: DRAINAGE BELOW GROUND**								
R1264	**Drainage fittings**								
R126413	**Vitrified clay fittings; Hepworth Building Products; HepSeal**								
R126413E	150 mm rest bends	Nr	0.22	2.79	-	18.50	21.29	23.42	3.899
R126413F	150 x 100 mm junctions	Nr	0.25	3.17	-	39.89	43.06	47.37	3.402
R126413G	150 x 150 mm junctions	Nr	0.25	3.17	-	45.03	48.20	53.02	4.597
R126413H	225 mm bends	Nr	0.22	2.79	-	80.76	83.55	91.91	6.431
R126413I	225 mm rest bends	Nr	0.25	3.17	-	98.64	101.81	111.99	10.290
R126413J	225 x 100 mm junctions	Nr	0.27	3.43	-	112.72	116.15	127.77	9.518
R126413K	225 x 150 mm junctions	Nr	0.27	3.43	-	112.72	116.15	127.77	9.354
R126413L	300 mm bends	Nr	0.35	4.44	-	139.44	143.88	158.27	17.424
R126413M	300 mm rest bends	Nr	0.38	4.83	-	212.24	217.07	238.78	18.008
R126413N	300 x 100 mm junctions	Nr	0.40	5.08	-	219.47	224.55	247.01	20.910
R126413O	300 x 150 mm junctions	Nr	0.40	5.08	-	219.47	224.55	247.01	20.910
R126413P	400 mm bends	Nr	0.45	5.71	-	358.75	364.46	400.91	47.521
R126413R	400 x 100 mm junctions	Nr	0.50	6.35	-	470.62	476.97	524.67	47.521
R126413S	400 x 150 mm junctions	Nr	0.50	6.35	-	470.62	476.97	524.67	52.273
R126413T	450 mm bends	Nr	0.55	6.99	4.56	472.42	483.97	532.37	51.541
R126413V	450 x 100 mm junctions	Nr	0.60	7.62	4.56	470.62	482.80	531.08	51.541
R126413W	450 x 150 mm junctions	Nr	0.60	7.62	4.56	562.99	575.17	632.69	56.293
R126414	**Vitrified clay fittings; Hepworth Building Products; HepSeal**								
R126414A	500 mm bends; 90 deg	Nr	0.60	7.62	4.56	821.01	833.19	916.51	91.005
R126414C	500 mm bends; 45 deg	Nr	0.60	7.62	4.56	586.46	598.64	658.50	72.971
R126414D	500 x 150 mm junctions	Nr	0.68	8.64	4.56	707.49	720.69	792.76	104.985
R126414E	600 mm bends; 90 deg	Nr	0.70	8.89	4.56	845.64	859.09	945.00	98.253
R126414G	600 mm bends; 45 deg	Nr	0.78	9.91	4.56	573.07	587.54	646.29	101.314
R126414H	600 x 150 mm junctions	Nr	0.78	9.91	4.56	636.74	651.21	716.33	103.994
R126415	**Vitrified clay fittings; Hepworth Building Products; HepLine**								
R126415A	100 mm bends	Nr	0.20	2.54	-	10.77	13.31	14.64	2.022
R126415B	100 x 100 mm junctions	Nr	0.25	3.17	-	22.72	25.89	28.48	3.733
R126415C	150 mm bends	Nr	0.20	2.54	-	14.40	16.94	18.63	3.213
R126415D	150 x 100 mm junctions	Nr	0.25	3.17	-	39.89	43.06	47.37	3.402
R126415E	150 x 150 mm junctions	Nr	0.25	3.17	-	45.03	48.20	53.02	4.597
R126415F	225 mm bends	Nr	0.22	2.79	-	98.64	101.43	111.57	6.431
R126415G	225 x 100 mm junctions	Nr	0.27	3.43	-	112.72	116.15	127.77	9.518
R126415H	225 x 150 mm junctions	Nr	0.27	3.43	-	112.72	116.15	127.77	9.354
R126415I	300 mm bends	Nr	0.35	4.44	-	139.44	143.88	158.27	19.242
R126415J	300 x 100 mm junctions	Nr	0.40	5.08	-	219.47	224.55	247.01	19.058
R126415K	300 x 150 mm junctions	Nr	0.40	5.08	-	219.47	224.55	247.01	21.964
R126416	**Concrete fittings, BS 5911 Part 1, Class L**								
R126416A	150 mm bends	Nr	0.40	5.08	-	63.15	68.23	75.05	9.218
R126416B	150 x 150 mm junctions	Nr	0.50	6.35	-	44.21	50.56	55.62	24.387
R126416C	225 mm bends	Nr	0.45	5.71	-	94.73	100.44	110.48	20.741
R126416D	225 x 150 mm junctions	Nr	0.55	6.99	-	66.31	73.30	80.63	54.871
R126416E	300 mm bends	Nr	0.60	7.62	4.56	126.30	138.48	152.33	40.893
R126416F	300 x 150 mm junctions	Nr	0.70	8.89	4.56	88.41	101.86	112.05	101.567
R126416G	375 mm bends	Nr	0.75	9.52	4.56	155.83	169.91	186.90	48.606
R126416H	375 x 150 mm junctions	Nr	0.80	10.16	4.56	109.08	123.80	136.18	119.752
R126416I	450 mm bends	Nr	0.85	10.80	4.56	187.81	203.17	223.49	66.521
R126416J	450 x 150 mm junctions	Nr	0.90	11.43	4.56	131.47	147.46	162.21	168.254
R126416K	525 mm bends	Nr	1.00	12.70	5.70	239.48	257.88	283.67	79.800
R126416L	525 x 150 mm junctions	Nr	1.10	13.97	5.70	167.64	187.31	206.04	223.777
R126416M	600 mm bends	Nr	1.20	15.24	6.39	303.45	325.08	357.59	103.065
R126416N	600 x 150 mm junctions	Nr	1.30	16.51	6.39	212.42	235.32	258.85	285.340
R126417	**Cast iron fittings; Timesaver bolted joints**								
R126417A	100 mm bends	Nr	0.23	8.99	-	68.13	77.12	84.83	32.489
R126417B	100 x 100 mm junction	Nr	0.33	12.76	-	114.04	126.80	139.48	48.132
R126417C	150 mm bends	Nr	0.27	10.56	-	156.80	167.36	184.10	43.720
R126417D	150 x 100 mm junction	Nr	0.33	12.76	-	214.96	227.72	250.49	70.393
R126417E	150 x 150 mm junction	Nr	0.33	12.76	-	269.72	282.48	310.73	82.025
R126418	**PVC-u fittings; OsmaDrain**								
R126418A	82 mm bends	Nr	0.10	1.27	-	18.04	19.31	21.24	0.483
R126418B	82 x 82 mm junctions	Nr	0.15	1.90	-	26.26	28.16	30.98	1.484
R126418C	110 mm bends	Nr	0.13	1.65	-	17.14	18.79	20.67	0.950
R126418D	110 mm rest bends	Nr	0.15	1.90	-	32.84	34.74	38.21	0.950
R126418E	110 x 110 mm junctions	Nr	0.18	2.29	-	22.76	25.05	27.56	1.016
R126418F	160 mm bends	Nr	0.20	2.54	-	43.73	46.27	50.90	2.200
R126418G	160 x 110 mm junctions	Nr	0.25	3.17	-	57.28	60.45	66.50	4.725
R126418H	160 x 160 mm junctions	Nr	0.25	3.17	-	74.31	77.48	85.23	5.615

Disposal Systems

Major Works 2011		Unit	Labour Hours	Labour Net	Plant Net	Materials Net	Unit Net	Unit with 10%	CO₂
				£	£	£	£	£	Kg
R12	**R12: DRAINAGE BELOW GROUND**								
R1264	**Drainage fittings**								
R126419	**PVC-u fittings; UltraRib**								
R126419A	150 mm bends	Nr	0.28	3.56	–	19.52	23.08	25.39	1.916
R126419B	150 x 110 mm junctions	Nr	0.30	3.81	–	40.18	43.99	48.39	2.177
R126419C	150 x 150 mm junctions	Nr	0.30	3.81	–	47.20	51.01	56.11	4.778
R126419D	225 mm bends	Nr	0.32	4.06	–	83.21	87.27	96.00	6.221
R126419E	225 x 110 mm junctions	Nr	0.35	4.44	–	109.42	113.86	125.25	12.170
R126419F	225 x 150 mm junctions	Nr	0.35	4.44	–	112.73	117.17	128.89	13.619
R126419G	225 x 160 mm junctions	Nr	0.35	4.44	–	112.73	117.17	128.89	14.957
R126419H	225 x 225 mm junctions	Nr	0.35	4.44	–	156.65	161.09	177.20	17.351
R126419I	300 mm bends	Nr	0.34	4.32	–	166.20	170.52	187.57	12.075
R126419J	300 x 150 mm junctions	Nr	0.37	4.70	–	223.67	228.37	251.21	22.313
R126419K	300 x 160 mm junctions	Nr	0.37	4.70	–	238.59	243.29	267.62	23.651
R126419L	300 x 225 mm junctions	Nr	0.37	4.70	–	344.55	349.25	384.18	35.963
R126419M	300 x 300 mm junctions	Nr	0.37	4.70	–	299.41	304.11	334.52	29.321
R1267	**Drainage accessories including concrete surrounds and additional excavation**								
R126721	**Vitrified clay accessories; Hepworth Building Products; SuperSleve**								
R126721A	100 mm rodding eye and plate	Nr	0.40	5.08	–	34.37	39.45	43.40	9.619
R126721B	100 mm rodding eye with airtight sea	Nr	0.40	5.08	–	43.15	48.23	53.05	9.619
R126721C	150 mm rodding eye and plate	Nr	0.45	5.71	–	53.02	58.73	64.60	15.859
R126721D	100 mm polypropylene adaptor to soil waste or rainwater pipe	Nr	0.05	0.64	–	11.53	12.17	13.39	0.067
R126721E	100 mm one piece gulley and grid	Nr	0.60	7.62	–	48.79	56.41	62.05	10.247
R126721F	100 mm two piece back inlet gully and grid	Nr	0.95	12.07	–	40.72	52.79	58.07	10.978
R126721G	150 mm two piece back inlet gully and grid	Nr	1.05	13.33	–	68.75	82.08	90.29	24.886
R126721H	100 mm access gully and grid	Nr	0.60	7.62	–	48.20	55.82	61.40	13.887
R126721I	polypropylene trapped road gully; 510 mm dia x 840 mm deep with 150 mm outlet, grating and frame	Nr	3.50	44.45	–	291.39	335.84	369.42	83.716
R126722	**Vitrified clay accessories; Hepworth Building Products; HepSleve**								
R126722A	garage gully and bucket; Deans type; 100 mm outlet	Nr	2.50	31.75	–	88.21	119.96	131.96	31.774
R126722B	mud gully and bucket; Deans type; 100 mm outlet	Nr	2.80	35.56	–	85.17	120.73	132.80	31.774
R126722C	garage gully and bucket; Deans type; 150 mm outlet	Nr	2.50	31.75	–	106.35	138.10	151.91	47.374
R126722D	mud gully and bucket; Deans type; 150 mm outlet	Nr	2.80	35.56	–	103.31	138.87	152.76	47.374
R126722E	road gully; RGR1/2; 300 mm dia 600 mm deep; 100 or 150 mm outlet	Nr	2.50	31.75	–	120.53	152.28	167.51	72.937
R126722F	road gully; RGR3; 400 mm dia x 750 mm deep; 150 mm outlet	Nr	2.90	36.83	–	141.64	178.47	196.32	120.481
R126722G	road gully; RGR4; 450 mm dia x 900 mm deep; 150 mm outlet	Nr	3.30	41.91	–	190.17	232.08	255.29	152.676
R126722H	universal grease trap; 375 x 375 x 70 mm deep; 100 mm inlet and outlet	Nr	2.50	31.75	–	885.47	917.22	1,008.94	103.502
R126723	**Concrete accessories; BS 5911 Part 1, Class L**								
R126723A	road gully; 375 mm dia x 900 mm deep; with rodding eye and 150 mm outlet	Nr	3.50	44.45	6.84	201.86	253.15	278.47	79.898
R126724	**Cast iron accessories; Timesaver bolted joints**								
R126724A	trap with 100 mm inlet and outlet	Nr	0.65	25.59	–	48.90	74.49	81.94	56.068
R126725	**PVC-u accessories; OsmaDrain**								
R126725A	110 mm rodding eye with airtight sea	Nr	0.40	5.08	–	56.08	61.16	67.28	10.838
R126725B	110 mm one piece bottle gully	Nr	0.60	7.62	–	29.41	37.03	40.73	13.544
R126725C	110 mm two piece bottle gully	Nr	0.80	10.16	–	36.12	46.28	50.91	15.763

Major Works 2011		Unit	Labour Hours	Labour Net	Plant Net	Materials Net	Unit Net	Unit with 10%	CO$_2$
				£	£	£	£	£	Kg
R12	**R12: DRAINAGE BELOW GROUND**								
R1271	**Inspection chambers or the like**								
R127110	**Excavation by machine for manholes, inspection chambers, septic tanks and soakaways; in firm ground; depth not exceeding**								
R127110B	1.00 m	m^3	0.31	3.94	7.07	-	11.01	12.11	6.231
R127110C	2.00 m	m^3	0.35	4.44	7.98	-	12.42	13.66	7.035
R127110D	4.00 m	m^3	0.40	5.08	9.12	-	14.20	15.62	8.040
R127110E	6.00 m	m^3	0.44	5.59	10.04	-	15.63	17.19	8.844
R127120	**Disposal of excavated material; off site to tip; including lower rate Landfill Tax (rocks and soil); distance to tip**								
R127120A	10 km	m^3	-	-	23.90	-	23.90	26.29	2.747
R127120B	20 km	m^3	-	-	37.81	-	37.81	41.59	3.752
R127125	**Disposal of excavated material; on site depositing in spoil heaps; distance**								
R127125A	50 m	m^3	0.07	0.89	1.60	-	2.49	2.74	1.407
R127127	**Filling to excavations with materials arising from earthworks; compacting in 250 mm layers**								
R127127A	generally	m^3	0.30	3.81	6.22	-	10.03	11.03	5.668
R127129	**Filling to excavations with imported materials; compacting in 250 mm layers**								
R127129A	sand	m^3	0.30	3.81	5.08	23.59	32.48	35.73	18.663
R127129B	hardcore	m^3	0.35	4.44	8.58	24.67	37.69	41.46	24.585
R127129C	hoggin	m^3	0.30	3.81	7.36	24.15	35.32	38.85	21.233
R127129D	DTp type 1	m^3	0.33	4.19	8.55	26.95	39.69	43.66	22.863
R127129E	DTp type 2	m^3	0.33	4.19	8.55	24.25	36.99	40.69	22.863
R127130	**Timber earthwork support in firm ground to sides of excavation not exceeding 2.00 m apart; open boarded; depth not exceeding**								
R127130A	1.00 m	m^2	0.10	3.79	-	0.91	4.70	5.17	0.461
R127130B	2.00 m	m^2	0.12	4.57	-	1.21	5.78	6.36	0.613
R127130C	4.00 m	m^2	0.16	6.10	-	1.81	7.91	8.70	0.919
R127130D	6.00 m	m^2	0.23	9.15	-	2.42	11.57	12.73	1.225
R127131	**Timber earthwork support in firm ground to sides of excavation 2.00 - 4.00 m apart; open boarded; depth not exceeding**								
R127131A	1.00 m	m^2	0.14	5.32	-	1.51	6.83	7.51	0.765
R127131B	2.00 m	m^2	0.16	6.10	-	1.81	7.91	8.70	0.919
R127131C	4.00 m	m^2	0.20	7.62	-	2.42	10.04	11.04	1.225
R127131D	6.00 m	m^2	0.27	10.67	-	3.03	13.70	15.07	1.535
R127132	**Timber earthwork support in firm ground to sides of excavation over 4.00 m apart; open boarded; depth not exceeding**								
R127132A	1.00 m	m^2	0.12	4.57	-	0.91	5.48	6.03	0.461
R127132B	2.00 m	m^2	0.20	7.62	-	1.81	9.43	10.37	0.919
R127132C	4.00 m	m^2	0.23	9.15	-	3.02	12.17	13.39	1.532
R127132D	6.00 m	m^2	0.31	12.20	-	4.23	16.43	18.07	2.145
R127133	**Plain in situ concrete C10; 14 mm aggregate; in bases and surrounds**								
R127133A	in bases and benchings	m^3	1.90	24.13	-	74.70	98.83	108.71	327.600

Disposal Systems

		Unit	Labour Hours	Labour Net	Plant Net	Materials Net	Unit Net	Unit with 10%	CO₂
				£	£	£	£	£	Kg
R12	**R12: DRAINAGE BELOW GROUND**								
R1271	**Inspection chambers or the like**								
R127133	**Plain in situ concrete C10; 14 mm aggregate; in bases and surrounds**								
R127133B	in surrounds	m³	1.95	24.76	-	76.48	101.24	111.36	335.400
R127134	**Plain in situ concrete C20; 20 mm aggregate; not exceeding 150 mm thick**								
R127134A	in bases and benchings	m³	1.90	24.13	-	77.93	102.06	112.27	327.600
R127134B	in surrounds	m³	1.95	24.76	-	79.79	104.55	115.01	335.400
R127135	**Plain in situ concrete C25; 20 mm aggregate; in bases and benchings**								
R127135A	not exceeding 150 mm thick	m³	0.68	26.67	4.68	79.10	110.45	121.50	339.660
R127135B	150 - 450 mm thick	m³	0.50	19.71	3.43	79.10	102.24	112.46	336.444
R127135C	exceeding 450 mm thick	m³	0.34	13.33	2.34	79.10	94.77	104.25	333.630
R127136	**Reinforced in situ concrete C25; 20 mm aggregate; in suspended slabs**								
R127136A	not exceeding 150 mm thick	m³	0.68	26.67	4.68	79.10	110.45	121.50	339.660
R127136B	150 - 450 mm thick	m³	0.50	19.71	3.43	79.10	102.24	112.46	336.444
R127137	**Reinforcement bar; BS 4483; hot rolled high yield plain round steel; bent; nominal dia**								
R127137A	8 mm	Tonne	54.00	799.20	-	854.14	1,653.34	1,818.67	1,775.240
R127137B	10 mm	Tonne	44.00	651.20	-	799.18	1,450.38	1,595.42	1,756.960
R127137C	12 mm	Tonne	38.00	562.40	-	762.27	1,324.67	1,457.14	1,744.665
R127137D	16 mm	Tonne	30.00	444.00	-	711.06	1,155.06	1,270.57	1,735.525
R127137E	20 mm	Tonne	26.00	384.80	-	696.28	1,081.08	1,189.19	1,727.590
R127137F	25 mm	Tonne	23.00	340.40	-	673.54	1,013.94	1,115.33	1,722.160
R127138	**Reinforcement fabric; BS 4483; steel; cut, lapped and tied; laid horizontally over 300 mm wide; ref**								
R127138A	A98; 1.54 kg/m²	m²	0.02	0.30	-	1.54	1.84	2.02	3.366
R127138B	A142; 2.22 kg/m²	m²	0.03	0.46	-	1.93	2.39	2.63	4.808
R127138C	A193; 3.02 kg/m²	m²	0.03	0.44	-	2.55	2.99	3.29	6.506
R127139	**Formwork for in situ concrete; soffits of isolated slabs; slab thickness not exceeding 200 mm; height from base to soffit**								
R127139A	not exceeding 1.50 m	m²	1.16	17.21	0.56	6.62	24.39	26.83	5.733
R127139B	1.50 - 3.0 m	m²	1.40	20.26	0.56	6.62	27.44	30.18	5.733
R127140	**Formwork for in situ concrete; isolated surrounds and casings; vertical**								
R127140A	in flat plane	m²	1.56	23.15	1.46	6.30	30.91	34.00	5.416
R127140B	in curved plane	m²	1.94	27.98	1.46	6.61	36.05	39.66	5.684
R127141	**Vitrified clay inspection chambers; surrounding in concrete; Hepworth Iron Co; 100 mm SuperSleve**								
R127141A	225 mm dia base, raising piece, cover and frame; straight through	Nr	1.20	15.24	-	153.47	168.71	185.58	18.835
R127141B	225 mm dia base, raising piece, cover and frame; one branch	Nr	1.30	16.51	-	176.66	193.17	212.49	19.013
R127141C	225 mm dia base, raising piece, cover and frame; two branches	Nr	1.40	17.78	-	201.16	218.94	240.83	19.190
R127142	**Polypropylene inspection chambers; granular bed and surround; Hepworth Iron Co; 100 mm SuperSleve**								
R127142A	475 mm dia base, raising piece, cover and frame; 585 mm deep	Nr	1.75	22.22	-	146.52	168.74	185.61	10.055
R127142B	475 mm dia base, raising piece, cover and frame; 930 mm deep	Nr	1.80	22.86	-	216.99	239.85	263.84	15.949

Major Works 2011		Unit	Labour Hours	Labour Net	Plant Net	Materials Net	Unit Net	Unit with 10%	CO$_2$
				£	£	£	£	£	Kg
R12	**R12: DRAINAGE BELOW GROUND**								
R1271	**Inspection chambers or the like**								
R127143	**Construct manhole complete; excavation; disposal; earthwork support; 150 mm thick plain concrete bed; one brick thick class B engineering brick walls; cover and frame; depth to invert**								
R127143A	not exceeding 1.00 m	Nr	5.31	196.03	30.07	222.71	448.81	493.69	704.131
R127143B	1.00 - 1.25 m	Nr	6.68	251.74	37.03	270.42	559.19	615.11	860.060
R127143C	1.25 - 1.50 m	Nr	7.82	297.04	45.36	315.86	658.26	724.09	1,017.243
R127143D	1.50 - 1.75 m	Nr	8.90	341.53	52.32	360.24	754.09	829.50	1,169.689
R127143E	1.75 - 2.00 m	Nr	9.98	386.27	57.67	405.66	849.60	934.56	1,324.985
R127144	**Construct manhole complete; excavation; disposal; earthwork support; 150 mm thick plain concrete bed; 1050 mm dia precast concrete chamber rings with step irons; concrete cover slab; cover and frame; depth to invert**								
R127144A	1.50 - 2.00 m	Nr	10.45	245.48	114.66	376.28	736.42	810.06	975.861
R127144B	2.00 - 2.50 m	Nr	13.78	329.07	151.05	459.71	939.83	1,033.81	1,178.596
R127144C	2.50 - 3.00 m	Nr	16.23	411.04	171.75	506.19	1,088.98	1,197.88	1,355.463
R127144D	3.00 - 3.50 m	Nr	18.84	474.75	204.27	577.87	1,256.89	1,382.58	1,546.092
R127144E	3.50 - 4.00 m	Nr	20.68	528.86	224.96	625.06	1,378.88	1,516.77	1,726.062
R127145	**Construct manhole complete; excavation; disposal; earthwork support; 150 mm thick plain concrete bed; 1200 mm dia precast concrete chamber rings with step irons; concrete cover slab; cover and frame; depth to invert**								
R127145A	1.50 - 2.00 m	Nr	11.54	269.62	135.31	445.20	850.13	935.14	1,167.175
R127145B	2.00 - 2.50 m	Nr	15.88	393.15	176.91	563.31	1,133.37	1,246.71	1,408.976
R127145C	2.50 - 3.00 m	Nr	18.01	454.20	203.00	609.77	1,266.97	1,393.67	1,627.396
R127145D	3.00 - 3.50 m	Nr	20.84	523.92	240.08	714.85	1,478.85	1,626.74	1,856.023
R127145E	3.50 - 4.00 m	Nr	22.94	584.21	265.76	760.57	1,610.54	1,771.59	2,071.109
R127146	**Construct soakaway complete; excavation; disposal; earthwork support; 150 mm thick plain concrete bed; 1500 mm dia precast concrete perforated rings; cover slab; cover and frame; depth to invert**								
R127146A	not exceeding 1.00 m	Nr	5.11	133.78	100.96	594.76	829.50	912.45	577.303
R127146B	1.00 - 1.50 m	Nr	7.46	203.76	152.21	865.56	1,221.53	1,343.68	769.542
R127146C	1.50 - 2.00 m	Nr	9.28	256.07	189.61	1,132.66	1,578.34	1,736.17	948.056
R127146D	2.00 - 2.50 m	Nr	13.40	388.90	246.34	1,417.92	2,053.16	2,258.48	1,152.440
R127146E	2.50 - 3.00 m	Nr	15.64	456.12	284.87	1,688.21	2,429.20	2,672.12	1,333.360
R127147	**Extra over inspection chambers or the like for the following**								
R127147A	heavy duty cast iron cover and frame 600 x 450 mm	Nr	-	-	-	102.46	102.46	112.71	87.615
R127147B	medium duty cast iron cover and frame; 500 mm dia	Nr	-	-	-	97.40	97.40	107.14	80.535
R127147C	heavy duty cast iron cover and frame 500 mm dia	Nr	-	-	-	90.40	90.40	99.44	114.165
R127147D	150 mm dia half round straight channel	m	-	-	-	4.94	4.94	5.43	2.637
R127147E	225 mm dia half round straight channel	m	-	-	-	20.41	20.41	22.45	10.391
R127147F	100 mm dia half round curved channel	m	-	-	-	1.75	1.75	1.93	0.695
R127147G	150 mm dia half round curved channel	m	-	-	-	8.45	8.45	9.30	1.746
R127147H	225 mm dia half round curved channel	m	-	-	-	54.21	54.21	59.63	8.940

Disposal Systems

		Unit	Labour Hours	Labour Net £	Plant Net £	Materials Net £	Unit Net £	Unit with 10% £	CO$_2$ Kg
R12	**R12: DRAINAGE BELOW GROUND**								
R1271	**Inspection chambers or the like**								
R127147	**Extra over inspection chambers or the like for the following**								
R127147I	150 mm dia three quarter section branches	Nr	-	-	-	12.27	12.27	13.50	1.124
R127147J	225 mm dia three quarter section branches	Nr	-	-	-	92.65	92.65	101.92	5.309
R127155	**Manhole cover and frame; grey iron light duty single seal solid; BS EN124 Class A15 42 mm deep; clear opening size**								
R127155A	450 x 450 mm; MHC-5140	Nr	1.50	19.05	-	50.56	69.61	76.57	54.534
R127155B	600 x 450 mm; MHC-5145	Nr	1.55	19.68	-	50.66	70.34	77.37	62.526
R127155C	600 mm dia; MHC-5150	Nr	1.60	20.32	-	100.81	121.13	133.24	77.454
R127155D	600 x 600 mm; MHC-5155	Nr	1.60	20.32	-	78.07	98.39	108.23	81.626
R127155E	750 x 600 mm; MHC-5165	Nr	1.65	20.95	-	153.09	174.04	191.44	114.447
R127155F	900 x 600 mm; MHC-5175	Nr	1.70	21.59	-	167.71	189.30	208.23	148.827
R127156	**Manhole cover and frame; grey iron light duty double seal solid; BS EN124 Class A15 42 mm deep; clear opening size**								
R127156A	600 x 450 mm; MHC-5146	Nr	1.70	21.59	-	60.81	82.40	90.64	100.374
R127156B	600 x 600 mm; MHC-5156	Nr	1.80	22.86	-	95.55	118.41	130.25	119.826
R127157	**Manhole cover and frame; grey iron light duty single seal recessed; BS EN124 Class A15 65 mm deep; clear opening size**								
R127157A	600 x 450 mm; MHC-5147	Nr	1.70	21.59	-	111.67	133.26	146.59	96.554
R127157B	600 x 600 mm; MHC-5157	Nr	1.80	22.86	-	76.38	99.24	109.16	112.186
R127158	**Manhole cover and frame; grey iron light duty double seal recessed; BS EN124 Class A15 65 mm deep; clear opening size**								
R127158A	600 x 450 mm; MHC-5148	Nr	1.70	21.59	-	60.81	82.40	90.64	130.934
R127158B	600 x 600 mm; MHC-5158	Nr	1.80	22.86	-	140.57	163.43	179.77	154.206
R127159	**Manhole cover and frame; ductile iron medium duty single seal solid top; BS EN124 Class BA125 45 mm deep; clear opening size**								
R127159A	450 x 450 mm; MHC-5240	Nr	1.65	20.95	-	82.67	103.62	113.98	58.354
R127159B	600 x 450 mm; MHC-5245	Nr	1.70	21.59	-	76.90	98.49	108.34	73.986
R127159C	600 x 600 mm; MHC-5255	Nr	1.75	22.22	-	110.74	132.96	146.26	91.176
R127159D	750 x 600 mm; MHC-5265	Nr	1.80	22.86	-	180.96	203.82	224.20	118.267
R127159E	900 x 600 mm; MHC-5275	Nr	2.00	25.40	-	208.43	233.83	257.21	135.457
R127160	**Manhole cover and frame; ductile iron medium duty single seal solid top; BS EN124 Class B125 75 mm deep; clear opening size**								
R127160A	450 x 450 mm; MHC-5241	Nr	1.65	20.95	-	69.11	90.06	99.07	79.364
R127160B	600 x 450 mm; MHC-5246	Nr	1.70	21.59	-	74.53	96.12	105.73	79.716
R127160C	600 x 600 mm; MHC-5256	Nr	1.75	22.22	-	113.32	135.54	149.09	93.086
R127160D	750 x 600 mm; MHC-5266	Nr	1.80	22.86	-	200.17	223.03	245.33	110.627
R127160E	900 x 600 mm; MHC-5276	Nr	2.00	25.40	-	208.43	233.83	257.21	183.207
R127175	**Precast concrete manhole rings; BS 5911-200; bedding, jointing and pointing in cement and sand mortar (1:3); 900 mm nominal internal dia shaft rings; unit height**								
R127175A	250 mm	Nr	2.00	25.40	6.84	22.33	54.57	60.03	34.125
R127175B	500 mm	Nr	2.20	27.94	6.84	33.24	68.02	74.82	60.462
R127175C	750 mm	Nr	2.40	30.48	6.84	33.24	70.56	77.62	86.800
R127175D	1000 mm	Nr	2.60	33.02	6.84	44.15	84.01	92.41	113.137

Major Works 2011		Unit	Labour Hours	Labour Net	Plant Net	Materials Net	Unit Net	Unit with 10%	CO₂
				£	£	£	£	£	Kg
R12	**R12: DRAINAGE BELOW GROUND**								
R1271	Inspection chambers or the like								
R127176	Precast concrete manhole rings; BS 5911-200; bedding, jointing and pointing in cement and sand mortar (1:3); 1050 mm nominal internal dia shaft rings; unit height								
R127176A	250 mm	Nr	2.10	26.67	7.30	23.77	57.74	63.51	43.507
R127176B	500 mm	Nr	2.25	28.57	7.30	35.29	71.16	78.28	78.122
R127176C	750 mm	Nr	2.50	31.75	7.30	35.29	74.34	81.77	112.737
R127176D	1000 mm	Nr	2.70	34.29	7.30	46.82	88.41	97.25	147.352
R127177	Precast concrete manhole rings; BS 5911-200; bedding, jointing and pointing in cement and sand mortar (1:3); 1200 mm nominal internal dia shaft rings; unit height								
R127177A	250 mm	Nr	2.20	27.94	7.53	36.00	71.47	78.62	55.943
R127177B	500 mm	Nr	2.44	30.99	7.53	53.49	92.01	101.21	101.738
R127177C	750 mm	Nr	2.70	34.29	7.53	43.17	84.99	93.49	147.533
R127177D	1000 mm	Nr	3.00	38.10	7.53	70.97	116.60	128.26	193.328
R127178	Precast concrete manhole rings; BS 5911-200; bedding, jointing and pointing in cement and sand mortar (1:3); 1350 mm nominal internal dia shaft rings; unit height								
R127178B	500 mm	Nr	2.50	31.75	7.98	63.94	103.67	114.04	131.437
R127178C	750 mm	Nr	2.80	35.56	7.98	63.94	107.48	118.23	191.530
R127178D	1000 mm	Nr	3.10	39.37	7.98	84.85	132.20	145.42	251.622
R127179	Precast concrete manhole rings; BS 5911-200; bedding, jointing and pointing in cement and sand mortar (1:3); 1500 mm nominal internal dia shaft rings; unit height								
R127179B	500 mm	Nr	2.70	34.29	8.67	88.85	131.81	144.99	151.126
R127179C	750 mm	Nr	3.00	38.10	8.67	71.66	118.43	130.27	220.409
R127179D	1000 mm	Nr	3.30	41.91	8.67	117.99	168.57	185.43	289.693
R127180	Precast concrete manhole rings; BS 5911-200; bedding, jointing and pointing in cement and sand mortar (1:3); 1800 mm nominal internal dia shaft rings; unit height								
R127180B	500 mm	Nr	3.00	38.10	9.12	105.60	152.82	168.10	196.931
R127180C	750 mm	Nr	3.40	43.18	9.12	105.60	157.90	173.69	288.037
R127180D	1000 mm	Nr	3.80	48.26	9.12	140.15	197.53	217.28	379.143
R127181	Precast concrete manhole rings; BS 5911-200; bedding, jointing and pointing in cement and sand mortar (1:3); 2100 mm nominal internal dia shaft rings; unit height								
R127181B	500 mm	Nr	3.20	40.64	10.95	205.50	257.09	282.80	249.208
R127181C	750 mm	Nr	3.60	45.72	10.95	189.66	246.33	270.96	364.771
R127181D	1000 mm	Nr	4.00	50.80	10.95	273.17	334.92	368.41	480.333
R127182	Precast concrete manhole rings; BS 5911-200; bedding, jointing and pointing in cement and sand mortar (1:3); 2400 mm nominal internal dia shaft rings; unit height								
R127182B	500 mm	Nr	3.60	45.72	11.40	265.09	322.21	354.43	295.042
R127182C	750 mm	Nr	4.00	50.80	11.40	265.08	327.28	360.01	432.265
R127182D	1000 mm	Nr	4.50	57.15	11.40	352.42	420.97	463.07	569.489

Disposal Systems

		Unit	Labour Hours	Labour Net £	Plant Net £	Materials Net £	Unit Net £	Unit with 10% £	CO₂ Kg
R12	**R12: DRAINAGE BELOW GROUND**								
R1271	**Inspection chambers or the like**								
R127183	**Precast concrete manhole rings; BS 5911-200; bedding, jointing and pointing in cement and sand mortar (1:3); 2700 mm nominal internal dia shaft rings; unit height**								
R127183B	500 mm	Nr	4.10	52.07	12.55	308.82	373.44	410.78	350.987
R127183C	750 mm	Nr	4.50	57.15	12.55	308.82	378.52	416.37	514.978
R127183D	1000 mm	Nr	4.80	60.96	12.55	410.60	484.11	532.52	678.969
R127184	**Precast concrete manhole cover slabs; BS 5911-200; bedding, jointing and pointing in cement and sand mortar (1:3); heavy duty; to suit shaft ring nominal internal dia**								
R127184A	900 mm	Nr	2.40	30.48	6.84	46.50	83.82	92.20	37.160
R127184B	1050 mm	Nr	2.60	33.02	7.30	49.93	90.25	99.28	48.774
R127184C	1200 mm	Nr	2.80	35.56	7.53	62.16	105.25	115.78	61.858
R127184D	1350 mm	Nr	3.00	38.10	7.98	90.97	137.05	150.76	76.814
R127184E	1500 mm	Nr	3.20	40.64	8.67	110.85	160.16	176.18	93.642
R127184F	1800 mm	Nr	3.50	44.45	9.12	153.29	206.86	227.55	131.155
R127184G	2100 mm	Nr	3.80	48.26	10.95	225.73	284.94	313.43	176.557
R127184H	2400 mm	Nr	4.10	52.07	11.40	308.70	372.17	409.39	478.610
R127184I	2700 mm	Nr	4.50	57.15	12.55	427.96	497.66	547.43	659.491
R127190	**Class B engineering bricks in cement and sand mortar (1:3) in manhole walls and raising courses; flush pointing**								
R127190A	half brick thick	m²	1.11	51.75	-	22.12	73.87	81.26	92.287
R127190B	one brick thick	m²	1.88	87.91	-	44.34	132.25	145.48	184.926
R127190C	one and a half brick thick	m²	2.77	129.39	-	66.57	195.96	215.56	277.564
R127192	**Step irons; galvanised general purpose pattern; built into brickwork**								
R127192A	short tail	Nr	-	-	-	5.13	5.13	5.64	4.230
R127192B	long tail	Nr	-	-	-	6.54	6.54	7.19	4.230
R127193	**Manhole step rungs; cast into pc concrete manhole rings; galvanised mild steel; patterned finish**								
R127193A	single	Nr	-	-	-	5.13	5.13	5.64	4.230
R127193B	double	Nr	-	-	-	6.54	6.54	7.19	4.230
R127195	**Benching to manholes; concrete (1:3:6) to slopes to channels and branches; finished with 13 mm thick cement mortar (1:3) trowelled smooth; average thickness**								
R127195A	225 mm	m²	2.65	33.65	-	29.07	62.72	68.99	62.060
R127195B	300 mm	m²	3.31	42.04	-	38.21	80.25	88.28	80.952
R127196	**In situ finishings; cement and sand (1:3); steel trowelled; to brickwork; 13 mm thick in one coat**								
R127196A	over 300 mm wide	m²	0.25	4.25	-	1.34	5.59	6.15	4.569
R127197	**Vitrified clay half round; bedding and pointing in cement sand mortar (1:3); to manholes and chambers**								
R127197A	100 mm dia straight channel; 300 mm	Nr	0.32	4.06	-	3.88	7.94	8.73	0.594
R127197B	100 mm dia straight channel; 600 mm	Nr	0.33	4.19	-	5.25	9.44	10.38	0.675
R127197C	100 mm dia straight channel; 1000 mm	Nr	0.35	4.44	-	7.45	11.89	13.08	1.125
R127197D	150 mm dia straight channel; 300 mm	Nr	0.36	4.57	-	8.83	13.40	14.74	1.134
R127197E	150 mm dia straight channel; 600 mm	Nr	0.37	4.70	-	8.83	13.53	14.88	2.277

Major Works 2011		Unit	Labour Hours	Labour Net	Plant Net	Materials Net	Unit Net	Unit with 10%	CO₂
				£	£	£	£	£	Kg
R12	R12: DRAINAGE BELOW GROUND								
R1271	Inspection chambers or the like								
R127197	Vitrified clay half round; bedding and pointing in cement sand mortar (1:3); to manholes and chambers								
R127197F	150 mm dia straight channel; 1000 mm	Nr	0.39	4.95	-	12.39	17.34	19.07	3.762
R127197G	225 mm dia straight channel; 300 mm	Nr	0.40	5.08	-	25.45	30.53	33.58	4.096
R127197H	225 mm dia straight channel; 600 mm	Nr	0.42	5.33	-	25.45	30.78	33.86	7.056
R127197I	225 mm dia straight channel; 1000 mm	Nr	0.44	5.59	-	27.86	33.45	36.80	11.516
R127197J	300 mm dia straight channel; 300 mm	m	0.44	5.59	-	42.29	47.88	52.67	11.516
R127197K	300 mm dia straight channel; 600 mm	m	0.46	5.84	-	42.29	48.13	52.94	14.111
R127197L	300 mm dia straight channel; 1000 mm	m	0.49	6.22	-	47.71	53.93	59.32	21.167
R127197M	100 mm dia half round channel bend	Nr	0.30	3.81	-	5.51	9.32	10.25	1.090
R127197N	150 mm dia half round channel bend	Nr	0.36	4.57	-	9.52	14.09	15.50	1.719
R127197O	225 mm dia half section channel bend	Nr	0.40	5.08	-	36.92	42.00	46.20	6.027
R127197P	300 mm dia half section channel bend	Nr	0.44	5.59	-	75.28	80.87	88.96	14.527
R127197Q	100 mm dia half section branch channel bend	Nr	0.32	4.06	-	16.39	20.45	22.50	0.648
R127197R	150 mm dia half section branch channel bend	Nr	0.36	4.57	-	26.86	31.43	34.57	1.793
R127197S	225 mm dia half section branch channel bend	Nr	0.40	5.08	-	74.03	79.11	87.02	4.469
R127197T	100 mm dia three quarter section branch channel bend	Nr	0.34	4.32	-	18.07	22.39	24.63	0.963
R127197U	150 mm dia three quarter section branch channel bend	nr	0.40	5.08	-	30.34	35.42	38.96	2.087
R127197V	225 mm dia three quarter section branch channel bend	Nr	0.44	5.59	-	110.72	116.31	127.94	6.272
R127198	Building in ends of pipes into manhole walls; pipe dia								
R127198A	100 mm	Nr	0.09	1.53	-	0.31	1.84	2.02	1.054
R127198B	150 mm	Nr	0.12	2.04	-	0.51	2.55	2.81	1.757
R127198C	225 mm	Nr	0.16	2.72	-	0.93	3.65	4.02	3.163
R127198D	300 mm	Nr	0.22	3.74	-	1.23	4.97	5.47	4.217
R1273	Soakaways								
R127310	Soakaways; excavation; disposal off site; DTp type 1 fill; geotextile cover; topsoil return; capacity below pipe invert level								
R127310A	1.20 m³	Nr	1.26	16.05	62.88	41.91	120.84	132.92	55.895
R127310B	2.50 m³	Nr	2.40	30.44	123.39	82.30	236.13	259.74	107.646
R127310C	3.75 m³	Nr	3.56	45.17	183.81	122.61	351.59	386.75	159.990
R127310D	5.00 m³	Nr	5.19	65.91	259.52	173.03	498.46	548.31	230.029
R127310E	7.50 m³	Nr	6.89	87.50	360.59	240.39	688.48	757.33	311.641
R1275	Septic tank installation								
R127561	Klargester standard grade septic tank installation complete; excavation; disposal; earthwork support; 150 mm thick concrete bed; fibreglass tank; granular surround; cover and frame; capacity								
R127561A	2720 Litres	Nr	28.96	655.97	463.72	1,075.75	2,195.44	2,414.98	1,038.898
R127561B	3750 Litres	Nr	34.92	772.81	556.88	1,265.78	2,595.47	2,855.02	1,309.746

Disposal Systems

Major Works 2011		Unit	Labour Hours	Labour Net £	Plant Net £	Materials Net £	Unit Net £	Unit with 10% £	CO₂ Kg
R12	**R12: DRAINAGE BELOW GROUND**								
R1275	**Septic tank installation**								
R127562	**Klargester heavy duty septic tank installation complete; excavation; disposal; earthwork support; 150 mm thick plain concrete; fibreglass tank; concrete cover slab; cover and frame; capacity**								
R127562A	6000 Litres	Nr	63.32	1,287.77	1,111.86	1,810.19	4,209.82	4,630.80	1,966.269
R127562B	7500 Litres	Nr	68.22	1,350.00	1,229.58	1,997.65	4,577.23	5,034.95	2,279.022
R1286	**Connections to existing drains**								
R128651	**Break into existing live sewer; make new connection and make good; excavation; backfilling; reinstatement (excluding statutory authority fees)**								
R128651A	100 mm vitrified clay sewer; 100 x 100 mm junction; in garden; 1.00 m deep	Nr	7.80	133.34	3.62	56.23	193.19	212.51	8.205
R128651B	150 mm vitrified clay sewer; 150 x 100 mm junction; in footpath; 1.50 m deep	Nr	13.34	231.15	8.36	71.81	311.32	342.45	50.537
R128651C	225 mm vitrified clay sewer; 225 x 150 mm junction; in road; 2.00 m deep	Nr	18.38	315.72	8.23	196.63	520.58	572.64	83.843
R128651D	300 mm vitrified clay sewer; 300 x 150 mm junction; in road; 3.00 m deep	Nr	28.93	531.99	14.08	331.44	877.51	965.26	108.652
R128652	**Break into existing live manhole; build in end of new pipe and make good walls and benching; excavation; backfilling; reinstatement (excluding statutory authority fees)**								
R128652A	one brick thick engineering brick walls; 100 mm pipe; 225 mm concrete benching; in garden; 1.00 m deep	Nr	7.98	144.05	4.58	8.23	156.86	172.55	17.228
R128652B	one brick thick engineering brick walls: 150 mm pipe; 225 mm concrete benching; in footpath; 1.50 m deep	Nr	12.31	219.64	9.32	51.68	280.64	308.70	56.930
R128652C	one brick thick engineering brick walls; 150 mm pipe; 225 mm concrete benching; in road; 2.00 m deep	Nr	17.28	298.26	13.13	86.74	398.13	437.94	88.364
R128652D	precast concrete chamber rings with 150 mm concrete surround; 150 mm backdrop pipe; in road 1.50 m deep	Nr	15.07	237.75	14.05	175.98	427.78	470.56	169.414
R128652E	precast concrete chamber rings with 150 mm concrete surround; 225 mm backdrop pipe; in road 2.00 m deep	Nr	19.39	307.99	14.31	447.41	769.71	846.68	322.059

Piped Supply Systems

Major Works 2011		Unit	Labour Hours	Labour Net	Plant Net	Materials Net	Unit Net	Unit with 10%	CO$_2$
				£	£	£	£	£	Kg
S12	**S12: HOT AND COLD WATER (SMALL SCALE)**								
S1210	**Copper pipework and fittings**								
S121001	**Copper pipework; capillary joints; BS 2871 Part 1, Table X; fixing with standard clips to masonry backgrounds; pipe dia**								
S121001A	8 mm	m	0.20	8.01	-	1.88	9.89	10.88	0.191
S121001B	10 mm	m	0.21	8.41	-	2.50	10.91	12.00	0.272
S121001C	12 mm	m	0.23	9.25	-	2.74	11.99	13.19	0.373
S121001D	15 mm	m	0.24	9.65	-	2.81	12.46	13.71	0.555
S121001E	22 mm	m	0.27	10.85	-	5.44	16.29	17.92	1.141
S121001F	28 mm	m	0.31	12.45	-	9.12	21.57	23.73	1.818
S121001G	35 mm	m	0.36	14.45	-	16.65	31.10	34.21	2.814
S121031	**Copper pipe fittings; capillary joints; BS 2871 Part 1, Table X; elbows; to suit pipe dia**								
S121031A	8 mm	Nr	0.16	6.41	-	1.67	8.08	8.89	0.027
S121031B	10 mm	Nr	0.18	7.21	-	1.59	8.80	9.68	0.043
S121031C	12 mm	Nr	0.19	7.61	-	1.71	9.32	10.25	0.062
S121031D	15 mm	Nr	0.20	8.01	-	0.58	8.59	9.45	0.096
S121031E	22 mm	Nr	0.22	8.85	-	1.32	10.17	11.19	0.207
S121031F	28 mm	Nr	0.25	10.05	-	2.72	12.77	14.05	0.335
S121031G	35 mm	Nr	0.30	12.05	-	8.55	20.60	22.66	0.523
S121051	**Copper pipe fittings; capillary joints; BS 2871 Part 1, Table X; equal tees; to suit pipe dia**								
S121051A	8 mm	Nr	0.24	9.65	-	3.16	12.81	14.09	0.027
S121051B	10 mm	Nr	0.27	10.85	-	2.87	13.72	15.09	0.043
S121051C	12 mm	Nr	0.29	11.65	-	2.84	14.49	15.94	0.062
S121051D	15 mm	Nr	0.30	12.05	-	1.00	13.05	14.36	0.096
S121051E	22 mm	Nr	0.33	13.25	-	2.30	15.55	17.11	0.207
S121051F	28 mm	Nr	0.38	15.26	-	5.63	20.89	22.98	0.335
S121051G	35 mm	Nr	0.45	18.06	-	14.79	32.85	36.14	0.523
S121071	**Copper pipe fittings; capillary joints; BS 2871 Part 1, Table X; unequal tees; size**								
S121071A	15 x 15 x 8 mm	Nr	0.30	12.05	-	5.20	17.25	18.98	0.043
S121071B	15 x 15 x 10 mm	Nr	0.30	12.05	-	5.18	17.23	18.95	0.043
S121071C	15 x 15 x 12 mm	Nr	0.30	12.05	-	2.91	14.96	16.46	0.043
S121071D	22 x 22 x 8 mm	Nr	0.33	13.25	-	7.63	20.88	22.97	0.207
S121071E	22 x 22 x 10 mm	Nr	0.33	13.25	-	6.67	19.92	21.91	0.207
S121071F	22 x 22 x 12 mm	Nr	0.33	13.25	-	6.81	20.06	22.07	0.207
S121071G	22 x 22 x 15 mm	Nr	0.33	13.25	-	2.21	15.46	17.01	0.207
S121071H	28 x 28 x 15 mm	Nr	0.38	15.26	-	7.53	22.79	25.07	0.335
S121071I	28 x 28 x 22 mm	Nr	0.38	15.26	-	8.01	23.27	25.60	0.335
S121071J	35 x 35 x 15 mm	Nr	0.45	18.06	-	16.23	34.29	37.72	0.523
S121071K	35 x 35 x 22 mm	Nr	0.45	18.06	-	16.42	34.48	37.93	0.523
S121071L	35 x 35 x 28 mm	Nr	0.45	18.06	-	16.37	34.43	37.87	0.523
S1215	**Polythene pipework and fittings**								
S121501	**Polyethylene pipework; blue 12 bar medium duty; compression couplings; laying in trench; dia**								
S121501A	20 mm	m	0.15	6.01	-	1.78	7.79	8.57	0.090
S121501B	25 mm	m	0.17	6.81	-	2.45	9.26	10.19	0.142
S121501C	32 mm	m	0.18	7.21	-	4.08	11.29	12.42	0.228
S121501D	50 mm	m	0.21	8.41	-	6.28	14.69	16.16	0.562
S1220	**Gunmetal and brass accessories**								
S122001	**Stopcock valves; BS 1010; jointing to copper pipe; size**								
S122001A	15 mm	Nr	0.18	7.21	-	5.41	12.62	13.88	1.910
S122001B	22 mm	Nr	0.20	8.01	-	12.94	20.95	23.05	2.801
S122011	**Gate valves; BS 5154; jointing to copper pipe; size**								
S122011A	15 mm	Nr	0.18	7.21	-	6.98	14.19	15.61	1.910
S122011B	22 mm	Nr	0.20	8.01	-	11.62	19.63	21.59	2.801
S122011C	28 mm	Nr	0.22	8.85	-	27.34	36.19	39.81	3.565

Piped Supply Systems

Major Works 2011		Unit	Labour Hours	Labour Net	Plant Net	Materials Net	Unit Net	Unit with 10%	CO$_2$
				£	£	£	£	£	Kg
S12	**S12: HOT AND COLD WATER (SMALL SCALE)**								
S1220	**Gunmetal and brass accessories**								
S122021	**Isolating valves for central heating pumps; self colour; size**								
S122021A	22 mm	Nr	0.25	10.05	-	4.58	14.63	16.09	2.475
S122021B	28 mm	Nr	0.28	11.25	-	5.44	16.69	18.36	2.475
S122031	**Ball valves with plastic floats; drilling and fixing to tanks; size**								
S122031A	15 mm piston type	Nr	0.20	8.01	-	11.00	19.01	20.91	2.475
S122031B	22 mm piston type	Nr	0.22	8.85	-	17.36	26.21	28.83	3.094
S1222	**Water storage tanks and cylinders**								
S122201	**Plastic water storage cisterns with lids and insulation; BS 4213; capacity**								
S122201A	25 litre	Nr	0.75	30.11	-	31.32	61.43	67.57	18.975
S122201B	227 litre	Nr	1.25	50.17	-	156.99	207.16	227.88	172.293
S122221	**Copper hot water cylinders; BS 699; Grade 3 direct; insulation jacket; capacity**								
S122221A	120 litre	Nr	0.60	24.06	-	282.58	306.64	337.30	137.310
S122221B	210 litre	Nr	0.85	34.11	-	282.58	316.69	348.36	137.310
S122231	**Copper hot water cylinders; BS 1566; Grade 3 indirect; insulation jacket; capacity**								
S122231A	114 litre	Nr	1.00	40.12	-	289.62	329.74	362.71	146.340
S122231B	120 litre	Nr	1.00	40.12	-	289.62	329.74	362.71	146.340
S122251	**Copper hot water cylinders; BS 1566; indirect; Economy 7; ready lagged; capacity**								
S122251A	116 litre	Nr	0.95	38.12	-	169.42	207.54	228.29	114.380
S122251B	227 litre	Nr	1.15	46.13	-	300.64	346.77	381.45	195.650
S122271	**Copper combination hot water storage and cold water header tanks; BS 3198; with lids; direct; capacity**								
S122271A	115 litre hot, 45 litre cold	Nr	1.15	46.13	-	527.03	573.16	630.48	137.310
S122271B	115 litre hot, 115 litre cold	Nr	1.30	52.17	-	559.80	611.97	673.17	152.360
S122281	**Copper combination hot water storage and cold water header tanks; BS 3198; with lids; indirect; capacity**								
S122281A	115 litre hot, 45 litre cold	Nr	1.15	46.13	-	601.09	647.22	711.94	161.390
S122281B	115 litre hot, 115 litre cold	Nr	1.30	52.17	-	623.28	675.45	743.00	182.460
S1224	**Oil fuel storage tanks**								
S122401	**Mild steel tanks; BS 799; capacity**								
S122401A	1130 litre	Nr	0.75	30.11	-	251.53	281.64	309.80	1,145.190
S122401B	1360 litre	Nr	0.85	34.11	-	288.99	323.10	355.41	1,237.230
S122401C	2730 litre	Nr	0.95	38.12	-	412.07	450.19	495.21	1,955.850
S122401D	4550 litre	Nr	1.20	48.17	-	754.57	802.74	883.01	2,566.500
S1250	**Thermal insulation**								
S125001	**Rigid foam insulation to pipework; Armaflex or equal and approved; 9 mm wall thickness; fixing to pipes with tape: pipe dia**								
S125001A	15 mm	m	0.15	6.01	-	2.55	8.56	9.42	0.088
S125001B	22 mm	m	0.17	6.81	-	3.28	10.09	11.10	0.122
S125001C	28 mm	m	0.20	8.01	-	3.53	11.54	12.69	0.154

Major Works 2011		Unit	Labour Hours	Labour Net	Plant Net	Materials Net	Unit Net	Unit with 10%	CO₂
				£	£	£	£	£	Kg
S12	**S12: HOT AND COLD WATER (SMALL SCALE)**								
S1250	**Thermal insulation**								
S125002	**Crown pipe insulation for steel pipes; with aluminium foil facing; reinforced; 25 mm wall thickness; pipe dia**								
S125002A	32 mm	m	0.20	8.01	-	1.96	9.97	10.97	0.628
S125002B	50 mm	m	0.22	8.85	-	2.61	11.46	12.61	0.981
S125002C	100 mm	m	0.24	9.65	-	4.48	14.13	15.54	1.962
S125003	**Crown pipe insulation for copper pipes; with aluminium foil facing; reinforced; 25 mm wall thickness; pipe dia**								
S125003A	50 mm	m	0.22	8.85	-	2.25	11.10	12.21	0.981
S125003B	65 mm	m	0.23	9.25	-	2.90	12.15	13.37	1.276
S125003C	100 mm	m	0.25	10.05	-	4.36	14.41	15.85	1.962

Electrical Supply, Power and Lighting Systems

Major Works 2011		Unit	Labour Hours	Labour Net	Plant Net	Materials Net	Unit Net	Unit with 10%	CO$_2$
				£	£	£	£	£	Kg
V90	**V90: ELECTRICAL INSTALLATION (SMALL SCALE)**								
V9001	**Two storey housing installations**								
V900101	**Consumer unit, standard metal enclosure with 100A main switch, surface mounted to outside wall**								
V900101A	8 ways with miniature circuit breakers: 4 x 32A for power ring mains, 2 x 6A for lighting circuits, 1 x 40A cooker circuit, 1 x 16A immersion heater circuit	Nr	0.75	16.31	-	155.38	171.69	188.86	10.497
V900111	**Socket outlets, switched, flush mounted including associated concealed wiring and mounting box**								
V900111A	2 gang	Nr	0.83	17.94	-	32.63	50.57	55.63	8.259
V900111B	1 gang	Nr	0.84	15.50	-	29.02	44.52	48.97	8.112
V900111C	1 gang with RCD protection	Nr	0.88	16.33	-	118.87	135.20	148.72	9.381
V900112	**Socket outlets, unswitched, flush mounted including associated concealed wiring and mounting box**								
V900112A	Shaver socket, dual voltage with neon indicator	Nr	0.88	16.33	-	68.45	84.78	93.26	8.790
V900121	**Fused connection unit only, switched, for domestic equipment, flush mounted, including associated concealed wiring and mounting box**								
V900121A	13A	Nr	0.82	15.02	-	31.74	46.76	51.44	10.383
V900131	**Fused connection unit only, switched, for domestic equipment, flush mounted, with neon indicator, including associated concealed wiring and mounting box**								
V900131A	15A	Nr	3.90	70.57	-	113.61	184.18	202.60	37.221
V900141	**Cooker power units**								
V900141A	45A DP with integral 13A SP switched socket outlet and neon indicator, for domestic kitchen. Surface mounted, including associated concealed wiring and mounting box	Nr	2.17	39.50	-	144.48	183.98	202.38	27.851
V900151	**Lighting points, ceiling mounted, including associated concealed cabling and mounting boxes**								
V900151A	1-way switch control	Nr	1.45	27.67	-	22.62	50.29	55.32	6.903
V900151B	2 switches in 2-way switch control	Nr	2.97	56.84	-	72.82	129.66	142.63	18.525
V900151C	3 switches in intermediate switch control	Nr	4.84	92.33	-	74.36	166.69	183.36	24.534
V900152	**External lighting units**								
V900152A	Bulkhead light fitting for exterior of domestic premises, single 100W, surface mounted, including all associated concealed wiring and mounting boxes. 1-way switch control	Nr	1.67	30.62	-	33.11	63.73	70.10	7.129

Major Works 2011		Unit	Labour Hours	Labour Net	Plant Net	Materials Net	Unit Net	Unit with 10%	CO$_2$
				£	£	£	£	£	Kg
V90	**V90: ELECTRICAL INSTALLATION (SMALL SCALE)**								
V9001	**Two storey housing installations**								
V900161	**Extractor fan, domestic 3KW, for air intake and/or extraction, with fan controller, connection unit, fixing to structure and associated concealed wiring and mounting boxes. (Associated vent trunking measured separately)**								
V900161A	For WC/bathroom, manual pull cord, flush mounted in ceiling	Nr	1.65	31.00	-	208.48	239.48	263.43	30.723
V900161B	For WC/bathroom, automatic delay timer flush mounted in ceiling	Nr	1.70	30.69	-	181.90	212.59	233.85	27.345
V900161C	General purpose, manual 30W, flush mounted in wall	Nr	2.37	41.07	-	252.15	293.22	322.54	34.486
V900161D	General purpose, automatic delay timer 60W, flush mounted in wall	Nr	1.70	31.50	-	464.57	496.07	545.68	31.394
V900171	**Immersion water heater, 3KW domestic, with thermostat, controller, connection unit, fixing to structure and associated concealed wiring and mounting boxes. (Associated plumbing installations, pipework, lagging etc measured separately)**								
V900171A	Standard 27 inch, with 24 hour timeswitch	Nr	4.48	83.11	-	184.86	267.97	294.77	52.290
V900171B	Aqualoy 27 inch, with 24 hour timeswitch	Nr	4.43	82.10	-	191.35	273.45	300.80	53.403
V900171C	Standard 27 inch, with Newlec Economy 7 quartz timeswitch	Nr	4.53	84.16	-	211.29	295.45	325.00	61.154
V900181	**Fire detection and alarm systems, domestic, surface mounted and fixed to structure, including associated fire resistant wiring and accessories**								
V900181A	Fire alarm panel, self contained, 2 zone, Gent Ltd., complete with batteries and charger, mounted on wall in hallway	Nr	2.12	39.23	-	316.60	355.83	391.41	15.580
V900181B	smoke detector head, Ionisation type, surface mounted to ceiling	Nr	1.74	31.57	-	133.85	165.42	181.96	19.066
V900181C	Manual call point, surface mounted to wall	Nr	0.47	8.13	-	27.34	35.47	39.02	4.964
V900181D	Alarm sounder, indoor type, electronic, 24v polarised	Nr	1.71	31.09	-	75.53	106.62	117.28	14.426
V900181E	Alarm sounder, weatherproof, electronic, 24v polarised	Nr	1.68	30.50	-	106.43	136.93	150.62	16.648
V9010	**Domestic garage/outbuilding installations**								
V901001	**Lighting points, ceiling mounted, including associated concealed wiring and mounting boxes**								
V901001A	Heavy duty pendant, 1 way switch control	Nr	0.97	20.19	-	30.70	50.89	55.98	8.688
V901002	**External lighting units**								
V901002A	Bulkhead light fittings, rectangular 100W surface mounted, including associated concealed wiring, 1 way switch control	Nr	1.01	20.94	-	39.79	60.73	66.80	8.930

Major Works 2011		Unit	Labour Hours	Labour Net	Plant Net	Materials Net	Unit Net	Unit with 10%	CO$_2$
				£	£	£	£	£	Kg
V90	**V90: ELECTRICAL INSTALLATION (SMALL SCALE)**								
V9010	**Domestic garage/outbuilding installations**								
V901003	**Socket outlet, switched, surface mounted metalclad, including associated part concealed wiring and part wiring in PVC-u conduit with mounting box**								
V901003A	2 gang	Nr	1.51	29.42	-	58.85	88.27	97.10	25.181
V901003B	1 gang	Nr	1.47	28.57	-	47.41	75.98	83.58	24.951

Transport Systems

Major Works 2011		Unit	Labour Hours	Labour Net	Plant Net	Materials Net	Unit Net	Unit with 10%	CO$_2$
				£	£	£	£	£	Kg
X10	**X10: LIFTS**								
X1010	**Passenger lifts; hydraulic; standard finish; single opening; internal fireman's control; in-car telephone; controls; suitable for disabled people**								
X101010	**Wall mounted 6 person; 450 kg; size 850 x 1400 x 2200 mm; serving**								
X101010A	2 floors	Nr	228.28	17,917.54	-	18,110.76	36,028.30	39,631.13	5,576.051
X101010B	3 floors	Nr	252.74	19,837.80	-	20,056.03	39,893.83	43,883.21	5,576.051
X101010C	4 floors	Nr	271.84	21,336.64	-	22,241.27	43,577.91	47,935.70	5,576.051
X101015	**Wall mounted 8 person; 630 kg; size 1100 x 1400 x 2200 mm; serving**								
X101015A	2 floors	Nr	232.41	18,242.17	-	22,485.95	40,728.12	44,800.93	7,806.472
X101015B	3 floors	Nr	255.91	20,086.45	-	25,471.17	45,557.62	50,113.38	7,806.472
X101015C	4 floors	Nr	276.77	21,723.44	-	27,579.45	49,302.89	54,233.18	7,806.472
X101020	**Wall mounted 10 person; 800 kg; size 1300 x 1400 x 2200 mm; serving**								
X101020A	2 floors	Nr	236.99	18,601.35	-	21,914.02	40,515.37	44,566.91	9,912.980
X101020B	3 floors	Nr	251.51	19,741.10	-	23,666.11	43,407.21	47,747.93	9,912.980
X101020C	4 floors	Nr	282.31	22,158.67	-	25,799.87	47,958.54	52,754.39	9,912.980
X101025	**Wall mounted 13 person; 1000 kg; size 1100 x 2100 x 2200 mm; serving**								
X101025A	2 floors	Nr	241.66	18,967.50	-	23,362.88	42,330.38	46,563.42	11,709.708
X101025B	3 floors	Nr	266.30	20,901.49	-	25,471.17	46,372.66	51,009.93	11,709.708
X101025C	4 floors	Nr	287.94	22,600.72	-	27,579.18	50,179.90	55,197.89	11,709.708
X1020	**Goods lifts; hydraulic; twin opening; heavy duty finish with shutter gates; internal lighting**								
X102010	**Wall mounted lift; 1000 kg; car size 1400 x 1800 x 2000 mm; serving**								
X102010A	2 floors	Nr	211.21	16,577.56	-	26,483.29	43,060.85	47,366.94	12,165.930
X102010B	3 floors	Nr	232.30	18,233.54	-	29,128.70	47,362.24	52,098.46	12,165.930
X102010C	4 floors	Nr	253.43	19,891.72	-	31,777.76	51,669.48	56,836.43	18,876.503
X102015	**Wall mounted lift; 1500 kg; car size 1700 x 2000 x 2300 mm; serving**								
X102015A	2 floors	Nr	264.01	20,721.99	-	33,104.11	53,826.10	59,208.71	18,876.503
X102015B	3 floors	Nr	285.11	22,377.89	-	35,749.52	58,127.41	63,940.15	18,876.503
X102015C	4 floors	Nr	306.23	24,036.15	-	31,777.76	55,813.91	61,395.30	18,876.503
X102020	**Wall mounted lift; 3000 kg; car size 2000 x 3000 x 2300 mm; serving**								
X102020A	2 floors	Nr	422.38	33,152.92	-	52,962.92	86,115.84	94,727.42	33,311.475
X102020B	3 floors	Nr	443.51	34,811.10	-	55,611.98	90,423.08	99,465.39	33,311.475
X102020C	4 floors	Nr	464.64	36,469.28	-	58,261.05	94,730.33	104,203.36	33,311.475

Appendices

Indices

The following all-in tender price, building cost and mechanical + electrical cost indices are calculated through the analysis of a large number of projects and construction data. The costs of construction materials, plant and labour are regularly monitored and tracked to calculate the cost indices.

Building cost indices

The Building Cost Index measures changes in contractors' costs. It is constructed using a calculated weighting of wage rates, material costs and plant and overhead charges. The weighting represents the levels of resources used in a typical building project. Please note that variances in inflationary levels are likely to be recorded depending on the type and resource weighting of the building being adjusted.

Mechanical + electrical cost indices

Mechanical and Electrical (M+E) Cost Index measures changes in the M+E contractors' costs. It is constructed using a calculated weighting of wage rates, material costs and plant and overhead charges. The weighting represents the levels of resources used in a typical building project. Please note that variances in inflationary levels are likely to be recorded depending on the type and resource weighting of the building being adjusted.

All-in tender price indices

The All-in Tender Price Index measures the trend of contractors' pricing levels in accepted tenders, i.e. what the client has to pay for the building. It therefore takes into account building costs, but it also makes an allowance for market conditions and profit.

Please note:

Using one generic index to inflate your project, sector or market can be a risky assumption to make. The inflation profile attributed by a generic index is unlikely to represent the inflation profile of the cost drivers that you are trying to represent. Franklin + Andrews always recommend that a detailed indexation study is carried out which identifies the specific cost driver weightings associated with your project in order to create a project specific inflation profile. If required, please contact our specialist indexation team at Franklin + Andrews' Economic Research Unit at eru@franklinandrews.com for guidance on the choice and correct application of inflation statistics and to also understand what service options are available to improve your levels of accuracy and confidence with your specific inflation issues.

Franklin + Andrews' Indices

The following table refelcts the change in tender prices, building costs and M+E Costs in the UK construction market since 2000.

Base 2000 = 100

Quarter	Building cost index	M+E cost index	All-in tender price index
1Q00	98	99	97
2Q00	99	100	99
3Q00	101	100	101
4Q00	102	102	103
1Q01	103	104	105
2Q01	103	104	105
3Q01	104	104	109
4Q01	105	105	110
1Q02	105	106	112
2Q02	106	107	116
3Q02	109	107	119
4Q02	110	110	119
1Q03	112	111	121
2Q03	112	112	122
3Q03	114	112	124
4Q03	115	113	125
1Q04	116	116	129
2Q04	118	117	131
3Q04	122	118	132
4Q04	124	121	134
1Q05	125	123	137
2Q05	126	123	139
3Q05	129	124	140
4Q05	129	126	142
1Q06	131	128	144
2Q06	133	130	145
3Q06	136	132	147
4Q06	137	133	148
1Q07	138	134	150
2Q07	140	136	152
3Q07	142	137	157
4Q07	143	138	160
1Q08	144	139	160
2Q08	146	141	157
3Q08	151	143	156
4Q08	152	145	154
1Q09	150	145	151
2Q09	151	146	146
3Q09	151	146	141
4Q09	152	147	137
1Q10	153	149	137
2Q10	155	151	137

Location Factors

Regional price variations

FACTOR SECOND QUARTER 2010

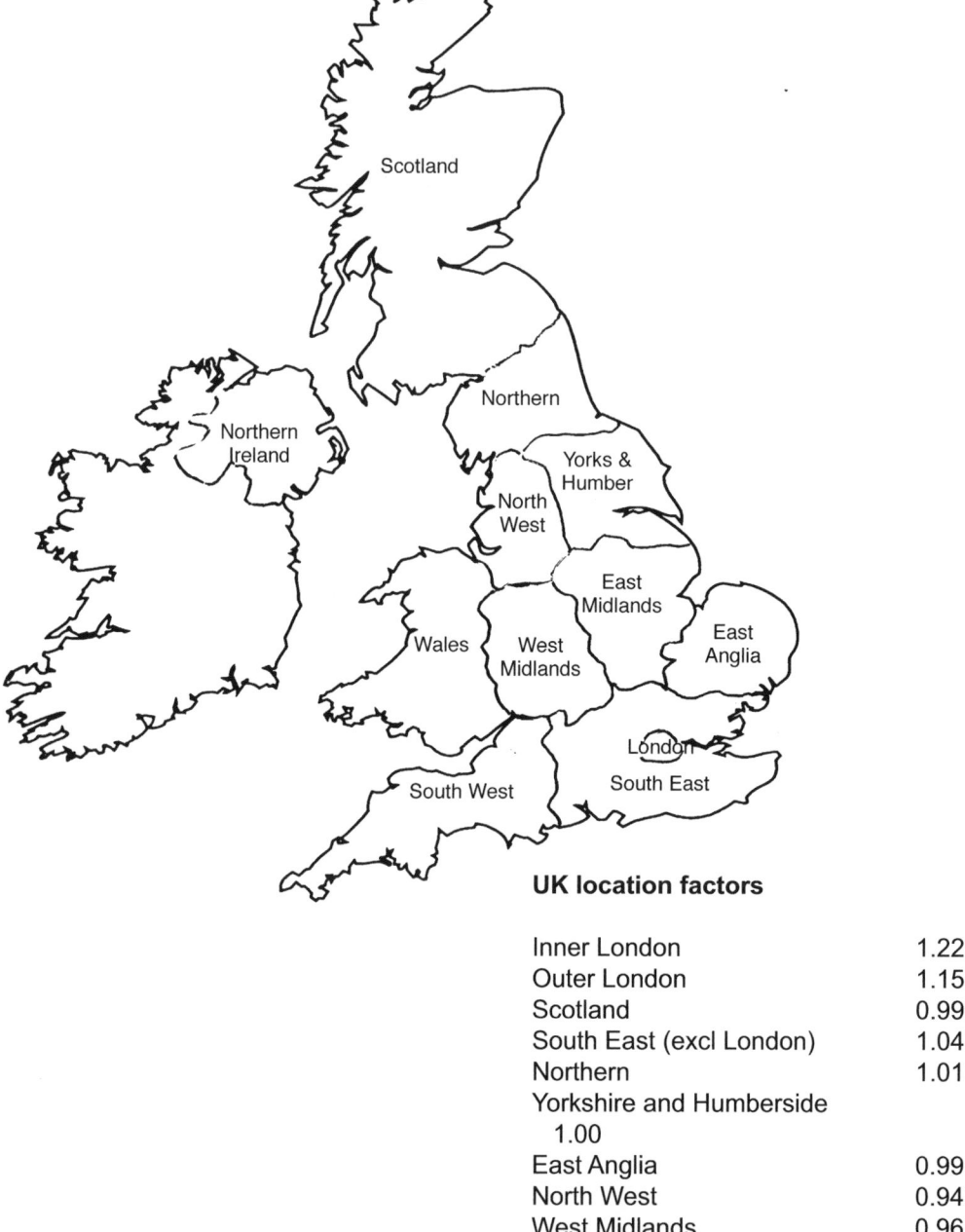

Scotland

Northern Ireland

Northern

Yorks & Humber

North West

East Midlands

Wales

West Midlands

East Anglia

London

South West

South East

UK location factors

Inner London	1.22
Outer London	1.15
Scotland	0.99
South East (excl London)	1.04
Northern	1.01
Yorkshire and Humberside	1.00
East Anglia	0.99
North West	0.94
West Midlands	0.96
South West	0.98
East Midlands	0.94
Northern Ireland	0.86
Wales	0.91

Indicative international location factors

By the analysis of similar projects throughout various locations around the world the following indicative international location factors have been calculated.

Care should be exercised when applying an international factor to another country's project. Procurement, technology, availability of materials, labour and plant may be different within any individual country, sometimes resulting in a project being factored that cannot actually be built in another part of the world.

These factors are presented as a guide only, a full study should be undertaken to obtain an accurate feasibility report in respect of any proposed project.

(Note: UK = 1.00)

	Location Factor				Location Factor		
	Mean	Low	High		Mean	Low	High
ARGENTINA	0.70	0.38	1.26	Shanghai	0.43		
AUSTRALIA	1.06	0.63	1.87	Macao	0.45		
Adelaide	0.93			**COLOMBIA**	0.72	0.35	1.98
Brisbane	0.90			**COTE D'IVOIRE**	0.88	0.39	1.75
Darwin	1.21			**CYPRUS**	0.87	0.47	1.60
Hobart	1.07			**CZECH REP**	0.70	0.22	1.20
Perth	0.92			Prague	0.70		
Sydney	1.06			Brno	0.67		
Melbourne	1.00			Liberec	0.65		
Queensland Islands	1.19			**DENMARK**	1.26	0.65	2.10
AUSTRIA	0.93	0.41	1.31	Copenhagen	1.26		
BAHRAIN	0.84	0.41	1.46	Odense	1.35		
BANGLADESH	0.76	0.22	1.53	Arhus	1.39		
BELGIUM	0.86	0.45	1.21	**EGYPT**	0.66	0.28	1.26
BOLIVIA	0.63	0.33	1.59	Alexandria	0.61		
BRAZIL	0.76	0.34	1.44	Cairo	0.66		
Rio de Janeiro	0.76			Port Said	0.61		
Sao Paulo	0.78			Suez	0.61		
Curitiba	0.78			Other Areas	0.56		
Salvador	0.80			**EL SALVADOR**	0.59	0.27	1.39
BULGARIA	0.60	0.27	1.20	**FINLAND**	0.99	0.43	1.63
CANADA	0.92	0.36	1.58	**FRANCE**	0.94	0.53	1.39
Edmonton	0.81			Paris	0.94		
Calgary	0.85			Ardenne	0.91		
Halifax	0.97			Picardie	0.90		
Montreal	0.83			Haute-Normandie	0.87		
Ottowa	0.90			Centre	0.92		
Quebec	0.83			Basse Normandie	0.93		
Toronto	0.92			Bourgogne	0.95		
St. Johns	1.04			Nord-Pas-de-Calais	0.90		
Vancouver	0.87			Lorraine	0.93		
Winnipeg	0.81			Alsace	0.94		
CHILE	0.77	0.30	1.34	Franche Comte	0.92		
CHINA	0.40	0.12	1.05	**GERMANY**	0.90	0.47	1.36
Shenzen	0.40			Baden - Stuttgart	0.95		
Beijing	0.42			Bavaria, Munich	0.95		

International Location Factors

	Location Factor				Location Factor		
	Mean	**Low**	**High**		**Mean**	**Low**	**High**
Berlin	1.08			Kobe / Kyoto	1.17		
Bremen	0.87			Nagoya	1.04		
Hamburg	0.87			Osaka	1.11		
Hannover	0.86			Sapporo	1.03		
Frankfurt	0.90			Tokyo	1.06		
Pomerania	0.86			**KENYA**	**0.52**	**0.14**	**1.07**
Cologne	0.92			**KOREA, SOUTH**	**0.64**	**0.33**	**1.46**
Ludwigshaven	0.93			Incheon	0.63		
Saarbrucken	0.96			Pusan	0.63		
GHANA	**0.87**	**0.38**	**1.71**	Seoul	0.64		
GREECE	**0.74**	**0.31**	**1.21**	Taegu	0.62		
HONG KONG	**0.75**	**0.24**	**0.96**	**KUWAIT**	**0.82**	**0.39**	**2.08**
HUNGARY	**0.68**	**0.24**	**1.04**	Kuwait	0.82		
Budapest	0.68			Al Jahrah	0.88		
INDIA	**0.52**	**0.14**	**0.99**	Ad Dawhah	0.93		
INDONESIA	**0.46**	**0.14**	**0.71**	Ash Shuaybah	1.02		
Bandung	0.43			**LIBYA**	**0.69**	**0.36**	**0.99**
Jakarta	0.46			**MALAWI**	**0.70**	**0.32**	**1.41**
Medan	0.43			**MALAYSIA**	**0.53**	**0.14**	**0.86**
Surabaya	0.41			Kuala Lumpur	0.53		
Other Areas	0.37			Johor Baharu	0.58		
IRELAND	**1.08**	**0.66**	**1.68**	**MEXICO**	**0.70**	**0.28**	**1.26**
Central Dublin	1.11			Ciudad Juarez	0.81		
Greater Dublin	1.08			Guadalajara	0.65		
Shannon	1.00			Merida	0.61		
Cork	1.03			Mexico City	0.70		
South West	0.98			Monterrey	0.67		
South East	1.00			Puebla	0.67		
Midlands East	1.00			**NETHERLANDS**	**0.97**	**0.55**	**1.42**
West	0.99			Arnhem	0.92		
North West	0.97			Amsterdam	0.97		
ITALY	**0.92**	**0.43**	**1.59**	Apeldorn	0.92		
Bari	0.83			Einhoven	0.90		
Bologna	0.90			Enschede	0.89		
Cagliari	0.79			Groningen	0.88		
Florence	0.93			Rotterdam	0.98		
Genoa	0.91			The Hague	0.99		
Milan	0.92			Utrecht	0.97		
Naples	0.83			**NEW ZEALAND**	**0.96**	**0.50**	**1.40**
Rome	0.87			**NIGERIA**	**0.75**	**0.35**	**1.56**
Palermo	0.79			Abuja	0.71		
Turin	0.93			Lagos	0.75		
Venice	0.93			Port Harcourt	0.71		
JAPAN	**1.06**	**0.34**	**1.70**	**NORWAY**	**0.99**	**0.46**	**2.21**
Fukuoka	0.93			Bergen	0.96		
Kitakyusha	0.93			Kristiansand	0.98		
Hiroshima	0.99			Oslo	0.99		
Kawasaki	1.02			Stavanger	0.97		
Yokohama	1.02			Trondheim	1.01		

	Location Factor				Location Factor		
	Mean	Low	High		Mean	Low	High
OMAN	0.80	0.32	1.41	Stockholm	1.19		
PAKISTAN	0.68	0.35	1.54	Uppsala	1.17		
PERU	0.61	0.27	1.18	**SWITZERLAND**	1.30	0.72	2.21
PHILIPPINES	0.45	0.09	0.87	**TAIWAN**	0.77	0.52	2.36
POLAND	0.70	0.24	1.58	**THAILAND**	0.49	0.19	0.78
Lodz	0.67			**TURKEY**	0.75	0.25	1.30
Krakow	0.68			Istanbul	0.67		
Poznan	0.67			Ankara	0.64		
Warsaw	0.70			Other Areas	0.54		
Other Areas	0.63			**UGANDA**	0.72	0.33	1.45
PORTUGAL	0.75	0.38	1.68	**UKRAINE**	0.77	0.35	1.54
Lisbon	0.75			**UNITED ARAB**			
Setubal	0.74			**EMIRATES**	0.85	0.31	1.26
Coimbra	0.71			**UNITED KINGDOM**	1.00	0.45	2.00
Braga	0.68			**USA**	0.98	0.56	2.26
Faro	0.86			Atlanta	0.86		
ROMANIA	0.68	0.33	1.28	Boston	1.06		
RUSSIAN FED.	1.08	0.59	1.94	Chicago	1.05	0.60	2.42
SAUDI ARABIA	0.77	0.35	1.93	Dallas	0.87		
Dammam / Dhahran	0.81			Los Angeles	1.09	0.62	2.51
Jeddah	0.73			New York City	1.20	0.68	2.76
Mecca	0.73			San Francisco	1.18		
Riyadh	0.77			Seattle	0.91		
Other Areas	0.69			Washington D.C	0.98		
SINGAPORE	0.63	0.23	1.04	**VENEZUELA**	0.76	0.38	1.71
SLOVENIA	0.66	0.25	1.09	**VIETNAM**	0.64	0.29	1.28
SOUTH AFRICA	0.75	0.25	1.25	**WEST INDIES**	1.03	0.46	2.05
Cape Town	0.72			**ZIMBABWE**	0.69	0.37	1.64
Durban	0.73						
Johannesburg	0.75						
Pretoria	0.74						
Port Elizabeth	0.74						
SPAIN	0.75	0.35	1.16				
Barcelona	0.77						
Bilbao	0.73						
Las Palmas							
de Gran Canaria	0.71						
Malaga	0.73						
Madrid	0.75						
Palma	0.74						
Valencia	0.74						
Seville	0.76						
SRI LANKA	0.76	0.31	1.38				
St. KITTS (Caribbean)	1.25	0.49	1.54				
SWEDEN	1.19	0.29	1.96				
Gothenburg	1.15						
Malmo	1.18						
Norrkoping	1.18						
Orebro	1.17						

Facility Benchmark Costs

Facility benchmark costs

The following facility rates and ranges are taken from high level analyses of a large number of projects.
As construction projects are homogenous in their nature we advise caution in the use of the figures without a fuller appraisal of the project and any likely cost drivers.

The costs are for a completed project at second quarter 2010 levels based on a UK average location but do not include VAT, fees or any site acquisition costs.

Although the figures are taken from a large number of existing projects it is possible for construction costs to fall outside the given range.

Facility type	Benchmark cost £/m² GFA	Low	High
Railway Stations	2,460	608	4,437
Railway Signal Boxes	1,258	822	1,687
Multi-storey Car Parks	373	197	615
Petrol Stations	2,165	806	4,978
Airport Terminal Buildings	2,137	950	4,166
Air Traffic Control Buildings	4,645	1,535	10,635
Recording Studios	1,543	770	3,050
Sorting Offices	988	328	2,154
Refuse Depots	599	325	929
Stables and the like	962	589	1,360
Chemicals Factories	1,053	444	2,391
Electronics Factories	1,170	733	1,899
Factories	669	208	2,737
Advanced Factories	583	274	2,191
Purpose Built Factories	839	257	2,737
Purpose Built Factories/Offices Mixed	783	333	1,898
Warehouses	621	172	2,338
Town Halls	1,472	1,042	2,705
Law Courts	1,793	784	2,605
Offices	1,412	399	3,657
Offices with Shops	1,485	353	3,492
Offices - Purpose Built	1,657	1,119	2,975
Offices - Speculative	1,741	1,045	2,438
Offices - Traditional	1,286	505	2,591
Banks / Building Societies	1,817	788	3,632
Retail Warehouses	587	224	2,097
Shopping Centres	916	359	1,796
Department Stores	1,119	386	2,127
Hypermarkets / Supermarkets	1,093	202	2,131
Shops	852	286	2,289
Cold Stores	991	279	1,886
Other Shops	954	459	2,398
Fire Stations	1,625	673	3,092

Facility Benchmark Costs

Facility type	Benchmark cost £/m² GFA	Low	High
Police Stations	1,698	985	2,752
Closed Prisons	1,897	972	2,593
Gynaecological Hospital Facilities	1,708	1,165	3,070
Paediatric Units	1,434	807	2,389
Ward Blocks	1,468	832	2,113
Outpatients / Casualty Units	1,768	1,191	2,533
Day Hospital	1,802	1,112	2,485
Intensive Care / Acute Wards	1,748	1,047	3,242
Health Centres	1,200	461	2,562
Nursing Homes	1,307	640	2,699
Homes for Mentally Handicapped	1,254	639	2,427
Homes for the Elderly	1,166	602	2,258
Day Centres	1,406	696	2,333
Veterinary Hospitals	1,545	1,313	1,854
Restaurants	1,785	834	3,900
Public Houses	1,419	757	2,563
Theatres	1,970	1,177	3,212
Cinemas	1,513	1,018	2,570
Community Centres	1,220	519	2,715
Clubs	1,170	623	1,774
Covered Swimming Pools	2,193	594	5,131
Sports Centres excl. Pools	1,140	473	2,542
Sports Centres incl. Pools	1,746	512	3,840
Sports Halls	1,050	343	2,107
Gymnasia	1,568	677	2,682
Squash Courts	1,119	792	2,253
Indoor Tennis Courts	462	276	730
Indoor Bowling Greens	587	329	1,042
Stadia	1,307	444	2,637
Golf Driving Ranges	845	416	1,464
Covered Ice Rinks	1,228	657	1,675
Pavilions / Sports Club Houses	1,240	329	4,710
Churches	1,474	628	2,957
Mission Halls	1,543	916	3,622
Crematoria	2,058	1,261	3,025
Schools	1,274	516	3,659
Nursey Schools	1,509	538	3,013
Primary Schools	1,240	517	2,635
Middle Schools	1,073	664	1,641
High Schools	1,152	579	3,659
Sixth Form Colleges	1,246	571	2,105
Special Schools	1,251	728	2,178
Universities	1,512	837	4,482
University Specialist Teaching Block	1,244	586	2,590
Colleges	1,330	594	2,588
Research Facilities	1,774	852	5,052
Laboratories	1,767	603	3,393

Facility type	Benchmark cost £/m² GFA	Low	High
Exhibition Buildings	1,896	1,212	4,322
Public Libraries	1,409	808	2,757
Estate Housing	822	363	1,966
Estate Housing - Detached	885	508	1,525
Estate Housing - Semi-detached	837	451	1,966
Estate Housing - Terraced	762	400	1,583
Flats	955	386	2,795
Housing - Detached	1,372	441	4,859
Housing - Semi-detached	961	625	1,442
Sheltered Housing	977	477	2,200
Hotels	1,358	803	2,585
Halls of Residence	1,360	771	2,808

Indicative refurbishment costs

Facility type	Benchmark cost £/m² GFA	Low	High
Offices	1,225	850	1,500
Banks	1,380	1,250	1,550
Factories/Warehouses	625	550	875
Warehouses/Storage Facilities	525	350	625
Sports Centres/Recreational Facilities	825	625	1,025
Hotels	1,225	975	1,500
Supermarkets	950	625	1,225
Shopping Centres/Malls	750	400	1,100
Hospitals	1,425	1,150	1,550
Educational Facilities	1,025	950	1,150

Indicative category B fit-out costs

Facility type	Benchmark cost £/m² GFA	Low	High
Legal	1,200	950	1,350
Banks	1,850	1,300	2,000
Accountancy	900	650	1,000
Media	1,000	650	1,100
Corporate	1,550	900	1,800

Elemental Analyses

Through the analysis of a large number of existing projects Elemental Benchmark proportions have been produced for the following 46 facility types.

When using any of the following information the reader should be aware of the need to take into account specific cost drivers applicable to the proposed project that may skew these percentage splits.

The following figures are provided as a guide only and a proper appraisal should be carried out during the preparation of any feasibility study.

Railway Stations	Public Houses
Multi-Storey Car Parks	Restaurants
Petrol Stations	Theatres
Airport Terminal Buildings	Community Centres
Chemical Factories	Covered Swimming Pools
Electronics Factories	Gymnasia
Factories	Sports Centres
Advanced Factories	Sports Centres incl pool
Warehouses	Sports Halls
Town Halls	Sports Stadia
Law Courts	Crematoria
Offices	Primary Schools
Offices with Shops	Middle Schools
Banks / Building Societies	High Schools
Shops	Sixth Form Colleges
Super / Hypermarkets	Universities
Department Stores	Laboratory Blocks
Shopping Centres	Research Facilities
Retail Warehouses	Detached Housing
General Hospitals	Semi-Detached Housing
Mixed Facility Hospitals	Estate Housing
Homes for Elderly	Hotels
Veterinary Surgeries	Halls of Residence

Elemental Analyses

Element		Railway Stations	Multi-Storey Car Parks	Petrol Stations	Airport Terminal Buildings
		%	%	%	%
1	**SUBSTRUCTURE**	**5.51%**	**17.27%**	**4.12%**	**2.79%**
2A	Frame	10.28%	9.14%	0.69%	12.27%
2B	Upper floors	2.60%	19.45%	0.00%	2.70%
2C	Roof	4.37%	3.75%	3.44%	2.14%
2D	Stairs	0.50%	1.17%	0.00%	0.36%
2E	External walls	2.81%	7.77%	4.73%	7.92%
2F	Windows and external doors	5.44%	1.38%	3.98%	0.20%
2G	Internal walls and partitions	4.88%	0.47%	0.69%	1.40%
2H	Internal doors	1.32%	0.44%	0.97%	1.07%
2	**SUPERSTRUCTURE**	**32.20%**	**43.57%**	**14.49%**	**28.07%**
3A	Wall finishes	3.22%	0.43%	0.95%	3.80%
3B	Floor finishes	2.41%	2.34%	1.46%	2.18%
3C	Ceiling finishes	1.10%	1.12%	0.93%	1.86%
3	**INTERNAL FINISHES**	**6.72%**	**3.89%**	**3.33%**	**7.85%**
4	**FITTINGS AND FURNISHINGS**	**2.25%**	**1.59%**	**3.56%**	**5.66%**
5A	Sanitary appliances	0.71%	0.10%	0.12%	0.38%
5B	Services equipment	0.18%	0.07%	0.00%	1.79%
5C	Disposal installations	0.65%	0.57%	0.51%	0.72%
5D	Water installations	0.00%	0.25%	0.17%	0.65%
5E	Heat source	5.68%	0.00%	0.00%	0.59%
5F	Space heating and air treatment	0.00%	0.01%	0.40%	6.30%
5G	Ventilating systems	0.00%	0.00%	0.96%	0.52%
5H	Electrical installations	4.32%	3.40%	6.55%	6.37%
5I	Gas installations	0.00%	0.00%	0.00%	0.05%
5J	Lift and conveyor installations	3.58%	1.28%	0.00%	1.48%
5K	Protective installations	0.00%	0.94%	0.02%	1.65%
5L	Communication installations	0.00%	1.26%	0.37%	2.14%
5M	Special Installations	0.00%	0.00%	0.59%	9.41%
5N	Builder's work in connection	1.78%	0.32%	0.61%	0.96%
5O	Builder's profit and attendance	0.42%	0.00%	0.01%	3.84%
5	**SERVICES**	**17.33%**	**8.17%**	**10.31%**	**36.85%**
	Building sub-total	**64.01%**	**74.48%**	**35.81%**	**81.22%**
6A	Site works	11.07%	10.27%	27.58%	11.08%
6B	Drainage	4.59%	2.22%	6.19%	0.33%
6C	External services	2.00%	0.66%	1.16%	1.44%
6D	Minor building works	5.44%	6.04%	19.69%	1.73%
6	**EXTERNAL WORKS**	**23.10%**	**19.20%**	**54.62%**	**14.59%**
7	**PRELIMINARIES**	**12.89%**	**6.32%**	**9.57%**	**4.20%**
	FACILITY	**100.00%**	**100.00%**	**100.00%**	**100.00%**

Element		Chemical Factories	Electronics Factories	Factories	Advanced Factories
		%	%	%	%
1	**SUBSTRUCTURE**	**10.22%**	**8.45%**	**13.45%**	**12.45%**
2A	Frame	14.62%	8.02%	9.29%	14.83%
2B	Upper floors	0.46%	0.88%	0.33%	0.00%
2C	Roof	10.42%	5.93%	8.98%	5.91%
2D	Stairs	0.23%	0.85%	0.51%	0.00%
2E	External walls	5.22%	8.55%	10.96%	6.19%
2F	Windows and external doors	2.33%	2.28%	4.94%	3.84%
2G	Internal walls and partitions	1.99%	3.13%	2.43%	2.44%
2H	Internal doors	0.89%	1.92%	0.97%	0.97%
2	**SUPERSTRUCTURE**	**36.14%**	**31.56%**	**38.41%**	**34.18%**
3A	Wall finishes	3.15%	1.27%	1.54%	2.24%
3B	Floor finishes	0.87%	3.30%	0.34%	0.39%
3C	Ceiling finishes	0.80%	1.12%	0.54%	0.28%
3	**INTERNAL FINISHES**	**4.83%**	**5.70%**	**2.42%**	**2.91%**
4	**FITTINGS AND FURNISHINGS**	**1.94%**	**1.09%**	**0.40%**	**0.19%**
5A	Sanitary appliances	0.18%	0.09%	0.83%	0.78%
5B	Services equipment	0.00%	0.25%	0.00%	0.00%
5C	Disposal installations	0.09%	0.10%	0.79%	0.38%
5D	Water installations	0.39%	1.77%	0.85%	1.18%
5E	Heat source	0.04%	0.15%	0.00%	0.26%
5F	Space heating and air treatment	4.03%	9.49%	1.20%	3.81%
5G	Ventilating systems	1.34%	3.20%	0.57%	0.24%
5H	Electrical installations	12.93%	9.26%	3.23%	9.92%
5I	Gas installations	0.00%	0.00%	0.08%	0.36%
5J	Lift and conveyor installations	0.30%	0.43%	0.00%	0.00%
5K	Protective installations	1.41%	1.70%	0.32%	0.39%
5L	Communication installations	0.00%	0.63%	0.00%	0.55%
5M	Special Installations	3.52%	0.08%	0.00%	1.26%
5N	Builder's work in connection	0.45%	1.48%	0.37%	0.88%
5O	Builder's profit and attendance	0.00%	0.02%	0.17%	0.09%
5	**SERVICES**	**24.69%**	**28.67%**	**8.41%**	**20.11%**
	Building sub-total	**77.81%**	**75.46%**	**63.10%**	**69.83%**
6A	Site works	10.52%	16.61%	13.19%	14.47%
6B	Drainage	4.32%	3.02%	7.75%	3.56%
6C	External services	0.72%	0.47%	6.16%	4.03%
6D	Minor building works	2.58%	0.75%	0.00%	1.20%
6	**EXTERNAL WORKS**	**18.15%**	**20.86%**	**27.11%**	**23.25%**
7	**PRELIMINARIES**	**4.03%**	**3.68%**	**9.80%**	**6.92%**
	FACILITY	**100.00%**	**100.00%**	**100.00%**	**100.00%**

Elemental Analyses

Element		Warehouses %	Law Courts %	Town Halls %	Offices %
1	**SUBSTRUCTURE**	**14.65%**	**4.68%**	**7.20%**	**7.28%**
2A	Frame	14.17%	5.16%	3.93%	3.90%
2B	Upper floors	1.01%	2.05%	3.85%	2.28%
2C	Roof	12.56%	5.84%	7.43%	6.91%
2D	Stairs	1.92%	1.92%	0.61%	1.02%
2E	External walls	6.09%	9.48%	5.50%	10.28%
2F	Windows and external doors	5.74%	3.81%	3.41%	4.37%
2G	Internal walls and partitions	2.35%	4.90%	1.91%	7.16%
2H	Internal doors	2.31%	3.90%	2.62%	3.72%
2	**SUPERSTRUCTURE**	**46.15%**	**37.06%**	**29.27%**	**39.64%**
3A	Wall finishes	4.16%	3.32%	0.75%	1.74%
3B	Floor finishes	1.33%	2.78%	4.31%	2.78%
3C	Ceiling finishes	1.22%	2.01%	3.97%	1.96%
3	**INTERNAL FINISHES**	**6.71%**	**8.12%**	**9.04%**	**6.48%**
4	**FITTINGS AND FURNISHINGS**	**0.52%**	**4.81%**	**4.37%**	**1.51%**
5A	Sanitary appliances	0.72%	0.79%	0.27%	0.71%
5B	Services equipment	0.00%	0.00%	0.72%	0.00%
5C	Disposal installations	0.00%	0.25%	0.08%	0.47%
5D	Water installations	0.00%	0.17%	0.33%	0.49%
5E	Heat source	0.00%	0.34%	1.22%	0.39%
5F	Space heating and air treatment	8.79%	10.39%	5.73%	5.78%
5G	Ventilating systems	0.00%	0.92%	4.84%	0.74%
5H	Electrical installations	5.01%	9.92%	7.73%	9.40%
5I	Gas installations	0.00%	2.23%	0.18%	0.06%
5J	Lift and conveyor installations	0.00%	1.66%	0.94%	1.61%
5K	Protective installations	0.00%	0.08%	0.17%	0.62%
5L	Communication installations	0.00%	0.36%	0.00%	0.58%
5M	Special Installations	0.00%	0.38%	0.31%	0.34%
5N	Builder's work in connection	0.00%	1.51%	1.51%	1.06%
5O	Builder's profit and attendance	0.00%	0.42%	0.50%	0.29%
5	**SERVICES**	**14.52%**	**29.43%**	**24.53%**	**22.53%**
	Building sub-total	**82.56%**	**84.10%**	**74.40%**	**77.45%**
6A	Site works	11.93%	4.95%	9.46%	7.60%
6B	Drainage	1.90%	1.06%	1.33%	3.85%
6C	External services	1.14%	0.26%	0.42%	2.83%
6D	Minor building works	0.00%	0.69%	2.22%	0.25%
6	**EXTERNAL WORKS**	**14.97%**	**6.96%**	**13.43%**	**14.53%**
7	**PRELIMINARIES**	**2.47%**	**8.94%**	**12.18%**	**8.02%**
	FACILITY	**100.00%**	**100.00%**	**100.00%**	**100.00%**

Element		Offices with Shops %	Banks / Building Societies %	Shops %	Super / Hypermarkets %
1	**SUBSTRUCTURE**	**7.22%**	**9.84%**	**17.49%**	**9.76%**
2A	Frame	5.92%	4.13%	6.41%	8.84%
2B	Upper floors	2.66%	0.78%	6.67%	0.31%
2C	Roof	7.16%	8.07%	13.25%	7.72%
2D	Stairs	2.33%	0.49%	2.91%	0.21%
2E	External walls	11.56%	5.09%	14.10%	4.65%
2F	Windows and external doors	6.18%	6.17%	3.62%	2.51%
2G	Internal walls and partitions	1.50%	2.61%	1.79%	1.17%
2H	Internal doors	3.96%	2.73%	2.93%	0.92%
2	**SUPERSTRUCTURE**	**41.27%**	**30.06%**	**51.69%**	**26.34%**
3A	Wall finishes	2.27%	1.66%	1.39%	1.28%
3B	Floor finishes	4.33%	3.04%	1.66%	2.79%
3C	Ceiling finishes	1.95%	1.41%	2.14%	1.57%
3	**INTERNAL FINISHES**	**8.55%**	**6.11%**	**5.19%**	**5.65%**
4	**FITTINGS AND FURNISHINGS**	**1.76%**	**8.85%**	**1.72%**	**1.19%**
5A	Sanitary appliances	0.58%	0.42%	0.39%	1.02%
5B	Services equipment	0.00%	0.00%	0.00%	0.00%
5C	Disposal installations	0.16%	0.73%	0.30%	0.08%
5D	Water installations	0.16%	0.31%	0.32%	0.23%
5E	Heat source	0.00%	0.00%	0.00%	1.26%
5F	Space heating and air treatment	8.76%	3.89%	1.24%	3.78%
5G	Ventilating systems	0.06%	1.70%	0.00%	0.14%
5H	Electrical installations	8.25%	13.41%	1.34%	5.06%
5I	Gas installations	0.02%	0.00%	0.00%	0.02%
5J	Lift and conveyor installations	1.57%	0.00%	0.00%	0.42%
5K	Protective installations	0.03%	0.00%	0.00%	1.59%
5L	Communication installations	0.00%	1.60%	0.00%	0.63%
5M	Special Installations	0.00%	0.00%	0.00%	6.71%
5N	Builder's work in connection	0.68%	0.92%	0.27%	1.30%
5O	Builder's profit and attendance	0.00%	0.00%	0.00%	0.05%
5	**SERVICES**	**20.28%**	**22.98%**	**3.85%**	**22.31%**
	Building sub-total	**79.08%**	**77.84%**	**79.93%**	**65.23%**
6A	Site works	2.93%	3.94%	6.42%	17.86%
6B	Drainage	1.46%	3.71%	2.71%	3.48%
6C	External services	1.41%	1.50%	1.58%	3.27%
6D	Minor building works	0.00%	3.64%	0.00%	0.37%
6	**EXTERNAL WORKS**	**5.80%**	**12.79%**	**10.71%**	**24.98%**
7	**PRELIMINARIES**	**15.12%**	**9.37%**	**9.36%**	**9.79%**
	FACILITY	**100.00%**	**100.00%**	**100.00%**	**100.00%**

Elemental Analyses

Element		Department Stores	Shopping Centres	Retail Warehouses	General Hospitals
		%	%	%	%
1	**SUBSTRUCTURE**	**10.95%**	**10.45%**	**15.85%**	**4.36%**
2A	Frame	16.39%	7.46%	15.49%	1.32%
2B	Upper floors	4.15%	4.26%	0.88%	2.93%
2C	Roof	9.33%	14.17%	7.04%	8.43%
2D	Stairs	0.82%	1.25%	0.31%	0.47%
2E	External walls	8.71%	7.66%	6.36%	3.91%
2F	Windows and external doors	2.04%	4.45%	3.43%	3.63%
2G	Internal walls and partitions	1.95%	3.98%	1.86%	2.72%
2H	Internal doors	0.69%	0.77%	0.60%	3.97%
2	**SUPERSTRUCTURE**	**44.08%**	**43.99%**	**35.99%**	**27.38%**
3A	Wall finishes	1.52%	3.88%	0.76%	2.34%
3B	Floor finishes	2.25%	2.95%	0.82%	2.63%
3C	Ceiling finishes	1.72%	1.71%	1.24%	1.75%
3	**INTERNAL FINISHES**	**5.50%**	**8.55%**	**2.83%**	**6.72%**
4	**FITTINGS AND FURNISHINGS**	**0.09%**	**0.64%**	**0.20%**	**4.12%**
5A	Sanitary appliances	0.11%	0.19%	0.21%	2.60%
5B	Services equipment	0.00%	0.00%	0.00%	0.04%
5C	Disposal installations	0.46%	1.21%	0.04%	0.97%
5D	Water installations	0.00%	0.40%	0.01%	3.84%
5E	Heat source	3.45%	0.00%	0.00%	0.17%
5F	Space heating and air treatment	0.00%	2.60%	2.16%	10.43%
5G	Ventilating systems	0.00%	0.39%	0.32%	2.91%
5H	Electrical installations	5.56%	3.52%	3.95%	8.84%
5I	Gas installations	0.00%	0.00%	0.00%	0.38%
5J	Lift and conveyor installations	4.34%	3.50%	0.81%	1.11%
5K	Protective installations	2.35%	1.46%	0.18%	0.40%
5L	Communication installations	0.00%	0.41%	0.00%	3.69%
5M	Special Installations	0.00%	0.31%	0.00%	2.17%
5N	Builder's work in connection	0.74%	0.33%	0.29%	1.53%
5O	Builder's profit and attendance	1.04%	0.48%	0.00%	0.00%
5	**SERVICES**	**18.05%**	**14.81%**	**7.99%**	**39.07%**
	Building sub-total	**78.66%**	**78.44%**	**62.85%**	**81.65%**
6A	Site works	7.74%	4.87%	23.43%	3.37%
6B	Drainage	2.52%	1.84%	4.81%	1.69%
6C	External services	0.51%	2.17%	1.62%	1.13%
6D	Minor building works	0.00%	0.41%	0.27%	2.13%
6	**EXTERNAL WORKS**	**10.77%**	**9.29**	**30.12%**	**8.32%**
7	**PRELIMINARIES**	**10.57%**	**12.27%**	**7.02%**	**10.03%**
	FACILITY	**100.00%**	**100.00%**	**100.00%**	**100.00%**

Element		Mixed Facility Hospitals %	Homes for Elderly %	Veterinary Surgeries %	Public Houses %
1	**SUBSTRUCTURE**	**6.01%**	**3.97%**	**12.45%**	**6.68%**
2A	Frame	4.81%	0.80%	0.00%	1.66%
2B	Upper floors	3.27%	2.87%	0.00%	0.85%
2C	Roof	4.06%	4.11%	7.30%	7.49%
2D	Stairs	0.50%	0.32%	0.00%	0.47%
2E	External walls	4.10%	6.15%	4.15%	4.82%
2F	Windows and external doors	3.57%	8.09%	7.46%	4.26%
2G	Internal walls and partitions	3.79%	3.96%	1.47%	2.49%
2H	Internal doors	3.38%	4.85%	0.00%	2.05%
2	**SUPERSTRUCTURE**	**27.47%**	**31.15%**	**20.37%**	**24.10%**
3A	Wall finishes	1.84%	3.42%	7.96%	3.03%
3B	Floor finishes	2.52%	3.49%	0.00%	3.72%
3C	Ceiling finishes	1.57%	3.27%	0.00%	2.20%
3	**INTERNAL FINISHES**	**5.93%**	**10.18%**	**7.96%**	**8.95%**
4	**FITTINGS AND FURNISHINGS**	**3.16%**	**6.86%**	**6.83%**	**12.98%**
5A	Sanitary appliances	1.49%	2.93%	2.35%	1.86%
5B	Services equipment	0.33%	0.73%	0.00%	2.78%
5C	Disposal installations	1.50%	0.58%	0.00%	0.16%
5D	Water installations	1.16%	0.00%	0.00%	0.00%
5E	Heat source	1.90%	0.00%	0.00%	0.00%
5F	Space heating and air treatment	17.13%	12.49%	12.97%	8.12%
5G	Ventilating systems	2.07%	0.00%	0.00%	0.64%
5H	Electrical installations	10.43%	13.37%	11.78%	6.49%
5I	Gas installations	0.27%	0.00%	0.00%	0.00%
5J	Lift and conveyor installations	1.19%	1.66%	0.00%	0.00%
5K	Protective installations	0.37%	0.00%	0.00%	0.15%
5L	Communication installations	1.05%	0.00%	0.00%	0.55%
5M	Special Installations	0.45%	0.00%	0.07%	0.32%
5N	Builder's work in connection	1.63%	0.93%	0.59%	0.92%
5O	Builder's profit and attendance	0.16%	0.00%	0.00%	0.00%
5	**SERVICES**	**41.13%**	**32.69%**	**27.77%**	**22.00%**
	Building sub-total	**83.70%**	**84.84%**	**75.37%**	**74.70%**
6A	Site works	4.30%	3.77%	9.12%	11.44%
6B	Drainage	2.10%	0.98%	3.15%	4.26%
6C	External services	1.29%	1.03%	0.00%	1.80%
6D	Minor building works	1.31%	0.00%	0.00%	0.61%
6	**EXTERNAL WORKS**	**8.99%**	**5.78%**	**12.27%**	**18.11%**
7	**PRELIMINARIES**	**7.30%**	**9.38%**	**12.36%**	**7.19%**
	FACILITY	**100.00%**	**100.00%**	**100.00%**	**100.00%**

Elemental Analyses

Element		Restaurants %	Theatres %	Community Centres %	Covered Swimming Pools %
1	SUBSTRUCTURE	5.09%	6.68%	9.98%	8.51%
2A	Frame	3.80%	9.74%	0.84%	7.08%
2B	Upper floors	0.75%	3.24%	0.26%	2.27%
2C	Roof	8.47%	6.25%	11.48%	6.56%
2D	Stairs	1.47%	1.21%	0.08%	1.55%
2E	External walls	6.44%	5.88%	5.53%	6.09%
2F	Windows and external doors	8.70%	2.83%	6.92%	2.23%
2G	Internal walls and partitions	2.82%	2.26%	2.26%	2.69%
2H	Internal doors	2.61%	1.83%	3.56%	0.98%
2	SUPERSTRUCTURE	35.06%	33.24%	30.93%	29.46%
3A	Wall finishes	2.17%	1.18%	2.26%	3.16%
3B	Floor finishes	2.92%	2.55%	3.59%	3.67%
3C	Ceiling finishes	1.47%	1.05%	1.51%	0.81%
3	INTERNAL FINISHES	6.56%	4.78%	7.36%	7.64%
4	FITTINGS AND FURNISHINGS	11.82%	11.15%	2.23%	6.92%
5A	Sanitary appliances	1.37%	0.51%	1.35%	0.45%
5B	Services equipment	3.78%	1.40%	0.00%	0.04%
5C	Disposal installations	0.55%	0.40%	0.31%	0.17%
5D	Water installations	11.34%	1.23%	0.51%	1.23%
5E	Heat source	1.31%	0.47%	0.27%	0.90%
5F	Space heating and air treatment	0.33%	9.28%	9.16%	5.46%
5G	Ventilating systems	0.49%	1.25%	0.00%	4.60%
5H	Electrical installations	7.99%	7.89%	7.27%	5.77%
5I	Gas installations	0.16%	0.02%	0.08%	0.16%
5J	Lift and conveyor installations	0.00%	0.36%	0.00%	0.17%
5K	Protective installations	0.16%	0.36%	0.15%	0.60%
5L	Communication installations	0.16%	0.93%	0.21%	0.16%
5M	Special Installations	0.33%	0.00%	0.00%	9.35%
5N	Builder's work in connection	1.01%	1.41%	0.85%	0.96%
5O	Builder's profit and attendance	0.00%	0.03%	0.00%	0.00%
5	SERVICES	28.98%	25.55%	20.15%	30.00%
	Building sub-total	87.53%	81.41%	70.65%	82.53%
6A	Site works	2.17%	2.94%	11.04%	4.58%
6B	Drainage	3.35%	1.24%	3.58%	1.94%
6C	External services	0.45%	1.45%	2.10%	0.66%
6D	Minor building works	0.00%	0.66%	0.00%	0.09%
6	EXTERNAL WORKS	5.97%	6.29%	16.72%	7.27%
7	PRELIMINARIES	6.50%	12.30%	12.62%	10.20%
	FACILITY	100.00%	100.00%	100.00%	100.00%

Element		Gymnasia	Sports Centres	Sports Centres incl. Pool	Sports Halls
		%	%	%	%
1	**SUBSTRUCTURE**	**6.62%**	**7.78%**	**7.51%**	**9.19%**
2A	Frame	9.11%	6.23%	6.57%	7.76%
2B	Upper floors	0.64%	1.43%	0.58%	0.62%
2C	Roof	6.62%	7.41%	7.62%	8.31%
2D	Stairs	0.59%	1.52%	0.78%	0.24%
2E	External walls	14.45%	7.14%	6.51%	7.77%
2F	Windows and external doors	2.13%	2.62%	2.31%	3.64%
2G	Internal walls and partitions	4.60%	1.39%	3.21%	2.59%
2H	Internal doors	1.25%	2.87%	1.22%	9.41%
2	**SUPERSTRUCTURE**	**39.38%**	**30.62%**	**28.79%**	**40.34%**
3A	Wall finishes	1.33%	2.37%	2.04%	3.12%
3B	Floor finishes	2.35%	5.16%	3.89%	3.82%
3C	Ceiling finishes	0.56%	1.55%	1.12%	1.56%
3	**INTERNAL FINISHES**	**4.24%**	**9.08%**	**7.05%**	**8.50%**
4	**FITTINGS AND FURNISHINGS**	**4.94%**	**4.45%**	**4.55%**	**3.10%**
5A	Sanitary appliances	0.83%	0.82%	0.63%	0.86%
5B	Services equipment	0.00%	0.09%	0.00%	0.00%
5C	Disposal installations	0.37%	0.49%	0.30%	0.61%
5D	Water installations	0.13%	0.57%	1.30%	0.41%
5E	Heat source	0.00%	0.00%	0.04%	1.78%
5F	Space heating and air treatment	9.14%	11.17%	14.37%	6.07%
5G	Ventilating systems	2.36%	0.85%	0.94%	2.15%
5H	Electrical installations	5.82%	7.69%	4.50%	7.50%
5I	Gas installations	0.00%	0.00%	0.00%	0.51%
5J	Lift and conveyor installations	0.70%	0.89%	0.54%	0.26%
5K	Protective installations	0.15%	0.16%	0.24%	0.02%
5L	Communication installations	0.80%	0.30%	0.66%	0.40%
5M	Special Installations	0.00%	3.02%	4.41%	0.00%
5N	Builder's work in connection	0.43%	0.80%	0.93%	0.62%
5O	Builder's profit and attendance	0.00%	0.00%	0.00%	0.00%
5	**SERVICES**	**20.73%**	**26.83%**	**28.86%**	**21.19%**
	Building sub-total	**75.91%**	**78.76%**	**76.75%**	**82.32%**
6A	Site works	7.74%	6.15%	6.28%	4.60%
6B	Drainage	2.62%	2.42%	3.01%	2.01%
6C	External services	0.58%	0.78%	1.61%	0.72%
6D	Minor building works	0.24%	0.73%	0.29%	0.17%
6	**EXTERNAL WORKS**	**11.17%**	**10.09%**	**11.18%**	**7.50%**
7	**PRELIMINARIES**	**12.92%**	**11.16%**	**12.07%**	**10.18%**
	FACILITY	**100.00%**	**100.00%**	**100.00%**	**100.00%**

Elemental Analyses

Element		Sports Stadia	Crematoria	Primary Schools	Middle Schools
		%	%	%	%
1	**SUBSTRUCTURE**	**10.34%**	**4.15%**	**10.34%**	**6.51%**
2A	Frame	8.85%	0.00%	2.12%	6.01%
2B	Upper floors	8.50%	0.00%	0.08%	0.72%
2C	Roof	5.00%	9.18%	10.05%	9.46%
2D	Stairs	1.36%	0.00%	0.01%	0.48%
2E	External walls	10.40%	9.59%	4.50%	7.49%
2F	Windows and external doors	2.34%	3.88%	6.10%	5.63%
2G	Internal walls and partitions	2.57%	2.04%	3.51%	3.84%
2H	Internal doors	1.62%	2.31%	2.26%	2.69%
2	**SUPERSTRUCTURE**	**40.64%**	**26.99%**	**28.63%**	**36.32%**
3A	Wall finishes	1.24%	0.81%	1.43%	1.69%
3B	Floor finishes	2.60%	1.49%	3.09%	4.14%
3C	Ceiling finishes	0.77%	2.46%	2.03%	3.31%
3	**INTERNAL FINISHES**	**4.61%**	**4.76%**	**6.55%**	**9.14%**
4	**FITTINGS AND FURNISHINGS**	**2.84%**	**2.24%**	**3.27%**	**4.33%**
5A	Sanitary appliances	1.08%	0.48%	1.36%	0.69%
5B	Services equipment	0.00%	0.00%	0.33%	0.28%
5C	Disposal installations	0.28%	0.34%	0.57%	0.30%
5D	Water installations	0.38%	0.00%	1.04%	1.17%
5E	Heat source	0.54%	0.00%	0.63%	2.25%
5F	Space heating and air treatment	6.40%	2.65%	8.57%	5.26%
5G	Ventilating systems	1.15%	0.00%	1.02%	0.59%
5H	Electrical installations	5.29%	5.30%	7.78%	5.20%
5I	Gas installations	0.05%	0.00%	0.07%	0.07%
5J	Lift and conveyor installations	0.24%	0.00%	0.00%	0.00%
5K	Protective installations	0.37%	0.00%	0.18%	0.15%
5L	Communication installations	0.51%	0.00%	1.32%	0.41%
5M	Special Installations	1.80%	14.97%	0.49%	0.16%
5N	Builder's work in connection	0.45%	0.60%	0.87%	0.64%
5O	Builder's profit and attendance	0.15%	0.00%	0.11%	0.14%
5	**SERVICES**	**18.68%**	**24.35%**	**24.34%**	**17.30%**
	Building sub-total	**77.11%**	**62.49%**	**73.13%**	**73.60%**
6A	Site works	8.32%	21.33%	10.07%	10.78%
6B	Drainage	3.59%	3.59%	3.52%	4.56%
6C	External services	1.96%	3.68%	1.59%	0.51%
6D	Minor building works	0.64%	1.23%	3.84%	1.31%
6	**EXTERNAL WORKS**	**14.52%**	**29.84%**	**19.01%**	**17.16%**
7	**PRELIMINARIES**	**8.37%**	**7.67%**	**7.85%**	**9.24%**
	FACILITY	**100.00%**	**100.00%**	**100.00%**	**100.00%**

Element		High Schools	Sixth Form Colleges	Universities	Laboratory Blocks
		%	%	%	%
1	**SUBSTRUCTURE**	**8.21%**	**9.09%**	**6.51%**	**3.31%**
2A	Frame	5.22%	5.80%	2.14%	1.74%
2B	Upper floors	0.93%	2.54%	2.85%	1.36%
2C	Roof	9.76%	7.08%	6.76%	4.19%
2D	Stairs	1.29%	0.91%	2.21%	0.41%
2E	External walls	5.64%	4.31%	22.84%	3.55%
2F	Windows and external doors	5.84%	11.89%	4.39%	1.32%
2G	Internal walls and partitions	3.54%	4.36%	2.00%	1.97%
2H	Internal doors	3.49%	2.89%	1.86%	0.94%
2	**SUPERSTRUCTURE**	**35.71%**	**39.78%**	**45.05%**	**15.48%**
3A	Wall finishes	1.78%	1.44%	1.80%	0.78%
3B	Floor finishes	3.44%	2.93%	2.70%	1.60%
3C	Ceiling finishes	1.32%	1.39%	2.62%	1.25%
3	**INTERNAL FINISHES**	**6.54%**	**5.75%**	**7.12%**	**3.63%**
4	**FITTINGS AND FURNISHINGS**	**3.46%**	**3.41%**	**4.40%**	**2.47%**
5A	Sanitary appliances	0.68%	2.89%	0.42%	0.47%
5B	Services equipment	0.00%	0.07%	0.17%	0.33%
5C	Disposal installations	0.30%	0.56%	0.82%	0.05%
5D	Water installations	0.00%	0.44%	0.41%	1.22%
5E	Heat source	0.00%	1.00%	0.38%	0.00%
5F	Space heating and air treatment	9.74%	5.76%	5.50%	4.62%
5G	Ventilating systems	0.00%	0.57%	0.84%	2.37%
5H	Electrical installations	9.04%	8.03%	5.42%	5.61%
5I	Gas installations	0.00%	0.00%	0.01%	0.24%
5J	Lift and conveyor installations	0.00%	0.31%	1.44%	0.33%
5K	Protective installations	0.03%	0.11%	0.18%	0.02%
5L	Communication installations	0.31%	0.23%	0.29%	1.08%
5M	Special Installations	0.18%	0.04%	0.00%	5.22%
5N	Builder's work in connection	1.25%	1.35%	0.97%	0.71%
5O	Builder's profit and attendance	0.00%	0.49%	0.04%	0.14%
5	**SERVICES**	**21.52%**	**21.85%**	**16.89%**	**22.40%**
	Building sub-total	**75.44%**	**79.87%**	**79.97%**	**47.29%**
6A	Site works	7.38%	6.90%	3.69%	2.40%
6B	Drainage	2.61%	1.99%	1.52%	0.86%
6C	External services	2.09%	1.60%	0.88%	0.70%
6D	Minor building works	0.94%	3.09%	1.79%	41.48%
6	**EXTERNAL WORKS**	**13.02%**	**13.58%**	**7.88%**	**45.44%**
7	**PRELIMINARIES**	**11.55%**	**6.55%**	**12.15%**	**7.27%**
	FACILITY	**100.00%**	**100.00%**	**100.00%**	**100.00%**

Elemental Analyses

Element		Research Facilities	Detached Housing	Semi-detached Housing	Estate Housing
		%	%	%	%
1	**SUBSTRUCTURE**	**8.71%**	**5.97%**	**8.88%**	**8.07%**
2A	Frame	10.01%	1.79%	0.00%	0.01%
2B	Upper floors	2.35%	2.17%	0.98%	1.42%
2C	Roof	4.24%	10.52%	11.20%	8.02%
2D	Stairs	1.83%	1.31%	0.60%	0.92%
2E	External walls	4.80%	6.67%	12.60%	11.40%
2F	Windows and external doors	4.12%	8.92%	8.23%	5.57%
2G	Internal walls and partitions	2.67%	2.01%	5.33%	2.65%
2H	Internal doors	1.35%	3.52%	3.73%	2.96%
2	**SUPERSTRUCTURE**	**31.37%**	**36.92%**	**42.67%**	**32.94%**
3A	Wall finishes	0.95%	3.48%	2.85%	4.39%
3B	Floor finishes	1.90%	2.25%	2.98%	2.91%
3C	Ceiling finishes	0.94%	2.30%	1.59%	1.67%
3	**INTERNAL FINISHES**	**3.79%**	**8.03%**	**7.42%**	**8.97%**
4	**FITTINGS AND FURNISHINGS**	**0.76%**	**6.00%**	**1.94%**	**1.92%**
5A	Sanitary appliances	0.25%	1.50%	3.38%	1.41%
5B	Services equipment	22.66%	0.00%	0.00%	0.00%
5C	Disposal installations	0.82%	1.17%	0.71%	0.45%
5D	Water installations	1.14%	0.41%	1.48%	0.57%
5E	Heat source	0.00%	0.89%	0.81%	0.00%
5F	Space heating and air treatment	5.74%	5.45%	3.06%	4.82%
5G	Ventilating systems	0.16%	0.00%	0.00%	0.07%
5H	Electrical installations	7.54%	3.77%	1.95%	2.74%
5I	Gas installations	0.05%	0.00%	0.05%	0.08%
5J	Lift and conveyor installations	0.81%	0.33%	0.00%	0.00%
5K	Protective installations	0.69%	0.00%	0.00%	0.03%
5L	Communication installations	0.66%	0.04%	0.00%	0.14%
5M	Special Installations	0.24%	1.83%	0.00%	0.03%
5N	Builder's work in connection	1.34%	0.44%	0.67%	0.90%
5O	Builder's profit and attendance	0.00%	0.10%	0.59%	0.02%
5	**SERVICES**	**42.11%**	**15.92%**	**12.70%**	**11.26%**
	Building sub-total	**86.74%**	**72.83%**	**73.61%**	**63.17%**
6A	Site works	4.59%	10.69%	14.48%	18.22%
6B	Drainage	1.06%	2.85%	4.44%	5.07%
6C	External services	0.13%	4.20%	4.21%	4.29%
6D	Minor building works	0.00%	0.54%	0.00%	0.26%
6	**EXTERNAL WORKS**	**5.79%**	**18.28%**	**23.13%**	**27.83%**
7	**PRELIMINARIES**	**7.48%**	**8.88%**	**3.26%**	**9.00%**
	FACILITY	**100.00%**	**100.00%**	**100.00%**	**100.00%**

Element		Hotels %	Halls of Residence %
1	**SUBSTRUCTURE**	**5.25%**	**5.10%**
2A	Frame	1.98%	2.85%
2B	Upper floors	4.92%	2.06%
2C	Roof	6.33%	5.81%
2D	Stairs	0.90%	1.93%
2E	External walls	4.85%	6.30%
2F	Windows and external doors	5.44%	5.50%
2G	Internal walls and partitions	4.69%	2.34%
2H	Internal doors	2.52%	5.47%
2	**SUPERSTRUCTURE**	**31.63%**	**32.26%**
3A	Wall finishes	3.90%	3.37%
3B	Floor finishes	3.42%	3.38%
3C	Ceiling finishes	2.30%	1.53%
3	**INTERNAL FINISHES**	**9.62%**	**8.29%**
4	**FITTINGS AND FURNISHINGS**	**4.69%**	**6.11%**
5A	Sanitary appliances	1.10%	7.83%
5B	Services equipment	0.02%	0.29%
5C	Disposal installations	0.00%	1.40%
5D	Water installations	0.00%	2.17%
5E	Heat source	3.27%	0.00%
5F	Space heating and air treatment	12.56%	7.01%
5G	Ventilating systems	0.00%	0.01%
5H	Electrical installations	9.23%	11.07%
5I	Gas installations	0.00%	0.04%
5J	Lift and conveyor installations	1.47%	0.08%
5K	Protective installations	0.00%	0.04%
5L	Communication installations	0.04%	1.37%
5M	Special Installations	1.48%	0.36%
5N	Builder's work in connection	0.87%	2.59%
5O	Builder's profit and attendance	0.00%	0.02%
5	**SERVICES**	**30.05%**	**34.27%**
	Building sub-total	**81.24%**	**86.03%**
6A	Site works	5.90%	3.50%
6B	Drainage	1.79%	1.58%
6C	External services	0.64%	1.43%
6D	Minor building works	0.98%	0.42%
6	**EXTERNAL WORKS**	**9.30%**	**6.93%**
7	**PRELIMINARIES**	**9.46%**	**7.04%**
	FACILITY	**100.00%**	**100.00%**

Sustainability

Sustainability is an environmental concept which embraces social and economic issues. In theory it is a way of configuring human activity so that society can meet its needs whilst preserving biodiversity and ecosystems for future generations, coupled with providing a comfortable, energy-saving and human-friendly environment.

Sustainability is increasingly accepted as a guideline for improvement and innovation in future development within the global construction sector. It is also becoming a more important issue as consumers become more ethical along with the requirement to meet increasingly stringent building legislation.

There a number of solutions which are currently being implemented and researched, and this section of the book provides budget costs for a host of solutions which are being adopted in society today."

The costs provided below are based on a domestic facility occupying 4 people. All costs exclude grants and maintenance.

Prices are all current at second quarter 2010 levels based on a UK average location.

Forms of renewable energy

There are various ways of generating renewable electricity, this section focuses on costs for heat pump installations and wind turbines. Photovoltaic (PV) panels are also considered and are listed later, under 'Roofing Systems'.

Ground Source Heat Pumps (GSHPs) include the cost for the unit and all associated pipework. Air Source Heat Pumps (ASHPs) include the cost for the unit and controller. GSHPs are approximately 60% more efficient than ASHPs at present, however ASHPs do not require piping and are an emerging solution as they are being further developed. Roof mounted wind turbines are significantly cheaper than standalone wind turbines, however they have a longer payback period as they are considerably less productive. The life expectancy of the systems below range between 25 - 30 years.

	Cost	Unit
GSHP - 8KW	£8,670 - £11,220	Per System
GSHP - 23KW	£14,280 - £17,850	Per System
ASHP - 8KW	£5,750 - £8,000	Per System
ASHP - 148KW	£6,800 - £9,000	Per System
Roof Mounted Wind Turbine - 1.0KW	£1,550 - £3,000	Per System
Standalone Wind Turbine - 1.2KW	£10,500 - £12,000	Per System
Standalone Wind Turbine - 2.5KW	£12,000 - £14,500	Per System
Standalone Wind Turbine - 6.0KW	£19,000 - £23,000	Per System
Standalone Wind Turbine - 15.0KW	£41,000 - £44,500	Per System

Wall construction

A number of sustainable methods for constructing walls to provide high insulation standards have been in existence for hundreds of years. These sustainable methods are continually being developed but are still a relatively rare solution, only tending to appeal to ethical-minded consumers.

Stabilised Rammed Earth (SRE) is formed by compressing a damp mixture of earth with quantities of sand, gravel and clay into formwork. Cob is formed in the same way as SRE but has a slightly different composition and utilises clay, sand, straw, water and earth. The straw bale wall cost includes three coats of lime render on both sides of the wall. The timber wall cost includes structural insulated panel (SIPs) and joists.

	Cost	Unit
Straw bale (533mm)	£75 - £125	£/m²
Timber Frame Incorporating SIPs (549mm)	£140 - £190	£/m²
Cob Blocks (499mm)	£115 - £165	£/m²
Insitu Cob (509mm)	£90 - £140	£/m²
Stabilised Rammed Earth - SRE (300mm) - Without encapsulated insulation used for internal partition walls or garden walls	£60 - £110	£/m²
Stabilised Rammed Earth - SRE (509mm) - Solid cavity walls with sufficient insulation to meet Building Regulations	£80 - £130	£/m²

Roofing systems

Photovoltaic (PV) panels
PV panels are another form of providing renewable energy and exploit light created by the sun. Monocrystalline systems typically last approximately 30 years and tend to be slightly more efficient than polycrystalline systems. Polycrystalline are significantly lighter than the Monocrystalline systems being approximately half the thickness and typically last 25 years.

	Cost	Unit
Monocrystalline Silicon-based System	£895 - £1050	£/m²
Polycrystalline Silicon-based System	£895 - £1050	£/m²

Solar hot water system options
Solar hot water systems facilitate the process of heating water, reducing the requirement for water heating. Solar hot water systems utilise the sun and are therefore better suited to sunnier climates. There are two main types of system employed in the United Kingdom; evacuated tube solar collectors and flat plate solar collectors. Flat plate solar collectors tend to comprise a thin absorber sheet backed by tubes containing water or antifreeze and are enclosed in an insulated shell, faced with glass. Evacuated tube solar collectors consist of a number of modular transparent glass tubes containing absorber tubes and are mounted in rows parallel to each other. Sunlight passes through the glass tubing and heats the absorber tube encased within them. For both systems the liquid within the tube is circulated and transported to a device which utilises the heated fluid, such as an insulated water tank or heat exchanger.

Evacuated tube collectors are more efficient, lighter and typically last around 25 - 30 years. Flat plate solar collectors panels are generally larger and last around 20 - 25 years.

Evacuated tube solar collectors

	Cost	Unit
20 tube twin coil system (1050mm x 450mm) Sufficient for 144 litres	£3,370 - £3,600	£/unit
30 tube twin coil system (1800mm x 400mm) Sufficient for 210 litres	£3,700 - £3,900	£/unit

Flat plate solar collectors

	Cost	Unit
2400mm x 1300mm, Sufficient for 210 litres	£3,450 - £3,700	£/unit

Landscaped roofs

Landscaped roofs, also known as green roofs, can be classified into three main categories; intensive, semi-intensive and extensive. Each category is classified by the amount of maintenance required and the depth of the soils. Intensive green roofs require a reasonable depth of soil to facilitate the growth of large plants and are labour-intensive. Extensive green roofs, by contrast, are designed to be virtually self-sustaining and require minimum maintenance. Semi-intensive green roofs fall in between extensive and intensive green roof systems. Some advantages associated with green roofs are; they utilise space and provide an amenity place for building users, they can reduce storm water run off, they advocate the habitat of wildlife and they can also reduce heating requirements because the high insulation standards they achieve.

	Cost	Unit
Intensive	£175 - £210	£/m²
Semi-Intensive	£165 - £190	£/m²
Extensive	£140 - £180	£/m²

Roof lights

Rooflights are an effective means of reducing the requirement of artificial lighting as they exploit the use of natural light from by the sun. The drawback associated with rooflights is they tend to have poorer insulation standards than the roof they occupy. The costs for the rooflights take into consideration the cost associated with cutting a hole in the roof and installing them.

	Cost	Unit
Stardome double skin polycarbonate dome with a PVC kerb - 600mm x 600mm	£395 - £450	£/Unit
- 1200mm x 1200mm	£790 - £900	£/Unit
- 1800mm x 1800mm	£1,350 - £1,600	£/Unit

Sunpipes

Sunpipes are another effective means of reducing the requirement of artificial lighting as they exploit the use of natural light created by the sun. Sunpipes can pipe natural daylight where daylight from windows cannot reach. A minor drawback associated with sunpipes is that they tend to have poorer insulation standards than the roof they occupy, but due to the size of the sunpipe the effect they have is minimal. The costs for the sunpipes take into consideration installation costs including forming the roof aperture to accommodate the unit.

		Cost	Unit
Pitched roof sunpipe	- 230mm	£415 - £550	£/Unit
	- 300mm	£475 - £700	£/Unit
	- 450mm	£565 - £800	£/Unit
	- 530mm	£615 - £950	£/Unit
Flat roof sunpipe	- 230mm	£450 - £550	£/Unit
	- 300mm	£525 - £600	£/Unit
	- 450mm	£655 - £750	£/Unit
	- 530mm	£732 - £800	£/Unit

Domestic rainwater recycling

Domestic rainwater recycling, also referred to as rainwater harvesting' is an effective way of reducing the requirement of mains water. Rainwater is collected from the roof of the house and drained into a storage tank. This water can be used for a range of system and if treated correctly can be potable. In the instance below we have considered systems which only use the water for partial main water use, such as for flushing toilets and washing laundry. The costs for the rainwater recycling systems take into consideration installation costs along with the cost for supplying a full working system.

Glass reinforced plastic (GRP) tank

	Cost	Unit
3000-litre - underground tank, partial mains water use	£3,250 - £3,600	£/unit
3000-litre - above-ground tank, partial mains water use	£3,500 - £3,900	£/unit

Concrete tank

	Cost	Unit
3000-litre - underground tank, partial mains water use	£3,450 - £3,800	£/unit
3000-litre - above-ground tank, partial mains water use	£3,750 - £4,300	£/unit

Compost toilet

Toilets traditionally account for approximately a quarter of water use within residential facilities. Compost toilets do not use water and therefore save on its use. Composting toilets provide an environment for waste to decompose naturally. Materials such as sawdust and straw are used to help absorb excess liquid and when the container is filled, the waste is removed. The costs for the compost toilet take into consideration the cost for supply and installation.

	Cost	Unit
Compost toilet	£3,950 - £4,800	£/unit

Memoranda

EXCAVATION
Excavated material bulking

Material	Bulking per m³
Loose sand	1.05
Loose gravel	1.10
Compacted sand	1.20
Compacted gravel	1.25
Soft clay	1.25
Firm clay	1.25
Loamy soil	1.25
Vegetable soil	1.25
Subsoil	1.25
Stiff clay	1.40
Hard boulder clay	1.50
Weathered rock	1.60
Solid chalk	1.75
Unweathered rock	1.75

CONCRETE WORK
Material quantities per cubic metre of concrete

Nominal concrete mix (by volume)	Cement (m³)	Moist sand (m³)	Coarse aggregate (m³)
1:1.5:3	0.273	0.545	0.818
1:2:4	0.214	0.572	0.857
1:3:6	0.150	0.600	0.900

Nominal concrete mix (by weight)	Cement (tonnes)	Moist sand (tonnes)	Coarse aggregate (tonnes)
1:1.5:3	0.393	0.687	1.227
1:2:4	0.308	0.721	1.286
1:3:6	0.216	0.756	1.350

REINFORCEMENT

Steel bar reinforcement

Bar diameter	Nominal weight (kg/m)	Length (m/tonne)	Sectional area (mm²)
6 mm	0.222	4505	28.27
8 mm	0.395	2532	50.27
10 mm	0.616	1623	78.54
12 mm	0.888	1126	113.10
16 mm	1.579	633	201.06
20 mm	2.466	406	314.16
25 mm	3.854	259	452.39
32 mm	6.313	158	804.25
40 mm	9.864	101	1256.64
50 mm	15.413	65	1963.50

Steel fabric reinforcement

BS 4483 reference	Nominal weight (kg/m²)	Mesh dimensions Main (mm)	Cross (mm)	Wire diameters Main (mm)	Cross (mm)
A 98	1.54	200	200	5	5
A 142	2.22	200	200	6	6
A 193	3.02	200	200	7	7
A 252	3.95	200	200	8	8
A 393	6.16	200	200	10	10
B 196	3.05	100	200	5	7
B 283	3.73	100	200	6	7
B 385	4.53	100	200	7	7
B 503	5.93	100	200	8	8
B 785	8.14	100	200	10	8
B 1131	10.90	100	200	12	8
C 283	2.61	100	400	6	5
C 385	3.41	100	400	7	5
C 503	4.34	100	400	8	5
C 636	5.55	80-130	400	8-10	6
C 785	6.72	100	400	10	6
D 49	0.77	100	100	2.5	2.5
D 98	1.54	200	200	5	5

BRICKWORK AND BLOCKWORK

Quantities of bricks and mortar per m² (excluding waste)

Basis: 215 x 102.5 x 65 mm size bricks

10 mm mortar joints, 4 courses = 300 mm
One snapped header per facing brick
Net quantities no allowance for waste

	Common bricks Nr/m²	Facing bricks Nr/m²	Mortar for brick types	
			Solid m³/m²	Single frog m³/m²
Unfaced walls				
102.5 mm	59.26	-	0.018	0.022
215 mm	118.52	-	0.045	0.054
327.5 mm	177.78	-	0.073	0.086
Faced walls				
102.5 mm in stretcher bond	-	59.3	0.018	0.022
102.5 mm in English bond with snapped headers	-	88.9	0.020	0.025
102.5 mm in Flemish bond with snapped headers	-	79.0	0.019	0.024
Walls in English bond				
215 mm - faced one side	29.6	88.9	0.045	0.054
327.5 mm - faced one side	88.9	88.9	0.073	0.086
Walls in English bond				
215 mm - faced both sides	-	118.5	0.045	0.054
327.5 mm - faced both sides	-	177.8	0.074	0.086
Walls in Flemish bond				
215 mm - faced one side	39.5	79.0	0.045	0.054
327.5 mm - faced one side	98.8	79.0	0.074	0.086
Walls in Flemish bond				
215 mm - faced both sides	-	118.5	0.045	0.054
327.5 mm - faced both sides	19.8	158.0	0.074	0.086

Quantities of blocks and mortar per m² (excluding waste)
Basis: 440 x 215 x nominated thickness work size blocks
10 mm mortar joints
Net quantities, no allowance for waste

Wall thickness	Blocks (Nr/m²)	Mortar (m³/m²)
60 mm	9.9	0.004
75 mm	9.9	0.005
90 mm	9.9	0.006
100 mm	9.9	0.007
140 mm	9.9	0.009
190 mm	9.9	0.013
215 mm	9.9	0.104
215 mm - 100 mm blocks laid flat	20.2	0.024
215 mm - 140 mm blocks laid flat	14.8	0.019

Mortar mixes
Basis: Cement 1440 kg/m³
Hydrated lime 500 kg/m³
Sand: 1260 kg/m³ moist
Net quantities, no allowance for waste
By volume (per m³ of mortar):

Mix	Cement m³	Lime m³	Sand (moist) m³
1:1	0.725	-	0.967
1:2	0.467	-	1.244
1:3	0.338	-	1.349
1:4	0.260	-	1.387
1:6	0.179	-	1.428
1:1:5	0.196	0.196	1.311
1:1:6	0.169	0.169	1.349
1:2:9	0.113	0.225	1.349

Mortar mixes
By weight (per m³ of mortar):

Mix	Cement kg	Lime kg	Sand (moist) kg
1:1	1044	-	1218
1:2	672	-	1567
1:3	487	-	1700
1:4	374	-	1748
1:6	258	-	1799
1:1:5	282	98	1652
1:1:6	243	85	1700
1:2:9	163	113	1700

STEELWORK
Structural steel sections

Universal beams - BS EN10025 1993 Grade 275JR

Size mm	Weight kg/m
1016 x 305	487.0
	438.0
	393.0
	349.0
	314.0
	272.0
	249.0
	222.0
914 x 419	388.0
	343.3
914 x 305	289.1
	253.4
	224.2
	200.9
838 x 292	226.5
	193.8
	175.9
762 x 267	196.8
	173.0
	146.9
	133.9
686 x 254	170.2
	152.4
	140.1
	125.2
610 x 305	238.1
	179.0
	149.1
610 X 229	139.9
	125.1
	113.0
	101.2
533 x 210	122.0
	109.0
	101.0
	92.1

Size mm	Weight kg/m
	82.2
457 x 191	98.3
	89.3
	82.0
	74.3
	67.1
457 x 152	82.1
	74.2
	67.2
	59.8
	52.3
406 x 178	74.2
	67.1
	60.1
	54.1
406 x 140	46.0
	39.0
356 x 171	67.1
	57.0
	51.0
	45.0
356 x 127	39.1
	33.1
305 x 165	54.0
	46.1
	40.3
305 x 127	48.1
	41.9
	37.0
305 x 102	32.8
	28.2
	24.8
254 x 146	43.0
	37.0
	31.1
254 x 102	28.3
	25.2
	22.0
203 x 133	30.0
	25.1

Size mm	Weight kg/m
203 x 102	23.1
178 x 102	19.0
152 x 89	16.0
127 x 76	13.0

Universal columns - BS EN10025 1993 Grade 275 JR

Size mm	Weight kg/m
356 x 406	633.9
	551.0
	467.0
	393.0
	339.9
	287.1
	235.1
356 X 368	201.9
	177.0
	152.9
	129.0
305 x 305	282.9
	240.0
	198.1
	158.1
	136.9
	117.9
	96.9
254 x 254	167.1
	132.0
	107.1
	88.9
	73.1
203 x 203	86.1
	71.0
	60.0
	52.0
	46.1

Structural steel sections (contd)

Size mm	Weight kg/m	Size mm	Weight kg/m	Size mm	Weight kg/m
152 x 152	37.0	Equal angles		45 x 45 x 3	2.09
	30.0			40 x 40 x 6	3.52
	23.0	200 x 200 x 24	71.1	40 x 40 x 5	2.97
		200 x 200 x 20	59.9	40 x 40 x 4	2.42
Joists		200 x 200 x 18	54.2	40 x 40 x 3	1.84
		200 x 200 x 16	48.5	30 x 30 x 5	2.18
254 x 203	82.0	150 x 150 x 18	40.1	30 x 30 x 4	1.78
203 x 152	53.3	150 x 150 x 15	33.8	30 x 30 x 3	1.36
152 x 127	37.3	150 x 150 x 12	27.3	25 x 25 x 5	1.77
127 x 114	29.3	150 x 150 x 10	23.0	25 x 25 x 4	1.45
127 x 114	27.1	120 x 120 x 15	26.6	25 x 25 x 3	1.11
102 x 102	23.0	120 x 120 x 12	21.6		
102 x 44	7.5	120 x 120 x 10	18.2	**Unequal angles**	
89 x 89	19.5	120 x 120 x 8	14.7		
76 x 76	12.8	100 x 100 x 15	21.9	200 x 150 x 18	47.1
		100 x 100 x 12	17.8	200 x 150 x 15	39.6
Channels		100 x 100 x 10	15.0	200 x 150 x 12	32.0
		100 x 100 x 8	12.2	200 x 100 x 15	33.7
430 x 100	64.4	90 x 90 x 12	15.9	200 x 100 x 12	27.3
		90 x 90 x 10	13.4	200 x 100 x 10	23.0
380 x 100	54.0	90 x 90 x 8	10.9		
300 x 100	45.5	90 x 90 x 7	9.61	150 x 90 x 15	26.6
300 x 90	41.4	90 x 90 x 6	8.30	150 x 90 x 12	21.6
		80 x 80 x 10	11.9	150 x 90 x 10	18.2
260 x 90	34.8	80 x 80 x 8	9.63	150 x 75 x 15	24.8
260 x 75	27.6	80 x 80 x 6	7.34	150 x 75 x 12	20.2
230 x 90	32.2	70 x 70 x 10	10.3	150 x 75 x 10	17.0
230xX 75	25.7	70 x 70 x 8	8.36	125 x 75 x 12	17.8
200 x 90	29.7	70 x 70 x 6	6.38	125 x 75 x 10	15.0
200 x 75	23.4	60 x 60 x 10	8.69	125 x 75 x 8	12.2
		60 x 60 x 8	7.09	100 x 75 x 12	15.4
180 x 90	26.1	60 x 60 x 6	5.42	100 x 75 x 10	13.0
180 x 75	20.3	60 x 60 x 5	4.57	100 x 75 x 8	10.6
150 x 90	23.9	50 x 50 x 8	5.82	100 x 65 x 10	12.3
150 x 75	17.9	50 x 50 x 6	4.47	100 x 65 x 8	9.94
125 x 65	14.8	50 x 50 x 5	3.77	100 x 65 x 7	8.77
100 x 50	10.2	50 x 50 x 4	3.06		
		50 x 50 x 3	2.33	80 x 60 x 8	8.34
		45 x 45 x 6	4.00	80 x 60 x 7	7.36
		45 x 45 x 5	3.38	80 x 60 x 6	6.37
		45 x 45 x 4	2.74	75 x 50 x 8	7.39

Structural steel sections (contd)

Size mm	Weight kg/m	Size mm	Weight kg/m	Size mm	Weight kg/m
75 x 50 x 6	5.65	273 x 25	153	88.9 x 5	10.3
65 x 50 x 8	6.75	273 x 20	125	88.9 x 4	8.38
65 x 50 x 6	5.16	273 x 16	101	88.9 x 3.2	6.76
65 x 50 x 5	4.35	273 x 12.5	80.3	76.1 x 5	8.77
60 x 30 x 6	3.99	273 x 10	64.9	76.1 x 4	7.11
60 x 30 x 5	3.37	273 x 8	52.3	76.1 x 3.2	5.75
40 x 25 x 4	1.93	273 x 6.3	41.4	60.3 x 5	6.82
		244.5 x 20	111	60.3 x 4	5.55
Circular hollow sections		244.5 x 16	90.2	60.3 x 3.2	4.51
- EN 10210		244.5 x 12.5	71.5	48.3 x 5	5.34
		244.5 x 10	57.8	48.3 x 4	4.37
457 x 40	411	244.5 x 8	46.7	48.3 x 3.2	3.56
457 x 32	335	244.5 x 6.3	37.0	42.4 x 4	3.79
457 x 25	266	219.1 x 20	98.2	42.4 x 3.2	3.09
457 x 20	216	219.1 x 16	80.1	42.4 x 2.5	2.46
457 x 16	174	219.1 x 12.5	63.7	33.7 x 4	2.93
457 x 12.5	137	219.1 x 10	51.6	33.7 x 3.2	2.41
457 x 10	110	219.1 x 8	41.6	33.7 x 2.5	1.92
406.4 x 32	295	219.1 x 6.3	33.1	26.9 x 3.2	1.87
406.4 x 25	235			21.3 x 3.2	1.43
406.4 x 20	191	193.7 x 16	70.1		
406.4 x 16	154	193.7 x 12.5	55.9	**Rectangular hollow**	
406.4 x 12.5	121	193.7 x 10	45.3	**sections**	
406.4 x 10	97.8	193.7 x 8	36.6		
		193.7 x 6.3	29.1	450 x 250 x 16	166
355.6 x 25	204	193.7 x 5.0	23.3	450 x 250 x 12.5	131
355.6 x 20	166			450 x 250 x 10	106
355.6 x 16	134			400 x 200 x16	141
355.6 x 12.5	106	168.3 x 10	39.0	400 x 200 x 12.5	112
355.6 x 10	85.2	168.3 x 8	31.6	400 x 200 x 10	90.2
355.6 x 8	68.6	168.3 x 6.3	25.2		
323.9 x 25	184	168.3 x 5	20.1	300 x 200 x 16	115
323.9 x 20	150	139.7 x 10	32.0	300 x 200 x 12.5	91.9
323.9 x 16	121	139.7 x 8	26.0	300 x 200 x 10	74.5
323.9 x 12.5	96.0	139.7 x 6.3	20.7	300 x 200 x 8	60.3
323.9 x 10	77.4	139.7 x 5	16.6	300 x 200 x 6.5	47.9
323.9 x 8	62.3	114.3 x 6.3	16.8		
		114.3 x 5	13.5		
		114.3 x 3.6	9.83		

Structural steel sections (contd)

Size mm	Weight kg/m	Size mm	Weight kg/m	Size mm	Weight kg/m
250 x 150 x 16	90.3	80 x 40 x 4	6.90	150 x 150 x 16	65.2
250 x 150 x 12.5	72.3	80 x 40 x 3.2	5.62	150 x 150 x 12.5	52.7
250 x 150 x 10	58.8	60 x 40 x 4	5.64	150 x 150 x 10	43.1
250 x 150 x 8	47.7	60 x 40 x 3.2	4.62	150 x 150 x 8	35.1
250 x 150 x 6.3	38.0	50 x 30 x 3.2	3.61	150 x 150 x 6.3	28.1
200 x 100 x 16	65.2	50 x 30 x 2.5	2.89	150 x 150 x 5	22.6
200 x 100 x 12.5	52.7			120 x 120 x 10	33.7
200 x 100 x 10	43.1	**Square hollow sections**		120 x 120 x 8	27.6
200 x 100 x 8	35.1	**- EN 10210**		120 x 120 x 6.3	22.2
200 x 100 x 6.3	28.1			120 x 120 x 5	17.8
200 x 100 x 5	22.6	400 x 400 x 12.5	151	100 x 100 x 10	27.4
		400 x 400 x 10	122	100 x 100 x 8	22.6
160 x 80 x 10	33.7			100 x 100 x 6.3	18.2
160 x 80 x 8	27.6	350 x 350 x 16	166	100 x 100 x 5	14.7
160 x 80 x 6.3	22.2	350 x 350 x 12.5	131	100 x 100 x 4	11.9
160 x 80 x 5	17.8	350 x 350 x 10	106		
150 x 100 x 10	35.3	300 x 300 x 16	141	90 x 90 x 6.3	16.2
150 x 100 x 8	28.9	300 x 300 x 12.5	112	90 x 90 x 5	13.1
150 x 100 x 6.3	23.1	300 x 300 x 10	90.2	90 x 90 x 3.6	9.66
150 x 100 x 5	18.6			80 x 80 x 6.3	14.2
120 x 80 x 10	27.4	250 x 250 x 16	115	80 x 80 x 5	11.6
120 x 80 x 8	22.6	250 x 250 x 12.5	91.9	80 x 80 x 3.6	8.53
120 x 80 x 6.3	18.2	250 x 250 x 10	74.5	70 x 70 x 5	9.99
120 x 80 x 5	14.7	250 x 250 x 8	60.3	70 x 70 x 3.6	7.40
		250 x 250 x 6.3	47.9	60 x 60 x 5	8.42
120 x 60 x 6.3	16.2	200 x 200 x 16	90.3	60 x 60 x 4	6.90
120 x 60 x 5	13.1	200 x 200 x 12.5	72.3	60 x 60 x 3.2	5.62
120 x 60 x 3.6	9.72	200 x 200 x 10	58.8	50 x 50 x 5	6.85
100 x 60 x 6.3	14.2	200 x 200 x 8	47.7	50 x 50 x 4	5.64
100 x 60 x 5	11.6	200 x 200 x 6.3	38.0	50 x 50 x 3.2	4.62
100 x 60 x 3.6	8.53			40 x 40 x 4	4.39
100 x 50 x 5	10.8	180 x 180 x 16	80.2	40 x 40 x 3.2	3.61
100 x 50 x 4	8.78	180 x 180 x 12.5	64.4	40 x 40 x 2.6	2.89
100 x 50 x 3.2	7.13	180 x 180 x 10	52.5	30 x 30 x 3.2	2.65
		180 x 180 x 8	42.7	30 x 30 x 2.6	2.21
90 x 50 x 5	9.99	180 x 180 x 6.3	34.0	20 x 20 x 2.6	1.39
90 x 50 x 3.6	7.40			20 x 20 x 2	1.12

ROOFING

Slating and tiling quantities per m²

Basis: Lap is length of cover of one tile/slate over unit under
Gauge is tiling/slating batten centres and length of tile/slate exposed

Centre nailed slates

Slate size mm	Lap mm	Gauge mm	Slates Nr/m²	Battens m/m²
610 x 305	76	267	12.3	3.7
610 x 305	100	255	12.9	3.9
600 x 300	76	262	12.7	3.8
600 x 300	100	250	13.3	4.0
510 x 255	76	217	18.1	4.6
510 x 255	100	205	19.1	4.9
500 x 250	76	212	18.9	4.7
500 x 250	100	200	20.0	5.0
405 x 205	75	165	29.6	6.1
405 x 205	95	155	31.5	6.5
400 x 200	70	165	30.3	6.1
400 x 200	90	155	32.3	6.5

Plain tiles

Tile size mm	Lap mm	Gauge mm	Tiles Nr/m²	Battens m/m²
265 x 165	38	114	53.2	8.8
265 x 165	65	100	60.6	10.0

Single lap tiles

Tile size mm	Cover width mm	Lap mm	Gauge mm	Tiles Nr/m²	Battens m/m²
430 x 380	343	75	355	8.2	2.8
430 x 380	343	100	330	8.8	3.0
420 x 332	300	75	345	9.7	2.9
420 x 332	300	100	320	10.4	3.1
413 x 330	292	75	338	10.1	3.0
413 x 330	292	100	313	10.9	3.2
380 x 230	200	75	305	16.4	3.3
380 x 230	200	100	280	17.9	3.6

Nail quantities per kilogramme

Round lost head nails

Aluminium		Copper		Steel	
Length x shank		**Length x shank**		**Length x shank**	
mm	Nr/kg	mm	Nr/kg	mm	Nr/kg
75 x 3.75	448	65 x 3.75	178	75 x 3.75	160
65 x 3.35	672	65 x 3.35	194	65 x 3.35	240
60 x 3.35	756	50 x 3.35	292	65 x 3.00	270
50 x 3.35	860	50 x 3.00	308	60 x 3.35	270
50 x 3.00	1008	40 x 2.65	474	60 x 3.00	330
40 x 2.65	1390	40 x 2.36	554	50 x 3.00	360
40 x 2.36	2128	50 x 2.65	420	40 x 2.36	760

Extra large head felt nails

Aluminium		Copper		Steel	
Length x shank		**Length x shank**		**Length x shank**	
mm	Nr/kg	mm	Nr/kg	mm	Nr/kg
25 x 3.35	1296	25 x 3.35	440	40 x 3.00	350
25 x 3.00	1636	25 x 3.00	517	30 x 3.00	420
20 x 3.35	1848	20 x 3.35	544	25 x 3.00	485
20 x 3.00	2130	20 x 3.00	627	20 x 3.00	580
15 x 3.35	1840	15 x 3.00	691	15 x 3.00	650
15 x 3.00	2283	13 x 3.00	880	13 x 3.00	780

Memoranda

Clout, slate or tile nails

Aluminium		Copper		Steel	
Length x shank		Length x shank		Length x shank	
mm	Nr/kg	mm	Nr/kg	mm	Nr/kg
65 x 3.75	504	65 x 3.75	170	100 x 4.50	75
60 x 3.75	550	65 x 3.35	195	90 x 4.50	85
60 x 3.35	680	50 x 3.35	241	75 x 3.75	150
50 x 3.75	644	50 x 3.00	276	65 x 3.75	180
50 x 3.35	812	50 x 2.65	327	50 x 3.75	230
50 x 3.00	952	45 x 3.35	308	50 x 3.35	290
45 x 3.35	924	45 x 3.00	366	50 x 3.00	340
45 x 3.00	1060	45 x 2.65	456	50 x 2.65	430
40 x 3.35	980	40 x 3.35	335	45 x 3.35	330
40 x 3.00	1200	40 x 3.00	398	45 x 2.65	460
40 x 2.65	1596	40 x 2.65	460	40 x 3.35	350
40 x 2.36	1960	40 x 2.36	553	40 x 2.65	570
30 x 3.00	1512	30 x 3.35	448	40 x 2.36	700
30 x 2.65	1848	30 x 3.00	550	30 x 3.00	540
30 x 2.36	2324	30 x 2.65	621	30 x 2.65	660
30 x 2.00	3000	30 x 2.36	748	30 x 2.36	830
25 x 3.35	1540	25 x 2.65	740	25 x 2.65	815
25 x 3.00	1750	20 x 2.65	920	20 x 2.65	1035
25 x 2.65	2282			15 x 2.36	1540
25 x 2.00	3800			15 x 2.00	2380
20 x 3.00	2300				
20 x 2.65	2898				

Sheet metal information

Sheet lead

Thickness mm	BS Code	Colour Code
1.32	3	Green
1.80	4	Blue
2.24	5	Red
2.65	6	Black
3.15	7	White
3.55	8	Orange

Sheet zinc

Thickness mm	ZG
0.45	9
0.65	12
0.80	14

Sheet copper

Thickness mm	SWG
0.45	26
0.55	24
0.70	22

Sheet aluminium

Thickness mm	SWG
0.60	23
0.80	21

Sawn timber lengths per m³

Basis: No allowance for saw cut waste

Timber section size mm x mm

x	16	19	22	25	32	44	50	63	75	100	125	150	175	200	225	250	275	300
16	3906	3289	2841	2500	1953	1420	1250	992	833	625	500	417	357	313	278	250	227	208
19	3289	2770	2392	2105	1645	1196	1053	835	702	526	421	351	301	263	234	211	191	175
22	2841	2392	2066	1818	1420	1033	909	722	606	455	364	303	260	227	202	182	165	152
25	2500	2105	1818	1600	1250	909	800	635	533	400	320	267	229	200	178	160	145	133
32	1953	1645	1420	1250	977	710	625	496	417	313	250	208	179	156	139	125	114	104
44	1420	1196	1033	909	710	517	455	361	303	227	182	152	130	114	101	91	83	76
50	1250	1053	909	800	625	455	400	317	267	200	160	133	114	100	89	80	73	67
63	992	835	722	635	496	361	317	252	212	159	127	106	91	79	71	63	58	53
75	833	702	606	533	417	303	267	212	178	133	107	89	76	67	59	53	48	44
100	625	526	455	400	313	227	200	159	133	100	80	67	57	50	44	40	36	33
125	500	421	364	320	250	182	160	127	107	80	64	53	46	40	36	32	29	27
150	417	351	303	267	208	152	133	106	89	67	53	44	38	33	30	27	24	22
175	357	301	260	229	179	130	114	91	76	57	46	38	33	29	25	23	21	19
200	313	263	227	200	156	114	100	79	67	50	40	33	29	25	22	20	18	17
225	278	234	202	178	139	101	89	71	59	44	36	30	25	22	20	18	16	15
250	250	211	182	160	125	91	80	63	53	40	32	27	23	20	18	16	15	13
275	227	191	165	145	114	83	73	58	48	36	29	24	21	18	16	15	13	12
300	208	175	152	133	104	76	67	53	44	33	27	22	19	17	15	13	12	11

WOODWORK
Standard sawn softwood lengths

1.8 m			
2.1 m	2.4 m	2.7 m	
3.0 m	3.3 m	3.6 m	3.9 m
4.2 m	4.5 m	4.8 m	
5.1 m	5.4 m	5.7 m	
6.0 m	6.3 m	6.6 m	6.9 m
7.2 m			

Timber boarding quantities per m²
Basis: No allowance for waste

Cover width mm	Length m/m²
75	13.33
100	10.00
125	8.00
150	6.67
175	5.71
200	5.00

FINISHES

Plaster coverage per tonne
Basis: No allowance for waste

Thickness of coating

Type	2 mm m²/tonne	3 mm m²/tonne	5 mm m²/tonne	8 mm m²/tonne	11 mm m²/tonne
Thistle plaster					
Undercoat	-	-	-	160	115
Finish	400	260	165	-	-
Carlite plaster					
Browning	-	-	-	-	140
Metal lathing	-	-	-	-	65
Bonding coat	-	-	-	135	90
Finish coat	450	-	-	-	-

Render coverings per m³
Basis: No allowance for waste

Thickness of coating

	6 mm m²/m³	10 mm m²/m³	13 mm m²/m³	16 mm m²/m³	20 mm m²/m³
Background					
Blockwork (non-grooved or keyless faces)	109	72	58	48	40
Brickwork (grooved face or raked joints)	87	62	51	43	36
Rubble substrate	72	54	46	40	33

PAINTING and DECORATING
Coverage of decorating materials

Surface finish

	Plaster m²/litre	Render m²/litre	Concrete m²/litre	Brickwork m²/litre	Blockwork m²/litre	Joinery m²/litre
Water thinned primer as primer	13 - 15	-	-	-	-	10 - 14
Water thinned primer as u/coat	-	-	-	-	-	12 - 15
Oil wood primer	-	-	-	-	-	8 - 11
Emulsion - contract	10 - 12	7 - 11	10 - 12	7 - 10	5 - 9	10 - 12
Emulsion - standard	12 - 15	8 - 12	11 - 14	8 - 12	6 - 10	10 - 12
Plaster primer	9 - 11	8 - 12	9 - 11	7 - 9	5 - 7	-
Alkali resistant primer	7 - 11	6 - 8	7 - 11	6 - 8	5 - 7	-
External wall primer sealer	6 - 8	6 - 7	6 - 8	5 - 7	4 - 6	-
Undercoat	11 - 14	7 - 9	7 - 9	6 - 8	6 - 8	11 - 14
Gloss top coat	11 - 14	8 - 10	8 - 10	7 - 9	6 - 8	11 - 14
Eggshell (oil based)	11 - 14	9 - 11	11 - 14	8 - 10	7 - 9	11 - 14
Masonry paint	5 - 7	4 - 6	5 - 7	4 - 6	3 - 5	-

	m²/kg	m²/kg	m²/kg	m²/kg	m²/kg
Cement based paint	-	4 - 6	6 - 7	3 - 6	3 - 6
Oil bound water paint	7 - 9	4 - 6	7 - 9	4 - 6	5 - 7

DRAINAGE
Pipe bedding and coverings per m length
Basis: No allowance for waste

Pipe internal diameter	100 mm	150 mm	225 mm	300 mm
Width of bed	450 mm	525 mm	600 mm	750 mm

Material requirements (m³/m):

	100 mm	150 mm	225 mm	300 mm
50 mm bed	0.023	0.026	0.030	0.038
100 mm bed	0.045	0.053	0.060	0.075
150 mm bed	0.068	0.079	0.090	0.113
100 mm bed and haunching	0.070	0.089	0.113	0.158
150 mm bed and haunching	0.093	0.116	0.143	0.196
100 mm bed and surround	0.140	0.179	0.225	0.316
150 mm bed and surround	0.185	0.231	0.285	0.391

Index

Small Works Index

Index

Index

Major Works Index